Modern Business Statistics

with Microsoft® Excel®

8e

Jeffrey D. Camm
Wake Forest University

James J. Cochran
University of Alabama

Michael J. Fry
University of Cincinnati

Jeffrey W. Ohlmann
University of Iowa

David R. Anderson
University of Cincinnati

Dennis J. Sweeney
University of Cincinnati

Thomas A. Williams
Rochester Institute of Technology

Cengage

Australia • Brazil • Canada • Mexico • Singapore • United Kingdom • United States

Cengage

Modern Business Statistics with Microsoft® Excel®, 8e

Jeffrey D. Camm, James J. Cochran, Michael J. Fry, Jeffrey W. Ohlmann, David R. Anderson, Dennis J. Sweeney, Thomas A. Williams

SVP, Product: Cheryl Costantini

VP, Product: Thais Alencar

Portfolio Product Director: Joe Sabatino

Senior Portfolio Product Manager: Aaron Arnsparger

Product Assistant: Flannery Cowan

Senior Learning Designer: Brandon Foltz

Content Manager: Jennifer Ziegler, Ramkumar Palani

Subject-Matter Expert: Deborah Cernauskas

Digital Project Manager: Andrew Southwell

VP, Product Marketing: Jason Sakos

Director, Product Marketing: Danae April

Product Marketing Manager: Colin Kramer

Content Acquisition Analyst: Rida Syed

Production Service: MPS Limited

Designer: Chris Doughman

Cover Image Source: shunli zhao/Moment/ Getty Images

Interior image Source: cmillerdesign

Previous edition(s): © 2021, © 2018, © 2016

Library of Congress Control Number: 2024930046

Student Edition:
ISBN: 978-0-357-92988-9

Loose-leaf Edition:
ISBN: 978-0-357-92989-6

Cengage
5191 Natorp Boulevard
Mason, OH 45040
USA

Printed at CLDPC, USA, 02-24

Brief Contents

About the Authors xviii
Preface xxi

Chapter 1	Data and Statistics 1
Chapter 2	Descriptive Statistics: Tabular and Graphical Displays 35
Chapter 3	Descriptive Statistics: Numerical Measures 115
Chapter 4	Introduction to Probability 185
Chapter 5	Discrete Probability Distributions 233
Chapter 6	Continuous Probability Distributions 289
Chapter 7	Sampling and Sampling Distributions 321
Chapter 8	Interval Estimation 373
Chapter 9	Hypothesis Tests 415
Chapter 10	Inference About Means and Proportions with Two Populations 465
Chapter 11	Inferences About Population Variances 509
Chapter 12	Tests of Goodness of Fit, Independence, and Multiple Proportions 537
Chapter 13	Experimental Design and Analysis of Variance 571
Chapter 14	Simple Linear Regression 625
Chapter 15	Multiple Regression 711
Chapter 16	Regression Analysis: Model Building 761
Chapter 17	Time Series Analysis and Forecasting 807
Chapter 18	Nonparametric Methods 877
Chapter 19	Statistical Methods for Quality Control 919
Chapter 20	Decision Analysis 951
Chapter 21	Sample Survey 985
Appendix A	References and Bibliography 1024
Appendix B	Tables 1026
Appendix C	Summation Notation 1037
Appendix D	Microsoft Excel and Tools for Statistical Analysis 1039
Appendix E	Microsoft Excel Online and Tools for Statistical Analysis 1047
Appendix F	Solutions to Even-Numbered Exercises (Cengage eBook)
Index	1055

Contents

About the Authors xviii
Preface xxi

Chapter 1 Data and Statistics 1

Statistics in Practice: Bloomberg Businessweek 2

1.1 Applications in Business and Economics 3
- Accounting 3
- Finance 3
- Marketing 4
- Production 4
- Economics 4
- Information Systems 4

1.2 Data 5
- Elements, Variables, and Observations 5
- Scales of Measurement 5
- Categorical and Quantitative Data 7
- Cross-Sectional and Time Series Data 8

1.3 Data Sources 10
- Existing Sources 10
- Observational Study 11
- Experiment 12
- Time and Cost Issues 13
- Data Acquisition Errors 13

1.4 Descriptive Statistics 13
1.5 Statistical Inference 15
1.6 Statistical Analysis Using Microsoft Excel 16
1.7 Analytics 19
1.8 Big Data and Data Mining 20
1.9 Ethical Guidelines for Statistical Practice 22

Summary 24
Glossary 24
Supplementary Exercises 25
Available in the Cengage eBook:
- Appendix: Getting Started with R and RStudio
- Appendix: Basic Data Manipulation in R

Chapter 2 Descriptive Statistics: Tabular and Graphical Displays 35

Statistics in Practice: Colgate-Palmolive Company 36

2.1 Summarizing Data for a Categorical Variable 37
- Frequency Distribution 37
- Relative Frequency and Percent Frequency Distributions 38
- Bar Charts and Pie Charts 41

2.2 Summarizing Data for a Quantitative Variable 48
- Frequency Distribution 48
- Relative Frequency and Percent Frequency Distributions 50

Dot Plot 52
Histogram 53
Cumulative Distributions 56
Stem-and-Leaf Display 57
2.3 Summarizing Data for Two Variables Using Tables 66
Crosstabulation 67
Simpson's Paradox 71
2.4 Summarizing Data for Two Variables Using Graphical Displays 77
Scatter Diagram and Trendline 77
Side-by-Side and Stacked Bar Charts 80
2.5 Visualizing Geospatial Data 86
Choropleth Maps 86
Cartograms 89
2.6 Data Visualization: Best Practices in Creating Effective Graphical Displays 92
Data-Ink Ratio 93
Creating Effective Graphical Displays 95
Choosing the Type of Graphical Display 96
Data Dashboards 97
Data Visualization in Practice: Cincinnati Zoo and Botanical Garden[2] 98
Summary 101
Glossary 102
Key Formulas 103
Supplementary Exercises 103
Case Problem 1: Pelican Stores 110
Case Problem 2: Movie Theater Releases 111
Case Problem 3: Queen City 111
Case Problem 4: Cut-Rate Machining, Inc. 112
Available in the Cengage eBook:
Appendix: Creating Tabular and Graphical Presentations with R

Chapter 3 Descriptive Statistics: Numerical Measures 115
Statistics in Practice: Small Fry Design 116
3.1 Measures of Location 117
Mean 117
Median 119
Mode 120
Weighted Mean 122
Geometric Mean 123
Percentiles 125
Quartiles 126
3.2 Measures of Variability 134
Range 135
Interquartile Range 135
Variance 135
Standard Deviation 137
Coefficient of Variation 138

3.3 Measures of Distribution Shape, Relative Location, and Detecting Outliers 143
Distribution Shape 143
z-Scores 145
Chebyshev's Theorem 146
Empirical Rule 147
Detecting Outliers 147
3.4 Five-Number Summaries and Boxplots 151
Five-Number Summary 151
Boxplot 152
Comparative Analysis Using Boxplots 153
3.5 Measures of Association Between Two Variables 157
Covariance 158
Interpretation of the Covariance 159
Correlation Coefficient 160
Interpretation of the Correlation Coefficient 162
3.6 Data Dashboards: Adding Numerical Measures to Improve Effectiveness 167
Summary 170
Glossary 170
Key Formulas 172
Supplementary Exercises 173
Case Problem 1: Pelican Stores 178
Case Problem 2: Movie Theater Releases 179
Case Problem 3: Business Schools of Asia-Pacific 180
Case Problem 4: Heavenly Chocolates Website Transactions 180
Case Problem 5: African Elephant Populations 183
Available in the Cengage eBook:
Appendix: Descriptive Statistics in R

Chapter 4 Introduction to Probability 185
Statistics in Practice: National Aeronautics and Space Administration 186
4.1 Experiments, Counting Rules, and Assigning Probabilities 187
Counting Rules, Combinations, and Permutations 188
Assigning Probabilities 192
Probabilities for the KP&L Project 193
4.2 Events and Their Probabilities 197
4.3 Some Basic Relationships of Probability 201
Complement of an Event 201
Addition Law 202
4.4 Conditional Probability 207
Independent Events 210
Multiplication Law 211
4.5 Bayes' Theorem 215
Tabular Approach 218
Summary 221
Glossary 221
Key Formulas 222
Supplementary Exercises 223

Case Problem 1: Hamilton County Judges 228
Case Problem 2: Rob's Market 230

Chapter 5 Discrete Probability Distributions 233
Statistics in Practice: Voter Waiting Times in Elections 234
5.1 Random Variables 235
Discrete Random Variables 235
Continuous Random Variables 235
5.2 Developing Discrete Probability Distributions 238
5.3 Expected Value and Variance 243
Expected Value 243
Variance 243
5.4 Bivariate Distributions, Covariance, and Financial Portfolios 249
A Bivariate Empirical Discrete Probability Distribution 249
Financial Applications 252
Summary 255
5.5 Binomial Probability Distribution 258
A Binomial Experiment 258
Martin Clothing Store Problem 260
Expected Value and Variance for the Binomial Distribution 265
5.6 Poisson Probability Distribution 268
An Example Involving Time Intervals 269
An Example Involving Length or Distance Intervals 270
5.7 Hypergeometric Probability Distribution 274
Summary 278
Glossary 279
Key Formulas 280
Supplementary Exercises 281
Case Problem 1: *Go Bananas*! Breakfast Cereal 285
Case Problem 2: McNeil's Auto Mall 286
Case Problem 3: Grievance Committee at Tuglar Corporation 286
Case Problem 4: Sagittarius Casino 287
Available in the Cengage eBook:
Appendix: Discrete Probability Distributions with R

Chapter 6 Continuous Probability Distributions 289
Statistics in Practice: Procter & Gamble 290
6.1 Uniform Probability Distribution 291
Area as a Measure of Probability 292
6.2 Normal Probability Distribution 295
Normal Curve 295
Standard Normal Probability Distribution 297
Computing Probabilities for Any Normal Probability Distribution 301
Grear Tire Company Problem 302
6.3 Exponential Probability Distribution 309
Computing Probabilities for the Exponential Distribution 310
Relationship Between the Poisson and Exponential Distributions 311

Summary 314
Glossary 314
Key Formulas 314
Supplementary Exercises 315
Case Problem 1: Specialty Toys 318
Case Problem 2: Gebhardt Electronics 319
Available in the Cengage eBook:
Appendix: Continuous Probability Distributions with R

Chapter 7 Sampling and Sampling Distributions 321

Statistics in Practice: The Food and Agriculture Organization 322
7.1 The Electronics Associates Sampling Problem 324
7.2 Selecting a Sample 324
Sampling from a Finite Population 325
Sampling from an Infinite Population 329
7.3 Point Estimation 332
Practical Advice 333
7.4 Introduction to Sampling Distributions 336
7.5 Sampling Distribution of $\bar{x}$ 338
Expected Value of $\bar{x}$ 338
Standard Deviation of $\bar{x}$ 339
Form of the Sampling Distribution of $\bar{x}$ 340
Sampling Distribution of $\bar{x}$ for the EAI Problem 342
Practical Value of the Sampling Distribution of $\bar{x}$ 342
Relationship Between the Sample Size and the Sampling Distribution of $\bar{x}$ 344
7.6 Sampling Distribution of $\bar{p}$ 348
Expected Value of $\bar{p}$ 348
Standard Deviation of $\bar{p}$ 349
Form of the Sampling Distribution of $\bar{p}$ 349
Practical Value of the Sampling Distribution of $\bar{p}$ 350
7.7 Other Sampling Methods 353
Stratified Random Sampling 354
Cluster Sampling 354
Systematic Sampling 355
Convenience Sampling 355
Judgment Sampling 356
7.8 Practical Advice: Big Data and Errors in Sampling 356
Sampling Error 356
Nonsampling Error 356
Big Data 358
Understanding What Big Data Is 358
Implications of Big Data for Sampling Error 359
Summary 365
Glossary 365
Key Formulas 366
Supplementary Exercises 367
Case Problem 1: Marion Dairies 370

Case Problem 2: Profitability of Small Restaurants 371
Available in the Cengage eBook:
Appendix: Random Sampling with JMP
Appendix: Random Sampling with R

Chapter 8 Interval Estimation 373
Statistics in Practice: Food Lion 374
8.1 Population Mean: σ Known 375
Margin of Error and the Interval Estimate 375
Practical Advice 380
8.2 Population Mean: σ Unknown 382
Margin of Error and the Interval Estimate 383
Practical Advice 387
Using a Small Sample 387
Summary of Interval Estimation Procedures 389
8.3 Determining the Sample Size 392
8.4 Population Proportion 395
Determining the Sample Size 398
8.5 Practical Advice: Big Data and Interval Estimation 402
Big Data and the Precision of Confidence Intervals 402
Implications of Big Data for Confidence Intervals 403
Summary 405
Glossary 406
Key Formulas 406
Supplementary Exercises 407
Case Problem 1: *Young Professional* Magazine 410
Case Problem 2: Gulf Real Estate Properties 411
Case Problem 3: Garza Research, Inc. 413
Case Problem 4: Go-Fer Meal Delivery Service 414
Available in the Cengage eBook:
Appendix: Interval Estimation of a Population Mean, Known Standard Deviation with R
Appendix: Interval Estimation of a Population Mean, Unknown Standard Deviation with R
Appendix: Interval Estimation of a Population Proportion with R

Chapter 9 Hypothesis Tests 415
Statistics in Practice: John Morrell & Company 416
9.1 Developing Null and Alternative Hypotheses 417
The Alternative Hypothesis as a Research Hypothesis 417
The Null Hypothesis as an Assumption to Be Challenged 418
Summary of Forms for Null and Alternative Hypotheses 419
9.2 Type I and Type II Errors 420
9.3 Population Mean: σ Known 423
One-Tailed Test 423
Two-Tailed Test 428
Summary and Practical Advice 432
Relationship Between Interval Estimation and Hypothesis Testing 433

9.4 Population Mean: σ Unknown 438
One-Tailed Test 439
Two-Tailed Test 440
Summary and Practical Advice 443
9.5 Population Proportion 446
Summary 449
9.6 Practical Advice: Big Data and Hypothesis Testing 452
Big Data, Hypothesis Testing, and *p*-Values 452
Implications of Big Data in Hypothesis Testing 454
Summary 455
Glossary 456
Key Formulas 456
Supplementary Exercises 457
Case Problem 1: Quality Associates, Inc. 460
Case Problem 2: Ethical Behavior of Students at Bayview University 461
Case Problem 3: New Product Development at Baxter Barnes Gelato 462
Available in the Cengage ebook:
Appendix: Hypothesis Testing of a Population Mean, Known Standard Deviation with R
Appendix: Hypothesis Testing of a Population Mean, Unknown Standard Deviation with R
Appendix: Hypothesis Testing of a Population Proportion with R

Chapter 10 **Inference About Means and Proportions with Two Populations 465**

Statistics in Practice: U.S. Food and Drug Administration 466
10.1 Inferences About the Difference Between Two Population Means: σ_1 and σ_2 Known 467
Interval Estimation of $\mu_1 - \mu_2$ 467
Hypothesis Tests About $\mu_1 - \mu_2$ 471
Practical Advice 474
10.2 Inferences About the Difference Between Two Population Means: σ_1 and σ_2 Unknown 476
Interval Estimation of $\mu_1 - \mu_2$ 477
Hypothesis Tests About $\mu_1 - \mu_2$ 480
Practical Advice 483
10.3 Inferences About the Difference Between Two Population Means: Matched Samples 487
10.4 Inferences About the Difference Between Two Population Proportions 494
Interval Estimation of $p_1 - p_2$ 494
Hypothesis Tests About $p_1 - p_2$ 497
Summary 503
Glossary 503
Key Formulas 503
Supplementary Exercises 505
Case Problem: Par, Inc. 508
Available in the Cengage ebook:
Appendix: Inferences About Two Populations with R

Chapter 11 **Inferences About Population Variances 509**
Statistics in Practice: U.S. Government Accountability Office 510
11.1 Inferences About a Population Variance 511
Interval Estimation 511
Hypothesis Testing 516
11.2 Inferences About Two Population Variances 523
Summary 531
Key Formulas 531
Supplementary Exercises 531
Case Problem 1: Air Force Training Program 534
Case Problem 2: Meticulous Drill & Reamer 535
Available in the Cengage ebook:
Appendix: Population Variances with R

Chapter 12 **Tests of Goodness of Fit, Independence, and Multiple Proportions 537**
Statistics in Practice: United Way 538
12.1 Goodness-of-Fit Test 539
Multinomial Probability Distribution 539
12.2 Test of Independence 545
12.3 Testing for Equality of Three or More Population Proportions 554
A Multiple Comparison Procedure 558
Summary 563
Glossary 564
Key Formulas 564
Supplementary Exercises 565
Case Problem 1: A Bipartisan Agenda for Change 568
Case Problem 2: Fuentes Salty Snacks, Inc. 568
Case Problem 3: Fresno Board Games 569
Available in the Cengage ebook:
Appendix: Chi-Square Tests with R

Chapter 13 **Experimental Design and Analysis of Variance 571**
Statistics in Practice: Burke, Inc. 572
13.1 An Introduction to Experimental Design and Analysis of Variance 573
Data Collection 574
Assumptions for Analysis of Variance 576
Analysis of Variance: A Conceptual Overview 576
13.2 Analysis of Variance and the Completely Randomized Design 578
Between-Treatments Estimate of Population Variance 579
Within-Treatments Estimate of Population Variance 580
Comparing the Variance Estimates: The *F* Test 581
ANOVA Table 582
Testing for the Equality of *k* Population Means: An Observational Study 584
13.3 Multiple Comparison Procedures 590
Fisher's LSD 590
Type I Error Rates 592

14.8 Residual Analysis: Validating Model Assumptions 671
Residual Plot Against x 672
Residual Plot Against $\hat{y}$ 673
Standardized Residuals 675
Normal Probability Plot 680
14.9 Outliers and Influential Observations 683
Detecting Outliers 683
Detecting Influential Observations 686
14.10 Practical Advice: Big Data and Hypothesis Testing in Simple Linear Regression 690
Summary 691
Glossary 691
Key Formulas 692
Supplementary Exercises 694
Case Problem 1: Measuring Stock Market Risk 704
Case Problem 2: U.S. Department of Transportation 705
Case Problem 3: Selecting a Point-and-Shoot Digital Camera 705
Case Problem 4: Finding the Best Car Value 707
Case Problem 5: Buckeye Creek Amusement Park 708
Appendix 14.1: Calculus-Based Derivation of Least Squares Formulas 709
Appendix 14.2: A Test for Significance Using Correlation 710
Available in the Cengage ebook:
Appendix: Simple Linear Regression with R

Chapter 15 Multiple Regression 711
Statistics in Practice: International Paper 712
15.1 Multiple Regression Model 713
Regression Model and Regression Equation 713
Estimated Multiple Regression Equation 714
15.2 Least Squares Method 715
An Example: Butler Trucking Company 715
Note on Interpretation of Coefficients 719
15.3 Multiple Coefficient of Determination 724
15.4 Model Assumptions 727
15.5 Testing for Significance 729
F Test 729
t Test 731
Multicollinearity 732
15.6 Using the Estimated Regression Equation for Estimation and Prediction 735
15.7 Categorical Independent Variables 737
An Example: Johnson Filtration, Inc. 737
Interpreting the Parameters 739
More Complex Categorical Variables 740
15.8 Residual Analysis 745
Residual Plot Against $\hat{y}$ 745
Standardized Residual Plot Against $\hat{y}$ 746

15.9 Practical Advice: Big Data and Hypothesis Testing in Multiple Regression 749
Summary 750
Glossary 750
Key Formulas 751
Supplementary Exercises 752
Case Problem 1: Consumer Research, Inc. 757
Case Problem 2: Predicting Winnings for NASCAR Drivers 758
Case Problem 3: Finding the Best Car Value 760
Available in the Cengage ebook:
Appendix: Multiple Linear Regression with R

Chapter 16 Regression Analysis: Model Building 761
Statistics in Practice: BASF 762
16.1 General Linear Model 763
Modeling Curvilinear Relationships 763
Interaction 765
Transformations Involving the Dependent Variable 769
Nonlinear Models That Are Intrinsically Linear 773
16.2 Determining When to Add or Delete Variables 778
General Case 779
16.3 Variable Selection Procedures 783
Regression Analysis of Cravens Example 784
Stepwise Regression 787
Forward Selection 787
Backward Elimination 788
Best-Subsets Regression 788
16.4 Multiple Regression Approach to Experimental Design 788
16.5 Autocorrelation and the Durbin–Watson Test 793
Jefe de Cocina Example 796
Summary 799
Glossary 800
Key Formulas 800
Supplementary Exercises 801
Case Problem 1: Analysis of LPGA Tour Statistics 804
Case Problem 2: Rating Wines from the Piedmont Region of Italy 804
Available in the Cengage ebook:
Appendix: Linear Regression Variable Selection Procedures with R

Chapter 17 Time Series Analysis and Forecasting 807
Statistics in Practice: Nevada Occupational Health Clinic 808
17.1 Time Series Patterns 809
Horizontal Pattern 810
Trend Pattern 812
Seasonal Pattern 813
Trend and Seasonal Pattern 815
Cyclical Pattern 816
Selecting a Forecasting Method 817

17.2 Forecast Accuracy 817
17.3 Moving Averages and Exponential Smoothing 822
Moving Averages 822
Weighted Moving Averages 825
Exponential Smoothing 826
17.4 Trend Projection 833
Linear Trend Regression 833
Nonlinear Trend Regression 838
17.5 Seasonality and Trend 848
Seasonality Without Trend 848
Seasonality and Trend 851
Models Based on Monthly Data 854
17.6 Time Series Decomposition 858
Calculating the Seasonal Indexes 859
Deseasonalizing the Time Series 863
Using the Deseasonalized Time Series to Identify Trend 863
Seasonal Adjustments 864
Models Based on Monthly Data 865
Cyclical Component 865
Summary 868
Glossary 868
Key Formulas 869
Supplementary Exercises 870
Case Problem 1: Forecasting Food and Beverage Sales 874
Case Problem 2: Forecasting Lost Sales 875
Available in the Cengage ebook:
Appendix: Forecasting with R

Chapter 18 **Nonparametric Methods 877**
Statistics in Practice: West Shell Realtors 878
18.1 Sign Test 879
Hypothesis Test About a Population Median 879
Hypothesis Test with Matched Samples 883
18.2 Wilcoxon Signed-Rank Test 888
18.3 Mann–Whitney–Wilcoxon Test 893
18.4 Kruskal–Wallis Test 903
18.5 Rank Correlation 907
Summary 912
Glossary 913
Key Formulas 913
Supplementary Exercises 914
Case: RainOrShine.Com 917
Available in the Cengage ebook:
Appendix: The Sign Test with R
Appendix: The Wilcoxon Signed-Rank Test with R
Appendix: The Mann-Whitney-Wilcoxon Test with R
Appendix: The Kruskal-Wallis Test with R
Appendix: The Spearman Rank Correlation Coefficient with R

Chapter 19 **Statistical Methods for Quality Control 919**

Statistics in Practice: Ocean Spray 920

19.1 Philosophies and Frameworks 921
- Malcolm Baldrige National Quality Award 922
- ISO 9001 922
- Six Sigma 922
- Quality in the Service Sector 924

19.2 Statistical Process Control 925
- Control Charts 926
- $\overline{x}$ Chart: Process Mean and Standard Deviation Known 927
- $\overline{x}$ Chart: Process Mean and Standard Deviation Unknown 929
- *R* Chart 931
- *p* Chart 932
- *np* Chart 935
- Interpretation of Control Charts 935

19.3 Acceptance Sampling 938
- KALI, Inc.: An Example of Acceptance Sampling 939
- Computing the Probability of Accepting a Lot 940
- Selecting an Acceptance Sampling Plan 942
- Multiple Sampling Plans 943

Summary 946
Glossary 946
Key Formulas 947
Supplementary Exercises 948
Available in the Cengage ebook:
Appendix: Control Charts with R

Chapter 20 **Decision Analysis 951**

Statistics in Practice: U.S. Centers for Disease Control and Prevention 952

20.1 Problem Formulation 952
- Payoff Tables 953
- Decision Trees 954

20.2 Decision Making with Probabilities 955
- Expected Value Approach 955
- Expected Value of Perfect Information 957

20.3 Decision Analysis with Sample Information 963
- Decision Tree 963
- Decision Strategy 966
- Expected Value of Sample Information 967

20.4 Computing Branch Probabilities Using Bayes' Theorem 973

Summary 977
Glossary 977
Key Formulas 978
Supplementary Exercises 978
Case Problem 1: Lawsuit Defense Strategy 982
Case Problem 2: Property Purchase Strategy 983

Chapter 21 **Sample Survey** 985
Statistics in Practice: Duke Energy 986
21.1 Terminology Used in Sample Surveys 986
21.2 Types of Surveys and Sampling Methods 987
21.3 Survey Errors 988
Nonsampling Error 989
Sampling Error 989
21.4 Simple Random Sampling 990
Population Mean 990
Population Total 991
Population Proportion 992
Using Excel for Simple Random Sampling 992
Determining the Sample Size 994
21.5 Stratified Simple Random Sampling 997
Population Mean 997
Using Excel: Population Mean 998
Population Total 1000
Population Proportion 1001
Using Excel: Population Proportion 1002
Determining the Sample Size 1002
21.6 Cluster Sampling 1006
Population Mean 1008
Population Total 1009
Population Proportion 1010
Using Excel for Cluster Sampling 1011
Determining the Sample Size 1012
21.7 Systematic Sampling 1014
Summary 1014
Glossary 1015
Key Formulas 1015
Simple Random Sampling 1015
Stratified Simple Random Sampling 1016
Cluster Sampling 1017
Supplementary Exercises 1018
Case: Medicament's Predicament 1020

Appendix A References and Bibliography 1024

Appendix B Tables 1026

Appendix C Summation Notation 1037

Appendix D Microsoft Excel and Tools for Statistical Analysis 1039

Appendix E Microsoft Excel Online and Tools for Statistical Analysis 1047

Appendix F Solutions to Even-Numbered Exercises (Cengage eBook)

Index 1055

About the Authors

Jeffrey D. Camm. Jeffrey D. Camm is the Inmar Presidential Chair and Senior Associate Dean for Faculty and Research in the School of Business at Wake Forest University. Born in Cincinnati, Ohio, he holds a B.S. from Xavier University (Ohio) and a Ph.D. from Clemson University. Prior to joining the faculty at Wake Forest, he was on the faculty of the University of Cincinnati. He has also been a visiting scholar at Stanford University and a visiting professor of business administration at the Tuck School of Business at Dartmouth College.

Dr. Camm has published over 45 papers in the general area of optimization applied to problems in operations management and marketing. He has published his research in *Science*, *Management Science*, *Operations Research*, *Interfaces*, and other professional journals. Dr. Camm was named the Dornoff Fellow of Teaching Excellence at the University of Cincinnati and he was the 2006 recipient of the INFORMS Prize for the Teaching of Operations Research Practice. A firm believer in practicing what he preaches, he has served as an operations research consultant to numerous companies and government agencies. From 2005 to 2010 he served as editor-in-chief of the *INFORMS Journal on Applied Analytics* (formerly *Interfaces*).

James J. Cochran. James J. Cochran is Professor of Applied Statistics and the Mike and Kathy Mouron Research Chair at The University of Alabama. Born in Dayton, Ohio, he earned his B.S., M.S., and M.B.A. degrees from Wright State University and a Ph.D. from the University of Cincinnati. He has been at The University of Alabama since 2014 and has been a visiting scholar at Stanford University, Universidad de Talca, the University of South Africa, Pôle Universitaire Léonard de Vinci, and University College London.

Professor Cochran has published over 50 papers in the development and application of operations research and statistical methods. He has published his research in *Management Science*, *The American Statistician*, *Communications in Statistics—Theory and Methods*, *Annals of Operations Research*, *European Journal of Operational Research*, *Journal of Combinatorial Optimization*, *Interfaces*, *Statistics and Probability Letters*, and other professional journals. He was the 2008 recipient of the INFORMS Prize for the Teaching of Operations Research Practice and the 2010 recipient of the Mu Sigma Rho Statistical Education Award. Professor Cochran was elected to the International Statistics Institute in 2005, was named a Fellow of the American Statistical Association in 2011, and was named a Fellow of INFORMS in 2017. He also received the Founders Award in 2014 and the Karl E. Peace Award in 2015 from the American Statistical Association as well as the President's Award in 2018 from INFORMS and the William G. Hunter Award Award from the American Society of Quality. A strong advocate for effective operations research and statistics education as a means of improving the quality of applications to real problems, Professor Cochran has organized and chaired teaching effectiveness workshops in Uruguay, South Africa, Colombia, India, Argentina, Kenya, Cuba, Croatia, Cameroon, Nepal, Moldova, Bulgaria, Grenada, and Sri Lanka. He has served as a statistical consultant to numerous companies and not-for-profit organizations. He served as editor-in-chief of *INFORMS Transactions on Education* from 2006 to 2012 and is on the editorial board of *INFORMS Journal on Applied Analytics* (formerly *Interfaces*), *International Transactions in Operational Research*, and *Significance*.

Michael J. Fry. Michael J. Fry is Professor of Operations, Business Analytics, and Information Systems (OBAIS), Lindner Research Fellow, and Managing Director of the Center for Business Analytics in the Carl H. Lindner College of Business at the University of Cincinnati. Born in Killeen, Texas, he earned a B.S. from Texas A&M University, and M.S.E. and Ph.D. degrees from the University of Michigan. He has been at the University of Cincinnati since 2002, where he served as Department Head. He has also been a visiting professor at the Samuel Curtis Johnson Graduate School of Management at Cornell University and the Sauder School of Business at the University of British Columbia.

Professor Fry has published more than 25 research papers in journals such as *Operations Research*, *M&SOM*, *Production & Operations Management, Transportation Science*, *Naval Research Logistics*, *IISE Transactions*, *Critical Care Medicine*, and *INFORMS Journal on Applied Analytics*. He serves on editorial boards for journals such as *Production and Operations Management*, *INFORMS Journal on Applied Analytics*, and *Journal of Quantitative Analysis in Sports*. His research interests are in applying analytics to the areas of supply chain management, sports, and public-policy operations. He has worked with many different organizations for his research, including Dell, Inc., Starbucks Coffee Company, Great American Insurance Group, the Cincinnati Fire Department, the State of Ohio Election Commission, the Cincinnati Bengals, and the Cincinnati Zoo & Botanical Garden. He was named a finalist for the Daniel H. Wagner Prize for Excellence in Operations Research Practice, and he has been recognized for both his research and teaching excellence at the University of Cincinnati. In 2019, he led the team that was awarded the INFORMS UPS George D. Smith Prize on behalf of the OBAIS Department at the University of Cincinnati.

Jeffrey W. Ohlmann. Jeffrey W. Ohlmann is Associate Professor of Business Analytics and Huneke Research Fellow in the Tippie College of Business at the University of Iowa. Born in Valentine, Nebraska, he earned a B.S. from the University of Nebraska, and M.S. and Ph.D. degrees from the University of Michigan. He has been at the University of Iowa since 2003.

Professor Ohlmann's research on the modeling and solution of decision-making problems has produced more than two dozen research papers in journals such as *Operations Research*, *Mathematics of Operations Research*, *INFORMS Journal on Computing*, *Transportation Science*, and *European Journal of Operational Research.* He has collaborated with companies such as Transfreight, LeanCor, Cargill, the Hamilton County Board of Elections, and three National Football League franchises. Because of the relevance of his work to industry, he was bestowed the George B. Dantzig Dissertation Award and was recognized as a finalist for the Daniel H. Wagner Prize for Excellence in Operations Research Practice.

David R. Anderson. David R. Anderson is Professor Emeritus in the Carl H. Lindner College of Business at the University of Cincinnati. Born in Grand Forks, North Dakota, he earned his B.S., M.S., and Ph.D. degrees from Purdue University. Professor Anderson has served as Head of the Department of Quantitative Analysis and Operations Management and as Associate Dean of the College of Business Administration at the University of Cincinnati. In addition, he was the coordinator of the College's first Executive Program.

At the University of Cincinnati, Professor Anderson has taught introductory statistics for business students as well as graduate-level courses in regression analysis, multivariate analysis, and management science. He has also taught statistical courses at the Department of Labor in Washington, D.C. He has been honored with nominations and awards for excellence in teaching and excellence in service to student organizations.

Professor Anderson has coauthored 10 textbooks in the areas of statistics, management science, linear programming, and production and operations management. He is an active consultant in the field of sampling and statistical methods.

Dennis J. Sweeney. Dennis J. Sweeney is Professor Emeritus in the Carl H. Lindner College of Business at the University of Cincinnati. Born in Des Moines, Iowa, he earned a B.S.B.A. degree from Drake University and his M.B.A. and D.B.A. degrees from Indiana University, where he was an NDEA Fellow. Professor Sweeney has worked in the management science group at Procter & Gamble and spent a year as a visiting professor at Duke University. Professor Sweeney served as Head of the Department of Quantitative Analysis and as Associate Dean of the College of Business Administration at the University of Cincinnati.

Professor Sweeney has published more than 30 articles and monographs in the area of management science and statistics. The National Science Foundation, IBM, Procter & Gamble, Federated Department Stores, Kroger, and Duke Energy have funded his research, which has been published in *Management Science*, *Operations Research*, *Mathematical Programming*, *Decision Sciences*, and other journals.

Professor Sweeney has coauthored 10 textbooks in the areas of statistics, management science, linear programming, and production and operations management.

Thomas A. Williams. Thomas A. Williams is Professor Emeritus of Management Science in the College of Business at Rochester Institute of Technology. Born in Elmira, New York, he earned his B.S. degree at Clarkson University. He did his graduate work at Rensselaer Polytechnic Institute, where he received his M.S. and Ph.D. degrees.

Before joining the College of Business at RIT, Professor Williams served for seven years as a faculty member in the College of Business Administration at the University of Cincinnati, where he developed the undergraduate program in Information Systems and then served as its coordinator. At RIT he was the first chairman of the Decision Sciences Department. He has taught courses in management science and statistics, as well as graduate courses in regression and decision analysis.

Professor Williams is the coauthor of 11 textbooks in the areas of management science, statistics, production and operations management, and mathematics. He has been a consultant for numerous *Fortune* 500 companies and has worked on projects ranging from the use of data analysis to the development of large-scale regression models.

Preface

This text is the eighth edition of *Modern Business Statistics with Microsoft® Excel®*. The purpose of *Modern Business Statistics with Microsoft Excel* is to give students, primarily those in the fields of business administration and economics, a conceptual introduction to the field of statistics and its many applications. The text is applications oriented and written with the needs of the nonmathematician in mind; the mathematical prerequisite is knowledge of algebra.

Applications of data analysis and statistical methodology are an integral part of the organization and presentation of the text material. The discussion and development of each technique is presented in an applications setting, with the statistical results providing insights to decisions and solutions to applied problems.

Although the book is applications oriented, we have taken care to provide sound methodological development and to use notation that is generally accepted for the topic being covered. Hence, students will find that this text provides good preparation for the study of more advanced statistical material. A bibliography to guide further study is included as an appendix.

Use of Microsoft Excel for Statistical Analysis

Modern Business Statistics with Microsoft Excel is first and foremost a statistics textbook that emphasizes statistical concepts and applications. But since most practical problems are too large to be solved using hand calculations, some type of statistical software package is required to solve these problems. There are several excellent statistical packages available today. However, because most students and potential employers value spreadsheet experience, many schools use a spreadsheet package in their statistics courses. Microsoft Excel is the most widely used spreadsheet package in business as well as in colleges and universities. We have written *Modern Business Statistics with Microsoft Excel* especially for statistics courses in which Microsoft Excel is used as the software package.

Excel has been integrated within each of the chapters and plays an integral part in providing an application orientation. Although we assume that readers using this text are familiar with Excel basics such as selecting cells, entering formulas, and copying, we do not assume that readers are familiar with Excel or Excel's tools for statistical analysis. As a result, we have included Appendix D, which provides an introduction to Excel and tools for statistical analysis, and Appendix E, which provides an introduction to Microsoft Excel Online and Tools for Statistical Analysis.

Throughout the text, the discussion of using Excel to perform a statistical procedure appears in a subsection immediately following the discussion of the statistical procedure. We believe that this style enables us to fully integrate the use of Excel throughout the text while maintaining the primary emphasis on the statistical methodology being discussed. In each of these subsections, we use a standard format for using Excel for statistical analysis. There are four primary tasks: Enter/Access Data, Enter Functions and Formulas, Apply Tools, and Editing Options. We believe a consistent framework for applying Excel helps users to focus on the statistical methodology without getting bogged down in the details of using Excel.

In presenting worksheet figures, we often use a nested approach in which the worksheet shown in the background of the figure displays the formulas and the worksheet shown in the foreground shows the values computed using the formulas.

Changes in the Eighth Edition

We appreciate the acceptance and positive response to the previous editions of *Modern Business Statistics with Microsoft Excel*. Accordingly, in making modifications for this new edition, we have maintained the presentation style and readability of those editions. The significant changes in the new edition are summarized here.

- **Expanded Coverage of Data Visualization.** We have expanded our coverage of data visualization concepts and tools in Chapter 2 of the textbook. We have added a new section that covers the visualization of geospatial data using maps. We introduce both choropleth maps and cartograms, and we explain how to create choropleth maps in Excel. We have also added to our existing coverage of best practices for data visualization by expanding our discussion of the use of the data-ink ratio and decluttering to create effective visualizations.
- **Extended Coverage of Regression Modeling.** In Chapter 16, we have slightly reorganized the chapter and elaborated on a few topics. First, we added a discussion about comparing a regression model with a transformed dependent variable to a regression model using the untransformed dependent variable in the original units. Second, we added an example to illustrate the use of the Durbin-Watson statistic to test the presence of first-order autocorrelation.
- **Learning objectives.** We have added Learning Objectives (LOs) to the beginning of each chapter. These LOs explain the key concepts that are covered in each chapter. The LOs are also mapped onto each problem so instructors can easily identify which LOs are covered by each problem.
- **New Examples and Exercises Based on Real Data.** In this edition, we have added over 90 new examples and exercises based on real data and referenced sources. By using data from sources also used by *The Wall Street Journal*, *USA Today*, *The Financial Times*, *Forbes*, and others, we have drawn from actual studies and applications to develop explanations and create exercises that demonstrate the many uses of statistics in business and economics. We believe that the use of real data from interesting and relevant problems generates greater student interest in the material and enables the student to more effectively learn about both statistical methodology and its application.
- **Case Problems.** We have added four new case problems to this edition. Over 50 case problems in the text provide students with the opportunity to analyze somewhat larger data sets and prepare managerial reports based on the results of their analysis.
- **Appendixes for Use of R.** We now provide appendixes in the Cengage eBook for many chapters that demonstrate the use of the popular open-source software R and RStudio for statistical applications. The use of R is not required to solve any problems or cases in the textbook, but the appendixes provide an introduction to R and RStudio for interested instructors and students.

Features and Pedagogy

Authors Camm, Cochran, Fry, and Ohlmann have continued many of the features that appeared in previous editions. Important features for students are noted here.

Methods Exercises and Applications Exercises

The end-of-section exercises are split into two parts: Methods and Applications. The Methods exercises require students to use the formulas and make the necessary computations. The Applications exercises require students to use the chapter material in real-world situations. Thus, students first focus on the computational "nuts and bolts" and then move on to the subtleties of statistical application and interpretation. Both the Methods and the Applications exercises now include notations indicating which learning objectives are covered in each exercise.

Margin Annotations and Notes and Comments

Margin annotations that highlight key points and provide additional insights for the student are a key feature of this text. These annotations, which appear in the margins, are designed to provide emphasis and enhance understanding of the terms and concepts being presented in the text.

At the end of many sections, we provide Notes and Comments that are designed to give the student additional insights about the statistical methodology and its application. Notes and Comments include warnings about or limitations of the methodology, recommendations for application, brief descriptions of additional technical considerations, and other matters.

Data Files Accompany the Text

Over 500 data files are available on the website that accompanies the text. DATAfile logos are used in the text to identify the data sets that are available on the website. Data sets for all case problems as well as data sets for larger exercises are included.

MindTap

MindTap, featuring Excel Online integration powered by Microsoft, is a complete digital solution for the business statistics course. It has enhancements that take students from learning basic statistical concepts to actively engaging in critical thinking applications, while learning valuable software skills for their future careers. The R appendixes for many of the chapters in the text are also accessible through MindTap.

MindTap is a customizable digital course solution that includes an interactive eBook and autograded, algorithmic exercises from the textbook. All of these materials offer students better access to understand the materials within the course. For more information on MindTap, please contact your Cengage representative.

Instructor and Student Resources

Additional instructor and student resources for this product are available online. Instructor assets include a Solutions and Answers Guide, Instructor's Manual, MindTap Educator's Guide, PowerPoint® slides, and a test bank powered by Cognero®. Student assets include data sets for chapter examples and problems. Sign up or sign in at **www.cengage.com** to search for and access this product and its online resources.

Acknowledgments

A special thanks goes to our associates from business and industry who supplied the Statistics in Practice features. We recognize them individually by a credit line in each of the articles. We are also indebted to our senior product manager, Aaron Arnsparger; our content managers, Jennifer Ziegler and Ramkumar Palani; senior learning designer, Brandon Foltz; digital project manager, Andrew Southwell; and our senior project manager at MPS Limited, Prashant Kumar Das, for their editorial counsel and support during the preparation of this text.

We would like to acknowledge the work of our reviewers who provided comments and suggestions of ways to continue to improve our text. Thanks to:

Jamal Abdul-Hafidh
University of Missouri–St. Louis

Chris Adalikwu
Concordia College

Eugene Allevato
Woodbury University

Solomon Antony
Murray State University

Glen Archibald
University of Mississippi

Ardavan Asef-Vaziri
California State University, Northridge

S. Scott Bailey
Troy University

Robert J. Banis
University of Missouri–St. Louis

Wayne Bedford
University of West Alabama

Enoch K. Beraho
South Carolina State University

Timothy M. Bergquist
Northwest Christian College

Darl Bien
University of Denver

William H. Bleuel
Pepperdine University

Gary Bliss
Florida State University–Panama City

Leslie M. Bobb
New York Institute of Technology

Michelle Boddy
Baker College

Thomas W. Bolland
Ohio University

Derrick S. Boone, Sr.
Wake Forest University

Lawrence Bos
Cornerstone University

Mike Bourke
Houston Baptist University

Alan Brokaw
Michigan Tech University

Nancy Brooks
University of Vermont

Yvonne Brown
Pima Community College

Peter Bryant
University of Colorado

Dawn Bulriss
Maricopa Community Colleges

Robert Burgess
Georgia Tech

Von L. Burton
Athens State University

Terri L. Byczkowski
University of Cincinnati

John R. Carpenter
Cornerstone University

Robert Carver
Stonehill College

Jasmine Chang
Georgia State University

Si Chen
Murray State University

Alan S. Chesen
Wright State University

Ying Chien
University of Scranton

Michael Cicero
Highline Community College

Robert Cochran
University of Wyoming

Robert Collins
Marquette University

Murray Côté
University of Florida

David W. Cravens
Texas Christian University

Tom Dahlstrom
Eastern College

Ping Deng
Maryville University

Sarvanan Devaraj
Notre Dame University

Terry Dielman
Texas Christian University

Cassandra DiRienzo
Elon University

Anne Drougas
Dominican University

Jianjun Du
University of Houston, Victoria

John N. Dyer
Georgia Southern University

Hossein Eftekari
University of Wisconsin–River Falls

Ronald Ehresman
Baldwin-Wallace College

Mohammed A. El-Saidi
Ferris State University

Robert M. Escudero
Pepperdine University

Allessandra Faggian
Ohio State University

Nicolas Farnum
California State University, Fullerton

Abe Feinberg
California State University, Northridge

Maggie Williams Flint
Northeast State Tech Community College

Alfonso Flores-Lagunes
University of Arizona

James Flynn
Cleveland State University

Alan F. Foltz
Drury University

Michael Ford
Rochester Institute of Technology

Ronald L. Friesen
Bluffton College

Phil Fry
Boise State University

Richard Gebhart
University of Tulsa

Paul Gentine
Bethany College

Deborah J. Gougeon
University of Scranton

Jeffrey Gropp
DePauw University

V. Daniel Guide
Duquesne University

Paul Guy
California State University, Chico

Rhonda Hensley
North Carolina A&T University

Erick Hofacker
University of Wisconsin–River Falls

Amy C. Hooper
Gettysburg College

Paul Hudec
Milwaukee School of Engineering

Alan Humphrey
University of Rhode Island

Ann Hussein
Philadelphia College of Textiles and Science

Ben Isselhardt
Rochester Institute of Technology

Wade Jackson
University of Memphis

Timmy James
Northwest Shoals Community College

Jeffery Jarrett
University of Rhode Island

Eugene Jones
The Ohio State University

Naser Kamleh
Wallace Community College

Mark P. Karscig
Central Missouri State University

Howard Kittleson
Riverland Community College

Kenneth Klassen
California State University, Northridge

Eileen Quinn Knight
St. Xavier University, Chicago

Bharat Kolluri
University of Hartford

Joseph Kosler
Indiana University of Pennsylvania

David A. Kravitz
George Mason University

Laura Kuhl
University of Phoenix, Cleveland Campus

June Lapidus
Roosevelt University

John Lawrence
California State University, Fullerton

Tenpao Lee
Niagara University

Daniel Light
Northwest State College

Robert Lindsey
College of Charleston

B. Lucas
A&M College

Michael Machiorlatti
City College of San Francisco

Malik B. Malik
University of Maryland Eastern Shore

Lee McClain
Western Washington University

Timothy E. McDaniel
Buena Vista University

Kim I. Melton
North Georgia College & State University

Brian Metz
Cabrini College

John M. Miller
Sam Houston State University

Patricia A. Mullins
University of Wisconsin–Madison

Jack Muryn
University of Wisconsin, Washington County

Muhammad Mustafa
South Carolina State University

Aravind Narasipur
Chennai Business School

Anthony Narsing
Macon State College

Kenneth F. O'Brien
Farmingdale State College

Ceyhun Ozgur
Valparaiso University

Michael Parzen
Emory University

Barry Pasternack
California State University, Fullerton

Lynne Pastor
Carnegie Mellon University

Ranjna Patel
Bethune-Cookman College

Tremaine Pimperl
Faulkner State Community College

Jennifer M. Platania
Elon University

Von Roderick Plessner
Northwest State Community College

Glenn Potts
University of Wisconsin–River Falls

Irene Powell
Grinnell College

Leonard Presby
William Paterson University

W. N. Pruitt
South Carolina State University

Narseeyappa Rajanikanth
Mississippi Valley State University

Elizabeth L. Rankin
Centenary College of Louisiana

Tim Raynor
Albertus Magnus College

Carolyn Renier
Pellissippi State Tech Community College

Ronny Richardson
Southern Polytechnic State University

Leonard E. Ross
California State University, Pomona

Probir Roy
University of Missouri, Kansas City

Randall K. Russell
Yavapai College

Alan Safer
California State University, Long Beach

David Satava
University of Houston, Victoria

Richard W. Schrader
Bellarmine University

Larry Seifert
Webster University

John Seydel
Arkansas State University

Philip Shaw
Fairfield University

Jim Shi
Robinson College of Business
Georgia State University

Robert Simoneau
Keene State College

Harvey A. Singer
George Mason University

Donald R. Smith
Monmouth University

Toni M. Somers
Wayne State University

Clifford Sowell
Berea College

Keith Starcher
Indiana Wesleyan University

William Stein
Texas A&M University

Jason Stine
Troy University

William Struning
Seton Hall University

Timothy S. Sullivan
Southern Illinois University, Edwardsville

Peter Wibawa Sutanto
Prairie View A&M University

Lee Tangedahk
University of Montana

Sudhir Thakur
California State University, Sacramento

Alexander Thomson
Schoolcraft College

Suzanne Tilleman
Montana State University–Northern

Daniel Tschopp
Daemen College (NY)

Sushila Umashankar
University of Arizona

Jack Vaughn
University of Texas, El Paso

Dave Vinson
Pellissippi State Community College

John Vogt
Newman University

Geoffrey L. Wallace
University of Wisconsin, Madison

Michael Wiemann
Metro Community Colleges

Charles Wilf
Duquesne University

John Wiorkowski
University of Texas, Dallas

Joyce A. Zadzilka
Morrisville State College

Guoqiang Peter Zhang
Georgia Southern University

Zhe George Zhang
Western Washington University

Deborah G. Ziegler
Hannibal-LaGrange College

Chapter 1

Data and Statistics

Contents

Statistics in Practice:
Bloomberg Businessweek

1.1 Applications in Business and Economics
- Accounting
- Finance
- Marketing
- Production
- Economics
- Information Systems

1.2 Data
- Elements, Variables, and Observations
- Scales of Measurement
- Categorical and Quantitative Data
- Cross-Sectional and Time Series Data

1.3 Data Sources
- Existing Sources
- Observational Study
- Experiment
- Time and Cost Issues
- Data Acquisition Errors

1.4 Descriptive Statistics

1.5 Statistical Inference

1.6 Statistical Analysis Using Microsoft Excel
- Data Sets and Excel Worksheets
- Using Excel for Statistical Analysis

1.7 Analytics

1.8 Big Data and Data Mining

1.9 Ethical Guidelines for Statistical Practice

Summary 24
Glossary 24
Supplementary Exercises 25

Available in the Cengage eBook:
Appendix: Getting Started with R and RStudio
Appendix: Basic Data Manipulation in R

Learning Objectives

After completing this chapter, you will be able to

LO 1 Identify the elements, variables, and observations in a data set.

LO 2 Identify categorical, quantitative, cross-sectional, and time-series data and their scale of measurement.

LO 3 Identify and create descriptive statistics for a data set.

LO 4 Distinguish between a population and a sample and identify the population being studied.

LO 5 Distinguish between data generated from a survey versus an experiment and when each is appropriate.

LO 6 Describe the data and sources of data that might be needed to answer a question.

LO 7 Make an inference based on descriptive statistics.

Statistics in Practice

Bloomberg Businessweek*

New York, New York

Bloomberg Businessweek is one of the most widely read business magazines in the world. Along with feature articles on current topics, the magazine contains articles on international business, economic analysis, information processing, and science and technology. Information in the feature articles and the regular sections helps readers stay abreast of current developments and assess the impact of those developments on business and economic conditions.

Most issues of *Bloomberg Businessweek* provide an in-depth report on a topic of current interest. Often, the in-depth reports contain statistical facts and summaries that help the reader understand the business and economic information. Examples of articles and reports include the impact of businesses moving important work to cloud computing, the crisis facing the U.S. Postal Service, and why the debt crisis is even worse than we think. In addition, *Bloomberg Businessweek* provides a variety of statistics about the state of the economy, including production indexes, stock prices, mutual funds, and interest rates.

Bloomberg Businessweek also uses statistics and statistical information in managing its own business. For example, an annual survey of subscribers helps the company learn about subscriber demographics, reading habits, likely purchases, lifestyles, and so on. *Bloomberg Businessweek* managers use statistical summaries from the survey to provide better services to subscribers and advertisers. One North American subscriber survey indicated that 64% of *Bloomberg Businessweek* subscribers are involved with computer purchases at work. Such statistics alert *Bloomberg Businessweek* managers to subscriber interest in articles about new developments in computers. The results of the subscriber survey are also made available to potential advertisers. The high percentage of subscribers involved with computer purchases at work would be an incentive for a computer manufacturer to consider advertising in *Bloomberg Businessweek*.

Bloomberg Businessweek *uses statistical facts and summaries in many of its articles. AP Images/Weng lei-Imaginechina*

In this chapter, we discuss the types of data available for statistical analysis and describe how the data are obtained. We introduce descriptive statistics and statistical inference as ways of converting data into meaningful and easily interpreted statistical information.

*The authors are indebted to Charlene Trentham, Research Manager, for providing this Statistics in Practice.

Frequently, we see the following types of statements on websites, in newspapers, and in magazines:

- When 544 U.S. college students and recent graduates were recently asked by the Generation Lab what they would miss if they worked remotely, 74% cited the office community and 41% said mentoring (*Harvard Business Review*, January-February, 2023).
- U.S. stocks rose Friday but finished the week with losses. The S&P 500, Nasdaq, and Dow lost 3.3%, 5.6%, and 1.4%, respectively, this week (*The Wall Street Journal*, Saturday, November 5–6, 2022).
- Founded in 2003 in Silicon Valley as a platform for professional networking, and purchased in 2016 by Microsoft for $26 billion, it (LinkedIn) has become a fixture of corporate cyberspace, with more than 800 million registered users worldwide (*The Economist*, December 24, 2022).

- The number of built-to-rent homes, single-family homes constructed expressly for the purpose of renting, increased by 30% from 2019 to 2020 (*The New York Times*, October 24, 2021).
- Americans say they need $1.25 million to retire comfortably, a 20% jump from 2021, according to a recent Northwestern Mutual Poll (*The Wall Street Journal*, December 6, 2022).

The numerical facts in the preceding statements—544, 74%, 41%, 3.3%, 5.6%, 1.4%, $26 billion, 800 million, 30%, $1.25 million, and 20%—are called **statistics**. In this usage, the term *statistics* refers to numerical facts such as averages, medians, percentages, and maximums that help us understand a variety of business and economic situations. However, as you will see, the subject of statistics involves much more than numerical facts. In a broader sense, statistics is the art and science of collecting, analyzing, presenting, and interpreting data. Particularly in business and economics, the information provided by collecting, analyzing, presenting, and interpreting data gives managers and decision makers a better understanding of the business and economic environment and thus enables them to make more informed and better decisions. In this text, we emphasize the use of statistics for business and economic decision making.

Chapter 1 begins with some illustrations of the applications of statistics in business and economics. In Section 1.2 we define the term *data* and introduce the concept of a data set. This section also introduces key terms such as *variables* and *observations,* discusses the difference between quantitative and categorical data, and illustrates the uses of cross-sectional and time series data. Section 1.3 discusses how data can be obtained from existing sources or through survey and experimental studies designed to obtain new data. The uses of data in developing descriptive statistics and in making statistical inferences are described in Sections 1.4 and 1.5. The last four sections of Chapter 1 provide the role of the computer in statistical analysis, an introduction to business analytics and the role statistics plays in it, an introduction to big data and data mining, and a discussion of ethical guidelines for statistical practice.

1.1 Applications in Business and Economics

In today's global business and economic environment, anyone can access vast amounts of statistical information. The most successful managers and decision makers understand the information and know how to use it effectively. In this section, we provide examples that illustrate some of the uses of statistics in business and economics.

Accounting

Public accounting firms use statistical sampling procedures when conducting audits for their clients. For instance, suppose an accounting firm wants to determine whether the amount of accounts receivable shown on a client's balance sheet fairly represents the actual amount of accounts receivable. Usually the large number of individual accounts receivable makes reviewing and validating every account too time-consuming and expensive. As common practice in such situations, the audit staff selects a subset of the accounts called a sample. After reviewing the accuracy of the sampled accounts, the auditors draw a conclusion as to whether the accounts receivable amount shown on the client's balance sheet is acceptable.

Finance

Financial analysts use a variety of statistical information to guide their investment recommendations. In the case of stocks, analysts review financial data such as price/earnings ratios and dividend yields. By comparing the information for an individual stock with information about the stock market averages, an analyst can begin to draw a conclusion as to whether the stock is a good investment. For example, the average dividend yield for the S&P 500 companies for 2021 was 1.29%. Over the same period, the average dividend yield for Microsoft was 0.81% (*Yahoo Finance*). In this case, the statistical information on dividend yield indicates a lower dividend yield for Microsoft than the average dividend yield for the S&P 500 companies. This and other information about Microsoft would help the analyst make an informed buy, sell, or hold recommendation for Microsoft stock.

Marketing

Electronic scanners at retail checkout counters collect data for a variety of marketing research applications. For example, data suppliers such as The Nielsen Company and IRI purchase point-of-sale scanner data from grocery stores, process the data, and then sell statistical summaries of the data to manufacturers. Manufacturers spend hundreds of thousands of dollars per product category to obtain this type of scanner data. Manufacturers also purchase data and statistical summaries on promotional activities such as special pricing and the use of in-store displays. Brand managers can review the scanner statistics and the promotional activity statistics to gain a better understanding of the relationship between promotional activities and sales. Such analyses often prove helpful in establishing future marketing strategies for the various products.

Production

Today's emphasis on quality makes quality control an important application of statistics in production. A variety of statistical quality control charts are used to monitor the output of a production process. In particular, an x-bar chart can be used to monitor the average output. Suppose, for example, that a machine fills containers with 12 ounces of a soft drink. Periodically, a production worker selects a sample of containers and computes the average number of ounces in the sample. This average, or x-bar value, is plotted on an x-bar chart. A plotted value above the chart's upper control limit indicates overfilling, and a plotted value below the chart's lower control limit indicates underfilling. The process is termed "in control" and allowed to continue as long as the plotted x-bar values fall between the chart's upper and lower control limits. Properly interpreted, an x-bar chart can help determine when adjustments are necessary to correct a production process.

Economics

Economists frequently provide forecasts about the future of the economy or some aspect of it. They use a variety of statistical information in making such forecasts. For instance, in forecasting inflation rates, economists use statistical information on such indicators as the Producer Price Index, the unemployment rate, and manufacturing capacity utilization. Often these statistical indicators are entered into computerized forecasting models that predict inflation rates.

Information Systems

Information systems administrators are responsible for the day-to-day operation of an organization's computer networks. A variety of statistical information helps administrators assess the performance of computer networks, including local area networks (LANs), wide area networks (WANs), network segments, intranets, and other data communication systems. Statistics such as the mean number of users on the system, the proportion of time any component of the system is down, and the proportion of bandwidth utilized at various times of the day, are examples of statistical information that help the system administrator better understand and manage the computer network.

Applications of statistics such as those described in this section are an integral part of this text. Such examples provide an overview of the breadth of statistical applications. To supplement these examples, practitioners in the fields of business and economics provided chapter-opening Statistics in Practice articles that introduce the material covered in each chapter. The Statistics in Practice applications show the importance of statistics in a wide variety of business and economic situations.

1.2 Data

Data are the facts and figures collected, analyzed, and summarized for presentation and interpretation. All the data collected in a particular study are referred to as the **data set** for the study. Table 1.1 shows a data set containing information for 60 nations that participate in the World Trade Organization (WTO). The WTO encourages the free flow of international trade and provides a forum for resolving trade disputes.

Elements, Variables, and Observations

Elements are the entities on which data are collected. Each nation listed in Table 1.1 is an element with the nation or element name shown in the first column. With 60 nations, the data set contains 60 elements.

A **variable** is a characteristic of interest for the elements. The data set in Table 1.1 includes the following five variables:

- WTO Status: The nation's membership status in the World Trade Organization; this can be either as a member or as an observer.
- Per Capita Gross Domestic Product (GDP) ($): The total market value ($) of all goods and services produced by the nation divided by the number of people in the nation; this is commonly used to compare economic productivity of the nations.
- Fitch Rating: The nation's sovereign credit rating as appraised by the Fitch Group;[1] the credit ratings range from a high of AAA to a low of F and can be modified by + or −.
- Fitch Outlook: An indication of the direction the credit rating is likely to move over the upcoming two years; the outlook can be negative, stable, or positive.

Measurements collected on each variable for every element in a study provide the data. The set of measurements obtained for a particular element is called an **observation**. Referring to Table 1.1, we see that the first observation (Armenia) contains the following measurements: Member, 4,267, B+, and Stable. The second observation (Australia) contains the following measurements: Member, 51,812, AAA, Negative, and so on. A data set with 60 elements contains 60 observations.

Scales of Measurement

Data collection requires one of the following scales of measurement: nominal, ordinal, interval, or ratio. The scale of measurement determines the amount of information contained in the data and indicates the most appropriate data summarization and statistical analyses.

When the data for a variable consist of labels or names used to identify an attribute of the element, the scale of measurement is considered a **nominal scale**. For example, referring to the data in Table 1.1, the scale of measurement for the WTO Status variable is nominal because the data "member" and "observer" are labels used to identify the status category for the nation. In cases where the scale of measurement is nominal, a numerical code as well as a nonnumerical label may be used. For example, to facilitate data collection and to prepare the data for entry into a computer database, we might use a numerical code for the WTO Status variable by letting 1 denote a member nation in the World Trade Organization and 2 denote an observer nation. The scale of measurement is nominal even though the data appear as numerical values.

The scale of measurement for a variable is considered an **ordinal scale** if the data exhibit the properties of nominal data and in addition, the order or rank of the data is meaningful. For example, referring to the data in Table 1.1, the scale of measurement for the Fitch Rating is ordinal, because the rating labels which range from AAA to F can be rank ordered from best credit rating AAA to poorest credit rating F. The rating letters provide

[1]The Fitch Group is one of three nationally recognized statistical rating organizations designated by the U.S. Securities and Exchange Commission. The other two are Standard and Poor's and Moody's investor service.

DATA*file*

nations

Data sets such as nations are available on the companion site for this title.

Table 1.1 Data Set for 60 Nations in the World Trade Organization

Nation	WTO Status	Per Capita GDP ($)	Fitch Rating	Fitch Outlook
Armenia	Member	4,267	B+	Stable
Australia	Member	51,812	AAA	Negative
Austria	Member	48,328	AA+	Stable
Azerbaijan	Observer	4,214	BB+	Stable
Bahrain	Member	28,608	B+	Stable
Belgium	Member	44,594	AA−	Negative
Brazil	Member	6,797	BB−	Negative
Bulgaria	Member	9,976	BBB	Positive
Canada	Member	43,258	AA+	Stable
Cape Verde	Member	43,258	B−	Stable
Chile	Member	13,232	A−	Stable
China	Member	10,500	A+	Stable
Colombia	Member	5,333	BBB−	Negative
CoStable Rica	Member	12,077	B	Negative
Croatia	Member	13,828	BBB−	Stable
Cyprus	Member	26,624	BBB−	Stable
Czech Republic	Member	22,932	AA−	Stable
Denmark	Member	61,063	AAA	Stable
Ecuador	Member	5,600	B−	Stable
Egypt	Member	5,600	B+	Stable
El Salvador	Member	3,799	B−	Negative
Estonia	Member	23,027	AA−	Stable
France	Member	39,030	AA	Negative
Georgia	Member	4,279	BB	Negative
Germany	Member	46,208	AAA	Stable
Hungary	Member	15,899	BBB	Stable
Iceland	Member	59,270	A	Negative
Ireland	Member	85,268	A+	Stable
Israel	Member	43,611	A+	Stable
Italy	Member	31,676	BBB−	Stable
Japan	Member	39,539	A	Negative
Kazakhstan	Member	9,056	BBB	Stable
Kenya	Member	1,838	B+	Negative
Latvia	Member	17,620	A−	Stable
Iraq	Observer	4,157	B−	Stable
Lithuania	Member	19,998	A	Stable
Malaysia	Member	10,402	BBB+	Stable
Mexico	Member	8,347	BBB−	Stable
Peru	Member	6,127	BBB+	Stable
Philippines	Member	3,299	BBB	Negative
Poland	Member	15,656	A−	Stable
Portugal	Member	22,437	BBB	Positive
South Korea	Member	1,805	AA−	Stable
Romania	Member	12,896	BBB−	Negative
Russia	Member	12,896	BBB	Stable
Rwanda	Member	798	B+	Stable
Serbia	Observer	7,666	BB+	Stable
Singapore	Member	59,798	AAA	Stable
Slovakia	Member	19,157	A	Negative

Slovenia	Member	25,517	A	Stable
South Africa	Member	5,091	BB−	Negative
Spain	Member	27,063	A−	Stable
Sweden	Member	52,259	AAA	Stable
Switzerland	Member	87,097	AAA	Stable
Thailand	Member	7,189	BBB+	Stable
Turkey	Member	8,538	BB−	Stable
United Kingdom	Member	40,285	AA−	Negative
Uruguay	Member	15,438	BBB−	Negative
United States	Member	63,544	AAA	Negative
Vietnam	Member	2,786	BB	Positive

the labels similar to nominal data, but in addition, the data can also be ranked or ordered based on the credit rating, which makes the measurement scale ordinal. Ordinal data can also be recorded by a numerical code, for example, your class rank in school.

The scale of measurement for a variable is an **interval scale** if the data have all the properties of ordinal data and the interval between values is expressed in terms of a fixed unit of measure. Interval data are always numeric. College admission SAT scores are an example of interval-scaled data. For example, three students with SAT math scores of 620, 550, and 470 can be ranked or ordered in terms of best performance to poorest performance in math. In addition, the differences between the scores are meaningful. For instance, student 1 scored $620 - 550 = 70$ points more than student 2, while student 2 scored $550 - 470 = 80$ points more than student 3.

The scale of measurement for a variable is a **ratio scale** if the data have all the properties of interval data and the ratio of two values is meaningful. Variables such as distance, height, weight, and time use the ratio scale of measurement. This scale requires that a zero value be included to indicate that nothing exists for the variable at the zero point. For example, consider the cost of an automobile. A zero value for the cost would indicate that the automobile has no cost and is free. In addition, if we compare the cost of $30,000 for one automobile to the cost of $15,000 for a second automobile, the ratio property shows that the first automobile is $30,000/$15,000 = 2 times, or twice, the cost of the second automobile.

Categorical and Quantitative Data

Data can be classified as either categorical or quantitative. Data that can be grouped by specific categories are referred to as **categorical data**. Categorical data use either the nominal or ordinal scale of measurement. Data that use numeric values to indicate how much or how many are referred to as **quantitative data**. Quantitative data are obtained using either the interval or ratio scale of measurement.

The statistical method appropriate for summarizing data depends upon whether the data are categorical or quantitative.

A **categorical variable** is a variable with categorical data, and a **quantitative variable** is a variable with quantitative data. The statistical analysis appropriate for a particular variable depends upon whether the variable is categorical or quantitative. If the variable is categorical, the statistical analysis is limited. We can summarize categorical data by counting the number of observations in each category or by computing the proportion of the observations in each category. However, even when the categorical data are identified by a numerical code, arithmetic operations such as addition, subtraction, multiplication, and division do not provide meaningful results. Section 2.1 discusses ways of summarizing categorical data.

Arithmetic operations provide meaningful results for quantitative variables. For example, quantitative data may be added and then divided by the number of observations to compute the average value. This average is usually meaningful and easily interpreted. In general, more alternatives for statistical analysis are possible when data are quantitative. Section 2.2 and Chapter 3 provide ways of summarizing quantitative data.

Cross-Sectional and Time Series Data

For purposes of statistical analysis, distinguishing between cross-sectional data and time series data is important. **Cross-sectional data** are data collected at the same or approximately the same point in time. The data in Table 1.1 are cross-sectional because they describe the five variables for the 60 World Trade Organization nations at the same point in time. **Time series data** are data collected over several time periods. For example, the time series in Figure 1.1 shows the U.S. average price per gallon of conventional regular gasoline from 2018 to 2022. The lowest average price was $1.72 in April of 2020. This occurred early in the COVID-19 pandemic when travel was sharply curtailed. The average price per gallon increased after April 2020 to a peak of $4.76 per gallon in June 2022, and then declined the last half of 2022.

Graphs of time series data are frequently found in business and economic publications. Such graphs help analysts understand what happened in the past, identify any trends over time, and project future values for the time series. The graphs of time series data can take on a variety of forms, as shown in Figure 1.2. With a little study, these graphs are usually easy to understand and interpret. For example, Panel (A) in Figure 1.2 is a graph that shows the Dow Jones Industrial Average Index from January 2012 to December 2022. The price of the index exhibits a general upward trend with a precipitous drop in early 2020, followed by a climb to a peak of 36,338 in December 2021.

The graph in Panel (B) shows the net income of McDonald's Inc. from 2012 to 2021. The chart shows that net income was lower in the period 2014–2016, then increased from 2017 to 2019 before dropping in 2020. The peak net income over this 10-year period occurred in 2021.

Panel (C) shows the time series for the occupancy rate of hotels in South Florida over a one-year period. The highest occupancy rates, 95% and 98%, occur during the months of February and March when the climate of South Florida is attractive to tourists. In fact,

Figure 1.1 U.S. Average Price per Gallon for Conventional Regular Gasoline

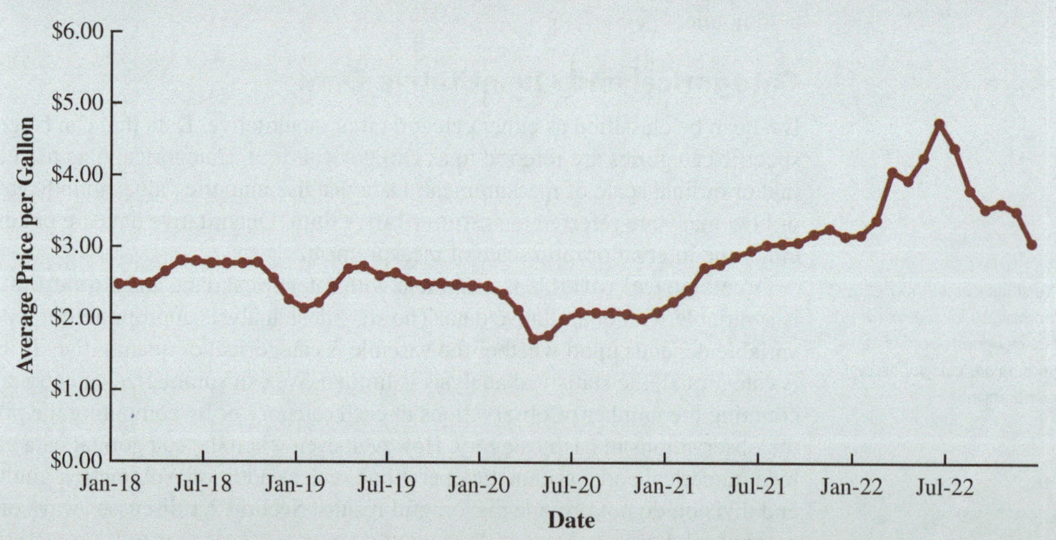

Source: *Energy Information Administration, U.S. Department of Energy.*

Figure 1.2 A Variety of Graphs of Time Series Data

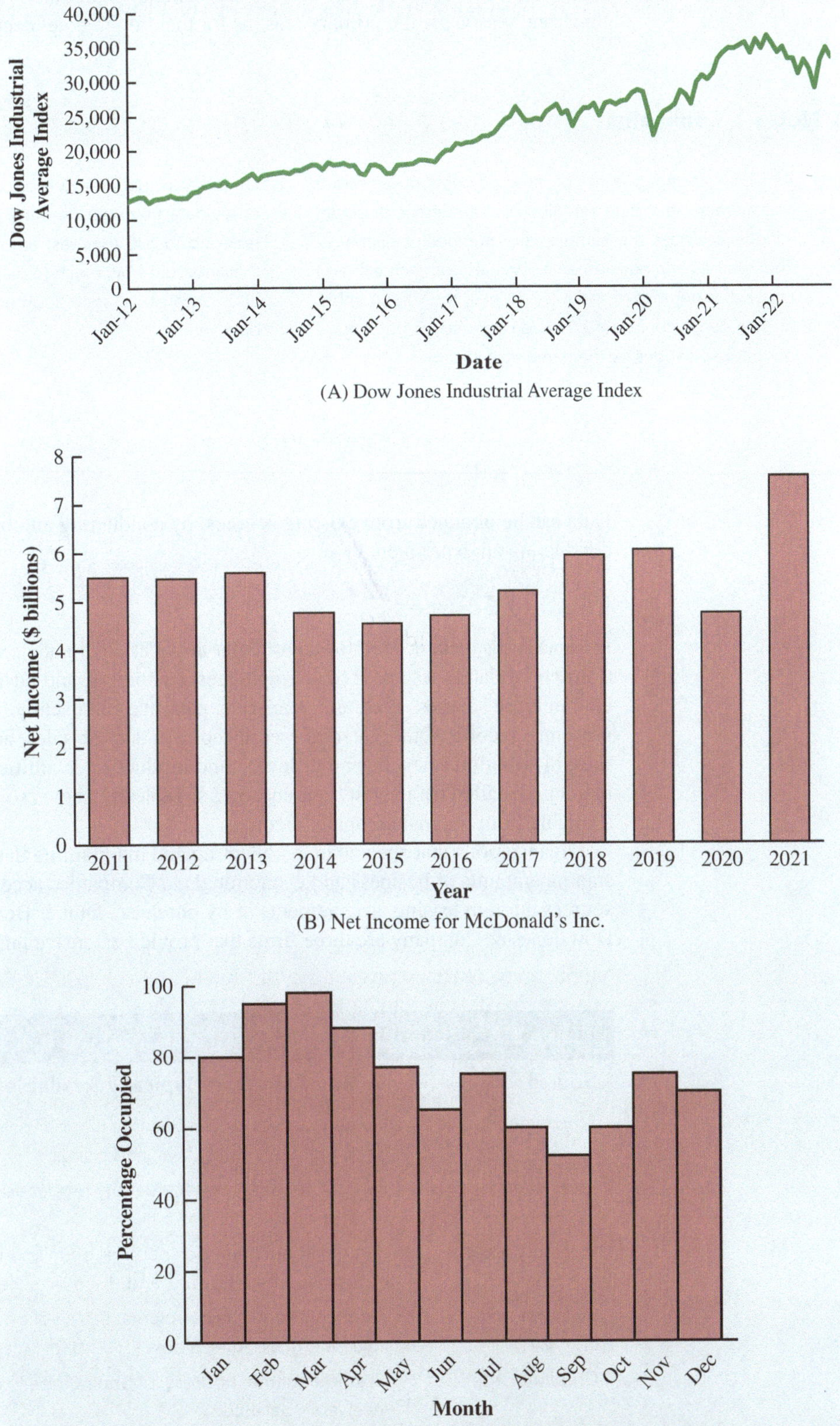

(A) Dow Jones Industrial Average Index

(B) Net Income for McDonald's Inc.

(C) Occupancy Rate of South Florida Hotels

January to April of each year is typically the high-occupancy season for South Florida hotels. On the other hand, note the low occupancy rates during the months of August to October, with the lowest occupancy rate of 50% occurring in September. High temperatures and the hurricane season are the primary reasons for the drop in hotel occupancy during this period.

Notes + Comments

1. An observation is the set of measurements obtained for one element in a data set. Hence, the number of observations is always the same as the number of elements. The number of measurements obtained for each element equals the number of variables. Hence, the total number of data items can be determined by multiplying the number of observations by the number of variables.
2. Quantitative data may be discrete or continuous. Quantitative data that measure how many (e.g., number of calls received in five minutes) are discrete. Quantitative data that measure how much (e.g., weight or time) are continuous because no separation occurs between the possible data values.

1.3 Data Sources

Data can be obtained from existing sources, by conducting an observational study, or by conducting an experiment.

Existing Sources

In some cases, data needed for a particular application already exist. Companies maintain a variety of databases about their employees, customers, and business operations. Data on employee salaries, ages, and years of experience can usually be obtained from internal personnel records. Other internal records contain data on sales, advertising expenditures, distribution costs, inventory levels, and production quantities. Most companies also maintain detailed data about their customers. Table 1.2 shows some of the data commonly available from internal company records.

Organizations that specialize in collecting and maintaining data make available substantial amounts of business and economic data. Companies access these external data sources through leasing arrangements or by purchase. Dun & Bradstreet, Bloomberg, and Dow Jones & Company are three firms that provide extensive business database services

Table 1.2 Examples of Data Available from Internal Company Records

Source	Some of the Data Typically Available
Employee records	Name, address, Social Security number, salary, number of vacation days, number of sick days, and bonus
Production records	Part or product number, quantity produced, direct labor cost, and materials cost
Inventory records	Part or product number, number of units on hand, reorder level, economic order quantity, and discount schedule
Sales records	Product number, sales volume, sales volume by region, and sales volume by customer type
Credit records	Customer name, address, phone number, credit limit, and accounts receivable balance
Customer profile	Age, gender, income level, household size, address, and preferences

Table 1.3 Examples of Data Available from Selected Government Agencies

Government Agency	Some of the Data Available
Census Bureau	Population data, number of households, and household income
Federal Reserve Board	Data on the money supply, installment credit, exchange rates, and discount rates
Office of Management and Budget	Data on revenue, expenditures, and debt of the federal government
Department of Commerce	Data on business activity, value of shipments by industry, level of profits by industry, and growing and declining industries
Bureau of Labor Statistics	Consumer spending, hourly earnings, unemployment rate, safety records, and international statistics
DATA.GOV	More than 250,000 data sets including agriculture, consumer, education, health, and manufacturing data

to clients. The Nielsen Company and IRI built successful businesses collecting and processing data that they sell to advertisers and product manufacturers.

Data are also available from a variety of industry associations and special interest organizations. The U.S. Travel Association maintains travel-related information such as the number of tourists and travel expenditures by states. Such data would be of interest to firms and individuals in the travel industry. The Graduate Management Admission Council maintains data on test scores, student characteristics, and graduate management education programs. Most of the data from these types of sources are available to qualified users at a modest cost.

The Internet is an important source of data and statistical information. Almost all companies maintain websites that provide general information about the company as well as data on sales, number of employees, number of products, product prices, and product specifications. In addition, a number of companies now specialize in making information available over the Internet. As a result, one can obtain access to stock quotes, meal prices at restaurants, salary data, and an almost infinite variety of information.

Government agencies are another important source of existing data. For instance, the website DATA.GOV was launched by the U.S. government in 2009 to make it easier for the public to access data collected by the U.S. federal government. The DATA.GOV website includes over 250,000 data sets from a variety of U.S. federal departments and agencies, but there are many other federal agencies that maintain their own websites and data repositories. Table 1.3 lists selected governmental agencies and some of the data they provide. Figure 1.3 shows the home-page for the DATA.GOV website. Many state and local governments are also now providing data sets online. As examples, the states of California and Texas maintain open data portals at data.ca.gov and data.texas.gov, respectively. New York City's open data website is opendata.cityofnewyork.us and the city of Cincinnati, Ohio, is at data.cincinnati-oh.gov.

Observational Study

In an *observational study* we simply observe what is happening in a particular situation, record data on one or more variables of interest, and conduct a statistical analysis of the resulting data. For example, researchers might observe a randomly selected group of customers that enter a Walmart supercenter to collect data on variables such as the length of time the customer spends shopping, the gender of the customer, and the amount spent. Statistical analysis of the data may help management determine how factors such as the length of time shopping and the gender of the customer affect the amount spent.

Figure 1.3 DATA.GOV Homepage

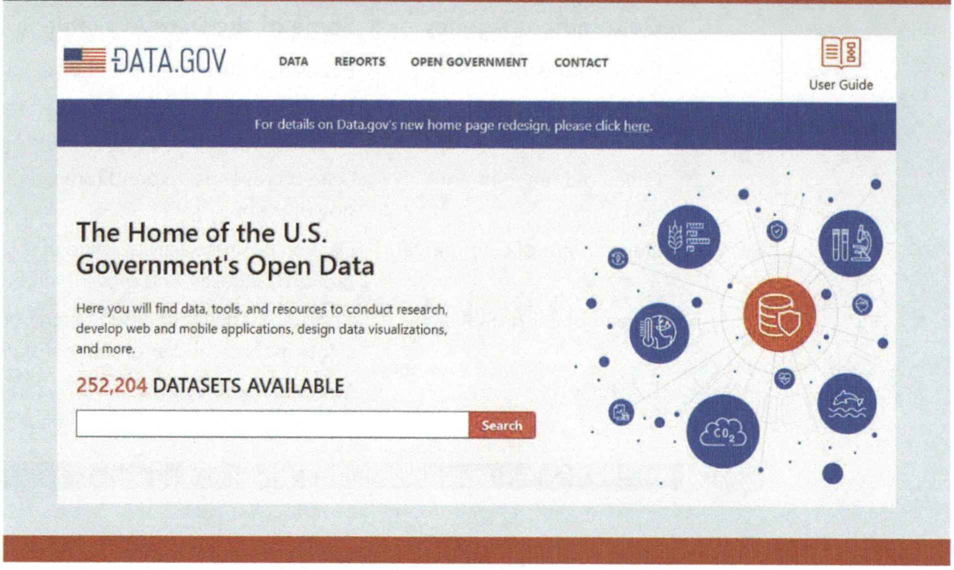

U.S. BUREAU OF LABOR STATISTICS HOMEPAGE

As another example of an observational study, suppose that researchers were interested in investigating the relationship between the gender of the CEO for a *Fortune* 500 company and the performance of the company as measured by the return on equity (ROE). To obtain data, the researchers selected a sample of companies and recorded the gender of the CEO and the ROE for each company. Statistical analysis of the data can help determine the relationship between performance of the company and the gender of the CEO. This example is an observational study because the researchers had no control over the gender of the CEO or the ROE at each of the companies that were sampled.

Surveys and public opinion polls are two other examples of commonly used observational studies. The data provided by these types of studies simply enable us to observe opinions of the respondents. For example, the New York State legislature commissioned a telephone survey in which residents were asked if they would support or oppose an increase in the state gasoline tax in order to provide funding for bridge and highway repairs. Statistical analysis of the survey results will assist the state legislature in determining if it should introduce a bill to increase gasoline taxes.

Experiment

The key difference between an observational study and an experiment is that an experiment is conducted under controlled conditions. As a result, the data obtained from a well-designed experiment can often provide more information as compared to the data obtained from existing sources or by conducting an observational study. For example, suppose a pharmaceutical company would like to learn about how a new drug it has developed affects blood pressure. To obtain data about how the new drug affects blood pressure, researchers selected a sample of individuals. Different groups of individuals are given different dosage levels of the new drug, and before and after data on blood pressure are collected for each group. Statistical analysis of the data can help determine how the new drug affects blood pressure.

In Chapter 13, we discuss statistical methods appropriate for analyzing the data from an experiment.

The types of experiments we deal with in statistics often begin with the identification of a particular variable of interest. Then one or more other variables are identified and controlled so that data can be obtained about how the other variables influence the primary variable of interest.

Time and Cost Issues

Anyone wanting to use data and statistical analysis as aids to decision making must be aware of the time and cost required to obtain the data. The use of existing data sources is desirable when data must be obtained in a relatively short period of time. If important data are not readily available from an existing source, the additional time and cost involved in obtaining the data must be taken into account. In all cases, the decision maker should consider the contribution of the statistical analysis to the decision-making process. The cost of data acquisition and the subsequent statistical analysis should not exceed the savings generated by using the information to make a better decision.

Data Acquisition Errors

Managers should always be aware of the possibility of data errors in statistical studies. Using erroneous data can be worse than not using any data at all. An error in data acquisition occurs whenever the data value obtained is not equal to the true or actual value that would be obtained with a correct procedure. Such errors can occur in a number of ways. For example, an interviewer might make a recording error, such as a transposition in writing the age of a 24-year-old person as 42, or the person answering an interview question might misinterpret the question and provide an incorrect response.

Experienced data analysts take great care in collecting and recording data to ensure that errors are not made. Special procedures can be used to check for internal consistency of the data. For instance, such procedures would indicate that the analyst should review the accuracy of data for a respondent shown to be 22 years of age but reporting 20 years of work experience. Data analysts also review data with unusually large and small values, called outliers, which are candidates for possible data errors.

In Chapter 3, we present some of the methods statisticians use to identify outliers.

Errors often occur during data acquisition. Blindly using any data that happen to be available or using data that were acquired with little care can result in misleading information and bad decisions. Thus, taking steps to acquire accurate data can help ensure reliable and valuable decision-making information.

1.4 Descriptive Statistics

Most of the statistical information in the media, company reports, and other publications consists of data that are summarized and presented in a form that is easy for the reader to understand. Such summaries of data, which may be tabular, graphical, or numerical, are referred to as **descriptive statistics**.

Refer to the data set in Table 1.1 showing data for 60 nations that participate in the World Trade Organization. Methods of descriptive statistics can be used to summarize these data. For example, consider the variable Fitch Outlook, which indicates the direction the nation's credit rating is likely to move over the next two years. The Fitch Outlook is recorded as being negative, stable, or positive. A tabular summary of the data showing the number of nations with each of the Fitch Outlook ratings is shown in Table 1.4. A graphical summary of the same data, called a bar chart, is shown in Figure 1.4. These types of summaries make the data easier to interpret. Referring to Table 1.4 and

Table 1.4 Frequencies and Percent Frequencies for the Fitch Credit Rating Outlook of 60 Nations

Fitch Outlook	Frequency	Percent Frequency (%)
Positive	3	5.0
Stable	39	65.0
Negative	18	30.0

Figure 1.4 Bar Chart for the Fitch Credit Rating Outlook for 60 Nations

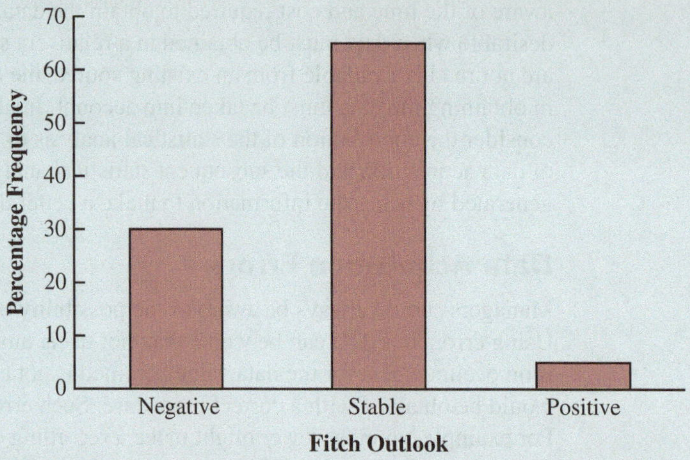

Figure 1.4, we can see that the majority of Fitch Outlook credit ratings are stable, with 65% of the nations having this rating. More nations have a negative outlook (30%) than a positive outlook (5%).

A graphical summary of the data for quantitative variable Per Capita GDP in Table 1.1, called a histogram, is provided in Figure 1.5. Using the histogram, it is easy to see that Per Capita GDP for the 60 nations ranges from $0 to $90,000, with the highest concentration between $0 and $10,000. There are no countries with Per Capita

Figure 1.5 Histogram of Per Capita GDP for 60 Nations

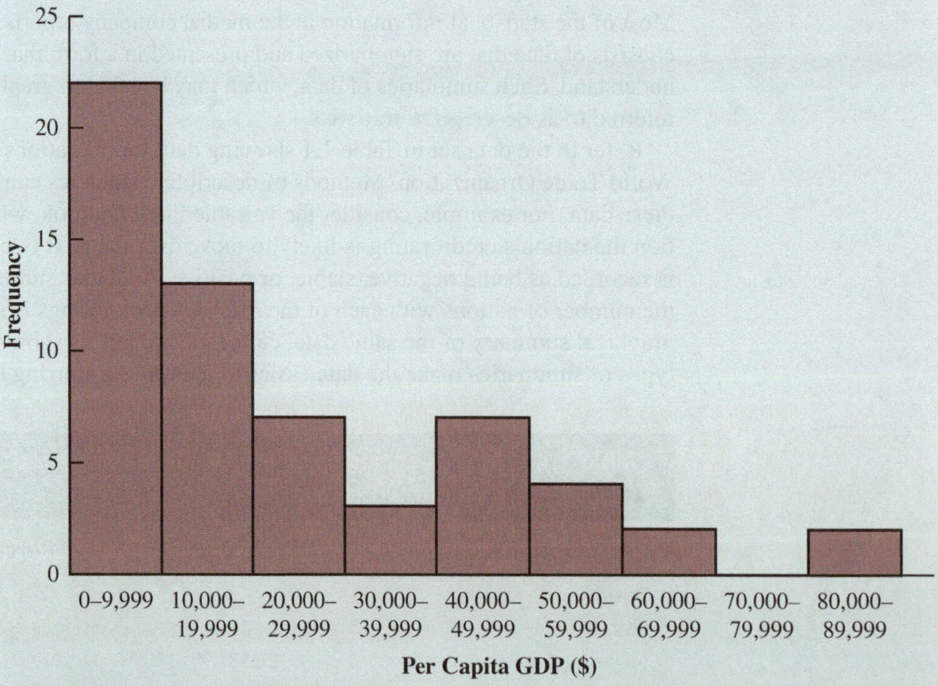

GDP in the range of \$70,000 to \$79,999 and two countries with Per Capita GDP over \$80,000.

In addition to tabular and graphical displays, numerical descriptive statistics are used to summarize data. The most common numerical measure is the average, or mean. Using the data on Per Capita GDP for the 60 nations in Table 1.1, we can compute the average by adding Per Capita GDP for all 60 nations and dividing the total by 60. Doing so provides an average Per Capita GDP of \$23,704. This average provides a measure of the central tendency, or central location of the data.

In Chapters 2 and 3, we discuss tabular, graphical, and numerical methods of descriptive statistics.

There is a great deal of interest in effective methods for developing and presenting descriptive statistics.

1.5 Statistical Inference

Many situations require information about a large group of elements (individuals, companies, voters, households, products, customers, and so on). But, because of time, cost, and other considerations, data can be collected from only a small portion of the group. The larger group of elements in a particular study is called the **population**, and the smaller group is called the **sample**. Formally, we use the following definitions:

Population

A population is the set of all elements of interest in a particular study.

Sample

A sample is a subset of the population.

The U.S. government conducts a census every 10 years. Market research firms conduct sample surveys every day.

The process of conducting a survey to collect data for the entire population is called a **census**. The process of conducting a survey to collect data for a sample is called a **sample survey**. As one of its major contributions, statistics uses data from a sample to make estimates and test hypotheses about the characteristics of a population through a process referred to as **statistical inference**.

As an example of statistical inference, let us consider the study conducted by Rogers Industries. Rogers manufactures lithium batteries used in rechargeable electronics such as laptop computers and tablets. In an attempt to increase battery life for its products, Rogers has developed a new solid-state lithium battery that should last longer and be safer to use. In this case, the population is defined as all lithium batteries that could be produced using the new solid-state technology. To evaluate the advantages of the new battery, a sample of 200 batteries manufactured with the new solid-state technology were tested. Data collected from this sample showed the number of hours each battery lasted before needing to be recharged under controlled conditions. See Table 1.5.

Suppose Rogers wants to use the sample data to make an inference about the average hours of battery life for the population of all batteries that could be produced with the new solid-state technology. Adding the 200 values in Table 1.5 and dividing the total by 200 provides the sample average battery life: 18.84 hours. We can use this sample result to estimate that the average lifetime for the batteries in the population is 18.84 hours. Figure 1.6 provides a graphical summary of the statistical inference process for Rogers Industries.

Whenever statisticians use a sample to estimate a population characteristic of interest, they usually provide a statement of the quality, or precision, associated with the estimate. For the Rogers Industries example, the statistician might state that the point estimate of the average battery life is 18.84 hours ± 0.68 hours. Thus, an interval estimate of the average battery life is 18.16 to 19.52 hours. The statistician can also state how confident they are that the interval from 18.16 to 19.52 hours contains the population average.

DATA*file*
rogers

Table 1.5 Hours Until Recharge for a Sample of 200 Batteries for the Rogers Industries Example

Battery Life (hours)									
19.49	18.18	18.65	19.45	19.89	18.94	17.72	18.35	18.66	18.23
19.08	19.92	19.01	18.84	17.73	19.70	18.37	18.69	19.98	18.80
19.11	18.26	19.05	17.89	19.61	18.52	18.10	19.08	18.27	18.29
19.55	18.81	18.68	17.43	20.34	17.73	17.66	18.52	19.90	19.33
18.81	19.12	18.39	19.27	19.43	19.29	19.11	18.96	19.65	18.20
19.18	20.07	18.54	18.37	18.13	18.29	19.11	20.22	18.07	18.91
18.44	19.04	18.88	19.51	18.84	20.98	18.82	19.40	19.00	17.53
18.74	19.04	18.35	19.01	17.54	18.14	19.82	19.23	19.20	20.02
20.14	17.75	18.50	19.85	18.93	19.07	18.83	18.54	17.85	18.51
18.74	18.74	19.06	19.00	18.77	19.12	19.58	18.75	18.67	20.71
18.35	19.42	19.42	19.41	19.85	18.23	18.31	18.44	17.61	19.21
17.71	18.04	19.53	18.87	19.11	19.28	18.55	18.58	17.33	18.75
18.52	19.06	18.54	18.41	19.86	17.24	18.32	19.27	18.34	18.89
18.78	18.88	18.67	18.19	19.07	20.12	17.69	17.92	19.49	19.52
19.91	18.46	18.98	19.18	19.01	18.79	17.90	18.43	18.35	19.02
18.06	19.11	19.40	18.71	18.91	18.95	18.51	19.27	20.39	19.72
17.48	17.49	19.29	18.49	17.93	19.42	19.19	19.46	18.56	18.41
18.24	17.83	18.28	19.51	18.17	18.64	18.57	18.65	18.61	17.97
18.73	19.32	19.37	18.60	19.16	19.44	18.28	19.20	17.88	18.90
19.66	19.00	18.43	19.54	19.15	18.62	19.64	18.87	18.31	19.54

Figure 1.6 The Process of Statistical Inference for the Rogers Industries Example

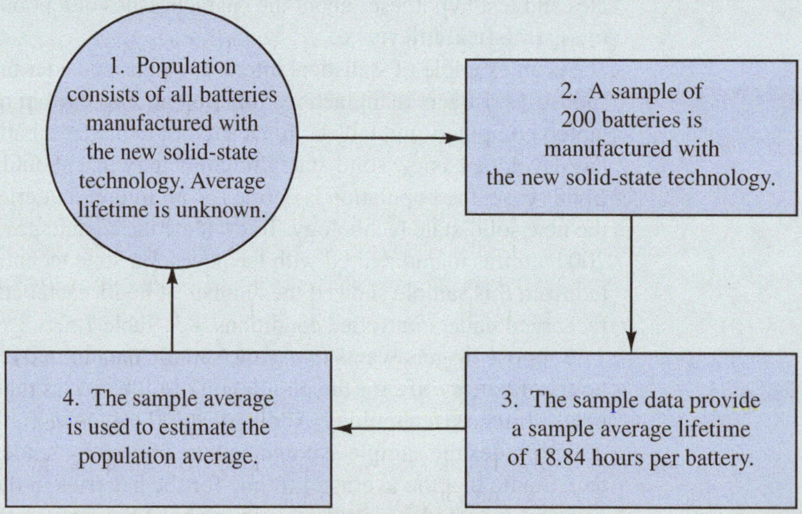

1.6 Statistical Analysis Using Microsoft Excel

Because statistical analysis typically involves working with large amounts of data, computer software is frequently used to conduct the analysis. In this book, we show how statistical analysis can be performed using Microsoft Excel.

We want to emphasize that this book is about statistics; it is not a book about spreadsheets. Our focus is on showing the appropriate statistical procedures for collecting, analyzing, presenting, and interpreting data. Because Excel is widely available in business organizations, you can expect to put the knowledge gained here to use in the setting where you currently, or soon will, work. If, in the process of studying this material, you become more proficient with Excel, so much the better.

We begin most sections with an application scenario in which a statistical procedure is useful. After showing what the statistical procedure is and how it is used, we turn to showing how to implement the procedure using Excel. Thus, you should gain an understanding of what the procedure is, the situation in which it is useful, and how to implement it using the capabilities of Excel.

Data Sets and Excel Worksheets

*To hide rows 15 through 54 of the Excel worksheet, first select rows 15 through 54. Then, right-click and choose the **Hide** option. To redisplay rows 15 through 54, just select rows 14 and 55, right-click, and select the **Unhide** option.*

Data sets are organized in Excel worksheets in much the same way as the data set for the 60 nations that participate in the World Trade Organization that appears in Table 1.1 is organized. Figure 1.7 shows an Excel worksheet for that data set. Note that row 1 and column A contain labels. Cells Bl:El contain the variable names; cells A2:A61 contain the observation names; and cells B2:E61 contain the data that were collected. Displaying a worksheet with this many rows on a single page of a textbook is not practical. In such cases, we will hide selected rows to conserve space. In the Excel worksheet shown in Figure 1.7, we have hidden rows 15 through 54 (observations 14 through 53) to conserve space.

The data are the focus of the statistical analysis. Except for the headings in row 1, each row of the worksheet corresponds to an observation and each column corresponds to a variable. For instance, row 2 of the worksheet contains the data for the first observation, Armenia; row 3 contains the data for the second observation, Australia; row 3 contains the data for the third observation, Austria; and so on. The names in column A provide a

Figure 1.7 Excel Worksheet for the 60 Nations That Participate in the World Trade Organization

Note: Rows 15–54 are hidden.

	A	B	C	D	E	F
1	**Nation**	**WTO Status**	**Per Capita GDP ($)**	**Fitch Rating**	**Fitch Outlook**	
2	Armenia	Member	4,267	B+	Stable	
3	Australia	Member	51,812	AAA	Negative	
4	Austria	Member	48,328	AA+	Stable	
5	Azerbaijan	Observer	4,214	BB+	Stable	
6	Bahrain	Member	28,608	B+	Stable	
7	Belgium	Member	44,594	AA-	Negative	
8	Brazil	Member	6,797	BB-	Negative	
9	Bulgaria	Member	9,976	BBB	Positive	
10	Canada	Member	43,258	AA+	Stable	
11	Cape Verde	Member	43,258	B-	Stable	
12	Chile	Member	13,232	A-	Stable	
13	China	Member	10,500	A+	Stable	
14	Colombia	Member	5,333	BBB-	Negative	
55	Switzerland	Member	87,097	AAA	Stable	
56	Thailand	Member	7,189	BBB+	Stable	
57	Turkey	Member	8,538	BB-	Stable	
58	United Kingdom	Member	40,285	AA-	Negative	
59	Uruguay	Member	15,438	BBB-	Negative	
60	United States	Member	63,544	AAA	Negative	
61	Vietnam	Member	2,786	BB	Positive	
62						
63						

Figure 1.8 Excel Worksheet for the Rogers Industries Data Set

	A	B	C
1	**Battery Life (hours)**		
2	19.49		
3	19.08		
4	19.11		
5	19.55		
6	18.81		
198	18.41		
199	17.97		
200	18.90		
201	19.54		
202			

DATA*file*
rogers

Note: Rows 7–197 are hidden

convenient way to refer to each of the 60 observations in the study. Note that column B of the worksheet contains the data for the variable WTO Status, column C contains the data for the Per Capita GDP ($), and so on.

Suppose now that we want to use Excel to analyze the Rogers Industries data shown in Table 1.5. The data in Table 1.5 are organized into 10 columns with 20 data values in each column so that the data would fit nicely on a single page of the text. Even though the table has several columns, it shows data for only one variable (hours until burnout). In statistical worksheets, it is customary to put all the data for each variable in a single column. Refer to the Excel worksheet shown in Figure 1.8. Note that rows 7 through 197 have been hidden to conserve space.

Using Excel for Statistical Analysis

To separate the discussion of a statistical procedure from the discussion of using Excel to implement the procedure, the material that discusses the use of Excel will usually be set apart in sections with headings such as Using Excel to Construct a Bar Chart and a Pie Chart, and Using Excel to Construct a Frequency Distribution. In using Excel for statistical analysis, four tasks may be needed: Enter/Access Data; Enter Functions and Formulas; Apply Tools; and Editing Options.

Enter/Access Data: Select cell locations for the data and enter the data along with appropriate labels; or open an existing Excel file such as one of the files that accompany the text.

Enter Functions and Formulas: Select cell locations, enter Excel functions and formulas, and provide descriptive labels to identify the results.

Apply Tools: Use Excel's tools for data analysis and presentation.

Editing Options: Edit the results to better identify the output or to create a different type of presentation. For example, when using Excel's chart tools, we can edit the chart that is created by adding, removing, or changing chart elements such as the title, legend, and data labels.

Our approach will be to describe how these tasks are performed each time we use Excel to implement a statistical procedure. It will always be necessary to enter data or open an existing Excel file. But, depending on the complexity of the statistical analysis, only one of the second or third tasks may be needed.

Figure 1.9 Computing the Average Lifetime of Batteries for Rogers Industries Using Excel's Average Function

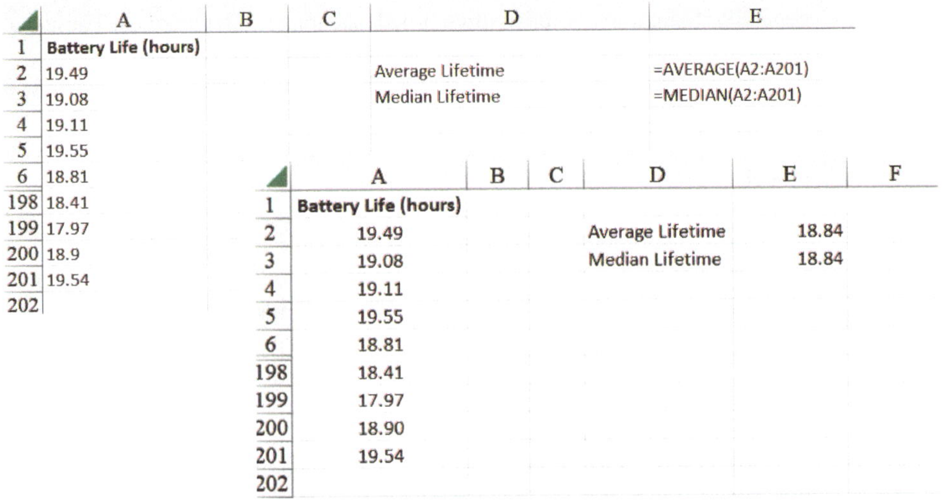

To illustrate how the discussion of Excel will appear throughout the book, we will show how to use Excel's AVERAGE function to compute the average lifetime for the 200 batteries in Table 1.5. Refer to Figure 1.9 as we describe the tasks involved. The worksheet shown in the foreground of Figure 1.9 displays the data for the problem and shows the results of the analysis. It is called the *value worksheet*. The worksheet shown in the background displays the Excel formula used to compute the average lifetime and is called the *formula worksheet*.

DATA*file*
rogers

Enter/Access Data: Open the file *rogers*. The data are in cells A2:A201 and the label is in cell A1.

Enter Functions and Formulas: Excel's AVERAGE function can be used to compute the mean by entering the following formula in cell E2:

=*AVERAGE(A2:A201)*

Similarly, the formula =*MEDIAN(A2:A201)* is entered in cell E3 to compute the median.

To identify the result, the label "Average Lifetime" is entered in cell D2 and the label "Median Lifetime" is entered into cell D3. Note that for this illustration the Apply Tools and Editing Options tasks were not required. The value worksheet shows that the value computed using the AVERAGE function is 18.84 hours and that the value computed using the MEDIAN function is also 18.84 hours.

1.7 Analytics

Because of the dramatic increase in available data, more cost-effective data storage, faster computer processing, and recognition by managers that data can be extremely valuable for understanding customers and business operations, there has been a dramatic increase in data-driven decision making. The broad range of techniques that may be used to support data-driven decisions comprise what has become known as analytics.

We adopt the definition of analytics developed by the Institute for Operations Research and the Management Sciences (INFORMS).

Analytics is the scientific process of transforming data into insights for making better decisions. Analytics is used for data-driven or fact-based decision making, which is often seen as more objective than alternative approaches to decision making. The tools of analytics can aid decision making by creating insights from data, improving our ability to more accurately forecast for planning, helping us quantify risk, and yielding better alternatives through analysis.

Analytics can involve a variety of techniques from simple reports to the most advanced optimization techniques (algorithms for finding the best course of action). Analytics is now generally thought to comprise three broad categories of techniques. These categories are descriptive analytics, predictive analytics, and prescriptive analytics.

Descriptive analytics encompasses the set of analytical techniques that describe what has happened in the past. Examples of these types of techniques are data queries, reports, descriptive statistics, data visualization, data dash boards, and basic what-if spreadsheet models.

Predictive analytics consists of analytical techniques that use models constructed from past data to predict the future or to assess the impact of one variable on another. For example, past data on sales of a product may be used to construct a mathematical model that predicts future sales. Such a model can account for factors such as the growth trajectory and seasonality of the product's sales based on past growth and seasonal patterns. Point-of-sale scanner data from retail outlets may be used by a packaged food manufacturer to help estimate the lift in unit sales associated with coupons or sales events. Survey data and past purchase behavior may be used to help predict the market share of a new product. Each of these is an example of predictive analytics. Linear regression, time series analysis, and forecasting models fall into the category of predictive analytics; these techniques are discussed later in this text. Simulation, which is the use of probability and statistical computer models to better understand risk, also falls under the category of predictive analytics.

Prescriptive analytics differs greatly from descriptive or predictive analytics. What distinguishes prescriptive analytics is that prescriptive models yield a best course of action to take. That is, the output of a prescriptive model is a best decision. Hence, **prescriptive analytics** is the set of analytical techniques that yield a course of action. Optimization models, which generate solutions that maximize or minimize some objective subject to a set of constraints, fall into the category of prescriptive models. The airline industry's use of revenue management is an example of a prescriptive model. The airline industry uses past purchasing data as inputs into a model that recommends the pricing strategy across all flights that will maximize revenue for the company.

How does the study of statistics relate to analytics? Most of the techniques in descriptive and predictive analytics come from probability and statistics. These include descriptive statistics, data visualization, probability and probability distributions, sampling, and predictive modeling, including regression analysis and time series forecasting. Each of these techniques is discussed in this text. The increased use of analytics for data-driven decision making makes it more important than ever for analysts and managers to understand statistics and data analysis. Companies are increasingly seeking data-savvy managers who know how to use descriptive and predictive models to make data-driven decisions.

At the beginning of this section, we mentioned the increased availability of data as one of the drivers of the interest in analytics. In the next section, we discuss this explosion in available data and how it relates to the study of statistics.

1.8 Big Data and Data Mining

With the aid of credit-card readers, bar code scanners, point-of-sale terminals, and online data collection, most organizations obtain large amounts of data on a daily basis. And, even for a small local restaurant that uses touch screen monitors to enter orders and handle billing, the amount of data collected can be substantial. For large retail companies, the sheer volume of data collected is hard to conceptualize, and figuring out how to effectively use these data to improve profitability is a challenge. Mass retailers such as Walmart capture data on 20 to 30 million transactions every day, telecommunication companies such as France Telecom and AT&T generate over 300 million call records per day, and Visa processes 6,800 payment transactions per second or approximately 600 million transactions per day.

In addition to the sheer volume and speed with which companies now collect data, more complicated types of data are now available and are proving to be of great value to businesses. Text data are collected by monitoring what is being said about a company's products or services on social media. Audio data are collected from service calls (on a service call, you will often hear "this call may be monitored for quality control"). Video data are collected by in-store video cameras to analyze shopping behavior. Analyzing information generated by these nontraditional sources is more complicated because of the complex process of transforming the information into data that can be analyzed.

Larger and more complex data sets are now often referred to as **big data**. Although there does not seem to be a universally accepted definition of *big data*, many think of it as a set of data that cannot be managed, processed, or analyzed with commonly available software in a reasonable amount of time. Many data analysts define *big data* by referring to the four V's of data: volume, velocity, variety, and veracity. *Volume* refers to the amount of available data (a typical unit of measure for data is now a terabyte, which is 10^{12} bytes); *velocity* refers to the speed at which data is collected and processed; *variety* refers to the different data types; and *veracity* refers to the reliability of the data generated.

The term *data warehousing* is used to refer to the process of capturing, storing, and maintaining the data. Computing power and data collection tools have reached the point where it is now feasible to store and retrieve extremely large quantities of data in seconds. Analysis of the data in the warehouse may result in decisions that will lead to new strategies and higher profits for the organization. For example, General Electric (GE) captures a large amount of data from sensors on its aircraft engines each time a plane takes off or lands. Capturing these data allows GE to offer an important service to its customers; GE monitors the engine performance and can alert its customer when service is needed or a problem is likely to occur.

The subject of **data mining** deals with methods for developing useful decision-making information from large databases. Using a combination of procedures from statistics, mathematics, and computer science, analysts "mine the data" in the warehouse to convert it into useful information, hence the name *data mining.* Dr. Kurt Thearling, a leading practitioner in the field, defines data mining as "the automated extraction of predictive information from (large) databases." The two key words in Dr. Thearling's definition are "automated" and "predictive." Data mining systems that are the most effective use automated procedures to extract information from the data using only the most general or even vague queries by the user. And data mining software automates the process of uncovering hidden predictive information that in the past required hands-on analysis.

The major applications of data mining have been made by companies with a strong consumer focus, such as retail businesses, financial organizations, and communication companies. Data mining has been successfully used to help retailers such as Amazon and Barnes & Noble determine one or more related products that customers who have already purchased a specific product are also likely to purchase. Then, when a customer logs on to the company's website and purchases a product, the website uses pop-ups to alert the customer about additional products that the customer is likely to purchase. In another application, data mining may be used to identify customers who are likely to spend more than $20 on a particular shopping trip. These customers may then be identified as the ones to receive special e-mail or regular mail discount offers to encourage them to make their next shopping trip before the discount termination date.

Statistical methods play an important role in data mining, both in terms of discovering relationships in the data and predicting future outcomes. However, a thorough coverage of data mining and the use of statistics in data mining is outside the scope of this text.

Data mining is a technology that relies heavily on statistical methodology such as multiple regression, logistic regression, and correlation. But it takes a creative integration of all these methods and computer science technologies involving artificial intelligence and machine learning to make data mining effective. A substantial investment in time and money is required to implement commercial data mining software packages developed by firms such as Oracle, Teradata, and SAS. However, open-source software such as R and Python are also very popular tools for performing data mining. The statistical concepts introduced in this text will be helpful in understanding the statistical methodology used by data mining software packages and enable you to better understand the statistical information that is developed.

Because statistical models play an important role in developing predictive models in data mining, many of the concerns that statisticians deal with in developing statistical models are also applicable. For instance, a concern in any statistical study involves the issue of model reliability. Finding a statistical model that works well for a particular sample of data does not necessarily mean that it can be reliably applied to other data. One of the common statistical approaches to evaluating model reliability is to divide the sample data set into two parts: a training data set and a test data set. If the model developed using the training data is able to accurately predict values in the test data, we say that the model is reliable. One advantage that data mining has over classical statistics is that the enormous amount of data available allows the data mining software to partition the data set so that a model developed for the training data set may be tested for reliability on other data. In this sense, the partitioning of the data set allows data mining to develop models and relationships and then quickly observe if they are repeatable and valid with new and different data. On the other hand, a warning for data mining applications is that with so much data available, there is a danger of overfitting the model to the point that misleading associations and cause/effect conclusions appear to exist. Careful interpretation of data mining results and additional testing will help avoid this pitfall.

1.9 Ethical Guidelines for Statistical Practice

Ethical behavior is something we should strive for in all that we do. Ethical issues arise in statistics because of the important role statistics plays in the collection, analysis, presentation, and interpretation of data. In a statistical study, unethical behavior can take a variety of forms including improper sampling, inappropriate analysis of the data, development of misleading graphs, use of inappropriate summary statistics, and/or a biased interpretation of the statistical results.

As you begin to do your own statistical work, we encourage you to be fair, thorough, objective, and neutral as you collect data, conduct analyses, make oral presentations, and present written reports containing information developed. As a consumer of statistics, you should also be aware of the possibility of unethical statistical behavior by others. When you see statistics in the media, it is a good idea to view the information with some skepticism, always being aware of the source as well as the purpose and objectivity of the statistics provided.

The American Statistical Association, the nation's leading professional organization for statistics and statisticians, developed the report "Ethical Guidelines for Statistical Practice"[2] to help statistical practitioners make and communicate ethical decisions and assist students in learning how to perform statistical work responsibly. The report contains guidelines organized into eight topic areas: Professional Integrity and Accountability; Integrity of Data and Methods; Responsibilities to Stakeholders; Responsibilities to Research Subjects, Data Subjects, or Those Directly Affected by Statistical Practices; Responsibilities to Members of Multidisciplinary Teams; Responsibilities to Fellow Statistical Practitioners and the Profession; Responsibilities of Leaders, Supervisors, and Mentors in Statistical Practice; and Responsibilities Regarding Potential Misconduct.

One of the ethical guidelines in the Professional Integrity and Accountability area addresses the issue of predetermining or influencing the analyses. Let us consider an

[2]American Statistical Association, "Ethical Guidelines for Statistical Practice," February 2022.

example. In Section 1.5, we discussed a statistical study conducted by Rogers Industries involving a sample of 200 lithium batteries manufactured with a new solid-state technology. The average battery life for the sample, 18.84 hours, provided an estimate of the average lifetime for all lithium batteries produced with the new solid-state technology. However, since Rogers selected a sample of batteries, it is reasonable to assume that another sample would have provided a different average battery life.

Suppose Rogers's management had hoped the sample results would enable them to claim that the average time until recharge for the new batteries was 20 hours or more. Suppose further that Rogers's management decides to continue the study by manufacturing and testing repeated samples of 200 batteries with the new solid-state technology until a sample mean of 20 hours or more is obtained. If the study is repeated enough times, a sample may eventually be obtained—by chance alone—that would provide the desired result and enable Rogers to make such a claim. In this case, consumers would be misled into thinking the new product is better than it actually is. Clearly, this type of behavior is unethical and represents a gross misuse of statistics in practice.

Several ethical guidelines in the Integrity of Data and Methods area deal with issues involving the handling of data. For instance, a statistician must account for all data considered in a study and explain the sample(s) actually used. In the Rogers Industries study, the average battery life for the 200 batteries in the original sample is 18.84 hours; this is less than the 20 hours or more that management hoped to obtain. Suppose now that after reviewing the results showing an 18.84-hour average battery life, Rogers discards all the observations with 18 or less hours until recharge, allegedly because these batteries contain imperfections caused by start-up problems in the manufacturing process. After discarding these batteries, the average lifetime for the remaining batteries in the sample turns out to be 22 hours. Would you be suspicious of Rogers' claim that the battery life for its new solid-state batteries is 22 hours?

If the Rogers batteries showing 18 or less hours until recharge were discarded to simply provide an average lifetime of 22 hours, there is no question that discarding the batteries with 18 or fewer hours until recharge is unethical. But, even if the discarded batteries contain imperfections due to startup problems in the manufacturing process—and, as a result, should not have been included in the analysis—the statistician who conducted the study must account for all the data that were considered and explain how the sample actually used was obtained. To do otherwise is potentially misleading and would constitute unethical behavior on the part of both the company and the statistician.

A guideline in the Professional Integrity and Accountability section of the American Statistical Association report states that statistical practitioners should avoid any tendency to slant statistical work toward predetermined outcomes. This type of unethical practice is often observed when unrepresentative samples are used to make claims. For instance, in many areas of the country smoking is not permitted in restaurants. Suppose, however, a lobbyist for the tobacco industry interviews people in restaurants where smoking is permitted in order to estimate the percentage of people who are in favor of allowing smoking in restaurants. The sample results show that 90% of the people interviewed are in favor of allowing smoking in restaurants. Based upon these sample results, the lobbyist claims that 90% of all people who eat in restaurants are in favor of permitting smoking in restaurants. In this case, we would argue that only sampling persons eating in restaurants that allow smoking has biased the results. If only the final results of such a study are reported, readers unfamiliar with the details of the study (i.e., that the sample was collected only in restaurants allowing smoking) can be misled.

The scope of the American Statistical Association's report is broad and includes ethical guidelines that are appropriate not only for a statistician, but also for consumers of statistical information. We encourage you to read the report to obtain a better perspective of ethical issues as you continue your study of statistics and to gain the background for determining how to ensure that ethical standards are met when you start to use statistics in practice.

Summary

Statistics is the art and science of collecting, analyzing, presenting, and interpreting data. Nearly every college student majoring in business or economics is required to take a course in statistics. We began the chapter by describing typical statistical applications for business and economics.

Data consist of the facts and figures that are collected and analyzed. The four scales of measurement used to obtain data on a particular variable are nominal, ordinal, interval, and ratio. The scale of measurement for a variable is nominal when the data are labels or names used to identify an attribute of an element. The scale is ordinal if the data demonstrate the properties of nominal data and the order or rank of the data is meaningful. The scale is interval if the data demonstrate the properties of ordinal data and the interval between values is expressed in terms of a fixed unit of measure. Finally, the scale of measurement is ratio if the data show all the properties of interval data and the ratio of two values is meaningful.

For purposes of statistical analysis, data can be classified as categorical or quantitative. Categorical data use labels or names to identify an attribute of each element. Categorical data use either the nominal or ordinal scale of measurement and may be nonnumeric or numeric. Quantitative data are numeric values that indicate how much or how many. Quantitative data use either the interval or ratio scale of measurement. Ordinary arithmetic operations are meaningful only if the data are quantitative. Therefore, statistical computations used for quantitative data are not always appropriate for categorical data.

In Sections 1.4 and 1.5, we introduced the topics of descriptive statistics and statistical inference. Descriptive statistics are the tabular, graphical, and numerical methods used to summarize data. The process of statistical inference uses data obtained from a sample to make estimates or test hypotheses about the characteristics of a population. The last four sections of the chapter provide information on the role of computers in statistical analysis, an introduction to the relatively new fields of analytics, data mining, and big data, and a summary of ethical guidelines for statistical practice.

Glossary

Analytics The scientific process of transforming data into insights for making better decisions.

Big data A set of data that cannot be managed, processed, or analyzed with commonly available software in a reasonable amount of time. Big data are characterized by great volume (a large amount of data), high velocity (fast collection and processing), or wide variety (could include nontraditional data such as video, audio, and text).

Categorical data Labels or names used to identify an attribute of each element. Categorical data use either the nominal or ordinal scale of measurement and may be nonnumeric or numeric.

Categorical variable A variable with categorical data.

Census A survey to collect data on the entire population.

Cross-sectional data Data collected at the same or approximately the same point in time.

Data The facts and figures collected, analyzed, and summarized for presentation and interpretation.

Data mining The process of using procedures from statistics and computer science to extract useful information from extremely large databases.

Data set All the data collected in a particular study.

Descriptive analytics Analytical techniques that describe what has happened in the past.

Descriptive statistics Tabular, graphical, and numerical summaries of data.

Elements The entities on which data are collected.

Interval scale The scale of measurement for a variable if the data demonstrate the properties of ordinal data and the interval between values is expressed in terms of a fixed unit of measure. Interval data are always numeric.

Nominal scale The scale of measurement for a variable when the data are labels or names used to identify an attribute of an element. Nominal data may be nonnumeric or numeric.
Observation The set of measurements obtained for a particular element.
Ordinal scale The scale of measurement for a variable if the data exhibit the properties of nominal data and the order or rank of the data is meaningful. Ordinal data may be nonnumeric or numeric.
Population The set of all elements of interest in a particular study.
Predictive analytics Analytical techniques that use models constructed from past data to predict the future or assess the impact of one variable on another.
Prescriptive analytics Analytical techniques that yield a course of action.
Quantitative data Numeric values that indicate how much or how many of something. Quantitative data are obtained using either the interval or ratio scale of measurement.
Quantitative variable A variable with quantitative data.
Ratio scale The scale of measurement for a variable if the data demonstrate all the properties of interval data and the ratio of two values is meaningful. Ratio data are always numeric.
Sample A subset of the population.
Sample survey A survey to collect data on a sample.
Statistical inference The process of using data obtained from a sample to make estimates or test hypotheses about the characteristics of a population.
Statistics The art and science of collecting, analyzing, presenting, and interpreting data.
Time series data Data collected over several time periods.
Variable A characteristic of interest for the elements.

Supplementary Exercises

1. ***Wall Street Journal Subscriber Characteristics.*** A *Wall Street Journal* subscriber survey asked 46 questions about subscriber characteristics and interests. State whether each of the following questions provides categorical or quantitative data. **LO 2**
   a. What is your age?
   b. Are you married?
   c. When did you first start reading the *WSJ*? High school, college, early career, midcareer, late career, or retirement?
   d. How long have you been in your present job or position?
   e. What type of vehicle are you considering for your next purchase? Nine response categories include sedan, sports car, SUV, minivan, and so on.
2. **Comparing Tablet Computers.** Tablet PC Comparison provides a wide variety of information about tablet computers. Their website enables consumers to easily compare different tablets using factors such as cost, type of operating system, display size, battery life, and CPU manufacturer. A sample of 10 tablet computers is shown in Table 1.6 (Tablet PC Comparison website). **LO 1, 2**
   a. How many elements are in this data set?
   b. How many variables are in this data set?
   c. Which variables are categorical and which variables are quantitative?
   d. What type of measurement scale is used for each of the variables?
3. **Tablet PCs: Cost, CPU, and Operating System.** Refer to Table 1.6. **LO 3**
   a. What is the average cost for the tablets?
   b. Compare the average cost of tablets with a Windows operating system to the average cost of tablets with an Android operating system.
   c. What percentage of tablets use a CPU manufactured by TI OMAP?
   d. What percentage of tablets use an Android operating system?
4. **Comparing Phones.** Table 1.7 shows data for eight phones (*Consumer Reports*). The Overall Score, a measure of the overall quality for the phone, ranges from 0 to 100. Voice Quality has possible ratings of poor, fair, good, very good, and excellent. Talk

Table 1.6 Product Information for 10 Tablet Computers

Tablet	Cost ($)	Operating System	Display Size (inches)	Battery Life (hours)	CPU Manufacturer
Acer Iconia W510	599	Windows	10.1	8.5	Intel
Amazon Kindle Fire HD	299	Android	8.9	9.0	TI OMAP
Apple iPad 4	499	iOS	9.7	11.0	Apple
HP Envy X2	860	Windows	11.6	8.0	Intel
Lenovo ThinkPad Tablet	668	Windows	10.1	10.5	Intel
Microsoft Surface Pro	899	Windows	10.6	4.0	Intel
Motorola Droid XYboard	530	Android	10.1	9.0	TI OMAP
Samsung Ativ Smart PC	590	Windows	11.6	7.0	Intel
Samsung Galaxy Tab	525	Android	10.1	10.0	Nvidia
Sony Tablet S	360	Android	9.4	8.0	Nvidia

Time is the manufacturer's claim of how long the phone can be used when it is fully charged. **LO 1, 2**

a. How many elements are in this data set?
b. For the variables Price, Overall Score, Voice Quality, and Talk Time, which variables are categorical and which variables are quantitative?
c. What scale of measurement is used for each variable?

5. **Summarizing Phone Data.** Refer to the data set in Table 1.7. **LO 3**
   a. What is the average price for the phones?
   b. What is the average talk time for the phones?
   c. What percentage of the phones have a voice quality of excellent?
6. **New Automobile Owners Survey.** J.D. Power and Associates surveys new automobile owners to learn about the quality of recently purchased vehicles. The following questions were asked in the J.D. Power Initial Quality Survey. Comment on whether each of the following questions provides categorical or quantitative data. **LO 2**
   a. Did you purchase or lease the vehicle?
   b. What price did you pay?
   c. What is the overall attractiveness of your vehicle's exterior? (Unacceptable, Average, Outstanding, or Truly Exceptional)
   d. What is your average number of miles per gallon?
   e. What is your overall rating of your new vehicle? (l- to 10-point scale with 1 Unacceptable and 10 Truly Exceptional)

Table 1.7 Data for Eight Phones

Brand	Model	Price ($)	Overall Score	Voice Quality	Talk Time (hours)
AT&T	CL84100	60	73	Excellent	7
AT&T	TL92271	80	70	Very Good	7
Panasonic	4773B	100	78	Very Good	13
Panasonic	6592T	70	72	Very Good	13
Uniden	D2997	45	70	Very Good	10
Uniden	D1788	80	73	Very Good	7
Vtech	DS6521	60	72	Excellent	7
Vtech	CS6649	50	72	Very Good	7

7. **Airline Customer Satisfaction.** Many service companies collect data via a follow-up survey of their customers. For example, to ascertain customer sentiment, Delta Air Lines sends an e-mail to customers immediately following a flight. Among other questions, Delta asks:

How likely are you to recommend Delta Air Lines to others?

The possible responses are:

Definitely Will	Probably Will	May or May Not	Probably Will Not	Definitely Will Not
❍	❍	❍	❍	❍

Use this information to answer the following questions. **LO 2, 4**

a. Are the data collected by Delta in this example quantitative or categorical?
b. What measurement scale is used?

8. **Readership Poll.** *The Tennessean*, an online newspaper located in Nashville, Tennessee, conducts a daily poll to obtain reader opinions on a variety of current issues. In a recent poll, 762 readers responded to the following question: "If a constitutional amendment to ban a state income tax is placed on the ballot in Tennessee, would you want it to pass?" Possible responses were Yes, No, or Not Sure (*The Tennessean* website). **LO 1, 2, 3**

a. What was the sample size for this poll?
b. Are the data categorical or quantitative?
c. Would it make more sense to use averages or percentages as a summary of the data for this question?
d. Of the respondents, 67% said Yes, they would want it to pass. How many individuals provided this response?

9. **College-Educated Workers.** Based on data from the U.S. Census Bureau, a Pew Research study showed that the percentage of employed individuals ages 25–29 who are college educated is at an all-time high. The study showed that the percentage of employed individuals aged 25–29 with at least a bachelor's degree in 2016 was 40%. In the year 2000, this percentage was 32%, in 1985 it was 25%, and in 1964 it was only 16% (Pew Research website). **LO 4**

a. What is the population being studied in each of the four years in which Pew has data?
b. What question was posed to each respondent?
c. Do responses to the question provide categorical or quantitative data?

10. **Driving with Cell Phones.** The Bureau of Transportation Statistics Omnibus Household Survey is conducted annually and serves as an information source for the U.S. Department of Transportation. In one part of the survey the person being interviewed was asked to respond to the following statement: "Drivers of motor vehicles should be allowed to talk on a handheld cell phone while driving." Possible responses were strongly agree, somewhat agree, somewhat disagree, and strongly disagree. Forty-four respondents said that they strongly agree with this statement, 130 said that they somewhat agree, 165 said they somewhat disagree, and 741 said they strongly disagree with this statement (Bureau of Transportation website). **LO 2, 3**

a. Do the responses for this statement provide categorical or quantitative data?
b. Would it make more sense to use averages or percentages as a summary of the responses for this statement?
c. What percentage of respondents strongly agree with allowing drivers of motor vehicles to talk on a handheld cell phone while driving?
d. Do the results indicate general support for or against allowing drivers of motor vehicles to talk on a handheld cell phone while driving?

11. **Driverless Cars Expected Soon.** A Gallup Poll utilizing a random sample of 1,503 adults ages 18 or older was conducted in April 2018. The survey indicated a majority

Figure 1.10 Histogram of Survey Results on Driverless Cars

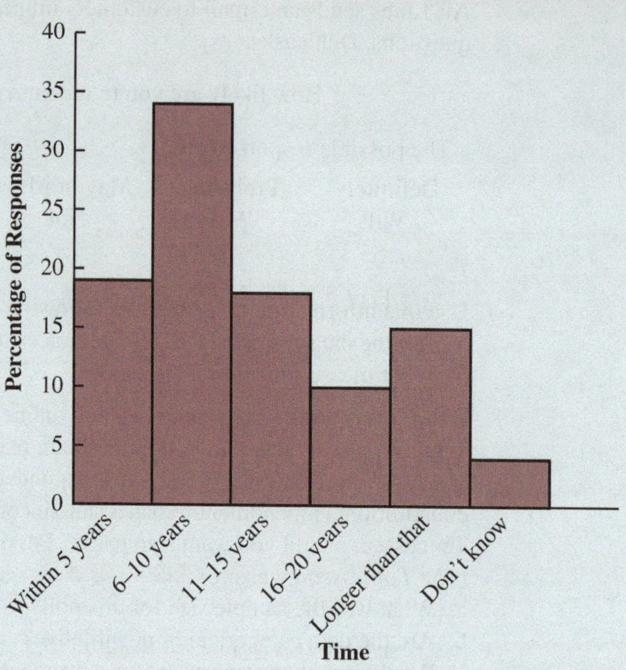

of Americans (53%) say driverless cars will be common in the next 10 years (Gallup). The question asked was:

> Thinking about fully automated, "driverless cars," cars that use technology to drive and do not need a human driver, based on what you have heard or read, how soon do you think driverless cars will be commonly used in the [United States]?

Figure 1.10 shows a summary of results of the survey in a histogram indicating the percentage of the total responses in different time intervals. **LO 2, 3**

a. Are the responses to the survey question quantitative or categorical?
b. How many of the respondents said that they expect driverless cars to be common in the next 10 years?
c. How many respondents answered in the range 16–20 years?

12. **Hawaii Visitors Poll.** The Hawaii Visitors Bureau collects data on visitors to Hawaii. The following questions were among 16 asked in a questionnaire handed out to passengers during incoming airline flights.

- This trip to Hawaii is my: 1st, 2nd, 3rd, 4th, etc.
- The primary reason for this trip is: (10 categories, including vacation, convention, honeymoon)
- Where I plan to stay: (11 categories, including hotel, apartment, relatives, camping)
- Total days in Hawaii

Use this information to answer the following questions. **LO 2, 4**

a. What is the population being studied?
b. Is the use of a questionnaire a good way to reach the population of passengers on incoming airline flights?
c. Comment on each of the four questions in terms of whether it will provide categorical or quantitative data.

Figure 1.11 Netflix Subscribers (millions)

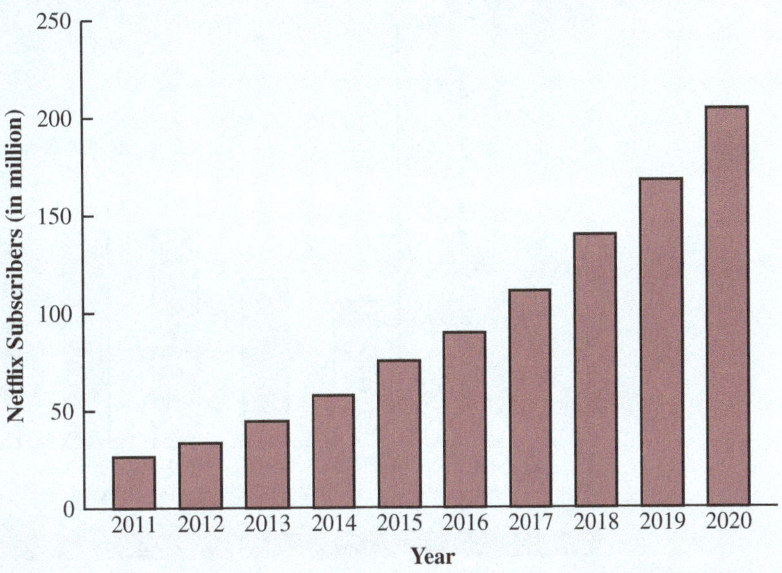

13. **Netflix Subscribers.** Figure 1.11 provides a bar chart showing the number of Netflix subscribers from 2011 to 2020 (*nscreenmedia.com*). **LO 1, 2**
    a. What is the variable of interest?
    b. Are the data categorical or quantitative?
    c. Are the data time series or cross-sectional?
    d. Comment on the trend in Facebook's annual advertising revenue over time.
14. **Rental Car Fleet Size.** The following data show the number of rental cars in service for three rental car companies: Hertz, Avis, and Dollar, over a four-year period. **LO 2**

	Cars in Service (1,000s)			
Company	**Year 1**	**Year 2**	**Year 3**	**Year 4**
Hertz	327	311	286	290
Dollar	167	140	106	108
Avis	204	220	300	270

    a. Construct a time series graph for the years 1 to 4 showing the number of rental cars in service for each company. Show the time series for all three companies on the same graph.
    b. Comment on who appears to be the market share leader and how the market shares are changing over time.
    c. Construct a bar chart showing rental cars in service for year 4. Is this chart based on cross-sectional or time series data?
15. **Worldwide Robot Supply.** The International Federation of Robotics estimates the worldwide supply of industrial robots each year. Figure 1.12 shows estimates of the worldwide supply of industrial robots for the years 2015 to 2021. **LO 1, 2**
    a. What is the variable of interest?
    b. Are the data quantitative or categorical?
    c. Are the data cross-sectional or time series?

Figure 1.12 Estimated Industrial Robot Supply (1,000s units)

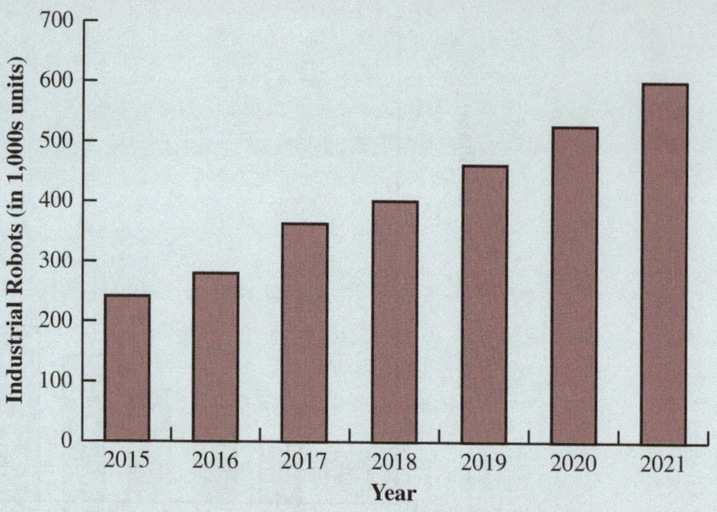

16. **Athletic Shoe Sales.** Skechers U.S.A., Inc., is a performance footwear company headquartered in Manhattan Beach, California. The sales revenue for Skechers over a four-year period are as follows:

Year	Sales ($ billions)
Year 1	2.30
Year 2	3.15
Year 3	3.56
Year 4	4.16

Use this information to answer the following questions. **LO 2, 3**

a. Are these cross-sectional or time-series data?
b. Construct a bar graph similar to Figure 1.12.
c. What can you say about how Skechers' sales are changing over these four years?

17. **Deciding on a Salary Increase.** A manager of a large corporation recommends a $10,000 raise be given to keep a valued subordinate from moving to another company. What internal and external sources of data might be used to decide whether such a salary increase is appropriate? **LO 5**

18. **Tax Survey.** A random telephone survey of 1021 adults (aged 18 and older) was conducted by Opinion Research Corporation on behalf of CompleteTax, an online tax preparation and e-filing service. The survey results showed that 684 of those surveyed planned to file their taxes electronically. **LO 3**

a. Develop a descriptive statistic that can be used to estimate the percentage of all taxpayers who file electronically.
b. The survey reported that the most frequently used method for preparing the tax return was to hire an accountant or professional tax preparer. If 60% of the people surveyed had their tax return prepared this way, how many people used an accountant or professional tax preparer?

c. Other methods that the person filing the return often used include manual preparation, use of an online tax service, and use of a software tax program. Would the data for the method for preparing the tax return be considered categorical or quantitative?

19. **Magazine Subscriber Survey.** A *Bloomberg Businessweek* North American subscriber study collected data from a sample of 2,861 subscribers. Fifty-nine percent of the respondents indicated an annual income of $75,000 or more, and 50% reported having an American Express credit card. **LO 2, 4, 5, 6**
    a. What is the population of interest in this study?
    b. Is annual income a categorical or quantitative variable?
    c. Is ownership of an American Express card a categorical or quantitative variable?
    d. Does this study involve cross-sectional or time series data?
    e. Describe any statistical inferences *Bloomberg Businessweek* might make on the basis of the survey.

20. **Investment Manager Survey.** A survey of 131 investment managers in *Barron's* Big Money poll revealed the following:
    - Forty-three percent of managers classified themselves as bullish or very bullish on the stock market.
    - The average expected return over the next 12 months for equities was 11.2%.
    - Twenty-one percent selected health care as the sector most likely to lead the market in the next 12 months.
    - When asked to estimate how long it would take for technology and telecom stocks to resume sustainable growth, the managers' average response was 2.5 years.

    Use this information to answer the following questions. **LO 3, 7**
    a. Cite two descriptive statistics.
    b. Make an inference about the population of all investment managers concerning the average return expected on equities over the next 12 months.
    c. Make an inference about the length of time it will take for technology and telecom stocks to resume sustainable growth.

21. **Cancer Research.** A seven-year medical research study reported that women whose mothers took the drug DES during pregnancy were twice as likely to develop tissue abnormalities that might lead to cancer as were women whose mothers did not take the drug. **LO 3, 4, 5**
    a. This study compared two populations. What were the populations?
    b. Do you suppose the data were obtained in a survey or an experiment?
    c. For the population of women whose mothers took the drug DES during pregnancy, a sample of 3,980 women showed that 63 developed tissue abnormalities that might lead to cancer. Provide a descriptive statistic that could be used to estimate the number of women out of 1,000 in this population who have tissue abnormalities.
    d. For the population of women whose mothers did not take the drug DES during pregnancy, what is the estimate of the number of women out of 1,000 who would be expected to have tissue abnormalities?
    e. Medical studies often use a relatively large sample (in this case, 3,980). Why?

22. **Why People Move.** A survey conducted by Better Homes and Gardens Real Estate LLC showed that one in five U.S. homeowners have either moved from their home or would like to move because their neighborhood or community isn't ideal for their lifestyle (Better Homes and Gardens Real Estate website). The top lifestyle priorities of respondents when searching for their next home include ease of commuting by car, access to health and safety services, family-friendly neighborhood, availability of retail stores, access to cultural activities, public transportation access, and nightlife and restaurant access. Suppose a real estate agency in Denver, Colorado, hired you to conduct a similar study to determine the top lifestyle priorities for clients that currently

have a home listed for sale with the agency or have hired the agency to help them locate a new home. **LO 4, 5**

a. What is the population for the survey you will be conducting?

b. How would you collect the data for this study?

23. **Investment in Cryptocurrency.** Pew Research Center is a nonpartisan polling organization that provides information about issues, attitudes, and trends. In a poll of 10,371 adults in the United States, Pew found that 16% of those polled have used, invested in, or traded, digital currency known as cryptocurrency. Of those who responded to the poll, 22% of men and 10% of women indicated that they had used, invested in, or traded cryptocurrency. **LO 4**

a. To what population does the statistic 16% refer?

b. To what population does the statistic 10% refer?

c. Do you think Pew researchers conducted a census or took a sample to obtain their results? Explain your answer.

24. **Midterm Grades.** A sample of midterm grades for five students showed the following results: 72, 65, 82, 90, 76. Which of the following statements are correct, and which should be challenged as being too generalized? **LO 3, 4**

a. The average midterm grade for the sample of five students is 77.

b. The average midterm grade for all students who took the exam is 77.

c. An estimate of the average midterm grade for all students who took the exam is 77.

d. More than half of the students who take this exam will score between 70 and 85.

e. If five other students are included in the sample, their grades will be between 65 and 90.

25. **Comparing Compact SUVs.** *Consumer Reports* evaluates products for consumers. The file *compactsuv* contains the data shown in Table 1.8 for 15 compact sports utility vehicles (SUVs) from the 2018 model line (*Consumer Reports* website):

DATA*file*
compactsuv

Make—manufacturer
Model—name of the model

Table 1.8 *Consumer Reports* Data Set for 15 Compact Sports Utility Vehicles

Make	Model	Overall Score	Recommended	Owner Satisfaction	Overall Miles per Gallon	Acceleration (0–60) Sec
Subaru	Forester	84	Yes	+	26	8.7
Honda	CRV	83	Yes	++	27	8.6
Toyota	Rav4	81	Yes	++	24	9.3
Nissan	Rogue	73	Yes	+	24	9.5
Mazda	CX-5	71	Yes	++	24	8.6
Kia	Sportage	71	Yes	+	23	9.6
Ford	Escape	69	Yes	0	23	10.1
Volkswagen	Tiguan Limited	67	No	0	21	8.5
Volkswagen	Tiguan	65	No	+	25	10.3
Mitsubishi	Outlander	63	No	0	24	10.0
Chevrolet	Equinox	63	No	0	31	10.1
Hyundai	Tucson	57	No	0	26	8.4
GMC	Terrain	57	No	0	22	7.2
Jeep	Cherokee	55	No	–	22	10.9
Jeep	Compass	50	No	0	24	9.8

Overall score—awarded based on a variety of measures, including those in this data set
Recommended—*Consumer Reports* recommends the vehicle or not
Owner satisfaction—satisfaction on a five-point scale based on the percentage of owners who would purchase the vehicle again ($- -$, $-$, 0, $+$, $++$).
Overall miles per gallon—miles per gallon achieved in a 150-mile test trip
Acceleration (0–60 sec)—time in seconds it takes vehicle to reach 60 miles per hour from a standstill with the engine idling

Use these data to answer the following questions. **LO 1, 2, 3**

a. How many variables are in the data set?
b. Which of the variables are categorical, and which are quantitative?
c. What percentage of these 15 vehicles are recommended?
d. What is the average of the overall miles per gallon across all 15 vehicles?

- Overall score — grades based on a variety of measures, including those in the data set
- Recommended — Consumer Reports recommends the vehicle or not
- Owner satisfaction — satisfaction on a five-point scale based on the percentage of owners who would purchase the vehicle again (– –, –, 0, +, ++)
- Overall miles per gallon — miles per gallon achieved in a 150-mile test trip
- Acceleration (0–60 sec) — time in seconds it takes vehicle to reach 60 miles per hour from a standstill with the engine idling

Consider the data set and answer the following questions. (LO 1, 2, 3, 4)

a. How many variables are in the data set?
b. Which of the variables are categorical and which are quantitative?
c. What percentage of these 16 vehicles are recommended?
d. What is the average of the overall miles per gallon across all 16 vehicles?

Chapter 2

Descriptive Statistics: Tabular and Graphical Displays

Contents

Statistics in Practice: *Colgate-Palmolive Company*

2.1 Summarizing Data for a Categorical Variable
- Frequency Distribution
- Relative Frequency and Percent Frequency Distributions
- Using Excel to Construct a Frequency Distribution, a Relative Frequency Distribution, and a Percent Frequency Distribution
- Bar Charts and Pie Charts
- Using Excel to Construct a Bar Chart

2.2 Summarizing Data for a Quantitative Variable
- Frequency Distribution
- Relative Frequency and Percent Frequency Distributions
- Using Excel to Construct a Frequency Distribution
- Dot Plot
- Histogram
- Using Excel's Recommended Charts Tool to Construct a Histogram
- Cumulative Distributions
- Stem-and-Leaf Display

2.3 Summarizing Data for Two Variables Using Tables
- Crosstabulation
- Using Excel's PivotTable Tool to Construct a Crosstabulation
- Simpson's Paradox

2.4 Summarizing Data for Two Variables Using Graphical Displays
- Scatter Diagram and Trendline
- Using Excel to Construct a Scatter Diagram and a Trendline
- Side-by-Side and Stacked Bar Charts
- Using Excel's Recommended Charts Tool to Construct Side-by-Side and Stacked Bar Charts

2.5 Visualizing Geospatial Data
- Choropleth Maps
- Using Excel to Construct a Choropleth Map
- Cartograms

2.6 Data Visualization: Best Practices in Creating Effective Graphical Displays
- Data-Ink Ratio
- Creating Effective Graphical Displays
- Choosing the Type of Graphical Display
- Data Dashboards
- Data Visualization in Practice: Cincinnati Zoo and Botanical Garden

Summary 101
Glossary 102
Key Formulas 103
Supplementary Exercises 103
Case Problem 1: Pelican Stores 110
Case Problem 2: Movie Theater Releases 111
Case Problem 3: Queen City 111
Case Problem 4: Cut-Rate Machining, Inc. 112

Available in the Cengage eBook:
Appendix: Creating Tabular and Graphical Presentations with R

Learning Objectives

After completing this chapter, you will be able to

LO 1 Construct and interpret frequency, relative frequency, and percent frequency distributions for categorical data.

LO 2 Construct and interpret bar graphs and pie charts for categorical data.

LO 3 Construct and interpret frequency, relative frequency, and percent frequency distributions for quantitative data.

LO 4 Construct and interpret cumulative frequency, cumulative relative frequency, and cumulative percent distributions for quantitative data.

LO 5 Construct and interpret dot plots, histograms, and stem-and-leaf displays for quantitative data.

LO 6 Interpret the shape of a distribution of data and identify positive skewness, negative skewness, and symmetric distributions.

LO 7 Construct and interpret cross-tabulations to summarize data for two variables.

LO 8 Construct and interpret a scatter diagram for two quantitative variables.

LO 9 Identify and explain Simpson's paradox from a crosstabulation.

LO 10 Construct and interpret side-by-side and stacked bar charts.

LO 11 Create and interpret choropleth maps and cartograms for applications to geospatial data.

LO 12 Apply concepts of data-ink ratio and decluttering to improve table and chart designs.

Statistics in Practice

Colgate-Palmolive Company*

New York, New York

The Colgate-Palmolive Company started as a small soap and candle shop in New York City in 1806. Today, Colgate-Palmolive employs more than 33,000 people working in nearly 200 countries and territories around the world. Although best known for its brand names of Colgate, Palmolive, and Softsoap, the company also markets Irish Spring, Hill's Science Diet, Softsoap, Ajax, Fabuloso, Hill's Pet Nutrition, and Tom's of Maine among other products.

The Colgate-Palmolive Company uses statistics in its quality assurance program for home laundry detergent products. One concern is customer satisfaction with the quantity of detergent in a carton. Every carton in each size category is filled with the same amount of detergent by weight, but the volume of detergent is affected by the density of the detergent powder. For instance, if the powder density is on the heavy side, a smaller volume of detergent is needed to reach the carton's specified weight. As a result, the carton may appear to be underfilled when opened by the consumer.

To control the problem of heavy detergent powder, limits are placed on the acceptable range of powder density. Statistical samples are taken periodically, and the density of each powder sample is measured. Data summaries are then provided for operating personnel so that corrective action can be taken if necessary to keep the density within the desired quality specifications.

A frequency distribution for the densities of 150 samples taken over a one-week period and a histogram are shown in the accompanying table and figure. Density levels above 0.40 are unacceptably high. The frequency distribution and histogram show that the operation is meeting its quality guidelines with all of the densities

The Colgate-Palmolive Company uses statistical summaries to help maintain the quality of its products.
Kurt Brady/Alamy Stock Photo

*The authors are indebted to William R. Fowle, Manager of Quality Assurance, Colgate-Palmolive Company, for providing this Statistics in Practice.

less than or equal to 0.40. Managers viewing these statistical summaries would be pleased with the quality of the detergent production process.

In this chapter, you will learn about tabular and graphical methods of descriptive statistics such as frequency distributions, bar charts, histograms, stem-and-leaf displays, crosstabulations, and others. The goal of these methods is to summarize data so that the data can be easily understood and interpreted.

Frequency Distribution of Density Data

Density	Frequency
0.29–0.30	30
0.31–0.32	75
0.33–0.34	32
0.35–0.36	9
0.37–0.38	3
0.39–0.40	1
Total	150

Histogram of Density Data

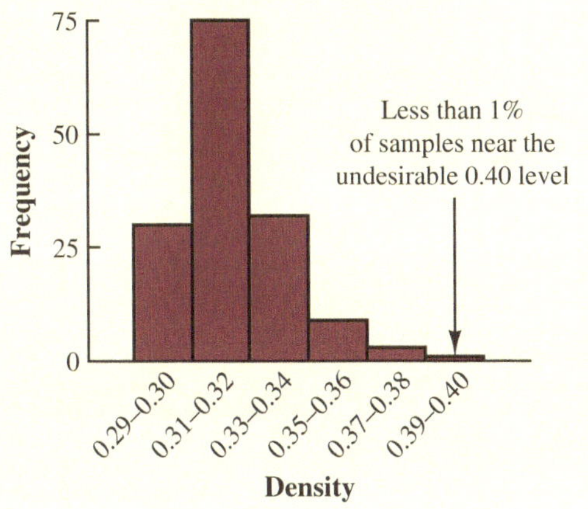

As discussed in Chapter 1, data can be classified as either categorical or quantitative. **Categorical data** use labels or names to identify categories of like items, and **quantitative data** are numerical values that indicate how much or how many. In this chapter, we introduce the use of tabular and graphical displays for summarizing both categorical and quantitative data. Tabular and graphical displays can be found in annual reports, newspaper articles, and research studies. Everyone is exposed to these types of presentations. Hence, it is important to understand how they are constructed and how they should be interpreted.

We begin with a discussion of the use of tabular and graphical displays to summarize the data for a single variable. This is followed by a discussion of the use of tabular and graphical displays to summarize the data for two variables in a way that reveals the relationship between the two variables. We also introduce several specialized graphical displays used for geospatial data to create maps based on data. **Data visualization** is a term often used to describe the use of graphical displays to summarize and present information about a data set. The last section of this chapter provides guidelines for creating effective graphical displays including a discussion of the use of the data-ink ratio and decluttering to improve visualizations.

2.1 Summarizing Data for a Categorical Variable

Frequency Distribution

We begin the discussion of how tabular and graphical displays can be used to summarize categorical data with the definition of a **frequency distribution**.

> **Frequency Distribution**
>
> A frequency distribution is a tabular summary of data showing the number (frequency) of observations in each of several nonoverlapping categories or classes.

Let us use the following example to demonstrate the construction and interpretation of a frequency distribution for categorical data. Coca-Cola, Diet Coke, Dr. Pepper, Pepsi, and Sprite are five popular soft drinks. Assume that the data in Table 2.1 show the soft drink selected in a sample of 50 soft drink purchases.

Table 2.1 Data from a Sample of 50 Soft Drink Purchases

Coca-Cola	Coca-Cola	Coca-Cola	Sprite	Coca-Cola
Diet Coke	Dr. Pepper	Diet Coke	Dr. Pepper	Diet Coke
Pepsi	Sprite	Coca-Cola	Pepsi	Pepsi
Diet Coke	Coca-Cola	Sprite	Diet Coke	Pepsi
Coca-Cola	Diet Coke	Pepsi	Pepsi	Pepsi
Coca-Cola	Coca-Cola	Coca-Cola	Coca-Cola	Pepsi
Dr. Pepper	Coca-Cola	Coca-Cola	Coca-Cola	Coca-Cola
Diet Coke	Sprite	Coca-Cola	Coca-Cola	Dr. Pepper
Pepsi	Coca-Cola	Pepsi	Pepsi	Pepsi
Pepsi	Diet Coke	Coca-Cola	Dr. Pepper	Sprite

DATA*file*
softdrink

To develop a frequency distribution for these data, we count the number of times each soft drink appears in Table 2.1. Coca-Cola appears 19 times, Diet Coke appears 8 times, Dr. Pepper appears 5 times, Pepsi appears 13 times, and Sprite appears 5 times. These counts are summarized in the frequency distribution in Table 2.2.

This frequency distribution provides a summary of how the 50 soft drink purchases are distributed across the five soft drinks. This summary offers more insight than the original data shown in Table 2.1. Viewing the frequency distribution, we see that Coca-Cola is the leader, Pepsi is second, Diet Coke is third, and Sprite and Dr. Pepper are tied for fourth. The frequency distribution summarizes information about the popularity of the five soft drinks.

Relative Frequency and Percent Frequency Distributions

A frequency distribution shows the number (frequency) of observations in each of several nonoverlapping classes. However, we are often interested in the proportion, or percentage, of observations in each class. The *relative frequency* of a class equals the fraction or proportion of observations belonging to a class. For a data set with n observations, the relative frequency of each class can be determined as follows:

Relative Frequency

$$\text{Relative frequency of a class} = \frac{\text{Frequency of the class}}{n} \tag{2.1}$$

The *percent frequency* of a class is the relative frequency multiplied by 100.

A **relative frequency distribution** gives a tabular summary of data showing the relative frequency for each class. A **percent frequency distribution** summarizes the percent frequency of the data for each class. Table 2.3 shows a relative frequency distribution and

Table 2.2 Frequency Distribution of Soft Drink Purchases

Soft Drink	Frequency
Coca-Cola	19
Diet Coke	8
Dr. Pepper	5
Pepsi	13
Sprite	5
Total	50

Table 2.3 Relative Frequency and Percent Frequency Distributions of Soft Drink Purchases

Soft Drink	Relative Frequency	Percent Frequency
Coca-Cola	0.38	38
Diet Coke	0.16	16
Dr. Pepper	0.10	10
Pepsi	0.26	26
Sprite	0.10	10
Total	1.00	100

a percent frequency distribution for the soft drink data. In Table 2.3 we see that the relative frequency for Coca-Cola is 19/50 = 0.38, the relative frequency for Diet Coke is 8/50 = 0.16, and so on. From the percent frequency distribution, we see that 38% of the purchases were Coca-Cola, 16% of the purchases were Diet Coke, and so on. We can also note that 38% + 26% + 16% = 80% of the purchases were for the top three soft drinks.

Using Excel to Construct a Frequency Distribution, a Relative Frequency Distribution, and a Percent Frequency Distribution

DATA*file*
softdrink

We can use Excel's Recommended PivotTables tool to construct a frequency distribution for the sample of 50 soft drink purchases. Two tasks are involved: Enter/Access Data and Apply Tools.

Enter/Access Data: Open the file *softdrink*. The data are in cells A2:A51 and a label is in cell A1.

Apply Tools: The following steps describe how to use Excel's Recommended PivotTables tool to construct a frequency distribution for the sample of 50 soft drink purchases.

Step 1. Select any cell in the data set (cells A1:A51)
Step 2. Click the **Insert** tab on the Ribbon
Step 3. In the **Tables** group click **Recommended PivotTables**; a preview showing the frequency distribution appears
Step 4. Click **OK**; the frequency distribution will appear in a new worksheet

The worksheet in Figure 2.1 shows the frequency distribution for the 50 soft drink purchases created using these steps. Also shown is the PivotTable Fields task pane, a key component of every PivotTable report. We will discuss the use of the PivotTable Fields task pane later in the chapter.

Editing Options: You can easily change the column headings in the frequency distribution output. For instance, to change the current heading in cell A3 (Row Labels) to "Soft Drink," click cell A3 and type *Soft Drink*; to change the current heading in cell B3 (Count of Brand Purchased) to "Frequency," click cell B3 and type *Frequency*; and to change the current heading in A9 (Grand Total) to "Total," click cell A9 and type *Total*. Figure 2.2 contains the revised headings; in addition, the headings "Relative Frequency" and "Percent Frequency" were entered into cells C3 and D3. We will now show how to construct the relative frequency and percent frequency distributions.

Enter Functions and Formulas: Refer to Figure 2.2 as we describe how to create the relative and percent frequency distributions for the soft drink purchases. The formula worksheet is in the background and the value worksheet in the foreground. To compute the relative frequency for Coca-Cola using equation (2.1), we entered the formula *=B4/$B$9* in cell C4; the result, 0.38, is the relative frequency for Coca-Cola. Copying cell C4 to cells C5:C8 computes

Figure 2.1 Frequency Distribution of Soft Drink Purchases Constructed Using Excel's Recommended PivotTables Tool

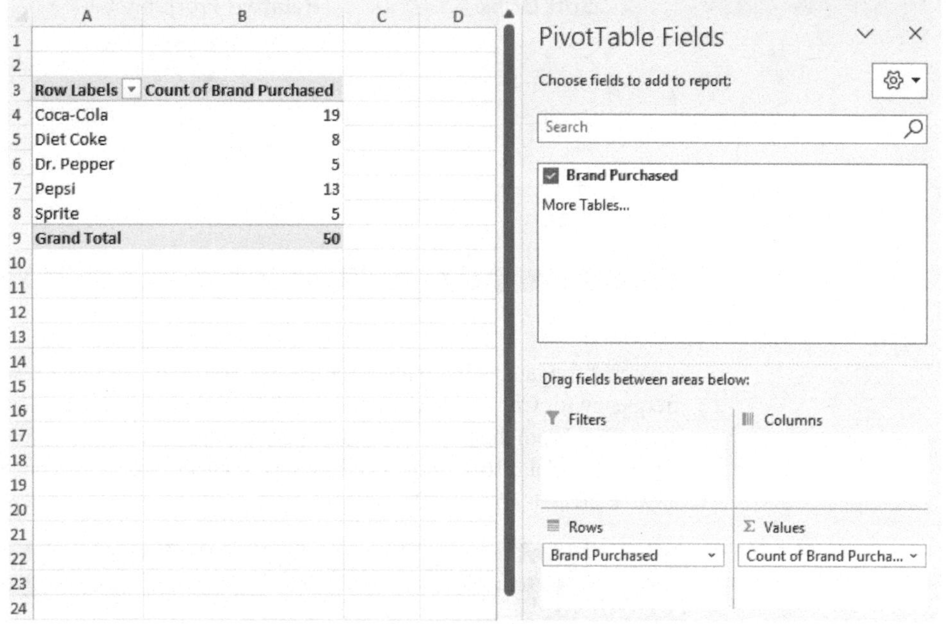

	A	B
3	Row Labels	Count of Brand Purchased
4	Coca-Cola	19
5	Diet Coke	8
6	Dr. Pepper	5
7	Pepsi	13
8	Sprite	5
9	Grand Total	50

the relative frequencies, for each of the other soft drinks. To compute the percent frequency for Coca-Cola, we entered the formula $=C4*100$ in cell D4. The result, 38, indicates that 38% of the soft drink purchases were Coca-Cola. Copying cell D4 to cells D5:D8 computes the percent frequencies for each of the other soft drinks. To compute the total of the relative and percent frequencies, we used Excel's SUM function in cells C9 and D9.

Figure 2.2 Relative Frequency and Percent Frequency Distributions of Soft Drink Purchases Constructed Using Excel's Recommended PivotTables Tool

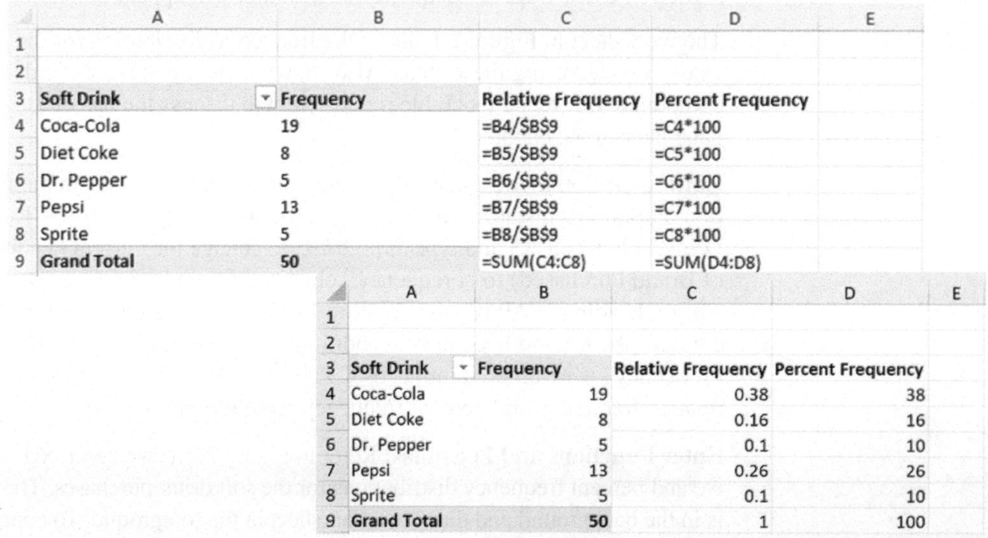

	A	B	C	D
3	Soft Drink	Frequency	Relative Frequency	Percent Frequency
4	Coca-Cola	19	=B4/$B$9	=C4*100
5	Diet Coke	8	=B5/$B$9	=C5*100
6	Dr. Pepper	5	=B6/$B$9	=C6*100
7	Pepsi	13	=B7/$B$9	=C7*100
8	Sprite	5	=B8/$B$9	=C8*100
9	Grand Total	50	=SUM(C4:C8)	=SUM(D4:D8)

	A	B	C	D
3	Soft Drink	Frequency	Relative Frequency	Percent Frequency
4	Coca-Cola	19	0.38	38
5	Diet Coke	8	0.16	16
6	Dr. Pepper	5	0.1	10
7	Pepsi	13	0.26	26
8	Sprite	5	0.1	10
9	Grand Total	50	1	100

Bar Charts and Pie Charts

A **bar chart** is a graphical display for depicting categorical data summarized in a frequency, relative frequency, or percent frequency distribution. On one axis of the graph, we specify the labels that are used for the classes (categories). A frequency, relative frequency, or percent frequency scale can be used for the other axis of the chart. Then, using a bar of fixed width drawn above or next to each class label, we extend the length of the bar until we reach the frequency, relative frequency, or percent frequency of the class. For categorical data, the bars should be separated to emphasize the fact that each class is separate. Figure 2.3 shows a bar chart of the frequency distribution for the 50 soft drink purchases. Note how the graphical presentation shows Coca-Cola, Pepsi, and Diet Coke to be the most preferred brands. We can make the brand preferences even more obvious by creating a sorted bar chart as in Figure 2.4. Here, we sort the drink categories: highest frequency on the left and lowest frequency on the right.

Figure 2.3 Bar Chart of Soft Drink Purchases

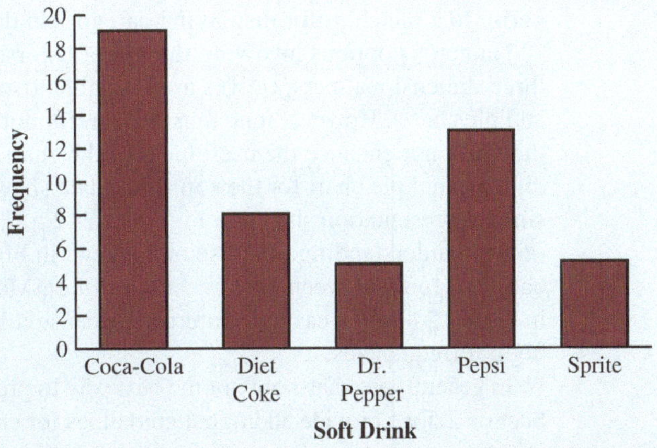

Figure 2.4 Sorted Bar Chart of Soft Drink Purchases

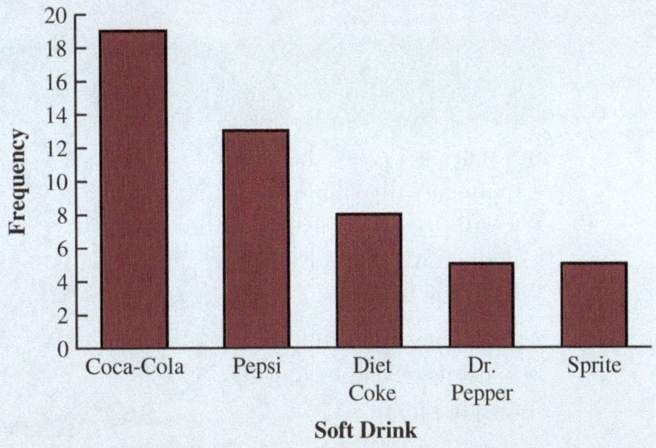

In Figures 2.3 and 2.4, the horizontal axis was used to specify the labels for the categories; thus, the bars of the chart appear vertically in the display. In Excel, this type of display is referred to as a *column chart*. We could also display the bars for the chart horizontally by using the vertical axis to display the labels; Excel refers to this type of display as a *bar chart*. The choice of whether to display the bars vertically or horizontally depends upon what you want the final chart to look like. Throughout the text we will refer to either type of display as a bar chart.

The **pie chart** provides another graphical display for presenting relative frequency and percent frequency distributions for categorical data. To construct a pie chart, we first draw a circle to represent all the data. Then we use the relative frequencies to subdivide the circle into sectors, or parts, that correspond to the relative frequency for each class. For example, because a circle contains 360 degrees and Coca-Cola shows a relative frequency of 0.38, the sector of the pie chart labeled Coca-Cola consists of $0.38(360) = 136.8$ degrees. The sector of the pie chart labeled Diet Coke consists of $0.16(360) = 57.6$ degrees. Similar calculations for the other classes yield the pie chart shown in Figure 2.5. The numerical values shown for each sector can be frequencies, relative frequencies, or percent frequencies. Although pie charts are common ways of visualizing data, many data visualization experts do not recommend their use because people have difficulty perceiving differences in area. In most cases, a bar chart is superior to a pie chart for displaying categorical data.

Numerous options involving the use of colors, shading, legends, text font, and three-dimensional perspectives are available to enhance the visual appearance of bar and pie charts. However, one must be careful not to overuse these options because they may not enhance the usefulness of the chart. For instance, consider the three-dimensional pie chart for the soft drink data shown in Figure 2.6. Compare it to the simpler presentation shown in Figures 2.3–2.5. The three-dimensional perspective adds no new understanding. The use of a legend in Figure 2.6 also forces your eyes to shift back and forth between the key and the chart. Most readers find the sorted bar chart in Figure 2.4 much easier to interpret because it is obvious which soft drinks have the highest frequencies.

In general, pie charts are not the best way to present percentages for comparison. In Section 2.5 we provide additional guidelines for creating effective visual displays.

Figure 2.5 Pie Chart of Soft Drink Purchases

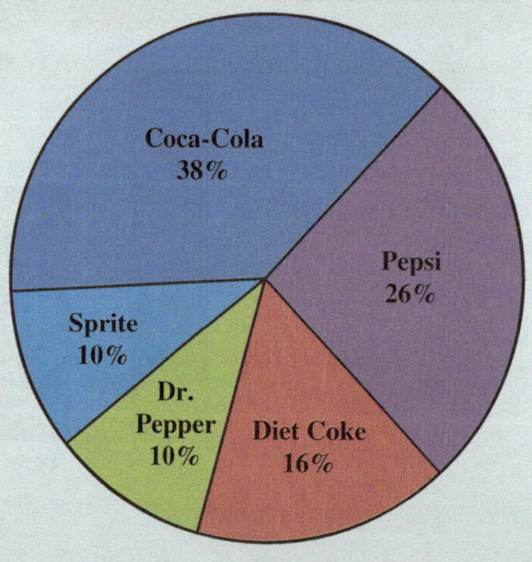

Figure 2.6 Three-Dimensional Pie Chart of Soft Drink Purchases

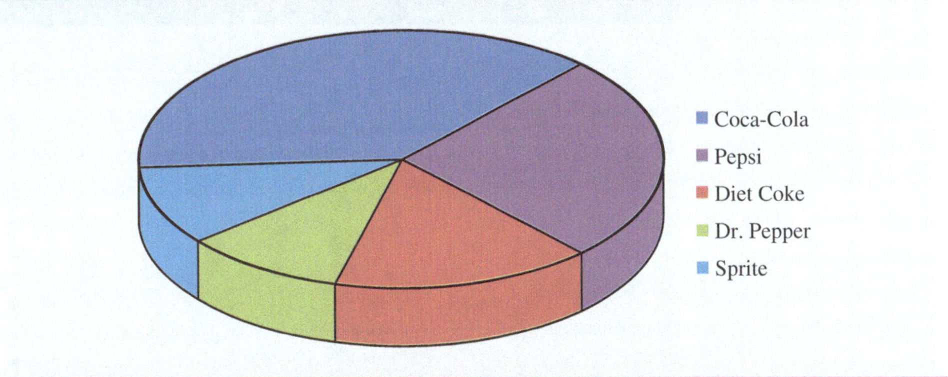

Using Excel to Construct a Bar Chart

DATA*file*
softdrink

We can use Excel's Recommended Charts tool to construct a bar chart for the sample of 50 soft drink purchases. Two tasks are involved: Enter/Access Data and Apply Tools.

Enter/Access Data: Open the file *softdrink*. The data are in cells A2:A51 and a label is in cell A1.

Apply Tools: The following steps describe how to use Excel's Recommended Charts tool to construct a bar chart for the sample of 50 soft drink purchases.

Step 1. Select any cell in the data set (cells A1:A51)
Step 2. Click the **Insert** tab on the Ribbon
Step 3. In the **Charts** group click **Recommended Charts**; a preview showing the bar chart appears
Step 4. Click **OK**; the bar chart will appear in a new worksheet

The worksheet in Figure 2.7 shows the bar chart for the 50 soft drink purchases created using these steps. Also shown are the frequency distribution and PivotTable Fields task pane that were created by Excel in order to construct the bar chart. Thus, using Excel's

Excel refers to the bar chart in Figure 2.7 as a Clustered Column chart.

Figure 2.7 Bar Chart of Soft Drink Purchases Constructed Using Excel's Recommended Charts Tool

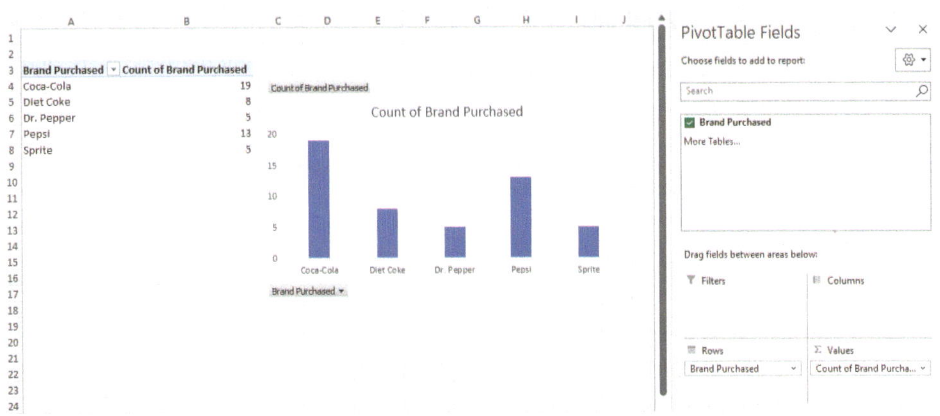

Figure 2.8 Edited Sorted Bar Chart of Soft Drink Purchases Constructed Using Excel's Recommended Charts Tool

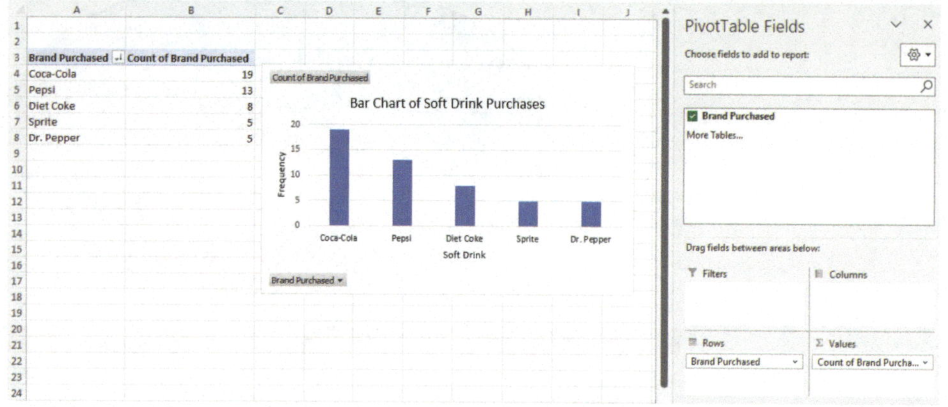

Recommended Charts tool you can construct a bar chart and a frequency distribution at the same time.

Editing Options: You can easily edit the bar chart to display a different chart title and add axis titles. For instance, suppose you would like to create a sorted bar chart to use "Bar Chart of Soft Drink Purchases" as the chart title, to use "Soft Drink" for the horizontal axis title and to use "Frequency" for the vertical axis title.

Step 1. Click the **Chart Title** and replace it with *Bar Chart of Soft Drink Purchases*
Step 2. Click the **Chart Elements** button
Step 3. When the list of chart elements appears:
Select the check box for **Axis Titles** (creates placeholders for the axis titles)
Step 4. Click the horizontal **Axis Title** placeholder and replace it with *Soft Drink*
Step 5. Click the vertical **Axis Title** placeholder and replace it with *Frequency*
Step 6. Right-click on any of the bars in the chart, select **Sort** and click **Sort Largest to Smallest**

The edited bar chart is shown in Figure 2.8.

Exercises

Methods

1. The response to a question has three alternatives: A, B, and C. A sample of 120 responses provides 60 A, 24 B, and 36 C. Show the frequency and relative frequency distributions. **LO 1**

2. A partial relative frequency distribution is given. **LO 1**

Class	Relative Frequency
A	0.22
B	0.18
C	0.40
D	

a. What is the relative frequency of class D?
b. The total sample size is 200. What is the frequency of class D?
c. Show the frequency distribution.
d. Show the percent frequency distribution.

3. A questionnaire provides 58 Yes, 42 No, and 20 No-Opinion answers. **LO 2**
   a. In the construction of a pie chart, how many degrees would be in the section of the pie showing the Yes answers?
   b. How many degrees would be in the section of the pie showing the No answers?
   c. Construct a pie chart.
   d. Construct a bar chart.

Applications

4. **Most Visited Websites.** In a recent report, the top five most-visited English-language websites were google.com (GOOG), facebook.com (FB), youtube.com (YT), yahoo.com (YAH), and wikipedia.com (WIKI). The most-visited websites for a sample of 50 Internet users are shown in the following table. **LO 1**

DATA*file*
websites

YAH	WIKI	YT	WIKI	GOOG
YT	YAH	GOOG	GOOG	GOOG
WIKI	GOOG	YAH	YAH	YAH
YAH	YT	GOOG	YT	YAH
GOOG	FB	FB	WIKI	GOOG
GOOG	GOOG	FB	FB	WIKI
FB	YAH	YT	YAH	YAH
YT	GOOG	YAH	FB	FB
WIKI	GOOG	YAH	WIKI	WIKI
YAH	YT	GOOG	GOOG	WIKI

   a. Are these data categorical or quantitative?
   b. Provide frequency and percent frequency distributions.
   c. On the basis of the sample, which website is most frequently visited website for Internet users? Which is second?

5. **Most Popular Baby Names for Females.** The most popular names for babies who are assigned a sex of female born in the United States in 2021 are Olivia, Emma, Ameilia, Ava, Sophia, and Charlotte (*www.babycenter.com*). Assume that a sample of 50 babies born in 2021 provides the following data:

DATA*file*
babynames2021

Olivia	Sophia	Sophia	Sophia	Olivia
Emma	Charlotte	Emma	Ava	Emma
Amelia	Emma	Olivia	Sophia	Ava
Ava	Emma	Emma	Ava	Olivia
Sophia	Amelia	Ava	Sophia	Ava
Sophia	Ava	Charlotte	Emma	Olivia
Ava	Emma	Emma	Olivia	Charlotte
Charlotte	Charlotte	Emma	Emma	Amelia
Amelia	Charlotte	Sophia	Amelia	Emma
Charlotte	Ava	Olivia	Ava	Amelia

   Summarize the data by constructing the following. **LO 1, 2**
   a. Relative and percent frequency distributions
   b. A bar chart
   c. A sorted bar chart

d. A pie chart

e. Based on these data, what are the three most common names for babies assigned a sex of female? Which type of chart makes this most apparent?

6. **Top-Rated Television Show Networks.** Nielsen Media Research provided the list of the 25 top-rated single shows in television history. The following data show the television network that produced each of these 25 top-rated shows. **LO 1, 2**

DATA*file*
tvnetworks

CBS	CBS	NBC	FOX	CBS
CBS	NBC	NBC	NBC	ABC
ABC	NBC	ABC	ABC	NBC
CBS	NBC	CBS	ABC	NBC
NBC	CBS	CBS	ABC	CBS

a. Construct a frequency distribution, percent frequency distribution, and bar chart for the data.

b. Which networks have done the best in terms of presenting top-rated television shows? Compare the performance of ABC, CBS, and NBC.

7. **Airline Customer Satisfaction Survey.** Many airlines use surveys to collect data on customer satisfaction related to flight experiences. After completing a flight, customers receive an e-mail asking them to go to the website and rate a variety of factors, including the reservation process, the check-in process, luggage policy, cleanliness of gate area, service by flight attendants, food/beverage selection, on-time arrival, and so on. A five-point scale, with Excellent (E), Very Good (V), Good (G), Fair (F), and Poor (P), is used to record customer ratings. Assume that passengers on a Delta Airlines flight from Myrtle Beach, South Carolina to Atlanta, Georgia provided the following ratings for the question "Please rate the airline based on your overall experience with this flight." The sample ratings are shown below. **LO 1, 2**

DATA*file*
airsurvey

E	E	G	V	V	E	V	V	V	E
E	G	V	E	E	V	E	E	E	V
V	V	V	F	V	E	V	E	G	E
G	E	V	E	V	E	V	V	V	V
E	E	V	V	E	P	E	V	P	V

a. Use a percent frequency distribution and a bar chart to summarize these data. What do these summaries indicate about the overall customer satisfaction with the Delta flight?

b. The online survey questionnaire enabled respondents to explain any aspect of the flight that failed to meet expectations. Would this be helpful information to a manager looking for ways to improve the overall customer satisfaction on Delta flights? Explain.

8. **Baseball Hall of Fame Positions.** Data for a sample of 55 members of the Baseball Hall of Fame in Cooperstown, New York are shown here. Each observation indicates the primary position played by the Hall of Famers: pitcher (P), catcher (H), first base (1), second base (2), third base (3), shortstop (S), left field (L), center field (C), and right field (R). **LO 1**

DATA*file*
baseballhall

L	P	C	H	2	P	R	1	S	S	1	L	P	R	P
P	P	P	R	C	S	L	R	P	C	C	P	P	R	P
2	3	P	H	L	P	1	C	P	P	P	S	1	L	R
R	1	2	H	S	3	H	2	L	P					

a. Construct frequency and relative frequency distributions to summarize the data.

b. What position provides the most Hall of Famers?

c. What position provides the fewest Hall of Famers?
d. What outfield position (L, C, or R) provides the most Hall of Famers?
e. Compare infielders (1, 2, 3, and S) to outfielders (L, C, and R).

9. **Degrees Awarded Annually.** Nearly 1.9 million bachelor's degrees and over 758,000 master's degrees are awarded annually by U.S. postsecondary institutions as of 2018 (National Center for Education Statistics website). The Department of Education tracks the field of study for these graduates in the following categories: Business (B), Computer Sciences and Engineering (CSE), Education (E), Humanities (H), Natural Sciences and Mathematics (NSM), Social and Behavioral Sciences (SBS), and Other (O). A sample of 100 graduates follows. **LO 1**

DATA*file*
majors

Bachelor's Degree Field of Study

SBS	H	H	H	E	B	O	SBS	NSM	CSE
O	B	B	O	O	H	B	O	SBS	O
H	CSE	CSE	O	CSE	B	H	O	O	SBS
SBS	SBS	B	H	NSM	B	B	O	SBS	SBS
B	H	SBS	O	B	B	O	O	B	O
O	H	SBS	H	CSE	CSE	B	E	CSE	SBS
SBS	NSM	NSM	CSE	H	H	E	E	SBS	CSE
NSM	NSM	SBS	O	H	H	B	SBS	SBS	NSM
H	B	B	O	O	O	NSM	H	E	B
E	B	O	B	B	B	O	O	O	O

Master's Degree Field of Study

O	O	B	O	B	E	B	H	E	B
O	E	SBS	B	CSE	H	B	E	E	O
O	B	B	O	E	CSE	NSM	O	B	E
H	H	B	E	SBS	E	E	B	O	E
SBS	B	B	CSE	H	B	B	CSE	SBS	B
CSE	B	E	CSE	B	E	CSE	O	E	O
B	O	E	O	B	NSM	H	E	B	E
B	E	B	O	E	E	H	O	O	O
CSE	O	O	H	B	O	B	E	CSE	O
E	O	SBS	E	E	O	SBS	B	B	O

a. Provide a percent frequency distribution of field of study for each degree.
b. Construct a bar chart for field of study for each degree.
c. What is the lowest percentage field of study for each degree?
d. What is the highest percentage field of study for each degree?
e. Which field of study has the largest increase in percentage from bachelor's to master's?

10. **Online Hotel Ratings.** TripAdvisor is one of many online websites that provides ratings for hotels throughout the world. Ratings provided by 649 guests at the Lakeview Lodge can be found in the file *hotelratings*. Possible responses were Excellent, Very Good, Average, Poor, and Terrible. **LO 1, 2**

DATA*file*
hotelratings

a. Construct a frequency distribution.
b. Construct a percent frequency distribution.
c. Construct a bar chart for the percent frequency distribution.
d. Comment on how guests rate their stay at the Lakeview Lodge.
e. Suppose that results for 1,679 guests who stayed at the Timber Hotel provided the following frequency distribution.

Rating	Frequency
Excellent	807
Very Good	521
Average	200
Poor	107
Terrible	44

Compare the ratings for the Timber Hotel with the results obtained for the Lakeview Lodge.

2.2 Summarizing Data for a Quantitative Variable

Frequency Distribution

As defined in Section 2.1, a frequency distribution is a tabular summary of data showing the number (frequency) of observations in each of several nonoverlapping categories or classes. This definition holds for quantitative as well as categorical data. However, with quantitative data, we must be more careful in defining the nonoverlapping classes to be used in the frequency distribution.

For example, consider the quantitative data in Table 2.4. These data show the time in days required to complete year-end audits for a sample of 20 clients of Sanderson and Clifford, a small public accounting firm. The three steps necessary to define the classes for a frequency distribution with quantitative data are as follows:

1. Determine the number of nonoverlapping classes.
2. Determine the width of each class.
3. Determine the class limits.

Let us demonstrate these steps by developing a frequency distribution for the audit time data in Table 2.4.

Number of classes Classes are formed by specifying ranges that will be used to group the data. As a general guideline, we recommend using between 5 and 20 classes. For a small number of data items, as few as five or six classes may be used to summarize the data. For a larger number of data items, a larger number of classes is usually required. The goal is to use enough classes to show the variation in the data, but not so many classes that some contain only a few data items. Because the number of data items in Table 2.4 is relatively small ($n = 20$), we chose to develop a frequency distribution with five classes.

Making the classes the same width reduces the chance of inappropriate interpretations by the user.

Width of the classes The second step in constructing a frequency distribution for quantitative data is to choose a width for the classes. As a general guideline, we recommend that the width be the same for each class. Thus the choices of the number of classes and the width of classes are not independent decisions. A larger number of classes means a smaller class width, and vice versa. To determine an approximate class width, we begin by

DATA*file*
audit

Table 2.4 Year-End Audit Times (In Days)

12	14	19	18
15	15	18	17
20	27	22	23
22	21	33	28
14	18	16	13

identifying the largest and smallest data values. Then, with the desired number of classes specified, we can use the following expression to determine the approximate class width.

$$\text{Approximate class width} = \frac{\text{Largest data value} - \text{Smallest data value}}{\text{Number of classes}} \tag{2.2}$$

The approximate class width given by equation (2.2) can be rounded to a more convenient value based on the preference of the person developing the frequency distribution. For example, an approximate class width of 9.28 might be rounded to 10 simply because 10 is a more convenient class width to use in presenting a frequency distribution.

For the data involving the year-end audit times, the largest data value is 33 and the smallest data value is 12. Because we decided to summarize the data with five classes, using equation (2.2) provides an approximate class width of $(33 - 12)/5 = 4.2$. We therefore decided to round up and use a class width of five days in the frequency distribution.

No single frequency distribution is best for a data set. Different people may construct different, but equally acceptable, frequency distributions. The goal is to reveal the natural grouping and variation in the data.

In practice, the number of classes and the appropriate class width are determined by trial and error. Once a possible number of classes is chosen, equation (2.2) is used to find the approximate class width. The process can be repeated for a different number of classes. Ultimately, the analyst uses judgment to determine the combination of the number of classes and class width that provides the best frequency distribution for summarizing the data.

For the audit time data in Table 2.4, after deciding to use five classes, each with a width of five days, the next task is to specify the class limits for each of the classes.

Class limits Class limits must be chosen so that each data item belongs to one and only one class. The *lower class limit* identifies the smallest possible data value assigned to the class. The *upper class limit* identifies the largest possible data value assigned to the class. In developing frequency distributions for categorical data, we did not need to specify class limits because each data item naturally fell into a separate class. But with quantitative data, such as the audit times in Table 2.4, class limits are necessary to determine where each data value belongs.

Using the audit time data in Table 2.4, we selected 10 days as the lower class limit and 14 days as the upper class limit for the first class. This class is denoted 10–14 in Table 2.5. The smallest data value, 12, is included in the 10–14 class. We then selected 15 days as the lower class limit and 19 days as the upper class limit of the next class. We continued defining the lower and upper class limits to obtain a total of five classes: 10–14, 15–19, 20–24, 25–29, and 30–34. The largest data value, 33, is included in the 30–34 class. The difference between the lower class limits of adjacent classes is the class width. Using the first two lower class limits of 10 and 15, we see that the class width is $15 - 10 = 5$.

Table 2.5 Frequency Distribution for the Audit Time Data

Audit Time (days)	Frequency
10–14	4
15–19	8
20–24	5
25–29	2
30–34	1
Total	20

Table 2.6 Relative Frequency and Percent Frequency Distributions for the Audit Time Data

Audit Time (days)	Relative Frequency	Percent Frequency
10–14	0.20	20
15–19	0.40	40
20–24	0.25	25
25–29	0.10	10
30–34	0.05	5
Total	1.00	100

With the number of classes, class width, and class limits determined, a frequency distribution can be obtained by counting the number of data values belonging to each class. For example, the data in Table 2.4 show that four values—12, 14, 14, and 13—belong to the 10–14 class. Thus, the frequency for the 10–14 class is 4. Continuing this counting process for the 15–19, 20–24, 25–29, and 30–34 classes provides the frequency distribution in Table 2.5. Using this frequency distribution, we can observe the following:

1. The most frequently occurring audit times are in the class of 15–19 days. Eight of the 20 audit times belong to this class.
2. Only one audit required 30 or more days.

Other conclusions are possible, depending on the interests of the person viewing the frequency distribution. The value of a frequency distribution is that it provides insights about the data that are not easily obtained by viewing the data in their original unorganized form.

Class midpoint In some applications, we want to know the midpoints of the classes in a frequency distribution for quantitative data. The **class midpoint** is the value halfway between the lower and upper class limits. For the audit time data, the five class midpoints are 12, 17, 22, 27, and 32.

Relative Frequency and Percent Frequency Distributions

We define the relative frequency and percent frequency distributions for quantitative data in the same manner as for categorical data. First, recall that the relative frequency is the proportion of the observations belonging to a class. With n observations,

$$\text{Relative frequency of class} = \frac{\text{Frequency of the class}}{n}$$

The percent frequency of a class is the relative frequency multiplied by 100.

Based on the class frequencies in Table 2.5 and with $n = 20$, Table 2.6 shows the relative frequency distribution and percent frequency distribution for the audit time data. Note that 0.40 of the audits, or 40%, required from 15 to 19 days. Only 0.05 of the audits, or 5%, required 30 or more days. Again, additional interpretations and insights can be obtained by using Table 2.6.

Using Excel to Construct a Frequency Distribution

We can use Excel's PivotTable tool to construct a frequency distribution for the audit time data. Two tasks are involved: Enter/Access Data and Apply Tools.

DATA*file*
audit

Enter/Access Data: Open the file *audit*. The data are in cells A2:A21 and a label is in cell A1.

Apply Tools: The following steps describe how to use Excel's PivotTable tool to construct a frequency distribution for the audit time data. When using Excel's PivotTable tool, each column of data is referred to as a *"field."* Thus, for the audit time example, the data appearing in cells A2:A21 and the label in cell A1 are referred to as the Audit Time field.

Step 1. Select any cell in the data set (cells A1:A21)
Step 2. Click the **Insert** tab on the Ribbon
Step 3. In the **Tables** group, click **PivotTable**
Step 4. When the **Create PivotTable** dialog box appears:
Click **OK**; a **PivotTable** and **PivotTable Fields** task pane will appear in a new worksheet
Step 5. In the **PivotTable Fields** task pane:
Drag **Audit Time** to the **Rows** area
Drag **Audit Time** to the **Values** area
Step 6. Click on **Sum of Audit Time** in the **Values** area
Step 7. Select **Value Field Settings...** from the list of options that appears
Step 8. When the **Value Field Settings** dialog box appears:
Under **Summarize value field by**, choose **Count**
Click **OK**

Figure 2.9 shows the resulting PivotTable Fields task pane and the corresponding PivotTable. To construct the frequency distribution shown in Table 2.5, we must group the rows containing the audit times. The following steps accomplish this.

Step 1. Right-click cell A4 in the PivotTable or any other cell containing an audit time
Step 2. Choose **Group** from the list of options that appears
Step 3. When the Grouping dialog box appears:
Enter *10* in the **Starting at:** box
Enter *34* in the **Ending at:** box
Enter *5* in the **By:** box
Click **OK**

Figure 2.9 PivotTable Fields Task Pane and Initial PivotTable Used to Construct a Frequency Distribution for the Audit Time Data

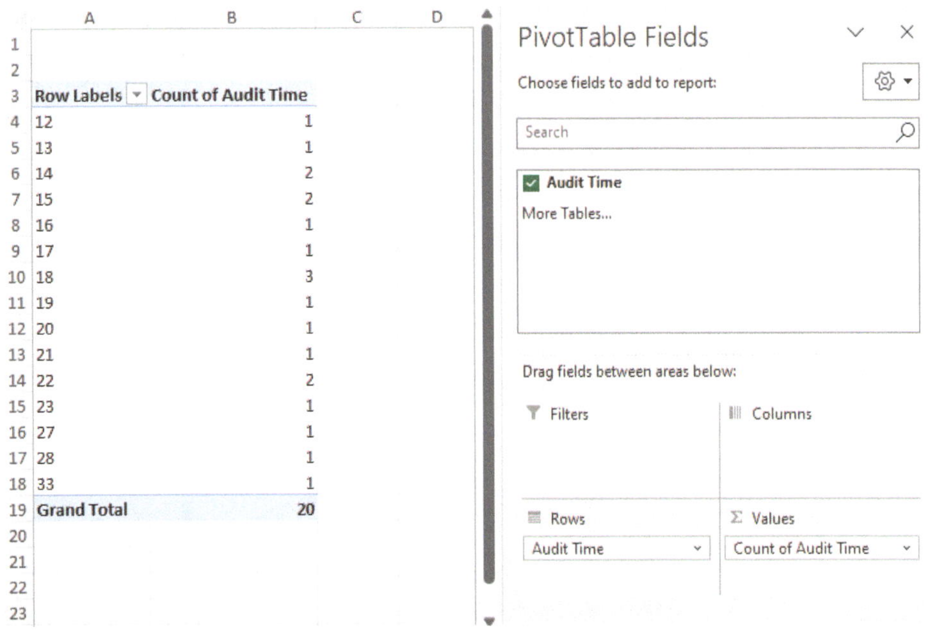

Figure 2.10 shows the completed PivotTable Fields task pane and the corresponding PivotTable. We see that with the exception of the column headings, the PivotTable provides the same information as the frequency distribution shown in Table 2.5.

The same Excel procedures we followed in the previous section can now be used to develop relative and percent frequency distributions if desired.

Editing Options: You can easily change the labels in the PivotTable to match the labels in Table 2.5. For instance, to change the current heading in cell A3 (Row Labels) to "Audit Time (days)," click in cell A3 and type *Audit Time (days)*; to change the current heading in cell B3 (Count of Audit Time) to "Frequency," click in cell B3 and type *Frequency*; and to change the current heading in A9 (Grand Total) to *Total*, click in cell A9 and type *Total*.

In smaller data sets or when there are a large number of classes, some classes may have no data values. In such cases, Excel's PivotTable tool will remove these classes when constructing the frequency distribution. For presentation, however, we recommend editing the results to show all the classes, including those with no data values. The following steps show how this can be done.

Step 1. Right-click on any cell in the **Row Labels** column of the PivotTable
Step 2. Click **Field Settings...**
Step 3. When the **Field Settings** dialog box appears:
Click the **Layout & Print** tab
Choose **Show items with no data**
Click **OK**

Dot Plot

One of the simplest graphical summaries of data is a **dot plot**. A horizontal axis shows the range for the data. Each data value is represented by a dot placed above the axis. Figure 2.11 is the dot plot for the audit time data in Table 2.4. The three dots located

Figure 2.10 Frequency Distribution for the Audit Time Data Constructed Using Excel's PivotTable Tool

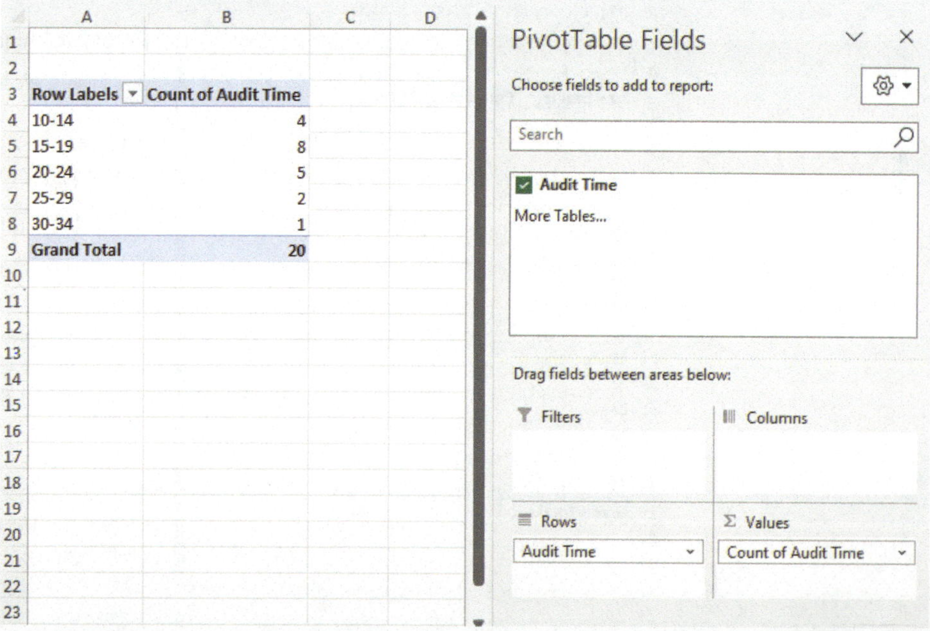

Figure 2.11 Dot Plot for the Audit Time Data

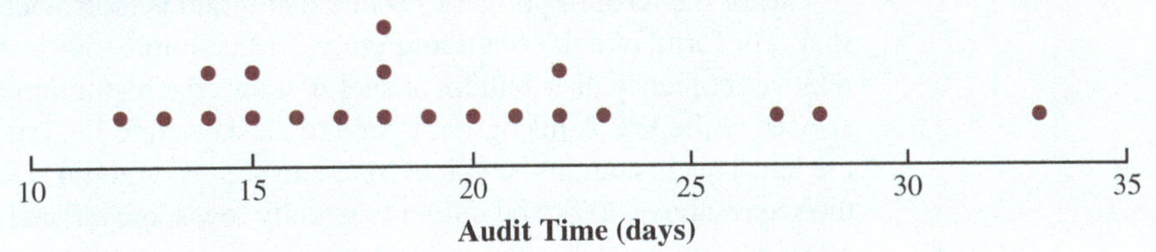

above 18 on the horizontal axis indicate that an audit time of 18 days occurred three times. Dot plots show the details of the data and are useful for comparing the distribution of the data for two or more variables.

Histogram

A common graphical display of quantitative data is a **histogram**. This graphical display can be prepared for data previously summarized in either a frequency, relative frequency, or percent frequency distribution. A histogram is constructed by placing the variable of interest on the horizontal axis and the frequency, relative frequency, or percent frequency on the vertical axis. The frequency, relative frequency, or percent frequency of each class is shown by drawing a rectangle whose base is determined by the class limits on the horizontal axis and whose height is the corresponding frequency, relative frequency, or percent frequency.

Figure 2.12 is a histogram for the audit time data. Note that the class with the greatest frequency is shown by the rectangle appearing above the class of 15–19 days. The height of the rectangle shows that the frequency of this class is 8. A histogram for the relative or percent frequency distribution of these data would look the same as the histogram in Figure 2.12 with the exception that the vertical axis would be labeled with relative or percent frequency values.

As Figure 2.12 shows, the adjacent rectangles of a histogram touch one another. Unlike a bar chart, a histogram contains no natural separation between the rectangles of adjacent classes. This format is the usual convention for histograms. Because the classes for the audit time data are stated as 10–14, 15–19, 20–24, 25–29, and 30–34, one-unit spaces of 14 to 15, 19 to 20, 24 to 25, and 29 to 30 would seem to be needed between the classes. These spaces are eliminated when constructing a histogram. Eliminating the spaces between

Figure 2.12 Histogram for the Audit Time Data

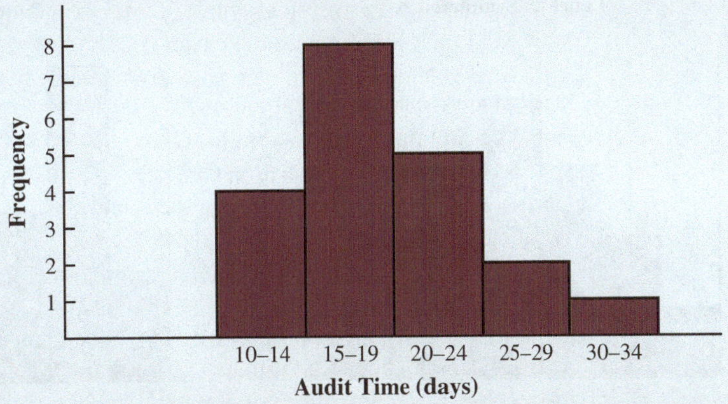

classes in a histogram for the audit time data helps show that all values between the lower limit of the first class and the upper limit of the last class are possible.

One of the most important uses of a histogram is to provide information about the shape, or form, of a distribution. Figure 2.13 contains four histograms constructed from relative frequency distributions. Panel A shows the histogram for a set of data moderately skewed to the left. A histogram is said to be skewed to the left if its tail extends farther to the left. This histogram is typical for exam scores, with no scores above 100%, most of the scores above 70%, and only a few really low scores. Panel B shows the histogram for a set of data moderately skewed to the right. A histogram is said to be skewed to the right if its tail extends farther to the right. An example of this type of histogram would be for data such as housing prices; a few expensive houses create the skewness in the right tail.

Panel C shows a symmetric histogram. In a symmetric histogram, the left tail mirrors the shape of the right tail. Histograms for data found in applications are never perfectly symmetric, but the histogram for many applications may be roughly symmetric. Data for SAT scores, heights and weights of people, and so on lead to histograms that are roughly symmetric. Panel D shows a histogram highly skewed to the right. This histogram was constructed from data on the dollar amount of customer purchases over one day at a clothing store. Data from applications in business and economics often lead to histograms that are skewed to the right. For instance, data on housing prices, salaries, purchase amounts, and so on often result in histograms skewed to the right.

Figure 2.13 Histograms Showing Differing Levels of Skewness

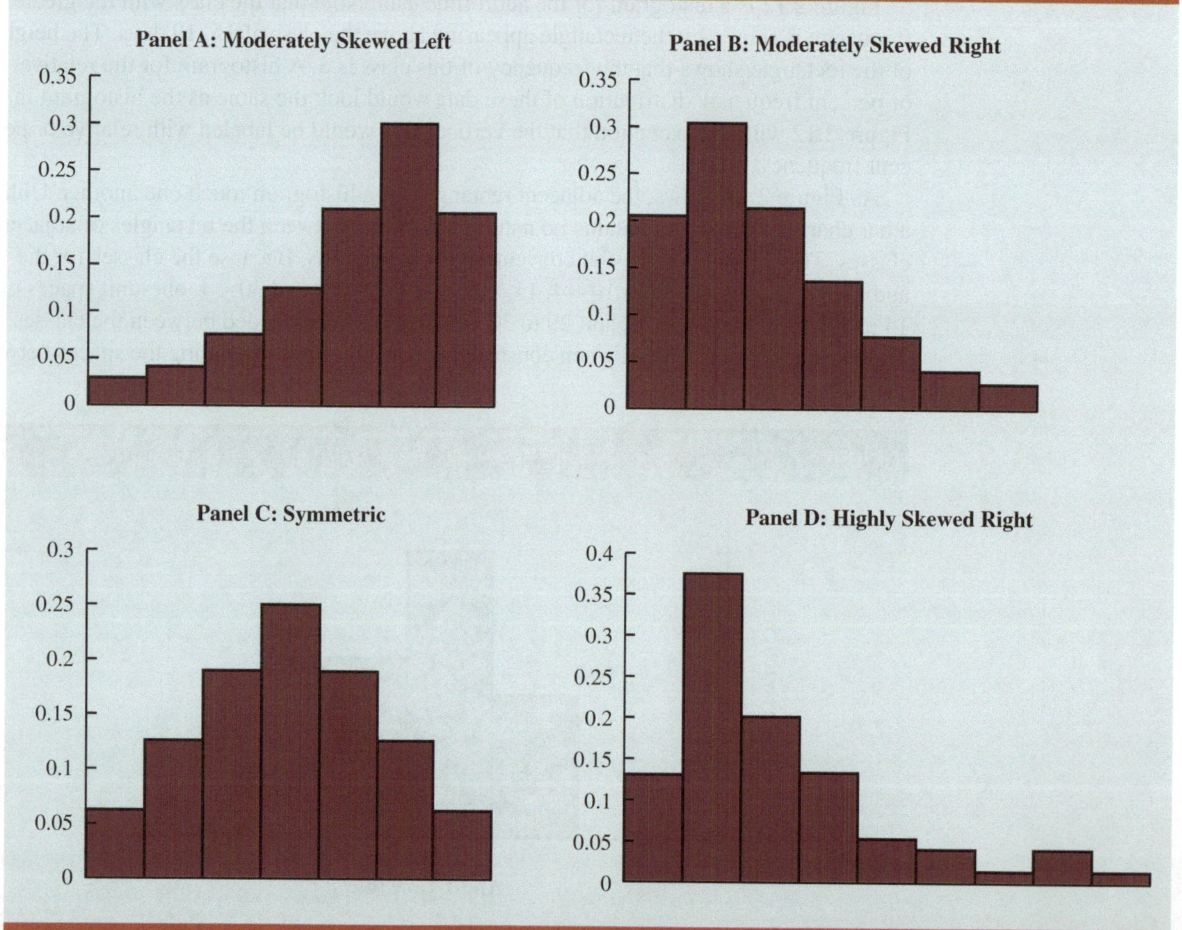

Using Excel's Recommended Charts Tool to Construct a Histogram

In Figure 2.10, we showed the results of using Excel's PivotTable tool to construct a frequency distribution for the audit time data. We will use these results to illustrate how Excel's Recommended Charts tool can be used to construct a histogram for depicting quantitative data summarized in a frequency distribution. Refer to Figure 2.14 as we describe the steps involved.

Apply Tools: The following steps describe how to use Excel's Recommended Charts tool to construct a histogram for the audit time data.

Step 1. Select any cell in the PivotTable report (cells A3:B9)
Step 2. Click the **Insert** tab on the Ribbon
Step 3. In the **Charts** group, click **Recommended Charts**; a preview showing the recommended chart appears
Step 4. Click **OK**

The worksheet in Figure 2.14 shows the chart for the audit time data created using these steps. With the exception of the gaps separating the bars, this resembles the histogram for the audit time data shown in Figure 2.12. We can easily edit this chart to remove the gaps between the bars and enter more descriptive axis labels and a chart heading.

Editing Options: In addition to removing the gaps between the bars, suppose you would like to use "Histogram for Audit Time Data" as the chart title and insert "Audit Time (days)" for the horizontal axis title and "Frequency" for the vertical axis title.

Step 1. Right-click any bar in the chart and choose **Format Data Series...** from the list of options that appears
Step 2. When the **Format Data Series** task pane appears:
Click **Series Options** to display the options
Set the **Gap Width** to *0*
Click the **Close** button × at the top right of the task pane
Step 3. Click the **Chart Title** and replace it with *Histogram for Audit Time Data*
Step 4. Click the **Chart Elements** button +
Step 5. When the list of chart elements appears:
Select the check box for **Axis Titles** (creates placeholders for the axis titles)
Deselect the check box for **Legend**
Deselect the check box for **Gridlines**

Figure 2.14 Initial Chart Used to Construct a Histogram for the Audit Time Data

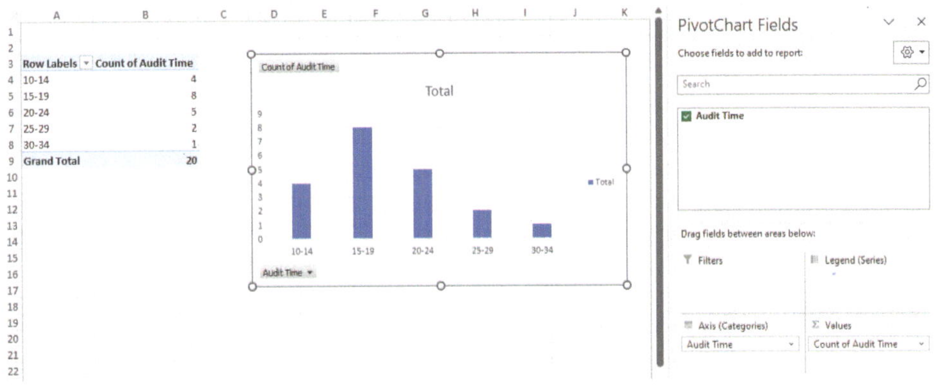

Figure 2.15 Histogram for the Audit Time Data Created Using Excel's Recommended Charts Tool

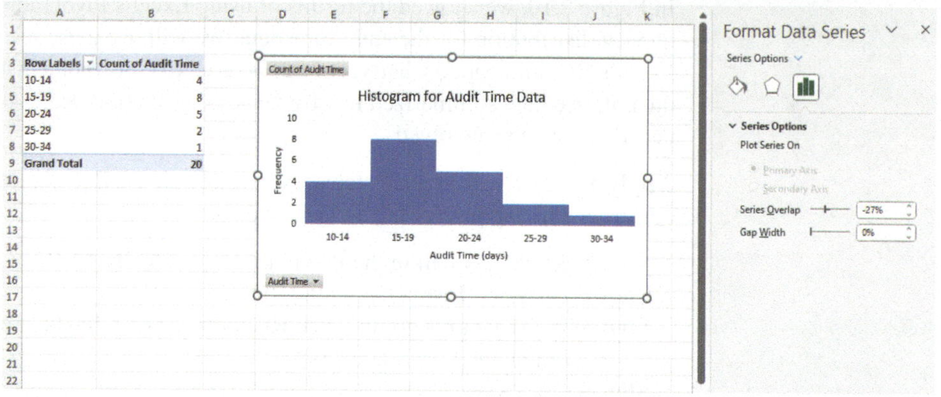

Step 6. Click the horizontal **Axis Title** placeholder and replace it with *Audit Time (days)*
Step 7. Click the vertical **Axis Title** placeholder and replace it with *Frequency*

The edited histogram for the audit time data is shown in Figure 2.15.

In smaller data sets or when there are a large number of classes, some classes may have no data values. In such cases, Excel's PivotTable tool will automatically remove these classes when constructing the frequency distribution, and the histogram created using Excel's Recommended Charts tool will not show the classes with no data values. For presentation, however, we recommend editing the results to show all the classes, including those with no data values. The following steps show how this can be done by editing the PivotTable tool output before constructing the histogram.

Step 1. Right-click on any cell in the **Row Labels** column of the PivotTable
Step 2. Click **Field Settings...**
Step 3. When the **Field Settings** dialog box appears:
Click the **Layout & Print** tab
Choose **Show items with no data**
Click **OK**

After performing steps 1–3, the PivotTable will display all classes, including those with no data values. Using the Recommended Charts tool will then create a histogram that displays all classes.

Cumulative Distributions

A variation of the frequency distribution that provides another tabular summary of quantitative data is the **cumulative frequency distribution**. The cumulative frequency distribution uses the number of classes, class widths, and class limits developed for the frequency distribution. However, rather than showing the frequency of each class, the cumulative frequency distribution shows the number of data items with values *less than or equal to the upper class limit* of each class. The first two columns of Table 2.7 provide the cumulative frequency distribution for the audit time data.

To understand how the cumulative frequencies are determined, consider the class with the description "less than or equal to 24." The cumulative frequency for this class is simply the sum of the frequencies for all classes with data values less than or equal to 24. For the frequency distribution in Table 2.5, the sum of the frequencies for classes 10–14, 15–19, and 20–24 indicates that $4 + 8 + 5 = 17$ data values are less than or equal to 24.

Table 2.7 Cumulative Frequency, Cumulative Relative Frequency, and Cumulative Percent Frequency Distributions for the Audit Time Data

Audit Time (days)	Cumulative Frequency	Cumulative Relative Frequency	Cumulative Percent Frequency
Less than or equal to 14	4	0.20	20
Less than or equal to 19	12	0.60	60
Less than or equal to 24	17	0.85	85
Less than or equal to 29	19	0.95	95
Less than or equal to 34	20	1.00	100

Hence, the cumulative frequency for this class is 17. In addition, the cumulative frequency distribution in Table 2.7 shows that four audits were completed in 14 days or less and 19 audits were completed in 29 days or less.

As a final point, we note that a **cumulative relative frequency distribution** shows the proportion of data items, and a **cumulative percent frequency distribution** shows the percentage of data items with values less than or equal to the upper limit of each class. The cumulative relative frequency distribution can be computed either by summing the relative frequencies in the relative frequency distribution or by dividing the cumulative frequencies by the total number of items. Using the latter approach, we found the cumulative relative frequencies in column 3 of Table 2.7 by dividing the cumulative frequencies in column 2 by the total number of items ($n = 20$). The cumulative percent frequencies were again computed by multiplying the relative frequencies by 100. The cumulative relative and percent frequency distributions show that 0.85 of the audits, or 85%, were completed in 24 days or less, 0.95 of the audits, or 95%, were completed in 29 days or less, and so on.

Stem-and-Leaf Display

A **stem-and-leaf display** is a graphical display used to show simultaneously the rank order and shape of a distribution of data. To illustrate the use of a stem-and-leaf display, consider the data in Table 2.8. These data result from a 150-question aptitude test given to 50 individuals recently interviewed for a position at Haskens Technology. The data indicate the number of questions answered correctly.

To develop a stem-and-leaf display, we first arrange the leading digits of each data value to the left of a vertical line. To the right of the vertical line, we record the last digit for each

DATA*file*
aptitudetest

Table 2.8 Number of Questions Answered Correctly on an Aptitude Test

112	72	69	97	107
73	92	76	86	73
126	128	118	127	124
82	104	132	134	83
92	108	96	100	92
115	76	91	102	81
95	141	81	80	106
84	119	113	98	75
68	98	115	106	95
100	85	94	106	119

data value. Based on the top row of data in Table 2.8 (112, 72, 69, 97, and 107), the first five entries in constructing a stem-and-leaf display would be as follows:

6	9
7	2
8	
9	7
10	7
11	2
12	
13	
14	

For example, the data value 112 shows the leading digits 11 to the left of the line and the last digit 2 to the right of the line. Similarly, the data value 72 shows the leading digit 7 to the left of the line and last digit 2 to the right of the line. Continuing to place the last digit of each data value on the line corresponding to its leading digit(s) provides the following:

6	9	8								
7	2	3	6	3	6	5				
8	6	2	3	1	1	0	4	5		
9	7	2	2	6	2	1	5	8	8	5	4
10	7	4	8	0	2	6	6	0	6	
11	2	8	5	9	3	5	9			
12	6	8	7	4						
13	2	4								
14	1									

With this organization of the data, sorting the digits on each line into rank order is simple. Doing so provides the stem-and-leaf display shown here.

6	8	9									
7	2	3	3	5	6	6					
8	0	1	1	2	3	4	5	6			
9	1	2	2	2	4	5	5	6	7	8	8
10	0	0	2	4	6	6	6	7	8		
11	2	3	5	5	8	9	9				
12	4	6	7	8							
13	2	4									
14	1										

The numbers to the left of the vertical line (6, 7, 8, 9, 10, 11, 12, 13, and 14) form the *stem*, and each digit to the right of the vertical line is a *leaf.* For example, consider the first row with a stem value of 6 and leaves of 8 and 9.

6 | 8 9

This row indicates that two data values have a first digit of six. The leaves show that the data values are 68 and 69. Similarly, the second row

7 | 2 3 3 5 6 6

indicates that six data values have a first digit of seven. The leaves show that the data values are 72, 73, 73, 75, 76, and 76.

To focus on the shape indicated by the stem-and-leaf display, let us use a rectangle to contain the leaves of each stem. Doing so, we obtain the following:

6	8 9
7	2 3 3 5 6 6
8	0 1 1 2 3 4 5 6
9	1 2 2 2 4 5 5 6 7 8 8
10	0 0 2 4 6 6 6 7 8
11	2 3 5 5 8 9 9
12	4 6 7 8
13	2 4
14	1

Rotating this page counterclockwise onto its side provides a picture of the data that is similar to a histogram with classes of 60–69, 70–79, 80–89, and so on.

Although the stem-and-leaf display may appear to offer the same information as a histogram, it has two primary advantages.

1. The stem-and-leaf display is easier to construct by hand.
2. Within a class interval, the stem-and-leaf display provides more information than the histogram because the stem-and-leaf shows the actual data.

Just as a frequency distribution or histogram has no absolute number of classes, neither does a stem-and-leaf display have an absolute number of rows or stems. If we believe that our original stem-and-leaf display condensed the data too much, we can easily stretch the display by using two or more stems for each leading digit. For example, to use two stems for each leading digit, we would place all data values ending in 0, 1, 2, 3, and 4 in one row and all values ending in 5, 6, 7, 8, and 9 in a second row. The following stretched stem-and-leaf display illustrates this approach.

In a stretched stem-and-leaf display, whenever a stem value is stated twice, the first value corresponds to leaf values of 0–4, and the second value corresponds to leaf values of 5–9.

6	8 9
7	2 3 3
7	5 6 6
8	0 1 1 2 3 4
8	5 6
9	1 2 2 2 4
9	5 5 6 7 8 8
10	0 0 2 4
10	6 6 6 7 8
11	2 3
11	5 5 8 9 9
12	4
12	6 7 8
13	2 4
13	
14	1

Note that values 72, 73, and 73 have leaves in the 0–4 range and are shown with the first stem value of 7. The values 75, 76, and 76 have leaves in the 5–9 range and are shown with the second stem value of 7. This stretched stem-and-leaf display is similar to a frequency distribution with intervals of 65–69, 70–74, 75–79, and so on.

The preceding example showed a stem-and-leaf display for data with as many as three digits. Stem-and-leaf displays for data with more than three digits are possible. For example, consider the following data on the number of hamburgers sold by a fast-food restaurant for each of 15 weeks.

1,565	1,852	1,644	1,766	1,888	1,912	2,044	1,812
1,790	1,679	2,008	1,852	1,967	1,954	1,733	

A stem-and-leaf display of these data follows.

Leaf unit = 10

15	6
16	4 7
17	3 6 9
18	1 5 5 8
19	1 5 6
20	0 4

A single digit is used to define each leaf in a stem-and-leaf display. The leaf unit indicates how to multiply the stem-and-leaf numbers in order to approximate the original data. Leaf units may be 100, 10, 1, 0.1, and so on.

Note that a single digit is used to define each leaf and that only the first three digits of each data value have been used to construct the display. At the top of the display we have specified Leaf unit = 10. To illustrate how to interpret the values in the display, consider the first stem, 15, and its associated leaf, 6. Combining these numbers, we obtain 156. To reconstruct an approximation of the original data value, we must multiply this number by 10, the value of the *leaf unit*. Thus, $156 \times 10 = 1{,}560$ is an approximation of the original data value used to construct the stem-and-leaf display. Although it is not possible to reconstruct the exact data value from this stem-and-leaf display, the convention of using a single digit for each leaf enables stem-and-leaf displays to be constructed for data having a large number of digits. For stem-and-leaf displays where the leaf unit is not shown, the leaf unit is assumed to equal 1.

Notes + Comments

1. A bar chart and a histogram are essentially the same thing; both are graphical displays of the data in a frequency distribution. A histogram is just a bar chart with no separation between bars. For some discrete quantitative data, a separation between bars is also appropriate. Consider, for example, the number of classes in which a college student is enrolled. The data may only assume integer values. Intermediate values such as 1.5 and 2.73 are not possible. With continuous quantitative data, however, such as the audit times in Table 2.4, a separation between bars is not appropriate.
2. The appropriate values for the class limits with quantitative data depend on the level of accuracy of the data. For instance, with the audit time data of Table 2.4 the limits used were integer values. If the data were rounded to the nearest tenth of a day (e.g., 12.3 and 14.4), then the limits would be stated in tenths of days. For instance, the first class would be 10.0–14.9. If the data were recorded to the nearest hundredth of a day (e.g., 12.34 and 14.45), the limits would be stated in hundredths of days. For instance, the first class would be 10.00–14.99.
3. An *open-end* class requires only a lower class limit or an upper class limit. For example, in the audit time data of Table 2.4, suppose two of the audits had taken 58 and 65 days. Rather than continue with the classes of width 5 with classes 35–39, 40–44, 45–49, and so on, we could simplify the frequency distribution to show an open-end class of "35 or more." This class would have a frequency of 2. Most often the open-end class appears at the upper end of the distribution. Sometimes an open-end class appears at the lower end of the distribution, and occasionally such classes appear at both ends.
4. The last entry in a cumulative frequency distribution always equals the total number of observations. The last entry in a cumulative relative frequency distribution always equals 1.00 and the last entry in a cumulative percent frequency distribution always equals 100.

Exercises

Methods

11. Consider the following data. **LO 3**

DATA*file* frequency

14	21	23	21	16
19	22	25	16	16
24	24	25	19	16
19	18	19	21	12
16	17	18	23	25
20	23	16	20	19
24	26	15	22	24
20	22	24	22	20

a. Develop a frequency distribution using classes of 12–14, 15–17, 18–20, 21–23, and 24–26.
b. Develop a relative frequency distribution and a percent frequency distribution using the classes in part (a).

12. Consider the following frequency distribution. **LO 4**

Class	Frequency
10–19	10
20–29	14
30–39	17
40–49	7
50–59	2

Construct a cumulative frequency distribution and a cumulative relative frequency distribution.

13. Construct a histogram for the data in problem 12. **LO 5**
14. Consider the following data. **LO 3, 5**

8.9	10.2	11.5	7.8	10.0	12.2	13.5	14.1	10.0	12.2
6.8	9.5	11.5	11.2	14.9	7.5	10.0	6.0	15.8	11.5

a. Construct a dot plot.
b. Construct a frequency distribution.
c. Construct a percent frequency distribution.

15. Construct a stem-and-leaf display for the following data. **LO 5**

11.3	9.6	10.4	7.5	8.3	10.5	10.0
9.3	8.1	7.7	7.5	8.4	6.3	8.8

16. Construct a stem-and-leaf display for the following data. Use a leaf unit of 10. **LO 5**

1,161	1,206	1,478	1,300	1,604	1,725	1,361	1,422
1,221	1,378	1,623	1,426	1,557	1,730	1,706	1,689

Applications

DATA*file* patientwaiting

17. **Patient Waiting Times.** A doctor's office staff studied the waiting times for patients who arrive at the office with a request for emergency service. The following data with waiting times in minutes were collected over a one-month period. **LO 3, 4**

2 5 10 12 4 4 5 17 11 8 9 8 12 21 6 8 7 13 18 3

Use classes of 0–4, 5–9, and so on in the following:
a. Show the frequency distribution.
b. Show the relative frequency distribution.
c. Show the cumulative frequency distribution.
d. Show the cumulative relative frequency distribution.
e. What proportion of patients needing emergency service wait 9 minutes or less?

18. **NBA Total Player Ratings.** CBSSports.com developed the Total Player Ratings system to rate players in the National Basketball Association (NBA) based upon various offensive and defensive statistics. The following data show the average number of points scored per game (PPG) for 50 players with the highest ratings for a portion of an NBA season (*CBSSports.com*). **LO 3, 4, 5, 6**

DATA*file*
nbaplayerpts

27.0	28.8	26.4	27.1	22.9	28.4	19.2	21.0	20.8	17.6
21.1	19.2	21.2	15.5	17.2	16.7	17.6	18.5	18.3	18.3
23.3	16.4	18.9	16.5	17.0	11.7	15.7	18.0	17.7	14.6
15.7	17.2	18.2	17.5	13.6	16.3	16.2	13.6	17.1	16.7
17.0	17.3	17.5	14.0	16.9	16.3	15.1	12.3	18.7	14.6

Use classes starting at 10 and ending at 30 in increments of 2 for PPG in the following.
a. Show the frequency distribution.
b. Show the relative frequency distribution.
c. Show the cumulative percent frequency distribution.
d. Develop a histogram for the average number of points scored per game.
e. Do the data appear to be skewed? Explain.
f. What percentage of the players averaged at least 20 points per game?

19. **Busiest Container Ports in the United States.** The amount of cargo processed by container ports is often measured in 20-foot equivalent units (TEUs). The following is a list of the 30 busiest container ports in the United States in 2020 (*Logistics Management*). **LO 3, 5**

DATA*file*
containerports

Container Port	TEUs Processed (1,000s)
Baltimore, MD	525
Boston, MA	165
Charleston, SC	1,174
Chester, PA	125
Everett, WA	32
Freeport, TX	51
Gulfport, MS	86
Houston, TX	1,996
Jacksonville, FL	237
Long Beach, CA	4,288
Los Angeles, CA	4,999
Miami, FL	737
Mobile, AL	251
New Orleans, LA	316
Newark, NJ	4,600
Norfolk, VA	1,285
Oakland, CA	1,102
Philadelphia, PA	389
Port Everglades, FL	499
Port Hueneme, CA	90
Port Manatee, FL	53

San Diego, CA	74
San Juan, PR	296
Savannah, GA	2,431
Seattle, WA	1,429
Tacoma, WA	1,316
Tampa, FL	76
West Palm Beach, FL	139
Wilmington, DE	205
Wilmington, NC	131

a. Which is busiest container port in terms of TEUs processed? Which is the least busy container port in terms of TEUs processed?
b. Using a class width of 500, develop a frequency distribution of the data starting with 0–499, 500–999, 1,000–1,499, and so on.
c. Prepare a histogram. Interpret the histogram.

20. **CEO Time in Meetings.** The London School of Economics and the Harvard Business School have conducted studies of how chief executive officers (CEOs) spend their time. These studies have found that CEOs spend many hours per week in meetings, not including conference calls, business meals, and public events (*The Wall Street Journal*). Shown below is the time spent per week in meetings (hours) for a sample of 25 CEOs. **LO 3, 5**

DATA*file*
ceotime

14	15	18	23	15
19	20	13	15	23
23	21	15	20	21
16	15	18	18	19
19	22	23	21	12

a. What is the least amount of time spent per week on meetings? The highest?
b. Use a class width of two hours to prepare a frequency distribution and a percent frequency distribution for the data.
c. Prepare a histogram and comment on the shape of the distribution.

21. **Average Annual Precipitation by State.** The following table displays the average annual precipitation for each of the 50 states in the United States. **LO 3, 4, 5, 6**

DATA*file*
stateprecipitation

State	Inches	State	Inches
Alabama	58.3	Kansas	28.9
Alaska	22.5	Kentucky	48.9
Arizona	13.6	Louisiana	60.1
Arkansas	50.6	Maine	42.2
California	22.2	Maryland	44.5
Colorado	15.9	Massachusetts	47.7
Connecticut	50.3	Michigan	32.8
Delaware	45.7	Minnesota	27.3
Florida	54.5	Mississippi	59.0
Georgia	50.7	Missouri	42.2
Hawaii	63.7	Montana	15.3
Idaho	18.9	Nebraska	23.6
Illinois	39.2	Nevada	9.5
Indiana	41.7	New Hampshire	43.4
Iowa	34.0	New Jersey	47.1

New Mexico	14.6	South Dakota	20.1
New York	41.8	Tennessee	54.2
North Carolina	50.3	Texas	28.9
North Dakota	17.8	Utah	12.2
Ohio	39.1	Vermont	42.7
Oklahoma	36.5	Virginia	44.3
Oregon	27.4	Washington	38.4
Pennsylvania	42.9	West Virginia	45.2
Rhode Island	47.9	Wisconsin	32.6
South Carolina	49.8	Wyoming	12.9

Summarize the data by constructing the following:

a. A frequency distribution (classes 0–4.99, 5–9.99, 10–14.99, 15–19.99, and so on).
b. A relative frequency distribution.
c. A cumulative frequency distribution.
d. A cumulative relative frequency distribution.
e. What do these distributions tell you about the average annual rainfall in different states?
f. Construct a histogram. Comment on the shape of the distribution.

22. **Top U.S. Franchises.** *Entrepreneur* magazine ranks franchises using performance measures such as growth rate, number of locations, start-up costs, and financial stability. The number of locations for the top 20 U.S. franchises follow (*The World Almanac*).

DATA*file*
franchise

Franchise	No. U.S. Locations	Franchise	No. U.S. Locations
Hampton Inn	1,864	Jan-Pro Franchising Intl. Inc.	12,394
ampm	3,183	Hardee's	1,901
McDonald's	32,805	Pizza Hut Inc.	13,281
7-Eleven Inc.	37,496	Kumon Math & Reading Centers	25,199
Supercuts	2,130	Dunkin' Donuts	9,947
Days Inn	1,877	KFC Corp.	16,224
Vanguard Cleaning Systems	2,155	Jazzercise Inc.	7,683
Servpro	1,572	Anytime Fitness	1,618
Subway	34,871	Matco Tools	1,431
Denny's Inc.	1,668	Stratus Building Solutions	5,018

Use classes 0–4,999, 5,000–9,999, 10,000–14,999, and so forth to answer the following questions. **LO 3, 5, 6**

a. Construct a frequency distribution and a percent frequency distribution of the number of U.S. locations for these top-ranked franchises.
b. Construct a histogram of these data.
c. Comment on the shape of the distribution.

23. **Percent Change in Stock Market Indexes.** The following data show the year-to-date percent change (YTD % Change) for 30 stock-market indexes from around the world (*The Wall Street Journal*). **LO 3, 5**

DATA*file*
marketindexes

Country	Index	YTD % Change
Australia	S&P/ASX200	10.2
Belgium	Bel-20	12.6
Brazil	São Paulo Bovespa	−14.4
Canada	S&P/TSX Comp	2.6
Chile	Santiago IPSA	−16.3
China	Shanghai Composite	−9.3
Eurozone	EURO Stoxx	10.0
France	CAC 40	11.8
Germany	DAX	10.6
Hong Kong	Hang Seng	−3.5
India	S&P BSE Sensex	−4.7
Israel	Tel Aviv	1.3
Italy	FTSE MIB	6.6
Japan	Nikkei	31.4
Mexico	IPC All-Share	−6.4
Netherlands	AEX	9.3
Singapore	Straits Times	−2.5
South Korea	Kospi	−6.4
Spain	IBEX 35	6.4
Sweden	SX All Share	13.8
Switzerland	Swiss Market	17.4
Taiwan	Weighted	2.3
U.K.	FTSE 100	10.1
U.S.	S&P 500	16.6
U.S.	DJIA	14.5
U.S.	Dow Jones Utility	6.6
U.S.	Nasdaq 100	17.4
U.S.	Nasdaq Composite	21.1
World	DJ Global ex U.S.	4.2
World	DJ Global Index	9.9

a. What index has the largest positive YTD % Change?
b. Using a class width of 5 beginning with −20 and going to 40, develop a frequency distribution for the data.
c. Prepare a histogram. Interpret the histogram, including a discussion of the general shape of the histogram.
d. Use *The Wall Street Journal* or another media source to find the current percent changes for these stock market indexes in the current year. Which index has had the largest percent increase? Which index has had the smallest percent decrease? Prepare a summary of the data.

DATA*file*
engineeringsalary

24. **Engineering School Graduate Salaries.** The file *engineeringsalary* contains the median starting salary and median mid-career salary (measured 10 years after graduation) for graduates from 19 engineering schools (*The Wall Street Journal*). Develop a stem-and-leaf display for both the median starting salary and the median mid-career salary. Comment on any differences you observe. **LO 5**

25. **Best Paying College Degrees.** Each year *America.edu* ranks the best paying college degrees in America. The following data show the median starting salary, the mid-career salary, and the percentage increase from starting salary to mid-career salary for the 20 college degrees with the highest mid-career salary (*America.edu* website). **LO 3, 5, 6**

Degree	Starting Salary	Mid-Career Salary	% Increase
Aerospace engineering	59,400	108,000	82
Applied mathematics	56,400	101,000	79
Biomedical engineering	54,800	101,000	84
Chemical engineering	64,800	108,000	67
Civil engineering	53,500	93,400	75
Computer engineering	61,200	87,700	43
Computer science	56,200	97,700	74
Construction management	50,400	87,000	73
Economics	48,800	97,800	100
Electrical engineering	60,800	104,000	71
Finance	47,500	91,500	93
Government	41,500	88,300	113
Information systems	49,300	87,100	77
Management info. systems	50,900	90,300	77
Mathematics	46,400	88,300	90
Nuclear engineering	63,900	104,000	63
Petroleum engineering	93,000	157,000	69
Physics	50,700	99,600	96
Software engineering	56,700	91,300	61
Statistics	50,000	93,400	87

DATA*file*
bestpayingdegrees

a. Using a class width of 10, construct a histogram for the percentage increase in the starting salary.
b. Comment on the shape of the distribution.
c. Develop a stem-and-leaf display for the percentage increase in the starting salary.
d. What are the primary advantages of the stem-and-leaf display as compared to the histogram?

26. **Marathon Runner Ages.** The Flying Pig is a marathon (26.2 miles long) running race held every year in Cincinnati, Ohio. Suppose that the following data show the ages for a sample of 40 marathoners. **LO 5**

DATA*file*
marathon

49	33	40	37	56
44	46	57	55	32
50	52	43	64	40
46	24	30	37	43
31	43	50	36	61
27	44	35	31	43
52	43	66	31	50
72	26	59	21	47

a. Construct a stretched stem-and-leaf display.
b. What age group had the largest number of runners?
c. What age occurred most frequently?

2.3 Summarizing Data for Two Variables Using Tables

Thus far in this chapter, we have focused on using tabular and graphical displays to summarize the data for a single categorical or quantitative variable. Often a manager or decision maker needs to summarize the data for two variables in order to reveal the relationship—if any—between the variables. In this section, we show how to construct a tabular summary of the data for two variables.

Crosstabulation

A **crosstabulation** is a tabular summary of data for two variables. Although both variables can be either categorical or quantitative, crosstabulations in which one variable is categorical and the other variable is quantitative are just as common. We will illustrate this latter case by considering the following application based on data from Zagat's Restaurant Review. Data showing the quality rating and the typical meal price were collected for a sample of 300 restaurants in the Los Angeles area. Table 2.9 shows the data for the first 10 restaurants. Quality rating is a categorical variable with rating categories of Good, Very Good, and Excellent. Meal Price is a quantitative variable that ranges from $10 to $49.

Grouping the data for a quantitative variable enables us to treat the quantitative variable as if it were a categorical variable when creating a crosstabulation.

A crosstabulation of the data for this application is shown in Table 2.10. The labels shown in the margins of the table define the categories (classes) for the two variables. In the left margin, the row labels (Good, Very Good, and Excellent) correspond to the three rating categories for the quality rating variable. In the top margin, the column labels ($10–19, $20–29, $30–39, and $40–49) show that the Meal Price data have been grouped into four classes. Because each restaurant in the sample provides a quality rating and a meal price, each restaurant is associated with a cell appearing in one of the rows and one of the columns of the crosstabulation. For example, Table 2.9 shows restaurant 5 as having a Very Good quality rating and a Meal Price of $33. This restaurant belongs to the cell in row 2 and column 3 of the crosstabulation shown in Table 2.10. In constructing a crosstabulation, we simply count the number of restaurants that belong to each of the cells.

DATA*file*
restaurant

Table 2.9 Quality Rating and Meal Price Data for 300 Los Angeles Restaurants

Restaurant	Quality Rating	Meal Price ($)
1	Good	18
2	Very Good	22
3	Good	28
4	Excellent	38
5	Very Good	33
6	Good	28
7	Very Good	19
8	Very Good	11
9	Very Good	23
10	Good	13
.	.	.
.	.	.
.	.	.

Table 2.10 Crosstabulation of Quality Rating and Meal Price Data for 300 Los Angeles Restaurants

	Meal Price				
Quality Rating	**$10–19**	**$20–29**	**$30–39**	**$40–49**	**Total**
Good	42	40	2	0	84
Very Good	34	64	46	6	150
Excellent	2	14	28	22	66
Total	78	118	76	28	300

Although four classes of the Meal Price variable were used to construct the crosstabulation shown in Table 2.10, the crosstabulation of quality rating and meal price could have been developed using fewer or more classes for the meal price variable. The issues involved in deciding how to group the data for a quantitative variable in a crosstabulation are similar to the issues involved in deciding the number of classes to use when constructing a frequency distribution for a quantitative variable. For this application, four classes of meal price was considered a reasonable number of classes to reveal any relationship between quality rating and meal price.

In reviewing Table 2.10, we see that the greatest number of restaurants in the sample (64) have a very good rating and a meal price in the $20–29 range. Only two restaurants have an excellent rating and a meal price in the $10–19 range. Similar interpretations of the other frequencies can be made. In addition, note that the right and bottom margins of the crosstabulation provide the frequency distributions for quality rating and meal price separately. From the frequency distribution in the right margin, we see that data on quality ratings show 84 restaurants with a good quality rating, 150 restaurants with a very good quality rating, and 66 restaurants with an excellent quality rating. Similarly, the bottom margin shows the frequency distribution for the meal price variable.

Dividing the totals in the right margin of the crosstabulation by the total for that column provides a relative and percent frequency distribution for the quality rating variable.

Quality Rating	**Relative Frequency**	**Percent Frequency**
Good	0.28	28
Very Good	0.50	50
Excellent	0.22	22
Total	1.00	100

From the percent frequency distribution, we see that 28% of the restaurants were rated good, 50% were rated very good, and 22% were rated excellent.

Dividing the totals in the bottom row of the crosstabulation by the total for that row provides a relative and percent frequency distribution for the meal price variable.

Note that the sum of the values shown in the relative frequency column does not add exactly to 1.00 and the sum of the values shown in the percent frequency distribution does not add exactly to 100; the reason is that the values shown are rounded.

Meal Price	**Relative Frequency**	**Percent Frequency**
$10–19	0.26	26
$20–29	0.39	39
$30–39	0.25	25
$40–49	0.09	9
Total	1.00	100

From the percent frequency distribution, we see that 26% of the meal prices are in the lowest price class ($10–19), 39% are in the next higher class, and so on.

The frequency and relative frequency distributions constructed from the margins of a crosstabulation provide information about each of the variables individually, but they do not shed any light on the relationship between the variables. The primary value of a crosstabulation lies in the insight it offers about the relationship between the variables. A review of the crosstabulation in Table 2.10 reveals that restaurants with higher meal prices received higher quality ratings than restaurants with lower meal prices.

Converting the entries in a crosstabulation into row percentages or column percentages can provide more insight into the relationship between the two variables. For row percentages, the results of dividing each frequency in Table 2.10 by its corresponding row total are shown in Table 2.11. Each row of Table 2.11 is a percent frequency distribution of meal price for one of the quality rating categories. Of the restaurants with the

Table 2.11 Row Percentages for Each Quality Rating Category

	Meal Price				
Quality Rating	**$10–19**	**$20–29**	**$30–39**	**$40–49**	**Total**
Good	50.0	47.6	2.4	0.0	100
Very Good	22.7	42.7	30.6	4.0	100
Excellent	3.0	21.2	42.4	33.4	100

lowest quality rating (good), we see that the greatest percentages are for the less expensive restaurants (50% have $10–19 meal prices and 47.6% have $20–29 meal prices). Of the restaurants with the highest quality rating (excellent), we see that the greatest percentages are for the more expensive restaurants (42.4% have $30–39 meal prices and 33.4% have $40–49 meal prices). Thus, we continue to see that restaurants with higher meal prices received higher quality ratings.

Crosstabulations are widely used to investigate the relationship between two variables. In practice, the final reports for many statistical studies include a large number of crosstabulations. In the Los Angeles restaurant survey, the crosstabulation is based on one categorical variable (Quality Rating) and one quantitative variable (Meal Price). Crosstabulations can also be developed when both variables are categorical and when both variables are quantitative. When quantitative variables are used, however, we must first create classes for the values of the variable. For instance, in the restaurant example we grouped the meal prices into four classes ($10–19, $20–29, $30–39, and $40–49).

Using Excel's PivotTable Tool to Construct a Crosstabulation

Excel's PivotTable tool can be used to summarize the data for two or more variables simultaneously. We will illustrate the use of Excel's PivotTable tool by showing how to develop a crosstabulation of quality ratings and meal prices for the sample of 300 restaurants located in the Los Angeles area.

DATA*file*
restaurant

Enter/Access Data: Open the file *restaurant*. The data are in cells B2:C301 and labels are in column A and cells B1:C1.

Apply Tools: Each of the three columns in the file *restaurant* [labeled Restaurant, Quality Rating, and Meal Price ($)] is considered a field by Excel. Fields may be chosen to represent rows, columns, or values in the PivotTable. The following steps describe how to use Excel's PivotTable tool to construct a crosstabulation of quality ratings and meal prices.

Step 1. Select cell A1 or any cell in the data set
Step 2. Click the **Insert** tab on the Ribbon
Step 3. In the **Tables** group click **PivotTable**
Step 4. When the **Create PivotTable** dialog box appears:
Click **OK**; a **PivotTable** and **PivotTable Fields** task pane will appear in a new worksheet
Step 5. In the **PivotTable Fields** task pane:
Drag **Quality Rating** to the **Rows** area
Drag **Meal Price** to the **Columns** area
Drag **Restaurant** to the **Values** area
Step 6. Click on **Sum of Restaurant** in the **Values** area
Step 7. Select **Value Field Settings...** from the list of options that appears
Step 8. When the **Value Field Settings** dialog box appears:
Under **Summarize value field by**, choose **Count**
Click **OK**

Figure 2.16 Initial PivotTable Fields Task Pane and PivotTable for the Restaurant Data

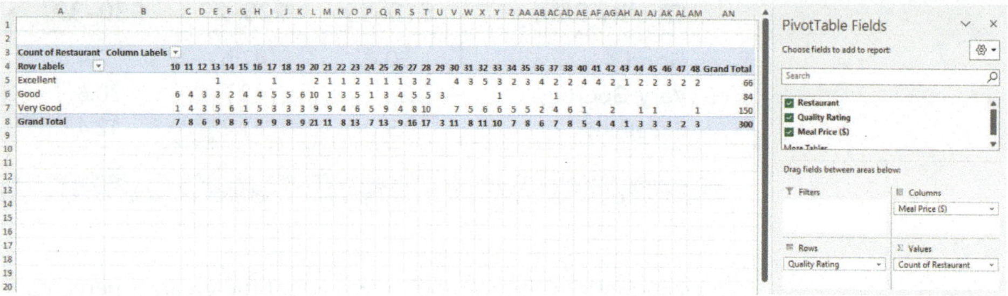

Figure 2.16 shows the PivotTable Fields task pane and the corresponding PivotTable created following the above steps. For readability, columns H:AC have been hidden.

Editing Options: To complete the PivotTable, we need to group the rows containing the meal prices and place the rows for quality rating in the proper order. The following steps accomplish this.

Step 1. Right-click cell B4 in the PivotTable or any other cell containing meal prices.
Step 2. Choose **Group** from the list of options that appears
Step 3. When the **Grouping** dialog box appears:
Enter *10* in the **Starting at:** box
Enter *49* in the **Ending at:** box
Enter *10* in the **By:** box
Click **OK**
Step 4. Right-click on **Excellent** in cell A5
Select **Move** and click **Move "Excellent" to End**

The final PivotTable is shown in Figure 2.17. Note that it provides the same information as the crosstabulation shown in Table 2.10.

Figure 2.17 Final PivotTable for the Restaurant Data

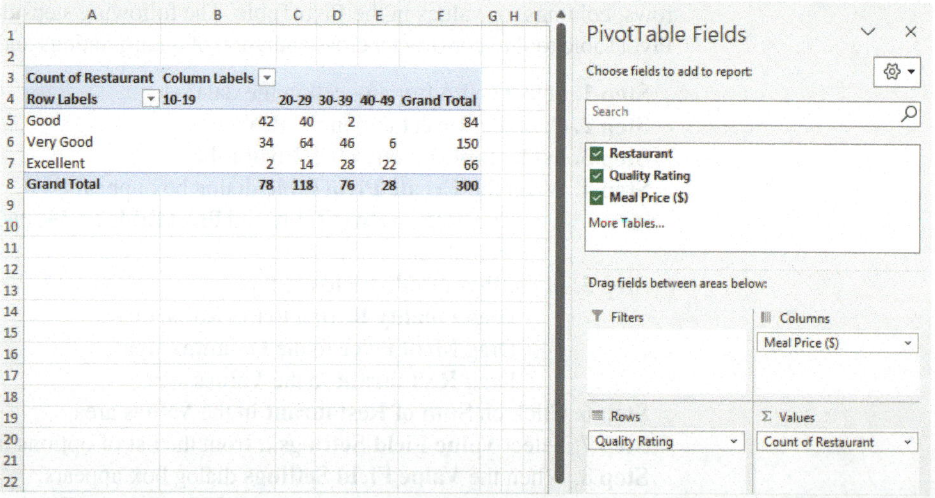

Simpson's Paradox

The data in two or more crosstabulations are often combined or aggregated to produce a summary crosstabulation showing how two variables are related. In such cases, conclusions drawn from two or more separate crosstabulations can be reversed when the data are aggregated into a single crosstabulation. The reversal of conclusions based on aggregate and disaggregated data is called **Simpson's paradox**. To provide an illustration of Simpson's paradox we consider an example involving the analysis of verdicts for two judges in two different courts.

Judges Susan Luckett and Dennis Kendall presided over cases in Common Pleas Court and Municipal Court during the past three years. Some of the verdicts they rendered were appealed. In most of these cases the appeals court upheld the original verdicts, but in some cases those verdicts were reversed. For each judge, a crosstabulation was developed based upon two variables: Verdict (upheld or reversed) and Type of Court (Common Pleas and Municipal). Suppose that the two crosstabulations were then combined by aggregating the type of court data. The resulting aggregated crosstabulation contains two variables: Verdict (upheld or reversed) and Judge (Luckett or Kendall). This crosstabulation shows the number of appeals in which the verdict was upheld and the number in which the verdict was reversed for both judges. The following crosstabulation shows these results, along with the column percentages in parentheses next to each value.

	Judge		
Verdict	Luckett	Kendall	Total
Upheld	129 (86%)	110 (88%)	239
Reversed	21 (14%)	15 (12%)	36
Total (%)	150 (100%)	125 (100%)	275

A review of the column percentages shows that 86% of the verdicts were upheld for Judge Luckett, whereas 88% of the verdicts were upheld for Judge Kendall. From this aggregated crosstabulation, we conclude that Judge Kendall is doing the better job because a greater percentage of Judge Kendall's verdicts are being upheld.

The following disaggregated crosstabulations show the cases tried by Judge Luckett and Judge Kendall in each court; column percentages are shown in parentheses next to each value.

Judge Luckett

Verdict	Common Pleas	Municipal Court	Total
Upheld	29 (91%)	100 (85%)	129
Reversed	3 (9%)	18 (15%)	21
Total (%)	32 (100%)	118 (100%)	150

Judge Kendall

Verdict	Common Pleas	Municipal Court	Total
Upheld	90 (90%)	20 (80%)	110
Reversed	10 (10%)	5 (20%)	15
Total (%)	100 (100%)	25 (100%)	125

From the crosstabulation and column percentages for Judge Luckett, we see that the verdicts were upheld in 91% of the Common Pleas Court cases and in 85% of the Municipal Court cases. From the crosstabulation and column percentages for Judge Kendall, we see that the verdicts were upheld in 90% of the Common Pleas Court cases and in 80% of the Municipal Court cases. Thus, when we disaggregate the data, we see that Judge Luckett has a better record because a greater percentage of Judge Luckett's verdicts are being upheld in both courts. This result contradicts the conclusion we reached with the aggregated data crosstabulation that showed Judge Kendall had the better record. This reversal of conclusions based on aggregated and disaggregated data illustrates Simpson's paradox.

The original crosstabulation was obtained by aggregating the data in the separate crosstabulations for the two courts. Note that for both judges the percentage of appeals that resulted in reversals was much higher in Municipal Court than in Common Pleas Court. Because Judge Luckett tried a much higher percentage of his cases in Municipal Court, the aggregated data favored Judge Kendall. When we look at the crosstabulations for the two courts separately, however, Judge Luckett shows the better record. Thus, for the original crosstabulation, we see that the *type of court* is a hidden variable that cannot be ignored when evaluating the records of the two judges.

Because of the possibility of Simpson's paradox, realize that the conclusion or interpretation may be reversed depending upon whether you are viewing disaggregated or aggregated crosstabulation data. Before drawing a conclusion, you may want to investigate whether the aggregate or disaggregate form of the crosstabulation provides the better insight and conclusion. Especially when the crosstabulation involves aggregated data, you should investigate whether a hidden variable could affect the results such that separate or disaggregated crosstabulations provide a different and possibly better insight and conclusion.

Exercises

Methods

27. The following data are for 30 observations involving two categorical variables, x and y. The categories for x are A, B, and C; the categories for y are 1 and 2. **LO 7**

DATA*file*
crosstab

Observation	x	y	Observation	x	y
1	A	1	16	B	2
2	B	1	17	C	1
3	B	1	18	B	1
4	C	2	19	C	1
5	B	1	20	B	1
6	C	2	21	C	2
7	B	1	22	B	1
8	C	2	23	C	2
9	A	1	24	A	1
10	B	1	25	B	1
11	A	1	26	C	2
12	B	1	27	C	2
13	C	2	28	A	1
14	C	2	29	B	1
15	C	2	30	B	2

a. Develop a crosstabulation for the data, with x as the row variable and y as the column variable.
b. Compute the row percentages.
c. Compute the column percentages.
d. What is the relationship, if any, between x and y?

28. The following observations are for two quantitative variables, x and y. **LO 7**

DATA*file*
crosstab2

Observation	x	y	Observation	x	y
1	28	72	11	13	98
2	17	99	12	84	21
3	52	58	13	59	32
4	79	34	14	17	81
5	37	60	15	70	34
6	71	22	16	47	64
7	37	77	17	35	68
8	27	85	18	62	67
9	64	45	19	30	39
10	53	47	20	43	28

a. Develop a crosstabulation for the data, with x as the row variable and y as the column variable. For x use classes of 10–29, 30–49, and so on; for y use classes of 40–59, 60–79, and so on.
b. Compute the row percentages.
c. Compute the column percentages.
d. What is the relationship, if any, between x and y?

Applications

29. **Average Speeds of Daytona 500 Winners by Automobile Makes.** The Daytona 500 is a 500-mile automobile race held annually at the Daytona International Speedway in Daytona Beach, Florida. The following crosstabulation shows the automobile make by average speed of the 25 winners from 1988 to 2012 (*The World Almanac*). **LO 7**

	Average Speed in Miles per Hour					
Make	**130–139.9**	**140–149.9**	**150–159.9**	**160–169.9**	**170–179.9**	**Total**
Buick	1					1
Chevrolet	3	5	4	3	1	16
Dodge		2				2
Ford	2	1	2	1		6
Total	6	8	6	4	1	25

a. Compute the row percentages.
b. What percentage of winners driving a Chevrolet won with an average speed of at least 150 miles per hour?
c. Compute the column percentages.
d. What percentage of winning average speeds 160–169.9 miles per hour were Chevrolets?

30. **Average Speeds of Daytona 500 Winners by Years.** The following crosstabulation shows the average speed of the 25 winners by year of the Daytona 500 automobile race (*The World Almanac*). **LO 7**
a. Calculate the row percentages.
b. What is the apparent relationship between average winning speed and year? What might be the cause of this apparent relationship?

	Year					
Average Speed	**1988–1992**	**1993–1997**	**1998–2002**	**2003–2007**	**2008–2012**	**Total**
130–139.9	1			2	3	6
140–149.9	2	2	1	2	1	8
150–159.9		3	1	1	1	6
160–169.9	2		2			4
170–179.9			1			1
Total	5	5	5	5	5	25

31. **Library Levy Voting Results.** Two nearby municipalities, Westminster and Southville, are voting on a joint ballot initiative to renew a library levy to provide funding to the libraries located in these two municipalities. The voting results for this library levy are summarized here. **LO 7, 9**

Westminster				**Southville**		
	Levy Voting Results				Levy Voting Results	
Party Affiliation	**For**	**Against**		**Party Affiliation**	**For**	**Against**
Republican	100	400		Republican	10	90
Democrat	250	250		Democrat	390	510

a. Combine these two crosstabulations into one with Westminster and Southville as the row labels and For and Against as the column labels. Which municipality has the highest percentage voting For the library levy?
b. Refer to the two initial crosstabulations. For Republicans, which municipality (Westminster or Southville) has the higher percentage of voters voting For the library levy?
c. Refer to the two initial crosstabulations. For Democrats, which municipality (Westminster or Southville) has the higher percentage of voters voting For the library levy?
d. What conclusions can you draw about the voting preferences in Westminster versus Southville? Are the conclusions you've drawn from part (a) consistent with the conclusions drawn from parts (b) and (c)? Explain any apparent inconsistencies.

32. **Household Income Levels.** The following crosstabulation shows the number of households (1,000s) in each of the four regions of the United States and the number of households at each income level (U.S. Census Bureau website). **LO 3, 5, 7**

	Income Level of Household							
Region	**Under $15,000**	**$15,000 to $24,999**	**$25,000 to $34,999**	**$35,000 to $49,999**	**$50,000 to $74,999**	**$75,000 to $99,999**	**$100,000 and Over**	**Number of Households (1,000s)**
Northeast	2,733	2,244	2,264	2,807	3,699	2,486	5,246	21,479
Midwest	3,273	3,326	3,056	3,767	5,044	3,183	4,742	26,391
South	6,235	5,657	5,038	6,476	7,730	4,813	7,660	43,609
West	3,086	2,796	2,644	3,557	4,804	3,066	6,104	26,057
Total	15,327	14,023	13,002	16,607	21,277	13,548	23,752	117,536

a. Compute the row percentages and identify the percent frequency distributions of income for households in each region.
b. What percentage of households in the West region have an income level of $50,000 or more? What percentage of households in the South region have an income level of $50,000 or more?
c. Construct percent frequency histograms for each region of households. Do any relationships between regions and income level appear to be evident in your findings?
d. Compute the column percentages. What information do the column percentages provide?
e. What percent of households with a household income of $100,000 and over are from the South region? What percentage of households from the South region have a household income of $100,000 and over? Why are these two percentages different?

33. **Value of World's Most Valuable Brands.** Each year *Forbes* ranks the world's most valuable brands. A portion of the data for 82 of the brands in the 2013 *Forbes* list is shown in Table 2.12. The data set includes the variables listed below. **LO 1, 3, 7**

Brand: The name of the brand.

Industry: The type of industry associated with the brand, labeled Automotive & Luxury, Consumer Packaged Goods, Financial Services, Other, Technology.

Brand Value ($ billions): A measure of the brand's value in billions of dollars developed by *Forbes* based on a variety of financial information about the brand.

1-Yr Value Change (%): The percentage change in the value of the brand over the previous year.

Brand Revenue ($ billions): The total revenue in billions of dollars for the brand.

a. Prepare a crosstabulation of the data on Industry (rows) and Brand Value ($ billions). Use classes of 0–9.9, 10–19.9, 20–29.9, 30–39.9, 40–49.9, and 50–60 for Brand Value ($ billions).
b. Prepare a frequency distribution for the data on Industry.
c. Prepare a frequency distribution for the data on Brand Value ($ billions).

DATA*file*
brandvalue

Table 2.12 Data for 82 of the Most Valuable Brands

Brand	Industry	Brand Value ($ billions)	1-Yr Value Change (%)	Brand Revenue ($ billions)
Accenture	Other	9.7	10	30.4
Adidas	Other	8.4	23	14.5
Allianz	Financial Services	6.9	5	130.8
Amazon.Com	Technology	14.7	44	60.6
⋮	⋮	⋮	⋮	⋮
Heinz	Consumer Packaged Goods	5.6	2	4.4
Hermès	Automotive & Luxury	9.3	20	4.5
⋮	⋮	⋮	⋮	⋮
Wells Fargo	Financial Services	9	−14	91.2
Zara	Other	9.4	11	13.5

Source: *Data from* Forbes, *2014.*

d. How has the crosstabulation helped in preparing the frequency distributions in parts (b) and (c)?

e. What conclusions can you draw about the type of industry and the brand value?

34. **Revenue of World's Most Valuable Brands.** Refer to Table 2.12. LO 3, 7

a. Prepare a crosstabulation of the data on Industry (rows) and Brand Revenue ($ billions). Use class intervals of 25 starting at 0 for Brand Revenue ($ billions).

b. Prepare a frequency distribution for the data on Brand Revenue ($ billions).

c. What conclusions can you draw about the type of industry and the brand revenue?

d. Prepare a crosstabulation of the data on Industry (rows) and the 1-Yr Value Change (%). Use class intervals of 20 starting at −60 for 1-Yr Value Change (%).

e. Prepare a frequency distribution for the data on 1-Yr Value Change (%).

f. What conclusions can you draw about the type of industry and the 1-year change in value?

35. **Car Fuel Efficiencies.** The U.S. Department of Energy's Fuel Economy Guide provides fuel efficiency data for cars and trucks (Fuel Economy website). A portion of the data from 2018 for 341 compact, midsize, and large cars is shown in Table 2.13. The data set contains the variables listed below.

Size: Compact, Midsize, and Large

Displacement: Engine size in liters

Cylinders: Number of cylinders in the engine

Drive: All wheel (A), front wheel (F), and rear wheel (R)

Fuel Type: Premium (P) or regular (R) fuel

City MPG: Fuel efficiency rating for city driving in terms of miles per gallon

Hwy MPG: Fuel efficiency rating for highway driving in terms of miles per gallon

The complete data set is contained in the file *fueldata2018*. LO 7

a. Prepare a crosstabulation of the data on Size (rows) and Hwy MPG (columns). Use classes of 20–24, 25–29, 30–34, 35–39, and 40–44 for Hwy MPG.

b. Comment on the relationship between Size and Hwy MPG.

DATA*file* fueldata2018

Table 2.13 Fuel Efficiency Data for 341 Cars

Car	Size	Displacement	Cylinders	Drive	Fuel Type	City MPG	Hwy MPG
1	Compact	1.4	4	F	R	27	40
2	Compact	1.4	4	F	R	27	35
3	Compact	1.4	4	F	R	28	38
•	•	•	•	•	•	•	•
•	•	•	•	•	•	•	•
•	•	•	•	•	•	•	•
190	Compact	2.5	4	F	R	27	36
191	Large	2.5	4	F	R	22	30
192	Midsize	2.5	4	F	R	21	32
•	•	•	•	•	•	•	•
•	•	•	•	•	•	•	•
•	•	•	•	•	•	•	•
339	Large	6.0	12	R	P	13	21
340	Large	6.0	12	R	P	13	22
341	Large	6.0	12	R	P	13	20

c. Prepare a crosstabulation of the data on Drive (rows) and City MPG (columns). Use classes of 10–14, 15–19, 20–24, 25–29, and 30–34 for City MPG.
d. Comment on the relationship between Drive and City MPG.
e. Prepare a crosstabulation of the data on Fuel Type (rows) and City MPG (columns). Use classes of 10–14, 15–19, 20–24, 25–29, and 30–34 for City MPG.
f. Comment on the relationship between Fuel Type and City MPG.

2.4 Summarizing Data for Two Variables Using Graphical Displays

In the previous section, we showed how a crosstabulation can be used to summarize the data for two variables and help reveal the relationship between the variables. In most cases, a graphical display is more useful for recognizing patterns and trends in the data.

In this section, we introduce a variety of graphical displays for exploring the relationships between two variables. Displaying data in creative ways can lead to powerful insights and allow us to make "common-sense inferences" based on our ability to visually compare, contrast, and recognize patterns. We begin with a discussion of scatter diagrams and trendlines.

Scatter Diagram and Trendline

A **scatter diagram** is a graphical display of the relationship between two quantitative variables, and a **trendline** is a line that provides an approximation of the relationship. As an illustration, consider the advertising/sales relationship for an electronics store in San Francisco. On 10 occasions during the past three months, the store used weekend television commercials to promote sales at its stores. The managers want to investigate whether a relationship exists between the number of commercials shown and sales at the store during the following week. Sample data for the 10 weeks with sales in hundreds of dollars are shown in Table 2.14.

Figure 2.18 shows the scatter diagram and the trendline[1] for the data in Table 2.14. The number of commercials (x) is shown on the horizontal axis and the sales (y) are shown on the vertical axis. For week 1, $x = 2$ and $y = 50$. A point with those coordinates is plotted on the scatter diagram. Similar points are plotted for the other nine weeks. Note that during two of the weeks one commercial was shown, during two of the weeks two commercials were shown, and so on.

DATA*file*
electronics

Table 2.14 Sample Data for the San Francisco Electronics Store

Week	Number of Commercials x	Sales ($100s) y
1	2	50
2	5	57
3	1	41
4	3	54
5	4	54
6	1	38
7	5	63
8	3	48
9	4	59
10	2	46

[1]The equation of the trendline is $y = 36.15 + 4.95x$. The slope of the trendline is 4.95 and the y-intercept (the point where the trendline intersects the y-axis) is 36.15. We will discuss in detail the interpretation of the slope and y-intercept for a linear trendline in Chapter 14 when we study simple linear regression.

Figure 2.18 Scatter Diagram and Trendline for the San Francisco Electronics Store

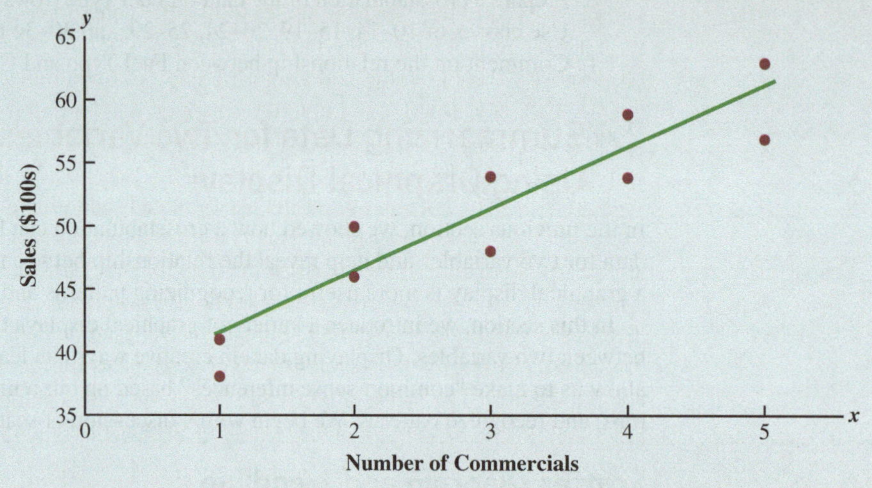

The scatter diagram in Figure 2.18 indicates a positive relationship between the number of commercials and sales. Higher sales are associated with a higher number of commercials. The relationship is not perfect in that all points are not on a straight line. However, the general pattern of the points and the trendline suggest that the overall relationship is positive.

Some general scatter diagram patterns and the types of relationships they suggest are shown in Figure 2.19. The top-left panel depicts a positive relationship similar to the one for the number of commercials and sales example. In the top-right panel, the scatter diagram shows no apparent relationship between the variables. The bottom panel depicts a negative relationship where y tends to decrease as x increases.

Using Excel to Construct a Scatter Diagram and a Trendline

We can use Excel to construct a scatter diagram and a trendline for the San Francisco electronics store data.

DATA*file*
electronics

Enter/Access Data: Open the file *electronics*. The data are in cells B2:C11 and labels are in column A and cells B1:C1.

Apply Tools: The following steps describe how to use Excel to construct a scatter diagram from the data in the worksheet.

Step 1. Select cells B1:C11
Step 2. Click the **Insert** tab on the Ribbon
Step 3. In the **Charts** group, click **Insert Scatter (X,Y) or Bubble Chart**
Step 4. When the list of scatter diagram subtypes appears:
Click **Scatter** (the chart in the upper-left corner)

The worksheet in Figure 2.20 shows the scatter diagram produced using these steps.

Editing Options: You can easily edit the scatter diagram to display a different chart title, add axis titles, and display the trendline. For instance, suppose you would like to use "Scatter Diagram for the San Francisco Electronics Store" as the chart title and insert "Number of Commercials" for the horizontal axis title and "Sales ($100s)" for the vertical axis title.

Figure 2.19 Types of Relationships Depicted by Scatter Diagrams

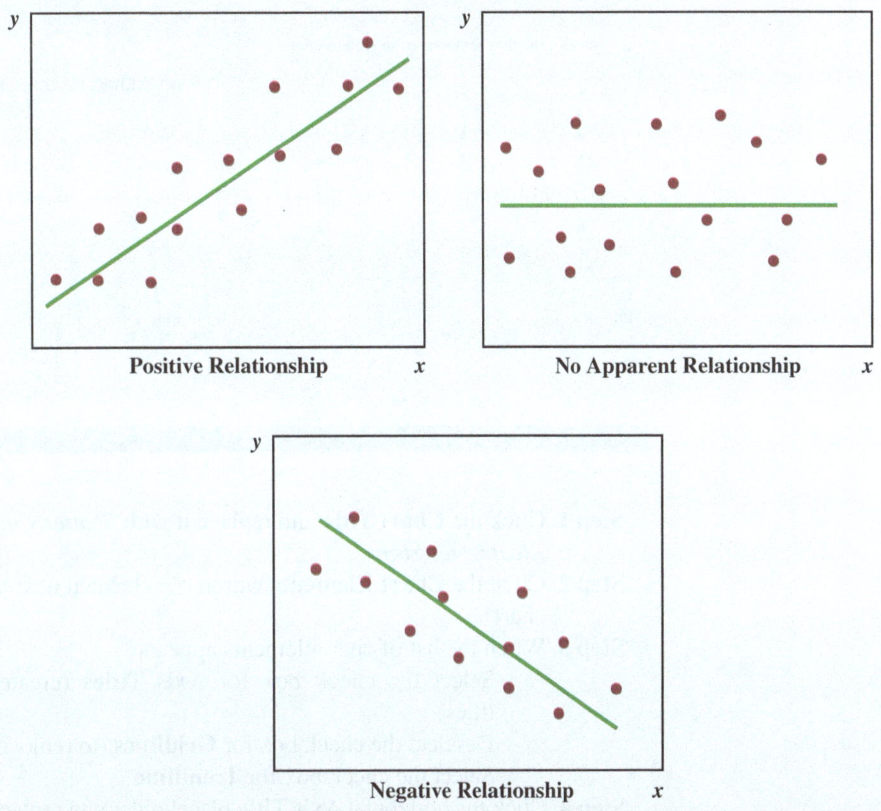

Figure 2.20 Initial Scatter Diagram for the San Francisco Electronics Store Using Excel's Recommended Charts Tool

	A	B	C
1	Week	Number of Commercials	Sales Volume
2	1	2	50
3	2	5	57
4	3	1	41
5	4	3	54
6	5	4	54
7	6	1	38
8	7	5	63
9	8	3	48
10	9	4	59
11	10	2	46

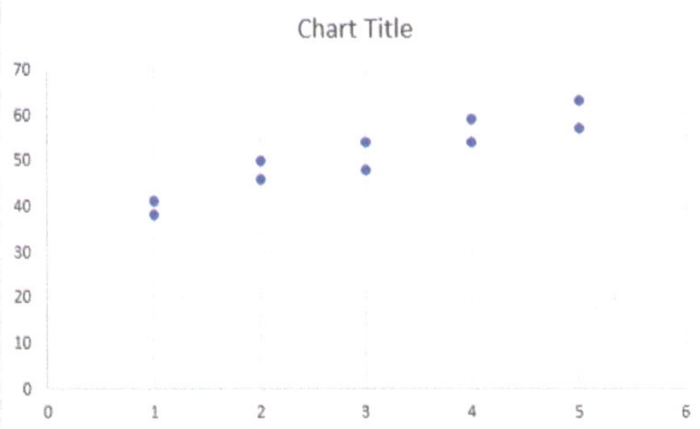

Figure 2.21 Edited Scatter Diagram and Trendline for the San Francisco Electronics Store Using Excel's Recommended Charts Tool

	A	B	C
1	Week	Number of Commercials	Sales Volume
2	1	2	50
3	2	5	57
4	3	1	41
5	4	3	54
6	5	4	54
7	6	1	38
8	7	5	63
9	8	3	48
10	9	4	59
11	10	2	46

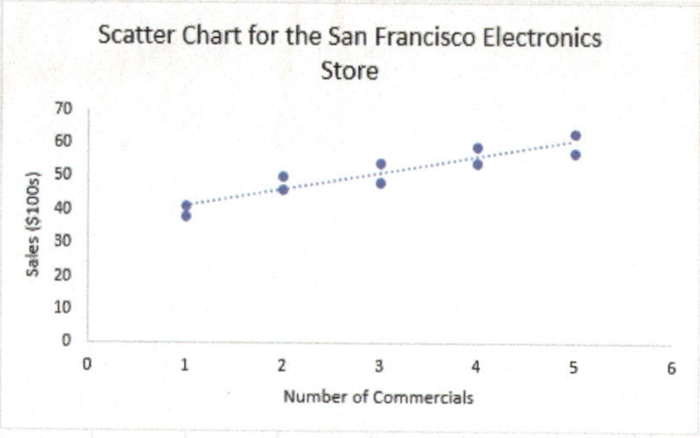

Step 1. Click the **Chart Title** and replace it with *Scatter Chart for the San Francisco Electronics Store*

Step 2. Click the **Chart Elements** button ＋ (located next to the top-right corner of the chart)

Step 3. When the list of chart elements appears:

Select the check box for **Axis Titles** (creates placeholders for the axis titles)

Deselect the check box for **Gridlines** (to remove the gridlines from the chart)

Select the check box for **Trendline**

Step 4. Click the horizontal **Axis Title** placeholder and replace it with *Number of Commercials*

Step 5. Click the vertical **Axis Title** placeholder and replace it with *Sales ($100s)*

The edited scatter diagram and trendline are shown in Figure 2.21.

Side-by-Side and Stacked Bar Charts

In Section 2.1, we said that a bar chart is a graphical display for depicting categorical data summarized in a frequency, relative frequency, or percent frequency distribution. Side-by-side bar charts and stacked bar charts are extensions of basic bar charts that are used to display and compare two variables. By displaying two variables on the same chart, we may better understand the relationship between the variables.

A **side-by-side bar chart** is a graphical display for depicting multiple bar charts on the same display. To illustrate the construction of a side-by-side chart, recall the application involving the quality rating and meal price data for a sample of 300 restaurants located in the Los Angeles area. Quality rating is a categorical variable with rating categories of Good, Very Good, and Excellent. Meal Price is a quantitative variable that ranges from $10 to $49. The crosstabulation displayed in Table 2.10 shows that the data for meal price were grouped into four classes: $10–19, $20–29, $30–39, and $40–49. We will use these classes to construct a side-by-side bar chart.

Figure 2.22 shows a side-by-side chart for the restaurant data. The color of each bar indicates the quality rating (light blue = good, medium blue = very good, and dark blue = excellent). Each bar is constructed by extending the bar to the point on the vertical axis that represents the frequency with which that quality rating occurred for each of the meal price categories. Placing each meal price category's quality rating frequency adjacent to one another allows us to quickly determine how a particular meal price category is rated. We

Figure 2.22 Side-by-Side Bar Chart for the Quality and Meal Price Data

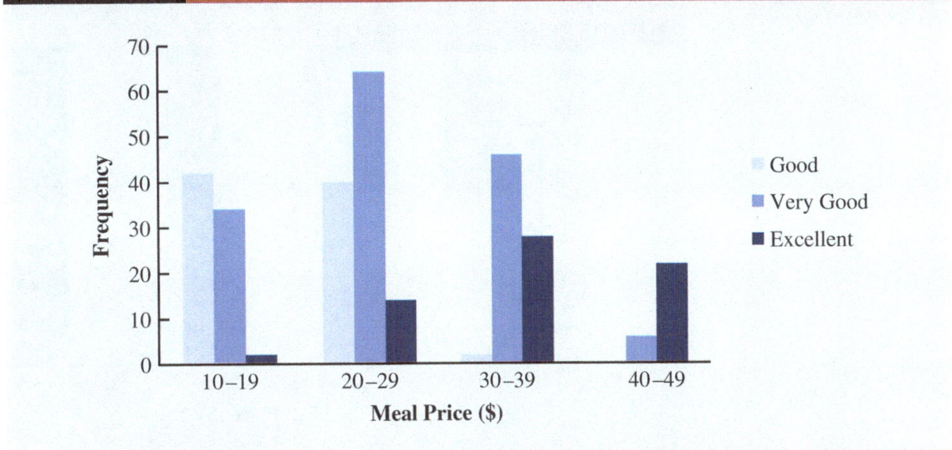

see that the lowest meal price category ($10–19) received mostly good and very good ratings, but very few excellent ratings. The highest price category ($40–49), however, shows a much different result. This meal price category received mostly excellent ratings, some very good ratings, but no good ratings.

Figure 2.22 also provides a good sense of the relationship between meal price and quality rating. Notice that as the price increases (left to right), the height of the light blue bars decreases and the height of the dark blue bars generally increases. This indicates that as price increases, the quality rating tends to be better. The very good rating, as expected, tends to be more prominent in the middle price categories as indicated by the dominance of the middle bar in the moderate price ranges of the chart.

Stacked bar charts are another way to display and compare two variables on the same display. A **stacked bar chart** is a bar chart in which each bar is broken into rectangular segments of a different color showing the relative frequency of each class in a manner similar to a pie chart. To illustrate a stacked bar chart, we will use the quality rating and meal price data summarized in the crosstabulation shown in Table 2.10.

We can convert the frequency data in Table 2.10 into column percentages by dividing each element in a particular column by the total for that column. For instance, 42 of the 78 restaurants with a meal price in the $10–19 range had a good quality rating. In other words, (42/78)100 or 53.8% of the 78 restaurants had a good rating. Table 2.15 shows the column percentages for each meal price category. Using the data in Table 2.15 we constructed the stacked bar chart shown in Figure 2.23. Because the stacked bar chart is based on percentages, Figure 2.23 shows even more clearly than Figure 2.22 the relationship between the variables. As we move from the low price category ($10–19) to the high price category ($40–49), the length of the light blue bars decreases and the length of the dark blue bars increases.

Table 2.15 Column Percentages for Each Meal Price Category

	Meal Price			
Quality Rating	**$10–19**	**$20–29**	**$30–39**	**$40–49**
Good	53.8%	33.9%	2.6%	0.0%
Very Good	43.6	54.2	60.5	21.4
Excellent	2.6	11.9	36.8	78.6
Total	100.0%	100.0%	100.0%	100.0%

Figure 2.23 Stacked Bar Chart for the Quality Rating and Meal Price Data

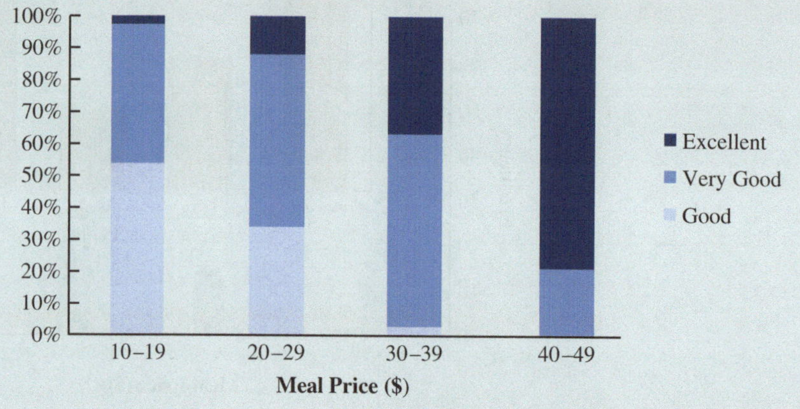

Using Excel's Recommended Charts Tool to Construct Side-by-Side and Stacked Bar Charts

In Figure 2.17, we showed the results of using Excel's PivotTable tool to construct a frequency distribution for the sample of 300 restaurants in the Los Angeles area. We will use these results to illustrate how Excel's Recommended Charts tool can be used to construct side-by-side and stacked bar charts for the restaurant data using the PivotTable output.

Apply Tools: The following steps describe how to use Excel's Recommended Charts tool to construct a side-by-side bar chart for the restaurant data using the PivotTable tool output shown in Figure 2.17.

Step 1. Select any cell in the PivotTable report (cells A3:F8)
Step 2. Click the **Insert** tab on the Ribbon
Step 3. In the **Charts** group, click **Recommended Charts**; a preview showing a bar chart with quality rating on the horizontal axis appears
Step 4. Click **OK** (alternatively, you can preview a different chart type by selecting one of the other chart types listed on the left side of the **Insert Chart** dialog box)
Step 5. Click the **Design** tab on the Ribbon
Step 6. In the **Data** group, click **Switch Row/Column**; a side-by-side bar chart with meal price on the horizontal axis appears

Excel refers to the bar chart in Figure 2.24 as a Clustered Column chart.

Editing Options: We can easily edit the side-by-side bar chart to change the bar colors and axis labels.

Step 1. Click the **Chart Elements** button + (located next to the top-right corner of the chart)
Step 2. When the list of chart elements appears:
Select the check box for **Axis Titles** (creates placeholder for the axis titles)
Deselect the check box for **Gridlines**
Step 3. Click the horizontal **Axis Title** placeholder and replace it with *Meal Price ($)*
Step 4. Click the vertical **Axis Title** placeholder and replace it with *Frequency*

The edited side-by-side chart is shown in Figure 2.24.

Figure 2.24 Edited Side-by-Side Bar Chart for the Restaurant Data Constructed Using Excel's Recommended Charts Tool

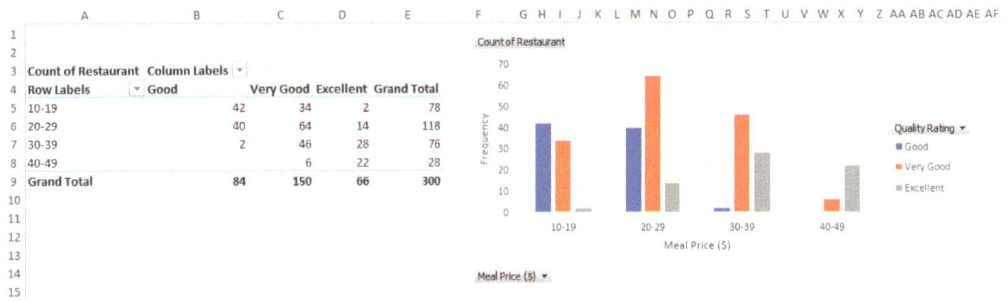

Count of Restaurant	Column Labels			
Row Labels	Good	Very Good	Excellent	Grand Total
10-19	42	34	2	78
20-29	40	64	14	118
30-39	2	46	28	76
40-49		6	22	28
Grand Total	84	150	66	300

Figure 2.25 Stacked Bar Chart for the Restaurant Data Constructed in Excel

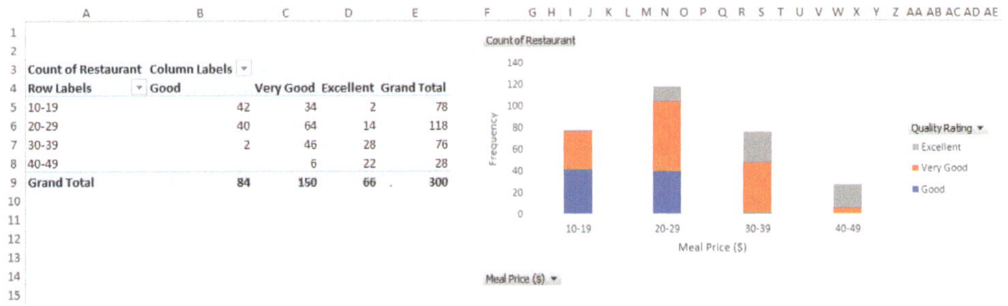

Count of Restaurant	Column Labels			
Row Labels	Good	Very Good	Excellent	Grand Total
10-19	42	34	2	78
20-29	40	64	14	118
30-39	2	46	28	76
40-49		6	22	28
Grand Total	84	150	66	300

You can easily change the side-by-side bar chart to a stacked bar chart using the following steps.

Step 5. Click on the bar chart
Click the **Design** tab on the Ribbon
In the **Type** group, click **Change Chart Type**

Step 6. When the **Change Chart Type** dialog box appears:
Select the **Stacked Columns** option
Click **OK**

The stacked bar chart appears in Figure 2.25.

Notes + Comments

1. A time series is a sequence of observations on a variable measured at successive points in time. A scatter diagram in which the value of time is shown on the horizontal axis and the time series values are shown on the vertical axis is referred to as a time series plot. We will discuss time series plots and how to analyze time series data in Chapter 17.
2. A stacked bar chart can also be used to display frequencies rather than percentage frequencies. In this case, the different color segments of each bar represent the contribution to the total for that bar, rather than the percentage contribution.

Exercises

Methods

36. The following 20 observations are for two quantitative variables, *x* and *y*. **LO 8**

DATA*file* scatter

Observation	x	y	Observation	x	y
1	−22	22	11	−37	48
2	−33	49	12	34	−29
3	2	8	13	9	−18
4	29	−16	14	−33	31
5	−13	10	15	20	−16
6	21	−28	16	−3	14
7	−13	27	17	−15	18
8	−23	35	18	12	17
9	14	−5	19	−20	−11
10	3	−3	20	−7	−22

a. Develop a scatter diagram for the relationship between *x* and *y*.
b. What is the relationship, if any, between *x* and *y*?

37. Consider the following data on two categorical variables. The first variable, *x*, can take on values A, B, C, or D. The second variable, *y*, can take on values I or II. The following table gives the frequency with which each combination occurs. **LO 10**

	y	
x	I	II
A	143	857
B	200	800
C	321	679
D	420	580

a. Construct a side-by-side bar chart with *x* on the horizontal axis.
b. Comment on the relationship between *x* and *y*.

38. The following crosstabulation summarizes the data for two categorical variables, *x* and *y*. The variable *x* can take on values Low, Medium, or High and the variable *y* can take on values Yes or No. **LO 10**

	y		
x	Yes	No	Total
Low	20	10	30
Medium	15	35	50
High	20	5	25
Total	55	50	105

a. Compute the row percentages.
b. Construct a stacked percent frequency bar chart with *x* on the horizontal axis.

Applications

39. **Driving Speed and Fuel Efficiency.** A study on driving speed (miles per hour) and fuel efficiency (miles per gallon) for midsize automobiles resulted in the data that follows. **LO 8**

DATA*file*
mpg

Driving Speed	30	50	40	55	30	25	60	25	50	55
Fuel Efficiency	28	25	25	23	30	32	21	35	26	25

a. Construct a scatter diagram with driving speed on the horizontal axis and fuel efficiency on the vertical axis.
b. Comment on any apparent relationship between these two variables.

DATA*file*
snow

40. **Low Temperatures and Snowfall.** The file *snow* contains average annual snowfall (inches) for 51 major U.S. cities over 30 years. For example, the average low temperature for Columbus, Ohio, is 44 degrees and the average annual snowfall is 27.5 inches. **LO 8**
   a. Construct a scatter diagram with the average annual low temperature on the horizontal axis and the average annual snowfall on the vertical axis.
   b. Does there appear to be any relationship between these two variables?
   c. Based on the scatter diagram, comment on any data points that seem unusual.

41. **Hypertension and Heart Disease.** People often wait until middle age to worry about having a healthy heart. However, recent studies have shown that earlier monitoring of risk factors such as blood pressure can be very beneficial (*The Wall Street Journal*). Having higher-than-normal blood pressure, a condition known as hypertension, is a major risk factor for heart disease. Suppose a large sample of male and female individuals of various ages was selected and that each individual's blood pressure was measured to determine if they have hypertension. For the sample data, the following table shows the percentage of individuals with hypertension. **LO 10**

DATA*file*
hypertension

	Percent with Hypertension	
Age	**Male**	**Female**
20–34	11.0	9.0
35–44	24.0	19.0
45–54	39.0	37.0
55–64	57.0	56.0
65–74	62.0	64.0
75+	73.3	79.0

   a. Develop a side-by-side bar chart with age on the horizontal axis, the percentage of individuals with hypertension on the vertical axis, and side-by-side bars based on gender.
   b. What does the display you developed in part (a) indicate about hypertension and age?
   c. Comment on differences by gender.

42. **4K TV.** 4K televisions (TVs) contain approximately four times as many pixels to display images as a 1080-display TV, and so they offer much higher picture resolution. Suppose that the following survey results show 4K TV ownership compared to ownership of 1080 TVs and other types of TVs by age. **LO 10**

DATA*file*
televisions

Age Category	4K TV (%)	1080 TV (%)	Other (%)
18–24	49	46	5
25–34	58	35	7
35–44	44	45	11
45–54	28	58	14
55–64	22	59	19
65+	11	45	44

a. Construct a stacked bar chart to display the above survey data on type of television ownership. Use age category as the variable on the horizontal axis.
b. Comment on the relationship between age and television ownership.
c. How would you expect the results of this survey to be different if conducted 10 years from now?

43. **Store Managers Time Study.** The Northwest regional manager of an outdoor equipment retailer conducted a study to determine how managers at three store locations are using their time. A summary of the results is shown in the following table. **LO 10**

DATA*file*
managertime

	Percentage of Manager's Work Week Spent On			
Store Location	**Meetings**	**Reports**	**Customers**	**Idle**
Bend	18	11	52	19
Portland	52	11	24	13
Seattle	32	17	37	14

a. Create a stacked bar chart with store location on the horizontal axis and percentage of time spent on each task on the vertical axis.
b. Create a side-by-side bar chart with store location on the horizontal axis and side-by-side bars of the percentage of time spent on each task.
c. Which type of bar chart (stacked or side-by-side) do you prefer for these data? Why?

2.5 Visualizing Geospatial Data

Geospatial data are data that include information on the geographic location of each record. When dealing with geospatial data, displaying them on a map can often help to discover patterns that would have been otherwise difficult to interpret. In this section, we consider two general types of geographic visualizations and discuss their use in data exploration.

Choropleth Maps

A **choropleth map** is a geographic visualization that uses shades of a color, different colors, or symbols to indicate the values of a quantitative or categorical variable associated with a geographic region or area. A familiar example of a choropleth map is a weather map, such as the one in Figure 2.26. In Figure 2.26, the preattentive attribute of color is used to depict the daily high temperature, with warmer colors (on the red end of the spectrum) representing higher temperatures and cooler colors (on the purple end of the spectrum) representing lower temperatures.

While choropleth maps may provide a good visual display of changes in a variable between geographic areas, they can also be misleading. If the location data are not granular enough so that the value of the displayed variable is relatively uniform over the respective areas over which it is displayed, then the values of the variable within regions and between regions may be misrepresented. The choropleth map may mask substantial variation of the variable within an area of the same color shading. Further, the choropleth map may suggest abrupt changes in the variable between region boundaries while the actual changes across boundaries may be more gradual.

Choropleth maps are the most reliable when the variable displayed is relatively constant within the different locations to be colored. If this is not the case, and a choropleth map is desired, the likelihood of the map to convey erroneous insights is mitigated when (1) variable measures are density based (quantity divided by land area or population) or (2) the colored regions are roughly equal-sized so there are no regions that are visually distracting.

Figure 2.26 Weather Map as an Example of a Choropleth Map

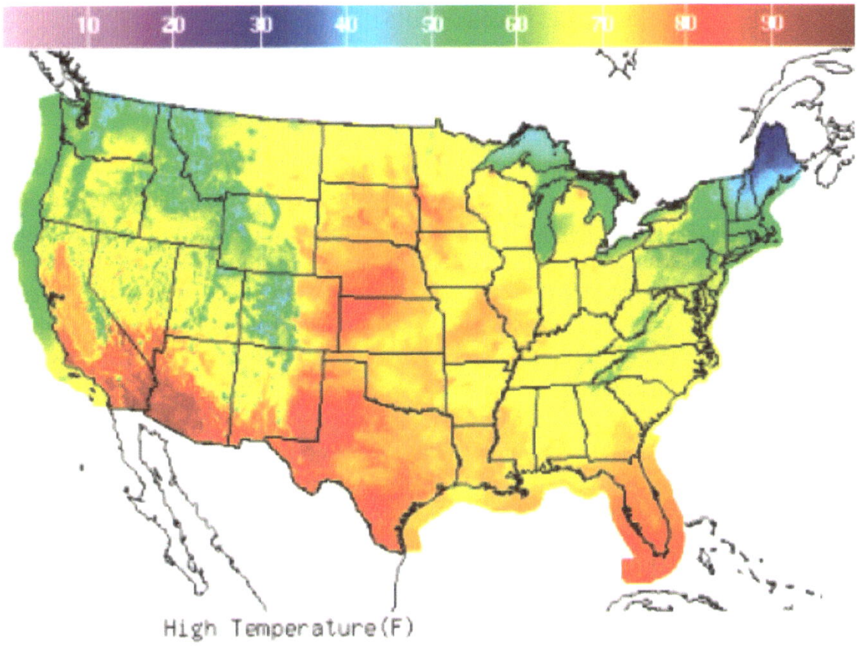

Using Excel to Construct a Choropleth Map

For data with variables representing geographical regions (e.g., countries, states, counties, postal codes), Excel has mapping functionality that will create a choropleth map. For example, data in Table 2.16 contains the median income for each state in the United States (these data are also in the file *incomestate*).

Table 2.16 Median Income Data by State

State	Median Income ($)	State	Median Income ($)	State	Median Income ($)	State	Median Income ($)	State	Median Income ($)
Alabama	49,881	Hawaii	80,527	Massachusetts	79,817	New Mexico	47,405	South Dakota	57,041
Alaska	74,912	Idaho	55,524	Michigan	56,640	New York	67,648	Tennessee	52,366
Arizona	59,079	Illinois	65,063	Minnesota	70,295	North Carolina	53,922	Texas	60,632
Arkansas	47,094	Indiana	55,725	Mississippi	44,740	North Dakota	65,250	Utah	71,381
California	75,250	Iowa	60,071	Missouri	54,412	Ohio	56,155	Vermont	60,917
Colorado	71,949	Kansas	58,150	Montana	55,248	Oklahoma	51,914	Virginia	72,600
Connecticut	76,366	Kentucky	50,189	Nebraska	59,724	Oregon	63,168	Washington	74,023
Delaware	65,467	Louisiana	48,021	Nevada	58,740	Pennsylvania	60,891	West Virginia	44,038
Florida	55,433	Maine	55,579	New Hampshire	75,322	Rhode Island	63,787	Wisconsin	60,779
Georgia	58,634	Maryland	83,076	New Jersey	81,777	South Carolina	52,449	Wyoming	62,259

DATA*file*
incomestate

Apply Tools to Show State-Level Data: The following steps use the file *incomestate* to create a choropleth map using shading to denote the median income in each state of the United States.

Step 1. Select cells A1:B51
Step 2. Click the **Insert** tab on the Ribbon
Step 3. In the **Charts** group, click the **Maps** button
Step 4. Select **Filled Map**

The preceding steps produce the choropleth map in Figure 2.27. As Figure 2.27 demonstrates, choropleth maps are typically better for displaying relative comparisons of magnitude than conveying absolute measures of magnitude. The value of median income for each state is difficult to estimate from Figure 2.27, but it is relatively easy to conclude that northeastern states have high median incomes relative to the rest of the country and many southern states have low median incomes. Indeed, the strength of a choropleth map is the identification of the high-level characteristics of a variable with respect to geographic positioning.

We also observe in Figure 2.27 that the relative size of the states plays a role in the audience's perception. For instance, Rhode Island is barely visible while larger states dominate the audience's field of vision. Another weakness of Figure 2.27 is that it masks the income distributions within each state.

DATA*file*
incomecounty

Apply Tools to Show Country-Level Data: The following steps use the file *incomecounty* to create a choropleth map using shading to denote the median income in the counties within each state of the United States.

Step 1. Select cells A1:C3148
Step 2. Click the **Insert** tab on the Ribbon
Step 3. In the **Charts** group, click the **Maps** button
Step 4. Select **Filled Map**

Figure 2.27 Choropleth Map of United States Displaying Median Income by State

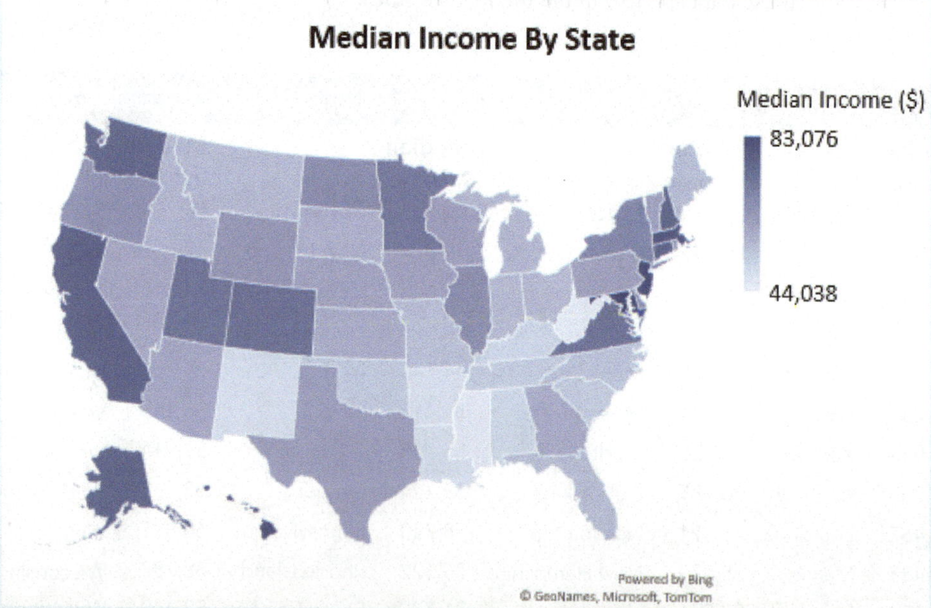

Figure 2.28 Choropleth Map of United States Displaying Median Income by Country

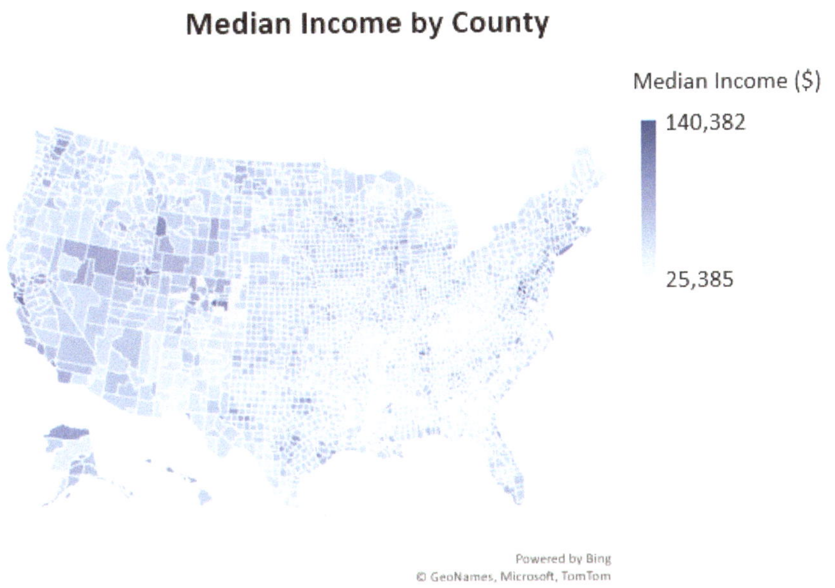

The preceding steps produce the choropleth map in Figure 2.28. (Note that It may take Excel several minutes to populate the county-level choropleth map.) The choice of choropleth map (state-level in Figure 2.27 or county level in Figure 2.28) depends on the insight intended to be delivered using the visualization. These two maps could also be used in tandem by first showing the state-level measure and then selecting one or more states to "zoom" in on and show the county-level measure.

Cartograms

Excel does not have the functionality to automatically generate cartograms.

Another type of geographic display is a cartogram. A **cartogram** is a map-like diagram that uses geographic positioning but purposefully represents map regions in a manner that does not necessarily correspond to land area. For example, Figure 2.29 contains a

Figure 2.29 Cartogram of United States Displaying State Population

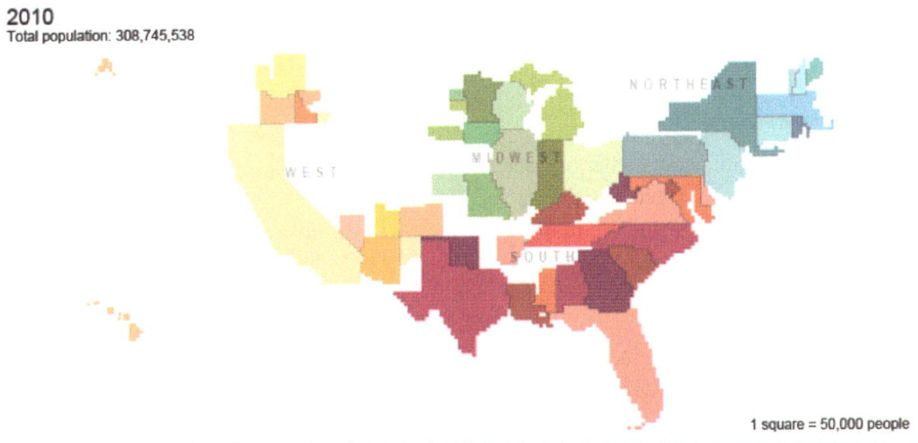

Figure 2.30 Equal-Area Cartogram of United States Displaying Median Income by State

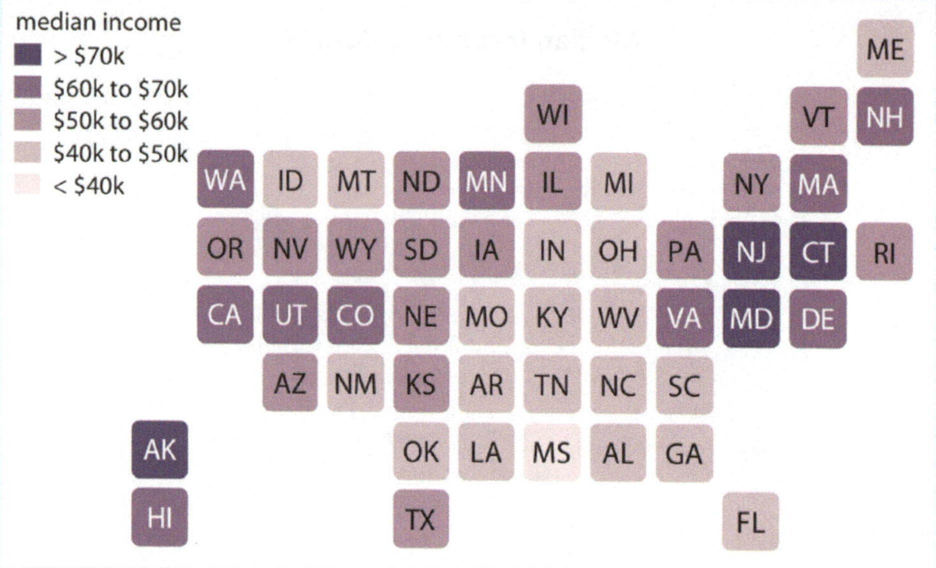

cartogram of the United States in which the area of each state is based on its population. A cartogram often leverages the audience's familiarity with the geography of the displayed regions to convey its message. In Figure 2.29, we observe the tiny size of many western states (Alaska, Nevada, Idaho, Nebraska, North Dakota, and South Dakota) and the white space paired with the audience's tacit knowledge of a standard U.S. map conveys the low population density in these areas.

A strength of a cartogram is that the area displayed is proportional to the variable being measured, thus avoiding any misleading impressions. A weakness of a cartogram is that the sizing of the regions according to the displayed variable may distort enough to render the relative geographic positioning meaningless and the standard area-based geography unrecognizable. Figure 2.30 contains a specific type of cartogram, known as an **equal-area cartogram**. In comparison to the choropleth in Figure 2.27, the equal-area cartogram provides a balanced visual representation of each state while still maintaining fidelity to relative geographic positioning.

Exercises

Methods

44. Indicate whether or not each of the following describe a limitation of using a choropleth map for geospatial data. **LO 11**
    a. A choropleth map may disguise variation within an area that has the same color of shading.
    b. A choropleth map can only be used for numerical values related the population of an area.
    c. A choropleth map distorts the size of geographic areas.
    d. A choropleth map may make small geographic areas difficult to interpret.
    e. A choropleth map may suggest larger changes across a geographic boundary than is true in reality.

45. Which of the following best describes the advantage of using an equal-are a cartogram compared to a non-equal-area cartogram? **LO 11**
   a. An equal size cartogram better shows the colors of differentiation based on the geospatial data.
   b. An equal-area cartogram prevents the distortion caused by areas representing small values of the corresponding data.
   c. An equal-area cartogram reduces the size of small-valued areas so they can effectively be ignored in the visualization.
   d. An equal-area cartogram can be used for time-series data while a non-equal-area cartogram cannot.

Applications

DATA*file*
species

46. **Biodiversity Preservation.** Ecologists often measure the biodiversity of a region by the number of distinct species that exist in the region. Nature reserves are lands specifically designated by the government to help maintain biodiversity. Care must be taken when setting up a network of nature reserves so that the maximum number of species can exist in the network. Geography matters as well, as putting reserves too close together might subject the entire network to risks, such as devastation from wildfires. The initial step in this type of planning usually involves mapping the number of species that exist in each region. The file *species* contains an estimate of the number of unique species that exist in each of the 50 states in the United States. **LO 11**
   a. Create a choropleth map that displays number of species by state. Add data labels to the choropleth map to show the number of species in each state.
   b. Comment on the distribution of species over the United States. Which regions of the United States have relatively many species? Which regions have relatively few species?
   c. Which two states have the most species? Why might this be expected?
   d. The choropleth map in part (a) helps to identify which states have the most species. However, how could one construct a choropleth map that identifies the states with the highest density of species?

47. **Electoral Vote Maps.** The President of the United States is elected based on the Electoral College. Each state in the United States has a specified number of electoral votes. Typically, the candidate that wins the popular vote in a state receives all the electoral votes assigned to that state (a few states like Maine and Nebraska split their electoral votes among the candidates based on the results of the popular vote). Suppose that a polling firm would like to create a visual for an upcoming Presidential election to show the relative standing of the Democratic and Republican candidates based on the most recent projections for the upcoming election. The first visualization shown below represents a choropleth map based on the latest projections. States that are shown in light (dark) blue are considered slightly (solidly) Democratic states. States that are shown in light (dark) red are considered slightly (solidly) Republican states. States that are shown in tan are considered to be toss-up states that could be won by either the Democratic or the Republican candidate. The second visualization represents a cartogram where each grid shown represents one electoral vote. Electoral votes are based on population, not geographic size. Thus, large states (in area) with small populations, like Montana (MT), are large in the choropleth map but small in the cartogram (because they have relatively few electoral votes). Compare the choropleth map to the cartogram. What advantages are provided by the cartogram compared to the choropleth map? **LO 11**

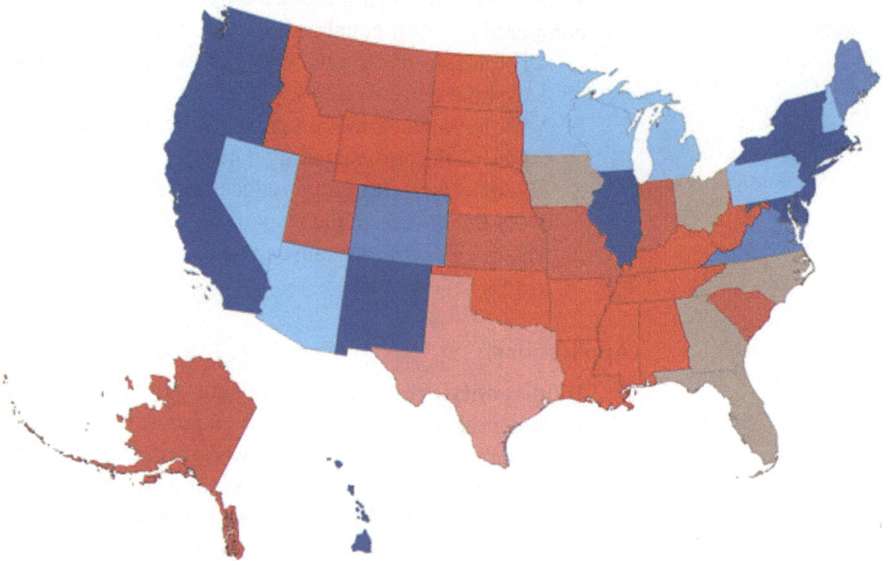

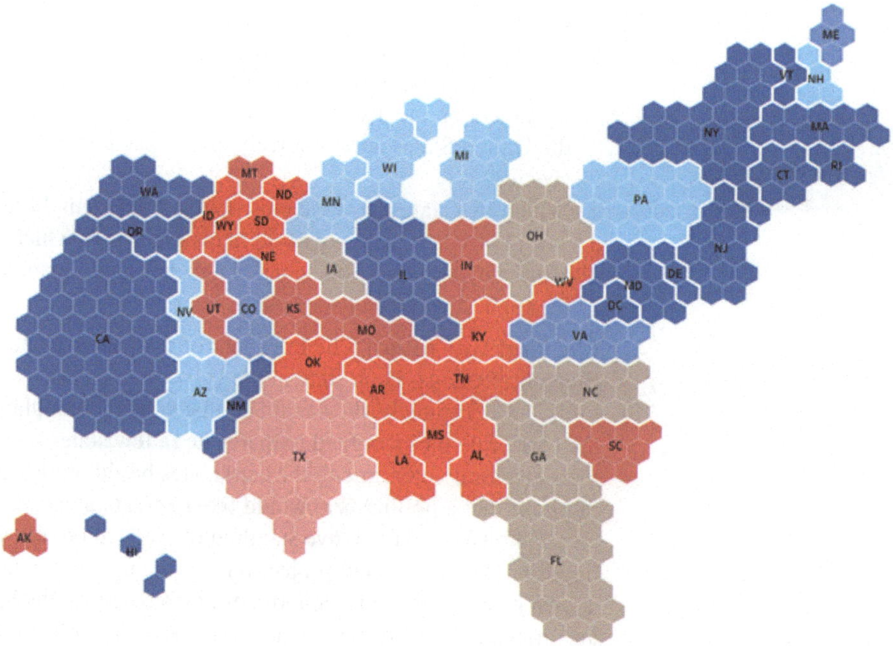

2.6 Data Visualization: Best Practices in Creating Effective Graphical Displays

Data visualization is a term used to describe the use of graphical displays to summarize and present information about a data set. The goal of data visualization is to communicate as effectively and clearly as possible the key information about the data. In this section, we provide guidelines for creating an effective graphical display, introduce the data-ink ratio as a measure of the effectiveness of visualizations, and discuss how to select an appropriate type of display given the purpose of the study. We also illustrate the use of data dashboards, and show how the Cincinnati Zoo and Botanical Garden uses data visualization techniques to improve decision making.

Data-Ink Ratio

Another helpful concept to keep in mind for creating effective tables and charts for data visualization is the idea of the **data-ink ratio**. The data-ink ratio measures the proportion of ink used in a table or chart that is necessary to convey the meaning to the audience (known as "data-ink") to the total ink used for the table or chart. Non-data-ink is ink used in a table or chart that serves no useful purpose in conveying the data to the audience. Overuse of non-data-ink increases the cognitive load required by the user to interpret the chart or table. A guiding principle for effective data visualizations is that the table or graph should illustrate the data to help the user generate insights and understanding. The table or graph should not be so cluttered as to disguise the data or be difficult to interpret.

Let us consider the case of Gossamer Industries, a firm that produces fine silk clothing products. Gossamer is interested in tracking the sales of one of its most popular items, a particular style of scarf. Table 2.17 and Figure 2.31 provide examples of a table and chart

Table 2.17 Example of Low Data-Ink Ratio Table

Scarf Sales			
Day	Sales (units)	Day	Sales (units)
1	150	11	170
2	170	12	160
3	140	13	290
4	150	14	200
5	180	15	210
6	180	16	110
7	210	17	90
8	230	18	140
9	140	19	150
10	200	20	230

Figure 2.31 Example of a Low Data-Ink Ratio Chart

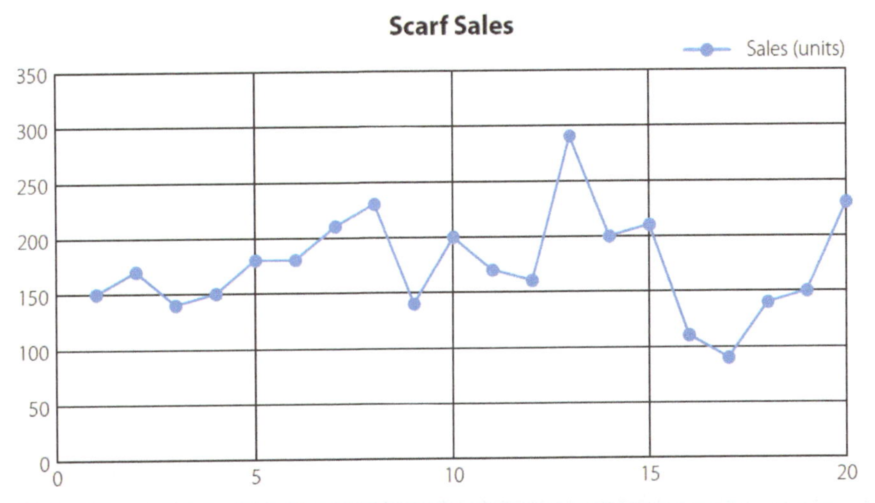

Table 2.18 Increasing the Data-Ink Ratio by Removing Unnecessary Gridlines

Scarf Sales

Day	Sales (units)	Day	Sales (units)
1	150	11	170
2	170	12	160
3	140	13	290
4	150	14	200
5	180	15	210
6	180	16	110
7	210	17	90
8	230	18	140
9	140	19	150
10	200	20	230

with low data-ink ratios used to display sales of this style of scarf. The data used in this table and figure represent product sales by day. Both of these examples are similar to tables and charts generated with Excel using common default settings. In Table 2.17, most of the grid lines serve no useful purpose. Likewise, in Figure 2.31, the horizontal lines in the chart also add little additional information. In both cases, most of these lines can be deleted without reducing the information conveyed. However, an important piece of information is missing from Figure 2.31: labels for axes. Unless both the meaning and the unit of measure are obvious, axes should always be labeled.

Table 2.18 shows a modified table in which all grid lines have been deleted except for those around the title of the table. Deleting the grid lines in Table 2.17 increases the data-ink ratio because a larger proportion of the ink in the table is used to convey the information (the actual numbers). Similarly, deleting the unnecessary horizontal and vertical grid lines in Figure 2.31, as shown in Figure 2.32, increases the data-ink ratio. Note that deleting these horizontal grid lines and removing (or reducing the size of) the markers at each data point can make it more difficult to determine the exact values plotted in the chart.

Figure 2.32 Increasing the Data-Ink Ratio by Adding Labels to Axes and Removing Unnecessary Lines and Labels

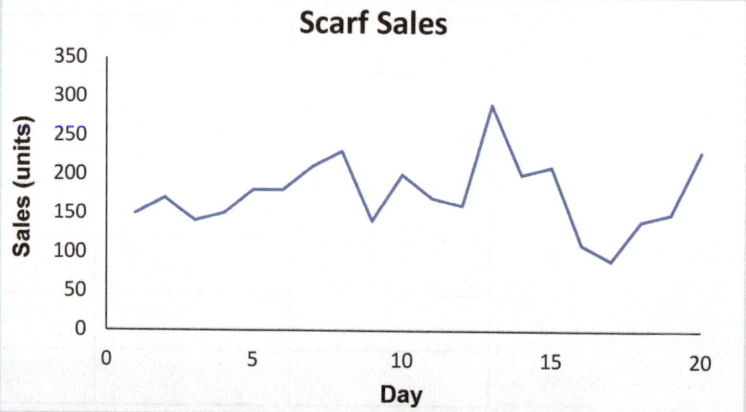

However, if it is important to convey the exact numerical values represented in the data, then it is generally better to use a table. Another form of non-value-added ink in tables and charts are unnecessary amounts of decimal places in numerical values. Only use the number of decimal places required to convey the amount of precision that is necessary. For very large numerical values, it may be preferable to express the values in "(millions)," or for large monetary values in "($ billions)," and then to round the numerical values appropriately in the table or chart.

In many cases, white space in a table or a chart can improve readability. This principle is similar to the idea of increasing the data-ink ratio. Consider Table 2.18 and Figure 2.32. Removing the unnecessary lines has increased the "white space," making it easier to read both the table and the chart. The process of increasing the data-ink ratio by adding whitespace is also known as **decluttering**. The fundamental idea in creating effective tables and charts is to make them as simple as possible in conveying information to the reader.

Creating Effective Graphical Displays

The data presented in Table 2.19 show the forecasted or planned value of sales ($1,000s) and the actual value of sales ($1,000s) by sales region in the United States for Gustin Chemical for the past year. Note that there are two quantitative variables (planned sales and actual sales) and one categorical variable (sales region). Suppose we would like to develop a graphical display that would enable management of Gustin Chemical to visualize how each sales region did relative to planned sales and simultaneously enable management to visualize sales performance across regions.

Figure 2.33 shows a side-by-side bar chart of the planned versus actual sales data. Note how this bar chart makes it very easy to compare the planned versus actual sales in a region,

Table 2.19 Planned and Actual Sales by Sales Region ($1,000s)

Sales Region	Planned Sales ($1,000s)	Actual Sales ($1,000s)
Northeast	540	447
Northwest	420	447
Southeast	575	556
Southwest	360	341

Figure 2.33 Side-by-Side Bar Chart for Planned Versus Actual Sales

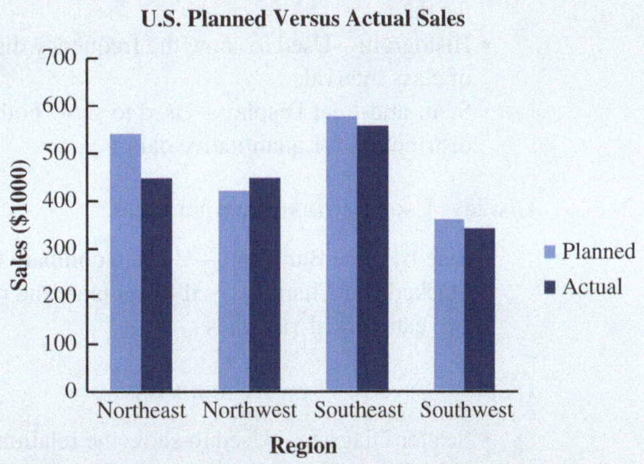

as well as across regions. This graphical display is simple, contains a title, is well labeled, and uses color to differentiate the two types of sales. Here, different shades of blue are used to prevent the chart from being distracting to the reader. Note also that the scale of the vertical axis begins at zero. The four sales regions are separated by space so that it is clear that they are distinct, whereas the planned versus actual sales values are side by side for easy comparison within each region. The side-by-side bar chart in Figure 2.33 makes it easy to see that the Southwest region is the lowest in both planned and actual sales and that the Northwest region slightly exceeded its planned sales.

Creating an effective graphical display is as much art as it is science. By following the general guidelines listed below you can increase the likelihood that your display will effectively convey the key information in the data.

- Give the display a clear and concise title.
- Keep the display simple by maximizing the data-ink ratio. Remove unnecessary gridlines and redundant labels. Do not use three dimensions when two dimensions are sufficient.
- Clearly label each axis and provide the units of measure.
- If color is used to distinguish categories, make sure the colors are distinct. Keep in mind that many people are color blind, so try to avoid colors that are not easily differentiated by those that are color blind (like red and green). Do not overuse color to the point it becomes distracting.
- If multiple colors or line types are used, use a legend to define how they are used and place the legend close to the representation of the data.

Choosing the Type of Graphical Display

In this chapter, we discussed a variety of graphical displays, including bar charts, pie charts, dot plots, histograms, stem-and-leaf plots, scatter diagrams, side-by-side bar charts, and stacked bar charts. Each of these types of displays was developed for a specific purpose. In order to provide guidelines for choosing the appropriate type of graphical display, we now provide a summary of the types of graphical displays categorized by their purpose. We note that some types of graphical displays may be used effectively for multiple purposes.

Displays Used to Show the Distribution of Data

- Bar Chart—Used to show the frequency distribution and relative frequency distribution for categorical data
- Pie Chart—Used to show the relative frequency and percent frequency for categorical data
- Dot Plot—Used to show the distribution for quantitative data over the entire range of the data
- Histogram—Used to show the frequency distribution for quantitative data over a set of class intervals
- Stem-and-Leaf Display—Used to show both the rank order and shape of the distribution for quantitative data

Displays Used to Make Comparisons

- Side-by-Side Bar Chart—Used to compare two variables
- Stacked Bar Charts—Used to compare the relative frequency or percent frequency of two categorical variables

Displays Used to Show Relationships

- Scatter Diagram—Used to show the relationship between two quantitative variables
- Trendline—Used to approximate the relationship of data in a scatter diagram
- Choropleth Map and Cartogram—Used to display geospatial data.

Data Dashboards

One of the most widely used data visualization tools is a **data dashboard**. If you drive a car, you are already familiar with the concept of a data dashboard. In an automobile, the car's dashboard contains gauges and other visual displays that provide the key information that is important when operating the vehicle. For example, the gauges used to display the car's speed, fuel level, engine temperature, and oil level are critical to ensure safe and efficient operation of the automobile. In some vehicles, this information is even displayed visually on the windshield to provide an even more effective display for the driver. Data dashboards play a similar role for managerial decision making.

Key performance indicators are sometimes referred to as key performance metrics (KPMs).

A data dashboard is a set of visual displays that organizes and presents information that is used to monitor the performance of a company or organization in a manner that is easy to read, understand, and interpret. Just as a car's speed, fuel level, engine temperature, and oil level are important information to monitor in a car, every business has key performance indicators (KPIs) that need to be monitored to assess how a company is performing. Examples of KPIs are inventory on hand, daily sales, percentage of on-time deliveries, and sales revenue per quarter. A data dashboard should provide timely summary information (potentially from various sources) on KPIs that is important to the user, and it should do so in a manner that informs rather than overwhelms its user.

To illustrate the use of a data dashboard in decision making, we will discuss an application involving the Grogan Oil Company. Grogan has offices located in three cities in Texas: Austin (its headquarters), Houston, and Dallas. Grogan's Information Technology (IT) call center, located in the Austin office, handles calls from employees regarding computer-related problems involving software, Internet, and e-mail issues. For example, if a Grogan employee in Dallas has a computer software problem, the employee can call the IT call center for assistance.

The data dashboard shown in Figure 2.34 was developed to monitor the performance of the call center. This data dashboard combines several displays to monitor the call center's KPIs. The data presented are for the current shift, which started at 8:00 A.M. The stacked bar chart in the upper-left-hand corner shows the call volume for each type of problem (software, Internet, or e-mail) over time. This chart shows that call volume is heavier during the first few hours of the shift, calls concerning e-mail issues appear to decrease over time, and volume of calls regarding software issues are highest at midmorning.

The bar chart in the upper-right-hand corner of the dashboard shows the percentage of time that call center employees spent on each type of problem or were idle (not working on a call). These top two charts are important displays in determining the optimal staffing levels. For instance, knowing the call mix and how stressed the system is, as measured by percentage of idle time, can help the IT manager make sure that enough call center employees are available with the right level of expertise.

The side-by-side bar chart title "Call Volume by Office" shows the call volume by type of problem for each of Grogan's offices. This allows the IT manager to quickly identify if there is a particular type of problem by location. For example, it appears that the office in Austin is reporting a relatively high number of issues with e-mail. If the source of the problem can be identified quickly, then the problem for many might be resolved quickly. Also, note that a relatively high number of software problems are coming from the Dallas office. The higher call volume in this case was simply due to the fact that the Dallas office is currently installing new software, and this has resulted in more calls to the IT call center. Because the IT manager was alerted to this by the Dallas office last week, the IT manager knew there would be an increase in calls coming from the Dallas office and was able to increase staffing levels to handle the expected increase in calls.

For each unresolved case that was received more than 15 minutes ago, the bar chart shown in the middle left-hand side of the data dashboard displays the length of time that each of these cases has been unresolved. This chart enables Grogan to quickly monitor the key problem cases and decide whether additional resources may be needed to resolve them. The worst case, T57, has been unresolved for over 300 minutes and is actually left over from the previous shift. Finally, the histogram at the bottom shows the distribution of the time to resolve the problem for all resolved cases for the current shift.

Figure 2.34 Grogan Oil Information Technology Call Center Data Dashboard

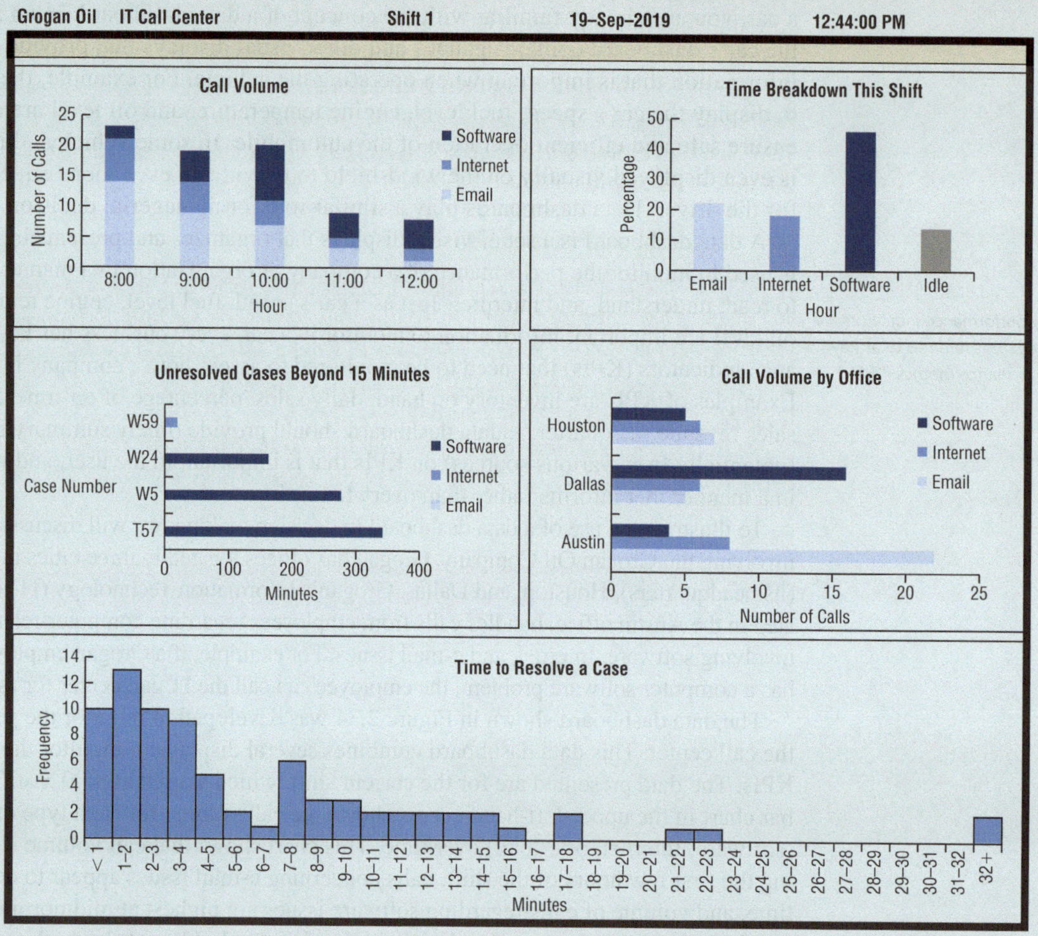

DATA*file*
grogan

The Grogan Oil data dashboard illustrates the use of a dashboard at the operational level. The data dashboard is updated in real time and used for operational decisions such as staffing levels. Data dashboards may also be used at the tactical and strategic levels of management. For example, a logistics manager might monitor KPIs for on-time performance and cost for its third-party carriers. This could assist in tactical decisions such as transportation mode and carrier selection. At the highest level, a more strategic dashboard would allow upper management to quickly assess the financial health of the company by monitoring more aggregate financial, service level, and capacity utilization information.

The guidelines for good data visualization discussed previously apply to the individual charts in a data dashboard, as well as to the entire dashboard. In addition to those guidelines, it is important to minimize the need for screen scrolling, avoid unnecessary use of color or three-dimensional displays, and use borders between charts to improve readability. As with individual charts, simpler is almost always better.

Data Visualization in Practice: Cincinnati Zoo and Botanical Garden[2]

The Cincinnati Zoo and Botanical Garden, located in Cincinnati, Ohio, is the second-oldest zoo in the world. In order to improve decision making by becoming more data-driven,

[2]The authors are indebted to John Lucas, formerly of the Cincinnati Zoo and Botanical Garden, for providing this application.

management decided they needed to link together the different facets of their business and provide nontechnical managers and executives with an intuitive way to better understand their data. A complicating factor is that when the zoo is busy, managers are expected to be on the grounds interacting with guests, checking on operations, and anticipating issues as they arise or before they become an issue. Therefore, being able to monitor what is happening on a real-time basis was a key factor in deciding what to do. Zoo management concluded that a data visualization strategy was needed to address the problem.

Because of its ease of use, real-time updating capability, and iPad compatibility, the Cincinnati Zoo decided to implement its data visualization strategy using IBM's Cognos advanced data visualization software. Using this software, the Cincinnati Zoo developed the data dashboard shown in Figure 2.35 to enable zoo management to track the following key performance indicators:

- Item Analysis (sales volumes and sales dollars by location within the zoo)
- Geoanalytics (using maps and displays of where the day's visitors are spending their time at the zoo)
- Customer Spending
- Cashier Sales Performance
- Sales and Attendance Data Versus Weather Patterns
- Performance of the Zoo's Loyalty Rewards Program

An iPad mobile application was also developed to enable the zoo's managers to be out on the grounds and still see and anticipate what is occurring on a real-time basis. The

Figure 2.35 Data Dashboard for the Cincinnati Zoo

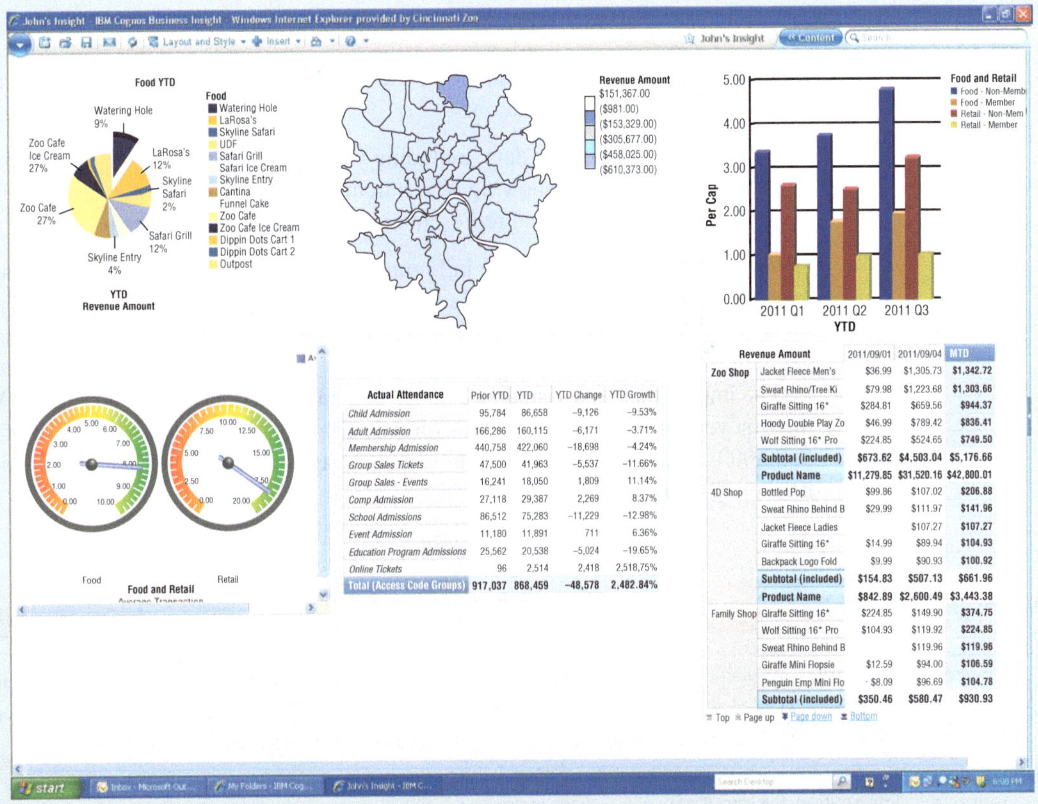

Figure 2.36 The Cincinnati Zoo iPad Data Dashboard

Cincinnati Zoo's iPad data dashboard, shown in Figure 2.36, provides managers with access to the following information:

- Real-time attendance data, including what types of guests are coming to the zoo
- Real-time analysis showing which items are selling the fastest inside the zoo
- Real-time geographical representation of where the zoo's visitors live

Having access to the data shown in Figures 2.35 and 2.36 allows the zoo managers to make better decisions on staffing levels within the zoo, which items to stock based upon weather and other conditions, and how to better target its advertising based on geodemographics.

The impact that data visualization has had on the zoo has been substantial. Within the first year of use, the system was directly responsible for revenue growth of over $500,000, increased visitation to the zoo, enhanced customer service, and reduced marketing costs.

Notes + Comments

1. A variety of software is available for data visualization. Among the more popular packages are Excel, Power BI, JMP, R, SAS Visual Analytics, Spotfire, and Tableau.
2. A very powerful tool for visualizing geographic data is a Geographic Information System (GIS). A GIS uses color, symbols, and text on a map to help you understand how variables are distributed geographically. Choropleth maps and cartograms are examples of GIS tools.

Summary

A set of data, even if modest in size, is often difficult to interpret directly in the form in which it is gathered. Tabular and graphical displays can be used to summarize and present data so that patterns are revealed and the data are more easily interpreted. Frequency distributions, relative frequency distributions, percent frequency distributions, bar charts, and pie charts were presented as tabular and graphical displays for summarizing the data for a single categorical variable. Frequency distributions, relative frequency distributions, percent frequency distributions, histograms, cumulative frequency distributions, cumulative relative frequency distributions, cumulative percent frequency distributions, and stem-and-leaf displays were presented as ways of summarizing the data for a single quantitative variable.

A crosstabulation was presented as a tabular display for summarizing the data for two variables, and a scatter diagram was introduced as a graphical display for summarizing the data for two quantitative variables. We showed that side-by-side bar charts and stacked bar charts are just extensions of basic bar charts that can be used to display and compare two categorical variables. We also showed how choropleth maps and cartograms can be used to display geospatial data. Guidelines for creating effective graphical displays, including a discussion of the data-ink ratio and decluttering, and how to choose the most appropriate type of display were discussed. Data dashboards were introduced to illustrate how a set of visual displays can be developed that organizes and presents information that is used to monitor a company's performance in a manner that is easy to read, understand, and interpret. Figure 2.37 provides a summary of the tabular and graphical methods presented in this chapter.

Figure 2.37 Tabular and Graphical Displays for Summarizing Data

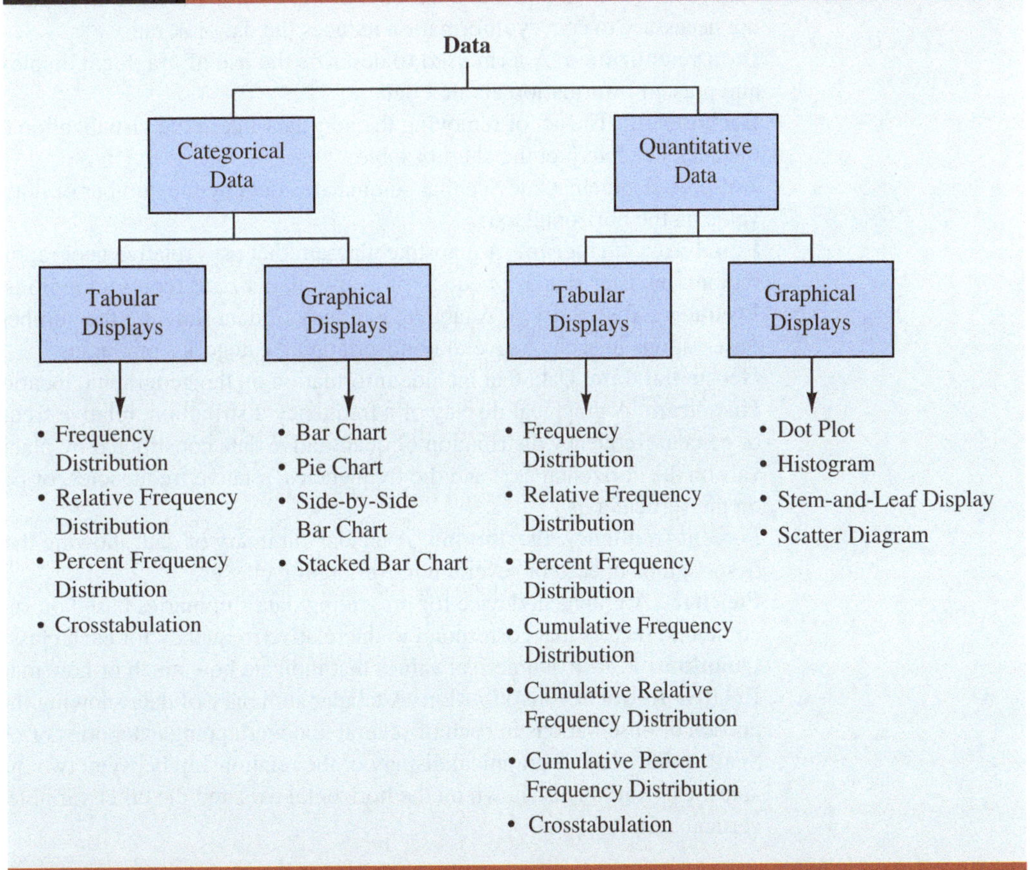

Glossary

Bar chart A graphical device for depicting categorical data that have been summarized in a frequency, relative frequency, or percent frequency distribution.

Cartogram A map-like diagram that uses geographic positioning but purposefully represents map regions in a manner that does not necessarily correspond to land area.

Categorical data Labels or names used to identify categories of like items.

Choropleth map A geographic visualization that uses shades of a color, different colors, or symbols to indicate the values of a variable associated with a region.

Class midpoint The value halfway between the lower and upper class limits.

Crosstabulation A tabular summary of data for two variables. The classes for one variable are represented by the rows; the classes for the other variable are represented by the columns.

Cumulative frequency distribution A tabular summary of quantitative data showing the number of data values that are less than or equal to the upper class limit of each class.

Cumulative percent frequency distribution A tabular summary of quantitative data showing the percentage of data values that are less than or equal to the upper class limit of each class.

Cumulative relative frequency distribution A tabular summary of quantitative data showing the fraction or proportion of data values that are less than or equal to the upper class limit of each class.

Data dashboard A set of visual displays that organizes and presents information that is used to monitor the performance of a company or organization in a manner that is easy to read, understand, and interpret.

Data-ink ratio The ratio of the amount of ink used in a table or chart that is necessary to convey information to the total amount of ink used in the table and chart. Ink used that is not necessary to convey information reduces the data-ink ratio.

Data visualization A term used to describe the use of graphical displays to summarize and present information about a data set.

Decluttering The act of removing the non-data-ink in the visualization that does not help the audience interpret the chart or table.

Dot plot A graphical device that summarizes data by the number of dots above each data value on the horizontal axis.

Equal-area cartogram A map-like diagram that uses relative geographic positioning of regions, but uses shapes of equal (or near-equal) size to represent regions.

Frequency distribution A tabular summary of data showing the number (frequency) of observations in each of several nonoverlapping categories or classes.

Geospatial data Data that include information on the geographic location of each record.

Histogram A graphical display of a frequency distribution, relative frequency distribution, or percent frequency distribution of quantitative data constructed by placing the class intervals on the horizontal axis and the frequencies, relative frequencies, or percent frequencies on the vertical axis.

Percent frequency distribution A tabular summary of data showing the percentage of observations in each of several nonoverlapping classes.

Pie chart A graphical device for presenting data summaries based on subdivision of a circle into sectors that correspond to the relative frequency for each class.

Quantitative data Numerical values that indicate how much or how many.

Relative frequency distribution A tabular summary of data showing the fraction or proportion of observations in each of several nonoverlapping categories or classes.

Scatter diagram A graphical display of the relationship between two quantitative variables. One variable is shown on the horizontal axis and the other variable is shown on the vertical axis.

Side-by-side bar chart A graphical display for depicting multiple bar charts on the same display.
Simpson's paradox Conclusions drawn from two or more separate crosstabulations that can be reversed when the data are aggregated into a single crosstabulation.
Stacked bar chart A bar chart in which each bar is broken into rectangular segments of a different color showing the relative frequency of each class in a manner similar to a pie chart.
Stem-and-leaf display A graphical display used to show simultaneously the rank order and shape of a distribution of data.
Trendline A line that provides an approximation of the relationship between two variables.

Key Formulas

Relative Frequency

$$\frac{\text{Frequency of the class}}{n} \tag{2.1}$$

Approximate Class Width

$$\frac{\text{Largest data value} - \text{Smallest data value}}{\text{Number of classes}} \tag{2.2}$$

Supplementary Exercises

DATA*file*
sat2021

48. **SAT Scores.** The SAT is a standardized test used by some colleges and universities in admission decisions. Approximately 1 million high school students took the SAT in 2021. The 2021 version of the SAT is composed of two sections: evidence-based reading and writing, and math. A perfect combined score for the SAT is 1600. A sample of SAT scores for the combined SAT is as follows. **LO 3, 5, 6**

740	1380	1260	940	1110
1210	600	1080	910	960
1310	850	800	920	1110
820	1270	1040	870	1160
1200	1080	1120	750	1040
900	1060	1420	1180	1030

a. Show a frequency distribution and histogram. Begin with the first class starting at 600 and use a class width of 100.
b. Comment on the shape of the distribution.
c. What other observations can be made about the SAT scores based on the tabular and graphical summaries?

DATA*file*
medianhousehold

49. **Median Household Incomes.** The file *medianhousehold* contains the median household income for a family with two earners for each of the 50 states (American Community Survey). **LO 3, 5, 6**
a. Construct a frequency and a percent frequency distribution of median household income. Begin the first class at 65.0 and use a class width of 5.
b. Construct a histogram.
c. Comment on the shape of the distribution.
d. Which state has the highest median income for two-earner households?
e. Which state has the lowest median income for two-earner households?

50. **State Populations.** Data showing the population by state in millions of people follow (*The World Almanac*). **LO 3, 6**

DATA*file*
population2012

State	Population	State	Population	State	Population
Alabama	4.8	Louisiana	4.5	Ohio	11.5
Alaska	0.7	Maine	1.3	Oklahoma	3.8
Arizona	6.4	Maryland	5.8	Oregon	4.3
Arkansas	2.9	Massachusetts	6.5	Pennsylvania	12.7
California	37.3	Michigan	9.9	Rhode Island	1.0
Colorado	5.0	Minnesota	5.3	South Carolina	4.6
Connecticut	3.6	Mississippi	3.0	South Dakota	0.8
Delaware	0.9	Missouri	6.0	Tennessee	6.3
Florida	18.8	Montana	0.9	Texas	25.1
Georgia	9.7	Nebraska	1.8	Utah	2.8
Hawaii	1.4	Nevada	2.7	Vermont	0.6
Idaho	1.6	New Hampshire	1.3	Virginia	8.0
Illinois	12.8	New Jersey	8.8	Washington	6.7
Indiana	6.5	New Mexico	2.0	West Virginia	1.9
Iowa	3.0	New York	19.4	Wisconsin	5.7
Kansas	2.9	North Carolina	9.5	Wyoming	0.6
Kentucky	4.3	North Dakota	0.7		

a. Develop a frequency distribution, a percent frequency distribution, and a histogram. Use a class width of 2.5 million.
b. Does there appear to be any skewness in the distribution? Explain.
c. What observations can you make about the population of the 50 states?

51. **Start-up Company Funds.** According to *The Wall Street Journal*, a startup company's ability to gain funding is a key to success. The funds raised (in millions of dollars) by 50 start-up companies follow. **LO 5**

DATA*file*
startups

81	61	103	166	168
80	51	130	77	78
69	119	81	60	20
73	50	110	21	60
192	18	54	49	63
91	272	58	54	40
47	24	57	78	78
154	72	38	131	52
48	118	40	49	55
54	112	129	156	31

a. Construct a stem-and-leaf display.
b. Comment on the display.

52. **Complaints Reported to BBB.** Consumer complaints are frequently reported to the Better Business Bureau (BBB). Some industries against whom the most complaints are reported to the BBB are banks, cable and satellite television companies, collection agencies, cellular phone providers, and new car dealerships (*USA Today*). The results for a sample of 200 complaints are contained in the file *bbb*. **LO 1, 2**

DATA*file*
bbb

a. Show the frequency and percent frequency of complaints by industry.
b. Construct a bar chart of the percent frequency distribution.
c. Which industry had the highest number of complaints?
d. Comment on the percentage frequency distribution for complaints.

53. **Stock Price Volatility.** The term "beta" refers to a measure of a stock's price volatility relative to the stock market as a whole. A beta of 1 means the stock's price moves exactly with the market. A beta of 1.6 means the stock's price would increase by 1.6% for an increase of 1% in the stock market. A larger beta means the stock price is more

Table 2.20 Betas for Stocks of Thirty Companies

DATA*file* stocksbeta

Company	Beta	Company	Beta
American Express Company	1.24	3M Company	1.23
The Boeing Company	0.99	Merck & Co. Inc.	0.56
Caterpillar Inc.	1.2	Microsoft Corporation	0.69
Cisco Systems, Inc.	1.36	Nike, Inc.	0.47
Chevron Corporation	1.11	Pfizer Inc.	0.72
Dow, Inc.	1.36	The Procter & Gamble Company	0.73
The Walt Disney Company	0.97	AT&T, Inc.	0.18
The Goldman Sachs Group, Inc.	1.79	The Travelers Companies, Inc.	0.86
The Home Depot, Inc.	1.22	UnitedHealth Group Incorporated	0.88
International Business Machines Corporation	0.92	United Technologies Corporation	1.22
Intel Corporation	0.9	Visa Inc.	0.82
Johnson & Johnson	0.84	Verizon Communications Inc.	0.04
JPMorgan Chase & Co.	1.84	Walgreens Boots Alliance	0.81
The Coca-Cola Company	0.68	Walmart Stores Inc.	0.26
McDonald's Corp.	0.62	ExxonMobil Corporation	1.1

volatile. The beta values for the stocks of 30 companies are shown in Table 2.20 (*Yahoo Finance*). **LO 3, 5, 6**

a. Construct a frequency distribution and percent frequency distribution.
b. Construct a histogram.
c. Comment on the shape of the distribution.
d. Which stock has the highest beta? Which has the lowest beta?

54. **Education Level and Household Income.** The U.S. Census Bureau serves as the leading source of quantitative data about the nation's people and economy. The following crosstabulation shows the number of households (1,000s) and the household income by the level of education for heads of household having received a high school degree or more education (U.S. Census Bureau website). **LO 1, 3, 7**

	Household Income				
Level of Education	Under $25,000	$25,000 to $49,999	$50,000 to $99,999	$100,000 and Over	Total
High School Graduate	9,880	9,970	9,441	3,482	32,773
Bachelor's Degree	2,484	4,164	7,666	7,817	22,131
Master's Degree	685	1,205	3,019	4,094	9,003
Doctoral Degree	79	160	422	1,076	1,737
Total	13,128	15,499	20,548	16,469	65,644

a. Construct a percent frequency distribution for the level of education variable. What percentage of heads of households have a master's or doctoral degree?
b. Construct a percent frequency distribution for the household income variable. What percentage of households have an income of $50,000 or more?
c. Convert the entries in the crosstabulation into column percentages. Compare the level of education of households with a household income of under $25,000 to the level of education of households with a household income of $100,000 or more. Comment on any other items of interest when reviewing the crosstabulation showing column percentages.

55. **Softball Players' Batting Averages.** Western University has only one women's softball scholarship remaining for the coming year. The final two players that Western is considering are Allison Fealey and Emily Janson. The coaching staff has concluded that the speed and defensive skills are virtually identical for the two players, and that the final decision will be based on which player has the best batting average. Crosstabulations of each player's batting performance in their junior and senior years of high school are as follows:

	Allison Fealey	
Outcome	Junior	Senior
Hit	15	75
No Hit	25	175
Total At-Bats	40	250

	Emily Janson	
Outcome	Junior	Senior
Hit	70	35
No Hit	130	85
Total At-Bats	200	120

A player's batting average is computed by dividing the number of hits a player has by the total number of at-bats. Batting averages are represented as a decimal number with three places after the decimal. **LO 7, 9**

a. Calculate the batting average for each player in her junior year. Then calculate the batting average of each player in her senior year. Using this analysis, which player should be awarded the scholarship? Explain.

b. Combine or aggregate the data for the junior and senior years into one crosstabulation as follows:

	Player	
Outcome	Fealey	Janson
Hit		
No Hit		
Total At-Bats		

Calculate each player's batting average for the combined two years. Using this analysis, which player should be awarded the scholarship? Explain.

c. Are the recommendations you made in parts (a) and (b) consistent? Explain any apparent inconsistencies.

DATA*file*
fortunebest100

56. **Best Places to Work.** *Fortune* magazine publishes an annual survey of the 100 best companies to work for. The data in the file *fortunebest100* shows the rank, company name, the size of the company, and the percentage job growth for full-time employees for 98 of the *Fortune* 100 companies for which percentage job growth data were available (*Fortune* magazine website). The column labeled "Rank" shows the rank of the company in the *Fortune* 100 list; the column labeled "Size" indicates whether the company is a small company (less than 2,500 employees), a midsized company (2,500 to 10,000 employees), or a large company (more than 10,000 employees); and the column labeled "Job Growth (%)" shows the percentage job growth for full-time employees. **LO 1, 3, 7**

a. Construct a crosstabulation with Job Growth (%) as the row variable and Size as the column variable. Use classes starting at −10 and ending at 70 in increments of 10 for Job Growth.

b. Show the frequency distribution for Job Growth (%) and the frequency distribution for Size.

c. Using the crosstabulation constructed in part (a), develop a crosstabulation showing column percentages.

DATA*file*
colleges

Table 2.21 Data for a Sample of Private Colleges and Universities

School	Year Founded	Tuition & Fees ($)	% Graduate
American University	1893	36,697	79.00
Baylor University	1845	29,754	70.00
Belmont University	1951	23,680	68.00
.	.	.	.
.	.	.	.
.	.	.	.
Wofford College	1854	31,710	82.00
Xavier University	1831	29,970	79.00
Yale University	1701	38,300	98.00

d. Using the crosstabulation constructed in part (a), develop a crosstabulation showing row percentages.

e. Comment on the relationship between the percentage job growth for full-time employees and the size of the company.

57. **Colleges' Year Founded and Cost.** Table 2.21 shows a portion of the data for a sample of 103 private colleges and universities. The complete data set is contained in the file *colleges*. The data include the name of the college or university, the year the institution was founded, the tuition and fees (not including room and board) for the most recent academic year, and the percentage of full-time, first-time bachelor's degree–seeking undergraduate students who obtain their degree in six years or less (*The World Almanac*). **LO 7**

a. Construct a crosstabulation with Year Founded as the row variable and Tuition & Fees as the column variable. Use classes starting with 1,600 and ending with 2,000 in increments of 50 for Year Founded. For Tuition & Fees, use classes starting with 1 and ending with 45,000 in increments of 5,000.

b. Compute the row percentages for the crosstabulation in part (a).

c. What relationship, if any, do you notice between Year Founded and Tuition & Fees?

58. **Colleges' Year Founded and Percent Graduated.** Refer to the data set in Table 2.21. **LO 7**

a. Construct a crosstabulation with Year Founded as the row variable and % Graduate as the column variable. Use classes starting with 1,600 and ending with 2,000 in increments of 50 for Year Founded. For % Graduate, use classes starting with 35% and ending with 100% in increments of 5%.

b. Compute the row percentages for your crosstabulation in part (a).

c. Comment on any relationship between the variables.

59. **Colleges' Year Founded and Cost.** Refer to the data set in Table 2.21. **LO 8**

a. Construct a scatter diagram to show the relationship between Year Founded and Tuition & Fees.

b. Comment on any relationship between the variables.

60. **Colleges' Cost and Percent Graduated.** Refer to the data set in Table 2.21. **LO 8**

a. Prepare a scatter diagram to show the relationship between Tuition & Fees and % Graduate.

b. Comment on any relationship between the variables.

61. **Electric Vehicle Sales.** Electric plug-in vehicle sales have been increasing worldwide. The table below displays data collected by the U.S. Department of Energy on electric plug-in vehicle sales in the world's top markets in 2013

and 2015. (Data compiled by Argonne National Laboratory, U.S. Department of Energy) **LO 10**

DATA*file*
electricvehicles

Region	2013	2015
China	15,004	214,283
Western Europe	71,233	184,500
United States	97,102	115,262
Japan	28,716	46,339
Canada	931	5,284

a. Construct a side-by-side bar chart with year as the variable on the horizontal axis. Comment on any trend in the display.
b. Convert the above table to percentage allocation for each year. Construct a stacked bar chart with year as the variable on the horizontal axis.
c. Is the display in part (a) or part (b) more insightful? Explain.

62. **Zoo Member Types and Attendance.** A zoo has categorized its visitors into three categories: member, school, and general. The member category refers to visitors who pay an annual fee to support the zoo. Members receive certain benefits such as discounts on merchandise and trips planned by the zoo. The school category includes faculty and students from day care and elementary and secondary schools; these visitors generally receive a discounted rate. The general category includes all other visitors. The zoo has been concerned about a recent drop in attendance. To help better understand attendance and membership, a zoo staff member has collected the following data. **LO 2, 10**

DATA*file*
zoo

	Attendance			
Visitor Category	Year 1	Year 2	Year 3	Year 4
General	153,713	158,704	163,433	169,106
Member	115,523	104,795	98,437	81,217
School	82,885	79,876	81,970	81,290
Total	352,121	343,375	343,840	331,613

a. Construct a bar chart of total attendance over time. Comment on any trend in the data.
b. Construct a side-by-side bar chart showing attendance by visitor category with year as the variable on the horizontal axis.
c. Comment on what is happening to zoo attendance based on the charts from parts (a) and (b).

63. **Omaha Steaks.** Omaha Steaks is a food retailing company that specializes in mail-order delivery of beef. The company is headquartered in Omaha, Nebraska, and was founded as a butcher shop in 1917. Omaha Steaks wants to create a visualization displaying the state's geographic distribution of beef cattle. Data on the number of beef cattle in each county in Nebraska and the size of each county (in square miles) are contained in the file *nebraskabeef.* **LO 11**

DATA*file*
nebraskabeef

a. Create a choropleth map that shades each county in Nebraska relative to the density of beef cattle (as measured by head per square mile).
b. Why might it be preferable to shade each county based on density of beef cattle (as measured by head per square mile) rather than just number of beef cattle?

64. **Sales Performance Bonuses.** A sales manager is trying to determine appropriate sales performance bonuses for the sales team this year. The following table contains the data relevant to determining the bonuses, but it is not easy to read and interpret. Reformat the table to improve readability using the principles of data-ink ratio and decluttering to help the sales manager make decisions about bonuses. **LO 12**

DATA*file*
salesbonuses

Salesperson	Total Sales ($)	Average Performance Bonus Previous Years ($)	Customer Accounts	Years with Company
Smith, Michael	325000.78	12499.3452	124	14
Yu, Joe	13678.21	239.9434	9	7
Reeves, Bill	452359.19	21987.2462	175	21
Hamilton, Joshua	87423.91	7642.9011	28	3
Harper, Derek	87654.21	1250.1393	21	4
Quinn, Dorothy	234091.39	14567.9833	48	9
Graves, Lorrie	379401.94	27981.4432	121	12
Sun, Yi	31733.59	672.9111	7	1
Thompson, Nicole	127845.22	13322.9713	17	3

65. **Gross Domestic Product Values.** The following table shows an example of gross domestic product values for five countries over six years in equivalent U.S. dollars ($). **LO 12**

Gross Domestic Product (US $)						
Country	Year 1	Year 2	Year 3	Year 4	Year 5	Year 6
Albania	7385937423	8105580293	9650128750	11592303225	10781921975	10569204154
Argentina	169725491092	198012474920	241037555661	301259040110	285070994754	339604450702
Australia	704453444387	758320889024	916931817944	982991358955	934168969952	1178776680167
Austria	272865358404	290682488352	336840690493	375777347214	344514388622	341440991770
Belgium	335571307765	355372712266	408482592257	451663134614	421433351959	416534140346

DATA*file*
gdp_years

a. How could you improve the readability of this table?

b. The file *gdp_years* contains sample data from the United Nations Statistics Division on 30 countries and their GDP values from Year 1 to Year 6 in US $. Create a table that provides all these data for a user. Format the table to make it as easy to read as possible. (*Hint:* It is generally not important for the user to know GDP to an exact dollar figure. It is typical to present GDP values in millions or billions of dollars.)

66. **Monthly Revenue Data.** The following table provides monthly revenue values for Tedstar, Inc., a company that sells valves to large industrial firms. The monthly revenue data have been graphed using a line chart in the following figure. **LO 12**

Month	Jan	Feb	Mar	Apr	May	Jun	Jul	Aug	Sep	Oct	Nov	Dec
Revenue ($)	145869	123576	143298	178505	186850	192850	134500	145286	154285	148523	139600	148235

DATA*file*
tedstar

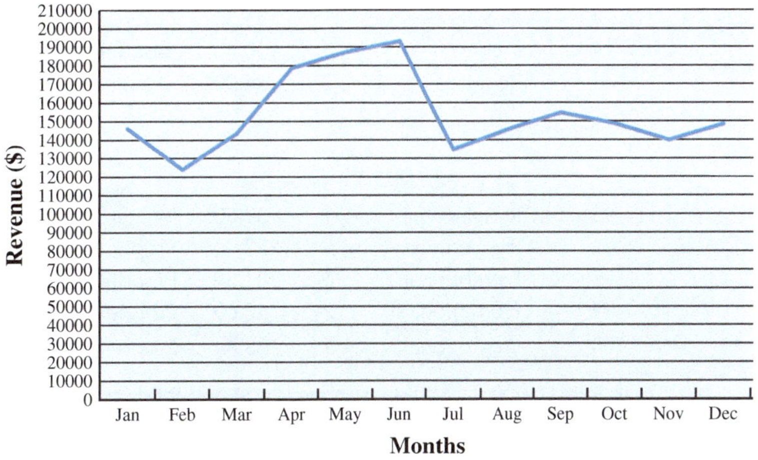

a. What are the problems with the layout and display of this line chart?
b. Create a new line chart for the monthly revenue data at Tedstar, Inc. using the principles of data-ink ratio and decluttering. Format the chart to make it easy to read and interpret.

Case Problem 1: Pelican Stores

Pelican Stores, a division of National Clothing, is a chain of clothing stores operating throughout the country. The chain recently ran a promotion in which discount coupons were sent to customers of other National Clothing stores. Data collected for a sample of 100 in-store credit card transactions at Pelican Stores during one day while the promotion was running are contained in the file *pelicanstores*. Table 2.22 shows a portion of the data set. The Proprietary Card method of payment refers to charges made using a National Clothing charge card. Customers who made a purchase using a discount coupon are referred to as promotional customers, and customers who made a purchase but did not use a discount coupon are referred to as regular customers. Because the promotional coupons were not sent to regular Pelican Stores customers, management considers the sales made to people presenting the promotional coupons as sales it would not otherwise make. Of course, Pelican also hopes that the promotional customers will continue to shop at its stores.

Most of the variables shown in Table 2.22 are self-explanatory, but two of the variables require some clarification.

Items	The total number of items purchased
Net Sales	The total amount ($) charged to the credit card

Pelican's management would like to use this sample data to learn about its customer base and to evaluate the promotion involving discount coupons. **LO 1, 2, 3, 7, 8**

Managerial Report

Use the tabular and graphical methods of descriptive statistics to help management develop a customer profile and to evaluate the promotional campaign. At a minimum, your report should include the following:

1. Percent frequency distribution for key variables.
2. A bar chart or pie chart showing the number of customer purchases attributable to the method of payment.

DATA*file*
pelicanstores

Table 2.22 Data for a Sample of 100 Credit Card Purchases at Pelican Stores

Customer	Type of Customer	Items	Net Sales	Method of Payment	College Graduate	Marital Status	Age
1	Regular	1	39.50	Discover	No	Married	32
2	Promotional	1	102.40	Proprietary Card	Yes	Married	36
3	Regular	1	22.50	Proprietary Card	Yes	Married	32
4	Promotional	5	100.40	Proprietary Card	Yes	Married	28
5	Regular	2	54.00	MasterCard	Yes	Married	34
.	.	.	.	.	.	.	.
.	.	.	.	.	.	.	.
.	.	.	.	.	.	.	.
96	Regular	1	39.50	MasterCard	Yes	Married	44
97	Promotional	9	253.00	Proprietary Card	Yes	Married	30
98	Promotional	10	287.59	Proprietary Card	Yes	Married	52
99	Promotional	2	47.60	Proprietary Card	Yes	Married	30
100	Promotional	1	28.44	Proprietary Card	Yes	Married	44

3. A crosstabulation of type of customer (regular or promotional) versus net sales. Comment on any similarities or differences present.
4. A scatter diagram to explore the relationship between net sales and customer age.

Case Problem 2: Movie Theater Releases

The movie industry is a competitive business. More than 50 studios produce hundreds of new movies for theater release each year, and the financial success of each movie varies considerably. The opening weekend gross sales ($ millions), the total gross sales ($ millions), the number of theaters the movie was shown in, and the number of weeks the movie was in release are common variables used to measure the success of a movie released to theaters. Data collected for the top 100 theater movies released in 2016 are contained in the file *movies2016* (Box Office Mojo website). Table 2.23 shows the data for the first 10 movies in this file. **LO 3, 8**

Managerial Report

Use the tabular and graphical methods of descriptive statistics to learn how these variables contribute to the success of a motion picture. Include the following in your report:

1. Tabular and graphical summaries for each of the four variables, along with a discussion of what each summary tells us about the movies that are released to theaters.
2. A scatter diagram to explore the relationship between Total Gross Sales and Opening Weekend Gross Sales. Discuss.
3. A scatter diagram to explore the relationship between Total Gross Sales and Number of Theaters. Discuss.
4. A scatter diagram to explore the relationship between Total Gross Sales and Number of Weeks in Release. Discuss.

Case Problem 3: Queen City

Cincinnati, Ohio, also known as the Queen City, has a population of just over 300,000 and is the third-largest city in the state of Ohio. The Cincinnati metropolitan area has a population of about 2.2 million. The city is governed by a mayor and a nine-member city council.

DATA*file*
movies2016

Table 2.23 Performance Data for Ten 2016 Movies Released to Theaters

Movie Title	Opening Gross Sales ($ millions)	Total Gross Sales ($ millions)	Number of Theaters	Weeks in Release
Rogue One: A Star Wars Story	155.08	532.18	4,157	20
Finding Dory	135.06	486.30	4,305	25
Captain America: Civil War	179.14	408.08	4,226	20
The Secret Life of Pets	104.35	368.38	4,381	25
The Jungle Book	103.26	364.00	4,144	24
Deadpool	132.43	363.07	3,856	18
Zootopia	75.06	341.27	3,959	22
Batman v Superman: Dawn of Justice	166.01	330.36	4,256	12
Suicide Squad	133.68	325.10	4,255	14
Sing	35.26	270.40	4,029	20

Table 2.24 Annual Expenditures for Queen City (First Four Entries)

Department	Department Description	Category	Fund	Expenditure ($)
121	Department of Human Resources	Fringe Benefits	050 - GENERAL FUND	7,085.21
121	Department of Human Resources	Fringe Benefits	050 - GENERAL FUND	102,678.64
121	Department of Human Resources	Fringe Benefits	050 - GENERAL FUND	79,112.85
121	Department of Human Resources	Contractual Services	050 - GENERAL FUND	3,572.50

The city manager, who is responsible for the day-to-day operation of the city, reports to the mayor and city council. The city manager recently created the Office of Performance and Data Analytics with the goal of improving the efficiency of city operations. One of the first tasks of this new office is to review the previous year's expenditures. The file *queencity* contains data on the previous year's expenditures, including the following:

DATA*file*
queencity

Department	The number of the department incurring the expenditure
Department Description	The name of the department incurring the description
Category	The category of the expenditure
Fund	The fund to which the expenditure was charged
Expenditure	The dollar amount of the expense

Table 2.24 shows the first four entries of the 5,427 expenditures for the year. The city manager would like to use this data to better understand how the city's budget is being spent. **LO 1, 2, 7**

Managerial Report

Use tabular and graphical methods of descriptive statistics to help the city manager get a better understanding of how the city is spending its funding. Your report should include the following:

1. Tables and/or graphical displays that show the amount of expenditures by category and percentage of total expenditures by category.
2. A table that shows the amount of expenditures by department and the percentage of total expenditures by department. Combine any department with less than 1% into a category named "Other."
3. A table that shows the amount of expenditures by fund and the percentage of total expenditures by fund. Combine any fund with less than 1% into a category named "Other."

Case Problem 4: Cut-Rate Machining, Inc.

Jon Weideman, first shift foreman for Cut-Rate Machining, Inc., is attempting to decide on a vendor from whom to purchase a drilling machine. Jon narrows his alternatives to four vendors: The Hole-Maker, Inc. (HM); Shafts & Slips, Inc. (SS); Judge's Jigs (JJ); and Drill-for-Bits, Inc. (DB). Each of these vendors is offering machines of similar capabilities at similar prices, so the effectiveness of the machines is the only selection criterion that can be used. Jon invites each vendor to ship one machine to the Richmond, Indiana, manufacturing facility for a test. Jon starts all four machines at 8:00 A.M. and lets them warm up for two hours before starting to use any of the machines. After the warmup period, one of Jon's employees will use each of the shipped machines to drill 3-centimeter-diameter holes in 25-centimeter-thick stainless-steel sheets for two hours. The widths of holes drilled with each machine are then measured and recorded. The results of the data collection are shown in Table 2.25.

Table 2.25 Data Collected for Drill-For-Bits, Inc. Vendor Selection

Shift	Time Period	Employee	Vendor	Measured Width (cm)
1	10:00 A.M. – noon	Airad	HM	3.50
1	10:00 A.M. – noon	Airad	HM	3.13
1	10:00 A.M. – noon	Airad	HM	3.39
1	10:00 A.M. – noon	Airad	HM	3.08
1	10:00 A.M. – noon	Airad	HM	3.22
1	10:00 A.M. – noon	Airad	HM	3.45
1	10:00 A.M. – noon	Airad	HM	3.32
1	10:00 A.M. – noon	Airad	HM	3.61
1	10:00 A.M. – noon	Airad	HM	3.10
1	10:00 A.M. – noon	Airad	HM	3.03
1	10:00 A.M. – noon	Airad	HM	3.67
1	10:00 A.M. – noon	Airad	HM	3.59
1	10:00 A.M. – noon	Airad	HM	3.33
1	10:00 A.M. – noon	Airad	HM	3.02
1	10:00 A.M. – noon	Airad	HM	3.55
1	10:00 A.M. – noon	Airad	HM	3.00
1	Noon – 2:00 P.M.	Airad	SS	2.48
1	Noon – 2:00 P.M.	Airad	SS	2.72
1	Noon – 2:00 P.M.	Airad	SS	2.99
1	Noon – 2:00 P.M.	Airad	SS	2.68
1	Noon – 2:00 P.M.	Airad	SS	2.75
1	Noon – 2:00 P.M.	Airad	SS	2.42
1	Noon – 2:00 P.M.	Airad	SS	2.92
1	Noon – 2:00 P.M.	Airad	SS	2.68
1	Noon – 2:00 P.M.	Airad	SS	2.98
1	Noon – 2:00 P.M.	Airad	SS	2.50
1	Noon – 2:00 P.M.	Airad	SS	2.45
1	Noon – 2:00 P.M.	Airad	SS	2.99
1	Noon – 2:00 P.M.	Airad	SS	2.31
1	Noon – 2:00 P.M.	Airad	SS	2.42
1	Noon – 2:00 P.M.	Airad	SS	2.91
1	Noon – 2:00 P.M.	Airad	SS	2.83
1	2:00 P.M. – 4:00 P.M.	Airad	JJ	2.66
1	2:00 P.M. – 4:00 P.M.	Airad	JJ	2.54
1	2:00 P.M. – 4:00 P.M.	Airad	JJ	2.61
1	2:00 P.M. – 4:00 P.M.	Airad	JJ	2.57
1	2:00 P.M. – 4:00 P.M.	Airad	JJ	2.71
1	2:00 P.M. – 4:00 P.M.	Airad	JJ	2.55
1	2:00 P.M. – 4:00 P.M.	Airad	JJ	2.59
1	2:00 P.M. – 4:00 P.M.	Airad	JJ	2.69

DATA*file*
cutrate

(Continued)

Table 2.25 *(Continued)*

Shift	Time Period	Employee	Vendor	Measured Width (cm)
1	2:00 P.M. – 4:00 P.M.	Airad	JJ	2.52
1	2:00 P.M. – 4:00 P.M.	Airad	JJ	2.57
1	2:00 P.M. – 4:00 P.M.	Airad	JJ	2.63
1	2:00 P.M. – 4:00 P.M.	Airad	JJ	2.60
1	2:00 P.M. – 4:00 P.M.	Airad	JJ	2.58
1	2:00 P.M. – 4:00 P.M.	Airad	JJ	2.61
1	2:00 P.M. – 4:00 P.M.	Airad	JJ	2.55
1	2:00 P.M. – 4:00 P.M.	Airad	JJ	2.62
2	4:00 P.M. – 6:00 P.M.	Sivaeb	DB	4.22
2	4:00 P.M. – 6:00 P.M.	Sivaeb	DB	2.68
2	4:00 P.M. – 6:00 P.M.	Sivaeb	DB	2.45
2	4:00 P.M. – 6:00 P.M.	Sivaeb	DB	1.84
2	4:00 P.M. – 6:00 P.M.	Sivaeb	DB	2.11
2	4:00 P.M. – 6:00 P.M.	Sivaeb	DB	3.95
2	4:00 P.M. – 6:00 P.M.	Sivaeb	DB	2.46
2	4:00 P.M. – 6:00 P.M.	Sivaeb	DB	3.79
2	4:00 P.M. – 6:00 P.M.	Sivaeb	DB	3.91
2	4:00 P.M. – 6:00 P.M.	Sivaeb	DB	2.22
2	4:00 P.M. – 6:00 P.M.	Sivaeb	DB	2.42
2	4:00 P.M. – 6:00 P.M.	Sivaeb	DB	2.09
2	4:00 P.M. – 6:00 P.M.	Sivaeb	DB	3.33
2	4:00 P.M. – 6:00 P.M.	Sivaeb	DB	4.07
2	4:00 P.M. – 6:00 P.M.	Sivaeb	DB	2.54
2	4:00 P.M. – 6:00 P.M.	Sivaeb	DB	3.96

Based on these results, from which vendor would you suggest Jon purchase his new machine? **LO 8**

Managerial Report

Use graphical methods of descriptive statistics to investigate the effectiveness of each vendor. Include the following in your report:

1. Scatter diagrams of the measured width of each hole (cm).
2. Based on the scatter diagrams a discussion of the effectiveness of each vendor and under which conditions (if any) that vendor would be acceptable.
3. A discussion of possible sources of error in the approach taken to assess these vendors.

Chapter 3

Descriptive Statistics: Numerical Measures

Contents

Statistics in Practice:
Small Fry Design

3.1 Measures of Location
- Mean
- Median
- Mode
- Using Excel to Compute the Mean, Median, and Mode
- Weighted Mean
- Geometric Mean
- Using Excel to Compute the Geometric Mean
- Percentiles
- Quartiles
- Using Excel to Compute Percentiles and Quartiles

3.2 Measures of Variability
- Range
- Interquartile Range
- Variance
- Standard Deviation
- Using Excel to Compute the Sample Variance and Sample Standard Deviation
- Coefficient of Variation
- Using Excel's Descriptive Statistics Tool

3.3 Measures of Distribution Shape, Relative Location, and Detecting Outliers
- Distribution Shape
- *z*-Scores
- Chebyshev's Theorem
- Empirical Rule
- Detecting Outliers

3.4 Five-Number Summaries and Boxplots
- Five-Number Summary
- Boxplot
- Using Excel to Construct a Boxplot
- Comparative Analysis Using Boxplots
- Using Excel to Construct a Comparative Analysis Using Boxplots

3.5 Measures of Association Between Two Variables
- Covariance
- Interpretation of the Covariance
- Correlation Coefficient
- Interpretation of the Correlation Coefficient
- Using Excel to Compute the Sample Covariance and Sample Correlation Coefficient

3.6 Data Dashboards: Adding Numerical Measures to Improve Effectiveness

Summary 170
Glossary 170
Key Formulas 172
Supplementary Exercises 173
Case Problem 1: Pelican Stores 178
Case Problem 2: Movie Theater Releases 179
Case Problem 3: Business Schools of Asia-Pacific 180
Case Problem 4: Heavenly Chocolates Website Transactions 180
Case Problem 5: African Elephant Populations 183

Available in the Cengage eBook:
Appendix: Descriptive Statistics in R

Learning Objectives

After completing this chapter, you will be able to

LO 1 Calculate and interpret measures of location for quantitative data such as the mean, weighted mean, median, geometric mean, and mode.

LO 2 Calculate and interpret percentiles and quartiles for quantitative data.

LO 3 Calculate and interpret measures of variability for quantitative data such as the range, interquartile range, variance, standard deviation, and coefficient of variation.

LO 4 Calculate and interpret *z*-scores for quantitative data.

LO 5 Apply and interpret Chebyshev's theorem and the empirical rule to quantitative data.

LO 6 Identify outliers in a set of quantitative data.

LO 7 Calculate and interpret a five-number summary for a set of quantitative data.

LO 8 Construct and interpret a boxplot.

LO 9 Calculate and interpret the covariance and the correlation coefficient for two quantitative variables.

Statistics in Practice

Small Fry Design*

Santa Ana, California

Founded in 1997, Small Fry Design was a toy and accessory company that designed and imported products for infants. The company's product line included teddy bears, mobiles, musical toys, rattles, and security blankets and featured high-quality soft toy designs with an emphasis on color, texture, and sound. The products were designed in the United States and manufactured in China.

Small Fry Design used independent representatives to sell the products to infant furnishing retailers, children's accessory and apparel stores, gift shops, upscale department stores, and major catalog companies. At one point, Small Fry Design products were distributed in more than 1,000 retail outlets throughout the United States.

Cash flow management was one of the most critical activities in the day-to-day operation of this company. Ensuring sufficient incoming cash to meet both current and ongoing debt obligations can mean the difference between business success and failure. A critical factor in cash flow management is the analysis and control of accounts receivable. By measuring the average age and dollar value of outstanding invoices, management can predict cash availability and monitor changes in the status of accounts receivable. The company set the following goals: The average age for outstanding invoices should not exceed 45 days, and the dollar value of invoices more than 60 days old should not exceed 5% of the dollar value of all accounts receivable.

Small Fry Design uses descriptive statistics to monitor its accounts receivable and incoming cash flow.
Robert Dant/Alamy Stock Photo

In a summary of accounts receivable status, the following descriptive statistics were provided for the age of outstanding invoices:

Mean	40 days
Median	35 days
Mode	31 days

Interpretation of these statistics shows that the mean or average age of an invoice is 40 days. The median shows that half of the invoices remain outstanding 35 days or more.

*The authors are indebted to John A. McCarthy, former President of Small Fry Design, for providing this Statistics in Practice.

The mode of 31 days, the most frequent invoice age, indicates that the most common length of time an invoice is outstanding is 31 days. The statistical summary also showed that only 3% of the dollar value of all accounts receivable was more than 60 days old. Based on the statistical information, management was satisfied that accounts receivable and incoming cash flow were under control.

In this chapter, you will learn how to compute and interpret some of the statistical measures used by Small Fry Design. In addition to the mean, median, and mode, you will learn about other descriptive statistics such as the range, variance, standard deviation, percentiles, and correlation. These numerical measures will assist in the understanding and interpretation of data.

In Chapter 2, we discussed tabular and graphical presentations used to summarize data. In this chapter, we present several numerical measures that provide additional alternatives for summarizing data.

We start by developing numerical summary measures for data sets consisting of a single variable. When a data set contains more than one variable, the same numerical measures can be computed separately for each variable. However, in the two-variable case, we will also develop measures of the relationship between the variables.

Point estimation is covered in more detail in Chapter 7.

Numerical measures of location, dispersion, shape, and association are introduced. If the measures are computed for data from a sample, they are called **sample statistics**. If the measures are computed for data from a population, they are called **population parameters**. In statistical inference, a sample statistic is referred to as the **point estimator** of the corresponding population parameter.

3.1 Measures of Location

Mean

The mean is sometimes referred to as the arithmetic mean.

Perhaps the most commonly used measure of location is the **mean**, or average value, for a variable. The mean provides a measure of central location for the data. If the data are for a sample, the mean is denoted by $\bar{x}$; if the data are for a population, the mean is denoted by the Greek lower case letter mu, or μ.

In statistical formulas, it is customary to denote the value of variable x for the first observation by x_1, the value of variable x for the second observation by x_2, and so on. In general, the value of variable x for the ith observation is denoted by x_i. For a sample with n observations, the formula for the sample mean is as follows.

The sample mean $\bar{x}$ is a sample statistic.

Sample Mean

$$\bar{x} = \frac{\Sigma x_i}{n} \tag{3.1}$$

The Greek capital letter sigma Σ is used to denote summation.

In the preceding formula, the numerator is the sum of the values of the n observations. That is,

$$\Sigma x_i = x_1 + x_2 + \cdots + x_n$$

To illustrate the computation of a sample mean, let us consider the following class size data for a sample of five college classes.

46 54 42 46 32

We use the notation x_1, x_2, x_3, x_4, x_5 to represent the number of students in each of the five classes.

$$x_1 = 46 \qquad x_2 = 54 \qquad x_3 = 42 \qquad x_4 = 46 \qquad x_5 = 32$$

Figure 3.1 The Mean as the Center of Balance for the Dot Plot of the Classroom Size Data

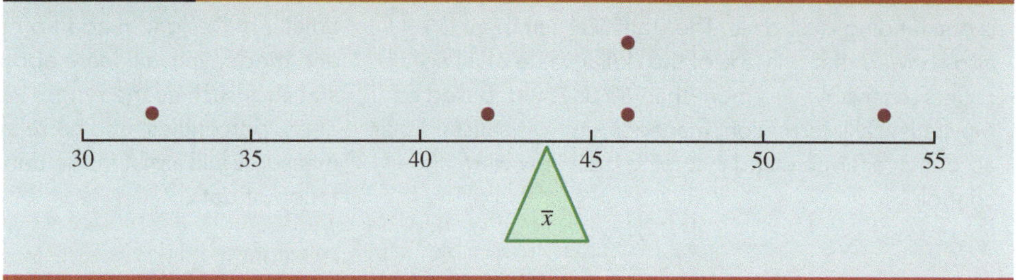

Hence, to compute the sample mean, we can write

$$\bar{x} = \frac{\Sigma x_i}{n} = \frac{x_1 + x_2 + x_3 + x_4 + x_5}{5} = \frac{46 + 54 + 42 + 46 + 32}{5} = 44$$

The sample mean class size is 44 students.

To provide a visual perspective of the mean and to show how it can be influenced by extreme values, consider the dot plot for the class size data shown in Figure 3.1. Treating the horizontal axis used to create the dot plot as a long, narrow board in which each of the dots has the same fixed weight, the mean is the point at which we would place a fulcrum or pivot point under the board in order to balance the dot plot. This is the same principle by which a see-saw on a playground works, the only difference being that the see-saw is pivoted in the middle so that as one end goes up, the other end goes down. In the dot plot we are locating the pivot point based upon the location of the dots. Now consider what happens to the balance if we increase the largest value from 54 to 114. We will have to move the fulcrum under the new dot plot in a positive direction in order to reestablish balance. To determine how far we would have to shift the fulcrum, we simply compute the sample mean for the revised class size data.

$$\bar{x} = \frac{\Sigma x_i}{n} = \frac{x_1 + x_2 + x_3 + x_4 + x_5}{5} = \frac{46 + 114 + 42 + 46 + 32}{5} = \frac{280}{5} = 56$$

Thus, the mean for the revised class size data is 56, an increase of 12 students. In other words, we have to shift the balance point 12 units to the right to establish balance under the new dot plot.

Another illustration of the computation of a sample mean is given in the following situation. Suppose that a college placement office sent a questionnaire to a sample of business school graduates requesting information on monthly starting salaries. Table 3.1 shows the

DATA*file*
startingsalaries

Table 3.1 Monthly Starting Salaries for a Sample of 12 Business School Graduates

Graduate	Monthly Starting Salary ($)	Graduate	Monthly Starting Salary ($)
1	5,850	7	5,890
2	5,950	8	6,130
3	6,050	9	5,940
4	5,880	10	6,325
5	5,755	11	5,920
6	5,710	12	5,880

collected data. The mean monthly starting salary for the sample of 12 business college graduates is computed as

$$\bar{x} = \frac{\Sigma x_i}{n} = \frac{x_1 + x_2 + \cdots + x_{12}}{12}$$

$$= \frac{5{,}850 + 5{,}950 + \cdots + 5{,}880}{12}$$

$$= \frac{71{,}280}{12} = 5{,}940$$

Equation (3.1) shows how the mean is computed for a sample with n observations. The formula for computing the mean of a population remains the same, but we use different notation to indicate that we are working with the entire population. The number of observations in a population is denoted by N and the symbol for a population mean is μ.

The sample mean $\bar{x}$ is a point estimator of the population mean μ.

Population Mean

$$\mu = \frac{\Sigma x_i}{N} \tag{3.2}$$

Median

The **median** is another measure of central location. The median is the value in the middle when the data are arranged in ascending order (smallest value to largest value). With an odd number of observations, the median is the middle value. An even number of observations has no single middle value. In this case, we follow convention and define the median as the average of the values for the middle two observations. For convenience, the definition of the median is restated as follows.

Median

Arrange the data in ascending order (smallest value to largest value).

(a) For an odd number of observations, the median is the middle value.
(b) For an even number of observations, the median is the average of the two middle values.

Let us apply this definition to compute the median class size for the sample of five college classes. Arranging the data in ascending order provides the following list.

32 42 46 46 54

Because $n = 5$ is odd, the median is the middle value. Thus the median class size is 46 students. Even though this data set contains two observations with values of 46, each observation is treated separately when we arrange the data in ascending order.

Suppose we also compute the median starting salary for the 12 business college graduates in Table 3.1. We first arrange the data in ascending order.

5,710 5,755 5,850 5,880 5,880 5,890 5,920 5,940 5,950 6,050 6,130 6,325

Middle Two Values (5,890 5,920)

Because $n = 12$ is even, we identify the middle two values: 5,890 and 5,920. The median is the average of these values.

$$\text{Median} = \frac{5{,}890 + 5{,}920}{2} = 5{,}905$$

The procedure we used to compute the median depends upon whether there is an odd number of observations or an even number of observations. Let us now describe a more conceptual and visual approach using the monthly starting salary for the 12 business college graduates. As before, we begin by arranging the data in ascending order.

5,710 5,755 5,850 5,880 5,880 5,890 5,920 5,940 5,950 6,050 6,130 6,325

Once the data are in ascending order, we trim pairs of extreme high and low values until no further pairs of values can be trimmed without completely eliminating all the data. For instance, after trimming the lowest observation (5,710) and the highest observation (6,325) we obtain a new data set with 10 observations.

~~5,710~~ 5,755 5,850 5,880 5,880 5,890 5,920 5,940 5,950 6,050 6,130 ~~6,325~~

We then trim the next lowest remaining value (5,755) and the next highest remaining value (6,130) to produce a new data set with eight observations.

~~5,710~~ ~~5,755~~ 5,850 5,880 5,880 5,890 5,920 5,940 5,950 6,050 ~~6,130~~ ~~6,325~~

Continuing this process, we obtain the following results.

~~5,710~~ ~~5,755~~ ~~5,850~~ 5,880 5,880 5,890 5,920 5,940 5,950 ~~6,050~~ ~~6,130~~ ~~6,325~~

~~5,710~~ ~~5,755~~ ~~5,850~~ ~~5,880~~ 5,880 5,890 5,920 5,940 ~~5,950~~ ~~6,050~~ ~~6,130~~ ~~6,325~~

~~5,710~~ ~~5,755~~ ~~5,850~~ ~~5,880~~ ~~5,880~~ 5,890 5,920 ~~5,940~~ ~~5,950~~ ~~6,050~~ ~~6,130~~ ~~6,325~~

At this point, no further trimming is possible without eliminating all the data. So, the median is just the average of the remaining two values. When there is an even number of observations, the trimming process will always result in two remaining values, and the average of these values will be the median. When there is an odd number of observations, the trimming process will always result in one final value, and this value will be the median. Thus, this method works whether the number of observations is odd or even.

The median is the measure of location most often reported for annual income and property value data because a few extremely large incomes or property values can inflate the mean. In such cases, the median is the preferred measure of central location.

Although the mean is the more commonly used measure of central location, in some situations the median is preferred. The mean is influenced by extremely small and large data values. For instance, suppose that the highest paid graduate (see Table 3.1) had a starting salary of $15,000 per month. If we change the highest monthly starting salary in Table 3.1 from $6,325 to $15,000 and recompute the mean, the sample mean changes from $5,940 to $6,663. The median of $5,905, however, is unchanged, because $5,890 and $5,920 are still the middle two values. With the extremely high starting salary included, the median provides a better measure of central location than the mean. We can generalize to say that whenever a data set contains extreme values, the median is often the preferred measure of central location.

Mode

Another measure of location is the **mode**. The mode is defined as follows.

Mode

The mode is the value that occurs with greatest frequency.

To illustrate the identification of the mode, consider the sample of five class sizes. The only value that occurs more than once is 46. Because this value, occurring with a frequency of 2, has the greatest frequency, it is the mode. As another illustration, consider the sample of starting salaries for the business school graduates. The only monthly starting salary that occurs more than once is $5,880. Because this value has the greatest frequency, it is the mode.

Situations can arise for which the greatest frequency occurs at two or more different values. In these instances, more than one mode exists. If the data contain exactly two modes, we say that the data are *bimodal*. If data contain more than two modes, we say that the data are *multimodal*. In multimodal cases, the mode is almost never reported because listing three or more modes would not be particularly helpful in describing a location for the data.

Using Excel to Compute the Mean, Median, and Mode

Excel provides functions for computing the mean, median, and mode. We illustrate the use of these functions by computing the mean, median, and mode for the starting salary data in Table 3.1. Refer to Figure 3.2 as we describe the tasks involved. The formula worksheet is in the background; the value worksheet is in the foreground.

DATA*file*
startingsalaries

Enter/Access Data: Open the file *startingsalaries*. The data are in cells B2:B13 and labels are in column A and cell B1.

Enter Functions and Formulas: Excel's AVERAGE function can be used to compute the mean by entering the following formula in cell E2:

=AVERAGE(B2:B13)

Similarly, the formulas *=MEDIAN(B2:B13)* and *=MODE.SNGL(B2:B13)* are entered in cells E3 and E4, respectively, to compute the median and the mode.

The formulas in cells E2:E4 are displayed in the background worksheet of Figure 3.2 and the values computed using the Excel functions are displayed in the foreground worksheet. Labels were also entered in cell D2:D4 to identify the output. Note that the mean (5,940), median (5,905), and mode (5,880) are the same as we computed earlier.

Figure 3.2 Excel Worksheet Used to Compute the Mean, Median, and Mode for the Starting Salary Data

	A	B	C	D	E
1	**Graduate**	**Monthly Starting Salary ($)**			
2	1	5850		**Mean**	=AVERAGE(B2:B13)
3	2	5950		**Median**	=MEDIAN(B2:B13)
4	3	6050		**Mode**	=MODE.SNGL(B2:B13)
5	4	5880			
6	5	5755			
7	6	5710			
8	7	5890			
9	8	6130			
10	9	5940			
11	10	6325			
12	11	5920			
13	12	5880			
14					

	A	B	C	D	E
1	**Graduate**	**Monthly Starting Salary ($)**			
2	1	5850		**Mean**	5940
3	2	5950		**Median**	5905
4	3	6050		**Mode**	5880
5	4	5880			
6	5	5755			
7	6	5710			
8	7	5890			
9	8	6130			
10	9	5940			
11	10	6325			
12	11	5920			
13	12	5880			
14					

Weighted Mean

In the formulas for the sample mean and population mean, each x_i is given equal importance or weight. For instance, the formula for the sample mean can be written as follows:

$$\bar{x} = \frac{\Sigma x_i}{n} = \frac{1}{n}\left(\sum x_i\right) = \frac{1}{n}(x_1 + x_2 + \cdots + x_n) = \frac{1}{n}(x_1) + \frac{1}{n}(x_2) + \cdots + \frac{1}{n}(x_n)$$

This shows that each observation in the sample is given a weight of $1/n$. Although this practice is most common, in some instances the mean is computed by giving each observation a weight that reflects its relative importance. A mean computed in this manner is referred to as a **weighted mean**. The weighted mean is computed as follows:

Weighted Mean

$$\bar{x} = \frac{\Sigma w_i x_i}{\Sigma w_i} \quad \textbf{(3.3)}$$

where

$$w_i = \text{weight for observation } i$$

When the data are from a sample, equation (3.3) provides the weighted sample mean. If the data are from a population, μ replaces $\bar{x}$ and equation (3.3) provides the weighted population mean.

As an example of the need for a weighted mean, consider the following sample of five purchases of a raw material over the past three months.

Purchase	Cost per Pound ($)	Number of Pounds
1	3.00	1,200
2	3.40	500
3	2.80	2,750
4	2.90	1,000
5	3.25	800

Note that the cost per pound varies from $2.80 to $3.40, and the quantity purchased varies from 500 to 2,750 pounds. Suppose that a manager wanted to know the mean cost per pound of the raw material. Because the quantities ordered vary, we must use the formula for a weighted mean. The five cost-per-pound data values are $x_1 = 3.00$, $x_2 = 3.40$, $x_3 = 2.80$, $x_4 = 2.90$, and $x_5 = 3.25$. The weighted mean cost per pound is found by weighting each cost by its corresponding quantity. For this example, the weights are $w_1 = 1{,}200$, $w_2 = 500$, $w_3 = 2{,}750$, $w_4 = 1{,}000$, and $w_5 = 800$. Based on equation (3.3), the weighted mean is calculated as follows:

$$\bar{x} = \frac{1{,}200(3.00) + 500(3.40) + 2{,}750(2.80) + 1{,}000(2.90) + 800(3.25)}{1{,}200 + 500 + 2{,}750 + 1{,}000 + 800}$$

$$= \frac{18{,}500}{6{,}250} = 2.96$$

Thus, the weighted mean computation shows that the mean cost per pound for the raw material is $2.96. Note that using equation (3.1) rather than the weighted mean formula in equation (3.3) would provide misleading results. In this case, the sample mean of the five cost-per-pound values is (3.00 + 3.40 + 2.80 + 2.90 + 3.25)/5 = 15.35/5 = $3.07, which overstates the actual mean cost per pound purchased.

The choice of weights for a particular weighted mean computation depends upon the application. An example that is well known to college students is the computation of a grade point average (GPA). In this computation, the data values generally used are 4 for an A grade, 3 for a B grade, 2 for a C grade, 1 for a D grade, and 0 for an F grade. The weights are the number of credit hours earned for each grade. In other weighted mean computations, quantities such as pounds, dollars, or volume are frequently used as weights. In any case, when observations vary in importance, the analyst must choose the weight that best reflects the importance of each observation in the determination of the mean.

Geometric Mean

The **geometric mean** is a measure of location that is calculated by finding the nth root of the product of n values. The general formula for the geometric mean, denoted $\bar{x}_g$, follows.

Geometric Mean

$$\bar{x}_g = \sqrt[n]{(x_1)(x_2)\cdots(x_n)} = [(x_1)(x_2)\cdots(x_n)]^{1/n} \tag{3.4}$$

The geometric mean is often used in analyzing growth rates in financial data. In these types of situations the arithmetic mean or average value will provide misleading results.

To illustrate the use of the geometric mean, consider Table 3.2, which shows the percentage annual returns, or growth rates, for a mutual fund over the past 10 years. Suppose we want to compute how much $100 invested in the fund at the beginning of Year 1 would be worth at the end of Year 10. Let's start by computing the balance in the fund at the end of Year 1. Because the percentage annual return for Year 1 was −22.1%, the balance in the fund at the end of Year 1 would be

$$\$100 - 0.221(\$100) = \$100(1 - 0.221) = \$100(0.779) = \$77.90$$

The growth factor for each year is 1 plus, 0.01 times the percentage return. A growth factor less than 1 indicates negative growth, while a growth factor greater than 1 indicates positive growth. The growth factor cannot be less than zero.

Note that 0.779 is identified as the growth factor for Year 1 in Table 3.2. This result shows that we can compute the balance at the end of Year 1 by multiplying the value invested in the fund at the beginning of Year 1 times the growth factor for Year 1.

The balance in the fund at the end of year 1, $77.90, now becomes the beginning balance in Year 2. So, with a percentage annual return for Year 2 of 28.7%, the balance at the end of Year 2 would be

$$\$77.90 + 0.287(\$77.90) = \$77.90(1 + 0.287) = \$77.90(1.287) = \$100.2573$$

DATA *file*
mutualfund

Table 3.2 Percentage Annual Returns and Growth Factors for the Mutual Fund Data

Year	Return (%)	Growth Factor
1	−22.1	0.779
2	28.7	1.287
3	10.9	1.109
4	4.9	1.049
5	15.8	1.158
6	5.5	1.055
7	−37.0	0.630
8	26.5	1.265
9	15.1	1.151
10	2.1	1.021

Note that 1.287 is the growth factor for Year 2. And, by substituting \$100(0.779) for \$77.90, we see that the balance in the fund at the end of Year 2 is

$$\$100(0.779)\,(1.287) = \$100.2573$$

In other words, the balance at the end of Year 2 is just the initial investment at the beginning of Year 1 times the product of the first two growth factors. This result can be generalized to show that the balance at the end of Year 10 is the initial investment times the product of all 10 growth factors.

$$\$100[(0.779)(1.287)(1.109)(1.049)(1.158)(1.055)(0.630)(1.265)(1.151)(1.021)] =$$

$$\$100(1.334493) = \$133.4493$$

So, a \$100 investment in the fund at the beginning of Year 1 would be worth \$133.4493 at the end of Year 10. Note that the product of the 10 growth factors is 1.334493. Thus, we can compute the balance at the end of Year 10 for any amount of money invested at the beginning of Year 1 by multiplying the value of the initial investment times 1.334493. For instance, an initial investment of \$2,500 at the beginning of Year 1 would be worth \$2,500(1.334493) or approximately \$3,336 at the end of Year 10.

What was the mean percentage annual return or mean rate of growth for this investment over the 10-year period? The geometric mean of the 10 growth factors can be used to answer to this question. Because the product of the 10 growth factors is 1.334493, the geometric mean is the 10th root of 1.334493 or

The nth root can be computed using most calculators or by using the POWER function in Excel. For instance, using Excel, the 10th root of 1.334493 =POWER(1.334493,1/10) or 1.029275.

$$\bar{x}_g = \sqrt[10]{1.334493} = 1.029275$$

The geometric mean tells us that annual returns grew at an average annual rate of $(1.029275 - 1)100\%$ or 2.9275%. In other words, with an average annual growth rate of 2.9275%, a \$100 investment in the fund at the beginning of Year 1 would grow to $\$100(1.029275)^{10} = \$133.4493$ at the end of 10 years.

It is important to understand that the arithmetic mean of the percentage annual returns does not provide the mean annual growth rate for this investment. The sum of the 10 annual percentage returns in Table 3.2 is 50.4. Thus, the arithmetic mean of the 10 percentage annual returns is $50.4/10 = 5.04\%$. A broker might try to convince you to invest in this fund by stating that the mean annual percentage return was 5.04%. Such a statement is not only misleading, it is inaccurate. A mean annual percentage return of 5.04% corresponds to an average growth factor of 1.0504. So, if the average growth factor were really 1.0504, \$100 invested in the fund at the beginning of Year 1 would have grown to $\$100(1.0504)^{10} = \$163.51$ at the end of 10 years. But, using the 10 annual percentage returns in Table 3.2, we showed that an initial \$100 investment is worth \$133.45 at the end of 10 years. The broker's claim that the mean annual percentage return is 5.04% grossly overstates the true growth for this mutual fund. The problem is that the sample mean is only appropriate for an additive process. For a multiplicative process, such as applications involving growth rates, the geometric mean is the appropriate measure of location.

While the applications of the geometric mean to problems in finance, investments, and banking are particularly common, the geometric mean should be applied any time you want to determine the mean rate of change over several successive periods. Other common applications include changes in populations of species, crop yields, pollution levels, and birth and death rates. Also note that the geometric mean can be applied to changes that occur over any number of successive periods of any length. In addition to annual changes, the geometric mean is often applied to find the mean rate of change over quarters, months, weeks, and even days.

Figure 3.3 Using Excel to Compute the Geometric Mean for the Mutual Fund Data

	A	B	C	D	E	F
1	Year	Return (%)	Growth Factor			
2	1	-22.1	=1+0.01*B2		Geometric Mean	=GEOMEAN(C2:C11)
3	2	28.7	=1+0.01*B3			
4	3	10.9	=1+0.01*B4			
5	4	4.9	=1+0.01*B5			
6	5	15.8	=1+0.01*B6			
7	6	5.5	=1+0.01*B7			
8	7	-37	=1+0.01*B8			
9	8	26.5	=1+0.01*B9			
10	9	15.1	=1+0.01*B10			
11	10	2.1	=1+0.01*B11			

	A	B	C	D	E	F
1	Year	Return (%)	Growth Factor			
2	1	-22.1	0.779		Geometric Mean	1.029275
3	2	28.7	1.287			
4	3	10.9	1.109			
5	4	4.9	1.049			
6	5	15.8	1.158			
7	6	5.5	1.055			
8	7	-37	0.63			
9	8	26.5	1.265			
10	9	15.1	1.151			
11	10	2.1	1.021			

Using Excel to Compute the Geometric Mean

DATA*file*
mutualfund

Excel's GEOMEAN function can be used to compute the geometric mean for the mutual fund data in Table 3.2. Refer to Figure 3.3 as we describe the tasks involved. The formula worksheet is in the background; the value worksheet is in the foreground.

Enter/Access Data: Open the file *mutualfund*. The data are in cells B2:B11 and labels are in column A and cell B2.

Enter Functions and Formulas: To compute the growth factor for the percentage return in cell B2 (-22.1) we entered the following formula in cell C2:

$$=1+.01*B2$$

To compute the growth factors for the other percentage returns we copied the same formula in cells C3:C11. Excel's GEOMEAN function can now be used to compute the geometric mean for the growth factors in cells C2:C11 by entering the following formula in cell F2:

$$=GEOMEAN(C2:C11)$$

The labels "Growth Factor" and "Geometric Mean" were entered in cells C1 and E2, respectively, to identify the output. Note that the geometric mean (1.029275) is the same value as we computed earlier.

Percentiles

A **percentile** provides information about how the data are spread over the interval from the smallest value to the largest value. For a data set containing n observations, the ***p*th percentile** divides the data into two parts: Approximately p% of the observations are less than the pth percentile, and approximately $(100 - p)$% of the observations are greater than the pth percentile.

Colleges and universities frequently report admission test scores in terms of percentiles. For instance, suppose an applicant obtains a score of 630 on the math portion of an admissions test. How this applicant performed in relation to others taking the same test may not be readily apparent. However, if the score of 630 corresponds to the 82nd percentile, we know that approximately that 82% of the applicants scored lower than this individual and approximately 18% of the applicants scored higher than this individual.

To calculate the pth percentile for a data set containing n observations, we must first arrange the data in ascending order (smallest value to largest value). The smallest value is in position 1, the next smallest value is in position 2, and so on. The location of the pth percentile, denoted L_p, is computed using the following equation.[1]

Several procedures can be used to compute the location of the pth percentile using sample data. All provide similar values, especially for large data sets. The procedure we show here is the procedure used by Excel's PERCENTILE.EXC function as well as several other statistical software packages.

Location of the pth Percentile

$$L_p = \frac{p}{100}(n + 1) \tag{3.5}$$

To illustrate the computation of the pth percentile, let us compute the 80th percentile for the starting salary data in Table 3.1. We begin by arranging the sample of 12 starting salaries in ascending order.

	5,710	5,755	5,850	5,880	5,880	5,890	5,920	5,940	5,950	6,050	6,130	6,325
Position	1	2	3	4	5	6	7	8	9	10	11	12

The position of each observation in the sorted data is shown directly below its value. For instance, the smallest value (5,710) is in position 1, the next smallest value (5,755) is in position 2, and so on. Using equation (3.5) with $p = 80$ and $n = 12$, the location of the 80th percentile is

$$L_{80} = \frac{p}{100}(n + 1) = \left(\frac{80}{100}\right)(12 + 1) = 10.4$$

The interpretation of $L_{80} = 10.4$ is that the 80th percentile is 40% of the way between the value in position 10 and the value in position 11. In other words, the 80th percentile is the value in position 10 (6,050) plus 0.4 times the difference between the value in position 11 (6,130) and the value in position 10 (6,050). Thus,

$$\text{80th percentile} = 6{,}050 + 0.4(6{,}130 - 6{,}050) = 6{,}050 + 0.4(80) = 6{,}082$$

Let us now compute the 50th percentile for the starting salary data. With $p = 50$ and $n = 12$, the location of the 50th percentile is

$$L_{50} = \frac{p}{100}(n + 1) = \left(\frac{50}{100}\right)(12 + 1) = 6.5$$

With $L_{50} = 6.5$, we see that the 50th percentile is 50% of the way between the value in position 6 (5,890) and the value in position 7 (5,920). Thus,

$$\text{50th percentile} = 5{,}890 + 0.5(5{,}920 - 5{,}890) = 5{,}890 + 0.5(30) = 5{,}905$$

Note that the 50th percentile is also the median.

Quartiles

Quartiles are specific percentiles; thus, the steps for computing percentiles can be applied directly in the computation of quartiles.

It is often desirable to divide a data set into four parts, with each part containing approximately one-fourth, or 25%, of the observations. These division points are referred to as the **quartiles** and are defined as follows:

Q_1 = first quartile, or 25th percentile

Q_2 = second quartile, or 50th percentile (also the median)

Q_3 = third quartile, or 75th percentile

[1]Note that Equation (3.5) cannot be used to find some extreme percentile values for small data sets. Specifically, the equation does not apply for $p < 100/(n + 1)$ or $p > 100n/(n + 1)$.

Because quartiles are just specific percentiles, the procedure for computing percentiles can be used to compute the quartiles.

To illustrate the computation of the quartiles for a data set consisting of n observations, we will compute the quartiles for the starting salary data in Table 3.1. Previously we showed that the 50th percentile for the starting salary data is 5,905; thus, the second quartile (median) is $Q_2 = 5{,}905$. To compute the first and third quartiles, we must find the 25th and 75th percentiles. The calculations follow.

For Q_1,

$$L_{25} = \frac{p}{100}(n + 1) = \left(\frac{25}{100}\right)(12 + 1) = 3.25$$

The first quartile, or 25th percentile, is 0.25 of the way between the value in position 3 (5,850) and the value in position 4 (5,880). Thus,

$$Q_1 = 5{,}850 + 0.25(5{,}880 - 5{,}850) = 5{,}850 + 0.25(30) = 5{,}857.5$$

For Q_3,

$$L_{75} = \frac{p}{100}(n + 1) = \left(\frac{75}{100}\right)(12 + 1) = 9.75$$

The third quartile, or 75th percentile, is 0.75 of the way between the value in position 9 (5,950) and the value in position 10 (6,050). Thus,

$$Q_3 = 5{,}950 + 0.75(6{,}050 - 5{,}950) = 5{,}950 + 0.75(100) = 6{,}025$$

We defined the quartiles as the 25th, 50th, and 75th percentiles. Thus, we computed the quartiles in the same way as percentiles. However, other conventions are sometimes used to compute quartiles, and the actual values reported for quartiles may vary slightly depending on the convention used. Nevertheless, the objective of all procedures for computing quartiles is to divide the data into four equal parts.

Using Excel to Compute Percentiles and Quartiles

DATA*file*
startingsalaries

Excel provides functions for computing percentiles and quartiles. We will illustrate the use of these functions by showing how to compute the pth percentile and the quartiles for the starting salary data in Table 3.1. Refer to Figure 3.4 as we describe the tasks involved. The formula worksheet is in the background; the value worksheet is in the foreground.

Enter/Access Data: Open the file *startingsalaries*. The data are in cells B2:B13 and labels are in column A and cell B1.

Enter Functions and Formulas: Excel's PERCENTILE.EXC function can be used to compute the pth percentile. For the starting salary data the general form of this function is

=PERCENTILE.EXC(B2:B13,*p*/100)

If we wanted to compute the 80th percentile for the starting salary data, we could enter the value of *80* into cell D2 and then enter the formula

=PERCENTILE.EXC(B2:B13,D2/100)

in cell E2.

Because the quartiles are just the 25th, 50th, and 75th percentiles, we could compute the quartiles for the starting salary data by using Excel's PERCENTILE.EXC function as

Figure 3.4 Using Excel to Compute Percentiles and Quartiles

	A	B	C	D	E
1	Graduate	Monthly Starting Salary ($)			
2	1	5850		Percentile	Value ($)
3	2	5950		80	=PERCENTILE.EXC(B2:B13,D3/100)
4	3	6050			
5	4	5880		Quartile	Value ($)
6	5	5755		1	=QUARTILE.EXC($B$2:$B$13,D6)
7	6	5710		2	=QUARTILE.EXC($B$2:$B$13,D7)
8	7	5890		3	=QUARTILE.EXC($B$2:$B$13,D8)
9	8	6130			
10	9	5940			
11	10	6325			
12	11	5920			
13	12	5880			
14					

	A	B	C	D	E
1	Graduate	Monthly Starting Salary ($)			
2	1	5850		Percentile	Value ($)
3	2	5950		80	6082.00
4	3	6050			
5	4	5880		Quartile	Value ($)
6	5	5755		1	5857.50
7	6	5710		2	5905.00
8	7	5890		3	6025.00
9	8	6130			
10	9	5940			
11	10	6325			
12	11	5920			
13	12	5880			
14					

described previously. But we can also use Excel's QUARTILE.EXC function to compute the quartiles. For the starting salary data, the general form of this function is

=QUARTILE.EXC(B2:B13,*quart*)

where *quart* = 1 for the first quartile, *quart* = 2 for the second quartile, and *quart* = 3 for the third quartile. To illustrate the use of this function for computing the quartiles, we entered the values *1*, *2*, and *3* in cells D5:D7 of the worksheet. To compute the first quartile, we entered the following function in cell E5:

=QUARTILE.EXC($B$2:$B$13,D5)

To compute the second and third quartiles, we copied the formula in cell E5 in cells E6 and E7. Labels were entered in cells D4 and E4 to identify the output. Note that the three quartiles (5,857.5, 5,905, and 6,025) are the same values as computed previously.

Notes + Comments

1. It is better to use the median than the mean as a measure of central location when a data set contains extreme values. Another measure that is sometimes used when extreme values are present is the trimmed mean. The trimmed mean is obtained by deleting a percentage of the smallest and largest values from a data set and then computing the mean of the remaining values. For example, the 5% trimmed mean is obtained by removing the smallest 5% and the largest 5% of the data values and then computing the mean of the remaining values. Using the sample with $n = 12$ starting salaries, $0.05(12) = 0.6$. Rounding this value to 1 indicates that the 5% trimmed mean is obtained by removing the smallest data value and the largest data value and then computing the mean of the remaining 10 values. For the starting salary data, the 5% trimmed mean is 5,924.50.
2. Other commonly used percentiles are the quintiles (the 20th, 40th, 60th, and 80th percentiles) and the deciles (the 10th, 20th, 30th, 40th, 50th, 60th, 70th, 80th, and 90th percentiles).

Exercises

Methods

1. Consider a sample with data values of 10, 20, 12, 17, and 16. Compute the mean and median. **LO 1**
2. Consider a sample with data values of 10, 20, 21, 17, 16, and 12. Compute the mean and median. **LO 1**
3. Consider the following data and corresponding weights. **LO 1**

x_i	Weight (w_i)
3.2	6
2.0	3
2.5	2
5.0	8

   a. Compute the weighted mean.
   b. Compute the sample mean of the four data values without weighting. Note the difference in the results provided by the two computations.

4. Consider the following data.

Period	Rate of Return (%)
1	−6.0
2	−8.0
3	−4.0
4	2.0
5	5.4

   What is the mean growth rate over these five periods? **LO 1**

5. Consider a sample with data values of 27, 25, 20, 15, 30, 34, 28, and 25. Compute the 20th, 25th, 65th, and 75th percentiles. **LO 2**
6. Consider a sample with data values of 53, 55, 70, 58, 64, 57, 53, 69, 57, 68, and 53. Compute the mean, median, and mode. **LO 1**

Applications

7. **eICU Waiting Times.** There is a severe shortage of critical care doctors and nurses to provide intensive-care services in hospitals. To offset this shortage, many hospitals, such as Emory Hospital in Atlanta, are using electronic intensive-care units (eICUs) to help provide this care to patients (Emory University News Center). eICUs use electronic monitoring tools and two-way communication through video and audio so that a centralized staff of specially trained doctors and nurses—who can be located as far away as Australia—can provide critical care services to patients located in remote hospitals without fully staffed ICUs. One of the most important metrics tracked by these eICUs is the time that a patient must wait for the first video interaction between the patient and the eICU staff. Consider the following sample of 40 patient waiting times until their first video interaction with the eICU staff. **LO 1, 2**

DATA*file*
eicu

Wait Time (minutes)			
40	46	49	44
45	45	38	51
42	46	41	45
49	41	48	42
49	40	42	43
43	42	41	41
55	43	42	40
42	40	49	43
44	45	61	37
40	37	39	43

a. Compute the mean waiting time for these 40 patients.
b. Compare the median waiting time.
c. Compute the mode.
d. Compute the first and third quartiles.

8. **Middle-Level Manager Salaries.** Suppose that an independent study of middle-level managers employed at companies located in Atlanta, Georgia, was conducted to compare the salaries of managers working at firms in Atlanta to the salaries of middle-level managers across the nation. The following data show the salary, in thousands of dollars, for a sample of 15 middle-level managers. **LO 1, 2**

108 83 106 73 53 85 80 63 67 75 124 55 93 118 77

a. Compute the median salary for the sample of 15 middle-level managers. Suppose the median salary of middle-level managers employed at companies located across the nation is $85,000. How does the median for middle-level managers in the Atlanta area compare to the median for managers across the nation?
b. Compute the mean annual salary for managers in the Atlanta area and discuss how and why it differs from the median computed in part (a).
c. Compute the first and third quartiles for salaries of middle-level managers in the Atlanta area.

9. **Advertising Spending.** Which companies spend the most money on advertising? *Business Insider* maintains a list of the top-spending companies. In 2014, Procter & Gamble spent more than any other company, $5 billion. In second place was Comcast, which spent $3.08 billion (*Business Insider* website). The top 12 companies and the amount each spent on advertising in billions of dollars are as follows. **LO 1, 2**

DATA*file*
advertisingspend

Company	Advertising ($ billions)	Company	Advertising ($ billions)
Procter & Gamble	5.00	American Express	2.19
Comcast	3.08	General Motors	2.15
AT&T	2.91	Toyota	2.09
Ford	2.56	Fiat Chrysler	1.97
Verizon	2.44	Walt Disney Company	1.96
L'Oreal	2.34	JPMorgan	1.88

a. What is the mean amount spent on advertising?
b. What is the median amount spent on advertising?
c. What are the first and third quartiles?

10. **Hardshell Jacket Ratings.** OutdoorGearLab is an organization that tests outdoor gear used for climbing, camping, mountaineering, and backpacking. Suppose that the following data show the ratings of hardshell jackets based on the breathability, durability, versatility, features, mobility, and weight of each jacket. The ratings range from 0 (lowest) to 100 (highest). LO 1, 2

DATA*file* jacketratings

42	66	67	71	78	62	61	76	71	67
61	64	61	54	83	63	68	69	81	53

a. Compute the mean, median, and mode.
b. Compute the first and third quartiles.
c. Compute and interpret the 90th percentile.

11. **Time Spent Watching Video on Electronic Devices.** The company Nielsen estimates that consumers spent an average of 5 hours and 43 minutes per day on their devices watching video in 2020. The devices used to watch video include televisions, computers, smartphones, and tablets. Suppose that the following data represent the amount of time spent watching video on their devices during a day for a sample of 28 consumers aged 18–29 and a sample of 33 consumers aged 30–45. LO 1, 2

DATA*file* watchingvideo

Hours Spent Watching Video

Consumers Aged 18–29	Consumers Aged 30–45	Consumers Aged 18–29	Consumers Aged 30–45
5.2	4.8	6.4	7.1
4.7	5.1	3.8	3.2
6.8	5.8	7.5	4.9
5.2	6.2	5.2	5.7
4.1	2.8	4.9	5.1
6.3	3.1	6.7	6.1
7.2	7.5	6.1	4.7
5.1	3.8	6.1	4.6
6.9	4.4	7.2	5.8
4.9	7.2	5.9	5.9
5.5	6.1	5.8	6.1
5.7	5.2		4.2
6.2	5.4		4.8
6.4	6.8		6.3
8.2	7.1		5.7
3.9	2.1		5.1
5.8	6.2		

12. **Online Multiplayer Game Downloads.** The creator of a new online multiplayer survival game has been tracking the monthly downloads of the game. The following table shows the monthly downloads (in 1,000s) for each month of the current and previous year. LO 1, 2

DATA*file* onlinegame

Month (previous year)	Downloads (1,000s)	Month (current year)	Downloads (1,000s)
February	33.0	January	37.0
March	34.0	February	37.0
April	34.0	March	37.0
May	32.0	April	38.0
June	32.0	May	37.0
July	35.0	June	36.0

(continued)

Month (previous year)	Downloads (1,000s)	Month (current year)	Downloads (1,000s)
August	34.0	July	37.0
September	37.0	August	35.0
October	37.0	September	33.0
November	35.0	October	32.0
December	33.0		

a. Compute the mean, median, and mode for number of downloads in the previous year.
b. Compute the mean, median, and mode for number of downloads in the current year.
c. Compute the first and third quartiles for downloads in the previous year.
d. Compute the first and third quartiles for downloads in the current year.
e. Compare the values calculated in parts (a) through (d) for the previous and current years. What does this tell you about the downloads of the game in the current year compared to the previous year?

DATA*file*
fuel

13. **Automobile Fuel Efficiencies.** In automobile mileage and gasoline-consumption testing, 13 automobiles were road tested for 300 miles in both city and highway driving conditions. The following data were recorded for miles-per-gallon performance.

City:	16.2	16.7	15.9	14.4	13.2	15.3	16.8	16.0	16.1	15.3	15.2	15.3	16.2
Highway:	19.4	20.6	18.3	18.6	19.2	17.4	17.2	18.6	19.0	21.1	19.4	18.5	18.7

Use the mean, median, and mode to make a statement about the difference in performance for city and highway driving. **LO 1**

DATA*file*
unemployment_rates

14. **Unemployment Rates by State.** The U.S. Bureau of Labor Statistics collects data on unemployment rates in each state. The data contained in the file *unemployment_rates* show the unemployment rate for every state over two consecutive years. **LO 1, 2**
a. To compare unemployment rates for the previous year with unemployment rates for the current year, compute the first quartile, the median, and the third quartile for the previous year unemployment data and the current year unemployment data.
b. What do these statistics suggest about the change in unemployment rates across the states over these two years?

15. **Motor Oil Prices.** Martinez Auto Supplies has retail stores located in eight cities in California. The price they charge for a particular product in each city varies because of differing competitive conditions. For instance, the price they charge for a case of a popular brand of motor oil in each city follows. Also shown are the number of cases that Martinez Auto sold last quarter in each city.

DATA*file*
motoroil

City	Price ($)	Sales (cases)
Bakersfield	34.99	501
Los Angeles	38.99	1,425
Modesto	36.00	294
Oakland	33.59	882
Sacramento	40.99	715
San Diego	38.59	1,088
San Francisco	39.59	1,644
San Jose	37.99	819

Compute the average sales price per case for this product during the last quarter. **LO 1**

16. **Calculating Grade Point Averages.** The grade point average for college students is based on a weighted mean computation. For most colleges, the grades are given the following data values: A (4), B (3), C (2), D (1), and F (0). After 60 credit hours of course work, a student at State University earned 9 credit hours of A, 15 credit hours of B, 33 credit hours of C, and 3 credit hours of D. **LO 1**
    a. Compute the student's grade point average.
    b. Students at State University must maintain a 2.5 grade point average for their first 60 credit hours of course work in order to be admitted to the business college. Will this student be admitted?

17. **Mutual Fund Rate of Return.** The following table shows the total return and the number of funds for four categories of mutual funds. **LO 1**

Type of Fund	Number of Funds	Total Return (%)
Domestic Equity	9,191	4.65
International Equity	2,621	18.15
Specialty Stock	1,419	11.36
Hybrid	2,900	6.75

    a. Using the number of funds as weights, compute the weighted average total return for these mutual funds.
    b. Is there any difficulty associated with using the "number of funds" as the weights in computing the weighted average total return in part (a)? Discuss. What else might be used for weights?
    c. Suppose you invested $10,000 in this group of mutual funds and diversified the investment by placing $2,000 in Domestic Equity funds, $4,000 in International Equity funds, $3,000 in Specialty Stock funds, and $1,000 in Hybrid funds. What is the expected return on the portfolio?

18. **Business School Ranking.** Based on a survey of master's programs in business administration, magazines such as *U.S. News & World Report* rank U.S. business schools. These types of rankings are based in part on surveys of business school deans and corporate recruiters. Each survey respondent is asked to rate the overall academic quality of the master's program on a scale from 1 "marginal" to 5 "outstanding." Use the sample of responses shown below to compute the weighted mean score for the business school deans and the corporate recruiters. Discuss. **LO 1**

DATA*file*
bschoolrankings

Quality Assessment	Business School Deans	Corporate Recruiters
5	44	31
4	66	34
3	60	43
2	10	12
1	0	0

19. **Revenue Growth Rate.** Annual revenue for Corning Supplies grew by 5.5% in 2014; 1.1% in 2015; −3.5% in 2016; −1.1% in 2017; and 1.8% in 2018. What is the mean growth annual rate over this period? **LO 1**

20. **Mutual Fund Comparison.** Suppose that at the beginning of Year 1 you invested $10,000 in the Stivers mutual fund and $5,000 in the Trippi mutual fund. The value of each investment at the end of each subsequent year is provided in the table below. Which mutual fund performed better? **LO 1**

DATA*file*
mutualfund_comp

Year	Stivers Value ($)	Trippi Value ($)
1	11,000	5,600
2	12,000	6,300
3	13,000	6,900
4	14,000	7,600
5	15,000	8,500
6	16,000	9,200
7	17,000	9,900
8	18,000	10,600

21. **Asset Growth Rate.** If an asset declines in value from $5,000 to $3,500 over nine years, what is the mean annual growth rate in the asset's value over these nine years? **LO 1**
22. **Company Value Growth Rate.** The current value of a company is $25 million. If the value of the company six years ago was $10 million, what is the company's mean annual growth rate over the past six years? **LO 1**

3.2 Measures of Variability

The variability in the delivery time creates uncertainty for production scheduling. Methods in this section help measure and understand variability.

In addition to measures of location, it is often desirable to consider measures of variability, or dispersion. For example, suppose that you are a purchasing agent for a large manufacturing firm and that you regularly place orders with two different suppliers. After several months of operation, you find that the mean number of days required to fill orders is 10 days for both of the suppliers. The histograms summarizing the number of working days required to fill orders from the suppliers are shown in Figure 3.5. Although the mean number of days is 10 for both suppliers, do the two suppliers demonstrate the same degree of reliability in terms of making deliveries on schedule? Note the dispersion, or variability, in delivery times indicated by the histograms. Which supplier would you prefer?

For most firms, receiving materials and supplies on schedule is important. The seven- or eight-day deliveries shown for J.C. Clark Distributors might be viewed favorably; however, a few of the slow 13- to 15-day deliveries could be disastrous in terms of

Figure 3.5 Historical Data Showing the Number of Days Required to Fill Orders

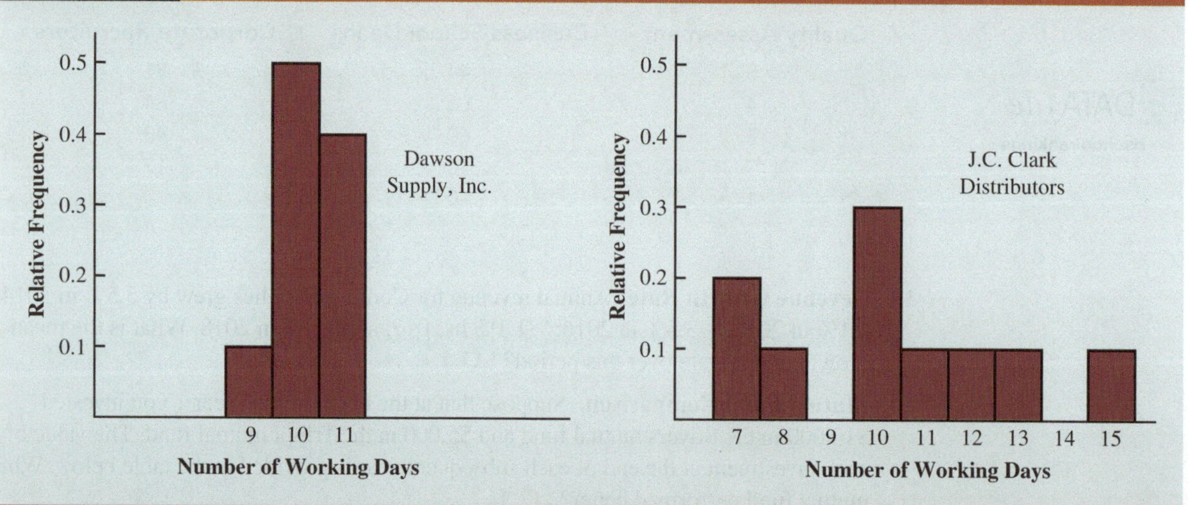

keeping a workforce busy and production on schedule. This example illustrates a situation in which the variability in the delivery times may be an overriding consideration in selecting a supplier. For most purchasing agents, the lower variability shown for Dawson Supply, Inc. would make Dawson the preferred supplier.

We turn now to a discussion of some commonly used measures of variability.

Range

The simplest measure of variability is the **range**.

Range

$$\text{Range} = \text{Largest value} - \text{Smallest value}$$

Let us refer to the data on starting salaries for business school graduates in Table 3.1. The largest starting salary is 6,325 and the smallest is 5,710. The range is 6,325 − 5,710 = 615.

Although the range is the easiest of the measures of variability to compute, it is seldom used as the only measure. The reason is that the range is based on only two of the observations and thus is highly influenced by extreme values. Suppose the highest-paid graduate received a starting salary of $15,000 per month. In this case, the range would be 15,000 − 5,710 = 9,290 rather than 615. This large value for the range would not be especially descriptive of the variability in the data because 11 of the 12 starting salaries are closely grouped between 5,710 and 6,130.

Interquartile Range

A measure of variability that overcomes the dependency on extreme values is the **interquartile range (IQR)**. This measure of variability is the difference between the third quartile, Q_3, and the first quartile, Q_1. In other words, the interquartile range is the range for the middle 50% of the data.

Interquartile Range

$$\text{IQR} = Q_3 - Q_1 \qquad \textbf{(3.6)}$$

For the data on monthly starting salaries, the quartiles are $Q_3 = 6{,}025$ and $Q_1 = 5{,}857.5$. Thus, the interquartile range is 6,025 − 5,857.5 = 167.5.

Variance

The **variance** is a measure of variability that utilizes all the data. The variance is based on the difference between the value of each observation (x_i) and the mean. The difference between each x_i and the mean ($\bar{x}$ for a sample, μ for a population) is called a *deviation about the mean.* For a sample, a deviation about the mean is written $(x_i - \bar{x})$; for a population, it is written $(x_i - \mu)$. In the computation of the variance, the deviations about the mean are *squared.*

If the data are for a population, the average of the squared deviations is called the *population variance.* The population variance is denoted by the square of the Greek lower case letter sigma, or σ^2. For a population of N observations and with μ denoting the population mean, the definition of the population variance is as follows.

Population Variance

$$\sigma^2 = \frac{\Sigma(x_i - \mu)^2}{N} \qquad \textbf{(3.7)}$$

In most statistical applications, the data being analyzed are for a sample. When we compute a sample variance, we are often interested in using it to estimate the population variance σ^2. Although a detailed explanation is beyond the scope of this text, it can be shown that if the sum of the squared deviations about the sample mean is divided by $n - 1$, and not n, the resulting sample variance provides an unbiased estimate of the population variance. For this reason, the *sample variance,* denoted by s^2, is defined as follows.

The sample variance s^2 is a point estimator of the population variance σ^2.

Sample Variance

$$s^2 = \frac{\Sigma(x_i - \bar{x})^2}{n - 1} \quad \textbf{(3.8)}$$

To illustrate the computation of the sample variance, we will use the data on class size for the sample of five college classes as presented in Section 3.1. A summary of the data, including the computation of the deviations about the mean and the squared deviations about the mean, is shown in Table 3.3. The sum of squared deviations about the mean is $\Sigma(x_i - \bar{x})^2 = 256$. Hence, with $n - 1 = 4$, the sample variance is

$$s^2 = \frac{\Sigma(x_i - \bar{x})^2}{n - 1} = \frac{256}{4} = 64$$

Before moving on, let us note that the units associated with the sample variance often cause confusion. Because the values being summed in the variance calculation, $(x_i - \bar{x})^2$, are squared, the units associated with the sample variance are also *squared.* For instance, the sample variance for the class size data is $s^2 = 64$ (students)^2. The squared units associated with variance make it difficult to develop an intuitive understanding and interpretation of the numerical value of the variance. We recommend that you think of the variance as a measure useful in comparing the amount of variability for two or more variables. In a comparison of the variables, the one with the largest variance shows the most variability. Further interpretation of the value of the variance may not be necessary.

The variance is useful in comparing the variability of two or more variables.

As another illustration of computing a sample variance, consider the starting salaries listed in Table 3.1 for the 12 business school graduates. In Section 3.1, we showed that the sample mean starting salary was 5,940. The computation of the sample variance ($s^2 = 27{,}440.91$) is shown in Table 3.4.

In Tables 3.3 and 3.4 we show both the sum of the deviations about the mean and the sum of the squared deviations about the mean. For any data set, the sum of the deviations about the mean will *always equal zero.* Note that in Tables 3.3 and 3.4, $\Sigma(x_i - \bar{x}) = 0$. The positive deviations and negative deviations cancel each other, causing the sum of the deviations about the mean to equal zero.

Table 3.3 Computation of Deviations and Squared Deviations About the Mean for the Class Size Data

Number of Students in Class (x_i)	Mean Class Size ($\bar{x}$)	Deviation About the Mean ($x_i - \bar{x}$)	Squared Deviation About the Mean ($x_i - \bar{x})^2$
46	44	2	4
54	44	10	100
42	44	−2	4
46	44	2	4
32	44	−12	144
		0	256
		$\Sigma(x_i - \bar{x})$	$\Sigma(x_i - \bar{x})^2$

Table 3.4 Computation of the Sample Variance for the Starting Salary Data

Monthly Salary (x_i)	Sample Mean ($\bar{x}$)	Deviation About the Mean ($x_i - \bar{x}$)	Squared Deviation About the Mean $(x_i - \bar{x})^2$
5,850	5,940	−90	8,100
5,950	5,940	10	100
6,050	5,940	110	12,100
5,880	5,940	−60	3,600
5,755	5,940	−185	34,225
5,710	5,940	−230	52,900
5,890	5,940	−50	2,500
6,130	5,940	190	36,100
5,940	5,940	0	0
6,325	5,940	385	148,225
5,920	5,940	−20	400
5,880	5,940	−60	3,600
		0	301,850
		$\Sigma(x_i - \bar{x})$	$\Sigma(x_i - \bar{x})^2$

Using equation (3.8),

$$s^2 = \frac{\Sigma(x_i - \bar{x})^2}{n - 1} = \frac{301,850}{11} = 27,440.91$$

Standard Deviation

The **standard deviation** is defined to be the positive square root of the variance. Following the notation we adopted for a sample variance and a population variance, we use s to denote the sample standard deviation and σ to denote the population standard deviation. The standard deviation is derived from the variance in the following way.

The sample standard deviation s is a point estimator of the population standard deviation σ.

Standard Deviation

$$\text{Sample standard deviation} = s = \sqrt{s^2} \quad \textbf{(3.9)}$$

$$\text{Population standard deviation} = \sigma = \sqrt{\sigma^2} \quad \textbf{(3.10)}$$

Recall that the sample variance for the sample of class sizes in five college classes is $s^2 = 64$. Thus, the sample standard deviation is $s = \sqrt{64} = 8$. For the data on starting salaries, the sample standard deviation is $s = \sqrt{27,440.91} = 165.65$.

The standard deviation is easier to interpret than the variance because the standard deviation is measured in the same units as the data.

What is gained by converting the variance to its corresponding standard deviation? Recall that the units associated with the variance are squared. For example, the sample variance for the starting salary data of business school graduates is $s^2 = 27,440.91$ (dollars)^2. Because the standard deviation is the square root of the variance, the units of the variance, dollars squared, are converted to dollars in the standard deviation. Thus, the standard deviation of the starting salary data is \$165.65. In other words, the standard deviation is measured in the same units as the original data. For this reason the standard deviation is more easily compared to the mean and other statistics that are measured in the same units as the original data.

Figure 3.6 Excel Worksheet Used to Compute the Sample Variance and the Sample Standard Deviation for the Starting Salary Data

	A	B	C	D	E
1	Graduate	Monthly Starting Salary ($)			
2	1	5850		Mean	=AVERAGE(B2:B13)
3	2	5950		Median	=MEDIAN(B2:B13)
4	3	6050		Mode	=MODE.SNGL(B2:B13)
5	4	5880		Variance	=VAR.S(B2:B13)
6	5	5755		Standard Deviation	=STDEV.S(B2:B13)
7	6	5710			
8	7	5890			
9	8	6130			
10	9	5940			
11	10	6325			
12	11	5920			
13	12	5880			

	A	B	C	D	E
1	Graduate	Monthly Starting Salary ($)			
2	1	5850		Mean	5940
3	2	5950		Median	5905
4	3	6050		Mode	5880
5	4	5880		Variance	27440.91
6	5	5755		Standard Deviation	165.65
7	6	5710			
8	7	5890			
9	8	6130			
10	9	5940			
11	10	6325			
12	11	5920			
13	12	5880			

Using Excel to Compute the Sample Variance and Sample Standard Deviation

Excel provides functions for computing the sample variance and sample standard deviation. We illustrate the use of these functions by computing the sample variance and sample standard deviation for the starting salary data in Table 3.1. Refer to Figure 3.6 as we describe the tasks involved. Figure 3.6 is an extension of Figure 3.2, where we showed how to use Excel functions to compute the mean, median, and mode. The formula worksheet is in the background; the value worksheet is in the foreground.

DATA*file*
startingsalaries

Enter/Access Data: Open the file *startingsalaries*. The data are in cells B2:B13 and labels appear in column A and cell B1.

Enter Functions and Formulas: Excel's AVERAGE, MEDIAN, and MODE.SNGL functions were entered in cells E2:E4, as described earlier. Excel's VAR.S function can be used to compute the sample variance by entering the following formula in cell E5:

=VAR.S(B2:B13)

Similarly, the formula *=STDEV.S(B2:B13)* is entered in cell E6 to compute the sample standard deviation.

The labels in cells D2:D6 identify the output. Note that the sample variance (27,440.91) and the sample standard deviation (165.65) are the same as we computed earlier using the definitions.

Coefficient of Variation

The coefficient of variation is a relative measure of variability; it measures the standard deviation relative to the mean.

In some situations we may be interested in a descriptive statistic that indicates how large the standard deviation is relative to the mean. This measure is called the **coefficient of variation** and is usually expressed as a percentage.

Coefficient of Variation

$$\left(\frac{\text{Standard deviation}}{\text{Mean}} \times 100\right)\% \qquad (3.11)$$

For the class size data, we found a sample mean of 44 and a sample standard deviation of 8. The coefficient of variation is $[(8/44) \times 100]\% = 18.2\%$. In words, the coefficient of variation tells us that the sample standard deviation is 18.2% of the value of the sample mean. For the starting salary data with a sample mean of 3,940 and a sample standard deviation of 165.65, the coefficient of variation, $[(165.65/3{,}940) \times 100]\% = 4.2\%$, tells us the sample standard deviation is only 4.2% of the value of the sample mean. In general, the coefficient of variation is a useful statistic for comparing the variability of variables that have different standard deviations and different means.

Using Excel's Descriptive Statistics Tool

As we have seen, Excel provides statistical functions to compute descriptive statistics for a data set. These functions can be used to compute one statistic at a time (e.g., mean, variance). Excel also provides a variety of data analysis tools. One of these, called Descriptive Statistics, allows the user to compute a variety of descriptive statistics at once. We will now show how Excel's Descriptive Statistics tool can be used for the starting salary data in Table 3.1. Refer to Figure 3.7 as we describe the tasks involved.

DATA*file*
startingsalaries

Enter/Access Data: Open the file *startingsalaries*. The data are in cells B2:B13 and labels appear in column A and in cell B1.

Apply Tools: The following steps describe how to use Excel's Descriptive Statistics tool for these data.

Step 1. Click the **Data** tab on the Ribbon
Step 2. In the **Analysis** group, click **Data Analysis**
Step 3. Choose **Descriptive Statistics** from the list of **Analysis Tools**

Figure 3.7 Dialog Box for Excel's Descriptive Statistics Tool

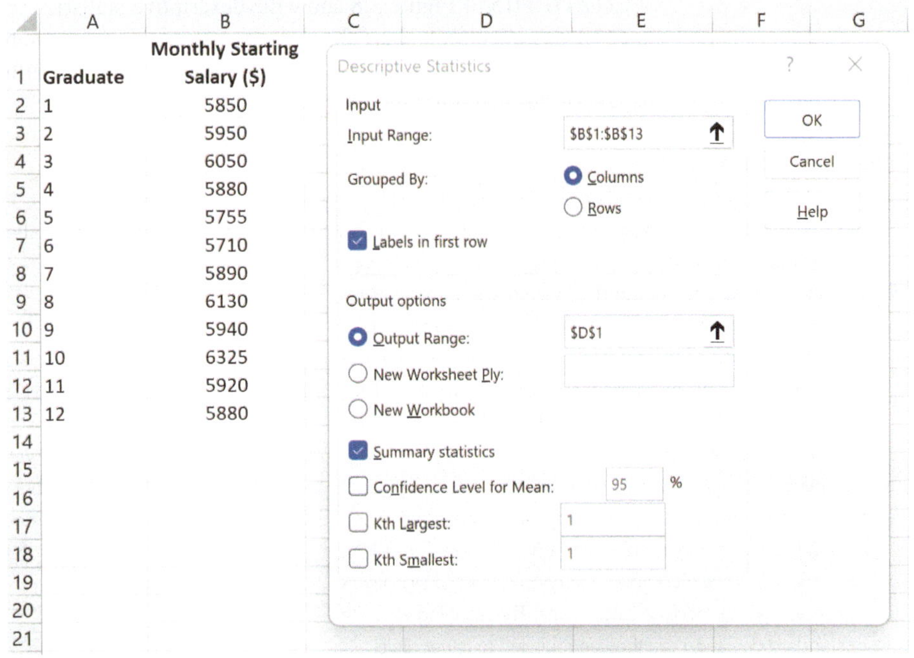

Figure 3.8 Descriptive Statistics Provided by Excel for the Starting Salary Data

	A	B	C	D	E
1	**Graduate**	**Monthly Starting Salary ($)**		*Monthly Starting Salary ($)*	
2	1	5850			
3	2	5950		**Mean**	5940
4	3	6050		Standard Error	47.82
5	4	5880		**Median**	5905
6	5	5755		**Mode**	5880
7	6	5710		**Standard Deviation**	165.65
8	7	5890		**Sample Variance**	27440.91
9	8	6130		Kurtosis	1.72
10	9	5940		Skewness	1.09
11	10	6325		**Range**	615
12	11	5920		**Minimum**	5710
13	12	5880		**Maximum**	6325
14				**Sum**	71280
15				**Count**	12
16					

Step 4. When the **Descriptive Statistics** dialog box appears (see Figure 3.7):
Enter *B1:B13* in the **Input Range:** box
Select **Columns** in the **Grouped By:** area
Select the check box for **Labels in First Row**
Select **Output Range:** in the **Output options** area
Enter *D1* in the **Output Range:** box (to identify the upper-left corner of the section of the worksheet where the descriptive statistics will appear)
Select the check box for **Summary Statistics**
Click **OK**

Cells D1:D15 of Figure 3.8 show the descriptive statistics provided by Excel. The boldfaced entries in column D are the descriptive statistics that we have already covered. The descriptive statistics that are not boldfaced in column D are either covered subsequently in the text or discussed in more advanced texts.

Notes + Comments

1. Statistical software packages and spreadsheets can be used to develop the descriptive statistics presented in this chapter. After the data are entered into a worksheet, a few simple commands can be used to generate the desired output.
2. Standard deviation is a commonly used measure of the risk associated with investing in stock and stock funds. It provides a measure of how monthly returns fluctuate around the long-run average return.
3. Rounding the value of the sample mean $\bar{x}$ and the values of the squared deviations $(x_i - \bar{x})^2$ may introduce errors when calculating the variance and standard deviation. To reduce rounding errors, we recommend carrying at least six significant digits during intermediate calculations. The resulting variance or standard deviation can then be rounded to fewer digits.
4. An alternative formula for the computation of the sample variance is

$$s^2 = \frac{\sum x_i^2 - n\bar{x}^2}{n-1}$$

where $\sum x_i^2 = x_1^2 + x_2^2 + \cdots + x_n^2$.
5. The mean absolute error (MAE) is another measure of variability that is computed by summing the absolute values of the deviations of the observations about the mean and dividing this sum by the number of observations. For a sample of size n, the MAE is computed as follows:

$$MAE = \frac{\sum |x_i - \bar{x}|}{n}$$

For the class size data presented in Section 3.1, $\bar{x} = 44$, $\sum |x_i - \bar{x}| = 28$, and the MAE $= 28/5 = 5.6$. You can learn more about the MAE and other measures of variability in Chapter 17.

Exercises

Methods

23. Consider a sample with data values of 10, 20, 12, 17, and 16. Compute the range and interquartile range. **LO 3**

24. Consider a sample with data values of 10, 20, 12, 17, and 16. Compute the variance and standard deviation. **LO 3**

25. Consider a sample with data values of 27, 25, 20, 15, 30, 34, 28, and 25. Compute the range, interquartile range, variance, and standard deviation. **LO 3**

Applications

26. **Price of Unleaded Gasoline.** Data collected by the Oil Price Information Service from more than 90,000 gasoline and convenience stores throughout the United States showed that the average price for a gallon of unleaded gasoline was $3.28 (MSN Auto website). The following data show the price per gallon ($) for a sample of 20 gasoline and convenience stores located in San Francisco. **LO 1, 3**

DATA*file*
sf_gasprices

3.59	3.59	4.79	3.56	3.55	3.71	3.65	3.60	3.75	3.56
3.57	3.59	3.55	3.99	4.15	3.66	3.63	3.73	3.61	3.57

a. Use the sample data to estimate the mean price for a gallon of unleaded gasoline in San Francisco.
b. Compute the sample standard deviation.
c. Compare the mean price per gallon for the sample data to the national average price. What conclusions can you draw about the cost of living in San Francisco?

27. **Round-Trip Flight Prices.** The following table displays round-trip flight prices from 14 major U.S. cities to Atlanta and Salt Lake City. **LO 1, 3**

DATA*file*
flights

	Round-Trip Cost ($)	
Departure City	**Atlanta**	**Salt Lake City**
Cincinnati	340.10	570.10
New York	321.60	354.60
Chicago	291.60	465.60
Denver	339.60	219.60
Los Angeles	359.60	311.60
Seattle	384.60	297.60
Detroit	309.60	471.60
Philadelphia	415.60	618.40
Washington, DC	293.60	513.60
Miami	249.60	523.20
San Francisco	539.60	381.60
Las Vegas	455.60	159.60
Phoenix	359.60	267.60
Dallas	333.90	458.60

a. Compute the mean price for a round-trip flight into Atlanta and the mean price for a round-trip flight into Salt Lake City. Is Atlanta less expensive to fly into than Salt Lake City? If so, what could explain this difference?
b. Compute the range, variance, and standard deviation for the two samples. What does this information tell you about the prices for flights into these two cities?

28. **Annual Sales Amounts.** Varatta Enterprises sells industrial plumbing valves. The following table lists the annual sales amounts for the different salespeople in the organization for the most recent fiscal year. **LO 1, 3**

DATA*file*
varattasales

Salesperson	Sales Amount ($1,000s)	Salesperson	Sales Amount ($1,000s)
Joseph	147	Wei	465
Jennifer	232	Samantha	410
Phillip	547	Erin	298
Stanley	328	Dominic	321
Luke	295	Charlie	190
Lexie	194	Amol	211
Margaret	368	Lenisa	413

a. Compute the mean, variance, and standard deviation for these annual sales values.
b. In the previous fiscal year, the average annual sales amount was $300,000 with a standard deviation of $95,000. Discuss any differences you observe between the annual sales amount in the most recent and previous fiscal years.

29. **Air Quality Index.** The *Los Angeles Times* regularly reports the air quality index for various areas of Southern California. A sample of air quality index values for Pomona provided the following data: 28, 42, 58, 48, 45, 55, 60, 49, and 50. **LO 3**
a. Compute the range and interquartile range.
b. Compute the sample variance and sample standard deviation.
c. A sample of air quality index readings for Anaheim provided a sample mean of 48.5, a sample variance of 136, and a sample standard deviation of 11.66. What comparisons can you make between the air quality in Pomona and that in Anaheim on the basis of these descriptive statistics?

30. **Reliability of Delivery Service.** The following data were used to construct the histograms of the number of days required to fill orders for Dawson Supply, Inc. and J.C. Clark Distributors (see Figure 3.5).

Dawson Supply Days for Delivery:	11	10	9	10	11	11	10	11	10	10
Clark Distributors Days for Delivery:	8	10	13	7	10	11	10	7	15	12

Use the range and standard deviation to support the previous observation that Dawson Supply provides the more consistent and reliable delivery times. **LO 3**

31. **Cellular Phone Spending.** According to the 2016 Consumer Expenditure Survey, Americans spend an average of $1,124 on cellular phone service annually (U.S. Bureau of Labor Statistics website). Suppose that we wish to determine if there are differences in cellular phone expenditures by age group. Therefore, samples of 10 consumers were selected for three age groups (18–34, 35–44, 45 and older). The annual expenditure for each person in the sample is provided in the table below. **LO 1, 3**

DATA*file*
cellphone_expenses

	Annual Expenditure ($)	
18–34	35–44	45 and Older
1,355	969	1,135
115	434	956
1,456	1,792	400
2,045	1,500	1,374
1,621	1,277	1,244
994	1,056	825
1,937	1,922	763
1,200	1,350	1,192
1,567	1,586	1,305
1,390	1,415	1,510

a. Compute the mean, variance, and standard deviation for each of these three samples.
b. What observations can be made based on these data?

DATA*file*
advertising

32. **Advertising Spend by Companies.** *Advertising Age* annually compiles a list of the 100 companies that spend the most on advertising. Consumer-goods company Procter & Gamble has often topped the list, spending billions of dollars annually. Consider the data found in the file *advertising*. It contains annual advertising expenditures for a sample of 20 companies in the automotive sector and 20 companies in the department store sector. **LO 1, 3**
    a. What is the mean advertising spent for each sector?
    b. What is the standard deviation for each sector?
    c. What is the range of advertising spent for each sector?
    d. What is the interquartile range for each sector?
    e. Based on this sample and your answers to parts (a) to (d), comment on any differences in the advertising spending in the automotive companies versus the department store companies.
33. **Stream Discharge Rates.** The amount of water flowing in a river or stream is typically measured by the discharge rate measured in units of cubic feet per second. Suppose that two possible measuring instruments are being compared by measuring the discharge rate at the same point in a stream when the discharge rate appears to be unchanging. The file *stream* contains the results of 12 recorded discharge rates for each instrument (A and B), as shown below. **LO 1, 3**

DATA*file*
stream

Instrument A Measurements (cubic feet per second):

720	750	760	740	760	810	710	690	750	770	730	740

Instrument B Measurements (cubic feet per second):

710	820	710	790	840	820	780	770	710	830	720	730

a. Calculate the mean and standard deviation of the discharge rates for Instrument A and for Instrument B.
b. Compare the mean and standard deviations for the two instruments. What can you determine from this comparison?

34. **Consistency of Running Times.** The following times were recorded by the quarter-mile and mile runners of a university track team (times are in minutes).

Quarter-Mile Times:	0.92	0.98	1.04	0.90	0.99
Mile Times:	4.52	4.35	4.60	4.70	4.50

After viewing this sample of running times, one of the coaches commented that the quarter-milers turned in the more consistent times. Use the standard deviation and the coefficient of variation to summarize the variability in the data. Does the use of the coefficient of variation indicate that the coach's statement should be modified? **LO 3**

3.3 Measures of Distribution Shape, Relative Location, and Detecting Outliers

We have described several measures of location and variability for data. In addition, it is often important to have a measure of the shape of a distribution. In Chapter 2, we noted that a histogram provides a graphical display showing the shape of a distribution. An important numerical measure of the shape of a distribution is called **skewness**.

Distribution Shape

Excel uses the function SKEW to compute the skewness of data.

Figure 3.9 shows four histograms constructed from relative frequency distributions. The histograms in Panels A and B are moderately skewed. The one in Panel A is skewed

Figure 3.9 Histograms Showing the Skewness for Four Distributions

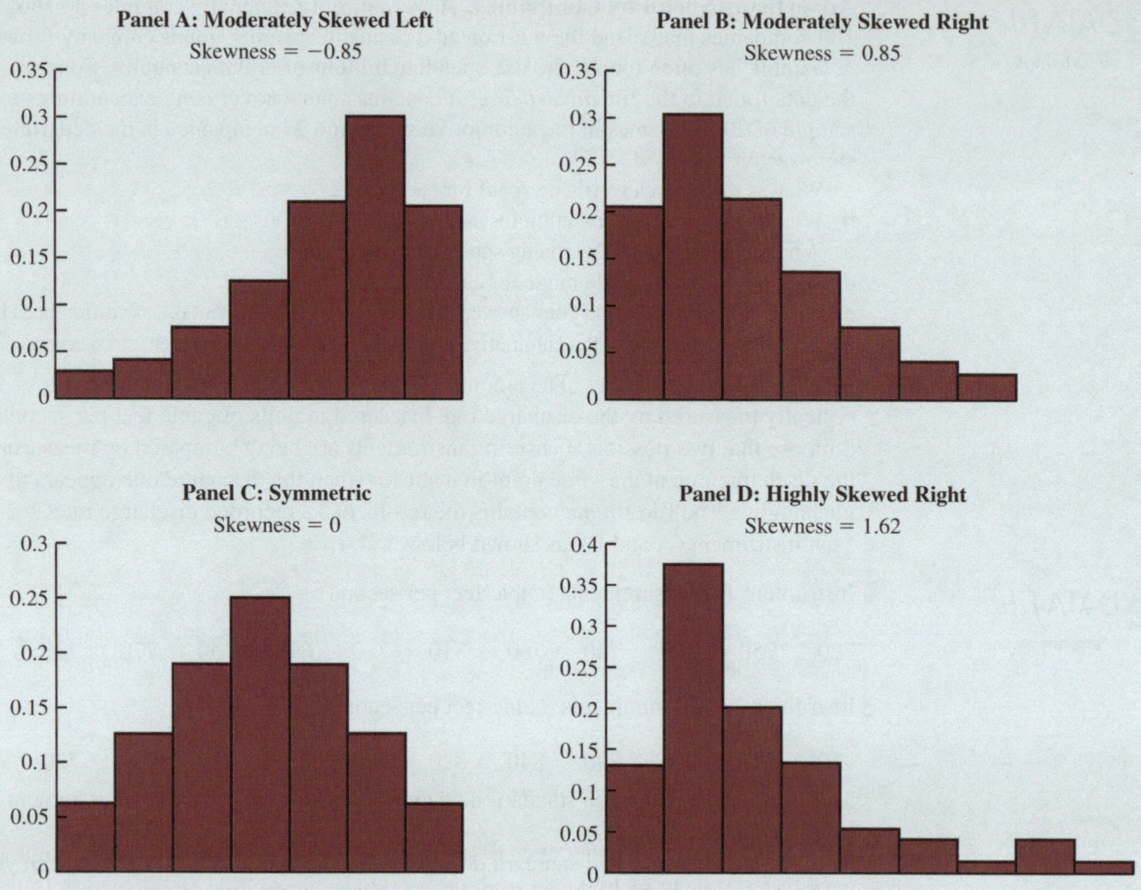

to the left; its skewness is -0.85. The histogram in Panel B is skewed to the right; its skewness is $+0.85$. The histogram in Panel C is symmetric; its skewness is zero. The histogram in Panel D is highly skewed to the right; its skewness is 1.62. The formula used to compute skewness is somewhat complex.[2] However, the skewness can easily be computed using statistical software. For data skewed to the left, the skewness is negative; for data skewed to the right, the skewness is positive. If the data are symmetric, the skewness is zero.

For a symmetric distribution, the mean and the median are equal. When the data are positively skewed, the mean will usually be greater than the median; when the data are negatively skewed, the mean will usually be less than the median. The data used to construct the histogram in Panel D are customer purchases at a women's apparel store. The mean purchase amount is \$77.60 and the median purchase amount is \$59.70. The relatively few large purchase amounts tend to increase the mean, whereas the median remains unaffected by the large purchase amounts. The median provides the preferred measure of location when the data are highly skewed.

[2]The formula for the skewness of sample data:

$$\text{Skewness} = \frac{n}{(n-1)(n-2)} \sum \left(\frac{x_i - \bar{x}}{s} \right)^3$$

z-Scores

In addition to measures of location, variability, and shape, we are also interested in the relative location of values within a data set. Measures of relative location help us determine how far a particular value is from the mean.

By using both the mean and standard deviation, we can determine the relative location of any observation. Suppose we have a sample of n observations, with the values denoted by $x_1, x_2, \ldots, x_n$. In addition, assume that the sample mean, $\bar{x}$, and the sample standard deviation, s, are already computed. Associated with each value, x_i, is another value called its **z-score**. Equation (3.12) shows how the z-score is computed for each x_i.

z-Score

$$z_i = \frac{x_i - \bar{x}}{s} \tag{3.12}$$

where

z_i = the z-score for x_i
$\bar{x}$ = the sample mean
s = the sample standard deviation

The z-score is often called the *standardized value*. The z-score, z_i, can be interpreted as the *number of standard deviations x_i is from the mean $\bar{x}$*. For example, $z_1 = 1.2$ would indicate that x_1 is 1.2 standard deviations greater than the sample mean. Similarly, $z_2 = -0.5$ would indicate that x_2 is 0.5, or 1/2, standard deviation less than the sample mean. A z-score greater than zero occurs for observations with a value greater than the mean, and a z-score less than zero occurs for observations with a value less than the mean. A z-score of zero indicates that the value of the observation is equal to the mean.

The z-score for any observation can be interpreted as a measure of the relative location of the observation in a data set. Thus, observations in two different data sets with the same z-score can be said to have the same relative location in terms of being the same number of standard deviations from their respective means.

The z-scores for the class size data from Section 3.1 are computed in Table 3.5. Recall the previously computed sample mean, $\bar{x} = 44$, and sample standard deviation, $s = 8$. The z-score of -1.50 for the fifth observation shows it is farthest from the mean; it is 1.50 standard deviations below the mean. Figure 3.10 provides a dot plot of the class size data with a graphical representation of the associated z-scores on the axis below.

Table 3.5 z-Scores for the Class Size Data

Number of Students in Class (x_i)	Deviation About the Mean ($x_i - \bar{x}$)	z-Score $\left(\frac{x_i - \bar{x}}{s}\right)$
46	2	2/8 = 0.25
54	10	10/8 = 1.25
42	−2	−2/8 = −0.25
46	2	2/8 = 0.25
32	−12	−12/8 = −1.50

Figure 3.10 Dot Plot Showing Class Size Data and z-Scores

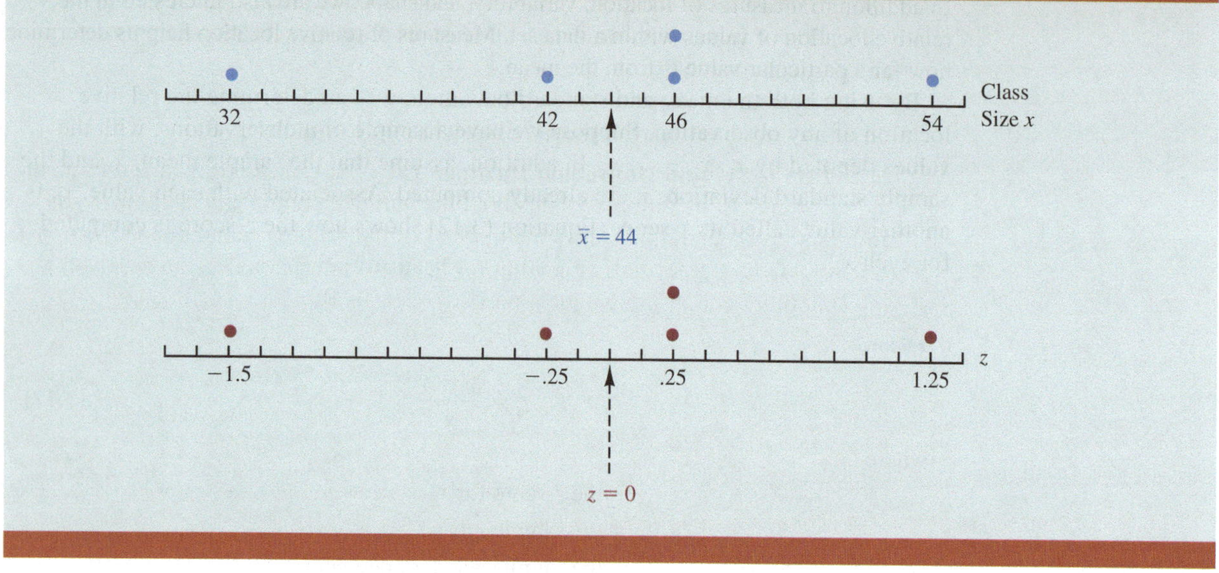

Chebyshev's Theorem

Chebyshev's theorem enables us to make statements about the proportion of data values that must be within a specified number of standard deviations of the mean.

> **Chebyshev's Theorem**
>
> At least $(1 - 1/z^2)$ of the data values must be within z standard deviations of the mean, where z is any value greater than 1.

Some of the implications of this theorem, with $z = 2$, 3, and 4 standard deviations, follow:

- At least 0.75, or 75%, of the data values must be within $z = 2$ standard deviations of the mean.
- At least 0.89, or 89%, of the data values must be within $z = 3$ standard deviations of the mean.
- At least 0.94, or 94%, of the data values must be within $z = 4$ standard deviations of the mean.

For an example using Chebyshev's theorem, suppose that the midterm test scores for 100 students in a college business statistics course had a mean of 70 and a standard deviation of 5. How many students had test scores between 60 and 80? How many students had test scores between 58 and 82?

For the test scores between 60 and 80, we note that 60 is two standard deviations below the mean and 80 is two standard deviations above the mean. Using Chebyshev's theorem, we see that at least 0.75, or at least 75%, of the observations must have values within two standard deviations of the mean. Thus, at least 75% of the students must have scored between 60 and 80.

Chebyshev's theorem requires $z > 1$, but z need not be an integer.

For the test scores between 58 and 82, we see that $(58 - 70)/5 = -2.4$ indicates 58 is 2.4 standard deviations below the mean and that $(82 - 70)/5 = +2.4$ indicates 82 is 2.4 standard deviations above the mean. Applying Chebyshev's theorem with $z = 2.4$, we have

$$\left(1 - \frac{1}{z^2}\right) = \left(1 - \frac{1}{(2.4)^2}\right) = 0.826$$

At least 82.6% of the students must have test scores between 58 and 82.

Figure 3.11 A Symmetric Mound-Shaped or Bell-Shaped Distribution

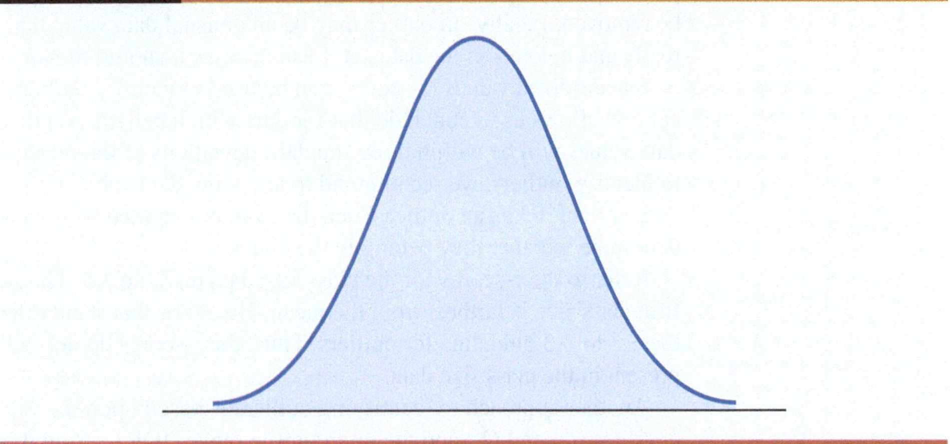

Empirical Rule

One of the advantages of Chebyshev's theorem is that it applies to any data set regardless of the shape of the distribution of the data. Indeed, it could be used with any of the distributions in Figure 3.9. In many practical applications, however, data sets exhibit a symmetric mound-shaped or bell-shaped distribution like the one shown in Figure 3.11. When the data are believed to approximate this distribution, the **empirical rule** can be used to determine the percentage of data values that must be within a specified number of standard deviations of the mean.

The empirical rule is based on the normal probability distribution, which is discussed in Chapter 6. The normal distribution is used extensively throughout this text.

Empirical Rule

For data having a bell-shaped distribution:

- Approximately 68% of the data values will be within one standard deviation of the mean.
- Approximately 95% of the data values will be within two standard deviations of the mean.
- Almost all (approximately 99.7%) of the data values will be within three standard deviations of the mean.

For example, liquid detergent cartons are filled automatically on a production line. Filling weights frequently have a bell-shaped distribution. If the mean filling weight is 16 ounces and the standard deviation is 0.25 ounces, we can use the empirical rule to draw the following conclusions:

- Approximately 68% of the filled cartons will have weights between 15.75 and 16.25 ounces (within one standard deviation of the mean).
- Approximately 95% of the filled cartons will have weights between 15.50 and 16.50 ounces (within two standard deviations of the mean).
- Almost all (approximately 99.7%) filled cartons will have weights between 15.25 and 16.75 ounces (within three standard deviations of the mean).

Detecting Outliers

Sometimes a data set will have one or more observations with unusually large or unusually small values. These extreme values are called **outliers**. Experienced statisticians take steps to identify outliers and then review each one carefully. An outlier may be a data value that has been incorrectly recorded. If so, it can be corrected before further analysis. An outlier may also be from an observation that was incorrectly included in the data set; if so, it can be removed. Finally, an outlier may be an unusual data value that has been recorded correctly and belongs in the data set. In such cases it should remain.

Standardized values (z-scores) can be used to identify outliers. Recall that the empirical rule allows us to conclude that for data with a bell-shaped distribution, almost all the data values will be within three standard deviations of the mean. Hence, in using z-scores to identify outliers, we recommend treating any data value with a z-score less than -3 or greater than $+3$ as an outlier. Such data values can then be reviewed for accuracy and to determine whether they belong in the data set.

Refer to the z-scores for the class size data in Table 3.5. The z-score of -1.50 shows the fifth class size is farthest from the mean. However, this standardized value is well within the -3 to $+3$ guideline for outliers. Thus, the z-scores do not indicate that outliers are present in the class size data.

Another approach to identifying outliers is based upon the values of the first and third quartiles (Q_1 and Q_3) and the interquartile range (IQR). Using this method, we first compute the following lower and upper limits:

$$\text{Lower Limit} = Q_1 - 1.5(\text{IQR})$$
$$\text{Upper Limit} = Q_3 + 1.5(\text{IQR})$$

The approach that uses the first and third quartiles and the IQR to identify outliers does not necessarily provide the same results as the approach based upon a z-score less than −3 or greater than +3. Either or both procedures may be used.

An observation is classified as an outlier if its value is less than the lower limit or greater than the upper limit. For the monthly starting salary data shown in Table 3.1, $Q_1 = 5{,}857.5$, $Q_3 = 6{,}025$, IQR $= 167.5$, and the lower and upper limits are

$$\text{Lower Limit} = Q_1 - 1.5(\text{IQR}) = 5{,}857.5 - 1.5(167.5) = 5{,}606.25$$
$$\text{Upper Limit} = Q_3 + 1.5(\text{IQR}) = 6{,}025 + 1.5(167.5) = 6{,}276.25$$

Looking at the data in Table 3.1 we see that there are no observations with a starting salary less than the lower limit of 5,606.25. But there is one starting salary, 6,325, that is greater than the upper limit of 6,276.25. Thus, 6,325 is considered to be an outlier using this alternate approach to identifying outliers.

Notes + Comments

1. Chebyshev's theorem is applicable for any data set and can be used to state the minimum number of data values that will be within a certain number of standard deviations of the mean. If the data are known to be approximately bell-shaped, more can be said. For instance, the empirical rule allows us to say that *approximately* 95% of the data values will be within two standard deviations of the mean; Chebyshev's theorem allows us to conclude only that at least 75% of the data values will be in that interval.
2. Before analyzing a data set, statisticians usually make a variety of checks to ensure the validity of data. In a large study it is not uncommon for errors to be made in recording data values or in entering the values into a computer. Identifying outliers is one tool used to check the validity of the data.

Exercises

Methods

35. Consider a sample with data values of 10, 20, 12, 17, and 16. Compute the z-score for each of the five observations. **LO 4**
36. Consider a sample with a mean of 500 and a standard deviation of 100. What are the z-scores for the following data values: 520, 650, 500, 450, and 280? **LO 4**
37. Consider a sample with a mean of 30 and a standard deviation of 5. Use Chebyshev's theorem to determine the percentage of the data within each of the ranges that follow. **LO 5**

a. 20 to 40
b. 15 to 45
c. 22 to 38
d. 18 to 42
e. 12 to 48

38. Suppose the data have a bell-shaped distribution with a mean of 30 and a standard deviation of 5. Use the empirical rule to determine the percentage of data within each of the ranges that follow. **LO 5**
a. 20 to 40
b. 15 to 45
c. 25 to 35

Applications

39. **Amount of Sleep per Night.** The results of a national survey showed that on average, adults sleep 6.9 hours per night. Suppose that the standard deviation is 1.2 hours. **LO 5**
a. Use Chebyshev's theorem to calculate the percentage of individuals who sleep between 4.5 and 9.3 hours.
b. Use Chebyshev's theorem to calculate the percentage of individuals who sleep between 3.9 and 9.9 hours.
c. Assume that the number of hours of sleep follows a bell-shaped distribution. Use the empirical rule to calculate the percentage of individuals who sleep between 4.5 and 9.3 hours per day. How does this result compare to the value that you obtained using Chebyshev's theorem in part (a)?

40. **Price per Gallon of Gasoline.** Suppose that mean retail price per gallon of regular-grade gasoline is \$3.43 with a standard deviation of \$0.10 and that the retail price per gallon has a bell-shaped distribution. **LO 5**
a. What percentage of regular grade gasoline sells for between \$3.33 and \$3.53 per gallon?
b. What percentage of regular grade gasoline sells for between \$3.33 and \$3.63 per gallon?
c. What percentage of regular grade gasoline sells for more than \$3.63 per gallon?

41. **GMAT Exam Scores.** The Graduate Management Admission Test (GMAT) is a standardized exam used by some universities as part of the assessment for admission to graduate study in business. The average GMAT score is 547 (*Magoosh* website). Assume that GMAT scores are bell-shaped with a standard deviation of 100. **LO 5**
a. What percentage of GMAT scores are 647 or higher?
b. What percentage of GMAT scores are 747 or higher?
c. What percentage of GMAT scores are between 447 and 547?
d. What percentage of GMAT scores are between 347 and 647?

42. **Cost of Backyard Structures.** Many families in California are using backyard structures for home offices, art studios, and hobby areas as well as for additional storage. Suppose that the mean price for a customized wooden, shingled backyard structure is \$3,100. Assume that the standard deviation is \$1,200. **LO 3, 6**
a. What is the z-score for a backyard structure costing \$2,300?
b. What is the z-score for a backyard structure costing \$4,900?
c. Interpret the z-scores in parts (a) and (b). Comment on whether either should be considered an outlier.
d. If the cost for a backyard shed-office combination built in Albany, California, is \$13,000, should this structure be considered an outlier? Explain.

43. **Best Places to Live.** Each year, *Money* magazine publishes a list of "Best Places to Live in the United States." These listings are based on affordability, educational performance, convenience, safety, and livability. The list on previous page shows the median household income of *Money* magazine's top city in each U.S. state for 2017 (*Money* magazine website). **LO 1, 2, 3, 6**

DATA*file* bestcities

City	Median Household Income ($)	City	Median Household Income ($)
Pelham, AL	66,772	Bozeman, MT	49,303
Juneau, AK	84,101	Papillion, NE	79,131
Paradise Valley, AZ	138,192	Sparks, NV	54,230
Fayetteville, AR	40,835	Nashua, NH	66,872
Monterey Park, CA	57,419	North Arlington, NJ	73,885
Lone Tree, CO	116,761	Rio Rancho, NM	58,982
Manchester, CT	64,828	Valley Stream, NY	88,693
Hockessin, DE	115,124	Concord, NC	54,579
St. Augustine, FL	47,748	Dickinson, ND	71,866
Vinings, GA	73,103	Wooster, OH	43,054
Kapaa, HI	62,546	Mustang, OK	66,714
Meridian, ID	62,899	Beaverton, OR	58,785
Schaumburg, IL	73,824	Lower Merion, PA	117,438
Fishers, IN	87,043	Warwick, RI	63,414
Council Bluffs, IA	46,844	Mauldin, SC	57,480
Lenexa, KS	76,505	Rapid City, SD	47,788
Georgetown, KY	58,709	Franklin, TN	82,334
Bossier City, LA	47,051	Allen, TX	104,524
South Portland, ME	56,472	Orem, UT	54,515
Rockville, MD	100,158	Colchester, VT	69,181
Waltham, MA	75,106	Reston, VA	112,722
Farmington Hills, MI	71,154	Mercer Island, WA	128,484
Woodbury, MN	99,657	Morgantown, WV	38,060
Olive Branch, MS	62,958	New Berlin, WI	74,983
St. Peters, MO	57,728	Cheyenne, WY	56,593

a. Compute the mean and median for these household income data.
b. Compare the mean and median values for these data. What does this indicate about the distribution of household income data?
c. Compute the range and standard deviation for these household income data.
d. Compute the first and third quartiles for these household income data.
e. Are there any outliers in these data? What does this suggest about the data?

44. **NCAA Basketball Game Scores.** A sample of 10 NCAA college basketball game scores provided the following data. **LO 1, 3, 5, 6**

DATA*file* ncaa

Winning Team	Points	Losing Team	Points	Winning Margin
Arizona	90	Oregon	66	24
Duke	85	Georgetown	66	19
Florida State	75	Wake Forest	70	5
Kansas	78	Colorado	57	21
Kentucky	71	Notre Dame	63	8
Louisville	65	Tennessee	62	3
Oklahoma State	72	Texas	66	6
Purdue	76	Michigan State	70	6
Stanford	77	Southern Cal	67	10
Wisconsin	76	Illinois	56	20

a. Compute the mean and standard deviation for the points scored by the winning team.
b. Assume that the points scored by the winning teams for all NCAA games follow a bell-shaped distribution. Using the mean and standard deviation found in part (a), estimate the percentage of all NCAA games in which the winning team scores 84 or more points. Estimate the percentage of NCAA games in which the winning team scores more than 90 points.
c. Compute the mean and standard deviation for the winning margin. Do the data contain outliers? Explain.

45. **Apple iPads in Schools.** *The New York Times* reported that Apple has unveiled a new iPad marketed specifically to school districts for use by students (*The New York Times* website). The 9.7-inch iPads will have faster processors and a cheaper price point in an effort to take market share away from Google Chromebooks in public school districts. Suppose that the following data represent the percentages of students currently using Apple iPads for a sample of 18 U.S. public school districts. **LO 1, 2, 3, 6**

DATA*file*
ipads

15 22 12 21 26 18 42 29 64 20 15 22 18 24 27
24 26 19

a. Compute the mean and median percentage of students currently using Apple iPads.
b. Compare the first and third quartiles for these data.
c. Compute the range and interquartile range for these data.
d. Compute the variance and standard deviation for these data.
e. Are there any outliers in these data?
f. Based on your calculated values, what can we say about the percentage of students using iPads in public school districts?

3.4 Five-Number Summaries and Boxplots

Summary statistics and easy-to-draw graphs based on summary statistics can be used to quickly summarize large quantities of data. In this section we show how five-number summaries and boxplots can be developed to identify several characteristics of a data set.

Five-Number Summary

In a **five-number summary**, five numbers are used to summarize the data:

1. Smallest value
2. First quartile (Q_1)
3. Median (Q_2)
4. Third quartile (Q_3)
5. Largest value

To illustrate the development of a five-number summary, we will use the monthly starting salary data in Table 3.1. Arranging the data in ascending order, we obtain the following results:

5,710 5,755 5,850 5,880 5,880 5,890 5,920 5,940 5,950 6,050 6,130 6,325

The smallest value is 5,710 and the largest value is 6,325. We showed how to compute the quartiles ($Q_1 = 5{,}857.5$; $Q_2 = 5{,}905$; and $Q_3 = 6{,}025$) in Section 3.1. Thus, the five-number summary for the monthly starting salary data is

5,710 5,857.5 5,905 6,025 6,325

The five-number summary indicates that the starting salaries in the sample are between 5,710 and 6,325 and that the median or middle value is 5,905. The first and third quartiles show that approximately 50% of the starting salaries are between 5,857.5 and 6,025.

Figure 3.12 Boxplot of the Monthly Starting Salary Data with Lines Showing the Lower and Upper Limits

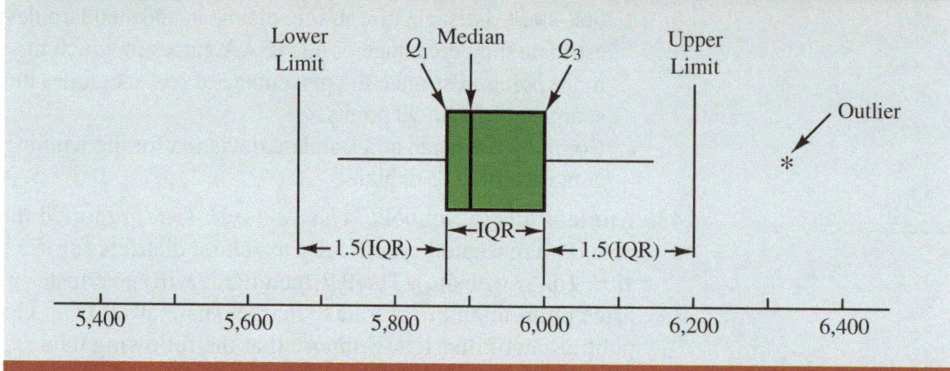

Boxplot

A **boxplot** is a graphical display of data based on a five-number summary. A key to the development of a boxplot is the computation of the interquartile range, IQR = $Q_3 - Q_1$. Figure 3.12 shows a boxplot for the monthly starting salary data. The steps used to construct the boxplot follow.

1. A box is drawn with the ends of the box located at the first and third quartiles. For the salary data, $Q_1 = 5{,}857.5$ and $Q_3 = 6{,}025$. This box contains the middle 50% of the data.
2. A vertical line is drawn in the box at the location of the median (5,905 for the salary data).
3. By using the interquartile range, IQR = $Q_3 - Q_1$, *limits* are located at 1.5(IQR) below Q_1, and 1.5(IQR) above Q_3. For the salary data, IQR = $Q_3 - Q_1 = 6{,}025 - 5{,}857.5 = 167.5$. Thus, the limits are $5{,}857.5 - 1.5(167.5) = 5{,}606.25$ and $6{,}025 + 1.5(167.5) = 6{,}276.25$. Data outside these limits are considered *outliers*.
4. The horizontal lines extending from each end of the box in Figure 3.12 are called *whiskers*. The whiskers are drawn from the ends of the box to the smallest and largest values *inside the limits* computed in step 3. Thus, the whiskers end at salary values of 5,710 and 6,130.
5. Finally, the location of each outlier is shown with a small dot. In Figure 3.12 we see one outlier, 6,325.

Boxplots provide another way to identify outliers, but they do not necessarily identify the same values as those with a z-score less than −3 or greater than +3. Either or both procedures may be used.

In Figure 3.12, we included lines showing the location of the upper and lower limits. These lines were drawn to show how the limits are computed and where they are located. Although the limits are always computed, generally they are not drawn on the boxplots.

Using Excel to Construct a Boxplot

In Excel, a boxplot is referred to as a box and whisker plot.

We can use Excel's Insert Statistic Chart to construct a boxplot of the monthly starting salary data as outlined below.

Enter/Access Data: Open the file *startingsalaries*. The data are in cells B2:B13.

DATA*file*
startingsalaries

Apply Tools: The following steps describe how to use Excel's Insert Statistic Chart to construct a histogram of the audit time data.

Step 1. Select cells B2:B13
Step 2. Click the **Insert** tab on the Ribbon

Figure 3.13 The Edited Boxplot Created in Excel for the Monthly Starting Salary Data

	A	B
1	Graduate	Monthly Starting Salary ($)
2	1	5850
3	2	5950
4	3	6050
5	4	5880
6	5	5755
7	6	5710
8	7	5890
9	8	6130
10	9	5940
11	10	6325
12	11	5920
13	12	5880
14		
15		

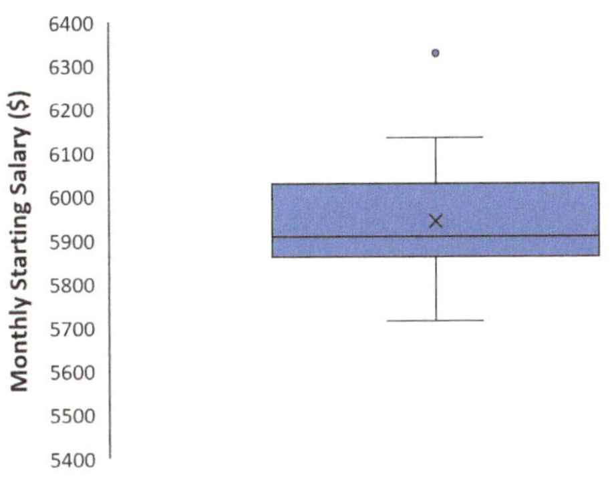

Step 3. In the **Charts** group, click **Insert Statistic Chart** and then click **Box and Whisker** to create the boxplot in Excel

Editing Options:

Step 1. Click on **Chart Title** and press the **Delete** key
Step 2. Click on the **1** below the horizontal axis and press the **Delete** key
Step 3. Click on the **Chart Elements** button
Step 4. When the list of chart elements appears:
Deselect **Gridlines** to remove the horizontal gridlines from the chart
Click **Axis Titles** to create placeholders for the axis titles
Click on the horizontal **Axis Title** and press the **Delete** key
Click on the vertical **Axis Title** placeholder and replace it with *Monthly Starting Salary ($)*

Figure 3.13 shows the resulting boxplot.

Comparative Analysis Using Boxplots

Boxplots can also be used to provide a graphical summary of two or more groups and facilitate visual comparisons among the groups. For example, suppose the placement office decided to conduct a follow-up study to compare monthly starting salaries by the graduate's major: accounting, finance, information systems, management, and marketing. The major and starting salary data for a new sample of 111 recent business school graduates are in the file *majorsalaries*.

Using Excel to Construct a Comparative Analysis Using Boxplots

DATA*file*
majorsalaries

We can use Excel's Insert Statistic Chart to construct a comparative boxplot of data on the monthly starting salary by major as outlined below.

Enter/Access Data: Open the file *majorsalaries*. The data are in cells A2:B112.

Apply Tools: The following steps describe how to use Excel's Insert Statistic Chart to construct boxplots of monthly salary by major.

Step 1. Select cells A2:B112
Step 2. Click the **Insert** tab on the Ribbon
Step 3. In the **Charts** group click **Insert Statistic Chart** and then click **Box and Whisker** to create the boxplot in Excel

Editing Options:

Step 1. Click on **Chart Title** and replace it with *Comparative Analysis of Monthly Starting Salary by Major*
Step 2. To put the majors in alphabetical order from left to right:
Select cells in the data set (A2:B112)
Select the **Data** tab on the Ribbon
Select **Sort** from the **Sort & Filter** group
From the **Sort by** drop-down menu in the **Sort** dialog box, select **Major**
From the **Order** drop-down menu in the **Sort** dialog box, select **A to Z**
Click **OK**
Step 3. Select the chart by clicking anywhere on the chart. Click on the **Chart Elements** button
Step 4. When the list of chart elements appears:
Deselect **Gridlines** to remove the horizontal gridlines from the chart
Click **Axis Titles** to create placeholders for the axis titles
Click on the horizontal **Axis Title** placeholder and replace it with *Major*
Click on the vertical **Axis Title** placeholder and replace it with *Monthly Starting Salary ($)*

Figure 3.14 shows the resulting boxplot comparative analysis.

What interpretations can you make from the boxplots in Figure 3.14? Specifically, we note the following:

- The higher salaries are in accounting; the lower salaries are in management and marketing.

Figure 3.14 The Edited Comparative Boxplots Created in Excel for the Monthly Starting Salary by Major Data

	A	B
1	Major	Monthly Starting Salary ($)
2	Accounting	6255
3	Accounting	5510
4	Accounting	6280
5	Accounting	6960
6	Accounting	5875
7	Accounting	6605
8	Accounting	6550
9	Accounting	5540
10	Accounting	6160
11	Accounting	6680
12	Accounting	5640
13	Accounting	6200
14	Accounting	7290
15	Accounting	6180
16	Accounting	5420
17	Accounting	7400
18	Accounting	6440

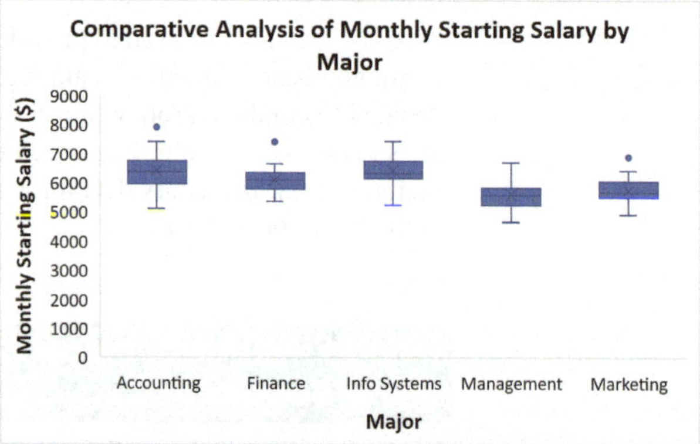

- Based on the medians, accounting and information systems have similar and higher median salaries than the other majors. Finance is next, with marketing and management showing lower median salaries.
- High salary outliers exist for accounting, finance, and marketing majors.

Perhaps you can see additional interpretations based on these boxplots.

Notes + Comments

1. There are several options with Excel's Box and Whisker chart. To invoke these options, right-click on the box part of the chart, select **Format Data Series**..., and the **Format Data Series** task pane will appear. This allows you to control what appears in the chart—for example, whether or not to show the mean marker, markers for outliers, and markers for all points. In the case of a comparative chart, you can control the gaps between categories and create a line connecting the means of the different categories.
2. In the **Format Data Series** task pane, there are two options for how quartiles are calculated: Inclusive median and Exclusive median. The default is Exclusive median; this option is consistent with the approach for calculating quartiles discussed in this text. We recommend that you leave this option at its default value of **Exclusive median**.

Exercises

Methods

46. Consider a sample with data values of 27, 25, 20, 15, 30, 34, 28, and 25. Provide the five-number summary for the data. **LO 7**
47. Show the boxplot for the data in exercise 46. **LO 8**
48. Show the five-number summary and the boxplot for the following data: 5, 15, 18, 10, 8, 12, 16, 10, 6. **LO 7**
49. A data set has a first quartile of 42 and a third quartile of 50. Compute the lower and upper limits for the corresponding boxplot. Should a data value of 65 be considered an outlier? **LO 6, 8**

Applications

DATA*file*
webpage_clicks

50. **A/B Testing and Number of Clicks.** A/B testing is a method for comparing two versions of a product in an attempt to determine which version is preferred by customers. A/B testing is often used in webpage design by randomly presenting one of two possible website designs and then measuring performance metrics for each webpage such as number of clicks on a particular link. Suppose that a company is performing an A/B test for two versions of a webpage: Version A and Version B. The company is measuring the number of clicks on each webpage version per day, and these data are contained in the file *webpage_clicks*. **LO 1, 7, 8**
    a. Compute the mean and median number of clicks per day for Version A and Version B of the webpage. Which version appears to be generating more clicks per day?
    b. Provide a five-number summary for the number of clicks per day generated by Version A and Version B.
    c. Construct boxplots for the number of clicks per day generated by Version A and Version B. Are there outliers for the number of clicks generated per day by Version A? Are there outliers for the number of clicks generated per day by Version B?

51. **Pharmaceutical Company Sales.** Annual sales, in millions of dollars, for 21 pharmaceutical companies follow. **LO 6, 7, 8**

DATA*file*
pharmacysales

Annual Sales ($ millions)					
8,408	1,374	1,872	8,879	2,459	11,413
608	14,138	6,452	1,850	2,818	1,356
10,498	7,478	4,019	4,341	739	2,127
3,653	5,794	8,305			

a. Provide a five-number summary.
b. Compute the lower and upper limits.
c. Do the data contain any outliers?
d. Johnson & Johnson's sales are the largest on the list of pharmaceutical companies at $14,138 million. Suppose a data entry error had been made and the sales had been entered as $41,138 million. Would the method of detecting outliers in part (c) identify this problem and allow for correction of the data entry error?
e. Show a boxplot.

52. **Cell Phone Companies Customer Satisfaction.** Suppose that an organization has measured overall customer satisfaction scores for AT&T, Dish Wireless, T-Mobile, and Verizon cell phone services in major metropolitan areas throughout the United States. The rating for each service reflects the overall customer satisfaction considering a variety of factors such as cost, connectivity problems, dropped calls, static interference, and customer support. A satisfaction scale from 0 to 100 was used with 0 indicating completely dissatisfied and 100 indicating completely satisfied. The ratings for the four cell phone services in 20 metropolitan areas are as shown. **LO 1, 6, 7, 8**

DATA*file*
cellservice

	Satisfaction Score			
Metropolitan Area	**AT&T**	**Dish Wireless**	**T-Mobile**	**Verizon**
Atlanta	70	66	71	79
Boston	69	64	74	76
Chicago	71	65	70	77
Dallas	75	65	74	78
Denver	71	67	73	77
Detroit	73	65	77	79
Jacksonville	73	64	75	81
Las Vegas	72	68	74	81
Los Angeles	66	65	68	78
Miami	68	69	73	80
Minneapolis	68	66	75	77
Philadelphia	72	66	71	78
Phoenix	68	66	76	81
San Antonio	75	65	75	80
San Diego	69	68	72	79
San Francisco	66	69	73	75
Seattle	68	67	74	77
St. Louis	74	66	74	79
Tampa	73	63	73	79
Washington, DC	72	68	71	76

a. Consider T-Mobile first. What is the median rating?
b. Develop a five-number summary for the T-Mobile service.
c. Are there outliers for T-Mobile? Explain.

d. Repeat parts (b) and (c) for the other three cell phone services.
e. Show the boxplots for the four cell phone services on one graph. Discuss what a comparison of the boxplots tells about the four services. Which service would be recommended as being best in terms of overall customer satisfaction?

DATA*file*
nfl_weight_height

53. **NFL Player Weights and Heights.** American football players in the National Football League (NFL) are highly specialized by position. Players who play at one position rarely play at another position. Two specific positions in the NFL are defensive tackle (DT) and quarterback (QB). The file *nfl_weight_height* contains data on the weights and heights of players at each of these positions in the NFL (*NFL.com*). Answer the following questions using these data. **LO 7, 8**
a. Calculate the five-number summary for the weights of DTs and the five-number summary for the weights of QBs. Which position tends to have players that weigh more?
b. Construct comparative boxplots showing the distribution of weights for DTs and QBs in the NFL. Are there outliers in the weights for DTs? Are there outliers in the weights for QBs?
c. Calculate the five-number summary for the heights of DTs and the five-number summary for the heights of QBs. Which position tends to have players that are taller?
d. Construct comparative boxplots showing the distribution of heights for DTs and QBs in the NFL. Are there outliers in the heights for DTs? Are there outliers in the heights for QBs?
e. Compare the boxplots from part (b) to the boxplots in part (d). What can you infer about the differences in the distributions of weight between DTs and QBs from the distributions of height between DTs and QBs?

DATA*file*
bordercrossings

54. **U.S. Border Crossings.** The Bureau of Transportation Statistics keeps track of all border crossings through ports of entry along the U.S.–Canadian and U.S.–Mexican borders. The data in the file *bordercrossings* show the most recently published figures for the number of personal vehicle crossings (rounded to the nearest 1,000) at the 50 busiest ports of entry during the month of August (U.S. Department of Transportation website). **LO 1, 2, 6, 7, 8**
a. What are the mean and median number of crossings for these ports of entry?
b. What are the first and third quartiles?
c. Provide a five-number summary.
d. Do the data contain any outliers? Show a boxplot.

3.5 Measures of Association Between Two Variables

Thus far, we have examined numerical methods used to summarize the data for *one variable at a time.* Often a manager or decision maker is interested in the *relationship between two variables.* In this section, we present covariance and correlation as descriptive measures of the relationship between two variables.

We begin by reconsidering the application concerning an electronics store in San Francisco, as presented in Section 2.4. The store's manager wants to determine the relationship between the number of weekend television commercials shown and the sales at the store during the following week. Sample data with sales expressed in hundreds of dollars are provided in Table 3.6. It shows 10 observations ($n = 10$), one for each week. The scatter diagram in Figure 3.15 shows a positive relationship, with higher sales (y) associated with a greater number of commercials (x). In fact, the scatter diagram suggests that a straight line could be used as an approximation of the relationship. In the following discussion, we introduce **covariance** as a descriptive measure of the linear association between two variables.

Table 3.6 Sample Data for the San Francisco Electronics Store

DATA*file* electronics

Week	Number of Commercials x	Sales ($100s) y
1	2	50
2	5	57
3	1	41
4	3	54
5	4	54
6	1	38
7	5	63
8	3	48
9	4	59
10	2	46

Figure 3.15 Scatter Diagram for the San Francisco Electronics Store

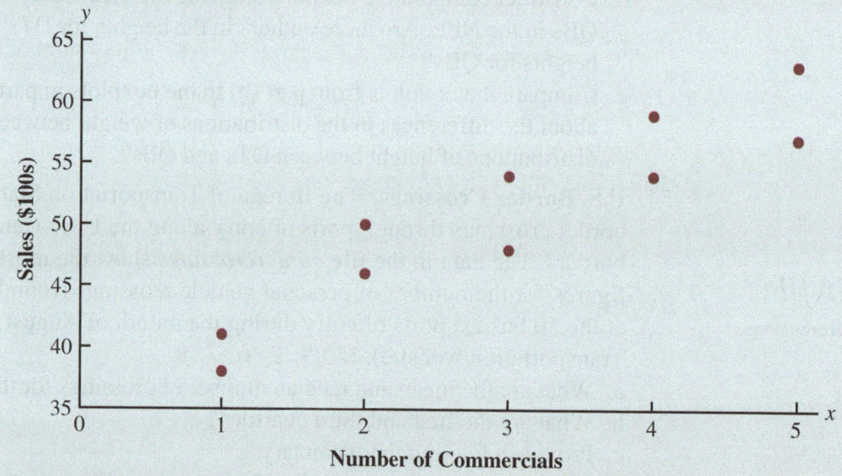

Covariance

For a sample of size n with the observations (x_1, y_1), (x_2, y_2), and so on, the sample covariance is defined as follows:

Sample Covariance

$$s_{xy} = \frac{\Sigma(x_i - \bar{x})(y_i - \bar{y})}{n - 1} \tag{3.13}$$

This formula pairs each x_i with a y_i. We then sum the products obtained by multiplying the deviation of each x_i from its sample mean $\bar{x}$ by the deviation of the corresponding y_i from its sample mean $\bar{y}$; this sum is then divided by $n - 1$.

To measure the strength of the linear relationship between the number of commercials x and the sales volume y in the San Francisco electronics store problem, we use equation (3.13) to compute the sample covariance. The calculations in Table 3.7 show the

Table 3.7 Calculations for the Sample Covariance

	x_i	y_i	$x_i - \bar{x}$	$y_i - \bar{y}$	$(x_i - \bar{x})(y_i - \bar{y})$
	2	50	−1	−1	1
	5	57	2	6	12
	1	41	−2	−10	20
	3	54	0	3	0
	4	54	1	3	3
	1	38	−2	−13	26
	5	63	2	12	24
	3	48	0	−3	0
	4	59	1	8	8
	2	46	−1	−5	5
Totals	30	510	0	0	99

$$s_{xy} = \frac{\Sigma(x_i - \bar{x})(y_i - \bar{y})}{n - 1} = \frac{99}{10 - 1} = 11$$

computation of $\Sigma(x_i - \bar{x})(y_i - \bar{y})$. Note that $\bar{x} = 30/10 = 3$ and $\bar{y} = 510/10 = 51$. Using equation (3.13), we obtain a sample covariance of

$$s_{xy} = \frac{\Sigma(x_i - \bar{x})(y_i - \bar{y})}{n - 1} = \frac{99}{9} = 11$$

The formula for computing the covariance of a population of size N is similar to equation (3.13), but we use different notation to indicate that we are working with the entire population.

Population Covariance

$$\sigma_{xy} = \frac{\Sigma(x_i - \mu_x)(y_i - \mu_y)}{N} \tag{3.14}$$

In equation (3.14), we use the notation μ_x for the population mean of the variable x and μ_y for the population mean of the variable y. The population covariance σ_{xy} is defined for a population of size N.

Interpretation of the Covariance

To aid in the interpretation of the sample covariance, consider Figure 3.16. It is the same as the scatter diagram of Figure 3.15, with a vertical dashed line at $\bar{x} = 3$ and a horizontal dashed line at $\bar{y} = 51$. The lines divide the graph into four quadrants. Points in quadrant I correspond to x_i greater than $\bar{x}$ and y_i greater than $\bar{y}$, points in quadrant II correspond to x_i less than $\bar{x}$ and y_i greater than $\bar{y}$, and so on. Thus, the value of $(x_i - \bar{x})(y_i - \bar{y})$ must be positive for points in quadrant I, negative for points in quadrant II, positive for points in quadrant III, and negative for points in quadrant IV.

The covariance is a measure of the linear association between two variables.

If the value of s_{xy} is positive, the points with the greatest influence on s_{xy} must be in quadrants I and III. Hence, a positive value for s_{xy} indicates a positive linear association between x and y; that is, as the value of x increases, the value of y increases. If the value of s_{xy} is negative, however, the points with the greatest influence on s_{xy} are in quadrants II and IV. Hence, a negative value for s_{xy} indicates a negative linear association between x and y; that is, as the value of x increases, the value of y decreases. Finally, if the points are evenly distributed across all four quadrants, the value of s_{xy} will be close to zero, indicating no

Figure 3.16 Partitioned Scatter Diagram for the San Francisco Electronics Store

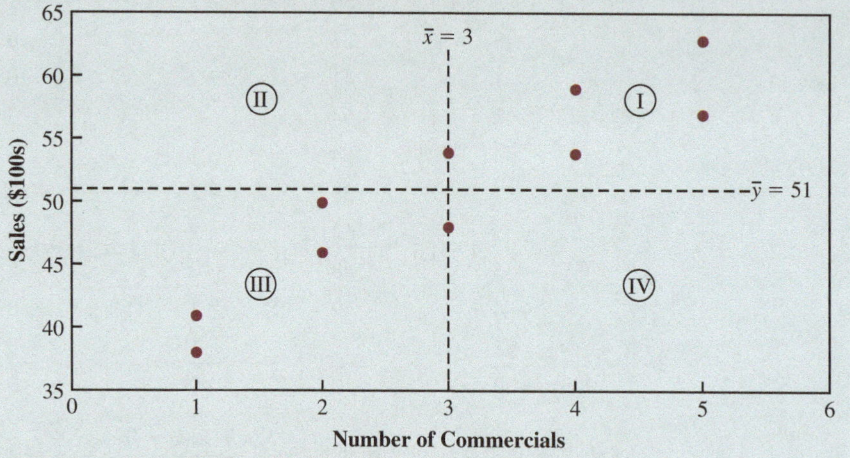

linear association between x and y. Figure 3.17 shows the values of s_{xy} that can be expected with three different types of scatter diagrams.

Referring again to Figure 3.16, we see that the scatter diagram for the electronics store follows the pattern in the top panel of Figure 3.17. As we should expect, the value of the sample covariance indicates a positive linear relationship with $s_{xy} = 11$.

From the preceding discussion, it might appear that a large positive value for the covariance indicates a strong positive linear relationship and that a large negative value indicates a strong negative linear relationship. However, one problem with using covariance as a measure of the strength of the linear relationship is that the value of the covariance depends on the units of measurement for x and y. For example, suppose we are interested in the relationship between height x and weight y for individuals. Clearly the strength of the relationship should be the same whether we measure height in feet or inches. Measuring the height in inches, however, gives us much larger numerical values for $(x_i - \bar{x})$ than when we measure height in feet. Thus, with height measured in inches, we would obtain a larger value for the numerator o$(x_i - \bar{x})(y_i - \bar{y})$ in equation (3.13)—and hence a larger covariance—when in fact the relationship does not change. A measure of the relationship between two variables that is not affected by the units of measurement for x and y is the **correlation coefficient**.

Correlation Coefficient

For sample data, the **Pearson product moment correlation coefficient** is defined as follows:

Pearson Product Moment Correlation Coefficient: Sample Data

$$r_{xy} = \frac{s_{xy}}{s_x s_y} \tag{3.15}$$

where

r_{xy} = sample correlation coefficient
s_{xy} = sample covariance
s_x = sample standard deviation of x
s_y = sample standard deviation of y

Figure 3.17 Interpretation of Sample Covariance

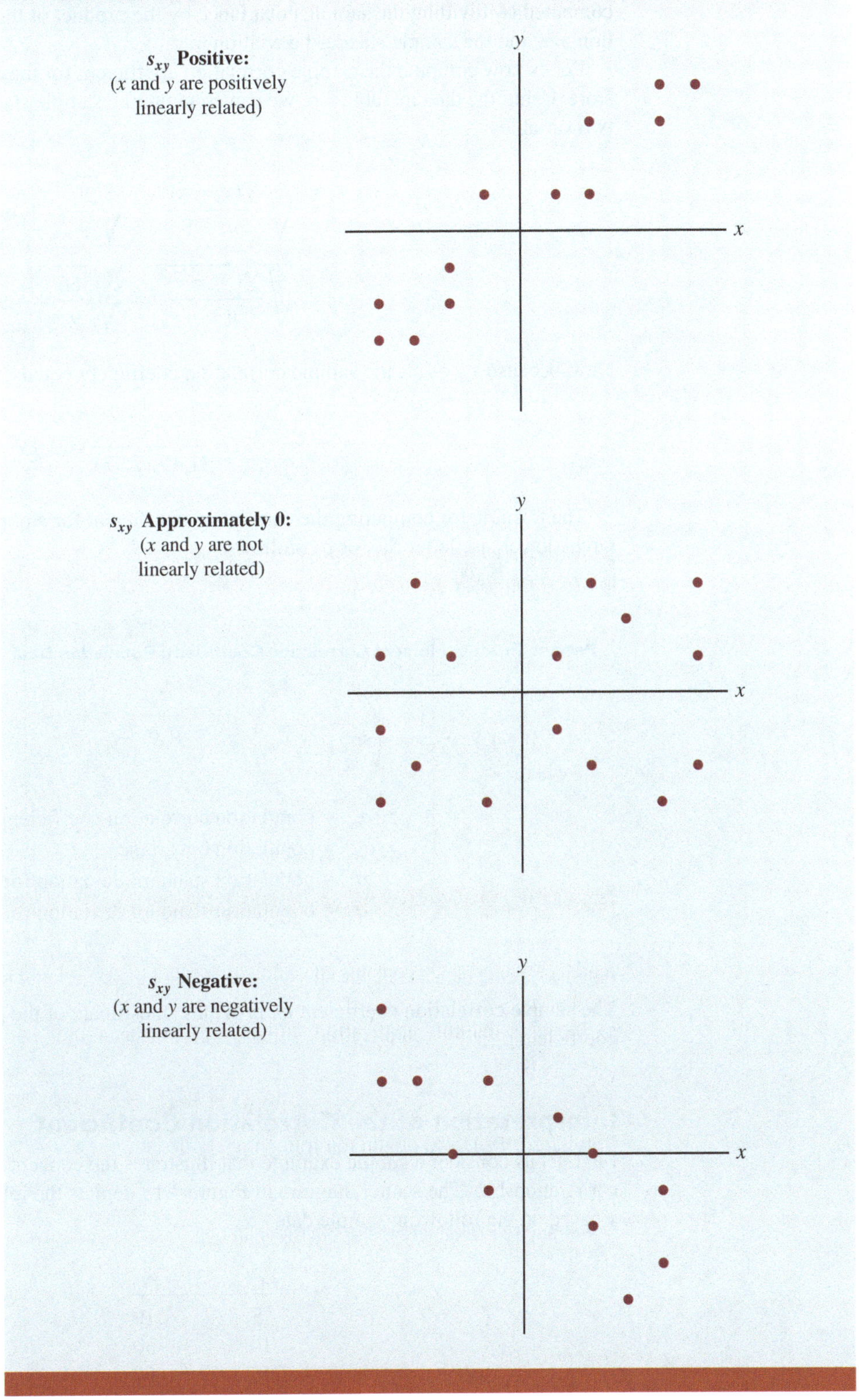

Equation (3.15) shows that the Pearson product moment correlation coefficient for sample data (commonly referred to more simply as the *sample correlation coefficient*) is computed by dividing the sample covariance by the product of the sample standard deviation of x and the sample standard deviation of y.

Let us now compute the sample correlation coefficient for the San Francisco electronics store. Using the data in Table 3.6, we can compute the sample standard deviations for the two variables:

$$s_x = \sqrt{\frac{\Sigma(x_i - \bar{x})^2}{n - 1}} = \sqrt{\frac{20}{9}} = 1.49$$

$$s_y = \sqrt{\frac{\Sigma(y_i - \bar{y})^2}{n - 1}} = \sqrt{\frac{566}{9}} = 7.93$$

Now, because $s_{xy} = 11$, the sample correlation coefficient equals

$$r_{xy} = \frac{s_{xy}}{s_x s_y} = \frac{11}{(1.49)(7.93)} = 0.93$$

The formula for computing the correlation coefficient for a population, denoted by the Greek lowercase letter rho, or ρ_{xy}, follows.

Pearson Product Moment Correlation Coefficient: Population Data

$$\rho_{xy} = \frac{\sigma_{xy}}{\sigma_x \sigma_y} \tag{3.16}$$

where

ρ_{xy} = population correlation coefficient
σ_{xy} = population covariance
σ_x = population standard deviation for x
σ_y = population standard deviation for y

The sample correlation coefficient r_{xy} provides an estimate of the population correlation coefficient ρ_{xy}.

Interpretation of the Correlation Coefficient

First, let us consider a simple example that illustrates the concept of a perfect positive linear relationship. The scatter diagram in Figure 3.18 depicts the relationship between x and y based on the following sample data.

x_i	y_i
5	10
10	30
15	50

The straight line drawn through each of the three points shows a perfect linear relationship between x and y. In order to apply equation (3.15) to compute the sample correlation, we must first compute s_{xy}, s_x, and s_y. Some of the computations are shown in Table 3.8.

Figure 3.18 Scatter Diagram Depicting a Perfect Positive Linear Relationship

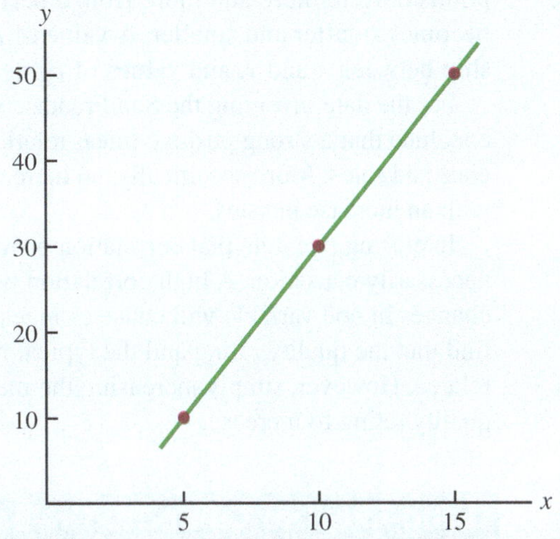

Table 3.8 Computations Used in Calculating the Sample Correlation Coefficient

	x_i	y_i	$x_i - \bar{x}$	$(x_i - \bar{x})^2$	$y_i - \bar{y}$	$(y_i - \bar{y})^2$	$(x_i - \bar{x})(y_i - \bar{y})$
	5	10	−5	25	−20	400	100
	10	30	0	0	0	0	0
	15	50	5	25	20	400	100
Totals	30	90	0	50	0	800	200
	$\bar{x} = 10$	$\bar{y} = 30$					

Using the results in this table, we find

$$s_{xy} = \frac{\Sigma(x_i - \bar{x})(y_i - \bar{y})}{n - 1} = \frac{200}{2} = 100$$

$$s_x = \sqrt{\frac{\Sigma(x_i - \bar{x})^2}{n - 1}} = \sqrt{\frac{50}{2}} = 5$$

$$s_y = \sqrt{\frac{\Sigma(y_i - \bar{y})^2}{n - 1}} = \sqrt{\frac{800}{2}} = 20$$

$$r_{xy} = \frac{s_{xy}}{s_x s_y} = \frac{100}{5(20)} = 1$$

Thus, we see that the value of the sample correlation coefficient is 1.

The correlation coefficient ranges from −1 to +1. Values close to −1 or +1 indicate a strong linear relationship. The closer the correlation is to zero, the weaker the relationship.

In general, it can be shown that if all the points in a data set fall on a positively sloped straight line, the value of the sample correlation coefficient is +1; that is, a sample correlation coefficient of +1 corresponds to a perfect positive linear relationship between x and y. Moreover, if the points in the data set fall on a straight line having a negative slope, the value of the sample correlation coefficient is −1; that is, a sample correlation coefficient of −1 corresponds to a perfect negative linear relationship between x and y.

Let us now suppose that a certain data set indicates a positive linear relationship between x and y but that the relationship is not perfect. The value of r_{xy} will be less than 1, indicating that the points in the scatter diagram are not all on a straight line. As the points deviate more and more from a perfect positive linear relationship, the value of r_{xy} becomes smaller and smaller. A value of r_{xy} equal to zero indicates no linear relationship between x and y, and values of r_{xy} near zero indicate a weak linear relationship.

For the data involving the San Francisco electronics store, $r_{xy} = 0.93$. Therefore, we conclude that a strong positive linear relationship occurs between the number of commercials and sales. More specifically, an increase in the number of commercials is associated with an increase in sales.

In closing, we note that correlation provides a measure of linear association and not necessarily causation. A high correlation between two variables does not mean that changes in one variable will cause changes in the other variable. For example, we may find that the quality rating and the typical meal price of restaurants are positively correlated. However, simply increasing the meal price at a restaurant will not cause the quality rating to increase.

Using Excel to Compute the Sample Covariance and Sample Correlation Coefficient

Excel provides functions that can be used to compute the covariance and correlation coefficient. We illustrate the use of these functions by computing the sample covariance and the sample correlation coefficient for the San Francisco electronics data in Table 3.6. Refer to Figure 3.19 as we describe the tasks involved. The formula worksheet is in the background; the value worksheet is in the foreground.

DATA*file*
electronics

Enter/Access Data: Open the file *electronics*. The data are in cells B2:C11 and labels are in column A and cells B1:C1.

Enter Functions and Formulas: Excel's COVARIANCE.S function can be used to compute the sample covariance by entering the following formula in cell F2:

$$=COVARIANCE.S(B2{:}B11,C2{:}C11)$$

Similarly, the formula $=CORREL(B2{:}B11,C2{:}C11)$ is entered in cell F3 to compute the sample correlation coefficient.

The labels in cells E2:E3 identify the output. Note that the sample covariance (11) and the sample correlation coefficient (0.93) are the same as we computed earlier using the definitions.

Figure 3.19 Using Excel to Compute the Covariance and Correlation Coefficient

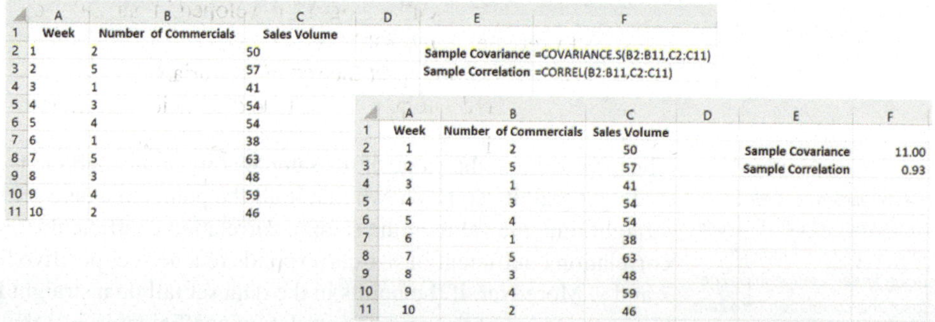

Notes + Comments

1. Because the correlation coefficient measures only the strength of the linear relationship between two quantitative variables, it is possible for the correlation coefficient to be near zero, suggesting no linear relationship, when the relationship between the two variables is nonlinear. For example, the following scatter diagram shows the relationship between the amount spent by a small retail store for environmental control (heating and cooling) and the daily high outside temperature over 100 days.

   The sample correlation coefficient for these data is $r_{xy} = -0.007$ and indicates there is no linear relationship between the two variables. However, the scatter diagram provides strong visual evidence of a nonlinear relationship. That is, we can see that as the daily high outside temperature increases, the money spent on environmental control first decreases as less heating is required and then increases as greater cooling is required.
2. While the correlation coefficient is useful in assessing the relationship between two quantitative variables, other measures—such as the Spearman rank-correlation coefficient—can be used to assess a relationship between two variables when at least one of the variables is nominal or ordinal. We discuss the use of the Spearman rank-correlation coefficient in Chapter 18.

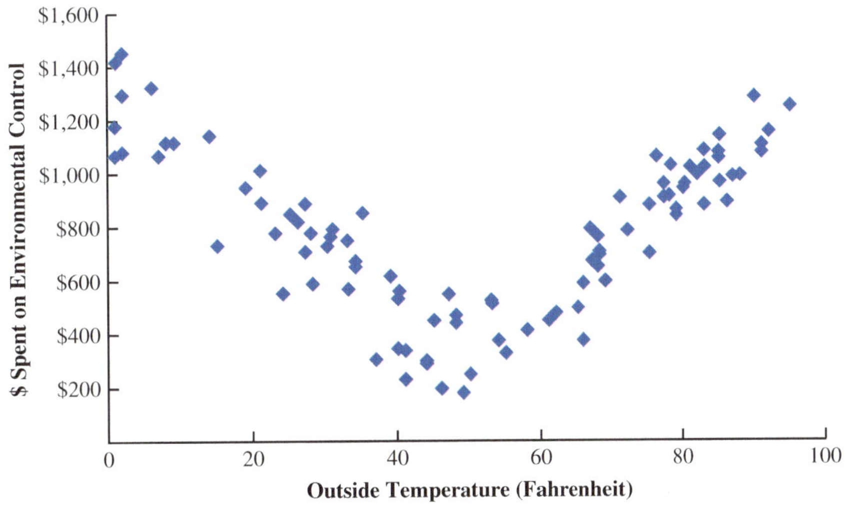

Exercises

Methods

55. Five observations taken for two variables follow. **LO 9**

x_i	4	6	11	3	16
y_i	50	50	40	60	30

   a. Develop a scatter diagram with x on the horizontal axis.
   b. What does the scatter diagram developed in part (a) indicate about the relationship between the two variables?
   c. Compute and interpret the sample covariance.
   d. Compute and interpret the sample correlation coefficient.

56. Five observations taken for two variables follow. **LO 9**

x_i	6	11	15	21	27
y_i	6	9	6	17	12

   a. Develop a scatter diagram for these data.
   b. What does the scatter diagram indicate about a relationship between x and y?
   c. Compute and interpret the sample covariance.
   d. Compute and interpret the sample correlation coefficient.

Applications

DATA*file* stockcomparison

57. **Stock Price Comparison.** The file *stockcomparison* contains monthly adjusted stock prices for technology company Apple, Inc., and consumer-goods company Procter & Gamble (P&G) from 2013 to 2018. LO 9
    a. Develop a scatter diagram with Apple stock price on the horizontal axis and P&G stock price on the vertical axis.
    b. What appears to be the relationship between these two stock prices?
    c. Compute and interpret the sample covariance.
    d. Compute the sample correlation coefficient. What does this value indicate about the relationship between the stock price of Apple and the stock price of P&G?

58. **Driving Speed and Fuel Efficiency.** A department of transportation's study on driving speed and miles per gallon for midsize automobiles resulted in the data that follows.

Speed (Miles per Hour)	30	50	40	55	30	25	60	25	50	55
Miles per Gallon	28	25	25	23	30	32	21	35	26	25

Compute and interpret the sample correlation coefficient. LO 9

DATA*file* smokedetectors

59. **Smoke Detector Use and Death Rates.** Over the past 40 years, the percentage of homes in the United States with smoke detectors has risen steadily and has plateaued at about 96% as of 2015 (*National Fire Protection Association* website). With this increase in the use of home smoke detectors, what has happened to the death rate from home fires? The file *smokedetectors* contains 17 years of data on the estimated percentage of homes with smoke detectors and the estimated home fire deaths per million of population. LO 9
    a. Do you expect a positive or negative relationship between smoke detector use and deaths from home fires? Why or why not?
    b. Compute and report the correlation coefficient. Is there a positive or negative correlation between smoke detector use and deaths from home fires? Comment.
    c. Show a scatter plot of the death rate per million of population and the percentage of homes with smoke detectors.

DATA*file* nasdaqdow

60. **Nasdaq Composite and Dow Jones Industrial Average Indexes Comparison.** The Nasdaq Composite is a stock market index based on the stock prices of nearly 3,500 companies that include many technology-based companies. The Dow Jones Industrial Average is based on 30 large companies. The file *nasdaqdow* gives the daily percentage returns for each of these stock indexes in 2021. LO 1, 3, 9
    a. Plot these percentage returns of the Nasdaq versus the percentage return of the Dow Jones using a scatter plot.
    b. Compute the sample mean and standard deviation for each index.
    c. Compute the sample correlation.
    d. Discuss similarities and differences in these two indexes.

DATA*file* bestprivatecolleges

61. **Best Private Colleges.** A random sample of 30 colleges from Kiplinger's list of the best values in private college provided the data shown in the file *bestprivatecolleges* (Kiplinger website). The variable Admit Rate (%) shows the percentage of students that applied to the college and were admitted, and the variable 4-yr Grad. Rate (%) shows the percentage of students that were admitted and graduated in four years. LO 9
    a. Develop a scatter diagram with Admit Rate (%) as the independent variable. What does the scatter diagram indicate about the relationship between the two variables?
    b. Compute the sample correlation coefficient. What does the value of the sample correlation coefficient indicate about the relationship between the Admit Rate (%) and the 4-yr Grad. Rate (%)?

3.6 Data Dashboards: Adding Numerical Measures to Improve Effectiveness

In Section 2.6, we provided an introduction to data visualization, a term used to describe the use of graphical displays to summarize and present information about a data set. The goal of data visualization is to communicate key information about the data as effectively and clearly as possible. One of the most widely used data visualization tools is a data dashboard, a set of visual displays that organizes and presents information that is used to monitor the performance of a company or organization in a manner that is easy to read, understand, and interpret. In this section, we extend the discussion of data dashboards to show how the addition of numerical measures can improve the overall effectiveness of the display.

The addition of numerical measures, such as the mean and standard deviation of key performance indicators (KPIs), to a data dashboard is critical because numerical measures often provide benchmarks or goals by which KPIs are evaluated. In addition, graphical displays that include numerical measures as components of the display are also frequently included in data dashboards. We must keep in mind that the purpose of a data dashboard is to provide information on the KPIs in a manner that is easy to read, understand, and interpret. Adding numerical measures and graphs that utilize numerical measures can help us accomplish these objectives.

DATA*file*
grogan

To illustrate the use of numerical measures in a data dashboard, recall the Grogan Oil Company application that we used in Section 2.6 to introduce the concept of a data dashboard. Grogan Oil has offices located in three cities in Texas: Austin (its headquarters), Houston, and Dallas. Grogan's Information Technology (IT) call center, located in the Austin office, handles calls regarding computer-related problems (software, Internet, and e-mail) from employees in the three offices. Figure 3.20 shows the data dashboard that Grogan developed to monitor the performance of the call center. The key components of this dashboard are as follows:

- The stacked bar chart in the upper left corner of the dashboard shows the call volume for each type of problem (software, Internet, or e-mail) over time.
- The bar chart in the upper-right corner of the dashboard shows the percentage of time that call center employees spent on each type of problem or not working on a call (idle).
- For each unresolved case that extended beyond 15 minutes, the bar chart shown in the middle-left portion of the dashboard shows the length of time that each of these cases has been unresolved.
- The bar chart in the middle-right portion of the dashboard shows the call volume by office (Houston, Dallas, Austin) for each type of problem.
- The histogram at the bottom of the dashboard shows the distribution of the time to resolve a case for all resolved cases for the current shift.

In order to gain additional insight into the performance of the call center, Grogan's IT manager has decided to expand the current dashboard by adding boxplots for the time required to resolve calls received for each type of problem (e-mail, Internet, and software). In addition, a graph showing the time to resolve individual cases has been added in the lower left portion of the dashboard. Finally, the IT manager added a display of summary statistics for each type of problem and summary statistics for each of the first few hours of the shift. The updated dashboard is shown in Figure 3.21.

The IT call center has set a target performance level or benchmark of 10 minutes for the mean time to resolve a case. Furthermore, the center has decided it is undesirable for the time to resolve a case to exceed 15 minutes. To reflect these benchmarks, a black horizontal line at the mean target value of 10 minutes and a red horizontal line at the maximum acceptable level of 15 minutes have been added to both the graph showing

Figure 3.20 Initial Grogan Oil Information Technology Call Center Data Dashboard

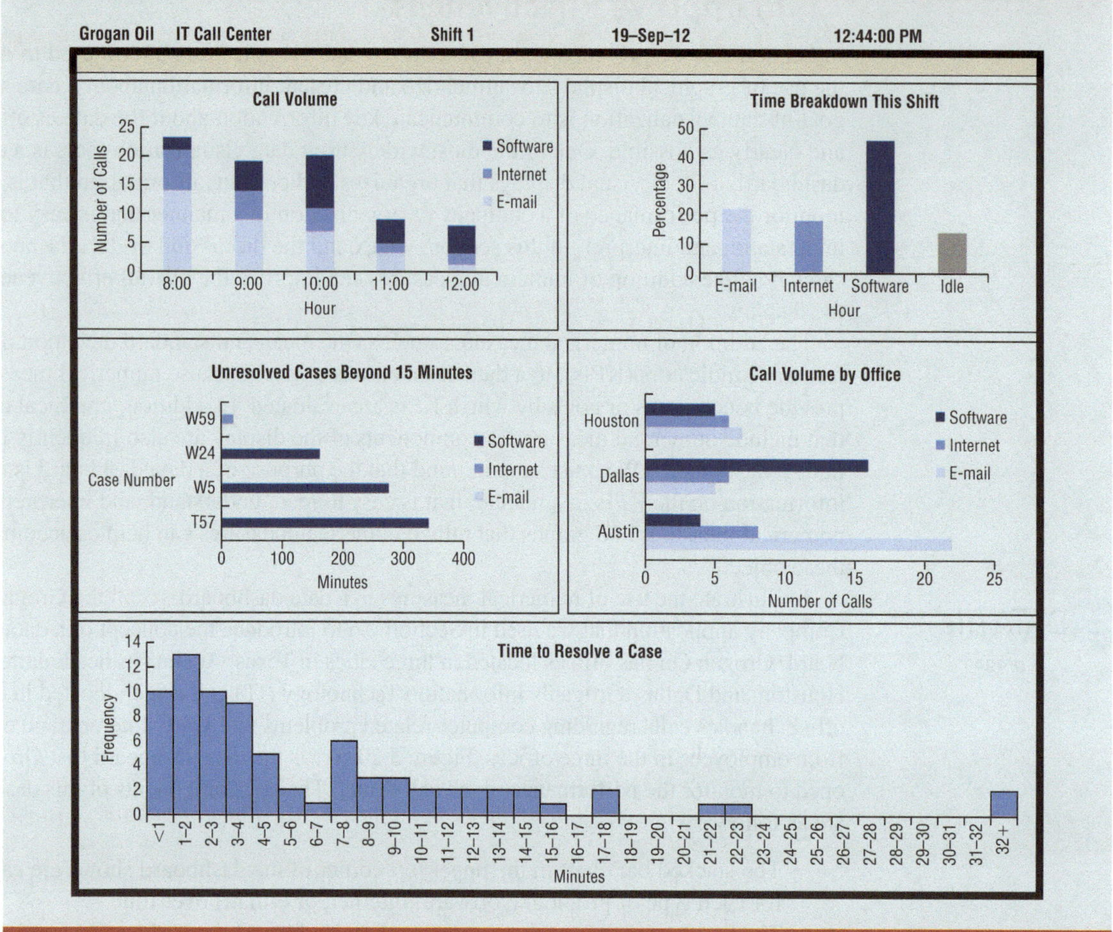

the time to resolve cases and the boxplots of the time required to resolve calls received for each type of problem.

The summary statistics in the dashboard in Figure 3.21 show that the mean time to resolve an e-mail case is 5.8 minutes, the mean time to resolve an Internet case is 3.0 minutes, and the mean time to resolve a software case is 5.4 minutes. Thus, the mean time to resolve each type of case is better than the target mean (10 minutes).

Reviewing the boxplots, we see that the box associated with the e-mail cases is *larger* than the boxes associated with the other two types of cases. The summary statistics also show that the standard deviation of the time to resolve e-mail cases is larger than the standard deviations of the times to resolve the other types of cases. This leads us to take a closer look at the e-mail cases in the two new graphs. The boxplot for the e-mail cases has a whisker that extends beyond 15 minutes and an outlier well beyond 15 minutes. The graph of the time to resolve individual cases (in the lower left position of the dashboard) shows that this is because of two calls on e-mail cases during the 9:00 hour that took longer than the target maximum time (15 minutes) to resolve. This analysis may lead the IT call center manager to further investigate why resolution times are more variable for e-mail cases than for Internet or software cases. Based on this analysis, the IT manager may also decide to investigate the circumstances that led to inordinately long resolution times for the two e-mail cases that took longer than 15 minutes to resolve.

Figure 3.21 Updated Grogan Oil Information Technology Call Center Data Dashboard

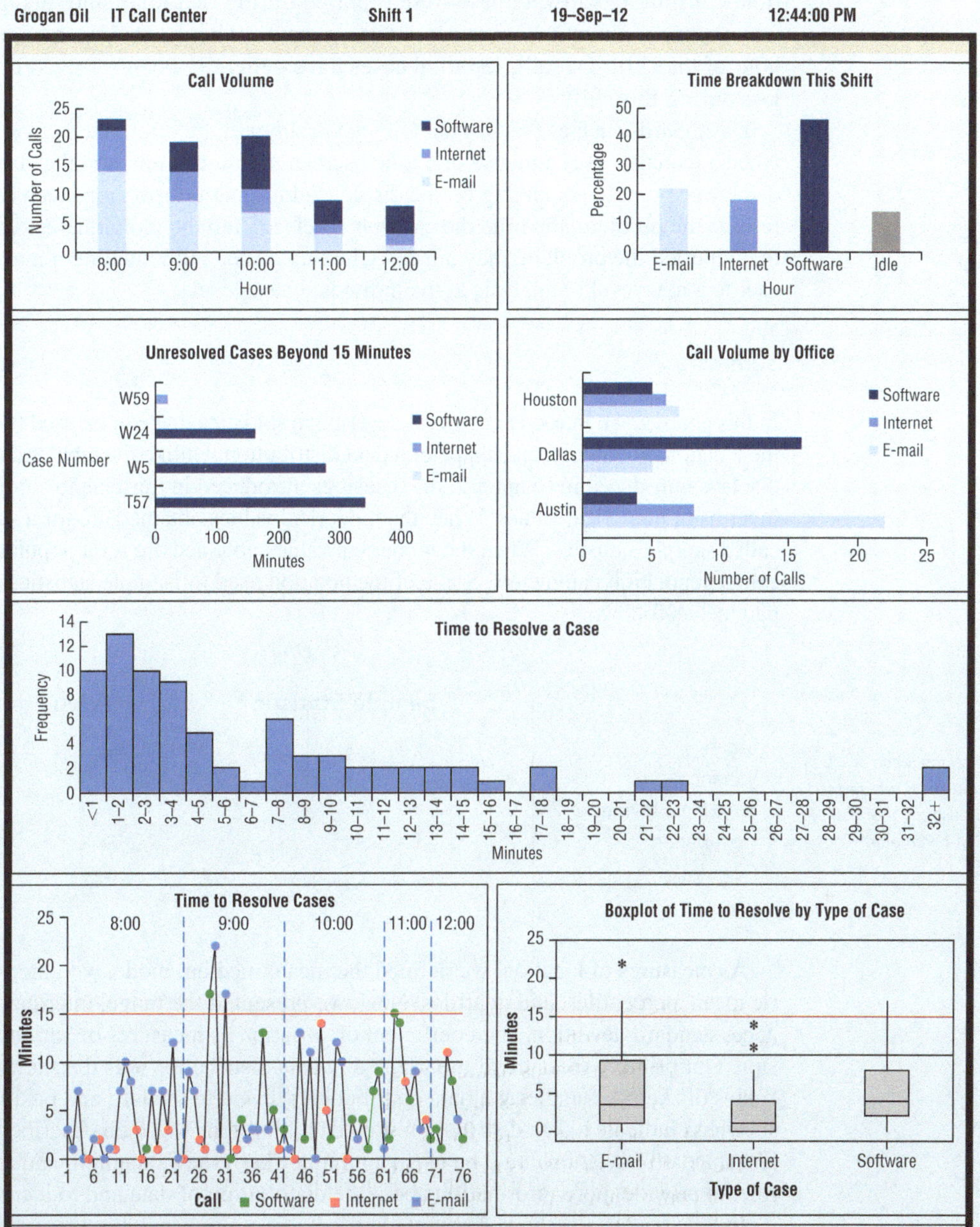

Type of Case	Cases	Mean	Median	Std. Dev
E-mail	34	5.8	3.5	5.4
Internet	19	3.0	1.0	4.0
Software	23	5.4	4.0	5.0

Hour	Cases	Mean	Median	Std. Dev
8:00	22	3.5	2.0	3.7
9:00	19	5.8	3.0	6.6
10:00	19	5.3	4.0	4.8
11:00	9	6.9	6.0	5.1
12:00	6	4.8	3.5	3.9

The graph of the time to resolve individual cases also shows that most calls received during the first hour of the shift were resolved relatively quickly; the graph also shows that the time to resolve cases increased gradually throughout the morning. This could be due to a tendency for complex problems to arise later in the shift or possibly to the backlog of calls that accumulates over time. Although the summary statistics suggest that cases submitted during the 9:00 hour take the longest to resolve, the graph of time to resolve individual cases shows that two time-consuming e-mail cases and one time-consuming software case were reported during that hour, and this may explain why the mean time to resolve cases during the 9:00 hour is larger than during any other hour of the shift. Overall, reported cases have generally been resolved in 15 minutes or less during this shift.

Drilling down refers to functionality in interactive data dashboards that allows the user to access information and analyses at an increasingly detailed level.

Dashboards such as the Grogan Oil data dashboard are often interactive. For instance, when a manager uses a mouse or a touch screen monitor to position the cursor over the display or point to something on the display, additional information, such as the time to resolve the problem, the time the call was received, and the individual and/or the location that reported the problem, may appear. Clicking on the individual item may also take the user to a new level of analysis at the individual case level.

Summary

In this chapter, we introduced several descriptive statistics that can be used to summarize the location, variability, and shape of a data distribution. Unlike the tabular and graphical displays introduced in Chapter 2, the measures introduced in this chapter summarize the data in terms of numerical values. When the numerical values obtained are for a sample, they are called sample statistics. When the numerical values obtained are for a population, they are called population parameters. Some of the notation used for sample statistics and population parameters follow.

In statistical inference, a sample statistic is referred to as a point estimator of the population parameter.

	Sample Statistic	Population Parameter
Mean	$\bar{x}$	μ
Variance	s^2	σ^2
Standard deviation	s	σ
Covariance	s_{xy}	σ_{xy}
Correlation	r_{xy}	ρ_{xy}

As measures of location, we defined the mean, median, mode, weighted mean, geometric mean, percentiles, and quartiles. Next, we presented the range, interquartile range, variance, standard deviation, and coefficient of variation as measures of variability or dispersion. Our primary measure of the shape of a data distribution was the skewness. Negative values of skewness indicate a data distribution skewed to the left, and positive values of skewness indicate a data distribution skewed to the right. We then described how the mean and standard deviation could be used, applying Chebyshev's theorem and the empirical rule, to provide more information about the distribution of data and to identify outliers.

In Section 3.4, we showed how to develop a five-number summary and a boxplot to provide simultaneous information about the location, variability, and shape of the distribution. In Section 3.5, we introduced covariance and the correlation coefficient as measures of association between two variables. In the final section, we showed how adding numerical measures can improve the effectiveness of data dashboards.

The descriptive statistics we discussed can be developed using statistical software packages and spreadsheets.

Glossary

Boxplot A graphical summary of data based on a five-number summary.

Chebyshev's theorem A theorem that can be used to make statements about the proportion of data values that must be within a specified number of standard deviations of the mean.

Coefficient of variation A measure of relative variability computed by dividing the standard deviation by the mean and multiplying by 100.
Correlation coefficient A measure of linear association between two variables that takes on values between −1 and +1. Values near +1 indicate a strong positive linear relationship; values near −1 indicate a strong negative linear relationship; and values near zero indicate the lack of a linear relationship.
Covariance A measure of linear association between two variables. Positive values indicate a positive relationship; negative values indicate a negative relationship.
Empirical rule A rule that can be used to compute the percentage of data values that must be within one, two, and three standard deviations of the mean for data that exhibit a bell-shaped distribution.
Five-number summary A technique that uses five numbers to summarize the data: smallest value, first quartile, median, third quartile, and largest value.
Geometric mean A measure of location that is calculated by finding the *n*th root of the product of *n* values.
Interquartile range (IQR) A measure of variability, defined as the difference between the third and first quartiles.
Mean A measure of central location computed by summing the data values and dividing by the number of observations.
Median A measure of central location provided by the value in the middle when the data are arranged in ascending order.
Mode A measure of location defined as the value that occurs with greatest frequency.
Outlier An unusually small or unusually large data value.
Pearson product moment correlation coefficient A measure of the linear relationship between two variables.
Percentile A value that provides information about how the data are spread over the interval from the smallest to the largest value.
Point estimator A sample statistic, such as $\bar{x}$, s^2, and s, used to estimate the corresponding population parameter.
Population parameter A numerical value used as a summary measure for a population (e.g., the population mean, μ, the population variance, σ^2, and the population standard deviation, σ).
***p*th percentile** For a data set containing n observations, the pth percentile divides the data into two parts: Approximately p% of the observation are less than the pth percentile and approximately $(100 - p)$% of the observations are greater than the pth percentile.
Quartiles The 25th, 50th, and 75th percentiles, referred to as the first quartile, the second quartile (median), and third quartile, respectively. The quartiles can be used to divide a data set into four parts, with each part containing approximately 25% of the data.
Range A measure of variability, defined to be the largest value minus the smallest value.
Sample statistic A numerical value used as a summary measure for a sample (e.g., the sample mean, $\bar{x}$, the sample variance, s^2, and the sample standard deviation, s).
Skewness A measure of the shape of a data distribution. Data skewed to the left result in negative skewness; a symmetric data distribution results in zero skewness; and data skewed to the right result in positive skewness.
Standard deviation A measure of variability computed by taking the positive square root of the variance.
Variance A measure of variability based on the squared deviations of the data values about the mean.
Weighted mean The mean obtained by assigning each observation a weight that reflects its importance.
***z*-score** A value computed by dividing the deviation about the mean $(x_i - \bar{x})$ by the standard deviation s. A z-score is referred to as a standardized value and denotes the number of standard deviations x_i is from the mean.

Key Formulas

Sample Mean

$$\bar{x} = \frac{\Sigma x_i}{n} \tag{3.1}$$

Population Mean

$$\mu = \frac{\Sigma x_i}{N} \tag{3.2}$$

Weighted Mean

$$\bar{x} = \frac{\Sigma w_i x_i}{\Sigma w_i} \tag{3.3}$$

Geometric Mean

$$\bar{x}_g = \sqrt[n]{(x_1)(x_2)\cdots(x_n)} = [(x_1)(x_2)\cdots(x_n)]^{1/n} \tag{3.4}$$

Location of the *p*th Percentile

$$L_p = \frac{p}{100}(n + 1) \tag{3.5}$$

Interquartile Range

$$\text{IQR} = Q_3 - Q_1 \tag{3.6}$$

Population Variance

$$\sigma^2 = \frac{\Sigma(x_i - \mu)^2}{N} \tag{3.7}$$

Sample Variance

$$s^2 = \frac{\Sigma(x_i - \bar{x})^2}{n - 1} \tag{3.8}$$

Sample Standard Deviation

$$s = \sqrt{s^2} \tag{3.9}$$

Population Standard Deviation

$$\sigma = \sqrt{\sigma^2} \tag{3.10}$$

Coefficient of Variation

$$\left(\frac{\text{Standard deviation}}{\text{Mean}} \times 100\right)\% \tag{3.11}$$

***z*-Score**

$$z_i = \frac{x_i - \bar{x}}{s} \tag{3.12}$$

Sample Covariance

$$s_{xy} = \frac{\Sigma(x_i - \bar{x})(y_i - \bar{y})}{n - 1} \tag{3.13}$$

Population Covariance

$$\sigma_{xy} = \frac{\Sigma(x_i - \mu_x)(y_i - \mu_y)}{N} \tag{3.14}$$

Pearson Product Moment Correlation Coefficient: Sample Data

$$r_{xy} = \frac{s_{xy}}{s_x s_y} \tag{3.15}$$

Pearson Product Moment Correlation Coefficient: Population Data

$$\rho_{xy} = \frac{\sigma_{xy}}{\sigma_x \sigma_y} \tag{3.16}$$

Supplementary Exercises

62. **Americans Dining Out.** Americans tend to dine out multiple times per week. The number of times a sample of 20 families dined out last week provides the following data. **LO 1, 2, 3, 6**

6	1	5	3	7	3	0	3	1	3
4	1	2	4	1	0	5	6	3	1

   a. Compute the mean and median.
   b. Compute the first and third quartiles.
   c. Compute the range and interquartile range.
   d. Compute the variance and standard deviation.
   e. The skewness measure for these data is 0.34. Comment on the shape of this distribution. Is it the shape you would expect? Why or why not?
   f. Do the data contain outliers?

63. **NCAA Football Coaches' Salaries.** A *USA Today* article reports that NCAA football coaches' salaries have continued to increase (*USA Today*). The annual base salaries for the previous head football coach and the new head football coach at 23 schools are given in the file *coaches*. **LO 1, 3**

DATA*file*
coaches

   a. Determine the median annual salary for a previous head football coach and a new head football coach.
   b. Compute the range for salaries for both previous and new head football coaches.
   c. Compute the standard deviation for salaries for both previous and new head football coaches.
   d. Based on your answers to (a) to (c), comment on any differences between the annual base salary a school pays a new head football coach compared to what it paid its previous head football coach.

64. **Physician Office Waiting Times.** The average waiting time for a patient at an El Paso physician's office is just over 29 minutes, well above the national average of 21 minutes. In order to address the issue of long patient wait times, some physician's offices are using wait tracking systems to notify patients of expected wait times. Patients can adjust their arrival times based on this information and spend less time in waiting rooms. The following data show wait times (minutes) for a sample of patients at offices that do not have an office tracking system and wait times for a sample of patients at offices with an office tracking system. **LO 1, 3, 4, 6**

DATA*file*
waittracking

Without Wait Tracking System	With Wait Tracking System
24	31
67	11
17	14
20	18
31	12
44	37
12	9
23	13
16	12
37	15

a. What are the mean and median patient wait times for offices with a wait tracking system? What are the mean and median patient wait times for offices without a wait tracking system?
b. What are the variance and standard deviation of patient wait times for offices with a wait tracking system? What are the variance and standard deviation of patient wait times for visits to offices without a wait tracking system?
c. Do offices with a wait tracking system have shorter patient wait times than offices without a wait tracking system? Explain.
d. Considering only offices without a wait tracking system, what is the z-score for the tenth patient in the sample?
e. Considering only offices with a wait tracking system, what is the z-score for the sixth patient in the sample? How does this z-score compare with the z-score you calculated for part (d)?
f. Based on z-scores, do the data for offices without a wait tracking system contain any outliers? Based on z-scores, do the data for offices with a wait tracking system contain any outliers?

65. **Worker Productivity and Insomnia.** According to a 2022 article from the Sleep Foundation, sleep deprivation of workers in the United States results in productivity losses of more than $136 billion per year. The following data show the number of hours of sleep attained during a recent night for a sample of 20 workers. **LO 1, 3**

DATA*file*
sleep

6	5	10	5	6	9	9	5	9	5
8	7	8	6	9	8	9	6	10	8

a. What is the mean number of hours of sleep for this sample?
b. What is the variance? Standard deviation?

66. **Smartphone Use.** Consider the following data indicating the number of minutes in a month spent interacting with others via a smartphone for a sample of 50 smartphone users. **LO 1, 3, 6**

DATA*file*
smartphone

353	458	404	394	416
437	430	369	448	430
431	469	446	387	445
354	468	422	402	360
444	424	441	357	435
461	407	470	413	351
464	374	417	460	352
445	387	468	368	430
384	367	436	390	464
405	372	401	388	367

a. What is the mean number of minutes spent interacting with others for this sample? How does it compare to the mean reported in the study?
b. What is the standard deviation for this sample?
c. Are there any outliers in this sample?

67. **Work Commuting Methods.** Public transportation and the automobile are two methods an employee can use to get to work each day. Samples of travel times recorded for each method are shown. Times are in minutes. **LO 1, 3, 8**

DATA*file*
transportation

Public Transportation:	28	29	32	37	33	25	29	32	41	34
Automobile:	29	31	33	32	34	30	31	32	35	33

a. Compute the sample mean time to get to work for each method.
b. Compute the sample standard deviation for each method.

c. On the basis of your results from parts (a) and (b), which method of transportation should be preferred? Explain.
d. Develop a boxplot for each method. Does a comparison of the boxplots support your conclusion in part (c)?

68. The following data represent a sample of 14 household incomes ($1,000s). Answer the following questions based on this sample. **LO 1, 2, 4, 6, 7**

49.4	52.4	53.4	51.3	52.1	48.7	52.1
52.2	64.5	51.6	46.5	52.9	52.5	51.2

a. What is the median household income for these sample data?
b. According to a previous survey, the median annual household income five years ago was $55,000. Based on the sample data above, estimate the percentage change in the median household income from five years ago to today.
c. Compute the first and third quartiles of the sample data.
d. Provide a five-number summary for the sample data.
e. Using the z-score approach, do the data contain any outliers? Does the approach that uses the values of the first and third quartiles and the interquartile range to detect outliers provide the same results?

DATA*file*
foodindustry

69. **Restaurant Chains' Sales per Store.** The data contained in the file *foodindustry* show the company/chain name, the average sales per store ($1,000s), and the food segment industry for 47 restaurant chains (*Quick Service Restaurant Magazine* website). **LO 1, 2, 7**
a. What is the mean U.S. sales per store for the 47 restaurant chains?
b. What are the first and third quartiles? What is your interpretation of the quartiles?
c. Show a boxplot for the level of sales and discuss if there are any outliers in terms of sales that would skew the results.
d. Develop a frequency distribution showing the average sales per store for each segment. Comment on the results obtained.

70. **Best Hotels.** *Travel + Leisure* magazine presented its annual list of the 500 best hotels in the world. The magazine provides a rating for each hotel along with a brief description that includes the size of the hotel, amenities, and the cost per night for a double room. A sample of 12 of the top-rated hotels in the United States follows. **LO 1, 9**

DATA*file*
travel

Hotel	Location	Rooms	Cost/Night ($)
Boulders Resort & Spa	Phoenix, AZ	220	499
Disney's Wilderness Lodge	Orlando, FL	727	340
Four Seasons Hotel Beverly Hills	Los Angeles, CA	285	585
Four Seasons Hotel	Boston, MA	273	495
Hay-Adams	Washington, DC	145	495
Inn on Biltmore Estate	Asheville, NC	213	279
Loews Ventana Canyon Resort	Phoenix, AZ	398	279
Mauna Lani Bay Hotel	Island of Hawaii	343	455
Montage Laguna Beach	Laguna Beach, CA	250	595
Sofitel Water Tower	Chicago, IL	414	367
St. Regis Monarch Beach	Dana Point, CA	400	675
The Broadmoor	Colorado Springs, CO	700	420

a. What is the mean number of rooms?
b. What is the mean cost per night for a double room?
c. Develop a scatter diagram with the number of rooms on the horizontal axis and the cost per night on the vertical axis. Does there appear to be a relationship between the number of rooms and the cost per night? Discuss.

d. What is the sample correlation coefficient? What does it tell you about the relationship between the number of rooms and the cost per night for a double room? Does this appear reasonable? Discuss.

71. **Dow Jones Industrial Average Companies Market Capitalizations and Revenues.** The market capitalization of a publicly traded company is calculated by multiplying the number of existing shares of stock for the company by the price per share. The table below displays the market capitalizations and the 2020 fiscal year revenues (both in $ billion) for the 30 companies that were included in the Dow Jones Industrial (DJI) Average stock index (Google Finance website). Use the data in this table to answer the following questions. **LO 1, 3, 6, 8, 9**

DATA*file*
marketcaprevenue

Company	Market Capitalization ($ billions)	2020 Fiscal Year Revenue ($ billions)
3M	102	32.2
American Express	130	36.1
Amgen	126	25.4
Apple	2,950	274.3
Boeing	119	58.2
Caterpillar	111	41.7
Chevron	228	94.5
Cisco	267	49.8
Coca-Cola	253	33
Dow	41	39
Goldman Sachs	130	44.6
Home Depot	421	132.1
Honeywell	142	32.7
IBM	118	73.6
Intel	210	77.9
Johnson & Johnson	445	82.6
JPMorgan Chase	466	123
McDonald's	200	19.2
Merck	192	48
Microsoft	2,560	44.3
Nike	264	37.4
P&G	392	76.1
Salesforce	252	17.1
Travelers	38	32
UnitedHealth	469	257
Verizon	218	23.9
Visa	458	21.8
Walgreens Boots Alliance	44	34.4
Walmart	389	141.7
Walt Disney	277	65.4

a. Calculate the mean and standard deviation for the market capitalizations and for the 2020 fiscal year revenues for the 30 companies included in the DJI.

b. Calculate the coefficient of variation for the market capitalization and for the 2020 fiscal year revenue. Which variable has the higher coefficient of variation?

c. Construct a boxplot for the market capitalization values. Are there any outliers for the market capitalization values?

d. Construct a boxplot for the 2020 fiscal year revenue values. Are there any outliers for the 2020 fiscal year revenue values? If so, are the companies that are outliers for 2020 fiscal year revenue values the same as the companies that are outliers for the market capitalization values?

e. Calculate the sample correlation coefficient for market capitalization and 2020 fiscal year revenues. What does this sample correlation coefficient value indicate about market capitalization and 2020 fiscal year revenues?

72. **Major League Baseball Team Winning Percentages.** Does a major league baseball team's record during spring training indicate how the team will play during the regular season? Over a six-year period, the correlation coefficient between a team's winning percentage in spring training and its winning percentage in the regular season is 0.18. Shown are the winning percentages for the 14 American League teams during a previous season. **LO 9**

DATA*file*
springtraining

Team	Spring Training	Regular Season	Team	Spring Training	Regular Season
Baltimore Orioles	0.407	0.422	Minnesota Twins	0.500	0.540
Boston Red Sox	0.429	0.586	New York Yankees	0.577	0.549
Chicago White Sox	0.417	0.546	Oakland A's	0.692	0.466
Cleveland Indians	0.569	0.500	Seattle Mariners	0.500	0.377
Detroit Tigers	0.569	0.457	Tampa Bay Rays	0.731	0.599
Kansas City Royals	0.533	0.463	Texas Rangers	0.643	0.488
Los Angeles Angels	0.724	0.617	Toronto Blue Jays	0.448	0.531

a. What is the correlation coefficient between the spring training and the regular season winning percentages?
b. What is your conclusion about a team's record during spring training indicating how the team will play during the regular season? What are some of the reasons why this occurs? Discuss.

73. **Money Market Funds Days to Maturity.** The days to maturity for a sample of five money market funds are shown here. The dollar amounts invested in the funds are provided. Use the weighted mean to determine the mean number of days to maturity for dollars invested in these five money market funds. **LO 1**

Days to Maturity	Dollar Value ($ millions)
20	20
12	30
7	10
5	15
6	10

74. **Automobile Speeds.** Automobiles traveling on a road with a posted speed limit of 55 miles per hour are checked for speed by a state police radar system. Following is a frequency distribution of speeds. **LO 1, 3**
a. What is the mean speed of the automobiles traveling on this road?
b. Compute the variance and the standard deviation.

Speed (miles per hour)	Frequency
45–49	10
50–54	40
55–59	150
60–64	175
65–69	75
70–74	15
75–79	10
Total	475

75. **Annual Returns for Panama Railroad Company Stock.** The Panama Railroad Company was established in 1850 to construct a railroad across the isthmus that would allow fast and easy access between the Atlantic and Pacific Oceans. The following table provides annual returns for Panama Railroad stock from 1853 through 1880. **LO 1**

DATA*file*
panama_railroad

Year	Return on Panama Railroad Company Stock (%)
1853	−1
1854	−9
1855	19
1856	2
1857	3
1858	36
1859	21
1860	16
1861	−5
1862	43
1863	44
1864	48
1865	7
1866	11
1867	23
1868	20
1869	−11
1870	−51
1871	−42
1872	39
1873	42
1874	12
1875	26
1876	9
1877	−6
1878	25
1879	31
1880	30

a. Create a graph of the annual returns on the stock. The New York Stock Exchange earned an annual average return of 8.4% from 1853 through 1880. Can you tell from the graph if the Panama Railroad Company stock outperformed the New York Stock Exchange?
b. Calculate the mean annual return on Panama Railroad Company stock from 1853 through 1880. Did the stock outperform the New York Stock Exchange over the same period?

Case Problem 1: Pelican Stores

Pelican Stores, a division of National Clothing, is a chain of women's apparel stores operating throughout the country. The chain recently ran a promotion in which discount coupons were sent to customers of other National Clothing stores. Data collected for a

Table 3.9 Sample of 100 Credit Card Purchases at Pelican Stores

Customer	Type of Customer	Items	Net Sales ($)	Method of Payment	College Graduate	Marital Status	Age
1	Regular	1	39.50	Discover	No	Married	32
2	Promotional	1	102.40	Proprietary Card	Yes	Married	36
3	Regular	1	22.50	Proprietary Card	Yes	Married	32
4	Promotional	5	100.40	Proprietary Card	Yes	Married	28
5	Regular	2	54.00	MasterCard	Yes	Married	34
.	.	.	.	.	.	.	.
.	.	.	.	.	.	.	.
.	.	.	.	.	.	.	.
96	Regular	1	39.50	MasterCard	Yes	Married	44
97	Promotional	9	253.00	Proprietary Card	Yes	Married	30
98	Promotional	10	287.59	Proprietary Card	Yes	Married	52
99	Promotional	2	47.60	Proprietary Card	Yes	Married	30
100	Promotional	1	28.44	Proprietary Card	Yes	Married	44

DATA*file*
pelicanstores

sample of 100 in-store credit card transactions at Pelican Stores during one day while the promotion was running are contained in the file *pelicanstores*. Table 3.9 shows a portion of the data set. The proprietary card method of payment refers to charges made using a National Clothing charge card. Customers who made a purchase using a discount coupon are referred to as promotional customers and customers who made a purchase but did not use a discount coupon are referred to as regular customers. Because the promotional coupons were not sent to regular Pelican Stores customers, management considers the sales made to people presenting the promotional coupons as sales it would not otherwise make. Of course, Pelican also hopes that the promotional customers will continue to shop at its stores.

Most of the variables shown in Table 3.9 are self-explanatory, but two of the variables require some clarification.

Items	The total number of items purchased
Net Sales	The total amount ($) charged to the credit card

Pelican's management would like to use this sample data to learn about its customer base and to evaluate the promotion involving discount coupons. **LO 1, 3, 9**

Managerial Report

Use the methods of descriptive statistics presented in this chapter to summarize the data and comment on your findings. At a minimum, your report should include the following:

1. Descriptive statistics on net sales and descriptive statistics on net sales by various classifications of customers.
2. Descriptive statistics concerning the relationship between age and net sales.

Case Problem 2: Movie Theater Releases

The movie industry is a competitive business. More than 50 studios produce hundreds of new movies for theater release each year, and the financial success of each movie varies considerably. The opening weekend gross sales ($ millions), the total gross sales ($ millions), the number of theaters the movie was shown in, and the number of weeks the movie was in release are common variables used to measure the success of a movie. Data on the top 100 grossing movies released in 2016 (Box Office Mojo website) are contained in the file *movies2016*. Table 3.10 shows the data for the first 10 movies in this file. **LO 1, 2, 3, 6, 9**

Table 3.10 Performance Data for Ten 2016 Movies Released to Theaters

Movie Title	Opening Gross Sales ($ millions)	Total Gross Sales ($ millions)	Number of Theaters	Weeks in Release
Rogue One: A Star Wars Story	155.08	532.18	4,157	20
Finding Dory	135.06	486.30	4,305	25
Captain America: Civil War	179.14	408.08	4,226	20
The Secret Life of Pets	104.35	368.38	4,381	25
The Jungle Book	103.26	364.00	4,144	24
Deadpool	132.43	363.07	3,856	18
Zootopia	75.06	341.27	3,959	22
Batman v Superman: Dawn of Justice	166.01	330.36	4,256	12
Suicide Squad	133.68	325.10	4,255	14
Sing	35.26	270.40	4,029	20

DATA*file*
movies2016

Managerial Report

Use the numerical methods of descriptive statistics presented in this chapter to learn how these variables contribute to the success of a movie. Include the following in your report:

1. Descriptive statistics for each of the four variables along with a discussion of what the descriptive statistics tell us about the movie industry.
2. What movies, if any, should be considered high-performance outliers? Explain.
3. Descriptive statistics showing the relationship between total gross sales and each of the other variables. Discuss.

Case Problem 3: Business Schools of Asia-Pacific

People around the world pursue higher education degrees in business. Many people who live in the Asia-Pacific region of the world are choosing to pursue an MBA. As a result, the number of applicants for MBA courses at Asia-Pacific schools continues to increase.

Courses in these Asia-Pacific schools are challenging, and include economics, banking, marketing, behavioral sciences, labor relations, decision making, strategic thinking, business law, and more. The data in Table 3.11, which can be found in the file *asia_mba*, shows some of the characteristics of the leading Asia-Pacific business schools. **LO 1, 2, 3**

DATA*file*
asia_mba

Managerial Report

Use the methods of descriptive statistics to summarize the data in Table 3.11. Discuss your findings. Your discussion should include a summary of each variable in the data set. What new insights do these descriptive statistics provide concerning Asia-Pacific business schools? You should also analyze differences between local and foreign tuition costs, between mean starting salaries for schools requiring and not requiring work experience, and between starting salaries for schools requiring and not requiring English tests.

Case Problem 4: Heavenly Chocolates Website Transactions

Heavenly Chocolates manufactures and sells quality chocolate products at its plant and retail store located in Saratoga Springs, New York. Two years ago the company developed

Table 3.11 Data for 25 Asia-Pacific Business Schools

Business School	Full-Time Enrollment	Students per Faculty	Local Tuition ($)	Foreign Tuition ($)	Age	% Foreign	GMAT	English Test	Work Experience	Starting Salary ($)
Melbourne Business School	200	5	24,420	29,600	28	47	Yes	No	Yes	71,400
University of New South Wales (Sydney)	228	4	19,993	32,582	29	28	Yes	No	Yes	65,200
Indian Institute of Management (Ahmedabad)	392	5	4,300	4,300	22	0	No	No	No	7,100
Chinese University of Hong Kong	90	5	11,140	11,140	29	10	Yes	No	No	31,000
International University of Japan (Niigata)	126	4	33,060	33,060	28	60	Yes	Yes	No	87,000
Asian Institute of Management (Manila)	389	5	7,562	9,000	25	50	Yes	No	Yes	22,800
Indian Institute of Management (Bangalore)	380	5	3,935	16,000	23	1	Yes	No	No	7,500
National University of Singapore	147	6	6,146	7,170	29	51	Yes	Yes	Yes	43,300
Indian Institute of Management (Calcutta)	463	8	2,880	16,000	23	0	No	No	No	7,400
Australian National University (Canberra)	42	2	20,300	20,300	30	80	Yes	Yes	Yes	46,600
Nanyang Technological University (Singapore)	50	5	8,500	8,500	32	20	Yes	No	Yes	49,300
University of Queensland (Brisbane)	138	17	16,000	22,800	32	26	No	No	Yes	49,600
Hong Kong University of Science and Technology	60	2	11,513	11,513	26	37	Yes	No	Yes	34,000
Macquarie Graduate School of Management (Sydney)	12	8	17,172	19,778	34	27	No	No	Yes	60,100
Chulalongkorn University (Bangkok)	200	7	17,355	17,355	25	6	Yes	No	Yes	17,600
Monash Mt. Eliza Business School (Melbourne)	350	13	16,200	22,500	30	30	Yes	Yes	Yes	52,500
Asian Institute of Management (Bangkok)	300	10	18,200	18,200	29	90	No	Yes	Yes	25,000
University of Adelaide	20	19	16,426	23,100	30	10	No	No	Yes	66,000
Massey University (Palmerston North, New Zealand)	30	15	13,106	21,625	37	35	No	Yes	Yes	41,400
Royal Melbourne Institute of Technology Business Graduate School	30	7	13,880	17,765	32	30	No	Yes	Yes	48,900
Jamnalal Bajaj Institute of Management Studies (Mumbai)	240	9	1,000	1,000	24	0	No	No	Yes	7,000
Curtin Institute of Technology (Perth)	98	15	9,475	19,097	29	43	Yes	No	Yes	55,000
Lahore University of Management Sciences	70	14	11,250	26,300	23	2.5	No	No	No	7,500
Universiti Sains Malaysia (Penang)	30	5	2,260	2,260	32	15	No	Yes	Yes	16,000
De La Salle University (Manila)	44	17	3,300	3,600	28	3.5	Yes	No	Yes	13,100

Table 3.12 A Sample of 50 Heavenly Chocolates Website Transactions

Customer	Day	Browser	Time (min)	Pages Viewed	Amount Spent ($)
1	Mon	Chrome	12.0	4	54.52
2	Wed	Other	19.5	6	94.90
3	Mon	Chrome	8.5	4	26.68
4	Tue	Firefox	11.4	2	44.73
5	Wed	Chrome	11.3	4	66.27
6	Sat	Firefox	10.5	6	67.80
7	Sun	Chrome	11.4	2	36.04
.	.	.	.	.	.
.	.	.	.	.	.
.	.	.	.	.	.
48	Fri	Chrome	9.7	5	103.15
49	Mon	Other	7.3	6	52.15
50	Fri	Chrome	13.4	3	98.75

DATA*file*
heavenlychocolates

a website and began selling its products over the Internet. Website sales have exceeded the company's expectations, and management is now considering strategies to increase sales even further. To learn more about the website customers, a sample of 50 Heavenly Chocolates transactions was selected from the previous month's sales. Data showing the day of the week each transaction was made, the type of browser the customer used, the time spent on the website, the number of website pages viewed, and the amount spent by each of the 50 customers are contained in the file *heavenlychocolates*. A portion of the data is shown in Table 3.12.

Heavenly Chocolates would like to use the sample data to determine if online shoppers who spend more time and view more pages also spend more money during their visit to the website. The company would also like to investigate the effect that the day of the week and the type of browser have on sales. **LO 1, 3, 9**

Managerial Report

Use the methods of descriptive statistics to learn about the customers who visit the Heavenly Chocolates website. Include the following in your report:

1. Graphical and numerical summaries for the length of time the shopper spends on the website, the number of pages viewed, and the mean amount spent per transaction. Discuss what you learn about Heavenly Chocolates' online shoppers from these numerical summaries.
2. Summarize the frequency, the total dollars spent, and the mean amount spent per transaction for each day of week. What observations can you make about Heavenly Chocolates' business based on the day of the week? Discuss.
3. Summarize the frequency, the total dollars spent, and the mean amount spent per transaction for each type of browser. What observations can you make about Heavenly Chocolates' business based on the type of browser? Discuss.
4. Develop a scatter diagram and compute the sample correlation coefficient to explore the relationship between the time spent on the website and the dollar amount spent. Use the horizontal axis for the time spent on the website. Discuss.
5. Develop a scatter diagram and compute the sample correlation coefficient to explore the relationship between the number of website pages viewed and the amount spent. Use the horizontal axis for the number of website pages viewed. Discuss.

6. Develop a scatter diagram and compute the sample correlation coefficient to explore the relationship between the time spent on the website and the number of pages viewed. Use the horizontal axis to represent the number of pages viewed. Discuss.

Case Problem 5: African Elephant Populations

Although millions of elephants once roamed across Africa, by the mid-1980s elephant populations in African nations had been devastated by poaching. Elephants are important to African ecosystems. In tropical forests, elephants create clearings in the canopy that encourage new tree growth. In savannas, elephants reduce bush cover to create an environment that is favorable to browsing and grazing animals. In addition, the seeds of many plant species depend on passing through an elephant's digestive tract before germination.

The status of the elephant now varies greatly across the continent. In some nations, strong measures have been taken to effectively protect elephant populations; for example, Kenya has destroyed over five tons of elephant ivory confiscated from poachers in an attempt to deter the growth of illegal ivory trade (Associated Press). In other nations, the elephant populations remain in danger due to poaching for meat and ivory, loss of habitat, and conflict with humans. Table 3.13 shows elephant populations for several African nations in 1979, 1989, 2007, and 2012 (*ElephantDatabase.org* website).

The David Sheldrick Wildlife Trust was established in 1977 to honor the memory of naturalist David Leslie William Sheldrick, who founded Warden of Tsavo East National Park in Kenya and headed the Planning Unit of the Wildlife Conservation and Management Department in that country. Management of the Sheldrick Trust would like to know what these data indicate about elephant populations in various African countries since 1979. **LO 1, 8**

DATA*file*
africanelephants

Table 3.13 Elephant Populations for Several African Nations in 1979, 1989, 2007, and 2012

	Elephant Population			
Country	**1979**	**1989**	**2007**	**2012**
Angola	12,400	12,400	2,530	2,530
Botswana	20,000	51,000	175,487	175,454
Cameroon	16,200	21,200	15,387	14,049
Cen African Rep	63,000	19,000	3,334	2,285
Chad	15,000	3,100	6,435	3,004
Congo	10,800	70,000	22,102	49,248
Dem Rep of Congo	377,700	85,000	23,714	13,674
Gabon	13,400	76,000	70,637	77,252
Kenya	65,000	19,000	31,636	36,260
Mozambique	54,800	18,600	26,088	26,513
Somalia	24,300	6,000	70	70
Tanzania	316,300	80,000	167,003	117,456
Zambia	150,000	41,000	29,231	21,589
Zimbabwe	30,000	43,000	99,107	100,291

Managerial Report

Use methods of descriptive statistics to summarize the data and comment on changes in elephant populations in African nations since 1979. At a minimum, your report should include the following:

1. The mean annual change in elephant population for each country in the 10 years from 1979 to 1989, and a discussion of which countries saw the largest changes in elephant population over this 10-year period.
2. The mean annual change in elephant population for each country from 1989 to 2007, and a discussion of which countries saw the largest changes in elephant population over this 18-year period.
3. The mean annual change in elephant population for each country from 2007 to 2012, and a discussion of which countries saw the largest changes in elephant population over this five-year period.
4. A comparison of your results from parts 1, 2, and 3, and a discussion of the conclusions you can draw from this comparison.

Chapter 4

Introduction to Probability

Contents

Statistics in Practice:
National Aeronautics and Space Administration

4.1 Experiments, Counting Rules, and Assigning Probabilities
Counting Rules, Combinations, and Permutations
Assigning Probabilities
Probabilities for the KP&L Project

4.2 Events and their Probabilities

4.3 Some Basic Relationships of Probability
Complement of an Event
Addition Law

4.4 Conditional Probability
Independent Events
Multiplication Law

4.5 Bayes' Theorem
Tabular Approach

Summary 221
Glossary 221
Key Formulas 222
Supplementary Exercises 223
Case Problem 1: Hamilton County Judges 228
Case Problem 2: Rob's Market 230

Learning Objectives

After completing this chapter, you will be able to

LO 1 Calculate the number of outcomes (sample points) for random experiments using tree diagrams, combinations, and permutations; list these outcomes.

LO 2 Assign probabilities to outcomes and events for a random experiment using the classical method, the relative frequency method, and the subjective method.

LO 3 Calculate and interpret the probability of the complement, the union, and the intersection of events.

LO 4 Calculate and interpret the conditional probability associated with two events.

LO 5 Identify and interpret mutually exclusive events and independent events.

LO 6 Create and interpret joint probability tables.

LO 7 Identify and interpret prior probabilities and posterior probabilities; apply Bayes' theorem to calculate posterior probabilities.

Statistics in Practice

National Aeronautics and Space Administration*

Washington, DC

The National Aeronautics and Space Administration (NASA) is the agency of the United States government that is responsible for the U.S. civilian space program and aeronautics and aerospace research. NASA is best known for its manned space exploration; its mission statement is to "drive advances in science, technology, aeronautics, and space exploration to enhance knowledge, education, innovation, economic vitality and stewardship of Earth." NASA, with more than 17,000 employees, oversees many different space-based missions including work on the International Space Station, exploration beyond our solar system with the Hubble telescope, and planning for possible future astronaut missions to the moon and Mars.

Although NASA's primary mission is space exploration, their expertise has been called upon to assist countries and organizations throughout the world. In one such situation, the San José copper and gold mine in Copiapó, Chile, caved in, trapping 33 miners more than 2000 feet underground. While it was important to bring the miners safely to the surface as quickly as possible, it was imperative that the rescue effort be carefully designed and implemented to save as many miners as possible. The Chilean government asked NASA to provide assistance in developing a rescue method. In response, NASA sent a four-person team consisting of an engineer, two physicians, and a psychologist with expertise in vehicle design and issues of long-term confinement.

The probability of success and failure of various rescue methods was prominent in the thoughts of everyone involved. Since there were no historical data available that applied to this unique rescue situation, NASA scientists developed subjective probability estimates for the success and failure of various rescue methods based on similar circumstances experienced by astronauts returning from short- and long-term space missions. The probability estimates provided by NASA guided officials in the selection of a rescue method and provided insight as to how the miners would survive the ascent in a rescue cage.

NASA scientists worked with the Chilean government to save all 33 miners trapped more than 2,000 feet underground. Source: Abaca Press/Alamy Stock Photo

The rescue method designed by the Chilean officials in consultation with the NASA team resulted in the construction of a 13-foot-long, 924-pound steel rescue capsule that would be used to bring up the miners one at a time. All miners were rescued, with the last miner emerging 68 days after the cave-in occurred.

In this chapter, you will learn about probability as well as how to compute and interpret probabilities for a variety of situations. In addition to subjective probabilities, you will learn about classical and relative frequency methods for assigning probabilities. The basic relationships of probability, conditional probability, and Bayes' theorem will be covered.

*The authors are indebted to Dr. Michael Duncan and Clinton Cragg at NASA for providing this Statistics in Practice.

Managers often base their decisions on an analysis of uncertainties such as the following:

1. What are the chances that sales will decrease if we increase prices?
2. What is the likelihood a new assembly method will increase productivity?
3. How likely is it that the project will be finished on time?
4. What is the chance that a new investment will be profitable?

Some of the earliest work on probability originated in a series of letters between Pierre de Fermat and Blaise Pascal in the 1650s.

Probability is a numerical measure of the likelihood that an event will occur. Thus, probabilities can be used as measures of the degree of uncertainty associated with the four events previously listed. If probabilities are available, we can determine the likelihood of each event occurring.

Figure 4.1 Probability as a Numerical Measure of the Likelihood of an Event Occurring

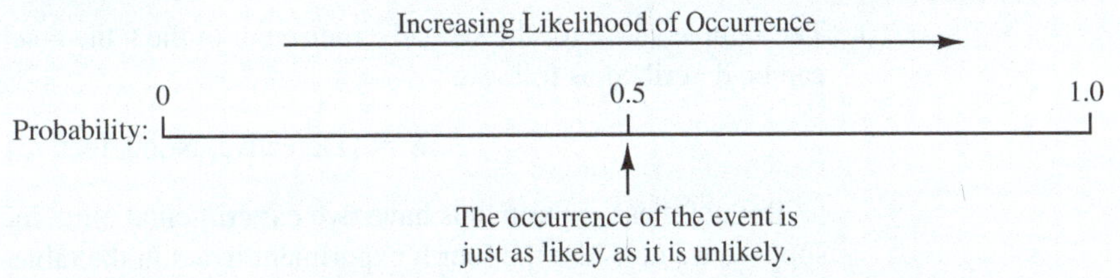

Probability values are always assigned on a scale from 0 to 1. A probability near zero indicates an event is unlikely to occur; a probability near 1 indicates an event is almost certain to occur. Other probabilities between 0 and 1 represent degrees of likelihood that an event will occur. For example, if we consider the event "rain tomorrow," we understand that when the weather report indicates "a near-zero probability of rain," it means almost no chance of rain. However, if a 0.90 probability of rain is reported, we know that rain is likely to occur. A 0.50 probability indicates that rain is just as likely to occur as not. Figure 4.1 depicts the view of probability as a numerical measure of the likelihood of an event occurring.

4.1 Experiments, Counting Rules, and Assigning Probabilities

In discussing probability, we define an **experiment** as a process that generates well-defined outcomes. On any single repetition of an experiment, one and only one of the possible experimental outcomes will occur. Several examples of experiments and their associated outcomes follow.

Experiment	Experimental Outcomes
Toss a coin	Head, tail
Select a part for inspection	Defective, nondefective
Conduct a sales call	Purchase, no purchase
Roll a die	1, 2, 3, 4, 5, 6
Play a football game	Win, lose, tie

By specifying all possible experimental outcomes, we identify the **sample space** for an experiment.

Sample Space

The sample space for an experiment is the set of all experimental outcomes.

Experimental outcomes are also called sample points.

An experimental outcome is also called a **sample point** to identify it as an element of the sample space.

Consider the first experiment in the preceding table—tossing a coin. The upward face of the coin—a head or a tail—determines the experimental outcomes (sample points).

If we let S denote the sample space, we can use the following notation to describe the sample space.

$$S = \{\text{Head, Tail}\}$$

The sample space for the second experiment in the table—selecting a part for inspection—can be described as follows:

$$S = \{\text{Defective, Nondefective}\}$$

Both of these experiments have two experimental outcomes (sample points). However, suppose we consider the fourth experiment listed in the table—rolling a die. The possible experimental outcomes, defined as the number of dots appearing on the upward face of the die, are the six points in the sample space for this experiment.

$$S = \{1, 2, 3, 4, 5, 6\}$$

Counting Rules, Combinations, and Permutations

Being able to identify and count the experimental outcomes is a necessary step in assigning probabilities. We now discuss three useful counting rules.

Multiple-Step Experiments The first counting rule applies to **multiple-step experiments**. Consider the experiment of tossing two coins. Let the experimental outcomes be defined in terms of the pattern of heads and tails appearing on the upward faces of the two coins. How many experimental outcomes are possible for this experiment? The experiment of tossing two coins can be thought of as a two-step experiment in which step 1 is the tossing of the first coin and step 2 is the tossing of the second coin. If we use H to denote a head and T to denote a tail, (H, H) indicates the experimental outcome with a head on the first coin and a head on the second coin. Continuing this notation, we can describe the sample space (S) for this coin-tossing experiment as follows:

$$S = \{(H, H), (H, T), (T, H), (T, T)\}$$

Thus, we see that four experimental outcomes are possible. In this case, we can easily list all the experimental outcomes.

The counting rule for multiple-step experiments makes it possible to determine the number of experimental outcomes without listing them.

Counting Rule for Multiple-Step Experiments

If an experiment can be described as a sequence of k steps with n_1 possible outcomes on the first step, n_2 possible outcomes on the second step, and so on, then the total number of experimental outcomes is given by $(n_1)\,(n_2)\ldots(n_k)$.

Viewing the experiment of tossing two coins as a sequence of first tossing one coin ($n_1 = 2$) and then tossing the other coin ($n_2 = 2$), we can see from the counting rule that $(2)(2) = 4$ distinct experimental outcomes are possible. As shown, they are $S = \{(H, H), (H, T), (T, H), (T, T)\}$. The number of experimental outcomes in an experiment involving tossing six coins is $(2)(2)(2)(2)(2)(2) = 64$.

Without the tree diagram, one might think only three experimental outcomes are possible for two tosses of a coin: 0 heads, 1 head, and 2 heads.

A **tree diagram** is a graphical representation that helps in visualizing a multiple-step experiment. Figure 4.2 shows a tree diagram for the experiment of tossing two coins. The sequence of steps moves from left to right through the tree. Step 1 corresponds to tossing the first coin, and step 2 corresponds to tossing the second coin. For each step, the two possible outcomes are head or tail. Note that for each possible outcome at step 1 two branches

Figure 4.2 Tree Diagram for the Experiment of Tossing Two Coins

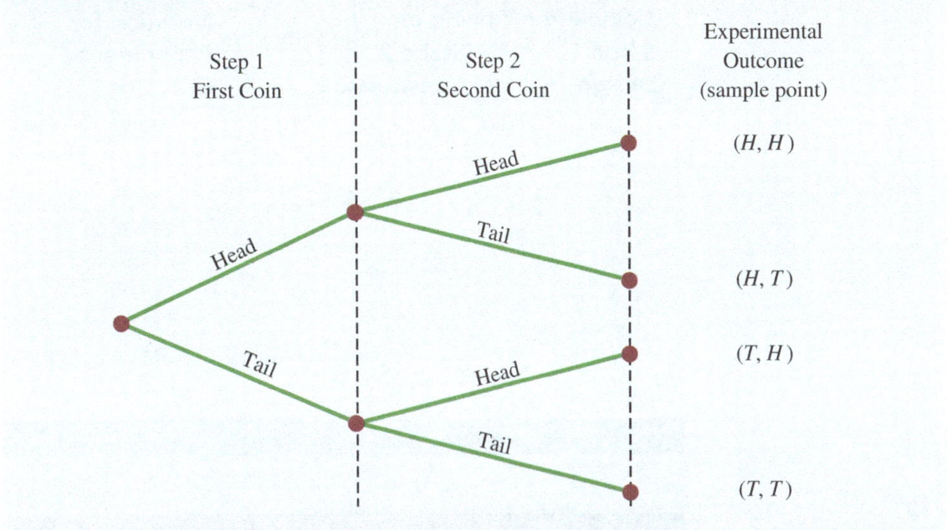

correspond to the two possible outcomes at step 2. Each of the points on the right end of the tree corresponds to an experimental outcome. Each path through the tree from left to right corresponds to a unique sequence of coin toss outcomes that lead to one of the four experimental outcomes.

Let us now see how the counting rule for multiple-step experiments can be used in the analysis of a capacity expansion project for the Kentucky Power & Light Company (KP&L). KP&L is starting a project designed to increase the generating capacity of one of its plants in northern Kentucky. The project is divided into two sequential stages or steps: stage 1 (design) and stage 2 (construction). Even though each stage will be scheduled and controlled as closely as possible, management cannot predict beforehand the exact time required to complete each stage of the project. An analysis of similar construction projects revealed possible completion times for the design stage of two, three, or four months and possible completion times for the construction stage of six, seven, or eight months. In addition, because of the critical need for additional electrical power, management set a goal of 10 months for the completion of the entire project.

Because this project has three possible completion times for the design stage (step 1) and three possible completion times for the construction stage (step 2), the counting rule for multiple-step experiments can be applied here to determine a total of $(3)(3) = 9$ experimental outcomes. To describe the experimental outcomes, we use a two-number notation; for instance, (2, 6) indicates that the design stage is completed in two months and the construction stage is completed in six months. This experimental outcome results in a total of $2 + 6 = 8$ months to complete the entire project. Table 4.1 summarizes the nine experimental outcomes for the KP&L problem. The tree diagram in Figure 4.3 shows how the nine outcomes (sample points) occur.

The counting rule and tree diagram help the project manager identify the experimental outcomes and determine the possible project completion times. From the information in Figure 4.3, we see that the project will be completed in 8 to 12 months, with six of the nine experimental outcomes providing the desired completion time of 10 months or less. Even though identifying the experimental outcomes may be helpful, we need to consider how probability values can be assigned to the experimental outcomes before making an assessment of the probability that the project will be completed within the desired 10 months.

Table 4.1 Experimental Outcomes (Sample Points) for the KP&L Project

Completion Time (months) Stage 1 Design	Stage 2 Construction	Notation for Experimental Outcome	Total Project Completion Time (months)
2	6	(2, 6)	8
2	7	(2, 7)	9
2	8	(2, 8)	10
3	6	(3, 6)	9
3	7	(3, 7)	10
3	8	(3, 8)	11
4	6	(4, 6)	10
4	7	(4, 7)	11
4	8	(4, 8)	12

Figure 4.3 Tree Diagram for the KP&L Project

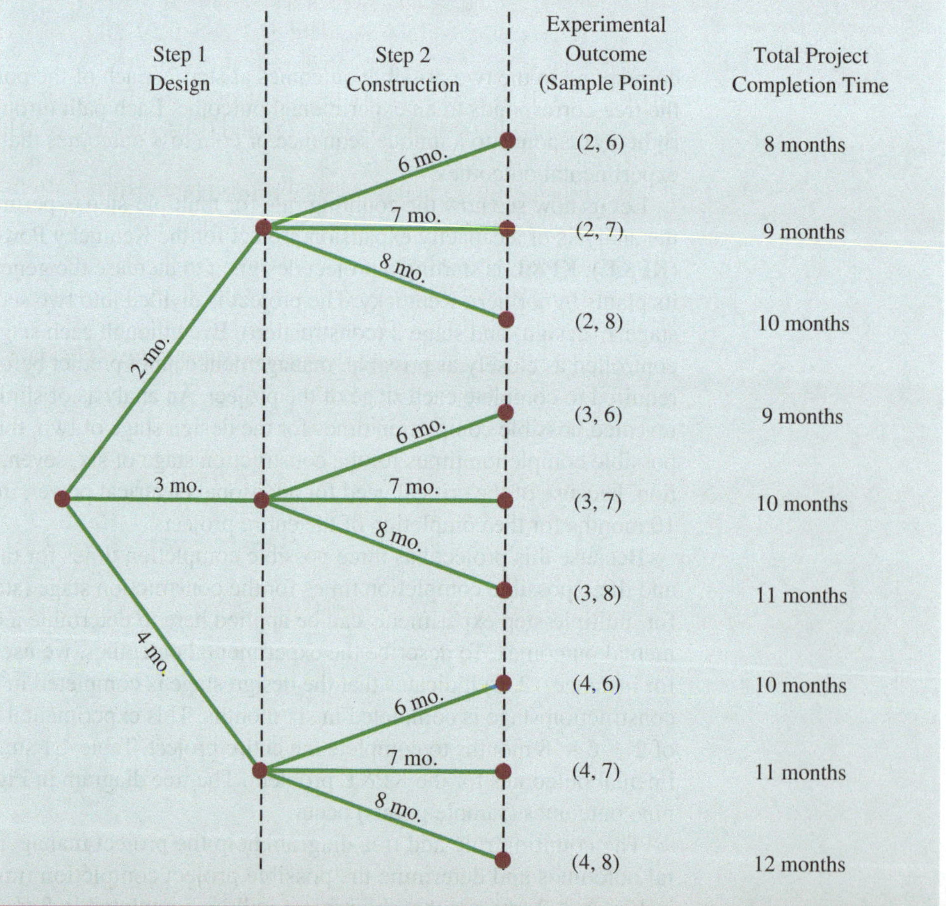

Combinations A second useful counting rule allows one to count the number of experimental outcomes when the experiment involves selecting x objects from a set of n objects. It is called the counting rule for **combinations**.

Counting Rule for Combinations

The number of combinations of n objects taken x at a time is

$$C_x^n = \binom{n}{x} = \frac{n!}{x!(n-x)!} \tag{4.1}$$

where

$$n! = n(n-1)(n-2)\cdots(2)(1)$$
$$x! = x(x-1)(x-2)\cdots(2)(1)$$

and, by definition,

$$0! = 1$$

The notation ! means factorial; for example, 5 factorial is 5! = (5)(4)(3)(2)(1) = 120.

As an illustration of the counting rule for combinations, consider a quality control procedure in which an inspector randomly selects two of five parts to test for defects. In a group of five parts, how many combinations of two parts can be selected? The counting rule in equation (4.1) shows that with $n = 5$ and $x = 2$, we have

In sampling from a finite population of size n, the counting rule for combinations is used to find the number of different samples of size x that can be selected.

$$C_2^5 = \binom{5}{2} = \frac{5!}{2!(5-2)!} = \frac{(5)(4)(3)(2)(1)}{(2)(1)(3)(2)(1)} = \frac{120}{12} = 10$$

Thus, 10 outcomes are possible for the experiment of randomly selecting two parts from a group of five. If we label the five parts as A, B, C, D, and E, the 10 combinations or experimental outcomes can be identified as AB, AC, AD, AE, BC, BD, BE, CD, CE, and DE.

As another example, consider a state lottery system that uses the random selection of 6 integers from a group of 53 to determine the weekly winner. The counting rule for combinations, equation (4.1), can be used to determine the number of ways 6 different integers can be selected from a group of 53.

$$\binom{53}{6} = \frac{53!}{6!(53-6)!} = \frac{53!}{6!47!} = \frac{(53)(52)(51)(50)(49)(48)}{(6)(5)(4)(3)(2)(1)} = 22{,}957{,}480$$

The counting rule for combinations tells us that almost 23 million experimental outcomes are possible in the lottery drawing. An individual who buys a lottery ticket has 1 chance in 22,957,480 of winning.

Permutations A third counting rule that is sometimes useful is the counting rule for **permutations**. It allows one to compute the number of experimental outcomes when x objects are to be selected from a set of n objects where the order of selection is important. The same x objects selected in a different order are considered a different experimental outcome.

Counting Rule for Permutations

The number of permutations of n objects taken x at a time is given by

$$P_x^n = x!\binom{n}{x} = \frac{n!}{(n-x)!} \tag{4.2}$$

The counting rule for permutations closely relates to the one for combinations; however, an experiment results in more permutations than combinations for the same number of objects because every selection of x objects can be ordered in $x!$ different ways.

As an example, consider again the quality control process in which an inspector selects two of five parts to inspect for defects. How many permutations may be selected? The counting rule in equation (4.2) shows that with $n = 5$ and $x = 2$, we have

$$P_2^5 = \frac{5!}{(5-2)!} = \frac{5!}{3!} = \frac{(5)(4)(3)(2)(1)}{(3)(2)(1)} = \frac{120}{6} = 20$$

Thus, 20 outcomes are possible for the experiment of randomly selecting two parts from a group of five when the order of selection must be taken into account. If we label the parts A, B, C, D, and E, the 20 permutations are AB, BA, AC, CA, AD, DA, AE, EA, BC, CB, BD, DB, BE, EB, CD, DC, CE, EC, DE, and ED.

Assigning Probabilities

Now let us see how probabilities can be assigned to experimental outcomes. The three approaches most frequently used are the classical, relative frequency, and subjective methods. Regardless of the method used, two **basic requirements for assigning probabilities** must be met.

Basic Requirements for Assigning Probabilities

1. The probability assigned to each experimental outcome must be between 0 and 1, inclusively. If we let E_i denote the ith experimental outcome and $P(E_i)$ its probability, then this requirement can be written as

$$0 \le P(E_i) \le 1 \text{ for all } i \tag{4.3}$$

2. The sum of the probabilities for all the experimental outcomes must equal 1.0. For n experimental outcomes, this requirement can be written as

$$P(E_1) + P(E_2) + \cdots + P(E_n) = 1 \tag{4.4}$$

The **classical method** of assigning probabilities is appropriate when all the experimental outcomes are equally likely. If n experimental outcomes are possible, a probability of $1/n$ is assigned to each experimental outcome. When using this approach, the two basic requirements for assigning probabilities are automatically satisfied.

For an example, consider the experiment of tossing a fair coin; the two experimental outcomes—head and tail—are equally likely. Because one of the two equally likely outcomes is a head, the probability of observing a head is 1/2, or 0.50. Similarly, the probability of observing a tail is also 1/2, or 0.50.

As another example, consider the experiment of rolling a die. It would seem reasonable to conclude that the six possible outcomes are equally likely, and hence each outcome is assigned a probability of 1/6. If $P(1)$ denotes the probability that one dot appears on the upward face of the die, then $P(1) = 1/6$. Similarly, $P(2) = 1/6$, $P(3) = 1/6$, $P(4) = 1/6$, $P(5) = 1/6$, and $P(6) = 1/6$. Note that these probabilities satisfy the two basic requirements of equations (4.3) and (4.4) because each of the probabilities is greater than or equal to zero and they sum to 1.0.

The **relative frequency method** of assigning probabilities is appropriate when data are available to estimate the proportion of the time the experimental outcome will occur if the experiment is repeated a large number of times. As an example, consider a study of waiting times in the X-ray department for a local hospital. A clerk recorded the number of patients waiting for service at 9:00 a.m. on 20 successive days and obtained the following results.

Number Waiting	Number of Days Outcome Occurred
0	2
1	5
2	6
3	4
4	3
Total	20

These data show that on 2 of the 20 days, zero patients were waiting for service; on 5 of the days, one patient was waiting for service; and so on. Using the relative frequency method, we would assign a probability of 2/20 = 0.10 to the experimental outcome of zero patients waiting for service, 5/20 = 0.25 to the experimental outcome of one patient waiting, 6/20 = 0.30 to two patients waiting, 4/20 = 0.20 to three patients waiting, and 3/20 = 0.15 to four patients waiting. As with the classical method, using the relative frequency method automatically satisfies the two basic requirements of equations (4.3) and (4.4).

The **subjective method** of assigning probabilities is most appropriate when one cannot realistically assume that the experimental outcomes are equally likely and when little relevant data are available. When the subjective method is used to assign probabilities to the experimental outcomes, we may use any information available, such as our experience or intuition. After considering all available information, a probability value that expresses our *degree of belief* (on a scale from 0 to 1) that the experimental outcome will occur is specified. Because subjective probability expresses a person's degree of belief, it is personal. Using the subjective method, different people can be expected to assign different probabilities to the same experimental outcome.

The subjective method requires extra care to ensure that the two basic requirements of equations (4.3) and (4.4) are satisfied. Regardless of a person's degree of belief, the probability value assigned to each experimental outcome must be between 0 and 1, inclusive, and the sum of all the probabilities for the experimental outcomes must equal 1.0.

Consider the case in which Tom and Judy Elsbernd make an offer to purchase a house. Two outcomes are possible:

$$E_1 = \text{their offer is accepted}$$
$$E_2 = \text{their offer is rejected}$$

Judy believes that the probability their offer will be accepted is 0.8; thus, Judy would set $P(E_1) = 0.8$ and $P(E_2) = 0.2$. Tom, however, believes that the probability that their offer will be accepted is 0.6; hence, Tom would set $P(E_1) = 0.6$ and $P(E_2) = 0.4$. Note that Tom's probability estimate for E_1 reflects a greater pessimism that their offer will be accepted.

Both Judy and Tom assigned probabilities that satisfy the two basic requirements. The fact that their probability estimates are different emphasizes the personal nature of the subjective method.

Bayes' theorem (see Section 4.5) provides a means for combining subjectively determined prior probabilities with probabilities obtained by other means to obtain revised, or posterior, probabilities.

Even in business situations where either the classical or the relative frequency approach can be applied, managers may want to provide subjective probability estimates. In such cases, the best probability estimates often are obtained by combining the estimates from the classical or relative frequency approach with subjective probability estimates.

Probabilities for the KP&L Project

To perform further analysis on the KP&L project, we must develop probabilities for each of the nine experimental outcomes listed in Table 4.1. On the basis of experience and judgment, management concluded that the experimental outcomes were not equally likely. Hence, the classical method of assigning probabilities could not be used. Management then decided to conduct a study of the completion times for similar projects undertaken by

Table 4.2 Completion Results for 40 KP&L Projects

Completion Time (months) Stage 1 Design	Stage 2 Construction	Sample Point	Number of Past Projects Having These Completion Times
2	6	(2, 6)	6
2	7	(2, 7)	6
2	8	(2, 8)	2
3	6	(3, 6)	4
3	7	(3, 7)	8
3	8	(3, 8)	2
4	6	(4, 6)	2
4	7	(4, 7)	4
4	8	(4, 8)	6
		Total	40

KP&L over the past three years. The results of a study of 40 similar projects are summarized in Table 4.2.

After reviewing the results of the study, management decided to employ the relative frequency method of assigning probabilities. Management could have provided subjective probability estimates but felt that the current project was quite similar to the 40 previous projects. Thus, the relative frequency method was judged best.

In using the data in Table 4.2 to compute probabilities, we note that outcome (2, 6)—stage 1 completed in two months and stage 2 completed in six months—occurred six times in the 40 projects. We can use the relative frequency method to assign a probability of $6/40 = 0.15$ to this outcome. Similarly, outcome (2, 7) also occurred in six of the 40 projects, providing a $6/40 = 0.15$ probability. Continuing in this manner, we obtain the probability assignments for the sample points of the KP&L project shown in Table 4.3. Note that $P(2, 6)$ represents the probability of the sample point (2, 6), $P(2, 7)$ represents the probability of the sample point (2, 7), and so on.

Table 4.3 Probability Assignments for the KP&L Project Based on the Relative Frequency Method

Sample Point	Project Completion Time	Probability of Sample Point
(2, 6)	8 months	$P(2, 6) = 6/40 = 0.15$
(2, 7)	9 months	$P(2, 7) = 6/40 = 0.15$
(2, 8)	10 months	$P(2, 8) = 2/40 = 0.05$
(3, 6)	9 months	$P(3, 6) = 4/40 = 0.10$
(3, 7)	10 months	$P(3, 7) = 8/40 = 0.20$
(3, 8)	11 months	$P(3, 8) = 2/40 = 0.05$
(4, 6)	10 months	$P(4, 6) = 2/40 = 0.05$
(4, 7)	11 months	$P(4, 7) = 4/40 = 0.10$
(4, 8)	12 months	$P(4, 8) = 6/40 = 0.15$
		Total 1.00

Notes + Comments

1. In statistics, the notion of an experiment differs somewhat from the notion of an experiment in the physical sciences. In the physical sciences, researchers usually conduct an experiment in a laboratory or a controlled environment in order to learn about cause and effect. In statistical experiments, probability determines outcomes. Even though the experiment is repeated in exactly the same way, an entirely different outcome may occur. Because of this influence of probability on the outcome, the experiments of statistics are sometimes called *random experiments*.
2. When drawing a random sample without replacement from a population of size n, the counting rule for combinations is used to find the number of different samples of size x that can be selected.

Exercises

Methods

1. An experiment has three steps with three outcomes possible for the first step, two outcomes possible for the second step, and four outcomes possible for the third step. How many experimental outcomes exist for the entire experiment? **LO 1**
2. How many ways can three items be selected from a group of six items? Use the letters A, B, C, D, E, and F to identify the items, and list each of the different combinations of three items. **LO 1**
3. How many permutations of three items can be selected from a group of six? Use the letters A, B, C, D, E, and F to identify the items, and list each of the permutations of items B, D, and F. **LO 1**
4. Consider the experiment of tossing a fair coin three times. **LO 1, 2**
   a. Develop a tree diagram for the experiment.
   b. List the experimental outcomes.
   c. What is the probability for each experimental outcome?
5. Suppose an experiment has five equally likely outcomes: E_1, E_2, E_3, E_4, E_5. Assign probabilities to each outcome and show that the requirements in equations (4.3) and (4.4) are satisfied. What method did you use? **LO 2**
6. An experiment with three outcomes has been repeated 50 times, and it was learned that E_1 occurred 20 times, E_2 occurred 13 times, and E_3 occurred 17 times. Assign probabilities to the outcomes. What method did you use? **LO 2**
7. A decision maker subjectively assigned the following probabilities to the four outcomes of an experiment: $P(E_1) = 0.10$, $P(E_2) = 0.15$, $P(E_3) = 0.40$, and $P(E_4) = 0.20$. Are these probability assignments valid? Explain. **LO 2**

Applications

8. **Zoning Changes.** In the city of Milford, applications for zoning changes go through a two-step process: a review by the planning commission and a final decision by the city council. At step 1, the planning commission reviews the zoning change request and makes a positive or negative recommendation concerning the change. At step 2, the city council reviews the planning commission's recommendation and then votes to approve or to disapprove the zoning change. Suppose the developer of an apartment complex submits an application for a zoning change. Consider the application process as an experiment. **LO 1**
   a. How many sample points are there for this experiment? List the sample points.
   b. Construct a tree diagram for the experiment.
9. **Sampling Bank Accounts.** Simple random sampling uses a sample of size n from a population of size N to obtain data that can be used to make inferences about the characteristics of a population. Suppose that, from a population of 50 bank accounts,

we want to take a random sample of four accounts in order to learn about the population. How many different random samples of four accounts are possible? **LO 1**

DATA*file*
codechurn

10. **Code Churn.** Code Churn is a common metric used to measure the efficiency and productivity of software engineers and computer programmers. It is usually measured as the percentage of a programmer's code that must be edited over a short period of time. Programmers with higher rates of code churn must rewrite code more often because of errors and inefficient programming techniques. The following table displays sample information for 10 computer programmers. **LO 2**

Programmer	Total Lines of Code Written	Number of Lines of Code Requiring Edits
Liwei	23,789	4,589
Andrew	17,962	2,780
Jaime	31,025	12,080
Sherae	26,050	3,780
Binny	19,586	1,890
Roger	24,786	4,005
Dong-Gil	24,030	5,785
Alex	14,780	1,052
Jay	30,875	3,872
Vivek	21,546	4,125

a. Use the data in the table above (which is also provided in the file *codechurn*) and the relative frequency method to determine probabilities that a randomly selected line of code will need to be edited for each programmer.
b. If you randomly select a line of code from Liwei, what is the probability that the line of code will require editing?
c. If you randomly select a line of code from Sherae, what is the probability that the line of code will *not* require editing?
d. Which programmer has the lowest probability of a randomly selected line of code requiring editing? Which programmer has the highest probability of a randomly selected line of code requiring editing?

11. **TikTok User Ages.** It is estimated that nearly half of all users in the United States of the social networking platform TikTok were between the ages of 10 and 29 in 2020 (*Statista.com*). Suppose that the results below were received from a survey sent to a random sample of people in the United States regarding their use of TikTok. **LO 2**

Age Range of Respondent	Uses TikTok	Does Not Use TikTok
10–19	36	44
20–29	87	52
30–39	42	89
40+	44	138
Total:	209	323

a. Use the sample data above to compute the probability that a respondent to this survey uses TikTok.
b. What is the probability of a respondent to this survey in each age range (10–19, 20–29, 30–39, 40+) using TikTok? Which age range has the highest probability of a respondent being a user of TikTok?

12. **Toothpaste Package Designs.** A company that manufactures toothpaste is studying five different package designs. Assuming that one design is just as likely to be selected by a consumer as any other design, what selection probability would you assign to each of the package designs? In an actual experiment, 100 consumers were asked to pick the design they preferred. The following data were obtained. Do the data confirm the belief that one design is just as likely to be selected as another? Explain. **LO 2**

Design	Number of Times Preferred
1	5
2	15
3	30
4	40
5	10

13. **Powerball Lottery.** The Powerball lottery is played twice each week in 45 states, the District of Columbia, Puerto Rico, and the Virgin Islands. To play Powerball, a participant must purchase a $2 ticket, select five numbers from the digits 1 through 69, and then select a Powerball number from the digits 1 through 26. To determine the winning numbers for each game, lottery officials draw 5 white balls out a drum of 69 white balls numbered 1 through 69 and 1 red ball out of a drum of 26 red balls numbered 1 through 26. To win the Powerball jackpot, a participant's numbers must match the numbers on the 5 white balls in any order and must also match the number on the red Powerball. The largest jackpots awarded in the Powerball lottery have exceeded $2 billion. (Powerball website). **LO 1, 2**
    a. How many Powerball lottery outcomes are possible? *Hint:* Consider this a two-step random experiment. Select the 5 white ball numbers and then select the 1 red Powerball number.
    b. What is the probability that a $2 lottery ticket wins the Powerball lottery?

4.2 Events and Their Probabilities

In the introduction to this chapter we used the term *event* much as it would be used in everyday language. Then, in Section 4.1, we introduced the concept of an experiment and its associated experimental outcomes or sample points. Sample points and events provide the foundation for the study of probability. As a result, we must now introduce the formal definition of an **event** as it relates to sample points. Doing so will provide the basis for determining the probability of an event.

Event

An event is a collection of sample points.

For an example, let us return to the KP&L project and assume that the project manager is interested in the event that the entire project can be completed in 10 months or less. Referring to Table 4.3, we see that six sample points—(2, 6), (2, 7), (2, 8), (3, 6), (3, 7), and (4, 6)—provide a project completion time of 10 months or less. Let C denote the event that the project is completed in 10 months or less; we write

$$C = \{(2, 6), (2, 7), (2, 8), (3, 6), (3, 7), (4, 6)\}$$

Event C is said to occur if *any one* of these six sample points appears as the experimental outcome.

Other events that might be of interest to KP&L management include the following:

L = The event that the project is completed in *less* than 10 months
M = The event that the project is completed in *more* than 10 months

Using the information in Table 4.3, we see that these events consist of the following sample points:

$$L = \{(2, 6), (2, 7), (3, 6)\}$$
$$M = \{(3, 8), (4, 7), (4, 8)\}$$

A variety of additional events can be defined for the KP&L project, but in each case the event must be identified as a collection of sample points for the experiment.

Given the probabilities of the sample points shown in Table 4.3, we can use the following definition to compute the probability of any event that KP&L management might want to consider.

Probability of an Event

The probability of any event is equal to the sum of the probabilities of the sample points in the event.

Using this definition, we calculate the probability of a particular event by adding the probabilities of the sample points (experimental outcomes) that make up the event. We can now compute the probability that the project will take 10 months or less to complete. Because this event is given by $C = \{(2, 6), (2, 7), (2, 8), (3, 6), (3, 7), (4, 6)\}$, the probability of event C, denoted $P(C)$, is given by

$$P(C) = P(2, 6) + P(2, 7) + P(2, 8) + P(3, 6) + P(3, 7) + P(4, 6)$$

Refer to the sample point probabilities in Table 4.3; we have

$$P(C) = 0.15 + 0.15 + 0.05 + 0.10 + 0.20 + 0.05 = 0.70$$

Similarly, because the event that the project is completed in less than 10 months is given by $L = \{(2, 6), (2, 7), (3, 6)\}$, the probability of this event is given by

$$\begin{aligned} P(L) &= P(2, 6) + P(2, 7) + P(3, 6) \\ &= 0.15 + 0.15 + 0.10 = 0.40 \end{aligned}$$

Finally, for the event that the project is completed in more than 10 months, we have $M = \{(3, 8), (4, 7), (4, 8)\}$ and thus

$$\begin{aligned} P(M) &= P(3, 8) + P(4, 7) + P(4, 8) \\ &= 0.05 + 0.10 + 0.15 = 0.30 \end{aligned}$$

Using these probability results, we can now tell KP&L management that there is a 0.70 probability that the project will be completed in 10 months or less, a 0.40 probability that the project will be completed in less than 10 months, and a 0.30 probability that the project will be completed in more than 10 months. This procedure of computing event probabilities can be repeated for any event of interest to the KP&L management.

Anytime that we can identify all the sample points of an experiment and assign probabilities to each, we can compute the probability of an event using the definition. However, in many experiments the large number of sample points makes the identification of the sample points, as well as the determination of their associated probabilities, extremely cumbersome, if not impossible. In the remaining sections of this chapter, we present some basic probability relationships that can be used to compute the probability of an event without knowledge of all the sample point probabilities.

Notes + Comments

1. The sample space, S, is an event. Because it contains all the experimental outcomes, it has a probability of 1; that is, $P(S) = 1.0$.
2. When the classical method is used to assign probabilities, the assumption is that the experimental outcomes are equally likely. In such cases, the probability of an event can be computed by counting the number of experimental outcomes in the event and dividing the result by the total number of experimental outcomes.

Exercises

Methods

14. An experiment has four equally likely outcomes: E_1, E_2, E_3, and E_4. **LO 2**
    a. What is the probability that E_2 occurs?
    b. What is the probability that any two of the outcomes occur (e.g., E_1 or E_3)?
    c. What is the probability that any three of the outcomes occur (e.g., E_1 or E_2 or E_4)?
15. Consider the experiment of selecting a playing card from a deck of 52 playing cards. A typical deck of playing cards contains cards labeled with four different suits (clubs, diamonds, hearts, spades). Each suit consists of 13 cards, which include three face cards (jack, queen, king), the ace, and cards labeled 2 through 10. Each card corresponds to a sample point with a 1/52 probability. **LO 1, 2**
    a. List the sample points in the event an ace is selected.
    b. List the sample points in the event a club is selected.
    c. List the sample points in the event a face card (jack, queen, or king) is selected.
    d. Find the probabilities associated with each of the events in parts (a), (b), and (c).
16. Consider the experiment of rolling a pair of six-sided dice. Suppose that we are interested in the sum of the face values showing on the dice. **LO 1, 2**
    a. How many sample points are possible? *Hint:* Use the counting rule for multiple-step experiments.
    b. List the sample points.
    c. What is the probability of obtaining a value of 7?
    d. What is the probability of obtaining a value of 9 or greater?
    e. Because each roll has six possible even values (2, 4, 6, 8, 10, and 12) and only five possible odd values (3, 5, 7, 9, and 11), the dice should show even values more often than odd values. Do you agree with this statement? Explain.
    f. What method did you use to assign the probabilities requested?

Applications

17. **KP&L Project Over Budget.** Refer to the KP&L sample points and sample point probabilities in Tables 4.2 and 4.3. **LO 1, 2**
    a. The design stage (stage 1) will run over budget if it takes four months to complete. List the sample points in the event the design stage is over budget.
    b. What is the probability that the design stage is over budget?
    c. The construction stage (stage 2) will run over budget if it takes eight months to complete. List the sample points in the event the construction stage is over budget.
    d. What is the probability that the construction stage is over budget?
    e. What is the probability that both stages are over budget?
18. **Corporate Headquarters Locations.** Each year *Fortune* magazine publishes an annual list of the 500 largest companies in the United States. The corporate headquarters for the 500 companies are located in 38 different states The following table shows the eight states with the largest number of *Fortune* 500 companies (*Money*/CNN website).

State	Number of Companies	State	Number of Companies
California	53	Ohio	28
Illinois	32	Pennsylvania	23
New Jersey	21	Texas	52
New York	50	Virginia	24

Suppose one of the 500 companies is selected at random for a follow-up questionnaire. **LO 2**

a. What is the probability that the company selected has its corporate headquarters in California?
b. What is the probability that the company selected has its corporate headquarters in California, New York, or Texas?
c. What is the probability that the company selected has its corporate headquarters in one of the eight states listed above?

19. **NCAA Basketball Championships.** Only 15 college basketball programs have won more than a single NCAA Basketball Championship. Those 15 colleges are shown below, along with their current NCAA Conference Affiliation and the number of NCAA Basketball Championships they have won. Suppose that the winner of one of these 60 NCAA Basketball Championships is selected at random. **LO 2**

DATA*file*
ncaabasketball

College	Current NCAA Conference Affiliation	Number of NCAA Basketball Championships
UCLA	Pac-12	11
Kentucky	SEC	8
North Carolina	ACC	6
Duke	ACC	5
Indiana	Big Ten	5
Kansas	Big 12	4
UConn	Big East	4
Villanova	Big East	3
Cincinnati	American	2
Florida	SEC	2
Louisville	ACC	2
Michigan State	Big Ten	2
NC State	ACC	2
Oklahoma State	Big 12	2
San Francisco	West Coast	2
	Total:	60

a. What is the probability that the selected winner is from UCLA?
b. What is the probability that the selected winner is from the Big Ten Conference?
c. What is the probability that the selected winner is from the ACC?
d. What is the probability that the selected winner is from either the Big Ten or the ACC?

20. **Age of Financial Independence.** Suppose that the following table represents a sample of 944 teenagers' responses to the question, "When do you think you will become financially independent?"

Age Financially Independent	Number of Responses
16 to 20	191
21 to 24	467
25 to 27	244
28 or older	42

Consider the experiment of randomly selecting a teenager from the population of teenagers aged 14 to 18. **LO 2**

a. Compute the probability of being financially independent for each of the four age categories.
b. What is the probability of being financially independent before the age of 25?
c. What is the probability of being financially independent after the age of 24?
d. Do the probabilities suggest that the teenagers may be somewhat unrealistic in their expectations about when they will become financially independent?

21. **Fatal Collisions with a Fixed Object.** The Insurance Institute for Highway Safety (IIHS) reports on traffic safety-related data. According to the IIHS, 8,884 fatal collisions in 2022 were the result of collisions with fixed objects (IIHS website). The following table provides more information on these collisions.

DATA*file*
iihs

Fixed Object Involved in Collision	Number of Collisions
Pole/post	1,004
Culvert/curb/ditch	561
Shrubbery/tree	3,964
Guardrail/fence	347
Embankment	423
Bridge/pier	208
Other	2,377

Assume that a collision will be randomly chosen from this population. **LO 2**

a. What is the probability of a fatal collision with a pole or post?
b. What is the probability of a fatal collision with a guardrail or fence?
c. What type of fixed object is least likely to be involved in a fatal collision? What is the probability associated with this type of fatal collision?
d. What type of object is most likely to be involved in a fatal collision? What is the probability associated with this type of fatal collision?

4.3 Some Basic Relationships of Probability

Complement of an Event

Given an event A, the **complement of A** is defined to be the event consisting of all sample points that are *not* in A. The complement of A is denoted by A^c. Figure 4.4 is a diagram, known as a **Venn diagram**, that illustrates the concept of a complement. The rectangular area represents the sample space for the experiment and as such contains all possible sample points. The circle represents event A and contains only the sample points that belong to A. The shaded

Figure 4.4 Complement of Event A Is Shaded

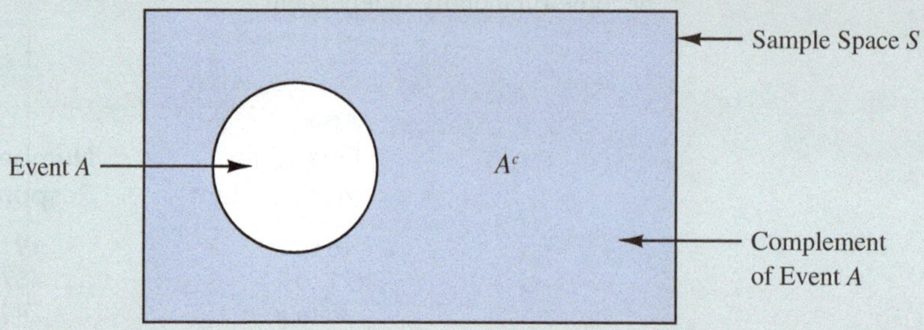

region of the rectangle contains all sample points not in event A and is by definition the complement of A.

In any probability application, either event A or its complement A^c must occur. Therefore, we have

$$P(A) + P(A^c) = 1$$

Solving for $P(A)$, we obtain the following result.

Computing Probability Using the Complement

$$P(A) = 1 - P(A^c) \tag{4.5}$$

Equation (4.5) shows that the probability of an event A can be computed easily if the probability of its complement, $P(A^c)$, is known.

As an example, consider the case of a sales manager who, after reviewing sales reports, states that 80% of new customer contacts result in no sale. By allowing A to denote the event of a sale and A^c to denote the event of no sale, the manager is stating that $P(A^c) = 0.80$. Using equation (4.5), we see that

$$P(A) = 1 - P(A^c) = 1 - 0.80 = 0.20$$

We can conclude that a new customer contact has a 0.20 probability of resulting in a sale.

In another example, a purchasing agent states a 0.90 probability that a supplier will send a shipment that is free of defective parts. Using the complement, we can conclude that there is a $1 - 0.90 = 0.10$ probability that the shipment will contain defective parts.

Addition Law

The addition law is helpful when we are interested in knowing the probability that at least one of two events occurs. That is, with events A and B we are interested in knowing the probability that event A or event B or both will occur.

Before we present the addition law, we need to discuss two concepts related to the combination of events: the *union* of events and the *intersection* of events. Given two events, A and B, the **union of A and B** is defined as follows.

Union of Two Events

The *union* of A and B is the event containing *all* sample points belonging to A *or* B *or both.* The union is denoted by $A \cup B$.

Figure 4.5 Union of Events *A* and *B* Is Shaded

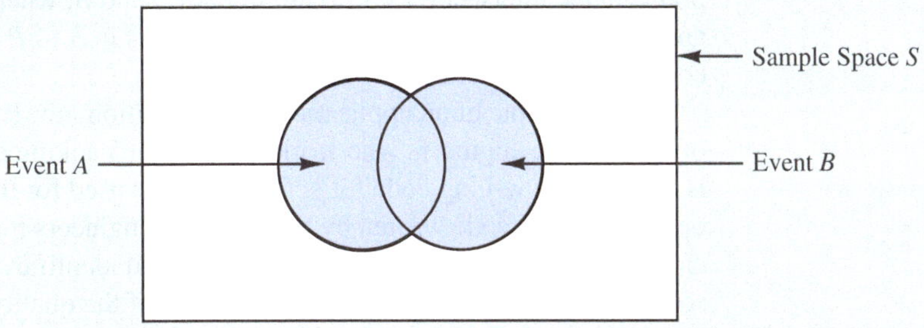

The Venn diagram in Figure 4.5 depicts the union of events *A* and *B*. Note that the two circles contain all the sample points in event *A* as well as all the sample points in event *B*. The fact that the circles overlap indicates that some sample points are contained in both *A* and *B*.

The definition of the **intersection of *A* and *B*** follows.

Intersection of Two Events

Given two events *A* and *B*, the *intersection* of *A* and *B* is the event containing the sample points belonging to *both A and B*. The intersection is denoted by $A \cap B$.

The Venn diagram depicting the intersection of events *A* and *B* is shown in Figure 4.6. The area where the two circles overlap is the intersection; it contains the sample points that are in both *A* and *B*.

Let us now continue with a discussion of the addition law. The **addition law** provides a way to compute the probability that event *A* or event *B* or both occur. In other words, the addition law is used to compute the probability of the union of two events. The addition law is written as follows.

Addition Law

$$P(A \cup B) = P(A) + P(B) - P(A \cap B) \quad \textbf{(4.6)}$$

Figure 4.6 Intersection of Events *A* and *B* Is Shaded

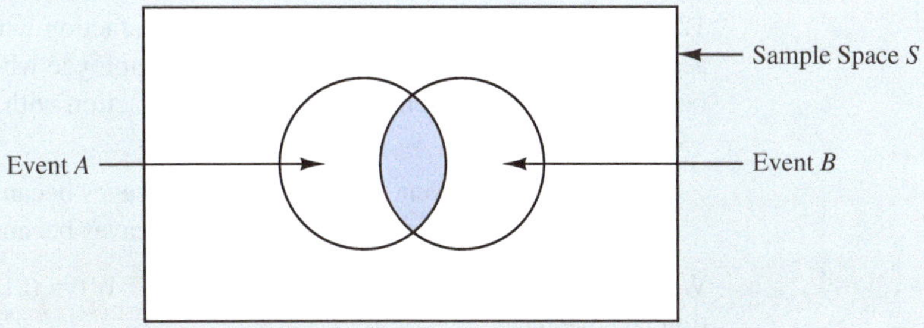

To understand the addition law intuitively, note that the first two terms in the addition law, $P(A) + P(B)$, account for all the sample points in $A \cup B$. However, because the sample points in the intersection $A \cap B$ are in both A and B, when we compute $P(A) + P(B)$, we are in effect counting each of the sample points in $A \cap B$ twice. We correct for this over-counting by subtracting $P(A \cap B)$.

As an example of an application of the addition law, let us consider the case of a group of 50 software engineers who work at an online banking company. Each software engineer is in charge of writing code for software that is used for the online banking company's operations. The code written by the software engineers must pass a quality assurance check that verifies the accuracy of the code and identifies errors. On occasion, some of the software engineers fail to meet the standards of the quality assurance check by either being late in completing their code or producing code that has errors. At the end of a performance evaluation period, the software engineering manager found that 5 of the 50 workers completed work late, 6 of the 50 workers produced code that contained errors, and 2 of the 50 workers both completed work late *and* produced code that contained errors.

Let

L = the event that the work is completed late
E = the event that the code produced contains errors

The relative frequency information leads to the following probabilities:

$$P(L) = \frac{5}{50} = 0.10$$

$$P(E) = \frac{6}{50} = 0.12$$

$$P(L \cap E) = \frac{2}{50} = 0.04$$

After reviewing the performance data, the software engineering manager decided to assign a poor performance rating to any employee whose work was either late or contained errors; thus the event of interest is $L \cup E$. What is the probability that the software engineering manager assigned an employee a poor performance rating?

Note that the probability question is about the union of two events. Specifically, we want to know $P(L \cup E)$. Using equation (4.6), we have

$$P(L \cup E) = P(L) + P(E) - P(L \cap E)$$

Knowing values for the three probabilities on the right side of this expression, we can write

$$P(L \cup E) = 0.10 + 0.12 - 0.04 = 0.18$$

This calculation tells us that there is a 0.18 probability that a randomly selected employee received a poor performance rating.

As another example of the addition law, consider a recent study conducted by the human resources manager of a large medical center. The study showed that 30% of the employees who left the medical center within two years did so primarily because they were dissatisfied with their salary, 20% left because they were dissatisfied with their work assignments, and 12% of the former employees indicated dissatisfaction with *both* their salary and their work assignments. What is the probability that an employee who leaves within two years does so because of dissatisfaction with salary, dissatisfaction with the work assignment, or both?

Let

S = the event that the employee leaves because of salary
W = the event that the employee leaves because of work assignment

We have $P(S) = 0.30$, $P(W) = 0.20$, and $P(S \cap W) = 0.12$. Using equation (4.6), the addition law, we have

$$P(S \cup W) = P(S) + P(W) - P(S \cap W) = 0.30 + 0.20 - 0.12 = 0.38$$

Figure 4.7 Mutually Exclusive Events

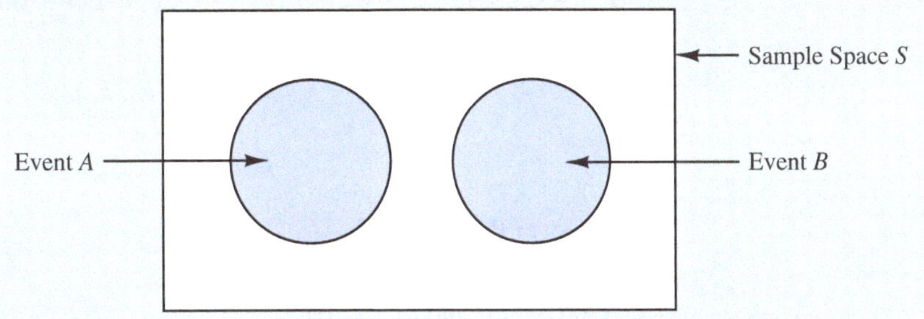

We find a 0.38 probability that an employee leaves for salary or work assignment reasons.

Before we conclude our discussion of the addition law, let us consider a special case that arises for **mutually exclusive events**.

Mutually Exclusive Events

Two events are said to be mutually exclusive if the events have no sample points in common.

Events A and B are mutually exclusive if, when one event occurs, the other cannot occur. Thus, a requirement for A and B to be mutually exclusive is that their intersection must contain no sample points. The Venn diagram depicting two mutually exclusive events A and B is shown in Figure 4.7. In this case $P(A \cap B) = 0$ and the addition law can be written as follows.

Addition Law for Mutually Exclusive Events

$$P(A \cup B) = P(A) + P(B)$$

Exercises

Methods

22. Suppose that we have a sample space with five equally likely experimental outcomes: E_1, E_2, E_3, E_4, E_5. Let

$$A = \{E_1, E_2\}$$
$$B = \{E_3, E_4\}$$
$$C = \{E_2, E_3, E_5\}$$

and answer the following. **LO 2, 3**

a. Find $P(A)$, $P(B)$, and $P(C)$.
b. Find $P(A \cup B)$. Are A and B mutually exclusive?
c. Find A^c, C^c, $P(A^c)$, and $P(C^c)$.
d. Find $A \cup B^c$ and $P(A \cup B^c)$.
e. Find $P(B \cup C)$.

23. Suppose that we have a sample space $S = \{E_1, E_2, E_3, E_4, E_5, E_6, E_7\}$, where E_1, $E_2, \ldots, E_7$ denote the sample points. The following probability assignments apply: $P(E_1) = 0.05$, $P(E_2) = 0.20$, $P(E_3) = 0.20$, $P(E_4) = 0.25$, $P(E_5) = 0.15$, $P(E_6) = 0.10$, and $P(E_7) = 0.05$. Let

$$A = \{E_1, E_4, E_6\}$$
$$B = \{E_2, E_4, E_7\}$$
$$C = \{E_2, E_3, E_5, E_7\}$$

and answer the following. **LO 2, 3**

a. Find $P(A)$, $P(B)$, and $P(C)$.
b. Find $A \cup B$ and $P(A \cup B)$.
c. Find $A \cap B$ and $P(A \cap B)$.
d. Are events A and C mutually exclusive?
e. Find B^c and $P(B^c)$.

Applications

24. **Clarkson University Alumni Survey.** Clarkson University surveyed alumni to learn more about what they think of Clarkson. One part of the survey asked respondents to indicate whether their overall experience at Clarkson fell short of expectations, met expectations, or surpassed expectations. The results showed that 4% of the respondents did not provide a response, 26% said that their experience fell short of expectations, and 65% of the respondents said that their experience met expectations. **LO 2, 3**
   a. If we chose an alumnus at random, what is the probability that the alumnus would say their experience *surpassed* expectations?
   b. If we chose an alumnus at random, what is the probability that the alumnus would say their experience met or surpassed expectations?

25. **Americans Using Facebook and LinkedIn.** A Pew Research Center survey (Pew Research website) examined the use of social media platforms in the United States. The survey found that there is a 0.68 probability that a randomly selected American will use Facebook and a 0.25 probability that a randomly selected American will use LinkedIn. In addition, there is a 0.22 probability that a randomly selected American will use both Facebook and LinkedIn. **LO 2, 3**
   a. What is the probability that a randomly selected American will use Facebook or LinkedIn?
   b. What is the probability that a randomly selected American will not use either social media platform?

26. **Morningstar Mutual Fund Ratings.** Information about mutual funds provided by Morningstar Investment Research includes the type of mutual fund (Domestic Equity, International Equity, or Fixed Income) and the Morningstar rating for the fund. The rating is expressed from 1-star (lowest rating) to 5-star (highest rating). Suppose a sample of 25 mutual funds provided the following counts:
   - Sixteen mutual funds were Domestic Equity funds.
   - Thirteen mutual funds were rated 3-star or less.
   - Seven of the Domestic Equity funds were rated 4-star.
   - Two of the Domestic Equity funds were rated 5-star.

   Assume that one of these 25 mutual funds will be randomly selected in order to learn more about the mutual fund and its investment strategy. **LO 2, 3**
   a. What is the probability of selecting a Domestic Equity fund?
   b. What is the probability of selecting a fund with a 4-star or 5-star rating?
   c. What is the probability of selecting a fund that is both a Domestic Equity fund *and* a fund with a 4-star or 5-star rating?
   d. What is the probability of selecting a fund that is a Domestic Equity fund *or* a fund with a 4-star or 5-star rating?

27. **Students at Mideastern University.** According to the National Center for Education Statistics (NCES), nearly 20% of the bachelor's degrees awarded in 2019 were business degrees (NCES website). Suppose that 24% of students at Mideastern University study business. Students at Mideastern University either live on campus or commute to campus. It is known that 38% of students commute to campus at Mideastern University and 59.5% of students are either business students or live on campus. **LO 3, 5**
    a. What is the probability that a randomly selected student at Mideastern University lives on campus?
    b. What is the probability that a randomly selected student at Mideastern University studies business and lives on campus?
    c. Is it true that a student studying business and a student commuting to campus at Mideastern University are mutually exclusive events? Explain.

28. **Survey on Car Rentals.** A survey of magazine subscribers showed that 45.8% rented a car during the past 12 months for business reasons, 54% rented a car during the past 12 months for personal reasons, and 30% rented a car during the past 12 months for both business and personal reasons. **LO 2, 3**
    a. What is the probability that a subscriber rented a car during the past 12 months for business or personal reasons?
    b. What is the probability that a subscriber did not rent a car during the past 12 months for either business or personal reasons?

29. **Ivy League Admissions.** High school seniors with strong academic records apply to the nation's most selective colleges in greater numbers each year. Because the number of slots remains relatively stable, some colleges reject more early applicants. Suppose that for a recent admissions class, an Ivy League college received 2,851 applications for early admission. Of this group, it admitted 1,033 students early, rejected 854 outright, and deferred 964 to the regular admission pool for further consideration. In the past, this school has admitted 18% of the deferred early admission applicants during the regular admission process. Counting the students admitted early and the students admitted during the regular admission process, the total class size was 2,375. Let E, R, and D represent the events that a student who applies for early admission is admitted early, rejected outright, or deferred to the regular admissions pool. **LO 2, 3**
    a. Use the data to estimate $P(E)$, $P(R)$, and $P(D)$.
    b. Are events E and D mutually exclusive? Find $P(E \cap D)$.
    c. For the 2,375 students who were admitted, what is the probability that a randomly selected student was accepted during early admission?
    d. Suppose a student applies for early admission. What is the probability that the student will be admitted for early admission or be deferred and later admitted during the regular admission process?

4.4 Conditional Probability

Often, the probability of an event is influenced by whether a related event already occurred. Suppose we have an event A with probability $P(A)$. If we obtain new information and learn that a related event, denoted by B, already occurred, we will want to take advantage of this information by calculating a new probability for event A. This new probability of event A is called a **conditional probability** and is written $P(A \mid B)$. We use the notation $\mid$ to indicate that we are considering the probability of event A *given* the condition that event B has occurred. Hence, the notation $P(A \mid B)$ reads "the probability of A given B."

As an illustration of the application of conditional probability, consider the situation of the promotion status of male and female officers of a major metropolitan police force in the eastern United States. The police force consists of 1,200 officers, 960 of whom self-identify as males, and 240 of whom self-identify as females. Over the past two

Table 4.4 Promotion Status of Police Officers Over the Past Two Years

	Male	Female	Total
Promoted	288	36	324
Not Promoted	672	204	876
Total	960	240	1,200

years, 324 officers on the police force received promotions. The specific breakdown of promotions for male and female officers is shown in Table 4.4.

After reviewing the promotion record, a committee of female officers raised a discrimination case on the basis that 288 male officers had received promotions, but only 36 female officers had received promotions. The police administration argued that the relatively low number of promotions for female officers was due not to discrimination, but to the fact that relatively few females are members of the police force. Let us show how conditional probability could be used to analyze the discrimination charge.

Let

$$
\begin{aligned}
M &= \text{event an officer is a male}\\
F &= \text{event an officer is a female}\\
A &= \text{event an officer is promoted}\\
A^c &= \text{event an officer is not promoted}
\end{aligned}
$$

Dividing the data values in Table 4.4 by the total of 1,200 officers enables us to summarize the available information with the following probability values.

$P(M \cap A) = 288/1{,}200 = 0.24$ probability that a randomly selected officer is male *and* is promoted

$P(M \cap A^c) = 672/1{,}200 = 0.56$ probability that a randomly selected officer is male *and* is not promoted

$P(F \cap A) = 36/1{,}200 = 0.03$ probability that a randomly selected officer is female *and* is promoted

$P(F \cap A^c) = 204/1{,}200 = 0.17$ probability that a randomly selected officer is female *and* is not promoted

Because each of these values gives the probability of the intersection of two events, the probabilities are called **joint probabilities**. Table 4.5, which provides a summary of the

Table 4.5 Joint Probability Table for Promotions

	Male (M)	Female (F)	Total
Promoted (A)	0.24	0.03	0.27
Not Promoted (A^c)	0.56	0.17	0.73
Total	0.80	0.20	1.00

Joint probabilities appear in the body of the table.

Marginal probabilities appear in the margins of the table.

probability information for the police officer promotion situation, is referred to as a *joint probability table.*

The values in the margins of the joint probability table provide the probabilities of each event separately. That is, $P(M) = 0.80$, $P(F) = 0.20$, $P(A) = 0.27$, and $P(A^c) = 0.73$. These probabilities are referred to as **marginal probabilities** because of their location in the margins of the joint probability table. We note that the marginal probabilities are found by summing the joint probabilities in the corresponding row or column of the joint probability table. For instance, the marginal probability of being promoted is $P(A) = P(M \cap A) + P(F \cap A) = 0.24 + 0.03 = 0.27$. From the marginal probabilities, we see that 80% of the force is male, 20% of the force is female, 27% of all officers received promotions, and 73% were not promoted.

Let us begin the conditional probability analysis by computing the probability that an officer is promoted given that the officer is male. In conditional probability notation, we are attempting to determine $P(A \mid M)$. To calculate $P(A \mid M)$, we first realize that this notation simply means that we are considering the probability of the event A (promotion) given that the condition designated as event M (the officer is male) is known to exist. Thus, $P(A \mid M)$ tells us that we are now concerned only with the promotion status of the 960 male officers. Because 288 of the 960 male officers received promotions, the probability of being promoted given that the officer is male is $288/960 = 0.30$. In other words, given that an officer is male, that officer had a 30% chance of receiving a promotion over the past two years.

This procedure was easy to apply because the values in Table 4.4 show the number of officers in each category. We now want to demonstrate how conditional probabilities such as $P(A \mid M)$ can be computed directly from related event probabilities rather than the frequency data of Table 4.4.

We have shown that $P(A \mid M) = 288/960 = 0.30$. Let us now divide both the numerator and denominator of this fraction by 1,200, the total number of officers in the study.

$$P(A \mid M) = \frac{288}{960} = \frac{288/1{,}200}{960/1{,}200} = \frac{0.24}{0.80} = 0.30$$

We now see that the conditional probability $P(A \mid M)$ can be computed as 0.24/0.80. Refer to the joint probability table (see Table 4.5). Note in particular that 0.24 is the joint probability of A and M; that is, $P(A \cap M) = 0.24$. Also note that 0.80 is the marginal probability that a randomly selected officer is male; that is, $P(M) = 0.80$. Thus, the conditional probability $P(A \mid M)$ can be computed as the ratio of the joint probability $P(A \cap M)$ to the marginal probability $P(M)$.

$$P(A \mid M) = \frac{P(A \cap M)}{P(M)} = \frac{0.24}{0.80} = 0.30$$

The fact that conditional probabilities can be computed as the ratio of a joint probability to a marginal probability provides the following general formula for conditional probability calculations for two events A and B.

Conditional Probability

$$P(A \mid B) = \frac{P(A \cap B)}{P(B)} \quad \textbf{(4.7)}$$

or

$$P(B \mid A) = \frac{P(A \cap B)}{P(A)} \quad \textbf{(4.8)}$$

The Venn diagram in Figure 4.8 is helpful in obtaining an intuitive understanding of conditional probability. The circle on the right shows that event B has occurred; the portion

Figure 4.8 Conditional Probability $P(A \mid B) = P(A \cap B)/P(B)$

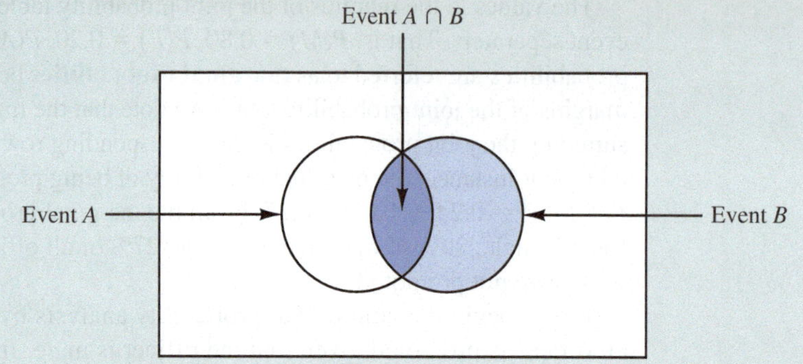

of the circle that overlaps with event A denotes the event $(A \cap B)$. We know that once event B has occurred, the only way that we can also observe event A is for the event $(A \cap B)$ to occur. Thus, the ratio $P(A \cap B)/P(B)$ provides the conditional probability that we will observe event A given that event B has already occurred.

Let us return to the issue of discrimination against the female officers. The marginal probability in row 1 of Table 4.5 shows that the probability of promotion of an officer is $P(A) = 0.27$ (regardless of whether that officer is male or female). However, the critical issue in the discrimination case involves the two conditional probabilities $P(A \mid M)$ and $P(A \mid F)$. That is, what is the probability of a promotion *given* that the officer is male, and what is the probability of a promotion *given* that the officer is female? If these two probabilities are equal, a discrimination argument has no basis because the chances of a promotion are the same for male and female officers. However, a difference in the two conditional probabilities will support the position that male and female officers are treated differently in promotion decisions.

We already determined that $P(A \mid M) = 0.30$. Let us now use the probability values in Table 4.5 and the basic relationship of conditional probability in equation (4.7) to compute the probability that an officer is promoted given that the officer is female; that is, $P(A \mid F)$. Using equation (4.7), with F replacing B, we obtain

$$P(A \mid F) = \frac{P(A \cap F)}{P(F)} = \frac{0.03}{0.20} = 0.15$$

What conclusion do you draw? The probability of a promotion given that the officer is male is 0.30, twice the 0.15 probability of a promotion given that the officer is female. Although the use of conditional probability does not in itself prove that discrimination exists in this case, the conditional probability values support the argument presented by the female officers.

Independent Events

In the preceding illustration, $P(A) = 0.27$, $P(A \mid M) = 0.30$, and $P(A \mid F) = 0.15$. We see that the probability of a promotion (event A) is affected or influenced by whether the officer is male or female. Particularly, because $P(A \mid M) \neq P(A)$, we would say that events A and M are dependent events. That is, the probability of event A (promotion) is altered or affected by knowing that event M (the officer is male) exists. Similarly, with $P(A \mid F) \neq P(A)$, we would say that events A and F are dependent events. However, if the probability of event A is not changed by the existence of event M—that is, $P(A \mid M) = P(A)$—we would say that events A and M are **independent events**. This situation leads to the following definition of the independence of two events.

Independent Events

Two events A and B are independent if

$$P(A \mid B) = P(A) \quad \textbf{(4.9)}$$

or

$$P(B \mid A) = P(B) \quad \textbf{(4.10)}$$

Otherwise, the events are dependent.

Multiplication Law

Whereas the addition law of probability is used to compute the probability of a union of two events, the multiplication law is used to compute the probability of the intersection of two events. The multiplication law is based on the definition of conditional probability. Using equations (4.7) and (4.8) and solving for $P(A \cap B)$, we obtain the **multiplication law**.

Multiplication Law

$$P(A \cap B) = P(B)P(A \mid B) \quad \textbf{(4.11)}$$

or

$$P(A \cap B) = P(A)P(B \mid A) \quad \textbf{(4.12)}$$

To illustrate the use of the multiplication law, consider a digital marketing company that tracks consumer usage of video streaming services. For a particular city, it is known that 84% of the households subscribe to the Netflix streaming service. If we let N denote the event that a household subscribes to Netflix streaming service, $P(N) = 0.84$. In addition, it is known that the probability that a household that already subscribes to Netflix streaming service also subscribes to Disney Plus streaming service (event D) is 0.75; that is, $P(D \mid N) = 0.75$. What is the probability that a household subscribes to both Netflix and Disney Plus streaming? Using the multiplication law, we compute the desired $P(D \cap N)$ as

$$P(D \cap N) = P(N)P(D \mid N) = 0.84(0.75) = 0.63$$

We now know that 63% of the households subscribe to both Netflix and Disney Plus streaming services.

Before concluding this section, let us consider the special case of the multiplication law when the events involved are independent. Recall that events A and B are independent whenever $P(A \mid B) = P(A)$ or $P(B \mid A) = P(B)$. Hence, using equations (4.11) and (4.12) for the special case of independent events, we obtain the following multiplication law.

Multiplication Law for Independent Events

$$P(A \cap B) = P(A)P(B) \quad \textbf{(4.13)}$$

To compute the probability of the intersection of two independent events, we simply multiply the corresponding probabilities. Note that the multiplication law for independent events provides another way to determine whether A and B are independent. That is, if $P(A \cap B) = P(A)P(B)$, then A and B are independent; if $P(A \cap B) \neq P(A)P(B)$, then A and B are dependent.

As an application of the multiplication law for independent events, consider the situation of a service station manager who knows from past experience that 80% of the customers use a credit card when they purchase gasoline. What is the probability that the next two customers purchasing gasoline will each use a credit card? If we let

A = the event that the first customer uses a credit card
B = the event that the second customer uses a credit card

then the event of interest is $A \cap B$. Given no other information, we can reasonably assume that A and B are independent events. Thus,

$$P(A \cap B) = P(A)P(B) = (0.80)(0.80) = 0.64$$

To summarize this section, we note that our interest in conditional probability is motivated by the fact that events are often related. In such cases, we say the events are dependent and the conditional probability formulas in equations (4.7) and (4.8) must be used to compute the event probabilities. If two events are not related, they are independent; in this case, neither event's probability is affected by whether the other event occurred.

Notes + Comments

Do not confuse the notion of mutually exclusive events with that of independent events. Two events with nonzero probabilities cannot be both mutually exclusive and independent. If one mutually exclusive event is known to occur, the other cannot occur; thus, the probability of the other event occurring is reduced to zero. They are, therefore, dependent.

Exercises

Methods

30. Suppose that we have two events, A and B, with $P(A) = 0.50$, $P(B) = 0.60$, and $P(A \cap B) = 0.40$. **LO 4**
    a. Find $P(A \mid B)$.
    b. Find $P(B \mid A)$.
    c. Are A and B independent? Why or why not?
31. Assume that we have two events, A and B, that are mutually exclusive. Assume further that we know $P(A) = 0.30$ and $P(B) = 0.40$. **LO 3, 4, 5**
    a. What is $P(A \cap B)$?
    b. What is $P(A \mid B)$?
    c. A student in statistics argues that the concepts of mutually exclusive events and independent events are really the same, and that if events are mutually exclusive they must be independent. Do you agree with this statement? Use the probability information in this problem to justify your answer.
    d. What general conclusion would you make about mutually exclusive and independent events given the results of this problem?

Applications

32. **Saving Enough to Retire.** Consider the following example survey results of 30–39-year-old and 40–49-year-old respondents in the United States, in response to the question, "Do you think you have saved enough to comfortably retire when you are 65 years old?" **LO 3, 4, 5**

	Yes	No	Totals
30–39 Years Old	95	142	237
40–49 Years Old	50	213	263
Totals	145	355	500

a. Develop the joint probability table for these data and use it to answer the following questions.
b. What are the marginal probabilities?
c. What is the probability that a 30–39-year-old respondent in the United States thinks they have saved enough to retire when they are 65 years old?
d. What is the probability that a 40–49-year-old respondent in the United States thinks they have saved enough to retire when they are 65 years old?

33. **Intent to Pursue MBA.** Students taking the Graduate Management Admissions Test (GMAT) were asked about their undergraduate major and intent to pursue their MBA as a full-time or part-time student. A summary of their responses follows. **LO 3, 4, 5, 6**

		Undergraduate Major			
		Business	Engineering	Other	Totals
Intended Enrollment Status	Full-Time	352	197	251	800
	Part-Time	150	161	194	505
	Totals	502	358	445	1,305

a. Develop a joint probability table for these data.
b. Use the marginal probabilities of undergraduate major (business, engineering, or other) to comment on which undergraduate major produces the most potential MBA students.
c. If a student intends to attend classes full-time in pursuit of an MBA degree, what is the probability that the student was an undergraduate engineering major?
d. If a student was an undergraduate business major, what is the probability that the student intends to attend classes full-time in pursuit of an MBA degree?
e. Let F denote the event that the student intends to attend classes full-time in pursuit of an MBA degree, and let B denote the event that the student was an undergraduate business major. Are events F and B independent? Justify your answer.

34. **On-Time Performance of Airlines.** The Bureau of Transportation Statistics reports on-time performance for airlines at major U.S. airports. JetBlue, United, and US Airways share Terminal C at Boston's Logan Airport. The percentage of on-time flights reported for a sample month were 76.8% for JetBlue, 71.5% for United, and 82.2% for US Airways. Assume that 30% of the flights arriving at Terminal C are JetBlue flights, 32% are United flights, and 38% US Airways flights. **LO 3, 4, 6**
a. Develop a joint probability table with three rows (the airlines) and two columns (on-time and late).
b. An announcement is made that Flight 1382 will be arriving at gate 20 of Terminal C. What is the probability that Flight 1382 will arrive on time?
c. What is the most likely airline for Flight 1382? What is the probability that Flight 1382 is by this airline?
d. Suppose that an announcement is made saying that Flight 1382 will now be arriving late. What is the most likely airline for this flight? What is the probability that Flight 1382 is by this airline?

35. **Age Ranges of Sports Fans.** According to a 2019 survey, the National Basketball Association (NBA) is most popular among younger fans (aged 18–29) while Major League Baseball (MLB) and the National Football League (NFL) are most popular for fans 30 years of age or older (*Statista.com*). Suppose that in a survey of 2500 randomly selected adults in the United States, respondents are asked to provide their favorite professional sports league out of NBA, MLB, and NFL. The results of the survey appear below. **LO 3, 4, 6**

	Favorite Professional Sports League		
Respondent's Age Range	**NBA**	**MLB**	**NFL**
18–29	230	120	240
30–54	180	260	665
55+	160	225	420

a. Develop a joint probability table and use it to answer the following questions.
b. Construct the marginal probabilities for each of the professional sports leagues (NBA, MLB, and NFL).
c. Given that a respondent is 18–29 years of age, what is the probability that the respondent's favorite professional sports league is MLB?
d. Given that a respondent is 55+ years of age, what is the probability that the respondent's favorite professional sports league is MLB?
e. Given that the respondent states that MLB is their favorite professional sports league, what is the probability that the respondent is 18–29 years of age?
f. Given that the respondent states that the NFL is their favorite professional sports league, are they more likely to be aged 18–29, 30–45, or 55+? What is the probability that the respondent is in this age range?

36. **NBA Free Throws.** Suppose that a particular NBA player makes 93% of free throws. Assume that late in a basketball game, this player is fouled and is awarded two free throws. **LO 2, 3**
a. What is the probability that the player will make both free throws?
b. What is the probability that the player will make at least one free throw?
c. What is the probability that the player will miss both free throws?
d. Late in a basketball game, a team often intentionally fouls an opposing player in order to stop the game clock. The usual strategy is to intentionally foul the other team's worst free-throw shooter. Assume that the team's worst free-throw shooter makes 58% of their free-throw shots. Calculate the probabilities for this player as shown in parts (a), (b), and (c), and show that intentionally fouling this player who makes 58% of his free throws is a better strategy than intentionally fouling the player who makes 93% of his free throws. Assume as in parts (a), (b), and (c) that two free throws will be awarded.

37. **Giving Up Electronics.** A 2018 Pew Research Center survey found that more Americans believe they could give up their televisions than could give up their cell phones (Pew Research website). Assume that the following table represents the joint probabilities of Americans who could give up their television or cell phone. **LO 3, 4**

		Could Give Up Television		
		Yes	**No**	
Could Give Up Cell Phone	**Yes**	0.31	0.17	0.48
	No	0.38	0.14	0.52
		0.69	0.31	

a. What is the probability that a person could give up her cell phone?
b. What is the probability that a person who could give up her cell phone could also give up television?
c. What is the probability that a person who could not give up her cell phone could give up television?
d. Is the probability a person could give up television higher if the person could not give up a cell phone or if the person could give up a cell phone?

38. **Payback of Student Loans.** The Institute for Higher Education Policy, a Washington, DC-based research firm, studied the payback of student loans for 1.8 million college students who had student loans that began to become due six years prior (*The Wall Street Journal*). The study found that 50% of the student loans were being paid back in a satisfactory fashion, and 50% of the student loans were delinquent. The following joint probability table shows the probabilities of a student's loan status and whether or not the student had received a college degree. **LO 2, 3, 4**

		College Degree		
		Yes	No	
Loan Status	Satisfactory	0.26	0.24	0.50
	Delinquent	0.16	0.34	0.50
		0.42	0.58	

a. What is the probability that a student with a student loan had received a college degree?
b. What is the probability that a student with a student loan had not received a college degree?
c. Given the student had received a college degree, what is the probability that the student has a delinquent loan?
d. Given the student had not received a college degree, what is the probability that the student has a delinquent loan?
e. What is the impact of dropping out of college without a degree for students who have a student loan?

4.5 Bayes' Theorem

In the discussion of conditional probability, we indicated that revising probabilities when new information is obtained is an important phase of probability analysis. Often, we begin the analysis with initial or **prior probability** estimates for specific events of interest. Then, from sources such as a sample, a special report, or a product test, we obtain additional information about the events. Given this new information, we update the prior probability values by calculating revised probabilities, referred to as **posterior probabilities. Bayes' theorem** provides a means for making these probability calculations. The steps in this probability revision process are shown in Figure 4.9.

Figure 4.9 Probability Revision Using Bayes' Theorem

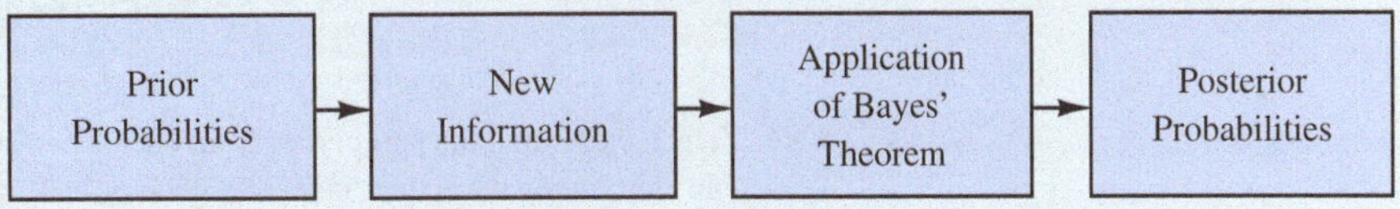

Table 4.6 Historical Quality Levels of Two Suppliers

	Percentage Good Parts	Percentage Bad Parts
Supplier 1	98	2
Supplier 2	95	5

As an application of Bayes' theorem, consider a manufacturing firm that receives shipments of parts from two different suppliers. Let A_1 denote the event that a part is from supplier 1 and A_2 denote the event that a part is from supplier 2. Currently, 65% of the parts purchased by the company are from supplier 1 and the remaining 35% are from supplier 2. Hence, if a part is selected at random, we would assign the prior probabilities $P(A_1) = 0.65$ and $P(A_2) = 0.35$.

The quality of the purchased parts varies with the source of supply. Historical data suggest that the quality ratings of the two suppliers are as shown in Table 4.6. If we let G denote the event that a part is good and B denote the event that a part is bad, the information in Table 4.6 provides the following conditional probability values.

$$P(G \mid A_1) = 0.98 \quad P(B \mid A_1) = 0.02$$
$$P(G \mid A_2) = 0.95 \quad P(B \mid A_2) = 0.05$$

The tree diagram in Figure 4.10 depicts the process of the firm receiving a part from one of the two suppliers and then discovering that the part is good or bad as a two-step experiment. We see that four experimental outcomes are possible; two correspond to the part being good and two correspond to the part being bad.

Each of the experimental outcomes is the intersection of two events, so we can use the multiplication rule to compute the probabilities. For instance,

$$P(A_1, G) = P(A_1 \cap G) = P(A_1)P(G \mid A_1)$$

The process of computing these joint probabilities can be depicted in what is called a probability tree (see Figure 4.11). From left to right through the tree, the probabilities for each branch at step 1 are prior probabilities and the probabilities for each branch at step 2 are conditional probabilities. To find the probabilities of each experimental outcome, we simply

Figure 4.10 Tree Diagram for Two-Supplier Example

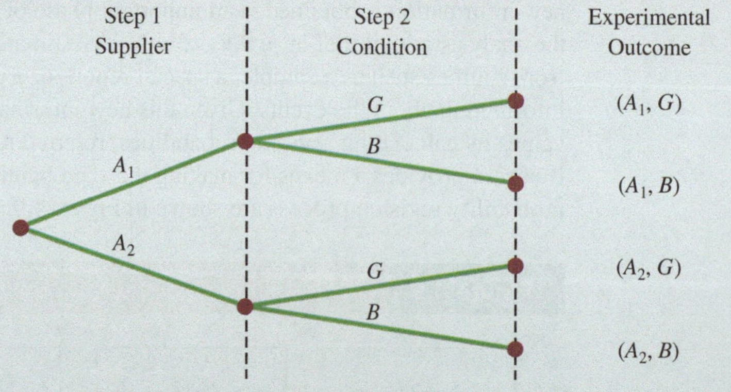

Note: Step 1 shows that the part comes from one of two suppliers, and step 2 shows whether the part is good or bad.

Figure 4.11 Probability Tree for Two-Supplier Example

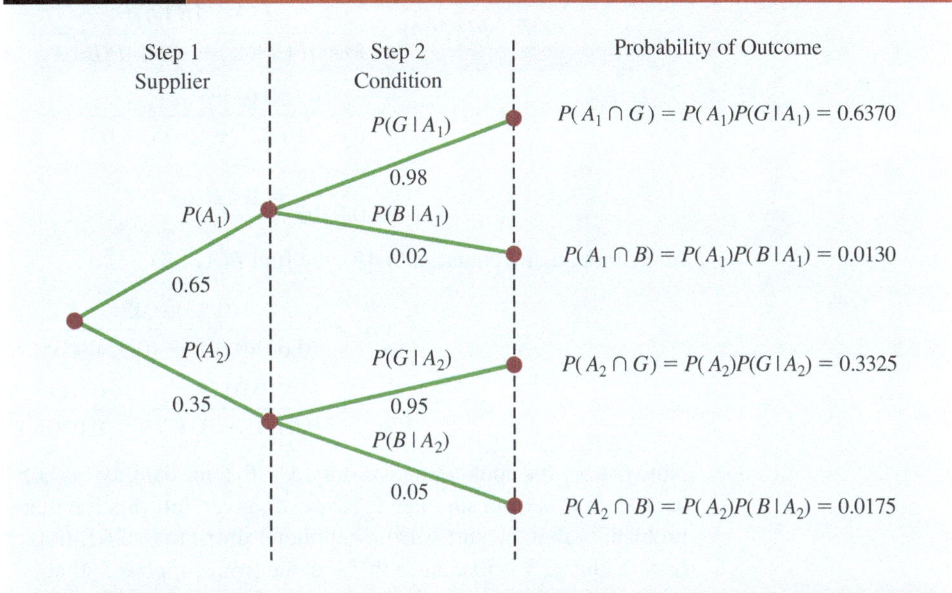

multiply the probabilities on the branches leading to the outcome. Each of these joint probabilities is shown in Figure 4.11, along with the known probabilities for each branch.

Suppose now that the parts from the two suppliers are used in the firm's manufacturing process and that a machine breaks down because it attempts to process a bad part. Given the information that the part is bad, what is the probability that it came from supplier 1 and what is the probability that it came from supplier 2? With the information in the probability tree (Figure 4.11), Bayes' theorem can be used to answer these questions.

Letting B denote the event that the part is bad, we are looking for the posterior probabilities $P(A_1 \mid B)$ and $P(A_2 \mid B)$. From the law of conditional probability, we know that

$$P(A_1 \mid B) = \frac{P(A_1 \cap B)}{P(B)} \tag{4.14}$$

Referring to the probability tree, we see that

$$P(A_1 \cap B) = P(A_1)P(B \mid A_1) \tag{4.15}$$

To find $P(B)$, we note that event B can occur in only two ways: $(A_1 \cap B)$ and $(A_2 \cap B)$. Therefore, we have

$$\begin{aligned} P(B) &= P(A_1 \cap B) + P(A_2 \cap B) \\ &= P(A_1)P(B \mid A_1) + P(A_2)P(B \mid A_2) \end{aligned} \tag{4.16}$$

Substituting from equations (4.15) and (4.16) into equation (4.14) and writing a similar result for $P(A_2 \mid B)$, we obtain Bayes' theorem for the case of two events.

The Reverend Thomas Bayes (1702–1761), a Presbyterian minister, is credited with the original work leading to the version of Bayes' theorem in use today.

Bayes' Theorem (Two-Event Case)

$$P(A_1 \mid B) = \frac{P(A_1)P(B \mid A_1)}{P(A_1)P(B \mid A_1) + P(A_2)P(B \mid A_2)} \tag{4.17}$$

$$P(A_2 \mid B) = \frac{P(A_2)P(B \mid A_2)}{P(A_1)P(B \mid A_1) + P(A_2)P(B \mid A_2)} \tag{4.18}$$

Using equation (4.17) and the probability values provided in the example, we have

$$P(A_1 \mid B) = \frac{P(A_1)P(B \mid A_1)}{P(A_1)P(B \mid A_1) + P(A_2)P(B \mid A_2)}$$

$$= \frac{(0.65)(0.02)}{(0.65)(0.02) + (0.35)(0.05)} = \frac{0.0130}{0.0130 + 0.0175}$$

$$= \frac{0.0130}{0.0305} = 0.4262$$

In addition, using equation (4.18), we find $P(A_2 \mid B)$.

$$P(A_2 \mid B) = \frac{(0.35)(0.05)}{(0.65)(0.02) + (0.35)(0.05)}$$

$$= \frac{0.0175}{0.0130 + 0.0175} = \frac{0.0175}{0.0305} = 0.5738$$

Note that in this application we started with a probability of 0.65 that a part selected at random was from supplier 1. However, given information that the part is bad, the probability that the part is from supplier 1 drops to 0.4262. In fact, if the part is bad, there is more than a 50–50 chance that it came from supplier 2; that is, $P(A_2 \mid B) = 0.5738$.

Bayes' theorem is applicable when the events for which we want to compute posterior probabilities are mutually exclusive and their union is the entire sample space.[1] For the case of n mutually exclusive events $A_1, A_2, \ldots, A_n$, whose union is the entire sample space, Bayes' theorem can be used to compute any posterior probability $P(A_i \mid B)$, as shown here.

Bayes' Theorem

$$P(A_i \mid B) = \frac{P(A_i)P(B \mid A_i)}{P(A_1)P(B \mid A_1) + P(A_2)P(B \mid A_2) + \cdots + P(A_n)P(B \mid A_n)} \quad \textbf{(4.19)}$$

With prior probabilities $P(A_1), P(A_2), \ldots, P(A_n)$ and the appropriate conditional probabilities $P(B \mid A_1), P(B \mid A_2), \ldots, P(B \mid A_n)$, equation (4.19) can be used to compute the posterior probability of the events $A_1, A_2, \ldots, A_n$.

Tabular Approach

A tabular approach is helpful in conducting the Bayes' theorem calculations. Such an approach is shown in Table 4.7 for the parts supplier problem. The computations shown there are done in the following steps.

Table 4.7 Tabular Approach to Bayes' Theorem Calculations for the Two-Supplier Problem

(1) Events A_i	(2) Prior Probabilities $P(A_i)$	(3) Conditional Probabilities $P(B \mid A_i)$	(4) Joint Probabilities $P(A_i \cap B)$	(5) Posterior Probabilities $P(A_i \mid B)$
A_1	0.65	0.02	0.0130	0.0130/0.0305 = 0.4262
A_2	0.35	0.05	0.0175	0.0175/0.0305 = 0.5738
	1.00		$P(B)$ = 0.0305	1.0000

[1] If the union of events is the entire sample space, the events are said to be collectively exhaustive.

Step 1. Prepare the following three columns:

Column 1—The mutually exclusive events A_i for which posterior probabilities are desired

Column 2—The prior probabilities $P(A_i)$ for the events

Column 3—The conditional probabilities $P(B \mid A_i)$ of the new information B given each event

Step 2. In column 4, compute the joint probabilities $P(A_i \cap B)$ for each event and the new information B by using the multiplication law. These joint probabilities are found by multiplying the prior probabilities in column 2 by the corresponding conditional probabilities in column 3; that is, $P(A_i \cap B) = P(A_i)P(B \mid A_i)$.

Step 3. Sum the joint probabilities in column 4. The sum is the probability of the new information, $P(B)$. Thus we see in Table 4.7 that there is a 0.0130 probability that the part came from supplier 1 and is bad and a 0.0175 probability that the part came from supplier 2 and is bad. Because these are the only two ways in which a bad part can be obtained, the sum 0.0130 + 0.0175 shows an overall probability of 0.0305 of finding a bad part from the combined shipments of the two suppliers.

Step 4. In column 5, compute the posterior probabilities using the basic relationship of conditional probability.

$$P(A_i \mid B) = \frac{P(A_i \cap B)}{P(B)}$$

Note that the joint probabilities $P(A_i \cap B)$ are in column 4 and the probability $P(B)$ is the sum of column 4.

Notes + Comments

1. Bayes' theorem is used extensively in decision analysis. The prior probabilities are often subjective estimates provided by a decision maker. Sample information is obtained and posterior probabilities are computed for use in choosing the best decision. We further explore the use of Bayes' theorem in decision analysis in Chapter 20.
2. An event and its complement are mutually exclusive, and their union is the entire sample space. Thus, Bayes' theorem is always applicable for computing posterior probabilities of an event and its complement.

Exercises

Methods

39. The prior probabilities for events A_1 and A_2 are $P(A_1) = 0.40$ and $P(A_2) = 0.60$. It is also known that $P(A_1 \cap A_2) = 0$. Suppose $P(B \mid A_1) = 0.20$ and $P(B \mid A_2) = 0.05$. **LO 3, 4, 5, 7**
    a. Are A_1 and A_2 mutually exclusive? Explain.
    b. Compute $P(A_1 \cap B)$ and $P(A_2 \cap B)$.
    c. Compute $P(B)$.
    d. Apply Bayes' theorem to compute $P(A_1 \mid B)$ and $P(A_2 \mid B)$.
40. The prior probabilities for events A_1, A_2, and A_3 are $P(A_1) = 0.20$, $P(A_2) = 0.50$, and $P(A_3) = 0.30$, respectively. The conditional probabilities of event B given A_1, A_2, and A_3 are $P(B \mid A_1) = 0.50$, $P(B \mid A_2) = 0.40$, and $P(B \mid A_3) = 0.30$. **LO 3, 4, 7**
    a. Compute $P(B \cap A_1)$, $P(B \cap A_2)$, and $P(B \cap A_3)$.
    b. Apply Bayes' theorem, equation (4.19), to compute the posterior probability $P(A_2 \mid B)$.
    c. Use the tabular approach to applying Bayes' theorem to compute $P(A_1 \mid B)$, $P(A_2 \mid B)$, and $P(A_3 \mid B)$.

Applications

41. **Consulting Firm Bids.** A consulting firm submitted a bid for a large research project. The firm's management initially felt they had a 50–50 chance of getting the project. However, the agency to which the bid was submitted subsequently requested additional information on the bid. Past experience indicates that for 75% of the successful bids and 40% of the unsuccessful bids the agency requested additional information. **LO 3, 4, 7**
    a. What is the prior probability of the bid being successful (that is, prior to the request for additional information)?
    b. What is the conditional probability of a request for additional information given that the bid will ultimately be successful?
    c. Compute the posterior probability that the bid will be successful given a request for additional information.

42. **Credit Card Defaults.** A local bank reviewed its credit card policy with the intention of recalling some of its credit cards. In the past approximately 5% of cardholders defaulted, leaving the bank unable to collect the outstanding balance. Hence, management established a prior probability of 0.05 that any particular cardholder will default. The bank also found that the probability of missing a monthly payment is 0.20 for customers who do not default. Of course, the probability of missing a monthly payment for those who default is 1. **LO 3, 4, 7**
    a. Given that a customer missed a monthly payment, compute the posterior probability that the customer will default.
    b. The bank would like to recall its credit card if the probability that a customer will default is greater than 0.20. Should the bank recall its credit card if the customer misses a monthly payment? Why or why not?

43. **Prostate Cancer Screening.** According to an article in *Esquire* magazine, approximately 70% of males over age 70 will develop cancerous cells in their prostate. Prostate cancer is second only to skin cancer as the most common form of cancer for males in the United States. One of the most common tests for the detection of prostate cancer is the prostate-specific antigen (PSA) test. However, this test is known to have a high false-positive rate (tests that come back positive for cancer when no cancer is present). Suppose there is a 0.02 probability that a male patient has prostate cancer before testing. The probability of a false-positive test is 0.75, and the probability of a false-negative (no indication of cancer when cancer is actually present) is 0.20. **LO 3, 4, 7**
    a. What is the probability that the male patient has prostate cancer if the PSA test comes back positive?
    b. What is the probability that the male patient has prostate cancer if the PSA test comes back negative?
    c. For older males, the prior probability of having cancer increases. Suppose that the prior probability of the male patient is 0.3 rather than 0.02. What is the probability that the male patient has prostate cancer if the PSA test comes back positive? What is the probability that the male patient has prostate cancer if the PSA test comes back negative?
    d. What can you infer about the PSA test from the results of parts (a), (b), and (c)?

44. **COVID-19 Testing.** More than 1.5 million tests for the COVID virus were performed each day in the United States during the COVID-19 pandemic in 2021. Many employers, schools, and government agencies required negative COVID-19 tests before allowing people on their premises. Suppose that for a particular COVID-19 test, the probability of a false negative (meaning that a person who is actually infected with the COVID-19 virus tests negative for the virus) is 0.1, and that the test always gives a negative result for someone who is not infected with COVID-19. Suppose also the probability that a randomly selected person is infected with COVID-19 is 0.05. Answer the following questions. **LO 3, 4, 7**

a. What is the probability that someone who tests negative for the COVID-19 virus actually has COVID-19?
b. Suppose that a large school system states that 2500 of its students have reported a negative COVID-19 test. Of these 2500 students who tested negative, how many would you expect to have COVID-19?
c. Suppose the incidence of COVID-19 pandemic is actually considerably higher and the probability of any randomly selected person having COVID-19 is 0.20. What is the probability in this case that someone who tests negative for the COVID-19 virus actually has COVID-19? Explain this change from part (a).

45. **Americans Without Health Insurance.** The National Center for Health Statistics, housed within the U.S. Centers for Disease Control and Prevention (CDC), tracks the number of adults in the United States who have health insurance. According to this agency, the uninsured rates for Americans in 2018 are as follows: 5.1% of those under the age of 18, 12.4% of those ages 18–64, and 1.1% of those 65 and older do not have health insurance (CDC website). Approximately 22.8% of Americans are under age 18, and 61.4% of Americans are ages 18–64. **LO 3, 4, 7**
a. What is the probability that a randomly selected person in the United States is 65 or older?
b. Given that the person is an uninsured American, what is the probability that the person is 65 or older?

Summary

In this chapter, we introduced basic probability concepts and illustrated how probability analysis can be used to provide helpful information for decision making. We described how probability can be interpreted as a numerical measure of the likelihood that an event will occur. In addition, we saw that the probability of an event can be computed either by summing the probabilities of the experimental outcomes (sample points) comprising the event or by using the relationships established by the addition, conditional probability, and multiplication laws of probability. For cases in which additional information is available, we showed how Bayes' theorem can be used to obtain revised or posterior probabilities.

Glossary

Addition law A probability law used to compute the probability of the union of two events. It is $P(A \cup B) = P(A) + P(B) - P(A \cap B)$. For mutually exclusive events, $P(A \cap B) = 0$; in this case the addition law reduces to $P(A \cup B) = P(A) + P(B)$.
Basic requirements for assigning probabilities Two requirements that restrict the manner in which probability assignments can be made: (1) For each experimental outcome E_i we must have $0 \leq P(E_i) \leq 1$; (2) considering all experimental outcomes, we must have $P(E_1) + P(E_2) + \cdots + P(E_n) = 1.0$.
Bayes' theorem A method used to compute posterior probabilities.
Classical method A method of assigning probabilities that is appropriate when all the experimental outcomes are equally likely.
Combination In an experiment we may be interested in determining the number of ways x objects may be selected from among n objects without regard to the order in which the x objects are selected. Each selection of x objects is called a combination and the total number of combinations of n objects taken x at a time is $C_x^n = \binom{n}{x} = \frac{n!}{x!(n-x)!}$ for $x = 0, 1, 2, \ldots, n$.
Complement of *A* The event consisting of all sample points that are not in A.
Conditional probability The probability of an event given that another event already occurred. The conditional probability of A given B is $P(A \mid B) = \frac{P(A \cap B)}{P(B)}$.

Event A collection of sample points.
Experiment A process that generates well-defined outcomes.
Independent events Two events A and B where $P(A \mid B) = P(A)$ or $P(B \mid A) = P(B)$; that is, the events have no influence on each other.
Intersection of *A* and *B* The event containing the sample points belonging to both A and B. The intersection is denoted $A \cap B$.
Joint probability The probability of two events both occurring; that is, the probability of the intersection of two events.
Marginal probability The values in the margins of a joint probability table that provide the probabilities of each event separately.
Multiple-step experiment An experiment that can be described as a sequence of steps. If a multiple-step experiment has k steps with n_1 possible outcomes on the first step, n_2 possible outcomes on the second step, and so on, the total number of experimental outcomes is given by $(n_1)(n_2) \ldots (n_k)$.
Multiplication law A probability law used to compute the probability of the intersection of two events. It is $P(A \cap B) = P(B)P(A \mid B)$ or $P(A \cap B) = P(A)P(B \mid A)$. For independent events it reduces to $P(A \cap B) = P(A)P(B)$.
Mutually exclusive events Events that have no sample points in common; that is, $A \cap B$ is empty and $P(A \cap B) = 0$.
Permutation In an experiment we may be interested in determining the number of ways x objects may be selected from among n objects when the order in which the x objects are selected is important. Each ordering of x objects is called a permutation and the total number of permutations of n objects taken x at a time is $P_x^n = x!\binom{n}{x} = \frac{n!}{(n-x)!}$ for $x = 0, 1, 2, \ldots, n$.
Posterior probabilities Revised probabilities of events based on additional information.
Prior probabilities Initial estimates of the probabilities of events.
Probability A numerical measure of the likelihood that an event will occur.
Relative frequency method A method of assigning probabilities that is appropriate when data are available to estimate the proportion of the time the experimental outcome will occur if the experiment is repeated a large number of times.
Sample point An element of the sample space. A sample point represents an experimental outcome.
Sample space The set of all experimental outcomes.
Subjective method A method of assigning probabilities on the basis of judgment.
Tree diagram A graphical representation that helps in visualizing a multiple-step experiment.
Union of *A* and *B* The event containing all sample points belonging to A or B or both. The union is denoted $A \cup B$.
Venn diagram A graphical representation for showing symbolically the sample space and operations involving events in which the sample space is represented by a rectangle and events are represented as circles within the sample space.

Key Formulas

Counting Rule for Combinations

$$C_x^n = \binom{n}{x} = \frac{n!}{x!(n-x)!} \qquad \textbf{(4.1)}$$

Counting Rule for Permutations

$$P_x^n = x!\binom{n}{x} = \frac{n!}{(n-x)!} \qquad \textbf{(4.2)}$$

Computing Probability Using the Complement

$$P(A) = 1 - P(A^c) \qquad \textbf{(4.5)}$$

Addition Law

$$P(A \cup B) = P(A) + P(B) - P(A \cap B) \tag{4.6}$$

Conditional Probability

$$P(A \mid B) = \frac{P(A \cap B)}{P(B)} \tag{4.7}$$

$$P(B \mid A) = \frac{P(A \cap B)}{P(A)} \tag{4.8}$$

Multiplication Law

$$P(A \cap B) = P(B)P(A \mid B) \tag{4.11}$$

$$P(A \cap B) = P(A)P(B \mid A) \tag{4.12}$$

Multiplication Law for Independent Events

$$P(A \cap B) = P(A)P(B) \tag{4.13}$$

Bayes' Theorem

$$P(A_i \mid B) = \frac{P(A_i)P(B \mid A_i)}{P(A_1)P(B \mid A_1) + P(A_2)P(B \mid A_2) + \cdots + P(A_n)P(B \mid A_n)} \tag{4.19}$$

Supplementary Exercises

46. **Time on Vacation Until Relaxed.** A *USA Today* survey of adults aged 18 and older conducted by Princess Cruises asked how many days into a vacation it takes until respondents feel truly relaxed. The responses were as follows. **LO 1, 2**

Days Until Relaxed	Frequency
≤ 1	422
2	181
3	80
$\geq 4, < \infty$	121
Never (∞)	201

a. How many adults participated in the Princess Cruises survey?
b. What response has the highest probability? What is the probability of this response?
c. What is the probability a respondent never feels truly relaxed on a vacation?
d. What is the probability it takes a respondent two or more days to feel truly relaxed?

47. **Financial Manager Investments.** A financial manager made two new investments—one in the oil industry and one in municipal bonds. After a one-year period, each of the investments will be classified as either successful or unsuccessful. Consider the making of the two investments as an experiment. **LO 1, 2, 3, 5**
a. How many sample points exist for this experiment?
b. Show a tree diagram and list the sample points.
c. Let O = the event that the oil industry investment is successful and M = the event that the municipal bond investment is successful. List the sample points in O and in M.
d. List the sample points in the union of the events ($O \cup M$).
e. List the sample points in the intersection of the events ($O \cap M$).
f. Are events O and M mutually exclusive? Explain.

48. **Opinions About Television Programs.** Below are the results of a survey of 1364 self-identifying females and males who were asked if they use social media to voice their opinions about television programs. **LO 2, 3, 4, 5**

	Uses Social Media to Voice Opinions About Television Programs	Doesn't Use Social Media to Voice Opinions About Television Programs
Female	395	291
Male	323	355

a. Show a joint probability table.
b. What is the probability a respondent is female?
c. What is the conditional probability a respondent uses social media to voice opinions about television programs given the respondent is female?
d. Let F denote the event that the respondent is female and A denote the event that the respondent uses social media to voice opinions about television programs. Are events F and A independent?

49. **Treatment-Caused Injuries.** A study of 31,000 hospital admissions in New York State found that 4% of the admissions led to treatment-caused injuries. One-seventh of these treatment-caused injuries resulted in death, and one-fourth were caused by negligence. Malpractice claims were filed in one out of 7.5 cases involving negligence, and payments were made in one out of every two claims. **LO 3, 4**
a. What is the probability a person admitted to the hospital will suffer a treatment-caused injury due to negligence?
b. What is the probability a person admitted to the hospital will die from a treatment-caused injury?
c. What is the probability a person admitted to the hospital will result in a malpractice claim that must be paid due to a negligent treatment that caused injury?

50. **Viewer Response to New Television Show.** A survey to determine viewer response to a new television show obtained the following data. **LO 2, 3**

Rating	Frequency
Poor	4
Below average	8
Average	11
Above average	14
Excellent	13

a. What is the probability that a randomly selected viewer will rate the new show as average or better?
b. What is the probability that a randomly selected viewer will rate the new show below average or worse?

51. **Highest Level of Education and Household Income.** The U.S. Census Bureau serves as the leading source of quantitative data about the nation's people and economy. The following crosstabulation shows the number of households 1,000s and the household income by the highest level of education for the head of household (U.S. Census Bureau website). Only households in which the head has a high school diploma or more are included. **LO 3, 4, 5, 6**

Highest Level of Education	Household Income Under $25,000	$25,000 to $49,999	$50,000 to $99,999	$100,000 and Over	Total
High school graduate	9,880	9,970	9,441	3,482	32,773
Bachelor's degree	2,484	4,164	7,666	7,817	22,131
Master's degree	685	1,205	3,019	4,094	9,003
Doctoral degree	79	160	422	1,076	1,737
Total	13,128	15,499	20,548	16,469	65,644

a. Develop a joint probability table.
b. What is the probability of the head of one of these households having a master's degree or more education?
c. What is the probability of a household headed by someone with a high school diploma earning $100,000 or more?
d. What is the probability of one of these households having an income below $25,000?
e. What is the probability of a household headed by someone with a bachelor's degree earning less than $25,000?
f. Is household income independent of educational level?

52. **MBA New-Matriculants Survey.** An MBA new-matriculants survey provided the following data for 2018 students. **LO 3, 6**

		Applied to More Than One School	
		Yes	No
Age Group	23 and under	207	201
	24–26	299	379
	27–30	185	268
	31–35	66	193
	36 and over	51	169

a. For a randomly selected MBA student, prepare a joint probability table for the experiment consisting of observing the student's age and whether the student applied to one or more schools.
b. What is the probability that a randomly selected applicant is 23 or under?
c. What is the probability that a randomly selected applicant is older than 26?
d. What is the probability that a randomly selected applicant applied to more than one school?

53. **MBA New-Matriculants Survey (revisited).** Refer again to the data from the MBA new matriculants survey in exercise 52. **LO 3, 4, 5, 6**
a. Given that a person applied to more than one school, what is the probability that the person is 24–26 years old?
b. Given that a person is in the 36-and-over age group, what is the probability that the person applied to more than one school?
c. What is the probability that a person is 24–26 years old or applied to more than one school?
d. Suppose a person is known to have applied to only one school. What is the probability that the person is 31 or more years old?
e. Is the number of schools applied to independent of age? Explain.

54. **Internet Sites Collecting User Information.** The Pew Internet & American Life project conducted a survey that included several questions about how Internet users feel about search engines and other websites collecting information about them and using this information either to shape search results or target advertising to them. In one question, participants were asked, "If a search engine kept track of what you search for, and then used that information to personalize your future search results, how would you feel about that?" Respondents could indicate either "Would *not* be okay with it because you feel it is an invasion of your privacy" or "Would be *okay* with it, even if it means they are gathering information about you." Joint probabilities of responses and age groups are summarized in the following table. **LO 3, 4, 5**

Age	Not Okay	Okay
18–29	0.1485	0.0604
30–49	0.2273	0.0907
50+	0.4008	0.0723

a. What is the probability a respondent will say they are *not okay* with this practice?
b. Given a respondent is 30–49 years old, what is the probability the respondent will say they are *okay* with this practice?
c. Given a respondent says they are *not okay* with this practice, what is the probability the respondent is 50+ years old?
d. Is the attitude about this practice independent of the age of the respondent? Why or why not?
e. Do attitudes toward this practice differ for respondents who are 18–29 years old and respondents who are 50+ years old?

55. **Advertisements and Product Purchases.** A large consumer goods company ran a television advertisement for one of its soap products. On the basis of a survey that was conducted, probabilities were assigned to the following events.

B = individual purchased the product
S = individual recalls seeing the advertisement
$B \cap S$ = individual purchased the product and recalls seeing the advertisement

The probabilities assigned were $P(B) = 0.20$, $P(S) = 0.40$, and $P(B \cap S) = 0.12$. **LO 3, 4**

a. What is the probability of an individual's purchasing the product given that the individual recalls seeing the advertisement? Does seeing the advertisement increase the probability that the individual will purchase the product? As a decision maker, would you recommend continuing the advertisement (assuming that the cost is reasonable)?
b. Assume that individuals who do not purchase the company's soap product buy from its competitors. What would be your estimate of the company's market share? Would you expect that continuing the advertisement will increase the company's market share? Why or why not?
c. The company also tested another advertisement and assigned it values of $P(S) = 0.30$ and $P(B \cap S) = 0.10$. What is $P(B \mid S)$ for this other advertisement? Which advertisement seems to have had the bigger effect on customer purchases?

56. **Days Listed Until Sold.** Cooper Realty is a small real estate company located in Albany, New York, specializing primarily in residential listings. They recently became interested in determining the likelihood of one of their listings being sold within a certain number of days. An analysis of company sales of 800 homes in previous years produced the following data. **LO 3, 4, 5**

		Days Listed Until Sold			
		Under 30	31–90	Over 90	Total
Initial Asking Price	Under $150,000	50	40	10	100
	$150,000–$199,999	20	150	80	250
	$200,000–$250,000	20	280	100	400
	Over $250,000	10	30	10	50
	Total	100	500	200	800

a. If A is defined as the event that a home is listed for more than 90 days before being sold, estimate the probability of A.
b. If B is defined as the event that the initial asking price is under $150,000, estimate the probability of B.
c. What is the probability of $A \cap B$?
d. Assuming that a contract was just signed to list a home with an initial asking price of less than $150,000, what is the probability that the home will take Cooper Realty more than 90 days to sell?
e. Are events A and B independent?

57. **Lost-Time Accidents.** A company studied the number of lost-time accidents occurring at its Brownsville, Texas, plant. Historical records show that 6% of the employees suffered lost-time accidents last year. Management believes that a special safety program will reduce such accidents to 5% during the current year. In addition, it estimates that 15% of employees who had lost-time accidents last year will experience a lost-time accident during the current year. **LO 3, 4**
    a. What percentage of the employees will experience lost-time accidents in both years?
    b. What percentage of the employees will suffer at least one lost-time accident over the two-year period?

58. **Corps of Cadets Students Joining the Military.** Southeastern Ohio University offers its students the option of joining the Corps of Cadets to receive specialized leadership and military training while in college. Many students who join the Corps of Cadets in college choose to serve in the military after graduation, but not all Corps of Cadets students do so. Suppose that 6% of Southeastern Ohio University students elect to serve in the military after graduation. Of those students from Southeastern Ohio University who elect to serve in the military after graduation, 87% of those students were part of the Corps of Cadets while in college. Of those students from Southeastern Ohio University who elect not to serve in the military after graduation, 4% of those students were part of the Corps of Cadets while in college. **LO 3, 4, 7**
    a. Given that a Southeastern Ohio University student is in the Corps of Cadets, what is the probability that the student will elect to join the military after graduation?
    b. Given that a Southeastern Ohio University student is not in the Corps of Cadets, what is the probability that the student will elect to join the military after graduation?
    c. If Southeastern Ohio University has 15,000 total students, approximately how many of these students are members of the Corps of Cadets?

59. **Finding Oil in Alaska.** An oil company purchased an option on land in Alaska. Preliminary geologic studies assigned the following prior probabilities.

$$P(\text{high-quality oil}) = 0.50$$
$$P(\text{medium-quality oil}) = 0.20$$
$$P(\text{no oil}) = 0.30$$

Use these prior probabilities to answer the following. **LO 3, 4, 7**

a. What is the probability of finding oil?
b. After 200 feet of drilling on the first well, a soil test is taken. The probabilities of finding the particular type of soil identified by the test follow.

$$P(\text{soil} \mid \text{high-quality oil}) = 0.20$$
$$P(\text{soil} \mid \text{medium-quality oil}) = 0.80$$
$$P(\text{soil} \mid \text{no oil}) = 0.20$$

How should the firm interpret the soil test? What are the revised probabilities, and what is the new probability of finding oil?

60. **Spam E-mail Filters.** A study by *Forbes* indicated that the five most common words appearing in spam e-mails are *shipping!, today!, here!, available,* and *fingertips!* Many spam filters separate spam from ham (e-mail not considered to be spam) through application of Bayes' theorem. Suppose that for one e-mail account, 1 in every 10 messages is spam and the proportions of spam messages that have the five most common words in spam e-mail are given below.

shipping!	0.051
today!	0.045
here!	0.034
available	0.014
fingertips!	0.014

Also suppose that the proportions of ham messages that have these words are

shipping!	0.0015
today!	0.0022
here!	0.0022
available	0.0041
fingertips!	0.0011

Use the information above and Bayes' theorem to answer the following. **LO 3, 4, 7**

a. If a message includes the word *shipping!,* what is the probability the message is spam? If a message includes the word *shipping!,* what is the probability the message is ham? Should messages that include the word *shipping!* be flagged as spam?
b. If a message includes the word *today!,* what is the probability the message is spam? If a message includes the word *here!,* what is the probability the message is spam? Which of these two words is a stronger indicator that a message is spam? Why?
c. If a message includes the word *available*, what is the probability the message is spam? If a message includes the word *fingertips!*, what is the probability the message is spam? Which of these two words is a stronger indicator that a message is spam? Why?
d. What insights do the results of parts (b) and (c) yield about what enables a spam filter that uses Bayes' theorem to work effectively?

Case Problem 1: Hamilton County Judges

Hamilton County judges try thousands of cases per year. In an overwhelming majority of the cases disposed, the verdict stands as rendered. However, some cases are appealed, and of those appealed, some of the cases are reversed. Kristen DelGuzzi of *The Cincinnati Enquirer* conducted a study of cases handled by Hamilton County judges over a three-year period. Shown in Table 4.8 are the results for 182,908 cases handled (disposed) by 38 judges in Common Pleas Court, Domestic Relations Court, and Municipal Court. Two of the judges (Dinkelacker and Hogan) did not serve in the same court for the entire three-year period.

The purpose of the newspaper's study was to evaluate the performance of the judges. Appeals are often the result of mistakes made by judges, and the newspaper wanted to know which judges were doing a good job and which were making too many

DATA*file*
judge

Table 4.8 Total Cases Disposed, Appealed, and Reversed in Hamilton County Courts

Common Pleas Court

Judge	Total Cases Disposed	Appealed Cases	Reversed Cases
Fred Cartolano	3,037	137	12
Thomas Crush	3,372	119	10
Patrick Dinkelacker	1,258	44	8
Timothy Hogan	1,954	60	7
Robert Kraft	3,138	127	7
William Mathews	2,264	91	18
William Morrissey	3,032	121	22
Norbert Nadel	2,959	131	20
Arthur Ney, Jr.	3,219	125	14
Richard Niehaus	3,353	137	16
Thomas Nurre	3,000	121	6
John O'Connor	2,969	129	12
Robert Ruehlman	3,205	145	18
J. Howard Sundermann	955	60	10
Ann Marie Tracey	3,141	127	13
Ralph Winkler	3,089	88	6
Total	43,945	1,762	199

Domestic Relations Court

Judge	Total Cases Disposed	Appealed Cases	Reversed Cases
Penelope Cunningham	2,729	7	1
Patrick Dinkelacker	6,001	19	4
Deborah Gaines	8,799	48	9
Ronald Panioto	12,970	32	3
Total	30,499	106	17

Municipal Court

Judge	Total Cases Disposed	Appealed Cases	Reversed Cases
Mike Allen	6,149	43	4
Nadine Allen	7,812	34	6
Timothy Black	7,954	41	6
David Davis	7,736	43	5
Leslie Isaiah Gaines	5,282	35	13
Karla Grady	5,253	6	0
Deidra Hair	2,532	5	0
Dennis Helmick	7,900	29	5
Timothy Hogan	2,308	13	2
James Patrick Kenney	2,798	6	1
Joseph Luebbers	4,698	25	8
William Mallory	8,277	38	9
Melba Marsh	8,219	34	7
Beth Mattingly	2,971	13	1
Albert Mestemaker	4,975	28	9
Mark Painter	2,239	7	3
Jack Rosen	7,790	41	13
Mark Schweikert	5,403	33	6
David Stockdale	5,371	22	4
John A. West	2,797	4	2
Total	108,464	500	104

mistakes. You are called in to assist in the data analysis. Use your knowledge of probability and conditional probability to help with the ranking of the judges. You also may be able to analyze the likelihood of appeal and reversal for cases handled by different courts. **LO 2, 3, 4**

Managerial Report

Prepare a report with your rankings of the judges. Also, include an analysis of the likelihood of appeal and case reversal in the three courts. At a minimum, your report should include the following:

1. The probability of cases being appealed and reversed in the three different courts.
2. The probability of a case being appealed for each judge.
3. The probability of a case being reversed for each judge.
4. The probability of reversal given an appeal for each judge.
5. Rank the judges within each court. State the criteria you used and provide a rationale for your choice.

Case Problem 2: Rob's Market

Rob's Market (RM) is a regional food store chain in the southwest United States. David Crawford, director of Business Intelligence for RM, would like to initiate a study of the purchase behavior of customers who use the RM loyalty card (a card that customers scan at checkout to qualify for discounted prices). The use of the loyalty card allows RM to capture what is known as "point-of-sale" data, that is, a list of products purchased by a given customer as he/she checks out of the market. David feels that better understanding of which products tend to be purchased together could lead to insights for better pricing and display strategies as well as a better understanding of sales and the potential impact of different levels of coupon discounts. This type of analysis is known as *market basket analysis*, as it is a study of what different customers have in their shopping baskets as they check out of the store.

As a prototype study, David wants to investigate customer buying behavior with regard to bread, jelly, and peanut butter. RM's Information Technology (IT) group, at David's request, has provided a data set of purchases by 1,000 customers over a one-week period. The data set in the file *marketbasket* contains the following variables for each customer:

DATA*file*
marketbasket

- Bread—wheat, white, or none
- Jelly—grape, strawberry, or none
- Peanut butter—creamy, natural, or none

The variables appear in the above order from left to right in the data set, where each row is a customer. For example, the first record of the data set is

white grape none

which means that customer 1 purchased white bread, grape jelly, and no peanut butter. The second record is

white strawberry none

which means that customer 2 purchased white bread, strawberry jelly, and no peanut butter. The sixth record in the data set is

none none none

which means that the sixth customer did not purchase bread, jelly, or peanut butter.

Other records are interpreted in a similar fashion.

David would like you to do an initial study of the data to get a better understanding of RM customer behavior with regard to these three products. **LO 2, 3, 4**

Managerial Report

Prepare a report that gives insight into the purchase behavior of customers who use the RM loyalty card. At a minimum your report should include estimates of the following.

One way to answer these questions is to use pivot tables (discussed in Chapter 2) to obtain absolute frequencies and use the pivot table results to calculate the relevant probabilities.

1. The probability that a random customer does not purchase any of the three products (bread, jelly, or peanut butter).
2. The probability that a random customer purchases white bread.
3. The probability that a random customer purchases wheat bread.
4. The probability that a random customer purchases grape jelly given that they purchase white bread.
5. The probability that a random customer purchases strawberry jelly given that they purchase white bread.
6. The probability that a random customer purchases creamy peanut butter given that they purchase white bread.
7. The probability that a random customer purchases natural peanut butter given that they purchase white bread.
8. The probability that a random customer purchases creamy peanut butter given that they purchase wheat bread.
9. The probability that a random customer purchases natural peanut butter given that they purchase wheat bread.
10. The probability that a random customer purchases white bread, grape jelly, and creamy peanut butter.

Managerial Report

Prepare a report that uses [illegible] the purchase behavior of customers who used the [illegible]

1. The probability that a [illegible]
2. The probability that [illegible]
3. The probability that [illegible]
4. The probability that a random [illegible]
5. The probability that a [illegible]
6. The probability [illegible]
7. The probability that a random [illegible]
8. The probability that [illegible]
9. The probability that [illegible]
10. The probability that a random [illegible]

Chapter 5

Discrete Probability Distributions

Contents

Statistics in Practice:
Voter Waiting Times in Elections

5.1 Random Variables
Discrete Random Variables
Continuous Random Variables

5.2 Developing Discrete Probability Distributions

5.3 Expected Value and Variance
Expected Value
Variance
Using Excel to Compute the Expected Value, Variance, and Standard Deviation

5.4 Bivariate Distributions, Covariance, and Financial Portfolios
A Bivariate Empirical Discrete Probability Distribution
Financial Applications
Summary

5.5 Binomial Probability Distribution
A Binomial Experiment
Martin Clothing Store Problem
Using Excel to Compute Binomial Probabilities
Expected Value and Variance for the Binomial Distribution

5.6 Poisson Probability Distribution
An Example Involving Time Intervals
An Example Involving Length or Distance Intervals
Using Excel to Compute Poisson Probabilities

5.7 Hypergeometric Probability Distribution
Using Excel to Compute Hypergeometric Probabilities

Summary 278
Glossary 279
Key Formulas 280
Supplementary Exercises 281
Case Problem 1: *Go Bananas*! Breakfast Cereal 285
Case Problem 2: McNeil's Auto Mall 286
Case Problem 3: Grievance Committee at Tuglar Corporation 286
Case Problem 4: Sagittarius Casino 287

Available in the Cengage ebook:
Appendix: Discrete Probability Distributions with R

Learning Objectives

After completing this chapter, you will be able to

- **LO 1** Define and identify discrete and continuous random variables.
- **LO 2** Develop, graph, and interpret valid probability distributions for discrete random variables.
- **LO 3** Calculate and interpret the expected value, variance, and standard deviation for discrete random variables.
- **LO 4** Develop and interpret the bivariate probability distribution for two discrete random variables.
- **LO 5** Calculate and interpret the covariance and correlation coefficient for two discrete random variables.
- **LO 6** Calculate and interpret the expected value and variance of a linear combination of two random variables.
- **LO 7** Identify and use the binomial probability function to compute the probability of a specified number of successes out of a given number of trials.
- **LO 8** Calculate and interpret the expected value, variance, and standard deviation for binomial experiments.
- **LO 9** Identify and use the Poisson probability function to compute the probability of a specified number of occurrences over a given interval.
- **LO 10** Calculate and interpret the expected value, variance, and standard deviation for Poisson experiments.
- **LO 11** Identify and use the hypergeometric probability function to compute the probability of a specified number of successes out of a given number of trials.
- **LO 12** Calculate and interpret the expected value, variance, and standard deviation for hypergeometric experiments.

Statistics in Practice

Voter Waiting Times in Elections*

Historically, most people in the United States who voted during an election did so by arriving to a specific location known as a precinct polling location and casting a ballot in person. The number of voters who cast a ballot by mail has increased and is the primary means of voting in states such as California, Colorado, Hawaii, Nevada, Oregon, Utah, Vermont, and Washington. However, many voters still vote in person, particularly outside these states. In recent elections, some voters have experienced extremely long waiting times to cast their ballots in person. This has been a cause of some concern because it could potentially disenfranchise voters who cannot wait in line to cast their ballots.

Statisticians have developed models for elections that estimate the arrivals to precinct polling locations and wait times for voters. These models use mathematical equations from the field of queueing theory to estimate wait times for voters. The wait time depends on many factors, including how many voting machines or voting booths are available at the polling precinct location, the length of the election ballot, and the arrival rate of voters.

Data collected on voter arrivals show that voter arrivals follow a probability distribution known as the *Poisson distribution*. Using the properties of the Poisson distribution, statisticians can compute the probabilities for the number of voters arriving during any time period. For example, let x = the number of voters arriving to a particular precinct polling location during a one-minute period. Assuming that this location has a mean arrival rate of two voters per minute, the following table shows the probabilities for the number of voters arriving during a one-minute period.

x	Probability
0	0.1353
1	0.2707
2	0.2707
3	0.1804
4	0.0902
5 or more	0.0527

Using these probabilities as inputs into their models, the statisticians use queueing theory to estimate voter wait times at each precinct polling location. The statisticians can then make recommendations on how many voting machines or voting booths to place at each precinct polling location to control voter waiting times.

Discrete probability distributions, such as the Poisson distribution used to model voter arrivals to precinct polling locations, are the topic of this chapter. In addition to the Poisson distribution, you will learn about the binomial and the hypergeometric distributions and how they can be used to provide helpful probability information.

*This Statistics in Practice is based on research done by Muer Yang, Michael J. Fry, Ted Allen, and W. David Kelton.

In this chapter, we extend the study of probability by introducing the concepts of random variables and probability distributions. Random variables and probability distributions are models for populations of data. The focus of this chapter is on probability distributions for discrete data, that is, discrete probability distributions.

We will introduce two types of discrete probability distributions. The first type is a table with one column for the values of the random variable and a second column for the associated probabilities. We will see that the rules for assigning probabilities to experimental outcomes introduced in Chapter 4 are used to assign probabilities for such a distribution. The second type of discrete probability distribution uses a special mathematical function to compute the probabilities for each value of the random variable. We present three probability distributions of this type that are widely used in practice: the binomial, Poisson, and hypergeometric distributions.

5.1 Random Variables

A random variable provides a means for describing experimental outcomes using numerical values. Random variables must assume numerical values.

The concept of an experiment and its associated experimental outcomes are discussed in Chapter 4.

Random Variable

A **random variable** is a numerical description of the outcome of an experiment.

In effect, a random variable associates a numerical value with each possible experimental outcome. The particular numerical value of the random variable depends on the outcome of the experiment. A random variable can be classified as being either *discrete* or *continuous* depending on the numerical values it assumes.

Discrete Random Variables

A random variable that may assume either a finite number of values or an infinite sequence of values such as 0, 1, 2, . . . is referred to as a **discrete random variable**. For example, consider the experiment of an accountant taking the certified public accountant (CPA) examination. The examination has four parts. We can define a random variable as $x =$ the number of parts of the CPA examination passed. It is a discrete random variable because it may assume the finite number of values 0, 1, 2, 3, or 4.

As another example of a discrete random variable, consider the experiment of patients arriving to a hospital's emergency room. The random variable of interest is $x =$ the number of patients who arrive to the emergency room in a one-day period. The possible values for x come from the sequence of integers 0, 1, 2, and so on. Hence, x is a discrete random variable assuming one of the values in this infinite sequence.

Although the outcomes of many experiments can naturally be described by numerical values, others cannot. For example, a survey question might ask an individual to recall the message in a recent television commercial. This experiment would have two possible outcomes: The individual cannot recall the message and the individual can recall the message. We can still describe these experimental outcomes numerically by defining the discrete random variable x as follows: Let $x = 0$ if the individual cannot recall the message and $x = 1$ if the individual can recall the message. The numerical values for this random variable are arbitrary (we could use 5 and 10), but they are acceptable in terms of the definition of a random variable—namely, x is a random variable because it provides a numerical description of the outcome of the experiment.

Table 5.1 provides some additional examples of discrete random variables. Note that in each example the discrete random variable assumes a finite number of values or an infinite sequence of values such as 0, 1, 2, ... These types of discrete random variables are discussed in detail in this chapter.

Continuous Random Variables

A random variable that may assume any numerical value in an interval or collection of intervals is called a **continuous random variable**. Experimental outcomes based on measurement scales such as time, weight, distance, and temperature can be described by

Table 5.1 Examples of Discrete Random Variables

Random Experiment	Random Variable (x)	Possible Values for the Random Variable
Flip a coin	Face of coin showing	1 if heads; 0 if tails
Roll a die	Number of dots showing on top of die	1, 2, 3, 4, 5, 6
Contact five customers	Number of customers who place an order	0, 1, 2, 3, 4, 5
Operate a healthcare clinic for one day	Number of patients who arrive	0, 1, 2, 3, . . .
Offer a customer the choice of two products	Product chosen by customer	0 if none; 1 if choose product A; 2 if choose product B

continuous random variables. For example, consider an experiment of monitoring incoming telephone calls to the claims office of a major insurance company. Suppose the random variable of interest is x = the time between consecutive incoming calls in minutes. This random variable may assume any value in the interval $x \geq 0$. In fact, an infinite number of values are possible for x, including values such as 1.26 minutes, 2.751 minutes, and 4.3333 minutes. As another example, consider a 90-mile section of interstate highway I-75 north of Atlanta, Georgia. For an emergency ambulance service located in Atlanta, we might define the random variable as x = number of miles to the location of the next traffic accident along this section of I-75. In this case, x would be a continuous random variable assuming any value in the interval $0 \leq x \leq 90$. Additional examples of continuous random variables are listed in Table 5.2. Note that each example describes a random variable that may assume any value in an interval of values.

Continuous random variables and their probability distributions are covered in Chapter 6.

Table 5.2 Examples of Continuous Random Variables

Random Experiment	Random Variable (x)	Possible Values for the Random Variable
Customer visits a website	Time customer spends on website in minutes	$x \geq 0$
Fill a soft drink can (max capacity = 12.1 ounces)	Number of ounces	$0 \leq x \leq 12.1$
Test a new chemical process	Temperature when the desired reaction takes place (min temperature = 150°F; max temperature = 212°F)	$150 \leq x \leq 212$
Invest $10,000 in the stock market	Value of investment after one year	$x \geq 0$

Notes + Comments

One way to determine whether a random variable is discrete or continuous is to think of the values of the random variable as points on a line segment. Choose two points representing values of the random variable. If the entire line segment between the two points also represents possible values for the random variable, then the random variable is continuous.

Exercises

Methods

1. Consider the experiment of tossing a coin twice. **LO 1**
   a. List the experimental outcomes.
   b. Define a random variable that represents the number of heads occurring on the two tosses.
   c. Show what value the random variable would assume for each of the experimental outcomes.
   d. Is this random variable discrete or continuous?
2. Consider the experiment of a worker assembling a product. **LO 1**
   a. Define a random variable that represents the time in minutes required to assemble the product.
   b. What values may the random variable assume?
   c. Is the random variable discrete or continuous?

Applications

3. **Interviews at Brookwood Institute.** Three students scheduled interviews for summer employment at the Brookwood Institute. In each case, the interview results in either an offer for a position or no offer. Experimental outcomes are defined in terms of the results of the three interviews. **LO 1**
   a. List the experimental outcomes.
   b. Define a random variable that represents the number of offers made. Is the random variable continuous?
   c. Show the value of the random variable for each of the experimental outcomes.
4. **Unemployment in Northeastern States.** The Census Bureau includes nine states in what it defines as the Northeast region of the United States. Assume that the government is interested in tracking unemployment in these nine states and that the random variable of interest is the number of northeastern states with an unemployment rate that is less than 3.5%. What values may this random variable assume? **LO 1**
5. **Blood Test Analysis.** To perform a certain type of blood analysis, lab technicians must perform two procedures. The first procedure requires either one or two separate steps, and the second procedure requires one, two, or three steps. **LO 1**
   a. List the experimental outcomes associated with performing the blood analysis.
   b. If the random variable of interest is the total number of steps required to do the complete analysis (both procedures), show what value the random variable will assume for each of the experimental outcomes.
6. **Types of Random Variables.** Listed below is a series of experiments and associated random variables. In each case, identify the values that the random variable can assume and state whether the random variable is discrete or continuous. **LO 1**

Experiment	Random Variable (x)
a. Take a 20-question examination	Number of questions answered correctly
b. Observe cars arriving at a tollbooth for 1 hour	Number of cars arriving at tollbooth
c. Audit 50 tax returns	Number of returns containing errors
d. Observe an employee's work	Number of nonproductive hours in an eight-hour workday
e. Weigh a shipment of goods	Number of kilograms

5.2 Developing Discrete Probability Distributions

The classical, subjective, and relative frequency methods are introduced in Chapter 4.

The **probability distribution** for a random variable describes how probabilities are distributed over the values of the random variable. For a discrete random variable x, a **probability function**, denoted by $f(x)$, provides the probability for each value of the random variable. The classical, subjective, and relative frequency methods of assigning probabilities can be used to develop discrete probability distributions. Application of this methodology leads to what we call tabular discrete probability distributions, that is, probability distributions that are presented in a table.

The classical method of assigning probabilities to values of a random variable is applicable when the experimental outcomes generate values of the random variable that are equally likely. For instance, consider the experiment of rolling a die and observing the number on the upward face. It must be one of the numbers 1, 2, 3, 4, 5, or 6, and each of these outcomes is equally likely. Thus, if we let x = number obtained on one roll of a die and $f(x)$ = the probability of x, the probability distribution of x is given in Table 5.3.

The subjective method of assigning probabilities can also lead to a table of values of the random variable together with the associated probabilities. With the subjective method the individual developing the probability distribution uses their best judgment to assign each probability. So, unlike probability distributions developed using the classical method, different people can be expected to obtain different probability distributions.

The relative frequency method of assigning probabilities to values of a random variable is applicable when reasonably large amounts of data are available. We then treat the data as if they were the population and use the relative frequency method to assign probabilities to the experimental outcomes. The use of the relative frequency method to develop discrete probability distributions leads to what is called an **empirical discrete distribution**. With the large amounts of data available today (e.g., scanner data, credit card data, online social media data), this type of probability distribution is becoming more widely used in practice. Let us illustrate by considering the sale of automobiles at a dealership.

We will use the relative frequency method to develop a probability distribution for the number of cars sold per day at DiCarlo Motors in Saratoga, New York. Over the past 300 days, DiCarlo has experienced 54 days with no automobiles sold, 117 days with 1 automobile sold, 72 days with 2 automobiles sold, 42 days with 3 automobiles sold, 12 days with 4 automobiles sold, and 3 days with 5 automobiles sold. Suppose we consider the experiment of observing a day of operations at DiCarlo Motors and define the random variable of interest as x = the number of automobiles sold during a day. Using the relative frequencies to assign probabilities to the values of the random variable x, we can develop the probability distribution for x.

In probability function notation, $f(0)$ provides the probability of 0 automobiles sold, $f(1)$ provides the probability of 1 automobile sold, and so on. Because historical data show 54 of 300 days with 0 automobiles sold, we assign the relative frequency $54/300 = 0.18$ to $f(0)$, indicating that the probability of 0 automobiles being sold during a day is 0.18. Similarly, because 117 of 300 days had 1 automobile sold, we assign the relative frequency $117/300 = 0.39$ to $f(1)$, indicating that the probability of exactly 1 automobile being sold during a day

Table 5.3 Probability Distribution for Number Obtained on One Roll of a Die

Number Obtained x	Probability of x $f(x)$
1	1/6
2	1/6
3	1/6
4	1/6
5	1/6
6	1/6

Table 5.4 Probability Distribution for the Number of Automobiles Sold During a Day at DiCarlo Motors

x	$f(x)$
0	0.18
1	0.39
2	0.24
3	0.14
4	0.04
5	0.01
Total	1.00

is 0.39. Continuing in this way for the other values of the random variable, we compute the values for $f(2)$, $f(3)$, $f(4)$, and $f(5)$ as shown in Table 5.4.

A primary advantage of defining a random variable and its probability distribution is that once the probability distribution is known, it is relatively easy to determine the probability of a variety of events that may be of interest to a decision maker. For example, using the probability distribution for DiCarlo Motors as shown in Table 5.4, we see that the most probable number of automobiles sold during a day is 1 with a probability of $f(1) = 0.39$. In addition, the probability of selling 3 or more automobiles during a day is $f(3) + f(4) + f(5) = 0.14 + 0.04 + 0.01 = 0.19$. These probabilities, plus others the decision maker may ask about, provide information that can help the decision maker understand the process of selling automobiles at DiCarlo Motors.

In the development of a probability function for any discrete random variable, the following two conditions must be satisfied.

These conditions are the analogs to the two basic requirements for assigning probabilities to experimental outcomes presented in Chapter 4.

Required Conditions for a Discrete Probability Function

$$f(x) \geq 0 \qquad \textbf{(5.1)}$$

$$\Sigma f(x) = 1 \qquad \textbf{(5.2)}$$

Table 5.4 shows that the probabilities for the random variable x satisfy equation (5.1); $f(x)$ is greater than or equal to 0 for all values of x. In addition, because the probabilities sum to 1, equation (5.2) is satisfied. Thus, the DiCarlo Motors probability function is a valid discrete probability function.

We can also show the DiCarlo Motors probability distribution graphically. In Figure 5.1, the values of the random variable x for DiCarlo Motors are shown on the horizontal axis and the probability associated with these values is shown on the vertical axis.

In addition to the probability distributions shown in tables, a formula that gives the probability function, $f(x)$, for every value of x is often used to describe probability distributions. The simplest example of a discrete probability distribution given by a formula is the **discrete uniform probability distribution**. Its probability function is defined by equation (5.3).

Discrete Uniform Probability Function

$$f(x) = 1/n \qquad \textbf{(5.3)}$$

where

n = the number of values the random variable may assume

Figure 5.1 Graphical Representation of the Probability Distribution for the Number of Automobiles Sold During a Day at DiCarlo Motors

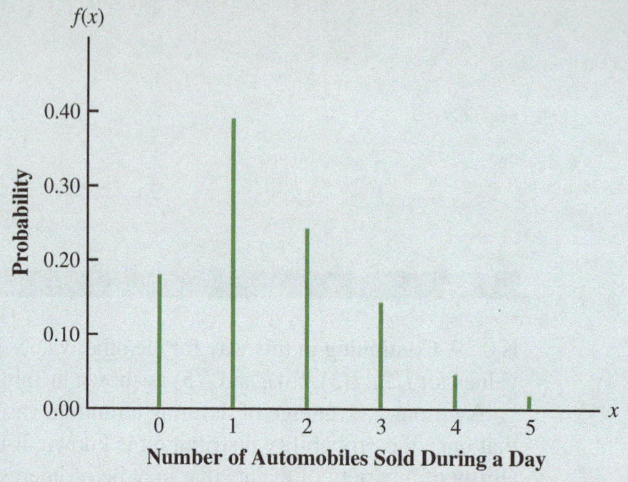

For example, consider again the experiment of rolling a die. We define the random variable x to be the number of dots on the upward face. For this experiment, $n = 6$ values are possible for the random variable; $x = 1, 2, 3, 4, 5, 6$. We showed earlier how the probability distribution for this experiment can be expressed as a table. Since the probabilities are equally likely, the discrete uniform probability function can also be used. The probability function for this discrete uniform random variable is

$$f(x) = 1/6 \qquad x = 1, 2, 3, 4, 5, 6$$

Several widely used discrete probability distributions are specified by formulas. Three important cases are the binomial, Poisson, and hypergeometric distributions; these distributions are discussed later in the chapter.

Exercises

Methods

7. The probability distribution for the random variable x follows. **LO 2**

x	f(x)
20	0.20
25	0.15
30	0.25
35	0.40

a. Is this probability distribution valid? Explain.
b. What is the probability that $x = 30$?
c. What is the probability that x is less than or equal to 25?
d. What is the probability that x is greater than 30?

Applications

8. **Operating Room Use.** The following data were collected by counting the number of operating rooms in use at Tampa General Hospital over a 20-day period: On three

of the days only one operating room was used, on five of the days two were used, on eight of the days three were used, and on four days all four of the hospital's operating rooms were used. **LO 2**

a. Use the relative frequency approach to construct an empirical discrete probability distribution for the number of operating rooms in use on any given day.
b. Draw a graph of the probability distribution.
c. Show that your probability distribution satisfies the required conditions for a valid discrete probability distribution.

9. **Employee Retention.** Employee retention is a major concern for many companies. A survey of Americans asked how long they have worked for their current employer (Bureau of Labor Statistics website). Consider the following example of sample data of 2,000 college graduates who graduated five years ago. **LO 2**

Time with Current Employer (years)	Number
1	506
2	390
3	310
4	218
5	576

Let x be the random variable indicating the number of years the respondent has worked for their current employer.

a. Use the data to develop an empirical discrete probability distribution for x.
b. Show that your probability distribution satisfies the conditions for a valid discrete probability distribution.
c. What is the probability that a respondent has been at her/his current place of employment for more than three years?

10. **Job Satisfaction of Information-Systems Managers.** The percent frequency distributions of job satisfaction scores for a sample of information-systems (IS) senior executives and middle managers are as follows. The job satisfaction scores range from a low of 1 (very dissatisfied) to a high of 5 (very satisfied). **LO 2**

Job Satisfaction Score	IS Senior Executives (%)	IS Middle Managers (%)
1	5	4
2	9	10
3	3	12
4	42	46
5	41	28

a. Develop a probability distribution for the job satisfaction score of a senior executive.
b. Develop a probability distribution for the job satisfaction score of a middle manager.
c. What is the probability a senior executive will report a job satisfaction score of 4 or 5?
d. What is the probability a middle manager is very satisfied?
e. Compare the overall job satisfaction of senior executives and middle managers.

11. **Magnetic Resonance Imaging Machine Malfunctions.** A technician services magnetic resonance imaging (MRI) machines at hospitals in the Phoenix area. Depending

on the type of malfunction, the service call can take 1, 2, 3, or 4 hours. The different types of malfunctions of the MRI machines occur at about the same frequency. **LO 2**

a. Develop a probability distribution for the duration of a service call.
b. Draw a graph of the probability distribution.
c. Show that your probability distribution satisfies the conditions required for a discrete probability function.
d. What is the probability a service call for an MRI machine will take 3 hours?
e. A service call for an MRI machine has just come in, but the type of malfunction is unknown. It is 3:00 P.M. and service technicians usually get off at 5:00 P.M. What is the probability the service technician will have to work overtime to fix the machine today?

12. **New Subscribers.** Spectrum provides cable television and Internet service to millions of customers. Suppose that the management of Spectrum subjectively assesses a probability distribution for the number of new subscribers next year in the state of New York as follows. **LO 2**

x	f(x)
100,000	0.10
200,000	0.20
300,000	0.25
400,000	0.30
500,000	0.10
600,000	0.05

a. Is this probability distribution valid? Explain.
b. What is the probability Spectrum will obtain more than 400,000 new subscribers?
c. What is the probability Spectrum will obtain fewer than 200,000 new subscribers?

13. **Insects on a Tomato Plant Leaf.** Botanists are studying a particular type of insect that attacks tomato plants. The botanists have performed a study to count the number of insects per leaf on tomato plants in their greenhouse. They have found that the number of insects on a leaf of the tomato plants is either one, two, three, or four. They have also determined that the following probability function describes the probability of the number of insects on a leaf on the tomato plants: $f(x) = \frac{x}{10}$ for $x = 1, 2, 3,$ or 4. **LO 1, 2**

a. Is the number of insects on a tomato-plant leaf a discrete or continuous random variable?
b. Is this probability function valid? Explain.
c. What is the probability that the botanists will find exactly one insect on a tomato-plant leaf?
d. What is the probability that the botanists will find exactly four insects on a tomato-plant leaf?
e. What is the probability that the botanists will find less than three insects on a tomato-plant leaf?

14. **MRA Company Projected Profits.** The following table is a partial probability distribution for the MRA Company's projected profits (x = profit in \$1,000s) for the first year of operation (the negative value denotes a loss). **LO 2**

x	f(x)
−100	0.10
0	0.20
50	0.30
100	0.25
150	0.10
200	

a. What is the proper value for $f(200)$? What is your interpretation of this value?
b. What is the probability that MRA will be profitable?
c. What is the probability that MRA will make at least $100,000?

5.3 Expected Value and Variance

Expected Value

The **expected value**, or mean, of a random variable is a measure of the central location for the random variable. The formula for the expected value of a discrete random variable x follows.

The expected value is a weighted average of the values of the random variable where the weights are the probabilities.

Expected Value of a Discrete Random Variable

$$E(x) = \mu = \sum xf(x) \tag{5.4}$$

Both the notations $E(x)$ and μ are used to denote the expected value of a random variable.

Equation (5.4) shows that to compute the expected value of a discrete random variable, we must multiply each value of the random variable by the corresponding probability $f(x)$ and then add the resulting products. Using the DiCarlo Motors automobile sales example from Section 5.2, we show the calculation of the expected value for the number of automobiles sold during a day in Table 5.5. The sum of the entries in the $xf(x)$ column shows that the expected value is 1.50 automobiles per day. We therefore know that although sales of 0, 1, 2, 3, 4, or 5 automobiles are possible on any one day, over time DiCarlo can anticipate selling an average of 1.50 automobiles per day. Assuming 30 days of operation during a month, we can use the expected value of 1.50 to forecast average monthly sales of 30(1.50) = 45 automobiles.

The expected value does not have to be a value the random variable can assume.

Variance

The expected value provides a measure of central tendency for a random variable, but we often also want a measure of variability, or dispersion. Just as we used the variance in Chapter 3 to summarize the variability in data, we now use **variance** to summarize the variability in the values of a random variable. The formula for the variance of a discrete random variable follows.

The variance is a weighted average of the squared deviations of a random variable from its mean. The weights are the probabilities.

Variance of a Discrete Random Variable

$$Var(x) = \sigma^2 = \sum(x - \mu)^2 f(x) \tag{5.5}$$

Table 5.5 Calculation of the Expected Value for the Number of Automobiles Sold During a Day at DiCarlo Motors

x	f(x)	xf(x)
0	0.18	0(0.18) = 0.00
1	0.39	1(0.39) = 0.39
2	0.24	2(0.24) = 0.48
3	0.14	3(0.14) = 0.42
4	0.04	4(0.04) = 0.16
5	0.01	5(0.01) = 0.05
		1.50

$E(x) = \mu = \sum xf(x)$

Table 5.6 Calculation of the Variance for the Number of Automobiles Sold During a Day at DiCarlo Motors

x	$x - \mu$	$(x - \mu)^2$	$f(x)$	$(x - \mu)^2 f(x)$
0	$0 - 1.50 = -1.50$	2.25	0.18	$2.25(0.18) = 0.4050$
1	$1 - 1.50 = -0.50$	0.25	0.39	$0.25(0.39) = 0.0975$
2	$2 - 1.50 = 0.50$	0.25	0.24	$0.25(0.24) = 0.0600$
3	$3 - 1.50 = 1.50$	2.25	0.14	$2.25(0.14) = 0.3150$
4	$4 - 1.50 = 2.50$	6.25	0.04	$6.25(0.04) = 0.2500$
5	$5 - 1.50 = 3.50$	12.25	0.01	$12.25(0.01) = 0.1225$
				1.2500

$\sigma^2 = \Sigma(x - \mu)^2 f(x)$

As equation (5.5) shows, an essential part of the variance formula is the deviation, $x - \mu$, which measures how far a particular value of the random variable is from the expected value, or mean, μ. In computing the variance of a random variable, the deviations are squared and then weighted by the corresponding value of the probability function. The sum of these weighted squared deviations for all values of the random variable is referred to as the variance. The notations $Var(x)$ and σ^2 are both used to denote the variance of a random variable.

The calculation of the variance for the probability distribution of the number of automobiles sold during a day at DiCarlo Motors is summarized in Table 5.6. We see that the variance is 1.25. The **standard deviation**, σ, is defined as the positive square root of the variance. Thus, the standard deviation for the number of automobiles sold during a day is

$$\sigma = \sqrt{1.25} = 1.118$$

The standard deviation is measured in the same units as the random variable ($\sigma = 1.118$ automobiles) and, therefore, is often preferred in describing the variability of a random variable. The variance σ^2 is measured in squared units and is thus more difficult to interpret.

Using Excel to Compute the Expected Value, Variance, and Standard Deviation

The calculations involved in computing the expected value and variance for a discrete random variable can easily be made in an Excel worksheet. One approach is to enter the formulas necessary to make the calculations in Tables 5.4 and 5.5. An easier way, however, is to make use of Excel's SUMPRODUCT function. In this subsection we show how to use the SUMPRODUCT function to compute the expected value and variance for daily automobile sales at DiCarlo Motors. Refer to Figure 5.2 as we describe the tasks involved. The formula worksheet is in the background; the value worksheet is in the foreground.

Enter/Access Data: The data needed are the values for the random variable and the corresponding probabilities. Labels, values for the random variable, and the corresponding probabilities are entered in cells A1:B7.

Enter Functions and Formulas: The SUMPRODUCT function multiplies each value in one range by the corresponding value in another range and sums the products. To use

Figure 5.2 Excel Worksheet for Expected Value, Variance, and Standard Deviation

	A	B	C	D
1	Sales	Probability	Squared Deviation from Mean	
2	0	0.18	=(A2-$B$9)^2	
3	1	0.39	=(A3-$B$9)^2	
4	2	0.24	=(A4-$B$9)^2	
5	3	0.14	=(A5-$B$9)^2	
6	4	0.04	=(A6-$B$9)^2	
7	5	0.01	=(A7-$B$9)^2	
8				
9	Mean	=SUMPRODUCT(A2:A7,B2:B7)		
10				
11	Variance	=SUMPRODUCT(C2:C7,B2:B7)		
12				
13	Std Deviation	=SQRT(B11)		
14				

	A	B	C	D
1	Sales	Probability	Squared Deviation from Mean	
2	0	0.18	2.25	
3	1	0.39	0.25	
4	2	0.24	0.25	
5	3	0.14	2.25	
6	4	0.04	6.25	
7	5	0.01	12.25	
8				
9	Mean	1.500		
10				
11	Variance	1.250		
12				
13	Std Deviation	1.118		
14				

the SUMPRODUCT function to compute the expected value of daily automobile sales at DiCarlo Motors, we entered the following formula in cell B9:

$$=SUMPRODUCT(A2{:}A7{,}B2{:}B7)$$

Note that the first range, A2:A7, contains the values for the random variable, daily automobile sales. The second range, B2:B7, contains the corresponding probabilities. Thus, the SUMPRODUCT function in cell B9 is computing A2*B2 + A3*B3 + A4*B4 + A5*B5 + A6*B6 + A7*B7; hence, it is applying the formula in equation (5.4) to compute the expected value. The result, shown in cell B9 of the value worksheet, is 1.500.

The formulas in cells C2:C7 are used to compute the squared deviations from the expected value or mean of 1.500 (the mean is in cell B9). The results, shown in the value worksheet, are the same as the results shown in Table 5.5. The formula necessary to compute the variance for daily automobile sales was entered in cell B11. It uses the SUMPRODUCT function to multiply each value in the range C2:C7 by each corresponding value in the range B2:B7 and sums the products. The result, shown in the value worksheet, is 1.250. Because the standard deviation is the square root of the variance, we entered the formula =*SQRT(B11)* in cell B13 to compute the standard deviation for daily automobile sales. The result, shown in the value worksheet, is 1.118.

Exercises

Methods

15. The following table provides a probability distribution for the random variable x. **LO 3**

x	$f(x)$
3	0.25
6	0.50
9	0.25

a. Compute $E(x)$, the expected value of x.
b. Compute σ^2, the variance of x.
c. Compute σ, the standard deviation of x.

16. The following table provides a probability distribution for the random variable y. **LO 3**

y	$f(y)$
2	0.20
4	0.30
7	0.40
8	0.10

a. Compute $E(y)$.
b. Compute $Var(y)$ and σ.

Applications

17. **Financial Statement Audits.** Internal auditors are often used to review an organization's financial statements such as balance sheets, income statements, and cash flow statements prior to public filings. Auditors seek to verify that the financial statements accurately represent the financial position of the organization and that the statements follow accepted accounting principles. Many errors that are discovered by auditors are minor errors that are easily corrected. However, some errors are serious and require substantial time to rectify. Suppose that the financial statements of 567 public companies are audited. The file *InternalAudit* contains the number of errors discovered during the internal audit of each of these 567 public companies that were classified as "serious." Use the data in the file *InternalAudit* to answer the following. **LO 2, 3**

DATA*file*
internalaudit

a. Construct an empirical discrete probability distribution for the number of serious errors discovered during the internal audits of these 567 public companies.
b. What is the probability that a company has no serious errors in its financial statements?
c. What is the probability that a company has four or more serious errors in its financial statements?
d. What is the expected number of serious errors in a company's financial statements?
e. What is the variance of the number of serious errors in a company's financial statements?
f. What is the standard deviation of the number of serious errors in a company's financial statements?

18. **Water Supply Stoppages.** The following data have been collected on the number of times that owner-occupied and renter-occupied units had a water supply stoppage lasting 6 or more hours over a 3-month period. **LO 2, 3**

	Number of Units (1,000s)	
Number of Times	**Owner Occupied**	**Renter Occupied**
0	439	394
1	1,100	760
2	249	221
3	98	92
4 times or more	120	111

a. Define a random variable x = number of times that owner-occupied units had a water supply stoppage lasting 6 or more hours in the past 3 months and develop a probability distribution for the random variable. (Let $x = 4$ represent 4 or more times.)
b. Compute the expected value and variance for x.

c. Define a random variable y = number of times that renter-occupied units had a water supply stoppage lasting 6 or more hours in the past 3 months and develop a probability distribution for the random variable. (Let $y = 4$ represent 4 or more times.)
d. Compute the expected value and variance for y.
e. What observations can you make from a comparison of the number of water supply stoppages reported by owner-occupied units versus renter-occupied units?

19. **New Tax Accounting Clients.** New legislation passed in 2017 by the U.S. Congress changed tax laws that affect how many people file their taxes, which required many people to seek tax advice from their accountants (*The New York Times*). Backen and Hayes LLC is an accounting firm in New York State. The accounting firm believes that it may have to hire additional accountants to assist with the increased demand in tax advice for the upcoming tax season. Backen and Hayes LLC has developed the following probability distribution for x = number of new clients seeking tax advice. **LO 2, 3**

x	$f(x)$
20	0.05
25	0.20
30	0.25
35	0.15
40	0.15
45	0.10
50	0.10

a. Is this a valid probability distribution? Explain.
b. What is the probability that Backen and Hayes LLC will obtain 40 or more new clients?
c. What is the probability that Backen and Hayes LLC will obtain fewer than 35 new clients?
d. Compute the expected value, variance, and standard deviation of x.

20. **Automobile Insurance Damage Claims.** The probability distribution for damage claims paid by the Newton Automobile Insurance Company on collision insurance follows. **LO 3**

Payment ($)	Probability
0	0.85
500	0.04
1,000	0.04
3,000	0.03
5,000	0.02
8,000	0.01
10,000	0.01

a. Use the expected collision payment to determine the collision insurance premium that would enable the company to break even.
b. The insurance company charges an annual rate of $520 for the collision coverage. What is the expected value of the collision policy for a policyholder? (*Hint:* It is the expected payments from the company minus the cost of coverage.) Why does the policyholder purchase a collision policy with this expected value?

21. **Information-Systems Managers Job Satisfaction.** The following probability distributions of job satisfaction scores for a sample of information-systems (IS) senior executives and middle managers range from a low of 1 (very dissatisfied) to a high of 5 (very satisfied). **LO 3**

Job Satisfaction Score	Probability IS Senior Executives	IS Middle Managers
1	0.05	0.04
2	0.09	0.10
3	0.03	0.12
4	0.42	0.46
5	0.41	0.28

a. What is the expected value of the job satisfaction score for senior executives?
b. What is the expected value of the job satisfaction score for middle managers?
c. Compute the variance of job satisfaction scores for executives and middle managers.
d. Compute the standard deviation of job satisfaction scores for both probability distributions.
e. Compare the overall job satisfaction of senior executives and middle managers.

22. **Carolina Industries Product Demand.** The demand for a product of Carolina Industries varies greatly from month to month. The probability distribution in the following table, based on the past two years of data, shows the company's monthly demand. **LO 3**

Unit Demand	Probability
300	0.20
400	0.30
500	0.35
600	0.15

a. If the company bases monthly orders on the expected value of the monthly demand, what should Carolina's monthly order quantity be for this product?
b. Assume that each unit demanded generates $70 in revenue and that each unit ordered costs $50. How much will the company gain or lose in a month if it places an order based on your answer to part (a) and the actual demand for the item is 300 units?

23. **Coffee Consumption.** In Gallup's Annual Consumption Habits Poll, telephone interviews were conducted for a random sample of 1,014 adults aged 18 and over. One of the questions was, "How many cups of coffee, if any, do you drink on an average day?" The following table shows the results obtained (Gallup website).

Number of Cups per Day	Number of Responses
0	365
1	264
2	193
3	91
4 or more	101

Define a random variable x = number of cups of coffee consumed on an average day. Let $x = 4$ represent four or more cups. **LO 2, 3**
a. Develop a probability distribution for x.
b. Compute the expected value of x.

c. Compute the variance of x.
d. Suppose we are only interested in adults who drink at least one cup of coffee on an average day. For this group, let y = the number of cups of coffee consumed on an average day. Compute the expected value of y and compare it to the expected value of x.

24. **Computer Company Plant Expansion.** The J. R. Ryland Computer Company is considering a plant expansion to enable the company to begin production of a new computer product. The company's president must determine whether to make the expansion a medium- or large-scale project. Demand for the new product is uncertain, which for planning purposes may be low demand, medium demand, or high demand. The probability estimates for demand are 0.20, 0.50, and 0.30, respectively. Letting x and y indicate the annual profit in thousands of dollars, the firm's planners developed the following profit forecasts for the medium- and large-scale expansion projects. **LO 3**

		Medium-Scale Expansion Profit		Large-Scale Expansion Profit	
		x	$f(x)$	y	$f(y)$
Demand	Low	50	0.20	0	0.20
	Medium	150	0.50	100	0.50
	High	200	0.30	300	0.30

a. Compute the expected value for the profit associated with the two expansion alternatives. Which decision is preferred for the objective of maximizing the expected profit?
b. Compute the variance for the profit associated with the two expansion alternatives. Which decision is preferred for the objective of minimizing the risk or uncertainty?

5.4 Bivariate Distributions, Covariance, and Financial Portfolios

A probability distribution involving two random variables is called a **bivariate probability distribution**. In discussing bivariate probability distributions, it is useful to think of a bivariate experiment. Each outcome for a bivariate experiment consists of two values, one for each random variable. For example, consider the bivariate experiment of rolling a pair of dice. The outcome consists of two values, the number obtained with the first die and the number obtained with the second die. As another example, consider the experiment of observing the financial markets for a year and recording the percentage gain for a stock fund and a bond fund. Again, the experimental outcome provides a value for two random variables, the percent gain in the stock fund and the percent gain in the bond fund. When dealing with bivariate probability distributions, we are often interested in the relationship between the random variables. In this section, we introduce bivariate distributions and show how the covariance and correlation coefficient can be used as a measure of linear association between the random variables. We shall also see how bivariate probability distributions can be used to construct and analyze financial portfolios.

A Bivariate Empirical Discrete Probability Distribution

Recall that in Section 5.2 we developed an empirical discrete distribution for daily sales at the DiCarlo Motors automobile dealership in Saratoga, New York. DiCarlo has another dealership in Geneva, New York. Table 5.7 shows the number of cars sold at each of the

Table 5.7 Number of Automobiles Sold at DiCarlo's Saratoga and Geneva Dealerships over 300 Days

	Saratoga Dealership						
Geneva Dealership	**0**	**1**	**2**	**3**	**4**	**5**	**Total**
0	21	30	24	9	2	0	86
1	21	36	33	18	2	1	111
2	9	42	9	12	3	2	77
3	3	9	6	3	5	0	26
Total	54	117	72	42	12	3	300

dealerships over a 300-day period. The numbers in the bottom row (labeled "Total") are the frequencies we used to develop an empirical probability distribution for daily sales at DiCarlo's Saratoga dealership in Section 5.2. The numbers in the right-most column (labeled "Total") are the frequencies of daily sales for the Geneva dealership. Entries in the body of the table give the number of days the Geneva dealership had a level of sales indicated by the row, when the Saratoga dealership had the level of sales indicated by the column. For example, the entry of 33 in the Geneva dealership row labeled "1" and the Saratoga column labeled "2" indicates that for 33 days out of the 300, the Geneva dealership sold 1 car and the Saratoga dealership sold 2 cars.

Suppose we consider the bivariate experiment of observing a day of operations at DiCarlo Motors and recording the number of cars sold. Let us define x = number of cars sold at the Geneva dealership and y = the number of cars sold at the Saratoga dealership. We can now divide all of the frequencies in Table 5.7 by the number of observations (300) to develop a bivariate empirical discrete probability distribution for automobile sales at the two DiCarlo dealerships. Table 5.8 shows this bivariate discrete probability distribution. The probabilities in the lower margin provide the marginal distribution for the DiCarlo Motors Saratoga dealership. The probabilities in the right margin provide the marginal distribution for the DiCarlo Motors Geneva dealership.

The probabilities in the body of the table provide the bivariate probability distribution for sales at both dealerships. Bivariate probabilities are often called joint probabilities. We see that the joint probability of selling 0 automobiles at Geneva and 1 automobile at Saratoga on a typical day is $f(0, 1) = 0.1000$, the joint probability of selling 1 automobile at Geneva and 4 automobiles at Saratoga on a typical day is 0.0067, and so on. Note that there is one bivariate probability for each experimental outcome. With 4 possible values for x and 6 possible values for y, there are 24 experimental outcomes and bivariate probabilities.

Suppose we would like to know the probability distribution for total sales at both DiCarlo dealerships and the expected value and variance of total sales. We can define $s = x + y$

Table 5.8 Bivariate Empirical Discrete Probability Distribution for Daily Sales at DiCarlo Dealerships in Saratoga and Geneva

	Saratoga Dealership						
Geneva Dealership	**0**	**1**	**2**	**3**	**4**	**5**	**Total**
0	0.0700	0.1000	0.0800	0.0300	0.0067	0.0000	0.2867
1	0.0700	0.1200	0.1100	0.0600	0.0067	0.0033	0.3700
2	0.0300	0.1400	0.0300	0.0400	0.0100	0.0067	0.2567
3	0.0100	0.0300	0.0200	0.0100	0.0167	0.0000	0.0867
Total	0.1800	0.3900	0.2400	0.1400	0.0400	0.0100	1.0000

Table 5.9 Calculation of the Expected Value and Variance for Total Daily Sales at DiCarlo Motors

s	$f(s)$	$sf(s)$	$s - E(s)$	$(s - E(s))^2$	$(s - E(s))^2 f(s)$
0	0.0700	0.0000	−2.6433	6.9872	0.4891
1	0.1700	0.1700	−1.6433	2.7005	0.4591
2	0.2300	0.4600	−0.6433	0.4139	0.0952
3	0.2900	0.8700	0.3567	0.1272	0.0369
4	0.1267	0.5067	1.3567	1.8405	0.2331
5	0.0667	0.3333	2.3567	5.5539	0.3703
6	0.0233	0.1400	3.3567	11.2672	0.2629
7	0.0233	0.1633	4.3567	18.9805	0.4429
8	0.0000	0.0000	5.3567	28.6939	0.0000
		$E(s) = 2.6433$			$Var(s) = 2.3895$

Computing covariance and correlation coefficients for sample data are discussed in Chapter 3.

as total sales for DiCarlo Motors. Working with the bivariate probabilities in Table 5.8, we see that $f(s = 0) = 0.0700$, $f(s = 1) = 0.0700 + 0.1000 = 0.1700$, $f(s = 2) = 0.0300 + 0.1200 + 0.0800 = 0.2300$, and so on. We show the complete probability distribution for $s = x + y$ along with the computation of the expected value and variance in Table 5.9. The expected value is $E(s) = 2.6433$ and the variance is $Var(s) = 2.3895$.

With bivariate probability distributions, we often want to know the relationship between the two random variables. The covariance and/or correlation coefficient are good measures of association between two random variables. The formula we will use for computing the covariance between two random variables x and y is given below.

Covariance of Random Variables x and y (see footnote 1)

$$\sigma_{xy} = [Var(x + y) - Var(x) - Var(y)]/2 \tag{5.6}$$

We have already computed $Var(s) = Var(x + y)$ and, in Section 5.2, we computed $Var(y)$. Now we need to compute $Var(x)$ before we can use equation (5.6) to compute the covariance of x and y. Using the probability distribution for x (the right margin of Table 5.8), we compute $E(x)$ and $Var(x)$ in Table 5.10.

Table 5.10 Calculation of the Expected Value and Variance of Daily Automobile Sales at DiCarlo Motors' Geneva Dealership

x	$f(x)$	$xf(x)$	$x - E(x)$	$[(x - E(x)]^2$	$[x - E(x)]^2 f(x)$
0	0.2867	0.0000	−1.1435	1.3076	0.3749
1	0.3700	0.3700	−0.1435	0.0206	0.0076
2	0.2567	0.5134	0.8565	0.8565	0.1883
3	0.0867	0.2601	1.8565	1.8565	0.2988
		$E(x) = 1.1435$			$Var(x) = 0.8696$

[1]Another formula is often used to compute the covariance of x and y when $Var(x + y)$ is not known. It is $\sigma_{xy} = \sum_{i,j} [x_i - E(x_i)]\,[y_j - E(y_j)]\, f(x_i, y_j)$.

We can now use equation (5.6) to compute the covariance of the random variables x and y.

$$\sigma_{xy} = [Var(x + y) - Var(x) - Var(y)]/2 = (2.3895 - 0.8696 - 1.25)/2 = 0.1350$$

A covariance of 0.1350 indicates that daily sales at DiCarlo's two dealerships have a positive relationship. To get a better sense of the strength of the relationship we can compute the correlation coefficient. The correlation coefficient for the two random variables x and y is given by equation (5.7).

Correlation between Random Variables x and y

$$\rho_{xy} = \frac{\sigma_{xy}}{\sigma_x \sigma_y} \tag{5.7}$$

From equation (5.7), we see that the correlation coefficient for two random variables is the covariance divided by the product of the standard deviations for the two random variables.

Let us compute the correlation coefficient between daily sales at the two DiCarlo dealerships. First, we compute the standard deviations for sales at the Saratoga and Geneva dealerships by taking the square root of the variance.

$$\sigma_x = \sqrt{0.8696} = 0.9325$$

$$\sigma_y = \sqrt{1.25} = 1.1180$$

Now we can compute the correlation coefficient as a measure of the linear association between the two random variables.

$$\rho_{xy} = \frac{\sigma_{xy}}{\sigma_x \sigma_y} = \frac{0.1350}{(0.9325)(1.1180)} = 0.1295$$

The correlation coefficient is a measure of the linear association between two variables. Values near $+1$ indicate a strong positive linear relationship; values near -1 indicate a strong negative linear relationship; and values near zero indicate a lack of a linear relationship. This interpretation is also valid for random variables. The correlation coefficient of 0.1295 indicates there is a weak positive relationship between the random variables representing daily sales at the two DiCarlo dealerships. If the correlation coefficient is equal to zero, we would conclude that daily sales at the two dealerships are independent.

Financial Applications

Let us now see how what we have learned can be useful in constructing financial portfolios that provide a good balance of risk and return. A financial advisor is considering four possible economic scenarios for the coming year and has developed a probability distribution showing the percent return, x, for investing in a large-cap stock fund and the percent return, y, for investing in a long-term government bond fund given each of the scenarios. The bivariate probability distribution for x and y is shown in Table 5.11. Table 5.11 is simply a list with a separate row for each experimental outcome (economic scenario). Each row contains the joint probability for the experimental outcome and a value for each random variable. Since there are only four joint probabilities, the tabular form used in Table 5.11 is simpler than the one we used for DiCarlo Motors where there were (4)(6) = 24 joint probabilities.

Using the formula in Section 5.3 for computing the expected value of a single random variable, we can compute the expected percent return for investing in the stock fund, $E(x)$, and the expected percent return for investing in the bond fund, $E(y)$.

$$E(x) = 0.10(-40) + 0.25(5) + 0.5(15) + 0.15(30) = 9.25$$

$$E(y) = 0.10(30) + 0.25(5) + 0.5(4) + 0.15(2) = 6.55$$

Table 5.11 Probability Distribution of Percent Returns for Investing in a Large-Cap Stock Fund, x, and Investing in a Long-Term Government Bond Fund, y

Economic Scenario	Probability $f(x, y)$	Large-Cap Stock Fund (x)	Long-Term Government Bond Fund (y)
Recession	0.10	−40	30
Weak growth	0.25	5	5
Stable growth	0.50	15	4
Strong growth	0.15	30	2

Using this information, we might conclude that investing in the stock fund is a better investment. It has a higher expected return, 9.25%. But financial analysts recommend that investors also consider the risk associated with an investment. The standard deviation of percent return is often used as a measure of risk. To compute the standard deviation, we must first compute the variance. Using the formula in Section 5.3 for computing the variance of a single random variable, we can compute the variance of the percent returns for the stock and bond fund investments.

$$Var(x) = 0.1(-40 - 9.25)^2 + 0.25(5 - 9.25)^2 + 0.50(15 - 9.25)^2 + 0.15(30 - 9.25)^2 = 328.1875$$

$$Var(y) = 0.1(30 - 6.55)^2 + 0.25(5 - 6.55)^2 + 0.50(4 - 6.55)^2 + 0.15(2 - 6.55)^2 = 61.9475$$

The standard deviation of the return from an investment in the stock fund is $\sigma_x = \sqrt{328.1875} = 18.1159\%$ and the standard deviation of the return from an investment in the bond fund is $\sigma_y = \sqrt{61.9475} = 7.8707\%$. So, we can conclude that investing in the bond fund is less risky. It has the smaller standard deviation. We have already seen that the stock fund offers a greater expected return, so if we want to choose between investing in either the stock fund or the bond fund it depends on our attitude toward risk and return. An aggressive investor might choose the stock fund because of the higher expected return; a conservative investor might choose the bond fund because of the lower risk. But there are other options. What about the possibility of investing in a portfolio consisting of both an investment in the stock fund and an investment in the bond fund?

Suppose we would like to consider three alternatives: investing solely in the large-cap stock fund, investing solely in the long-term government bond fund, and splitting our funds equally between the stock fund and the bond fund (one-half in each). We have already computed the expected value and standard deviation for investing solely in the stock fund and the bond fund. Let us now evaluate the third alternative: constructing a portfolio by investing equal amounts in the large-cap stock fund and in the long-term government bond fund.

To evaluate this portfolio, we start by computing its expected return. We have previously defined x as the percent return from an investment in the stock fund and y as the percent return from an investment in the bond fund so the percent return for our portfolio is $r = 0.5x + 0.5y$. To find the expected return for a portfolio with one-half invested in the stock fund and one-half invested in the bond fund, we want to compute $E(r) = E(0.5x + 0.5y)$. The expression $0.5x + 0.5y$ is called a linear combination of the random variables x and y. Equation (5.8) provides an easy method for computing the expected value of a linear combination of the random variables x and y when we already know $E(x)$ and $E(y)$. In equation (5.8), a represents the coefficient of x and b represents the coefficient of y in the linear combination.

Expected Value of a Linear Combination of Random Variables x and y

$$E(ax + by) = aE(x) + bE(y) \tag{5.8}$$

Since we have already computed $E(x) = 9.25$ and $E(y) = 6.55$, we can use equation (5.8) to compute the expected value of our portfolio.

$$E(0.5x + 0.5y) = 0.5E(x) + 0.5E(y) = 0.5(9.25) + 0.5(6.55) = 7.9$$

We see that the expected return for investing in the portfolio is 7.9%. With \$100 invested, we would expect a return of \$100(0.079) = \$7.90; with \$1,000 invested we would expect a return of \$1,000(0.079) = \$79.00; and so on. But what about the risk? As mentioned previously, financial analysts often use the standard deviation as a measure of risk.

Our portfolio is a linear combination of two random variables, so we need to be able to compute the variance and standard deviation of a linear combination of two random variables in order to assess the portfolio risk. When the covariance between two random variables is known, the formula given by equation (5.9) can be used to compute the variance of a linear combination of two random variables.

Variance of a Linear Combination of Two Random Variables, *x* and *y*

$$Var(ax + by) = a^2Var(x) + b^2Var(y) + 2ab\sigma_{xy} \tag{5.9}$$

where σ_{xy} is the covariance of x and y

From equation (5.9), we see that both the variance of each random variable individually and the covariance between the random variables are needed to compute the variance of a linear combination of two random variables and hence the variance of our portfolio.

We computed Var(x + y) = 119.46 the same way we did for DiCarlo Motors in the previous subsection.

We have already computed the variance of each random variable individually: $Var(x) = 328.1875$ and $Var(y) = 61.9475$. Also, it can be shown that $Var(x + y) = 119.46$. So, using equation (5.6), the covariance of the random variables x and y is

$$\sigma_{xy} = [Var(x + y) - Var(x) - Var(y)]/2 = [119.46 - 328.1875 - 61.9475]/2 = -135.3375$$

A negative covariance between x and y, such as this, means that when x tends to be above its mean, y tends to be below its mean and vice versa.

We can now use equation (5.9) to compute the variance of return for our portfolio.

$$Var(0.5x + 0.5y) = 0.5^2(328.1875) + 0.5^2(61.9475) + 2(0.5)(0.5)(-135.3375) = 29.865$$

The standard deviation of our portfolio is then given by $\sigma_{0.5x + 0.5y} = \sqrt{29.865} = 5.4650\%$. This is our measure of risk for the portfolio consisting of investing 50% in the stock fund and 50% in the bond fund.

Perhaps we would now like to compare the three investment alternatives: investing solely in the stock fund, investing solely in the bond fund, or creating a portfolio by dividing our investment amount equally between the stock and bond funds. Table 5.12 shows the expected returns, variances, and standard deviations for each of the three alternatives.

Table 5.12 Expected Values, Variances, and Standard Deviations for Three Investment Alternatives

Investment Alternative	Expected Return (%)	Variance of Return	Standard Deviation of Return (%)
100% in Stock Fund	9.25	328.1875	18.1159
100% in Bond Fund	6.55	61.9475	7.8707
Portfolio (50% in Stock Fund, 50% in Bond Fund)	7.90	29.865	5.4650

Which of these alternatives would you prefer? The expected return is highest for investing 100% in the stock fund, but the risk is also highest. The standard deviation is 18.1159%. Investing 100% in the bond fund has a lower expected return, but a significantly smaller risk. Investing 50% in the stock fund and 50% in the bond fund (the portfolio) has an expected return that is halfway between that of the stock fund alone and the bond fund alone. But note that it has less risk than investing 100% in either of the individual funds. Indeed, it has both a higher return and less risk (smaller standard deviation) than investing solely in the bond fund. So we would say that investing in the portfolio dominates the choice of investing solely in the bond fund.

Whether you would choose to invest in the stock fund or the portfolio depends on your attitude toward risk. The stock fund has a higher expected return. But the portfolio has significantly less risk and also provides a fairly good return. Many would choose it. It is the negative covariance between the stock and bond funds that has caused the portfolio risk to be so much smaller than the risk of investing solely in either of the individual funds.

The portfolio analysis we just performed was for investing 50% in the stock fund and the other 50% in the bond fund. How would you calculate the expected return and the variance for other portfolios? Equations (5.8) and (5.9) can be used to make these calculations easily.

Suppose we wish to create a portfolio by investing 25% in the stock fund and 75% in the bond fund. What are the expected value and variance of this portfolio? The percent return for this portfolio is $r = 0.25x + 0.75y$, so we can use equation (5.8) to get the expected value of this portfolio:

$$E(0.25x + 0.75y) = 0.25E(x) + 0.75E(y) = 0.25(9.25) + 0.75(6.55) = 7.225$$

Likewise, we may calculate the variance of the portfolio using equation (5.9):

$$\begin{aligned} Var(0.25x + 0.75y) &= (0.25)^2 Var(x) + (0.75)^2\, Var(y) + 2(0.25)(0.75)\sigma_{xy} \\ &= 0.0625(328.1875) + (0.5625)(61.9475) + (0.375)(-135.3375) \\ &= 4.6056 \end{aligned}$$

The standard deviation of the new portfolio is $\sigma_{0.25x + 0.75y} = \sqrt{4.6056} = 2.1461$.

Summary

We have introduced bivariate discrete probability distributions in this section. Since such distributions involve two random variables, we are often interested in a measure of association between the variables. The covariance and the correlation coefficient are the two measures we introduced and showed how to compute. A correlation coefficient near 1 or -1 indicates a strong correlation between the two random variables, and a correlation coefficient near zero indicates a weak correlation between the variables. If two random variables are independent, the covariance and the correlation coefficient will equal zero.

We also showed how to compute the expected value and variance of linear combinations of random variables. From a statistical point of view, financial portfolios are linear combinations of random variables. They are actually a special kind of linear combination called a weighted average. The coefficients are nonnegative and add to 1. The portfolio example we presented showed how to compute the expected value and variance for a portfolio consisting of an investment in a stock fund and a bond fund. The same methodology can be used to compute the expected value and variance of a portfolio consisting of any two financial assets. It is the effect of covariance between the individual random variables on the variance of the portfolio that is the basis for much of the theory of reducing portfolio risk by diversifying across investment alternatives.

Notes + Comments

1. Equations (5.8) and (5.9) for computing the expected value and variance of a linear combination of two random variables can be extended to three or more random variables. The extension of equation (5.8) is straightforward; one more term is added for each additional random variable. The extension of equation (5.9) is more complicated because a separate term is needed for the covariance between all pairs of random variables. We leave these extensions to more advanced texts.
2. Equations (5.8) and (5.9), along with their extensions to three or more random variables, are key building blocks in financial portfolio construction and analysis.
3. The covariance term of equation (5.9) shows why negatively correlated random variables (investment alternatives) reduce the variance and, hence, the risk of a portfolio.

Exercises

Methods

25. Given below is a bivariate distribution for the random variables x and y. **LO 3, 5, 6**

$f(x, y)$	x	y
0.2	50	80
0.5	30	50
0.3	40	60

a. Compute the expected value and the variance for x and y.
b. Develop a probability distribution for $x + y$.
c. Using the result of part (b), compute $E(x + y)$ and $Var(x + y)$.
d. Compute the covariance and correlation for x and y. Are x and y positively related, negatively related, or unrelated?
e. Is the variance of the sum of x and y bigger than, smaller than, or the same as the sum of the individual variances? Why?

26. A person is interested in constructing a portfolio. Two stocks are being considered. Let x = percent return for an investment in Stock 1, and y = percent return for an investment in Stock 2. The expected return and variance for Stock 1 are $E(x) = 8.45\%$ and $Var(x) = 25$. The expected return and variance for Stock 2 are $E(y) = 3.20\%$ and $Var(y) = 1$. The covariance between the returns is $\sigma_{xy} = -3$. **LO 3, 5, 6**
a. What is the standard deviation for an investment in Stock 1 and for an investment in Stock 2? Using the standard deviation as a measure of risk, which of these stocks is the riskier investment?
b. What is the expected return and standard deviation, in dollars, for a person who invests $500 in Stock 1?
c. What is the expected percent return and standard deviation for a person who constructs a portfolio by investing 50% in each stock?
d. What is the expected percent return and standard deviation for a person who constructs a portfolio by investing 70% in Stock 1 and 30% in Stock 2?
e. Compute the correlation coefficient for x and y and comment on the relationship between the returns for the two stocks.

Applications

27. **Vancouver Restaurant Ratings.** The Chamber of Commerce in Vancouver, British Columbia, has conducted an evaluation of 300 restaurants in its metropolitan area. Each restaurant received a rating on a 3-point scale on typical meal price (1 least expensive to 3 most expensive) and quality (1 lowest quality to 3 greatest quality). A crosstabulation of the rating data is shown. Forty-two of the restaurants received a rating of 1 on quality and

1 on meal price, 39 of the restaurants received a rating of 1 on quality and 2 on meal price, and so on. Forty-eight of the restaurants received the highest rating of 3 on both quality and meal price. **LO 3, 4, 5, 6**

	Meal Price (y)			
Quality (x)	1	2	3	Total
1	42	39	3	84
2	33	63	54	150
3	3	15	48	66
Total	78	117	105	300

a. Develop a bivariate probability distribution for quality and meal price of a randomly selected restaurant in Vancouver. Let x = quality rating and y = meal price.
b. Compute the expected value and variance for quality rating, x.
c. Compute the expected value and variance for meal price, y.
d. The $Var(x + y) = 1.6691$. Compute the covariance of x and y. What can you say about the relationship between quality and meal price? Is this what you would expect?
e. Compute the correlation coefficient between quality and meal price? What is the strength of the relationship? Do you suppose it is likely to find a low-cost restaurant in this city that is also high quality? Why or why not?

28. **Printer Manufacturing Costs.** PortaCom has developed a design for a high-quality portable printer. The two key components of manufacturing cost are direct labor and parts. During a testing period, the company has developed prototypes and conducted extensive product tests with the new printer. PortaCom's engineers have developed the following bivariate probability distribution for the manufacturing costs. Parts cost (in dollars) per printer is represented by the random variable x and direct labor cost (in dollars) per printer is represented by the random variable y. Management would like to use this probability distribution to estimate manufacturing costs. **LO 3, 4, 5**

	Direct Labor (y)			
Parts (x)	43	45	48	Total
85	0.05	0.2	0.2	0.45
95	0.25	0.2	0.1	0.55
Total	0.30	0.4	0.3	1.00

a. Show the marginal distribution of direct labor cost and compute its expected value, variance, and standard deviation.
b. Show the marginal distribution of parts cost and compute its expected value, variance, and standard deviation.
c. Total manufacturing cost per unit is the sum of direct labor cost and parts cost. Show the probability distribution for total manufacturing cost per unit.
d. Compute the expected value, variance, and standard deviation of total manufacturing cost per unit.
e. Are direct labor and parts costs independent? Why or why not? If you conclude that they are not, what is the relationship between direct labor and parts cost?
f. PortaCom produced 1,500 printers for its product introduction. The total manufacturing cost was $198,350. Is that about what you would expect? If it is higher or lower, what do you think may be the reason?

29. **Investing in Stocks and Bonds.** The Vanguard Group is one of the largest investment firms in the world with approximately $7 trillion in assets in 2021. Vanguard offers

investment funds in stocks, bonds, annuities, and many other forms. Vanguard estimates the average correlation between the returns offered by stocks and bonds to be −0.32 (Vanguard Research Report, September 2021). Suppose that a particular stock index fund offered by Vanguard has an expected return of 4.78% with a standard deviation of 18.04%, and an investment-grade bond fund offered by Vanguard has an expected return of 5.33% with a standard deviation of 2.65%. **LO 3, 5, 6**

a. Based on the information provided, what is the covariance between this stock index fund and the investment-grade bond fund?
b. What is the expected return and standard deviation for a portfolio composed of 60% invested in the stock index fund and 40% invested in the investment-grade bond fund?
c. What is the expected return and standard deviation for a portfolio composed of 40% invested in the stock index fund and 60% invested in the investment-grade bond fund?
d. Which of the portfolios in part (b) or (c) has the highest expected return? Which portfolio has the lowest standard deviation?
e. Which portfolio would you prefer to invest in? Is the portfolio you chose guaranteed to perform better than the other portfolio in any given year?

30. **Investing in Stocks and Bonds (revisited).** Suppose that in addition to the stock index fund and investment-grade bond fund described in Problem 29, that Vanguard also offers the ability to invest in a real-estate fund. The real-estate fund has an expected return of 11.98% and a standard deviation of 25.76%. The correlation between the stock index fund and the real-estate fund is 0.64, and the correlation between the investment-grade bond fund and the real-estate fund is −0.19. **LO 3, 5, 6**
    a. Based on the information provided, what is the covariance between the stock index fund and the real-estate fund? What is the covariance between the investment-grade bond fund and the real-estate fund?
    b. What is the expected return and standard deviation for a portfolio composed of 50% invested in the stock index fund and 50% invested in the real-estate fund?
    c. What is the expected return and standard deviation for a portfolio composed of 50% invested in the investment-grade bond fund and 50% invested in the real-estate fund?
    d. Consider the portfolios described in Problem 29 as well as the portfolios from parts (b) and (c) of this problem. Which portfolio would be most appropriate for a conservative investor? Which portfolio would be most appropriate for an aggressive investor?

5.5 Binomial Probability Distribution

The binomial probability distribution is a discrete probability distribution that has many applications. It is associated with a multiple-step experiment that we call the binomial experiment.

A Binomial Experiment

A **binomial experiment** exhibits the following four properties.

Properties of a Binomial Experiment

1. The experiment consists of a sequence of n identical trials.
2. Two outcomes are possible on each trial. We refer to one outcome as a *success* and the other outcome as a *failure.*
3. The probability of a success, denoted by p, does not change from trial to trial. Consequently, the probability of a failure, denoted by $1 - p$, does not change from trial to trial.
4. The trials are independent.

Jakob Bernoulli (1654–1705), the first of the Bernoulli family of Swiss mathematicians, published a treatise on probability that contained the theory of permutations and combinations, as well as the binomial theorem.

If properties 2, 3, and 4 are present, we say the trials are generated by a Bernoulli process. If, in addition, property 1 is present, we say we have a binomial experiment. Figure 5.3 depicts one possible sequence of successes and failures for a binomial experiment involving eight trials.

In a binomial experiment, our interest is in the *number of successes occurring in the* n *trials*. If we let x denote the number of successes occurring in the n trials, we see that x can assume the values of 0, 1, 2, 3, . . . , n. Because the number of values is finite, x is a *discrete* random variable. The probability distribution associated with this random variable is called the **binomial probability distribution**. For example, consider the experiment of tossing a coin five times and on each toss observing whether the coin lands with a head or a tail on its upward face. Suppose we want to count the number of heads appearing over the five tosses. Does this experiment show the properties of a binomial experiment? What is the random variable of interest? Note that

1. The experiment consists of five identical trials; each trial involves the tossing of one coin.
2. Two outcomes are possible for each trial: a head or a tail. We can designate head a success and tail a failure.
3. The probability of a head and the probability of a tail are the same for each trial, with $p = 0.5$ and $1 - p = 0.5$.
4. The trials or tosses are independent because the outcome on any one trial is not affected by what happens on other trials or tosses.

Thus, the properties of a binomial experiment are satisfied. The random variable of interest is $x =$ the number of heads appearing in the five trials. In this case, x can assume the values of 0, 1, 2, 3, 4, or 5.

As another example, consider an insurance salesperson who visits 10 randomly selected families. The outcome associated with each visit is classified as a success if the family purchases an insurance policy and a failure if the family does not. From past experience, the salesperson knows the probability that a randomly selected family will purchase an insurance policy is 0.10. Checking the properties of a binomial experiment, we observe that

1. The experiment consists of 10 identical trials; each trial involves contacting one family.
2. Two outcomes are possible on each trial: the family purchases a policy (success) or the family does not purchase a policy (failure).
3. The probabilities of a purchase and a nonpurchase are assumed to be the same for each sales call, with $p = 0.10$ and $1 - p = 0.90$.
4. The trials are independent because the families are randomly selected.

Figure 5.3 One Possible Sequence of Successes and Failures for an Eight-Trial Binomial Experiment

Property 1: The experiment consists of $n = 8$ identical trials.

Property 2: Each trial results in either success (S) or failure (F).

Trials →	1	2	3	4	5	6	7	8
Outcomes →	S	F	F	S	S	F	S	S

Because the four assumptions are satisfied, this example is a binomial experiment. The random variable of interest is the number of sales obtained in contacting the 10 families. In this case, x can assume the values of 0, 1, 2, 3, 4, 5, 6, 7, 8, 9, and 10.

Property 3 of the binomial experiment is called the *stationarity assumption* and is sometimes confused with property 4, *independence of trials*. To see how they differ, consider again the case of the salesperson calling on families to sell insurance policies. If, as the day wore on, the salesperson got tired and lost enthusiasm, the probability of success (selling a policy) might drop to 0.05, for example, by the 10th call. In such a case, property 3 (stationarity) would not be satisfied, and we would not have a binomial experiment. Even if property 4 held—that is, the purchase decisions of each family were made independently—it would not be a binomial experiment if property 3 was not satisfied.

In applications involving binomial experiments, a special mathematical formula, called the *binomial probability function,* can be used to compute the probability of x successes in the n trials.

This example illustrates how the formula for the binomial probability function is developed using concepts from Chapter 4.

Martin Clothing Store Problem

Let us consider the purchase decisions of the next three customers who enter the Martin Clothing Store. On the basis of past experience, the store manager estimates the probability that any one customer will make a purchase is 0.30. What is the probability that two of the next three customers will make a purchase?

Using a tree diagram (Figure 5.4), we can see that the experiment of observing the three customers each making a purchase decision has eight possible outcomes. Using S to denote success (a purchase) and F to denote failure (no purchase), we are interested in experimental outcomes involving two successes in the three trials (purchase decisions). Next, let

Figure 5.4 Tree Diagram for the Martin Clothing Store Problem

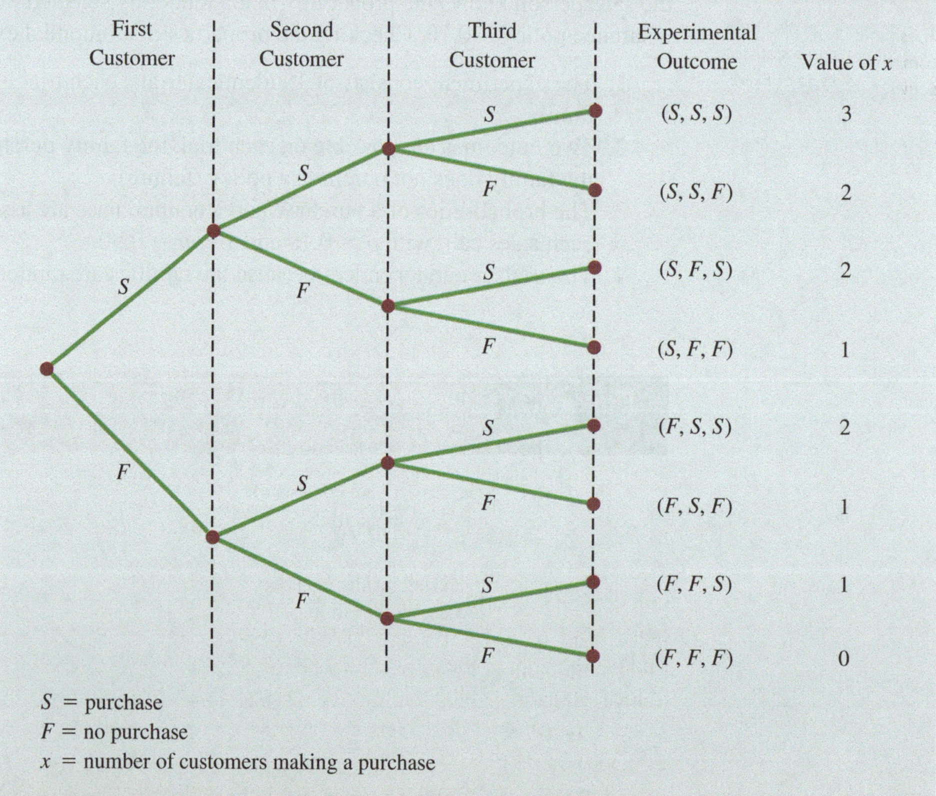

us verify that the experiment involving the sequence of three purchase decisions can be viewed as a binomial experiment. Checking the four requirements for a binomial experiment, we note that

1. The experiment can be described as a sequence of three identical trials, one trial for each of the three customers who will enter the store.
2. Two outcomes—the customer makes a purchase (success) or the customer does not make a purchase (failure)—are possible for each trial.
3. The probability that the customer will make a purchase (0.30) or will not make a purchase (0.70) is assumed to be the same for all customers.
4. The purchase decision of each customer is independent of the decisions of the other customers.

Hence, the properties of a binomial experiment are present.

The number of experimental outcomes resulting in exactly x successes in n trials can be computed using the following formula.[2]

Number of Experimental Outcomes Providing Exactly x Successes in n Trials

$$\binom{n}{x} = \frac{n!}{x!(n-x)!} \tag{5.10}$$

where

$$n! = n(n-1)(n-2)\cdots(2)(1)$$

and, by definition,

$$0! = 1$$

Now let us return to the Martin Clothing Store experiment involving three customer purchase decisions. Equation (5.10) can be used to determine the number of experimental outcomes involving two purchases; that is, the number of ways of obtaining $x = 2$ successes in the $n = 3$ trials. From equation (5.10) we have

$$\binom{n}{x} = \binom{3}{2} = \frac{3!}{2!(3-2)!} = \frac{(3)(2)(1)}{(2)(1)(1)} = \frac{6}{2} = 3$$

Equation (5.10) shows that three of the experimental outcomes yield two successes. From Figure 5.3 we see that these three outcomes are denoted by (S, S, F), (S, F, S), and (F, S, S).

Using equation (5.10) to determine how many experimental outcomes have three successes (purchases) in the three trials, we obtain

$$\binom{n}{x} = \binom{3}{3} = \frac{3!}{3!(3-3)!} = \frac{3!}{3!0!} = \frac{(3)(2)(1)}{3(2)(1)(1)} = \frac{6}{6} = 1$$

From Figure 5.4 we see that the one experimental outcome with three successes is identified by (S, S, S).

We know that equation (5.10) can be used to determine the number of experimental outcomes that result in x successes in n trials. If we are to determine the probability of x successes in n trials, however, we must also know the probability associated with each of these experimental outcomes. Because the trials of a binomial experiment are independent, we can simply multiply the probabilities associated with each trial outcome to find the probability of a particular sequence of successes and failures.

[2]This formula, introduced in Chapter 4, determines the number of combinations of n objects selected x at a time. For the binomial experiment, this combinatorial formula provides the number of experimental outcomes (sequences of n trials) resulting in x successes.

The probability of purchases by the first two customers and no purchase by the third customer, denoted (S, S, F), is given by

$$(p)(p)(1 - p)$$

With a 0.30 probability of a purchase on any one trial, the probability of a purchase on the first two trials and no purchase on the third is given by

$$(0.30)(0.30)(0.70) = (0.30)^2(0.70) = 0.063$$

Two other experimental outcomes also result in two successes and one failure. The probabilities for all three experimental outcomes involving two successes follow.

Trial Outcomes				
1st Customer	**2nd Customer**	**3rd Customer**	**Experimental Outcome**	**Probability of Experimental Outcome**
Purchase	Purchase	No purchase	(S, S, F)	$(p)(p)(1 - p) = p^2(1 - p)$ $= (0.30)^2(0.70) = 0.063$
Purchase	No purchase	Purchase	(S, F, S)	$(p)(1 - p)(p) = p^2(1 - p)$ $= (0.30)^2(0.70) = 0.063$
No purchase	Purchase	Purchase	(F, S, S)	$(1 - p)(p)(p) = p^2(1 - p)$ $= (0.30)^2(0.70) = 0.063$

Observe that all three experimental outcomes with two successes have exactly the same probability. This observation holds in general. In any binomial experiment, all sequences of trial outcomes yielding x successes in n trials have the *same probability* of occurrence. The probability of each sequence of trials yielding x successes in n trials follows.

$$\begin{array}{l}\text{Probability of a particular} \\ \text{sequence of trial outcomes} \\ \text{with } x \text{ successes in } n \text{ trials}\end{array} = p^x(1 - p)^{(n-x)} \qquad \textbf{(5.11)}$$

For the Martin Clothing Store, this formula shows that any experimental outcome with two successes has a probability of $p^2(1 - p)^{(3-2)} = p^2(1 - p)^1 = (0.30)^2(0.70)^1 = 0.063$.

Because equation (5.10) shows the number of outcomes in a binomial experiment with x successes and equation (5.11) gives the probability for each sequence involving x successes, we combine equations (5.10) and (5.11) to obtain the following **binomial probability function**.

Binomial Probability Function

$$f(x) = \binom{n}{x} p^x(1 - p)^{(n-x)} \qquad \textbf{(5.12)}$$

where

$$\begin{aligned} x &= \text{the number of successes} \\ p &= \text{the probability of a success on one trial} \\ n &= \text{the number of trials} \\ f(x) &= \text{the probability of } x \text{ successes in } n \text{ trials} \\ \binom{n}{x} &= \frac{n!}{x!(n - x)!} \end{aligned}$$

For the binomial probability distribution, x is a discrete random variable with the probability function $f(x)$ applicable for values of $x = 0, 1, 2, \ldots, n$.

Table 5.13 Probability Distribution for the Number of Customers Making a Purchase

x	$f(x)$
0	$\frac{3!}{0!3!}(0.30)^0(0.70)^3 = 0.343$
1	$\frac{3!}{1!2!}(0.30)^1(0.70)^2 = 0.441$
2	$\frac{3!}{2!1!}(0.30)^2(0.70)^1 = 0.189$
3	$\frac{3!}{3!0!}(0.30)^3(0.70)^0 = 0.027$
	1.000

In the Martin Clothing Store example, let us use equation (5.12) to compute the probability that no customer makes a purchase, exactly one customer makes a purchase, exactly two customers make a purchase, and all three customers make a purchase. The calculations are summarized in Table 5.13, which gives the probability distribution of the number of customers making a purchase. Figure 5.5 is a graph of this probability distribution.

The binomial probability function can be applied to *any* binomial experiment. If we are satisfied that a situation demonstrates the properties of a binomial experiment and if we know the values of n and p, we can use equation (5.12) to compute the probability of x successes in the n trials.

If we consider variations of the Martin experiment, such as 10 customers rather than 3 entering the store, the binomial probability function given by equation (5.12) is still applicable. Suppose we have a binomial experiment with $n = 10$, $x = 4$, and $p = 0.30$. The probability of making exactly four sales to 10 customers entering the store is

$$f(4) = \frac{10!}{4!6!}(0.30)^4(0.70)^6 = 0.2001$$

Figure 5.5 Graphical Representation of the Probability Distribution for the Number of Customers Making a Purchase

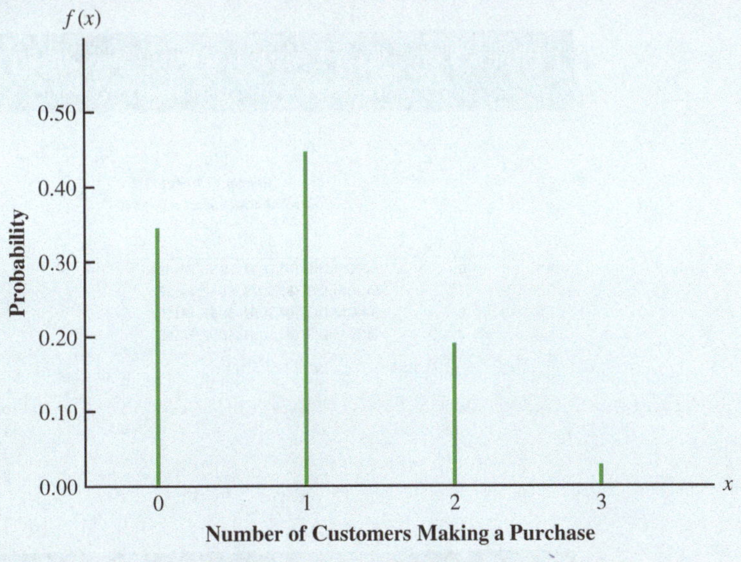

Using Excel to Compute Binomial Probabilities

For many probability functions that can be specified as formulas, Excel provides functions for computing probabilities and cumulative probabilities. In this section, we show how Excel's BINOM.DIST function can be used to compute binomial probabilities and cumulative binomial probabilities. We begin by showing how to compute the binomial probabilities for the Martin Clothing Store example shown in Table 5.13. Refer to Figure 5.6 as we describe the tasks involved. The formula worksheet is in the background; the value worksheet is in the foreground.

Enter/Access Data: To compute a binomial probability we must know the number of trials (n), the probability of success (p), and the value of the random variable (x). For the Martin Clothing Store example, the number of trials is 3; this value has been entered in cell D1. The probability of success is 0.3; this value has been entered in cell D2. Because we want to compute the probability for $x = 0, 1, 2,$ and 3, these values were entered in cells B5:B8.

Enter Functions and Formulas: The BINOM.DIST function has four inputs: The first is the value of x, the second is the value of n, the third is the value of p, and the fourth is FALSE or TRUE. We choose FALSE for the fourth input if a probability is desired and TRUE if a cumulative probability is desired. The formula *=BINOM.DIST(B5,$D$1,$D$2, FALSE)* has been entered in cell C5 to compute the probability of 0 successes in 3 trials. Note in the value worksheet that the probability computed for $f(0)$, 0.343, is the same as that shown in Table 5.13. The formula in cell C5 is copied to cells C6:C8 to compute the probabilities for $x = 1, 2,$ and 3 successes, respectively.

We can also compute cumulative probabilities using Excel's BINOM.DIST function. To illustrate, let us consider the case of 10 customers entering the Martin Clothing Store and compute the probabilities and cumulative probabilities for the number of customers making a purchase. Recall that the cumulative probability for $x = 1$ is the probability of 1 or fewer purchases, the cumulative probability for $x = 2$ is the probability of 2 or fewer purchases, and so on. So, the cumulative probability for $x = 10$ is 1. Refer to Figure 5.7 as we describe the tasks involved in computing these cumulative probabilities. The formula worksheet is in the background; the value worksheet is in the foreground.

Enter/Access Data: We entered the number of trials (*10*) in cell D1, the probability of success (*0.3*) in cell D2, and the values for the random variable in cells B5:B15.

Enter Functions and Formulas: The binomial probabilities for each value of the random variable are computed in column C and the cumulative probabilities are computed in

Figure 5.6 Excel Worksheet for Computing Binomial Probabilities of Number of Customers Making a Purchase

	A	B	C	D	E
1			Number of Trials (*n*)	3	
2			Probability of Success (*p*)	0.3	
3					
4		*x*	*f(x)*		
5		0	=BINOM.DIST(B5,$D$1,$D$2, FALSE)		
6		1	=BINOM.DIST(B6,$D$1, $D$2, FALSE)		
7		2	=BINOM.DIST(B7,$D$1, $D$2, FALSE)		
8		3	=BINOM.DIST(B8,$D$1, $D$2, FALSE)		
9					

	A	B	C	D	E
1			Number of Trials (*n*)	3	
2			Probability of Success (*p*)	0.3	
3					
4		*x*	*f(x)*		
5		0	0.343		
6		1	0.441		
7		2	0.189		
8		3	0.027		
9					

Figure 5.7 Excel Worksheet for Computing Probabilities and Cumulative Probabilities for Number of Purchases with 10 Customers

	A	B	C	D	E
1			Number of Trials (*n*)	10	
2			Probability of Success (*p*)	0.3	
3					
4		*x*	*f*(*x*)	Cumulative Probability	
5		0	=BINOM.DIST(B5,$D$1, $D$2, FALSE)	=BINOM.DIST(B5,$D$1, $D$2, TRUE)	
6		1	=BINOM.DIST(B6,$D$1, $D$2, FALSE)	=BINOM.DIST(B6,$D$1, $D$2, TRUE)	
7		2	=BINOM.DIST(B7,$D$1, $D$2, FALSE)	=BINOM.DIST(B7,$D$1, $D$2, TRUE)	
8		3	=BINOM.DIST(B8,$D$1, $D$2, FALSE)	=BINOM.DIST(B8,$D$1, $D$2, TRUE)	
9		4	=BINOM.DIST(B9,$D$1, $D$2, FALSE)	=BINOM.DIST(B9,$D$1, $D$2, TRUE)	
10		5	=BINOM.DIST(B10,$D$1, $D$2, FALSE)	=BINOM.DIST(B10,$D$1, $D$2, TRUE)	
11		6	=BINOM.DIST(B11,$D$1, $D$2, FALSE)	=BINOM.DIST(B11,$D$1, $D$2, TRUE)	
12		7	=BINOM.DIST(B12,$D$1, $D$2, FALSE)	=BINOM.DIST(B12,$D$1, $D$2, TRUE)	
13		8	=BINOM.DIST(B13,$D$1, $D$2, FALSE)	=BINOM.DIST(B13,$D$1, $D$2, TRUE)	
14		9	=BINOM.DIST(B14,$D$1, $D$2, FALSE)	=BINOM.DIST(B14,$D$1, $D$2, TRUE)	
15		10	=BINOM.DIST(B15,$D$1, $D$2, FALSE)	=BINOM.DIST(B15,$D$1, $D$2, TRUE)	
16					

	A	B	C	D	E
1			Number of Trials (*n*)	10	
2			Probability of Success (*p*)	0.3	
3					
4		*x*	*f*(*x*)	Cumulative Probability	
5		0	0.0282	0.0282	
6		1	0.1211	0.1493	
7		2	0.2335	0.3828	
8		3	0.2668	0.6496	
9		4	0.2001	0.8497	
10		5	0.1029	0.9527	
11		6	0.0368	0.9894	
12		7	0.0090	0.9984	
13		8	0.0014	0.9999	
14		9	0.0001	1.0000	
15		10	0.0000	1.0000	
16					

column D. We entered the formula *=BINOM.DIST(B5,$D$1,$D$2,FALSE)* in cell C5 to compute the probability of 0 successes in 10 trials. Note that we used *FALSE* as the fourth input in the BINOM.DIST function. The probability (0.0282) is shown in cell C5 of the value worksheet. The formula in cell C5 is simply copied to cells C6:C15 to compute the remaining probabilities.

To compute the cumulative probabilities, we start by entering the formula *=BINOM.DIST(B5,$D$1,$D$2,TRUE)* in cell D5. Note that we used *TRUE* as the fourth input in the BINOM.DIST function. The formula in cell D5 is then copied to cells D6:D15 to compute the remaining cumulative probabilities. In cell D5 of the value worksheet we see that the cumulative probability for $x = 0$ is the same as the probability for $x = 0$. Each of the remaining cumulative probabilities is the sum of the previous cumulative probability and the individual probability in column C. For instance, the cumulative probability for $x = 4$ is given by $0.6496 + 0.2001 = 0.8497$. Note also that the cumulative probability for $x = 10$ is also shown to be 1 in Figure 5.7. The cumulative probability of $x = 9$ is also 1 in Figure 5.7 because the probability of $x = 10$ is zero to four decimal places of accuracy.

Expected Value and Variance for the Binomial Distribution

In Section 5.3, we provided formulas for computing the expected value and variance of a discrete random variable. In the special case where the random variable has a binomial distribution with a known number of trials n and a known probability of success p, the general formulas for the expected value and variance can be simplified. The results follow.

Expected Value and Variance for the Binomial Distribution

$$E(x) = \mu = np \tag{5.13}$$

$$Var(x) = \sigma^2 = np(1 - p) \tag{5.14}$$

For the Martin Clothing Store problem with three customers, we can use equation (5.13) to compute the expected number of customers who will make a purchase.

$$E(x) = np = 3(0.30) = 0.9$$

Suppose that for the next month the Martin Clothing Store forecasts 1,000 customers will enter the store. What is the expected number of customers who will make a purchase? The answer is $\mu = np = (1{,}000)(0.3) = 300$. Thus, to increase the expected number of purchases, Martin Clothing Store must induce more customers to enter the store and/or somehow increase the probability that any individual customer will make a purchase after entering.

For the Martin Clothing Store problem with three customers, we see that the variance and standard deviation for the number of customers who will make a purchase are

$$\sigma^2 = np(1 - p) = 3(0.3)(0.7) = 0.63$$
$$\sigma = \sqrt{0.63} = 0.79$$

For the next 1,000 customers entering the store, the variance and standard deviation for the number of customers who will make a purchase are

$$\sigma^2 = np(1 - p) = 1{,}000(0.3)(0.7) = 210$$
$$\sigma = \sqrt{210} = 14.49$$

Exercises

Methods

31. Consider a binomial experiment with two trials and $p = 0.4$. **LO 7, 8**
    a. Draw a tree diagram for this experiment (see Figure 5.3).
    b. Compute the probability of one success, $f(1)$.
    c. Compute $f(0)$.
    d. Compute $f(2)$.
    e. Compute the probability of at least one success.
    f. Compute the expected value, variance, and standard deviation.
32. Consider a binomial experiment with $n = 10$ and $p = 0.10$. **LO 7, 8**
    a. Compute $f(0)$.
    b. Compute $f(2)$.
    c. Compute $P(x \leq 2)$.
    d. Compute $P(x \geq 1)$.
    e. Compute $E(x)$.
    f. Compute $Var(x)$ and σ.
33. Consider a binomial experiment with $n = 20$ and $p = 0.70$. **LO 7, 8**
    a. Compute $f(12)$.
    b. Compute $f(16)$.
    c. Compute $P(x \geq 16)$.
    d. Compute $P(x \leq 15)$.
    e. Compute $E(x)$.
    f. Compute $Var(x)$ and σ.

Applications

34. **Listening to News through Smart Speakers.** A smart speaker is an Internet-enabled speaker with which the user can interact with the speaker through voice commands. Amazon, Google, and Sonos are companies that produce some of the most popular smart speakers. A 2018 survey from Nielsen estimates that 68% of smart-speaker users listen to the news on a regular basis through their smart speakers (Nielsen website). Suppose eight smart-speaker users are randomly selected to be interviewed, which can be considered a binomial experiment. **LO 7**
    a. What is the probability that none of the eight smart-speaker users listen to the news through their smart speaker?
    b. What is the probability that all eight smart-speaker users listen to the news through their smart speaker?
    c. What is the probability that five of the eight smart-speaker users listen to the news through their smart speaker?

d. What is the probability that six or more of the eight smart-speaker users listen to the news through their smart speaker.

35. **Appeals for Medicare Service.** The Center for Medicare and Medical Services reported that there were 295,000 appeals for hospitalization and other Part A Medicare service. For this group, 40% of first-round appeals were successful (*The Wall Street Journal*). Suppose 10 first-round appeals have just been received by a Medicare appeals office. **LO 7**
    a. Compute the probability that none of the appeals will be successful.
    b. Compute the probability that exactly one of the appeals will be successful.
    c. What is the probability that at least two of the appeals will be successful?
    d. What is the probability that more than half of the appeals will be successful?

36. **Number of Defective Parts.** When a new machine is functioning properly, only 3% of the items produced are defective. Assume that we will randomly select two parts produced on the machine and that we are interested in the number of defective parts found. **LO 7**
    a. Describe the conditions under which this situation would be a binomial experiment.
    b. Draw a tree diagram similar to Figure 5.4 showing this problem as a two-trial experiment.
    c. How many experimental outcomes result in exactly one defect being found?
    d. Compute the probabilities associated with finding no defects, exactly one defect, and two defects.

37. **Americans Saving for Retirement.** According to a 2018 survey by *Bankrate.com*, 20% of adults in the United States save nothing for retirement (CNBC website). Suppose that 15 adults in the United States are selected randomly. **LO 7**
    a. Is the selection of the 15 adults a binomial experiment? Explain.
    b. What is the probability that all of the selected adults save nothing for retirement?
    c. What is the probability that exactly five of the selected adults save nothing for retirement?
    d. What is the probability that at least one of the selected adults saves nothing for retirement?

38. **Detecting Missile Attacks.** Military radar and missile detection systems are designed to warn a country of an enemy attack. A reliability question is whether a detection system will be able to identify an attack and issue a warning. Assume that a particular detection system has a 0.90 probability of detecting a missile attack. Use the binomial probability distribution to answer the following questions. **LO 7**
    a. What is the probability that a single detection system will detect an attack?
    b. If two detection systems are installed in the same area and operate independently, what is the probability that at least one of the systems will detect the attack?
    c. If three systems are installed, what is the probability that at least one of the systems will detect the attack?
    d. Would you recommend that multiple detection systems be used? Explain.

39. **Dog Food Marketing Focus Group.** According to the American Veterinary Medical Association (AVMA), 38.4% of households in the United States own a dog as a pet (AVMA website). Suppose that a company that sells dog food would like to establish a focus group to gather input on a new dog food marketing campaign. The company plans to contact 25 randomly selected households to invite people to join the focus group. **LO 7, 8**
    a. Compute the probability that 10 of these 25 households own a dog as a pet.
    b. Compute the probability that 2 or fewer of these 25 households own a dog as a pet.
    c. For the sample of 25 households, compute the expected number of households who own a dog as a pet.
    d. For the sample of 25 households, compute the variance and standard deviation of households who own a dog as a pet.

40. **Contributing to Household Income.** A study conducted by the Pew Research Center showed that 75% of 18- to 34-year-olds living with their parents say they contribute

to household expenses (*The Wall Street Journal*). Suppose that a random sample of fifteen 18- to 34-year-olds living with their parents is selected and asked if they contribute to household expenses. **LO 7**

a. Is the selection of the fifteen 18- to 34-year-olds living with their parents a binomial experiment? Explain.
b. If the sample shows that none of the fifteen 18- to 34-year-olds living with their parents contributes to household expenses, would you question the results of the Pew Research study? Explain.
c. What is the probability that at least 10 of the fifteen 18- to 34-year-olds living with their parents contribute to household expenses?

41. **Introductory Statistics Course Withdrawals.** A university found that 20% of its students withdraw without completing the introductory statistics course. Assume that 20 students registered for the course. **LO 7, 8**
   a. Compute the probability that 2 or fewer will withdraw.
   b. Compute the probability that exactly 4 will withdraw.
   c. Compute the probability that more than 3 will withdraw.
   d. Compute the expected number of withdrawals.
42. **State of the Nation Survey.** A Gallup Poll showed that 30% of Americans are satisfied with the way things are going in the United States (Gallup website). Suppose a sample of 20 Americans is selected as part of a study of the state of the nation. The Americans in the sample are asked whether or not they are satisfied with the way things are going in the United States. **LO 7, 8**
   a. Compute the probability that exactly 4 of the 20 Americans surveyed are satisfied with the way things are going in the United States.
   b. Compute the probability that at least 2 of the Americans surveyed are satisfied with the way things are going in the United States.
   c. For the sample of 20 Americans, compute the expected number of Americans who are satisfied with the way things are going in the United States.
   d. For the sample of 20 Americans, compute the variance and standard deviation of the number of Americans who are satisfied with the way things are going in the United States.
43. **Tracked E-mails.** According to a 2017 *Wired* magazine article, 40% of e-mails that are received are tracked using software that can tell the e-mail sender when, where, and on what type of device the e-mail was opened (*Wired* magazine website). Suppose we randomly select 50 received e-mails. **LO 8**
   a. What is the expected number of these e-mails that are tracked?
   b. What are the variance and standard deviation for the number of these e-mails that are tracked?

5.6 Poisson Probability Distribution

The Poisson probability distribution is often used to model random arrivals in waiting line situations.

In this section, we consider a discrete random variable that is often useful in estimating the number of occurrences over a specified interval of time or space. For example, the random variable of interest might be the number of arrivals to a hospital emergency room, the number of repairs needed in 10 miles of highway, or the number of leaks in 100 miles of pipeline. If the following two properties are satisfied, the number of occurrences is a random variable described by the **Poisson probability distribution**.

Properties of a Poisson Experiment

1. The probability of an occurrence is the same for any two intervals of equal length.
2. The occurrence or nonoccurrence in any interval is independent of the occurrence or nonoccurrence in any other interval.

Siméon Poisson taught mathematics at the Ecole Polytechnique in Paris from 1802 to 1808. In 1837, he published a work entitled "Researches on the Probability of Criminal and Civil Verdicts," which includes a discussion of what later became known as the Poisson distribution.

The **Poisson probability function** is defined by equation (5.15).

Poisson Probability Function

$$f(x) = \frac{\mu^x e^{-\mu}}{x!} \tag{5.15}$$

where

$f(x)$ = the probability of x occurrences in an interval
μ = expected value or mean number of occurrences in an interval
$e \approx 2.71828$

For the Poisson probability distribution, x is a discrete random variable indicating the number of occurrences in the interval. Since there is no stated upper limit for the number of occurrences, the probability function $f(x)$ is applicable for values $x = 0, 1, 2, \ldots$ without limit. In practical applications, x will eventually become large enough so that $f(x)$ is approximately zero and the probability of any larger values of x becomes negligible.

An Example Involving Time Intervals

Suppose that we are interested in the number of patients who arrive at an emergency room of a large hospital during a 15-minute period on weekday mornings. If we can assume that the probability of a patient arriving is the same for any two time periods of equal length and that the arrival or nonarrival of a patient in any time period is independent of the arrival or nonarrival in any other time period, the Poisson probability function is applicable. Suppose these assumptions are satisfied and an analysis of historical data shows that the average number of patients arriving in a 15-minute period of time is 10; in this case, the following probability function applies.

$$f(x) = \frac{10^x e^{-10}}{x!}$$

The random variable here is x = number of patients arriving in any 15-minute period.

If management wanted to know the probability of exactly five arrivals in 15 minutes, we would set $x = 5$ and thus obtain

$$\begin{array}{l}\text{Probability of exactly} \\ \text{5 arrivals in 15 minutes}\end{array} = f(5) = \frac{10^5 e^{-10}}{5!} = 0.0378$$

The probability of five arrivals in 15 minutes was obtained by using a calculator to evaluate the probability function. Excel also provides a function called POISSON.DIST for computing Poisson probabilities and cumulative probabilities. This function is easier to use when numerous probabilities and cumulative probabilities are desired. At the end of this section, we show how to compute these probabilities with Excel.

In the preceding example, the mean of the Poisson distribution is $\mu = 10$ arrivals per 15-minute period. A property of the Poisson distribution is that the mean of the distribution and the variance of the distribution are *equal*. Thus, the variance for the number of arrivals during 15-minute periods is $\sigma^2 = 10$. The standard deviation is $\sigma = \sqrt{10} = 3.16$.

Our illustration involves a 15-minute period, but other time periods can be used. Suppose we want to compute the probability of one arrival in a 3-minute period. Because 10 is the expected number of arrivals in a 15-minute period, we see that $10/15 = 2/3$ is the expected number of arrivals in a 1-minute period and that $(2/3)(3 \text{ minutes}) = 2$ is the expected number of arrivals in a 3-minute period. Thus, the probability of x arrivals in a 3-minute time period with $\mu = 2$ is given by the following Poisson probability function.

$$f(x) = \frac{2^x e^{-2}}{x!}$$

The probability of one arrival in a 3-minute period is calculated as follows:

$$\text{Probability of exactly} \atop \text{1 arrival in 3 minutes} = f(1) = \frac{2^1 e^{-2}}{1!} = 0.2707$$

One might expect that because (5 arrivals)/5 = 1 arrival and (15 minutes)/5 = 3 minutes, the probability of one arrival during a 3-minute period and the probability of five arrivals during a 15-minute period would be identical. Earlier we computed the probability of five arrivals in a 15-minute period to be 0.0378. However, note that the probability of one arrival in a 3-minute period (0.2707) is not the same. When computing a Poisson probability for a different time interval, we must first convert the mean arrival rate to the time period of interest and then compute the probability.

An Example Involving Length or Distance Intervals

Let us illustrate an application not involving time intervals in which the Poisson distribution is useful. Suppose we are concerned with the occurrence of major defects in a highway one month after resurfacing. We will assume that the probability of a defect is the same for any two highway intervals of equal length and that the occurrence or nonoccurrence of a defect in any one interval is independent of the occurrence or nonoccurrence of a defect in any other interval. Hence, the Poisson distribution can be applied.

Suppose we learn that major defects one month after resurfacing occur at the average rate of two per mile. Let us find the probability of no major defects in a particular 3-mile section of the highway. Because we are interested in an interval with a length of 3 miles, $\mu = (2 \text{ defects/mile})(3 \text{ miles}) = 6$ represents the expected number of major defects over the 3-mile section of highway. Using equation (5.11), the probability of no major defects is $f(0) = 6^0 e^{-6}/0! = 0.0025$. Thus, it is unlikely that no major defects will occur in the 3-mile section. In fact, this example indicates a $1 - 0.0025 = 0.9975$ probability of at least one major defect in the 3-mile highway section.

Using Excel to Compute Poisson Probabilities

The Excel function for computing Poisson probabilities and cumulative probabilities is called POISSON.DIST. It works in much the same way as the Excel function for computing binomial probabilities. Here we show how to use it to compute Poisson probabilities and cumulative probabilities. To illustrate, we use the example introduced earlier in this section: cars arrive at a bank drive-up teller window at the mean rate of 10 per 15-minute time interval. Refer to Figure 5.8 as we describe the tasks involved.

Enter/Access Data: To compute a Poisson probability, we must know the mean number of occurrences (μ) per time period and the number of occurrences for which we want to compute the probability (x). For the drive-up teller window example, the occurrences of interest are the arrivals of cars. The mean arrival rate is *10*, which has been entered in cell D1. Earlier in this section, we computed the probability of 5 arrivals. But suppose we now want to compute the probability of 0 up through 20 arrivals. To do so, we enter the values *0, 1, 2, . . . , 20* in cells A4:A24.

Enter Functions and Formulas: The POISSON.DIST function has three inputs: The first is the value of x, the second is the value of μ, and the third is FALSE or TRUE. We choose FALSE for the third input if a probability is desired and TRUE if a cumulative probability is desired. The formula *=POISSON.DIST(A4,$D$1,FALSE)* has been entered in cell B4 to compute the probability of 0 arrivals in a 15-minute period. The value worksheet in the foreground shows that the probability of 0 arrivals is 0.0000. The formula in cell B4 is copied to cells B5:B24 to compute the probabilities for 1 through 20 arrivals. Note, in cell B9 of the value worksheet, that the probability of 5 arrivals is 0.0378. This result is the same as we calculated earlier in the text.

Figure 5.8 Excel Worksheet for Computing Poisson Probabilities

	A	B	C	D
1			Mean Number of Occurrences	10
2				
3	Number of Arrivals	Probability *f(x)*		
4	0	=POISSON.DIST(A4,$D$1,FALSE)		
5	1	=POISSON.DIST(A5,$D$1,FALSE)		
6	2	=POISSON.DIST(A6,$D$1,FALSE)		
7	3	=POISSON.DIST(A7,$D$1,FALSE)		
8	4	=POISSON.DIST(A8,$D$1,FALSE)		
9	5	=POISSON.DIST(A9,$D$1,FALSE)		
10	6	=POISSON.DIST(A10,$D$1,FALSE)		
11	7	=POISSON.DIST(A11,$D$1,FALSE)		
12	8	=POISSON.DIST(A12,$D$1,FALSE)		
13	9	=POISSON.DIST(A13,$D$1,FALSE)		
14	10	=POISSON.DIST(A14,$D$1,FALSE)		
15	11	=POISSON.DIST(A15,$D$1,FALSE)		
16	12	=POISSON.DIST(A16,$D$1,FALSE)		
17	13	=POISSON.DIST(A17,$D$1,FALSE)		
18	14	=POISSON.DIST(A18,$D$1,FALSE)		
19	15	=POISSON.DIST(A19,$D$1,FALSE)		
20	16	=POISSON.DIST(A20,$D$1,FALSE)		
21	17	=POISSON.DIST(A21,$D$1,FALSE)		
22	18	=POISSON.DIST(A22,$D$1,FALSE)		
23	19	=POISSON.DIST(A23,$D$1,FALSE)		
24	20	=POISSON.DIST(A24,$D$1,FALSE)		
25				

	A	B	C	D
1	Mean Number of Occurrences			10
2				
3	Number of Arrivals	Probability *f(x)*		
4	0	0.0000		
5	1	0.0005		
6	2	0.0023		
7	3	0.0076		
8	4	0.0189		
9	5	0.0378		
10	6	0.0631		
11	7	0.0901		
12	8	0.1126		
13	9	0.1251		
14	10	0.1251		
15	11	0.1137		
16	12	0.0948		
17	13	0.0729		
18	14	0.0521		
19	15	0.0347		
20	16	0.0217		
21	17	0.0128		
22	18	0.0071		
23	19	0.0037		
24	20	0.0019		
25				

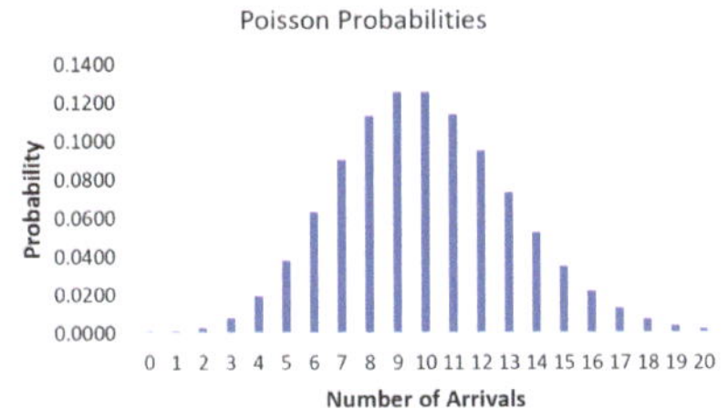

Notice how easy it was to compute all the probabilities for 0 through 20 arrivals using the POISSON.DIST function. These calculations would take quite a bit of work using a calculator. We have also used Excel's chart tools to develop a graph of the Poisson probability distribution of arrivals. See the value worksheet in Figure 5.8. This chart gives a nice graphical presentation of the probabilities for the various number of arrival possibilities in a 15-minute interval. We can quickly see that the most likely number of arrivals is 9 or 10 and that the probabilities fall off rather smoothly for smaller and larger values.

Let us now see how cumulative probabilities are generated using Excel's POISSON.DIST function. It is really a simple extension of what we have already done. We again use the example of arrivals at a drive-up teller window. Refer to Figure 5.9 as we describe the tasks involved.

Enter/Access Data: To compute cumulative Poisson probabilities we must provide the mean number of occurrences (μ) per time period and the values of x that we are interested in. The mean arrival rate (*10*) has been entered in cell D1. Suppose we want to compute the cumulative probabilities for a number of arrivals ranging from zero up through 20. To do so, we enter the values *0, 1, 2, . . . , 20* in cells A4:A24.

Enter Functions and Formulas: Refer to the formula worksheet in the background of Figure 5.8. The formulas we enter in cells B4:B24 of Figure 5.9 are the same as in Figure 5.8, with one exception. Instead of FALSE for the third input, we enter the word *TRUE* to obtain cumulative probabilities. After entering these formulas in cells B4:B24 of the worksheet in Figure 5.9, the cumulative probabilities shown were obtained.

Note, in Figure 5.9, that the probability of 5 or fewer arrivals is 0.0671 and that the probability of 4 or fewer arrivals is 0.0293. Thus, the probability of exactly 5 arrivals is the difference in these two numbers: $f(5) = 0.0671 - 0.0293 = 0.0378$. We computed this probability earlier in this section and in Figure 5.8. Using these cumulative probabilities, it is easy to compute the probability that a random variable lies within a certain interval. For instance, suppose we wanted to know the probability of more than 5 and fewer than 16 arrivals. We would just find the cumulative probability of 15 arrivals and subtract from that the cumulative probability for 5 arrivals. Referring to Figure 5.9 to obtain the appropriate probabilities, we obtain $0.9513 - 0.0671 = 0.8842$. With such a high probability, we

Figure 5.9 Excel Worksheet for Computing Cumulative Poisson Probabilities

	A	B	C	D
1			Mean Number of Occurrences	10
2				
3	Number of Arrivals	Probability *f(x)*		
4	0	=POISSON.DIST(A4,$D$1,TRUE)		
5	1	=POISSON.DIST(A5,$D$1,TRUE)		
6	2	=POISSON.DIST(A6,$D$1,TRUE)		
7	3	=POISSON.DIST(A7,$D$1,TRUE)		
8	4	=POISSON.DIST(A8,$D$1,TRUE)		
9	5	=POISSON.DIST(A9,$D$1,TRUE)		
10	6	=POISSON.DIST(A10,$D$1,TRUE)		
11	7	=POISSON.DIST(A11,$D$1,TRUE)		
12	8	=POISSON.DIST(A12,$D$1,TRUE)		
13	9	=POISSON.DIST(A13,$D$1,TRUE)		
14	10	=POISSON.DIST(A14,$D$1,TRUE)		
15	11	=POISSON.DIST(A15,$D$1,TRUE)		
16	12	=POISSON.DIST(A16,$D$1,TRUE)		
17	13	=POISSON.DIST(A17,$D$1,TRUE)		
18	14	=POISSON.DIST(A18,$D$1,TRUE)		
19	15	=POISSON.DIST(A19,$D$1,TRUE)		
20	16	=POISSON.DIST(A20,$D$1,TRUE)		
21	17	=POISSON.DIST(A21,$D$1,TRUE)		
22	18	=POISSON.DIST(A22,$D$1,TRUE)		
23	19	=POISSON.DIST(A23,$D$1,TRUE)		
24	20	=POISSON.DIST(A24,$D$1,TRUE)		
25				

	A	B	C	D
1		Mean Number of Occurrences		10
2				
3	Number of Arrivals	Probability *f(x)*		
4	0	0.0000		
5	1	0.0005		
6	2	0.0028		
7	3	0.0103		
8	4	0.0293		
9	5	0.0671		
10	6	0.1301		
11	7	0.2202		
12	8	0.3328		
13	9	0.4579		
14	10	0.5830		
15	11	0.6968		
16	12	0.7916		
17	13	0.8645		
18	14	0.9165		
19	15	0.9513		
20	16	0.9730		
21	17	0.9857		
22	18	0.9928		
23	19	0.9965		
24	20	0.9984		
25				

could conclude that 6 to 15 cars will arrive in most 15-minute intervals. Using the cumulative probability for 20 arrivals, we can also conclude that the probability of more than 20 arrivals in a 15-minute period is $1 - 0.9984 = 0.0016$; thus, there is almost no chance of more than 20 cars arriving.

Exercises

Methods

44. Consider a Poisson distribution with $\mu = 3$. **LO 9**
    a. Write the appropriate Poisson probability function.
    b. Compute $f(2)$.
    c. Compute $f(1)$.
    d. Compute $P(x \geq 2)$.
45. Consider a Poisson distribution with a mean of two occurrences per time period. **LO 9, 10**
    a. Write the appropriate Poisson probability function.
    b. What is the expected number of occurrences in three time periods?
    c. Write the appropriate Poisson probability function to determine the probability of x occurrences in three time periods.
    d. Compute the probability of two occurrences in one time period.
    e. Compute the probability of six occurrences in three time periods.
    f. Compute the probability of five occurrences in two time periods.

Applications

46. **Regional Airways Calls.** Phone calls arrive at the rate of 48 per hour at the reservation desk for Regional Airways. **LO 9**
    a. Compute the probability of receiving three calls in a 5-minute interval of time.
    b. Compute the probability of receiving exactly 10 calls in 15 minutes.
    c. Suppose no calls are currently on hold. If the agent takes 5 minutes to complete the current call, how many callers do you expect to be waiting by that time? What is the probability that none will be waiting?
    d. If no calls are currently being processed, what is the probability that the agent can take 3 minutes for personal time without being interrupted by a call?
47. **Computer Code Errors.** The book *Code Complete* by Steve McDonnell estimates that there are 15 to 50 errors per 1,000 lines of delivered code for computer programs. Assume that for a particular software package, the error rate is 25 per 1,000 lines of code and that the number of errors per 1,000 lines of code follows a Poisson distribution. **LO 9, 10**
    a. What is the probability that a portion of code for this computer package that contains 250 lines of code contains no errors?
    b. What is the probability of there being exactly 30 errors in 1,000 lines of code?
    c. What is the probability of more than three errors in 100 lines of code?
    d. What is the expected number of errors in a portion of code that contains 25,000 lines of code?
48. **Motor Vehicle Accidents in New York City.** In a one-year period, New York City had a total of 11,232 motor vehicle accidents that occurred on Monday through Friday between the hours of 3 P.M. and 6 P.M. (New York State Department of Motor Vehicles website). This corresponds to a mean of 14.4 accidents per hour. Assume the number of vehicle accidents that occur follows a Poisson distribution and answer the following. **LO 9**
    a. Compute the probability of no accidents in a 15-minute period.
    b. Compute the probability of at least one accident in a 15-minute period.
    c. Compute the probability of four or more accidents in a 15-minute period.
49. **Airport Passenger-Screening Facility.** Airline passengers arrive randomly and independently at the passenger-screening facility at a major international airport. The mean arrival rate is 10 passengers per minute, and passenger arrivals follow a Poisson distribution. **LO 9**.
    a. Compute the probability of no arrivals in a one-minute period.
    b. Compute the probability that three or fewer passengers arrive in a one-minute period.
    c. Compute the probability of no arrivals in a 15-second period.
    d. Compute the probability of at least one arrival in a 15-second period.
50. **Tornadoes in Colorado.** According to the National Oceanic and Atmospheric Administration (NOAA), the state of Colorado averages 18 tornadoes every June (NOAA website). Assume the number of tornadoes that occur in Colorado follows a Poisson distribution and answer the following. (*Note*: There are 30 days in June.) **LO 9, 10**
    a. Compute the mean number of tornadoes per day.
    b. Compute the probability of no tornadoes during a day.
    c. Compute the probability of exactly one tornado during a day.
    d. Compute the probability of more than one tornado during a day.
51. **E-mails Received.** According to a 2017 survey conducted by the technology market research firm The Radicati Group, U.S. office workers receive an average of 121 e-mails per day (*Entrepreneur* magazine website). Assume the number of e-mails received per hour follows a Poisson distribution and that the average number of e-mails received per hour is five. **LO 9, 10**
    a. What is the probability of receiving no e-mails during an hour?
    b. What is the probability of receiving at least three e-mails during an hour?
    c. What is the expected number of e-mails received during 15 minutes?
    d. What is the probability that no e-mails are received during 15 minutes?

5.7 Hypergeometric Probability Distribution

The **hypergeometric probability distribution** is closely related to the binomial distribution. The two probability distributions differ in two key ways. With the hypergeometric distribution, the trials are not independent, and the probability of success changes from trial to trial.

In the usual notation for the hypergeometric distribution, r denotes the number of elements in the population of size N labeled success, and $N - r$ denotes the number of elements in the population labeled failure. The **hypergeometric probability function** is used to compute the probability that in a random selection of n elements, selected without replacement, we obtain x elements labeled success and $n - x$ elements labeled failure. For this outcome to occur, we must obtain x successes from the r successes in the population and $n - x$ failures from the $N - r$ failures. The following hypergeometric probability function provides $f(x)$, the probability of obtaining x successes in n trials.

Hypergeometric Probability Function

$$f(x) = \frac{\binom{r}{x}\binom{N-r}{n-x}}{\binom{N}{n}} \tag{5.16}$$

where

x = the number of successes
n = the number of trials
$f(x)$ = the probability of x successes in n trials
N = the number of elements in the population
r = the number of elements in the population labeled success

Note that $\binom{N}{n}$ represents the number of ways n elements can be selected from a population of size N; $\binom{r}{x}$ represents the number of ways that x successes can be selected from a total of r successes in the population; and $\binom{N-r}{n-x}$ represents the number of ways that $n - x$ failures can be selected from a total of $N - r$ failures in the population.

For the hypergeometric probability distribution, x is a discrete random variable and the probability function $f(x)$ given by equation (5.16) is usually applicable for values of $x = 0, 1, 2, \ldots, n$. However, only values of x where the number of observed successes is *less than or equal* to the number of successes in the population ($x \leq r$) and where the number of observed failures is *less than or equal to* the number of failures in the population ($n - x \leq N - r$) are valid. If these two conditions do not hold for one or more values of x, the corresponding $f(x) = 0$ indicating that the probability of this value of x is zero.

To illustrate the computations involved in using equation (5.16), let us consider the following quality control application. Electric fuses produced by Ontario Electric are packaged in boxes of 12 units each. Suppose an inspector randomly selects 3 of the 12 fuses in a box for testing. If the box contains exactly 5 defective fuses, what is the probability that the inspector will find exactly 1 of the 3 fuses defective? In this application, $n = 3$ and $N = 12$. With $r = 5$ defective fuses in the box, the probability of finding $x = 1$ defective fuse is

$$f(1) = \frac{\binom{5}{1}\binom{7}{2}}{\binom{12}{3}} = \frac{\left(\frac{5!}{1!4!}\right)\left(\frac{7!}{2!5!}\right)}{\left(\frac{12!}{3!9!}\right)} = \frac{(5)(21)}{220} = 0.4773$$

Now suppose that we wanted to know the probability of finding *at least* 1 defective fuse. The easiest way to answer this question is to first compute the probability that the inspector does not find any defective fuses. The probability of $x = 0$ is

$$f(0) = \frac{\binom{5}{0}\binom{7}{3}}{\binom{12}{3}} = \frac{\left(\frac{5!}{0!5!}\right)\left(\frac{7!}{3!4!}\right)}{\left(\frac{12!}{3!9!}\right)} = \frac{(1)(35)}{220} = 0.1591$$

With a probability of zero defective fuses $f(0) = 0.1591$, we conclude that the probability of finding at least 1 defective fuse must be $1 - 0.1591 = 0.8409$. Thus, there is a reasonably high probability that the inspector will find at least 1 defective fuse.

The mean and variance of a hypergeometric distribution are as follows.

$$E(x) = \mu = n\left(\frac{r}{N}\right) \tag{5.17}$$

$$Var(x) = \sigma^2 = n\left(\frac{r}{N}\right)\left(1 - \frac{r}{N}\right)\left(\frac{N-n}{N-1}\right) \tag{5.18}$$

In the preceding example $n = 3$, $r = 5$, and $N = 12$. Thus, the mean and variance for the number of defective fuses are

$$\mu = n\left(\frac{r}{N}\right) = 3\left(\frac{5}{12}\right) = 1.25$$

$$\sigma^2 = n\left(\frac{r}{N}\right)\left(1 - \frac{r}{N}\right)\left(\frac{N-n}{N-1}\right) = 3\left(\frac{5}{12}\right)\left(1 - \frac{5}{12}\right)\left(\frac{12-3}{12-1}\right) = 0.60$$

The standard deviation is $\sigma = \sqrt{0.60} = 0.77$.

Using Excel to Compute Hypergeometric Probabilities

The Excel function for computing hypergeometric probabilities is HYPGEOM.DIST. This function's usage is similar to that of BINOM.DIST for the binomial distribution and POISSON.DIST for the Poisson distribution. To illustrate we reconsider the example of selecting 3 fuses for inspection from a fuse box containing 12 fuses, 5 of which are defective. Refer to Figure 5.10 as we describe the tasks involved.

Enter/Access Data: To compute the probability of x selected fuses being defective, we must enter the number of fuses selected (n), the number of defective fuses in a box (r), and the number of fuses in a box (N). We enter these values in cells D1:D3, as shown in Figure 5.10. Suppose we want to know the probability of 0, 1, 2, and 3 of the 3 selected fuses being defective. To calculate this, we enter *0, 1, 2, 3* in cells A6:A9.

Enter Functions and Formulas: The HYPGEOM.DIST function has five inputs: the first is the value of x, the second is the value of n, the third is the value of r, the fourth is the value of N, and the fifth is FALSE or TRUE. We choose FALSE if a probability is desired and TRUE if a cumulative probability is desired. The formula *=HYPGEOM.DIST(A6, $D$1, $D$2, $D$3, FALSE)* is entered in cell B6 to calculate the probability that none of the 3 selected fuses is defective. The value in the worksheet is 0.1581, indicating that the probability that

Figure 5.10 Excel Worksheet for Computing Hypergeometric Probabilities

	A	B	C	D	E
1			Number fuses selected, *n*	3	
2			Number defective fuses in box, *r*	5	
3			Number fuses in box, *N*	12	
4					
5	Number selected fuses defective, *x*	Probability f(x)			
6	0	=HYPGEOM.DIST(A6,$D$1,$D$2,$D$3,FALSE)			
7	1	=HYPGEOM.DIST(A7,$D$1,$D$2,$D$3,FALSE)			
8	2	=HYPGEOM.DIST(A8,$D$1,$D$2,$D$3,FALSE)			
9	3	=HYPGEOM.DIST(A9,$D$1,$D$2,$D$3,FALSE)			
10					

	A	B	C	D	E
1		Number fuses selected, *n*		3	
2		Number defective fuses in box, *r*		5	
3		Number fuses in box, *N*		12	
4					
5		Number selected fuses defective, *x*	Probability f(x)		
6		0	0.1591		
7		1	0.4773		
8		2	0.3182		
9		3	0.0455		
10					

Figure 5.11 Excel Worksheet for Computing Cumulative Hypergeometric Probabilities

	A	B	C	D	E
1			Number fuses selected, *n*	3	
2			Number defective fuses in box, *r*	5	
3			Number fuses in box, *N*	12	
4					
5	Number selected fuses defective, *x*	Probability f(x)			
6	0	=HYPGEOM.DIST(A6,$D$1,$D$2,$D$3,TRUE)			
7	1	=HYPGEOM.DIST(A7,$D$1,$D$2,$D$3,TRUE)			
8	2	=HYPGEOM.DIST(A8,$D$1,$D$2,$D$3,TRUE)			
9	3	=HYPGEOM.DIST(A9,$D$1,$D$2,$D$3,TRUE)			
10					

	A	B	C	D	E
1		Number fuses selected, *n*		3	
2		Number defective fuses in box, *r*		5	
3		Number fuses in box, *N*		12	
4					
5	Number selected fuses defective, *x*	Probability f(x)			
6	0	0.1591			
7	1	0.6364			
8	2	0.9545			
9	3	1.0000			
10					

none of the 3 selected fuses is defective is 0.1581. The formula in cell D6 is then copied to cells D7:D9 to calculate the probability that 1, 2, and 3 of the 3 selected fuses are defective.

To calculate the cumulative probabilities for 0, 1, 2, and 3 of the selected fuses being defective, we change the value of the fifth argument in the HYPGEOM.DIST function from FALSE to TRUE. The results of these calculations are shown in Figure 5.11.

Notes + Comments

Consider a hypergeometric distribution with n trials. Let $p = (r/N)$ denote the probability of a success on the first trial. If the population size is large, the term $(N - n)/(N - 1)$ in equation (5.18) approaches 1. As a result, the expected value and variance can be written $E(x) = np$ and $Var(x) = np(1 - p)$. Note that these expressions are the same as the expressions used to compute the expected value and variance of a binomial distribution, as in equations (5.13) and (5.14). When the population size is large, a hypergeometric distribution can be approximated by a binomial distribution with n trials and a probability of success $p = (r/N)$.

Exercises

Methods

52. Suppose $N = 10$ and $r = 3$. Compute the hypergeometric probabilities for the following values of n and x. **LO 11**
   a. $n = 4, x = 1$.
   b. $n = 2, x = 2$.
   c. $n = 2, x = 0$.
   d. $n = 4, x = 2$.
   e. $n = 4, x = 4$.
53. Suppose $N = 15$ and $r = 4$. What is the probability of $x = 3$ for $n = 10$? **LO 11**

Applications

54. **Online Holiday Shopping.** More and more shoppers prefer to do their holiday shopping online from companies such as Amazon. Suppose we have a group of 10 shoppers; 7 prefer to do their holiday shopping online and 3 prefer to do their holiday shopping in stores. A random sample of 3 of these 10 shoppers is selected for a more in-depth study of how the economy has impacted their shopping behavior. **LO 11**
   a. What is the probability that exactly 2 prefer shopping online?
   b. What is the probability that the majority (either 2 or 3) prefer shopping online?
55. **Playing Blackjack.** Blackjack, or twenty-one as it is frequently called, is a popular gambling game played in casinos. A player is dealt two cards. Face cards (jacks, queens, and kings) and tens have a point value of 10. Aces have a point value of 1 or 11. A 52-card deck contains 16 cards with a point value of 10 (jacks, queens, kings, and tens) and four aces. **LO 11**
   a. What is the probability that both cards dealt are aces or 10-point cards?
   b. What is the probability that both of the cards are aces?
   c. What is the probability that both of the cards have a point value of 10?
   d. A blackjack is a 10-point card and an ace for a value of 21. Use your answers to parts (a), (b), and (c) to determine the probability that a player is dealt blackjack. (*Hint:* Part (d) is not a hypergeometric problem. Develop your own logical relationship as to how the hypergeometric probabilities from parts (a), (b), and (c) can be combined to answer this question.)
56. **Computer Company Benefits Questionnaire.** Axline Computers manufactures personal computers at two plants, one in Texas and the other in Hawaii. The Texas plant has 40 employees; the Hawaii plant has 20. A random sample of 10 employees is asked to fill out a benefits questionnaire. **LO 11**
   a. What is the probability that none of the employees in the sample work at the plant in Hawaii?
   b. What is the probability that 1 of the employees in the sample works at the plant in Hawaii?
   c. What is the probability that 2 or more of the employees in the sample work at the plant in Hawaii?
   d. What is the probability that 9 of the employees in the sample work at the plant in Texas?
57. **Business Meal Reimbursement.** The Zagat Restaurant Survey provides food, decor, and service ratings for some of the top restaurants across the United States. For 15 restaurants located in Boston, the average price of a dinner, including one drink and tip, was $48.60. You are leaving on a business trip to Boston and will eat dinner at three of these restaurants. Your company will reimburse you for a maximum of $50 per dinner. Business associates familiar with these restaurants have told you that the meal cost at one-third of these restaurants will exceed $50. Suppose that you randomly select three of these restaurants for dinner. **LO 11**
   a. What is the probability that none of the meals will exceed the cost covered by your company?

b. What is the probability that one of the meals will exceed the cost covered by your company?
c. What is the probability that two of the meals will exceed the cost covered by your company?
d. What is the probability that all three of the meals will exceed the cost covered by your company?

58. **TARP Funds.** The Troubled Asset Relief Program (TARP), passed by the U.S. Congress in October 2008, provided $700 billion in assistance for the struggling U.S. economy. Over $200 billion was given to troubled financial institutions with the hope that there would be an increase in lending to help jump-start the economy. But three months later, a Federal Reserve survey found that two-thirds of the banks that had received TARP funds had tightened terms for business loans (*The Wall Street Journal*). Of the 10 banks that were the biggest recipients of TARP funds, only 3 had actually increased lending during this period.

Increased Lending	Decreased Lending
BB&T	Bank of America
Sun Trust Banks	Capital One
U.S. Bancorp	Citigroup
	Fifth Third Bancorp
	JPMorgan Chase
	Regions Financial
	Wells Fargo

For the purposes of this exercise, assume that you will randomly select 3 of these 10 banks for a study that will continue to monitor bank lending practices. Let x be a random variable indicating the number of banks in the study that had increased lending. **LO 11, 12**

a. What is $f(0)$? What is your interpretation of this value?
b. What is $f(3)$? What is your interpretation of this value?
c. Compute $f(1)$ and $f(2)$. Show the probability distribution for the number of banks in the study that had increased lending. What value of x has the highest probability?
d. What is the probability that the study will have at least one bank that had increased lending?
e. Compute the expected value, variance, and standard deviation for the random variable.

Summary

A random variable provides a numerical description of the outcome of an experiment. The probability distribution for a random variable describes how the probabilities are distributed over the values the random variable can assume. For any discrete random variable x, the probability distribution is defined by a probability function, denoted by $f(x)$, which provides the probability associated with each value of the random variable.

We introduced two types of discrete probability distributions. One type involved providing a list of the values of the random variable and the associated probabilities in a table. We showed how the relative frequency method of assigning probabilities could be used to develop empirical discrete probability distributions of this type. Bivariate empirical distributions were also discussed. With bivariate distributions, interest focuses on the relationship between two random variables. We showed how to compute the covariance and correlation coefficient as measures of such a relationship. We also showed how bivariate distributions involving market returns on financial assets could be used to create financial portfolios.

The second type of discrete probability distribution we discussed involved the use of a mathematical function to provide the probabilities for the random variable. The binomial,

Poisson, and hypergeometric distributions discussed were all of this type. The binomial distribution can be used to determine the probability of x successes in n trials whenever the experiment has the following properties:

1. The experiment consists of a sequence of n identical trials.
2. Two outcomes are possible on each trial, one called success and the other failure.
3. The probability of a success p does not change from trial to trial. Consequently, the probability of failure, $1 - p$, does not change from trial to trial.
4. The trials are independent.

When the four properties hold, the binomial probability function can be used to determine the probability of obtaining x successes in n trials. Formulas were also presented for the mean and variance of the binomial distribution.

The Poisson distribution is used when it is desirable to determine the probability of obtaining x occurrences over an interval of time or space. The following assumptions are necessary for the Poisson distribution to be applicable:

1. The probability of an occurrence of the event is the same for any two intervals of equal length.
2. The occurrence or nonoccurrence of the event in any interval is independent of the occurrence or nonoccurrence of the event in any other interval.

A third discrete probability distribution, the hypergeometric, was introduced in Section 5.7. Like the binomial, it is used to compute the probability of x successes in n trials. But, in contrast to the binomial, the probability of success changes from trial to trial.

Glossary

Binomial experiment An experiment having the following four properties: (1) the experiment consists of a sequence of n identical trials; (2) two outcomes are possible on each trial, either a success or a failure; (3) the probability of a success (and equivalently, a failure) does not change from trial to trial; (4) the trials are independent.

Binomial probability distribution A probability distribution showing the probability of x successes in n trials of a binomial experiment.

Binomial probability function The function used to compute binomial probabilities.

Bivariate probability distribution A probability distribution involving two random variables. A discrete bivariate probability distribution provides a probability for each pair of values that may occur for the two random variables.

Continuous random variable A random variable that may assume any numerical value in an interval or collection of intervals.

Discrete random variable A random variable that may assume either a finite number of values or an infinite sequence of values.

Discrete uniform probability distribution A probability distribution for which each possible value of the random variable has the same probability.

Empirical discrete distribution A discrete probability distribution for which the relative frequency method is used to assign the probabilities.

Expected value A measure of the central location, or mean, of a random variable.

Hypergeometric probability distribution A probability distribution showing the probability of x successes in n trials from a population with r successes and $N - r$ failures.

Hypergeometric probability function The function used to compute hypergeometric probabilities.

Poisson probability distribution A probability distribution showing the probability of x occurrences of an event over a specified interval of time or space.

Poisson probability function The function used to compute Poisson probabilities.

Probability distribution A description of how the probabilities are distributed over the values of the random variable.

Probability function A function, denoted by $f(x)$, that provides the probability that x assumes a particular value for a discrete random variable.
Random variable A numerical description of the outcome of an experiment.
Standard deviation The positive square root of the variance.
Variance A measure of the variability, or dispersion, of a random variable.

Key Formulas

Discrete Uniform Probability Function

$$f(x) = 1/n \tag{5.3}$$

Expected Value of a Discrete Random Variable

$$E(x) = \mu = \Sigma x f(x) \tag{5.4}$$

Variance of a Discrete Random Variable

$$Var(x) = \sigma^2 = \Sigma(x - \mu)^2 f(x) \tag{5.5}$$

Covariance of Random Variables x and y

$$\sigma_{xy} = [Var(x + y) - Var(x) - Var(y)]/2 \tag{5.6}$$

Correlation between Random Variables x and y

$$\rho_{xy} = \frac{\sigma_{xy}}{\sigma_x \sigma_y} \tag{5.7}$$

Expected Value of a Linear Combination of Random Variables x and y

$$E(ax + by) = aE(x) + bE(y) \tag{5.8}$$

Variance of a Linear Combination of Two Random Variables x and y

$$Var(ax + by) = a^2Var(x) + b^2Var(y) + 2ab\sigma_{xy} \tag{5.9}$$

where σ_{xy} is the covariance of x and y

Number of Experimental Outcomes Providing Exactly x Successes in n Trials

$$\binom{n}{x} = \frac{n!}{x!(n - x)!} \tag{5.10}$$

Binomial Probability Function

$$f(x) = \binom{n}{x} p^x (1 - p)^{(n - x)} \tag{5.12}$$

Expected Value for the Binomial Distribution

$$E(x) = \mu = np \tag{5.13}$$

Variance for the Binomial Distribution

$$Var(x) = \sigma^2 = np(1 - p) \tag{5.14}$$

Poisson Probability Function

$$f(x) = \frac{\mu^x e^{-\mu}}{x!} \tag{5.15}$$

Hypergeometric Probability Function

$$f(x) = \frac{\binom{r}{x}\binom{N - r}{n - x}}{\binom{N}{n}} \tag{5.16}$$

Expected Value for the Hypergeometric Distribution

$$E(x) = \mu = n\left(\frac{r}{N}\right) \tag{5.17}$$

Variance for the Hypergeometric Distribution

$$Var(x) = \sigma^2 = n\left(\frac{r}{N}\right)\left(1 - \frac{r}{N}\right)\left(\frac{N-n}{N-1}\right) \tag{5.18}$$

Supplementary Exercises

59. **Wind Conditions and Boating Accidents.** The U.S. Coast Guard (USCG) provides a wide variety of information on boating accidents including the wind condition at the time of the accident. The following table shows the results obtained for 4,401 accidents (USCG website).

Wind Condition	Percentage of Accidents
None	9.6
Light	57.0
Moderate	23.8
Strong	7.7
Storm	1.9

Let x be a random variable reflecting the known wind condition at the time of each accident. Set $x = 0$ for none, $x = 1$ for light, $x = 2$ for moderate, $x = 3$ for strong, and $x = 4$ for storm. **LO 2, 3**

a. Develop a probability distribution for x.
b. Compute the expected value of x.
c. Compute the variance and standard deviation for x.
d. Comment on what your results imply about the wind conditions during boating accidents.

60. **Wait Times at Car Repair Garages.** The Car Repair Ratings website provides consumer reviews and ratings for garages in the United States and Canada. The time customers wait for service to be completed is one of the categories rated. The following table provides a summary of the wait-time ratings (1 = Slow/Delays; 10 = Quick/On Time) for 40 randomly selected garages located in the province of Ontario, Canada. **LO 2, 3**

Wait-Time Rating	Number of Garages
1	6
2	2
3	3
4	2
5	5
6	2
7	4
8	5
9	5
10	6

a. Develop a probability distribution for x = wait-time rating.
b. Any garage that receives a wait-time rating of at least 9 is considered to provide outstanding service. If a consumer randomly selects one of the 40 garages for their next car service, what is the probability the garage selected will provide outstanding wait-time service?
c. What is the expected value and variance for x?
d. Suppose that seven of the 40 garages reviewed were new car dealerships. Of the seven new car dealerships, two were rated as providing outstanding wait-time service. Compare the likelihood of a new car dealership achieving an outstanding wait-time service rating as compared to other types of service providers.

61. **Expense Forecasts.** The budgeting process for a midwestern college resulted in expense forecasts for the coming year (in $ millions) of $9, $10, $11, $12, and $13. Because the actual expenses are unknown, the following respective probabilities are assigned: 0.3, 0.2, 0.25, 0.05, and 0.2. **LO 2, 3**
a. Show the probability distribution for the expense forecast.
b. What is the expected value of the expense forecast for the coming year?
c. What is the variance of the expense forecast for the coming year?
d. If income projections for the year are estimated at $12 million, comment on the financial position of the college.

62. **Bookstore Customer Purchases.** A bookstore at the Hartsfield-Jackson Airport in Atlanta sells reading materials (books, newspapers, magazines) as well as snacks (peanuts, pretzels, candy, etc.). A point-of-sale terminal collects a variety of information about customer purchases. The following table shows the number of snack items and the number of items of reading material purchased by the most recent 600 customers. **LO 4, 5**

	Reading Material		
Snacks	**0**	**1**	**2**
0	0	60	18
1	240	90	30
2	120	30	12

a. Using the data in the table construct an empirical discrete bivariate probability distribution for x = number of snack items and y = number of reading materials for a randomly selected customer purchase. What is the probability of a customer purchase consisting of one item of reading materials and two snack items? What is the probability of a customer purchasing one snack item only? Why is the probability $f(x = 0, y = 0) = 0$? **LO 2, 3**
b. Show the marginal probability distribution for the number of snack items purchased. Compute the expected value and variance.
c. What is the expected value and variance for the number of reading materials purchased by a customer?
d. Show the probability distribution for t = total number of items for a randomly selected customer purchase. Compute its expected value and variance.
e. Compute the covariance and correlation coefficient between x and y. What is the relationship, if any, between the number of reading materials and number of snacks purchased?

63. **Creating a Diversified Investment Portfolio.** The Knowles/Armitage (KA) group at Merrill Lynch advises clients on how to create a diversified investment portfolio. One of the investment alternatives they make available to clients is the All World Fund composed of global stocks with good dividend yields. One of their clients is interested

in a portfolio consisting of investment in the All World Fund and a treasury bond fund. The expected percent return of an investment in the All World Fund is 7.80% with a standard deviation of 18.90%. The expected percent return of an investment in a treasury bond fund is 5.50% and the standard deviation is 4.60%. The covariance of an investment in the All World Fund with an investment in a treasury bond fund is −12.4. **LO 3, 6**

a. Which of the funds would be considered the more risky? Why?
b. If KA recommends that the client invest 75% in the All World Fund and 25% in the treasury bond fund, what is the expected percent return and standard deviation for such a portfolio? What would be the expected return and standard deviation, in dollars, for a client investing $10,000 in such a portfolio?
c. If KA recommends that the client invest 25% in the All World Fund and 75% in the treasury bond fund, what is the expected return and standard deviation for such a portfolio? What would be the expected return and standard deviation, in dollars, for a client investing $10,000 in such a portfolio?
d. Which of the portfolios in parts (b) and (c) would you recommend for an aggressive investor? Which would you recommend for a conservative investor? Why?

64. **Party Affiliation.** According to 2022 Gallup polling, 24% of Americans identify their political party affiliation as Republican, 28% identify as Democratic, and 46% identify as Independents (Gallup website). **LO 7, 8**
a. If a random sample of 10 Americans is chosen, what is the probability that exactly three people in the sample will identify as Republican?
b. If a random sample of 10 Americans is chosen, what is the probability that more than five people in the sample will identify as Democratic?
c. If a random sample of 5,000 Americans is chosen, what is the expected number in the sample that will identify as being Independents?
d. If a random sample of 5,000 Americans is chosen, what is the variance and standard deviation of the number of people in the sample that will identify as being Independents?
e. If a new, and unverified, polling firm reports that their polling found that a random sample of 100 people contained 76 people that identified as Republican, do you think this poll could be considered reliable? Explain.

65. **Investing in the Stock Market.** According to a 2017 Gallup survey, the percentage of individuals in the United States who are invested in the stock market by age is as shown in the following table (Gallup website).

Age Range	Percent of Individuals Invested in Stock Market
18 to 29	31
30 to 49	62
50 to 64	62
65+	54

Suppose Gallup wishes to complete a follow-up survey to find out more about the specific type of stocks people in the United States are purchasing. **LO 7, 8**
a. How many 18- to 29-year-olds must be sampled to find at least 50 who invest in the stock market?
b. How many people 65 years of age and older must be sampled to find at least 50 who invest in the stock market?
c. If 1,000 individuals are randomly sampled, what is the expected number of 18- to 29-year-olds who invest in the stock market in this sample? What is the standard deviation of the number of 18- to 29-year-olds who invest in the stock market?

d. If 1,000 individuals are randomly sampled, what is the expected number of those 65 years of age and older who invest in the stock market in this sample? What is the standard deviation of the number of those 65 years of age and older who invest in the stock market?

66. **Acceptance Sampling.** Many companies use a quality control technique called acceptance sampling to monitor incoming shipments of parts, raw materials, and so on. In the electronics industry, component parts are commonly shipped from suppliers in large lots. Inspection of a sample of n components can be viewed as the n trials of a binomial experiment. The outcome for each component tested (trial) will be that the component is classified as good or defective. Reynolds Electronics accepts a lot from a particular supplier if the defective components in the lot do not exceed 1%. Suppose a random sample of five items from a recent shipment is tested. **LO 7**
   a. Assume that 1% of the shipment is defective. Compute the probability that no items in the sample are defective.
   b. Assume that 1% of the shipment is defective. Compute the probability that exactly one item in the sample is defective.
   c. What is the probability of observing one or more defective items in the sample if 1% of the shipment is defective?
   d. Would you feel comfortable accepting the shipment if one item was found to be defective? Why or why not?

67. **Poverty Rate in the United States.** According to the U.S. Census Bureau, the poverty rate in the United States in 2020 was 11.4% (*Census.gov* website). Suppose that 500 people in the United States are randomly selected. **LO 8**
   a. What is the expected number of people in the selected sample that are classified as living in poverty?
   b. What is the variance and standard deviation for the number of people in the selected sample that are classified as living in poverty?

68. **Choosing a Home Builder.** Mahoney Custom Home Builders, Inc. of Canyon Lake, Texas, asked visitors to their website what is most important when choosing a home builder. Possible responses were quality, price, customer referral, years in business, and special features. Results showed that 23.5% of the respondents chose price as the most important factor (Mahoney Custom Homes website). Suppose a sample of 200 potential home buyers in the Canyon Lake area was selected. **LO 7, 8**
   a. How many people would you expect to choose price as the most important factor when choosing a home builder?
   b. What is the standard deviation of the number of respondents who would choose price as the most important factor in selecting a home builder?
   c. What is the standard deviation of the number of respondents who do not list price as the most important factor in selecting a home builder?

69. **Arrivals to a Car Wash.** Cars arrive at a car wash randomly and independently; the probability of an arrival is the same for any two time intervals of equal length. The mean arrival rate is 15 cars per hour. What is the probability that 20 or more cars will arrive during any given hour of operation? **LO 9**

70. **Production Process Breakdowns.** A new automated production process averages 1.5 breakdowns per day. Because of the cost associated with a breakdown, management is concerned about the possibility of having 3 or more breakdowns during a day. Assume that breakdowns occur randomly, that the probability of a breakdown is the same for any two time intervals of equal length, and that breakdowns in one period are independent of breakdowns in other periods. What is the probability of having 3 or more breakdowns during a day? **LO 9**

71. **Small Business Failures.** A regional director responsible for business development in the state of Pennsylvania is concerned about the number of small business failures. If the mean number of small business failures per month is 10, what is the probability that exactly 4 small businesses will fail during a given month? Assume that the probability of a failure is the same for any two months and that the occurrence

or nonoccurrence of a failure in any month is independent of failures in any other month. **LO 9**

72. **Bank Customer Arrivals.** Customer arrivals at a bank are random and independent; the probability of an arrival in any one-minute period is the same as the probability of an arrival in any other one-minute period. Answer the following questions, assuming a mean arrival rate of 3 customers per minute. **LO 9**
    a. What is the probability of exactly 3 arrivals in a one-minute period?
    b. What is the probability of at least 3 arrivals in a one-minute period?

73. **Poker Hands.** A deck of playing cards contains 52 cards, four of which are aces. What is the probability that the deal of a five-card poker hand provides the following cards? **LO 11**
    a. A pair of aces
    b. Exactly one ace
    c. No aces
    d. At least one ace

74. **Business School Student GPAs.** According to *U.S. News & World Reports,* 7 of the top 10 graduate schools of business have students with an average undergraduate grade point average (GPA) of 3.50 or higher. Suppose that we randomly select 2 of the top 10 graduate schools of business. **LO 11**
    a. What is the probability that exactly one school has students with an average undergraduate GPA of 3.50 or higher?
    b. What is the probability that both schools have students with an average undergraduate GPA of 3.50 or higher?
    c. What is the probability that neither school has students with an average undergraduate GPA of 3.50 or higher?

Case Problem 1: *Go Bananas*! Breakfast Cereal

Great Grasslands Grains, Inc. (GGG) manufactures and sells a wide variety of breakfast cereals. GGG's product development lab recently created a new cereal that consists of rice flakes and banana-flavored marshmallows. The company's marketing research department has tested the new cereal extensively and has found that consumers are enthusiastic about the cereal when 16-ounce boxes contain at least 1.6 ounces and no more than 2.4 ounces of the banana-flavored marshmallows.

As GGG prepares to begin producing and selling 16-ounce boxes of the new cereal, which it has named *Go Bananas!*, management is concerned about the amount of banana-flavored marshmallows. It wants to be careful not to include less than 1.6 ounces or more than 2.4 ounces of banana-flavored marshmallows in each 16-ounce box of *Go Bananas!*. Tina Finkel, VP of Production for GGG, has suggested that the company measure the weight of banana-flavored marshmallows in a random sample of 25 boxes of *Go Bananas!* on a weekly basis. Each week, GGG can count the number of boxes out of the 25 boxes in the sample that contain less than 1.6 ounces or more than 2.4 ounces of banana-flavored marshmallows; if the number of boxes that fail to meet the standard weight of banana-flavored marshmallows is too high, production will be shut down and inspected.

Ms. Finkel and her staff have designed the production process so that only 8% of all 16-ounce boxes of *Go Bananas!* fail to meet the standard weight of banana-flavored marshmallows. After much debate, GGG management has decided to shut down production of *Go Bananas!* if at least five boxes in a weekly sample fail to meet the standard weight of banana-flavored marshmallows. **LO 7, 8**

Managerial Report

Prepare a managerial report that addresses the following issues.

1. Calculate the probability that a weekly sample will result in a shutdown of production if the production process is working properly. Comment on GGG management's policy for deciding when to shut down production of *Go Bananas!*.

2. GGG management wants to shut down production of *Go Bananas!* no more than 1% of the time when the production process is working properly. Suggest the appropriate number of boxes in the weekly sample that must fail to meet the standard weight of banana-flavored marshmallows in order for production to be shut down if this goal is to be achieved.
3. Ms. Finkel has suggested that if given sufficient resources, they could redesign the production process to reduce the percentage of 16-ounce boxes of *Go Bananas!* that fail to meet the standard weight of banana-flavored marshmallows when the process is working properly. To what level must Ms. Finkel reduce the percentage of 16-ounce boxes of *Go Bananas!* that fail to meet the standard weight of banana-flavored marshmallows when the process is working properly in order for them to reduce the probability at least five of the sampled boxes fail to meet the standard to 0.01 or less?

Case Problem 2: McNeil's Auto Mall

Harriet McNeil, proprietor of McNeil's Auto Mall, believes that it is good business for her automobile dealership to have more customers on the lot than can be served, as Harriet believes this creates an impression that demand for the automobiles on the lot is high. However, Harriet also understands that if there are far more customers on the lot than can be served by salespeople, the dealership may lose sales to customers who become frustrated and leave without making a purchase.

Harriet is primarily concerned about the staffing of salespeople on the lot on Saturday mornings (8:00 A.M. to noon), which are the busiest time of the week for McNeil's Auto Mall. On Saturday mornings, an average of 6.8 customers arrive per hour. The customers arrive randomly at a constant rate throughout the morning, and a salesperson spends an average of one hour with a customer. Harriet believes that if there are two more customers on the lot than can be served at any time on a Saturday morning, the automobile dealership achieves the optimal balance of creating an impression of high demand without losing too many customers who become frustrated and leave without making a purchase.

Harriet now wants to determine how many salespeople to have on the lot on Saturday mornings in order to achieve the goal of having two more customers on the lot than can be served at any time. Harriet understands that occasionally the number of customers on the lot will exceed the number of salespeople by more than two, and Harriet is willing to accept such an occurrence no more than 10% of the time. **LO 9, 10**

Managerial Report

Harriet has asked you to determine the number of salespeople she should have on the lot on Saturday mornings in order to satisfy the stated criteria. In answering Harriet's question, consider the following three questions:

1. How is the number of customers who arrive on the lot on a Saturday morning distributed?
2. Suppose Harriet currently uses five salespeople on the lot on Saturday mornings. Using the probability distribution you identified in (1), what is the probability that the number of customers who arrive on the lot will exceed the number of salespeople by more than two? Does the current Saturday morning employment strategy satisfy Harriet's stated objective? Why or why not?
3. What is the minimum number of salespeople Harriet should have on the lot on Saturday mornings to achieve the stated objective?

Case Problem 3: Grievance Committee at Tuglar Corporation

Several years ago, management at Tuglar Corporation established a grievance committee composed of employees who volunteered to work toward the amicable resolution of disputes between Tuglar management and its employees. Each year management issues a call for volunteers to serve on the grievance committee, and 10 of the respondents are randomly selected to serve on the committee for the upcoming year.

Employees in the Accounting Department are distressed because no member of their department has served on the Tuglar grievance committee in the past five years. Management has assured its employees in the Accounting Department that the selections have been made randomly, but these assurances have not quelled suspicions that management has intentionally omitted accountants from the committee. The table below summarizes the total number of volunteers and the number of employees from the Accounting Department who have volunteered for the grievance committee in each of the past five years:

	Year 1	Year 2	Year 3	Year 4	Year 5
Total Number of Volunteers	29	31	23	26	28
Number of Volunteers from the Accounting Department	1	1	1	2	1

In its defense, management has provided these numbers to the Accounting Department. Given these numbers, is the lack of members of the Accounting Department on the grievance committee for the past five years suspicious (i.e., unlikely)? **LO 11**

Managerial Report

In addressing the issue of whether or not the committee selection process is random, consider the following questions:

1. How is the number of members of the Accounting Department who are selected to serve on the grievance committee distributed?
2. Using the probability distribution you identified in (1), what is the probability for each of these five years that no members of the Accounting Department have been selected to serve?
3. Using the probabilities you identified in (2), what is the probability that no members of the Accounting Department have been selected to serve during the past five years?
4. What is the cause of the lack of Accounting Department representation on the grievance committee over the past five years? What can be done to increase the probability that a member of the Accounting Department will be selected to serve on the grievance committee using the current selection method?

Case Problem 4: Sagittarius Casino

The Sagittarius Casino's strategy for establishing a competitive advantage over its competitors is to periodically create unique and interesting new games for its customers to play. Sagittarius management feels it is time for the casino to once again introduce a new game to excite its customer base, and Sagittarius's Director of Research and Development, Lou Zerbit, believes the casino staff have developed a new game that will accomplish this goal. The game, which they have named ***POSO!*** (an acronym for **P**ayouts **O**n **S**elected **O**utcomes), is to be played in the following manner. A player will select two different values from 1, 2, 3, 4, 5, and 6. Two dice are then rolled. If the first number the player selected comes up on at least one of the two dice, the player wins \$5.00; if the second number the player selected comes up on both of the dice, the player wins \$10.00. If neither of these events occurs, the player wins nothing.

For example, suppose a player fills out the following card for one game of ***POSO!***

POSO!	
First Number (select one number from 1, 2, 3, 4, 5, or 6)	Second Number (select a different number from 1, 2, 3, 4, 5, or 6)
4	2
If this number comes up on at least one die, ***you win $5.00!***	If this number comes up on both dice, *you* ***win $10.00!***

When the two dice are rolled, if at least one die comes up 4 the player will win $5.00, if both dice come up 2 the player will win $10.00, and if any other outcome occurs the player wins nothing. **LO 2, 7, 8**

Managerial Report

Sagittarius management now has three questions about ***POSO!*** These questions should be addressed in your report.

1. Although they certainly do not want to pay out more than they take in, casinos like to offer games in which players win frequently; casino managers believe this keeps players excited about playing the game. What is the probability a player will win if they play a single game of ***POSO!***?
2. What is the expected amount a player will win when playing one game of ***POSO!***?
3. Sagittarius managers want to take in more than they pay out on average for a game of ***POSO!***. Furthermore, casinos such as Sagittarius are often looking for games that provide their customers with an opportunity to play for a small bet, and Sagittarius management would like to charge players $2.00 to play one game of ***POSO!***. What will be the expected profit earned by Sagittarius Casino on a single play if a player has to pay $2.00 for a single play of ***POSO!***? Will Sagittarius Casino expect to earn or lose money on ***POSO!*** if a player pays $2.00 for a single play? What is the minimum amount Sagittarius Casino can charge a player for a single play of ***POSO!*** and still expect to earn money?

Chapter 6

Continuous Probability Distributions

Contents

Statistics in Practice:
Procter & Gamble

6.1 Uniform Probability Distribution
Area as a Measure of Probability

6.2 Normal Probability Distribution
Normal Curve
Standard Normal Probability Distribution
Computing Probabilities for Any Normal Probability Distribution
Grear Tire Company Problem
Using Excel to Compute Normal Probabilities

6.3 Exponential Probability Distribution
Computing Probabilities for the Exponential Distribution
Relationship Between the Poisson and Exponential Distributions
Using Excel to Compute Exponential Probabilities

Summary 314
Glossary 314
Key Formulas 314
Supplementary Exercises 315
Case Problem 1: Specialty Toys 318
Case Problem 2: Gebhardt Electronics 319

Available in the Cengage eBook:
Appendix: Continuous Probability Distributions with R

Learning Objectives

After completing this chapter, you will be able to

LO 1 Define, graph, and interpret the probability density function for a random variable that has a uniform probability distribution.

LO 2 Calculate and interpret the probability a random variable that has a uniform probability distribution assumes a value within a specified interval.

LO 3 Calculate and interpret the expected value, variance, and standard deviation for a random variable that has a uniform probability distribution.

LO 4 Graph the probability density function for a random variable that has a normal (or standard normal) probability distribution.

LO 5 Calculate and interpret the probability a random variable that has a normal (or standard normal) probability distribution assumes a value within a specified interval.

LO 6 Find and interpret the value of the random variable (or *z* value) corresponding to a specified probability for a normal (or standard normal) probability distribution.

LO 7 Calculate and interpret the probability a random variable that has an exponential probability distribution assumes a value within a specified interval.

LO 8 Define, graph, and interpret the probability density function for a random variable that has an exponential probability distribution function.

Statistics in Practice

Procter & Gamble*

Cincinnati, Ohio

Procter & Gamble (P&G) produces and markets such products as detergents, disposable diapers, razors, toothpastes, soaps, mouthwashes, and paper towels. Worldwide, it has the leading brand in more categories than any other consumer products company.

As a leader in the application of statistical methods in decision making, P&G employs people with diverse academic backgrounds: engineering, statistics, operations research, analytics and business. The major quantitative technologies for which these people provide support are probabilistic decision and risk analysis, advanced simulation, quality improvement, and quantitative methods (e.g., linear programming, data analytics, probability analysis, machine learning).

The Chemicals Division of P&G is a major supplier of fatty alcohols derived from natural substances such as coconut oil and from petroleum-based derivatives. The division wanted to know the economic risks and opportunities of expanding its fatty-alcohol production facilities, so it called in P&G's experts in probabilistic decision and risk analysis to help. After structuring and modeling the problem, they determined that the key to profitability was the cost difference between the petroleum- and coconut-based raw materials. Future costs were unknown, but the analysts were able to approximate them with the following continuous random variables.

x = the coconut oil price per pound of fatty alcohol

and

y = the petroleum raw material price per pound of fatty alcohol

Because the key to profitability was the difference between these two random variables, a third random variable, $d = x - y$, was used in the analysis. Experts were interviewed to determine the probability distributions for x and y. In turn, this information was used to develop a probability distribution for the difference in prices d. This continuous probability distribution showed a 0.90 probability that the price difference would be \$0.0655 or less and a 0.50 probability that the price difference would be \$0.035 or less. In addition, there was only a 0.10 probability that the price difference would be \$0.0045 or less.†

Procter & Gamble is a leader in the application of statistical methods in decision making. John Sommers II/Reuters

The Chemicals Division thought that being able to quantify the impact of raw material price differences was key to reaching a consensus. The probabilities obtained were used in a sensitivity analysis of the raw material price difference. The analysis yielded sufficient insight to form the basis for a recommendation to management.

The use of continuous random variables and their probability distributions was helpful to P&G in analyzing the economic risks associated with its fatty-alcohol production. In this chapter, you will gain an understanding of continuous random variables and their probability distributions, including one of the most important probability distributions in statistics, the normal distribution.

*The authors are indebted to Joel Kahn of Procter & Gamble for providing this Statistics in Practice.

†The price differences stated here have been modified to protect proprietary data.

In the preceding chapter, we discussed discrete random variables and their probability distributions. In this chapter, we turn to the study of continuous random variables. Specifically, we discuss three continuous probability distributions: the uniform, the normal, and the exponential.

A fundamental difference separates discrete and continuous random variables in terms of how probabilities are computed. For a discrete random variable, the probability function $f(x)$ provides the probability that the random variable assumes a particular value. With continuous random variables, the counterpart of the probability function is the **probability density function**, also denoted by $f(x)$. The difference is that the probability density function does not directly provide probabilities. However, the area under the graph of $f(x)$ corresponding to a given interval does provide the probability that the continuous random variable x assumes a value in that interval. So, when we compute probabilities for continuous random variables, we are computing the probability that the random variable assumes any value in an interval.

Because the area under the graph of $f(x)$ at any particular point is zero, one of the implications of the definition of probability for continuous random variables is that the probability of any particular value of the random variable is zero. In Section 6.1, we demonstrate these concepts for a continuous random variable that has a uniform distribution.

Much of the chapter is devoted to describing and showing applications of the normal distribution. The normal distribution is of major importance because of its wide applicability and its extensive use in statistical inference. The chapter closes with a discussion of the exponential distribution. The exponential distribution is useful in applications involving such factors as waiting times and service times.

6.1 Uniform Probability Distribution

Consider the random variable x representing the flight time of an airplane traveling from Chicago to New York. Suppose the flight time can be any value in the interval from 120 to 140 minutes. Because the random variable x can assume any value in that interval, x is a continuous rather than a discrete random variable. Let us assume that sufficient actual flight data are available to conclude that the probability of a flight time within any one-minute interval is the same as the probability of a flight time within any other one-minute interval contained in the larger interval from 120 to 140 minutes. With every one-Δminute interval being equally likely, the random variable x is said to have a **uniform probability distribution**. The probability density function, which defines the uniform distribution for the flight-time random variable, is

$$f(x) = \begin{cases} 1/20 & \text{for } 120 \le x \le 140 \\ 0 & \text{elsewhere} \end{cases}$$

Figure 6.1 is a graph of this probability density function. In general, the uniform probability density function for a random variable x is defined by the following formula.

Uniform Probability Density Function

$$f(x) = \begin{cases} \dfrac{1}{b-a} & \text{for } a \le x \le b \\ 0 & \text{elsewhere} \end{cases} \tag{6.1}$$

For the flight-time random variable, $a = 120$ and $b = 140$.

As noted in the introduction, for a continuous random variable, we consider probability only in terms of the likelihood that a random variable assumes a value within a specified interval. In the flight time example, an acceptable probability question is: What is the probability that the flight time is between 120 and 130 minutes? That is, what is $P(120 \le x \le 130)$? Because the flight time must be between 120 and 140 minutes and because the probability is described as being uniform over this interval, we feel comfortable saying that $P(120 \le x \le 130) = 0.50$. In the following subsection we show that this probability can be computed as the area under the graph of $f(x)$ from 120 to 130 (see Figure 6.2).

Figure 6.1 Uniform Probability Distribution for Flight Time

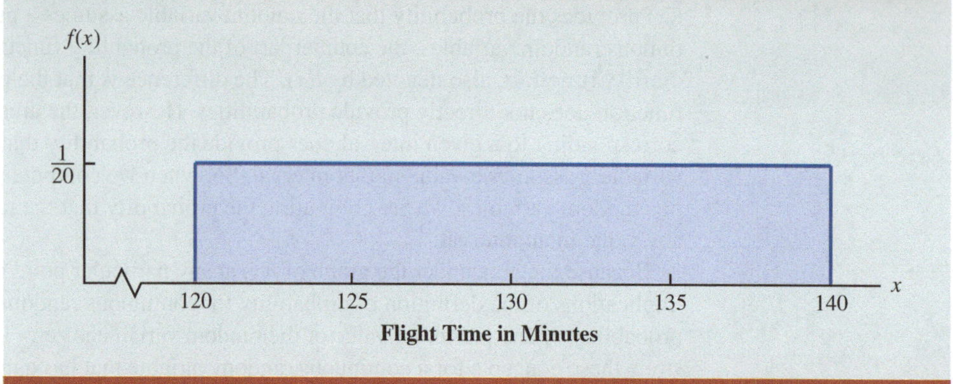

Figure 6.2 Area Provides Probability of a Flight Time Between 120 and 130 Minutes

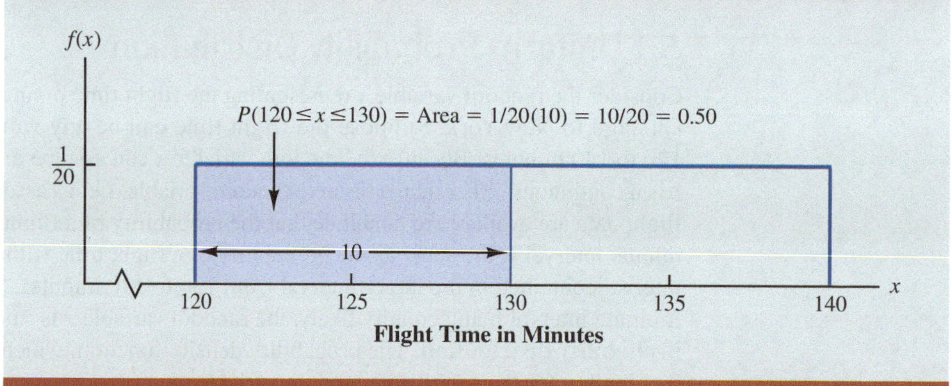

Area as a Measure of Probability

Let us make an observation about the graph in Figure 6.2. Consider the area under the graph of $f(x)$ in the interval from 120 to 130. The area is rectangular, and the area of a rectangle is simply the width multiplied by the height. With the width of the interval equal to $130 - 120 = 10$ and the height equal to the value of the probability density function $f(x) = 1/20$, we have area = width $\times$ height $= 10(1/20) = 10/20 = 0.50$.

Note that the area under the graph of $f(x)$ and the probability are identical. Indeed, this observation is valid for all continuous random variables. Once a probability density function $f(x)$ is identified, the probability that x takes a value between some lower value x_1 and some higher value x_2 can be found by computing the area under the graph of $f(x)$ over the interval from x_1 to x_2.

Given the uniform distribution for flight time and using the interpretation of area as probability, we can answer any number of probability questions about flight times. For example, what is the probability of a flight time between 128 and 136 minutes? The width of the interval is $136 - 128 = 8$. With the uniform height of $f(x) = 1/20$, we see that $P(128 \le x \le 136) = 8(1/20) = 0.40$.

Note that $P(120 \le x \le 140) = 20(1/20) = 1$; that is, the total area under the graph of $f(x)$ is equal to 1. This property holds for all continuous probability distributions and is the analog of the condition that the sum of the probabilities must equal 1 for a discrete probability function. For a continuous probability density function, we must also require that $f(x) \geq 0$ for all values of x. This requirement is the analog of the requirement that $f(x) \geq 0$ for discrete probability functions.

Two major differences stand out between the treatment of continuous random variables and the treatment of their discrete counterparts.

To see that the probability of any single point is 0, refer to Figure 6.2 and compute the probability of a single point, say, x = 125. P(x = 125) = P(125 ≤ x ≤ 125) = 0(1/20) = 0.

1. We no longer talk about the probability of the random variable assuming a particular value. Instead, we talk about the probability of the random variable assuming a value within some given interval.
2. The probability of a continuous random variable assuming a value within some given interval from x_1 to x_2 is defined to be the area under the graph of the probability density function between x_1 and x_2. Because a single point is an interval of zero width, this implies that the probability of a continuous random variable assuming any particular value exactly is zero. It also means that the probability of a continuous random variable assuming a value in any interval is the same whether or not the endpoints are included.

The calculation of the expected value and variance for a continuous random variable is analogous to that for a discrete random variable. However, because the computational procedure involves integral calculus, we leave the derivation of the appropriate formulas to more advanced texts.

For the uniform continuous probability distribution introduced in this section, the formulas for the expected value and variance are

$$E(x) = \frac{a + b}{2}$$

$$Var(x) = \frac{(b - a)^2}{12}$$

In these formulas, a is the smallest value and b is the largest value that the random variable may assume.

Applying these formulas to the uniform distribution for flight times from Chicago to New York, we obtain

$$E(x) = \frac{(120 + 140)}{2} = 130$$

$$Var(x) = \frac{(140 - 120)^2}{12} = 33.33$$

The standard deviation of flight times can be found by taking the square root of the variance. Thus, $\sigma = 5.77$ minutes.

Notes + Comments

To see more clearly why the height of a probability density function is not a probability, think about a random variable with the following uniform probability distribution.

$$f(x) = \begin{cases} 2 & \text{for } 0 \leq x \leq 0.5 \\ 0 & \text{elsewhere} \end{cases}$$

The height of the probability density function, $f(x)$, is 2 for values of x between 0 and 0.5. However, we know probabilities can never be greater than 1. Thus, we see that $f(x)$ cannot be interpreted as the probability of x.

Exercises

Methods

1. The random variable x is known to be uniformly distributed between 1.0 and 1.5.
   a. Show the graph of the probability density function. **LO 1, 2**
   b. Compute $P(x = 1.25)$.
   c. Compute $P(1.0 \leq x \leq 1.25)$.
   d. Compute $P(1.20 < x < 1.5)$.

2. The random variable x is known to be uniformly distributed between 10 and 20.
   a. Show the graph of the probability density function. **LO 1, 2, 3**
   b. Compute $P(x < 15)$.
   c. Compute $P(12 \leq x \leq 18)$.
   d. Compute $E(x)$.
   e. Compute $Var(x)$.

Applications

3. **Cincinnati to Tampa Flight Time.** Delta Airlines quotes a flight time of 2 hours, 5 minutes for its flights from Cincinnati to Tampa. Suppose we believe that actual flight times are uniformly distributed between 2 hours and 2 hours, 20 minutes. **LO 1, 2, 3**
   a. Show the graph of the probability density function for flight time.
   b. What is the probability that the flight will be no more than five minutes late?
   c. What is the probability that the flight will be more than 10 minutes late?
   d. What is the expected flight time?

4. **Excel RAND Function.** Most computer languages include a function that can be used to generate random numbers. In Excel, the RAND function can be used to generate random numbers between 0 and 1. If we let x denote a random number generated using RAND, then x is a continuous random variable with the following probability density function. **LO 1, 2**

$$f(x) = \begin{cases} 1 & \text{for } 0 \leq x \leq 1 \\ 0 & \text{elsewhere} \end{cases}$$

   a. Graph the probability density function.
   b. What is the probability of generating a random number between 0.25 and 0.75?
   c. What is the probability of generating a random number with a value less than or equal to 0.30?
   d. What is the probability of generating a random number with a value greater than 0.60?
   e. Generate 50 random numbers by entering =*RAND()* into 50 cells of an Excel worksheet.
   f. Compute the mean and standard deviation for the random numbers in part (e).

5. **Tesla Battery Recharge Time.** The electric-vehicle manufacturing company Tesla estimates that a driver who commutes 50 miles per day in a Model S will require a nightly charge time of around 1 hour and 45 minutes (105 minutes) to recharge the vehicle's battery (Tesla company website). Assume that the actual recharging time required is uniformly distributed between 90 and 120 minutes. **LO 1, 2**
   a. Give a mathematical expression for the probability density function of battery recharging time for this scenario.
   b. What is the probability that the recharge time will be less than 110 minutes?
   c. What is the probability that the recharge time required is at least 100 minutes?
   d. What is the probability that the recharge time required is between 95 and 110 minutes?

6. **Daily Discretionary Spending.** A Gallup Daily Tracking Survey found that the mean daily discretionary spending by Americans earning over $90,000 per year

was \$136 per day. The discretionary spending excluded home purchases, vehicle purchases, and regular monthly bills. Let $x =$ the discretionary spending per day and assume that a uniform probability density function applies with $f(x) = 0.00625$ for $a \leq x \leq b$. **LO 1, 2**

a. Find the values of a and b for the probability density function.
b. What is the probability that consumers in this group have daily discretionary spending between \$100 and \$200?
c. What is the probability that consumers in this group have daily discretionary spending of \$150 or more?
d. What is the probability that consumers in this group have daily discretionary spending of \$80 or less?

7. **Bidding on Land.** Suppose we are interested in bidding on a piece of land and we know one other bidder is interested. The seller announced that the highest bid in excess of \$10,000 will be accepted. Assume that the competitor's bid x is a random variable that is uniformly distributed between \$10,000 and \$15,000. **LO 2**
   a. Suppose you bid \$12,000. What is the probability that your bid will be accepted?
   b. Suppose you bid \$14,000. What is the probability that your bid will be accepted?
   c. What amount should you bid to maximize the probability that you get the property?
   d. Suppose you know someone who is willing to pay you \$16,000 for the property. Would you consider bidding less than the amount in part (c)? Why or why not?

6.2 Normal Probability Distribution

Abraham de Moivre, a French mathematician, derived the normal distribution in the 18th century.

The most commonly used probability distribution for describing a continuous random variable is the **normal probability distribution**. The normal distribution has been used in a wide variety of practical applications in which the random variables are heights and weights of people, test scores, scientific measurements, amounts of rainfall, and other similar values. It is also widely used in statistical inference, which is the major topic of the remainder of this book. In such applications, the normal distribution provides a description of the likely results obtained through sampling.

Normal Curve

The form, or shape, of the normal distribution is illustrated by the bell-shaped normal curve in Figure 6.3. The probability density function that defines the bell-shaped curve of the normal distribution follows.

Figure 6.3 Bell-Shaped Curve for the Normal Distribution

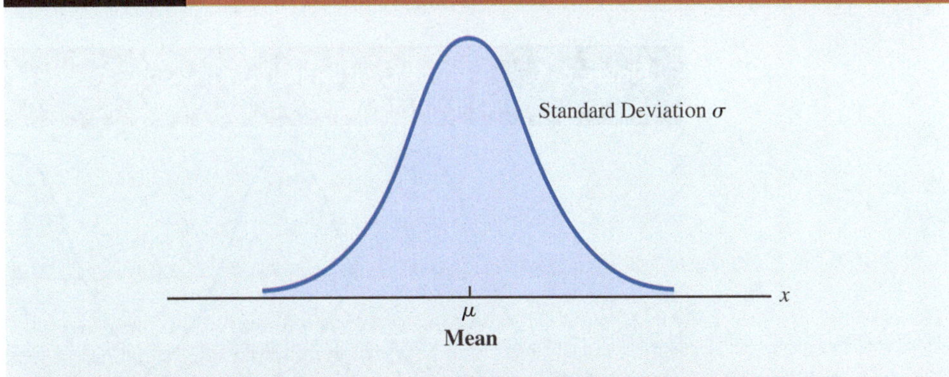

Normal Probability Density Function

$$f(x) = \frac{1}{\sigma\sqrt{2\pi}} e^{-\frac{1}{2}\left(\frac{x-\mu}{\sigma}\right)^2} \quad (6.2)$$

where

μ = mean
σ = standard deviation
π = 3.14159
e = 2.71828

We make several observations about the characteristics of the normal distribution.

The normal curve has two parameters, μ and σ. They determine the location and shape of the normal distribution.

1. The entire family of normal distributions is differentiated by two parameters: the mean μ and the standard deviation σ.
2. The highest point on the normal curve is at the mean, which is also the median and mode of the distribution.
3. The mean of the distribution can be any numerical value: negative, zero, or positive. Three normal distributions with the same standard deviation but three different means (−10, 0, and 20) are shown in Figure 6.4.
4. The normal distribution is symmetric, with the shape of the normal curve to the left of the mean a mirror image of the shape of the normal curve to the right of the mean. The tails of the normal curve extend to infinity in both directions and theoretically never touch the horizontal axis. Because it is symmetric, the normal distribution is not skewed; its skewness measure is zero.
5. The standard deviation determines how flat and wide the normal curve is. Larger values of the standard deviation result in wider, flatter curves, showing more variability in the data. Two normal distributions with the same mean but with different standard deviations are shown in Figure 6.5.
6. Probabilities for the normal random variable are given by areas under the normal curve. The total area under the curve for the normal distribution is 1. Because the distribution is symmetric, the area under the curve to the left of the mean is 0.50 and the area under the curve to the right of the mean is 0.50.
7. The percentage of values in some commonly used intervals are
   a. 68.3% of the values of a normal random variable are within plus or minus one standard deviation of its mean;
   b. 95.4% of the values of a normal random variable are within plus or minus two standard deviations of its mean;
   c. 99.7% of the values of a normal random variable are within plus or minus three standard deviations of its mean.

These percentages are the basis for the empirical rule introduced in Section 3.3.

Figure 6.6 shows properties (a), (b), and (c) graphically.

Figure 6.4 Normal Distributions with Same Standard Deviation and Different Means

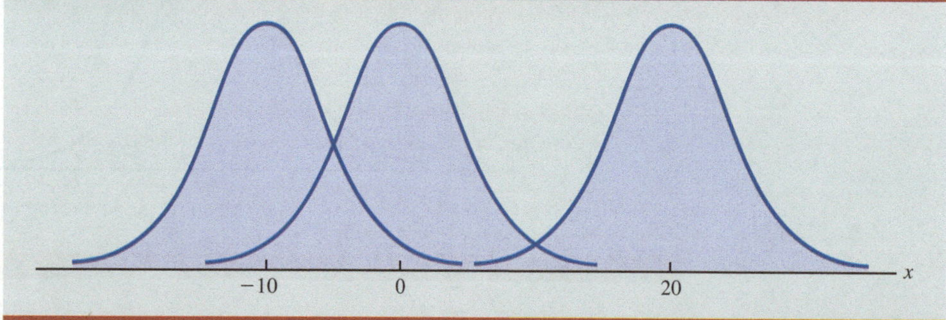

Figure 6.5 Normal Distributions with Same Mean and Different Standard Deviations

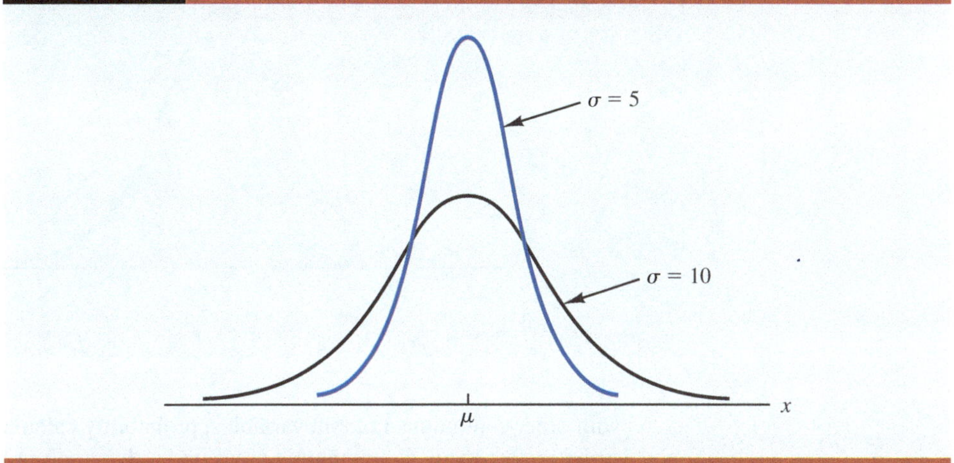

Figure 6.6 Areas Under the Curve for Any Normal Distribution

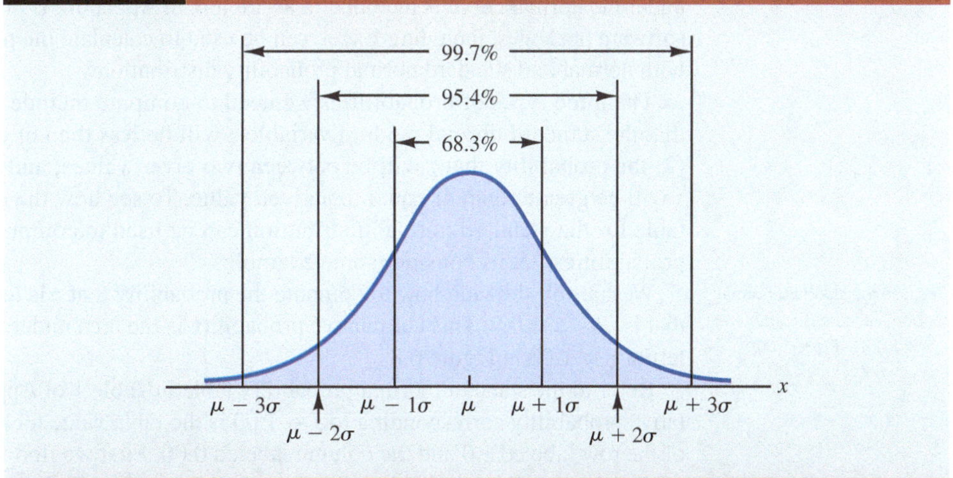

Standard Normal Probability Distribution

A random variable that has a normal distribution with a mean of zero and a standard deviation of one is said to have a **standard normal probability distribution**. The letter z is commonly used to designate this particular normal random variable. Figure 6.7 is the graph of the standard normal distribution. It has the same general appearance as other normal distributions, but with the special properties of $\mu = 0$ and $\sigma = 1$.

Because $\mu = 0$ and $\sigma = 1$, the formula for the standard normal probability density function is a simpler version of equation (6.2).

Standard Normal Density Function

$$f(z) = \frac{1}{\sqrt{2\pi}} e^{-\frac{z^2}{2}}$$

Figure 6.7 The Standard Normal Distribution

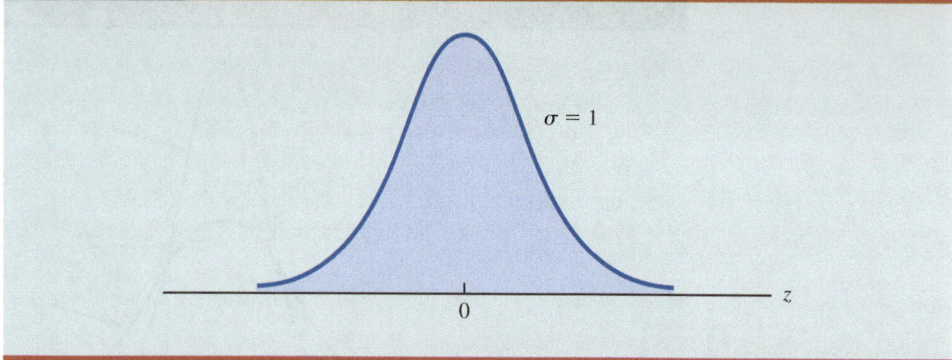

As with other continuous random variables, probability calculations with any normal distribution are made by computing areas under the graph of the probability density function. Thus, to find the probability that a normal random variable is within any specific interval, we must compute the area under the normal curve over that interval.

For the standard normal distribution, areas under the normal curve have been computed and are available in tables that can be used to compute probabilities. Such a table of areas under the normal curve is included in as Table 1 in Appendix B of this textbook. Statistical software packages, including Excel, can be used to calculate the probabilities associated with normal and standard normal probability distributions.

The three types of probabilities we need to compute include (1) the probability that the standard normal random variable z will be less than or equal to a given value; (2) the probability that z will be between two given values; and (3) the probability that z will be greater than or equal to a given value. To see how the cumulative probability table for the standard normal distribution can be used to compute these three types of probabilities, let us consider some examples.

Because the standard normal random variable is continuous, $P(z \leq 1.00) = P(z < 1.00)$.

We start by showing how to compute the probability that z is less than or equal to 1.00; that is, $P(z \leq 1.00)$. This cumulative probability is the area under the normal curve to the left of $z = 1.00$ in Figure 6.8.

Refer to the standard normal probability table in Table 1 of Appendix B. The cumulative probability corresponding to $z = 1.00$ is the table value located at the intersection of the row labeled 1.0 and the column labeled 0.00. First we find 1.0 in the left column of the table and then find 0.00 in the top row of the table. By looking in the body of the table, we find that the 1.0 row and the 0.00 column intersect at the value of 0.8413; thus,

Figure 6.8 Cumulative Probability for Standard Normal Distribution Corresponding to $P(z \leq 1.00)$

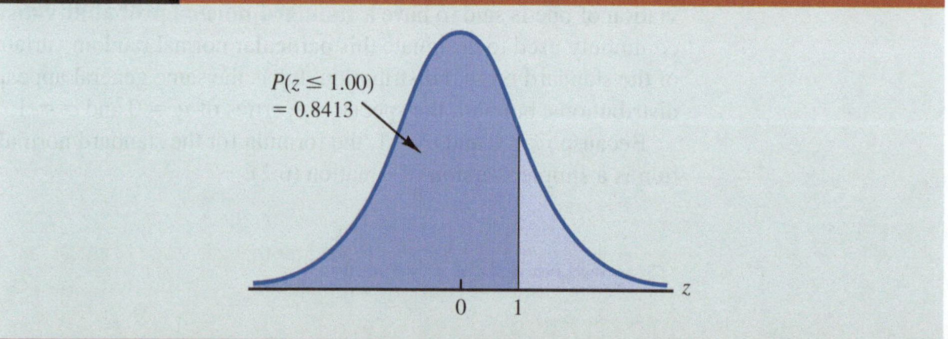

$P(z \leq 1.00) = 0.8413$. The following excerpt from the standard normal probability table shows these steps.

z	**0.00**	**0.01**	**0.02**
.			
.			
.			
0.9	0.8159	0.8186	0.8212
1.0	**0.8413**	0.8438	0.8461
1.1	0.8643	0.8665	0.8686
1.2	0.8849	0.8869	0.8888
.			
.			
.			

$P(z \leq 1.00)$

These values can also be computed using a statistical software package or Excel.

To illustrate the second type of probability calculation, we show how to compute the probability that z is in the interval between -0.50 and 1.25; that is, $P(-0.50 \leq z \leq 1.25)$. Figure 6.9 shows this area, or probability.

Three steps are required to compute this probability. First, we find the area under the normal curve to the left of $z = 1.25$. Second, we find the area under the normal curve to the left of $z = -0.50$. Finally, we subtract the area to the left of $z = -0.50$ from the area to the left of $z = 1.25$ to find $P(-0.50 \leq z \leq 1.25)$.

To find the area under the normal curve to the left of $z = 1.25$, we first locate the 1.2 row in the standard normal probability table and then move across to the 0.05 column. Because the table value in the 1.2 row and the 0.05 column is 0.8944, $P(z \leq 1.25) = 0.8944$. Similarly, to find the area under the curve to the left of $z = -0.50$, we use the left-hand page of the table to locate the table value in the -0.5 row and the 0.00 column; with a table value of 0.3085, $P(z \leq -0.50) = 0.3085$. Thus, $P(-0.50 \leq z \leq 1.25) = P(z \leq 1.25) - P(z \leq -0.50) = 0.8944 - 0.3085 = 0.5859$.

Let us consider another example of computing the probability that z is in the interval between two given values. Often it is of interest to compute the probability that a normal random variable assumes a value within a certain number of standard deviations of the mean. Suppose we want to compute the probability that the standard normal random variable is within one standard deviation of the mean; that is, $P(-1.00 \leq z \leq 1.00)$. To compute this probability, we must find the area under the curve between -1.00 and 1.00. Earlier we found that $P(z \leq 1.00) = 0.8413$. Referring again to the standard normal probability table

Figure 6.9 Probability for Standard Normal Distribution Corresponding to $P(-0.50 \leq z \leq 1.25)$

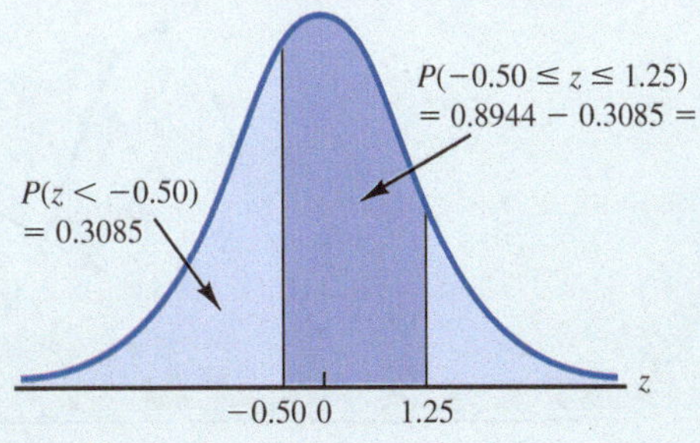

Figure 6.10 Probability for Standard Normal Distribution Corresponding to $P(-1.00 \le z \le 1.00)$

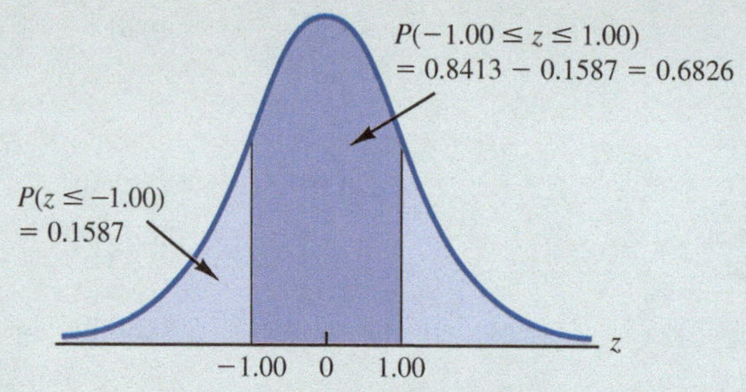

from Table 1 of Appendix B, we find that the area under the curve to the left of $z = -1.00$ is 0.1587, so $P(z \le -1.00) = 0.1587$. Therefore, $P(-1.00 \le z \le 1.00) = P(z \le 1.00) - P(z \le -1.00) = 0.8413 - 0.1587 = 0.6826$. This probability is shown graphically in Figure 6.10.

To illustrate how to make the third type of probability computation, suppose we want to compute the probability of obtaining a z value of at least 1.58; that is, $P(z \ge 1.58)$. The value in the $z = 1.5$ row and the 0.08 column of the cumulative normal table is 0.9429; thus, $P(z < 1.58) = 0.9429$. However, because the total area under the normal curve is 1, $P(z \ge 1.58) = 1 - 0.9429 = 0.0571$. This probability is shown in Figure 6.11.

In the preceding illustrations, we showed how to compute probabilities given specified z values. In some situations, we are given a probability and are interested in working backward to find the corresponding z value. Suppose we want to find a z value such that the probability of obtaining a larger z value is 0.10. Figure 6.12 shows this situation graphically.

This problem is the inverse of those in the preceding examples. Previously, we specified the z value of interest and then found the corresponding probability, or area. In this example, we are given the probability, or area, and asked to find the corresponding z value. To do so, we use the standard normal probability table somewhat differently.

Recall that the standard normal probability table gives the area under the curve to the left of a particular z value. We have been given the information that the area in the upper tail of the curve is 0.10. Hence, the area under the curve to the left of the unknown z value must equal 0.9000. Scanning the body of Table 1 in Appendix B, we

Figure 6.11 Probability for Standard Normal Distribution Corresponding to $P(z \ge 1.58)$

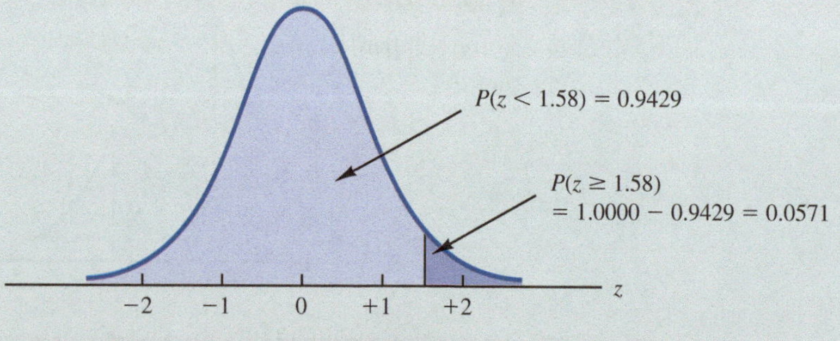

Figure 6.12 Finding z Value Such That Probability of Obtaining a Larger z Value Is 0.10

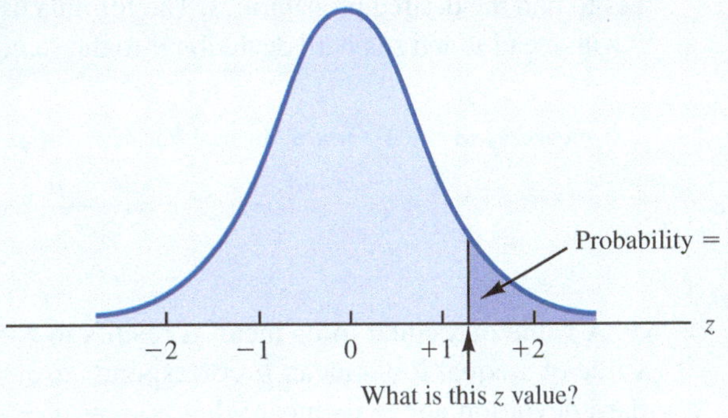

find that 0.8997 is the cumulative probability value closest to 0.9000. The section of the table providing this result follows.

Given a probability, we can use the standard normal table in an inverse fashion to find the corresponding z value.

z	**0.06**	**0.07**	**0.08**	**0.09**
.				
.				
.				
1.0	0.8554	0.8577	0.8599	0.8621
1.1	0.8770	0.8790	0.8810	0.8830
1.2	0.8962	0.8980	0.8997	0.9015
1.3	0.9131	0.9147	0.9162	0.9177
1.4	0.9279	0.9292	0.9306	0.9319
.				
.				
.				

Cumulative probability value closest to 0.9000

Reading the z value from the leftmost column and the top row of the table, we find that the corresponding z value is 1.28. Thus, an area of approximately 0.9000 (actually 0.8997) will be to the left of $z = 1.28$.[2] In terms of the question originally asked, there is an approximately 0.10 probability of a z value larger than 1.28.

The examples illustrate that the table of cumulative probabilities for the standard normal probability distribution can be used to find probabilities associated with values of the standard normal random variable z. Two types of questions can be asked. The first type of question specifies a value, or values, for z and asks us to use the table to determine the corresponding areas or probabilities. The second type of question provides an area, or probability, and asks us to use the table to determine the corresponding z value. Thus, we need to be flexible in using the standard normal probability table to answer the desired probability question. In most cases, sketching a graph of the standard normal probability distribution and shading the appropriate area will help to visualize the situation and aid in determining the correct answer.

Computing Probabilities for Any Normal Probability Distribution

The reason for discussing the standard normal distribution so extensively is that probabilities for all normal distributions are computed by using the standard normal distribution. That is,

[2] We could use interpolation in the body of the table to get a better approximation of the z value that corresponds to an area of 0.9000. Doing so to provide one more decimal place of accuracy would yield a z value of 1.282. However, in most practical situations, sufficient accuracy is obtained simply by using the table value closest to the desired probability. And if additional accuracy is needed, one can use most any statistical software to calculate the z value. Later in this chapter, we show how to calculate z values using Excel.

when we have a normal distribution with any mean μ and any standard deviation σ, we answer probability questions about the distribution by first converting to the standard normal distribution. Then we can use the standard normal probability table and the appropriate z values to find the desired probabilities. The formula used to convert any normal random variable x with mean μ and standard deviation σ to the standard normal random variable z follows.

The formula for the standard normal random variable is similar to the formula we introduced in Chapter 3 for computing z-scores for a data set.

Converting to the Standard Normal Random Variable

$$z = \frac{x - \mu}{\sigma} \tag{6.3}$$

A value of x equal to its mean μ results in $z = (\mu - \mu)/\sigma = 0$. Thus, we see that a value of x equal to its mean μ corresponds to $z = 0$. Now suppose that x is one standard deviation above its mean; that is, $x = \mu + \sigma$. Applying equation (6.3), we see that the corresponding z value is $z = [(\mu + \sigma) - \mu]/\sigma = \sigma/\sigma = 1$. Thus, an x value that is one standard deviation above its mean corresponds to $z = 1$. In other words, *we can interpret* z *as the number of standard deviations that the normal random variable* x *is from its mean* μ.

To see how this conversion enables us to compute probabilities for any normal distribution, suppose we have a normal distribution with $\mu = 10$ and $\sigma = 2$. What is the probability that the random variable x is between 10 and 14? Using equation (6.3), we see that at $x = 10$, $z = (x - \mu)/\sigma = (10 - 10)/2 = 0$ and that at $x = 14$, $z = (14 - 10)/2 = 4/2 = 2$. Thus, the answer to our question about the probability of x being between 10 and 14 is given by the equivalent probability that z is between 0 and 2 for the standard normal distribution. In other words, the probability that we are seeking is the probability that the random variable x is between its mean and two standard deviations above the mean. Using $z = 2.00$ and the standard normal probability table in Table 1 of Appendix B for this text, we see that $P(z \leq 2) = 0.9772$. Because $P(z \leq 0) = 0.5000$, we can compute $P(0.00 \leq z \leq 2.00) = P(z \leq 2) - P(z \leq 0) = 0.9772 - 0.5000 = 0.4772$. Hence, the probability that x is between 10 and 14 is 0.4772.

Grear Tire Company Problem

We turn now to an application of the normal probability distribution. Suppose the Grear Tire Company developed a new steel-belted radial tire to be sold through a national chain of discount stores. Because the tire is a new product, Grear's managers believe that the mileage guarantee offered with the tire will be an important factor in the acceptance of the product. Before finalizing the tire mileage guarantee policy, Grear's managers want probability information about the number of miles the tires will last. Let x denote the number of miles the tire lasts.

From actual road tests with the tires, Grear's engineering group estimated that the mean tire mileage is $\mu = 36{,}500$ miles and that the standard deviation is $\sigma = 5{,}000$. In addition, the data collected indicate that a normal distribution is a reasonable assumption. What percentage of the tires can be expected to last more than 40,000 miles? In other words, what is the probability that the tire mileage, x, will exceed 40,000? This question can be answered by finding the area of the darkly shaded region in Figure 6.13.

At $x = 40{,}000$, we have

$$z = \frac{x - \mu}{\sigma} = \frac{40{,}000 - 36{,}500}{5{,}000} = \frac{3{,}500}{5{,}000} = 0.70$$

Refer now to the bottom of Figure 6.13. We see that a value of $x = 40{,}000$ on the Grear Tire normal distribution corresponds to a value of $z = 0.70$ on the standard normal distribution. Using the standard normal probability table, we see that the area under the standard normal curve to the left of $z = 0.70$ is 0.7580. Thus, $1.000 - 0.7580 = 0.2420$ is the

Figure 6.13 Grear Tire Company Mileage Distribution

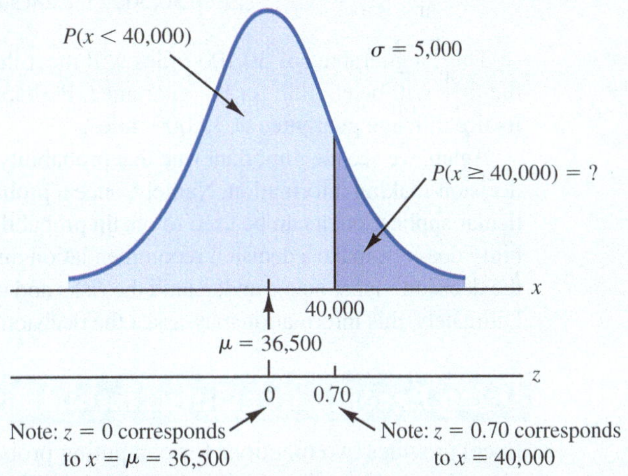

probability that z will exceed 0.70 and hence x will exceed 40,000. We can conclude that about 24.2% of the tires will exceed 40,000 in mileage.

Let us now assume that Grear is considering a guarantee that will provide a discount on replacement tires if the original tires do not provide the guaranteed mileage. What should the guaranteed mileage be if Grear wants no more than 10% of the tires to be eligible for the discount guarantee? This question is interpreted graphically in Figure 6.14.

According to Figure 6.14, the area under the curve to the left of the unknown guaranteed mileage must be 0.10. So, we must first find the z value that cuts off an area of 0.10 in the left tail of a standard normal distribution. Using the standard normal probability table, we see that $z = -1.28$ cuts off an area of 0.10 in the lower tail. Hence, $z = -1.28$ is the value of the standard normal random variable corresponding to the desired mileage guarantee on the Grear Tire normal distribution. To find the value of x corresponding to $z = -1.28$, we have

The guaranteed mileage we need to find is 1.28 standard deviations below the mean. Thus, $x = \mu - 1.28\sigma$.

$$z = \frac{x - \mu}{\sigma} = -1.28$$

$$x - \mu = -1.28\sigma$$

$$x = \mu - 1.28\sigma$$

Figure 6.14 Grear's Discount Guarantee

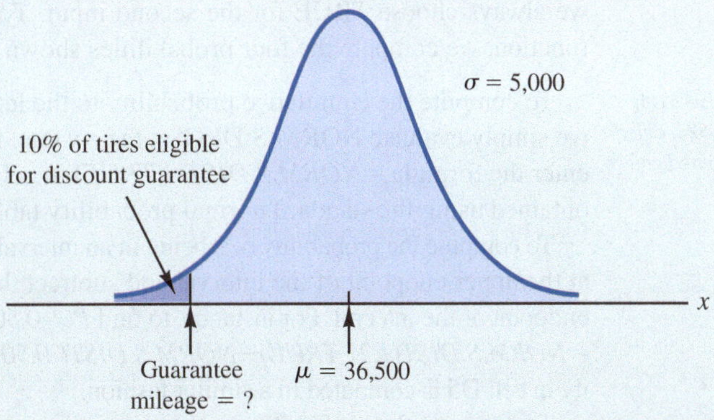

With $\mu = 36{,}500$ and $\sigma = 5{,}000$,

$$x = 36{,}500 - 1.28(5{,}000) = 30{,}100$$

With the guarantee set at 30,000 miles, the actual percentage eligible for the guarantee will be 9.68%.

Thus, a guarantee of 30,100 miles will meet the requirement that approximately 10% of the tires will be eligible for the guarantee. Perhaps, with this information, the firm will set its tire mileage guarantee at 30,000 miles.

Again, we see the important role that probability distributions play in providing decision-making information. Namely, once a probability distribution is established for a particular application, it can be used to obtain probability information about the problem. Probability does not make a decision recommendation directly, but it provides information that helps the decision maker better understand the risks and uncertainties associated with the problem. Ultimately, this information may assist the decision maker in reaching a good decision.

Using Excel to Compute Normal Probabilities

Excel provides two functions for computing probabilities and z values for a standard normal probability distribution: NORM.S.DIST and NORM.S.INV. The NORM.S.DIST function computes the cumulative probability given a z value, and the NORM.S.INV function computes the z value given a cumulative probability. Two similar functions, NORM.DIST and NORM.INV, are available for computing the cumulative probability and the x value for any normal distribution. We begin by showing how to use the NORM.S.DIST and NORM.S.INV functions.

The letter S that appears in the name of the NORM.S.DIST and NORM.S.INV functions reminds us that these functions relate to the standard normal probability distribution.

The NORM.S.DIST function provides the area under the standard normal curve to the left of a given z value; thus, it provides the same cumulative probability we would obtain if we used the standard normal probability table from the online supplemental materials for this text. Using the NORM.S.DIST function is just like having Excel look up cumulative normal probabilities for you. The NORM.S.INV function is the inverse of the NORM.S.DIST function; it takes a cumulative probability as input and provides the z value corresponding to that cumulative probability.

Let's see how both of these functions work by computing the probabilities and z values obtained earlier in this section using the standard normal probability table. Refer to Figure 6.15 as we describe the tasks involved. The formula worksheet is in the background; the value worksheet is in the foreground.

Enter/Access Data: Open a blank worksheet. No data are entered in the worksheet. We will simply enter the appropriate z values and probabilities directly into the formulas as needed.

Enter Functions and Formulas: The NORM.S.DIST function has two inputs: the z value and a value of TRUE or FALSE. For the second input we enter TRUE if a cumulative probability is desired, and we enter FALSE if the height of the standard normal curve is desired. Because we will always be using NORM.S.DIST to compute cumulative probabilities, we always choose TRUE for the second input. To illustrate the use of the NORM.S.DIST function, we compute the four probabilities shown in cells D3:D6 of Figure 6.15.

The probabilities in cells D4, 0.5858, and D5, 0.6827, differ from what we computed earlier due to rounding.

To compute the cumulative probability to the left of a given z value (area in lower tail), we simply evaluate NORM.S.DIST at the z value. For instance, to compute $P(z \leq 1)$ we enter the formula *=NORM.S.DIST(1,TRUE)* in cell D3. The result, 0.8413, is the same as obtained using the standard normal probability table.

To compute the probability of z being in an interval, we compute the value of NORM.S.DIST at the upper endpoint of the interval and subtract the value of NORM.S.DIST at the lower endpoint of the interval. For instance, to find $P(-0.50 \leq z \leq 1.25)$, we enter the formula *=NORM.S.DIST(1.25,TRUE)−NORM.S.DIST(-0.50,TRUE)* in cell D4. The interval probability in cell D5 is computed in a similar fashion.

To compute the probability to the right of a given z value (upper tail area), we must subtract the cumulative probability represented by the area under the curve below the

Figure 6.15 Excel Worksheet for Computing Probabilities and z Values for the Standard Normal Distribution

	A	B	C	D	E
1			Probabilities: Standard Normal Distribution		
2					
3			P(z ≤ 1)	=NORM.S.DIST(1, TRUE)	
4			P(-0.50 ≤ z ≤ 1.25)	=NORM.S.DIST(1.25, TRUE) - NORM.S.DIST(-0.5, TRUE)	
5			P(-1.00 ≤ z ≤ 1.00)	=NORM.S.DIST(1,TRUE) - NORM.S.DIST(-1, TRUE)	
6			P(z ≥ 1.58)	=1 - NORM.S.DIST(1.58, TRUE)	
7					
8					
9			Finding z-values Given Probabilities		
10					
11			z value with 0.10 in upper tail	=NORM.S.INV(0.9)	
12			z value with 0.025 in upper tail	=NORM.S.INV(0.975)	
13			z value with 0.025 in lower tail	=NORM.S.INV(0.025)	
14					

	A	B	C	D	E
1		Probabilities: Standard Normal Distribution			
2					
3			P(z ≤ 1)	0.8413	
4			P(-0.50 ≤ z ≤ 1.25)	0.5858	
5			P(-1.00 ≤ z ≤ 1.00)	0.6827	
6			P(z ≥ 1.58)	0.0571	
7					
8					
9		Finding z-values Given Probabilities			
10					
11			z value with 0.10 in upper tail	1.28	
12			z value with 0.025 in upper tail	1.96	
13			z value with 0.025 in lower tail	-1.96	
14					

z value (lower tail area) from 1. For example, to compute $P(z \geq 1.58)$, we enter the formula *=1−NORM.S.DIST(1.58,TRUE)* in cell D6.

To compute the z value for a given cumulative probability (lower tail area), we use the NORM.S.INV function. To find the z value corresponding to an upper tail probability of 0.10, we note that the corresponding lower tail area is 0.90 and enter the formula *=NORM.S.INV(0.9)* in cell D11. Actually, NORM.S.INV(0.9) gives us the z value providing a cumulative probability (lower tail area) of 0.9. But it is also the z value associated with an upper tail area of $1 - 0.9 = 0.10$.

Two other z values are computed in Figure 6.15. These z values will be used extensively in succeeding chapters. To compute the z value corresponding to an upper tail probability of 0.025, we enter the formula *=NORM.S.INV(0.975)* in cell D12. To compute the z value corresponding to a lower tail probability of 0.025, we enter the formula *=NORM.S.INV(0.025)* in cell D13. We see that $z = 1.96$ corresponds to an upper tail probability of 0.025, and $z = -1.96$ corresponds to a lower tail probability of 0.025.

Let us now turn to the Excel functions for computing cumulative probabilities and x values for any normal distribution. The NORM.DIST function provides the area under the normal curve to the left of a given value of the random variable x; thus, it provides cumulative probabilities. The NORM.INV function is the inverse of the NORM.DIST function; it takes a cumulative probability as input and provides the value of x corresponding to that cumulative probability. The NORM.DIST and NORM.INV functions do the same thing for any normal distribution that the NORM.S.DIST and NORM.S.INV functions do for the standard normal distribution.

Let's see how both of these functions work by computing probabilities and x values for the Grear Tire Company example introduced earlier in this section. Recall that the lifetime of a Grear tire has a mean of 36,500 miles and a standard deviation of 5,000 miles. Refer to Figure 6.16 as we describe the tasks involved. The formula worksheet is in the background; the value worksheet is in the foreground.

Enter/Access Data: Open a blank worksheet. No data are entered in the worksheet. We simply enter the appropriate x values and probabilities directly into the formulas as needed.

Enter Functions and Formulas: The NORM.DIST function has four inputs: (1) the x value we want to compute the cumulative probability for, (2) the mean, (3) the standard deviation, and (4) a value of TRUE or FALSE. For the fourth input, we enter TRUE if a cumulative probability is desired, and we enter FALSE if the height of the curve is desired.

Figure 6.16 Excel Worksheet for Computing Probabilities and x Values for the Normal Distribution

	A	B	C	D
1			**Probabilities: Normal Distribution**	
2				
3			***P*(*x* ≤ 20,000)**	=NORM.DIST(20000, 36500, 5000, TRUE)
4			***P*(20,000 ≤ *x* ≤ 40,000)**	=NORM.DIST(40000, 36500, 5000, TRUE) - NORM.DIST(20000, 36500, 5000, TRUE)
5			***P*(*x* ≥ 40,000)**	=1 - NORM.DIST(40000, 36500, 5000, TRUE)
6				
7			**Finding *x* values Given Probabilities**	
8				
9			***x* value with 0.10 in lower tail**	=NORM.INV(0.1, 36500, 5000)
10			***x* value with 0.025 in upper tail**	=NORM.INV(0.975, 36500, 5000)
11				

	A	B	C	D
1			**Probabilities: Normal Distribution**	
2				
3			***P*(*x* ≤ 20,000)**	0.0005
4			***P*(20,000 ≤ *x* ≤ 40,000)**	0.7576
5			***P*(*x* ≥ 40,000)**	0.2420
6				
7			**Finding *x* values Given Probabilities**	
8				
9			***x* value with 0.10 in lower tail**	30092.24
10			***x* value with 0.025 in upper tail**	46299.82
11				

Because we will always be using NORM.DIST to compute cumulative probabilities, we will always choose TRUE for the fourth input.

To compute the cumulative probability to the left of a given x value (lower tail area), we simply evaluate NORM.DIST at the x value. For instance, to compute the probability that a Grear tire will last 20,000 miles or less, we enter the formula *=NORM.DIST(20000,36500,5000,TRUE)* in cell D3. The value worksheet shows that this cumulative probability is 0.0005. So, we can conclude that almost all Grear tires will last at least 20,000 miles.

To compute the probability of x being in an interval we compute the value of NORM.DIST at the upper endpoint of the interval and subtract the value of NORM.DIST at the lower endpoint of the interval. The formula in cell D4 provides the probability that a tire's lifetime is between 20,000 and 40,000 miles, $P(20{,}000 \leq x \leq 40{,}000)$. In the value worksheet, we see that this probability is 0.7576.

To compute the probability to the right of a given x value (upper tail area), we must subtract the cumulative probability represented by the area under the curve below the x value (lower tail area) from 1. The formula in cell D5 computes the probability that a Grear tire will last for at least 40,000 miles. We see that this probability is 0.2420.

To compute the x value for a given cumulative probability, we use the NORM.INV function. The NORM.INV function has only three inputs. The first input is the cumulative probability; the second and third inputs are the mean and standard deviation. For instance, to compute the tire mileage corresponding to a lower tail area of 0.1 for Grear Tire, we enter the formula *=NORM.INV(0.1,36500,5000)* in cell D9. From the value worksheet, we see that 10% of the Grear tires will last for 30,092.24 miles or less.

To compute the minimum tire mileage for the top 2.5% of Grear tires, we want to find the value of x corresponding to an area of 0.025 in the upper tail. This calculation is the same as finding the x value that provides a cumulative probability of 0.975. Thus we enter the formula *=NORM.INV(0.975,36500,5000)* in cell D10 to compute this tire mileage. From the value worksheet, we see that 2.5% of the Grear tires will last at least 46,299.82 miles.

Exercises

Methods

8. Using Figure 6.6 as a guide, sketch a normal curve for a random variable x that has a mean of $\mu = 100$ and a standard deviation of $\sigma = 10$. Label the horizontal axis with values of 70, 80, 90, 100, 110, 120, and 130. **LO 4**

9. A random variable is normally distributed with a mean of $\mu = 50$ and a standard deviation of $\sigma = 5$. **LO 4, 5**
   a. Sketch a normal curve for the probability density function. Label the horizontal axis with values of 35, 40, 45, 50, 55, 60, and 65. Figure 6.6 shows that the normal curve almost touches the horizontal axis at three standard deviations below and at three standard deviations above the mean (in this case at 35 and 65).
   b. What is the probability that the random variable will assume a value between 45 and 55?
   c. What is the probability that the random variable will assume a value between 40 and 60?

10. Draw a graph for the standard normal distribution. Label the horizontal axis at values of −3, −2, −1, 0, 1, 2, and 3. Then compute the following probabilities. **LO 4, 5**
   a. $P(z \leq 1.5)$
   b. $P(z \leq 1)$
   c. $P(1 \leq z \leq 1.5)$
   d. $P(0 < z < 2.5)$

11. Given that z is a standard normal random variable, compute the following probabilities. **LO 5**
   a. $P(z \leq -1.0)$
   b. $P(z \geq -1)$
   c. $P(z \geq -1.5)$
   d. $P(-2.5 \leq z)$
   e. $P(-3 < z \leq 0)$

12. Given that z is a standard normal random variable, compute the following probabilities. **LO 5**
   a. $P(0 \leq z \leq 0.83)$
   b. $P(-1.57 \leq z \leq 0)$
   c. $P(z > 0.44)$
   d. $P(z \geq -0.23)$
   e. $P(z < 1.20)$
   f. $P(z \leq -0.71)$

13. Given that z is a standard normal random variable, compute the following probabilities. **LO 5**
   a. $P(-1.98 \leq z \leq 0.49)$
   b. $P(0.52 \leq z \leq 1.22)$
   c. $P(-1.75 \leq z \leq -1.04)$

14. Given that z is a standard normal random variable, find z for each situation. **LO 6**
   a. The area to the left of z is 0.9750.
   b. The area between 0 and z is 0.4750.
   c. The area to the left of z is 0.7291.
   d. The area to the right of z is 0.1314.
   e. The area to the left of z is 0.6700.
   f. The area to the right of z is 0.3300.

15. Given that z is a standard normal random variable, find z for each situation. **LO 6**
   a. The area to the left of z is 0.2119.
   b. The area between $-z$ and z is 0.9030.
   c. The area between $-z$ and z is 0.2052.
   d. The area to the left of z is 0.9948.
   e. The area to the right of z is 0.6915.

16. Given that z is a standard normal random variable, find z for each situation. **LO 6**
   a. The area to the right of z is 0.01.
   b. The area to the right of z is 0.025.

c. The area to the right of z is 0.05.
d. The area to the right of z is 0.10.

Applications

17. **Height of Dutch Males.** Those assigned the sex of male at birth in the Netherlands are the tallest, on average, in the world with an average height of 183 centimeters (cm) (BBC News website). Assume that the height of males in the Netherlands is normally distributed with a mean of 183 cm and standard deviation of 10.5 cm. **LO 5**
 a. What is the probability that a Dutch male is shorter than 175 cm?
 b. What is the probability that a Dutch male is taller than 195 cm?
 c. What is the probability that a Dutch male is between 173 and 193 cm?
 d. Out of a random sample of 1,000 Dutch males, how many would we expect to be taller than 190 cm?
18. **Large-Cap Domestic Stock Fund.** The average return for large-cap domestic stock funds over three years was 14.4%. Assume the three-year returns were normally distributed across funds with a standard deviation of 4.4%. **LO 5, 6**
 a. What is the probability an individual large-cap domestic stock fund had a three-year return of at least 20%?
 b. What is the probability an individual large-cap domestic stock fund had a three-year return of 10% or less?
 c. How big does the return have to be to put a domestic stock fund in the top 10% for the three-year period?
19. **Automobile Repair Costs.** Automobile repair costs continue to rise with the average cost now at $367 per repair (*U.S. News & World Report* website). Assume that the cost for an automobile repair is normally distributed with a standard deviation of $88. Answer the following questions about the cost of automobile repairs. **LO 5, 6**
 a. What is the probability that the cost will be more than $450?
 b. What is the probability that the cost will be less than $250?
 c. What is the probability that the cost will be between $250 and $450?
 d. If the cost for your car repair is in the lower 5% of automobile repair charges, what is your cost?
20. **Basketball Game.** Suppose that the Fort Wayne Mad Ants are playing the Cleveland Charge in a basketball game. The number of points scored in a game by the Mad Ants is normally distributed with a mean of 107 and standard deviation of 13. The number of points scored in a game by the Charge is normally distributed with a mean of 111 and standard deviation of 19. **LO 5**
 a. What is the probability that the Mad Ants will score more than 100 points in a game?
 b. What percentage of games would you expect the Charge to score more than 120 points in a game?
 c. What is the probability that the Mad Ants will score more points in a game than the mean number of points scored by the Charge?
21. **Leadtime Quotes for Steel Production.** A certain cold-rolled steel product requires a production lead time that is normally distributed with a mean of 7.6 days and standard deviation of 2.8 days. If the company that produces this steel product wants to quote a lead time to a customer such that the company is 90% confident that it will produce the product in less than the quoted lead time, what lead time should it quote to the customer? **LO 6**
22. **Screen Time.** Suppose that the mean time someone spends using a device with a screen such as a smartphone, computer, or television is 8.35 hours. Use a normal probability distribution with a standard deviation of 2.5 hours to answer the following questions about daily screen time. **LO 5, 6**
 a. What is the probability that a randomly selected person has between 5 and 10 hours of screen time a day?

b. How many hours of screen time must a person have in order to be in the top 3% of all screen time values?
c. What is the probability that a person has more than three hours of screen time a day?

23. **Time to Complete Final Exam.** The time needed to complete a final examination in a particular college course is normally distributed with a mean of 80 minutes and a standard deviation of 10 minutes. Answer the following questions. **LO 5**
    a. What is the probability of completing the exam in one hour or less?
    b. What is the probability that a student will complete the exam in more than 60 minutes but less than 75 minutes?
    c. Assume that the class has 60 students and that the examination period is 90 minutes in length. How many students do you expect will be unable to complete the exam in the allotted time?

24. **Amount of Sleep.** The United States Centers for Disease Control and Prevention (CDC) recommends that adults sleep 7 to 9 hours per night (CDC.gov). However, many adults in the United States sleep less than seven hours per night. Suppose that the amount of sleep for an adult in the United States follows a normal distribution with a mean of 8.0 hours and standard deviation of 1.7 hours. **LO 5, 6**
    a. What is the probability that an adult in the United States sleeps less than 7.0 hours?
    b. What is the probability that an adult in the United States sleeps between 7.0 and 9.0 hours?
    c. How many hours of sleep would an adult in the United States get if they are in the 10th percentile of this distribution?

25. **Real per Capita Income by State**. Nominal income refers to an income value that is not adjusted for inflation. Real income adjusts the nominal value for the rate of inflation. Real income per capita is considered a good measure of the buying power of an individual in a particular area because it adjusts for both the number of people in the area and the relative inflation of the area. According to Forbes magazine, the state with the highest annual real income per capita in 2020 is Connecticut with a real per capita income of $68,533. Suppose that the annual real income of individuals in Connecticut follows a normal distribution with a mean of $68,533 and standard deviation of $23,480. **LO 5, 6**
    a. What is the probability that an individual in Connecticut has an annual real income of $50,000 or more?
    b. What is the probability that an individual in Connecticut has an annual real income of $30,000 or less?
    c. What is the probability that an individual in Connecticut has an annual real income between $60,000 and $80,000?
    d. What is the annual real income of a person in the 99th percentile of annual real income in Connecticut?

6.3 Exponential Probability Distribution

The **exponential probability distribution** may be used for random variables such as the time between arrivals at a car wash, the time required to load a truck, and the distance between major defects in a highway. The exponential probability density function follows.

Exponential Probability Density Function

$$f(x) = \frac{1}{\mu} e^{-x/\mu} \quad \text{for } x \geq 0 \tag{6.4}$$

where

μ = expected value or mean

e = 2.71828

Figure 6.17 Exponential Distribution for the Schips Loading Dock Example

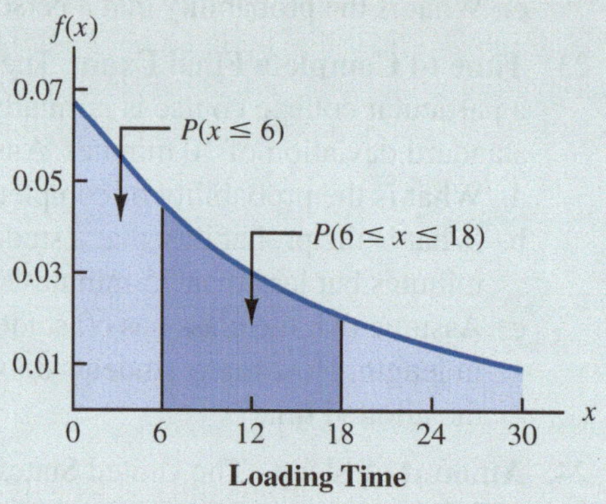

As an example of the exponential distribution, suppose that x represents the loading time for a truck at the Schips loading dock and follows such a distribution. If the mean, or average, loading time is 15 minutes ($\mu = 15$), the appropriate probability density function for x is

$$f(x) = \frac{1}{15} e^{-x/15}$$

Figure 6.17 is the graph of this probability density function.

Computing Probabilities for the Exponential Distribution

In waiting line applications, the exponential distribution is often used for service time.

As with any continuous probability distribution, the area under the curve corresponding to an interval provides the probability that the random variable assumes a value in that interval. In the Schips loading dock example, the probability that loading a truck will take six minutes or less $P(x \leq 6)$ is defined to be the area under the curve in Figure 6.17 from $x = 0$ to $x = 6$. Similarly, the probability that the loading time will be 18 minutes or less $P(x \leq 18)$ is the area under the curve from $x = 0$ to $x = 18$. Note also that the probability that the loading time will be between 6 and 18 minutes $P(6 \leq x \leq 18)$ is given by the area under the curve from $x = 6$ to $x = 18$.

To compute exponential probabilities such as those just described, we use the following formula. It provides the cumulative probability of obtaining a value for the exponential random variable of less than or equal to some specific value denoted by x_0.

Exponential Distribution: Cumulative Probabilities

$$P(x \leq x_0) = 1 - e^{-x_0/\mu} \qquad \textbf{(6.5)}$$

For the Schips loading dock example, x = loading time in minutes and μ = 15 minutes. Using equation (6.5),

$$P(x \leq x_0) = 1 - e^{-x_0/15}$$

Hence, the probability that loading a truck will take six minutes or less is

$$P(x \leq 6) = 1 - e^{-6/15} = 0.3297$$

Using equation (6.5), we calculate the probability of loading a truck in 18 minutes or less.

$$P(x \leq 18) = 1 - e^{-18/15} = 0.6988$$

Thus, the probability that loading a truck will take between 6 and 18 minutes is equal to $0.6988 - 0.3297 = 0.3691$. Probabilities for any other interval can be computed similarly.

In the preceding example, the mean time it takes to load a truck is $\mu = 15$ minutes. A property of the exponential distribution is that the mean of the distribution and the standard deviation of the distribution are *equal.* Thus, the standard deviation for the time it takes to load a truck is $\sigma = 15$ minutes. The variance is $\sigma^2 = (15)^2 = 225$.

Relationship Between the Poisson and Exponential Distributions

In Section 5.5, we introduced the Poisson distribution as a discrete probability distribution that is often useful in examining the number of occurrences of an event over a specified interval of time or space. Recall that the Poisson probability function is

$$f(x) = \frac{\mu^x e^{-\mu}}{x!}$$

where

μ = expected value or mean number of occurrences over a specified interval

The continuous exponential probability distribution is related to the discrete Poisson distribution. If the Poisson distribution provides an appropriate description of the number of occurrences per interval, the exponential distribution provides a description of the length of the interval between occurrences.

To illustrate this relationship, suppose the number of cars that arrive at a car wash during one hour is described by a Poisson probability distribution with a mean of 10 cars per hour. The Poisson probability function that gives the probability of x arrivals per hour is

$$f(x) = \frac{10^x e^{-10}}{x!}$$

Because the average number of arrivals is 10 cars per hour, the average time between cars arriving is

$$\frac{1 \text{ hour}}{10 \text{ cars}} = 0.1 \text{ hour/car}$$

Thus, the corresponding exponential distribution that describes the time between the arrivals has a mean of $\mu = 0.1$ hour per car; as a result, the appropriate exponential probability density function is

$$f(x) = \frac{1}{0.1} e^{-x/0.1} = 10e^{-10x}$$

Using Excel to Compute Exponential Probabilities

Excel's EXPON.DIST function can be used to compute exponential probabilities. We will illustrate by computing probabilities associated with the time it takes to load a truck at the Schips loading dock. This example was introduced at the beginning of the section. Refer to Figure 6.18 as we describe the tasks involved. The formula worksheet is in the background; the value worksheet is in the foreground.

Enter/Access Data: Open a blank worksheet. No data are entered in the worksheet. We simply enter the appropriate values for the exponential random variable into the formulas as needed. The random variable is x = loading time.

Figure 6.18 Excel Worksheet for Computing Probabilities for the Exponential Probability Distribution

	A	B	C	D	E
1				Probabilities: Exponential Distribution	
2					
3			P(x ≤ 18)	=EXPON.DIST(18, 1/15, TRUE)	
4			P(6 ≤ x ≤ 18)	=EXPON.DIST(18, 1/15, TRUE) - EXPON.DIST(6, 1/15, TRUE)	
5			P(x ≥ 8)	=1 - EXPON.DIST(8, 1/15, TRUE)	
6					

	A	B	C	D	E
1	Probabilities: Exponential Distribution				
2					
3			P(x ≤ 18)	0.6988	
4			P(6 ≤ x ≤ 18)	0.3691	
5			P(x ≥ 8)	0.5866	
6					

Enter Functions and Formulas: The EXPON.DIST function has three inputs: The first is the value of x, the second is $1/\mu$, and the third is TRUE or FALSE. We choose TRUE for the third input if a cumulative probability is desired and FALSE if the height of the probability density function is desired. We will always use TRUE because we will be computing cumulative probabilities.

The first probability we compute is the probability that the loading time is 18 minutes or less. For the Schips problem, $1/\mu = 1/15$, so we enter the formula *=EXPON.DIST(18,1/15,TRUE)* in cell D3 to compute the desired cumulative probability. From the value worksheet, we see that the probability of loading a truck in 18 minutes or less is 0.6988.

The second probability we compute is the probability that the loading time is between 6 and 18 minutes. To find this probability, we first compute the cumulative probability for the upper endpoint of the time interval and subtract the cumulative probability for the lower endpoint of the interval. The formula we have entered in cell D4 calculates this probability. The value worksheet shows that this probability is 0.3691.

The last probability we calculate is the probability that the loading time is at least 8 minutes. Because the EXPON.DIST function computes only cumulative (lower tail) probabilities, we compute this probability by entering the formula *=1−EXPON.DIST(8,1/15,TRUE)* in cell D5. The value worksheet shows that the probability of a loading time of 8 minutes or more is 0.5866.

Notes + Comments

1. As we can see in Figure 6.17, the exponential distribution is skewed to the right. Indeed, the skewness measure for the exponential distribution is 2. The exponential distribution gives us a good idea what a skewed distribution looks like.
2. A property of the exponential distribution is that the mean and the standard deviation are equal.
3. If the number of arrivals in a specified time interval follows a Poisson distribution, the time between arrivals must follow an exponential distribution.

Exercises

Methods

26. Consider the following exponential probability density function. **LO 7**

$$f(x) = \frac{1}{8}e^{-x/8} \qquad \text{for } x \geq 0$$

a. Find $P(x \leq 6)$.
b. Find $P(x \leq 4)$.
c. Find $P(x \geq 6)$.
d. Find $P(4 \leq x \leq 6)$.

27. Consider the following exponential probability density function. **LO 7**

$$f(x) = \frac{1}{3}e^{-x/3} \quad \text{for } x \geq 0$$

a. Write the formula for $P(x \leq x_0)$.
b. Find $P(x \leq 2)$.
c. Find $P(x \geq 3)$.
d. Find $P(x \leq 5)$.
e. Find $P(2 \leq x \leq 5)$.

Applications

28. **Phone Battery Life.** Battery life between charges for a certain mobile phone is 20 hours when the primary use is talk time, and drops to 7 hours when the phone is primarily used for Internet applications over cellular. Assume that the battery life in both cases follows an exponential distribution. **LO 7, 8**
a. Show the probability density function for battery life for this phone when its primary use is talk time.
b. What is the probability that the battery charge for a randomly selected phone will last no more than 15 hours when its primary use is talk time?
c. What is the probability that the battery charge for a randomly selected phone will last more than 20 hours when its primary use is talk time?
d. What is the probability that the battery charge for a randomly selected phone will last no more than five hours when its primary use is Internet applications?

29. **Arrival of Vehicles to an Intersection.** The time between arrivals of vehicles at a particular intersection follows an exponential probability distribution with a mean of 12 seconds. **LO 7, 8**
a. Sketch this exponential probability distribution.
b. What is the probability that the arrival time between vehicles is 12 seconds or less?
c. What is the probability that the arrival time between vehicles is six seconds or less?
d. What is the probability of 30 or more seconds between vehicle arrivals?

30. **Comcast Service Operations.** Comcast Corporation is a global telecommunications company headquartered in Philadelphia, PA. Generally known for reliable service, the company periodically experiences unexpected service interruptions. When service interruptions do occur, Comcast customers who call the office receive a message providing an estimate of when service will be restored. Suppose that for a particular outage, Comcast customers are told that service will be restored in two hours. Assume that two hours is the mean time to do the repair and that the repair time has an exponential probability distribution. **LO 7**
a. What is the probability that the cable service will be repaired in one hour or less?
b. What is the probability that the repair will take between one hour and two hours?
c. For a customer who calls the Comcast office at 1:00 P.M., what is the probability that the cable service will not be repaired by 5:00 P.M.?

31. **Patient Length of Stays in ICUs.** Intensive care units (ICUs) generally treat the sickest patients in a hospital. ICUs are often the most expensive department in a hospital because of the specialized equipment and extensive training required to be an ICU doctor or nurse. Therefore, it is important to use ICUs as efficiently as possible in a hospital. According to a 2017 large-scale study of elderly ICU patients, the average length of stay in the ICU

is 3.4 days (*Critical Care Medicine* journal article). Assume that this length of stay in the ICU has an exponential distribution. **LO 7**

a. What is the probability that the length of stay in the ICU is one day or less?
b. What is the probability that the length of stay in the ICU is between two and three days?
c. What is the probability that the length of stay in the ICU is more than five days?

32. **Boston 911 Calls.** The Boston Fire Department receives 911 calls at a mean rate of 1.6 calls per hour (*Mass.gov* website). Suppose the number of calls per hour follows a Poisson probability distribution. **LO 7, 8**
    a. What is the mean time between 911 calls to the Boston Fire Department in minutes?
    b. Using the mean in part (a), show the probability density function for the time between 911 calls in minutes.
    c. What is the probability that there will be less than one hour between 911 calls?
    d. What is the probability that there will be 30 minutes or more between 911 calls?
    e. What is the probability that there will be more than 5 minutes but less than 20 minutes between 911 calls?

Summary

This chapter extended the discussion of probability distributions to the case of continuous random variables. The major conceptual difference between discrete and continuous probability distributions involves the method of computing probabilities. With discrete distributions, the probability function $f(x)$ provides the probability that the random variable x assumes various values. With continuous distributions, the probability density function $f(x)$ does not provide probability values directly. Instead, probabilities are given by areas under the curve or graph of the probability density function $f(x)$. Because the area under the curve above a single point is zero, we observe that the probability of any particular value is zero for a continuous random variable.

Three continuous probability distributions—the uniform, normal, and exponential distributions—were treated in detail. The normal distribution is used widely in statistical inference and will be used extensively throughout the remainder of the text.

Glossary

Exponential probability distribution A continuous probability distribution that is useful in computing probabilities for the time it takes to complete a task.
Normal probability distribution A continuous probability distribution. Its probability density function is bell shaped and determined by its mean μ and standard deviation σ.
Probability density function A function used to compute probabilities for a continuous random variable. The area under the graph of a probability density function over an interval represents probability.
Standard normal probability distribution A normal distribution with a mean of zero and a standard deviation of one.
Uniform probability distribution A continuous probability distribution for which the probability that the random variable will assume a value in any interval is the same for each interval of equal length.

Key Formulas

Uniform Probability Density Function

$$f(x) = \begin{cases} \dfrac{1}{b-a} & \text{for } a \leq x \leq b \\ 0 & \text{elsewhere} \end{cases} \tag{6.1}$$

Normal Probability Density Function

$$f(x) = \frac{1}{\sigma\sqrt{2\pi}} e^{-\frac{1}{2}\left(\frac{x-\mu}{\sigma}\right)^2} \tag{6.2}$$

Converting to the Standard Normal Random Variable

$$z = \frac{x - \mu}{\sigma} \tag{6.3}$$

Exponential Probability Density Function

$$f(x) = \frac{1}{\mu} e^{-x/\mu} \quad \text{for } x \geq 0 \tag{6.4}$$

Exponential Distribution: Cumulative Probabilities

$$P(x \leq x_0) = 1 - e^{-x_0/\mu} \tag{6.5}$$

Supplementary Exercises

33. **Selling a House.** A business executive, transferred from Chicago to Atlanta, needs to sell her house in Chicago quickly. The executive's employer has offered to buy the house for $310,000, but the offer expires at the end of the week. The executive does not currently have a better offer, but can afford to leave the house on the market for another month. From conversations with her realtor, the executive believes the price she will get by leaving the house on the market for another month is uniformly distributed between $300,000 and $325,000. **LO 1, 2**
    a. If she leaves the house on the market for another month, what is the mathematical expression for the probability density function of the sales price?
    b. If she leaves it on the market for another month, what is the probability that she will get at least $315,000 for the house?
    c. If she leaves it on the market for another month, what is the probability that she will get less than $310,000?
    d. Should the executive leave the house on the market for another month? Why or why not?

34. **Stock Returns**. Suppose the annual return for a certain class of stocks is normally distributed with a mean of 11.4% and a standard deviation of 9.6%. **LO 5, 6**
    a. What is the probability a randomly selected stock from this class of stocks with have an annual return of more than 15%?
    b. What is the probability a randomly selected stock from this class of stocks will have a negative annual return?
    c. What annual return would you expect from a stock in this class of stocks that outperforms 90% of all stocks in this class?

35. **Production Defects.** Motorola used the normal distribution to determine the probability of defects and the number of defects expected in a production process. Assume a production process produces items with a mean weight of 10 ounces. **LO 5**
    a. Suppose that the process standard deviation is 0.15, and the process control is set at plus or minus one standard deviation. Units with weights less than 9.85 or greater than 10.15 ounces will be classified as defects. Calculate the probability of a defect and the expected number of defects for a 1,000-unit production run.
    b. Suppose that through process design improvements, the process standard deviation can be reduced to 0.05. Assume the process control remains the same, with weights less than 9.85 or greater than 10.15 ounces being classified as defects. Calculate the probability of a defect and the expected number of defects for a 1,000-unit production run.

c. What is the advantage of reducing process variation, thereby causing process control limits to be at a greater number of standard deviations from the mean?

36. **Bringing Items to a Pawnshop.** One indicator of the level of economic hardship in a community is the number of people who bring items to a pawnshop. Assume the number of people bringing items to the pawnshop per day is normally distributed with a mean of 658. **LO 5, 6**
    a. Suppose you learn that on 3% of the days, 610 or fewer people brought items to the pawnshop. What is the standard deviation of the number of people bringing items to the pawnshop per day?
    b. On any given day, what is the probability that between 600 and 700 people bring items to the pawnshop?
    c. How many people bring items to the pawnshop on the busiest 3% of days?

37. **Amazon Alexa App Downloads.** Alexa is the popular virtual assistant developed by Amazon. Alexa interacts with users using artificial intelligence and voice recognition. It can be used to perform daily tasks such as making to-do lists, reporting the news and weather, and interacting with other smart devices in the home. In 2018, the Amazon Alexa app was downloaded some 2,800 times per day from the Google Play store (AppBrain website). Assume that the number of downloads per day of the Amazon Alexa app is normally distributed with a mean of 2,800 and standard deviation of 860. **LO 5, 6**
    a. What is the probability there are 2,000 or fewer downloads of Amazon Alexa in a day?
    b. What is the probability there are between 1,500 and 2,500 downloads of Amazon Alexa in a day?
    c. What is the probability there are more than 3,000 downloads of Amazon Alexa in a day?
    d. Assume that Google has designed its servers so there is probability 0.01 that the number of Amazon Alexa app downloads in a day exceeds the servers' capacity and more servers have to be brought online. How many Amazon Alexa app downloads per day are Google's servers designed to handle?

38. **Service Contract Offer.** Ward Doering Auto Sales is considering offering a special service contract that will cover the total cost of any service work required on leased vehicles. From experience, the company manager estimates that yearly service costs are approximately normally distributed, with a mean of $150 and a standard deviation of $25. **LO 5**
    a. If the company offers the service contract to customers for a yearly charge of $200, what is the probability that any one customer's service costs will exceed the contract price of $200?
    b. What is Ward's expected profit per service contract?

39. **Wedding Costs.** The XO Group Inc. conducted a survey of 13,000 brides and grooms married in the United States and found that the average cost of a wedding is $29,858 (XO Group website). Assume that the cost of a wedding is normally distributed with a mean of $29,858 and a standard deviation of $5,600. **LO 5, 6**
    a. What is the probability that a wedding costs less than $20,000?
    b. What is the probability that a wedding costs between $20,000 and $30,000?
    c. For a wedding to be among the 5% most expensive, how much would it have to cost?

40. **College Admissions Test Scores.** Assume that the test scores from a college admissions test are normally distributed, with a mean of 450 and a standard deviation of 100. **LO 5, 6**
    a. What percentage of the people taking the test score between 400 and 500?
    b. Suppose someone receives a score of 630. What percentage of the people taking the test score better? What percentage score worse?
    c. If a particular university will not admit anyone scoring below 480, what percentage of the persons taking the test would be acceptable to the university?

41. **College Graduates Starting Salaries.** According to *Forbes* magazine, the 2023 average starting salary for new college graduates in humanities was \$50,681. The average starting salary for new college graduates in engineering was \$73,922 (*Forbes.com* website). Assume that starting salaries are normally distributed and that the standard deviation for starting salaries for new college graduates in humanities is \$14,000. Assume that the standard deviation for starting salaries for new college graduates in engineering is \$19,000. **LO 5, 6**
    a. What is the probability that a new college graduate in engineering will earn a starting salary of at least \$80,000?
    b. What is the probability that a new college graduate in humanities will earn a starting salary of at least \$80,000?
    c. What is the probability that a new college graduate in humanities will earn a starting salary less than \$50,000?
    d. How much would a new college graduate in engineering have to earn in order to have a starting salary higher than 99% of all starting salaries of new college graduates in humanities? What percentage of engineering students are expected to earn a starting salary higher than 99% of all starting salaries of humanities graduates?
42. **Filling Weights.** A machine fills containers with a particular product. The standard deviation of filling weights is known from past data to be 0.6 ounce. If only 2% of the containers hold less than 18 ounces, what is the mean filling weight for the machine? That is, what must μ equal? Assume the filling weights have a normal distribution. **LO 6**
43. **Mean Time Between Failures.** The mean time between failures (MTBF) is a common metric used to measure the performance of manufacturing systems. MTBF is the elapsed time between failures of a system during normal operations. The failures could be caused by broken machines or computer errors, among other failures. Suppose that the MTBF for a new automated manufacturing system follows an exponential distribution with a mean of 12.7 hours. **LO 7**
    a. What is the probability that the automated manufacturing system runs for more than 15 hours without a failure?
    b. What is the probability that the automated manufacturing system runs for eight or fewer hours before failure?
    c. What is the probability that the automated manufacturing system runs for more than 6 hours but less than 10 hours before a failure?
44. **Website Traffic.** A website for bed and breakfast inns gets approximately seven visitors per minute. Suppose the number of website visitors per minute follows a Poisson probability distribution. **LO 7, 8**
    a. What is the mean time between visits to the website?
    b. Show the exponential probability density function for the time between website visits.
    c. What is the probability that no one will access the website in a one-minute period?
    d. What is the probability that no one will access the website in a 12-second period?
45. **Waiting in Line at Kroger.** Supermarket chain Kroger has used computer simulation and information technology to reduce the average waiting time for customers at 2,300 stores. Using a new system called *QueVision*, which allows Kroger to better predict when shoppers will be checking out, the company was able to decrease average customer waiting time to just 26 seconds (*InformationWeek* website). **LO 7**
    a. Assume that Kroger waiting times are exponentially distributed. Show the probability density function of waiting time at Kroger.
    b. What is the probability that a customer will have to wait between 15 and 30 seconds?
    c. What is the probability that a customer will have to wait more than two minutes?

46. **Calls to Insurance Claims Office.** The time (in minutes) between telephone calls at an insurance claims office has the following exponential probability distribution. **LO 7, 8**

$$f(x) = 0.50e^{-0.50x} \quad \text{for } x \geq 0$$

a. What is the mean time between telephone calls?
b. What is the probability of having 30 seconds or less between telephone calls?
c. What is the probability of having one minute or less between telephone calls?
d. What is the probability of having five or more minutes without a telephone call?

47. **Laffy Taffy Candy Production.** Laffy Taffy is a type of taffy candy made from corn syrup, sugar, palm oil, and other ingredients. Laffy Taffy comes in a variety of flavors including strawberry, banana, and cherry. Suppose that Laffy Taffy is produced as a continuous length of taffy on an extrusion machine. Defects can occur in the taffy including large air bubbles and tears. Assume that the distance between such defects follows an exponential distribution with a mean of 523 meters. **LO 7**
a. What is the probability that the machine will produce more than 1,000 meters of taffy before the next defect is observed?
b. What is the probability that the next defect will be observed before the machine produces 500 meters or less of taffy?

Case Problem 1: Specialty Toys

Specialty Toys, Inc. sells a variety of new and innovative children's toys. Management learned that the preholiday season is the best time to introduce a new toy, because many families use this time to look for new ideas for December holiday gifts. When Specialty discovers a new toy with good market potential, it chooses an October market entry date.

In order to get toys into its stores by October, Specialty places one-time orders with its manufacturers in June or July of each year. Demand for children's toys can be highly volatile. If a new toy catches on, a sense of shortage in the marketplace often increases the demand to high levels and large profits can be realized. However, new toys can also flop, leaving Specialty stuck with high levels of inventory that must be sold at reduced prices. The most important question the company faces is deciding how many units of a new toy should be purchased to meet anticipated sales demand. If too few are purchased, sales will be lost; if too many are purchased, profits will be reduced because of low prices realized in clearance sales.

For the coming season, Specialty plans to introduce a new product called Weather Teddy. This variation of a talking teddy bear is made by a company in Taiwan. When a child presses Teddy's hand, the bear begins to talk. A built-in barometer selects one of five responses that predict the weather conditions. The responses range from "It looks to be a very nice day! Have fun" to "I think it may rain today. Don't forget your umbrella." Tests with the product show that, even though it is not a perfect weather predictor, its predictions are surprisingly good. Several of Specialty's managers claimed Teddy gave predictions of the weather that were as good as those of many local television weather forecasters.

As with other products, Specialty faces the decision of how many Weather Teddy units to order for the coming holiday season. Members of the management team suggested order quantities of 15,000, 18,000, 24,000, or 28,000 units. The wide range of order quantities suggested indicates considerable disagreement concerning the market potential. The product management team asks you for an analysis of the stock-out probabilities for various order quantities, an estimate of the profit potential, and help with making an order quantity recommendation. Specialty expects to sell Weather Teddy for \$24 based on a cost of \$16 per unit. If inventory remains after the holiday season, Specialty will sell all surplus inventory for \$5 per unit. After reviewing the sales history of similar products, Specialty's senior sales forecaster predicted an expected demand of 20,000 units with a 0.95 probability that demand would be between 10,000 units and 30,000 units. **LO 3, 4, 5, 6**

Managerial Report

Prepare a managerial report that addresses the following issues and recommends an order quantity for the Weather Teddy product.

1. Use the sales forecaster's prediction to describe a normal probability distribution that can be used to approximate the demand distribution. Sketch the distribution and show its mean and standard deviation.
2. Compute the probability of a stock-out for the order quantities suggested by members of the management team.
3. Compute the projected profit for the order quantities suggested by the management team under three scenarios: worst case in which sales = 10,000 units, most likely case in which sales = 20,000 units, and best case in which sales = 30,000 units.
4. One of Specialty's managers felt that the profit potential was so great that the order quantity should have a 70% chance of meeting demand and only a 30% chance of any stock-outs. What quantity would be ordered under this policy, and what is the projected profit under the three sales scenarios?
5. Provide your own recommendation for an order quantity and note the associated profit projections. Provide a rationale for your recommendation.

Case Problem 2: Gebhardt Electronics

Gebhardt Electronics produces a wide variety of transformers that it sells directly to manufacturers of electronics equipment. For one component used in several models of its transformers, Gebhardt uses a 3-foot length of 0.20-mm diameter solid wire made of pure Oxygen-Free Electronic (OFE) copper. A flaw in the wire reduces its conductivity and increases the likelihood it will break, and this critical component is difficult to reach and repair after a transformer has been constructed. Therefore, Gebhardt wants to use primarily flawless lengths of wire in making this component. The company is willing to accept no more than a 1 in 20 chance that a three-foot length taken from a spool will be flawless. Gebhardt also occasionally uses smaller pieces of the same wire in the manufacture of other components, so the three-foot segments to be used for this component are essentially taken randomly from a long spool of 0.20-mm diameter solid OFE copper wire.

Gebhardt is now considering a new supplier for copper wire. This supplier claims that its spools of 0.20-mm diameter solid OFE copper wire average 50 inches between flaws. Gebhardt now must determine whether the new supply will be satisfactory if the supplier's claim is valid. **LO 7, 8**

Managerial Report

In making this assessment for Gebhardt Electronics, consider the following three questions:

1. If the new supplier does provide spools of 0.20-mm solid OFE copper wire that average 50 inches between flaws, how is the length of wire between two consecutive flaws distributed?
2. Using the probability distribution you identified in (1), what is the probability that Gebhardt's criteria will be met (i.e., a 1 in 20 chance that a randomly selected three-foot segment of wire provided by the new supplier will be flawless)?
3. In inches, what is the minimum mean length between consecutive flaws that would result in satisfaction of Gebhardt's criteria?
4. In inches, what is the minimum mean length between consecutive flaws that would result in a 1 in 100 chance that a randomly selected three-foot segment of wire provided by the new supplier will be flawless?

Chapter 7

Sampling and Sampling Distributions

Contents

Statistics in Practice:
The Food and Agriculture Organization

7.1 The Electronics Associates Sampling Problem

7.2 Selecting a Sample
Sampling from a Finite Population
Sampling from an Infinite Population

7.3 Point Estimation
Practical Advice

7.4 Introduction to Sampling Distributions

7.5 Sampling Distribution of $\bar{x}$
Expected Value of $\bar{x}$
Standard Deviation of $\bar{x}$
Form of the Sampling Distribution of $\bar{x}$
Sampling Distribution of $\bar{x}$ for the EAI Problem
Practical Value of the Sampling Distribution of $\bar{x}$
Relationship Between the Sample Size and the Sampling Distribution of $\bar{x}$

7.6 Sampling Distribution of $\bar{p}$
Expected Value of $\bar{p}$
Standard Deviation of $\bar{p}$
Form of the Sampling Distribution of $\bar{p}$
Practical Value of the Sampling Distribution of $\bar{p}$

7.7 Other Sampling Methods
Stratified Random Sampling
Cluster Sampling
Systematic Sampling
Convenience Sampling
Judgment Sampling

7.8 Practical Advice: Big Data and Errors in Sampling
Sampling Error
Nonsampling Error
Big Data
Understanding What Big Data Is
Implications of Big Data for Sampling Error

Summary 365
Glossary 365
Key Formulas 366
Supplementary Exercises 367
Case Problem 1: Marion Dairies 370
Case Problem 2: Profitability of Small Restaurants 371

Available in the Cengage eBook:
Appendix: Random Sampling with JMP
Appendix: Random Sampling with R

Learning Objectives

After completing this chapter, you will be able to

LO 1 Select a simple random sample from a finite population.

LO 2 Identify when a sample is being drawn from a finite or an infinite population and explain how to construct a corresponding frame.

LO 3 Use sample data to calculate the point estimate of the population mean.

LO 4 Use sample data to calculate the point estimate of the population standard deviation.

LO 5 Use sample data to calculate the point estimate of the population proportion.

LO 6 Calculate $\sigma_{\bar{x}}$, the standard deviation of the sample mean, for a sample of size n taken from a population with a known mean μ and standard deviation σ, and use the finite population correction factor when appropriate.

LO 7 Describe and explain the distribution form and parameters of the sampling distribution of the sample mean for a sample of size n taken from a population with a known mean μ and standard deviation σ.

LO 8 Use the sampling distribution of the sample mean to calculate the probability the sample mean will fall between two specified values.

LO 9 Calculate $\sigma_{\bar{p}}$, the standard error of the proportion, for a sample of size n taken from a population with a known proportion p.

LO 10 Describe and explain the distribution form and parameters of the sampling distribution of the sample proportion for a sample of size n taken from a population with a known proportion p.

LO 11 Use the sampling distribution of the sample proportion to calculate the probability the sample proportion will fall between two specified values.

Statistics in Practice

The Food and Agriculture Organization

Rome, Italy

The Food and Agriculture Organization (FAO) is a specialized agency of the United Nations that leads international efforts to achieve food security and ensure that people have regular access to sufficient high-quality food to lead active, healthy lives. The FAO includes over 190 member states and the organization is active in over 130 countries worldwide.

As part of its mission, the FAO engages in national forest assessments that require it to gather information that is useful in efforts to fight deforestation and the resulting land degradation (which reduces a nation's ability to grow food crops). These national forest assessments require reliable and accurate information about a nation's timberlands and forests. What is the present volume in the forests? What is the past growth of the forests? What is the projected future growth of the forests? With answers to these important questions, the FAO can assess the conditions of a nation's forest inventory, assist the nation in developing strategies and plans for the future (including long-term planting and harvesting schedules for the trees), and slow or eliminate deforestation and land degradation.

Random sampling of its forest holdings enables the FAO assist nations in the management of their forest inventories. Robert Crum/Shutterstock.com

The FAO uses a cluster sampling methodology to obtain the information it needs about a nation's vast forest holdings. Once the forest population is defined, it is divided into plots of a prespecified size and shape and the variables to be measured are identified. A random sample of these plots is selected, and measurements are taken from each selected plot.

The use of cluster sampling reduces the travel required for data collection while still providing a sample that enables the FAO to obtain national estimates of the total area of forest categorized into various forest types and conditions. The FAO also collects the wood volume and distribution of trees by species and size, estimates of changes in forest attributes, and indicators of biodiversity. The sampling plan further allows the FAO to obtain sufficiently precise estimates for selected geographic regions, collect sufficient information to satisfy international reporting requirements, and achieve an acceptable balance between cost and precision.

In this chapter, you will learn about various random sampling (including cluster sampling) and the sample selection process. In addition, you will learn how statistics such as the sample mean and sample proportion are used to estimate the population mean and population proportion. The important concept of sampling distribution is also introduced.

McRoberts, R.E., Tomppo, E.O., Czaplewski, R.L. "Sampling Designs for National Forest Assessments," Food and Agriculture Organization of the United Nations, http://www.fao.org/forestry/44859-02cf95ef26dfdcb86c6be2720f8b938a8.pdf.

In Chapter 1, we presented the following definitions of an element, a population, and a sample.

- An *element* is the entity on which data are collected.
- A *population* is the collection of all the elements of interest.
- A *sample* is a subset of the population.

The reason we select a sample is to collect data to make an inference and answer research questions about a population.

Let us begin by citing two examples in which sampling was used to answer a research question about a population.

1. Members of a political party in Texas were considering supporting a particular candidate for election to the U.S. Senate, and party leaders wanted to estimate the proportion of registered voters in the state favoring the candidate. A sample of 400 registered voters in Texas was selected and 160 of the 400 voters indicated a preference for the candidate. Thus, an estimate of the proportion of the population of registered voters favoring the candidate is $160/400 = 0.40$.
2. A tire manufacturer is considering producing a new tire designed to provide an increase in mileage over the firm's current line of tires. To estimate the mean useful life of the new tires, the manufacturer produced a sample of 120 tires for testing. The test results provided a sample mean of 36,500 miles. Hence, an estimate of the mean useful life for the population of new tires was 36,500 miles.

A sample mean provides an estimate of a population mean, and a sample proportion provides an estimate of a population proportion. With estimates such as these, some estimation error can be expected. This chapter provides the basis for determining how large that error might be.

It is important to realize that sample results provide only *estimates* of the values of the corresponding population characteristics. We do not expect exactly 0.40, or 40%, of the population of registered voters to favor the candidate, nor do we expect the sample mean of 36,500 miles to exactly equal the mean mileage for the population of all new tires produced. The reason is simply that the sample contains only a portion of the population. Some sampling error is to be expected. With proper sampling methods, the sample results will provide "good" estimates of the population parameters. But how good can we expect the sample results to be? Fortunately, statistical procedures are available for answering this question.

Let us define some of the terms used in sampling. The **sampled population** is the population from which the sample is drawn, and a **frame** is a list of the elements from which the sample will be selected. In the first example, the sampled population is all registered voters in Texas, and the frame is a list of all the registered voters in Texas. Because the number of registered voters in Texas is a finite number, the first example is an illustration of sampling from a finite population. In Section 7.2, we discuss how a simple random sample can be selected when sampling from a finite population.

The sampled population for the tire mileage example is more difficult to define because the sample of 120 tires was obtained from a production process at a particular point in time. We can think of the sampled population as the conceptual population of all the tires that could have been made by the production process at that particular point in time. In this sense, the sampled population is considered infinite, making it impossible to construct a frame from which to draw the sample. In Section 7.2, we discuss how to select a random sample in such a situation.

In this chapter, we show how simple random sampling can be used to select a sample from a finite population and describe how a random sample can be taken from an infinite population that is generated by an ongoing process. We then show how data obtained from a sample can be used to compute estimates of a population mean, a population standard deviation, and a population proportion. In addition, we introduce the important concept of a sampling distribution. As we will show, knowledge of the appropriate sampling distribution enables us to make statements about how close the sample estimates are to the corresponding population parameters. In Section 7.7, we discuss some alternatives to simple random sampling that are often employed in practice. In the last section, we discuss sampling and nonsampling error, and how these relate to large samples.

7.1 The Electronics Associates Sampling Problem

The director of personnel for Electronics Associates, Inc. (EAI) has been assigned the task of developing a profile of the company's 2,500 employees. The characteristics to be identified include the mean annual salary for the employees and the proportion of employees having completed the company's management training program.

DATA*file*
eai

Using the 2,500 employees as the population for this study, we can find the annual salary and the training program status for each individual by referring to the firm's personnel records. The data set containing this information for all 2,500 employees in the population is in the file *eai*.

Using the EAI data and the formulas presented in Chapter 3, we compute the population mean and the population standard deviation for the annual salary data.

$$\text{Population mean: } \mu = \$71{,}800$$

$$\text{Population standard deviation: } \sigma = \$4{,}000$$

The data for the training program status show that 1,500 of the 2,500 employees completed the training program.

Numerical characteristics of a population are called **parameters**. Letting p denote the proportion of the population that completed the training program, we see that $p = 1{,}500/2{,}500 = 0.60$. The population mean annual salary ($\mu = \$71{,}800$), the population standard deviation of annual salary ($\sigma = \$4{,}000$), and the population proportion that completed the training program ($p = 0.60$) are parameters of the population of EAI employees.

Often the cost of collecting information from a sample is substantially less than from a population, especially when personal interviews must be conducted to collect the information.

Now, suppose that the necessary information on all the EAI employees was not readily available in the company's database. The question we now consider is how the firm's director of personnel can obtain estimates of the population parameters by using a sample of employees rather than all 2,500 employees in the population. Suppose that a sample of 30 employees will be used. Clearly, the time and the cost of developing a profile would be substantially less for 30 employees than for the entire population. If the personnel director could be assured that a sample of 30 employees would provide adequate information about the population of 2,500 employees, working with a sample would be preferable to working with the entire population. Let us explore the possibility of using a sample for the EAI study by first considering how we can identify a sample of 30 employees.

7.2 Selecting a Sample

In this section we describe how to select a sample. We first describe how to sample from a finite population and then describe how to select a sample from an infinite population.

Sampling from a Finite Population

Statisticians recommend selecting a probability sample when sampling from a finite population because a probability sample allows them to make valid statistical inferences about the population. The simplest type of probability sample is one in which each sample of size n has the same probability of being selected. It is called a simple random sample. A simple random sample of size n from a finite population of size N is defined as follows.

Simple Random Sample (Finite Population)

A **simple random sample** of size n from a finite population of size N is a sample selected such that each possible sample of size n has the same probability of being selected.

The random numbers generated using Excel's RAND function follow a uniform probability distribution between 0 and 1.

The procedures used to select a simple random sample from a finite population are based upon the use of random numbers. We can use Excel's RAND function to generate a random number between 0 and 1 by entering the formula =*RAND()* into any cell in a worksheet. The number generated is called a random number because the mathematical procedure used by the RAND function guarantees that every number between 0 and 1 has the same probability of being selected. Let us see how these random numbers can be used to select a simple random sample.

Our procedure for selecting a simple random sample of size n from a population of size N involves two steps.

Step 1. Assign a random number to each element of the population.
Step 2. Select the n elements corresponding to the n smallest random numbers.

Because each set of n elements in the population has the same probability of being assigned the n smallest random numbers, each set of n elements has the same probability of being selected for the sample. If we select the sample using this two-step procedure, every sample of size n has the same probability of being selected; thus, the sample selected satisfies the definition of a simple random sample.

Let us consider an example involving selecting a simple random sample of size $n = 5$ from a population of size $N = 15$. Table 7.1 contains a list of the 15 teams in the 2019 National Baseball League. Suppose we want to select a simple random sample of five teams to conduct in-depth interviews about how they manage their minor league franchises.

Step 1 of our simple random sampling procedure requires that we assign a random number to each of the 15 teams in the population. Figure 7.1 shows a worksheet used to generate a random number corresponding to each of the 15 teams in the population. The names of the baseball teams are in column A, and the random numbers generated are in column B. From the formula worksheet in the background we see that the formula =RAND() has been entered in cells B2:B16 to generate the random numbers between 0 and 1. From the value worksheet in the foreground we see that Arizona is assigned the random number 0.850862, Atlanta has been assigned the random number 0.706245, and so on.

Table 7.1 2019 National Baseball League Teams

Arizona	Los Angeles	Pittsburgh
Atlanta	Miami	San Diego
Chicago	Milwaukee	San Francisco
Cincinnati	New York	St. Louis
Colorado	Philadelphia	Washington

Figure 7.1 Worksheet Used to Generate a Random Number Corresponding to Each Team

	A	B	C
1	**Team**	**Random Numbers**	
2	Arizona	=RAND()	
3	Atlanta	=RAND()	
4	Chicago	=RAND()	
5	Cincinnati	=RAND()	
6	Colorado	=RAND()	
7	Los Angeles	=RAND()	
8	Miami	=RAND()	
9	Milwaukee	=RAND()	
10	New York	=RAND()	
11	Philadelphia	=RAND()	
12	Pittsburgh	=RAND()	
13	San Diego	=RAND()	
14	San Francisco	=RAND()	
15	St. Louis	=RAND()	
16	Washington	=RAND()	
17			
18			

	A	B	C
1	**Team**	**Random Numbers**	
2	Arizona	0.850862	
3	Atlanta	0.706245	
4	Chicago	0.724789	
5	Cincinnati	0.614784	
6	Colorado	0.553815	
7	Los Angeles	0.857324	
8	Miami	0.179123	
9	Milwaukee	0.525636	
10	New York	0.471490	
11	Philadelphia	0.523103	
12	Pittsburgh	0.851552	
13	San Diego	0.806185	
14	San Francisco	0.327713	
15	St. Louis	0.374168	
16	Washington	0.066942	
17			
18			

DATA*file*
nationalleague

The second step is to select the five teams corresponding to the five smallest random numbers as our sample. Looking through the random numbers in Figure 7.1, we see that the team corresponding to the smallest random number (0.066942) is Washington, and that the four teams corresponding to the next four smallest random numbers are Miami, San Francisco, St. Louis, and New York. Thus, these five teams make up the simple random sample.

Searching through the list of random numbers in Figure 7.1 to find the five smallest random numbers is tedious, and it is easy to make mistakes. Excel's Sort procedure simplifies this step. We illustrate by sorting the list of baseball teams in Figure 7.1 to find the five teams corresponding to the five smallest random numbers. Refer to the foreground worksheet in Figure 7.1 as we describe the steps involved.

Step 1. Select any cell in the range B2:B16
Step 2. Click the **Home** tab on the Ribbon
Step 3. In the **Editing** group, click **Sort & Filter**
Step 4. Choose **Sort Smallest to Largest**

Figure 7.2 Using Excel's Sort Procedure to Select the Simple Random Sample of Five Teams

	A	B	C
1	Team	Random Numbers	
2	Washington	0.066942	
3	Miami	0.179123	
4	San Francisco	0.327713	
5	St. Louis	0.374168	
6	New York	0.471490	
7	Philadelphia	0.523103	
8	Milwaukee	0.525636	
9	Colorado	0.553815	
10	Cincinnati	0.614784	
11	Atlanta	0.706245	
12	Chicago	0.724789	
13	San Diego	0.806185	
14	Arizona	0.850862	
15	Pittsburgh	0.851552	
16	Los Angeles	0.857324	
17			
18			

After completing these steps we obtain the worksheet shown in Figure 7.2.[1] The teams listed in rows 2–6 are the ones corresponding to the smallest five random numbers; they are our simple random sample. Note that the random numbers shown in Figure 7.2 are in ascending order, and that the teams are not in their original order. For instance, Washington is the last team listed in Figure 7.1, but it is the first team selected in the simple random sample. Miami, the second team in our sample, is the seventh team in the original list, and so on.

The Excel Sort procedure for identifying the employees associated with the 30 smallest random numbers is especially valuable with such a large population.

We now use this simple random sampling procedure to select a simple random sample of 30 EAI employees from the population of 2,500 EAI employees. We begin by generating 2,500 random numbers, one for each employee in the population. Then we select the 30 employees corresponding to the 30 smallest random numbers as our sample. Refer to Figure 7.3 as we describe the steps involved.

Enter/Access Data: Open the file *eai*. The first three columns of the worksheet in the background show the annual salary data and training program status for the first 30 employees in the population of 2,500 EAI employees. (The complete worksheet contains all 2,500 employees.)

Enter Functions and Formulas: In the background worksheet, the label **Random Numbers** has been entered in cell D1 and the formula =*RAND()* has been entered in cells D2:D2501 to generate a random number between 0 and 1 for each of the 2,500 EAI employees. The random number generated for the first employee is 0.820711, the random number generated for the second employee is 0.292880, and so on.

Apply Tools: All that remains is to find the employees associated with the 30 smallest random numbers. To do so, we sort the data in columns A through D into ascending order by the random numbers in column D.

Step 1. Select any cell in the range D2:D2501
Step 2. Click the **Home** tab on the Ribbon

[1]In order to show the random numbers from Figure 7.1 in ascending order in this worksheet, we turned off the automatic recalculation option prior to sorting for illustrative purposes. If the recalculation option were not turned off, a new set of random numbers would have been generated when the sort was completed.

Step 3. In the **Editing** group, click **Sort & Filter**
Step 4. Choose **Sort Smallest to Largest**

After completing these steps we obtain the worksheet shown in the foreground of Figure 7.3. The employees listed in rows 2–31 are the ones corresponding to the smallest 30 random numbers that were generated. Hence, this group of 30 employees is a simple random sample. Note that the random numbers shown in the foreground of Figure 7.3 are in ascending order, and that the employees are not in their original order. For instance, employee 648 in the population is associated with the smallest random number and is the

Figure 7.3 Using Excel to Select a Simple Random Sample

	A	B	C	D	E	F	G
1	Manager	Annual Salary	Training Program	Random Numbers			
2	1	75769.50	No	0.820711			
3	2	70823.00	Yes	0.292880			
4	3	68408.20	No	0.811446			
5	4	69787.50	No	0.243200			
6	5	72801.60	Yes	0.399899			
7	6	71767.70	No	0.070882			
8	7	78346.60	Yes	0.635444			
9	8	66670.20	No	0.586243			
10	9	70246.80	Yes	0.532798			
11	10	71255.00	No	0.837563			
12	11	72546.60	No	0.263176			
13	12	69512.50	Yes	0.889819			
14	13	71753.00	Yes	0.006145			
15	14	73547.10	No	0.848728			
16	15	68052.20	No	0.570196			
17	16	64652.50	Yes	0.393356			
18	17	71764.90	Yes	0.742566			
19	18	65187.80	Yes	0.693885			
20	19	69867.50	Yes	0.526144			
21	20	73706.30	Yes	0.697304			
22	21	72039.50	Yes	0.244056			
23	22	72973.60	No	0.532791			
24	23	73372.50	No	0.615720			
25	24	74592.00	Yes	0.799402			
26	25	75738.10	Yes	0.842918			
27	26	72975.10	Yes	0.021609			
28	27	72386.20	Yes	0.878803			
29	28	71051.60	Yes	0.904844			
30	29	72095.60	Yes	0.016513			
31	30	64956.50	No	0.474088			

The formula in cells D2:D2501 is =RAND().

	A	B	C	D	E
1	Manager	Annual Salary	Training Program	Random Numbers	
2	648	67809.80	No	0.000157	
3	1728	75439.50	Yes	0.000303	
4	1488	74614.80	Yes	0.000674	
5	2232	70934.50	Yes	0.000684	
6	996	75234.90	No	0.000969	
7	2054	80352.80	Yes	0.001075	
8	359	75698.70	No	0.001179	
9	1409	73007.30	Yes	0.001477	
10	1627	71326.50	No	0.001553	
11	297	70811.70	No	0.001733	
12	1430	68584.60	No	0.002515	
13	1411	73263.90	Yes	0.002531	
14	2463	68063.70	No	0.002888	
15	972	71905.10	No	0.002965	
16	753	71382.60	No	0.003297	
17	1633	70164.20	No	0.004987	
18	277	65401.50	Yes	0.005049	
19	1255	66543.70	No	0.005159	
20	414	71258.10	Yes	0.005606	
21	13	71753.00	Yes	0.006145	
22	811	67616.70	No	0.006642	
23	739	78524.20	Yes	0.007294	
24	1694	70673.40	Yes	0.007454	
25	353	67137.30	Yes	0.007551	
26	2248	74293.30	Yes	0.008297	
27	1490	71873.30	No	0.008908	
28	408	65962.40	Yes	0.009536	
29	2429	73279.80	Yes	0.009569	
30	1052	71175.40	No	0.009628	
31	404	77161.60	Yes	0.009842	

Note: Rows 32-2501 are not shown.

first element in the sample, and employee 13 in the population (see row 14 of the background worksheet) has been included as the 20th observation in the sample (row 21 of the foreground worksheet).

Sampling from an Infinite Population

Sometimes we want to select a sample from a population, but the population is infinitely large or the elements of the population are being generated by an ongoing process for which there is no limit on the number of elements that can be generated. Thus, it is not possible to develop a list of all the elements in the population. This is considered the infinite population case. With an infinite population, we cannot select a simple random sample because we cannot construct a frame consisting of all the elements. In the infinite population case, statisticians recommend selecting what is called a random sample.

Random Sample (Infinite Population)

A **random sample** of size *n* from an infinite population is a sample selected such that the following conditions are satisfied.

1. Each element selected comes from the same population.
2. Each element is selected independently.

Care and judgment must be exercised in implementing the selection process for obtaining a random sample from an infinite population. Each case may require a different selection procedure. Let us consider two examples to see what we mean by the conditions: (1) Each element selected comes from the same population and (2) each element is selected independently.

A common quality control application involves a production process where there is no limit on the number of elements that can be produced. The conceptual population we are sampling from is all the elements that could be produced (not just the ones that are produced) by the ongoing production process. Because we cannot develop a list of all the elements that could be produced, the population is considered infinite. To be more specific, let us consider a production line designed to fill boxes of a breakfast cereal with a mean weight of 24 ounces of breakfast cereal per box. Samples of 12 boxes filled by this process are periodically selected by a quality control inspector to determine if the process is operating properly or if, perhaps, a machine malfunction has caused the process to begin underfilling or overfilling the boxes.

With a production operation such as this, the biggest concern in selecting a random sample is to make sure that condition 1 (the sampled elements are selected from the same population) is satisfied. To ensure that this condition is satisfied, the boxes must be selected at approximately the same point in time. This way the inspector avoids the possibility of selecting some boxes when the process is operating properly and other boxes when the process is not operating properly and is underfilling or overfilling the boxes. With a production process such as this, the second condition (each element is selected independently) is satisfied by designing the production process so that each box of cereal is filled independently. With this assumption, the quality control inspector only needs to worry about satisfying the same population condition.

As another example of selecting a random sample from an infinite population, consider the population of customers arriving at a fast-food restaurant. Suppose an employee is asked to select and interview a sample of customers in order to develop a profile of customers who visit the restaurant. The customer arrival process is ongoing and there is no way to obtain a list of all customers in the population. So, for practical purposes, the population for this ongoing process is considered infinite. As long as a sampling procedure is designed so that all the elements in the sample are customers of the restaurant and they are selected independently, a random sample will be obtained. In this case, the employee collecting the sample needs to select the sample from people who come into the restaurant and make a purchase to ensure that the same population condition is satisfied. If, for instance, the employee selected someone for the sample who came into the restaurant just to use the restroom, that person would not be a customer and the same population condition would be violated. So, as long as the interviewer selects the sample from people making a purchase at the restaurant, condition 1 is satisfied. Ensuring that the customers are selected independently can be more difficult.

The purpose of the second condition of the random sample selection procedure (each element is selected independently) is to prevent selection bias. In this case, selection bias would occur if the interviewer were free to select customers for the sample arbitrarily. The interviewer might feel more comfortable selecting customers in a particular age group and might avoid customers in other age groups. Selection bias would also occur if the interviewer selected a group of five customers who entered the restaurant together and asked all of them to participate in the sample. Such a group of customers would be likely to exhibit similar characteristics, which might provide misleading information about the population of customers. Selection bias such as this can be avoided by ensuring that the selection of a particular customer does not influence the selection of any other customer. In other words, the elements (customers) are selected independently.

McDonald's, the fast-food restaurant leader, implemented a random sampling procedure for this situation. The sampling procedure was based on the fact that some customers presented discount coupons. Whenever a customer presented a discount coupon, the next customer served was asked to complete a customer profile questionnaire. Because arriving customers presented discount coupons randomly and independently of other customers, this sampling procedure ensured that customers were selected independently. As a result, the sample satisfied the requirements of a random sample from an infinite population.

Situations involving sampling from an infinite population are usually associated with a process that operates over time. Examples include parts being manufactured on a production line, repeated experimental trials in a laboratory, transactions occurring at a bank, telephone calls arriving at a technical support center, and customers entering a retail store. In each case, the situation may be viewed as a process that generates elements from an infinite population. As long as the sampled elements are selected from the same population and are selected independently, the sample is considered a random sample from an infinite population.

Notes + Comments

1. In this section, we have been careful to define two types of samples: a simple random sample from a finite population and a random sample from an infinite population. In the remainder of the text, we will generally refer to both of these as either a *random sample* or simply a *sample*. We will not make a distinction of the sample being a "simple" random sample unless it is necessary for the exercise or discussion.
2. Statisticians who specialize in sample surveys from finite populations use sampling methods that provide probability samples. With a probability sample, each possible sample has a known probability of selection and a random process is used to select the elements for the sample. Simple random sampling is one of these methods. In Section 7.7, we describe some other probability sampling methods: stratified random sampling, cluster sampling, and systematic sampling. We use the term *simple* in simple random sampling to clarify that this is the probability sampling method that assures each sample of size n has the same probability of being selected.
3. The number of different simple random samples of size n that can be selected from a finite population of size N is

$$\frac{N!}{n!(N-n)!}$$

In this formula, $N!$ and $n!$ are the factorial formulas discussed in Chapter 4. For the EAI problem with $N = 2{,}500$ and $n = 30$, this expression can be used to show that approximately 2.75×10^{69} different simple random samples of 30 EAI employees can be obtained.

Exercises

Methods

1. Consider a finite population with five elements labeled A, B, C, D, and E. Ten possible simple random samples of size 2 can be selected. **LO 1**
   a. List the 10 samples beginning with AB, AC, and so on.
   b. Using simple random sampling, what is the probability that each sample of size 2 is selected?
   c. Suppose we use Excel's RAND function to assign random numbers to the five elements: A (0.7266), B (0.0476), C (0.2459), D (0.0957), E (0.9408). List the simple random sample of size 2 that will be selected by using these random numbers.
2. Assume a finite population has 10 elements. Number the elements from 1 to 10 and use the following 10 random numbers to select a sample of size 4. **LO 1**

0.7545 0.0936 0.0341 0.3242 0.1449 0.9060 0.2420 0.9773 0.5428 0.0729

Applications

3. **Randomly Sampling American League Teams.** The 2019 American League consists of 15 baseball teams. Suppose a sample of five teams is to be selected to conduct player interviews. The following table lists the 15 teams and the random numbers assigned by Excel's RAND function. Use these random numbers to select a sample of size 5. **LO 1**

DATA*file*
americanleague

Team	Random Number	Team	Random Number	Team	Random Number
Baltimore	0.578370	Chicago	0.562178	Anaheim	0.895267
Boston	0.290197	Cleveland	0.960271	Houston	0.657999
New York	0.178624	Detroit	0.253574	Oakland	0.288287
Tampa Bay	0.867778	Kansas City	0.326836	Seattle	0.839071
Toronto	0.965807	Minnesota	0.811810	Texas	0.500879

4. **Randomly Sampling PGA Golfers.** The U.S. Golf Association has instituted a ban on long and belly putters. This has caused a great deal of controversy among both amateur golfers and members of the Professional Golf Association (PGA). Shown below are the names of the top 10 finishers in the recent PGA Tour RSM Classic golf tournament. (Note that two golfers tied for fourth place and four golfers tied for seventh place.)

1. Charles Howell III	6. Cameron Champ
2. Patrick Rodgers	7. Zach Johnson
3. Webb Simpson	8. Peter Uihlein
4. Luke List	9. Chase Wright
5. Ryan Blaum	10. Kevin Kisner

Select a simple random sample of three of these players to assess their opinions on the use of long and belly putters. **LO 1**

DATA*file*
eai

5. **Randomly Sampling EAI Employees.** In this section we used a two-step procedure to select a simple random sample of 30 EAI employees. Use this procedure to select a simple random sample of 50 EAI employees. **LO 1**
6. **Finite vs. Infinite Populations.** Indicate which of the following situations involve sampling from a finite population and which involve sampling from an infinite

population. In cases where the sampled population is finite, describe how you would construct a frame. **LO 2**

a. Select a sample of licensed drivers in the state of New York.
b. Select a sample of boxes of cereal off the production line for the Breakfast Choice Company.
c. Select a sample of cars crossing the Golden Gate Bridge on a typical weekday.
d. Select a sample of students in a statistics course at Indiana University.
e. Select a sample of the orders being processed by a mail-order firm.

7.3 Point Estimation

Now that we have described how to select a simple random sample, let us return to the EAI problem. A simple random sample of 30 employees and the corresponding data on annual salary and management training program participation are as shown in Table 7.2. The notation x_1, x_2, and so on is used to denote the annual salary of the first employee in the sample, the annual salary of the second employee in the sample, and so on. Participation in the management training program is indicated by Yes in the management training program column.

To estimate the value of a population parameter, we compute a corresponding characteristic of the sample, referred to as a **sample statistic**. For example, to estimate the population mean μ and the population standard deviation σ for the annual salary of EAI employees, we use the data in Table 7.2 to calculate the corresponding sample statistics: the sample mean and the sample standard deviation s. Using the formulas for a sample mean and a sample standard deviation presented in Chapter 3, the sample mean is

$$\bar{x} = \frac{\Sigma x_i}{n} = \frac{2{,}154{,}420}{30} = \$71{,}814$$

and the sample standard deviation is

$$s = \sqrt{\frac{\Sigma(x_i - \bar{x})^2}{n - 1}} = \sqrt{\frac{325{,}009{,}260}{29}} = \$3{,}348$$

Table 7.2 Annual Salary and Training Program Status for a Simple Random Sample of 30 EAI Managers

Annual Salary ($)	Management Training Program	Annual Salary ($)	Management Training Program
x_1 = 69,094.30	Yes	x_{16} = 71,766.00	Yes
x_2 = 73,263.90	Yes	x_{17} = 72,541.30	No
x_3 = 69,643.50	Yes	x_{18} = 64,980.00	Yes
x_4 = 69,894.90	Yes	x_{19} = 71,932.60	Yes
x_5 = 67,621.60	No	x_{20} = 72,973.00	Yes
x_6 = 75,924.00	Yes	x_{21} = 65,120.90	Yes
x_7 = 69,092.30	Yes	x_{22} = 71,753.00	Yes
x_8 = 71,404.40	Yes	x_{23} = 74,391.80	No
x_9 = 70,957.70	Yes	x_{24} = 70,164.20	No
x_{10} = 75,109.70	Yes	x_{25} = 72,973.60	No
x_{11} = 65,922.60	Yes	x_{26} = 70,241.30	No
x_{12} = 77,268.40	No	x_{27} = 72,793.90	No
x_{13} = 75,688.80	Yes	x_{28} = 70,979.40	Yes
x_{14} = 71,564.70	No	x_{29} = 75,860.90	Yes
x_{15} = 76,188.20	No	x_{30} = 77,309.10	No

To estimate p, the proportion of employees in the population who completed the management training program, we use the corresponding sample proportion $\bar{p}$. Let x denote the number of employees in the sample who completed the management training program. The data in Table 7.2 show that $x = 19$. Thus, with a sample size of $n = 30$, the sample proportion is

$$\bar{p} = \frac{x}{n} = \frac{19}{30} = 0.63$$

By making the preceding computations, we perform the statistical procedure called *point estimation*. We refer to the sample mean $\bar{x}$ as the **point estimator** of the population mean μ, the sample standard deviation s as the point estimator of the population standard deviation σ, and the sample proportion $\bar{p}$ as the point estimator of the population proportion p. The numerical value obtained for $\bar{x}$, s, or $\bar{p}$ is called the **point estimate**. Thus, for the simple random sample of 30 EAI employees shown in Table 7.2, $71,814 is the point estimate of μ, $3,348 is the point estimate of σ, and 0.63 is the point estimate of p. Table 7.3 summarizes the sample results and compares the point estimates to the actual values of the population parameters.

As is evident from Table 7.3, the point estimates differ somewhat from the corresponding population parameters. This difference is to be expected because a sample, and not a census of the entire population, is being used to develop the point estimates.

In Chapter 8, we discuss how to construct an interval estimate in order to provide information about how close the point estimate is to the population parameter.

Practical Advice

The subject matter of much of the rest of the book is concerned with statistical inference. Point estimation is a form of statistical inference. We use a sample statistic to make an inference about a population parameter. When making inferences about a population based on a sample, it is important to have a close correspondence between the sampled population and the target population. The **target population** is the population we want to make inferences about, while the sampled population is the population from which the sample is actually taken. In this section, we have described the process of drawing a simple random sample from the population of EAI employees and making point estimates of characteristics of that same population. So the sampled population and the target population are identical, which is the desired situation. But in other cases, it is not as easy to obtain a close correspondence between the sampled and target populations.

Consider the case of an amusement park selecting a sample of its customers to learn about characteristics such as age and time spent at the park. Suppose all the sample elements were selected on a day when park attendance was restricted to employees of a large company. Then the sampled population would be composed of employees of that company

Table 7.3 Summary of Point Estimates Obtained from a Simple Random Sample of 30 EAI Employees

Population Parameter	Parameter Value	Point Estimator	Point Estimate
μ = Population mean annual salary	$71,800	$\bar{x}$ = Sample mean annual salary	$71,814
σ = Population standard deviation for annual salary	$4,000	s = Sample standard deviation for annual salary	$3,348
p = Population proportion having completed the management training program	0.60	$\bar{p}$ = Sample proportion having completed the management training program	0.63

and members of their families. If the target population we wanted to make inferences about were typical park customers over a typical summer, then we might encounter a significant difference between the sampled population and the target population. In such a case, we would question the validity of the point estimates being made. Park management would be in the best position to know whether a sample taken on a particular day was likely to be representative of the target population.

In summary, whenever a sample is used to make inferences about a population, we should make sure that the study is designed so that the sampled population and the target population are in close agreement. Good judgment is a necessary ingredient of sound statistical practice.

Exercises

Methods

7. The following data are from a simple random sample. **LO 3, 4**

   5 8 10 7 10 14

   a. What is the point estimate of the population mean?
   b. What is the point estimate of the population standard deviation?

8. A survey question for a sample of 150 individuals yielded 75 Yes responses, 55 No responses, and 20 No Opinions. **LO 5**
   a. What is the point estimate of the proportion in the population who respond Yes?
   b. What is the point estimate of the proportion in the population who respond No?

Applications

9. **Monthly Sales Data.** A simple random sample of five months of sales data provided the following information. **LO 3, 4**

Month:	1	2	3	4	5
Units Sold:	94	100	85	94	92

   a. Develop a point estimate of the population mean number of units sold per month.
   b. Develop a point estimate of the population standard deviation.

DATA*file*
morningstar

10. **Morningstar Stock Data.** Morningstar publishes ratings data on 1208 company stocks. A sample of 40 of these stocks is contained in the file *morningstar*. Use the data set to answer the following questions. **LO 5**
    a. Develop a point estimate of the proportion of the stocks that receive Morningstar's highest rating of 5 stars.
    b. Develop a point estimate of the proportion of the Morningstar stocks that are rated Above Average with respect to business risk.
    c. Develop a point estimate of the proportion of the Morningstar stocks that are rated 2 stars or less.

11. **Rating Wines.** According to Wine-Searcher, wine critics generally use a wine-scoring scale to communicate their opinions on the relative quality of wines. Wine scores range from 0 to 100, with a score of 95–100 indicating a great wine, 90–94 indicating an outstanding wine, 85–89 indicating a very good wine, 80–84 indicating a good wine, 75–79 indicating a mediocre wine, and below 75 indicating that the wine is not recommended. Random ratings of a pinot noir recently produced by a newly established vineyard in 2018 follow. **LO 3, 4**

87	91	86	82	72	91
60	77	80	79	83	96

    a. Develop a point estimate of mean wine score for this pinot noir.
    b. Develop a point estimate of the standard deviation for wine scores received by this pinot noir.

12. **AARP Survey.** AARP is an interest group based in the United States that focuses on issues affecting adults age 50 and older. In a sample of 426 U.S. adults age 50 and older, AARP asked how important a variety of issues were in choosing whom to vote for in the most recent presidential election. **LO 5**
    a. What is the sampled population for this study?
    b. Social Security and Medicare were cited as "very important" by 350 respondents. Estimate the proportion of the population of U.S. adults age 50 and over who believe this issue is very important.
    c. Education was cited as "very important" by 74% of the respondents. Estimate the number of respondents who believe this issue is very important.
    d. Job Growth was cited as "very important" by 354 respondents. Estimate the proportion of U.S. adults age 50 and over who believe job growth is very important.
    e. What is the target population for the inferences being made in parts (b) and (d)? Is it the same as the sampled population you identified in part (a)? Suppose you later learn that the sample was restricted to members of the AARP. Would you still feel the inferences being made in parts (b) and (d) are valid? Why or why not?

13. **Attitudes Toward Automated Vehicles.** The American Automobile Association (AAA) annual automated vehicle survey includes a series of questions about automobile automation technology. The 1,010 interviews completed in the 2021 survey showed that 222 respondents feel manufacturers should focus on developing self-driving vehicles. In addition, 808 respondents want current vehicle safety systems (such as automatic emergency braking and lane keeping assistance) to work better, and 586 respondents want these systems in the next vehicle they purchase. **LO 5**
    a. Develop a point estimate of the proportion of respondents who feel manufacturers should focus on developing self-driving vehicles.
    b. Develop a point estimate of the proportion of respondents who want current vehicle safety systems (such as automatic emergency braking and lane keeping assistance) to work better.
    c. Develop a point estimate of the proportion of respondents who want current vehicle safety systems (such as automatic emergency braking and lane keeping assistance) in the next vehicle they purchase.

14. **Teen Attitudes on Social Media.** In 2018, the Pew Internet & American Life Project asked 743 teens aged 13 to 17 several questions about their attitudes toward social media. The results showed that 602 say social media makes them feel more connected to what is going on in their friends' lives; 513 say social media helps them interact with a more diverse group of people; and 275 feel pressure to post content that will get a lot of likes and comments. **LO 5**
    a. Develop a point estimate of the proportion of teens aged 13 to 17 who say social media makes them feel more connected to what is going on in their friends' lives.
    b. Develop a point estimate of the proportion of teens aged 13 to 17 who say social media helps them interact with a more diverse group of people.
    c. Develop a point estimate of the proportion of teens aged 13 to 17 who feel pressure to post content that will get a lot of likes and comments.

DATA*file*
eai

15. **Point Estimates for EAI Employees.** In this section we showed how a simple random sample of 30 EAI employees can be used to develop point estimates of the population mean annual salary, the population standard deviation for annual salary, and the population proportion having completed the management training program. **LO 3, 4, 5**
    a. Use Excel to select a simple random sample of 50 EAI employees.
    b. Develop a point estimate of the mean annual salary.
    c. Develop a point estimate of the population standard deviation for annual salary.
    d. Develop a point estimate of the population proportion having completed the management training program.

7.4 Introduction to Sampling Distributions

In the preceding section we said that the sample mean $\bar{x}$ is the point estimator of the population mean μ, and the sample proportion $\bar{p}$ is the point estimator of the population proportion p. For the simple random sample of 30 EAI employees shown in Table 7.2, the point estimate of μ is $\bar{x} = \$71{,}814$ and the point estimate of p is $\bar{p} = 0.63$. Suppose we select another simple random sample of 30 EAI employees and obtain the following point estimates:

$$\text{Sample mean: } \bar{x} = \$72{,}670$$
$$\text{Sample proportion: } \bar{p} = 0.70$$

Note that different values of $\bar{x}$ and $\bar{p}$ were obtained. Indeed, a second simple random sample of 30 EAI employees cannot be expected to provide the same point estimates as the first sample.

The ability to understand the material in subsequent chapters depends heavily on the ability to understand and use the sampling distributions presented in this chapter.

Now, suppose we repeat the process of selecting a simple random sample of 30 EAI employees over and over again, each time computing the values of $\bar{x}$ and $\bar{p}$. Table 7.4 contains a portion of the results obtained for 500 simple random samples, and Table 7.5 shows the frequency and relative frequency distributions for the 500 $\bar{x}$ values. Figure 7.4 shows the relative frequency histogram for the $\bar{x}$ values.

In Chapter 5, we defined a random variable as a numerical description of the outcome of an experiment. If we consider the process of selecting a simple random sample as an

Table 7.4 Values of $\bar{x}$ and $\bar{p}$ from 500 Simple Random Samples of 30 EAI Employees

Sample Number	Sample Mean ($\bar{x}$)	Sample Proportion ($\bar{p}$)
1	71,814	0.63
2	72,670	0.70
3	71,780	0.67
4	71,588	0.53
.	.	.
.	.	.
.	.	.
500	71,752	0.50

Table 7.5 Frequency and Relative Frequency Distributions of $\bar{x}$ from 500 Simple Random Samples of 30 EAI Employees

Mean Annual Salary ($)	Frequency	Relative Frequency
69,500.00–69,999.99	2	0.004
70,000.00–70,499.99	16	0.032
70,500.00–70,999.99	52	0.104
71,000.00–71,499.99	101	0.202
71,500.00–71,999.99	133	0.266
72,000.00–72,499.99	110	0.220
72,500.00–72,999.99	54	0.108
73,000.00–73,499.99	26	0.052
73,500.00–73,999.99	6	0.012
Totals	500	1.000

Figure 7.4 Relative Frequency Histogram of $\bar{x}$ Values from 500 Simple Random Samples of Size 30 Each

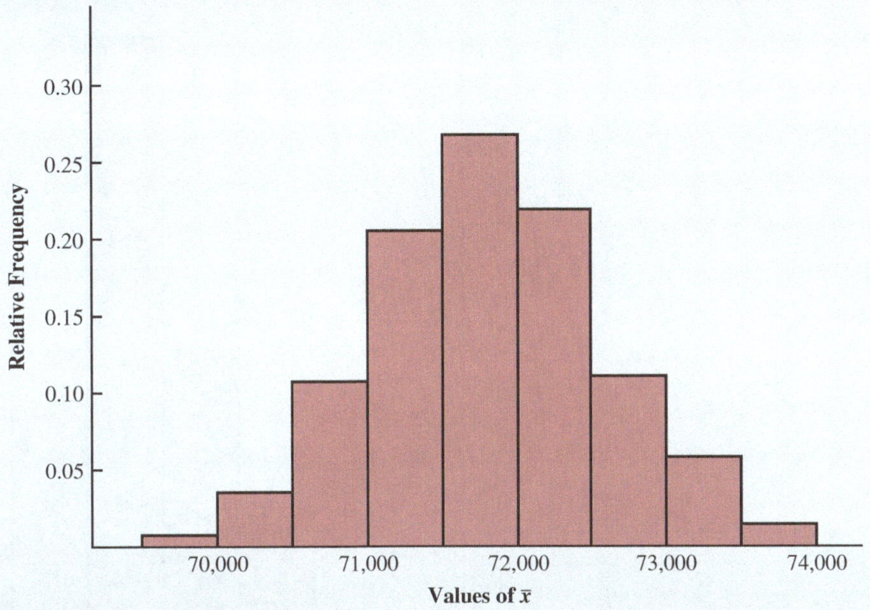

experiment, the sample mean $\bar{x}$ is the numerical description of the outcome of the experiment. Thus, the sample mean $\bar{x}$ is a random variable. As a result, just like other random variables, $\bar{x}$ has a mean or expected value, a standard deviation, and a probability distribution. Because the various possible values of $\bar{x}$ are the result of different simple random samples, the probability distribution of $\bar{x}$ is called the **sampling distribution** of $\bar{x}$. Knowledge of this sampling distribution and its properties will enable us to make probability statements about how close the sample mean $\bar{x}$ is to the population mean μ.

Let us return to Figure 7.4. We would need to enumerate every possible sample of 30 employees and compute each sample mean to completely determine the sampling distribution of $\bar{x}$. However, the histogram of 500 $\bar{x}$ values gives an approximation of this sampling distribution. From the approximation we observe the bell-shaped appearance of the distribution. We note that the largest concentration of the $\bar{x}$ values and the mean of the 500 $\bar{x}$ values is near the population mean $\mu = \$71,800$. We will describe the properties of the sampling distribution of $\bar{x}$ more fully in the next section.

The 500 values of the sample proportion $\bar{p}$ are summarized by the relative frequency histogram in Figure 7.5. As in the case of $\bar{x}$, $\bar{p}$ is a random variable. If every possible sample of size 30 were selected from the population and if a value of $\bar{p}$ were computed for each sample, the resulting probability distribution would be the sampling distribution of $\bar{p}$. The relative frequency histogram of the 500 sample values in Figure 7.5 provides a general idea of the appearance of the sampling distribution of $\bar{p}$.

In practice, we select only one simple random sample from the population. We repeated the sampling process 500 times in this section simply to illustrate that many different samples are possible and that the different samples generate a variety of values for the sample statistics $\bar{x}$ and $\bar{p}$. The probability distribution of any particular sample statistic is called the sampling distribution of the statistic. In Section 7.5, we discuss the characteristics of the sampling distribution of $\bar{x}$. In Section 7.6, we discuss the characteristics of the sampling distribution of $\bar{p}$.

Figure 7.5 Relative Frequency Histogram of $\bar{p}$ Values from 500 Simple Random Samples of Size 30 Each

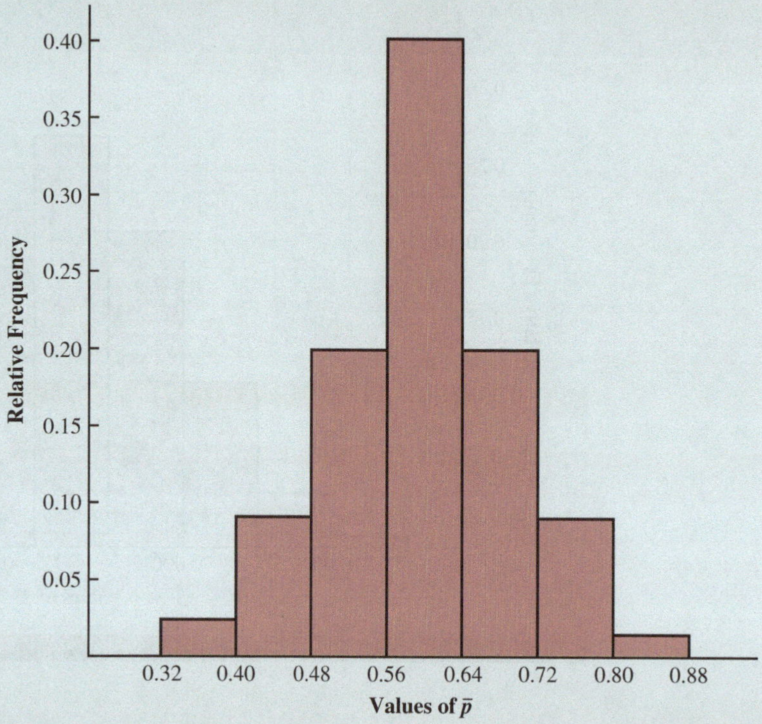

7.5 Sampling Distribution of $\bar{x}$

In the previous section we said that the sample mean $\bar{x}$ is a random variable and its probability distribution is called the sampling distribution of $\bar{x}$.

Sampling Distribution of $\bar{x}$

The sampling distribution of $\bar{x}$ is the probability distribution of all possible values of the sample mean $\bar{x}$.

This section describes the properties of the sampling distribution of $\bar{x}$. Just as with other probability distributions we studied, the sampling distribution of $\bar{x}$ has an expected value or mean, a standard deviation, and a characteristic shape or form. Let us begin by considering the mean of all possible $\bar{x}$ values, which is referred to as the expected value of $\bar{x}$.

Expected Value of $\bar{x}$

In the EAI sampling problem we saw that different simple random samples result in a variety of values for the sample mean $\bar{x}$. Because many different values of the random variable $\bar{x}$ are possible, we are often interested in the mean of all possible values of $\bar{x}$ that can be generated by the various simple random samples. The mean of the $\bar{x}$ random variable is the expected value of $\bar{x}$. Let $E(\bar{x})$ represent the expected value of $\bar{x}$ and μ represent the mean of the population from which we are selecting a simple random sample. It can be shown that with simple random sampling, $E(\bar{x})$ and μ are equal.

The expected value of $\bar{x}$ equals the mean of the population from which the sample is selected.

Expected Value of $\bar{x}$

$$E(\bar{x}) = \mu \tag{7.1}$$

where

$$E(\bar{x}) = \text{the expected value of } \bar{x}$$
$$\mu = \text{the population mean}$$

This result shows that with simple random sampling, the expected value or mean of the sampling distribution of $\bar{x}$ is equal to the mean of the population. In Section 7.1, we saw that the mean annual salary for the population of EAI employees is $\mu = \$71{,}800$. Thus, according to equation (7.1), the mean of all possible sample means for the EAI study is also \$71,800.

When the expected value of a point estimator equals the population parameter, we say the point estimator is **unbiased**. Thus, equation (7.1) shows that $\bar{x}$ is an unbiased estimator of the population mean μ.

Standard Deviation of $\bar{x}$

Let us define the standard deviation of the sampling distribution of $\bar{x}$. We will use the following notation.

$$\sigma_{\bar{x}} = \text{the standard deviation of } \bar{x}$$
$$\sigma = \text{the standard deviation of the population}$$
$$n = \text{the sample size}$$
$$N = \text{the population size}$$

It can be shown that the formula for the standard deviation of $\bar{x}$ depends on whether the population is finite or infinite. The two formulas for the standard deviation of $\bar{x}$ follow.

Standard Deviation of $\bar{x}$

Finite Population	Infinite Population	
$\sigma_{\bar{x}} = \sqrt{\frac{N-n}{N-1}}\left(\frac{\sigma}{\sqrt{n}}\right)$	$\sigma_{\bar{x}} = \frac{\sigma}{\sqrt{n}}$	**(7.2)**

In comparing the two formulas in equation (7.2), we see that the factor $\sqrt{(N-n)/(N-1)}$ is required for the finite population case but not for the infinite population case. This factor is commonly referred to as the **finite population correction factor**. In many practical sampling situations, we find that the population involved, although finite, is "large," whereas the sample size is relatively "small." In such cases the finite population correction factor $\sqrt{(N-n)/(N-1)}$ is close to 1. As a result, the difference between the values of the standard deviation of $\bar{x}$ for the finite and infinite population cases becomes negligible. Then, $\sigma_{\bar{x}} = \sigma/\sqrt{n}$ becomes a good approximation to the standard deviation of $\bar{x}$ even though the population is finite. This observation leads to the following general guideline, or rule of thumb, for computing the standard deviation of $\bar{x}$.

Use the Following Expression to Compute the Standard Deviation of $\bar{x}$

$$\sigma_{\bar{x}} = \frac{\sigma}{\sqrt{n}} \tag{7.3}$$

whenever

1. The population is infinite; or
2. The population is finite *and* the sample size is less than or equal to 5% of the population size; that is, $n/N \le 0.05$.

In cases where $n/N > 0.05$, the finite population version of formula (7.2) should be used in the computation of $\sigma_{\bar{x}}$. Unless otherwise noted, throughout the text we will assume that the population size is "large," $n/N \le 0.05$, and expression (7.3) can be used to compute $\sigma_{\bar{x}}$.

The term standard error is used throughout statistical inference to refer to the standard deviation of a point estimator.

To compute $\sigma_{\bar{x}}$, we need to know σ, the standard deviation of the population. To further emphasize the difference between $\sigma_{\bar{x}}$ and σ, we refer to the standard deviation of $\bar{x}$, $\sigma_{\bar{x}}$, as the **standard error** of the mean. In general, the term *standard error* refers to the standard deviation of a point estimator. Later we will see that the value of the standard error of the mean is helpful in determining how far the sample mean may be from the population mean. Let us now return to the EAI example and compute the standard error of the mean associated with simple random samples of 30 EAI employees.

In Section 7.1, we saw that the standard deviation of annual salary for the population of 2,500 EAI employees is $\sigma = 4{,}000$. In this case, the population is finite, with $N = 2{,}500$. However, with a sample size of 30, we have $n/N = 30/2{,}500 = 0.012$. Because the sample size is less than 5% of the population size, we can ignore the finite population correction factor and use equation (7.3) to compute the standard error.

$$\sigma_{\bar{x}} = \frac{\sigma}{\sqrt{n}} = \frac{4{,}000}{\sqrt{30}} = 730.3$$

Form of the Sampling Distribution of $\bar{x}$

The preceding results concerning the expected value and standard deviation for the sampling distribution of $\bar{x}$ are applicable for any population. The final step in identifying the characteristics of the sampling distribution of $\bar{x}$ is to determine the form or shape of the sampling distribution. We will consider two cases: (1) The population has a normal distribution; and (2) the population does not have a normal distribution.

Population Has a Normal Distribution In many situations it is reasonable to assume that the population from which we are selecting a random sample has a normal, or nearly normal, distribution. When the population has a normal distribution, the sampling distribution of $\bar{x}$ is normally distributed for any sample size.

Population Does Not Have a Normal Distribution When the population from which we are selecting a random sample does not have a normal distribution, the **central limit theorem** is helpful in identifying the shape of the sampling distribution of $\bar{x}$. A statement of the central limit theorem as it applies to the sampling distribution of $\bar{x}$ follows.

Central Limit Theorem

In selecting random samples of size n from a population, the sampling distribution of the sample mean $\bar{x}$ can be approximated by a *normal distribution* as the sample size becomes large.

Figure 7.6 Illustration of the Central Limit Theorem for Three Populations

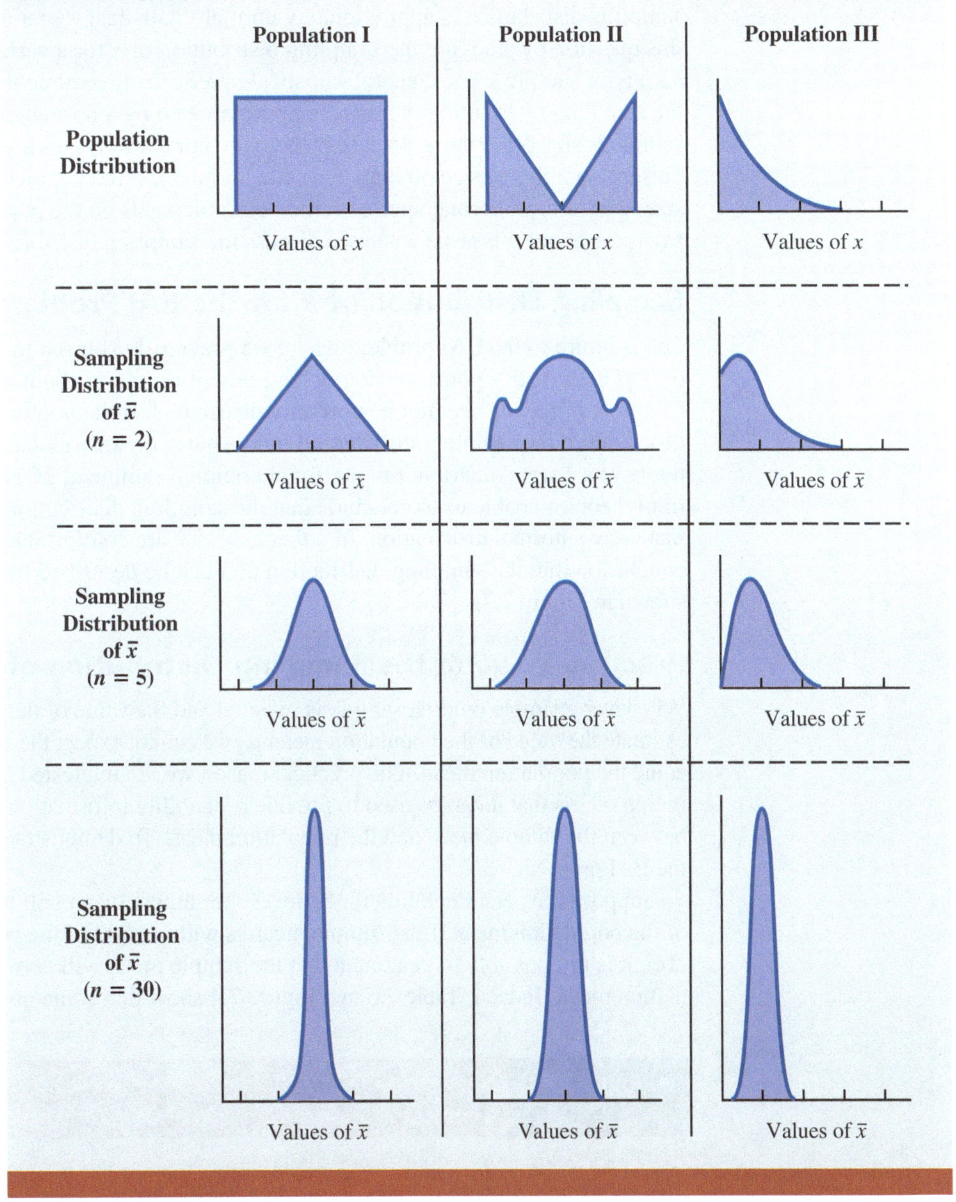

Figure 7.6 shows how the central limit theorem works for three different populations; each column refers to one of the populations. The top panel of the figure shows that none of the populations are normally distributed. Population I follows a uniform distribution. Population II is often called the rabbit-eared distribution. It is symmetric, but the more likely values fall in the tails of the distribution. Population III is shaped like the exponential distribution; it is skewed to the right.

The bottom three panels of Figure 7.6 show the shape of the sampling distribution for samples of size $n = 2$, $n = 5$, and $n = 30$. When the sample size is 2, we see that the shape of each sampling distribution is different from the shape of the corresponding population distribution. For samples of size 5, we see that the shapes of the sampling distributions for populations I and II begin to look similar to the shape of a normal distribution. Even though the shape of the sampling distribution for population III begins to look similar to the shape of a normal distribution, some skewness to the right is still present. Finally, for samples of size 30, the shapes of each of the three sampling distributions are approximately normal.

From a practitioner standpoint, we often want to know how large the sample size needs to be before the central limit theorem applies and we can assume that the shape of the sampling distribution is approximately normal. Statistical researchers have investigated this question by studying the sampling distribution of $\bar{x}$ for a variety of populations and a variety of sample sizes. General statistical practice is to assume that, for most applications, the sampling distribution of $\bar{x}$ can be approximated by a normal distribution whenever the sample is size 30 or more. In cases where the population is highly skewed or outliers are present, samples of size 50 may be needed. Finally, if the population is discrete, the sample size needed for a normal approximation often depends on the population proportion. We say more about this issue when we discuss the sampling distribution of $\bar{p}$ in Section 7.6.

Sampling Distribution of $\bar{x}$ for the EAI Problem

Let us return to the EAI problem where we previously showed that $E(\bar{x}) = \$71{,}800$ and $\sigma_{\bar{x}} = 730.3$. At this point, we do not have any information about the population distribution; it may or may not be normally distributed. If the population has a normal distribution, the sampling distribution of $\bar{x}$ is normally distributed. If the population does not have a normal distribution, the simple random sample of 30 employees and the central limit theorem enable us to conclude that the sampling distribution of $\bar{x}$ can be approximated by a normal distribution. In either case, we are comfortable proceeding with the conclusion that the sampling distribution of $\bar{x}$ can be described by the normal distribution shown in Figure 7.7.

Practical Value of the Sampling Distribution of $\bar{x}$

Whenever a simple random sample is selected and the value of the sample mean is used to estimate the value of the population mean μ, we cannot expect the sample mean to exactly equal the population mean. The practical reason we are interested in the sampling distribution of $\bar{x}$ is that it can be used to provide probability information about the difference between the sample mean and the population mean. To demonstrate this use, let us return to the EAI problem.

Suppose the personnel director believes the sample mean will be an acceptable estimate of the population mean if the sample mean is within \$500 of the population mean. However, it is not possible to guarantee that the sample mean will be within \$500 of the population mean. Indeed, Table 7.5 and Figure 7.4 show that some of the 500 sample means

Figure 7.7 Sampling Distribution of $\bar{x}$ for the Mean Annual Salary of a Simple Random Sample of 30 EAI Employees

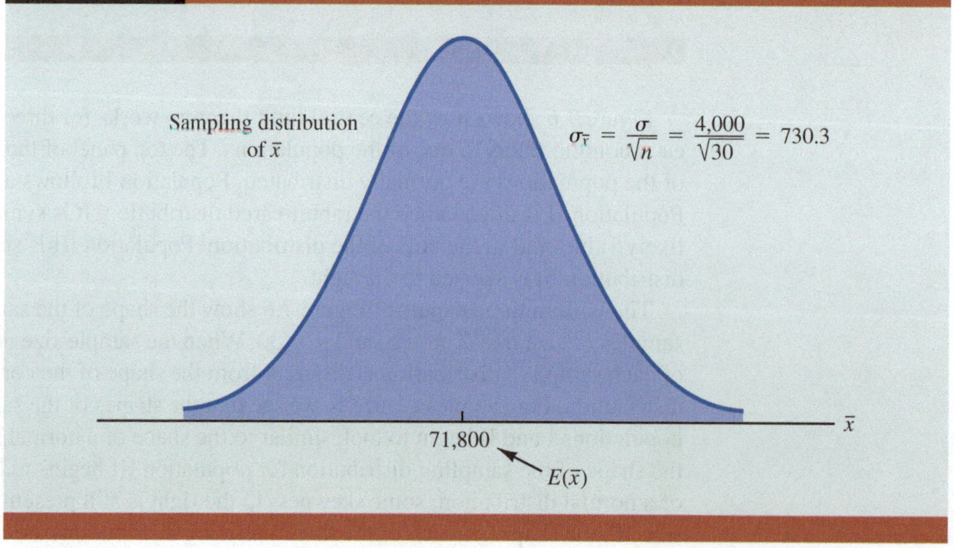

Figure 7.8 Probability of a Sample Mean Being Within $500 of the Population Mean for a Simple Random Sample of 30 EAI Employees

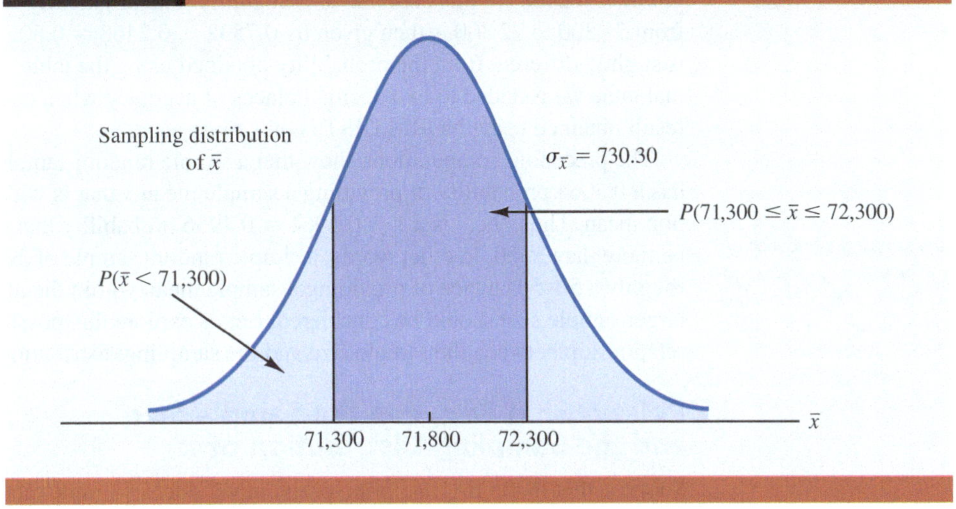

differed by more than $2,000 from the population mean. So we must think of the personnel director's request in probability terms. That is, the personnel director is concerned with the following question: What is the probability that the sample mean computed using a simple random sample of 30 EAI employees will be within $500 of the population mean?

Because we have identified the properties of the sampling distribution of $\bar{x}$ (see Figure 7.7), we will use this distribution to answer the probability question. Refer to the sampling distribution of $\bar{x}$ shown again in Figure 7.8. With a population mean of $71,800, the personnel director wants to know the probability that $\bar{x}$ is between $71,300 and $72,300. This probability is given by the darkly shaded area of the sampling distribution shown in Figure 7.8. Because the sampling distribution is normally distributed, with mean 71,800 and standard error of the mean 730.3, we can use the standard normal probability table to find the area or probability.

We first calculate the z value at the upper endpoint of the interval (72,300) and use the table to find the cumulative probability at that point (left tail area). Then we compute the z value at the lower endpoint of the interval (71,300) and use the table to find the area under the curve to the left of that point (another left tail area). Subtracting the second tail area from the first gives us the desired probability.

At $\bar{x} = 72,300$, we have

$$z = \frac{72,300 - 71,800}{730.30} = 0.68$$

Referring to the standard normal probability table, we find a cumulative probability (area to the left of $z = 0.68$) of 0.7517.

At $\bar{x} = 71,300$, we have

$$z = \frac{71,300 - 71,800}{730.30} = -0.68$$

The area under the curve to the left of $z = -0.68$ is 0.2483. Therefore, $P(71,300 \leq \bar{x} \leq 72,300) = P(z \leq 0.68) - P(z < -0.68) = 0.7517 - 0.2483 = 0.5034$.

Using Excel's NORM.DIST function is easier and provides more accurate results than using the tables with rounded values for z.

The desired probability can also be computed using Excel's NORM.DIST function. The advantage of using the NORM.DIST function is that we do not have to make a separate computation of the z value. Evaluating the NORM.DIST function at the upper endpoint of the interval provides the cumulative probability at 72,300. Entering the formula *=NORM.DIST(72300,71800,730.30,TRUE)* in a cell of an Excel worksheet provides

0.7532 for this cumulative probability. Evaluating the NORM.DIST function at the lower endpoint of the interval provides the area under the curve to the left of 71,300. Entering the formula *=NORM.DIST(71300,71800,730.30,TRUE)* in a cell of an Excel worksheet provides 0.2468 for this cumulative probability. The probability of $\bar{x}$ being in the interval from 71,300 to 72,300 is then given by $0.7532 - 0.2468 = 0.5064$. We note that this result is slightly different from the probability obtained using the table, because in using the normal table we rounded to two decimal places of accuracy when computing the z value. The result obtained using NORM.DIST is thus more accurate.

The preceding computations show that a simple random sample of 30 EAI employees has a 0.5064 probability of providing a sample mean $\bar{x}$ that is within \$500 of the population mean. Thus, there is a $1 - 0.5064 = 0.4936$ probability that the sampling error will be more than \$500. In other words, a simple random sample of 30 EAI employees has roughly a 50–50 chance of providing a sample mean within the allowable \$500. Perhaps a larger sample size should be considered. Let us explore this possibility by considering the relationship between the sample size and the sampling distribution of $\bar{x}$.

The sampling distribution of $\bar{x}$ can be used to provide probability information about how close the sample mean $\bar{x}$ is to the population mean μ.

Relationship Between the Sample Size and the Sampling Distribution of $\bar{x}$

Suppose that in the EAI sampling problem we select a simple random sample of 100 EAI employees instead of the 30 originally considered. Intuitively, it would seem that with more data provided by the larger sample size, the sample mean based on $n = 100$ should provide a better estimate of the population mean than the sample mean based on $n = 30$. To see how much better, let us consider the relationship between the sample size and the sampling distribution of $\bar{x}$.

First note that $E(\bar{x}) = \mu$ regardless of the sample size. Thus, the mean of all possible values of $\bar{x}$ is equal to the population mean μ regardless of the sample size n. However, note that the standard error of the mean, $\sigma_{\bar{x}} = \sigma/\sqrt{n}$, is related to the square root of the sample size. Whenever the sample size is increased, the standard error of the mean $\sigma_{\bar{x}}$ decreases. With $n = 30$, the standard error of the mean for the EAI problem is 730.3. However, with the increase in the sample size to $n = 100$, the standard error of the mean is decreased to

$$\sigma_{\bar{x}} = \frac{\sigma}{\sqrt{n}} = \frac{4{,}000}{\sqrt{100}} = 400$$

The sampling distributions of $\bar{x}$ with $n = 30$ and $n = 100$ are shown in Figure 7.9. Because the sampling distribution with $n = 100$ has a smaller standard error, the values of $\bar{x}$ have less variation and tend to be closer to the population mean than the values of $\bar{x}$ with $n = 30$.

We can use the sampling distribution of $\bar{x}$ for the case with $n = 100$ to compute the probability that a simple random sample of 100 EAI employees will provide a sample mean that is within \$500 of the population mean. In this case the sampling distribution is normal with a mean of 71,800 and a standard deviation of 400 (see Figure 7.10). Again, we could compute the appropriate z values and use the standard normal probability distribution table to make this probability calculation. However, Excel's NORM.DIST function is easier to use and provides more accurate results. Entering the formula *=NORM.DIST(72300,71800,400,TRUE)* in a cell of an Excel worksheet provides the cumulative probability corresponding to $\bar{x} = 72{,}300$. The value provided by Excel is 0.8944. Entering the formula = *NORM.DIST (71300,71800,400,TRUE)* in a cell of an Excel worksheet provides the cumulative probability corresponding to $\bar{x} = 71{,}300$. The value provided by Excel is 0.1056. Thus, the probability of $\bar{x}$ being in the interval from 71,300 to 72,300 is given by $0.8944 - 0.1056 = 0.7888$. By increasing the sample size from 30 to 100 EAI employees, we increase the probability that the sampling error will be \$500 or less; that is, the probability of obtaining a sample mean within \$500 of the population mean increases from 0.5064 to 0.7888.

The important point in this discussion is that as the sample size increases, the standard error of the mean decreases. As a result, a larger sample size will provide a higher probability that the sample mean falls within a specified distance of the population mean.

Figure 7.9 A Comparison of the Sampling Distributions of $\bar{x}$ for Simple Random Samples of $n = 30$ and $n = 100$ EAI Employees

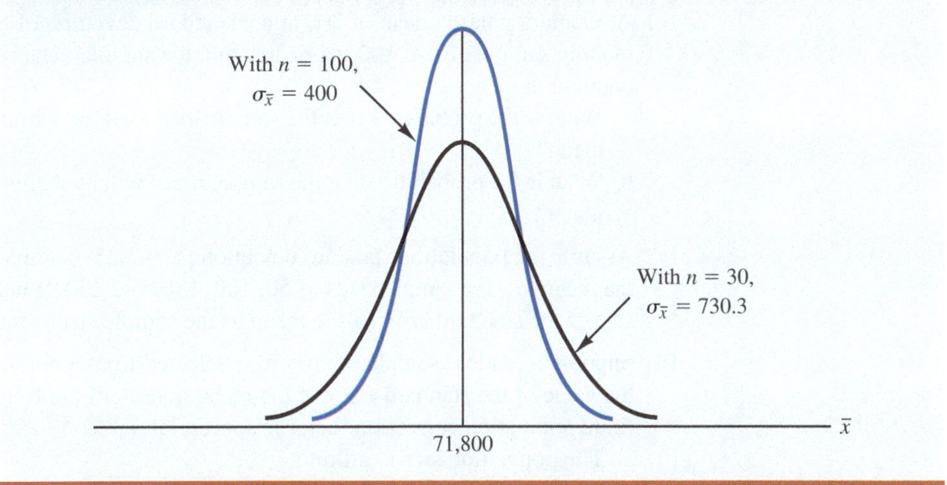

Figure 7.10 Probability of a Sample Mean Being Within $500 of the Population Mean for a Simple Random Sample of 100 EAI Employees

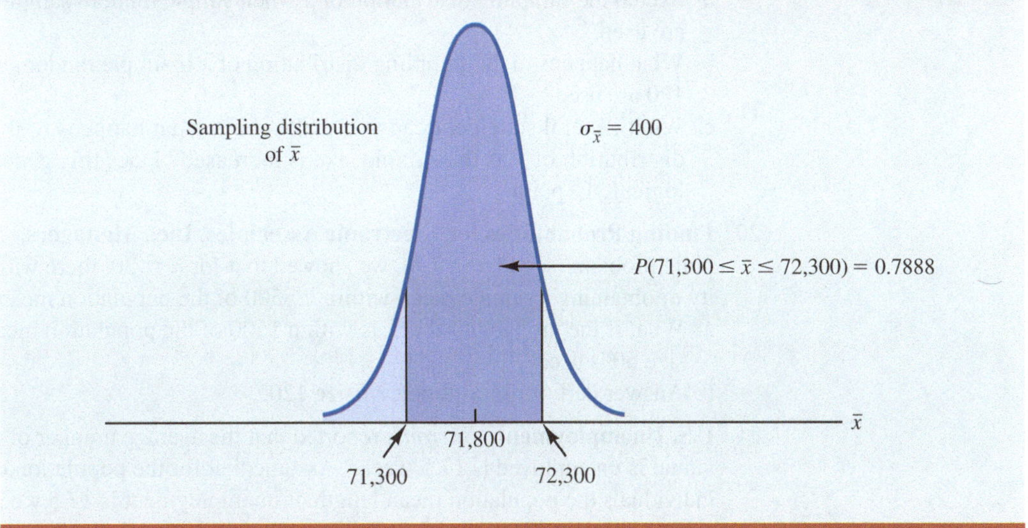

Note + Comment

In presenting the sampling distribution of $\bar{x}$ for the EAI problem, we took advantage of the fact that the population mean $\mu = 71{,}800$ and the population standard deviation $\sigma = 4{,}000$ were known. However, usually the values of the population mean μ and the population standard deviation σ that are needed to determine the sampling distribution of $\bar{x}$ will be unknown. In Chapter 8 we show how the sample mean $\bar{x}$ and the sample standard deviation s are used when μ and σ are unknown.

Exercises

Methods

16. A population has a mean of 200 and a standard deviation of 50. Suppose a simple random sample of size 100 is selected and the sample mean $\bar{x}$ is used to estimate the population mean μ. **LO 6, 7**
    a. What is the probability that the sample mean will be within ± 5 of the population mean?
    b. What is the probability that the sample mean will be within ± 10 of the population mean?

17. Assume the population standard deviation is $\sigma = 25$. Compute the standard error of the mean, $\sigma_{\bar{x}}$, for sample sizes of 50, 100, 150, and 200. What can you say about the size of the standard error of the mean as the sample size is increased? **LO 6**

18. Suppose a random sample of size 50 is selected from a population with $\sigma = 10$. Find the value of the standard error of the mean in each of the following cases (use the finite population correction factor if appropriate). **LO 6**
    a. The population size is infinite.
    b. The population size is $N = 50{,}000$.
    c. The population size is $N = 5{,}000$.
    d. The population size is $N = 500$.

Applications

19. **Sampling Distribution for Electronic Associates, Inc., Managers.** Refer to the EAI sampling problem. Suppose a simple random sample of 60 employees is used. **LO 6, 7**
    a. Sketch the sampling distribution of $\bar{x}$ when simple random samples of size 60 are used.
    b. What happens to the sampling distribution of $\bar{x}$ if simple random samples of size 120 are used?
    c. What general statement can you make about what happens to the sampling distribution of $\bar{x}$ as the sample size is increased? Does this generalization seem logical? Explain.

20. **Finding Probabilities for Electronic Associates, Inc., Managers.** In the EAI sampling problem (see Figure 7.8), we showed that for $n = 30$, there was 0.5064 probability of obtaining a sample mean within $\pm\$500$ of the population mean. **LO 6, 8**
    a. What is the probability that $\bar{x}$ is within \$500 of the population mean if a sample of size 60 is used?
    b. Answer part (a) for a sample of size 120.

21. **U.S. Unemployment.** *Barron's* reported that the average number of weeks an individual is unemployed is 17.5 weeks. Assume that for the population of all unemployed individuals the population mean length of unemployment is 17.5 weeks and that the population standard deviation is four weeks. Suppose you would like to select a random sample of 50 unemployed individuals for a follow-up study. **LO 6, 7, 8**
    a. Describe the sampling distribution of $\bar{x}$, the sample mean average for a sample of 50 unemployed individuals, by specifying its distribution form and parameters.
    b. What is the probability that a simple random sample of 50 unemployed individuals will provide a sample mean within one week of the population mean?
    c. What is the probability that a simple random sample of 50 unemployed individuals will provide a sample mean within 1/2 week of the population mean?

22. **SAT Scores.** In March 2021, PrepScholar reported the following mean scores for two parts of the Scholastic Aptitude Test (SAT):

Evidence-Based Reading and Writing	523
Mathematics	528

Assume that the population standard deviation on each part of the test is $\sigma = 100$. **LO 6, 7, 8**

a. What is the probability a sample of 90 test takers will provide a sample mean test score within 10 points of the population mean of 523 on the Evidence-Based Reading and Writing part of the test?
b. What is the probability a sample of 90 test takers will provide a sample mean test score within 10 points of the population mean of 528 on the Mathematics part of the test?
c. Comment on the differences between the values computed in parts (a) and (b).

23. **Federal Income Tax Returns.** *The Wall Street Journal* reported that 33% of taxpayers with adjusted gross incomes between \$30,000 and \$60,000 itemized deductions on their federal income tax return. The mean amount of deductions for this population of taxpayers was \$16,642. Assume the standard deviation is $\sigma = \$2{,}400$. **LO 6, 7, 8**
    a. What is the probability that a sample of taxpayers from this income group who have itemized deductions will show a sample mean within \$200 of the population mean for each of the following sample sizes: 30, 50, 100, and 400?
    b. What is the advantage of a larger sample size when attempting to estimate the population mean?
24. **College Graduate-Level Wages.** The Economic Policy Institute periodically issues reports on workers' wages. The institute reported that mean wages for male college graduates were \$37.39 per hour and for female college graduates were \$27.83 per hour in 2017. Assume the standard deviation is \$4.60 for male graduates and \$4.10 for female graduates. **LO 6, 7, 8**
    a. What is the probability that a sample of 50 male graduates will provide a sample mean within \$1.00 of the population mean, \$37.39?
    b. What is the probability that a sample of 50 female graduates will provide a sample mean within \$1.00 of the population mean, \$27.83?
    c. In which of the preceding two cases, part (a) or part (b), do we have a higher probability of obtaining a sample estimate within \$1.00 of the population mean? Why?
    d. What is the probability that a sample of 120 female graduates will provide a sample mean more than \$.60 below the population mean, 27.83?
25. **State Rainfalls.** According to the Current Results website, the state of California has a mean annual rainfall of 22 inches, whereas the state of New York has a mean annual rainfall of 42 inches. Assume that the standard deviation for both states is 4 inches. A sample of 30 years of rainfall for California and a sample of 45 years of rainfall for New York have been taken. **LO 6, 7, 8**
    a. Describe the probability distribution of the sample mean annual rainfall for California by specifying its distribution form and parameters.
    b. What is the probability that the sample mean is within 1 inch of the population mean for California?
    c. What is the probability that the sample mean is within 1 inch of the population mean for New York?
    d. In which case, part (b) or part (c), is the probability of obtaining a sample mean within 1 inch of the population mean greater? Why?
26. **Income Tax Return Preparation Fees.** AccountingToday reports that the mean preparation fee for an itemized 1040 and state return in 2020 was \$302. Use this price as the population mean and assume the population standard deviation of preparation fees is \$100. **LO 6, 7, 8**
    a. What is the probability that the mean price for a sample of 30 federal income tax returns is within \$16 of the population mean?
    b. What is the probability that the mean price for a sample of 50 federal income tax returns is within \$16 of the population mean?

c. What is the probability that the mean price for a sample of 100 federal income tax returns is within \$16 of the population mean?
d. Which, if any, of the sample sizes in parts (a), (b), and (c) would you recommend to ensure at least a 0.95 probability that the sample mean is within \$16 of the population mean?

27. **Employee Ages.** To estimate the mean age for a population of 4,000 employees, a simple random sample of 40 employees is selected. **LO 6, 8**
   a. Would you use the finite population correction factor in calculating the standard error of the mean? Explain.
   b. If the population standard deviation is $\sigma = 8.2$ years, compute the standard error both with and without the finite population correction factor. What is the rationale for ignoring the finite population correction factor whenever $n/N \leq 0.05$?
   c. What is the probability that the sample mean age of the employees will be within ± 2 years of the population mean age?

7.6 Sampling Distribution of $\bar{p}$

The sample proportion $\bar{p}$ is the point estimator of the population proportion p. The formula for computing the sample proportion is

$$\bar{p} = \frac{x}{n}$$

where

$x =$ the number of elements in the sample that possess the characteristic of interest
$n =$ sample size

As noted in Section 7.4, the sample proportion $\bar{p}$ is a random variable and its probability distribution is called the sampling distribution of $\bar{p}$.

Sampling Distribution of $\bar{p}$

The sampling distribution of $\bar{p}$ is the probability distribution of all possible values of the sample proportion $\bar{p}$.

To determine how close the sample proportion $\bar{p}$ is to the population proportion p, we need to understand the properties of the sampling distribution of $\bar{p}$: the expected value of $\bar{p}$, the standard deviation of $\bar{p}$, and the shape or form of the sampling distribution of $\bar{p}$.

Expected Value of $\bar{p}$

The expected value of $\bar{p}$, the mean of all possible values of $\bar{p}$, is equal to the population proportion p.

Expected Value of $\bar{p}$

$$E(\bar{p}) = p \qquad (7.4)$$

where

$E(\bar{p}) =$ the expected value of $\bar{p}$
$p =$ the population proportion

Because $E(\bar{p}) = p$, $\bar{p}$ is an unbiased estimator of p. Recall from Section 7.1 where we noted that $p = 0.60$ for the EAI population, where p is the proportion of the population of employees who participated in the company's management training program. Thus, the expected value of $\bar{p}$ for the EAI sampling problem is 0.60.

Standard Deviation of $\bar{p}$

Just as we found for the standard deviation of $\bar{x}$, the standard deviation of $\bar{p}$ depends on whether the population is finite or infinite. The two formulas for computing the standard deviation of $\bar{p}$ follow.

Standard Deviation of $\bar{p}$

Finite Population *Infinite Population*

$$\sigma_{\bar{p}} = \sqrt{\frac{N-n}{N-1}}\sqrt{\frac{p(1-p)}{n}} \qquad \sigma_{\bar{p}} = \sqrt{\frac{p(1-p)}{n}} \tag{7.5}$$

Comparing the two formulas in equation (7.5), we see that the only difference is the use of the finite population correction factor $\sqrt{(N-n)/(N-1)}$.

As was the case with the sample mean $\bar{x}$, the difference between the expressions for the finite population and the infinite population becomes negligible if the size of the finite population is large in comparison to the sample size. We follow the same rule of thumb that we recommended for the sample mean. That is, if the population is finite with $n/N \leq 0.05$, we will use $\sigma_{\bar{p}} = \sqrt{p(1-p)/n}$. However, if the population is finite with $n/N > 0.05$, the finite population correction factor should be used. Again, unless specifically noted, throughout the text we will assume that the population size is large in relation to the sample size and thus the finite population correction factor is unnecessary.

In Section 7.5, we used the term *standard error of the mean* to refer to the standard deviation of $\bar{x}$. We stated that in general the term *standard error* refers to the standard deviation of a point estimator. Thus, for proportions we use *standard error of the proportion* to refer to the standard deviation of $\bar{p}$. Let us now return to the EAI example and compute the standard error of the proportion associated with simple random samples of 30 EAI employees.

For the EAI study we know that the population proportion of employees who participated in the management training program is $p = 0.60$. With $n/N = 30/2{,}500 = 0.012$, we can ignore the finite population correction factor when we compute the standard error of the proportion. For the simple random sample of 30 employees, $\sigma_{\bar{p}}$ is

$$\sigma_{\bar{p}} = \sqrt{\frac{p(1-p)}{n}} = \sqrt{\frac{0.60(1-0.60)}{30}} = 0.0894$$

Form of the Sampling Distribution of $\bar{p}$

Now that we know the mean and standard deviation of the sampling distribution of $\bar{p}$, the final step is to determine the form or shape of the sampling distribution. The sample proportion is $\bar{p} = x/n$. For a simple random sample from a large population, the value of x is a binomial random variable indicating the number of elements in the sample with the characteristic of interest. Because n is a constant, the probability of x/n is the same as the binomial probability of x, which means that the sampling distribution of $\bar{p}$ is also a discrete probability distribution and that the probability for each value of x/n is the same as the probability of x.

Statisticians have shown that a binomial distribution can be approximated by a normal distribution whenever the sample size is large enough to satisfy the following two conditions:

$$np \geq 5 \quad \text{and} \quad n(1-p) \geq 5$$

Assuming these two conditions are satisfied, the probability distribution of x in the sample proportion, $\bar{p} = x/n$, can be approximated by a normal distribution. And because n is a constant, the sampling distribution of $\bar{p}$ can also be approximated by a normal distribution. This approximation is stated as follows:

> The sampling distribution of $\bar{p}$ can be approximated by a normal distribution whenever $np \geq 5$ and $n(1 - p) \geq 5$.

In practical applications, when an estimate of a population proportion is desired, we find that sample sizes are almost always large enough to permit the use of a normal approximation for the sampling distribution of $\bar{p}$.

Recall that for the EAI sampling problem we know that the population proportion of employees who participated in the training program is $p = 0.60$. With a simple random sample of size 30, we have $np = 30(0.60) = 18$ and $n(1 - p) = 30(0.40) = 12$. Thus, the sampling distribution of $\bar{p}$ can be approximated by the normal distribution shown in Figure 7.11.

Practical Value of the Sampling Distribution of $\bar{p}$

The practical value of the sampling distribution of $\bar{p}$ is that it can be used to provide probability information about the difference between the sample proportion and the population proportion. For instance, suppose that in the EAI problem the personnel director wants to know the probability of obtaining a value of $\bar{p}$ that is within 0.05 of the population proportion of EAI employees who participated in the training program. That is, what is the probability of obtaining a sample with a sample proportion $\bar{p}$ between 0.55 and 0.65? The darkly shaded area in Figure 7.12 shows this probability. Using the fact that the sampling distribution of $\bar{p}$ can be approximated by a normal probability distribution with a mean of 0.60 and a standard error of $\sigma_{\bar{p}} = 0.0894$, we can use Excel's NORM.DIST function to make this calculation. Entering the formula *=NORM.DIST(.65,.60,.0894,TRUE)* in a cell of an Excel worksheet provides the cumulative probability corresponding to $\bar{p} = 0.65$. The value calculated by Excel is 0.7120. Entering the formula *=NORM.DIST(.55,.60,.0894,TRUE)* in a cell of an Excel worksheet provides the cumulative probability corresponding to $\bar{p} = 0.55$. The value calculated by Excel is 0.2880. Thus, the probability of $\bar{p}$ being in the interval from 0.55 to 0.65 is given by $0.7120 - 0.2880 = 0.4240$.

Figure 7.11 Sampling Distribution of $\bar{p}$ for the Proportion of EAI Employees Who Participated in the Management Training Program

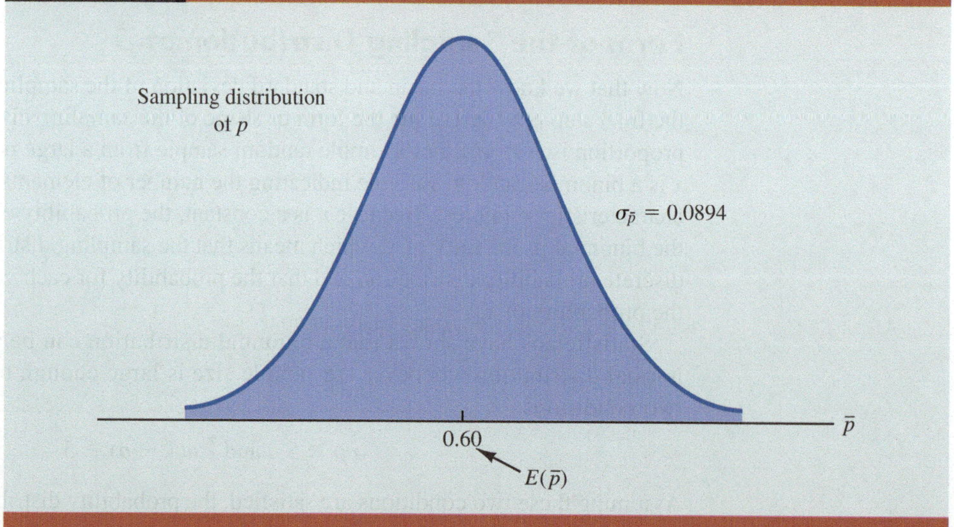

Figure 7.12 Probability of Obtaining $\bar{p}$ Between 0.55 and 0.65

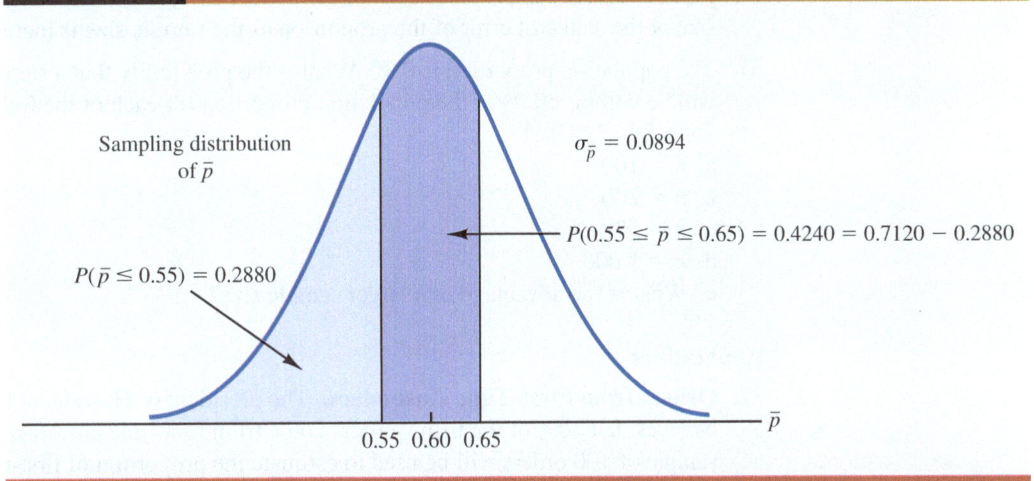

If we consider increasing the sample size to $n = 100$, the standard error of the proportion becomes

$$\sigma_{\bar{p}} = \sqrt{\frac{0.60(1 - 0.60)}{100}} = 0.0490$$

With a sample size of 100 EAI employees, the probability of the sample proportion having a value within 0.05 of the population proportion can now be computed. Because the sampling distribution is approximately normal, with mean 0.60 and standard deviation 0.0490, we can use Excel's NORM.DIST function to make this calculation. Entering the formula *=NORM.DIST(.65,.60,.0490,TRUE)* in a cell of an Excel worksheet provides the cumulative probability corresponding to $\bar{p} = 0.65$. The value calculated by Excel is 0.8462. Entering the formula *=NORM.DIST(.55,.60,.0490,TRUE)* in a cell of an Excel worksheet provides the cumulative probability corresponding to $\bar{p} = 0.55$. The value calculated by Excel is 0.1538. Thus, the probability of $\bar{p}$ being in the interval from 0.55 to 0.65 is given by $0.8462 - 0.1538 = 0.6924$. Increasing the sample size increases the probability that the sampling error will be less than or equal to 0.05 by 0.2684 (from 0.4240 to 0.6924).

Exercises

Methods

28. A random sample of size 100 is selected from a population with $p = 0.40$. **LO 9, 10**
    a. What is the expected value of $\bar{p}$?
    b. What is the standard error of $\bar{p}$?
    c. Describe the sampling distribution of $\bar{p}$.
    d. What does the sampling distribution of $\bar{p}$ show?

29. A population proportion is 0.40. A random sample of size 200 will be taken and the sample proportion $\bar{p}$ will be used to estimate the population proportion. **LO 9, 11**
    a. What is the probability that the sample proportion will be within ± 0.03 of the population proportion?
    b. What is the probability that the sample proportion will be within ± 0.05 of the population proportion?

30. Assume that the population proportion is 0.55. Compute the standard error of the proportion, $\sigma_{\bar{p}}$, for sample sizes of 100, 200, 500, and 1,000. What can you say about the size of the standard error of the proportion as the sample size is increased? **LO 9**

31. The population proportion is 0.30. What is the probability that a sample proportion will be within ±0.04 of the population proportion for each of the following sample sizes. **LO 9, 10, 11**
    a. $n = 100$
    b. $n = 200$
    c. $n = 500$
    d. $n = 1{,}000$
    e. What is the advantage of a larger sample size?

Applications

32. **Orders from First-Time Customers.** The president of Howahkan Distributors, Inc. believes that 30% of the firm's orders come from first-time customers. A random sample of 100 orders will be used to estimate the proportion of first-time customers. **LO 9, 10, 11**
    a. Assume that the president is correct and $p = 0.30$. Describe the sampling distribution of $\bar{p}$ for this study by specifying its distribution form and parameters.
    b. What is the probability that the sample proportion $\bar{p}$ will be between 0.20 and 0.40?
    c. What is the probability that the sample proportion will be between 0.25 and 0.35?

33. **Ages of Entrepreneurs.** *The Wall Street Journal* reported that the age at first start-up for 55% of entrepreneurs was 29 years or less and the age at first start-up for 45% of entrepreneurs was 30 years or more. **LO 9, 10, 11**
    a. Suppose a sample of 200 entrepreneurs will be taken to learn about the most important qualities of entrepreneurs. Specify the distribution form and parameters of the sampling distribution of $\bar{p}$ where $\bar{p}$ is the sample proportion of entrepreneurs whose first start-up was at 29 years of age or less.
    b. What is the probability that the sample proportion in part (a) will be within ±0.05 of its population proportion?
    c. Suppose a sample of 200 entrepreneurs will be taken to learn about the most important qualities of entrepreneurs. Describe the sampling distribution of $\bar{p}$ where $\bar{p}$ is now the sample proportion of entrepreneurs whose first start-up was at 30 years of age or more.
    d. What is the probability that the sample proportion in part (c) will be within ±0.05 of its population proportion?
    e. Is the probability different in parts (b) and (d)? Why?
    f. Answer part (b) for a sample of size 400. Is the probability smaller? Why?

34. **Food Waste.** In 2017, the Restaurant Hospitality website reported that only 10% of surplus food is being recovered in the food-service and restaurant sector, leaving approximately 1.5 billion meals per year uneaten. Assume this is the true population proportion and that you plan to take a sample survey of 525 companies in the food service and restaurant sector to further investigate their behavior. **LO 9, 10, 11**
    a. Specify the distribution form and parameters of the sampling distribution of $\bar{p}$, the proportion of food recovered by your sample respondents.
    b. What is the probability that your survey will provide a sample proportion within ±0.03 of the population proportion?
    c. What is the probability that your survey will provide a sample proportion within ±0.015 of the population proportion?

35. **Unnecessary Medical Care.** According to *Reader's Digest*, 42% of primary care doctors think their patients receive unnecessary medical care. **LO 9, 10, 11**
    a. Suppose a sample of 300 primary care doctors was taken. Describe the sampling distribution of the proportion of the doctors who think their patients receive unnecessary medical care.

b. What is the probability that the sample proportion will be within ± 0.03 of the population proportion?
c. What is the probability that the sample proportion will be within ± 0.05 of the population proportion?
d. What would be the effect of taking a larger sample on the probabilities in parts (b) and (c)? Why?

36. **Better Business Bureau Complaints.** In 2016, the Better Business Bureau settled 80% of complaints they received in the United States. Suppose you have been hired by the Better Business Bureau to investigate the complaints they received this year involving new car dealers. You plan to select a sample of new car dealer complaints to estimate the proportion of complaints the Better Business Bureau is able to settle. Assume the population proportion of complaints settled for new car dealers is 0.80, the same as the overall proportion of complaints settled in 2016. **LO 9, 10, 11**
a. Suppose you select a sample of 200 complaints involving new car dealers. Specify the distribution form and parameters of the sampling distribution of $\bar{p}$.
b. Based upon a sample of 200 complaints, what is the probability that the sample proportion will be within 0.04 of the population proportion?
c. Suppose you select a sample of 450 complaints involving new car dealers. Describe the sampling distribution of $\bar{p}$.
d. Based upon the larger sample of 450 complaints, what is the probability that the sample proportion will be within 0.04 of the population proportion?
e. As measured by the increase in probability, how much do you gain in precision by taking the larger sample in part (d)?

37. **Product Labeling.** The Grocery Manufacturers of America reported that 76% of consumers read the ingredients listed on a product's label. Assume the population proportion is $p = 0.76$ and a sample of 400 consumers is selected from the population. **LO 9, 10, 11**
a. Specify the distribution form and parameters of the sampling distribution of the sample proportion $\bar{p}$, where $\bar{p}$ is the proportion of the sampled consumers who read the ingredients listed on a product's label.
b. What is the probability that the sample proportion will be within ± 0.03 of the population proportion?
c. Answer part (b) for a sample of 750 consumers.

38. **Household Grocery Expenditures.** The Food Marketing Institute shows that 17% of households spend more than \$100 per week on groceries. Assume the population proportion is $p = 0.17$ and a simple random sample of 800 households will be selected from the population. **LO 9, 10, 11**
a. Specify the distribution form and parameters of the sampling distribution of $\bar{p}$, the sample proportion of households spending more than \$100 per week on groceries.
b. What is the probability that the sample proportion will be within ± 0.02 of the population proportion?
c. Answer part (b) for a sample of 1,600 households.

7.7 Other Sampling Methods

This section provides a brief introduction to survey sampling methods other than simple random sampling.

We described simple random sampling as a procedure for sampling from a finite population and discussed the properties of the sampling distributions of $\bar{x}$ and $\bar{p}$ when simple random sampling is used. Other methods such as stratified random sampling, cluster sampling, and systematic sampling provide advantages over simple random sampling in some of these situations. In this section we briefly introduce these alternative sampling methods.

Figure 7.13 Diagram for Stratified Random Sampling

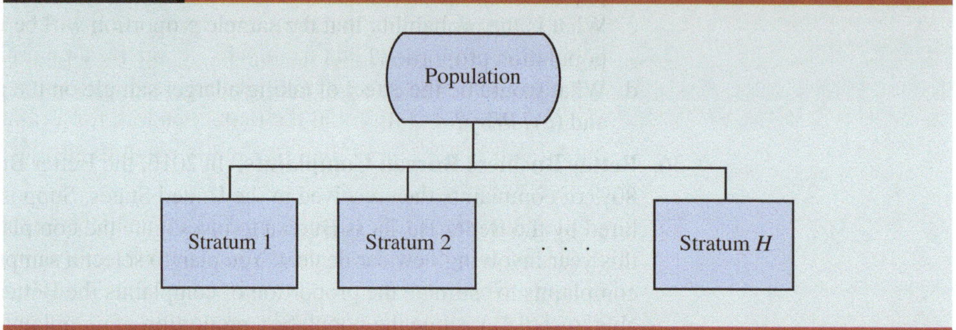

Stratified Random Sampling

Stratified random sampling works best when the variance among elements in each stratum is relatively small.

In **stratified random sampling**, the elements in the population are first divided into groups called *strata,* such that each element in the population belongs to one and only one stratum. The basis for forming the strata, such as department, location, age, and industry type, is at the discretion of the designer of the sample. However, the best results are obtained when the elements within each stratum are as much alike as possible. Figure 7.13 is a diagram of a population divided into *H* strata.

After the strata are formed, a simple random sample is taken from each stratum. Formulas are available for combining the results for the individual stratum samples into one estimate of the population parameter of interest. The value of stratified random sampling depends on how homogeneous the elements are within the strata. If elements within strata are alike, the strata will have low variances. Thus, relatively small sample sizes can be used to obtain good estimates of the strata characteristics. If strata are homogeneous, the stratified random sampling procedure provides results just as precise as those of simple random sampling by using a smaller total sample size.

Cluster Sampling

Cluster sampling works best when each cluster provides a small-scale representation of the population.

In **cluster sampling**, the elements in the population are first divided into separate groups called *clusters*. Each element of the population belongs to one and only one cluster (see Figure 7.14). A simple random sample of the clusters is then taken. All elements within each sampled cluster form the sample. Cluster sampling tends to provide the best results when the elements within the clusters are not alike. In the ideal case, each cluster is a representative small-scale version of the entire population. The value of cluster sampling depends on how representative each cluster is of the entire population. If all clusters are

Figure 7.14 Diagram for Cluster Sampling

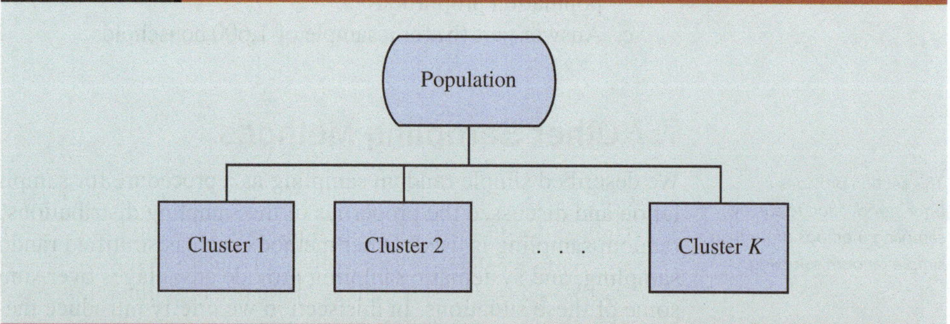

alike in this regard, sampling a small number of clusters will provide good estimates of the population parameters.

One of the primary applications of cluster sampling is area sampling, where clusters are city blocks or other well-defined areas. Cluster sampling generally requires a larger total sample size than either simple random sampling or stratified random sampling. However, it can result in cost savings because when an interviewer is sent to a sampled cluster (e.g., a city-block location), many sample observations can be obtained in a relatively short time. Hence, a larger sample size may be obtainable with a significantly lower total cost.

Systematic Sampling

In some sampling situations, especially those with large populations, it is time-consuming to select a simple random sample by first finding a random number and then counting or searching through the list of the population until the corresponding element is found. An alternative to simple random sampling is **systematic sampling**. For example, if a sample size of 50 is desired from a population containing 5,000 elements, we will sample one element for every 5,000/50 = 100 elements in the population. A systematic sample for this case involves selecting randomly one of the first 100 elements from the population list. Other sample elements are identified by starting with the first sampled element and then selecting every 100th element that follows in the population list. In effect, the sample of 50 is identified by moving systematically through the population and identifying every 100th element after the first randomly selected element. The sample of 50 usually will be easier to identify in this way than it would be if simple random sampling were used. Because the first element selected is a random choice, a systematic sample is usually assumed to have the properties of a simple random sample. This assumption is especially applicable when the list of elements in the population is a random ordering of the elements.

Convenience Sampling

The sampling methods discussed thus far are referred to as *probability sampling* techniques. Elements selected from the population have a known probability of being included in the sample. The advantage of probability sampling is that the sampling distribution of the appropriate sample statistic generally can be identified. Formulas such as the ones for simple random sampling presented in this chapter can be used to determine the properties of the sampling distribution. Then, the sampling distribution can be used to make probability statements about the error associated with using the sample results to make inferences about the population.

Convenience sampling is a *nonprobability sampling* technique. As the name implies, the sample is identified primarily by convenience. Elements are included in the sample without prespecified or known probabilities of being selected. For example, a professor conducting research at a university may use student volunteers to constitute a sample simply because they are readily available and will participate as subjects for little or no cost. Similarly, an inspector may sample a shipment of oranges by selecting oranges haphazardly from among several crates. Labeling each orange and using a probability method of sampling would be impractical. Samples such as wildlife captures and volunteer panels for consumer research are also convenience samples.

Convenience samples have the advantage of relatively easy sample selection and data collection; however, it is impossible to evaluate the "goodness" of the sample in terms of its representativeness of the population. A convenience sample may provide good results or it may not; no statistically justified procedure allows a probability analysis and inference about the quality of the sample results. Sometimes researchers apply statistical methods designed for probability samples to a convenience sample, arguing that the convenience sample can be treated as though it were a probability sample. However, this argument cannot be supported, and we should be cautious in interpreting the results of convenience samples that are used to make inferences about populations.

Judgment Sampling

Judgment sampling is another nonprobability sampling technique. In this approach, the person most knowledgeable on the subject of the study selects elements of the population that he or she feels are most representative of the population. Often this method is a relatively easy way of selecting a sample. For example, a reporter may sample two or three senators, judging that those senators reflect the general opinion of all senators. However, the quality of the sample results depends on the judgment of the person selecting the sample. Again, great caution is warranted in drawing conclusions based on judgment samples used to make inferences about populations.

Note + Comment

We recommend using probability sampling methods when sampling from finite populations: simple random sampling, stratified random sampling, cluster sampling, or systematic sampling. For these methods, formulas are available for evaluating the "goodness" of the sample results in terms of the closeness of the results to the population parameters being estimated. An evaluation of the goodness cannot be made with convenience or judgment sampling. Thus, great care should be used in interpreting the results based on nonprobability sampling methods.

7.8 Practical Advice: Big Data and Errors in Sampling

The purpose of collecting a sample is to make inferences and answer research questions about a population. Therefore, it is important that the sample look like, or be representative of, the population being investigated. In practice, individual samples always, to varying degrees, fail to be perfectly representative of the populations from which they have been taken. There are two general reasons a sample may fail to be representative of the population of interest: sampling error and nonsampling error.

Sampling Error

One reason a sample may fail to represent the population from which it has been taken is **sampling error**, or deviation of the sample from the population that results from random sampling. If repeated independent random samples of the same size are collected from the population of interest using a probability sampling technique, on average the samples will be representative of the population. This is the justification for collecting sample data randomly. However, the random collection of sample data does not ensure that any single sample will be perfectly representative of the population of interest; when collecting a sample randomly, the data in the sample cannot be expected to be perfectly representative of the population from which it has been taken. Sampling error is unavoidable when collecting a random sample; this is a risk we must accept when we chose to collect a random sample rather than incur the costs associated with taking a census of the population.

As expressed by equations (7.2) and (7.5), the standard errors of the sampling distributions of the sample mean $\bar{x}$ and the sample proportion $\bar{p}$ reflect the potential for sampling error when using sample data to estimate the population mean μ and the population proportion p, respectively. As the sample size n increases, the potential impact of extreme values on the statistic decreases, so there is less variation in the potential values of the statistic produced by the sample and the standard errors of these sampling distributions decrease. Because these standard errors reflect the potential for sampling error when using sample data to estimate the population mean μ and the population proportion p, we see that for an extremely large sample there may be little potential for sampling error.

Nonsampling Error

Although the standard error of a sampling distribution decreases as the sample size n increases, this does not mean that we can conclude that an extremely large sample will always provide reliable information about the population of interest; this is because sampling error is not the sole reason a sample may fail to represent the target population. Deviations of the sample from the population that occur for reasons other than random sampling are referred to as **nonsampling error**. Nonsampling error can occur for a variety of reasons.

Consider the online news service PenningtonDailyTimes.com (PDT). Because PDT's primary source of revenue is the sale of advertising, the news service is intent on collecting sample data on the behavior of visitors to its website in order to support its advertising sales. Prospective advertisers are willing to pay a premium to advertise on websites that have long visit times, so PDT's management is keenly interested in the amount of time customers spend during their visits to PDT's website. Advertisers are also concerned with how frequently visitors to a website click on any of the ads featured on the website, so PDT is also interested in whether visitors to its website clicked on any of the ads featured on PenningtonDailyTimes.com.

From whom should PDT collect its data? Should it collect data on current visits to PenningtonDailyTimes.com? Should it attempt to attract new visitors and collect data on these visits? If so, should it measure the time spent at its website by visitors it has attracted from competitors' websites or from visitors who do not routinely visit online news sites? The answers to these questions depend on PDT's research objectives. Is the company attempting to evaluate its current market, assess the potential of customers it can attract from competitors, or explore the potential of an entirely new market such as individuals who do not routinely obtain their news from online news services? If the research objective and the population from which the sample is to be drawn are not aligned, the data that PDT collects will not help the company accomplish its research objective. This type of error is referred to as a **coverage error**.

Nonsampling error can occur in a sample or a census.

Even when the sample is taken from the appropriate population, nonsampling error can occur when segments of the target population are systematically underrepresented or overrepresented in the sample. This may occur because the study design is flawed or because some segments of the population are either more likely or less likely to respond. Suppose PDT implements a pop-up questionnaire that opens when a visitor leaves PenningtonDailyTimes.com. Visitors to PenningtonDailyTimes.com who have installed pop-up blockers will be likely underrepresented, and visitors to PenningtonDailyTimes.com who have not installed pop-up blockers will likely be overrepresented. If the behavior of PenningtonDailyTimes.com visitors who have installed pop-up blockers differs from the behaviors of PenningtonDailyTimes.com visitors who have not installed pop-up blockers, attempting to draw conclusions from this sample about how all visitors to the PDT website behave may be misleading. This type of error is referred to as a **nonresponse error**.

Another potential source of nonsampling error is incorrect measurement of the characteristic of interest. If PDT asks questions that are ambiguous or difficult for respondents to understand, the responses may not accurately reflect how the respondents intended to respond. For example, respondents may be unsure how to respond if PDT asks, *"Are the news stories on PenningtonDailyTimes.com compelling and accurate?"*. How should a visitor respond if she or he feels the news stories on PenningtonDailyTimes.com are compelling but erroneous? What response is appropriate if the respondent feels the news stories on PenningtonDailyTimes.com are accurate but dull? A similar issue can arise if a question is asked in a biased or leading way. If PDT asks, *"Many readers find the news stories on PenningtonDailyTimes.com to be compelling and accurate. Do you find the news stories on PenningtonDailyTimes.com to be compelling and accurate?"*, the qualifying statement PDT makes prior to the actual question will likely result in a bias toward positive responses. Incorrect measurement of the characteristic of interest can also occur when respondents provide incorrect answers; this may be due to a respondent's poor recall or unwillingness to respond honestly. This type of error is referred to as a **measurement error**.

Errors that are introduced by interviewers or during the recording and preparation of the data are other types of nonsampling error. These types of error are referred to as interviewer errors and processing errors, respectively.

Nonsampling error can introduce bias into the estimates produced using the sample, and this bias can mislead decision makers who use the sample data in their decision-making processes. No matter how small or large the sample, we must contend with this limitation of sampling whenever we use sample data to gain insight into a population of interest. Although sampling error decreases as the size of the sample increases, an extremely large sample can still suffer from nonsampling error and fail to be representative of the population of interest. When sampling, care must be taken to ensure that we minimize the introduction of nonsampling error into the data collection process. This can be done by carrying out the following steps:

- Carefully define the target population before collecting sample data, and subsequently design the data collection procedure so that a probability sample is drawn from this target population.
- Carefully design the data collection process and train the data collectors.
- Pretest the data collection procedure to identify and correct for potential sources of nonsampling error prior to final data collection.
- Use stratified random sampling when population-level information about an important qualitative variable is available to ensure that the sample is representative of the population with respect to that qualitative characteristic.
- Use cluster sampling when the population can be divided into heterogeneous subgroups or clusters.
- Use systematic sampling when population-level information about an important quantitative variable is available to ensure that the sample is representative of the population with respect to that quantitative characteristic.

Finally, recognize that every random sample (even an extremely large random sample) will suffer from some degree of sampling error, and eliminating all potential sources of nonsampling error may be impractical. Understanding these limitations of sampling will enable us to be more realistic and pragmatic when interpreting sample data and using sample data to draw conclusions about the target population.

Big Data

Recent estimates state that approximately 2.5 quintillion bytes of data are created worldwide each day. This represents a dramatic increase from the estimated 100 gigabytes (GB) of data generated worldwide per day in 1992, the 100 GB of data generated worldwide per hour in 1997, and the 100 GB of data generated worldwide per second in 2002. Every minute, there is an average of 216,000 Instagram posts, 204,000,000 e-mails sent, 12 hours of footage uploaded to YouTube, and 277,000 tweets posted on Twitter. Without question, the amount of data that is now generated is overwhelming, and this trend is certainly expected to continue.

In each of these cases the data sets that are generated are so large or complex that current data processing capacity and/or analytic methods are not adequate for analyzing the data. Thus, each is an example of **big data**. There are myriad other sources of big data. Sensors and mobile devices transmit enormous amounts of data. Internet activities, digital processes, and social media interactions also produce vast quantities of data.

The amount of data has increased so rapidly that our vocabulary for describing a data set by its size must expand. A few years ago, a petabyte of data seemed almost unimaginably large, but we now routinely describe data in terms of yottabytes. Table 7.6 summarizes terminology for describing the size of data sets.

Understanding What Big Data Is

The processes that generate big data can be described by four attributes or dimensions that are referred to as the four Vs:

- **Volume**—the amount of data generated
- **Variety**—the diversity in types and structures of data generated
- **Veracity**—the reliability of the data generated
- **Velocity**—the speed at which the data are generated

Table 7.6 Terminology for Describing the Size of Data Sets

Number of Bytes	Metric	Name
1000^1	kB	kilobyte
1000^2	MB	megabyte
1000^3	GB	gigabyte
1000^4	TB	terabyte
1000^5	PB	petabyte
1000^6	EB	exabyte
1000^7	ZB	zettabyte
1000^8	YB	yottabyte

A high degree of any of these attributes individually is sufficient to generate big data, and when they occur at high levels simultaneously the resulting amount of data can be overwhelmingly large. Technological advances and improvements in electronic (and often automated) data collection make it easy to collect millions, or even billions, of observations in a relatively short time. Businesses are collecting greater volumes of an increasing variety of data at a higher velocity than ever.

To understand the challenges presented by big data, we consider its structural dimensions. Big data can be **tall data**; a data set that has so many observations that traditional statistical inference has little meaning. For example, producers of consumer goods collect information on the sentiment expressed in millions of social media posts each day to better understand consumer perceptions of their products. Such data consist of the sentiment expressed (the variable) in millions (or over time, even billions) of social media posts (the observations). Big data can also be **wide data**; a data set that has so many variables that simultaneous consideration of all variables is infeasible. For example, a high-resolution image can comprise millions or billions of pixels. The data used by facial recognition algorithms consider each pixel in an image when comparing an image to other images in an attempt to find a match. Thus, these algorithms make use of the characteristics of millions or billions of pixels (the variables) for relatively few high-resolution images (the observations). Of course, big data can be both tall and wide, and the resulting data set can again be overwhelmingly large.

Statistics are useful tools for understanding the information embedded in a big data set, but we must be careful when using statistics to analyze big data. It is important that we understand the limitations of statistics when applied to big data and we temper our interpretations accordingly. Because tall data are the most common form of big data used in business, we focus on this structure in the discussions throughout the remainder of this section.

Implications of Big Data for Sampling Error

Let's revisit the data collection problem of online news service PenningtonDailyTimes.com (PDT). Because PDT's primary source of revenue is the sale of advertising, PDT's management is interested in the amount of time customers spend during their visits to PDT's website. From historical data, PDT has estimated that the standard deviation of the time spent by individual customers when they visit PDT's website is $\sigma = 20$ seconds. Table 7.7 shows how the standard error of the sampling distribution of the sample mean time spent by individual customers when they visit PDT's website decreases as the sample size increases.

PDT also wants to collect information from its sample respondents on whether a visitor to its website clicked on any of the ads featured on the website. From its historical data, PDT knows that 51% of past visitors to its website clicked on any ad featured on

Table 7.7 Standard Error of the Sample Mean $\bar{x}$ when s = 20 at Various Sample Sizes

Sample Size n	Standard Error $\sigma_{\bar{x}} = \sigma/\sqrt{n}$
10	6.32456
100	2.00000
1,000	0.63246
10,000	0.20000
100,000	0.06325
1,000,000	0.02000
10,000,000	0.00632
100,000,000	0.00200
1,000,000,000	0.00063

the website, so it will use this value as $\bar{p}$ to estimate the standard error. Table 7.8 shows how the standard error of the sampling distribution of the proportion of the sample that clicked on any of the ads featured on PenningtonDailyTimes.com decreases as the sample size increases.

A sample of one million or more visitors might seem unrealistic, but keep in mind that Amazon.com had over 2.7 billion visitors in June of 2021.

The PDT example illustrates the general relationship between standard errors and the sample size. We see in Table 7.7 that the standard error of the sample mean decreases as the sample size increases. For a sample of $n = 10$, the standard error of the sample mean is 6.32456; when we increase the sample size to $n = 100{,}000$, the standard error of the sample mean decreases to 0.06325; and at a sample size of $n = 1{,}000{,}000{,}000$, the standard error of the sample mean decreases to only 0.00063. In Table 7.8, we see that the standard error of the sample proportion also decreases as the sample size increases. For a sample of $n = 10$, the standard error of the sample proportion is 0.15811; when we increase the sample size to $n = 100{,}000$, the standard error of the sample proportion decreases to 0.00158; and at a sample size of $n = 1{,}000{,}000{,}000$, the standard error of the sample mean decreases to only 0.00002. In both Tables 7.7 and 7.8, the standard error when $n = 1{,}000{,}000{,}000$ is *one ten-thousandth of the standard error when $n = 10$.*

Suppose that last year the mean time spent by all visitors to the PDT website was 84 seconds. Further suppose that the mean time has not changed since last year and that PDT now collects a sample of 1,000,000 visitors to its website. With $n = 1{,}000{,}000$ and

Table 7.8 Standard Error of the Sample Proportion $\bar{p}$ when p = 0.51 at Various Sample Sizes

Sample Size n	Standard Error $\sigma_{\bar{p}} = \sqrt{p(1-p)/n}$
10	0.15811
100	0.05000
1,000	0.01581
10,000	0.00500
100,000	0.00158
1,000,000	0.00050
10,000,000	0.00016
100,000,000	0.00005
1,000,000,000	0.00002

the assumed known value of $\sigma = 20$ seconds for the population standard deviation, the standard error will be $\sigma_{\bar{x}} = \sigma/\sqrt{n} = 20/\sqrt{1{,}000{,}000} = 0.02$. Note that because of the very large sample size, the sampling distribution of the sample mean $\bar{x}$ will be normally distributed. PDT can use this information to calculate the probability the sample mean $\bar{x}$ will fall within 0.15 of the population mean, or within the interval 84 ± 0.15. At $\bar{x} = 83.85$

$$z = \frac{83.85 - 84}{0.02} = -7.5$$

and at $\bar{x} = 84.15$,

$$z = \frac{84.15 - 84}{0.02} = 7.5$$

Because $P(z \leq -7.5) \approx 0.0000$ and $P(z \leq 7.5) \approx 1.0000$, the probability the sample mean $\bar{x}$ will fall within 1.5 of the population mean μ is

$$P(-7.5 \leq z \leq 7.5) \approx 1.0000 - 0.0000 = 1.0000$$

Using Excel, we find

NORM.DIST(84.15,84,.02,TRUE) − NORM.DIST(83.85,84,.02,TRUE) = 1.000

Now, suppose that for the new sample of 1,000,000 visitors the sample mean time spent by all visitors to the PDT website is 88 seconds. What could PDT conclude? Its calculations show that the probability the sample mean will be between 83.85 and 84.15 is approximately 1.0000, and yet the mean of PDT's sample is 88. There are three possible reasons that PDT's sample mean differs so substantially from the population mean for last year:

- sampling error
- nonsampling error
- the population mean has changed since last year

Because the sample size is extremely large, the sample should have very little sampling error, and so sampling error cannot explain the substantial difference between PDT's sample mean of $\bar{x} = 88$ seconds and the population mean of $\mu = 84$ seconds for last year. Nonsampling error is a possible explanation and should be investigated. If PDT determines that it introduced little or no nonsampling error into its sample data, the only remaining plausible explanation for the substantial difference between PDT's sample mean and the population mean for last year is that the population mean has changed since last year. If the sample was collected properly, it provides evidence of a potentially important change in behavior of visitors to the PDT website that could have tremendous implications for PDT.

No matter how small or large the sample, we must contend with the limitations of sampling whenever we use sample data to learn about a population of interest. Although sampling error decreases as the size of the sample increases, an extremely large sample can indeed suffer from failure to be representative of the population of interest because of nonsampling error.

Finally, recognize that every random sample (even an extremely large sample) will suffer from some degree of sampling error, and eliminating all potential sources of nonsampling error may be impractical. Understanding these limitations of sampling will enable us to be more realistic when interpreting sample data and using sample data to draw conclusions about the target population. In the next several chapters, we will explore statistical methods for dealing with these issues in greater detail.

Notes + Comments

1. In the previous section of this chapter, we explained that one reason probability sampling methods are generally preferred over nonprobability sampling methods is that formulas are available for evaluating the "goodness" of the sample results in terms of the closeness of the results to the population parameters being estimated for sample data collected using probability sampling methods. This evaluation cannot be made with convenience or judgment sampling. Another reason for the general preference of probability sampling methods over nonprobability sampling methods is that probability sampling methods are less likely than nonprobability sampling methods to introduce nonsampling error. Although nonsampling can occur when either a probability sampling method or a nonprobability sampling method is used, nonprobability sampling methods such as convenience sampling and judgment sampling frequently introduce nonsampling error into the sample data. This is because of the manner in which sample data are collected when using a nonprobability sampling method.
2. Several approaches to statistical inference (interval estimation and hypothesis testing) are introduced in subsequent chapters of this book. These approaches assume nonsampling error has not been introduced into the sample data. The reliability of the results of statistical inference decreases as greater nonsampling error is introduced into the sample data.

Exercises

Methods

39. A population has a mean of 400 and a standard deviation of 100. A sample of size 100,000 will be taken, and the sample mean $\bar{x}$ will be used to estimate the population mean. **LO 6, 7**
    a. What is the expected value of $\bar{x}$?
    b. What is the standard deviation of $\bar{x}$?
    c. Describe the sampling distribution of $\bar{x}$.
    d. What does the sampling distribution of $\bar{x}$ show?
40. Assume the population standard deviation is $\sigma = 25$. Compute the standard error of the mean, $\sigma_{\bar{x}}$, for sample sizes of 500,000; 1,000,000; 5,000,000; 10,000,000; and 100,000,000. What can you say about the size of the standard error of the mean as the sample size is increased? **LO 6**
41. A sample of size 100,000 is selected from a population with $p = 0.75$. **LO 9, 10**
    a. What is the expected value of $\bar{p}$?
    b. What is the standard error of $\bar{p}$?
    c. Describe the sampling distribution of $\bar{p}$.
    d. What does the sampling distribution of $\bar{p}$ show?
42. Assume that the population proportion is 0.44. Compute the standard error of the proportion, $\sigma_{\bar{p}}$, for sample sizes of 500,000; 1,000,000; 5,000,000; 10,000,000; and 100,000,000. What can you say about the size of the standard error of the sample proportion as the sample size is increased? **LO 9**

Applications

43. **Sampling Distribution of App Users.** Martina Levitt, director of marketing for the messaging app Spontanversation, has been assigned the task of profiling users of this app. Assume that individuals who have downloaded Spontanversation use the app an average of 30 times per day with a standard deviation of 6. **LO 6, 7**
    a. What is the sampling distribution of $\bar{x}$ if a random sample of 50 individuals who have downloaded Spontanversation is used?
    b. What is the sampling distribution of $\bar{x}$ if a random sample of 500,000 individuals who have downloaded Spontanversation is used?

c. What general statement can you make about what happens to the sampling distribution of $\bar{x}$ as the sample size becomes extremely large? Does this generalization seem logical? Explain.

44. **Profiling App Users.** Consider the Spontanversation sampling problem for which individuals who have downloaded Spontanversation use the app an average of 30 times per day with a standard deviation of 6. **LO 6, 8**
    a. What is the probability that $\bar{x}$ is within 1.7 of the population mean if a random sample of 50 individuals who have downloaded Spontanversation is used?
    b. What would you conclude if the mean of the sample collected in part (a) is 30.2?
    c. What is the probability that $\bar{x}$ is within 0.017 of the population mean if a sample of 500,000 individuals who have downloaded Spontanversation is used?
    d. What would you conclude if the mean of the sample collected in part (c) is 30.2?

45. **Vacation Hours Earned by Blue-Collar and Service Employees.** The U.S. Bureau of Labor Statistics (BLS) reported that the mean annual number of hours of vacation time earned by blue-collar and service employees who work for small private establishments and have at least 10 years of service is 100. Assume that for this population the standard deviation for the annual number of vacation hours earned is 48. Suppose the BLS would like to select a sample of 15,000 individuals from this population for a follow-up study. **LO 6, 7, 8**
    a. Specify the distribution form and parameters of the sampling distribution of $\bar{x}$, the sample mean for a sample of 15,000 individuals from this population.
    b. What is the probability that a simple random sample of 15,000 individuals from this population will provide a sample mean that is within one hour of the population mean?
    c. Suppose the mean annual number of hours of vacation time earned for a sample of 15,000 blue-collar and service employees who work for small private establishments and have at least 10 years of service differs from the population mean μ by more than one hour. Considering your results for part (b), how would you interpret this result?

46. **MPG for New Cars.** *The New York Times* reported that 17.2 million new cars and light trucks were sold in the United States in 2021, and the U.S. Environmental Protection Agency projects the average efficiency for these vehicles to be 25.7 miles per gallon. Assume that the population standard deviation in miles per gallon for these automobiles is $\sigma = 6$. **LO 6, 7, 8**
    a. What is the probability a sample of 70,000 new cars and light trucks sold in the United States in 2021 will provide a sample mean miles per gallon that is within 0.05 miles per gallon of the population mean of 25.7?
    b. What is the probability a sample of 70,000 new cars and light trucks sold in the United States in 2021 will provide a sample mean miles per gallon that is within 0.01 miles per gallon of the population mean of 25.7? Compare this probability to the value computed in part (a).
    c. What is the probability a sample of 90,000 new cars and light trucks sold in the United States in 2021 will provide a sample mean miles per gallon that is within 0.01 of the population mean of 25.7? Comment on the differences between this probability and the value computed in part (b).
    d. Suppose the mean miles per gallon for a sample of 70,000 new cars and light trucks sold in the United States in 2021 differs from the population mean μ by more than one gallon. How would you interpret this result?

47. **Genders of Entrepreneurs.** *The Wall Street Journal* reported that 37% of all entrepreneurs who opened new U.S. businesses in the previous year were female. **LO 9, 10, 11**
    a. Suppose a random sample of 300 entrepreneurs who opened new U.S. businesses in the previous year will be taken to learn about which industries are most appealing to entrepreneurs. Describe the sampling distribution of $\bar{p}$, where $\bar{p}$ is the sample

proportion of entrepreneurs who opened new U.S. businesses in the previous year that are female.

b. What is the probability that the sample proportion in part (a) will be within ± 0.05 of its population proportion?

c. Suppose a random sample of 30,000 entrepreneurs who opened new U.S. businesses in the previous year will be taken to learn about which industries are most appealing to entrepreneurs. Describe the sampling distribution of $\bar{p}$ where $\bar{p}$ is the sample proportion of entrepreneurs who opened new U.S. businesses last year that are female.

d. What is the probability that the sample proportion in part (c) will be within ± 0.05 of its population proportion?

e. Is the probability different in parts (b) and (d)? Why?

48. **Customers' Ages.** The vice president of sales for Blasterman Cosmetics, Inc. believes that 40% of the company's orders come from customers who are less than 30 years old. A random sample of 10,000 orders will be used to estimate the proportion of customers who are less than 30 years old. **LO 9, 10, 11**

a. Assume that the vice president of sales is correct and $p = 0.40$. What is the sampling distribution of $\bar{p}$ for this study?

b. What is the probability that the sample proportion will be between 0.37 and 0.43?

c. What is the probability that the sample proportion will be between 0.39 and 0.41?

d. What would you conclude if the sample proportion is 0.36?

49. **Repeat Purchases.** The president of Velez.com, Inc., believes that 42% of the firm's orders come from customers who have purchased from Velez.com in the past. A random sample of 108,700 orders from the past six months will be used to estimate the proportion of orders placed by repeat customers. **LO 9, 10, 11**

a. Assume that Velez.com's president is correct and the population proportion $p = 0.42$. What is the sampling distribution of $\bar{p}$ for this study?

b. What is the probability that the sample proportion $\bar{p}$ will be within 0.1% of the population proportion?

c. What is the probability that the sample proportion $\bar{p}$ will be within 0.25% of the population proportion? Comment on the difference between this probability and the value computed in part (b).

d. Suppose the proportion of orders placed by repeat customers for a sample of 108,700 orders from the past six months differs from the population proportion p by more than 1%. How would you interpret this result?

50. **Landline Telephone Service.** According to the Centers for Disease Control and Prevention's National Health Interview Survey, only 40% of homes in the United States used landline telephone service in 2021. **LO 9, 10, 11**

a. Suppose a sample of 207,000 U.S. homes will be taken to learn about home telephone usage. Specify the distribution form and parameters of the sampling distribution of $\bar{p}$ where $\bar{p}$ is the sample proportion of homes that use landline phone service.

b. What is the probability that the sample proportion in part (a) will be within $\pm$ 0.002 of the population proportion?

c. Suppose a sample of 86,800 U.S. homes will be taken to learn about home telephone usage. Describe the sampling distribution of $\bar{p}$ where $\bar{p}$ is the sample proportion of homes that use landline phone service.

d. What is the probability that the sample proportion in part (c) will be within $\pm$ 0.002 of the population proportion?

e. Are the probabilities different in parts (b) and (d)? Why or why not?

Summary

In this chapter, we presented the concepts of sampling and sampling distributions. We demonstrated how a simple random sample can be selected from a finite population and how a random sample can be selected from an infinite population. The data collected from such samples can be used to develop point estimates of population parameters. Because different samples provide different values for the point estimators, point estimators such as $\bar{x}$ and $\bar{p}$ are random variables. The probability distribution of such a random variable is called a sampling distribution. In particular, we described in detail the sampling distributions of the sample mean $\bar{x}$ and the sample proportion $\bar{p}$.

In considering the characteristics of the sampling distributions of $\bar{x}$ and $\bar{p}$, we stated that $E(\bar{x}) = \mu$ and $E(\bar{p}) = p$. After developing the standard deviation or standard error formulas for these estimators, we described the conditions necessary for the sampling distributions of $\bar{x}$ and $\bar{p}$ to follow a normal distribution. Other sampling methods including stratified random sampling, cluster sampling, systematic sampling, convenience sampling, and judgment sampling were discussed. Finally, we discussed the concept of big data and the ramifications of extremely large samples on the sampling distributions of the sample mean and the sample proportion.

Glossary

Big data Any set of data that is too large or too complex to be handled by standard data-processing techniques and typical desktop software.

Central limit theorem A theorem that enables one to use the normal probability distribution to approximate the sampling distribution of $\bar{x}$ whenever the sample size is large.

Cluster sampling A probability sampling method in which the population is first divided into clusters and then a simple random sample of the clusters is taken.

Convenience sampling A nonprobability method of sampling whereby elements are selected for the sample on the basis of convenience.

Coverage error Nonsampling error that results when the research objective and the population from which the sample is to be drawn are not aligned.

Finite population correction factor The term $\sqrt{(N - n)/(N - 1)}$ that is used in the formulas for $\sigma_{\bar{x}}$ and $\sigma_{\bar{p}}$ whenever a finite population, rather than an infinite population, is being sampled. The generally accepted rule of thumb is to ignore the finite population correction factor whenever $n/N \leq 0.05$.

Frame A listing of the elements the sample will be selected from.

Judgment sampling A nonprobability method of sampling whereby elements are selected for the sample based on the judgment of the person doing the study.

Measurement error Nonsampling error that results from the incorrect or imprecise measurement of the population characteristic of interest.

Nonresponse error Nonsampling error that results when potential respondents that belong to some segment(s) of the population are less likely to respond to the survey mechanism than potential respondents that belong to other segments of the population.

Nonsampling error All types of errors other than sampling error, such as coverage error, nonresponse error, measurement error, interviewer error, and processing error.

Parameter A numerical characteristic of a population, such as a population mean μ, a population standard deviation σ, or a population proportion p.

Point estimate The value of a point estimator used in a particular instance as an estimate of a population parameter.

Point estimator The sample statistic, such as $\bar{x}$, s, or $\bar{p}$, that provides the point estimate of the population parameter.

Random sample A random sample from an infinite population is a sample selected such that the following conditions are satisfied: (1) Each element selected comes from the same population; (2) each element is selected independently.

Sample statistic A sample characteristic, such as a sample mean $\bar{x}$, a sample standard deviation s, or a sample proportion $\bar{p}$. The value of the sample statistic is used to estimate the value of the corresponding population parameter.
Sampled population The population from which the sample is taken.
Sampling distribution A probability distribution consisting of all possible values of a sample statistic.
Sampling error The error that occurs because a sample, and not the entire population, is used to estimate a population parameter.
Simple random sample A simple random sample of size n from a finite population of size N is a sample selected such that each possible sample of size n has the same probability of being selected.
Standard error The standard deviation of a point estimator.
Stratified random sampling A probability sampling method in which the population is first divided into strata and a simple random sample is then taken from each stratum.
Systematic sampling A probability sampling method in which we randomly select one of the first k elements and then select every kth element thereafter.
Tall data A data set that has so many observations that traditional statistical inference has little meaning.
Target population The population for which statistical inferences such as point estimates are made. It is important for the target population to correspond as closely as possible to the sampled population.
Unbiased A property of a point estimator that is present when the expected value of the point estimator is equal to the population parameter it estimates.
Variety The diversity in types and structures of the data generated.
Velocity The speed at which the data are generated.
Veracity The reliability of the data generated.
Volume The amount of data generated.
Wide data A data set that has so many variables that simultaneous consideration of all variables is infeasible.

Key Formulas

Expected Value of $\bar{x}$

$$E(\bar{x}) = \mu \tag{7.1}$$

Standard Deviation of $\bar{x}$ (Standard Error)

Finite Population *Infinite Population*

$$\sigma_{\bar{x}} = \sqrt{\frac{N-n}{N-1}}\left(\frac{\sigma}{\sqrt{n}}\right) \qquad \sigma_{\bar{x}} = \frac{\sigma}{\sqrt{n}} \tag{7.2}$$

Expected Value of $\bar{p}$

$$E(\bar{p}) = p \tag{7.4}$$

Standard Deviation of $\bar{p}$ (Standard Error)

Finite Population *Infinite Population*

$$\sigma_{\bar{p}} = \sqrt{\frac{N-n}{N-1}}\sqrt{\frac{p(1-p)}{n}} \qquad \sigma_{\bar{p}} = \sqrt{\frac{p(1-p)}{n}} \tag{7.5}$$

Supplementary Exercises

DATA*file*
shadowstocks

51. **Shadow Stocks.** Jack Lawler, a financial analyst, wants to prepare an article on the Shadow Stock portfolio developed by the American Association of Individual Investors (AAII). A list of the 30 companies in the Shadow Stock portfolio as of March 2014 is contained in the file *shadowstocks* (AAII website). Jack would like to select a simple random sample of five of these companies for an interview concerning management practices. **LO 1**
    a. In the file *shadowstocks*, the Shadow Stock companies are listed in column A of an Excel worksheet. In column B we have generated a random number for each of the companies. Use these random numbers to select a simple random sample of five of these companies for Jack.
    b. Generate a new set of random numbers and use them to select a new simple random sample. Did you select the same companies?
52. **Personal Health Expenditures.** Data made available through the Centers for Medicare & Medicaid Services showed health expenditures were \$12,530 per person in the United States. Use \$12,530 as the population mean and suppose a survey research firm will take a sample of 100 people to investigate the nature of their health expenditures. Assume the population standard deviation is \$2,500. **LO 6, 7, 8**
    a. Specify the distribution form and parameters of the sampling distribution of the mean amount of health care expenditures for a sample of 100 people.
    b. What is the probability the sample mean will be within ±\$200 of the population mean?
    c. What is the probability the sample mean will be greater than \$14,000? If the survey research firm reports a sample mean greater than \$14,000, would you question whether the firm followed correct sampling procedures? Why or why not?
53. **Foot Locker Store Productivity.** According to a report in *The Wall Street Journal*, Foot Locker uses sales per square foot as a measure of store productivity. Sales are currently running at an annual rate of \$406 per square foot. You have been asked by management to conduct a study of a sample of 64 Foot Locker stores. Assume the standard deviation in annual sales per square foot for the population of all 3,400 Foot Locker stores is \$80. **LO 6, 7, 8**
    a. Specify the distribution form and parameters of the sampling distribution of $\bar{x}$, the sample mean annual sales per square foot for a sample of 64 Foot Locker stores.
    b. What is the probability that the sample mean will be within \$15 of the population mean?
    c. Suppose you find a sample mean of \$380. What is the probability of finding a sample mean of \$380 or less? Would you consider such a sample to be an unusually low performing group of stores?
54. **Airline Fares.** The Bureau of Transportation Statistics reports that the mean airfare for flights departing from Buffalo Niagara International Airport during the first three months of 2021 was \$279.19. Assume the standard deviation for this population of fares is known to be \$80. Suppose a random sample of 60 flights departing from Buffalo Niagara International Airport during the first three months of 2022 is taken. **LO 6, 8**
    a. If the mean and standard deviation of the population of airfares for flights departing from Buffalo Niagara International Airport didn't changed between the first three months of 2021 and the first three months of 2022, what is the probability the sample mean will be within \$20 of the population mean cost per flight?
    b. What is the probability the sample mean will be within \$10 of the population mean cost per flight?
55. **University Costs.** The average cost to attend the University of Southern California (USC) is \$78,951. Assume the population standard deviation is \$7,400. Suppose that a random sample of 60 USC students will be taken from this population. **LO 6, 7, 8**

a. What is the value of the standard error of the mean?
b. What is the probability that the sample mean will be more than $78,951?
c. What is the probability that the sample mean will be within $1,000 of the population mean?
d. How would the probability in part (c) change if the sample size were increased to 100?

56. **Inventory Costs.** Three firms carry inventories that differ in size. Firm A's inventory contains 2,000 items, firm B's inventory contains 5,000 items, and firm C's inventory contains 10,000 items. The population standard deviation for the cost of the items in each firm's inventory is $\sigma = 144$. A statistical consultant recommends that each firm take a sample of 50 items from its inventory to provide statistically valid estimates of the average cost per item. Employees of the small firm state that because it has the smallest population, it should be able to make the estimate from a much smaller sample than that required by the larger firms. However, the consultant states that to obtain the same standard error and thus the same precision in the sample results, all firms should use the same sample size regardless of population size. **LO 6, 8**
a. Using the finite population correction factor, compute the standard error for each of the three firms given a sample of size 50.
b. What is the probability that for each firm the sample mean $\bar{x}$ will be within ± 25 of the population mean μ?

57. **Survey Research Results.** A researcher reports survey results by stating that the standard error of the mean is 20. The population standard deviation is 500. **LO 6, 8**
a. How large was the sample used in this survey?
b. What is the probability that the point estimate was within ± 25 of the population mean?

58. **Production Quality Control.** A production process is checked periodically by a quality control inspector. The inspector selects simple random samples of 30 finished products and computes the sample mean product weights $\bar{x}$. If test results over a long period of time show that 5% of the $\bar{x}$ values are over 2.1 pounds and 5% are under 1.9 pounds, what are the mean and the standard deviation for the population of products produced with this process? **LO 6, 8**

59. **Australians and Smoking.** Reuters reports that 15% of Australians smoke. By introducing tough laws banning brand labels on cigarette packages, Australia hopes to reduce the percentage of people smoking to 10%. Answer the following questions based on a sample of 240 Australians. **LO 9, 10, 11**
a. Specify the distribution form and parameters of the sampling distribution of $\bar{p}$, the proportion of Australians who are smokers.
b. What is the probability the sample proportion will be within ± 0.04 of the population proportion?
c. What is the probability the sample proportion will be within ± 0.02 of the population proportion?

60. **Marketing Research Telephone Surveys.** A market research firm conducts telephone surveys with a 40% historical response rate. What is the probability that in a new sample of 400 telephone numbers, at least 150 individuals will cooperate and respond to the questions? In other words, what is the probability that the sample proportion will be at least $150/400 = 0.375$? **LO 9, 10, 11**

61. **Internet Advertising.** Advertisers contract with Internet service providers and search engines to place ads on websites. They pay a fee based on the number of potential customers who click on their ad. Unfortunately, click fraud—the practice of someone clicking on an ad solely for the purpose of driving up advertising revenue—has become a problem. According to *BusinessWeek*, 40% of advertisers claim they have been a victim of click fraud. Suppose a simple random sample of 380 advertisers will be taken to learn more about how they are affected by this practice. **LO 9, 11**

a. What is the probability that the sample proportion will be within ±0.04 of the population proportion experiencing click fraud?
b. What is the probability that the sample proportion will be greater than 0.45?

62. **Traffic Tickets.** The proportion of individuals insured by the All-Driver Automobile Insurance Company who received at least one traffic ticket during a five-year period is 0.15. **LO 9, 10, 11**
a. Specify the distribution form and parameters of the sampling distribution of $\bar{p}$ if a random sample of 150 insured individuals is used to estimate the proportion having received at least one ticket.
b. What is the probability that the sample proportion will be within ±0.03 of the population proportion?

63. **Textbook Publishing.** Lori Jeffrey is a successful sales representative for a major publisher of college textbooks. Historically, Lori obtains a book adoption on 25% of their sales calls. Viewing Lori's sales calls for one month as a sample of all possible sales calls, assume that a statistical analysis of the data yields a standard error of the proportion of 0.0625. **LO 9, 10, 11**
a. How large was the sample used in this analysis? That is, how many sales calls did Lori make during the month?
b. Let $\bar{p}$ indicate the sample proportion of book adoptions obtained during the month. Specify the distribution form and parameters of the sampling distribution of $\bar{p}$.
c. Using the sampling distribution of $\bar{p}$, compute the probability that Lori will obtain book adoptions on 30% or more of her sales calls during a one-month period.

64. **Life of Compact Fluorescent Lights.** In 2018, the Simple Dollar website reported that the mean life of 14-watt compact fluorescent lights (CFLs) is 8,000 hours. Assume that for this population the standard deviation for CFL life is 480. Suppose the U.S. Department of Energy would like to select a random sample of 35,000 from the population of 14-watt CFLs for a follow-up study. **LO 6, 7, 8**
a. Specify the distribution form and parameters of the sampling distribution of $\bar{x}$, the sample mean for a sample of 35,000 individuals from this population.
b. What is the probability that a simple random sample of 35,000 individuals from this population will provide a sample mean that is within four hours of the population mean?
c. What is the probability that a simple random sample of 35,000 individuals from this population will provide a sample mean that is within one hour of the population mean?
d. Suppose the mean life of a sample of 35,000 14-watt CFLs differs from the population mean life by more than four hours. How would you interpret this result?

65. **Typical Home Internet Usage.** According to USC Annenberg, the mean time spent by Americans on the Internet in their home per week is 17.6 hours. Assume that the standard deviation for the time spent by Americans on the Internet in their home per week is 5.1 hours. Suppose the Florida Department of State plans to select a random sample of 85,020 of the state's residents for a study of Floridians' Internet usage. **LO 6, 7, 8**
a. Using the U.S. population figures provided in the problem (the population mean and standard deviation of time spent by Americans on the Internet in their home per week are 17.6 hours and 5.1 hours, respectively), specify the distribution form and parameters of is the sampling distribution of the sample mean for the sample of 85,020 Floridians.
b. Using the sampling distribution from part (a), what is the probability that a random sample of 85,020 Floridians will provide a sample mean that is within three minutes of the population mean?
c. Suppose the mean time spent on the Internet in their home per week by the sample of 85,020 Floridians differs from the U.S. population mean by more than three minutes? How would you interpret this result?

66. **Undeliverable Mail Pieces.** Of the 155 billion mailpieces the U.S. Postal Service (USPS) processed and delivered in 2017, 4.3% were undeliverable as addressed. Suppose that a brief questionnaire about USPS service is attached to each mailpiece in a random sample of 114,250 mailpieces. **LO 9, 10, 11**
    a. Specify the distribution form and parameters of is the sampling distribution of the sample proportion of undeliverable mailpieces $\bar{p}$ for this study.
    b. What is the probability that the sample proportion of undeliverable mailpieces $\bar{p}$ will be within 0.1% of the population proportion of undeliverable mailpieces?
    c. What is the probability that the sample proportion of undeliverable mailpieces $\bar{p}$ will be within 0.05% of the population proportion of undeliverable mailpieces? Comment on the difference between this probability and the probability computed in part (b).
67. **U.S. Drivers and Speeding.** ABC News reports that 58% of U.S. drivers admit to speeding. Suppose that a new satellite technology can instantly measure the speed of any vehicle on a U.S. road and determine whether the vehicle is speeding, and this satellite technology was used to take a random sample of 20,000 vehicles at 6 P.M. EST on a recent Tuesday afternoon. **LO 9, 10, 11**
    a. For this investigation, specify the distribution form and parameters of the sampling distribution for sample proportion of vehicles on U.S. roads that speed.
    b. What is the probability that the sample proportion of speeders $\bar{p}$ will be within 1% of the population proportion of speeders?
    c. Suppose the sample proportion of speeders $\bar{p}$ differs from the U.S. population proportion of seeders by more than 1%? How would you interpret this result?

Case Problem 1: Marion Dairies

Last year Marion Dairies decided to enter the yogurt market, and it began cautiously by producing, distributing, and marketing a single flavor—a blueberry-flavored yogurt that it calls Blugurt. The company's initial venture into the yogurt market has been very successful; sales of Blugurt are higher than expected, and consumers' ratings of the product have a mean of 80 and a standard deviation of 25 on a 100-point scale for which 100 is the most favorable score and zero is the least favorable score. Past experience has also shown Marion Dairies that a consumer who rates one of its products with a score greater than 75 on this scale will consider purchasing the product, and a score of 75 or less indicates the consumer will not consider purchasing the product.

Emboldened by the success and popularity of its blueberry-flavored yogurt, Marion Dairies management is now considering the introduction of a second flavor. Marion's marketing department is pressing to extend the product line through the introduction of a strawberry-flavored yogurt that would be called Strawgurt, but senior managers are concerned about whether or not Strawgurt will increase Marion's market share by appealing to potential customers who do not like Blugurt. That is, the goal in offering the new product is to increase Marion's market share rather than cannibalize existing sales of Blugurt. The marketing department has proposed giving tastes of both Blugurt and Strawgurt to a simple random sample of 50 customers and asking each of them to rate the two flavors of yogurt on the 100-point scale. If the mean score given to Blugurt by this sample of consumers is 75 or less, Marion's senior management believes the sample can be used to assess whether Strawgurt will appeal to potential customers who do not like Blugurt. **LO 6, 7, 8**

Managerial Report

Prepare a managerial report that addresses the following issues.

1. Calculate the probability the mean score of Blugurt given by the simple random sample of Marion Dairies customers will be 75 or less.

2. If the Marketing Department increases the sample size to 150, what is the probability the mean score of Blugurt given by the simple random sample of Marion Dairies customers will be 75 or less?
3. Explain to Marion Dairies senior management why the probability that the mean score of Blugurt for a random sample of Marion Dairies customers will be 75 or less is different for samples of 50 and 150 Marion Dairies customers.

Case Problem 2: Profitability of Small Restaurants

Lucía Pérez, a data analyst employed by the Small Business/Big Economy (SBBE) think tank, is performing an analysis of the profitability of restaurants in the United States with 50 or fewer employees during the previous year. In the course of the analysis, they have learned from the Small Business Association (SBA) that 78% of all businesses in the United States with 50 or fewer employees reported a profit during the most recent year.

As part of the analysis, SBBE has asked Ms. Pérez to compare the profitability of restaurants in the United States with 50 or fewer employees to all businesses in the United States with 50 or fewer employees during the most recent year. After spending a great deal of time trying to develop a way to measure the proportion of the 135,000+ restaurants in the United States with no more than 50 employees that reported a profit last year, they find the results of a recent SBBE online survey that they believe will be useful. The survey was distributed to a list of 98,731 U.S. restaurants with 50 or fewer employees, and one question on the survey asked whether the restaurant was profitable during the previous year.

Of the 98,731 restaurants surveyed, 37,918 responded. Of the restaurants that responded, 29,007 indicated they were profitable during the previous year. **LO 9, 10, 11**

Managerial Report

Prepare a managerial report that addresses the following issues.

1. Use the results of the SBBE online sample to estimate the proportion of restaurants with no more than 50 employees that reported a profit during the previous year.
2. Assuming the proportion of restaurants with no more than 50 employees that was profitable during the previous year is equal to the proportion of all businesses in the United States with 50 or fewer employees that were profitable during the past year, provide the sampling distribution of the sample proportion of restaurants with no more than 50 employees that were profitable for the previous year.
3. Assuming the proportion of restaurants with no more than 50 employees that was profitable during the previous year is identical to the proportion of all businesses in the United States with 50 or fewer employees that were profitable during the past year, calculate the probability that the proportion of a sample of 37,918 restaurants with 50 or fewer employees that was profitable last year does not exceed 0.765.
4. Explain the implications of the results of your response to part 3.
5. Express any concerns you have over the collection of the sample of restaurants in the United States with no more than 50 employees.

Chapter 8

Interval Estimation

Contents

Statistics in Practice:
Food Lion

8.1 Population Mean: σ Known
Margin of Error and the Interval Estimate
Using Excel
Practical Advice

8.2 Population Mean: σ Unknown
Margin of Error and the Interval Estimate
Using Excel
Practical Advice
Using a Small Sample
Summary of Interval Estimation Procedures

8.3 Determining the Sample Size

8.4 Population Proportion
Using Excel
Determining the Sample Size

8.5 Practical Advice: Big Data and Interval Estimation
Big Data and the Precision of Confidence Intervals
Implications of Big Data for Confidence Intervals

Summary 405
Glossary 406
Key Formulas 406
Supplementary Exercises 407
Case Problem 1: *Young Professional* Magazine 410
Case Problem 2: Gulf Real Estate Properties 411
Case Problem 3: Garza Research, Inc. 413
Case Problem 4: Go-Fer Meal Delivery Service 414

Available in the Cengage ebook:
Appendix: Interval Estimation of a Population Mean, Known Standard Deviation with R
Appendix: Interval Estimation of a Population Mean, Unknown Standard Deviation with R
Appendix: Interval Estimation of a Population Proportion with R

Learning Objectives

After completing this chapter, you will be able to

LO 1 Calculate and interpret the margin of error and the interval estimate at a given level of confidence for a mean when the population standard deviation σ is known.

LO 2 Describe and explain the distribution form and parameters of the sampling distribution of the sample mean in the cases when the population standard deviation is unknown.

LO 3 Calculate and interpret the margin of error and the interval estimate at a given level of confidence for a mean when the population standard deviation σ is unknown.

LO 4 Determine the sample size necessary to provide an interval estimate of the mean at a desired margin of error at a specified confidence level.

LO 5 Calculate and interpret the margin of error, and the interval estimate at a given level of confidence for a proportion.

LO 6 Determine the sample size necessary to provide an interval estimate of the proportion at a desired margin of error at a specified confidence level.

Statistics in Practice

Food Lion*

Salisbury, North Carolina

Founded in 1957 as Food Town, Food Lion is one of the largest supermarket chains in the United States, with over 1,100 stores in 10 Southeastern and Mid-Atlantic states. The company sells more than 24,000 different products and offers nationally and regionally advertised brand-name merchandise, as well as a growing number of high-quality private label products manufactured especially for Food Lion. The company maintains its low-price leadership and quality assurance through operating efficiencies such as standard store formats, innovative warehouse design, energy-efficient facilities, and data synchronization with suppliers. Food Lion looks to a future of continued innovation, growth, price leadership, and service to its customers.

Being in an inventory-intense business, Food Lion made the decision to adopt the LIFO (last-in, first-out) method of inventory valuation. This method matches current costs against current revenues, which minimizes the effect of radical price changes on profit and loss results. In addition, the LIFO method reduces net income, thereby reducing income taxes during periods of inflation.

Food Lion establishes a LIFO index for each of seven inventory pools: Grocery, Paper/Household, Pet Supplies, Health & Beauty Aids, Dairy, Cigarettes/Tobacco, and Beer/Wine. For example, a LIFO index of 1.008 for the Grocery pool would indicate that the company's grocery inventory value at current costs reflects a 0.8% increase due to inflation over the most recent one-year period.

A LIFO index for each inventory pool requires that the year-end inventory count for each product be valued at the current year-end cost and at the preceding year-end cost. To avoid excessive time and expense associated with counting the inventory in all store locations, Food Lion selects a random sample of 50 stores. Year-end physical inventories are taken in each of the sample stores. The current-year and preceding-year costs for each item are then used to construct the required LIFO indexes for each inventory pool.

© Davis Turner/Bloomberg/Getty Images

For a recent year, the sample estimate of the LIFO index for the Health & Beauty Aids inventory pool was 1.015. Using a 95% confidence level, Food Lion computed a margin of error of 0.006 for the sample estimate. Thus, the interval from 1.009 to 1.021 provided a 95% confidence interval estimate of the population LIFO index. This level of precision was judged to be very good.

In this chapter, you will learn how to compute the margin of error associated with sample estimates. You will also learn how to use this information to construct and interpret interval estimates of a population mean and a population proportion.

*The authors are indebted to Keith Cunningham, Tax Director, and Bobby Harkey, Staff Tax Accountant, at Food Lion for providing this Statistics in Practice.

In Chapter 7, we stated that a point estimator is a sample statistic used to estimate a population parameter. For instance, the sample mean $\bar{x}$ is a point estimator of the population mean μ and the sample proportion $\bar{p}$ is a point estimator of the population proportion p. Because a point estimator cannot be expected to provide the exact value of the population parameter, an **interval estimate** is often computed by adding and subtracting a value, called the **margin of error**, to the point estimate. The general form of an interval estimate is as follows:

$$\text{Point estimate} \pm \text{Margin of error}$$

The purpose of an interval estimate is to provide information about how close the point estimate, provided by the sample, is to the value of the population parameter.

In this chapter, we show how to compute interval estimates of a population mean μ and a population proportion p. The general form of an interval estimate of a population mean is

$$\bar{x} \pm \text{Margin of error}$$

Similarly, the general form of an interval estimate of a population proportion is

$$\bar{p} \pm \text{Margin of error}$$

The sampling distributions of $\bar{x}$ and $\bar{p}$ play key roles in computing these interval estimates.

8.1 Population Mean: σ Known

In order to develop an interval estimate of a population mean, either the population standard deviation σ or the sample standard deviation s must be used to compute the margin of error. In most applications σ is not known, and s is used to compute the margin of error. In some applications, however, large amounts of relevant historical data are available and can be used to estimate the population standard deviation prior to sampling. Also, in quality control applications where a process is assumed to be operating correctly, or "in control," it is appropriate to treat the population standard deviation as known. We refer to such cases as **σ known** cases. In this section we introduce an example in which it is reasonable to treat σ as known and show how to construct an interval estimate for this case.

Each week, Lloyd's Department Store selects a simple random sample of 100 customers in order to learn about the amount spent per shopping trip. With x representing the amount spent per shopping trip, the sample mean $\bar{x}$ provides a point estimate of μ, the mean amount spent per shopping trip for the population of all Lloyd's customers. Lloyd's has been using the weekly survey for several years. Based on the historical data, Lloyd's now assumes a known value of $\sigma = \$20$ for the population standard deviation. The historical data also indicate that the population follows a normal distribution.

DATA*file*
lloyds

During the most recent week, Lloyd's surveyed 100 customers ($n = 100$) and obtained a sample mean of $\bar{x} = \$82$. The sample mean amount spent provides a point estimate of the population mean amount spent per shopping trip, μ. In the discussion that follows, we show how to compute the margin of error for this estimate and develop an interval estimate of the population mean.

Margin of Error and the Interval Estimate

In Chapter 7, we showed that the sampling distribution of $\bar{x}$ can be used to compute the probability that $\bar{x}$ will be within a given distance of μ. In the Lloyd's example, the historical data show that the population of amounts spent is normally distributed with a standard deviation of $\sigma = 20$. So, using what we learned in Chapter 7, we can conclude that the sampling distribution of $\bar{x}$ follows a normal distribution with a standard error of $\sigma_{\bar{x}} = \sigma/\sqrt{n} = 20/\sqrt{100} = 2$. This sampling distribution is shown in Figure 8.1.[1] Because the sampling distribution shows how values of $\bar{x}$ are distributed around the population mean μ, the sampling distribution of $\bar{x}$ provides information about the possible differences between $\bar{x}$ and μ.

Using the standard normal probability table, we find that 95% of the values of any normally distributed random variable are within ± 1.96 standard deviations of the mean. Thus, when the sampling distribution of $\bar{x}$ is normally distributed, 95% of the $\bar{x}$ values must be within $\pm 1.96\sigma_{\bar{x}}$ of the mean μ. In the Lloyd's example, we know that the sampling distribution of $\bar{x}$ is normally distributed with a standard error of $\sigma_{\bar{x}} = 2$. Because $\pm 1.96\sigma_{\bar{x}} = 1.96(2) = 3.92$, we can conclude that 95% of all $\bar{x}$ values obtained using a sample size of $n = 100$ will be within ± 3.92 of the population mean μ. See Figure 8.2.

[1] We use the fact that the population of amounts spent has a normal distribution to conclude that the sampling distribution of $\bar{x}$ has a normal distribution. If the population did not have a normal distribution, we could rely on the central limit theorem and the sample size of $n = 100$ to conclude that the sampling distribution of $\bar{x}$ is approximately normal. In either case, the sampling distribution of $\bar{x}$ would appear as shown in Figure 8.1.

Figure 8.1 Sampling Distribution of the Sample Mean Amount Spent from Simple Random Samples of 100 Customers

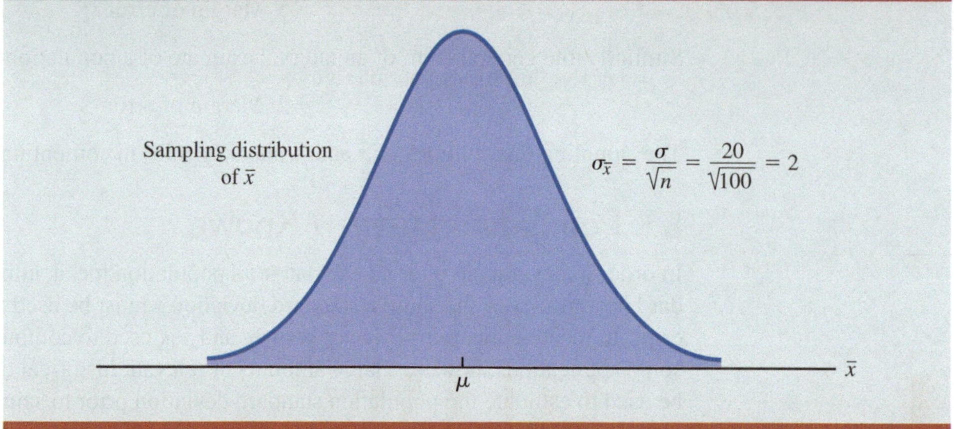

Figure 8.2 Sampling Distribution of $\bar{x}$ Showing the Location of Sample Means That Are Within 3.92 of μ

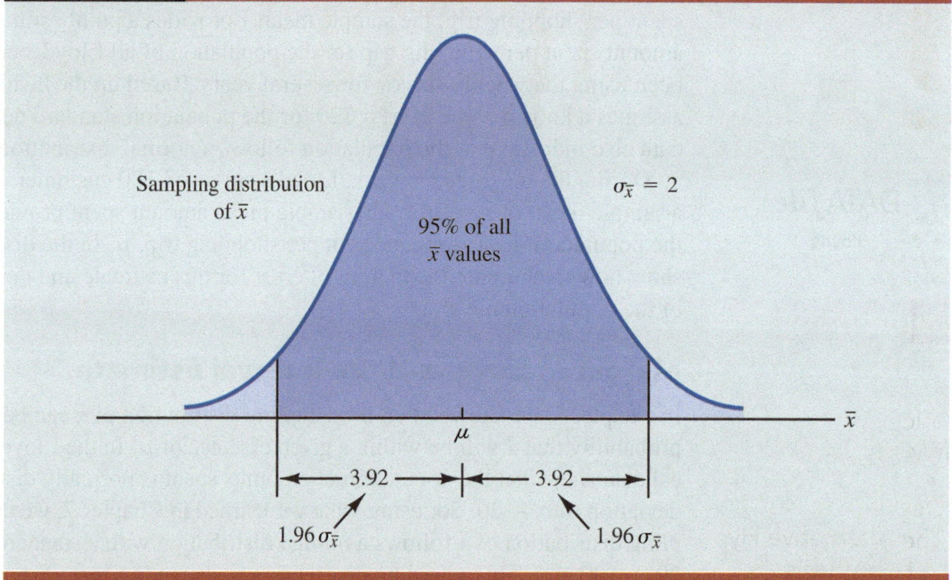

In the introduction to this chapter, we said that the general form of an interval estimate of the population mean μ is $\bar{x} \pm$ margin of error. For the Lloyd's example, suppose we set the margin of error equal to 3.92 and compute the interval estimate of μ using $\bar{x} \pm 3.92$. To provide an interpretation for this interval estimate, let us consider the values of $\bar{x}$ that could be obtained if we took three *different* simple random samples, each consisting of 100 Lloyd's customers. The first sample mean might turn out to have the value shown as $\bar{x}_1$ in Figure 8.3. In this case, Figure 8.3 shows that the interval formed by subtracting 3.92 from $\bar{x}_1$ and adding 3.92 to $\bar{x}_1$ includes the population mean μ. Now consider what happens if the second sample mean turns out to have the value shown as $\bar{x}_2$ in Figure 8.3. Although this sample mean differs from the first sample mean, we see that the interval formed by subtracting 3.92 from $\bar{x}_2$ and adding 3.92 to $\bar{x}_2$ also includes the population mean μ. However, consider what happens if the third sample mean turns out to have the

Figure 8.3 Intervals Formed from Selected Sample Means at Locations $\bar{x}_1$, $\bar{x}_2$, and $\bar{x}_3$

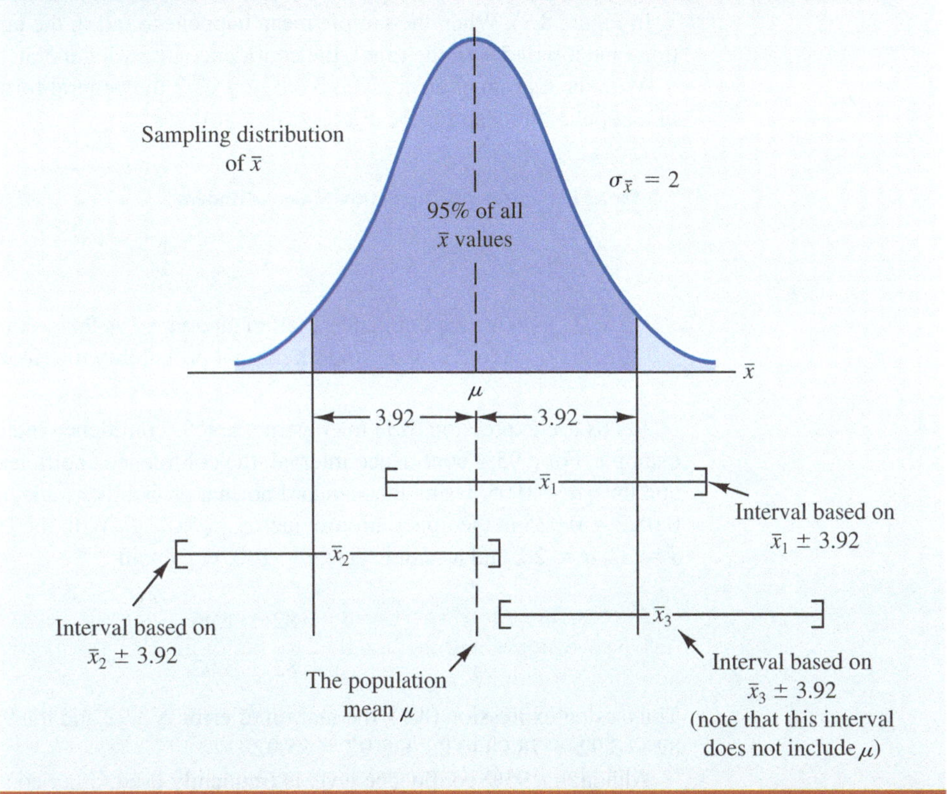

value shown as $\bar{x}_3$ in Figure 8.3. In this case, the interval formed by subtracting 3.92 from $\bar{x}_3$ and adding 3.92 to $\bar{x}_3$ does not include the population mean μ. Because $\bar{x}_3$ falls in the upper tail of the sampling distribution and is farther than 3.92 from μ, subtracting and adding 3.92 to $\bar{x}_3$ forms an interval that does not include μ.

Any sample mean $\bar{x}$ that is within the darkly shaded region of Figure 8.3 will provide an interval that contains the population mean μ. Because 95% of all possible sample means are in the darkly shaded region, 95% of all intervals formed by subtracting 3.92 from $\bar{x}$ and adding 3.92 to $\bar{x}$ will include the population mean μ.

Recall that during the most recent week, the quality assurance team at Lloyd's surveyed 100 customers and obtained a sample mean amount spent of $\bar{x} = 82$. Using $\bar{x} \pm 3.92$ to construct the interval estimate, we obtain 82 ± 3.92. Thus, the specific interval estimate of μ based on the data from the most recent week is $82 - 3.92 = 78.08$ to $82 + 3.92 = 85.92$. Because 95% of all the intervals constructed using $\bar{x} \pm 3.92$ will contain the population mean, we say that we are 95% confident that the interval 78.08 to 85.92 includes the population mean μ. We say that this interval has been established at the 95% **confidence level**. The value 0.95 is referred to as the **confidence coefficient**, and the interval 78.08 to 85.92 is called the 95% **confidence interval**.

This discussion provides insight as to why the interval is called a 95% confidence interval.

Another term sometimes associated with an interval estimate is the **level of significance**. The level of significance associated with an interval estimate is denoted by the Greek letter α. The level of significance and the confidence coefficient are related as follows:

$$\alpha = \text{Level of significance} = 1 - \text{Confidence coefficient}$$

The level of significance is the probability that the interval estimation procedure will generate an interval that does not contain μ. For example, the level of significance corresponding to a 0.95 confidence coefficient is $\alpha = 1 - 0.95 = 0.05$. In the Lloyd's case, the level of significance ($\alpha = 0.05$) is the probability of drawing a sample, computing the sample mean, and finding that $\bar{x}$ lies in one of the tails of the sampling distribution (see $\bar{x}_3$ in Figure 8.3). When the sample mean happens to fall in the tail of the sampling distribution (and it will 5% of the time), the confidence interval generated will not contain μ.

With the margin of error given by $(z_{\alpha/2}\sigma/\sqrt{n})$, the general form of an interval estimate of a population mean for the σ known case follows.

Interval Estimate of a Population Mean: σ Known

$$\bar{x} \pm z_{\alpha/2}\frac{\sigma}{\sqrt{n}} \quad \textbf{(8.1)}$$

where $(1 - \alpha)$ is the confidence coefficient and $z_{\alpha/2}$ is the z value providing an area of $\alpha/2$ in the upper tail of the standard normal probability distribution.

Let us use expression (8.1) to construct a 95% confidence interval for the Lloyd's example. For a 95% confidence interval, the confidence coefficient is $(1 - \alpha) = 0.95$ and thus, $\alpha = 0.05$. Using the standard normal probability table, an area of $\alpha/2 = 0.05/2 = 0.025$ in the upper tail provides $z_{0.025} = 1.96$. With the Lloyd's sample mean $\bar{x} = 82$, $\sigma = 20$, and a sample size $n = 100$, we obtain

$$82 \pm 1.96\frac{20}{\sqrt{100}}$$
$$82 \pm 3.92$$

Thus, using expression (8.1), the margin of error is 3.92 and the 95% confidence interval is $82 - 3.92 = 78.08$ to $82 + 3.92 = 85.92$.

Although a 95% confidence level is frequently used, other confidence levels such as 90% and 99% may be considered. Values of $z_{\alpha/2}$ for the most commonly used confidence levels are shown in Table 8.1. Using these values and expression (8.1), the 90% confidence interval for the Lloyd's example is

$$82 \pm 1.645\frac{20}{\sqrt{100}}$$
$$82 \pm 3.29$$

Thus, at 90% confidence, the margin of error is 3.29 and the confidence interval is $82 - 3.29 = 78.71$ to $82 + 3.29 = 85.29$. Similarly, the 99% confidence interval is

$$82 \pm 2.576\frac{20}{\sqrt{100}}$$
$$82 \pm 5.15$$

Thus, at 99% confidence, the margin of error is 5.15 and the confidence interval is $82 - 5.15 = 76.85$ to $82 + 5.15 = 87.15$.

Comparing the results for the 90%, 95%, and 99% confidence levels, we see that in order to have a higher level of confidence, the margin of error and thus the width of the confidence interval must be larger.

Table 8.1 Values of $z_{\alpha/2}$ for the Most Commonly Used Confidence Levels

Confidence Level	α	$\alpha/2$	$z_{\alpha/2}$
90%	0.10	0.05	1.645
95%	0.05	0.025	1.960
99%	0.01	0.005	2.576

Using Excel

We will use the Lloyd's Department Store data to illustrate how Excel can be used to construct an interval estimate of the population mean for the σ known case. Refer to Figure 8.4 as we describe the tasks involved. The formula worksheet is in the background; the value worksheet appears in the foreground.

Enter/Access Data: Open the file *lloyds*. A label and the sales data are entered in cells A1:A101.

Enter Functions and Formulas: The sample size and sample mean are computed in cells D4:D5 using Excel's COUNT and AVERAGE functions, respectively. The value worksheet shows that the sample size is 100 and the sample mean is 82. The value of the known population standard deviation (*20*) is entered in cell D7 and the desired confidence coefficient (*0.95*) is entered in cell D8. The level of significance is computed in cell D9 by entering the formula *=1-D8*; the value worksheet shows that the level of significance associated with a confidence coefficient of 0.95 is 0.05. The margin of error is computed in cell D11 using Excel's CONFIDENCE.NORM function. The CONFIDENCE.NORM function has three inputs: the level of significance (cell D9); the population standard deviation (cell D7); and the sample size (cell D4). Thus, to compute the margin of error associated with a 95% confidence interval, the following formula is entered in cell D11:

=CONFIDENCE.NORM(D9,D7,D4)

The resulting value of 3.92 is the margin of error associated with the interval estimate of the population mean amount spent per week.

Cells D13:D15 provide the point estimate and the lower and upper limits for the confidence interval. Because the point estimate is just the sample mean, the formula *=D5* is entered in cell D13. To compute the lower limit of the 95% confidence interval, $\bar{x}$ − (margin of error), we enter the formula *=D13-D11* in cell D14. To compute the upper limit of the 95% confidence interval, $\bar{x}$ + (margin of error), we enter the formula *=D13 + D11* in cell D15. The value worksheet shows a lower limit of 78.08 and an upper limit of 85.92. In other words, the 95% confidence interval for the population mean is from 78.08 to 85.92.

Figure 8.4 Excel Worksheet: Constructing a 95% Confidence Interval for Lloyd's Department Store

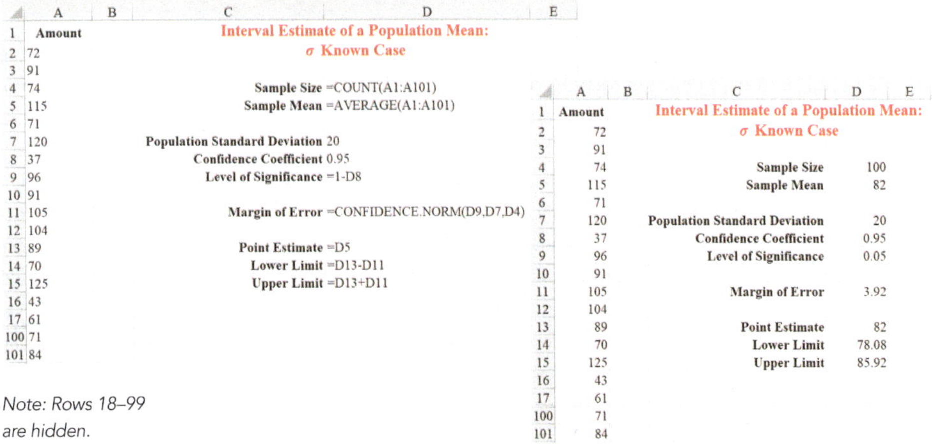

Note: Rows 18–99 are hidden.

A Template for Other Problems To use this worksheet as a template for another problem of this type, we must first enter the new problem data in column A. Then, the cell formulas in cells D4 and D5 must be updated with the new data range and the known population standard deviation must be entered in cell D7. After doing so, the point estimate and a 95% confidence interval will be displayed in cells D13:D15. If a confidence interval with a different confidence coefficient is desired, we simply change the value in cell D8.

We can further simplify the use of Figure 8.4 as a template for other problems by eliminating the need to enter new data ranges in cells D4 and D5. To do so, we rewrite the cell formulas as follows:

Cell D4: =*COUNT(A:A)*
Cell D5: =*AVERAGE(A:A)*

The Lloyd's data set includes a worksheet entitled Template that uses the A:A method for entering the data ranges.

With the A:A method of specifying data ranges, Excel's COUNT function will count the number of numerical values in column A and Excel's AVERAGE function will compute the average of the numerical values in column A. Thus, to solve a new problem it is only necessary to enter the new data into column A and enter the value of the known population standard deviation in cell D7.

This worksheet can also be used as a template for text exercises in which the sample size, sample mean, and the population standard deviation are given. In this type of situation we simply replace the values in cells D4, D5, and D7 with the given values of the sample size, sample mean, and the population standard deviation.

Practical Advice

If the population follows a normal distribution, the confidence interval provided by expression (8.1) is exact. In other words, if expression (8.1) were used repeatedly to generate 95% confidence intervals, exactly 95% of the intervals generated would contain the population mean. If the population does not follow a normal distribution, the confidence interval provided by expression (8.1) will be approximate. In this case, the quality of the approximation depends on both the distribution of the population and the sample size.

In most applications, a sample size of $n \geq 30$ is adequate when using expression (8.1) to develop an interval estimate of a population mean. If the population is not normally distributed, but is roughly symmetric, sample sizes as small as 15 can be expected to provide good approximate confidence intervals. With smaller sample sizes, expression (8.1) should only be used if the analyst believes, or is willing to assume, that the population distribution is at least approximately normal.

Notes + Comments

1. The interval estimation procedure discussed in this section is based on the assumption that the population standard deviation σ is known. By σ known, we mean that historical data or other information are available that permit us to obtain a good estimate of the population standard deviation prior to taking the sample that will be used to develop an estimate of the population mean. So, technically we don't mean that σ is actually known with certainty. We just mean that we obtained a good estimate of the standard deviation prior to sampling and thus we won't be using the same sample to estimate both the population mean and the population standard deviation.
2. The sample size n appears in the denominator of the interval estimation expression (8.1). Thus, if a particular sample size provides too wide an interval to be of any practical use, we may want to consider increasing the sample size. With n in the denominator, a larger sample size will provide a smaller margin of error, a narrower interval, and greater precision. The procedure for determining the size of a simple random sample necessary to obtain a desired precision is discussed in Section 8.3.
3. When developing a confidence interval for the mean with a sample size that is at least 5% of the population size (that is, $n/N \geq 0.05$), the finite population correction factor should be used when calculating the standard error of the sampling distribution of $\bar{x}$ when σ is known, i.e., $\sigma_{\bar{x}} = \sqrt{\frac{N-n}{N-1}}\left(\frac{\sigma}{\sqrt{n}}\right)$.

Exercises

Methods

1. A simple random sample of 40 items resulted in a sample mean of 25. The population standard deviation is $\sigma = 5$. **LO 1**
   a. What is the standard error of the mean, $\sigma_{\bar{x}}$?
   b. At 95% confidence, what is the margin of error?

2. A simple random sample of 50 items from a population with $\sigma = 6$ resulted in a sample mean of 32. **LO 1**
   a. Provide a 90% confidence interval for the population mean.
   b. Provide a 95% confidence interval for the population mean.
   c. Provide a 99% confidence interval for the population mean.

3. A simple random sample of 60 items resulted in a sample mean of 80. The population standard deviation is $\sigma = 15$. **LO 1**
   a. Compute the 95% confidence interval for the population mean.
   b. Assume that the same sample mean was obtained from a sample of 120 items. Provide a 95% confidence interval for the population mean.
   c. What is the effect of a larger sample size on the interval estimate?

4. A 95% confidence interval for a population mean was reported to be 152 to 160. If $\sigma = 15$, what sample size was used in this study? **LO 4**

Applications

DATA*file* houston

5. **Restaurant Bills.** Data were collected on the amount spent by 64 customers for lunch at a major Houston restaurant. These data are contained in the file *houston*. Based upon past studies the population standard deviation is known with $\sigma = \$6$. **LO 1**
   a. At 99% confidence, what is the margin of error?
   b. Develop a 99% confidence interval estimate of the mean amount spent for lunch.

DATA*file* traveltax

6. **Travel Taxes.** In an attempt to assess total daily travel taxes in various cities, the Global Business Travel Association conducted a study of daily travel taxes on lodging, rental car, and meals. The data contained in the file *traveltax* are consistent with the findings of that study for business travel to Chicago. Assume the population standard deviation is known to be \$8.50 and develop a 95% confidence interval of the population mean total daily travel taxes for Chicago. **LO 1**

DATA*file* setters

7. **Cost of Dog Ownership**. *Money* reports that the average annual cost of the first year of owning and caring for a large dog in 2017 is \$1,448. The Irish Red and White Setter Association of America has requested a study to estimate the annual first-year cost for owners of this breed. A sample of 50 will be used. Based on past studies, the population standard deviation is assumed known with $\sigma = \$255$. **LO 1**
   a. What is the margin of error for a 95% confidence interval of the mean cost of the first year of owning and caring for this breed?
   b. The file *setters* contains data collected from fifty owners of Irish Setters on the cost of the first year of owning and caring for their dogs. Use this data set to compute the sample mean. Using this sample, what is the 95% confidence interval for the mean cost of the first year of owning and caring for an Irish Red and White Setter?

8. **Cost of Massage Therapy Sessions.** *The Wall Street Journal* reported on several studies that show massage therapy has a variety of health benefits and it is not too expensive. A sample of 10 typical one-hour massage therapy sessions showed an average charge of \$59. The population standard deviation for a one-hour session is $\sigma = \$5.50$. **LO 1**
   a. What assumptions about the population should we be willing to make if a margin of error is desired?
   b. Using 95% confidence, what is the margin of error?
   c. Using 99% confidence, what is the margin of error?

DATA*file*
tobaccofires

9. **Cost to Repair Fire Damage.** The mean cost to repair the smoke and fire damage that result from home fires of all causes is \$11,389 (HomeAdvisor). How does the damage that results from home fires caused by careless use of tobacco compare? The file *tobaccofires* provides the cost to repair smoke and fire damage associated with a sample of 55 fires caused by careless use of tobacco products. Using past years' data, the population standard deviation can be assumed known with $\sigma = \$3{,}027$. What is the 95% confidence interval estimate of the mean cost to repair smoke and fire damage that results from home fires caused by careless use of tobacco? How does this compare with the mean cost to repair the smoke and fire damage that result from home fires of all causes? **LO 1**

10. **Assisted-Living Facility Rent.** Costs are rising for all kinds of medical care. The mean monthly rent at assisted-living facilities was reported to have increased 17% over the last five years to \$3,486. Assume this cost estimate is based on a sample of 120 facilities and, from past studies, it can be assumed that the population standard deviation is $\sigma = \$650$. **LO 1**
    a. Develop a 90% confidence interval estimate of the population mean monthly rent.
    b. Develop a 95% confidence interval estimate of the population mean monthly rent.
    c. Develop a 99% confidence interval estimate of the population mean monthly rent.
    d. What happens to the width of the confidence interval as the confidence level is increased? Does this seem reasonable? Explain.

8.2 Population Mean: σ Unknown

When developing an interval estimate of a population mean, we usually do not have a good estimate of the population standard deviation either. In these cases, we must use the same sample to estimate both μ and σ. This situation represents the **σ unknown** case. When s is used to estimate σ, the margin of error and the interval estimate for the population mean are based on a probability distribution known as the ***t* distribution**. Although the mathematical development of the t distribution is based on the assumption of a normal distribution for the population we are sampling from, research shows that the t distribution can be successfully applied in many situations where the population deviates significantly from normal. Later in this section, we provide guidelines for using the t distribution if the population is not normally distributed.

William Sealy Gosset, writing under the name "Student," is the founder of the t distribution. Gosset, an Oxford graduate in mathematics, worked for the Guinness Brewery in Dublin, Ireland. He developed the t distribution while working on small-scale materials and temperature experiments.

The t distribution is a family of similar probability distributions, with a specific t distribution depending on a parameter known as the **degrees of freedom**. The t distribution with 1 degree of freedom is unique, as is the t distribution with 2 degrees of freedom, with 3 degrees of freedom, and so on. As the number of degrees of freedom increases, the difference between the t distribution and the standard normal distribution becomes smaller and smaller. Figure 8.5 shows t distributions with 10 and 20 degrees of freedom and their relationship to the standard normal probability distribution. Note that a t distribution with more degrees of freedom exhibits less variability and more closely resembles the standard normal distribution. Note also that the mean of the t distribution is zero.

We place a subscript on t to indicate the area in the upper tail of the t distribution. For example, just as we used $z_{0.025}$ to indicate the z value providing a 0.025 area in the upper tail of a standard normal distribution, we will use $t_{0.025}$ to indicate a 0.025 area in the upper tail of a t distribution. In general, we will use the notation $t_{\alpha/2}$ to represent a t value with an area of $\alpha/2$ in the upper tail of the t distribution. See Figure 8.6.

As the degrees of freedom increase, the t distribution approaches the standard normal distribution.

Table 2 in Appendix B (available online) contains a table for the t distribution. A portion of this table is shown in Table 8.2. Each row in the table corresponds to a separate t distribution with the degrees of freedom shown. For example, for a t distribution with 9 degrees of freedom, $t_{0.025} = 2.262$. Similarly, for a t distribution with 60 degrees of freedom, $t_{0.025} = 2.000$. As the degrees of freedom continue to increase, $t_{0.025}$ approaches $z_{0.025} = 1.96$. In fact, the standard normal distribution z values can be found in the infinite degrees of freedom row (labeled ∞) of the t distribution table. If the degrees of freedom exceed 100, the infinite degrees of freedom row can be used to approximate the actual

Figure 8.5 Comparison of the Standard Normal Distribution with t Distributions Having 10 and 20 Degrees of Freedom

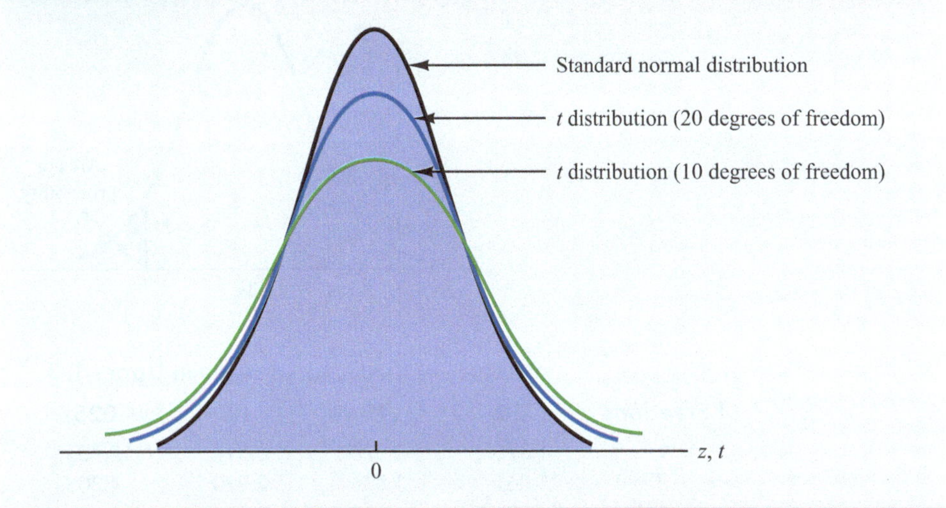

Figure 8.6 t Distribution with $\alpha/2$ Area or Probability in the Upper Tail

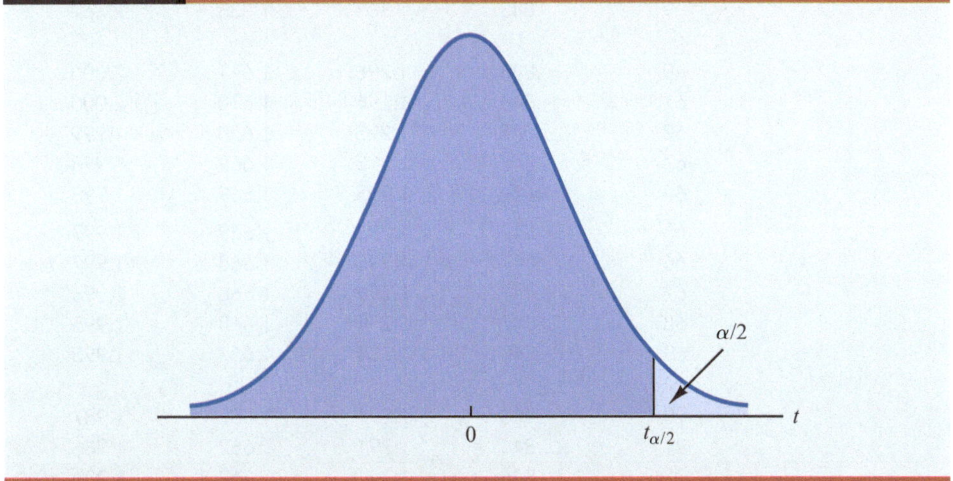

t value; in other words, for more than 100 degrees of freedom, the standard normal z value provides a good approximation to the t value.

Margin of Error and the Interval Estimate

In Section 8.1, we showed that an interval estimate of a population mean for the σ known case is

$$\bar{x} \pm z_{\alpha/2}\frac{\sigma}{\sqrt{n}}$$

To compute an interval estimate of μ for the σ unknown case, the sample standard deviation s is used to estimate σ, and $z_{\alpha/2}$ is replaced by the t distribution value $t_{\alpha/2}$. The margin

Table 8.2 Selected Values from the *t* Distribution Table*

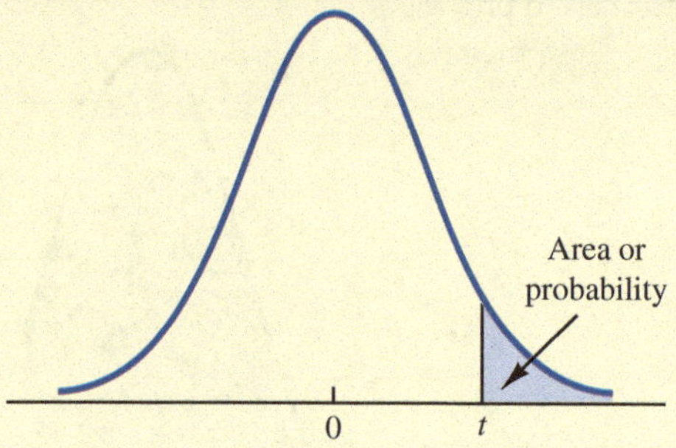

Degrees of Freedom	Area in Upper Tail .20	.10	.05	.025	.01	.005
1	1.376	3.078	6.314	12.706	31.821	63.656
2	1.061	1.886	2.920	4.303	6.965	9.925
3	.978	1.638	2.353	3.182	4.541	5.841
4	.941	1.533	2.132	2.776	3.747	4.604
5	.920	1.476	2.015	2.571	3.365	4.032
6	.906	1.440	1.943	2.447	3.143	3.707
7	.896	1.415	1.895	2.365	2.998	3.499
8	.889	1.397	1.860	2.306	2.896	3.355
9	.883	1.383	1.833	2.262	2.821	3.250
⋮	⋮	⋮	⋮	⋮	⋮	⋮
60	.848	1.296	1.671	2.000	2.390	2.660
61	.848	1.296	1.670	2.000	2.389	2.659
62	.847	1.295	1.670	1.999	2.388	2.657
63	.847	1.295	1.669	1.998	2.387	2.656
64	.847	1.295	1.669	1.998	2.386	2.655
65	.847	1.295	1.669	1.997	2.385	2.654
66	.847	1.295	1.668	1.997	2.384	2.652
67	.847	1.294	1.668	1.996	2.383	2.651
68	.847	1.294	1.668	1.995	2.382	2.650
69	.847	1.294	1.667	1.995	2.382	2.649
⋮	⋮	⋮	⋮	⋮	⋮	⋮
90	.846	1.291	1.662	1.987	2.368	2.632
91	.846	1.291	1.662	1.986	2.368	2.631
92	.846	1.291	1.662	1.986	2.368	2.630
93	.846	1.291	1.661	1.986	2.367	2.630
94	.845	1.291	1.661	1.986	2.367	2.629
95	.845	1.291	1.661	1.985	2.366	2.629
96	.845	1.290	1.661	1.985	2.366	2.628
97	.845	1.290	1.661	1.985	2.365	2.627
98	.845	1.290	1.661	1.984	2.365	2.627
99	.845	1.290	1.660	1.984	2.364	2.626
100	.845	1.290	1.660	1.984	2.364	2.626
∞	.842	1.282	1.645	1.960	2.326	2.576

**Note:* A more extensive table is provided as Table 2 of Appendix B (available online).

of error is then given by $t_{\alpha/2}s/\sqrt{n}$. With this margin of error, the general expression for an interval estimate of a population mean when σ is unknown follows.

Interval Estimate of a Population Mean: σ Unknown

$$\bar{x} \pm t_{\alpha/2}\frac{s}{\sqrt{n}} \tag{8.2}$$

where s is the sample standard deviation, $(1 - \alpha)$ is the confidence coefficient, and $t_{\alpha/2}$ is the t value providing an area of $\alpha/2$ in the upper tail of the t distribution with $n - 1$ degrees of freedom.

The reason the number of degrees of freedom associated with the t value in expression (8.2) is $n - 1$ concerns the use of s as an estimate of the population standard deviation σ. The expression for the sample standard deviation is

$$s = \sqrt{\frac{\Sigma(x_i - \bar{x})^2}{n - 1}}$$

Degrees of freedom refer to the number of independent pieces of information that go into the computation of $\Sigma(x_i - \bar{x})^2$. The n pieces of information involved in computing $\Sigma(x_i - \bar{x})^2$ are as follows: $x_1 - \bar{x}, x_2 - \bar{x}, \ldots, x_n - \bar{x}$. In Section 3.2, we indicated that $\Sigma(x_i - \bar{x}) = 0$ for any data set. Thus, only $n - 1$ of the $x_i - \bar{x}$ values are independent; that is, if we know $n - 1$ of the values, the remaining value can be determined exactly by using the condition that the sum of the $x_i - \bar{x}$ values must be 0. Thus, $n - 1$ is the number of degrees of freedom associated with $\Sigma(x_i - \bar{x})^2$ and hence the number of degrees of freedom for the t distribution in expression (8.2).

To illustrate the interval estimation procedure for the σ unknown case, we will consider a study designed to estimate the mean credit card debt for the population of U.S. households. A sample of $n = 70$ households provided the credit card balances shown in Table 8.3. For this situation, no previous estimate of the population standard deviation σ is available. Thus, the sample data must be used to estimate both the population mean and the population standard deviation. Using the data in Table 8.3, we compute the sample mean $\bar{x} = \$9,312$ and the sample standard deviation $s = \$4,007$. With 95% confidence and $n - 1 = 69$ degrees of freedom, Table 8.2 can be used to obtain the appropriate value for $t_{0.025}$. We want the t value in the row with 69 degrees of freedom, and the column corresponding to 0.025 in the upper tail. The value shown is $t_{0.025} = 1.995$.

DATA*file*
newbalance

Table 8.3 Credit Card Balances for a Sample of 70 Households ($)

9,430	14,661	7,159	9,071	9,691	11,032
7,535	12,195	8,137	3,603	11,448	6,525
4,078	10,544	9,467	16,804	8,279	5,239
5,604	13,659	12,595	13,479	5,649	6,195
5,179	7,061	7,917	14,044	11,298	12,584
4,416	6,245	11,346	6,817	4,353	15,415
10,676	13,021	12,806	6,845	3,467	15,917
1,627	9,719	4,972	10,493	6,191	12,591
10,112	2,200	11,356	615	12,851	9,743
6,567	10,746	7,117	13,627	5,337	10,324
13,627	12,744	9,465	12,557	8,372	
18,719	5,742	19,263	6,232	7,445	

We use expression (8.2) to compute an interval estimate of the population mean credit card balance.

$$9{,}312 \pm 1.995 \frac{4{,}007}{\sqrt{70}}$$

$$9{,}312 \pm 955$$

The point estimate of the population mean is \$9,312, the margin of error is \$955, and the 95% confidence interval is 9,312 − 955 = \$8,357 to 9,312 + 955 = \$10,267. Thus, we are 95% confident that the mean credit card balance for the population of all households is between \$8,357 and \$10,267.

Using Excel

We will use the credit card balances in Table 8.3 to illustrate how Excel can be used to construct an interval estimate of the population mean for the σ unknown case. We start by summarizing the data using Excel's Descriptive Statistics tool described in Chapter 3. Refer to Figure 8.7 as we describe the tasks involved. The formula worksheet is in the background; the value worksheet is in the foreground.

Enter/Access Data: Open the file *newbalance*. A label and the credit card balances are entered in cells A1:A71.

Figure 8.7 Excel Worksheet: 95% Confidence Interval for Credit Card Balances

	A	B	C	D	E
1	NewBalance		*NewBalance*		
2	9430				
3	7535		Mean	9312	
4	4078		Standard Error	478.928085819952	
5	5604		Median	9466	
6	5179		Mode	13627	
7	4416		Standard Deviation	4006.99984990035	
8	10676		Sample Variance	16056047.7971014	
9	1627		Kurtosis	-0.296002497492274	
10	10112		Skewness	0.187919587444176	
11	6567		Range	18648	
12	13627		Minimum	615	
13	18719		Maximum	19263	
14	14661		Sum	651840	
15	12195		Count	70	
16	10544		Confidence Level(95.0%)	955.435388972598	
17	13659				
18	7061		Point Estimate	=D3	
19	6245		Lower Limit	=D18-D16	
20	13021		Upper Limit	=D18+D16	
70	9743				
71	10324				

	A	B	C	D	E	F
1	NewBalance		*NewBalance*			
2	9430					
3	7535		Mean	9312	Point Estimate	
4	4078		Standard Error	478.9280858		
5	5604		Median	9466		
6	5179		Mode	13627		
7	4416		Standard Deviation	4006.99985		
8	10676		Sample Variance	16056047.8		
9	1627		Kurtosis	-0.296002497		
10	10112		Skewness	0.187919587		
11	6567		Range	18648		
12	13627		Minimum	615		
13	18719		Maximum	19263		
14	14661		Sum	651840		
15	12195		Count	70		
16	10544		Confidence Level(95.0%)	955.435389	Margin of Error	
17	13659					
18	7061		Point Estimate	9312		
19	6245		Lower Limit	8356.564611		
20	13021		Upper Limit	10267.43539		
70	9743					
71	10324					

Note: Rows 21–69 are hidden.

Apply Analysis Tools: The following steps describe how to use Excel's Descriptive Statistics tool for these data:

Step 1. Click the **Data** tab on the Ribbon
Step 2. In the **Analysis** group, click **Data Analysis**
Step 3. Choose **Descriptive Statistics** from the list of Analysis Tools
Step 4. When the **Descriptive Statistics** dialog box appears:
Enter *A1:A71* in the **Input Range:** box
Select **Columns** in the **Grouped By:** area
Select the check box for **Labels in First Row**
Select **Output Range:** in the **Output Options** area
Enter *C1* in the **Output Range:** box
Select the check box for **Summary Statistics**
Select the check box for **Confidence Level for Mean:**
Enter *95* in the **Confidence Level for Mean:** box
Click **OK**

The sample mean ($\bar{x}$) is in cell D3. The margin of error, labeled **Confidence Level(95%)**, appears in cell D16. The value worksheet shows $\bar{x}$ = 9,312 and a margin of error equal to 955.

Enter Functions and Formulas: Cells D18:D20 provide the point estimate and the lower and upper limits for the confidence interval. Because the point estimate is just the sample mean, the formula =*D3* is entered in cell D18. To compute the lower limit of the 95% confidence interval, $\bar{x}$ − (margin of error), we enter the formula =*D18-D16* in cell D19. To compute the upper limit of the 95% confidence interval, $\bar{x}$ + (margin of error), we enter the formula =*D18+D16* in cell D20. The value worksheet shows a lower limit of 8,357 and an upper limit of 10,267. In other words, the 95% confidence interval for the population mean is from 8,357 to 10,267.

Practical Advice

If the population follows a normal distribution, the confidence interval provided by expression (8.2) is exact and can be used for any sample size. If the population does not follow a normal distribution, the confidence interval provided by expression (8.2) will be approximate. In this case, the quality of the approximation depends on both the distribution of the population and the sample size.

Larger sample sizes are needed if the distribution of the population is highly skewed or includes outliers.

In most applications, a sample size of $n \geq 30$ is adequate when using expression (8.2) to develop an interval estimate of a population mean. However, if the population distribution is highly skewed or contains outliers, most statisticians would recommend increasing the sample size to 50 or more. If the population is not normally distributed but is roughly symmetric, sample sizes as small as 15 can be expected to provide good approximate confidence intervals. With smaller sample sizes, expression (8.2) should only be used if the analyst believes, or is willing to assume, that the population distribution is at least approximately normal.

Using a Small Sample

In the following example, we develop an interval estimate for a population mean when the sample size is small. As we already noted, an understanding of the distribution of the population becomes a factor in deciding whether the interval estimation procedure provides acceptable results.

Scheer Industries is considering a new computer-assisted program to train maintenance employees to do machine repairs. In order to fully evaluate the program, the director of manufacturing requested an estimate of the population mean time required for maintenance employees to complete the computer-assisted training.

Table 8.4 Training Time in Days for a Sample of 20 Scheer Industries Employees

52	59	54	42
44	50	42	48
55	54	60	55
44	62	62	57
45	46	43	56

DATA*file*
scheer

A sample of 20 employees is selected, with each employee in the sample completing the training program. Data on the training time in days for the 20 employees are shown in Table 8.4. A histogram of the sample data appears in Figure 8.8. What can we say about the distribution of the population based on this histogram? First, the sample data do not support the conclusion that the distribution of the population is normal, yet we do not see any evidence of skewness or outliers. Therefore, using the guidelines in the previous subsection, we conclude that an interval estimate based on the t distribution appears acceptable for the sample of 20 employees.

We continue by computing the sample mean and sample standard deviation as follows.

$$\bar{x} = \frac{\Sigma x_i}{n} = \frac{1{,}030}{20} = 51.5 \text{ days}$$

$$s = \sqrt{\frac{\Sigma(x_i - \bar{x})^2}{n - 1}} = \sqrt{\frac{889}{20 - 1}} = 6.84 \text{ days}$$

Figure 8.8 Histogram of Training Times for the Scheer Industries Sample

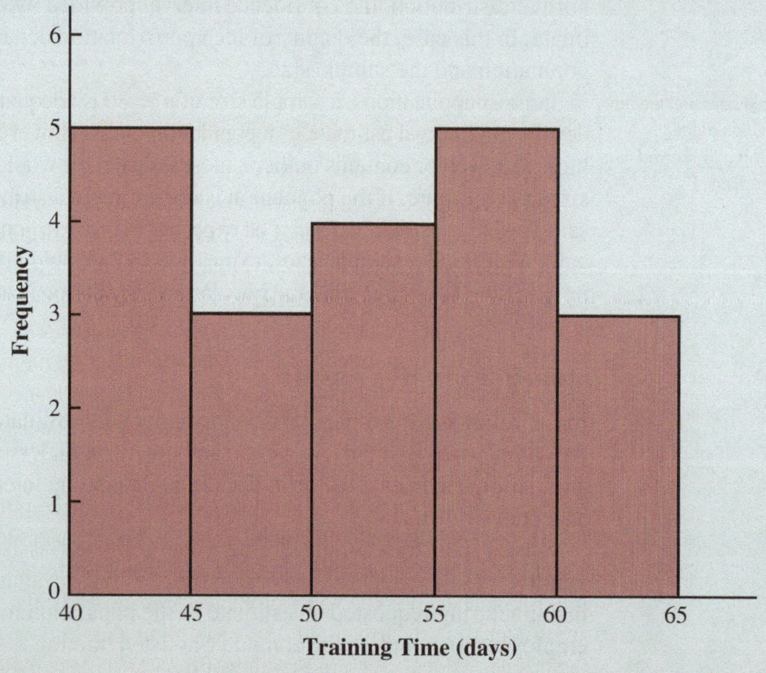

For a 95% confidence interval, we use Table 2 of Appendix B (available online) and $n - 1 = 19$ degrees of freedom to obtain $t_{0.025} = 2.093$. Expression (8.2) provides the interval estimate of the population mean.

$$51.5 \pm 2.093\left(\frac{6.84}{\sqrt{20}}\right)$$

$$51.5 \pm 3.2$$

The point estimate of the population mean is 51.5 days. The margin of error is 3.2 days and the 95% confidence interval is $51.5 - 3.2 = 48.3$ days to $51.5 + 3.2 = 54.7$ days.

Using a histogram of the sample data to learn about the distribution of a population is not always conclusive, but in many cases it provides the only information available. The histogram, along with judgment on the part of the analyst, can often be used to decide whether expression (8.2) can be used to develop the interval estimate.

Summary of Interval Estimation Procedures

We provided two approaches to developing an interval estimate of a population mean. For the σ known case, σ and the standard normal distribution are used in expression (8.1) to compute the margin of error and to develop the interval estimate. For the σ unknown case, the sample standard deviation s and the t distribution are used in expression (8.2) to compute the margin of error and to develop the interval estimate.

A summary of the interval estimation procedures for the two cases is shown in Figure 8.9. In most applications, a sample size of $n \geq 30$ is adequate. If the population has a normal or approximately normal distribution, however, smaller sample sizes may be used. For the σ unknown case, a sample size of $n \geq 50$ is recommended if the population distribution is believed to be highly skewed or has outliers.

Figure 8.9 Summary of Interval Estimation Procedures for a Population Mean

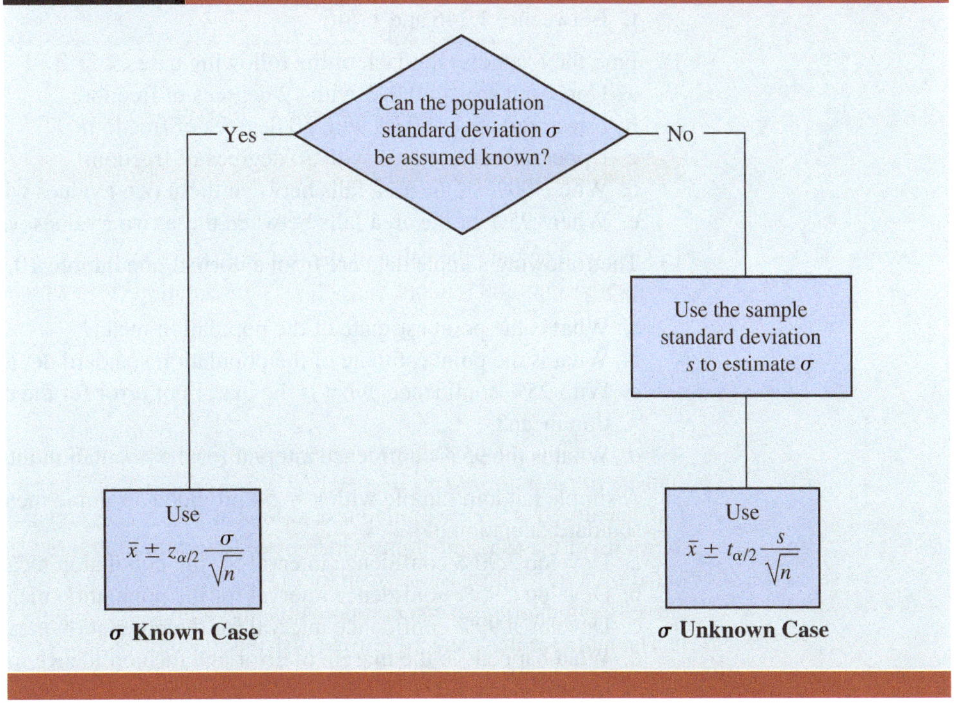

Notes + Comments

1. When σ is known, the margin of error, $z_{\alpha/2}(\sigma/\sqrt{n})$, is fixed and is the same for all samples of size n. When σ is unknown, the margin of error, $t_{\alpha/2}(s/\sqrt{n})$, varies from sample to sample. This variation occurs because the sample standard deviation s varies depending upon the sample selected. A large value for s provides a larger margin of error, while a small value for s provides a smaller margin of error.
2. What happens to confidence interval estimates when the population is skewed? Consider a population that is skewed to the right with large data values stretching the distribution to the right. When such skewness exists, the sample mean $\bar{x}$ and the sample standard deviation s are positively correlated. Larger values of s tend to be associated with larger values of $\bar{x}$. Thus, when $\bar{x}$ is larger than the population mean, s tends to be larger than σ. This skewness causes the margin of error, $t_{\alpha/2}(s/\sqrt{n})$, to be larger than it would be with σ known. The confidence interval with the larger margin of error tends to include the population mean μ more often than it would if the true value of σ were used. But when $\bar{x}$ is smaller than the population mean, the correlation between $\bar{x}$ and s causes the margin of error to be small. In this case, the confidence interval with the smaller margin of error tends to miss the population mean more than it would if we knew σ and used it. For this reason, we recommend using larger sample sizes with highly skewed population distributions.
3. When developing a confidence interval for the mean with a sample size that is at least 5% of the population size (that is, $n/N \geq 0.05$), the finite population correction factor should be used when calculating the standard error of the sampling distribution of $\bar{x}$ when σ is unknown, i.e.,

$$s_{\bar{x}} = \sqrt{\frac{N-n}{N-1}}\left(\frac{s}{\sqrt{n}}\right).$$

Exercises

Methods

11. For a t distribution with 16 degrees of freedom, find the area, or probability, in each region. **LO 2**
    a. To the right of 2.120
    b. To the left of 1.337
    c. To the left of −1.746
    d. To the right of 2.583
    e. Between −2.120 and 2.120
    f. Between −1.746 and 1.746
12. Find the t value(s) for each of the following cases. **LO 2**
    a. Upper tail area of 0.025 with 12 degrees of freedom
    b. Lower tail area of 0.05 with 50 degrees of freedom
    c. Upper tail area of 0.01 with 30 degrees of freedom
    d. Where 90% of the area falls between these two t values with 25 degrees of freedom
    e. Where 95% of the area falls between these two t values with 45 degrees of freedom
13. The following sample data are from a normal population: 10, 8, 12, 15, 13, 11, 6, 5. **LO 2, 3**
    a. What is the point estimate of the population mean?
    b. What is the point estimate of the population standard deviation?
    c. With 95% confidence, what is the margin of error for the estimation of the population mean?
    d. What is the 95% confidence interval for the population mean?
14. A simple random sample with $n = 54$ provided a sample mean of 22.5 and a sample standard deviation of 4.4. **LO 2, 3**
    a. Develop a 90% confidence interval for the population mean.
    b. Develop a 95% confidence interval for the population mean.
    c. Develop a 99% confidence interval for the population mean.
    d. What happens to the margin of error and the confidence interval as the confidence level is increased?

Applications

15. **Weekly Sales Reports.** Sales personnel for Skillings Distributors submit weekly reports listing the customer contacts made during the week. A sample of 65 weekly reports showed a sample mean of 19.5 customer contacts per week. The sample standard deviation was 5.2. Provide 90% and 95% confidence intervals for the population mean number of weekly customer contacts for the sales personnel. **LO 2, 3**

DATA*file* corporatebonds

16. **Years to Bond Maturity.** A sample of years to maturity and yield for 40 corporate bonds taken from *Barron's* is in the file *corporatebonds*. **LO 2, 3**
    a. What is the sample mean years to maturity for corporate bonds and what is the sample standard deviation?
    b. Develop a 95% confidence interval for the population mean years to maturity.
    c. What is the sample mean yield on corporate bonds and what is the sample standard deviation?
    d. Develop a 95% confidence interval for the population mean yield on corporate bonds.

DATA*file* miami

17. **Quality Ratings of Airports.** The International Air Transport Association surveys business travelers to develop quality ratings for transatlantic gateway airports. The maximum possible rating is 10. Suppose a simple random sample of 50 business travelers is selected and each traveler is asked to provide a rating for the Miami International Airport. The file *miami* contains the ratings obtained from the sample of 50 business travelers. Develop a 95% confidence interval estimate of the population mean rating for Miami. **LO 2, 3**

DATA*file* jobsearch

18. **Employment in Older Workers.** Older people often have a hard time finding work. AARP reported on the number of weeks it takes a worker aged 55 plus to find a job. The data on number of weeks spent searching for a job contained in the file *jobsearch* are consistent with the AARP findings. **LO 2, 3**
    a. Provide a point estimate of the population mean number of weeks it takes a worker aged 55 plus to find a job.
    b. At 95% confidence, what is the margin of error?
    c. What is the 95% confidence interval estimate of the mean?
    d. Discuss the degree of skewness found in the sample data. What suggestion would you make for a repeat of this study?

DATA*file* hongkongmeals

19. **Meal Cost in Hong Kong.** The mean cost of a meal for two in a mid-range restaurant in Tokyo is $40. How do prices for comparable meals in Hong Kong compare? The file *hongkongmeals* contains the costs for a sample of 42 recent meals for two in Hong Kong mid-range restaurants. **LO 2, 3**
    a. With 95% confidence, what is the margin of error?
    b. What is the 95% confidence interval estimate of the population mean?
    c. How do prices for meals for two in mid-range restaurants in Hong Kong compare to prices for comparable meals in Tokyo restaurants?

DATA*file* autoinsurance

20. **Automobile Insurance Premiums.** The average annual premium for automobile insurance in the United States is $1,503. The file *autoinsurance* contains annual premiums ($) that are representative of the website's findings for the state of Michigan. Assume the population of annual premiums is approximately normal. **LO 2, 3**
    a. Provide a point estimate of the mean annual automobile insurance premium in Michigan.
    b. Develop a 95% confidence interval for the mean annual automobile insurance premium in Michigan.
    c. Does the 95% confidence interval for the annual automobile insurance premium in Michigan include the national average for the United States? What is your interpretation of the relationship between auto insurance premiums in Michigan and the national average?

DATA*file* telehealth

21. **Telemedicine.** As healthcare costs continue to increase, the number of employers who offer their employees telehealth options is growing. In 2021, net cost savings is

estimated to be $19–$121 per telemedicine visit, depending on where the employee would have otherwise sought care (First Stop Health). The data in the file *telehealth* are consistent with the dollar savings per visit reported by First Stop Health. Assuming the population is roughly symmetric, construct a 95% confidence interval for the mean savings for a televisit to the doctor as opposed to an office visit. **LO 2, 3**

DATA*file*
eternals

22. **Movie Ticket Sales.** Marvel Studio's motion picture *Eternals* opened over the first weekend in November 2021 with $71 million in ticket sales revenue in North America. The ticket sales revenue in dollars for a sample of 30 theaters during these dates is provided in the file *eternals*. **LO 2, 3**
    a. What is the 95% confidence interval estimate for the mean ticket sales revenue per theater? Interpret this result.
    b. Using the movie ticket price of $10.00 per ticket, what is the estimate of the mean number of customers per theater?
    c. The movie was shown in 4,090 theaters during its opening weekend. Estimate the total box office ticket sales for the weekend.

8.3 Determining the Sample Size

If a desired margin of error is selected prior to sampling, the procedures in this section can be used to determine the sample size necessary to satisfy the margin of error requirement.

In providing practical advice in the two preceding sections, we commented on the role of the sample size in providing good approximate confidence intervals when the population is not normally distributed. In this section, we focus on another aspect of the sample size issue. We describe how to choose a sample size large enough to provide a desired margin of error. To understand how this process works, we return to the σ known case presented in Section 8.1. Using expression (8.1), the interval estimate is

$$\bar{x} \pm z_{\alpha/2}\frac{\sigma}{\sqrt{n}}$$

The quantity $z_{\alpha/2}(\sigma/\sqrt{n})$ is the margin of error. Thus, we see that $z_{\alpha/2}$, the population standard deviation σ, and the sample size n combine to determine the margin of error. Once we select a confidence coefficient $1 - \alpha$, $z_{\alpha/2}$ can be determined. Then, if we have a value for σ, we can determine the sample size n needed to provide any desired margin of error. Development of the formula used to compute the required sample size n follows.

Let E = the desired margin of error:

$$E = z_{\alpha/2}\frac{\sigma}{\sqrt{n}}$$

Solving for $\sqrt{n}$, we have

$$\sqrt{n} = \frac{z_{\alpha/2}\sigma}{E}$$

Squaring both sides of this equation, we obtain the following expression for the sample size.

Equation (8.3) can be used to provide a good sample size recommendation. However, judgment on the part of the analyst should be used to determine whether the final sample size should be adjusted upward.

Sample Size for an Interval Estimate of a Population Mean

$$n = \frac{(z_{\alpha/2})^2\sigma^2}{E^2} \tag{8.3}$$

This sample size provides the desired margin of error at the chosen confidence level.

In equation (8.3), E is the margin of error that the user is willing to accept, and the value of $z_{\alpha/2}$ follows directly from the confidence level to be used in developing the interval estimate. Although user preference must be considered, 95% confidence is the most frequently chosen value ($z_{0.025} = 1.96$).

Finally, use of equation (8.3) requires a value for the population standard deviation σ. However, even if σ is unknown, we can use equation (8.3) provided we have a preliminary or *planning value* for σ. In practice, one of the following procedures can be chosen.

A planning value for the population standard deviation σ must be specified before the sample size can be determined. Three methods of obtaining a planning value for σ are discussed here.

1. Use the estimate of the population standard deviation computed from data of previous studies as the planning value for σ.
2. Use a pilot study to select a preliminary sample. The sample standard deviation from the preliminary sample can be used as the planning value for σ.
3. Use judgment or a "best guess" for the value of σ. For example, we might begin by estimating the largest and smallest data values in the population. The difference between the largest and smallest values provides an estimate of the range for the data. Finally, the range divided by 4 is often suggested as a rough approximation of the standard deviation and thus an acceptable planning value for σ.

Let us demonstrate the use of equation (8.3) to determine the sample size by considering the following example. A previous study that investigated the cost of renting automobiles in the United States found a mean cost of approximately $55 per day for renting a midsize automobile. Suppose that the organization that conducted this study would like to conduct a new study in order to estimate the population mean daily rental cost for a midsize automobile in the United States. In designing the new study, the project director specifies that the population mean daily rental cost be estimated with a margin of error of $2 and a 95% level of confidence.

The project director specified a desired margin of error of $E = 2$, and the 95% level of confidence indicates $z_{0.025} = 1.96$. Thus, we only need a planning value for the population standard deviation σ in order to compute the required sample size. At this point, an analyst reviewed the sample data from the previous study and found that the sample standard deviation for the daily rental cost was $9.65. Using 9.65 as the planning value for σ, we obtain

Equation (8.3) provides the minimum sample size needed to satisfy the desired margin of error requirement. If the computed sample size is not an integer, rounding up to the next integer value will provide a margin of error slightly smaller than required.

$$n = \frac{(z_{\alpha/2})^2\sigma^2}{E^2} = \frac{(1.96)^2(9.65)^2}{2^2} = 89.43$$

Thus, the sample size for the new study needs to be at least 89.43 midsize automobile rentals in order to satisfy the project director's $2 margin-of-error requirement. In cases where the computed n is not an integer, we round up to the next integer value; hence, the recommended sample size is 90 midsize automobile rentals.

Note + Comment

Equation (8.3) provides the recommended sample size n for an infinite population as well as for a large finite population of size N provided $n/N \le 0.05$. This is fine for most statistical studies. However, if we have a finite population such that $n/N > 0.05$, a smaller sample size can be used to obtain the desired margin of error. The smaller sample size, denoted by n', can be computed using the following equation:

$$n' = \frac{n}{(1 + n/N)}$$

For example, suppose that the example presented in this section showing $n = 89.43$ was computed for a population of size $N = 500$. With $n/N = 89.43/500 = 0.18 > 0.05$, a smaller sample size can be computed by

$$n' = \frac{n}{1 + n/N} = \frac{89.43}{1 + 89.43/500} = 75.86$$

Thus, for the finite population of $N = 500$, the sample size required to obtain the desired margin of error $E = 2$ would be reduced from 90 to 76.

Exercises

Methods

23. How large a sample should be selected to provide a 95% confidence interval with a margin of error of 10? Assume that the population standard deviation is 40. **LO 4**
24. The range for a set of data is estimated to be 36. **LO 4**
    a. What is the planning value for the population standard deviation?
    b. At 95% confidence, how large a sample would provide a margin of error of 3?
    c. At 95% confidence, how large a sample would provide a margin of error of 2?

Applications

25. **Computer-Assisted Training.** Refer to the Scheer Industries example in Section 8.2. Use 6.84 days as a planning value for the population standard deviation. **LO 4**
    a. Assuming 95% confidence, what sample size would be required to obtain a margin of error of 1.5 days?
    b. If the precision statement was made with 90% confidence, what sample size would be required to obtain a margin of error of 2 days?
26. **Gasoline Prices.** The U.S. Energy Information Administration (U.S. EIA) reported that the average price for a gallon of regular gasoline is \$3.16. The U.S. EIA updates its estimates of average gas prices on a weekly basis. Assume the standard deviation is \$0.25 for the price of a gallon of regular gasoline and recommend the appropriate sample size for the U.S. EIA to use if they wish to report each of the following margins of error at 95% confidence. **LO 4**
    a. The desired margin of error is \$0.10.
    b. The desired margin of error is \$0.07.
    c. The desired margin of error is \$0.05.
27. **Salaries of Business Graduates.** Annual starting salaries for college graduates with degrees in business administration are generally expected to be between \$45,000 and \$60,000. Assume that a 95% confidence interval estimate of the population mean annual starting salary is desired? **LO 4**
    a. What is the planning value for the population standard deviation?
    b. How large a sample should be taken if the desired margin of error is \$500? \$200? \$100?
    c. Would you recommend trying to achieve the \$100 margin of error? Explain.
28. **Beef Consumption.** Many medical professionals believe that eating too much red meat increases the risk of heart disease and cancer. Suppose you would like to conduct a survey to determine the yearly consumption of beef by a typical American and want to use 3 pounds as the desired margin of error for a confidence interval estimate of the population mean amount of beef consumed annually. Use 25 pounds as a planning value for the population standard deviation and recommend a sample size for each of the following situations. **LO 4**
    a. A 90% confidence interval is desired for the mean amount of beef consumed.
    b. A 95% confidence interval is desired for the mean amount of beef consumed.
    c. A 99% confidence interval is desired for the mean amount of beef consumed.
    d. When the desired margin of error is set, what happens to the sample size as the confidence level is increased? Would you recommend using a 99% confidence interval in this case? Discuss.
29. **Length of Theater Previews.** Customers arrive at a movie theater at the advertised movie time only to find that they have to sit through several previews and prepreview ads before the movie starts. Many complain that the time devoted to previews is too long. A preliminary sample conducted by *The Wall Street Journal* showed that the standard deviation of the amount of time devoted to previews was 4 minutes. Use that as a planning value for the standard deviation in answering the following questions. **LO 4**

a. If we want to estimate the population mean time for previews at movie theaters with a margin of error of 75 seconds, what sample size should be used? Assume 95% confidence.
b. If we want to estimate the population mean time for previews at movie theaters with a margin of error of 1 minute, what sample size should be used? Assume 95% confidence.

30. **Miles Driven by Young Drivers.** There has been a trend toward less driving in the last few years, especially by young people. Over the past eight years, the annual vehicle miles traveled by people from 16 to 34 years of age decreased from 10,300 to 7,900 miles per person. Assume the standard deviation is now 2,000 miles. Suppose you would like to conduct a survey to develop a 95% confidence interval estimate of the annual vehicle-miles per person for people 16 to 34 years of age at the current time. A margin of error of 100 miles is desired. How large a sample should be used for the current survey? **LO 4**

8.4 Population Proportion

In the introduction to this chapter, we said that the general form of an interval estimate of a population proportion p is

$$\bar{p} \pm \text{Margin of error}$$

The sampling distribution of $\bar{p}$ plays a key role in computing the margin of error for this interval estimate.

In Chapter 7, we said that the sampling distribution of $\bar{p}$ can be approximated by a normal distribution whenever $np \geq 5$ and $n(1 - p) \geq 5$. Figure 8.10 shows the normal approximation of the sampling distribution of $\bar{p}$. The mean of the sampling distribution of $\bar{p}$ is the population proportion p, and the standard error of $\bar{p}$ is

$$\sigma_{\bar{p}} = \sqrt{\frac{p(1-p)}{n}} \tag{8.4}$$

Figure 8.10 Normal Approximation of the Sampling Distribution of $\bar{p}$

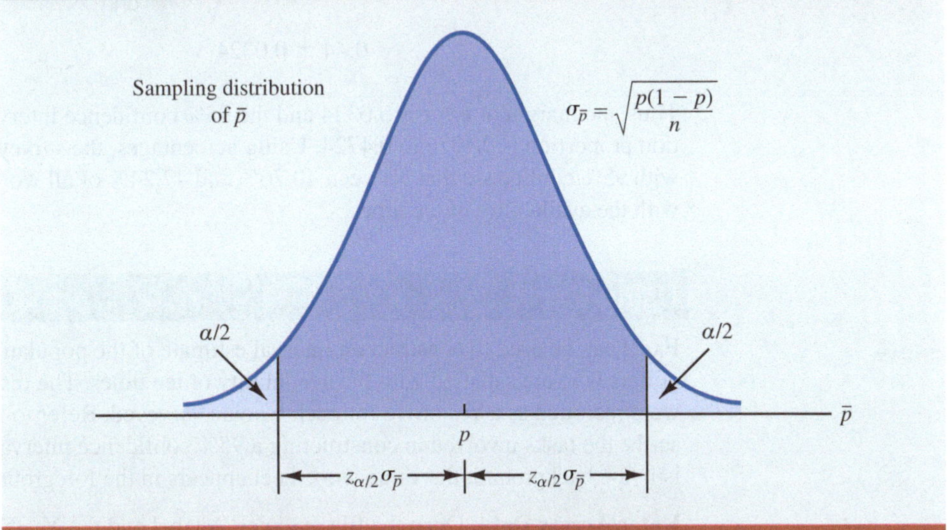

Because the sampling distribution of $\bar{p}$ is normally distributed, if we choose $z_{\alpha/2}\sigma_{\bar{p}}$ as the margin of error in an interval estimate of a population proportion, we know that $100(1 - \alpha)\%$ of the intervals generated will contain the true population proportion. But $\sigma_{\bar{p}}$ cannot be used directly in the computation of the margin of error because p will not be known; p is what we are trying to estimate. So $\bar{p}$ is substituted for p and the margin of error for an interval estimate of a population proportion is given by

$$\text{Margin of error} = z_{\alpha/2}\sqrt{\frac{\bar{p}(1-\bar{p})}{n}} \tag{8.5}$$

With this margin of error, the general expression for an interval estimate of a population proportion is as follows.

When developing confidence intervals for proportions, the quantity $z_{\alpha/2}\sqrt{\bar{p}(1-\bar{p})/n}$ provides the margin of error.

Interval Estimate of a Population Proportion

$$\bar{p} \pm z_{\alpha/2}\sqrt{\frac{\bar{p}(1-\bar{p})}{n}} \tag{8.6}$$

where $1 - \alpha$ is the confidence coefficient and $z_{\alpha/2}$ is the z value providing an area of $\alpha/2$ in the upper tail of the standard normal distribution.

DATA*file*
teetimes

The following example illustrates the computation of the margin of error and interval estimate for a population proportion. A national survey of 900 women golfers was conducted to learn how women golfers view their treatment at golf courses in the United States. The survey found that 396 of the women golfers were satisfied with the availability of tee times. Thus, the point estimate of the proportion of the population of women golfers who are satisfied with the availability of tee times is 396/900 = 0.44. Using expression (8.6) and a 95% confidence level,

$$\bar{p} \pm z_{\alpha/2}\sqrt{\frac{\bar{p}(1-\bar{p})}{n}}$$

$$0.44 \pm 1.96\sqrt{\frac{0.44(1-0.44)}{900}}$$

$$0.44 \pm 0.0324$$

Thus, the margin of error is 0.0324 and the 95% confidence interval estimate of the population proportion is 0.4076 to 0.4724. Using percentages, the survey results enable us to state with 95% confidence that between 40.76% and 47.24% of all women golfers are satisfied with the availability of tee times.

Using Excel

Excel can be used to construct an interval estimate of the population proportion of women golfers who are satisfied with the availability of tee times. The responses in the survey were recorded as a Yes or No for each woman surveyed. Refer to Figure 8.11 as we describe the tasks involved in constructing a 95% confidence interval. The formula worksheet is in the background; the value worksheet appears in the foreground.

Enter/Access Data: Open the file *teetimes*. A label and the Yes/No data for the 900 women golfers are entered in cells A1:A901.

Figure 8.11 Excel Worksheet: 95% Confidence Interval for Survey of Women Golfers

DATA*file*

teetimes

	A	B	C	D
1	Response		Interval Estimate of a Population Proportion	
2	Yes			
3	No		Sample Size	=COUNTA(A2:A901)
4	Yes		Response of Interest	Yes
5	Yes		Count for Response	=COUNTIF(A2:A901,D4)
6	No		Sample Proportion	=D5/D3
7	No			
8	No		Confidence Coefficient	0.95
9	Yes		Level of Significance (alpha)	=1-D8
10	Yes		z Value	=NORM.S.INV(1-D9/2)
11	Yes			
12	No		Standard Error	=SQRT(D6*(1-D6)/D3)
13	No		Margin of Error	=D10*D12
14	Yes			
15	No		Point Estimate	=D6
16	No		Lower Limit	=D15-D13
17	Yes		Upper Limit	=D15+D13
18	No			
900	Yes			
901	Yes			

Note: Rows 19 to 899 are hidden.

	A	B	C	D	E	F	G
1	Response		Interval Estimate of a Population Proportion				
2	Yes						
3	No		Sample Size	900	Enter Yes as the		
4	Yes		Response of Interest	Yes	Response of Interest		
5	Yes		Count for Response	396			
6	No		Sample Proportion	0.44			
7	No						
8	No		Confidence Coefficient	0.95			
9	Yes		Level of Significance (alpha)	0.05			
10	Yes		z Value	1.959964			
11	Yes						
12	No		Standard Error	0.0165			
13	No		Margin of Error	0.0324			
14	Yes						
15	No		Point Estimate	0.44			
16	No		Lower Limit	0.4076			
17	Yes		Upper Limit	0.4724			
18	No						
900	Yes						
901	Yes						

Enter Functions and Formulas: The descriptive statistics we need and the response of interest are provided in cells D3:D6. Because Excel's COUNT function works only with numerical data, we used the COUNTA function in cell D3 to compute the sample size. The response for which we want to develop an interval estimate, Yes or No, is entered in cell D4. Figure 8.11 shows that Yes has been entered in cell D4, indicating that we want to develop an interval estimate of the population proportion of women golfers who are satisfied with the availability of tee times. If we had wanted to develop an interval estimate of the population proportion of women golfers who are not satisfied with the availability of tee times, we would have entered No in cell D4. With Yes entered in cell D4, the COUNTIF function in cell D5 counts the number of Yes responses in the sample. The sample proportion is then computed in cell D6 by dividing the number of Yes responses in cell D5 by the sample size in cell D3.

Cells D8:D10 are used to compute the appropriate z value. The confidence coefficient (*0.95*) is entered in cell D8 and the level of significance (α) is computed in cell D9 by entering the formula *=1-D8*. The z value corresponding to an upper tail area of $\alpha/2$ is computed by entering the formula *=NORM.S.INV(1-D9/2)* in cell D10. The value worksheet shows that $z_{0.025} = 1.96$.

Cells D12:D13 provide the estimate of the standard error and the margin of error. In cell D12, we entered the formula *=SQRT(D6*(1-D6)/D3)* to compute the standard error using the sample proportion and the sample size as inputs. The formula *=D10*D12* is entered in cell D13 to compute the margin of error.

Cells D15:D17 provide the point estimate and the lower and upper limits for a confidence interval. The point estimate in cell D15 is the sample proportion. The lower and upper limits in cells D16 and D17 are obtained by subtracting and adding the margin of error to the point estimate. We note that the 95% confidence interval for the proportion of women golfers who are satisfied with the availability of tee times is 0.4076 to 0.4724.

A Template for Other Problems The worksheet in Figure 8.11 can be used as a template for developing confidence intervals about a population proportion p. To use this worksheet for another problem of this type, we must first enter the new problem data in column A. The response of interest would then be typed in cell D4 and the ranges for the formulas in cells D3 and D5 would be revised to correspond to the new data. After doing so, the point estimate and a 95% confidence interval will be displayed in cells D15:D17. If a confidence interval with a different confidence coefficient is desired, we simply change the value in cell D8.

Determining the Sample Size

Let us consider the question of how large the sample size should be to obtain an estimate of a population proportion at a specified level of precision. The rationale for the sample size determination in developing interval estimates of p is similar to the rationale used in Section 8.3 to determine the sample size for estimating a population mean.

Previously in this section we said that the margin of error associated with an interval estimate of a population proportion is $z_{\alpha/2}\sqrt{\bar{p}(1-\bar{p})/n}$. The margin of error is based on the value of $z_{\alpha/2}$, the sample proportion $\bar{p}$, and the sample size n. Larger sample sizes provide a smaller margin of error and better precision.

Let E denote the desired margin of error.

$$E = z_{\alpha/2}\sqrt{\frac{\bar{p}(1-\bar{p})}{n}}$$

Solving this equation for n provides a formula for the sample size that will provide a margin of error of size E.

$$n = \frac{(z_{\alpha/2})^2\bar{p}(1-\bar{p})}{E^2}$$

Note, however, that we cannot use this formula to compute the sample size that will provide the desired margin of error because $\bar{p}$ will not be known until after we select the sample. What we need, then, is a planning value for $\bar{p}$ that can be used to make the computation. Using p^* to denote the planning value for $\bar{p}$, the following formula can be used to compute the sample size that will provide a margin of error of size E.

Sample Size for an Interval Estimate of a Population Proportion

$$n = \frac{(z_{\alpha/2})^2 p^*(1-p^*)}{E^2} \tag{8.7}$$

In practice, the planning value p^* can be chosen by one of the following procedures.

1. Use the sample proportion from a previous sample of the same or similar units.
2. Use a pilot study to select a preliminary sample. The sample proportion from this sample can be used as the planning value, p^*.
3. Use judgment or a "best guess" for the value of p^*.
4. If none of the preceding alternatives applies, use a planning value of $p^* = 0.50$.

Let us return to the survey of women golfers and assume that the company is interested in conducting a new survey to estimate the current proportion of the population of women golfers who are satisfied with the availability of tee times. How large should the sample be if the survey director wants to estimate the population proportion with a margin of error of 0.025 at 95% confidence? With $E = 0.025$ and $z_{\alpha/2} = 1.96$, we need a planning value p^* to answer the sample size question. Using the previous survey result of $\bar{p} = 0.44$ as the planning value p^*, equation (8.7) shows that

$$n = \frac{(z_{\alpha/2})^2 p^*(1-p^*)}{E^2} = \frac{(1.96)^2(0.44)(1-0.44)}{(0.025)^2} = 1{,}514.5$$

Thus, the sample size must be at least 1,514.5 women golfers to satisfy the margin of error requirement. Rounding up to the next integer value indicates that a sample of 1,515 women golfers is recommended to satisfy the margin of error requirement.

Table 8.5 Some Possible Values for $p^*(1 - p^*)$

p^*	$p^*(1 - p^*)$	
0.10	(0.10)(0.90) = 0.09	
0.30	(0.30)(0.70) = 0.21	
0.40	(0.40)(0.60) = 0.24	
0.50	(0.50)(0.50) = 0.25	← Largest value for $p^*(1 - p^*)$
0.60	(0.60)(0.40) = 0.24	
0.70	(0.70)(0.30) = 0.21	
0.90	(0.90)(0.10) = 0.09	

The fourth alternative suggested for selecting a planning value p^* is to use $p^* = 0.50$. This value of p^* is frequently used when no other information is available. To understand why, note that the numerator of equation (8.7) shows that the sample size is proportional to the quantity $p^*(1 - p^*)$. A larger value for the quantity $p^*(1 - p^*)$ will result in a larger sample size. Table 8.5 gives some possible values of $p^*(1 - p^*)$. Note that the largest value of $p^*(1 - p^*)$ occurs when $p^* = 0.50$. Thus, in case of any uncertainty about an appropriate planning value, we know that $p^* = 0.50$ will provide the largest sample size recommendation. In effect, we play it safe by recommending the largest necessary sample size. If the sample proportion turns out to be different from the 0.50 planning value, the margin of error will be smaller than anticipated. Thus, in using $p^* = 0.50$, we guarantee that the sample size will be sufficient to obtain the desired margin of error.

In the survey of women golfers example, a planning value of $p^* = 0.50$ would have provided the sample size

$$n = \frac{(z_{\alpha/2})^2 p^*(1 - p^*)}{E^2} = \frac{(1.96)^2(0.50)(1 - 0.50)}{(0.025)^2} = 1{,}536.6$$

Thus, a slightly larger sample size of 1,537 women golfers would be recommended.

Notes + Comments

1. The desired margin of error for estimating a population proportion is almost always 0.10 or less. In national public opinion polls conducted by organizations such as Gallup and Harris, a 0.03 or 0.04 margin of error is common. With such margins of error, equation (8.7) will almost always provide a sample size that is large enough to satisfy the requirements of $np \geq 5$ and $n(1 - p) \geq 5$ for using a normal distribution as an approximation for the sampling distribution of $\bar{x}$.
2. When developing a confidence interval for the proportion with a sample size that is at least 5% of the population size (that is, $n/N \geq 0.05$), the finite population correction factor should be used when calculating the standard error of the sampling distribution of $\bar{p}$, i.e., $s_{\bar{p}} = \sqrt{\frac{N - n}{N - 1}}\sqrt{\frac{\bar{p}(1 - \bar{p})}{n}}$.
3. Equation (8.7) provides the recommended sample size n for an infinite population as well as for a large finite population of size N provided $n/N < 0.05$. This is fine for most statistical studies. However, if we have a finite population such that $n/N > 0.05$, a smaller sample size can be used to obtain the desired margin of error. The smaller sample size denoted by n' can be computed using the following equation.

$$n' = \frac{n}{(1 + n/N)}$$

For example, suppose that the example presented in this section showing $n = 1{,}536.6$ was computed for a population of size $N = 2{,}500$. With $n/N = 1{,}536.6/2{,}500 = 0.61 > 0.05$, a smaller sample size can be computed by

$$n' = \frac{n}{(1 + n/N)} = \frac{1{,}536.6}{(1 + 1{,}536.6/2{,}500)} = 951.67$$

Thus, for the finite population of $N = 2{,}500$, the sample size required to obtain the desired margin of error $E = 0.025$ would be reduced from 1,537 to 952.

Exercises

Methods

31. A simple random sample of 400 individuals provides 100 Yes responses. **LO 5**
    a. What is the point estimate of the proportion of the population that would provide Yes responses?
    b. What is your estimate of the standard error of the proportion, $\sigma_{\bar{p}}$?
    c. Compute the 95% confidence interval for the population proportion.

32. A simple random sample of 800 elements generates a sample proportion $\bar{p} = 0.70$. **LO 5**
    a. Provide a 90% confidence interval for the population proportion.
    b. Provide a 95% confidence interval for the population proportion.

33. In a survey, the planning value for the population proportion is $p^* = 0.35$. How large a sample should be taken to provide a 95% confidence interval with a margin of error of 0.05? **LO 6**

34. At 95% confidence, how large a sample should be taken to obtain a margin of error of 0.03 for the estimation of a population proportion? Assume that past data are not available for developing a planning value for p^*. **LO 6**

Applications

35. **Healthcare Survey.** In the spring of 2017, the Consumer Reports National Research Center conducted a survey of 1,007 adults to learn about their major healthcare concerns. The survey results showed that 574 of the respondents lack confidence they will be able to afford health insurance in the future. **LO 5**
    a. What is the point estimate of the population proportion of adults who lack confidence they will be able to afford health insurance in the future.
    b. At 90% confidence, what is the margin of error?
    c. Develop a 90% confidence interval for the population proportion of adults who lack confidence they will be able to afford health insurance in the future.
    d. Develop a 95% confidence interval for this population proportion.

36. **Automobile Insurance Coverage.** According to statistics reported on CNBC, a surprising number of motor vehicles are not covered by insurance. Sample results, consistent with the CNBC report, showed 46 of 200 vehicles were not covered by insurance. **LO 5**
    a. What is the point estimate of the proportion of vehicles not covered by insurance?
    b. Develop a 95% confidence interval for the population proportion.

DATA*file*
rightdirection

37. **Voter Sentiment.** One of the questions Rasmussen Reports included on a 2018 survey of 2,500 likely voters asked if the country is headed in the right direction. Representative data are shown in the file *rightdirection*. A response of Yes indicates that the respondent does think the country is headed in the right direction. A response of No indicates that the respondent does not think the country is headed in the right direction. Respondents may also give a response of Not Sure. **LO 5**
    a. What is the point estimate of the proportion of the population of likely voters who do think that the country is headed in the right direction?
    b. At 95% confidence, what is the margin of error?
    c. What is the 95% confidence interval for the proportion of likely voters who do think that the country is headed in the right direction?
    d. What is the 95% confidence interval for the proportion of likely voters who do not think that the country is headed in the right direction?
    e. Which of the confidence intervals in parts (c) and (d) has the smaller margin of error? Why?

DATA*file*
casualdining

38. **Franchise Profits.** According to *Franchise Business Review*, over 50% of all food franchises earn a profit of less than $50,000 a year. In the sample of 142 casual dining

restaurants contained in the file *casualdining*, 81 earned a profit of less than $50,000 last year. **LO 5**

a. What is the point estimate of the proportion of casual dining restaurants that earned a profit of less than $50,000 last year?
b. Determine the margin of error and provide a 95% confidence interval for the proportion of casual dining restaurants that earned a profit of less than $50,000 last year.
c. How large a sample is needed if the desired margin of error is 0.03?

39. **Stay-at-Home Parenting.** In November 2018, Pew Research reported that in 17% of all homes with a stay-at-home parent, the father is the stay-at-home parent. An independent research firm has been charged with conducting a sample survey to obtain more current information. **LO 6**
    a. What sample size is needed if the research firm's goal is to estimate the current proportion of homes with a stay-at-home parent in which the father is the stay-at-home parent with a margin of error of 0.03? Use a 95% confidence level.
    b. Repeat part (a) using a 99% confidence level.

40. **Employee Contributions to Healthcare Coverage.** For many years businesses have struggled with the rising cost of health care. But recently, the increases have slowed due to less inflation in healthcare prices and employees paying for a larger portion of healthcare benefits. A recent Mercer survey showed that 52% of U.S. employers were likely to require higher employee contributions for healthcare coverage in the upcoming year. Suppose the survey was based on a sample of 800 companies. Compute the margin of error and a 95% confidence interval for the proportion of companies likely to require higher employee contributions for healthcare coverage in the upcoming year. **LO 5**

41. **Driver's License Rates.** Fewer young people are driving. In 1995, 63.9% of people under 20 years old who were eligible had a driver's license. The Federal Highway Administration reported that percentage had dropped to 41.5% in 2020. Suppose these results are based on a random sample of 1,200 people under 20 years old who were eligible to have a driver's license in 1995 and again in 2020. **LO 5**
    a. At 95% confidence, what is the margin of error and the interval estimate of the number of eligible people under 20 years old who had a driver's license in 1995?
    b. At 95% confidence, what is the margin of error and the interval estimate of the number of eligible people under 20 years old who had a driver's license in 2020?
    c. Is the margin of error the same in parts (a) and (b)? Why or why not?

42. **Voter Intent.** A poll for the presidential campaign sampled 491 potential voters in June. A primary purpose of the poll was to obtain an estimate of the proportion of potential voters who favored each candidate. Assume a planning value of $p^* = 0.50$ and a 95% confidence level. **LO 5, 6**
    a. For $p^* = 0.50$, what was the planned margin of error for the June poll?
    b. Closer to the November election, better precision and smaller margins of error are desired. Assume the following margins of error are requested for surveys to be conducted during the presidential campaign. Compute the recommended sample size for each survey.

Survey	Margin of Error
September	0.04
October	0.03
Early November	0.02
Pre–Election Day	0.01

43. **Internet Usage.** In 2012, the Pew Research Center Internet Project conducted a survey of 1,502 Internet users that provided a variety of statistics on Internet users. For instance, in 2021, 93% of American adults were Internet users. In 1995, only 14% of American adults used the Internet. **LO 5**
   a. Develop a 95% confidence interval for the proportion of American adults who identified as Internet users in 2021.
   b. The sample survey showed that 77% of respondents said they have a broadband connection at home. Develop a 95% confidence interval for the proportion of American adults who say they have a broadband connection at home.
   c. The sample survey showed that 15% of American adults say their smartphones are their primary means of online access at home. Develop a 95% confidence interval for the proportion of American adults who say their smartphones are their primary means of online access at home.
   d. Compare the margin of error for the interval estimates in parts (a), (b), and (c). How is the margin of error related to the sample proportion?

8.5 Practical Advice: Big Data and Interval Estimation

We have seen that confidence intervals are powerful tools for making inferences about population parameters. We now consider the ramifications of big data on confidence intervals for means and proportions, and we return to the data-collection problem of online news service PenningtonDailyTimes.com (PDT). Recall that PDT's primary source of revenue is the sale of advertising, so PDT's management is concerned about the time customers spend during their visits to PDT's website and whether visitors click on any of the ads featured on the website.

Big Data and the Precision of Confidence Intervals

A review of equations (8.2) and (8.6) shows that confidence intervals for the population mean μ and population proportion p become more narrow as the size of the sample increases. Therefore, the potential sampling error also decreases as the sample size increases. To illustrate the rate at which interval estimates narrow for a given confidence level, we consider the online news service PenningtonDailyTimes.com (PDT).

Prospective advertisers are willing to pay a premium to advertise on websites that have long visit times, so the time customers spend during their visits to PDT's website has a substantial impact on PDT's advertising revenues. Suppose PDT's management wants to develop a 95% confidence interval estimate of the mean amount of time customers spend during their visits to PDT's website. Table 8.6 shows how the margin of error at the 95% confidence level decreases as the sample size increases when $s = 20$.

Table 8.6 Margin of Error for Interval Estimates of the Population Mean at the 95% Confidence Level for Various Sample Sizes

Sample Size n	Margin of Error $t_{\alpha/2}s_{\bar{x}}$
10	14.30714
100	3.96843
1,000	1.24109
10,000	0.39204
100,000	0.12396
1,000,000	0.03920
10,000,000	0.01240
100,000,000	0.00392
1,000,000,000	0.00124

Table 8.7 Margin of Error for Interval Estimates of the Population Proportion at the 95% Confidence Level for Various Sample Sizes

Sample Size n	Margin of Error $z_{\alpha/2}\sigma_{\bar{p}}$
10	0.30984
100	0.09798
1,000	0.03098
10,000	0.00980
100,000	0.00310
1,000,000	0.00098
10,000,000	0.00031
100,000,000	0.00010
1,000,000,000	0.00003

Suppose that in addition to estimating the population mean amount of time customers spend during their visits to PDT's website, PDT would like to develop a 95% confidence interval estimate of the proportion of its website visitors that click on an ad. Table 8.7 shows how the margin of error for a 95% confidence interval estimate of the population proportion decreases as the sample size increases when the sample proportion is $\bar{p} = 0.51$.

The PDT example illustrates the relationship between the precision of interval estimates and the sample size. We see in Tables 8.6 and 8.7 that at a given confidence level, the margins of error decrease as the sample sizes increase. As a result, if the sample mean time spent by customers when they visit PDT's website is 84.1 seconds, the 95% confidence interval estimate of the population mean time spent by customers when they visit PDT's website decreases from (69.79286, 98.40714) for a sample of $n = 10$ to (83.97604, 84.22396) for a sample of $n = 100{,}000$ to (84.09876, 84.10124) for a sample of $n = 1{,}000{,}000{,}000$. Similarly, if the sample proportion of its website visitors who clicked on an ad is 0.51, the 95% confidence interval estimate of the population proportion of its website visitors who clicked on an ad decreases from (0.20016, 0.81984) for a sample of $n = 10$ to (0.50690, 0.51310) for a sample of $n = 100{,}000$ to (0.50997, 0.51003) for a sample of $n = 1{,}000{,}000{,}000$. In both instances, as the sample size becomes extremely large, the margin of error becomes extremely small and the resulting confidence intervals become extremely narrow.

Implications of Big Data for Confidence Intervals

Last year the mean time spent by all visitors to PenningtonDailyTimes.com was 84 seconds. Suppose that PDT wants to assess whether the population mean time has changed since last year. PDT now collects a new sample of 1,000,000 visitors to its website and calculates the sample mean time spent by these visitors to the PDT website to be $\bar{x} = 84.1$ seconds. The estimated population standard deviation is $s = 20$ seconds, so the standard error is $s_{\bar{x}} = s/\sqrt{n} = 0.02000$. Furthermore, the sample is sufficiently large to ensure that the sampling distribution of the sample mean will be normally distributed. Thus, the 95% confidence interval estimate of the population mean is

$$\bar{x} \pm t_{\alpha/2}s_{\bar{x}} = 84.1 \pm 0.0392 = (84.06080, 84.13920)$$

What could PDT conclude from these results? There are three possible reasons that PDT's sample mean of 84.1 seconds differs from last year's population mean of 84 seconds: (1) sampling error, (2) nonsampling error, or (3) the population mean has changed since last year. The 95% confidence interval estimate of the population mean does not include the value for the mean time spent by all visitors to the PDT website for last year (84 seconds), suggesting that the difference between PDT's sample mean for the new sample (84.1 seconds) and the mean from last year (84 seconds) is not likely to be exclusively a consequence of sampling error. Nonsampling error is a possible explanation and should be investigated as the results of statistical inference become less reliable as nonsampling error is introduced into the sample data. If PDT determines that it introduced little or no nonsampling error into its sample data, the only remaining plausible explanation for a difference of this magnitude is that the population mean has changed since last year.

If PDT concludes that the sample has provided reliable evidence and the population mean has changed since last year, management must still consider the potential impact of the difference between the sample mean and the mean from last year. If a 0.1 second difference in the time spent by visitors to PenningtonDailyTimes.com has a consequential effect on what PDT can charge for advertising on its site, this result could have practical business implications for PDT. Otherwise, there may be no **practical significance** of the 0.1 second difference in the time spent by visitors to PenningtonDailyTimes.com.

Confidence intervals are extremely useful, but as with any other statistical tool, they are only effective when properly applied. Because interval estimates become increasingly precise as the sample size increases, extremely large samples will yield extremely precise estimates. However, no interval estimate, no matter how precise, will accurately reflect the parameter being estimated unless the sample is relatively free of nonsampling error. Therefore, when using interval estimation, it is always important to carefully consider whether a random sample of the population of interest has been taken.

Note + Comment

When taking an extremely large sample, it is conceivable that the sample size is at least 5% of the population size; that is, $n/N \geq 0.05$. Under these conditions it is necessary to use the finite population correction factor when calculating the standard error of the sampling distribution.

Exercises

Applications

DATA*file* fedtaxerrors

44. **Federal Tax Return Errors.** Suppose a sample of 10,001 erroneous Federal income tax returns from last year has been taken and is provided in the file *fedtaxerrors*. A positive value indicates the taxpayer underpaid and a negative value indicates that the taxpayer overpaid. Also suppose the IRS has established that the standard deviation of errors made on Federal income tax returns is $\sigma = 12{,}300$. **LO 2, 3**
    a. What is the point estimate for the mean error made on erroneous Federal income tax returns last year?
    b. Using 95% confidence, what is the margin of error?
    c. Using the results from parts (a) and (b), develop the 95% confidence interval estimate of the mean error made on erroneous Federal income tax returns last year.

DATA*file* fedsickhours

45. **Federal Government Employee Sick Hours.** According to the Census Bureau, 2,475,780 people are employed by the federal government in the United States as of 2018. Suppose that a random sample of 3,500 of these federal employees was selected and the number of sick hours each of these employees took last year was collected from an electronic personnel database. The data collected in this survey are provided in the file *fedsickhours*. Based on historical data, the population standard deviation can be assumed to be known with $\sigma = 34.5$. **LO 2, 3**
    a. What is the point estimate for the mean number of sick hours taken by federal employees last year?
    b. Using 99% confidence, what is the margin of error?
    c. Using the results from parts (a) and (b), develop the 99% confidence interval estimate of the mean number of sick hours taken by federal employees last year.
    d. If the mean sick hours federal employees took two years ago was 62.2, what would the confidence interval in part (c) lead you to conclude about last year?

46. **Web Browser Satisfaction.** Internet users were recently asked online to rate their satisfaction with the web browser they use most frequently. Of 102,519 respondents, 65,120 indicated they were very satisfied with the web browser they use most frequently. **LO 5**
   a. What is the point estimate for the proportion of Internet users who are very satisfied with the web browser they use most frequently?
   b. Using 95% confidence, what is the margin of error?
   c. Using the results from parts (a) and (b), develop the 95% confidence interval estimate of the proportion of Internet users who are very satisfied with the web browser they use most frequently.

47. **Speeding Drivers.** In 2017, ABC News reports that 58% of U.S. drivers admit to speeding. Suppose that a new satellite technology can instantly measure the speed of any vehicle on a U.S. road and determine whether the vehicle is speeding, and this satellite technology was used to take a sample of 20,000 vehicles at 6:00 P.M. EST on a recent Tuesday afternoon. Of these 20,000 vehicles, 9,252 were speeding. **LO 5**
   a. What is the point estimate for the proportion of vehicles on U.S. roads that speed?
   b. Using 99% confidence, what is the margin of error?
   c. Using the results from parts (a) and (b), develop the 99% confidence interval estimate of the proportion of vehicles on U.S. roads that speed.
   d. What the confidence interval in part (c) lead you to conclude about the ABC News report?

Summary

In this chapter, we presented methods for developing interval estimates of a population mean and a population proportion. A point estimator may or may not provide a good estimate of a population parameter. The use of an interval estimate provides a measure of the precision of an estimate. Both the interval estimate of the population mean and the population proportion are of the form: point estimate $\pm$ margin of error.

We presented interval estimates for a population mean for two cases. In the σ known case, historical data or other information is used to develop an estimate of σ prior to taking a sample. Analysis of new sample data then proceeds based on the assumption that σ is known. In the σ unknown case, the sample data are used to estimate both the population mean and the population standard deviation. The final choice of which interval estimation procedure to use depends upon the analyst's understanding of which method provides the best estimate of σ.

In the σ known case, the interval estimation procedure is based on the assumed value of σ and the use of the standard normal distribution. In the σ unknown case, the interval estimation procedure uses the sample standard deviation s and the t distribution. In both cases the quality of the interval estimates obtained depends on the distribution of the population and the sample size. If the population is normally distributed the interval estimates will be exact in both cases, even for small sample sizes. If the population is not normally distributed, the interval estimates obtained will be approximate. Larger sample sizes will provide better approximations, but the more highly skewed the population is, the larger the sample size needs to be to obtain a good approximation. Practical advice about the sample size necessary to obtain good approximations was included in Sections 8.1 and 8.2. In most cases a sample of size 30 or more will provide good approximate confidence intervals.

The general form of the interval estimate for a population proportion is $\bar{p} \pm$ margin of error. In practice the sample sizes used for interval estimates of a population proportion are generally large. Thus, the interval estimation procedure is based on the standard normal distribution.

Often a desired margin of error is specified prior to developing a sampling plan. We showed how to choose a sample size large enough to provide the desired precision. Finally, we discussed the ramifications of extremely large samples on the precision of confidence interval estimates of the mean and proportion.

Glossary

Confidence coefficient The confidence level expressed as a decimal value. For example, 0.95 is the confidence coefficient for a 95% confidence level.
Confidence interval Another name for an interval estimate.
Confidence level The confidence associated with an interval estimate. For example, if an interval estimation procedure provides intervals such that 95% of the intervals formed using the procedure will include the population parameter, the interval estimate is said to be constructed at the 95% confidence level.
Degrees of freedom A parameter of the t distribution. When the t distribution is used in the computation of an interval estimate of a population mean, the appropriate t distribution has $n - 1$ degrees of freedom, where n is the size of the sample.
Interval estimate An estimate of a population parameter that provides an interval believed to contain the value of the parameter. For the interval estimates in this chapter, it has the form: point estimate ± margin of error.
Level of significance The probability that the interval estimation procedure will generate an interval that does not contain μ.
Margin of error The ± value added to and subtracted from a point estimate in order to develop an interval estimate of a population parameter.
Practical significance The real-world impact the result of statistical inference will have on business decisions.
σ known The case when historical data or other information provide a good value for the population standard deviation prior to taking a sample. The interval estimation procedure uses this known value of σ in computing the margin of error.
σ unknown The more common case when no good basis exists for estimating the population standard deviation prior to taking the sample. The interval estimation procedure uses the sample standard deviation s in computing the margin of error.
***t* distribution** A family of probability distributions that can be used to develop an interval estimate of a population mean whenever the population standard deviation σ is unknown and is estimated by the sample standard deviation s.

Key Formulas

Interval Estimate of a Population Mean: σ Known

$$\bar{x} \pm z_{\alpha/2} \frac{\sigma}{\sqrt{n}} \tag{8.1}$$

Interval Estimate of a Population Mean: σ Unknown

$$\bar{x} \pm t_{\alpha/2} \frac{s}{\sqrt{n}} \tag{8.2}$$

Sample Size for an Interval Estimate of a Population Mean

$$n = \frac{(z_{\alpha/2})^2 \sigma^2}{E^2} \tag{8.3}$$

Interval Estimate of a Population Proportion

$$\bar{p} \pm z_{\alpha/2} \sqrt{\frac{\bar{p}(1 - \bar{p})}{n}} \tag{8.6}$$

Sample Size for an Interval Estimate of a Population Proportion

$$n = \frac{(z_{\alpha/2})^2 p^*(1 - p^*)}{E^2} \tag{8.7}$$

Supplementary Exercises

48. **Discount Brokerage Trade Fees.** A sample survey of 54 discount brokers showed that the mean price charged for a trade of 100 shares at $50 per share was $33.77. The survey is conducted annually. With the historical data available, assume a known population standard deviation of $15. **LO 1**
    a. Using the sample data, what is the margin of error associated with a 95% confidence interval?
    b. Develop a 95% confidence interval for the mean price charged by discount brokers for a trade of 100 shares at $50 per share.

49. **Family Vacation Expenses.** A survey conducted by the American Automobile Association (AAA) showed that a family of four spends an average of $215.60 per day while on vacation. Suppose a sample of 64 families of four vacationing at Niagara Falls resulted in a sample mean of $252.45 per day and a sample standard deviation of $74.50. **LO 2, 3**
    a. Develop a 95% confidence interval estimate of the mean amount spent per day by a family of four visiting Niagara Falls.
    b. Based on the confidence interval from part (a), does it appear that the population mean amount spent per day by families visiting Niagara Falls differs from the mean reported by the American Automobile Association? Explain.

50. **Annual Restaurant Expenditures.** The 92 million Americans of age 50 and over control 50% of all discretionary income. AARP estimated that the average annual expenditure on restaurants and carryout food was $1,873 for individuals in this age group. Suppose this estimate is based on a sample of 80 persons and that the sample standard deviation is $550. **LO 2, 3**
    a. At 95% confidence, what is the margin of error?
    b. What is the 95% confidence interval for the population mean amount spent on restaurants and carryout food?
    c. What is your estimate of the total amount spent by Americans of age 50 and over on restaurants and carryout food?
    d. If the amount spent on restaurants and carryout food is skewed to the right, would you expect the median amount spent to be greater or less than $1,873?

DATA *file*
sleephabits

51. **Healthy Sleep Duration.** The Centers for Disease Control and Prevention (CDC) defines a healthy sleep duration to be at least seven hours per day. The CDC reports that the percentage of people who report a healthy sleep duration varies by marital status. The CDC also reports that in 2018, 67% of those who are married report a healthy sleep duration; 62% of those who have never been married report a healthy sleep duration; and 56% of those who are divorced, widowed, or separated report a healthy sleep duration. The file *sleephabits* contains sample data on the sleeping habits of people who have never been married that are consistent with the CDC's findings. Use these data to answer the following questions. **LO 5**
    a. Develop a point estimate and a 95% confidence interval for the proportion of those who have never been married who report a healthy sleep duration.
    b. Develop a point estimate and a 95% confidence interval for the mean number of hours of sleep for those who have never been married.
    c. For those who have never been married, estimate the number of hours of sleep per day for those who report a healthy sleep duration.

DATA *file*
drugcost

52. **Healthcare Expenditures.** The Health Care Cost Institute tracks healthcare expenditures for beneficiaries under the age of 65 who are covered by employer-sponsored private health insurance. The data contained in the file *drugcost* are consistent with the institute's findings concerning annual prescription costs per employee. Analyze the data using Excel and answer the following questions. **LO 2, 3**
    a. Develop a 90% confidence interval for the annual cost of prescription drugs.
    b. Develop a 90% confidence interval for the amount of out-of-pocket expense per employee.

c. What is your point estimate of the proportion of employees who incurred no prescription drug costs?
d. Which, if either, of the confidence intervals in parts (a) and (b) has a larger margin of error. Why?

DATA*file*
obesity

53. **Obesity.** Obesity is a risk factor for many health problems such as type 2 diabetes, high blood pressure, joint problems, and gallstones. Using data collected in 2018 through the National Health and Nutrition Examination Survey, the National Institute of Diabetes and Digestive and Kidney Diseases estimates that 37.7% of all adults in the United States have a body mass index (BMI) in excess of 30 and so are categorized as obese. The data in the file *obesity* are consistent with these findings. **LO 2, 3**
a. Use the *obesity* data set to develop a point estimate of the BMI for adults in the United States. Are adults in the United States obese on average?
b. What is the sample standard deviation?
c. Develop a 95% confidence interval for the BMI of adults in the United States.

54. **Automobile Mileage Tests.** Mileage tests are conducted for a particular model of automobile. If a 98% confidence interval with a margin of error of 1 mile per gallon is desired, how many automobiles should be used in the test? Assume that preliminary mileage tests indicate the standard deviation is 2.6 miles per gallon. **LO 4**

55. **Patient Treatment Times.** In developing patient appointment schedules, a medical center wants to estimate the mean time that a staff member spends with each patient. How large a sample should be taken if the desired margin of error is two minutes at a 95% level of confidence? How large a sample should be taken for a 99% level of confidence? Use a planning value for the population standard deviation of eight minutes. **LO 4**

56. **CEO Compensation.** Annual salary plus bonus data for chief executive officers are presented in an annual pay survey. A preliminary sample showed that the standard deviation is $675 with data provided in thousands of dollars. How many chief executive officers should be in a sample if we want to estimate the population mean annual salary plus bonus with a margin of error of $100,000? (*Note:* The desired margin of error would be $E = 100$ if the data are in thousands of dollars.) Use 95% confidence. **LO 4**

57. **Paying for College Tuition.** The National Center for Education Statistics reported that 47% of college students work to pay for tuition and living expenses. Assume that a sample of 450 college students was used in the study. **LO 5**
a. Provide a 95% confidence interval for the population proportion of college students who work to pay for tuition and living expenses.
b. Provide a 99% confidence interval for the population proportion of college students who work to pay for tuition and living expenses.
c. What happens to the margin of error as the confidence is increased from 95% to 99%?

58. **Parenting Time.** A *USA Today*/CNN/Gallup survey of 369 working parents found 200 who said they spend too little time with their children because of work commitments. **LO 5**
a. What is the point estimate of the proportion of the population of working parents who feel they spend too little time with their children because of work commitments?
b. At 95% confidence, what is the margin of error?
c. What is the 95% confidence interval estimate of the population proportion of working parents who feel they spend too little time with their children because of work commitments?

59. **Social Media Usage.** The Pew Research Center has conducted extensive research on social media usage. One finding, reported in June 2018, was that 78% of adults aged 18 to 24 use Snapchat. Another finding was that 45% of those aged 18 to 24 use Twitter. Assume the sample size associated with both findings is 500. **LO 5**
a. Develop a 95% confidence interval for the proportion of adults aged 18 to 24 who use Snapchat.

b. Develop a 99% confidence interval for the proportion of adults aged 18 to 24 who use Twitter.

c. In which case, part (a) or part (b), is the margin of error larger? Explain why.

60. **Importance of Economy to Voters.** A survey of 750 likely voters in Ohio was conducted by the Rasmussen Poll just prior to the general election. The state of the economy was thought to be an important determinant of how people would vote. Among other things, the survey found that 165 of the respondents rated the economy as good or excellent and 315 rated the economy as poor. **LO 5**

a. Develop a point estimate of the proportion of likely voters in Ohio who rated the economy as good or excellent.

b. Construct a 95% confidence interval for the proportion of likely voters in Ohio who rated the economy as good or excellent.

c. Construct a 95% confidence interval for the proportion of likely voters in Ohio who rated the economy as poor.

d. Which of the confidence intervals in parts (b) and (c) is wider? Why?

61. **Smoking.** In 2023, the *Centers for Disease Control and Prevention* reported the percentage of people 18 years of age and older who smoke. Suppose that a study designed to collect new data on smokers and nonsmokers uses a preliminary estimate of the proportion who smoke of 0.30. **LO 5, 6**

a. How large a sample should be taken to estimate the proportion of smokers in the population with a margin of error of 0.02? Use 95% confidence?

b. Assume that the study uses your sample size recommendation in part (a) and finds 520 smokers. What is the point estimate of the proportion of smokers in the population?

c. What is the 95% confidence interval for the proportion of smokers in the population?

62. **Credit Card Balances.** A well-known bank credit card firm wishes to estimate the proportion of credit card holders who carry a nonzero balance at the end of the month and incur an interest charge. Assume that the desired margin of error is 0.03 at 98% confidence. **LO 6**

a. How large a sample should be selected if it is anticipated that roughly 70% of the firm's card holders carry a nonzero balance at the end of the month?

b. How large a sample should be selected if no planning value for the proportion could be specified?

63. **Credit Card Ownership.** Credit card ownership varies across age groups. In 2018, CreditCards.com estimated that the percentage of people who own at least one credit card is 67% in the 18–24 age group, 83% in the 25–34 age group, 76% in the 35–49 age group, and 78% in the 50+ age group. Suppose these estimates are based on 455 randomly selected people from each age group. **LO 5, 6**

a. Construct a 95% confidence interval for the proportion of people in each of these age groups who owns at least one credit card.

b. Assuming the same sample size will be used in each age group, how large would the sample need to be to ensure that the margin of error is 0.03 or less for each of the four confidence intervals?

64. **Factors in Choosing an Airline.** Although airline schedules and cost are important factors for business travelers when choosing an airline carrier, a *USA Today* survey found that business travelers list an airline's frequent flyer program as the most important factor. From a sample of $n = 1{,}993$ business travelers who responded to the survey, 618 listed a frequent flyer program as the most important factor. **LO 5, 6**

a. What is the point estimate of the proportion of the population of business travelers who believe a frequent flyer program is the most important factor when choosing an airline carrier?

b. Develop a 95% confidence interval estimate of the population proportion.
c. How large a sample would be required to report the margin of error of 0.01 at 95% confidence? Would you recommend that *USA Today* attempt to provide this degree of precision? Why or why not?

DATA*file* 35mph

65. **Driving Speeds.** Huston Systems Private Limited reports that smart traffic signals and signs can measure a passing vehicle's speed. Consider the speeds of 15,717 vehicles collected as they passed 35 MPH speed limit signs throughout the United States in 2018 that are provided in the file *35mph.* **LO 2, 3**
a. What is the sample mean speed of U.S. drivers in a 35-mph zone?
b. Using 95% confidence, what is the margin of error?
c. Using the results from parts (a) and (b), develop the 95% confidence interval estimate of the mean speed of U.S. drivers in a 35 MPH zone.

DATA*file* underemployed

66. **Underemployment.** A recent survey by PayScale found that 46% of U.S. workers—roughly 22 million—are underemployed, either working part-time or at jobs that don't allow them to use their education or skills. Suppose that the numbers of hours worked in the past week were collected from a random sample of 28,585 of these workers. The data collected in this survey are provided in the file *underemployed.* **LO 2, 3**
a. What is the sample mean number of hours worked by underemployed U.S. workers?
b. Using 99% confidence, what is the margin of error?
c. Using the results from parts (a) and (b), develop the 99% confidence interval estimate of the mean number of hours worked by underemployed U.S. workers.
d. If the mean hours worked by underemployed U.S. workers during the same week one year ago was 35.6, what would the confidence interval in part (c) lead you to conclude about last week?

DATA*file* floridafraud

67. **FTC Fraud Reports.** In 2017, 42.54% of the nearly 2.7 million reports taken nationwide by the Federal Trade Commission's Consumer Sentinel Network dealt with instances of fraud. Consider results of a random sample of 42,296 of the reports taken by the Consumer Sentinel Network from Florida that are provided the file *floridafraud.* **LO 5**
a. What is the sample proportion of reports filed from Florida that dealt with instances of fraud?
b. Using 95% confidence, what is the margin of error?
c. Using the results from parts (a) and (b), develop the 95% confidence interval estimate of the proportion reports filed from Florida that dealt with instances of fraud. What do you conclude about Florida from these results?

68. **Structurally Deficient Bridges.** The Infrastructure Report Card (IRC) reports that of 614,387 U.S. bridges, 9.1% were structurally deficient as of last year. The IRC also reports that more than 1,300 California bridges fall under this category. How does California compare to the nation? Consider a random sample of 8,749 bridges in California that includes 490 structurally deficient bridges. **LO 5**
a. What is the sample proportion of structurally deficient bridges in California?
b. Using 90% confidence, what is the margin of error?
c. Using the results from parts (a) and (b), develop the 90% confidence interval estimate of the proportion of structurally deficient bridges in California.
d. What does the confidence interval in part (c) lead you to conclude about California bridges?

Case Problem 1: *Young Professional* Magazine

Young Professional magazine was developed for a target audience of recent college graduates who are in their first 10 years in a business/professional career. In its two years of publication, the magazine has been fairly successful. Now the publisher is interested in expanding the magazine's advertising base. Potential advertisers continually ask about the demographics and interests of subscribers to *Young Professional*. To collect this information, the magazine commissioned a

Table 8.8 Partial Survey Results for *Young Professional* Magazine

Age	Gender	Real Estate Purchases	Value of Investments ($)	Number of Transactions	Internet Access	Household Income ($)	Children
38	Female	No	12,200	4	Yes	75,200	Yes
30	Male	No	12,400	4	Yes	70,300	Yes
41	Female	No	26,800	5	Yes	48,200	No
28	Female	Yes	19,600	6	No	95,300	No
31	Female	Yes	15,100	5	No	73,300	Yes
⋮	⋮	⋮	⋮	⋮	⋮	⋮	⋮

survey to develop a profile of its subscribers. The survey results will be used to help the magazine choose articles of interest and provide advertisers with a profile of subscribers. As a new employee of the magazine, you have been asked to help analyze the survey results.

Some of the survey questions follow:

1. What is your age?
2. Are you: Male_________ Female___________
3. Do you plan to make any real estate purchases in the next two years?
   Yes______ No______
4. What is the approximate total value of financial investments, exclusive of your home, owned by you or members of your household?
5. How many stock/bond/mutual fund transactions have you made in the past year?
6. Do you have broadband access to the Internet at home? Yes______ No______
7. Please indicate your total household income last year.
8. Do you have children? Yes______ No______

DATA*file*
professional

The file *professional* contains the responses to these questions. Table 8.8 shows the portion of the file pertaining to the first five survey respondents. **LO 5**

Managerial Report

Prepare a managerial report summarizing the results of the survey. In addition to statistical summaries, discuss how the magazine might use these results to attract advertisers. You might also comment on how the survey results could be used by the magazine's editors to identify topics that would be of interest to readers. Your report should address the following issues, but do not limit your analysis to just these areas.

1. Develop appropriate descriptive statistics to summarize the data.
2. Develop 95% confidence intervals for the mean age and household income of subscribers.
3. Develop 95% confidence intervals for the proportion of subscribers who have Internet access at home and the proportion of subscribers who have children.
4. Would *Young Professional* be a good advertising outlet for online brokers? Justify your conclusion with statistical data.
5. Would this magazine be a good place to advertise for companies selling educational software and computer games for young children?
6. Comment on the types of articles you believe would be of interest to readers of *Young Professional*.

Case Problem 2: Gulf Real Estate Properties

Gulf Real Estate Properties, Inc. is a real estate firm located in southwest Florida. The company, which advertises itself as "expert in the real estate market," monitors condominium sales by collecting data on location, list price, sale price, and number of days it takes to sell each unit. Each condominium is classified as *Gulf View* if it is located directly on the

Gulf of Mexico or *No Gulf View* if it is located on the bay or a golf course, near but not on the Gulf. Sample data from the Multiple Listing Service in Naples, Florida, provided sales data for 40 Gulf View condominiums and 18 No Gulf View condominiums.* Prices are in thousands of dollars. The data are shown in Table 8.9. **LO 2, 3**

DATA*file*
gulfprop

Table 8.9 Sales Data for Gulf Real Estate Properties

Gulf View Condominiums			No Gulf View Condominiums		
List Price ($ thousands)	Sale Price ($ thousands)	Days to Sell	List Price ($ thousands)	Sale Price ($ thousands)	Days to Sell
495.0	475.0	130	217.0	217.0	182
379.0	350.0	71	148.0	135.5	338
529.0	519.0	85	186.5	179.0	122
552.5	534.5	95	239.0	230.0	150
334.9	334.9	119	279.0	267.5	169
550.0	505.0	92	215.0	214.0	58
169.9	165.0	197	279.0	259.0	110
210.0	210.0	56	179.9	176.5	130
975.0	945.0	73	149.9	144.9	149
314.0	314.0	126	235.0	230.0	114
315.0	305.0	88	199.8	192.0	120
885.0	800.0	282	210.0	195.0	61
975.0	975.0	100	226.0	212.0	146
469.0	445.0	56	149.9	146.5	137
329.0	305.0	49	160.0	160.0	281
365.0	330.0	48	322.0	292.5	63
332.0	312.0	88	187.5	179.0	48
520.0	495.0	161	247.0	227.0	52
425.0	405.0	149			
675.0	669.0	142			
409.0	400.0	28			
649.0	649.0	29			
319.0	305.0	140			
425.0	410.0	85			
359.0	340.0	107			
469.0	449.0	72			
895.0	875.0	129			
439.0	430.0	160			
435.0	400.0	206			
235.0	227.0	91			
638.0	618.0	100			
629.0	600.0	97			
329.0	309.0	114			
595.0	555.0	45			
339.0	315.0	150			
215.0	200.0	48			
395.0	375.0	135			
449.0	425.0	53			
499.0	465.0	86			
439.0	428.5	158			

*Data based on condominium sales reported in the Naples MLS (Coldwell Banker, June 2000).

Managerial Report

1. Use appropriate descriptive statistics to summarize each of the three variables for the 40 Gulf View condominiums.
2. Use appropriate descriptive statistics to summarize each of the three variables for the 18 No Gulf View condominiums.
3. Compare your summary results. Discuss any specific statistical results that would help a real estate agent understand the condominium market.
4. Develop a 95% confidence interval estimate of the population mean sales price and population mean number of days to sell for Gulf View condominiums. Interpret your results.
5. Develop a 95% confidence interval estimate of the population mean sales price and population mean number of days to sell for No Gulf View condominiums. Interpret your results.
6. Assume the branch manager requested estimates of the mean selling price of Gulf View condominiums with a margin of error of $40,000 and the mean selling price of No Gulf View condominiums with a margin of error of $15,000. Using 95% confidence, how large should the sample sizes be?
7. Gulf Real Estate Properties just signed contracts for two new listings: a Gulf View condominium with a list price of $589,000 and a No Gulf View condominium with a list price of $285,000. What is your estimate of the final selling price and number of days required to sell each of these units?

Case Problem 3: Garza Research, Inc.

Garza Research, Inc., a consumer research organization, conducts surveys designed to evaluate a wide variety of products and services available to consumers. In one particular study, Garza looked at consumer satisfaction with the performance of automobiles produced by a major Detroit manufacturer. A questionnaire sent to owners of one of the manufacturer's full-sized cars revealed several complaints about early transmission problems. To learn more about the transmission failures, Garza used a sample of actual transmission repairs provided by a transmission repair firm in the Detroit area. The following data show the actual number of miles driven for 50 vehicles at the time of transmission failure. **LO 3, 4**

DATA*file*
auto

85,092	32,609	59,465	77,437	32,534	64,090	32,464	59,902
39,323	89,641	94,219	116,803	92,857	63,436	65,605	85,861
64,342	61,978	67,998	59,817	101,769	95,774	121,352	69,568
74,276	66,998	40,001	72,069	25,066	77,098	69,922	35,662
74,425	67,202	118,444	53,500	79,294	64,544	86,813	116,269
37,831	89,341	73,341	85,288	138,114	53,402	85,586	82,256
77,539	88,798						

Managerial Report

1. Use appropriate descriptive statistics to summarize the transmission failure data.
2. Develop a 95% confidence interval for the mean number of miles driven until transmission failure for the population of automobiles with transmission failure. Provide a managerial interpretation of the interval estimate.
3. Discuss the implication of your statistical findings in terms of the belief that some owners of the automobiles experienced early transmission failures.
4. How many repair records should be sampled if the research firm wants the population mean number of miles driven until transmission failure to be estimated with a margin of error of 5,000 miles? Use 95% confidence.
5. What other information would you like to gather to evaluate the transmission failure problem more fully?

Case Problem 4: Go-Fer Meal Delivery Service

Go-Fer is a company that maintains, markets, and operates a mobile app that is used to by its customers arrange for food delivery from restaurants and supermarkets to their homes. Go-Fer management wants to understand the income and dwelling status (owner or renter) of the users of its app better, so it collects data from 854,528 orders Go-Fer has filled through its app over the past six months. The company then purchases access to a large demographic database service and uses the address to which the food was delivered for each of these 854,528 orders to link its data to the demographic data. As a result, Go-Fer has the household income and dwelling status for each of these 854,528 deliveries. The file *gofer* contains these data. **LO 2, 3, 5**

DATA*file*
gofer

Managerial Report

1. Calculate the sample mean and sample standard deviation for annual household income for Go-Fer management.
2. Calculate the sample proportion of respondents who own their homes for Go-Fer management.
3. Develop a 99% confidence interval estimate of the population mean annual household income for Go-Fer customers.
4. Go-Fer management believes the population mean annual household income for its customers is at least $93,000. Based on the interval estimate of the population mean annual household income for Go-Fer customers you calculated in part (3), explain to Go-Fer management whether these data support their belief.
5. Develop a 99% confidence interval estimate of the population proportion of Go-Fer customers who are homeowners. Interpret your results.
6. Go-Fer management believes the population proportion of Go-Fer customers who are homeowners is at least 0.64. Based on the interval estimate of the population proportion of Go-Fer customers who are homeowners you calculated in part (5), explain to Go-Fer management whether these data support their belief.

Chapter 9

Hypothesis Tests

Contents

Statistics in Practice:
John Morrell & Company

9.1 Developing Null and Alternative Hypotheses
The Alternative Hypothesis as a Research Hypothesis
The Null Hypothesis as an Assumption to Be Challenged
Summary of Forms for Null and Alternative Hypotheses

9.2 Type I and Type II Errors

9.3 Population Mean: σ Known
One-Tailed Test
Two-Tailed Test
Using Excel
Summary and Practical Advice
Relationship Between Interval Estimation and Hypothesis Testing

9.4 Population Mean: σ Unknown
One-Tailed Test
Two-Tailed Test
Using Excel
Summary and Practical Advice

9.5 Population Proportion
Using Excel
Summary

9.6 Practical Advice: Big Data and Hypothesis Testing
Big Data, Hypothesis Testing, and *p*-Values
Implications of Big Data in Hypothesis Testing

Summary 455
Glossary 456
Key Formulas 456
Supplementary Exercises 457
Case Problem 1: Quality Associates, Inc. 460
Case Problem 2: Ethical Behavior of Students at Bayview University 461
Case Problem 3: New Product Development at Baxter Barnes Gelato 462

Available in the Cengage ebook:
Appendix: Hypothesis Testing of a Population Mean, Known Standard Deviation with R
Appendix: Hypothesis Testing of a Population Mean, Unknown Standard Deviation with R
Appendix: Hypothesis Testing of a Population Proportion with R

Learning Objectives

After completing this chapter, you will be able to

LO 1 Formulate appropriate one- and two-tailed null and alternative hypotheses for problem scenarios and interpret the results.

LO 2 Interpret the results of a hypothesis test.

LO 3 Identify the Type I error and Type II error associated with a hypothesis test and explain their potential consequences.

LO 4 Test one- and two-tailed hypotheses about a population mean when the population standard deviation σ is known using the *p*-value approach, critical value approach, and the confidence interval approach.

LO 5 Test one- and two-tailed hypotheses about a population mean when the population standard deviation σ is unknown using the *p*-value approach, critical value approach, and the confidence interval approach.

LO 6 Test one- and two-tailed hypotheses about a population proportion using the *p*-value approach, critical value approach, and the confidence interval approach.

LO 7 Calculate the probability of making a Type II error for a hypothesis test.

LO 8 Determine the sample size for a hypothesis test about a population mean.

LO 9 Distinguish between statistical significance and practical significance and identify when statistically significant results may lack practical significance.

Statistics in Practice

John Morrell & Company*

Cincinnati, Ohio

John Morrell & Company, which began in England in 1827, is considered the oldest continuously operating meat manufacturer in the United States. It is a wholly owned and independently managed subsidiary of Smithfield Foods, Smithfield, Virginia. John Morrell & Company offers an extensive product line of processed meats and fresh pork to consumers under 13 regional brands, including John Morrell, E-Z-Cut, Tobin's First Prize, Dinner Bell, Hunter, Kretschmar, Rath, Rodeo, Shenson, Farmers Hickory Brand, Iowa Quality, and Peyton's. Each regional brand enjoys high brand recognition and loyalty among consumers.

Market research at Morrell provides management with up-to-date information on the company's various products and how the products compare with competing brands of similar products. A recent study compared a Beef Pot Roast made by Morrell to similar beef products from two major competitors. In the three-product comparison test, a sample of consumers was used to indicate how the products rated in terms of taste, appearance, aroma, and overall preference.

One research question concerned whether the Beef Pot Roast made by Morrell was the preferred choice of more than 50% of the consumer population. Letting p indicate the population proportion preferring Morrell's product, the hypothesis test for the research question is as follows:

$$H_0: p \le 0.50$$
$$H_a: p > 0.50$$

The null hypothesis H_0 indicates that the preference for Morrell's product is less than or equal to 50%. If the sample data support rejecting H_0 in favor of the alternative hypothesis H_a, Morrell will draw the research conclusion that in a three-product comparison, its Beef Pot Roast is preferred by more than 50% of the consumer population.

Hypothesis testing helps John Morrell & Company analyze market research about its products.
Jeffrey Isaac Greenberg 11+/Alamy Stock Photo

In an independent taste test study using a sample of 224 consumers in Cincinnati, Milwaukee, and Los Angeles, 150 consumers selected the Beef Pot Roast made by Morrell as the preferred product. Using statistical hypothesis testing procedures, the null hypothesis H_0 was rejected. The study provided statistical evidence supporting H_a and the conclusion that the Morrell product is preferred by more than 50% of the consumer population.

The point estimate of the population proportion was $\bar{p} = 150/224 = 0.67$. Thus, the sample data provided support for a food magazine advertisement showing that in a three-product taste comparison, Beef Pot Roast made by Morrell was "preferred 2 to 1 over the competition."

In this chapter we will discuss how to formulate hypotheses and how to conduct tests like the one used by Morrell. Through the analysis of sample data, we will be able to determine whether a hypothesis should or should not be rejected.

*The authors are indebted to Marty Butler, Vice President of Marketing, John Morrell, for providing this Statistics in Practice.

In Chapters 7 and 8, we showed how a sample could be used to develop point and interval estimates of population parameters. In this chapter, we continue the discussion of statistical inference by showing how hypothesis testing can be used to determine whether a statement about the value of a population parameter should or should not be rejected.

In hypothesis testing, we begin by making a tentative assumption about a population parameter. This tentative assumption is called the **null hypothesis** and is denoted by H_0. We then define another hypothesis, called the **alternative hypothesis**, which is the opposite of what is stated in the null hypothesis. The alternative hypothesis is denoted by H_a.

The hypothesis testing procedure uses data from a sample to test the two competing statements indicated by H_0 and H_a.

This chapter shows how hypothesis tests can be conducted about a population mean and a population proportion. We begin by providing examples that illustrate approaches to developing null and alternative hypotheses.

9.1 Developing Null and Alternative Hypotheses

It is not always obvious how the null and alternative hypotheses should be formulated. Care must be taken to structure the hypotheses appropriately so that the hypothesis testing conclusion provides the information the researcher or decision maker wants. The context of the situation is very important in determining how the hypotheses should be stated. All hypothesis testing applications involve collecting a sample and using the sample results to provide evidence for drawing a conclusion. Good questions to consider when formulating the null and alternative hypotheses are: What is the purpose of collecting the sample? What conclusions are we hoping to make?

Learning to formulate hypotheses correctly will take some practice. Expect some initial confusion over the proper choice of the null and alternative hypotheses. The examples in this section are intended to provide guidelines.

In the chapter introduction, we stated that the null hypothesis H_0 is a tentative assumption about a population parameter such as a population mean or a population proportion. The alternative hypothesis H_a is a statement that is the opposite of what is stated in the null hypothesis. In some situations, it is easier to identify the alternative hypothesis first and then develop the null hypothesis. In other situations, it is easier to identify the null hypothesis first and then develop the alternative hypothesis. We will illustrate these situations in the following examples.

The Alternative Hypothesis as a Research Hypothesis

Many applications of hypothesis testing involve an attempt to gather evidence in support of a research hypothesis. In these situations, it is often best to begin with the alternative hypothesis and make it the conclusion that the researcher hopes to support. Consider a particular automobile that currently attains a fuel efficiency of 24 miles per gallon in city driving. A product research group has developed a new fuel injection system designed to increase the miles-per-gallon rating. The group will run controlled tests with the new fuel injection system looking for statistical support for the conclusion that the new fuel injection system provides more miles per gallon than the current system.

Several new fuel injection units will be manufactured, installed in test automobiles, and subjected to research-controlled driving conditions. The sample mean miles per gallon for these automobiles will be computed and used in a hypothesis test to determine whether it can be concluded that the new system provides more than 24 miles per gallon. In terms of the population mean miles per gallon μ, the research hypothesis $\mu > 24$ becomes the alternative hypothesis. Since the current system provides an average or mean of 24 miles per gallon, we will make the tentative assumption that the new system is not any better than the current system and choose $\mu \le 24$ as the null hypothesis. The null and alternative hypotheses are:

$$H_0\colon \mu \le 24$$
$$H_a\colon \mu > 24$$

If the sample results lead to the conclusion to reject H_0, the inference can be made that $H_a\colon \mu > 24$ is true. The researchers have the statistical support to state that the new fuel injection system increases the mean number of miles per gallon. The production of automobiles with the new fuel injection system should be considered. However, if the sample results lead to the conclusion that H_0 cannot be rejected, the researchers cannot conclude that the new fuel injection system is better than the current system. Production of automobiles with the new fuel injection system on the basis of better gas mileage cannot be justified. Perhaps more research and further testing can be conducted.

The conclusion that the research hypothesis is true is made if the sample data provide sufficient evidence to show that the null hypothesis can be rejected.

Successful companies stay competitive by developing new products, new methods, new systems, and the like that are better than what is currently available. Before adopting something new, it is desirable to conduct research to determine whether there is statistical support for the conclusion that the new approach is indeed better. In such cases, the research hypothesis is stated as the alternative hypothesis. For example, a new teaching method is developed that is believed to be better than the current method. The alternative hypothesis is that the new method is better. The null hypothesis is that the new method is no better than the old method. A new sales force bonus plan is developed in an attempt to increase sales. The alternative hypothesis is that the new bonus plan increases sales. The null hypothesis is that the new bonus plan does not increase sales. A new drug is developed with the goal of lowering blood pressure more than an existing drug. The alternative hypothesis is that the new drug lowers blood pressure more than the existing drug. The null hypothesis is that the new drug does not provide lower blood pressure than the existing drug. In each case, rejection of the null hypothesis H_0 provides statistical support for the research hypothesis. We will see many examples of hypothesis tests in research situations such as these throughout this chapter and in the remainder of the text.

The Null Hypothesis as an Assumption to Be Challenged

Of course, not all hypothesis tests involve research hypotheses. In the following discussion we consider applications of hypothesis testing where we begin with a belief or an assumption that a statement about the value of a population parameter is true. We will then use a hypothesis test to challenge the assumption and determine whether there is statistical evidence to conclude that the assumption is incorrect. In these situations, it is helpful to develop the null hypothesis first. The null hypothesis H_0 expresses the belief or assumption about the value of the population parameter. The alternative hypothesis H_a is that the belief or assumption is incorrect.

As an example, consider the situation of a manufacturer of soft drink products. The label on a soft drink bottle states that it contains 67.6 fluid ounces. We consider the label correct provided the population mean filling volume for the bottles is *at least* 67.6 fluid ounces. Without any reason to believe otherwise, we would give the manufacturer the benefit of the doubt and assume that the statement provided on the label is correct. Thus, in a hypothesis test about the population mean fluid ounces per bottle, we would begin with the assumption that the label is correct and state the null hypothesis as $\mu \geq 67.6$. The challenge to this assumption would imply that the label is incorrect and the bottles are being underfilled. This challenge would be stated as the alternative hypothesis $\mu < 67.6$. Thus, the null and alternative hypotheses are:

$$H_0\colon \mu \geq 67.6$$
$$H_a\colon \mu < 67.6$$

A manufacturer's product information is usually assumed to be true and stated as the null hypothesis. The conclusion that the information is incorrect can be made if the null hypothesis is rejected.

A government agency with the responsibility for validating manufacturing labels could select a sample of soft drink bottles, compute the sample mean fluid ounces, and use the sample results to test the preceding hypotheses. If the sample results lead to the conclusion to reject H_0, the inference that $H_a\colon \mu < 67.6$ is true can be made. With this statistical support, the agency is justified in concluding that the label is incorrect and underfilling of the bottles is occurring. Appropriate action to force the manufacturer to comply with labeling standards would be considered. However, if the sample results indicate H_0 cannot be rejected, the assumption that the manufacturer's labeling is correct cannot be rejected. With this conclusion, no action would be taken.

Let us now consider a variation of the soft drink bottle-filling example by viewing the same situation from the manufacturer's point of view. The bottle-filling operation has been designed to fill soft drink bottles with 67.6 fluid ounces as stated on the label. The company does not want to underfill the containers because that could result in an underfilling complaint from customers or, perhaps, a government agency. However, the company does not want to overfill containers either because putting more soft drink than necessary into the containers would be an unnecessary cost. The company's goal would be to adjust the bottle-filling operation so that the population mean filling weight per bottle is 67.6 fluid ounces as specified on the label.

Although this is the company's goal, from time to time any production process can get out of adjustment. If this occurs in our example, underfilling or overfilling of the soft drink bottles will occur. In either case, the company would like to know about it in order to correct the situation by readjusting the bottle-filling operation to the designed 67.6 fluid ounces. In this hypothesis testing application, we would begin with the assumption that the production process is operating correctly and state the null hypothesis as $\mu = 67.6$ fluid ounces. The alternative hypothesis that challenges this assumption is that $\mu \neq 67.6$, which indicates either overfilling or underfilling is occurring. The null and alternative hypotheses for the manufacturer's hypothesis test are

$$H_0\colon \mu = 67.6$$
$$H_a\colon \mu \neq 67.6$$

Suppose that the soft drink manufacturer uses a quality control procedure to periodically select a sample of bottles from the filling operation and computes the sample mean fluid ounces per bottle. If the sample results lead to the conclusion to reject H_0, the inference is made that $H_a\colon \mu \neq 67.6$ is true. We conclude that the bottles are not being filled properly and the production process should be adjusted to restore the population mean to 67.6 fluid ounces per bottle. However, if the sample results indicate H_0 cannot be rejected, the assumption that the manufacturer's bottle-filling operation is functioning properly cannot be rejected. In this case, no further action would be taken and the production operation would continue to run.

The two preceding forms of the soft drink manufacturing hypothesis test show that the null and alternative hypotheses may vary depending upon the point of view of the researcher or decision maker. To formulate hypotheses correctly, it is important to understand the context of the situation and structure the hypotheses to provide the information the researcher or decision maker wants.

Summary of Forms for Null and Alternative Hypotheses

The hypothesis tests in this chapter involve two population parameters: the population mean and the population proportion. Depending on the situation, hypothesis tests about a population parameter may take one of three forms: Two use inequalities in the null hypothesis; the third uses an equality in the null hypothesis. For hypothesis tests involving a population mean, we let μ_0 denote the hypothesized value and we must choose one of the following three forms for the hypothesis test.

The three possible forms of hypotheses H_0 and H_a are shown here. Note that the equality always appears in the null hypothesis H_0.

$$H_0\colon \mu \geq \mu_0 \qquad H_0\colon \mu \leq \mu_0 \qquad H_0\colon \mu = \mu_0$$
$$H_a\colon \mu < \mu_0 \qquad H_a\colon \mu > \mu_0 \qquad H_a\colon \mu \neq \mu_0$$

For reasons that will be clear later, the first two forms are called one-tailed tests. The third form is called a two-tailed test.

In many situations, the choice of H_0 and H_a is not obvious and judgment is necessary to select the proper form. However, as the preceding forms show, the equality part of the expression (either $\geq$, $\leq$, or $=$) *always* appears in the null hypothesis. In selecting the proper form of H_0 and H_a, keep in mind that the alternative hypothesis is often what the test is attempting to establish. Hence, asking whether the user is looking for evidence to support $\mu < \mu_0$, $\mu > \mu_0$, or $\mu \neq \mu_0$ will help determine H_a. The following exercises are designed to provide practice in choosing the proper form for a hypothesis test involving a population mean.

Exercises

1. **Hotel Guest Bills.** The manager of the Danvers-Hilton Resort Hotel stated that the mean guest bill for a weekend is $600 or less. A member of the hotel's accounting staff noticed that the total charges for guest bills have been increasing in recent months. The accountant will use a sample of future weekend guest bills to test the manager's claim. **LO 1, 2**
   a. Which form of the hypotheses should be used to test the manager's claim? Explain.

$$H_0\colon \mu \geq 600 \qquad H_0\colon \mu \leq 600 \qquad H_0\colon \mu = 600$$
$$H_a\colon \mu < 600 \qquad H_a\colon \mu > 600 \qquad H_a\colon \mu \neq 600$$

   b. What conclusion is appropriate when H_0 cannot be rejected?
   c. What conclusion is appropriate when H_0 can be rejected?

2. **Bonus Plan's Effect on Automobile Sales.** The manager of an automobile dealership is considering a new bonus plan designed to increase sales volume. Currently, the mean sales volume is 14 automobiles per month. The manager wants to conduct a research study to see whether the new bonus plan increases sales volume. To collect data on the plan, a sample of sales personnel will be allowed to sell under the new bonus plan for a one-month period. **LO 1, 2**
   a. Develop the null and alternative hypotheses most appropriate for this situation.
   b. Comment on the conclusion when H_0 cannot be rejected.
   c. Comment on the conclusion when H_0 can be rejected.

3. **Filling Detergent Cartons.** A production line operation is designed to fill cartons with laundry detergent to a mean weight of 32 ounces. A sample of cartons is periodically selected and weighed to determine whether underfilling or overfilling is occurring. If the sample data lead to a conclusion of underfilling or overfilling, the production line will be shut down and adjusted to obtain proper filling. **LO 1, 2**
   a. Formulate the null and alternative hypotheses that will help in deciding whether to shut down and adjust the production line.
   b. Comment on the conclusion and the decision when H_0 cannot be rejected.
   c. Comment on the conclusion and the decision when H_0 can be rejected.

4. **Process Improvement.** Because of high production-changeover time and costs, a director of manufacturing must convince management that a proposed manufacturing method reduces costs before the new method can be implemented. The current production method operates with a mean cost of $220 per hour. A research study will measure the cost of the new method over a sample production period. **LO 1, 2**
   a. Develop the null and alternative hypotheses most appropriate for this study.
   b. Comment on the conclusion when H_0 cannot be rejected.
   c. Comment on the conclusion when H_0 can be rejected.

9.2 Type I and Type II Errors

The null and alternative hypotheses are competing statements about the population. Either the null hypothesis H_0 is true or the alternative hypothesis H_a is true, but not both. Ideally the hypothesis testing procedure should lead to the acceptance of H_0 when H_0 is true and the rejection of H_0 when H_a is true. Unfortunately, the correct conclusions are not always possible. Because hypothesis tests are based on sample information, we must allow for the possibility of errors. Table 9.1 illustrates the two kinds of errors that can be made in hypothesis testing.

The first row of Table 9.1 shows what can happen if the conclusion is to accept H_0. If H_0 is true, this conclusion is correct. However, if H_a is true, we make a **Type II error**; that is, we accept H_0 when it is false. The second row of Table 9.1 shows what can happen if the conclusion is to reject H_0. If H_0 is true, we make a **Type I error**; that is, we reject H_0 when it is true. However, if H_a is true, rejecting H_0 is correct.

Recall the hypothesis testing illustration discussed in Section 9.1, in which an automobile product research group developed a new fuel injection system designed to increase the

Table 9.1 Errors and Correct Conclusions in Hypothesis Testing

		Population Condition	
		H_0 True	H_a True
Conclusion	Accept H_0	Correct Conclusion	Type II Error
	Reject H_0	Type I Error	Correct Conclusion

miles-per-gallon rating of a particular automobile. With the current model obtaining an average of 24 miles per gallon, the hypothesis test was formulated as follows.

$$H_0: \mu \leq 24$$
$$H_a: \mu > 24$$

The alternative hypothesis, H_a: $\mu > 24$, indicates that the researchers are looking for sample evidence to support the conclusion that the population mean miles per gallon with the new fuel injection system is greater than 24.

In this application, the Type I error of rejecting H_0 when it is true corresponds to the researchers claiming that the new system improves the miles-per-gallon rating ($\mu > 24$) when in fact the new system is not any better than the current system. In contrast, the Type II error of accepting H_0 when it is false corresponds to the researchers concluding that the new system is not any better than the current system ($\mu \leq 24$) when in fact the new system improves miles-per-gallon performance.

For the miles-per-gallon rating hypothesis test, the null hypothesis is H_0: $\mu \leq 24$. Suppose the null hypothesis is true as an equality; that is, $\mu = 24$. The probability of making a Type I error when the null hypothesis is true as an equality is called the **level of significance**. Thus, for the miles-per-gallon rating hypothesis test, the level of significance is the probability of rejecting H_0: $\mu \leq 24$ when $\mu = 24$. Because of the importance of this concept, we now restate the definition of level of significance.

Level of Significance

The level of significance is the probability of making a Type I error when the null hypothesis is true as an equality.

The Greek symbol α (alpha) is used to denote the level of significance, and common choices for α are 0.05 and 0.01.

In practice, the person responsible for the hypothesis test specifies the level of significance. By selecting α, that person is controlling the probability of making a Type I error. If the cost of making a Type I error is high, small values of α are preferred. If the cost of making a Type I error is not too high, larger values of α are typically used. Applications of hypothesis testing that only control for the Type I error are called *significance tests*. Many applications of hypothesis testing are of this type.

If the sample data are consistent with the null hypothesis H_0, we will follow the practice of concluding "do not reject H_0." This conclusion is preferred over "accept H_0," because the conclusion to accept H_0 puts us at risk of making a Type II error.

Although most applications of hypothesis testing control for the probability of making a Type I error, they do not always control for the probability of making a Type II error. Hence, if we decide to accept H_0, we cannot determine how confident we can be with that decision. Because of the uncertainty associated with making a Type II error when conducting significance tests, statisticians usually recommend that we use the statement "do not reject H_0" instead of "accept H_0." Using the statement "do not reject H_0" carries the recommendation to withhold both judgment and action. In effect, by not directly accepting H_0, the statistician avoids the risk of making a Type II error. Whenever the probability of making a Type II error has not been determined and controlled, we will not make the statement "accept H_0." In such cases, only two conclusions are possible: *do not reject* H_0 or *reject* H_0.

Although controlling for a Type II error in hypothesis testing is not common, it can be done. More advanced texts describe procedures for determining and controlling the probability of making a Type II error.[1] If proper controls have been established for this error, action based on the "accept H_0" conclusion can be appropriate.

Note + Comment

Walter Williams, syndicated columnist and professor of economics at George Mason University, points out that the possibility of making a Type I or a Type II error is always present in decision making (*The Cincinnati Enquirer*). He notes that the Food and Drug Administration runs the risk of making these errors in its drug approval process. The FDA must either approve a new drug or not approve it. Thus, the FDA runs the risk of making a Type I error by approving a new drug that is not safe and effective, or making a Type II error by failing to approve a new drug that is safe and effective. Regardless of the decision made, the possibility of making a costly error cannot be eliminated.

Exercises

5. **Beer and Cider Consumption.** According to the National Beer Wholesalers Association, U.S. consumers 21 years and older consumed 26.9 gallons of beer and cider per person during 2017. A distributor in Milwaukee believes that beer and cider consumption are higher in that city. A sample of consumers 21 years and older in Milwaukee will be taken, and the sample mean 2017 beer and cider consumption will be used to test the following null and alternative hypotheses that follow. **LO 2, 3**

$$H_0: \mu \leq 26.9$$
$$H_a: \mu > 26.9$$

   a. Assume the sample data led to rejection of the null hypothesis. What would be your conclusion about consumption of beer and cider in Milwaukee?
   b. What is the Type I error in this situation? What are the consequences of making this error?
   c. What is the Type II error in this situation? What are the consequences of making this error?

6. **Orange Juice Labels.** The label on a 3-quart container of orange juice states that the orange juice contains an average of 1 gram of fat or less. Answer the following questions for a hypothesis test that could be used to test the claim on the label.
   a. Develop the appropriate null and alternative hypotheses. **LO 1, 3**
   b. What is the Type I error in this situation? What are the consequences of making this error?
   c. What is the Type II error in this situation? What are the consequences of making this error?

7. **Carpet Salesperson Salaries.** Carpetland salespersons average $8,000 per week in sales. Steve Contois, the firm's vice president, proposes a compensation plan with new selling incentives. Steve hopes that the results of a trial selling period will enable him to conclude that the compensation plan increases the average sales per salesperson. **LO 1, 3**

[1]See, for example, D. R. Anderson, D. J. Sweeney, and T. A. Williams, *Statistics for Business and Economics*, 13th edition (Cincinnati: Cengage Learning, 2018).

a. Develop the appropriate null and alternative hypotheses.
b. What is the Type I error in this situation? What are the consequences of making this error?
c. What is the Type II error in this situation? What are the consequences of making this error?

8. **Production Operating Costs.** Suppose a new production method will be implemented if a hypothesis test supports the conclusion that the new method reduces the mean operating cost per hour. **LO 1, 3**
   a. State the appropriate null and alternative hypotheses if the mean cost for the current production method is \$220 per hour.
   b. What is the Type I error in this situation? What are the consequences of making this error?
   c. What is the Type II error in this situation? What are the consequences of making this error?

9.3 Population Mean: σ Known

In Chapter 8, we said that the σ known case corresponds to applications in which historical data and/or other information are available that enable us to obtain a good estimate of the population standard deviation prior to sampling. In such cases the population standard deviation can, for all practical purposes, be considered known. In this section we show how to conduct a hypothesis test about a population mean for the σ known case.

The methods presented in this section are exact if the sample is selected from a population that is normally distributed. In cases where it is not reasonable to assume the population is normally distributed, these methods are still applicable if the sample size is large enough. We provide some practical advice concerning the population distribution and the sample size at the end of this section.

One-Tailed Test

One-tailed tests about a population mean take one of the following two forms.

Lower Tail Test	Upper Tail Test
H_0: $\mu \geq \mu_0$	H_0: $\mu \leq \mu_0$
H_a: $\mu < \mu_0$	H_a: $\mu > \mu_0$

Let us consider an example involving a lower tail test.

The Federal Trade Commission (FTC) periodically conducts statistical studies designed to test the claims that manufacturers make about their products. For example, the label on a large can of Hilltop Coffee states that the can contains 3 pounds of coffee. The FTC knows that Hilltop's production process cannot place exactly 3 pounds of coffee in each can, even if the mean filling weight for the population of all cans filled is 3 pounds per can. However, as long as the population mean filling weight is at least 3 pounds per can, the rights of consumers will be protected. Thus, the FTC interprets the label information on a large can of coffee as a claim by Hilltop that the population mean filling weight is at least 3 pounds per can. We will show how the FTC can check Hilltop's claim by conducting a lower tail hypothesis test.

The first step is to develop the null and alternative hypotheses for the test. If the population mean filling weight is at least 3 pounds per can, Hilltop's claim is correct. This establishes the null hypothesis for the test. However, if the population mean weight is less than 3 pounds per can, Hilltop's claim is incorrect. This establishes the alternative hypothesis. With μ denoting the population mean filling weight, the null and alternative hypotheses are as follows:

$$H_0: \mu \geq 3$$
$$H_a: \mu < 3$$

Note that the hypothesized value of the population mean is $\mu_0 = 3$.

If the sample data indicate that H_0 cannot be rejected, the statistical evidence does not support the conclusion that a label violation has occurred. Hence, no action should be taken against Hilltop. However, if the sample data indicate that H_0 can be rejected, we will conclude that the alternative hypothesis, H_a: $\mu < 3$, is true. In this case, a conclusion of underfilling and a charge of a label violation against Hilltop would be justified.

Suppose a sample of 36 cans of coffee is selected and the sample mean $\bar{x}$ is computed as an estimate of the population mean μ. If the value of the sample mean $\bar{x}$ is less than 3 pounds, the sample results will cast doubt on the null hypothesis. What we want to know is how much less than 3 pounds must $\bar{x}$ be before we would be willing to declare the difference significant and risk making a Type I error by falsely accusing Hilltop of a label violation. A key factor in addressing this issue is the value the decision maker selects for the level of significance.

As noted in the preceding section, the level of significance, denoted by α, is the probability of making a Type I error by rejecting H_0 when the null hypothesis is true as an equality. The decision maker must specify the level of significance. If the cost of making a Type I error is high, a small value should be chosen for the level of significance. If the cost is not high, a larger value is more appropriate. In the Hilltop Coffee study, the director of the FTC's testing program made the following statement: "If the company is meeting its weight specifications at $\mu = 3$, I do not want to take action against them. But, I am willing to risk a 1% chance of making such an error." From the director's statement, we set the level of significance for the hypothesis test at $\alpha = 0.01$. Thus, we must design the hypothesis test so that the probability of making a Type I error when $\mu = 3$ is 0.01.

For the Hilltop Coffee study, by developing the null and alternative hypotheses and specifying the level of significance for the test, we carry out the first two steps required in conducting every hypothesis test. We are now ready to perform the third step of hypothesis testing: collect the sample data and compute the value of what is called a test statistic.

Test Statistic For the Hilltop Coffee study, previous FTC tests show that the population standard deviation can be assumed known with a value of $\sigma = 0.18$. In addition, these tests also show that the population of filling weights can be assumed to have a normal distribution. From the study of sampling distributions in Chapter 7, we know that if the population from which we are sampling is normally distributed, the sampling distribution of $\bar{x}$ will also be normally distributed. Thus, for the Hilltop Coffee study, the sampling distribution of $\bar{x}$ is normally distributed. With a known value of $\sigma = 0.18$ and a sample size of $n = 36$, Figure 9.1 shows the sampling distribution of $\bar{x}$ when the null hypothesis is true as an equality, that is, when $\mu = \mu_0 = 3$.[2] Note that the standard error of $\bar{x}$ is given by $\sigma_{\bar{x}} = \sigma/\sqrt{n} = 0.18/\sqrt{36} = 0.03$.

The standard error of $\bar{x}$ is the standard deviation of the sampling distribution of $\bar{x}$.

Figure 9.1 Sampling Distribution of $\bar{x}$ for the Hilltop Coffee Study When the Null Hypothesis Is True as an Equality ($\mu = 3$)

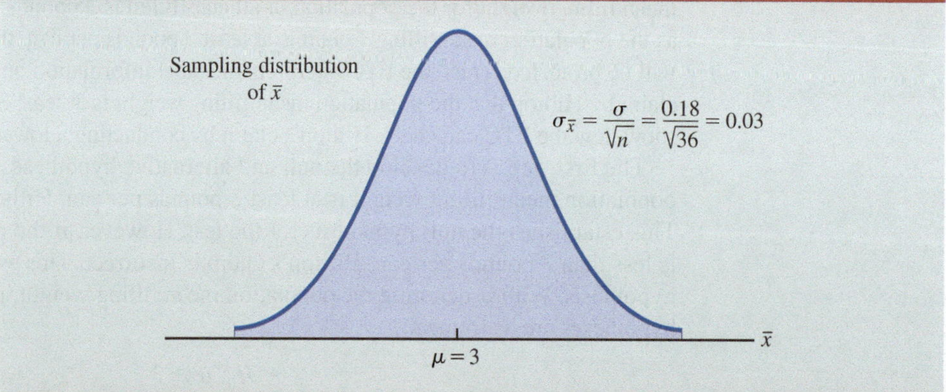

[2]In constructing sampling distributions for hypothesis tests, it is assumed that H_0 is satisfied as an equality.

Because the sampling distribution of $\bar{x}$ is normally distributed, the sampling distribution of

$$z = \frac{\bar{x} - \mu_0}{\sigma_{\bar{x}}} = \frac{\bar{x} - 3}{0.03}$$

is a standard normal distribution. A value of $z = -1$ means that the value of $\bar{x}$ is one standard error below the hypothesized value of the mean, a value of $z = -2$ means that the value of $\bar{x}$ is two standard errors below the hypothesized value of the mean, and so on. We can use the standard normal probability table to find the lower tail probability corresponding to any z value. For instance, the lower tail area at $z = -3.00$ is 0.0013. Hence, the probability of obtaining a value of z that is three or more standard errors below the mean is 0.0013. As a result, the probability of obtaining a value of $\bar{x}$ that is 3 or more standard errors below the hypothesized population mean $\mu_0 = 3$ is also 0.0013. Such a result is unlikely if the null hypothesis is true.

For hypothesis tests about a population mean in the σ known case, we use the standard normal random variable z as a **test statistic** to determine whether $\bar{x}$ deviates from the hypothesized value of μ enough to justify rejecting the null hypothesis. With $\sigma_{\bar{x}} = \sigma/\sqrt{n}$, the test statistic is as follows.

Test Statistic for Hypothesis Tests About a Population Mean: σ Known

$$z = \frac{\bar{x} - \mu_0}{\sigma/\sqrt{n}} \tag{9.1}$$

The key question for a lower tail test is, How small must the test statistic z be before we choose to reject the null hypothesis? Two approaches can be used to answer this question: the p-value approach and the critical value approach.

***p*-Value Approach** The p-value approach uses the value of the test statistic z to compute a probability called a ***p*-value**.

A small p-value indicates that the value of the test statistic is unusual given the assumption that H_0 is true.

p-Value

A p-value is a probability that provides a measure of the evidence against the null hypothesis provided by the sample. Smaller p-values indicate more evidence against H_0.

The p-value is used to determine whether the null hypothesis should be rejected.

Let us see how the p-value is computed and used. The value of the test statistic is used to compute the p-value. The method used depends on whether the test is a lower tail, an upper tail, or a two-tailed test. For a lower tail test, the p-value is the probability of obtaining a value for the test statistic as small as or smaller than that provided by the sample. Thus, to compute the p-value for the lower tail test in the σ known case, we must find, using the standard normal distribution, the probability that z is less than or equal to the value of the test statistic. After computing the p-value, we must then decide whether it is small enough to reject the null hypothesis; as we will show, this decision involves comparing the p-value to the level of significance.

DATA*file*
coffee

Let us now compute the p-value for the Hilltop Coffee lower tail test. Suppose the sample of 36 Hilltop coffee cans provides a sample mean of $\bar{x} = 2.92$ pounds. Is $\bar{x} = 2.92$ small enough to cause us to reject H_0? Because this is a lower tail test, the p-value is the area under the standard normal curve for values of $z \leq$ the value of the test statistic. Using $\bar{x} = 2.92$, $\sigma = 0.18$, and $n = 36$, we compute the value of the test statistic z.

$$z = \frac{\bar{x} - \mu_0}{\sigma/\sqrt{n}} = \frac{2.92 - 3}{0.18/\sqrt{36}} = -2.67$$

Figure 9.2 p-Value for the Hilltop Coffee Study When $\bar{x} = 2.92$ and $z = -2.67$

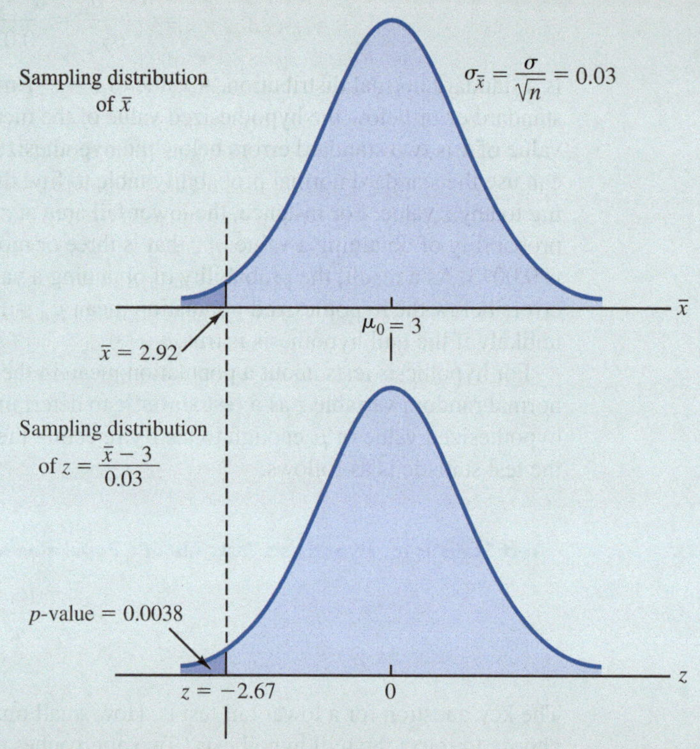

Thus, the p-value is the probability that z is less than or equal to -2.67 (the lower tail area corresponding to the value of the test statistic).

Using the standard normal probability table, we find that the lower tail area at $z = -2.67$ is 0.0038. Figure 9.2 shows that $\bar{x} = 2.92$ corresponds to $z = -2.67$ and a p-value = 0.0038. This p-value indicates a small probability of obtaining a sample mean of $\bar{x} = 2.92$ (and a test statistic of -2.67) or smaller when sampling from a population with $\mu = 3$. This p-value does not provide much support for the null hypothesis, but is it small enough to cause us to reject H_0? The answer depends upon the level of significance for the test.

As noted previously, the director of the FTC's testing program selected a value of 0.01 for the level of significance. The selection of $\alpha = 0.01$ means that the director is willing to tolerate a probability of 0.01 of rejecting the null hypothesis when it is true as an equality ($\mu_0 = 3$). The sample of 36 coffee cans in the Hilltop Coffee study resulted in a p-value = 0.0038, which means that the probability of obtaining a value of $\bar{x} = 2.92$ or less when the null hypothesis is true as an equality is 0.0038. Because 0.0038 is less than or equal to $\alpha = 0.01$, we reject H_0. Therefore, we find sufficient statistical evidence to reject the null hypothesis at the 0.01 level of significance.

We can now state the general rule for determining whether the null hypothesis can be rejected when using the p-value approach. For a level of significance α, the rejection rule using the p-value approach is as follows.

Rejection Rule Using p-Value

$$\text{Reject } H_0 \text{ if } p\text{-value} \leq \alpha$$

Figure 9.3 Critical Value = −2.33 for the Hilltop Coffee Hypothesis Test

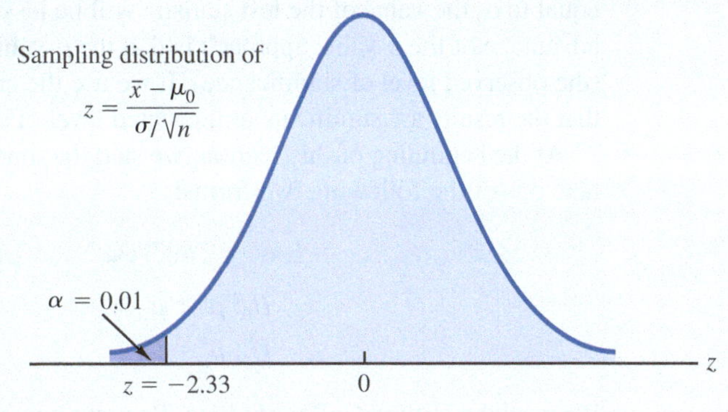

In the Hilltop Coffee test, the p-value of 0.0038 resulted in the rejection of the null hypothesis. Although the basis for making the rejection decision involves a comparison of the p-value to the level of significance specified by the FTC director, the observed p-value of 0.0038 means that we would reject H_0 for any value of $\alpha \geq 0.0038$. For this reason, the p-value is also called the *observed level of significance.*

Different decision makers may express different opinions concerning the cost of making a Type I error and may choose a different level of significance. By providing the p-value as part of the hypothesis testing results, another decision maker can compare the reported p-value to their own level of significance and possibly make a different decision with respect to rejecting H_0.

Critical Value Approach The critical value approach requires that we first determine a value for the test statistic called the **critical value**. For a lower tail test, the critical value serves as a benchmark for determining whether the value of the test statistic is small enough to reject the null hypothesis. It is the value of the test statistic that corresponds to an area of α (the level of significance) in the lower tail of the sampling distribution of the test statistic. In other words, the critical value is the largest value of the test statistic that will result in the rejection of the null hypothesis. Let us return to the Hilltop Coffee example and see how this approach works.

In the σ known case, the sampling distribution for the test statistic z is a standard normal distribution. Therefore, the critical value is the value of the test statistic that corresponds to an area of $\alpha = 0.01$ in the lower tail of a standard normal distribution. Using the standard normal probability table, we find that $z = -2.33$ provides an area of 0.01 in the lower tail (see Figure 9.3). Thus, if the sample results in a value of the test statistic that is less than or equal to -2.33, the corresponding p-value will be less than or equal to 0.01; in this case, we should reject the null hypothesis. Hence, for the Hilltop Coffee study the critical value rejection rule for a level of significance of 0.01 is

$$\text{Reject } H_0 \text{ if } z \leq -2.33$$

In the Hilltop Coffee example, $\bar{x} = 2.92$ and the test statistic is $z = -2.67$. Because $z = -2.67 < -2.33$, we can reject H_0 and conclude that Hilltop Coffee is underfilling cans.

We can generalize the rejection rule for the critical value approach to handle any level of significance. The rejection rule for a lower tail test follows.

Rejection Rule for a Lower Tail Test: Critical Value Approach

$$\text{Reject } H_0 \text{ if } z \leq -z_\alpha$$

where $-z_\alpha$ is the critical value; that is, the z value that provides an area of α in the lower tail of the standard normal distribution.

Summary The p-value approach to hypothesis testing and the critical value approach will always lead to the same rejection decision; that is, whenever the p-value is less than or equal to α, the value of the test statistic will be less than or equal to the critical value. The advantage of the p-value approach is that the p-value tells us *how* significant the results are (the observed level of significance). If we use the critical value approach, we only know that the results are significant at the stated level of significance.

At the beginning of this section, we said that one-tailed tests about a population mean take one of the following two forms:

Lower Tail Test	Upper Tail Test
H_0: $\mu \geq \mu_0$	H_0: $\mu \leq \mu_0$
H_a: $\mu < \mu_0$	H_a: $\mu > \mu_0$

We used the Hilltop Coffee study to illustrate how to conduct a lower tail test. We can use the same general approach to conduct an upper tail test. The test statistic z is still computed using equation (9.1). But, for an upper tail test, the p-value is the probability of obtaining a value for the test statistic as large as or larger than that provided by the sample. Thus, to compute the p-value for the upper tail test in the σ known case, we must use the standard normal distribution to compute the probability that z is greater than or equal to the value of the test statistic. Using the critical value approach causes us to reject the null hypothesis if the value of the test statistic is greater than or equal to the critical value z_α; in other words, we reject H_0 if $z \geq z_\alpha$.

Let us summarize the steps involved in computing p-values for one-tailed hypothesis tests.

Computation of *p*-values for One-Tailed Tests

1. Compute the value of the test statistic using equation (9.1).
2. **Lower tail test:** Using the standard normal distribution, compute the probability that z is less than or equal to the value of the test statistic (area in the lower tail).
3. **Upper tail test:** Using the standard normal distribution, compute the probability that z is greater than or equal to the value of the test statistic (area in the upper tail).

Two-Tailed Test

In hypothesis testing, the general form for a **two-tailed test** about a population mean is as follows:

$$H_0: \mu = \mu_0$$
$$H_a: \mu \neq \mu_0$$

In this subsection we show how to conduct a two-tailed test about a population mean for the σ known case. As an illustration, we consider the hypothesis testing situation facing MaxFlight, Inc.

The U.S. Golf Association (USGA) establishes rules that manufacturers of golf equipment must meet if their products are to be acceptable for use in USGA events. MaxFlight uses a high-technology manufacturing process to produce golf balls with a mean driving distance of 295 yards. Sometimes, however, the process gets out of adjustment and produces golf balls with a mean driving distance different from 295 yards. When the mean distance falls below 295 yards, the company worries about losing sales because the golf balls do not provide as much distance as advertised. When the mean distance passes 295 yards, MaxFlight's golf balls may be rejected by the USGA for exceeding the overall distance standard concerning carry and roll.

MaxFlight's quality control program involves taking periodic samples of 50 golf balls to monitor the manufacturing process. For each sample, a hypothesis test is conducted to determine whether the process has fallen out of adjustment. Let us develop the null and alternative hypotheses. We begin by assuming that the process is functioning correctly; that is, the golf balls being produced have a mean distance of 295 yards. This assumption establishes the null hypothesis. The alternative hypothesis is that the mean distance is not equal to 295 yards. With a hypothesized value of $\mu_0 = 295$, the null and alternative hypotheses for the MaxFlight hypothesis test are as follows:

$$H_0\text{: } \mu = 295$$
$$H_a\text{: } \mu \neq 295$$

If the sample mean $\bar{x}$ is significantly less than 295 yards or significantly greater than 295 yards, we will reject H_0. In this case, corrective action will be taken to adjust the manufacturing process. On the other hand, if $\bar{x}$ does not deviate from the hypothesized mean $\mu_0 = 295$ by a significant amount, H_0 will not be rejected and no action will be taken to adjust the manufacturing process.

The quality control team selected $\alpha = 0.05$ as the level of significance for the test. Data from previous tests conducted when the process was known to be in adjustment show that the population standard deviation can be assumed known with a value of $\sigma = 12$. Thus, with a sample size of $n = 50$, the standard error of $\bar{x}$ is

$$\sigma_{\bar{x}} = \frac{\sigma}{\sqrt{n}} = \frac{12}{\sqrt{50}} = 1.7$$

The Central Limit Theorem is discussed in Chapter 7.

Because the sample size is large, the central limit theorem allows us to conclude that the sampling distribution of $\bar{x}$ can be approximated by a normal distribution. Figure 9.4 shows the sampling distribution of $\bar{x}$ for the MaxFlight hypothesis test with a hypothesized population mean of $\mu_0 = 295$.

DATA*file*
golftest

Suppose that a sample of 50 golf balls is selected and that the sample mean is $\bar{x} = 297.6$ yards. This sample mean provides support for the conclusion that the population mean is larger than 295 yards. Is this value of $\bar{x}$ enough larger than 295 to cause us to reject H_0 at the 0.05 level of significance? In the previous section we described two approaches that can be used to answer this question: the p-value approach and the critical value approach.

p-Value Approach Recall that the p-value is a probability used to determine whether the null hypothesis should be rejected. For a two-tailed test, values of the test statistic in *either* tail provide evidence against the null hypothesis. For a two-tailed test, the p-value is the probability of obtaining a value for the test statistic *as unlikely as or more unlikely than* that provided by the sample. Let us see how the p-value is computed for the MaxFlight hypothesis test.

Figure 9.4 Sampling Distribution of $\bar{x}$ for the MaxFlight Hypothesis Test

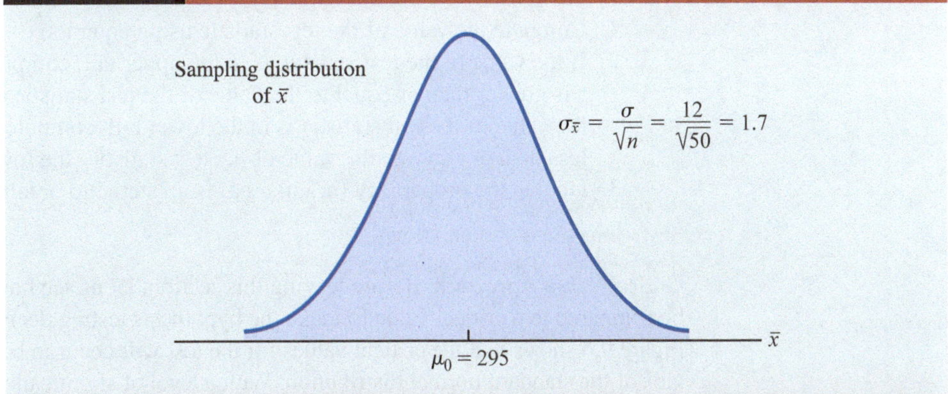

Figure 9.5 *p*-Value for the MaxFlight Hypothesis Test

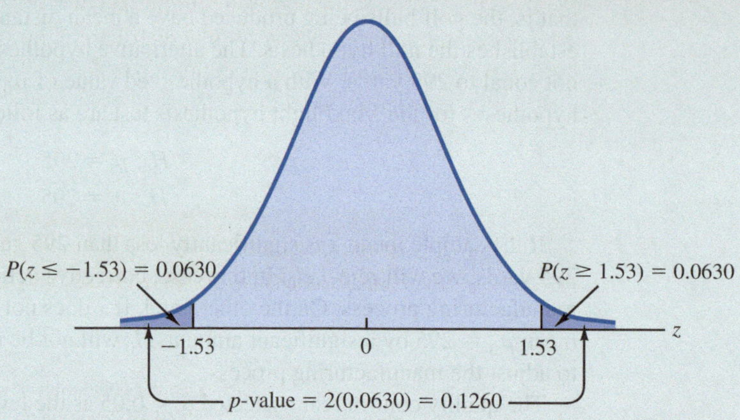

First we compute the value of the test statistic. For the σ known case, the test statistic z is a standard normal random variable. Using equation (9.1) with $\bar{x} = 297.6$, the value of the test statistic is

$$z = \frac{\bar{x} - \mu_0}{\sigma/\sqrt{n}} = \frac{297.6 - 295}{12/\sqrt{50}} = 1.53$$

Now to compute the p-value we must find the probability of obtaining a value for the test statistic *at least as unlikely as* $z = 1.53$. Clearly values of $z \geq 1.53$ are *at least as unlikely.* But, because this is a two-tailed test, values of $z \leq -1.53$ are also *at least as unlikely as* the value of the test statistic provided by the sample. In Figure 9.5, we see that the two-tailed p-value in this case is given by $P(z \leq -1.53) + P(z \geq 1.53)$. Because the normal curve is symmetric, we can compute this probability by finding $P(z \geq 1.53)$ and doubling it. The table for the standard normal distribution shows that $P(z < 1.53) = 0.9370$. Thus, the upper tail area is $P(z \geq 1.53) = 1.0000 - 0.9370 = 0.0630$. Doubling this, we find that the p-value for the MaxFlight two-tailed hypothesis test is p-value $= 2(0.0630) = 0.1260$.

Next, we compare the p-value to the level of significance to see whether the null hypothesis should be rejected. With a level of significance of $\alpha = 0.05$, we do not reject H_0 because the p-value $= 0.1260 > 0.05$. Because the null hypothesis is not rejected, no action will be taken to adjust the MaxFlight manufacturing process.

Let us summarize the steps involved in computing p-values for two-tailed hypothesis tests.

Computation of *p*-values for Two-Tailed Tests

1. Compute the value of the test statistic using equation (9.1).
2. If the value of the test statistic is in the upper tail, compute the probability that z is greater than or equal to the value of the test statistic (the upper tail area). If the value of the test statistic is in the lower tail, compute the probability that z is less than or equal to the value of the test statistic (the lower tail area).
3. Double the probability (or tail area) from step 2 to obtain the p-value.

Critical Value Approach Before leaving this section, let us see how the test statistic z can be compared to a critical value to make the hypothesis testing decision for a two-tailed test. Figure 9.6 shows that the critical values for the test will occur in both the lower and upper tails of the standard normal distribution. With a level of significance of $\alpha = 0.05$, the area in each tail corresponding to the critical values is $\alpha/2 = 0.05/2 = 0.025$. Using the standard

Figure 9.6 Critical Values for the MaxFlight Hypothesis Test

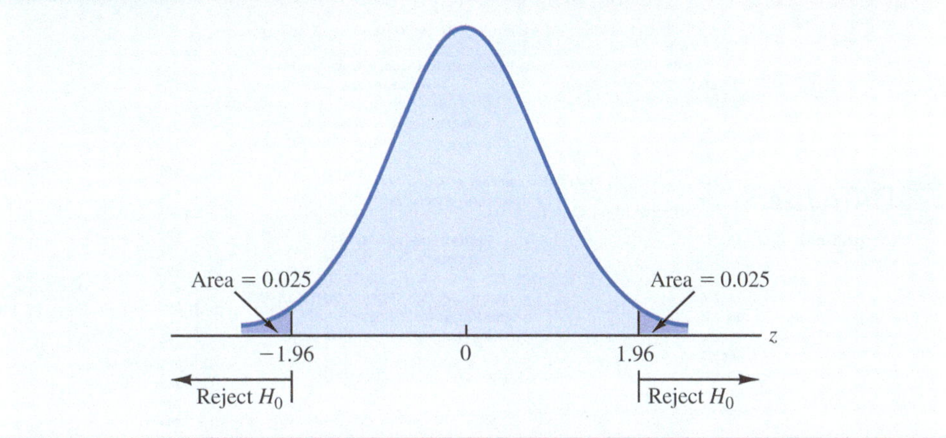

normal probability table, we find the critical values for the test statistic are $-z_{0.025} = -1.96$ and $z_{0.025} = 1.96$. Thus, using the critical value approach, the two-tailed rejection rule is

$$\text{Reject } H_0 \text{ if } z \leq -1.96 \text{ or if } z \geq 1.96$$

Because the value of the test statistic for the MaxFlight study is $z = 1.53$, the statistical evidence will not permit us to reject the null hypothesis at the 0.05 level of significance.

Using Excel

Excel can be used to conduct one-tailed and two-tailed hypothesis tests about a population mean for the σ known case using the p-value approach. Recall that the method used to compute a p-value depends upon whether the test is lower tail, upper tail, or two-tailed. Therefore, in the Excel procedure we describe we will use the sample results to compute three p-values: p-value (Lower Tail), p-value (Upper Tail), and p-value (Two Tail). The user can then choose α and draw a conclusion using whichever p-value is appropriate for the type of hypothesis test being conducted. We will illustrate using the MaxFlight two-tailed hypothesis test. Refer to Figure 9.7 as we describe the tasks involved. The formula worksheet is in the background; the value worksheet is in the foreground.

Enter/Access Data: Open the file *golftest*. A label and the distance data for the sample of 50 golf balls are entered in cells A1:A51.

Enter Functions and Formulas: The sample size and sample mean are computed in cells D4 and D5 using Excel's COUNT and AVERAGE functions, respectively. The value worksheet shows that the sample size is 50 and the sample mean is 297.6. The value of the known population standard deviation (*12*) is entered in cell D7, and the hypothesized value of the population mean (*295*) is entered in cell D8.

The standard error is obtained in cell D10 by entering the formula *=D7/SQRT(D4)*. The formula =(D5-D8)/D10 in cell D11 computes the test statistic z (1.5321). To compute the p-value for a lower tail test, we enter the formula *=NORM.S.DIST(D11,TRUE)* in cell D13. The p-value for an upper tail test is then computed in cell D14 as 1 minus the p-value for the lower tail test. Finally, the p-value for a two-tailed test is computed in cell D15 as two times the minimum of the two one-tailed p-values. The value worksheet shows that p-value (Lower Tail) = 0.9372, p-value (Upper Tail) = 0.0628, and p-value (Two Tail) = 0.1255.

The development of the worksheet is now complete. For the two-tailed MaxFlight problem we cannot reject H_0: $\mu = 295$ using $\alpha = 0.05$ because the p-value (Two Tail) = 0.1255

Figure 9.7 Excel Worksheet: Hypothesis Test for the σ Known Case

DATA*file*
golftest

	A	B	C	D	E
1	Yards		Hypothesis Test about a Population Mean:		
2	303		σ Known Case		
3	282				
4	289		Sample Size	=COUNT(A2:A51)	
5	298		Sample Mean	=AVERAGE(A2:A51)	
6	283				
7	317		Population Standard Deviation	12	
8	297		Hypothesized Value	295	
9	308				
10	317		Standard Error	=D7/SQRT(D4)	
11	293		Test Statistic z	=(D5-D8)/D10	
12	284				
13	290		p-value (Lower Tail)	=NORM.S.DIST(D11,TRUE)	
14	304		p-value (Upper Tail)	=1-D13	
15	290		p-value (Two Tail)	=2*(MIN(D13,D14))	
16	311				
50	301				
51	292				
52					

Note: Rows 17–49 are hidden.

	A	B	C	D	E
1	Yards		Hypothesis Test about a Population Mean:		
2	303		σ Known Case		
3	282				
4	289		Sample Size	50	
5	298		Sample Mean	297.6	
6	283				
7	317		Population Standard Deviation	12	
8	297		Hypothesized Value	295	
9	308				
10	317		Standard Error	1.6971	
11	293		Test Statistic z	1.5321	
12	284				
13	290		p-value (Lower Tail)	0.9372	
14	304		p-value (Upper Tail)	0.0628	
15	290		p-value (Two Tail)	0.1255	
16	311				
50	301				
51	292				
52					

is greater than α. Thus, the quality control manager has no reason to doubt that the manufacturing process is producing golf balls with a population mean distance of 295 yards.

A Template for Other Problems The worksheet in Figure 9.7 can be used as a template for conducting any one-tailed and two-tailed hypothesis tests for the σ known case. Just enter the appropriate data in column A, adjust the ranges for the formulas in cells D4 and D5, enter the population standard deviation in cell D7, and enter the hypothesized value in cell D8. The standard error, the test statistic, and the three p-values will then appear. Depending on the form of the hypothesis test (lower tail, upper tail, or two-tailed), we can then choose the appropriate p-value to make the rejection decision.

We can further simplify the use of Figure 9.7 as a template for other problems by eliminating the need to enter new data ranges in cells D4 and D5. To do so we rewrite the cell formulas as follows:

Cell D4: $=COUNT(A{:}A)$
Cell D5: $=AVERAGE(A{:}A)$

The file golftest includes a worksheet entitled Template that uses the A:A method for entering the data ranges.

With the A:A method of specifying data ranges, Excel's COUNT function will count the number of numerical values in column A and Excel's AVERAGE function will compute the average of the numerical values in column A. Thus, to solve a new problem it is only necessary to enter the new data in column A, enter the value of the known population standard deviation in cell D7, and enter the hypothesized value of the population mean in cell D8.

The worksheet can also be used as a template for text exercises in which n, $\bar{x}$, and σ are given. Just ignore the data in column A and enter the values for n, $\bar{x}$, and σ in cells D4, D5, and D7, respectively. Then enter the appropriate hypothesized value for the population mean in cell D8. The p-values corresponding to lower tail, upper tail, and two-tailed hypothesis tests will then appear in cells D13:D15.

Summary and Practical Advice

We presented examples of a lower tail test and a two-tailed test about a population mean. Based upon these examples, we can now summarize the hypothesis testing procedures about a population mean for the σ known case as shown in Table 9.2. Note that μ_0 is the hypothesized value of the population mean.

Table 9.2 Summary of Hypothesis Tests About a Population Mean: σ Known Case

	Lower Tail Test	Upper Tail Test	Two-Tailed Test
Hypotheses	$H_0: \mu \geq \mu_0$ $H_a: \mu < \mu_0$	$H_0: \mu \leq \mu_0$ $H_a: \mu > \mu_0$	$H_0: \mu = \mu_0$ $H_a: \mu \neq \mu_0$
Test Statistic	$z = \dfrac{\bar{x} - \mu_0}{\sigma/\sqrt{n}}$	$z = \dfrac{\bar{x} - \mu_0}{\sigma/\sqrt{n}}$	$z = \dfrac{\bar{x} - \mu_0}{\sigma/\sqrt{n}}$
Rejection Rule: *p*-Value Approach	Reject H_0 if p-value $\leq \alpha$	Reject H_0 if p-value $\leq \alpha$	Reject H_0 if p-value $\leq \alpha$
Rejection Rule: Critical Value Approach	Reject H_0 if $z \leq -z_\alpha$	Reject H_0 if $z \geq z_\alpha$	Reject H_0 if $z \leq -z_{\alpha/2}$ or if $z \geq z_{\alpha/2}$

The hypothesis testing steps followed in the two examples presented in this section are common to every hypothesis test.

Steps of Hypothesis Testing

Step 1. Develop the null and alternative hypotheses.
Step 2. Specify the level of significance.
Step 3. Collect the sample data and compute the value of the test statistic.

p-Value Approach

Step 4. Use the value of the test statistic to compute the p-value.
Step 5. Reject H_0 if the p-value $\leq \alpha$.
Step 6. Interpret the statistical conclusion in the context of the application.

Critical Value Approach

Step 4. Use the level of significance to determine the critical value and the rejection rule.
Step 5. Use the value of the test statistic and the rejection rule to determine whether to reject H_0.
Step 6. Interpret the statistical conclusion in the context of the application.

Practical advice about the sample size for hypothesis tests is similar to the advice we provided about the sample size for interval estimation in Chapter 8. In most applications, a sample size of $n \geq 30$ is adequate when using the hypothesis testing procedure described in this section. In cases where the sample size is less than 30, the distribution of the population from which we are sampling becomes an important consideration. If the population is normally distributed, the hypothesis testing procedure that we described is exact and can be used for any sample size. If the population is not normally distributed but is at least roughly symmetric, sample sizes as small as 15 can be expected to provide acceptable results.

Relationship Between Interval Estimation and Hypothesis Testing

In Chapter 8, we showed how to develop a confidence interval estimate of a population mean. For the σ known case, the $(1 - \alpha)\%$ confidence interval estimate of a population mean is given by

$$\bar{x} \pm z_{\alpha/2} \frac{\sigma}{\sqrt{n}}$$

In this chapter, we showed that a two-tailed hypothesis test about a population mean takes the following form:

$$H_0: \mu = \mu_0$$
$$H_a: \mu \neq \mu_0$$

where μ_0 is the hypothesized value for the population mean.

Suppose that we follow the procedure described in Chapter 8 for constructing a $100(1 - \alpha)\%$ confidence interval for the population mean. We know that $100(1 - \alpha)\%$ of the confidence intervals generated will contain the population mean and $100\alpha\%$ of the confidence intervals generated will not contain the population mean. Thus, if we reject H_0 whenever the confidence interval does not contain μ_0, we will be rejecting the null hypothesis when it is true ($\mu = \mu_0$) with probability α. Recall that the level of significance is the probability of rejecting the null hypothesis when it is true. So constructing a $100(1 - \alpha)\%$ confidence interval and rejecting H_0 whenever the interval does not contain μ_0 is equivalent to conducting a two-tailed hypothesis test with α as the level of significance. The procedure for using a confidence interval to conduct a two-tailed hypothesis test can now be summarized.

A Confidence Interval Approach to Testing a Hypothesis of the Form

$$H_0: \mu = \mu_0$$
$$H_a: \mu \neq \mu_0$$

1. Select a simple random sample from the population and use the value of the sample mean $\bar{x}$ to develop the confidence interval for the population mean μ.

$$\bar{x} \pm z_{\alpha/2}\frac{\sigma}{\sqrt{n}}$$

2. If the confidence interval contains the hypothesized value μ_0, do not reject H_0. Otherwise, reject[3] H_0.

For a two-tailed hypothesis test, the null hypothesis can be rejected if the confidence interval does not include μ_0.

Let us illustrate by conducting the MaxFlight hypothesis test using the confidence interval approach. The MaxFlight hypothesis test takes the following form:

$$H_0: \mu = 295$$
$$H_a: \mu \neq 295$$

To test these hypotheses with a level of significance of $\alpha = 0.05$, we sampled 50 golf balls and found a sample mean distance of $\bar{x} = 297.6$ yards. Recall that the population standard deviation is $\sigma = 12$. Using these results with $z_{0.025} = 1.96$, we find that the 95% confidence interval estimate of the population mean is

$$\bar{x} \pm z_{0.025}\frac{\sigma}{\sqrt{n}}$$
$$297.6 \pm 1.96\frac{12}{\sqrt{50}}$$
$$297.6 \pm 3.3$$

or

$$294.3 \text{ to } 300.9$$

This finding enables the quality control manager to conclude with 95% confidence that the mean distance for the population of golf balls is between 294.3 and 300.9 yards.

[3]To be consistent with the rule for rejecting H_0 when the p-value $\leq \alpha$, we would also reject H_0 using the confidence interval approach if μ_0 happens to be equal to one of the endpoints of the $100(1 - \alpha)\%$ confidence interval.

Because the hypothesized value for the population mean, $\mu_0 = 295$, is in this interval, the hypothesis testing conclusion is that the null hypothesis, H_0: $\mu = 295$, cannot be rejected.

Note that this discussion and example pertain to two-tailed hypothesis tests about a population mean. However, the same confidence interval and two-tailed hypothesis testing relationship exists for other population parameters. The relationship can also be extended to one-tailed tests about population parameters. Doing so, however, requires the development of one-sided confidence intervals, which are rarely used in practice.

Notes + Comments

1. We have shown how to use *p*-values. The smaller the *p*-value the greater the evidence against H_0 and the more the evidence in favor of H_a. Here are some guidelines statisticians suggest for interpreting small *p*-values.
   - Less than 0.01—Overwhelming evidence to conclude that H_a is true
   - Between 0.01 and 0.05—Strong evidence to conclude that H_a is true
   - Between 0.05 and 0.10—Weak evidence to conclude that H_a is true
   - Greater than 0.10—Insufficient evidence to conclude that H_a is true
2. When testing a hypothesis of the population mean with a sample size that is at least 5% of the population size (that is, $n/N \geq 0.05$), the finite population correction factor should be used when calculating the standard error of the sampling distribution of $\bar{x}$ when σ is known, that is, $\sigma_{\bar{x}} = \sqrt{\frac{N-n}{N-1}}\left(\frac{\sigma}{\sqrt{n}}\right)$.

Exercises

Note to Student: Some of the exercises that follow ask you to use the *p*-value approach and others ask you to use the critical value approach. Both methods will provide the same hypothesis testing conclusion. We provide exercises with both methods to give you practice using both. In later sections and in following chapters, we will generally emphasize the *p*-value approach as the preferred method, but you may select either based on personal preference.

Methods

9. Consider the following hypothesis test:

$$H_0: \mu \geq 20$$
$$H_a: \mu < 20$$

A sample of 50 provided a sample mean of 19.4. The population standard deviation is 2. **LO 2, 4**

a. Compute the value of the test statistic.
b. What is the *p*-value?
c. Using $\alpha = 0.05$, what is your conclusion?
d. What is the rejection rule using the critical value? What is your conclusion?

10. Consider the following hypothesis test:

$$H_0: \mu \leq 25$$
$$H_a: \mu > 25$$

A sample of 40 provided a sample mean of 26.4. The population standard deviation is 6. **LO 2, 4**

a. Compute the value of the test statistic.
b. What is the *p*-value?
c. At $\alpha = 0.01$, what is your conclusion?
d. What is the rejection rule using the critical value? What is your conclusion?

11. Consider the following hypothesis test:

$$H_0\colon \mu = 15$$
$$H_a\colon \mu \neq 15$$

A sample of 50 provided a sample mean of 14.15. The population standard deviation is 3. **LO 2, 4**

a. Compute the value of the test statistic.
b. What is the p-value?
c. At $\alpha = 0.05$, what is your conclusion?
d. What is the rejection rule using the critical value? What is your conclusion?

12. Consider the following hypothesis test:

$$H_0\colon \mu \geq 80$$
$$H_a\colon \mu < 80$$

A sample of 100 is used and the population standard deviation is 12. Compute the p-value and state your conclusion for each of the following sample results. Use $\alpha = 0.01$. **LO 2, 4**

a. $\bar{x} = 78.5$
b. $\bar{x} = 77$
c. $\bar{x} = 75.5$
d. $\bar{x} = 81$

13. Consider the following hypothesis test:

$$H_0\colon \mu \leq 50$$
$$H_a\colon \mu > 50$$

A sample of 60 is used and the population standard deviation is 8. Use the critical value approach to state your conclusion for each of the following sample results. Use $\alpha = 0.05$. **LO 2, 4**

a. $\bar{x} = 52.5$
b. $\bar{x} = 51$
c. $\bar{x} = 51.8$

14. Consider the following hypothesis test:

$$H_0\colon \mu = 22$$
$$H_a\colon \mu \neq 22$$

A sample of 75 is used and the population standard deviation is 10. Compute the p-value and state your conclusion for each of the following sample results. Use $\alpha = 0.01$. **LO 2, 4**

a. $\bar{x} = 23$
b. $\bar{x} = 25.1$
c. $\bar{x} - 20$

Applications

15. **Federal Tax Returns.** According to the IRS, individuals filing federal income tax returns prior to March 31 received an average refund of $1,056 in 2018. Consider the population of "last-minute" filers who mail their tax return during the last five days of the income tax period (typically April 10 to April 15). **LO 1, 2, 4**

a. A researcher suggests that a reason individuals wait until the last five days is that on average these individuals receive lower refunds than do early filers. Develop appropriate hypotheses such that rejection of H_0 will support the researcher's contention.
b. For a sample of 400 individuals who filed a tax return between April 10 and 15, the sample mean refund was $910. Based on prior experience, a population standard deviation of $\sigma = \$1,600$ may be assumed. What is the p-value?

c. At $\alpha = 0.05$, what is your conclusion?
d. Repeat the preceding hypothesis test using the critical value approach.

16. **Credit Card Use by Undergraduates.** In a study entitled How Undergraduate Students Use Credit Cards, *Sallie Mae* reported that undergraduate students have a mean credit card balance of \$3,173. This figure was an all-time high and had increased 44% over the previous five years. Assume that a current study is being conducted to determine whether it can be concluded that the mean credit card balance for undergraduate students has continued to increase compared to the April 2009 report. Based on previous studies, use a population standard deviation $\sigma = \$1,000$. **LO 1, 2**
    a. State the null and alternative hypotheses.
    b. What is the p-value for a sample of 180 undergraduate students with a sample mean credit card balance of \$3,325?
    c. Using a 0.05 level of significance, what is your conclusion?

17. **Use of Texting.** TextRequest reports that adults 18–24 years old send and receive 128 texts every day. Suppose we take a sample of 25–34-year-olds to see if their mean number of daily texts differs from the mean for 18–24-year-olds reported by TextRequest. **LO 1, 2, 4**
    a. State the null and alternative hypotheses we should use to test whether the population mean daily number of texts for 25–34-year-olds differs from the population daily mean number of texts for 18–24-year-olds.
    b. Suppose a sample of thirty 25–34-year-olds showed a sample mean of 118.6 texts per day. Assume a population standard deviation of 33.17 texts per day and compute the p-value.
    c. With $\alpha = 0.05$ as the level of significance, what is your conclusion?
    d. Repeat the preceding hypothesis test using the critical value approach.

18. **CPA Work Hours.** The American Institute of Certified Tax Planners reports that the average U.S. CPA works 60 hours per week during tax season. Do CPAs in states that have flat state income tax rates work fewer hours per week during tax season? Conduct a hypothesis test to determine if this is so. **LO 1, 2, 4**
    a. Formulate hypotheses that can be used to determine whether the mean hours worked per week during tax season by CPAs in states that have flat state income tax rates is less than the mean hours worked per week by all U.S. CPAs during tax season?
    b. Based on a sample, the mean number of hours worked per week during tax season by CPAs in states with flat tax rates was 55. Assume the sample size was 150 and that, based on past studies, the population standard deviation can be assumed to be $\sigma = 27.4$. Use the sample results to compute the test statistic and p-value for your hypothesis test.
    c. At $\alpha = 0.05$, what is your conclusion?

19. **Length of Calls to the IRS.** According to the IRS, taxpayers calling the IRS in 2017 waited 13 minutes on average for an IRS telephone assister to answer. Do callers who use the IRS help line early in the day have a shorter wait? Suppose a sample of 50 callers who placed their calls to the IRS in the first 30 minutes that the line is open during the day have a mean waiting time of 11 minutes before an IRS telephone assister answers. Based on data from past years, you decide that it is reasonable to assume that the standard deviation of waiting times is 8 minutes. Using these sample results, can you conclude that the waiting time for calls placed during the first 30 minutes the IRS help line is open each day is significantly less than the overall mean waiting time of 13 minutes? Use $\alpha = 0.05$. **LO 1, 2, 4**

20. **Prescription Drug Costs.** According to the Hospital Care Cost Institute, the annual expenditure for prescription drugs is \$838 per person in the Northeast region of the country. A sample of 60 individuals in the Midwest shows a per person annual expenditure for prescription drugs of \$745. Use a population standard deviation of \$300 to answer the following questions. **LO 1, 2, 4**

a. Formulate hypotheses for a test to determine whether the sample data support the conclusion that the population annual expenditure for prescription drugs per person is lower in the Midwest than in the Northeast.
b. What is the value of the test statistic?
c. What is the p-value?
d. At $\alpha = 0.01$, what is your conclusion?

DATA*file*
fowle

21. **Cost of Telephone Surveys.** Fowle Marketing Research, Inc. bases charges to a client on the assumption that telephone surveys can be completed in a mean time of 15 minutes or less. If a longer mean survey time is necessary, a premium rate is charged. A sample of 35 surveys provided the survey times shown in the file *fowle*. Based upon past studies, the population standard deviation is assumed known with $\sigma = 4$ minutes. Is the premium rate justified? **LO 1, 2, 4**
a. Formulate the null and alternative hypotheses for this application.
b. Compute the value of the test statistic.
c. What is the p-value?
d. At $\alpha = 0.01$, what is your conclusion?

22. **Time in Supermarket Checkout Lines.** CCN and ActMedia provided a television channel targeted to individuals waiting in supermarket checkout lines. The channel showed news, short features, and advertisements. The length of the program was based on the assumption that the population mean time a shopper stands in a supermarket checkout line is 8 minutes. A sample of actual waiting times will be used to test this assumption and determine whether actual mean waiting time differs from this standard. **LO 1, 2, 4**
a. Formulate the hypotheses for this application.
b. A sample of 120 shoppers showed a sample mean waiting time of 8.4 minutes. Assume a population standard deviation of $\sigma = 3.2$ minutes. What is the p-value?
c. At $\alpha = 0.05$, what is your conclusion?
d. Compute a 95% confidence interval for the population mean. Does it support your conclusion?

9.4 Population Mean: σ Unknown

In this section, we describe how to conduct hypothesis tests about a population mean for the σ unknown case. Because the σ unknown case corresponds to situations in which an estimate of the population standard deviation cannot be developed prior to sampling, the sample must be used to develop an estimate of both μ and σ. Thus, to conduct a hypothesis test about a population mean for the σ unknown case, the sample mean $\bar{x}$ is used as an estimate of μ and the sample standard deviation s is used as an estimate of σ.

The steps of the hypothesis testing procedure for the σ unknown case are the same as those for the σ known case described in Section 9.3. But, with σ unknown, the computation of the test statistic and p-value is a bit different. Recall that for the σ known case, the sampling distribution of the test statistic has a standard normal distribution. For the σ unknown case, however, the sampling distribution of the test statistic follows the t distribution; it has slightly more variability because the sample is used to develop estimates of both μ and σ.

In Section 8.2, we showed that an interval estimate of a population mean for the σ unknown case is based on a probability distribution known as the t distribution. Hypothesis tests about a population mean for the σ unknown case are also based on the t distribution. For the σ unknown case, the test statistic has a t distribution with $n - 1$ degrees of freedom.

Test Statistic for Hypothesis Tests About a Population Mean: σ Unknown

$$t = \frac{\bar{x} - \mu_0}{s/\sqrt{n}} \tag{9.2}$$

In Chapter 8, we said that the t distribution is based on an assumption that the population from which we are sampling has a normal distribution. However, research shows that this assumption can be relaxed considerably when the sample size is large enough. We provide some practical advice concerning the population distribution and sample size at the end of the section.

One-Tailed Test

DATA*file*
airrating

Let us consider an example of a one-tailed test about a population mean for the σ unknown case. A business travel magazine wants to classify transatlantic gateway airports according to the mean rating for the population of business travelers. A rating scale with a low score of 0 and a high score of 10 will be used, and airports with a population mean rating greater than 7 will be designated as superior service airports. The magazine staff surveyed a sample of 60 business travelers at each airport to obtain the ratings data. The sample for London's Heathrow Airport provided a sample mean rating of $\bar{x} = 7.25$ and a sample standard deviation of $s = 1.052$. Do the data indicate that Heathrow should be designated as a superior service airport?

We want to develop a hypothesis test for which the decision to reject H_0 will lead to the conclusion that the population mean rating for the Heathrow Airport is *greater* than 7. Thus, an upper tail test with H_a: $\mu > 7$ is required. The null and alternative hypotheses for this upper tail test are as follows:

$$H_0\colon \mu \le 7$$
$$H_a\colon \mu > 7$$

We will use $\alpha = 0.05$ as the level of significance for the test.

Using equation (9.2) with $\bar{x} = 7.25$, $\mu_0 = 7$, $s = 1.052$, and $n = 60$, the value of the test statistic is

$$t = \frac{\bar{x} - \mu_0}{s/\sqrt{n}} = \frac{7.25 - 7}{1.052/\sqrt{60}} = 1.84$$

The sampling distribution of t has $n - 1 = 60 - 1 = 59$ degrees of freedom. Because the test is an upper tail test, the p-value is $P(t \ge 1.84)$, that is, the upper tail area corresponding to the value of the test statistic.

The t distribution table provided in most textbooks will not contain sufficient detail to determine the exact p-value, such as the p-value corresponding to $t = 1.84$. For instance, using Table 2 in Appendix B (available online), the t distribution with 59 degrees of freedom provides the following information.

Area in Upper Tail	**0.20**	**0.10**	**0.05**	**0.025**	**0.01**	**0.005**
***t* Value (59 *df*)**	0.848	1.296	1.671	2.001	2.391	2.662

$t = 1.84$

We see that $t = 1.84$ is between 1.671 and 2.001. Although the table does not provide the exact p-value, the values in the "Area in Upper Tail" row show that the p-value must be less than 0.05 and greater than 0.025. With a level of significance of $\alpha = 0.05$, this placement is all we need to know to make the decision to reject the null hypothesis and conclude that Heathrow should be classified as a superior service airport.

It is cumbersome to use a t table to compute p-values, and only approximate values are obtained. We describe how to compute exact p-values using Excel's T.DIST function in the Using Excel subsection which follows. The exact upper tail p-value for the Heathrow Airport hypothesis test is 0.0354. With $0.0354 < 0.05$, we reject the null hypothesis and conclude that Heathrow should be classified as a superior service airport.

The decision whether to reject the null hypothesis in the σ unknown case can also be made using the critical value approach. The critical value corresponding to an area of $\alpha = 0.05$ in the upper tail of a t distribution with 59 degrees of freedom is $t_{0.05} = 1.671$. Thus the rejection rule using the critical value approach is to reject H_0 if $t \ge 1.671$. Because $t = 1.84 > 1.671$, H_0 is rejected. Heathrow should be classified as a superior service airport.

Two-Tailed Test

To illustrate how to conduct a two-tailed test about a population mean for the σ unknown case, let us consider the hypothesis testing situation facing Holiday Toys. The company manufactures and distributes its products through more than 1,000 retail outlets. In planning production levels for the coming winter season, Holiday must decide how many units of each product to produce prior to knowing the actual demand at the retail level. For this year's most important new toy, Holiday's marketing director is expecting demand to average 40 units per retail outlet. Prior to making the final production decision based upon this estimate, Holiday decided to survey a sample of 25 retailers in order to develop more information about the demand for the new product. Each retailer was provided with information about the features of the new toy along with the cost and the suggested selling price. Then each retailer was asked to specify an anticipated order quantity.

With μ denoting the population mean order quantity per retail outlet, the sample data will be used to conduct the following two-tailed hypothesis test:

$$H_0\colon \mu = 40$$
$$H_a\colon \mu \neq 40$$

If H_0 cannot be rejected, Holiday will continue its production planning based on the marketing director's estimate that the population mean order quantity per retail outlet will be $\mu = 40$ units. However, if H_0 is rejected, Holiday will immediately reevaluate its production plan for the product. A two-tailed hypothesis test is used because Holiday wants to reevaluate the production plan if the population mean quantity per retail outlet is less than anticipated or greater than anticipated. Because no historical data are available (it's a new product), the population mean μ and the population standard deviation must both be estimated using $\bar{x}$ and s from the sample data.

DATA*file*
orders

The sample of 25 retailers provided a mean of $\bar{x} = 37.4$ and a standard deviation of $s = 11.79$ units. Before going ahead with the use of the t distribution, the analyst constructed a histogram of the sample data in order to check on the form of the population distribution. The histogram of the sample data showed no evidence of skewness or any extreme outliers, so the analyst concluded that the use of the t distribution with $n - 1 = 24$ degrees of freedom was appropriate. Using equation (9.2) with $\bar{x} = 37.4$, $\mu_0 = 40$, $s = 11.79$, and $n = 25$, the value of the test statistic is

$$t = \frac{\bar{x} - \mu_0}{s/\sqrt{n}} = \frac{37.4 - 40}{11.79/\sqrt{25}} = -1.10$$

Because we have a two-tailed test, the p-value is two times the area under the curve of the t distribution for $t \leq -1.10$. Using Table 2 in Appendix B (available online), the t distribution table for 24 degrees of freedom provides the following information.

Area in Upper Tail	**0.20**	**0.10**	**0.05**	**0.025**	**0.01**	**0.005**
***t*-Value (24 *df*)**	0.857	1.318	1.711	2.064	2.492	2.797

$t = 1.10$

The t distribution table contains only positive t values (corresponding to areas in the upper tail). Because the t distribution is symmetric, however, the upper tail area for $t = 1.10$ is the same as the lower tail area for $t = -1.10$. We see that $t = 1.10$ is between 0.857 and 1.318. From the "Area in Upper Tail" row, we see that the area in the tail to the right of $t = 1.10$ is between 0.20 and 0.10. When we double these amounts, we see that the p-value must be between 0.40 and 0.20. With a level of significance of $\alpha = 0.05$, we now know that the p-value is greater than α. Therefore, H_0 cannot be rejected. Sufficient evidence is not available to conclude that Holiday should change its production plan for the coming season.

In the Using Excel subsection that follows, we show how to compute the exact p-value for this hypothesis test using Excel. The p-value obtained is 0.2811. With a level of significance of $\alpha = 0.05$, we cannot reject H_0 because $0.2811 > 0.05$.

The test statistic can also be compared to the critical value to make the two-tailed hypothesis testing decision. With $\alpha = 0.05$ and the t distribution with 24 degrees of freedom, $-t_{0.025} = -2.064$ and $t_{0.025} = 2.064$ are the critical values for the two-tailed test. The rejection rule using the test statistic is

$$\text{Reject } H_0 \text{ if } t \leq -2.064 \text{ or if } t \geq 2.064$$

Based on the test statistic $t = -1.10$, H_0 cannot be rejected. This result indicates that Holiday should continue its production planning for the coming season based on the expectation that $\mu = 40$.

Using Excel

Excel can be used to conduct one-tailed and two-tailed hypothesis tests about a population mean for the σ unknown case. The approach is similar to the procedure used in the σ known case. The sample data and the test statistic (t) are used to compute three p-values: p-value (Lower Tail), p-value (Upper Tail), and p-value (Two Tail). The user can then choose α and draw a conclusion using whichever p-value is appropriate for the type of hypothesis test being conducted.

Let's start by showing how to use Excel's T.DIST function to compute a lower tail p-value. The T.DIST function has three inputs; its general form is as follows:

T.DIST(test statistic, degrees of freedom, cumulative)

For the first input, we enter the value of the test statistic, for the second input we enter the number of degrees of freedom. For the third input, we enter *TRUE* if we want a cumulative probability and *FALSE* if we want the height of the curve. When we want to compute a lower tail p-value, we enter *TRUE*.

Once the lower tail p-value has been computed, it is easy to compute the upper tail and the two-tailed p-values. The upper tail p-value is just 1 minus the lower tail p-value. And the two-tailed p-value is given by two times the smaller of the lower and upper tail p-values.

Let us now construct an Excel worksheet to conduct the two-tailed hypothesis test for the Holiday Toys study. Refer to Figure 9.8 as we describe the tasks involved. The formula worksheet is in the background; the value worksheet is in the foreground.

Enter/Access Data: Open the file *orders*. A label and the order quantity data for the sample of 25 retailers are entered in cells A1:A26.

Enter Functions and Formulas: The sample size, sample mean, and sample standard deviation are computed in cells D4:D6 using Excel's COUNT, AVERAGE, and STDEV.S functions, respectively. The value worksheet shows that the sample size is 25, the sample mean is 37.4, and the sample standard deviation is 11.79. The hypothesized value of the population mean (*40*) is entered in cell D8.

Using the sample standard deviation as an estimate of the population standard deviation, an estimate of the standard error is obtained in cell D10 by dividing the sample standard deviation in cell D6 by the square root of the sample size in cell D4. The formula =*(D5-D8)/D10* entered in cell D11 computes the test statistic t (-1.1026). The degrees of freedom are computed in cell D12 as the sample size in cell D4 minus 1.

To compute the p-value for a lower tail test, we enter the following formula in cell D14:

=*T.DIST(D11,D12,TRUE)*

The p-value for an upper tail test is then computed in cell D15 as 1 minus the p-value for the lower tail test. Finally, the p-value for a two-tailed test is computed in cell D16 as two times the minimum of the two one-tailed p-values. The value worksheet shows that the three p-values are p-value (Lower Tail) = 0.1406, p-value (Upper Tail) = 0.8594, and p-value (Two Tail) = 0.2811.

Figure 9.8 Excel Worksheet: Hypothesis Test for the σ Unknown Case

	A	B	C	D	E
1	Units		Hypothesis Test about a Population Mean:		
2	26		σ Unknown Case		
3	23				
4	32		Sample Size	=COUNT(A2:A26)	
5	47		Sample Mean	=AVERAGE(A2:A26)	
6	45		Sample Standard Deviation	=STDEV.S(A2:A26)	
7	31				
8	47		Hypothesized Value	40	
9	59				
10	21		Standard Error	=D6/SQRT(D4)	
11	52		Test Statistic *t*	=(D5-D8)/D10	
12	45		Degrees of Freedom	=D4-1	
13	53				
14	34		*p*-value (Lower Tail)	=T.DIST(D11,D12,TRUE)	
15	45		*p*-value (Upper Tail)	=1-D14	
16	39		*p*-value (Two Tail)	=2*MIN(D14,D15)	
17	52				
25	30				
26	28				
27					

DATA*file*
orders

Note: Rows 18–24 are hidden.

	A	B	C	D	E
1	Units		Hypothesis Test about a Population Mean:		
2	26		σ Unknown Case		
3	23				
4	32		Sample Size	25	
5	47		Sample Mean	37.4	
6	45		Sample Standard Deviation	11.79	
7	31				
8	47		Hypothesized Value	40	
9	59				
10	21		Standard Error	2.3580	
11	52		Test Statistic *t*	-1.1026	
12	45		Degrees of Freedom	24	
13	53				
14	34		*p*-value (Lower Tail)	0.1406	
15	45		*p*-value (Upper Tail)	0.8594	
16	39		*p*-value (Two Tail)	0.2811	
17	52				
25	30				
26	28				
27					

The development of the worksheet is now complete. For the two-tailed Holiday Toys problem we cannot reject H_0: $\mu = 40$ using $\alpha = 0.05$ because the p-value (Two Tail) $= 0.2811$ is greater than α. This result indicates that Holiday should continue its production planning for the coming season based on the expectation that $\mu = 40$. The worksheet in Figure 9.8 can also be used for any one-tailed hypothesis test involving the t distribution. If a lower tail test is required, compare the p-value (Lower Tail) with α to make the rejection decision. If an upper tail test is required, compare the p-value (Upper Tail) with α to make the rejection decision.

A Template for Other Problems The worksheet in Figure 9.8 can be used as a template for any hypothesis tests about a population mean for the σ unknown case. Just enter the appropriate data in column A, adjust the ranges for the formulas in cells D4:D6, and enter the hypothesized value in cell D8. The standard error, the test statistic, and the three p-values will then appear. Depending on the form of the hypothesis test (lower tail, upper tail, or two-tailed), we can then choose the appropriate p-value to make the rejection decision.

We can further simplify the use of Figure 9.8 as a template for other problems by eliminating the need to enter new data ranges in cells D4:D6. To do so, we rewrite the cell formulas as follows:

Cell D4: =*COUNT(A:A)*

Cell D5: =*AVERAGE(A:A)*

Cell D6: =*STDEV(A:A)*

The file orders includes a worksheet entitled Template that uses the A:A method for entering the data ranges.

With the A:A method of specifying data ranges, Excel's COUNT function will count the number of numeric values in column A, Excel's AVERAGE function will compute the average of the numeric values in column A, and Excel's STDEV function will compute the standard deviation of the numeric values in Column A. Thus, to solve a new problem it is only necessary to enter the new data in column A and enter the hypothesized value of the population mean in cell D8.

Table 9.3 Summary of Hypothesis Tests About a Population Mean: σ Unknown Case

	Lower Tail Test	Upper Tail Test	Two-Tailed Test
Hypotheses	$H_0: \mu \geq \mu_0$ $H_a: \mu < \mu_0$	$H_0: \mu \leq \mu_0$ $H_a: \mu > \mu_0$	$H_0: \mu = \mu_0$ $H_a: \mu \neq \mu_0$
Test Statistic	$t = \dfrac{\bar{x} - \mu_0}{s/\sqrt{n}}$	$t = \dfrac{\bar{x} - \mu_0}{s/\sqrt{n}}$	$t = \dfrac{\bar{x} - \mu_0}{s/\sqrt{n}}$
Rejection Rule: *p*-Value Approach	Reject H_0 if p-value $\leq \alpha$	Reject H_0 if p-value $\leq \alpha$	Reject H_0 if p-value $\leq \alpha$
Rejection Rule: Critical Value Approach	Reject H_0 if $t \leq -t_\alpha$	Reject H_0 if $t \geq t_\alpha$	Reject H_0 if $t \leq -t_{\alpha/2}$ or if $t \geq t_{\alpha/2}$

Summary and Practical Advice

Table 9.3 provides a summary of the hypothesis testing procedures about a population mean for the σ unknown case. The key difference between these procedures and the ones for the σ known case is that s is used, instead of σ, in the computation of the test statistic. For this reason, the test statistic follows the t distribution.

The applicability of the hypothesis testing procedures of this section is dependent on the distribution of the population being sampled from and the sample size. When the population is normally distributed, the hypothesis tests described in this section provide exact results for any sample size. When the population is not normally distributed, the procedures are approximations. Nonetheless, we find that sample sizes of 30 or greater will provide good results in most cases. If the population is approximately normal, small sample sizes (e.g., $n < 15$) can provide acceptable results. If the population is highly skewed or contains outliers, sample sizes approaching 50 are recommended.

Note + Comment

When testing a hypothesis of the population mean with a sample size that is at least 5% of the population size (that is, $n/N \geq 0.05$), the finite population correction factor should be used when calculating the standard error of the sampling distribution of $\bar{x}$ when σ is unknown, i.e., $s_{\bar{x}} = \sqrt{\dfrac{N-n}{N-1}}\left(\dfrac{s}{\sqrt{n}}\right)$.

Exercises

Methods

23. Consider the following hypothesis test:

$$H_0: \mu \leq 12$$
$$H_a: \mu > 12$$

A sample of 25 provided a sample mean $\bar{x} = 14$ and a sample standard deviation $s = 4.32$. **LO 2, 5**

a. Compute the value of the test statistic.

b. Use the t distribution table (Table 2 in online Appendix B) to compute a range for the p-value.

c. At $\alpha = 0.05$, what is your conclusion?
d. What is the rejection rule using the critical value? What is your conclusion?

24. Consider the following hypothesis test:

$$H_0: \mu = 18$$
$$H_a: \mu \neq 18$$

A sample of 48 provided a sample mean $\bar{x} = 17$ and a sample standard deviation $s = 4.5$. **LO 2, 5**

a. Compute the value of the test statistic.
b. Use the t distribution table (Table 2 in online Appendix B) to compute a range for the p-value.
c. At $\alpha = 0.05$, what is your conclusion?
d. What is the rejection rule using the critical value? What is your conclusion?

25. Consider the following hypothesis test:

$$H_0: \mu \geq 45$$
$$H_a: \mu < 45$$

A sample of 36 is used. Identify the p-value and state your conclusion for each of the following sample results. Use $\alpha = 0.01$. **LO 2, 5**

a. $\bar{x} = 44$ and $s = 5.2$
b. $\bar{x} = 43$ and $s = 4.6$
c. $\bar{x} = 46$ and $s = 5.0$

26. Consider the following hypothesis test:

$$H_0: \mu = 100$$
$$H_a: \mu \neq 100$$

A sample of 65 is used. Identify the p-value and state your conclusion for each of the following sample results. Use $\alpha = 0.05$. **LO 2, 5**

a. $\bar{x} = 103$ and $s = 11.5$
b. $\bar{x} = 96.5$ and $s = 11.0$
c. $\bar{x} = 102$ and $s = 10.5$

Applications

27. **Price of Good Red Wine.** According to the Vivino website, the mean price for a bottle of red wine that scores 4.0 or higher on the Vivino Rating System is \$32.48. A New England–based lifestyle magazine wants to determine if red wines of the same quality are less expensive in Providence, and it has collected prices for 56 randomly selected red wines of similar quality from wine stores throughout Providence. The mean and standard deviation for this sample are \$30.15 and \$12, respectively. **LO 1, 2, 5**

a. Develop appropriate hypotheses for a test to determine whether the sample data support the conclusion that the mean price in Providence for a bottle of red wine that scores 4.0 or higher on the Vivino Rating System is less than the population mean of \$32.48.
b. Using the sample from the 56 bottles, what is the p-value?
c. At $\alpha = 0.05$, what is your conclusion?
d. Repeat the preceding hypothesis test using the critical value approach.

28. **CEO Tenure.** A shareholders' group, in lodging a protest, claimed that the mean tenure for a chief executive officer (CEO) was at least nine years. A survey of companies reported in *The Wall Street Journal* found a sample mean tenure of $\bar{x} = 7.27$ years for CEOs with a standard deviation of $s = 6.38$ years. **LO 1, 2, 5**

a. Formulate hypotheses that can be used to challenge the validity of the claim made by the shareholders' group.
b. Assume 85 companies were included in the sample. What is the p-value for your hypothesis test?
c. At $\alpha = 0.01$, what is your conclusion?

DATA*file*
residentialwater

29. **Cost of Residential Water.** On its municipal website, the city of Tulsa states that the rate it charges per 5 CCF of residential water is \$21.62. How do the residential water rates of other U.S. public utilities compare to Tulsa's rate? The file *residentialwater* contains the rate per 5 CCF of residential water for 42 randomly selected U.S. cities. **LO 1, 2, 5**
   a. Formulate hypotheses that can be used to determine whether the population mean rate per 5 CCF of residential water charged by U.S. public utilities differs from the \$21.62 rate charged by Tulsa.
   b. What is the p-value for your hypothesis test in part (a)?
   c. At $\alpha = 0.05$, can your null hypothesis be rejected? What is your conclusion?
   d. Repeat the preceding hypothesis test using the critical value approach.

DATA*file*
childcare

30. **Time in Child Care.** The time married men with children spend on child care averages 6.4 hours per week. You belong to a professional group on family practices that would like to do its own study to determine whether the time married men in your area spend on child care per week differs from the reported mean of 6.4 hours per week. A sample of 40 married couples will be used with the data collected showing the hours per week the husband spends on child care. The sample data are contained in the file *childcare*. **LO 1, 2, 5**
   a. What are the hypotheses if your group would like to determine whether the population mean number of hours married men are spending in child care differs from the mean reported by *Time* in your area?
   b. What is the sample mean and the p-value?
   c. Select your own level of significance. What is your conclusion?

31. **Chocolate Consumption.** The United States ranks ninth in the world in per capita chocolate consumption; *Forbes* reports that the average American eats 9.5 pounds of chocolate annually. Suppose you are curious whether chocolate consumption is higher in Hershey, Pennsylvania, the location of The Hershey Company's corporate headquarters. A sample of 36 individuals from the Hershey area showed a sample mean annual consumption of 10.05 pounds and a standard deviation of $s = 1.5$ pounds. Using $\alpha = 0.05$, do the sample results support the conclusion that mean annual consumption of chocolate is higher in Hershey than it is throughout the United States? **LO 1, 2, 5**

DATA*file*
usedcars

32. **Used Car Prices.** According to the Kelly Blue Book, the mean price for used cars is \$27,569 used car sales at the dealership in an attempt to determine whether the population mean price for used cars at this particular dealership differed from the national mean. The prices for the sample of 50 cars are shown in the file *usedcars*. **LO 1, 2, 5**
   a. Formulate the hypotheses that can be used to determine whether a difference exists in the mean price for used cars at the dealership.
   b. What is the p-value?
   c. At $\alpha = 0.05$, what is your conclusion?

33. **Automobile Insurance Premiums.** Insure.com reports that the mean annual premium for automobile insurance in the United States was \$1,365 in 2018. Being from Pennsylvania, you believe automobile insurance is cheaper there and wish to develop statistical support for your opinion. A sample of 25 automobile insurance policies from the state of Pennsylvania showed a mean annual premium of \$1,302 with a standard deviation of $s = \$165$. **LO 1, 2, 5**
   a. Develop a hypothesis test that can be used to determine whether the mean annual premium in Pennsylvania is lower than the national mean annual premium.
   b. What is a point estimate of the difference between the mean annual premium in Pennsylvania and the national mean?
   c. What is the p-value?
   d. At $\alpha = 0.05$, test for a significant difference. What is your conclusion?

34. **Landscaping Labor Costs.** Joan's Nursery specializes in custom-designed landscaping for residential areas. The estimated labor cost associated with a particular landscaping proposal is based on the number of plantings of trees, shrubs, and so on to be used for the project. For cost-estimating purposes, managers use two hours of labor time for the planting of a medium-sized tree. Actual times from a sample of 10 plantings during the past month follow (times in hours).

1.7	1.5	2.6	2.2	2.4	2.3	2.6	3.0	1.4	2.3

With a 0.05 level of significance, test to see whether the mean tree-planting time differs from two hours. **LO 1, 2, 5**

a. State the null and alternative hypotheses.
b. Compute the sample mean.
c. Compute the sample standard deviation.
d. What is the p-value?
e. What is your conclusion?

9.5 Population Proportion

In this section, we show how to conduct a hypothesis test about a population proportion p. Using p_0 to denote the hypothesized value for the population proportion, the three forms for a hypothesis test about a population proportion are as follows:

$$\begin{array}{lll} H_0\colon p \geq p_0 & H_0\colon p \leq p_0 & H_0\colon p = p_0 \\ H_a\colon p < p_0 & H_a\colon p > p_0 & H_a\colon p \neq p_0 \end{array}$$

The first form is called a lower tail test, the second form is called an upper tail test, and the third form is called a two-tailed test.

Hypothesis tests about a population proportion are based on the difference between the sample proportion $\bar{p}$ and the hypothesized population proportion p_0. The methods used to conduct the hypothesis test are similar to those used for hypothesis tests about a population mean. The only difference is that we use the sample proportion and its standard error to compute the test statistic. The p-value approach or the critical value approach is then used to determine whether the null hypothesis should be rejected.

Let us consider an example involving a situation faced by Pine Creek golf course. Over the past year, 20% of the players at Pine Creek were women. In an effort to increase the proportion of women players, Pine Creek implemented a special promotion designed to attract women golfers. One month after the promotion was implemented, the course manager requested a statistical study to determine whether the proportion of women players at Pine Creek had increased. Because the objective of the study is to determine whether the proportion of women golfers increased, an upper tail test with $H_a\colon p > 0.20$ is appropriate. The null and alternative hypotheses for the Pine Creek hypothesis test are as follows:

$$\begin{aligned} H_0&\colon p \leq 0.20 \\ H_a&\colon p > 0.20 \end{aligned}$$

If H_0 can be rejected, the test results will give statistical support for the conclusion that the proportion of women golfers increased and the promotion was beneficial. The course manager specified that a level of significance of $\alpha = 0.05$ be used in carrying out this hypothesis test.

The next step of the hypothesis testing procedure is to select a sample and compute the value of an appropriate test statistic. To show how this step is done for the Pine Creek upper tail test, we begin with a general discussion of how to compute the value of the test statistic for any form of a hypothesis test about a population proportion. The sampling distribution of $\bar{p}$, the point estimator of the population parameter p, is the basis for developing the test statistic.

When the null hypothesis is true as an equality, the expected value of $\bar{p}$ equals the hypothesized value p_0; that is, $E(\bar{p}) = p_0$. The standard error of $\bar{p}$ is given by

$$\sigma_{\bar{p}} = \sqrt{\frac{p_0(1 - p_0)}{n}}$$

In Chapter 7, we indicated that if $np \geq 5$ and $n(1 - p) \geq 5$, the sampling distribution of $\bar{p}$ can be approximated by a normal distribution.[4] Under these conditions, which usually apply in practice, the quantity

$$z = \frac{\bar{p} - p_0}{\sigma_{\bar{p}}} \tag{9.3}$$

has a standard normal probability distribution. With $\sigma_{\bar{p}} = \sqrt{p_0(1 - p_0)/n}$, the standard normal random variable z is the test statistic used to conduct hypothesis tests about a population proportion.

Test Statistic for Hypothesis Tests About a Population Proportion

$$z = \frac{\bar{p} - p_0}{\sqrt{\dfrac{p_0(1 - p_0)}{n}}} \tag{9.4}$$

DATA*file*
womengolf

We can now compute the test statistic for the Pine Creek hypothesis test. Suppose a random sample of 400 players was selected, and that 100 of the players were women. The proportion of women golfers in the sample is

$$\bar{p} = \frac{100}{400} = 0.25$$

Using equation (9.4), the value of the test statistic is

$$z = \frac{\bar{p} - p_0}{\sqrt{\dfrac{p_0(1 - p_0)}{n}}} = \frac{0.25 - 0.20}{\sqrt{\dfrac{0.20(1 - 0.20)}{400}}} = \frac{0.05}{0.02} = 2.50$$

Because the Pine Creek hypothesis test is an upper tail test, the p-value is the probability that z is greater than or equal to $z = 2.50$; that is, it is the upper tail area corresponding to $z \geq 2.50$. Using the standard normal probability table, we find that the lower tail area for $z = 2.50$ is 0.9938. Thus, the p-value for the Pine Creek test is $1.0000 - 0.9938 = 0.0062$. Figure 9.9 shows this p-value calculation.

Figure 9.9 Calculation of the *p*-Value for the Pine Creek Hypothesis Test

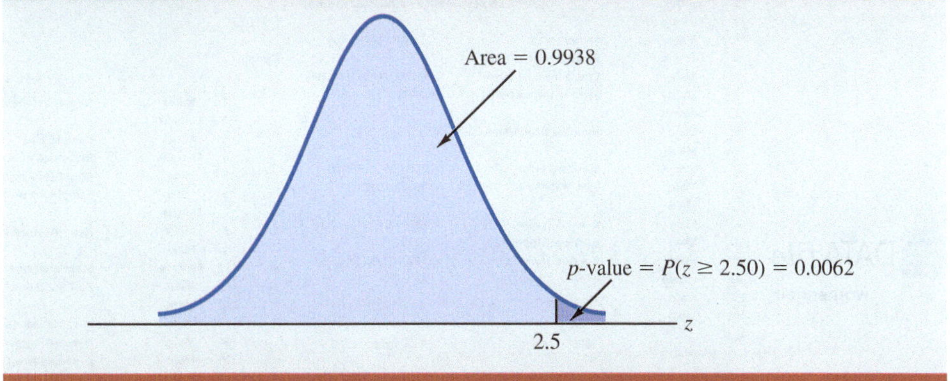

[4]In most applications involving hypothesis tests of a population proportion, sample sizes are large enough to use the normal approximation. The exact sampling distribution of $\bar{p}$ is discrete, with the probability for each value of $\bar{p}$ given by the binomial distribution. So hypothesis testing is a bit more complicated for small samples when the normal approximation cannot be used.

Recall that the course manager specified a level of significance of $\alpha = 0.05$. A p-value $= 0.0062 < 0.05$ gives sufficient statistical evidence to reject H_0 at the 0.05 level of significance. Thus, the test provides statistical support for the conclusion that the special promotion increased the proportion of women players at the Pine Creek golf course.

The decision whether to reject the null hypothesis can also be made using the critical value approach. The critical value corresponding to an area of 0.05 in the upper tail of a normal probability distribution is $z_{0.05} = 1.645$. Thus, the rejection rule using the critical value approach is to reject H_0 if $z \geq 1.645$. Because $z = 2.50 > 1.645$, H_0 is rejected.

Again, we see that the p-value approach and the critical value approach lead to the same hypothesis testing conclusion, but the p-value approach provides more information. With a p-value $= 0.0062$, the null hypothesis would be rejected for any level of significance greater than or equal to 0.0062.

Using Excel

Excel can be used to conduct one-tailed and two-tailed hypothesis tests about a population proportion using the p-value approach. The procedure is similar to the approach used with Excel in conducting hypothesis tests about a population mean. The primary difference is that the test statistic is based on the sampling distribution of $\bar{x}$ for hypothesis tests about a population mean and on the sampling distribution of $\bar{p}$ for hypothesis tests about a population proportion. Thus, although different formulas are used to compute the test statistic needed to make the hypothesis testing decision, the computations of the critical value and the p-value for the tests are identical.

We will illustrate the procedure by showing how Excel can be used to conduct the upper tail hypothesis test for the Pine Creek golf course study. Refer to Figure 9.10 as we describe the tasks involved. The formula worksheet is in the background; the value worksheet is in the foreground.

Enter/Access Data: Open the file *womengolf*. A label and the gender of each golfer in the study are entered in cells A1:A401.

Enter Functions and Formulas: The sample size, response count, and sample proportion are calculated in cells D3, D5, and D6. Because the data are not numeric, Excel's COUNTA function, not the COUNT function, is used in cell D3 to determine the sample size.

Figure 9.10 Excel Worksheet: Hypothesis Test for Pine Creek Golf Course

DATA*file*
womengolf

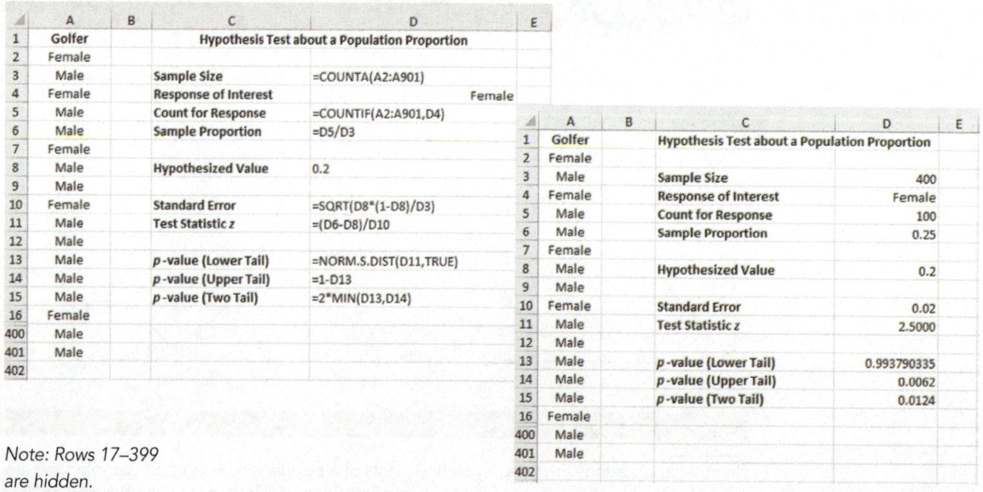

	A	B	C	D	E
1	Golfer		Hypothesis Test about a Population Proportion		
2	Female				
3	Male		Sample Size	=COUNTA(A2:A901)	
4	Female		Response of Interest	Female	
5	Male		Count for Response	=COUNTIF(A2:A901,D4)	
6	Male		Sample Proportion	=D5/D3	
7	Female				
8	Male		Hypothesized Value	0.2	
9	Male				
10	Female		Standard Error	=SQRT(D8*(1-D8)/D3)	
11	Male		Test Statistic z	=(D6-D8)/D10	
12	Male				
13	Male		p-value (Lower Tail)	=NORM.S.DIST(D11,TRUE)	
14	Male		p-value (Upper Tail)	=1-D13	
15	Male		p-value (Two Tail)	=2*MIN(D13,D14)	
16	Female				
400	Male				
401	Male				
402					

	A	B	C	D	E
1	Golfer		Hypothesis Test about a Population Proportion		
2	Female				
3	Male		Sample Size	400	
4	Female		Response of Interest	Female	
5	Male		Count for Response	100	
6	Male		Sample Proportion	0.25	
7	Female				
8	Male		Hypothesized Value	0.2	
9	Male				
10	Female		Standard Error	0.02	
11	Male		Test Statistic z	2.5000	
12	Male				
13	Male		p-value (Lower Tail)	0.993790335	
14	Male		p-value (Upper Tail)	0.0062	
15	Male		p-value (Two Tail)	0.0124	
16	Female				
400	Male				
401	Male				
402					

Note: Rows 17–399 are hidden.

We entered *Female* in cell D4 to identify the response for which we wish to compute a proportion. The COUNTIF function is then used in cell D5 to determine the number of responses of the type identified in cell D4. The sample proportion is then computed in cell D6 by dividing the response count by the sample size.

The hypothesized value of the population proportion (*0.20*) is entered in cell D8. The standard error is obtained in cell D10 by entering the formula *=SQRT(D8*(1-D8)/D3)*. The formula *=(D6-D8)/D10* entered in cell D11 computes the test statistic z (2.50). To compute the p-value for a lower tail test, we enter the formula *=NORM.S.DIST(D11,TRUE)* in cell D13. The p-value for an upper tail test is then computed in cell D14 as 1 minus the p-value for the lower tail test. Finally, the p-value for a two-tailed test is computed in cell D15 as two times the minimum of the two one-tailed p-values. The value worksheet shows that the three p-values are as follows: p-value (Lower Tail) = 0.9938; p-value (Upper Tail) = 0.0062; and p-value (Two Tail) = 0.0124.

The development of the worksheet is now complete. For the Pine Creek upper tail hypothesis test, we reject the null hypothesis that the population proportion is 0.20 or less because the p-value (Upper Tail) = 0.0062 is less than $\alpha = 0.05$. Indeed, with this p-value we would reject the null hypothesis for any level of significance of 0.0062 or greater.

A Template for Other Problems The worksheet in Figure 9.10 can be used as a template for hypothesis tests about a population proportion whenever $np \geq 5$ and $n(1 - p) \geq 5$. Just enter the appropriate data in column A, adjust the ranges for the formulas in cells D3 and D5, enter the appropriate response in cell D4, and enter the hypothesized value in cell D8. The standard error, the test statistic, and the three p-values will then appear. Depending on the form of the hypothesis test (lower tail, upper tail, or two-tailed), we can then choose the appropriate p-value to make the rejection decision.

Summary

The procedure used to conduct a hypothesis test about a population proportion is similar to the procedure used to conduct a hypothesis test about a population mean. Although we only illustrated how to conduct a hypothesis test about a population proportion for an upper tail test, similar procedures can be used for lower tail and two-tailed tests. Table 9.4 provides a summary of the hypothesis tests about a population proportion. We assume that $np \geq 5$ and $n(1 - p) \geq 5$; thus, the normal probability distribution can be used to approximate the sampling distribution of $\bar{p}$.

Table 9.4 Summary of Hypothesis Tests About a Population Proportion

	Lower Tail Test	Upper Tail Test	Two-Tailed Test
Hypotheses	H_0: $p \geq p_0$ H_a: $p < p_0$	H_0: $p \leq p_0$ H_a: $p > p_0$	H_0: $p = p_0$ H_a: $p \neq p_0$
Test Statistic	$z = \dfrac{\bar{p} - p_0}{\sqrt{\dfrac{p_0(1 - p_0)}{n}}}$	$z = \dfrac{\bar{p} - p_0}{\sqrt{\dfrac{p_0(1 - p_0)}{n}}}$	$z = \dfrac{\bar{p} - p_0}{\sqrt{\dfrac{p_0(1 - p_0)}{n}}}$
Rejection Rule: *p*-Value Approach	Reject H_0 if p-value $\leq \alpha$	Reject H_0 if p-value $\leq \alpha$	Reject H_0 if p-value $\leq \alpha$
Rejection Rule: Critical Value Approach	Reject H_0 if $z \leq -z_\alpha$	Reject H_0 if $z \geq z_\alpha$	Reject H_0 if $z \leq -z_{\alpha/2}$ or if $z \geq z_{\alpha/2}$

Note + Comment

When testing a hypothesis of the population proportion with a sample size that is at least 5% of the population size (that is, $n/N \geq 0.05$), the finite population correction factor should be used when calculating the standard error of the sampling distribution of $\bar{p}$, i.e., $s_{\bar{p}} = \sqrt{\frac{N-n}{N-1}}\sqrt{\frac{p_0(1-p_0)}{n}}$.

Exercises

Methods

35. Consider the following hypothesis test:

$$H_0: p = 0.20$$
$$H_a: p \neq 0.20$$

A sample of 400 provided a sample proportion $\bar{p} = 0.175$. **LO 2, 6**

a. Compute the value of the test statistic.
b. What is the p-value?
c. At $\alpha = 0.05$, what is your conclusion?
d. What is the rejection rule using the critical value? What is your conclusion?

36. Consider the following hypothesis test:

$$H_0: p \geq 0.75$$
$$H_a: p < 0.75$$

A sample of 300 items was selected. Compute the p-value and state your conclusion for each of the following sample results. Use $\alpha = 0.05$. **LO 2, 6**

a. $\bar{p} = 0.68$
b. $\bar{p} = 0.72$
c. $\bar{p} = 0.70$
d. $\bar{p} = 0.77$

Applications

37. **Union Membership.** The U.S. Bureau of Labor Statistics reports that 10.2% of U.S. workers belonged to unions in 2018. Suppose a sample of 400 U.S. workers is collected in 2019 to determine whether union efforts to organize have increased union membership. **LO 1, 2, 6**

a. Formulate the hypotheses that can be used to determine whether union membership increased in 2019.
b. If the sample results show that 48 of the workers belonged to unions, what is the p-value for your hypothesis test?
c. At $\alpha = 0.05$, what is your conclusion?

38. **Attitudes toward Supermarket Brands.** A study by *Consumer Reports* showed that 64% of supermarket shoppers believe supermarket brands to be as good as national name brands. To investigate whether this result applies to its own product, the manufacturer of a national name-brand ketchup asked a sample of shoppers whether they believed that supermarket ketchup was as good as the national brand ketchup. **LO 1, 2, 6**

a. Formulate the hypotheses that could be used to determine whether the percentage of supermarket shoppers who believe that the supermarket ketchup was as good as the national brand ketchup differed from 64%.
b. If a sample of 100 shoppers showed 52 stating that the supermarket brand was as good as the national brand, what is the p-value?
c. At $\alpha = 0.05$, what is your conclusion?
d. Should the national brand ketchup manufacturer be pleased with this conclusion? Explain.

DATA*file*
homestate

39. **Population Mobility.** What percentage of the population live in their state of birth? According to the U.S. Census Bureau's American Community Survey, the figure ranges from 25% in Nevada to 78.7% in Louisiana. The average percentage across all states and the District of Columbia is 57.7%. The data in the file *homestate* are consistent with the findings in the American Community Survey. The data represent a random sample of 120 Arkansas residents and for a random sample of 180 Virginia residents. **LO 1, 2, 6**
   a. Formulate hypotheses that can be used to determine whether the percentage of stay-at-home residents in the two states differs from the overall average of 57.7%.
   b. Estimate the proportion of stay-at-home residents in Arkansas. Does this proportion differ significantly from the mean proportion for all states? Use $\alpha = 0.05$.
   c. Estimate the proportion of stay-at-home residents in Virginia. Does this proportion differ significantly from the mean proportion for all states? Use $\alpha = 0.05$.
   d. Would you expect the proportion of stay-at-home residents to be higher in Virginia than in Arkansas? Support your conclusion with the results obtained in parts (b) and (c).
40. **Holiday Gifts from Employers.** Last year, 46% of business owners gave a holiday gift to their employees. A survey of business owners conducted this year indicated that 35% plan to provide a holiday gift to their employees. Suppose the survey results are based on a sample of 60 business owners. **LO 1, 2, 6**
   a. How many business owners in the survey plan to provide a holiday gift to their employees this year?
   b. Suppose the business owners in the sample do as they plan. Compute the p-value for a hypothesis test that can be used to determine whether the proportion of business owners providing holiday gifts has decreased from last year.
   c. Using a 0.05 level of significance, would you conclude that the proportion of business owners providing gifts has decreased? What is the smallest level of significance for which you could draw such a conclusion?
41. **Adequate Preparation for Retirement.** In 2018, RAND Corporation researchers found that 71% of all individuals ages 66 to 69 are adequately prepared financially for retirement. Many financial planners have expressed concern that a smaller percentage of those in this age group who did not complete high school are adequately prepared financially for retirement. **LO 1, 2, 6**
   a. Develop appropriate hypotheses such that rejection of H_0 will support the conclusion that the proportion of those who are adequately prepared financially for retirement is smaller for people in the 66–69 age group who did not complete high school than it is for the population of the 66–69 age group.
   b. In a random sample of 300 people from the 66–69 age group who did not complete high school, 165 are prepared financially for retirement. What is the p-value for your hypothesis test?
   c. At $\alpha = 0.01$, what is your conclusion?
42. **Returned Merchandise.** According to the University of Nevada Center for Logistics Management, 6% of all merchandise sold in the United States gets returned. A Houston department store sampled 80 items sold in January and found that 12 of the items were returned. **LO 1, 2, 6**
   a. Construct a point estimate of the proportion of items returned for the population of sales transactions at the Houston store.
   b. Construct a 95% confidence interval for the proportion of returns at the Houston store.
   c. Is the proportion of returns at the Houston store significantly different from the returns for the nation as a whole? Provide statistical support for your answer.

DATA*file*
eagle

43. **Coupon Usage.** Eagle Outfitters is a chain of stores specializing in outdoor apparel and camping gear. It is considering a promotion that involves mailing discount coupons to all its credit card customers. This promotion will be considered a success if more

than 10% of those receiving the coupons use them. Before going national with the promotion, coupons were sent to a sample of 100 credit card customers. **LO 1, 2, 6**

a. Develop hypotheses that can be used to test whether the population proportion of those who will use the coupons is sufficient to go national.
b. The file *eagle* contains the sample data. Develop a point estimate of the population proportion.
c. Use $\alpha = 0.05$ to conduct your hypothesis test. Should Eagle go national with the promotion?

DATA*file*
lawsuit

44. **Malpractice Suits.** One of the reasons healthcare costs have been rising rapidly in recent years is the increasing cost of malpractice insurance for physicians. Also, fear of being sued causes doctors to run more precautionary tests (possibly unnecessary) just to make sure they are not guilty of missing something. These precautionary tests also add to healthcare costs. Data in the file *lawsuit* are consistent with findings in a *Reader's Digest* article and can be used to estimate the proportion of physicians over the age of 55 who have been sued at least once. **LO 1, 2, 6**
    a. Formulate hypotheses that can be used to see if these data can support a finding that more than half of physicians over the age of 55 have been sued at least once.
    b. Use Excel and the file *lawsuit* to compute the sample proportion of physicians over the age of 55 who have been sued at least once. What is the p-value for your hypothesis test?
    c. At $\alpha = 0.01$, what is your conclusion?
45. **Bullish, Neutral, or Bearish.** The American Association of Individual Investors (AAII) conducts a weekly survey of its members to measure the percent who are bullish, bearish, and neutral on the stock market for the next six months. For the week ending March 27, 2019, the survey results showed 33.2% bullish, 39.6% neutral, and 27.2% bearish. Assume these results are based on a sample of 300 AAII members. **LO 1, 2, 5**
    a. Over the long term, the proportion of bullish AAII members is 0.385. Conduct a hypothesis test at the 5% level of significance to see if the current sample results show that bullish sentiment differs from its long-term average of 0.385. What are your findings?
    b. Over the long term, the proportion of bearish AAII members is 0.31. Conduct a hypothesis test at the 1% level of significance to see if the current sample results show that bearish sentiment is above its long-term average of 0.31. What are your findings?
    c. Would you feel comfortable extending these results to all investors? Why or why not?

9.6 Practical Advice: Big Data and Hypothesis Testing

We have seen that interval estimates of the population mean μ and the population proportion p narrow as the sample size increases. This occurs because the standard error of the associated sampling distributions decrease as the sample size increases. Now consider the relationship between interval estimation and hypothesis testing that we discussed earlier in this chapter. If we construct a $100(1 - \alpha)\%$ interval estimate for the population mean, we reject H_0: $\mu = \mu_0$ if the $100(1 - \alpha)\%$ interval estimate does not contain μ_0. Thus, for a given level of confidence, as the sample size increases we will reject H_0: $\mu = \mu_0$ for increasingly smaller differences between the sample mean $\bar{x}$ and the hypothesized population mean μ_0. We can see that when the sample size n is very large, almost any difference between the sample mean $\bar{x}$ and the hypothesized population mean μ_0 results in rejection of the null hypothesis.

Big Data, Hypothesis Testing, and p-Values

In this section, we will elaborate how big data affects hypothesis testing and the magnitude of p-values. Specifically, we will examine how rapidly the p-value associated with a given difference between a point estimate and a hypothesized value of a parameter decreases as the sample size increases.

Table 9.5 Values of the Test Statistic t and the p-Values for the Test of the Null Hypothesis H_0: $\mu \leq 84$ and Sample Mean $\bar{x} = 84.1$ Seconds for Various Sample Sizes

Sample Size n	t	p-Value
10	0.01581	0.49386
100	0.05000	0.48011
1,000	0.15811	0.43720
10,000	0.50000	0.30854
100,000	1.58114	0.05692
1,000,000	5.00000	2.87E-07
10,000,000	15.81139	1.30E-56
100,000,000	50.00000	0.00E+00
1,000,000,000	158.11388	0.00E+00

Let us consider the online news service PenningtonDailyTimes.com (PDT). PDT's primary source of revenue is the sale of advertising, and prospective advertisers are willing to pay a premium to advertise on websites that have long visit times. To promote its news service, PDT's management wants to promise potential advertisers that the mean time spent by customers when they visit PenningtonDailyTimes.com is greater than last year, that is, more than 84 seconds. PDT therefore decides to collect a sample tracking the amount of time spent by individual customers when they visit PDT's website in order to test its null hypothesis H_0: $\mu \leq 84$.

For a sample mean of 84.1 seconds and a sample standard deviation of $s = 20$ seconds, Table 9.5 provides the values of the test statistic t and the p-values for the test of the null hypothesis H_0: $\mu \leq 84$. The p-value for this hypothesis test is essentially 0 for all samples in Table 9.5 with at least $n = 1{,}000{,}000$.

PDT's management also wants to promise potential advertisers that the proportion of its website visitors who click on an ad this year exceeds the proportion of its website visitors who clicked on an ad last year, which was 0.50. PDT collects information from its sample on whether the visitor to its website clicked on any of the ads featured on the website, and it wants to use these data to test its null hypothesis H_0: $p \leq 0.50$.

For a sample proportion of 0.51, Table 9.6 provides the values of the test statistic z and the p-values for the test of the null hypothesis H_0: $p \leq 0.5$ p-value for this hypothesis test is essentially 0 for all samples in Table 9.6 with at least $n = 100{,}000$.

We see in Tables 9.5 and 9.6 that the p-value associated with a given difference between a point estimate and a hypothesized value of a parameter decreases as the sample size increases.

Table 9.6 Values of the Test Statistic z and the p-Values for the Test of the Null Hypothesis H_0: $p \leq 0.50$ and Sample Proportion $\bar{p} = 0.51$ for Various Sample Sizes

Sample Size n	z	p-Value
10	0.06325	0.47479
100	0.20000	0.42074
1,000	0.63246	0.26354
10,000	2.00000	0.02275
100,000	6.32456	1.27E-10
1,000,000	20.00000	0.00E+00
10,000,000	63.24555	0.00E+00
100,000,000	200.00000	0.00E+00
1,000,000,000	632.45553	0.00E+00

As a result, if the sample mean time spent by customers when they visit PDT's website is 84.1 seconds, PDT's null hypothesis H_0: $\mu \leq 84$ is not rejected at $\alpha = 0.01$ for samples with $n \leq 100{,}000$, and is rejected at $\alpha = 0.01$ for samples with $n \geq 1{,}000{,}000$. Similarly, if the sample proportion of visitors to its website clicked on an ad featured on the website is 0.51, PDT's null hypothesis H_0: $p \leq 0.50$ is not rejected at $\alpha = 0.01$ for samples with $n \leq 10{,}000$, and is rejected at $\alpha = 0.01$ for samples with $n \geq 100{,}000$. In both instances, as the sample size becomes extremely large the p-value associated with the given difference between a point estimate and the hypothesized value of the parameter becomes extremely small.

Implications of Big Data in Hypothesis Testing

Suppose PDT collects a sample of 1,000,000 visitors to its website and uses these data to test its null hypotheses H_0: $\mu \leq 84$ and H_0: $p \leq 0.50$ at the 0.05 level of significance. The sample mean is 84.1 and the sample proportion is 0.51, so the null hypothesis is rejected in both tests as Tables 9.5 and 9.6 show. As a result, PDT can promise potential advertisers that the mean time spent by individual customers who visit PDT's website exceeds 84 seconds and the proportion individual visitors to of its website who click on an ad exceeds 0.50. These results suggest that for each of these hypothesis tests, the difference between the point estimate and the hypothesized value of the parameter being tested is not likely solely a consequence of sampling error. However, the results of any hypothesis test, no matter the sample size, are only reliable if the sample is relatively free of nonsampling error. If nonsampling error is introduced in the data collection process, the likelihood of making a Type I or Type II error may be higher than if the sample data are free of nonsampling error. Therefore, when testing a hypothesis, it is always important to think carefully about whether a random sample of the population of interest has been taken.

If PDT determines that it has introduced little or no nonsampling error into its sample data, the only remaining plausible explanation for these results is that these null hypotheses are false. At this point, PDT and the companies that advertise on PenningtonDailyTimes.com should also consider whether these statistically significant differences between the point estimates and the hypothesized values of the parameters being tested are of **practical significance**. Although a 0.1 second increase in the mean time spent by customers when they visit PDT's website is statistically significant, it may not be meaningful to companies that might advertise on PenningtonDailyTimes.com. Similarly, although an increase of 0.01 in the proportion of visitors to its website that click on an ad is statistically significant, it may not be meaningful to companies that might advertise on PenningtonDailyTimes.com. Determining whether these statistically significant differences have meaningful implications for ensuing business decisions of PDT and its advertisers.

Ultimately, no business decision should be based solely on statistical inference. Practical significance should always be considered in conjunction with statistical significance. This is particularly important when the hypothesis test is based on an extremely large sample because even an extremely small difference between the point estimate and the hypothesized value of the parameter being tested will be statistically significant. When done properly, statistical inference provides evidence that should be considered in combination with information collected from other sources to make the most informed decision possible.

Notes + Comments

1. Nonsampling error can occur when either a probability sampling technique or a nonprobability sampling technique is used. However, nonprobability sampling techniques such as convenience sampling and judgment sampling often introduce nonsampling error into sample data because of the manner in which sample data are collected. Therefore, probability sampling techniques are preferred over nonprobability sampling techniques.
2. When taking an extremely large sample, it is conceivable that the sample size is at least 5% of the population size; that is, $n/N \geq 0.05$. Under these conditions, it is necessary to use the finite population correction factor when calculating the standard error of the sampling distribution to be used in confidence intervals and hypothesis testing.

Exercises

Applications

DATA*file*
fedemail

46. **Government Use of E-mail.** The Federal Government wants to determine whether the mean number of business e-mails sent and received per business day by its employees differs from the mean number of e-mails sent and received per day by corporate employees, which is 101.5. Suppose the department electronically collects information on the number of business e-mails sent and received on a randomly selected business day over the past year from each of 10,163 randomly selected federal employees. The results are provided in the file *fedemail*. Test the department's hypothesis at $\alpha = 0.01$. Discuss the practical significance of the results. **LO 1, 2, 5, 9**

DATA*file*
socialnetwork

47. **CEOs and Social Networks.** CEOs who belong to a popular business-oriented social networking service have an average of 930 connections. Do other members have fewer connections than CEOs? The number of connections for a random sample of 7,515 members who are not CEOs is provided in the file *socialnetwork*. Using this sample, test the hypothesis that other members have fewer connections than CEOs at $\alpha = 0.01$. Discuss the practical significance of the results. **LO 1, 2, 5, 9**

48. **French Fry Purchases.** The American Potato Growers Association (APGA) would like to test the claim that the proportion of fast-food orders this year that includes French fries exceeds the proportion of fast-food orders that included French fries last year. Suppose that a random sample of 49,581 electronic receipts for fast-food orders placed this year shows that 31,038 included French fries. Assuming that the proportion of fast-food orders that included French fries last year is 0.62, use this information to test APGA's claim at $\alpha = 0.05$. Discuss the practical significance of the results. **LO 1, 2, 6, 9**

49. **GPS Usage in Canada.** According to CNN, 55% of all U.S. smartphone users have used their GPS capability to get directions. Suppose a provider of wireless telephone service in Canada wants to know if GPS usage by its customers differs from U.S. smartphone users. The company collects usage records for this year for a random sample of 547,192 of its customers and determines that 302,050 of these customers have used their telephone's GPS capability this year. Use this information to test the Canadian company's claim at $\alpha = 0.01$. Discuss the practical significance of the results. **LO 1, 2, 6, 9**

Summary

Hypothesis testing is a statistical procedure that uses sample data to determine whether a statement about the value of a population parameter should or should not be rejected. The hypotheses are two competing statements about a population parameter. One statement is called the null hypothesis (H_0), and the other statement is called the alternative hypothesis (H_a). In Section 9.1, we provided guidelines for developing hypotheses for situations frequently encountered in practice.

Whenever historical data or other information provide a basis for assuming that the population standard deviation is known, the hypothesis testing procedure for the population mean is based on the standard normal distribution. Whenever σ is unknown, the sample standard deviation s is used to estimate σ and the hypothesis testing procedure is based on the t distribution. In both cases, the quality of results depends on both the form of the population distribution and the sample size. If the population has a normal distribution, both hypothesis testing procedures are applicable, even with small sample sizes. If the population is not normally distributed, larger sample sizes are needed. General guidelines about the sample size were provided in Sections 9.3 and 9.4. In the case of hypothesis tests about a population proportion, the hypothesis testing procedure uses a test statistic based on the standard normal distribution.

In all cases, the value of the test statistic can be used to compute a p-value for the test. A p-value is a probability used to determine whether the null hypothesis should be rejected. If the p-value is less than or equal to the level of significance α, the null hypothesis can be rejected.

Hypothesis testing conclusions can also be made by comparing the value of the test statistic to a critical value. For lower tail tests, the null hypothesis is rejected if the value of the test statistic is less than or equal to the critical value. For upper tail tests, the null hypothesis is rejected if the value of the test statistic is greater than or equal to the critical value. Two-tailed tests consist of two critical values: one in the lower tail of the sampling distribution and one in the upper tail. In this case, the null hypothesis is rejected if the value of the test statistic is less than or equal to the critical value in the lower tail or greater than or equal to the critical value in the upper tail. Finally, we discussed the ramifications of extremely large samples on hypothesis tests of the mean and proportion.

Glossary

Alternative hypothesis The hypothesis concluded to be true if the null hypothesis is rejected.
Critical value A value that is compared with the test statistic to determine whether H_0 should be rejected.
Level of significance The probability of making a Type I error when the null hypothesis is true as an equality.
Minimum significant difference The smallest difference between a point estimate and a hypothesized value of a parameter that will result in rejection of the null hypothesis for a given level of significance α.
Null hypothesis The hypothesis tentatively assumed true in the hypothesis testing procedure.
One-tailed test A hypothesis test in which rejection of the null hypothesis occurs for values of the test statistic in one tail of its sampling distribution.
Practical significance The usefulness or meaningfulness to a decision maker of the difference between a point estimate and the hypothesized value of a parameter.
***p*-value** A probability that provides a measure of the evidence against the null hypothesis provided by the sample. Smaller *p*-values indicate more evidence against H_0. For a lower tail test, the *p*-value is the probability of obtaining a value for the test statistic as small as or smaller than that provided by the sample. For an upper tail test, the *p*-value is the probability of obtaining a value for the test statistic as large as or larger than that provided by the sample. For a two-tailed test, the *p*-value is the probability of obtaining a value for the test statistic at least as unlikely as or more unlikely than that provided by the sample.
Test statistic A statistic whose value helps determine whether a null hypothesis should be rejected.
Two-tailed test A hypothesis test in which rejection of the null hypothesis occurs for values of the test statistic in either tail of its sampling distribution.
Type I error The error of rejecting H_0 when it is true.
Type II error The error of accepting H_0 when it is false.

Key Formulas

Test Statistic for Hypothesis Tests About a Population Mean: σ Known

$$z = \frac{\bar{x} - \mu_0}{\sigma/\sqrt{n}} \tag{9.1}$$

Test Statistic for Hypothesis Tests About a Population Mean: σ Unknown

$$t = \frac{\bar{x} - \mu_0}{s/\sqrt{n}} \tag{9.2}$$

Test Statistic for Hypothesis Tests About a Population Proportion

$$z = \frac{\bar{p} - p_0}{\sqrt{\dfrac{p_0(1 - p_0)}{n}}} \tag{9.4}$$

Supplementary Exercises

50. **Production Line Fill Weights.** A production line operates with a mean filling weight of 16 ounces per container. Overfilling or underfilling presents a serious problem and when detected requires the operator to shut down the production line to readjust the filling mechanism. From past data, a population standard deviation $\sigma = 0.8$ ounces is assumed. A quality control inspector selects a sample of 30 items every hour and at that time makes the decision of whether to shut down the line for readjustment. The level of significance is $\alpha = 0.05$. **LO 1, 2, 4**
    a. State the hypothesis test for this quality control application.
    b. If a sample mean of $\bar{x} = 16.32$ ounces were found, what is the p-value? What action would you recommend?
    c. If a sample mean of $\bar{x} = 15.82$ ounces were found, what is the p-value? What action would you recommend?
    d. Use the critical value approach. What is the rejection rule for the preceding hypothesis testing procedure? Repeat parts (b) and (c). Do you reach the same conclusion?

51. **Scholarship Examination Scores.** The historical mean of scholarship examination scores for freshman applications at Western University is 900. A historical population standard deviation $\sigma = 180$ is assumed known. Each year, the assistant dean uses a sample of applications to determine whether the mean examination score for the new freshman applications has changed. **LO 1, 2, 4**
    a. State the hypotheses.
    b. What is the 95% confidence interval estimate of the population mean examination score if a sample of 200 applications provided a sample mean of $\bar{x} = 935$?
    c. Use the confidence interval to conduct a hypothesis test. Using $\alpha = 0.05$, what is your conclusion?
    d. What is the p-value?

52. **Exposure to Background Television.** CNN reports that young children in the United States are exposed to an average of 4 hours of background television per day. Having the television on in the background while children are doing other activities may have adverse consequences on a child's well-being. You have a research hypothesis that children from low-income families are exposed to more than 4 hours of daily background television. In order to test this hypothesis, you have collected a random sample of 60 children from low-income families and found that these children were exposed to a sample mean of 4.5 hours of daily background television. **LO 1, 2, 4**
    a. Develop hypotheses that can be used to test your research hypothesis.
    b. Based on a previous study, you are willing to assume that the population standard deviation is $\sigma = 1.5$ hours. What is the p-value based on your sample of 60 children from low-income families?
    c. Use $\alpha = 0.01$ as the level of significance. What is your conclusion?

53. **Starting Salaries for Business Graduates.** ZipRecruiter reports that the average annual starting salary for graduates with bachelor's degrees in business in the United States was \$50,070 in 2022. The results for a sample of 100 business majors receiving a bachelor's degree who took jobs in Connecticut showed a mean starting salary of \$51,276 with a sample standard deviation of \$5,200 in 2022. Conduct a hypothesis test to determine whether the mean starting salary for business majors who took jobs in Connecticut is greater than the mean starting salary nationwide in 2022. Use $\alpha = 0.01$ as the level of significance. **LO 1, 2, 5**

DATA*file*
britainmarriages

54. **Age at British First Marriages.** According to the UK Parliament, the average age of the British who married for the first time in 2021 was 31 years. A news reporter noted that this represents a continuation of the trend of waiting until a later age to wed. A new sample of 47 British people who were wed for the first time this year provided their ages at the time of marriage. These data are contained in the file *britainmarriages*. Do these

data indicate that the average age of the British at the time of marriage exceeds the average age in 2021? Test this hypothesis at $\alpha = 0.05$. What is your conclusion? **LO 1, 2, 5**

DATA*file*
weeklyhsgradpay

55. **Wages of Workers Without High School Diploma.** SmartAsset reports that the average weekly earnings for workers who have not received a high school diploma is \$493 in 2018. Suppose you would like to determine if the average weekly earnings for workers who have received a high school diploma is significantly greater than average weekly earnings for workers who have not received a high school diploma. Data providing the weekly pay for a sample of 50 workers who have received a high school diploma are available in the file *weeklyhsgradpay*. These data are consistent with the findings reported by SmartAsset. **LO 1, 2, 5**
    a. State the hypotheses that should be used to test whether the mean weekly pay for workers who have received a high school diploma is significantly greater than the mean weekly pay for workers who have not received a high school diploma.
    b. Use the data in the file *weeklyhsgradpay* to compute the sample mean, the test statistic, and the p-value.
    c. Use $\alpha = 0.05$. What is your conclusion? Is this result surprising? Why did these data likely lead to this conclusion?
56. **Residential Property Values.** The chamber of commerce of a Florida Gulf Coast community advertises that area residential property is available at a mean cost of \$125,000 or less per lot. Suppose a sample of 32 properties provided a sample mean of \$130,000 per lot and a sample standard deviation of \$12,500. Use a 0.05 level of significance to test the validity of the advertising claim. **LO 1, 2, 5**
57. **Length of Time to Sell a Home.** According to the National Association of Realtors, it took an average of three weeks to sell a home in 2017. Data for the sale of 40 randomly selected homes sold in Greene County, Ohio, in 2017 showed a sample mean of 3.6 weeks with a sample standard deviation of 2 weeks. Conduct a hypothesis test to determine whether the number of weeks until a house sold in Greene County differed from the national average in 2017. Use $\alpha = 0.05$ for the level of significance, and state your conclusion. **LO 1, 2, 5**
58. **Sleeping on Flights.** According to Expedia, 52% of Americans report that they generally can sleep during flights. Are people who fly frequently more likely to be able to sleep during flights? Suppose we have a random sample of 510 individuals who flew at least 25,000 miles last year and 285 indicated that they were able to sleep during flights. **LO 1, 2, 6**
    a. Conduct a hypothesis test to determine whether the results justify concluding that people who fly frequently are more likely to be able to sleep during flights. Use $\alpha = 0.05$.
    b. Conduct the same hypothesis test you performed in part (a) at $\alpha = 0.01$. What is your conclusion?
59. **Using Laptops on Flights.** An airline promotion to business travelers is based on the assumption that two-thirds of business travelers use a laptop computer on overnight business trips. **LO 1, 2, 6**
    a. State the hypotheses that can be used to test the assumption.
    b. What is the sample proportion from an American Express sponsored survey that found 355 of 546 business travelers use a laptop computer on overnight business trips?
    c. What is the p-value?
    d. Use $\alpha = 0.05$. What is your conclusion?
60. **Millennial Dependency on Parents.** Members of the millennial generation continue to be dependent on their parents (either living with or otherwise receiving support from parents) into early adulthood. A family research organization has claimed that, in past generations, no more than 30% of individuals aged 18 to 32 continued to be dependent on their parents. Suppose that a sample of 400 individuals aged 18 to 32 showed that 136 of them continue to be dependent on their parents. **LO 1, 2, 6**
    a. Develop hypotheses for a test to determine whether the proportion of millennials continuing to be dependent on their parents is higher than for past generations.

b. What is your point estimate of the proportion of millennials that are continuing to be dependent on their parents?
c. What is the p-value provided by the sample data?
d. What is your hypothesis testing conclusion? Use $\alpha = 0.05$ as the level of significance.

61. **Using Social Media in a Job Search.** According to Inc.com, 79% of job seekers used social media in their job search in 2018. Many believe this number is inflated by the proportion of 22- to 30-year-old job seekers who use social media in their job search. A survey of 22- to 30-year-old job seekers showed that 310 of the 370 respondents use social media in their job search. In addition, 275 of the 370 respondents indicated they have electronically submitted a resume to an employer. **LO 1, 2, 6**
    a. Conduct a hypothesis test to determine if the results of the survey justify concluding the proportion of 22- to 30-year-old job seekers who use social media in their job search exceeds the proportion of the population that use social media in their job search. Use $\alpha = 0.05$.
    b. Conduct a hypothesis test to determine if the results of the survey justify concluding that more than 70% of 22- to 30-year-old job seekers have electronically submitted a resume to an employer. Using $\alpha = 0.05$, what is your conclusion?

62. **Hotel Availability over Holiday Weekend.** A radio station in Myrtle Beach announced that at least 90% of the hotels and motels would be full for the Memorial Day weekend. The station advised listeners to make reservations in advance if they planned to be in the resort over the weekend. On Saturday night a sample of 58 hotels and motels showed 49 with a no-vacancy sign and 9 with vacancies. What is your reaction to the radio station's claim after seeing the sample evidence? Use $\alpha = 0.05$ in making the statistical test. What is the p-value? **LO 1, 2, 6**

63. **Vegetarianism in the United States.** Vegetarians are much less common in the United States than in the rest of the world. In a 2018 survey of 11,000 people in the United States, VeganBits found 55 who are vegetarians. **LO 1, 2, 6**
    a. Develop a point estimate of the proportion of people in the United States who are vegetarians.
    b. Set up a hypothesis test so that the rejection of H_0 will allow you to conclude that the proportion of people in the United States who are vegetarians exceeds 0.004.
    c. Conduct your hypothesis test using $\alpha = 0.05$. What is your conclusion?

DATA*file*
channelsurfing

64. **Time Spent Channel Surfing.** According to an article published by *The US Sun* in 2021, the average person spends 24.4 minutes per day channel surfing. The file *channelsurfing* provides the number of minutes per day looking for something to watch on television for a random sample 8,783 people in December. Do these data support the conclusion that people spend less time channel surfing during December than they do throughout the year? Test this hypothesis at $\alpha = 0.01$. Discuss the practical significance of the results. **LO 1, 2, 5, 9**

65. **Potato Chip Quality Control.** NDC Technology's MM710e On-Line Snacks Gauge rapidly measures surface brownness of potato chips just before packaging. This allows for a high degree of control over this important characteristic of a potato chip; chips that are too brown are overfried, and chips that are not sufficiently brown are underfried. A potato chip manufacturer is now using the MM710e to assess the quality of the chips it produces; one of this manufacturer's goals is to produce less than 1 overfried chip in every 1,000 chips. In a recent random sample of 111,667 chips taken from the production lines of the manufacturer's production facilities nationwide, the MM710e found 98 overfried chips. Conduct a hypothesis test to determine if the sample data indicates the manufacturer is meeting its goal for overfried chips at $\alpha = 0.05$. **LO 1, 2, 6**

DATA*file*
tsawaittimes

66. **TSA Security Line Wait Times.** According to the U.S. Transportation Security Administration (TSA), 2% of the 771,556,886 travelers who utilized 440 federalized airports in 2017 waited more than 20 minutes in the TSA security line. The file *tsawaittimes* contains waiting times in TSA security lines at a major U.S. airport for

a recent random sample 10,531 travelers. Use these data to test the hypothesis that the proportion of travelers waiting more than 20 minutes in TSA security lines at this airport is the same as the national proportion at $\alpha = 0.05$. **LO 1, 2, 6**

Case Problem 1: Quality Associates, Inc.

Quality Associates, Inc., a consulting firm, advises its clients about sampling and statistical procedures that can be used to control their manufacturing processes. In one particular application, a client gave Quality Associates a sample of 800 observations taken during a time in which that client's process was operating satisfactorily. The sample standard deviation for these data was 0.21; hence, with so much data, the population standard deviation was assumed to be 0.21. Quality Associates then suggested that random samples of size 30 be taken periodically to monitor the process on an ongoing basis. By analyzing the new samples, the client could quickly learn whether the process was operating satisfactorily. When the process was not operating satisfactorily, corrective action could be taken to eliminate the problem. The design specification indicated the mean for the process should be 12. The hypothesis test suggested by Quality Associates follows.

$$H_0: \mu = 12$$
$$H_a: \mu \neq 12$$

Corrective action will be taken any time H_0 is rejected.

The samples on the following page were collected at hourly intervals during the first day of operation of the new statistical process control procedure. These data are available in the file *quality*. **LO 1, 2, 3, 4**

Managerial Report

1. Conduct a hypothesis test for each sample at the 0.01 level of significance and determine what action, if any, should be taken. Provide the test statistic and p-value for each test.
2. Compute the standard deviation for each of the four samples. Does the assumption of 0.21 for the population standard deviation appear reasonable?
3. Compute limits for the sample mean $\bar{x}$ around $\mu = 12$ such that, as long as a new sample mean is within those limits, the process will be considered to be operating satisfactorily. If $\bar{x}$ exceeds the upper limit or if $\bar{x}$ is below the lower limit, corrective action will be taken. These limits are referred to as upper and lower control limits for quality control purposes.
4. Discuss the implications of changing the level of significance to a larger value. What mistake or error could increase if the level of significance is increased?

DATA*file*
quality

Sample 1	Sample 2	Sample 3	Sample 4
11.55	11.62	11.91	12.02
11.62	11.69	11.36	12.02
11.52	11.59	11.75	12.05
11.75	11.82	11.95	12.18
11.90	11.97	12.14	12.11
11.64	11.71	11.72	12.07
11.64	11.71	11.72	12.07
11.80	11.87	11.61	12.05
12.03	12.10	11.85	11.64
11.94	12.01	12.16	12.39
11.92	11.99	11.91	11.65
12.13	12.20	12.12	12.11

Sample 1	Sample 2	Sample 3	Sample 4
12.09	12.16	11.61	11.90
11.93	12.00	12.21	12.22
12.21	12.28	11.56	11.88
12.32	12.39	11.95	12.03
11.93	12.00	12.01	12.35
11.85	11.92	12.06	12.09
11.76	11.83	11.76	11.77
12.16	12.23	11.82	12.20
11.77	11.84	12.12	11.79
12.00	12.07	11.60	12.30
12.04	12.11	11.95	12.27
11.98	12.05	11.96	12.29
12.30	12.37	12.22	12.47
12.18	12.25	11.75	12.03
11.97	12.04	11.96	12.17
12.17	12.24	11.95	11.94
11.85	11.92	11.89	11.97
12.30	12.37	11.88	12.23
12.15	12.22	11.93	12.25

Case Problem 2: Ethical Behavior of Students at Bayview University

There is evidence that academic dishonesty (including plagiarism, cheating on exams, and unauthorized collaboration on academic projects) is widespread among students at universities. For example, researchers with The International Center for Academic Integrity (ICAI) reported in March 2023 that 60% of all undergraduate students admitted to cheating in some manner.

Cheating has been a concern of Bayview University president Dr. Bhavna Jha for several years. Some faculty members at the university share Dr. Jha's belief that cheating is more widespread at Bayview than at other universities, while other faculty members think that cheating is not a major problem at Bayview. To resolve some of these issues, Dr. Jha commissioned a study to assess the current ethical behavior of business students at Bayview. As part of this study, an anonymous exit survey was administered to a sample of 90 business students from this year's graduating class. Responses to the following questions were used to obtain data regarding three types of cheating.

During your time at Bayview, did you ever present work copied off the Internet as your own?

Yes ________ No ________

During your time at Bayview, did you ever copy answers off another student's exam?

Yes ________ No ________

During your time at Bayview, did you ever collaborate with other students on projects that were supposed to be completed individually?

Yes ________ No ________

Any student who answered Yes to one or more of these questions was considered to have been involved in some type of cheating. A portion of the data collected follows. The complete data set is in the file *bayview*. **LO 1, 2, 6**

DATA*file*
bayview

Student	Copied from Internet	Copied on Exam	Collaborated on Individual Project	In-State or Out-of-State
1	No	No	No	In-State
2	No	No	No	Out-Of-State
3	Yes	No	Yes	Out-Of-State
4	Yes	Yes	No	Out-Of-State
5	No	No	Yes	Out-Of-State
6	Yes	No	No	In-State
.	.	.	.	.
.	.	.	.	.
.	.	.	.	.
88	No	No	No	Out-Of-State
89	No	Yes	Yes	Out-Of-State
90	No	No	No	In-State

Managerial Report

Prepare a report for Dr. Jha that summarizes your assessment of the nature of cheating by students at Bayview University. Be sure to include the following items in your report.

1. Use descriptive statistics to summarize the data and comment on your findings.
2. Develop 95% confidence intervals for the proportion of all students, the proportion of in-state students, and the proportion of out-of-state students who were involved in some type of cheating.
3. Conduct a hypothesis test to determine if the proportion of students at Bayview University who were involved in some type of cheating is less than that of students at other institutions as reported by the ICAI.
4. What advice would you give to Dr. Jha based upon your analysis of the data?

Case Problem 3: New Product Development at Baxter Barnes Gelato

Baxter Barnes Gelato (BBG) manufactures and distributes 15 unique flavors of premium gelato. BBG is known by consumers for its consistent high quality and its unique flavors. Its current line of flavors includes ricotta fig, cilantro kiwi, clementine mint, gooseberry cobbler, and ghost-peppered caramel. BBG adds at most one new flavor every two years, and it only does so if consumer testing of any of the new flavors it has recently developed in its lab achieves a favorable test response. As the scheduled date on which BBG is to announce its newest flavor approaches, social media typically fills with rumors about the new flavor and consumers of premium ice cream anxiously await BBG's announcement. BBG is due to make an announcement on its newest flavor in a few months.

Through its recent introductions of new gelato flavors, BBG management has learned that a new flavor will likely fail to meet the company's sales expectations unless more than three-fourths of consumers of premium ice cream indicate they will consider purchasing the flavor after tasting a sample. This year BBG's lab has developed three new flavors: Champaign grape, basil cantaloupe, and jalapeno lime. They produce batches of each new flavor and distribute the batches around the nation for use in consumer testing.

DATA*file*
bbg

BBG is ultimately able to secure ratings for each of the three new flavors from a random sample of 21,478 consumers of premium ice cream. Each consumer in the test was provided a sample of the three new flavors of gelato. For each flavor of gelato, a test consumer was asked if they would consider purchasing the flavor. The data collected through this consumer testing is provided in the file *bbg*. **LO 1, 2, 6, 9**

Managerial Report

1. For the new gelato flavors recently created by BBG's lab, what are the point estimates for the proportion of consumers of premium ice cream who indicate they would consider purchasing the respective flavor? Explain to BBG management why these results are or are not sufficient for making their decision on whether to add any of these new flavors to their existing product line.
2. For each new flavor, conduct separate hypothesis tests at $\alpha = 0.05$ to determine whether more than three quarters of consumers of premium ice cream will consider purchasing the respective new flavor.
3. Interpret the results of your hypothesis tests in part (2) for BBG management. Which of the new flavors do the results suggest BBG management should add to its current line of flavors? How do you suggest that BBG management proceed?

Chapter 10

Inference About Means and Proportions with Two Populations

Contents

Statistics in Practice:
U.S. Food and Drug Administration

10.1 Inferences About the Difference Between Two Population Means: σ_1 and σ_2 Known
Interval Estimation of $\mu_1 - \mu_2$
Using Excel to Construct a Confidence Interval
Hypothesis Tests About $\mu_1 - \mu_2$
Using Excel to Conduct a Hypothesis Test
Practical Advice

10.2 Inferences About the Difference Between Two Population Means: σ_1 and σ_2 Unknown
Interval Estimation of $\mu_1 - \mu_2$
Using Excel to Construct a Confidence Interval
Hypothesis Tests About $\mu_1 - \mu_2$
Using Excel to Conduct a Hypothesis Test
Practical Advice

10.3 Inferences About the Difference Between Two Population Means: Matched Samples
Using Excel to Conduct a Hypothesis Test

10.4 Inferences About The Difference Between Two Population Proportions
Interval Estimation of $p_1 - p_2$
Using Excel to Construct a Confidence Interval
Hypothesis Tests About $p_1 - p_2$
Using Excel to Conduct a Hypothesis Test

Summary 503
Glossary 503
Key Formulas 503
Supplementary Exercises 505
Case Problem: Par, Inc. 508

Available in the Cengage eBook:
Appendix: Inferences About Two Populations with R

Learning Objectives

After completing this chapter, you will be able to

LO 1 Describe and explain the distribution form and parameters of the sampling distribution of the difference between the sample means of two different populations.

LO 2 Calculate and interpret the interval estimate at a given level of confidence for a difference between two population means when the standard deviations of the two populations are known.

LO 3 Conduct a hypothesis test about the difference between two population means when the standard deviations of the two populations are known.

LO 4 Calculate and interpret the interval estimate at a given level of confidence for a difference between two population means when the standard deviations of the two populations are unknown.

LO 5 Conduct a hypothesis test about the difference between two population means when the standard deviations of the two populations are unknown.

LO 6 Conduct a hypothesis test about the difference between two population means when using a matched sample design.

LO 7 Calculate and interpret the interval estimate at a given level of confidence for a difference between two population means when using a matched sample design.

LO 8 Describe and explain the distribution form and parameters of the sampling distribution of the difference between the sample proportions of two different populations.

LO 9 Calculate and interpret the interval estimate at a given level of confidence for a difference between two population proportions.

LO 10 Conduct a hypothesis test about the difference between two population proportions.

Statistics in Practice

U.S. Food and Drug Administration

Washington, D.C.

It is the responsibility of the U.S. Food and Drug Administration (FDA), through its Center for Drug Evaluation and Research (CDER), to ensure that drugs are safe and effective. But CDER does not do the actual testing of new drugs itself. It is the responsibility of the company seeking to market a new drug to test it and submit evidence that it is safe and effective. CDER statisticians and scientists then review the evidence submitted.

Companies seeking approval of a new drug conduct extensive statistical studies to support their application. The testing process in the pharmaceutical industry usually consists of three stages: (1) preclinical testing, (2) testing for long-term usage and safety, and (3) clinical efficacy testing. At each successive stage, the chance that a drug will pass the rigorous tests decreases; however, the cost of further testing increases dramatically. Industry surveys indicate that on average the research and development for one new drug costs $250 million and takes 12 years. Hence, it is important to eliminate unsuccessful new drugs in the early stages of the testing process, as well as to identify promising ones for further testing.

Statistics plays a major role in pharmaceutical research, where government regulations are stringent and rigorously enforced. In preclinical testing, a two- or three-population statistical study typically is used to determine whether a new drug should continue to be studied in the long-term usage and safety program. The populations may consist of the new drug, a control, and a standard drug. The preclinical testing process begins when a new drug is sent to the pharmacology group for evaluation of efficacy—the capacity of the drug to produce the desired effects. As part of the process, a statistician is asked to design an experiment that can be used to test the new drug. The design must specify the sample size and the statistical methods of analysis. In a two-population study, one sample is used to obtain data on the efficacy of the new drug (population 1) and a second sample is used to obtain data on the efficacy of a standard drug (population 2). Depending on the intended use, the new and standard drugs are tested in such disciplines as neurology, cardiology, and immunology. In most studies, the statistical method involves hypothesis testing for the difference between the means of the new drug population and the standard drug population. If a new drug lacks efficacy or produces undesirable effects in comparison with the standard drug, the new drug is rejected and withdrawn from further testing. Only new drugs that show promising comparisons with the standard drugs are forwarded to the long-term usage and safety testing program.

Statistical methods are used to test and develop new drugs. © Lisa S./ShutterStock.com

Further data collection and multipopulation studies are conducted in the long-term usage and safety testing program and in the clinical testing programs. The FDA requires that statistical methods be defined prior to such testing to avoid data-related biases. In addition, to avoid human biases, some of the clinical trials are double or triple blind. That is, neither the subject nor the investigator knows what drug is administered to whom. If the new drug meets all requirements in relation to the standard drug, a new drug application (NDA) is filed with the FDA. The application is rigorously scrutinized by statisticians and scientists at the agency.

In this chapter, you will learn how to construct interval estimates and make hypothesis tests about means and proportions with two populations. Techniques will be presented for analyzing independent random samples as well as matched samples.

In Chapters 8 and 9, we show how to develop interval estimates and conduct hypothesis tests for situations involving a single population mean and a single population proportion.

In this chapter, we extend the discussion of statistical inference beyond single sample analyses of a population mean or population proportion by showing how interval estimates and hypothesis tests can be developed for situations involving two populations when the difference between the two population means or the two population proportions is of prime importance. For example, we may want to develop an interval estimate of the difference between the mean starting salary for a population of males and the mean starting salary for a population of females or conduct a hypothesis test to determine whether any difference is present between the proportion of defective parts in a population of parts produced by supplier A and the proportion of defective parts in a population of parts produced by supplier B. We begin our discussion of statistical inference about two populations by showing how to develop interval estimates and conduct hypothesis tests about the difference between the means of two populations when the standard deviations of the two populations can be assumed known.

10.1 Inferences About the Difference Between Two Population Means: σ_1 and σ_2 Known

Letting μ_1 denote the mean of population 1 and μ_2 denote the mean of population 2, we will focus on inferences about the difference between the means: $\mu_1 - \mu_2$. To make an inference about this difference, we select a random sample of n_1 units from population 1 and a second random sample of n_2 units from population 2. The two samples, taken separately and independently, are referred to as **independent random samples**. In this section, we assume that information is available such that the two population standard deviations, σ_1 and σ_2, can be assumed known prior to collecting the samples. We refer to this situation as the σ_1 and σ_2 known case. In the following example, we show how to compute a margin of error and develop an interval estimate of the difference between the two population means when σ_1 and σ_2 are known.

Interval Estimation of $\mu_1 - \mu_2$

HomeStyle sells furniture at two stores in Buffalo, New York: One is in the inner city and the other is in a suburban shopping center. The regional manager noticed that products that sell well in one store do not always sell well in the other. The manager believes this situation may be attributable to differences in customer demographics at the two locations. Customers may differ in age, education, income, and so on. Suppose the manager asks us to investigate the difference between the mean ages of the customers who shop at the two stores.

Let us define population 1 as all customers who shop at the inner-city store and population 2 as all customers who shop at the suburban store.

μ_1 = mean of population 1 (i.e., the mean age of all customers who shop at the inner-city store)

μ_2 = mean of population 2 (i.e., the mean age of all customers who shop at the suburban store)

The difference between the two population means is $\mu_1 - \mu_2$.

To estimate $\mu_1 - \mu_2$, we will select a random sample of n_1 customers from population 1 and a random sample of n_2 customers from population 2. We then compute the two sample means.

$\bar{x}_1$ = sample mean age for the random sample of n_1 inner-city customers
$\bar{x}_2$ = sample mean age for the random sample of n_2 suburban customers

The point estimator of the difference between the two population means is the difference between the two sample means.

Point Estimator of the Difference Between Two Population Means

$$\bar{x}_1 - \bar{x}_2 \tag{10.1}$$

Figure 10.1 provides an overview of the process used to estimate the difference between two population means based on two independent random samples.

Figure 10.1 Estimating the Difference Between Two Population Means

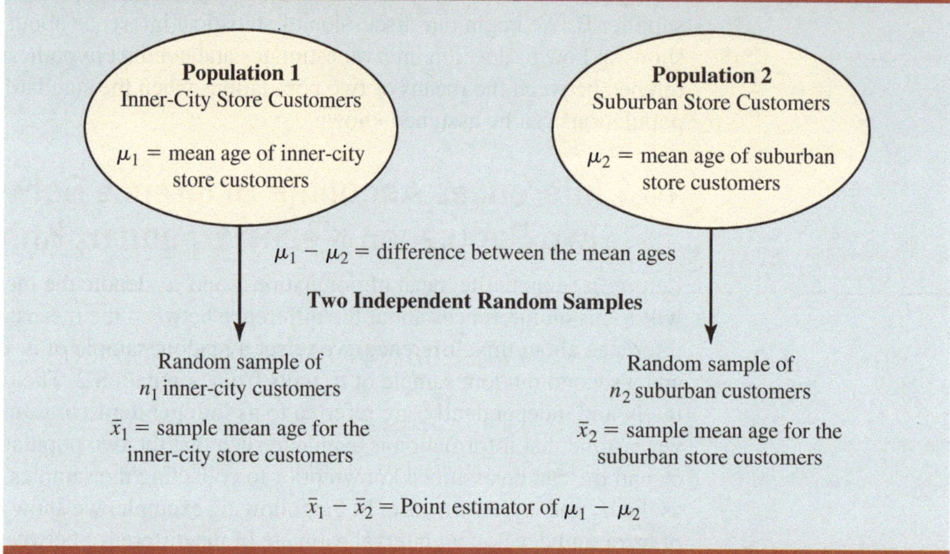

The standard error of $\bar{x}_1 - \bar{x}_2$ is the standard deviation of the sampling distribution of $\bar{x}_1 - \bar{x}_2$.

As with other point estimators, the point estimator $\bar{x}_1 - \bar{x}_2$ has a standard error that describes the variation in the sampling distribution of the estimator. With two independent random samples, the standard error of $\bar{x}_1 - \bar{x}_2$ is as follows.

Standard Error of $\bar{x}_1 - \bar{x}_2$

$$\sigma_{\bar{x}_1-\bar{x}_2} = \sqrt{\frac{\sigma_1^2}{n_1} + \frac{\sigma_2^2}{n_2}} \tag{10.2}$$

If both populations have a normal distribution, or if the sample sizes are large enough that the central limit theorem enables us to conclude that the sampling distributions of $\bar{x}_1$ and $\bar{x}_2$ can be approximated by a normal distribution, the sampling distribution of $\bar{x}_1 - \bar{x}_2$ will have a normal distribution with mean given by $\mu_1 - \mu_2$.

In general, an interval estimate is given by a point estimate ± a margin of error. In the case of estimation of the difference between two population means, an interval estimate will take the following form:

$$\bar{x}_1 - \bar{x}_2 \pm \text{Margin of error}$$

With the sampling distribution of $\bar{x}_1 - \bar{x}_2$ having a normal distribution, we can write the margin of error as follows:

The margin of error is given by multiplying the standard error by $z_{\alpha/2}$.

$$\text{Margin of error} = z_{\alpha/2}\sigma_{\bar{x}_1-\bar{x}_2} = z_{\alpha/2}\sqrt{\frac{\sigma_1^2}{n_1} + \frac{\sigma_2^2}{n_2}} \tag{10.3}$$

Thus, the interval estimate of the difference between two population means is as follows.

Interval Estimate of the Difference Between Two Population Means: σ_1 and σ_2 Known

$$\bar{x}_1 - \bar{x}_2 \pm z_{\alpha/2}\sqrt{\frac{\sigma_1^2}{n_1} + \frac{\sigma_2^2}{n_2}} \tag{10.4}$$

where $1 - \alpha$ is the confidence coefficient.

Let us return to the HomeStyle example. Based on data from previous customer demographic studies, the two population standard deviations are known with $\sigma_1 = 9$ years and $\sigma_2 = 10$ years. The data collected from the two independent random samples of HomeStyle customers provided the following results.

DATA*file*
homestyle_mod

	Inner-City Store	Suburban Store
Sample Size	$n_1 = 36$	$n_2 = 49$
Sample Mean	$\bar{x}_1 = 40$ years	$\bar{x}_2 = 35$ years

Using expression (10.1), we find that the point estimate of the difference between the mean ages of the two populations is $\bar{x}_1 - \bar{x}_2 = 40 - 35 = 5$ years. Thus, we estimate that the customers at the inner-city store have a mean age five years greater than the mean age of the suburban store customers. We can now use expression (10.4) to compute the margin of error and provide the interval estimate of $\mu_1 - \mu_2$. Using 95% confidence and $z_{\alpha/2} = z_{0.025} = 1.96$, we have

$$\bar{x}_1 - \bar{x}_2 \pm z_{\alpha/2}\sqrt{\frac{\sigma_1^2}{n_1} + \frac{\sigma_2^2}{n_2}}$$

$$40 - 35 \pm 1.96\sqrt{\frac{9^2}{36} + \frac{10^2}{49}}$$

$$5 \pm 4.06$$

Thus, the margin of error is 4.06 years and the 95% confidence interval estimate of the difference between the two population means is $5 - 4.06 = 0.94$ years to $5 + 4.06 = 9.06$ years.

Using Excel to Construct a Confidence Interval

Excel's data analysis tools do not provide a procedure for developing interval estimates involving two population means. However, we can develop an Excel worksheet that can be used as a template to construct interval estimates. We will illustrate by constructing an interval estimate of the difference between the population means in the HomeStyle Furniture Stores study. Refer to Figure 10.2 as we describe the tasks involved. The formula worksheet is in the background; the value worksheet is in the foreground.

Enter/Access Data: Open the file *homestyle_mod*. Column A contains the age data and a label for the random sample of 36 inner-city customers, and column B contains the age data and a label for the random sample of 49 suburban customers.

Enter Functions and Formulas: The descriptive statistics needed are provided in cells E5:F6. The known population standard deviations are entered into cells E8 and F8. Using the two population standard deviations and the sample sizes, the standard error of the point estimator $\bar{x}_1 - \bar{x}_2$ is computed using equation (10.2) by entering the following formula into cell E9:

=SQRT(E8^2/E5+F8^2/F5)

Cells E11:E14 are used to compute the appropriate z value and the margin of error. By entering *0.95* into cell E12 for the value of the confidence coefficient, the corresponding level of significance ($\alpha = 1 -$ confidence coefficient) is computed in cell E12. In cell E13, we used the NORM.S.INV function to compute the z value needed for the interval estimate. The margin of error is computed in cell E14 by multiplying the z value by the standard error.

In cell E16, the difference in the sample means is used to compute the point estimate of the difference in the two population means. The lower limit of the confidence interval is computed in cell E17 (0.94) and the upper limit is computed in cell E18 (9.06); thus, the 95% confidence interval estimate of the difference in the two population means is 0.94 to 9.06.

Figure 10.2 Excel Worksheet: Constructing a 95% Confidence Interval for Homestyle Furniture Stores

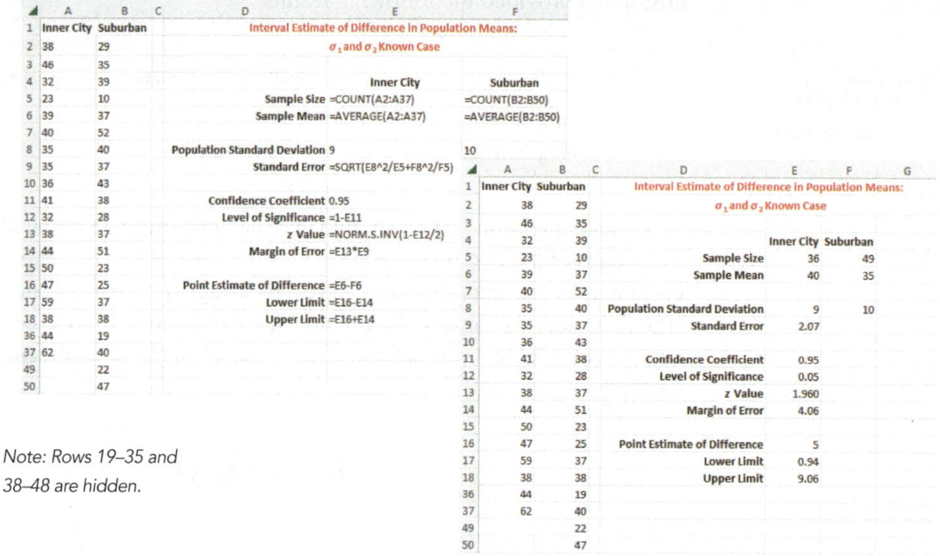

	A	B	C	D	E	F
1	Inner City	Suburban		Interval Estimate of Difference in Population Means:		
2	38	29		σ_1 and σ_2 Known Case		
3	46	35				
4	32	39			Inner City	Suburban
5	23	10		Sample Size	=COUNT(A2:A37)	=COUNT(B2:B50)
6	39	37		Sample Mean	=AVERAGE(A2:A37)	=AVERAGE(B2:B50)
7	40	52				
8	35	40		Population Standard Deviation	9	10
9	35	37		Standard Error	=SQRT(E8^2/E5+F8^2/F5)	
10	36	43				
11	41	38		Confidence Coefficient	0.95	
12	32	28		Level of Significance	=1-E11	
13	38	37		z Value	=NORM.S.INV(1-E12/2)	
14	44	51		Margin of Error	=E13*E9	
15	50	23				
16	47	25		Point Estimate of Difference	=E6-F6	
17	59	37		Lower Limit	=E16-E14	
18	38	38		Upper Limit	=E16+E14	
36	44	19				
37	62	40				
49		22				
50		47				

	A	B	C	D	E	F	G
1	Inner City	Suburban		Interval Estimate of Difference in Population Means:			
2	38	29		σ_1 and σ_2 Known Case			
3	46	35					
4	32	39			Inner City	Suburban	
5	23	10		Sample Size	36	49	
6	39	37		Sample Mean	40	35	
7	40	52					
8	35	40		Population Standard Deviation	9	10	
9	35	37		Standard Error	2.07		
10	36	43					
11	41	38		Confidence Coefficient	0.95		
12	32	28		Level of Significance	0.05		
13	38	37		z Value	1.960		
14	44	51		Margin of Error	4.06		
15	50	23					
16	47	25		Point Estimate of Difference	5		
17	59	37		Lower Limit	0.94		
18	38	38		Upper Limit	9.06		
36	44	19					
37	62	40					
49		22					
50		47					

Note: Rows 19–35 and 38–48 are hidden.

A Template for Other Problems This worksheet can be used as a template for developing interval estimates of the difference in population means when the population standard deviations are assumed known. For another problem of this type, we must first enter the new problem data in columns A and B. The data ranges in cells E5:F6 must be modified in order to compute the sample means and sample sizes for the new data. Also, the assumed known population standard deviations must be entered into cells E8 and F8. After doing so, the point estimate and a 95% confidence interval will be displayed in cells E16:E18. If a confidence interval with a different confidence coefficient is desired, we simply change the value in cell E11.

We can further simplify the use of Figure 10.2 as a template for other problems by eliminating the need to enter new data ranges in cells E5:F6. We rewrite the cell formulas as follows:

$$\text{Cell E5: } = COUNT(A{:}A)$$
$$\text{Cell F5: } = COUNT(B{:}B)$$
$$\text{Cell E6: } = AVERAGE(A{:}A)$$
$$\text{Cell F6: } = AVERAGE(B{:}B)$$

The file homestyle_mod *includes a worksheet titled Template that uses the A:A and B:B methods for entering the data ranges.*

Using the A:A method of specifying data ranges in cells E5 and E6, Excel's COUNT function will count the number of numerical values in column A and Excel's AVERAGE function will compute the average of the numerical values in column A. Similarly, using the B:B method of specifying data ranges in cells F5 and F6, Excel's COUNT function will count the number of numerical values in column B and Excel's AVERAGE function will compute the average of the numerical values in column B. Thus, to solve a new problem, it is only necessary to enter the new data into columns A and B and enter the known population standard deviations in cells E8 and F8.

This worksheet can also be used as a template for text exercises in which the sample sizes, sample means, and population standard deviations are given. In this type of situation, no change in the data is necessary. We simply replace the values in cells E5:F6 and E8:F8 with the given values of the sample sizes, sample means, and population standard deviations. If something other than a 95% confidence interval is desired, the confidence coefficient in cell E11 must also be changed.

Hypothesis Tests About $\mu_1 - \mu_2$

Let us consider hypothesis tests about the difference between two population means. Using D_0 to denote the hypothesized difference between μ_1 and μ_2, the three forms for a hypothesis test are as follows:

$$H_0: \mu_1 - \mu_2 \geq D_0 \qquad H_0: \mu_1 - \mu_2 \leq D_0 \qquad H_0: \mu_1 - \mu_2 = D_0$$
$$H_a: \mu_1 - \mu_2 < D_0 \qquad H_a: \mu_1 - \mu_2 > D_0 \qquad H_a: \mu_1 - \mu_2 \neq D_0$$

In many applications, $D_0 = 0$. Using the two-tailed test as an example, when $D_0 = 0$ the null hypothesis is H_0: $\mu_1 - \mu_2 = 0$. In this case, the null hypothesis is that μ_1 and μ_2 are equal. Rejection of H_0 leads to the conclusion that H_a: $\mu_1 - \mu_2 \neq 0$ is true; that is, μ_1 and μ_2 are not equal.

In Chapter 9, we introduce the general steps for hypothesis testing for a single population mean and single population proportion.

The general steps for conducting hypothesis tests are still applicable here. We must choose a level of significance, compute the value of the test statistic, and find the p-value to determine whether the null hypothesis should be rejected. With two independent random samples, we showed that the point estimator $\bar{x}_1 - \bar{x}_2$ has a standard error $\sigma_{\bar{x}_1 - \bar{x}_2}$ given by expression (10.2) and, when the sample sizes are large enough, the distribution of $\bar{x}_1 - \bar{x}_2$ can be described by a normal distribution. In this case, the test statistic for the difference between two population means when σ_1 and σ_2 are known is as follows.

Test Statistic for Hypothesis Tests About $\mu_1 - \mu_2$: σ_1 and σ_2 Known

$$z = \frac{(\bar{x}_1 - \bar{x}_2) - D_0}{\sqrt{\dfrac{\sigma_1^2}{n_1} + \dfrac{\sigma_2^2}{n_2}}} \tag{10.5}$$

Let us demonstrate the use of this test statistic in the following hypothesis testing example.

As part of a study to evaluate differences in education quality between two training centers, a standardized examination is given to individuals who are trained at the centers. The difference between the mean examination scores is used to assess quality differences between the centers. The population means for the two centers are as follows.

μ_1 = the mean examination score for the population of individuals trained at center A

μ_2 = the mean examination score for the population of individuals trained at center B

We begin with the tentative assumption that no difference exists between the training quality provided at the two centers. Hence, in terms of the mean examination scores, the null hypothesis is that $\mu_1 - \mu_2 = 0$. If sample evidence leads to the rejection of this hypothesis, we will conclude that the mean examination scores differ for the two populations. This conclusion indicates a quality differential between the two centers and suggests that a follow-up study investigating the reason for the differential may be warranted. The null and alternative hypotheses for this two-tailed test are written as follows.

$$H_0: \mu_1 - \mu_2 = 0$$
$$H_a: \mu_1 - \mu_2 \neq 0$$

The standardized examination given previously in a variety of settings always resulted in an examination score standard deviation near 10 points. Thus, we will use this information to assume that the population standard deviations are known with $\sigma_1 = 10$ and $\sigma_2 = 10$. An $\alpha = 0.05$ level of significance is specified for the study.

DATA *file*
examscores

Independent random samples of $n_1 = 30$ individuals from training center A and $n_2 = 40$ individuals from training center B are taken. The respective sample means are $\bar{x}_1 = 82$ and $\bar{x}_2 = 78$. Do these data suggest a significant difference between the population means at the two training centers? To help answer this question, we compute the test statistic using equation (10.5).

$$z = \frac{(\bar{x}_1 - \bar{x}_2) - D_0}{\sqrt{\frac{\sigma_1^2}{n_1} + \frac{\sigma_2^2}{n_2}}} = \frac{(82 - 78) - 0}{\sqrt{\frac{10^2}{30} + \frac{10^2}{40}}} = 1.66$$

Next, let us compute the p-value for this two-tailed test. Because the test statistic z is in the upper tail, we first compute the upper tail area corresponding to $z = 1.66$. Using the standard normal distribution table, the area to the left of $z = 1.66$ is 0.9515. Thus, the area in the upper tail of the distribution is $1.0000 - 0.9515 = 0.0485$. Because this test is a two-tailed test, we must double the tail area: p-value $= 2(0.0485) = 0.0970$. Following the usual rule to reject H_0 if p-value $\leq \alpha$, we see that the p-value of 0.0970 does not allow us to reject H_0 at the 0.05 level of significance. The sample results do not provide sufficient evidence to conclude that the training centers differ in quality.

In this chapter, we will use the p-value approach to hypothesis testing. However, if you prefer, the test statistic and the critical value rejection rule may be used. With $\alpha = 0.05$ and $z_{\alpha/2} = z_{0.025} = 1.96$, the rejection rule employing the critical value approach would be reject H_0 if $z \leq -1.96$ or if $z \geq 1.96$. With $z = 1.66$, we reach the same do not reject H_0 conclusion.

In the preceding example, we demonstrated a two-tailed hypothesis test about the difference between two population means. Lower tail and upper tail tests can also be considered. These tests use the same test statistic as given in equation (10.5). The procedure for computing the p-value and the rejection rules for these one-tailed tests are the same as those for hypothesis tests involving a single population mean and single population proportion.

Using Excel to Conduct a Hypothesis Test

Excel's z-Test: Two Sample for Means tool can be used to conduct the hypothesis test to determine whether there is a significant difference in population means when σ_1 and σ_2 are assumed known. We illustrate using the sample data for exam scores at center A and at center B. With an assumed known standard deviation of 10 points at each center, the known variance of exam scores for each of the two populations is equal to $10^2 = 100$. Refer to the Excel worksheets shown in Figure 10.3 and Figure 10.4 as we describe the tasks involved.

Enter/Access Data: Open the file *examscores*. Column A in Figure 10.3 contains the examination score data and a label for the random sample of 30 individuals trained at center A, and column B contains the examination score data and a label for the random sample of 40 individuals trained at center B.

Apply Tools: The following steps will provide the information needed to conduct the hypothesis test to see whether there is a significant difference in test scores at the two centers.

Step 1. Click the **Data** tab on the Ribbon
Step 2. In the **Analyze** group, click **Data Analysis**
Step 3. Choose **z-Test: Two Sample for Means** from the list of Analysis Tools
Step 4. When the **z-Test: Two Sample for Means** dialog box appears (Figure 10.3):
Enter *A1:A31* in the **Variable 1 Range:** box
Enter *B1:B41* in the **Variable 2 Range:** box
Enter *0* in the **Hypothesized Mean Difference:** box
Enter *100* in the **Variable 1 Variance (known):** box
Enter *100* in the **Variable 2 Variance (known):** box
Select the check box for **Labels**
Enter *0.05* in the **Alpha:** box
Select **Output Range:** and enter *D4* in the box
Click **OK**

Figure 10.3 Dialog Box for Excel's *z*-Test: Two Sample for Means Tool

Note: Rows 18–28 and 33–39 are hidden.

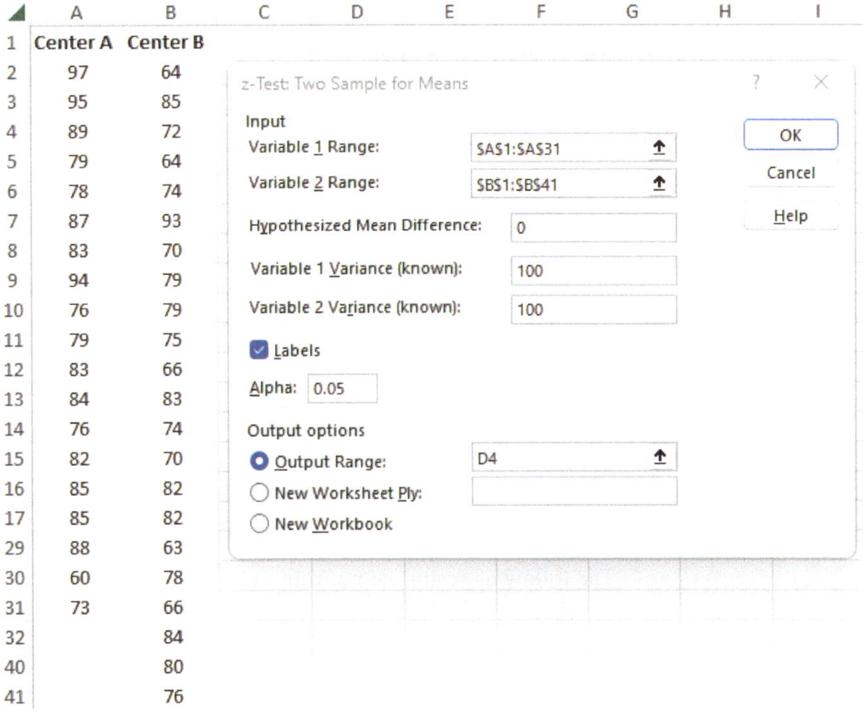

Source: Microsoft Corporation

Figure 10.4 Excel Results for the Hypothesis Test About Equality of Exam Scores at Two Training Centers

Note: Rows 18–28 and 33–39 are hidden.

	A	B
1	Center A	Center B
2	97	64
3	95	85
4	89	72
5	79	64
6	78	74
7	87	93
8	83	70
9	94	79
10	76	79
11	79	75
12	83	66
13	84	83
14	76	74
15	82	70
16	85	82
17	85	82
29	88	63
30	60	78
31	73	66
32		84
40		80
41		76

z-Test: Two Sample for Means

	Center A	*Center B*
Mean	82	78
Known Variance	100	100
Observations	30	40
Hypothesized Mean Difference	0	
z	1.6562	
P(Z<=z) one-tail	0.0488	
z Critical one-tail	1.6449	
P(Z<=z) two-tail	0.0977	
z Critical two-tail	1.9600	

The value of the test statistic shown here (1.6562) and the p-value (0.0977) differ slightly from those shown previously, because we rounded the test statistic to two places (1.66) in the text.

The results are shown in Figure 10.4. Descriptive statistics for the two samples are shown in cells E7:F9. The value of the test statistic, 1.6562, is shown in cell E11. The *p*-value for the test, labeled "P(Z<=*z*) two-tail," is shown in cell E14. Because the *p*-value, 0.0977, is greater than the level of significance, $\alpha = 0.05$, we cannot conclude that the means for the two populations are different.

The z-Test: Two Sample for Means tool can also be used to conduct one-tailed hypothesis tests. The only change required to make the hypothesis testing decision is that we need to use the *p*-value for a one-tailed test, labeled "P(Z<=*z*) one-tail" (see cell E12).

Practical Advice

In most applications of the interval estimation and hypothesis testing procedures presented in this section, random samples with $n_1 \geq 30$ and $n_2 \geq 30$ are adequate. In cases where either or both sample sizes are less than 30, the distributions of the populations become important considerations. In general, with smaller sample sizes, it is more important for the analyst to be satisfied that it is reasonable to assume that the distributions of the two populations are at least approximately normal.

Exercises

Methods

1. The following results come from two independent random samples taken of two populations. **LO 1, 2**

Sample 1	Sample 2
$n_1 = 50$	$n_2 = 35$
$\bar{x}_1 = 13.6$	$\bar{x}_2 = 11.6$
$\sigma_1 = 2.2$	$\sigma_2 = 3.0$

a. What is the point estimate of the difference between the two population means?
b. Provide a 90% confidence interval for the difference between the two population means.
c. Provide a 95% confidence interval for the difference between the two population means.

2. Consider the following hypothesis test.

$$H_0: \mu_1 - \mu_2 \leq 0$$
$$H_a: \mu_1 - \mu_2 > 0$$

The following results are for two independent samples taken from the two populations. **LO 3**

Sample 1	Sample 2
$n_1 = 40$	$n_2 = 50$
$\bar{x}_1 = 25.2$	$\bar{x}_2 = 22.8$
$\sigma_1 = 5.2$	$\sigma_2 = 6.0$

a. What is the value of the test statistic?
b. What is the *p*-value?
c. With $\alpha = 0.05$, what is your hypothesis testing conclusion?

3. Consider the following hypothesis test.

$$H_0: \mu_1 - \mu_2 = 0$$
$$H_a: \mu_1 - \mu_2 \neq 0$$

The following results are for two independent samples taken from the two populations. LO 3

Sample 1	Sample 2
$n_1 = 80$	$n_2 = 70$
$\bar{x}_1 = 104$	$\bar{x}_2 = 106$
$\sigma_1 = 8.4$	$\sigma_2 = 7.6$

a. What is the value of the test statistic?
b. What is the *p*-value?
c. With $\alpha = 0.05$, what is your hypothesis testing conclusion?

Applications

4. **Cruise Ship Ratings.** *Condé Nast Traveler* conducts an annual survey in which readers rate their favorite cruise ship. All ships are rated on a 100-point scale, with higher values indicating better service. A sample of 37 ships that carry fewer than 500 passengers resulted in an average rating of 85.36, and a sample of 44 ships that carry 500 or more passengers provided an average rating of 81.40. Assume that the population standard deviation is 4.55 for ships that carry fewer than 500 passengers and 3.97 for ships that carry 500 or more passengers. LO 1, 2
   a. What is the point estimate of the difference between the population mean rating for ships that carry fewer than 500 passengers and the population mean rating for ships that carry 500 or more passengers?
   b. At 95% confidence, what is the margin of error?
   c. What is a 95% confidence interval estimate of the difference between the population mean ratings for the two sizes of ships?

5. **Valentine's Day Expenditures.** *USA Today* reports that the average expenditure on Valentine's Day is \$100.89. Do male and female consumers differ in the amounts they spend? The average expenditure in a sample survey of 40 male consumers was \$135.67, and the average expenditure in a sample survey of 30 female consumers was \$68.64. Based on past surveys, the standard deviation for male consumers is assumed to be \$35, and the standard deviation for female consumers is assumed to be \$20. LO 1, 2
   a. What is the point estimate of the difference between the population mean expenditure for males and the population mean expenditure for females?
   b. At 99% confidence, what is the margin of error?
   c. Develop a 99% confidence interval for the difference between the two population means.

DATA*file*
hotel

6. **Hotel Price Comparison.** Suppose that you are responsible for making arrangements for a business convention and that you have been charged with choosing a city for the convention that has the least expensive hotel rooms. You have narrowed your choices to Atlanta and Houston. The file *hotel* contains samples of prices for rooms in Atlanta and Houston that are consistent with a *SmartMoney* survey conducted by Smith Travel Research. Because considerable historical data on the prices of rooms in both cities are available, the population standard deviations for the prices can be assumed to be \$20 in Atlanta and \$25 in Houston. Based on the sample data, can you conclude that the mean price of a hotel room in Atlanta is lower than one in Houston? LO 2, 3

7. **Supermarket Customer Satisfaction.** *Consumer Reports* uses a survey of readers to obtain customer satisfaction ratings for the nation's largest supermarkets (*Consumer Reports* website). Each survey respondent is asked to rate a specified supermarket based on a variety of factors such as quality of products, selection, value, checkout efficiency, service, and store layout. An overall satisfaction score summarizes the rating for each respondent with 100 meaning the respondent is completely satisfied in terms

of all factors. Sample data representative of independent samples of Publix and Trader Joe's customers are shown below. **LO 2, 3**

Publix	Trader Joe's
$n_1 = 250$	$n_2 = 300$
$\bar{x}_1 = 86$	$\bar{x}_2 = 85$

a. Formulate the null and alternative hypotheses to test whether there is a difference between the population mean customer satisfaction scores for the two retailers.
b. Assume that experience with the *Consumer Reports* satisfaction rating scale indicates that a population standard deviation of 12 is a reasonable assumption for both retailers. Conduct the hypothesis test and report the *p*-value. At a 0.05 level of significance what is your conclusion?
c. Which retailer, if either, appears to have the greater customer satisfaction? Provide a 95% confidence interval for the difference between the population mean customer satisfaction scores for the two retailers.

8. **Decreases in Customer Satisfaction.** Companies are concerned with the quality of their customer service as this is often highly correlated with a profitability. The following satisfaction scores of three companies for the fourth quarters of two consecutive years were obtained from the American Customer Satisfaction Index. Assume that the scores are based on a poll of 60 customers from each company. Historical polling data suggest that the standard deviation can be assumed to equal six points in each case. **LO 3**

Company	Current Year	Previous Year
Rite Aid	72	75
Costco	81	83
Bass Pro Shops	79	80

a. For Rite Aid, is the decrease in the satisfaction score over these two years statistically significant? Use $\alpha = 0.05$. What can you conclude?
b. Can you conclude that the current year score for Rite Aid is below the retail sector's national average of 75.5? Use $\alpha = 0.05$.
c. For Costco, is the decrease over these two years statistically significant? Use $\alpha = 0.05$.
d. When conducting a hypothesis test with the values given for the standard deviation, sample size, and α, how large must the decrease over these two years be for it to be statistically significant?
e. Use the result of part (d) to state whether the decrease for Bass Pro Shops over these two years is statistically significant.

10.2 Inferences About the Difference Between Two Population Means: σ_1 and σ_2 Unknown

In this section, we extend the discussion of inferences about the difference between two population means to the case when the two population standard deviations, σ_1 and σ_2, are unknown. In this case, we will use the sample standard deviations, s_1 and s_2, to estimate the unknown population standard deviations. When we use the sample standard deviations, the interval estimation and hypothesis testing procedures will be based on the *t* distribution rather than the standard normal distribution.

Interval Estimation of $\mu_1 - \mu_2$

In the following example, we show how to compute a margin of error and develop an interval estimate of the difference between two population means when σ_1 and σ_2 are unknown. Clearwater National Bank is conducting a study designed to identify differences between checking account practices by customers at two of its branch banks. A random sample of 28 checking accounts is selected from the Cherry Grove Branch and an independent random sample of 22 checking accounts is selected from the Beechmont Branch. The current checking account balance is recorded for each of the checking accounts. A summary of the account balances follows.

DATA*file*
checkacct_mod

	Cherry Grove	Beechmont
Sample Size	$n_1 = 28$	$n_2 = 22$
Sample Mean	$\bar{x}_1 = \$1,025$	$\bar{x}_2 = \$910$
Sample Standard Deviation	$s_1 = \$150$	$s_2 = \$125$

Clearwater National Bank would like to estimate the difference between the mean checking account balance maintained by the population of Cherry Grove customers and the population of Beechmont customers. Let us develop the margin of error and an interval estimate of the difference between these two population means.

In Section 10.1, we provided the following interval estimate for the case when the population standard deviations, σ_1 and σ_2, are known.

$$\bar{x}_1 - \bar{x}_2 \pm z_{\alpha/2}\sqrt{\frac{\sigma_1^2}{n_1} + \frac{\sigma_2^2}{n_2}}$$

When σ_1 and σ_2 are estimated by s_1 and s_2, the t distribution is used to make inferences about the difference between two population means.

With σ_1 and σ_2 unknown, we will use the sample standard deviations s_1 and s_2 to estimate σ_1 and σ_2 and replace $z_{\alpha/2}$ with $t_{\alpha/2}$. As a result, the interval estimate of the difference between two population means is given by the following expression.

Interval Estimate of the Difference Between Two Population Means: σ_1 and σ_2 Unknown

$$\bar{x}_1 - \bar{x}_2 \pm t_{\alpha/2}\sqrt{\frac{s_1^2}{n_1} + \frac{s_2^2}{n_2}} \tag{10.6}$$

where $1 - \alpha$ is the confidence coefficient.

In this expression, the use of the t distribution is an approximation, but it provides excellent results and is relatively easy to use. The only difficulty that we encounter in using expression (10.6) is determining the appropriate degrees of freedom for $t_{\alpha/2}$. Statistical software packages compute the appropriate degrees of freedom automatically. The formula used is as follows.

Degrees of Freedom: t Distribution with Two Independent Random Samples

$$df = \frac{\left(\frac{s_1^2}{n_1} + \frac{s_2^2}{n_2}\right)^2}{\frac{1}{n_1 - 1}\left(\frac{s_1^2}{n_1}\right)^2 + \frac{1}{n_2 - 1}\left(\frac{s_2^2}{n_2}\right)^2} \tag{10.7}$$

Let us return to the Clearwater National Bank example and show how to use expression (10.6) to provide a 95% confidence interval estimate of the difference between the population mean checking account balances at the two branch banks. The sample data show $n_1 = 28$, $\bar{x}_1 = \$1{,}025$, and $s_1 = \$150$ for the Cherry Grove branch, and $n_2 = 22$, $\bar{x}_2 = \$910$, and $s_2 = \$125$ for the Beechmont branch. The calculation for degrees of freedom for $t_{\alpha/2}$ is as follows:

$$df = \frac{\left(\dfrac{s_1^2}{n_1} + \dfrac{s_2^2}{n_2}\right)^2}{\dfrac{1}{n_1 - 1}\left(\dfrac{s_1^2}{n_1}\right)^2 + \dfrac{1}{n_2 - 1}\left(\dfrac{s_2^2}{n_2}\right)^2} = \frac{\left(\dfrac{150^2}{28} + \dfrac{125^2}{22}\right)^2}{\dfrac{1}{28 - 1}\left(\dfrac{150^2}{28}\right)^2 + \dfrac{1}{22 - 1}\left(\dfrac{125^2}{22}\right)^2} = 47.8$$

We round the noninteger degrees of freedom *down* to 47 to provide a larger t value and a more conservative interval estimate. Using the t distribution table with 47 degrees of freedom, we find $t_{0.025} = 2.012$. Using expression (10.6), we develop the 95% confidence interval estimate of the difference between the two population means as follows.

$$\bar{x}_1 - \bar{x}_2 \pm t_{.025}\sqrt{\frac{s_1^2}{n_1} + \frac{s_2^2}{n_2}}$$

$$1025 - 910 \pm 2.012\sqrt{\frac{150^2}{28} + \frac{125^2}{22}}$$

$$115 \pm 78$$

The point estimate of the difference between the population mean checking account balances at the two branches is \$115. The margin of error is \$78, and the 95% confidence interval estimate of the difference between the two population means is $115 - 78 = \$37$ to $115 + 78 = \$193$.

Using Excel to Construct a Confidence Interval

Excel's data analysis tools do not provide a procedure for developing interval estimates involving two population means. However, we can develop an Excel worksheet that can be used as a template to construct interval estimates. We will illustrate by constructing an interval estimate of the difference between the population means in the Clearwater National Bank study. Refer to Figure 10.5 as we describe the tasks involved. The formula worksheet is in the background; the value worksheet is in the foreground.

Enter/Access Data: Open the file *checkacct_mod.* Column A contains the account balances and a label for the random sample of 28 customers at the Cherry Grove Branch, and column B contains the account balances and a label for the random sample of 22 customers at the Beechmont Branch.

Enter Functions and Formulas: The descriptive statistics needed are provided in cells E5:F7. Using the two sample standard deviations and the sample sizes, an estimate of the variance of the point estimator $\bar{x}_1 - \bar{x}_2$ is computed by entering the following formula into cell E9:

=E7^2/E5+F7^2/F5

An estimate of the standard error is then computed in cell E10 by taking the square root of the variance.

Cells E12:E16 are used to compute the appropriate t value and the margin of error. By entering *0.95* into cell E12 for the value of the confidence coefficient, the corresponding level of significance is computed in cell E13 ($\alpha = 0.05$). In cell E14, we used formula (10.7) to compute the degrees of freedom (47.8). In cell E15, we used the T.INV.2T function to compute the t value needed for the interval estimate. The margin of error is computed in cell E16 by multiplying the t value by the standard error.

Figure 10.5 Excel Worksheet: Constructing a 95% Confidence Interval for Clearwater National Bank

	A	B	C	D	E	F
1	Cherry Grove	Beechmont		Interval Estimate of Difference in Population Means:		
2	1263	996.7		σ_1 and σ_2 Unknown Case		
3	897	897				
4	849	912			Cherry Grove	Beechmont
5	891	894.9		Sample Size	=COUNT(A2:A29)	=COUNT(B2:B23)
6	964	785		Sample Mean	=AVERAGE(A2:A29)	=AVERAGE(B2:B23)
7	810	750.7		Sample Standard Deviation	=STDEV.S(A2:A29)	=STDEV.S(B2:B23)
8	877	882.2				
9	899	1110		Estimate of Variance	=E7^2/E5+F7^2/F5	
10	847	907.2		Standard Error	=SQRT(E9)	
11	1070	1226.1				
12	1252	762.1		Confidence Coefficient	0.95	
13	920	835.5		Level of Significance	=1-E12	
14	1256	1048		Degrees of Freedom	=E9^2/((1/(E5-1))*(E7^2/E5)^2+(1/(F5-1)*(F7^2/F5)^2))	
15	1196	773.8		*t* Value	=T.INV.2T(E13,E14)	
16	1150	807		Margin of Error	=E15*E10	
17	1024	972				
18	1016	980		Point Estimate of Difference	=E6-F6	
19	1126	876.6		Lower Limit	=E18-E16	
20	1289	943		Upper Limit	=E18+E16	
21	1220	992.7				
22	912	704.3				
23	1026	962.9				
24	786					
25	989					
26	1133					
27	990					
28	999					
29	1049					

	A	B	C	D	E	F
1	Cherry Grove	Beechmont		Interval Estimate of Difference in Population Means:		
2	1263	997		σ_1 and σ_2 Unknown Case		
3	897	897				
4	849	912			Cherry Grove	Beechmont
5	891	895		Sample Size	28	22
6	964	785		Sample Mean	1025	910
7	810	751		Sample Standard Deviation	150	125
8	877	882				
9	899	1110		Estimate of Variance	1513.8550	
10	847	907		Standard Error	38.9083	
11	1070	1226				
12	1252	762		Confidence Coefficient	0.95	
13	920	836		Level of Significance	0.05	
14	1256	1048		Degrees of Freedom	47.8	
15	1196	774		*t* Value	2.012	
16	1150	807		Margin of Error	78	
17	1024	972				
18	1016	980		Point Estimate of Difference	115	
19	1126	877		Lower Limit	37	
20	1289	943		Upper Limit	193	
21	1220	993				
22	912	704				
23	1026	963				
24	786					
25	989					
26	1133					
27	990					
28	999					
29	1049					

In cell E18, the difference in the sample means is used to compute the point estimate of the difference in the two population means (115). The lower limit of the confidence interval is computed in cell E19 (37) and the upper limit is computed in cell E20 (193); thus, the 95% confidence interval estimate of the difference in the two population means is 37 to 193.

A Template for Other Problems This worksheet can be used as a template for developing interval estimates of the difference in population means when the population standard deviations are unknown. For another problem of this type, we must first enter the new problem data in columns A and B. The data ranges in cells E5:F7 must be modified in order to compute the sample means, sample sizes, and sample standard deviations for the new data. After doing so, the point estimate and a 95% confidence interval will be displayed in cells E18:E20. If a confidence interval with a different confidence coefficient is desired, we simply change the value in cell E12.

We can further simplify the use of Figure 10.5 as a template for other problems by eliminating the need to enter new data ranges in cells E5:F7. We rewrite the cell formulas as follows:

Cell E5: =*COUNT*(*A*:*A*)
Cell F5: =*COUNT*(*B*:*B*)
Cell E6: =*AVERAGE*(*A*:*A*)
Cell F6: =*AVERAGE*(*B*:*B*)
Cell E7: =*STDEV.S*(*A*:*A*)
Cell F7: =*STDEV.S*(*B*:*B*)

The file checkacct_mod *includes a worksheet titled* Template *that uses the A:A and B:B methods for entering the data ranges.*

Using the A:A method of specifying data ranges in cells E5:E7, Excel's COUNT function will count the number of numeric values in column A, Excel's AVERAGE function will compute the average of the numeric values in column A, and Excel's

STDEV.S function will compute the standard deviation of the numeric values in column A. Similarly, using the B:B method of specifying data ranges in cells F5:F7, Excel's COUNT function will count the number of numeric values in column B, Excel's AVERAGE function will compute the average of the numeric values in column B, and Excel's STDEV.S function will compute the standard deviation of the numeric values in column B. Thus, to solve a new problem, it is only necessary to enter the new data into columns A and B.

This worksheet can also be used as a template for text exercises in which the sample sizes, sample means, and sample standard deviations are given. In this type of situation, no change in the data is necessary. We simply replace the values in cells E5:F7 with the given values of the sample sizes, sample means, and sample standard deviations. If something other than a 95% confidence interval is desired, the confidence coefficient in cell E12 must also be changed.

Hypothesis Tests About $\mu_1 - \mu_2$

Let us now consider hypothesis tests about the difference between the means of two populations when the population standard deviations σ_1 and σ_2 are unknown. Letting D_0 denote the hypothesized difference between μ_1 and μ_2, Section 10.1 showed that the test statistic used for the case where σ_1 and σ_2 are known is as follows.

$$z = \frac{(\bar{x}_1 - \bar{x}_2) - D_0}{\sqrt{\dfrac{\sigma_1^2}{n_1} + \dfrac{\sigma_2^2}{n_2}}}$$

The test statistic, z, follows the standard normal distribution.

When σ_1 and σ_2 are unknown, we use s_1 as an estimator of σ_1 and s_2 as an estimator of σ_2. Substituting these sample standard deviations for σ_1 and σ_2 provides the following test statistic when σ_1 and σ_2 are unknown.

Test Statistic for Hypothesis Tests About $\mu_1 - \mu_2$: σ_1 and σ_2 Unknown

$$t = \frac{(\bar{x}_1 - \bar{x}_2) - D_0}{\sqrt{\dfrac{s_1^2}{n_1} + \dfrac{s_2^2}{n_2}}} \qquad \textbf{(10.8)}$$

The degrees of freedom for t are given by equation (10.7).

Let us demonstrate the use of this test statistic in the following hypothesis testing example.

Consider a new computer software package developed to help systems analysts reduce the time required to design, develop, and implement an information system. To evaluate the benefits of the new software package, a random sample of 24 systems analysts is selected. Each analyst is given specifications for a hypothetical information system. Then, 12 of the analysts are instructed to produce the information system by using current technology. The other 12 analysts are trained in the use of the new software package and then instructed to use it to produce the information system.

This study involves two populations: a population of systems analysts using the current technology and a population of systems analysts using the new software package. In terms of the time required to complete the information system design project, the population means are as follow.

Table 10.1 Completion Time Data and Summary Statistics for the Software Testing Study

DATA*file*
softwaretest

	Current Technology	New Software
	300	274
	280	220
	344	308
	385	336
	372	198
	360	300
	288	315
	321	258
	376	318
	290	310
	301	332
	283	263
Summary Statistics		
Sample size	$n_1 = 12$	$n_2 = 12$
Sample mean	$\bar{x}_1 = 325$ hours	$\bar{x}_2 = 286$ hours
Sample standard deviation	$s_1 = 40$	$s_2 = 44$

μ_1 = the mean project completion time for systems analysts using the current technology

μ_2 = the mean project completion time for systems analysts using the new software package

The researcher in charge of the new software evaluation project hopes to show that the new software package will provide a shorter mean project completion time. Thus, the researcher is looking for evidence to conclude that μ_2 is less than μ_1; in this case, the difference between the two population means, $\mu_1 - \mu_2$, will be greater than zero. The research hypothesis $\mu_1 - \mu_2 > 0$ is stated as the alternative hypothesis. Thus, the hypothesis test becomes

$$H_0: \mu_1 - \mu_2 \leq 0$$
$$H_a: \mu_1 - \mu_2 > 0$$

We will use $\alpha = 0.05$ as the level of significance.

Suppose that the 24 analysts complete the study with the results shown in Table 10.1. Using the test statistic in equation (10.8), we have

$$t = \frac{(\bar{x}_1 - \bar{x}_2) - D_0}{\sqrt{\dfrac{s_1^2}{n_1} + \dfrac{s_2^2}{n_2}}} = \frac{(325 - 286) - 0}{\sqrt{\dfrac{40^2}{12} + \dfrac{44^2}{12}}} = 2.27$$

Computing the degrees of freedom using equation (10.7), we have

$$df = \frac{\left(\dfrac{s_1^2}{n_1} + \dfrac{s_2^2}{n_2}\right)^2}{\dfrac{1}{n_1 - 1}\left(\dfrac{s_1^2}{n_1}\right)^2 + \dfrac{1}{n_2 - 1}\left(\dfrac{s_2^2}{n_2}\right)^2} = \frac{\left(\dfrac{40^2}{12} + \dfrac{44^2}{12}\right)^2}{\dfrac{1}{12 - 1}\left(\dfrac{40^2}{12}\right)^2 + \dfrac{1}{12 - 1}\left(\dfrac{44^2}{12}\right)^2} = 21.8$$

Rounding down, we will use a t distribution with 21 degrees of freedom. This row of the t distribution table is as follows:

Area in Upper Tail	**0.20**	**0.10**	**0.05**	**0.025**	**0.01**	**0.005**
***t*-Value (21 *df*)**	0.859	1.323	1.721	2.080	2.518	2.831

$t = 2.27$

Using the t distribution table, we can only determine a range for the p-value. Use of Excel (see Figure 10.7) shows the exact p-value = 0.017.

With an upper tail test, the p-value is the area in the upper tail to the right of $t = 2.27$. From the above results, we see that the p-value is between 0.025 and 0.01. Thus, the p-value is less than $\alpha = 0.05$ and H_0 is rejected. The sample results enable the researcher to conclude that $\mu_1 - \mu_2 > 0$, or $\mu_1 > \mu_2$. Thus, the research study supports the conclusion that the new software package provides a smaller population mean completion time.

Using Excel to Conduct a Hypothesis Test

Excel's t-Test: Two-Sample Assuming Unequal Variances tool can be used to conduct a hypothesis test to determine whether there is a significant difference in population means when the population standard deviations are unknown. We illustrate using the sample data for the software evaluation study. Twelve systems analysts developed an information system using current technology, and 12 systems analysts developed an information system using a new software package. A one-tailed hypothesis test is to be conducted to see whether the mean completion time is shorter using the new software package. Refer to the Excel worksheets shown in Figure 10.6 and Figure 10.7 as we describe the tasks involved.

Enter/Access Data: Open the file *softwaretest*. Column A in Figure 10.6 contains the completion time data and a label for the random sample of 12 individuals using the current technology, and column B contains the completion time data and a label for the random sample of 12 individuals using the new software.

Figure 10.6 Dialog Box for Excel's t-Test: Two-Sample Assuming Unequal Variances Tool

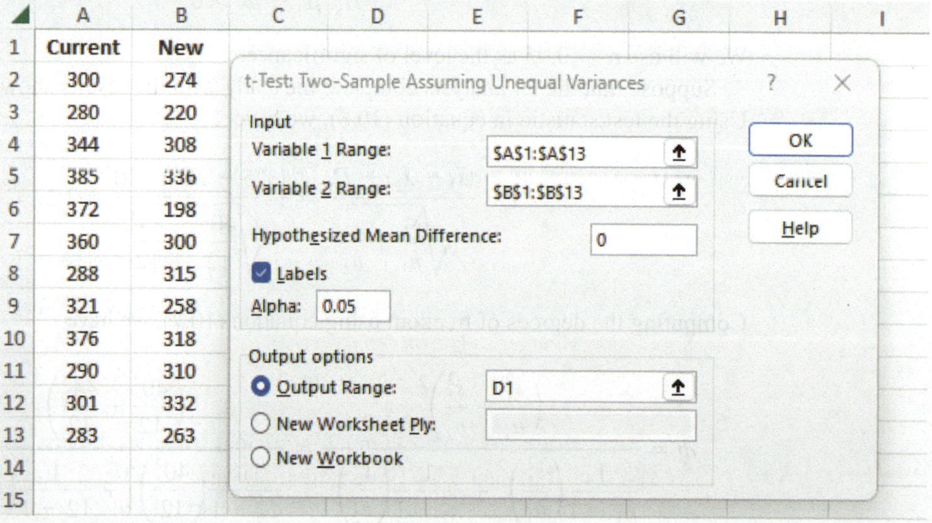

Source: Microsoft Corporation

Figure 10.7 Excel Results for the Hypothesis Test About Equality of Mean Project Completion Times

	A	B	C	D	E	F
1	**Current**	**New**		t-Test: Two-Sample Assuming Unequal Variances		
2	300	274				
3	280	220			*Current*	*New*
4	344	308		Mean	325	286
5	385	336		Variance	1599.6364	1935.8182
6	372	198		Observations	12	12
7	360	300		Hypothesized Mean Difference	0	
8	288	315		df	22	
9	321	258		t Stat	2.2721	
10	376	318		P(T<=t) one-tail	0.0166	
11	290	310		t Critical one-tail	1.7171	
12	301	332		P(T<=t) two-tail	0.0332	
13	283	263		t Critical two-tail	2.0739	

Apply Tools: The following steps will provide the information needed to conduct the hypothesis test to see whether there is a significant difference in favor of the new software.

Step 1. Click the **Data** tab on the Ribbon
Step 2. In the **Analyze** group, click **Data Analysis**
Step 3. Choose **t-Test: Two-Sample Assuming Unequal Variances** from the list of Analysis Tools
Step 4. When the **t-Test: Two-Sample Assuming Unequal Variances** dialog box appears (Figure 10.6):
    Enter *A1:A13* in the **Variable 1 Range:** box
    Enter *B1:B13* in the **Variable 2 Range:** box
    Enter *0* in the **Hypothesized Mean Difference:** box
    Select the check box for **Labels**
    Enter *0.05* in the **Alpha:** box
    Select **Output Range:** and enter *D1* in the box
    Click **OK**

The results are shown in Figure 10.7. Descriptive statistics for the two samples are shown in cells E4:F6. The value of the test statistic, 2.2721, is shown in cell E9. The p-value for the test, labeled "P(T<=t) one-tail," is shown in cell E10. Because the p-value, 0.0166, is less than the level of significance $\alpha = 0.05$, we can conclude that the mean completion time for the population using the new software package is smaller.

The t-Test: Two-Sample Assuming Unequal Variances tool can also be used to conduct two-tailed hypothesis tests. The only change required to make the hypothesis testing decision is that we need to use the p-value for a two-tailed test, labeled "P(T<=t) two-tail" (see cell E12).

Practical Advice

Whenever possible, equal sample sizes, $n_1 = n_2$, are recommended.

The interval estimation and hypothesis testing procedures presented in this section are robust and can be used with relatively small sample sizes. In most applications, equal or nearly equal sample sizes such that the total sample size $n_1 + n_2$ is at least 20 can be expected to provide very good results even if the populations are not normal. Larger sample sizes are recommended if the distributions of the populations are highly skewed or contain outliers. Smaller sample sizes should only be used if the analyst is satisfied that the distributions of the populations are at least approximately normal.

Note + Comment

Another approach used to make inferences about the difference between two population means when σ_1 and σ_2 are unknown is based on the assumption that the two population standard deviations are *equal* ($\sigma_1 = \sigma_2 = \sigma$). Under this assumption, the two sample standard deviations are combined to provide the following *pooled sample variance:*

$$s_p^2 = \frac{(n_1 - 1)s_1^2 + (n_2 - 1)s_2^2}{n_1 + n_2 - 2}$$

The *t*-test statistic becomes

$$t = \frac{(\bar{x}_1 - \bar{x}_2) - D_0}{s_p\sqrt{\dfrac{1}{n_1} + \dfrac{1}{n_2}}}$$

and has $n_1 + n_2 - 2$ degrees of freedom. At this point, the computation of the *p*-value and the interpretation of the sample results are identical to the procedures discussed earlier in this section.

A difficulty with this procedure is that the assumption that the two population standard deviations are equal is usually difficult to verify. Unequal population standard deviations are frequently encountered. Using the pooled procedure may not provide satisfactory results, especially if the sample sizes n_1 and n_2 are quite different.

The *t* procedure that we presented in this section does not require the assumption of equal population standard deviations and can be applied whether the population standard deviations are equal or not. It is a more general procedure and is recommended for most applications.

Exercises

Methods

9. The following results are for independent random samples taken from two populations. **LO 1, 4**

Sample 1	Sample 2
$n_1 = 20$	$n_2 = 30$
$\bar{x}_1 = 22.5$	$\bar{x}_2 = 20.1$
$s_1 = 2.5$	$s_2 = 4.8$

a. What is the point estimate of the difference between the two population means?
b. What is the degrees of freedom for the *t* distribution?
c. At 95% confidence, what is the margin of error?
d. What is the 95% confidence interval for the difference between the two population means?

10. Consider the following hypothesis test.

$$H_0: \mu_1 - \mu_2 = 0$$
$$H_a: \mu_1 - \mu_2 \neq 0$$

The following results are from independent samples taken from two populations. **LO 5**

Sample 1	Sample 2
$n_1 = 35$	$n_2 = 40$
$\bar{x}_1 = 13.6$	$\bar{x}_2 = 10.1$
$s_1 = 5.2$	$s_2 = 8.5$

a. What is the value of the test statistic?
b. What is the degrees of freedom for the *t* distribution?
c. What is the *p*-value?
d. At $\alpha = 0.05$, what is your conclusion?

11. Consider the following data for two independent random samples taken from two normal populations. **LO 1, 4**

Sample 1	10	7	13	7	9	8
Sample 2	8	7	8	4	6	9

a. Compute the two sample means.
b. Compute the two sample standard deviations.
c. What is the point estimate of the difference between the two population means?
d. What is the 90% confidence interval estimate of the difference between the two population means?

Applications

12. **Miles Driven Per Day.** The U.S. Department of Transportation provides the number of miles that residents of the 75 largest metropolitan areas travel per day in a car. Suppose that for a random sample of 50 Buffalo residents the mean is 22.5 miles a day and the standard deviation is 8.4 miles a day, and for an independent random sample of 40 Boston residents the mean is 18.6 miles a day and the standard deviation is 7.4 miles a day. **LO 1, 4**
a. What is the point estimate of the difference between the mean number of miles that Buffalo residents travel per day and the mean number of miles that Boston residents travel per day?
b. What is the 95% confidence interval for the difference between the two population means?

13. **Annual Cost of College.** According to the Bureau of Labor Statistics, the growth in annual cost to attend college (including tuition, room, board, books, and fees) has outpaced inflation for several decades. The following random samples show the annual cost of attending private and public colleges. Data are in thousands of dollars. **LO 1, 4**

DATA*file*
collegecosts

Private Colleges

52.8	43.2	45.0	33.3	44.0	
30.6	45.8	37.8	50.5	42.0	

Public Colleges

20.3	22.0	28.2	15.6	24.1	28.5
22.8	25.8	18.5	25.6	14.4	21.8

a. Compute the sample mean and sample standard deviation for private and public colleges.
b. What is the point estimate of the difference between the two population means? Interpret this value in terms of the annual cost of attending private and public colleges.
c. Develop a 95% confidence interval of the difference between the mean annual cost of attending private and public colleges.

14. **Salaries of Recent College Graduates.** The Tippie College of Business obtained the following results on the salaries of a recent graduating class. **LO 5**

Finance Majors	Business Analytics Majors
$n_1 = 110$	$n_2 = 30$
$\bar{x}_1 = \$48,537$	$\bar{x}_2 = \$55,317$
$s_1 = \$18,000$	$s_2 = \$10,000$

a. Formulate a hypothesis so that, if the null hypothesis is rejected, we can conclude that salaries for Finance majors are significantly lower than the salaries of Business Analytics majors. Use $\alpha = 0.05$.
b. What is the value of the test statistic?
c. What is the p-value?
d. What is your conclusion?

DATA*file*
inthotels

15. **Hotel Prices.** Hotel room pricing changes over time, but is there a difference between Europe hotel prices and U.S. hotel prices? The file *inthotels* contains changes in the hotel prices for 47 major European cities and 53 major U.S. cities. **LO 5**
a. On the basis of the sample results, can we conclude that the mean change in hotel rates in Europe and the United States are different? Develop appropriate null and alternative hypotheses.
b. Use $\alpha = 0.01$. What is your conclusion?

16. **Effect of Parents' Education on Student SAT Scores.** The College Board provided comparisons of Scholastic Aptitude Test (SAT) scores based on the highest level of education attained by the test taker's parents. A research hypothesis was that students whose parents had attained a higher level of education would on average score higher on the SAT. The overall mean SAT math score was 514. SAT math scores for independent samples of students follow. The first sample shows the SAT math test scores for students whose parents are college graduates with a bachelor's degree. The second sample shows the SAT math test scores for students whose parents are high school graduates but do not have a college degree. **LO 1, 5**

DATA*file*
satmath

Students' Parents

College Grads		High School Grads	
485	487	442	492
534	533	580	478
650	526	479	425
554	410	486	485
550	515	528	390
572	578	524	535
497	448		
592	469		

a. Formulate the hypotheses that can be used to determine whether the sample data support the hypothesis that students show a higher population mean math score on the SAT if their parents attained a higher level of education.
b. What is the point estimate of the difference between the means for the two populations?
c. Compute the p-value for the hypothesis test.
d. At $\alpha = 0.05$, what is your conclusion?

17. **Comparing Financial Consultant Ratings.** Periodically, Merrill Lynch customers are asked to evaluate Merrill Lynch financial consultants and services. Higher ratings on the client satisfaction survey indicate better service, with 7 the maximum service rating. Independent samples of service ratings for two financial consultants are summarized here. Consultant A has 10 years of experience, whereas consultant B has 1 year of experience. Use $\alpha = 0.05$ and test to see whether the consultant with more experience has the higher population mean service rating. **LO 5**

Consultant A	Consultant B
$n_1 = 16$	$n_2 = 10$
$\bar{x}_1 = 6.82$	$\bar{x}_2 = 6.25$
$s_1 = 0.64$	$s_2 = 0.75$

a. State the null and alternative hypotheses.
b. Compute the value of the test statistic.
c. What is the p-value?
d. What is your conclusion?

18. **Comparing Length of Flight Delays.** The success of an airline depends heavily on its ability to provide a pleasant customer experience. One dimension of customer service on which airlines compete is on-time arrival. The file *lateflights* contains a sample of data from delayed flights showing the number of minutes each delayed flight was late for two different airlines, Delta and Southwest. **LO 5**

DATA*file*
lateflights

a. Formulate the hypotheses that can be used to test for a difference between the population mean minutes late for delayed flights by these two airlines.
b. What is the sample mean number of minutes late for delayed flights for each of these two airlines?
c. Using a 0.05 level of significance, what is the p-value and what is your conclusion?

10.3 Inferences About the Difference Between Two Population Means: Matched Samples

Suppose employees at a manufacturing company can use two different methods to perform a production task. To maximize production output, the company wants to identify the method with the smaller population mean completion time. Let μ_1 denote the population mean completion time for production method 1 and μ_2 denote the population mean completion time for production method 2. With no preliminary indication of the preferred production method, we begin by tentatively assuming that the two production methods have the same population mean completion time. Thus, the null hypothesis is H_0: $\mu_1 - \mu_2 = 0$. If this hypothesis is rejected, we can conclude that the population mean completion times differ. In this case, the method providing the smaller mean completion time would be recommended. The null and alternative hypotheses are written as follows.

$$H_0: \mu_1 - \mu_2 = 0$$
$$H_a: \mu_1 - \mu_2 \neq 0$$

In choosing the sampling procedure that will be used to collect production time data and test the hypotheses, we consider two alternative designs. One is based on independent samples and the other is based on **matched samples**.

1. *Independent sample design:* A random sample of workers is selected and each worker in the sample uses method 1. A second independent random sample of workers is selected and each worker in this sample uses method 2. The test of the difference between population means is based on the procedures in Section 10.2.
2. *Matched sample design:* One random sample of workers is selected. Each worker first uses one method and then uses the other method. The order of the two methods is assigned randomly to the workers, with some workers performing method 1 first and others performing method 2 first. Each worker provides a pair of data values, one value for method 1 and another value for method 2.

In the matched sample design, the two production methods are tested under similar conditions (i.e., with the same workers); hence this design often leads to a smaller sampling error than the independent sample design. The primary reason is that in a matched sample design, variation between workers is eliminated because the same workers are used for both production methods.

Let us demonstrate the analysis of a matched sample design by assuming it is the method used to test the difference between population means for the two production methods. A random sample of six workers is used. The data on completion times for the six workers are given in Table 10.2. Note that each worker provides a pair of data values, one for each

Table 10.2 Task Completion Times for a Matched Sample Design

Worker	Completion Time for Method 1 (minutes)	Completion Time for Method 2 (minutes)	Difference in Completion Times (d_i)
1	6.0	5.4	0.6
2	5.0	5.2	−0.2
3	7.0	6.5	0.5
4	6.2	5.9	0.3
5	6.0	6.0	0.0
6	6.4	5.8	0.6

DATA*file*
matched

production method. Also note that the last column contains the difference in completion times d_i for each worker in the sample.

The key to the analysis of the matched sample design is to realize that we consider only the column of differences. Therefore, we have six data values (0.6, −0.2, 0.5, 0.3, 0.0, and 0.6) that will be used to analyze the difference between population means of the two production methods.

Let μ_d = the mean of the *difference* in values for the population of workers. With this notation, the null and alternative hypotheses are rewritten as follows.

$$H_0\text{: } \mu_d = 0$$
$$H_a\text{: } \mu_d \neq 0$$

Other than the use of the d notation, the formulas for the sample mean and sample standard deviation are the same ones used previously in the text.

If H_0 is rejected, we can conclude that the population mean completion times differ.

The d notation is a reminder that the matched sample provides *difference* data. The sample mean and sample standard deviation for the six difference values in Table 10.2 follow.

$$\bar{d} = \frac{\sum d_i}{n} = \frac{1.8}{6} = 0.30$$

$$s_d = \sqrt{\frac{\sum(d_i - \bar{d})^2}{n-1}} = \sqrt{\frac{0.56}{5}} = 0.335$$

It is not necessary to make the assumption that the population has a normal distribution if the sample size is large. In Chapters 8 and 9, we present guidelines for using the t distribution.

With the small sample of $n = 6$ workers, we need to make the assumption that the population of differences has a normal distribution. This assumption is necessary so that we may use the t distribution for hypothesis testing and interval estimation procedures. Based on this assumption, the following test statistic has a t distribution with $n - 1$ degrees of freedom.

Test Statistic for Hypothesis Tests Involving Matched Samples

$$t = \frac{\bar{d} - \mu_d}{s_d/\sqrt{n}} \qquad \textbf{(10.9)}$$

Once the difference data are computed, the t distribution procedure for matched samples is the same as the one-population estimation and hypothesis testing procedures described in Chapters 8 and 9.

Let us use equation (10.9) to test the hypotheses H_0: $\mu_d = 0$ and H_a: $\mu_d \neq 0$, using $\alpha = 0.05$. Substituting the sample results $\bar{d} = 0.30$, $s_d = 0.335$, and $n = 6$ into equation (10.9), we compute the value of the test statistic.

$$t = \frac{\bar{d} - \mu_d}{s_d/\sqrt{n}} = \frac{0.30 - 0}{0.335/\sqrt{6}} = 2.20$$

Now let us compute the p-value for this two-tailed test. Because $t = 2.20 > 0$, the test statistic is in the upper tail of the t distribution. With $t = 2.20$, the area in the upper tail to the right of the test statistic can be found by using the t distribution table with degrees of freedom $= n - 1 = 6 - 1 = 5$. Information from the 5 degrees of freedom row of the t distribution table is as follows:

Area in Upper Tail	**0.20**	**0.10**	**0.05**	**0.025**	**0.01**	**0.005**
***t*-Value (5 *df*)**	0.920	1.476	2.015	2.571	3.365	4.032

$t = 2.20$

Thus, we see that the area in the upper tail is between 0.05 and 0.025. Because this test is a two-tailed test, we double these values to conclude that the p-value is between 0.10 and 0.05. This p-value is greater than $\alpha = 0.05$. Thus, the null hypothesis H_0: $\mu_d = 0$ is not rejected. Using Excel and the data in Table 10.2, we find the exact p-value $= 0.0795$.

Chapter 8 discusses the construction of an interval estimate for a single population mean.

In addition we can obtain an interval estimate of the difference between the two population means by using the single population methodology. At 95% confidence, the calculation follows.

$$\bar{d} \pm t_{0.025}\frac{s_d}{\sqrt{n}}$$

$$0.3 \pm 2.571\left(\frac{0.335}{\sqrt{6}}\right)$$

$$0.3 \pm 0.35$$

Thus, the margin of error is 0.35 and the 95% confidence interval for the difference between the population means of the two production methods is −0.05 minutes to 0.65 minutes.

Using Excel to Conduct a Hypothesis Test

Excel's t-Test: Paired Two Sample for Means tool can be used to conduct a hypothesis test about the difference between the population means when a matched sample design is used. We illustrate by conducting the hypothesis test involving the two production methods. Refer to the Excel worksheets shown in Figure 10.8 and Figure 10.9 as we describe the tasks involved.

Enter/Access Data: Open the file *matched*. Column A in Figure 10.8 is used to identify each of the six workers who participated in the study. Column B contains the completion time data for each worker using method 1, and column C contains the completion time data for each worker using method 2.

Apply Tools: The following steps describe how to use Excel's t-Test: Paired Two Sample for Means tool to conduct the hypothesis test about the difference between the means of the two production methods

Step 1. Click the **Data** tab on the Ribbon
Step 2. In the **Analyze** group, click **Data Analysis**
Step 3. Choose **t-Test: Paired Two Sample for Means** from the list of Analysis Tools
Step 4. When the **t-Test: Paired Two Sample for Means** dialog box appears (Figure 10.8):
Enter *B1:B7* in the **Variable 1 Range:** box
Enter *C1:C7* in the **Variable 2 Range:** box
Enter *0* in the **Hypothesized Mean Difference:** box
Select the check box for **Labels**

Enter *0.05* in the **Alpha:** box
Select **Output Range** in the **Output options** area
Enter *E1* in the **Output Range:** box
Click **OK**

The results are shown in cells E1:G14 of the worksheet shown in Figure 10.9. The p-value for the test, labeled "P(T<=t) two-tail," is shown in cell F13. Because the p-value, 0.0795, is greater than the level of significance $\alpha = 0.05$, we cannot reject the null hypothesis that the mean completion times are equal.

The same procedure can also be used to conduct one-tailed hypothesis tests. The only change required to make the hypothesis testing decision is that we need to use the p-value for a one-tailed test, labeled "P(T<=t) one-tail" (see cell F11).

Figure 10.8 Dialog Box for Excel's *t*-Test: Paired Two Sample for Means Tool

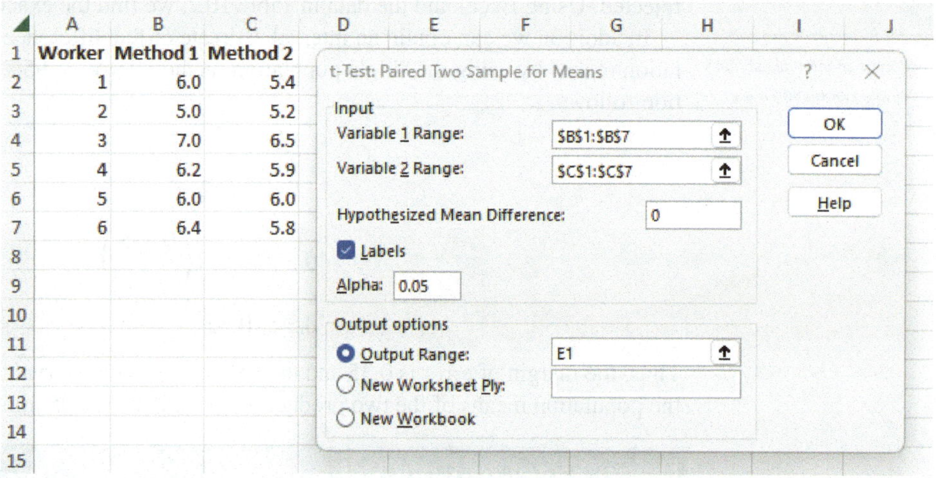

Source: Microsoft Corporation

Figure 10.9 Excel Results for the Hypothesis Test in the Matched Samples Study

	A	B	C	D	E	F	G
1	Worker	Method 1	Method 2		t-Test: Paired Two Sample for Means		
2	1	6.0	5.4				
3	2	5.0	5.2			*Method 1*	*Method 2*
4	3	7.0	6.5		Mean	6.1	5.8
5	4	6.2	5.9		Variance	0.428	0.212
6	5	6.0	6.0		Observations	6	6
7	6	6.4	5.8		Pearson Correlation	0.8764	
8					Hypothesized Mean Difference	0	
9					df	5	
10					t Stat	2.1958	
11					P(T<=t) one-tail	0.0398	
12					t Critical one-tail	2.0150	
13					P(T<=t) two-tail	0.0795	
14					t Critical two-tail	2.5706	

Notes + Comments

1. In the example presented in this section, workers performed the production task with first one method and then the other method. This example illustrates a matched sample design in which each sampled element (worker) provides a pair of data values. It is also possible to use different but "similar" elements to provide the pair of data values. For example, a worker at one location could be matched with a similar worker at another location (similarity based on age, education, gender, experience, etc.). The pairs of workers would provide the difference data that could be used in the matched sample analysis.
2. A matched sample procedure for inferences about two population means generally provides better precision than the independent sample approach; therefore it is the recommended design. However, in some applications, the matching cannot be achieved, or perhaps the time and cost associated with matching are excessive. In such cases, the independent sample design should be used.

Exercises

Methods

19. Consider the following hypothesis test.

$$H_0: \mu_d \leq 0$$
$$H_a: \mu_d > 0$$

The following data are from matched samples taken from two populations. **LO 6**

	Population	
Element	**1**	**2**
1	21	20
2	28	26
3	18	18
4	20	20
5	26	24

a. Compute the difference value for each element.
b. Compute $\bar{d}$.
c. Compute the standard deviation s_d.
d. Conduct a hypothesis test using $\alpha = 0.05$. What is your conclusion?

20. The following data are from matched samples taken from two populations. **LO 7**

	Population	
Element	**1**	**2**
1	11	8
2	7	8
3	9	6
4	12	7
5	13	10
6	15	15
7	15	14

a. Compute the difference value for each element.
b. Compute $\bar{d}$.
c. Compute the standard deviation s_d.

d. What is the point estimate of the difference between the two population means?
e. Provide a 95% confidence interval for the difference between the two population means.

Applications

21. **Television Commercials and Product Purchase Potential.** A market research firm used a sample of individuals to rate the purchase potential of a particular product before and after the individuals saw a new television commercial about the product. The purchase potential ratings were based on a 0 to 10 scale, with higher values indicating a higher purchase potential. The null hypothesis stated that the mean rating "after" would be less than or equal to the mean rating "before." Rejection of this hypothesis would show that the commercial improved the mean purchase potential rating. Use $\alpha = 0.05$ and the following data to test the hypothesis and comment on the value of the commercial. **LO 6**

	Purchase Rating			Purchase Rating	
Individual	After	Before	Individual	After	Before
1	6	5	5	3	5
2	6	4	6	9	8
3	7	7	7	7	5
4	4	3	8	6	6

22. **First Quarter Stock Market Performance.** The price per share of stock for a sample of 25 companies was recorded at the beginning of the first financial quarter and then again at the end of the first financial quarter. How stocks perform during the first quarter is an indicator of what is ahead for the stock market and the economy. Use the sample data in the file *stockquarter* to answer the following. **LO 7**

DATA*file*
stockquarter

a. Let d_i denote the percentage change in price per share for company i where

$$d_i = \frac{\textit{end of } 1^{st} \textit{quarter price per share} - \textit{beginning of } 1^{st} \textit{ quarter price per share}}{\textit{beginning of } 1^{st} \textit{ quarter price per share}}$$

Use the sample mean of these values to estimate the percentage change in the stock price over the first quarter.

b. What is the 95% confidence interval estimate of the population mean percentage change in the price per share of stock during the first quarter? Interpret this result.

23. **Credit Card Expenditures.** Bank of America's Consumer Spending Survey collected data on annual credit card charges in seven different categories of expenditures: transportation, groceries, dining out, household expenses, home furnishings, apparel, and entertainment. Using data from a sample of 42 credit card accounts, assume that each account was used to identify the annual credit card charges for groceries (population 1) and the annual credit card charges for dining out (population 2). Using the difference data, the sample mean difference was $\bar{d} = \$850$, and the sample standard deviation was $s_d = \$1{,}123$. **LO 6, 7**

a. Formulate the null and alternative hypotheses to test for no difference between the population mean credit card charges for groceries and the population mean credit card charges for dining out.
b. Use a 0.05 level of significance. Can you conclude that the population means differ? What is the p-value?
c. Which category, groceries or dining out, has a higher population mean annual credit card charge? What is the point estimate of the difference between the population means? What is the 95% confidence interval estimate of the difference between the population means?

24. **Domestic Airfare.** The Global Business Travel Association reported the domestic airfare for business travel for the current year and the previous year. Below is a sample of 12 flights with their domestic airfares shown for both years. **LO 6**

DATA*file*
businesstravel

Current Year	Previous Year	Current Year	Previous Year
345	315	635	585
526	463	710	650
420	462	605	545
216	206	517	547
285	275	570	508
405	432	610	580

a. Formulate the hypotheses and test for a significant increase in the mean domestic airfare for business travel for the one-year period. What is the p-value? Using a 0.05 level of significance, what is your conclusion?
b. What is the sample mean domestic airfare for business travel for each year?
c. What is the percentage change in the airfare for the one-year period?

25. **SAT Scores.** The College Board SAT college entrance exam consists of two sections: math and evidence-based reading and writing (EBRW). Sample data showing the math and EBRW scores for a sample of 12 students who took the SAT follow. **LO 6**

DATA*file*
testscores

Student	Math	EBRW	Student	Math	EBRW
1	540	474	7	480	430
2	432	380	8	499	459
3	528	463	9	610	615
4	574	612	10	572	541
5	448	420	11	390	335
6	502	526	12	593	613

a. Use a 0.05 level of significance and test for a difference between the population mean for the math scores and the population mean for the EBRW scores. What is the p-value and what is your conclusion?
b. What is the point estimate of the difference between the mean scores for the two tests? What are the estimates of the population mean scores for the two tests? Which test reports the higher mean score?

26. **PGA Tour Scores.** Scores in the first and fourth (final) rounds for a sample of 20 golfers who competed in PGA tournaments are shown in the following table. Suppose you would like to determine whether the mean score for the first round of a PGA Tour event is significantly different than the mean score for the fourth and final round. Does the pressure of playing in the final round cause scores to go up? Or does the increased player concentration cause scores to come down? **LO 6, 7**

DATA*file*
golfscores

Player	First Round	Final Round	Player	First Round	Final Round
Michael Letzig	70	72	Aron Price	72	72
Scott Verplank	71	72	Charles Howell	72	70
D. A. Points	70	75	Jason Dufner	70	73
Jerry Kelly	72	71	Mike Weir	70	77
Soren Hansen	70	69	Carl Pettersson	68	70
D. J. Trahan	67	67	Bo Van Pelt	68	65
Bubba Watson	71	67	Ernie Els	71	70
Reteif Goosen	68	75	Cameron Beckman	70	68
Jeff Klauk	67	73	Nick Watney	69	68
Kenny Perry	70	69	Tommy Armour III	67	71

a. Use $\alpha = 0.10$ to test for a statistically significantly difference between the population means for first- and fourth-round scores. What is the p-value? What is your conclusion?
b. What is the point estimate of the difference between the two population means? For which round is the population mean score lower?
c. What is the margin of error for a 90% confidence interval estimate for the difference between the population means? Could this confidence interval have been used to test the hypothesis in part (a)? Explain.

27. **Price Comparison of Smoothie Blenders.** A personal fitness company produces both a deluxe and a standard model of a smoothie blender for home use. Selling prices obtained from a sample of retail outlets follow. **LO 6, 7**

	Model Price ($)			Model Price ($)	
Retail Outlet	Deluxe	Standard	Retail Outlet	Deluxe	Standard
1	39	27	5	40	30
2	39	28	6	39	34
3	45	35	7	35	29
4	38	30			

a. The manufacturer's suggested retail prices for the two models show a $10 price differential. Use a 0.05 level of significance and test that the mean difference between the prices of the two models is $10.
b. What is the 95% confidence interval for the difference between the mean prices of the two models?

10.4 Inferences About the Difference Between Two Population Proportions

Letting p_1 denote the proportion for population 1 and p_2 denote the proportion for population 2, we next consider inferences about the difference between the two population proportions: $p_1 - p_2$. To make an inference about this difference, we will select two independent random samples consisting of n_1 units from population 1 and n_2 units from population 2.

Interval Estimation of $p_1 - p_2$

In the following example, we show how to compute a margin of error and develop an interval estimate of the difference between two population proportions.

A tax preparation firm is interested in comparing the quality of work at two of its regional offices. By randomly selecting samples of tax returns prepared at each office and verifying the sample returns' accuracy, the firm will be able to estimate the proportion of erroneous returns prepared at each office. Of particular interest is the difference between these proportions.

$$p_1 = \text{proportion of erroneous returns for population 1 (office 1)}$$
$$p_2 = \text{proportion of erroneous returns for population 2 (office 2)}$$
$$\bar{p}_1 = \text{sample proportion for a random sample from population 1}$$
$$\bar{p}_2 = \text{sample proportion for a random sample from population 2}$$

The difference between the two population proportions is given by $p_1 - p_2$. The point estimator of $p_1 - p_2$ is as follows.

Point Estimator of the Difference Between Two Population Proportions

$$\bar{p}_1 - \bar{p}_2 \qquad \textbf{(10.10)}$$

Thus, the point estimator of the difference between two population proportions is the difference between the sample proportions of two independent random samples.

As with other point estimators, the point estimator $\bar{p}_1 - \bar{p}_2$ has a sampling distribution that reflects the possible values of $\bar{p}_1 - \bar{p}_2$ if we repeatedly took two independent random samples. The mean of this sampling distribution is $p_1 - p_2$ and the standard error of $\bar{p}_1 - \bar{p}_2$ is as follows:

Standard Error of $\bar{p}_1 - \bar{p}_2$

$$\sigma_{\bar{p}_1 - \bar{p}_2} = \sqrt{\frac{p_1(1 - p_1)}{n_1} + \frac{p_2(1 - p_2)}{n_2}} \tag{10.11}$$

Sample sizes involving proportions are usually large enough to use this approximation.

If the sample sizes are large enough that n_1p_1, $n_1(1 - p_1)$, n_2p_2, and $n_2(1 - p_2)$ are all greater than or equal to 5, the sampling distribution of $\bar{p}_1 - \bar{p}_2$ can be approximated by a normal distribution.

As we showed previously, an interval estimate is given by a point estimate $\pm$ a margin of error. In the estimation of the difference between two population proportions, an interval estimate will take the following form:

$$\bar{p}_1 - \bar{p}_2 \pm \text{Margin of error}$$

With the sampling distribution of $\bar{p}_1 - \bar{p}_2$ approximated by a normal distribution, we would like to use $z_{\alpha/2}\sigma_{\bar{p}_1 - \bar{p}_2}$ as the margin of error. However, $\sigma_{\bar{p}_1 - \bar{p}_2}$ given by equation (10.11) cannot be used directly because the two population proportions, p_1 and p_2, are unknown. Using the sample proportion $\bar{p}_1$ to estimate p_1 and the sample proportion $\bar{p}_2$ to estimate p_2, the margin of error is as follows:

$$\text{Margin of error} = z_{\alpha/2}\sqrt{\frac{\bar{p}_1(1 - \bar{p}_1)}{n_1} + \frac{\bar{p}_2(1 - \bar{p}_2)}{n_2}} \tag{10.12}$$

The general form of an interval estimate of the difference between two population proportions is as follows.

Interval Estimate of the Difference Between Two Population Proportions

$$\bar{p}_1 - \bar{p}_2 \pm z_{\alpha/2}\sqrt{\frac{\bar{p}_1(1 - \bar{p}_1)}{n_1} + \frac{\bar{p}_2(1 - \bar{p}_2)}{n_2}} \tag{10.13}$$

where $1 - \alpha$ is the confidence coefficient.

Returning to the tax preparation example, we find that independent random samples from the two offices provide the following information.

DATA*file*
taxprep_mod

Office 1	Office 2
$n_1 = 250$	$n_2 = 300$
Number of returns with errors = 35	Number of returns with errors = 27

The sample proportions for the two offices follow.

$$\bar{p}_1 = \frac{35}{250} = 0.14$$

$$\bar{p}_2 = \frac{27}{300} = 0.09$$

The point estimate of the difference between the proportions of erroneous tax returns for the two populations is $\bar{p}_1 - \bar{p}_2 = 0.14 - 0.09 = 0.05$. Thus, we estimate that office 1 has a 0.05, or 5%, greater error rate than office 2.

Expression (10.13) can now be used to provide a margin of error and interval estimate of the difference between the two population proportions. Using a 90% confidence interval with $z_{\alpha/2} = z_{0.05} = 1.645$, we have

$$\bar{p}_1 - \bar{p}_2 \pm z_{\alpha/2}\sqrt{\frac{\bar{p}_1(1-\bar{p}_1)}{n_1} + \frac{\bar{p}_2(1-\bar{p}_2)}{n_2}}$$

$$0.14 - 0.09 \pm 1.645\sqrt{\frac{0.14(1-0.14)}{250} + \frac{0.09(1-0.09)}{300}}$$

$$0.05 \pm 0.045$$

Thus, the margin of error is 0.045, and the 90% confidence interval is 0.005 to 0.095.

Using Excel to Construct a Confidence Interval

We can create a worksheet for developing an interval estimate of the difference between population proportions. Let us illustrate by developing an interval estimate of the difference between the proportions of erroneous tax returns at the two offices of the tax preparation firm. Refer to Figure 10.10 as we describe the tasks involved. The formula worksheet is in the background; the value worksheet appears in the foreground.

Enter/Access Data: Open the file *taxprep_mod*. Columns A and B contain headings and Yes or No data that indicate which of the tax returns from each office contain an error.

Figure 10.10 Constructing a 90% Confidence Interval for the Difference in the Proportion of Erroneous Tax Returns Prepared by Two Offices

	A	B	C	D	E	F
1	Office 1	Office 2			Interval Estimate of Difference	
2	No	No			in Population Proportions	
3	No	No				
4	No	No			Office 1	Office 2
5	No	No		Sample Size	=COUNTA(A2:A251)	=COUNTA(B2:B301)
6	No	No		Response of Interest	Yes	Yes
7	Yes	No		Count for Response	=COUNTIF(A2:A251,E6)	=COUNTIF(B2:B301,F6)
8	No	No		Sample Proportion	=E7/E5	=F7/F5
9	No	No				
10	No	No		Confidence Coefficient	0.9	
11	No	No		Level of Significance	=1-E10	
12	No	No		z Value	=NORM.S.INV(1-E11/2)	
13	No	No				
14	No	No		Standard Error	=SQRT(E8*(1-E8)/E5+F8*(1-F8)/F5)	
15	No	No		Margin of Error	=E12*E14	
16	No	No				
17	No	Yes		Point Estimate of Difference	=E8-F8	
18	Yes	No		Lower Limit	=E17-E15	
19	No	No		Upper Limit	=E17+E15	
250	Yes	No				
251	No	No				
300		No				
301		No				

	A	B	C	D	E	F
1	Office 1	Office 2			Interval Estimate of Difference	
2	No	No			in Population Proportions	
3	No	No				
4	No	No			Office 1	Office 2
5	No	No		Sample Size	250	300
6	No	No		Response of Interest	Yes	Yes
7	Yes	No		Count for Response	35	27
8	No	No		Sample Proportion	0.14	0.09
9	No	No				
10	No	No		Confidence Coefficient	0.9	
11	No	No		Level of Significance	0.1	
12	No	No		z Value	1.645	
13	No	No				
14	No	No		Standard Error	0.0275	
15	No	No		Margin of Error	0.0452	
16	No	No				
17	No	Yes		Point Estimate of Difference	0.05	
18	Yes	No		Lower Limit	0.0048	
19	No	No		Upper Limit	0.0952	
250	Yes	No				
251	No	No				
300		No				
301		No				

Note: Rows 20–249 and 252–299 are hidden.

The Excel function COUNTA counts all cells that are not empty, i.e., it counts "anything," while the Excel function COUNT only counts cells with numeric values.

Enter Functions and Formulas: The descriptive statistics needed are provided in cells E5:F5 and E7:F8. Note that Excel's COUNTA function is used in cells E5 and F5 to count the number of observations for each of the samples. The value worksheet indicates 250 returns in the sample from office 1 and 300 returns in the sample from office 2. In cells E6 and F6, we type *Yes* to indicate the response of interest (an erroneous return). Excel's COUNTIF function is used in cells E7 and F7 to count the number of Yes responses from each office. Formulas entered into cells E8 and F8 compute the sample proportions. Entering *0.9* into cell E10 for the value of the confidence coefficient, the corresponding level of significance ($\alpha = 0.10$) is computed in cell E11. In cell E12, we use the NORM.S.INV function to compute the z value needed to compute the margin of error for the interval estimate.

In cell E14, a point estimate of $\sigma_{\bar{p}_1-\bar{p}_2}$, the standard error of the point estimator $\bar{p}_1 - \bar{p}_2$, is computed based on the two sample proportions (E8 and F8) and sample sizes (E5 and F5). The margin of error is then computed in cell E15 by multiplying the z value by the estimate of the standard error.

The point estimate of the difference in the two population proportions is computed in cell E17 as the difference in the sample proportions; the result, shown in the value worksheet, is 0.05. The lower limit of the confidence interval is computed in cell E18 by subtracting the margin of error from the point estimate. The upper limit is computed in cell E19 by adding the margin of error to the point estimate. The value worksheet shows that the 90% confidence interval estimate of the difference in the two population proportions is 0.0048 to 0.0952.

A Template for Other Problems This worksheet can be used as a template for other problems requiring an interval estimate of the difference in population proportions. The new data must be entered in columns A and B. The data ranges in the cells used to compute the sample size (E5:F5) and the cells used to compute a count of the response of interest (E7:F7) must be changed to correctly indicate the location of the new data. The response of interest must be typed into cells E6:F6. The 90% confidence interval for the new data will then appear in cells E17:E19. If an interval estimate with a different confidence coefficient is desired, simply change the entry in cell E10.

This worksheet can also be used as a template for solving text exercises in which the sample data have already been summarized. No change in the data section is necessary. Simply type the values for the given sample sizes in cells E5:F5 and type the given values for the sample proportions in cells E8:F8. The 90% confidence interval will then appear in cells E17:E19. If an interval estimate with a different confidence coefficient is desired, simply change the entry in cell E10.

Hypothesis Tests About $p_1 - p_2$

Let us now consider hypothesis tests about the difference between the proportions of two populations. We focus on tests involving no difference between the two population proportions. In this case, the three forms for a hypothesis test are as follows:

All hypotheses considered use 0 as the difference of interest.

$$\begin{array}{lll} H_0\colon p_1 - p_2 \geq 0 & H_0\colon p_1 - p_2 \leq 0 & H_0\colon p_1 - p_2 = 0 \\ H_a\colon p_1 - p_2 < 0 & H_a\colon p_1 - p_2 > 0 & H_a\colon p_1 - p_2 \neq 0 \end{array}$$

When we assume H_0 is true as an equality, we have $p_1 - p_2 = 0$, which is the same as saying that the population proportions are equal, $p_1 = p_2$.

We will base the test statistic on the sampling distribution of the point estimator $\bar{p}_1 - \bar{p}_2$. In equation (10.11), we showed that the standard error of $\bar{p}_1 - \bar{p}_2$ is given by

$$\sigma_{\bar{p}_1 - \bar{p}_2} = \sqrt{\frac{p_1(1-p_1)}{n_1} + \frac{p_2(1-p_2)}{n_2}}$$

Under the assumption H_0 is true as an equality, the population proportions are equal and $p_1 = p_2 = p$. In this case, $\sigma_{\bar{p}_1 - \bar{p}_2}$ becomes

Standard Error of $\bar{p}_1 - \bar{p}_2$ when $p_1 = p_2 = p$

$$\sigma_{\bar{p}_1 - \bar{p}_2} = \sqrt{\frac{p(1-p)}{n_1} + \frac{p(1-p)}{n_2}} = \sqrt{p(1-p)\left(\frac{1}{n_1} + \frac{1}{n_2}\right)} \qquad \textbf{(10.14)}$$

With p unknown, we pool, or combine, the point estimators from the two samples ($\bar{p}_1$ and $\bar{p}_2$) to obtain a single point estimator of p as follows:

Pooled Estimator of p When $p_1 = p_2 = p$

$$\bar{p} = \frac{n_1\bar{p}_1 + n_2\bar{p}_2}{n_1 + n_2} \qquad \textbf{(10.15)}$$

This **pooled estimator of p** is a weighted average of $\bar{p}_1$ and $\bar{p}_2$.

Substituting $\bar{p}$ for p in equation (10.14), we obtain an estimate of the standard error of $\bar{p}_1 - \bar{p}_2$. This estimate of the standard error is used in the test statistic. The general form of the test statistic for hypothesis tests about the difference between two population proportions is the point estimator divided by the estimate of $\sigma_{\bar{p}_1 - \bar{p}_2}$.

Test Statistic for Hypothesis Tests About $p_1 - p_2$

$$z = \frac{(\bar{p}_1 - \bar{p}_2)}{\sqrt{\bar{p}(1-\bar{p})\left(\frac{1}{n_1} + \frac{1}{n_2}\right)}} \qquad \textbf{(10.16)}$$

This test statistic applies to large sample situations where n_1p_1, $n_1(1 - p_1)$, n_2p_2, and $n_2(1 - p_2)$ are all greater than or equal to 5.

Let us return to the tax preparation firm example and assume that the firm wants to use a hypothesis test to determine whether the error proportions differ between the two offices. A two-tailed test is required. The null and alternative hypotheses are as follows:

$$H_0\colon p_1 - p_2 = 0$$
$$H_a\colon p_1 - p_2 \neq 0$$

If H_0 is rejected, the firm can conclude that the error rates at the two offices differ. We will use $\alpha = 0.10$ as the level of significance.

The sample data previously collected showed $\bar{p}_1 = 0.14$ for the $n_1 = 250$ returns sampled at office 1 and $\bar{p}_2 = 0.09$ for the $n_2 = 300$ returns sampled at office 2. We continue by computing the pooled estimate of p.

$$\bar{p} = \frac{n_1\bar{p}_1 + n_2\bar{p}_2}{n_1 + n_2} = \frac{250(0.14) + 300(0.09)}{250 + 300} = 0.1127$$

Using this pooled estimate and the difference between the sample proportions, the value of the test statistic is as follows.

$$z = \frac{(\bar{p}_1 - \bar{p}_2)}{\sqrt{\bar{p}(1-\bar{p})\left(\frac{1}{n_1} + \frac{1}{n_2}\right)}} = \frac{(0.14 - 0.09)}{\sqrt{0.1127(1 - 0.1127)\left(\frac{1}{250} + \frac{1}{300}\right)}} = 1.85$$

In computing the p-value for this two-tailed test, we first note that $z = 1.85$ is in the upper tail of the standard normal distribution. Using $z = 1.85$ and the standard normal distribution table, we find the area in the upper tail is $1.0000 - 0.9678 = 0.0322$. Doubling this area for a two-tailed test, we find the p-value $= 2(0.0322) = 0.0644$. With the p-value less than $\alpha = 0.10$, H_0 is rejected at the 0.10 level of significance. The firm can conclude that the error rates differ between the two offices. This hypothesis testing conclusion is consistent with the earlier interval estimation results that showed the interval estimate of the difference between the population error rates at the two offices to be 0.005 to 0.095, with office 1 having the higher error rate.

Using Excel to Conduct a Hypothesis Test

We can create a worksheet for conducting a hypothesis test about the difference between population proportions. Let us illustrate by testing to see whether there is a significant difference between the proportions of erroneous tax returns at the two offices of the tax preparation firm. Refer to Figure 10.11 as we describe the tasks involved. The formula worksheet is in the background; the value worksheet is in the foreground.

Enter/Access Data: Open the file *taxprep_mod*. Columns A and B contain headings and Yes or No data that indicate which of the tax returns from each office contain an error.

Enter Functions and Formulas: The descriptive statistics needed to perform the hypothesis test are provided in cells E5:F5 and E7:F8. They are the same as the ones used for an interval estimate (see Figure 10.10). The hypothesized value of the difference between the two populations is zero; it is entered into cell E10. In cell E11, the difference in the sample proportions is used to compute a point estimate of the difference in the two population proportions. Using the two sample proportions and sample sizes, a pooled estimate of the population proportion p is computed in cell E13; its value is 0.1127. Then, in cell E14, an estimate of $\sigma_{\bar{p}_1 - \bar{p}_2}$ is computed using equation (10.14), with the pooled estimate of p and the sample sizes.

Figure 10.11 Hypothesis Test Concerning Difference in Proportion of Erroneous Tax Returns Prepared by Two Offices

	A	B	C	D	E	F
1	Office 1	Office 2			Hypothesis Test Concerning Difference Between Population Proportions	
2	No	No				
3	No	No				
4	No	No			Office 1	Office 2
5	No	No		Sample Size	=COUNTA(A2:A251)	=COUNTA(B2:B301)
6	No	No		Response of Interest	Yes	Yes
7	Yes	No		Count for Response	=COUNTIF(A2:A251,E6)	=COUNTIF(B2:B301,F6)
8	No	No		Sample Proportion	=E7/E5	=F7/F5
9	No	No				
10	No	No		Hypothesized Value	0	
11	No	No		Point Estimate of Difference	=E8-F8	
12	No	No				
13	No	No		Pooled Estimate of *p*	=(E5*E8+F5*F8)/(E5+F5)	
14	No	No		Standard Error	=SQRT(E13*(1-E13)*(1/E5+1/F5))	
15	No	No		Test Statistic	=(E11-E10)/E14	
16	No	No				
17	No	Yes		*p*-value (Lower Tail)	=NORM.S.DIST(E15,TRUE)	
18	Yes	No		*p*-value (Upper Tail)	=1-NORM.S.DIST(E15,TRUE)	
19	No	No		*p*-value (Two Tail)	=2*MIN(E17,E18)	
250	Yes	No				
251	No	No				
300		No				
301		No				

	A	B	C	D	E	F
1	Office 1	Office 2		Hypothesis Test Concerning Difference Between Population Proportions		
2	No	No				
3	No	No				
4	No	No			Office 1	Office 2
5	No	No		Sample Size	250	300
6	No	No		Response of Interest	Yes	Yes
7	Yes	No		Count for Response	35	27
8	No	No		Sample Proportion	0.14	0.09
9	No	No				
10	No	No		Hypothesized Value	0	
11	No	No		Point Estimate of Difference	0.05	
12	No	No				
13	No	No		Pooled Estimate of *p*	0.1127	
14	No	No		Standard Error	0.0271	
15	No	No		Test Statistic	1.8462	
16	No	No				
17	No	Yes		*p*-value (Lower Tail)	0.9676	
18	Yes	No		*p*-value (Upper Tail)	0.0324	
19	No	No		*p*-value (Two Tail)	0.0649	
250	Yes	No				
251	No	No				
300		No				
301		No				

Note: Rows 20–249 and 252–299 are hidden.

The p-value here (0.0649) differs from the one we found using the cumulative normal probability tables (0.0644) due to rounding.

The formula =*(E11-E10)/E14* entered into cell E15 computes the test statistic z (1.8462). The NORM.S.DIST function is then used to compute the p-value (Lower Tail) and the p-value (Upper Tail) in cells E17 and E18. The p-value (Two Tail) is computed in cell E19 as twice the minimum of the two one-tailed p-values. The value worksheet shows that p-value (Two Tail) = 0.0649. Because the p-value = 0.0649 is less than the level of significance, $\alpha = 0.10$, we have sufficient evidence to reject the null hypothesis and conclude that the population proportions are not equal.

This worksheet can be used as a template for hypothesis testing problems involving differences between population proportions. The new data can be entered into columns A and B. The ranges for the new data and the response of interest need to be revised in cells E5:F7. The remainder of the worksheet will then be updated as needed to conduct the hypothesis test. If a hypothesized difference other than 0 is to be used, the new value must be entered in cell E10.

To use this worksheet for exercises in which the sample statistics are given, just type in the given values for cells E5:F5 and E7:F8. The remainder of the worksheet will then be updated to conduct the hypothesis test. If a hypothesized difference other than 0 is to be used, the new value must be entered in cell E10.

Exercises

Methods

28. Consider the following results for independent samples taken from two populations. **LO 8, 9**

Sample 1	Sample 2
$n_1 = 400$	$n_2 = 300$
$\bar{p}_1 = 0.48$	$\bar{p}_2 = 0.36$

a. What is the point estimate of the difference between the two population proportions?
b. Develop a 90% confidence interval for the difference between the two population proportions.
c. Develop a 95% confidence interval for the difference between the two population proportions.

29. Consider the hypothesis test

$$H_0: p_1 - p_2 \leq 0$$
$$H_a: p_1 - p_2 > 0$$

The following results are for independent samples taken from the two populations. **LO 10**

Sample 1	Sample 2
$n_1 = 200$	$n_2 = 300$
$\bar{p}_1 = 0.22$	$\bar{p}_2 = 0.16$

a. What is the p-value?
b. With $\alpha = 0.05$, what is your hypothesis testing conclusion?

Applications

30. **Corporate Hiring Outlook.** A *BusinessWeek/Harris* poll asked senior executives at large corporations their opinions about the economic outlook for the future. One question was, "Do you think that there will be an increase in the number of full-time employees at your company over the next 12 months?" In the current survey, 220 of 400 executives answered Yes, while in a previous year survey, 192 of 400 executives had answered Yes. Provide a 95% confidence interval estimate for the difference

between the proportions at the two points in time. What is your interpretation of the interval estimate? **LO 9**

31. **Impact of Pinterest on Purchase Decisions.** *Forbes* reports that females trust recommendations from Pinterest more than recommendations from any other social network platform (*Forbes.com*). But does trust in Pinterest differ by sex? The following sample data show the number of females and males who stated in a recent sample that they trust recommendations made on Pinterest. **LO 8, 9**

	Females	Males
Sample	150	170
Trust Recommendations Made on Pinterest	117	102

a. What is the point estimate of the proportion of females who trust recommendations made on Pinterest?
b. What is the point estimate of the proportion of males who trust recommendations made on Pinterest?
c. Provide a 95% confidence interval estimate of the difference between the proportion of females and males who trust recommendations made on Pinterest.

32. **Mislabeling of Fish.** Researchers with Oceana, a group dedicated to preserving the ocean ecosystem, reported finding that 33% of fish sold in retail outlets, grocery stores, and sushi bars throughout the United States had been mislabeled (*San Francisco Chronicle*). Does this mislabeling differ for different species of fish? The following data show the number labeled incorrectly for samples of tuna and mahi mahi. **LO 8, 9**

	Tuna	Mahi Mahi
Sample	220	160
Mislabeled	99	56

a. What is the point estimate of the proportion of tuna that is mislabeled?
b. What is the point estimate of the proportion of mahi mahi that is mislabeled?
c. Provide a 95% confidence interval estimate of the difference between the proportions of tuna and mahi mahi that is mislabeled.

33. **Voter Turnout.** Minnesota had the highest turnout rate of any state for the 2016 presidential election (United States Election Project website). Political analysts wonder if turnout in rural Minnesota was higher than turnout in the urban areas of the state. A sample shows that 663 of 884 registered voters from rural Minnesota voted in the 2016 presidential election, while 414 out of 575 registered voters from urban Minnesota voted. **LO 10**
a. Formulate the null and alternative hypotheses that can be used to test whether registered voters in rural Minnesota were more likely than registered voters in urban Minnesota to vote in the 2016 presidential election.
b. What is the proportion of sampled registered voters in rural Minnesota that voted in the 2016 presidential election?
c. What is the proportion of sampled registered voters in urban Minnesota that voted in the 2016 presidential election?
d. At $\alpha = 0.05$, test the political analysts' hypothesis. What is the p-value, and what conclusion do you draw from your results?

34. **Wearable Fitness Trackers.** Fitness trackers are devices that monitor the wearer's heart rate, sleep duration, body temperature, and activity level. In a recent survey, Gallup asked Americans about their use of wearable fitness trackers. The table below cross tabulates survey data based on whether the respondents wear fitness trackers and whether they have annual incomes below $100,000. **LO 8, 10**

	Income ≥ \$100,000	Income < \$100,000
Wear Tracker	445	425
Do Not Wear Tracker	990	2411

a. Formulate the null and alternative hypotheses that can be used to test whether individuals in the higher income category are more likely to wear fitness trackers than individuals in the lower income category.
b. What is the point estimate of the proportion of higher income individuals who wear fitness trackers?
c. What is the point estimate of the proportion of lower income individuals who wear fitness trackers?
d. What is the *p*-value of your hypothesis test? At $\alpha = 0.05$, what conclusion do you draw from your results?

35. **Hotel Occupancy Rates.** Tourism is extremely important to the economy of Florida. Hotel occupancy is an often-reported measure of visitor volume and visitor activity (*Orlando Sentinel,* May 19, 2018). Hotel occupancy data for February in two consecutive years are as follows. **LO 8, 9, 10**

	Current Year	Previous Year
Occupied Rooms	1,470	1,458
Total Rooms	1,750	1,800

a. Formulate the hypothesis test that can be used to determine whether there has been an increase in the proportion of rooms occupied over the one-year period.
b. What is the estimated proportion of hotel rooms occupied each year?
c. Using a 0.05 level of significance, what is your hypothesis test conclusion? What is the *p*-value?
d. What is the 95% confidence interval estimate of the change in occupancy for the one-year period? Do you think area officials would be pleased with the results?

36. **Differences in Raise or Promotion Expectations by Sex.** The Adecco Workplace Insights Survey sampled male and female workers and asked if they expected to get a raise or promotion this year (*USA Today*). Suppose the survey sampled 200 males and 200 females. If 104 of the males replied Yes and 74 of the females replied Yes, are the results statistically significant in that you can conclude a greater proportion of men are expecting to get a raise or a promotion this year? **LO 8, 10**
a. State the hypothesis test in terms of the population proportion of males and the population proportion of females?
b. What is the sample proportion for males? For females?
c. Use a 0.01 level of significance. What is the *p*-value and what is your conclusion?

37. **Default Rates on Bank Loans.** Carl Allen and Norm Nixon are two loan officers at Brea Federal Savings and Loan Bank. The bank manager is interested in comparing the default rate on the loans approved by Carl to the default rate on the loans approved by Norm. In the sample of loans collected, there are 60 loans approved by Carl (9 of which defaulted) and 80 loans approved by Norm (7 of which defaulted). **LO 8, 10**
a. State the hypothesis test that the default rates are the same for the two loan officers.
b. What is the sample default proportion for Carl? For Norm?
c. Use a 0.05 level of significance. What is the *p*-value and what is your conclusion?

Summary

In this chapter, we discussed procedures for developing interval estimates and conducting hypothesis tests involving two populations. First, we showed how to make inferences about the difference between two population means when independent random samples are selected. We first considered the case where the population standard deviations σ_1 and σ_2 could be assumed known. The standard normal distribution z was used to develop the interval estimate and served as the test statistic for hypothesis tests. We then considered the case where the population standard deviations were unknown and estimated by the sample standard deviations s_1 and s_2. In this case, the t distribution was used to develop the interval estimate and the t value served as the test statistic for hypothesis tests.

Inferences about the difference between two population means were then discussed for the matched sample design. In the matched sample design, each element provides a pair of data values, one from each population. The difference between the paired data values is then used in the statistical analysis. The matched sample design is generally preferred to the independent sample design because the matched sample procedure often improves the precision of the estimate.

Finally, interval estimation and hypothesis testing about the difference between two population proportions were discussed. Statistical procedures for analyzing the difference between two population proportions are similar to the procedures for analyzing the difference between two population means.

We showed how Excel can be used to develop the interval estimates and conduct the hypothesis tests discussed in the chapter. Many of the worksheets can be used as templates to solve problems encountered in practice as well as the exercises and case problems found in the text.

Glossary

Independent random samples Samples selected from two populations in such a way that the elements making up one sample are chosen independently of the elements making up the other sample.

Matched samples Samples in which each data value of one sample is matched with a corresponding data value of the other sample.

Pooled estimator of *p* An estimator of a population proportion obtained by computing a weighted average of the point estimators obtained from two independent samples.

Key Formulas

Point Estimator of the Difference Between Two Population Means

$$\bar{x}_1 - \bar{x}_2 \tag{10.1}$$

Standard Error of $\bar{x}_1 - \bar{x}_2$

$$\sigma_{\bar{x}_1 - \bar{x}_2} = \sqrt{\frac{\sigma_1^2}{n_1} + \frac{\sigma_2^2}{n_2}} \tag{10.2}$$

Interval Estimate of the Difference Between Two Population Means: σ_1 and σ_2 Known

$$\bar{x}_1 - \bar{x}_2 \pm z_{\alpha/2}\sqrt{\frac{\sigma_1^2}{n_1} + \frac{\sigma_2^2}{n_2}} \tag{10.4}$$

Test Statistic for Hypothesis Tests About $\mu_1 - \mu_2$: σ_1 and σ_1 Known

$$z = \frac{(\bar{x}_1 - \bar{x}_2) - D_0}{\sqrt{\frac{\sigma_1^2}{n_1} + \frac{\sigma_2^2}{n_2}}} \tag{10.5}$$

Interval Estimate of the Difference Between Two Population Means: σ_1 and σ_2 Unknown

$$\bar{x}_1 - \bar{x}_2 \pm t_{\alpha/2}\sqrt{\frac{s_1^2}{n_1} + \frac{s_2^2}{n_2}} \tag{10.6}$$

Degrees of Freedom: *t* Distribution with Two Independent Random Samples

$$df = \frac{\left(\dfrac{s_1^2}{n_1} + \dfrac{s_2^2}{n_2}\right)^2}{\dfrac{1}{n_1 - 1}\left(\dfrac{s_1^2}{n_1}\right)^2 + \dfrac{1}{n_2 - 1}\left(\dfrac{s_2^2}{n_2}\right)^2} \tag{10.7}$$

Test Statistic for Hypothesis Tests About $\mu_1 - \mu_2$: σ_1 and σ_2 Unknown

$$t = \frac{(\bar{x}_1 - \bar{x}_2) - D_0}{\sqrt{\dfrac{s_1^2}{n_1} + \dfrac{s_2^2}{n_2}}} \tag{10.8}$$

Test Statistic for Hypothesis Tests Involving Matched Samples

$$t = \frac{\bar{d} - \mu_d}{s_d/\sqrt{n}} \tag{10.9}$$

Point Estimator of the Difference Between Two Population Proportions

$$\bar{p}_1 - \bar{p}_2 \tag{10.10}$$

Standard Error of $p_1 - p_2$

$$\sigma_{\bar{p}_1 - \bar{p}_2} = \sqrt{\frac{p_1(1 - p_1)}{n_1} + \frac{p_2(1 - p_2)}{n_2}} \tag{10.11}$$

Interval Estimate of the Difference Between Two Population Proportions

$$\bar{p}_1 - \bar{p}_2 \pm z_{\alpha/2}\sqrt{\frac{\bar{p}_1(1 - \bar{p}_1)}{n_1} + \frac{\bar{p}_2(1 - \bar{p}_2)}{n_2}} \tag{10.13}$$

Standard Error of $p_1 - p_2$ When $p_1 = p_2 = p$

$$\sigma_{\bar{p}_1 - \bar{p}_2} = \sqrt{p(1 - p)\left(\frac{1}{n_1} + \frac{1}{n_2}\right)} \tag{10.14}$$

Pooled Estimator of p When $p_1 = p_2 = p$

$$\bar{p} = \frac{n_1\bar{p}_1 + n_2\bar{p}_2}{n_1 + n_2} \tag{10.15}$$

Test Statistic for Hypothesis Tests About $p_1 - p_2$

$$z = \frac{(\bar{p}_1 - \bar{p}_2)}{\sqrt{\bar{p}(1 - \bar{p})\left(\dfrac{1}{n_1} + \dfrac{1}{n_2}\right)}} \tag{10.16}$$

Supplementary Exercises

38. **Supermarket Checkout Lane Design.** Safegate Foods, Inc., is redesigning the checkout lanes in its supermarkets throughout the country and is considering two designs. Tests on customer checkout times conducted at two stores where the two new systems have been installed result in the following summary of the data.

System A	System B
$n_1 = 120$	$n_2 = 100$
$\bar{x}_1 = 4.1$ minutes	$\bar{x}_2 = 3.4$ minutes
$\sigma_1 = 2.2$ minutes	$\sigma_2 = 1.5$ minutes

Test at the 0.05 level of significance to determine whether the population mean checkout times of the two systems differ. Which system is preferred? **LO 3**

DATA*file*
carpriceinversion

39. **Car Price Inversion.** In most circumstances, the price of a new car is higher than the price of a slightly used car of the same make and model. However, disruptions in the supply chains of automobile manufacturers can reduce the availability of new cars to such a degree that a slightly used version of the same car can actually sell for a higher price. The file *carpriceinversion* contains the selling price for 46 randomly selected slightly-used Tesla Model 3's and 33 randomly selected new Tesla Model 3's. **LO 1, 4**
   a. Provide and interpret a point estimate of the difference between the population mean sale price between a slightly-used Tesla Model 3 and the new Tesla Model 3.
   b. Develop a 99% confidence interval estimate of the difference between the mean sale price between a slightly-used Tesla Model 3 and a new Tesla Model 3. Would you feel justified in concluding that sale price of a slightly-used Tesla Model 3 is higher than a new Tesla Model 3? Why or why not?

40. **Load versus No-Load Mutual Funds.** Mutual funds are classified as *load* or *no-load* funds. Load funds require an investor to pay an initial fee based on a percentage of the amount invested in the fund. The no-load funds do not require this initial fee. Some financial advisors argue that the load mutual funds may be worth the extra fee because these funds provide a higher mean rate of return than the no-load mutual funds. A sample of 30 load mutual funds and a sample of 30 no-load mutual funds were selected. Data in the file *mutual* were collected on the annual return for the funds over a five-year period. The data for the first five load and first five no-load mutual funds are as follows. **LO 5**

DATA*file*
mutual

Mutual Funds—Load	Return	Mutual Funds—No-Load	Return
American National Growth	15.51	Amana Income Fund	13.24
Arch Small Cap Equity	14.57	Berger One Hundred	12.13
Bartlett Cap Basic	17.73	Columbia International Stock	12.17
Calvert World International	10.31	Dodge & Cox Balanced	16.06
Colonial Fund A	16.23	Evergreen Fund	17.61

   a. Formulate H_0 and H_a such that rejection of H_0 leads to the conclusion that the load mutual funds have a higher mean annual return over the five-year period.
   b. Conduct the hypothesis test. What is the *p*-value? At $\alpha = 0.05$, what is your conclusion?

41. **Kitchen Versus Bedroom Remodeling Costs.** The National Association of Home Builders provided data on the cost of the most popular home remodeling projects.

Sample data on cost in thousands of dollars for two types of remodeling projects are as follows. **LO 1, 4**

Kitchen	Master Bedroom	Kitchen	Master Bedroom
25.2	18.0	23.0	17.8
17.4	22.9	19.7	24.6
22.8	26.4	16.9	21.0
21.9	24.8	21.8	
19.7	26.9	23.6	

a. Develop a point estimate of the difference between the population mean remodeling costs for the two types of projects.
b. Develop a 90% confidence interval for the difference between the two population means.

42. **Effect of Siblings on SAT Scores.** In *Born Together—Reared Apart: The Landmark Minnesota Twin Study*, Nancy Segal discusses the efforts of research psychologists at the University of Minnesota to understand similarities and differences between twins by studying sets of twins who were raised separately. Below are evidence-based reading and writing (EBRW) SAT scores for several pairs of identical twins (twins who share all of their genes) and were raised separately, one of whom was raised in a family with no other children (no siblings) and one of whom was raised in a family with other children (with siblings). **LO 6, 7**

DATA*file*
twins

No Siblings		With Siblings	
Name	EBRW SAT Score	Name	EBRW SAT Score
Bob	440	Donald	420
Matthew	610	Ronald	540
Shannon	590	Kedriana	630
Tyler	390	Kevin	430
Michelle	410	Erin	460
Darius	430	Michael	490
Wilhelmina	510	Josephine	460
Donna	620	Jasmine	540
Drew	510	Kraig	460
Lucinda	680	Bernadette	650
Barry	580	Larry	450
Julie	610	Jennifer	640
Hannah	510	Diedra	460
Roger	630	Latishia	580
Garrett	570	Bart	490
Roger	630	Kara	640
Nancy	530	Rachel	560
Sam	590	Joey	610
Simon	500	Drew	520
Megan	610	Annie	640

a. What is the mean difference between the EBRW SAT scores for the twins raised with no siblings and the twins raised with siblings?
b. Provide a 90% confidence interval estimate of the mean difference between the EBRW SAT scores for the twins raised with no siblings and the twins raised with siblings.

c. Conduct a hypothesis test of equality of the critical reading SAT scores for the twins raised with no siblings and the twins raised with siblings at $\alpha = 0.01$. What is your conclusion?

43. **Change in Financial Security.** Country Financial, a financial services company, uses surveys of adults age 18 and older to determine whether personal financial fitness is changing over time. A recent sample of 1,000 adults showed 410 indicating that their financial security was more than fair. Just a year prior, a sample of 900 adults showed 315 indicating that their financial security was more than fair. **LO 9, 10**
    a. State the hypotheses that can be used to test for a significant difference between the population proportions for the two years.
    b. Conduct the hypothesis test and compute the *p*-value. At a 0.05 level of significance, what is your conclusion?
    c. What is the 95% confidence interval estimate of the difference between the two population proportions? What is your conclusion?

44. **Differences in Insurance Claims Based on Marital Status.** A large automobile insurance company selected samples of single and married male policyholders and recorded the number who made an insurance claim over the preceding three-year period. **LO 9, 10**

Single Policyholders	Married Policyholders
$n_1 = 400$	$n_2 = 900$
Number making claims = 76	Number making claims = 90

    a. Use $\alpha = 0.05$. Test to determine whether the claim rates differ between single and married male policyholders.
    b. Provide a 95% confidence interval for the difference between the proportions for the two populations.

45. **Drug-Resistant Gonorrhea.** Each year, over two million people in the United States become infected with bacteria that are resistant to antibiotics. In particular, the Centers of Disease Control and Prevention has launched studies of drug-resistant gonorrhea (*CDC.gov* website). Of 142 cases tested in Alabama, 9 were found to be drug-resistant. Of 268 cases tested in Texas, 5 were found to be drug-resistant. Do these data suggest a statistically significant difference between the proportions of drug-resistant cases in the two states? Use a 0.02 level of significance. What is the *p*-value, and what is your conclusion? **LO 10**

DATA*file*
computernews

46. **News Access Via Computer.** The American Press Institute reports that almost 70% of all American adults use a computer to gain access to news. Suppose you suspect that the proportion of American adults under 30 years old who use a computer to gain access to news exceeds the proportion of Americans at least 30 years old who use a computer to gain access to news. Data in the file *computernews* represent responses to the question "Do you use a computer to gain access to news?" given by random samples of American adults under 30 years old and Americans who are at least 30 years old. **LO 8, 9**
    a. Estimate the proportion of American adults under 30 years old who use a computer to gain access to news and the proportion of Americans at least 30 years old who use a computer to gain access to news.
    b. Provide a 95% confidence interval for the difference in these proportions.
    c. On the basis of your findings, does it appear the proportion of American adults under 30 years old who use a computer to gain access to news exceeds the proportion of Americans who are at least 30 years old that use a computer to gain access to news?

Case Problem: Par, Inc.

Par, Inc., is a major manufacturer of golf equipment. Management believes that Par's market share could be increased with the introduction of a cut-resistant, longer-lasting golf ball. Therefore, the research group at Par has been investigating a new golf ball coating designed to resist cuts and provide a more durable ball. The tests with the coating have been promising.

One of the researchers voiced concern about the effect of the new coating on driving distances. Par would like the new cut-resistant ball to offer driving distances comparable to those of the current-model golf ball. To compare the driving distances for the two balls, 40 balls of both the new and current models were subjected to distance tests. The testing was performed with a mechanical hitting machine so that any difference between the mean distances for the two models could be attributed to a difference in the two models. The results of the tests, with distances measured to the nearest yard, follow. These data are available in the file *golf*. **LO 4, 5**

DATA*file*
golf

Model		Model		Model		Model	
Current	New	Current	New	Current	New	Current	New
264	277	270	272	263	274	281	283
261	269	287	259	264	266	274	250
267	263	289	264	284	262	273	253
272	266	280	280	263	271	263	260
258	262	272	274	260	260	275	270
283	251	275	281	283	281	267	263
258	262	265	276	255	250	279	261
266	289	260	269	272	263	274	255
259	286	278	268	266	278	276	263
270	264	275	262	268	264	262	279

Managerial Report

1. Formulate and present the rationale for a hypothesis test that Par could use to compare the driving distances of the current and new golf balls.
2. Analyze the data to provide the hypothesis testing conclusion. What is the p-value for your test? What is your recommendation for Par, Inc.?
3. Provide descriptive statistical summaries of the data for each model.
4. What is the 95% confidence interval for the population mean driving distance of each model, and what is the 95% confidence interval for the difference between the means of the two populations?
5. Do you see a need for larger sample sizes and more testing with the golf balls? Discuss.

Chapter 11

Inferences About Population Variances

Contents

Statistics in Practice:
U.S. Government Accountability Office

11.1 Inferences About a Population Variance
- Interval Estimation
- Using Excel to Construct a Confidence Interval
- Hypothesis Testing
- Using Excel to Conduct a Hypothesis Test

11.2 Inferences About Two Population Variances
- Using Excel to Conduct a Hypothesis Test

Summary 531
Key Formulas 531
Supplementary Exercises 531
Case Problem 1: Air Force Training Program 534
Case Problem 2: Meticulous Drill & Reamer 535

Available in the Cengage eBook:
Appendix: Population Variances with R

Learning Objectives

After completing this chapter, you will be able to

LO 1 Describe the distribution form and parameters of the sampling distribution of the sample variance and report values from this distribution.

LO 2 Calculate and interpret the interval estimate at a given level of confidence for a population variance and a population standard deviation.

LO 3 Conduct a hypothesis test about the population variance using either the *p*-value approach or the critical value approach.

LO 4 Describe the distribution form and parameters of the sampling distribution of the ratio of the sample variances of two different populations, and report values from this distribution.

LO 5 Conduct a hypothesis test about the ratio between two population variances using either the *p*-value approach or the critical value approach.

Statistics in Practice

U.S. Government Accountability Office*

Washington, D.C.

The U.S. Government Accountability Office (GAO) is an independent, nonpolitical audit organization in the legislative branch of the federal government. GAO evaluators determine the effectiveness of current and proposed federal programs. To carry out their duties, evaluators must be proficient in records review, legislative research, and statistical analysis techniques.

In one case, GAO evaluators studied a Department of Interior program established to help clean up the nation's rivers and lakes. As part of this program, federal grants were made to small cities throughout the United States. Congress asked the GAO to determine how effectively the program was operating. To do so, the GAO examined records and visited the sites of several waste treatment plants.

One objective of the GAO audit was to ensure that the effluent (treated sewage) at the plants met certain standards. Among other things, the audits reviewed sample data on the oxygen content, the pH level, and the amount of suspended solids in the effluent. A requirement of the program was that a variety of tests be taken daily at each plant and that the collected data be sent periodically to the state engineering department. The GAO's investigation of the data showed whether various characteristics of the effluent were within acceptable limits.

For example, the mean or average pH level of the effluent was examined carefully. In addition, the variance in the reported pH levels was reviewed. The following hypothesis test was conducted about the variance in pH level for the population of effluent.

$$H_0: \sigma^2 = \sigma_0^2$$
$$H_a: \sigma^2 \neq \sigma_0^2$$

In this test, σ_0^2 is the population variance in pH level expected at a properly functioning plant. In one particular plant, the null hypothesis was rejected. Further analysis showed that this plant had a variance in pH level that was significantly less than normal.

The auditors visited the plant to examine the measuring equipment and to discuss their statistical findings with the plant manager. The auditors found that the measuring equipment was not being used because the operator did not know how to work it. Instead, the operator had been told by an engineer what level of pH was acceptable and had simply recorded similar values without actually conducting the test. The unusually low variance in this plant's data resulted in rejection of H_0. The GAO suspected that other plants might have similar problems and recommended an operator training program to improve the data collection aspect of the pollution control program.

In this chapter, you will learn how to conduct statistical inferences about the variances of one and two populations. Two new distributions, the chi-square distribution and the F distribution, will be introduced and used to make interval estimates and hypothesis tests about population variances.

Effluent at this facility must fall within a statistically determined pH range. Avatar_023/Shutterstock.com

*The authors thank Mr. Art Foreman and Mr. Dale Ledman of the U.S. Government Accountability Office for providing this Statistics in Practice.

In this chapter, we examine methods of statistical inference involving population variances. As an example of a case in which a variance can provide important decision-making information, consider the production process of filling containers with a liquid detergent product. The filling mechanism for the process is adjusted so that the mean filling weight is 16 ounces per container. Although a mean of 16 ounces is desired, the variance of the filling weights is also critical. That is, even with the filling mechanism properly adjusted for the mean of 16 ounces, we cannot expect every container to have exactly 16 ounces.

By selecting a sample of containers, we can compute a sample variance for the number of ounces placed in a container. This value will serve as an estimate of the variance for the population of containers being filled by the production process. If the sample variance is modest, the production process will be continued. However, if the sample variance is excessive, overfilling and underfilling may be occurring even though the mean is correct at 16 ounces. In this case, the filling mechanism will be readjusted in an attempt to reduce the filling variance for the containers.

In many manufacturing applications, controlling the process variance is extremely important in maintaining quality.

In the first section we consider inferences about the variance of a single population. Subsequently, we will discuss procedures that can be used to make inferences about the variances of two populations.

11.1 Inferences About a Population Variance

The sample variance

$$s^2 = \frac{\Sigma(x_i - \bar{x})^2}{n - 1} \tag{11.1}$$

is the point estimator of the population variance σ^2. In using the sample variance as a basis for making inferences about a population variance, the sampling distribution of the quantity $(n - 1)s^2/\sigma^2$ is helpful. This sampling distribution is described as follows.

Sampling Distribution of $(n - 1)s^2/\sigma^2$

Whenever a random sample of size n is selected from a normal population, the sampling distribution of

$$\frac{(n - 1)s^2}{\sigma^2} \tag{11.2}$$

has a chi-square distribution with $n - 1$ degrees of freedom.

The chi-square distribution is based on sampling from a normal population.

Figure 11.1 shows some possible forms of the sampling distribution of $(n - 1)s^2/\sigma^2$.

Because the sampling distribution of $(n - 1)s^2/\sigma^2$ is known to have a chi-square distribution whenever a random sample of size n is selected from a normal population, we can use the chi-square distribution to develop interval estimates and conduct hypothesis tests about a population variance.

Interval Estimation

To show how the chi-square distribution can be used to develop a confidence interval estimate of a population variance σ^2, suppose that we are interested in estimating the population variance for the production filling process mentioned at the beginning of this chapter. A sample of 20 containers is taken, and the sample variance for the filling quantities is found to be $s^2 = 0.0025$. However, we know we cannot expect the variance of a sample of 20 containers to provide the exact value of the variance for the population of containers filled by the production process. Hence, our interest will be in developing an interval estimate for the population variance.

We will use the notation χ^2_α to denote the value for the chi-square distribution that provides an area or probability of α to the *right* of the χ^2_α value. For example, in Figure 11.2 the chi-square distribution with 19 degrees of freedom is shown with $\chi^2_{0.025} = 32.852$ indicating that 2.5% of the chi-square values are to the right of 32.852, and $\chi^2_{0.975} = 8.907$ indicating that 97.5% of the chi-square values are to the right of 8.907. Tables of areas or probabilities are readily available for the chi-square

Figure 11.1 Examples of the Sampling Distribution of $(n - 1)s^2/\sigma^2$ (a Chi-Square Distribution)

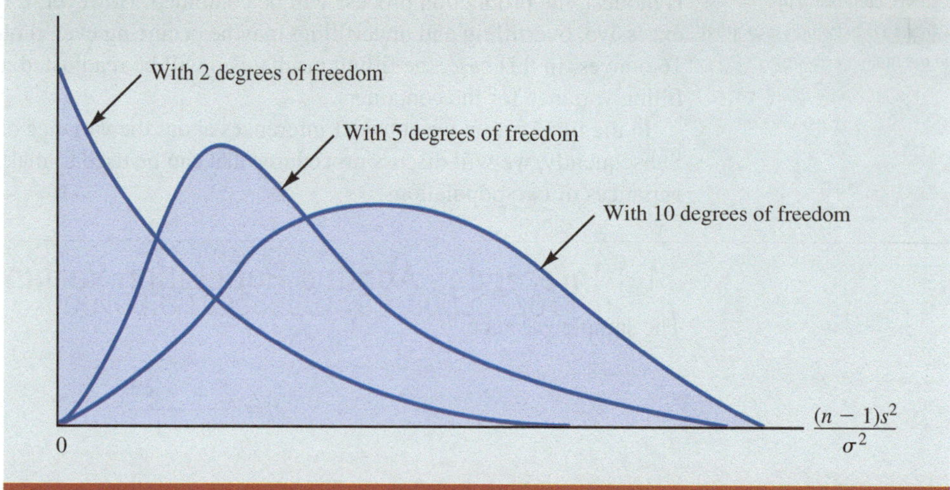

Figure 11.2 A Chi-Square Distribution with 19 Degrees of Freedom

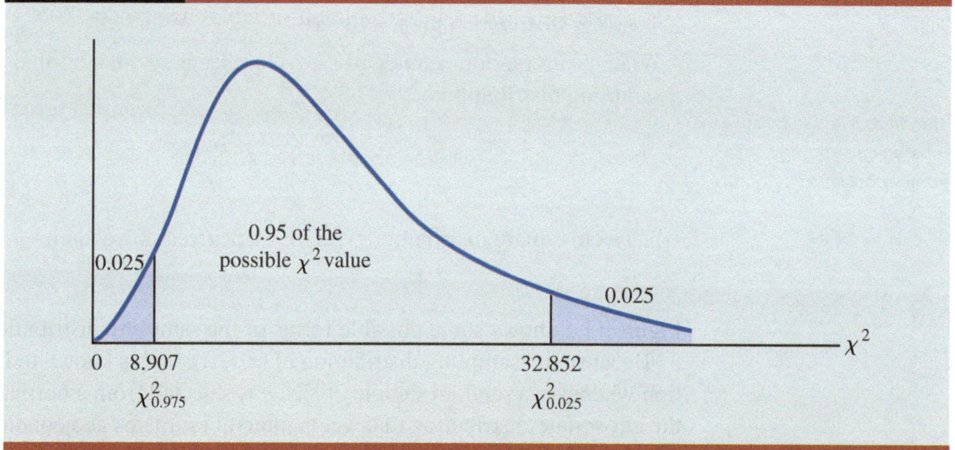

distribution. Refer to Table 11.1 and verify that these chi-square values with 19 degrees of freedom (19th row of the table) are correct. Table 3 of Appendix B (available online) provides a more extensive table of chi-square values.

From the graph in Figure 11.2 we see that 0.95, or 95%, of the chi-square values are between $\chi^2_{0.975}$ and $\chi^2_{0.025}$. That is, there is a 0.95 probability of obtaining a χ^2 value such that

$$\chi^2_{0.975} \le \chi^2 \le \chi^2_{0.025}$$

We stated in expression (11.2) that $(n - 1)s^2/\sigma^2$ follows a chi-square distribution; therefore, we can substitute $(n - 1)s^2/\sigma^2$ for χ^2 and write

$$\chi^2_{0.975} \le \frac{(n-1)s^2}{\sigma^2} \le \chi^2_{0.025} \qquad \textbf{(11.3)}$$

In effect, expression (11.3) provides an interval estimate in that 0.95, or 95%, of all possible values for $(n - 1)s^2/\sigma^2$ will be in the interval $\chi^2_{0.975}$ to $\chi^2_{0.025}$. We now need to do

Table 11.1 Selected Values from the Chi-Square Distribution Table*

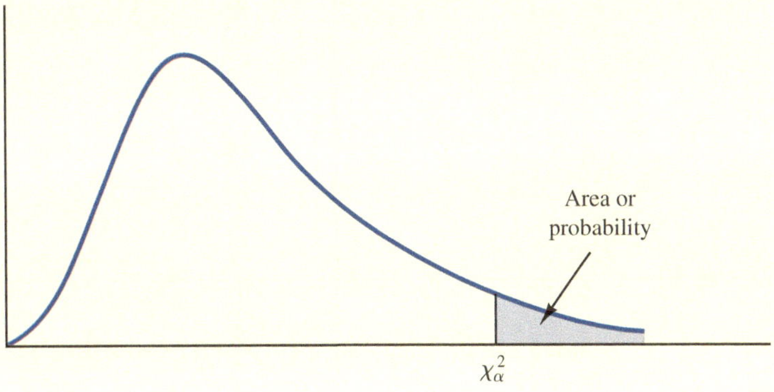

Degrees of Freedom	Area in Upper Tail 0.99	0.975	0.95	0.90	0.10	0.05	0.025	0.01
1	0.000	0.001	0.004	0.016	2.706	3.841	5.024	6.635
2	0.020	0.051	0.103	0.211	4.605	5.991	7.378	9.210
3	0.115	0.216	0.352	0.584	6.251	7.815	9.348	11.345
4	0.297	0.484	0.711	1.064	7.779	9.488	11.143	13.277
5	0.554	0.831	1.145	1.610	9.236	11.070	12.832	15.086
6	0.872	1.237	1.635	2.204	10.645	12.592	14.449	16.812
7	1.239	1.690	2.167	2.833	12.017	14.067	16.013	18.475
8	1.647	2.180	2.733	3.490	13.362	15.507	17.535	20.090
9	2.088	2.700	3.325	4.168	14.684	16.919	19.023	21.666
10	2.558	3.247	3.940	4.865	15.987	18.307	20.483	23.209
11	3.053	3.816	4.575	5.578	17.275	19.675	21.920	24.725
12	3.571	4.404	5.226	6.304	18.549	21.026	23.337	26.217
13	4.107	5.009	5.892	7.041	19.812	22.362	24.736	27.688
14	4.660	5.629	6.571	7.790	21.064	23.685	26.119	29.141
15	5.229	6.262	7.261	8.547	22.307	24.996	27.488	30.578
16	5.812	6.908	7.962	9.312	23.542	26.296	28.845	32.000
17	6.408	7.564	8.672	10.085	24.769	27.587	30.191	33.409
18	7.015	8.231	9.390	10.865	25.989	28.869	31.526	34.805
19	7.633	8.907	10.117	11.651	27.204	30.144	32.852	36.191
20	8.260	9.591	10.851	12.443	28.412	31.410	34.170	37.566
21	8.897	10.283	11.591	13.240	29.615	32.671	35.479	38.932
22	9.542	10.982	12.338	14.041	30.813	33.924	36.781	40.289
23	10.196	11.689	13.091	14.848	32.007	35.172	38.076	41.638
24	10.856	12.401	13.848	15.659	33.196	36.415	39.364	42.980
25	11.524	13.120	14.611	16.473	34.382	37.652	40.646	44.314
26	12.198	13.844	15.379	17.292	35.563	38.885	41.923	45.642
27	12.878	14.573	16.151	18.114	36.741	40.113	43.195	46.963
28	13.565	15.308	16.928	18.939	37.916	41.337	44.461	48.278
29	14.256	16.047	17.708	19.768	39.087	42.557	45.722	49.588
30	14.953	16.791	18.493	20.599	40.256	43.773	46.979	50.892
40	22.164	24.433	26.509	29.051	51.805	55.758	59.342	63.691
60	37.485	40.482	43.188	46.459	74.397	79.082	83.298	88.379
80	53.540	57.153	60.391	64.278	96.578	101.879	106.629	112.329
100	70.065	74.222	77.929	82.358	118.498	124.342	129.561	135.807

**Note:* A more extensive table is provided as Table 3 of Appendix B (available online).

some algebraic manipulations with expression (11.3) to develop an interval estimate for the population variance σ^2. Working with the leftmost inequality in expression (11.3), we have

$$\chi^2_{0.975} \le \frac{(n-1)s^2}{\sigma^2}$$

Thus

$$\sigma^2\chi^2_{0.975} \le (n-1)s^2$$

or

$$\sigma^2 \le \frac{(n-1)s^2}{\chi^2_{0.975}} \quad \textbf{(11.4)}$$

Performing similar algebraic manipulations with the rightmost inequality in expression (11.3) gives

$$\frac{(n-1)s^2}{\chi^2_{0.025}} \le \sigma^2 \quad \textbf{(11.5)}$$

The results of expressions (11.4) and (11.5) can be combined to provide

$$\frac{(n-1)s^2}{\chi^2_{0.025}} \le \sigma^2 \le \frac{(n-1)s^2}{\chi^2_{0.975}} \quad \textbf{(11.6)}$$

Because expression (11.3) is true for 95% of the $(n-1)s^2/\sigma^2$ values, expression (11.6) provides a 95% confidence interval estimate for the population variance σ^2.

Let us return to the problem of providing an interval estimate for the population variance of filling quantities. Recall that the sample of 20 containers provided a sample variance of $s^2 = 0.0025$. With a sample size of 20, we have 19 degrees of freedom. As shown in Figure 11.2, we have already determined that $\chi^2_{0.975} = 8.907$ and $\chi^2_{0.025} = 32.852$. Using these values in expression (11.6) provides the following interval estimate for the population variance.

$$\frac{(19)(0.0025)}{32.852} \le \sigma^2 \le \frac{(19)(0.0025)}{8.907}$$

or

$$0.0014 \le \sigma^2 \le 0.0053$$

Taking the square root of these values provides the following 95% confidence interval for the population standard deviation.

$$0.0380 \le \sigma \le 0.0730$$

Thus, we illustrated the process of using the chi-square distribution to establish interval estimates of a population variance and a population standard deviation. Note specifically that because $\chi^2_{0.975}$ and $\chi^2_{0.025}$ were used, the interval estimate has a 0.95 confidence coefficient. Extending expression (11.6) to the general case of any confidence coefficient, we have the following interval estimate of a population variance.

Interval Estimate of a Population Variance

$$\frac{(n-1)s^2}{\chi^2_{\alpha/2}} \le \sigma^2 \le \frac{(n-1)s^2}{\chi^2_{(1-\alpha/2)}} \quad \textbf{(11.7)}$$

where the χ^2 values are based on a chi-square distribution with $n-1$ degrees of freedom and where $1-\alpha$ is the confidence coefficient.

Using Excel to Construct a Confidence Interval

Excel can be used to construct a 95% confidence interval of the population variance for the example involving filling containers with a liquid detergent product. Refer to Figure 11.3 as we describe the tasks involved. The formula worksheet is in the background; the value worksheet is in the foreground.

DATA*file*
detergent_mod

Enter/Access Data: Open the file *detergent_mod*. Column A shows the number of ounces of detergent for each of the 20 containers.

Enter Functions and Formulas: The descriptive statistics needed are provided in cells D3:D4. Excel's COUNT and VAR.S functions are used to compute the sample size and the sample variance, respectively.

Cells D6:D9 are used to compute the appropriate chi-square values. The confidence coefficient was entered in cell D6 and the level of significance (α) was computed in cell D7 by entering the formula =*1-D6*. Excel's CHISQ.INV function was used to compute the lower tail chi-square value. The form of the CHISQ.INV function is CHISQ.INV (lower tail probability, degrees of freedom). The formula =*CHISQ.INV(D7/2,D3-1)* was entered in cell D8 to compute the chi-square value in the lower tail. The value worksheet shows that the chi-square value for 19 degrees of freedom is $\chi^2_{0.975} = 8.9065$. Then, to compute the chi-square value corresponding to an upper tail probability of 0.025, the formula =*CHISQ.INV.RT(D7/2,D3-1)* was entered in cell D9. The value worksheet shows that the chi-square value obtained is $\chi^2_{0.025} = 32.8523$.

Cells D11:D13 provide the point estimate and the lower and upper limits for the confidence interval. Because the point estimate is just the sample variance, we entered the

Figure 11.3 Excel Worksheet for the Liquid Detergent Filling Process

	A	B	C	D
1	Ounces		Interval Estimate of a Population Variance	
2	15.92			
3	16.02		Sample Size	=COUNT(A2:A21)
4	15.99		Variance	=VAR.S(A2:A21)
5	16.02			
6	15.91		Confidence Coefficient	0.95
7	15.98		Level of Significance (alpha)	=1-D6
8	16.06		Chi-Square Value (lower tail)	=CHISQ.INV(D7/2,D3-1)
9	15.97		Chi-Square Value (upper tail)	=CHISQ.INV.RT(D7/2,D3-1)
10	15.97			
11	16.07		Point Estimate	=D4
12	15.94		Lower Limit	=((D3-1)*D4)/D9
13	15.96		Upper Limit	=((D3-1)*D4)/D8
14	16.04			
15	16.01			
16	16.07			
17	16.01			
18	15.9			
19	15.96			
20	16			
21	15.99			

	A	B	C	D
1	Ounces		Interval Estimate of a Population Variance	
2	15.92			
3	16.02		Sample Size	20
4	15.99		Variance	0.0025
5	16.02			
6	15.91		Confidence Coefficient	0.95
7	15.98		Level of Significance (alpha)	0.05
8	16.06		Chi-Square Value (lower tail)	8.9065
9	15.97		Chi-Square Value (upper tail)	32.8523
10	15.97			
11	16.07		Point Estimate	0.0025
12	15.94		Lower Limit	0.0014
13	15.96		Upper Limit	0.0053
14	16.04			
15	16.01			
16	16.07			
17	16.01			
18	15.90			
19	15.96			
20	16.00			
21	15.99			

formula =*D4* in cell D11. Inequality (11.7) shows that the lower limit of the 95% confidence interval is

$$\frac{(n-1)s^2}{\chi^2_{\alpha/2}} = \frac{(n-1)s^2}{\chi^2_{0.025}}$$

Thus, to compute the lower limit of the 95% confidence interval, the formula =*((D3-1)*D4)/D9* was entered in cell D12. Inequality (11.7) also shows that the upper limit of the confidence interval is

$$\frac{(n-1)s^2}{\chi^2_{(1-\alpha/2)}} = \frac{(n-1)s^2}{\chi^2_{0.975}}$$

Thus, to compute the upper limit of the 95% confidence interval, the formula =*((D3-1)*D4)/D8* was entered in cell D13. The value worksheet shows a lower limit of 0.0014 and an upper limit of 0.0053. In other words, the 95% confidence interval estimate of the population variance is from 0.0014 to 0.0053.

Hypothesis Testing

Using σ_0^2 to denote the hypothesized value for the population variance, the three forms for a hypothesis test about a population variance are as follows:

$$\begin{array}{lll} H_0: \sigma^2 \geq \sigma_0^2 & H_0: \sigma^2 \leq \sigma_0^2 & H_0: \sigma^2 = \sigma_0^2 \\ H_a: \sigma^2 < \sigma_0^2 & H_a: \sigma^2 > \sigma_0^2 & H_a: \sigma^2 \neq \sigma_0^2 \end{array}$$

We discuss hypothesis tests about population means and proportions in Chapters 9 and 10.

These three forms are similar to the three forms used to conduct one-tailed and two-tailed hypothesis tests about population means and proportions.

The procedure for conducting a hypothesis test about a population variance uses the hypothesized value for the population variance σ_0^2 and the sample variance s^2 to compute the value of a χ^2 test statistic. Assuming that the population has a normal distribution, the test statistic is as follows.

Test Statistic for Hypothesis Tests About a Population Variance

$$\chi^2 = \frac{(n-1)s^2}{\sigma_0^2} \tag{11.8}$$

where χ^2 has a chi-square distribution with $n - 1$ degrees of freedom.

After computing the value of the χ^2 test statistic, either the p-value approach or the critical value approach may be used to determine whether the null hypothesis can be rejected.

Let us consider the following example. The St. Louis Metro Bus Company wants to promote an image of reliability by encouraging its drivers to maintain consistent schedules. As a standard policy the company would like arrival times at bus stops to have low variability. In terms of the variance of arrival times, the company standard specifies an arrival time variance of 4 or less when arrival times are measured in minutes. The following hypothesis test is formulated to help the company determine whether the arrival time population variance is excessive.

$$H_0: \sigma^2 \leq 4$$
$$H_a: \sigma^2 > 4$$

In tentatively assuming H_0 is true, we are assuming that the population variance of arrival times is within the company guideline. We reject H_0 if the sample evidence indicates that the population variance exceeds the guideline. In this case, follow-up steps should be taken to reduce the population variance. We conduct the hypothesis test using a level of significance of $\alpha = 0.05$.

DATA*file*
bustimes_mod

Suppose that a random sample of 24 bus arrivals taken at a downtown intersection provides a sample variance of $s^2 = 4.9$. Assuming that the population distribution of arrival times is approximately normal, the value of the test statistic is as follows:

$$\chi^2 = \frac{(n-1)s^2}{\sigma_0^2} = \frac{(24-1)(4.9)}{4} = 28.18$$

The chi-square distribution with $n - 1 = 24 - 1 = 23$ degrees of freedom is shown in Figure 11.4. Because this is an upper tail test, the area under the curve to the right of the test statistic $\chi^2 = 28.18$ is the p-value for the test.

Like the t distribution table, the chi-square distribution table does not contain sufficient detail to enable us to determine the p-value exactly. However, we can use the chi-square distribution table to obtain a range for the p-value. For example, using Table 11.1, we find the following information for a chi-square distribution with 23 degrees of freedom.

Area in Upper Tail	0.10	0.05	0.025	0.01
χ^2 Value (23 *df*)	32.007	35.172	38.076	41.638

$\chi^2 = 28.18$

Using Excel, p-value = CHISQ.DIST.RT(28.18,23) = 0.2091.

Because $\chi^2 = 28.18$ is less than 32.007, the area in the upper tail (the p-value) is greater than 0.10. With the p-value $> \alpha = 0.05$, we cannot reject the null hypothesis. The sample does not support the conclusion that the population variance of the arrival times is excessive.

As with other hypothesis testing procedures, the critical value approach can also be used to draw the hypothesis testing conclusion. With $\alpha = 0.05$, $\chi^2_{0.05}$ provides the critical value for the upper tail hypothesis test. Using Table 11.1 and 23 degrees of freedom, $\chi^2_{0.05} = 35.172$. Thus, the rejection rule for the bus arrival time example is as follows:

$$\text{Reject } H_0 \text{ if } \chi^2 \geq 35.172$$

Because the value of the test statistic is $\chi^2 = 28.18$, we cannot reject the null hypothesis.

In practice, upper tail tests as presented here are the most frequently encountered tests about a population variance. In situations involving arrival times, production times, filling weights, part dimensions, and so on, low variances are desirable, whereas large variances are unacceptable. With a statement about the maximum allowable population variance, we can test the null hypothesis that the population variance is less than or equal to the maximum allowable value against the alternative hypothesis that the population variance is greater than the

Figure 11.4 Chi-Square Distribution for the St. Louis Metro Bus Example

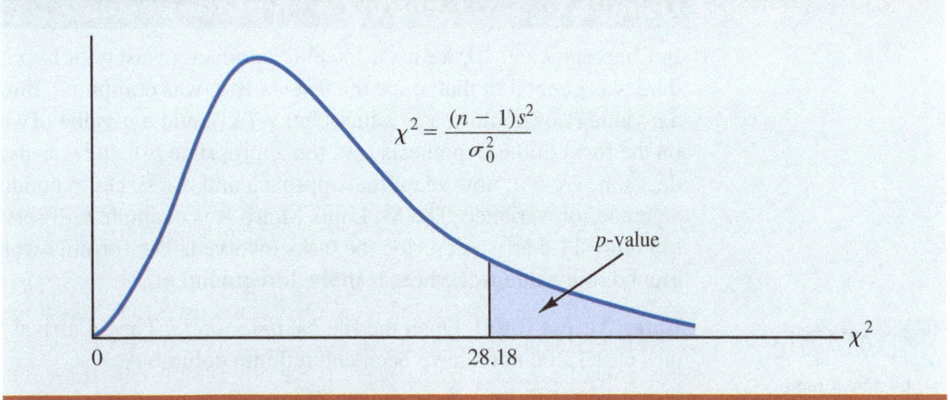

maximum allowable value. With this test structure, corrective action will be taken whenever rejection of the null hypothesis indicates the presence of an excessive population variance.

As we saw with population means and proportions, other forms of hypothesis tests can be developed. Let us demonstrate a two-tailed test about a population variance by considering a situation faced by a bureau of motor vehicles. Historically, the variance in test scores for individuals applying for driver's licenses has been $\sigma^2 = 100$. A new examination with new test questions has been developed. Administrators of the bureau of motor vehicles would like the variance in the test scores for the new examination to remain at the historical level. To evaluate the variance in the new examination test scores, the following two-tailed hypothesis test has been proposed.

$$H_0: \sigma^2 = 100$$
$$H_a: \sigma^2 \neq 100$$

Rejection of H_0 will indicate that a change in the variance has occurred and suggest that some questions in the new examination may need revision to make the variance of the new test scores similar to the variance of the old test scores. A sample of 30 applicants for driver's licenses will be given the new version of the examination. We will use a level of significance $\alpha = 0.05$ to conduct the hypothesis test.

The sample of 30 examination scores provided a sample variance $s^2 = 162$. The value of the chi-square test statistic is as follows:

$$\chi^2 = \frac{(n-1)s^2}{\sigma_0^2} = \frac{(30-1)(162)}{100} = 46.98$$

Now, let us compute the p-value. Using Table 11.1 and $n - 1 = 30 - 1 = 29$ degrees of freedom, we find the following:

Area in Upper Tail	**0.10**	**0.05**	**0.025**	**0.01**
χ^2 Value (29 *df*)	39.087	42.557	45.722	49.588

↑ $\chi^2 = 46.98$ (between 45.722 and 49.588)

Using Excel, p-value = 2*CHISQ.DIST.RT(46.98,29) = 0.0374.

Thus, the value of the test statistic $\chi^2 = 46.98$ provides an area between 0.025 and 0.01 in the upper tail of the chi-square distribution. Doubling these values shows that the two-tailed p-value is between 0.05 and 0.02. Excel can be used to show that $\chi^2 = 46.98$ provides a p-value $= 0.0374$. With p-value $\leq \alpha = 0.05$, we reject H_0 and conclude that the new examination test scores have a population variance different from the historical variance of $\sigma^2 = 100$. A summary of the hypothesis testing procedures for a population variance is shown in Table 11.2.

Using Excel to Conduct a Hypothesis Test

In Chapters 9 and 10, we used Excel to conduct a variety of hypothesis tests. The procedure was general in that, once the test statistic was computed, three p-values were obtained: a p-value (Lower Tail), a p-value (Upper Tail), and a p-value (Two Tail). Then, depending on the form of the hypothesis test, the appropriate p-value was used to make the rejection decision. We will now adapt that approach and use Excel to conduct a hypothesis test about a population variance. The St. Louis Metro Bus example will serve as an illustration. Refer to Figure 11.5 as we describe the tasks involved. The formula worksheet is in the background; the value worksheet is in the foreground.

DATA*file* bustimes_mod

Enter/Access Data: Open the file *bustimes_mod*. The 24 arrival times in number of minutes past 12:00 noon have been entered into column A.

Enter Functions and Formulas: The descriptive statistics we need are provided in cells D3:D5. Excel's COUNT function has been used to compute the sample size and Excel's

Table 11.2 Summary of Hypothesis Tests About a Population Variance

	Lower Tail Test	Upper Tail Test	Two-Tailed Test
Hypotheses	$H_0\colon \sigma^2 \geq \sigma_0^2$ $H_a\colon \sigma^2 < \sigma_0^2$	$H_0\colon \sigma^2 \leq \sigma_0^2$ $H_a\colon \sigma^2 > \sigma_0^2$	$H_0\colon \sigma^2 = \sigma_0^2$ $H_a\colon \sigma^2 \neq \sigma_0^2$
Test Statistic	$\chi^2 = \frac{(n-1)s^2}{\sigma_0^2}$	$\chi^2 = \frac{(n-1)s^2}{\sigma_0^2}$	$\chi^2 = \frac{(n-1)s^2}{\sigma_0^2}$
Rejection Rule: *p*-Value Approach	Reject H_0 if p-value $\leq \alpha$	Reject H_0 if p-value $\leq \alpha$	Reject H_0 if p-value $\leq \alpha$
Rejection Rule: Critical Value Approach	Reject H_0 if $\chi^2 \leq \chi^2_{(1-\alpha)}$	Reject H_0 if $\chi^2 \geq \chi^2_{\alpha}$	Reject H_0 if $\chi^2 \leq \chi^2_{(1-\alpha/2)}$ or if $\chi^2 \geq \chi^2_{\alpha/2}$

AVERAGE and VAR.S functions have been used to compute the sample mean and sample variance. The value worksheet shows $n = 24$, $\bar{x} = 14.76$, and $s^2 = 4.9$.

The hypothesized value of the population variance, $\sigma_0^2 = 4$, was entered in cell D7. The formula *=(D3-1)*D5/D7* was entered in cell D9 to compute the χ^2 test statistic (28.18), and the formula *=D3-1* was entered in cell D10 to compute the degrees of freedom associated with the test statistic.

Figure 11.5 Hypothesis Test for Variance in Bus Arrival Times

	A	B	C	D
1	Times		Hypothesis Test About a Population Variance	
2	15.7			
3	16.9		Sample Size	=COUNT(A:A)
4	12.8		Sample Mean	=AVERAGE(A:A)
5	15.6		Sample Variance	=VAR.S(A:A)
6	14			
7	16.2		Hypothesized Value	4
8	14.8			
9	19.8		Test Statistic	=(D3-1)*D5/D7
10	13.2		Degrees of Freedom	=D3-1
11	15.3			
12	14.7		*p*-value (Lower Tail)	=CHISQ.DIST(D9,D10,TRUE)
13	10.2		*p*-value (Upper Tail)	=CHISQ.DIST.RT(D9,D10)
14	16.7		*p*-value (Two Tail)	=2*MIN(D12,D13)
15	13.6			
25	12.7			

	A	B	C	D
1	Times		Hypothesis Test About a Population Variance	
2	15.7			
3	16.9		Sample Size	24
4	12.8		Sample Mean	14.76
5	15.6		Sample Variance	4.9
6	14.0			
7	16.2		Hypothesized Value	4
8	14.8			
9	19.8		Test Statistic	28.18
10	13.2		Degrees of Freedom	23
11	15.3			
12	14.7		*p*-value (Lower Tail)	0.7909
13	10.2		*p*-value (Upper Tail)	0.2091
14	16.7		*p*-value (Two Tail)	0.4181
15	13.6			
25	12.7			

Note: Rows 16–24 are hidden.

The lower and upper tail p-values are computed in cells D12 and D13. The CHISQ.DIST function is used to compute the lower tail p-value in cell D12. To compute the p-value for a one-tailed hypothesis test in which the rejection region is in the lower tail, we entered the formula =*CHISQ.DIST(D9,D10,TRUE)* in cell D12. The CHISQ.DIST.RT function is used to compute the upper tail p-value in cell D13. To compute the p-value for a one-tailed hypothesis test in which the rejection region is in the upper tail, we entered the formula =*CHISQ.DIST.RT(D9,D10)* in cell D13. Finally, to compute the p-value for a two-tailed test, we entered the formula =*2*MIN(D12,D13)* in cell D14. The value worksheet shows that p-value (Lower Tail) = 0.7909, p-value (Upper Tail) = 0.2091, and p-value (Two Tail) = 0.4181. The rejection region for the St. Louis Metro Bus example is in the upper tail; thus, the appropriate p-value is 0.2091. At a 0.05 level of significance, we cannot reject H_0 because $0.2091 > 0.05$. Hence, the sample variance of $s^2 = 4.9$ is insufficient evidence to conclude that the arrival time variance is not meeting the company standard.

To avoid having to revise the cell ranges for functions in cells D3:D5, the A:A method of specifying cell ranges can be used.

This worksheet can be used as a template for other hypothesis tests about a population variance. Enter the data in column A, revise the ranges for the functions in cells D3:D5 as appropriate for the data, and type the hypothesized value σ_0^2 in cell D7. The p-value appropriate for the test can then be selected from cells D12:D14. The worksheet can also be used for exercises in which the sample size, sample variance, and hypothesized value are given. For instance, in the previous subsection we conducted a two-tailed hypothesis test about the variance in scores on a new examination given by the bureau of motor vehicles. The sample size was 30, the sample variance was $s^2 = 162$, and the hypothesized value for the population variance was $\sigma_0^2 = 100$. Using the worksheet in Figure 11.5, we can type *30* in cell D3, *162* in cell D5, and *100* in cell D7. The correct two-tailed p-value will then be given in cell D14 as 0.0374.

Exercises

Methods

1. Find the following chi-square distribution values from Table 11.1 or Table 3 of Appendix B (available online). **LO 1**
   a. $\chi^2_{0.05}$ with $df = 5$
   b. $\chi^2_{0.025}$ with $df = 15$
   c. $\chi^2_{0.975}$ with $df = 20$
   d. $\chi^2_{0.01}$ with $df = 10$
   e. $\chi^2_{0.95}$ with $df = 18$
2. A sample of 20 items provides a sample standard deviation of 5. **LO 2**
   a. Compute the 90% confidence interval estimate of the population variance.
   b. Compute the 95% confidence interval estimate of the population variance.
   c. Compute the 95% confidence interval estimate of the population standard deviation.
3. A sample of 16 items provides a sample standard deviation of 9.5. Test the following hypotheses using $\alpha = 0.05$. What is your conclusion? Use both the p-value approach and the critical value approach. **LO 3**

$$H_0: \sigma^2 \leq 50$$
$$H_a: \sigma^2 > 50$$

Applications

4. **Package Delivery by Drones.** Amazon.com is testing the use of drones to deliver packages for same-day delivery. In order to quote narrow time windows, the variability in delivery times must be sufficiently small. Consider a sample of 24 drone deliveries with sample variance of $s^2 = 0.81$. **LO 2**
   a. Construct a 90% confidence interval estimate of the population variance for the drone delivery time.
   b. Construct a 90% confidence interval estimate of the population standard deviation.
5. **College Basketball Coaches' Salaries.** In 2023, John Calipari topped the list of highest paid college basketball coaches (*Sports Illustrated* website). The following sample

shows the head basketball coach's salary for a sample of 10 schools playing NCAA Division I basketball. Salary data are in millions of dollars. **LO 2**

DATA*file*
coachsalary

University	Coach's Salary	University	Coach's Salary
North Carolina State	2.2	Miami (FL)	1.5
Iona	0.5	Creighton	1.3
Texas A&M	2.4	Texas Tech	1.5
Oregon	2.7	South Dakota State	0.3
Iowa State	2.0	New Mexico State	0.3

a. Use the sample mean for the 10 schools to estimate the population mean annual salary for head basketball coaches at colleges and universities playing NCAA Division I basketball.
b. Use the data to estimate the population standard deviation for the annual salary for head basketball coaches.
c. What is the 95% confidence interval for the population variance?
d. What is the 95% confidence interval for the population standard deviation?

6. **Volatility of General Electric Stock.** To analyze the risk, or volatility, associated with investing in General Electric common stock, consider a sample of the eight quarterly percent total returns. The percent total return includes the stock price change plus the dividend payment for the quarter. **LO 2**

20.0	−20.5	12.2	12.6	10.5	−5.8	−18.7	15.3

a. What is the value of the sample mean? What is its interpretation?
b. Compute the sample variance and sample standard deviation as measures of volatility for the quarterly return for General Electric.
c. Construct a 95% confidence interval for the population variance.
d. Construct a 95% confidence interval for the population standard deviation.

7. **Halloween Spending.** In 2017, Americans spent a record-high $9.1 billion on Halloween-related purchases (*the balance* website). Sample data showing the amount, in dollars, that 16 adults spent on a Halloween costume are as follows. **LO 2**

DATA*file*
halloween

12	69	22	64
33	36	31	44
52	16	13	98
45	32	63	26

a. What is the estimate of the population mean amount adults spend on a Halloween costume?
b. What is the sample standard deviation?
c. Provide a 95% confidence interval estimate of the population standard deviation for the amount adults spend on a Halloween costume.

8. **Variability in Daily Change in Stock Price.** Consider a day when the Dow Jones Industrial Average went up 149.82 points. The following table shows the stock price changes for a sample of 12 companies on that day. **LO 2**

DATA*file*
stockpricechange

Company	Price Change ($)	Company	Price Change ($)
Aflac	0.81	Johnson & Johnson	1.46
Altice USA	0.41	Loews Corporation	0.92
Bank of America	−0.05	Nokia Corporation	0.21
Diageo plc	1.32	Sempra Energy	0.97
Fluor Corporation	2.37	Sunoco LP	0.52
Goodrich Petroleum	0.3	Tyson Foods, Inc.	0.12

a. Compute the sample variance for the daily price change.
b. Compute the sample standard deviation for the price change.
c. Provide 95% confidence interval estimates of the population variance and the population standard deviation.

9. **Aerospace Part Manufacturing.** The competitive advantage of some small American factories such as In Tolerance Contract Manufacturing lies in their ability to produce parts with very narrow requirements, or tolerances, that are typical in the aerospace industry. Consider a product with specifications that call for a maximum variance in the lengths of the parts of 0.0004. Suppose the sample variance for 30 parts turns out to be $s^2 = 0.0005$. Use $\alpha = 0.05$ to test whether the population variance specification is being violated. **LO 3**

10. **Costco Customer Satisfaction.** *Consumer Reports* uses a 100-point customer satisfaction score to rate the nation's major chain stores. Assume that from past experience with the satisfaction rating score, a population standard deviation of $\sigma = 12$ is expected. In 2012, Costco with its 432 warehouses in 40 states was the only chain store to earn an outstanding rating for overall quality. A sample of 15 Costco customer satisfaction scores follows. **LO 3**

DATA*file*
costco

95	90	83	75	95
98	80	83	82	93
86	80	94	64	62

a. What is the sample mean customer satisfaction score for Costco?
b. What is the sample variance?
c. What is the sample standard deviation?
d. Construct a hypothesis test to determine whether the population standard deviation of $\sigma = 12$ should be rejected for Costco. With a 0.05 level of significance, what is your conclusion?

DATA*file*
econgmat

11. **Variability in GMAT Scores.** In 2016, the Graduate Management Admission Council reported that the variance in GMAT scores was 14,660. At a recent summit, a group of economics professors met to discuss the GMAT performance of undergraduate students majoring in economics. Some expected the variability in GMAT scores achieved by undergraduate economics students to be greater than the variability in GMAT scores of the general population of GMAT takers. However, others took the opposite view. The file *econgmat* contains GMAT scores for 51 randomly selected undergraduate students majoring in economics. **LO 3**
a. Compute the mean, variance, and standard deviation of the GMAT scores for the 51 randomly selected undergraduate students majoring in economics.
b. Develop hypotheses to test whether the sample data indicate that the variance in GMAT scores for undergraduate students majoring in economics differs from the general population of GMAT takers.
c. Use $\alpha = 0.05$ to conduct the hypothesis test formulated in part (b). What is your conclusion?

12. **Vehicle Ownership by *Fortune* Magazine Subscribers.** A *Fortune* study found that the variance in the number of vehicles owned or leased by subscribers to *Fortune* magazine is 0.94. Assume a sample of 12 subscribers to another magazine provided the following data on the number of vehicles owned or leased: 2, 1, 2, 0, 3, 2, 2, 1, 2, 1, 0, and 1. **LO 3**
a. Compute the sample variance in the number of vehicles owned or leased by the 12 subscribers.
b. Test the hypothesis H_0: $\sigma^2 = 0.94$ to determine whether the variance in the number of vehicles owned or leased by subscribers of the other magazine differs from $\sigma^2 = 0.94$ for *Fortune*. At a 0.05 level of significance, what is your conclusion?

11.2 Inferences About Two Population Variances

In some statistical applications, we may want to compare the variances in product quality resulting from two different production processes, the variances in assembly times for two assembly methods, or the variances in temperatures for two heating devices. In making comparisons about the two population variances, we will be using data collected from two independent random samples, one from population 1 and another from population 2. The two sample variances s_1^2 and s_2^2 will be the basis for making inferences about the two population variances σ_1^2 and σ_2^2. Whenever the variances of two normal populations are equal ($\sigma_1^2 = \sigma_2^2$), the sampling distribution of the ratio of the two sample variances s_1^2/s_2^2 is as follows.

Sampling Distribution of s_1^2/s_2^2 When $\sigma_1^2 = \sigma_2^2$

Whenever independent random samples of sizes n_1 and n_2 are selected from two normal populations with equal variances, the sampling distribution of

$$\frac{s_1^2}{s_2^2} \tag{11.9}$$

The F distribution is based on sampling from two normal populations.

has an F distribution with $n_1 - 1$ degrees of freedom for the numerator and $n_2 - 1$ degrees of freedom for the denominator; s_1^2 is the sample variance for the random sample of n_1 items from population 1 and s_2^2 is the sample variance for the random sample of n_2 items from population 2.

Figure 11.6 is a graph of the F distribution with 20 degrees of freedom for both the numerator and denominator. As indicated by this graph, the F distribution is not symmetric, and the F values can never be negative. The shape of any particular F distribution depends on its numerator and denominator degrees of freedom.

We will use F_α to denote the value of F that provides an area or probability of α in the upper tail of the distribution. For example, as noted in Figure 11.6, $F_{0.05}$ denotes the upper tail area of 0.05 for an F distribution with 20 degrees of freedom for the numerator and 20 degrees of freedom for the denominator. The specific value of $F_{0.05}$ can be found by referring to the F distribution table, a portion of which is shown in Table 11.3. Using 20 degrees of freedom for the numerator, 20 degrees of freedom for the denominator, and the row corresponding to an area of 0.05 in the upper tail, we find $F_{0.05} = 2.12$. Note that

Figure 11.6 F Distribution with 20 Degrees of Freedom for the Numerator and 20 Degrees of Freedom for the Denominator

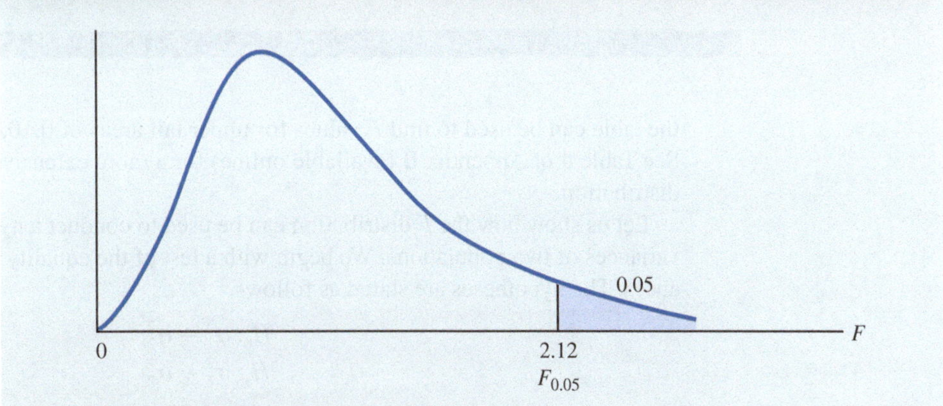

Table 11.3 Selected Values from the *F* Distribution Table*

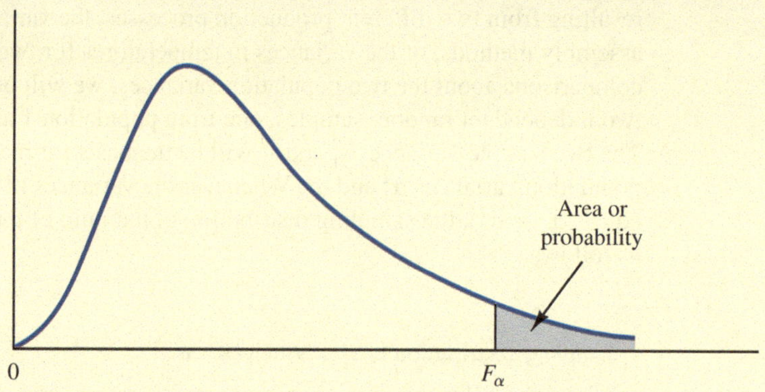

Denominator Degrees of Freedom	Area in Upper Tail	Numerator Degrees of Freedom 10	15	20	25	30
10	0.10	2.32	2.24	2.20	2.17	2.16
	0.05	2.98	2.85	2.77	2.73	2.70
	0.025	3.72	3.52	3.42	3.35	3.31
	0.01	4.85	4.56	4.41	4.31	4.25
15	0.10	2.06	1.97	1.92	1.89	1.87
	0.05	2.54	2.40	2.33	2.28	2.25
	0.025	3.06	2.86	2.76	2.69	2.64
	0.01	3.80	3.52	3.37	3.28	3.21
20	0.10	1.94	1.84	1.79	1.76	1.74
	0.05	2.35	2.20	2.12	2.07	2.04
	0.025	2.77	2.57	2.46	2.40	2.35
	0.01	3.37	3.09	2.94	2.84	2.78
25	0.10	1.87	1.77	1.72	1.68	1.66
	0.05	2.24	2.09	2.01	1.96	1.92
	0.025	2.61	2.41	2.30	2.23	2.18
	0.01	3.13	2.85	2.70	2.60	2.54
30	0.10	1.82	1.72	1.67	1.63	1.61
	0.05	2.16	2.01	1.93	1.88	1.84
	0.025	2.51	2.31	2.20	2.12	2.07
	0.01	2.98	2.70	2.55	2.45	2.39

**Note:* A more extensive table is provided as Table 4 of Appendix B (available online).

the table can be used to find *F* values for upper tail areas of 0.10, 0.05, 0.025, and 0.01. See Table 4 of Appendix B (available online) for a more extensive table for the *F* distribution.

Let us show how the *F* distribution can be used to conduct a hypothesis test about the variances of two populations. We begin with a test of the equality of two population variances. The hypotheses are stated as follows.

$$H_0: \sigma_1^2 = \sigma_2^2$$
$$H_a: \sigma_1^2 \neq \sigma_2^2$$

We make the tentative assumption that the population variances are equal. If H_0 is rejected, we will draw the conclusion that the population variances are not equal.

The procedure used to conduct the hypothesis test requires two independent random samples, one from each population. The two sample variances are then computed. We refer to the population providing the *larger* sample variance as population 1. Thus, a sample size of n_1 and a sample variance of s_1^2 correspond to population 1, and a sample size of n_2 and a sample variance of s_2^2 correspond to population 2. Based on the assumption that both populations have a normal distribution, the ratio of sample variances provides the following F test statistic.

Test Statistic for Hypothesis Tests About Population Variances with $\sigma_1^2 = \sigma_2^2$

$$F = \frac{s_1^2}{s_2^2} \tag{11.10}$$

Denoting the population with the larger sample variance as population 1, the test statistic has an F distribution with $n_1 - 1$ degrees of freedom for the numerator and $n_2 - 1$ degrees of freedom for the denominator.

We always denote the population with the larger sample variance as population 1.

Because the F test statistic is constructed with the larger sample variance s_1^2 in the numerator, the value of the test statistic will be in the upper tail of the F distribution. Therefore, the F distribution table as shown in Table 11.3 and in Table 4 of Appendix B (available online) need only provide upper tail areas or probabilities. If we did not construct the test statistic in this manner, lower tail areas or probabilities would be needed. In this case, additional calculations or more extensive F distribution tables would be required. Let us now consider an example of a hypothesis test about the equality of two population variances.

Dullus County Schools is renewing its school bus service contract for the coming year and must select one of two bus companies, the Milbank Company or the Gulf Park Company. We will use the variance of the arrival or pickup/delivery times as a primary measure of the quality of the bus service. Low variance values indicate the more consistent and higher-quality service. If the variances of arrival times associated with the two services are equal, Dullus School administrators will select the company offering the better financial terms. However, if the sample data on bus arrival times for the two companies indicate a significant difference between the variances, the administrators may want to give special consideration to the company with the better or lower variance service. The appropriate hypotheses follow.

$$H_0: \sigma_1^2 = \sigma_2^2$$
$$H_a: \sigma_1^2 \neq \sigma_2^2$$

If H_0 can be rejected, the conclusion of unequal service quality is appropriate. We will use a level of significance of $\alpha = 0.10$ to conduct the hypothesis test.

DATA*file*
schoolbus

A sample of 26 arrival times for the Milbank service provides a sample variance of 48 and a sample of 16 arrival times for the Gulf Park service provides a sample variance of 20. Because the Milbank sample provided the larger sample variance, we will denote Milbank as population 1. Using equation (11.10), we find the value of the test statistic:

$$F = \frac{s_1^2}{s_2^2} = \frac{48}{20} = 2.40$$

The corresponding F distribution has $n_1 - 1 = 26 - 1 = 25$ numerator degrees of freedom and $n_2 - 1 = 16 - 1 = 15$ denominator degrees of freedom.

As with other hypothesis testing procedures, we can use the p-value approach or the critical value approach to obtain the hypothesis testing conclusion. Table 11.3 shows the following areas in the upper tail and corresponding F values for an F distribution with 25 numerator degrees of freedom and 15 denominator degrees of freedom.

Area in Upper Tail	0.10	0.05	0.025	0.01
F Value ($df_1 = 25, df_2 = 15$)	1.89	2.28	2.69	3.28

$F = 2.40$

Because $F = 2.40$ is between 2.28 and 2.69, the area in the upper tail of the distribution is between 0.05 and 0.025. For this two-tailed test, we double the upper tail area, which results in a p-value between 0.10 and 0.05. Because we selected $\alpha = 0.10$ as the level of significance, the p-value $< \alpha = 0.10$. Thus, the null hypothesis is rejected. This finding leads to the conclusion that the two bus services differ in terms of pickup/delivery time variances. The recommendation is that the Dullus County School administrators give special consideration to the better or lower variance service offered by the Gulf Park Company.

*Using Excel, 2*F.DIST.RT(2.4,25,15) = 0.0812.*

We can use Excel to show that the test statistic $F = 2.40$ provides a two-tailed p-value $= 0.0812$. With $0.0812 < \alpha = 0.10$, the null hypothesis of equal population variances is rejected.

To use the critical value approach to conduct the two-tailed hypothesis test at the $\alpha = 0.10$ level of significance, we would select critical values with an area of $\alpha/2 = 0.10/2 = 0.05$ in each tail of the distribution. Because the value of the test statistic computed using equation (11.10) will always be in the upper tail, we only need to determine the upper tail critical value. From Table 11.3, we see that $F_{0.05} = 2.28$. Thus, even though we use a two-tailed test, the rejection rule is stated as follows.

$$\text{Reject } H_0 \text{ if } F \geq 2.28$$

Because the test statistic $F = 2.40$ is greater than 2.28, we reject H_0 and conclude that the two bus services differ in terms of pickup/delivery time variances.

One-tailed tests involving two population variances are also possible. In this case, we use the F distribution to determine whether one population variance is significantly greater than the other. A one-tailed hypothesis test about two population variances will always be formulated as an *upper tail* test:

$$H_0: \sigma_1^2 \leq \sigma_2^2$$
$$H_a: \sigma_1^2 > \sigma_2^2$$

A one-tailed hypothesis test about two population variances can always be formulated as an upper tail test. This approach eliminates the need for lower tail F values.

This form of the hypothesis test always places the p-value and the critical value in the upper tail of the F distribution. As a result, only upper tail F values will be needed, simplifying both the computations and the table for the F distribution.

Let us demonstrate the use of the F distribution to conduct a one-tailed test about the variances of two populations by considering a public opinion survey. Samples of 31 men and 41 women will be used to study attitudes about current political issues. The researcher conducting the study wants to test to see whether the sample data indicate that women show a greater variation in attitude on political issues than men. In the form of the one-tailed hypothesis test given previously, women will be denoted as population 1 and men will be denoted as population 2. The hypothesis test will be stated as follows.

$$H_0: \sigma^2_{\text{women}} \leq \sigma^2_{\text{men}}$$
$$H_a: \sigma^2_{\text{women}} > \sigma^2_{\text{men}}$$

A rejection of H_0 gives the researcher the statistical support necessary to conclude that women show a greater variation in attitude on political issues.

With the sample variance for women in the numerator and the sample variance for men in the denominator, the F distribution will have $n_1 - 1 = 41 - 1 = 40$ numerator degrees of freedom and $n_2 - 1 = 31 - 1 = 30$ denominator degrees of freedom. We will use a level of significance $\alpha = 0.05$ to conduct the hypothesis test. The survey results provide a

Table 11.4 Summary of Hypothesis Tests About Two Population Variances

	Upper Tail Test	Two-Tailed Test
Hypotheses	$H_0: \sigma_1^2 \le \sigma_2^2$ $H_a: \sigma_1^2 > \sigma_2^2$	$H_0: \sigma_1^2 = \sigma_2^2$ $H_a: \sigma_1^2 \ne \sigma_2^2$ Note: Population 1 has the larger sample variance
Test Statistic	$F = \frac{s_1^2}{s_2^2}$	$F = \frac{s_1^2}{s_2^2}$
Rejection Rule: *p*-Value Approach	Reject H_0 if *p*-value $\le \alpha$	Reject H_0 if *p*-value $\le \alpha$
Rejection Rule: Critical Value Approach	Reject H_0 if $F \ge F_\alpha$	Reject H_0 if $F \ge F_{\alpha/2}$

sample variance of $s_1^2 = 120$ for women and a sample variance of $s_2^2 = 80$ for men. The test statistic is as follows.

$$F = \frac{s_1^2}{s_2^2} = \frac{120}{80} = 1.50$$

Using Excel, p-value = F.DIST.RT(1.5,40,30) = 0.1256.

Referring to Table 4 in Appendix B (available online), we find that an F distribution with 40 numerator degrees of freedom and 30 denominator degrees of freedom has $F_{0.10} = 1.57$. Because the test statistic $F = 1.50$ is less than 1.57, the area in the upper tail must be greater than 0.10. Thus, we can conclude that the p-value is greater than 0.10. Excel can be used to show that $F = 1.50$ provides a p-value $= 0.1256$. Because the p-value $> \alpha = 0.05$, H_0 cannot be rejected. Hence, the sample results do not support the conclusion that women show greater variation in attitude on political issues than men. Table 11.4 provides a summary of hypothesis tests about two population variances.

Using Excel to Conduct a Hypothesis Test

Excel's F-Test Two-Sample for Variances tool can be used to conduct a hypothesis test comparing the variances of two populations. We illustrate by using Excel to conduct the two-tailed hypothesis test for the Dullus County School Bus study. Refer to the Excel worksheets in Figure 11.7 and in Figure 11.8 as we describe the tasks involved.

DATA*file*
schoolbus

Enter/Access Data: Open the file *schoolbus*. Column A contains the sample of 26 arrival times for the Milbank Company and column B contains the sample of 16 arrival times for the Gulf Park Company.

Apply Tools: The following steps describe how to use Excel's F-Test Two-Sample for Variances tool.

Step 1. Click the **Data** tab on the Ribbon
Step 2. In the **Analyze** group, click **Data Analysis**
Step 3. When the **Data Analysis** dialog box appears:
Choose **F-Test Two-Sample for Variances** from the list of Analysis Tools
Step 4. When the **F-Test Two-Sample for Variances** dialog box appears (Figure 11.7):
Enter *A1:A27* in the **Variable 1 Range:** box
Enter *B1:B17* in the **Variable 2 Range:** box

Select the check box for **Labels**
Enter *0.05* in the **Alpha:** box
(*Note:* This Excel procedure uses alpha as the area in the upper tail.)
Select **Output Range:** and enter *D1* in the box
Click **OK**

The value of 0.0405 in cell E9, labeled "P(F<=f) one-tail," is the one-tail area associated with the test statistic $F = 2.401$. Thus, the two-tailed p-value is $2(0.0405) = 0.081$; we

Figure 11.7 Dialog Box for *F*-Test Two-Sample for Variances

Note: Rows 12–15 and 19–25 are hidden.

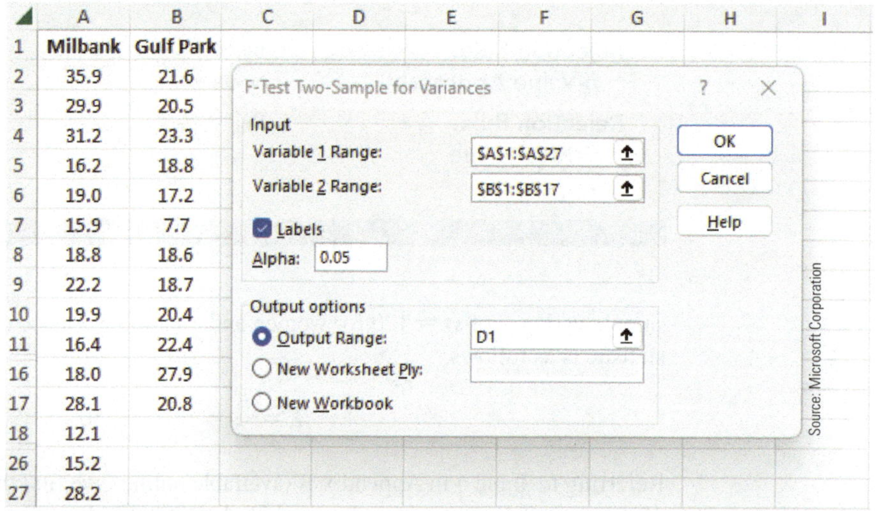

Source: Microsoft Corporation

Figure 11.8 Excel Results for Hypothesis Test Comparing Variance in Pickup Times for Two School Bus Services

	A	B	C	D	E	F
1	Milbank	Gulf Park		F-Test Two-Sample for Variances		
2	35.9	21.6				
3	29.9	20.5			*Milbank*	*Gulf Park*
4	31.2	23.3		Mean	20.2308	20.2438
5	16.2	18.8		Variance	48.0206	20.0000
6	19.0	17.2		Observations	26	16
7	15.9	7.7		df	25	15
8	18.8	18.6		F	2.4010	
9	22.2	18.7		P(F<=f) one-tail	0.0405	
10	19.9	20.4		F Critical one-tail	2.2797	
11	16.4	22.4				
16	18.0	27.9				
17	28.1	20.8				
18	12.1					
26	15.2					
27	28.2					

reject the null hypothesis at the 0.10 level of significance. If the hypothesis test had been a one-tail test (with $\alpha = 0.05$), the one-tail area in cell E9 would provide the p-value directly. We would not need to double it.

Note + Comment

Research confirms the fact that the F distribution is sensitive to the assumption of normal populations. The F distribution should not be used unless it is reasonable to assume that both populations are at least approximately normally distributed.

Exercises

Methods

13. Find the following F distribution values from Table 4 of Appendix B (available online). **LO 4**
    a. $F_{0.05}$ with degrees of freedom 5 and 10
    b. $F_{0.025}$ with degrees of freedom 20 and 15
    c. $F_{0.01}$ with degrees of freedom 8 and 12
    d. $F_{0.10}$ with degrees of freedom 10 and 20
14. A sample of 16 items from population 1 has a sample variance $s_1^2 = 5.8$ and a sample of 21 items from population 2 has a sample variance $s_2^2 = 2.4$. Test the following hypotheses at the 0.05 level of significance. **LO 5**

$$H_0: \sigma_1^2 \leq \sigma_2^2$$
$$H_a: \sigma_1^2 > \sigma_2^2$$

    a. What is your conclusion using the p-value approach?
    b. Repeat the test using the critical value approach.
15. Consider the following hypothesis test. **LO 5**

$$H_0: \sigma_1^2 = \sigma_2^2$$
$$H_a: \sigma_1^2 \neq \sigma_2^2$$

    a. What is your conclusion if $n_1 = 21$, $s_1^2 = 8.2$, $n_2 = 26$, and $s_2^2 = 4.0$? Use $\alpha = 0.05$ and the p-value approach.
    b. Repeat the test using the critical value approach.

Applications

16. **Comparing Risk of Mutual Funds.** Investors commonly use the standard deviation of the monthly percentage return for a mutual fund as a measure of the risk for the fund; in such cases, a fund that has a larger standard deviation is considered more risky than a fund with a lower standard deviation. The standard deviation for the American Century Equity Growth fund and the standard deviation for the Fidelity Growth Discovery fund were recently reported to be 15.0% and 18.9%, respectively. Assume that each of these standard deviations is based on a sample of 60 months of returns. Do the sample results support the conclusion that the Fidelity fund has a larger population variance than the American Century fund? Which fund is more risky? **LO 5**
17. **Repair Costs as Automobiles Age.** In its 2016 Auto Reliability Survey, *Consumer Reports* asked subscribers to report their maintenance and repair costs. Most individuals are aware of the fact that the average annual repair cost for an automobile depends on the age of the automobile. A researcher is interested in finding out whether the variance of the annual repair costs also increases with the age of the automobile. A sample of 26 four-year old automobiles showed a sample standard

deviation for annual repair costs of $170 and a sample of 25 two-year old automobiles old showed a sample standard deviation for annual repair costs of $100. **LO 5**

a. State the null and alternative versions of the research hypothesis that the variance in annual repair costs is larger for the older automobiles.
b. At a 0.01 level of significance, what is your conclusion? What is the *p*-value? Discuss the reasonableness of your findings.

18. **Variance in Fund Amounts: Merrill Lynch Versus Morgan Stanley.** Barron's has collected data on the top 1,000 financial advisors. Merrill Lynch and Morgan Stanley have many of their advisors on this list. A sample of 16 of the Merrill Lynch advisers and 10 of the Morgan Stanley advisers showed that the advisers managed many very large accounts with a large variance in the total amount of funds managed. The standard deviation of the amount managed by the Merrill Lynch advisers was $s_1 = \$587$ million. The standard deviation of the amount managed by the Morgan Stanley advisers was $s_2 = \$489$ million. Conduct a hypothesis test at $\alpha = 0.10$ to determine whether there is a significant difference in the population variances for the amounts managed by the two companies. What is your conclusion about the variability in the amount of funds managed by advisers from the two firms? **LO 5**

19. **Bag-Filling Machines at Jelly Belly.** The variance in a production process is an important measure of the quality of the process. A large variance often signals an opportunity for improvement in the process by finding ways to reduce the process variance. Jelly Belly Candy Company is testing two machines that use different technologies to fill three pound bags of jelly beans. The file *bags* contains a sample of data on the weights of bags (in pounds) filled by each machine. Conduct a statistical test to determine whether there is a significant difference between the variances in the bag weights for two machines. Use a 0.05 level of significance. What is your conclusion? Which machine, if either, provides the greater opportunity for quality improvements? **LO 5**

DATA*file*
bags

20. **Salaries at Public Accounting Firms.** On the basis of data provided by a Romac salary survey, the variance in annual salaries for senior partners in public accounting firms is approximately 2.1 and the variance in annual salaries for managers in public accounting firms is approximately 11.1. The salary data were provided in thousands of dollars. Assuming that the salary data were based on samples of 25 senior partners and 26 managers, test the hypothesis that the population variances in the salaries are equal. At a 0.05 level of significance, what is your conclusion? **LO 5**

21. **Smartphone Battery Life.** Battery life is an important issue for many smartphone owners. Public health studies have examined "low-battery anxiety" and acute anxiety called "nomophobia" that results when a smartphone user's phone battery charge runs low and then dies (*Wall Street Journal*, May 5, 2018). Battery life between charges for the Samsung Galaxy S9 averages 31 hours when the primary use is talk time and 10 hours when the primary use is Internet applications. Because the mean hours for talk time usage is greater than the mean hours for Internet usage, the question was raised as to whether the variance in hours of usage is also greater when the primary use is talk time. Sample data showing battery life between charges for the two applications follows. **LO 5**

DATA*file*
batterylife

Primary Use: Talking

35.8	22.2	24.0	32.6	18.5	42.5
28.0	23.8	30.0	22.8	20.3	35.5

Primary Use: Internet

14.0	12.5	16.4	11.9	9.9	3.1
5.4	11.0	15.2	4.0	4.7	

a. Formulate hypotheses about the two population variances that can be used to determine whether the population variance in battery life is greater for the talk time application.
b. What are the standard deviations of battery life for the two samples?
c. Conduct the hypothesis test and compute the p-value. Using a 0.05 level of significance, what is your conclusion?

22. **Stopping Distances of Automobiles.** A research hypothesis is that the variance of stopping distances of automobiles on wet pavement is substantially greater than the variance of stopping distances of automobiles on dry pavement. In the research study, 16 automobiles traveling at the same speeds are tested for stopping distances on wet pavement and then tested for stopping distances on dry pavement. On wet pavement, the standard deviation of stopping distances is 32 feet. On dry pavement, the standard deviation is 16 feet. **LO 5**
    a. At a 0.05 level of significance, do the sample data justify the conclusion that the variance in stopping distances on wet pavement is greater than the variance in stopping distances on dry pavement? What is the p-value?
    b. What are the implications of your statistical conclusions in terms of driving safety recommendations?

Summary

In this chapter, we presented statistical procedures that can be used to make inferences about population variances. In the process we introduced two new probability distributions: the chi-square distribution and the F distribution. The chi-square distribution can be used as the basis for interval estimation and hypothesis tests about the variance of a normal population.

We illustrated the use of the F distribution in hypothesis tests about the variances of two normal populations. In particular, we showed that with independent random samples of sizes n_1 and n_2 selected from two normal populations with equal variances $\sigma_1^2 = \sigma_2^2$, the sampling distribution of the ratio of the two sample variances s_1^2/s_2^2 has an F distribution with $n_1 - 1$ degrees of freedom for the numerator and $n_2 - 1$ degrees of freedom for the denominator.

Key Formulas

Interval Estimate of a Population Variance

$$\frac{(n-1)s^2}{\chi^2_{\alpha/2}} \leq \sigma^2 \leq \frac{(n-1)s^2}{\chi^2_{(1-\alpha/2)}} \qquad \textbf{(11.7)}$$

Test Statistic for Hypothesis Tests About a Population Variance

$$\chi^2 = \frac{(n-1)s^2}{\sigma_0^2} \qquad \textbf{(11.8)}$$

Test Statistic for Hypothesis Tests About Population Variances with $\sigma_1^2 = \sigma_2^2$

$$F = \frac{s_1^2}{s_2^2} \qquad \textbf{(11.10)}$$

Supplementary Exercises

23. **Daily Hotel Room Occupancy.** Because of staffing decisions, managers of the Gibson-Marimont Hotel are interested in the variability in the number of rooms occupied per day during a particular season of the year. A sample of 20 days of

operation shows a sample mean of 290 rooms occupied per day and a sample standard deviation of 30 rooms. **LO 2**

a. What is the point estimate of the population variance?
b. Provide a 90% confidence interval estimate of the population variance.
c. Provide a 90% confidence interval estimate of the population standard deviation.

24. **Pricing of Initial Public Offerings.** Initial public offerings (IPOs) of stocks are on average underpriced. The standard deviation measures the dispersion, or variation, in the underpricing-overpricing indicator. A sample of 13 Canadian IPOs that were subsequently traded on the Toronto Stock Exchange had a standard deviation of 14.95. Develop a 95% confidence interval estimate of the population standard deviation for the underpricing-overpricing indicator. **LO 2**

25. **Business Travel Costs.** According to the 2017 Corporate Travel Index compiled by *Business Travel News*, the average daily cost for business travel in the United States rose to $321 per day. The file *travel* contains sample data for an analogous study on the estimated daily living costs for an executive traveling to various international cities. The estimates include a single room at a four-star hotel, beverages, breakfast, taxi fares, and incidental costs. **LO 2**

DATA*file*
travel

City	Daily Living Cost ($)	City	Daily Living Cost ($)
Bangkok	242.87	Mexico City	212.00
Bogotá	260.93	Milan	284.08
Cairo	194.19	Mumbai	139.16
Dublin	260.76	Paris	436.72
Frankfurt	355.36	Rio de Janeiro	240.87
Hong Kong	346.32	Seoul	310.41
Johannesburg	165.37	Tel Aviv	223.73
Lima	250.08	Toronto	181.25
London	326.76	Warsaw	238.20
Madrid	283.56	Washington, DC	250.61

a. Compute the sample mean.
b. Compute the sample standard deviation.
c. Compute a 95% confidence interval for the population standard deviation.

26. **Manufacturing of Ball Bearings.** Ball bearing manufacturing is a very precise business and minimal part variability is critical. Large variances in the size of the ball bearings cause bearing failure and rapid wearout. Production standards call for a maximum variance of 0.0001 inches^2. Gerry Liddy has gathered a sample of 15 bearings that shows a sample standard deviation of 0.014 inches. **LO 2, 3**

a. Use $\alpha = 0.10$ to determine whether the sample indicates that the maximum acceptable variance is being exceeded.
b. Compute the 90% confidence interval estimate of the variance of the ball bearings in the population.

27. **Count Chocula Cereal.** Filling boxes with consistent amounts of its cereals are critical to General Mills' success. The filling variance for boxes of Count Chocula cereal is designed to be 0.02 ounces^2 or less. A sample of 41 boxes of Count Chocula shows a sample standard deviation of 0.16 ounces. Use $\alpha = 0.05$ to determine whether the variance in the cereal box fillings is exceeding the design specification. **LO 3**

28. **Grubhub Food Delivery.** Grubhub is a service that delivers food that its customers order online from participating restaurants. Grubhub claims consistent delivery

times for its deliveries. A sample of 22 meal deliveries shows a sample variance of 1.5. Test to determine whether H_0: $\sigma^2 \leq 1$ can be rejected. Use $\alpha = 0.10$. **LO 3**

29. **Daily Patient Volume at Dental Clinic.** A sample of 9 days over the past six months showed that Philip Sherman, DDS, treated the following numbers of patients at this dental clinic: 22, 25, 20, 18, 15, 22, 24, 19, and 26. If the number of patients seen per day is normally distributed, would an analysis of these sample data reject the hypothesis that the variance in the number of patients seen per day is equal to 10? Use a 0.10 level of significance. What is your conclusion? **LO 3**

30. **Passenger Volume on Allegiant Airlines.** A sample standard deviation for the number of passengers taking a particular Allegiant Airlines flight is 8. A 95% confidence interval estimate of the population standard deviation is 5.86 passengers to 12.62 passengers. **LO 1, 2**
    a. Was a sample size of 10 or 15 used in the statistical analysis?
    b. Suppose the sample standard deviation of $s = 8$ was based on a sample of 25 flights. What change would you expect in the confidence interval for the population standard deviation? Compute a 95% confidence interval estimate of σ with a sample size of 25.

31. **Golf Scores.** Is there any difference in the variability in golf scores for players on the LPGA Tour (the women's professional golf tour) and players on the PGA Tour (the men's professional golf tour)? A sample of 20 tournament scores from LPGA events showed a standard deviation of 2.4623 strokes, and a sample of 30 tournament scores from PGA events showed a standard deviation of 2.2118. Conduct a hypothesis test for equal population variances to determine whether there is any statistically significant difference in the variability of golf scores for male and female professional golfers. Use $\alpha = 0.10$. What is your conclusion? **LO 5**

32. **Grade Point Average Comparison.** The grade point averages of 352 students who completed a college course in financial accounting have a standard deviation of 0.940. The grade point averages of 73 students who dropped out of the same course have a standard deviation of 0.797. Do the data indicate a difference between the variances of grade point averages for students who completed a financial accounting course and students who dropped out? Use a 0.05 level of significance. (*Note:* $F_{0.025}$ with 351 and 72 degrees of freedom is 1.466.) **LO 5**

33. **Weekly Cost Reporting.** Stable cost reporting in a manufacturing setting is typically a sign that operations are running smoothly. The accounting department at Rockwell Collins, an avionics manufacturer, analyzes the variance of the weekly costs reported by two of its production departments. A sample of 16 cost reports for each of the two departments shows cost variances of 2.3 and 5.4, respectively. Is this sample sufficient to conclude that the two production departments differ in terms of weekly cost variance? Use $\alpha = 0.10$. **LO 5**

34. **Lean Process Improvement at the New York City Food Bank.** In an effort to make better use of its resources, the New York City Food Bank engaged in lean process improvement. This employee-driven kaizen effort resulted in a new method for packing meals for distribution to needy families. One goal of the process improvement effort was to reduce the variability in the meal-packing time. The following table summarizes information from a sample of data using the current method and the new method. Did the kaizen event successfully reduce the population variation? Use $\alpha = 0.10$ and formulate the appropriate hypothesis test. **LO 5**

	Current Method	New Method
Sample Size	$n_1 = 31$	$n_2 = 25$
Sample Variance	$s_1^2 = 25$	$s_2^2 = 12$

Case Problem 1: Air Force Training Program

An Air Force introductory course in electronics uses a personalized system of instruction whereby each student views a videotaped lecture and then is given a programmed instruction text. The students work independently with the text until they have completed the training and passed a test. Of concern is the varying pace at which the students complete this portion of their training program. Some students are able to cover the programmed instruction text relatively quickly, whereas other students work much longer with the text and require additional time to complete the course. The fast students wait until the slow students complete the introductory course before the entire group proceeds together with other aspects of their training.

A proposed alternative system involves use of computer-assisted instruction. In this method, all students view the same videotaped lecture and then each is assigned to a computer terminal for further instruction. The computer guides the student, working independently, through the self-training portion of the course.

To compare the proposed and current methods of instruction, an entering class of 122 students was assigned randomly to one of the two methods. One group of 61 students used the current programmed-text method and the other group of 61 students used the proposed computer-assisted method. The time in hours was recorded for each student in the study. The following data are provided in the file named *training*. **LO 5**

DATA*file*
training

Course Completion Times (hours) for Current Training Method

76	76	77	74	76	74	74	77	72	78	73
78	75	80	79	72	69	79	72	70	70	81
76	78	72	82	72	73	71	70	77	78	73
79	82	65	77	79	73	76	81	69	75	75
77	79	76	78	76	76	73	77	84	74	74
69	79	66	70	74	72					

Course Completion Times (hours) for Proposed Computer-Assisted Method

74	75	77	78	74	80	73	73	78	76	76
74	77	69	76	75	72	75	72	76	72	77
73	77	69	77	75	76	74	77	75	78	72
77	78	78	76	75	76	76	75	76	80	77
76	75	73	77	77	77	79	75	75	72	82
76	76	74	72	78	71					

Managerial Report

We discuss interval estimation and hypothesis testing on the difference between population means in Chapter 10.

1. Use appropriate descriptive statistics to summarize the training time data for each method. What similarities or differences do you observe from the sample data?
2. Conduct a hypothesis test on the difference between the population means for the two methods. Discuss your findings.
3. Compute the standard deviation and variance for each training method. Conduct a hypothesis test about the equality of population variances for the two training methods. Discuss your findings.
4. What conclusion can you reach about any differences between the two methods? What is your recommendation? Explain.
5. Can you suggest other data or testing that might be desirable before making a final decision on the training program to be used in the future?

Case Problem 2: Meticulous Drill & Reamer

Meticulous Drill & Reamer (MD&R) specializes in drilling and boring precise holes in hard metals (e.g., steel alloys, tungsten carbide, and titanium). The company recently contracted to drill holes with three-centimeter diameters in large carbon-steel alloy disks, and it will have to purchase a special drill to complete this job. MD&R has eliminated all but two of the drills it has been considering: Davis Drills' T2005 and Worth Industrial Tools' AZ100. These producers have each agreed to allow MD&R to use a T2005 and an AZ100 for one week to determine which drill it will purchase. During the one-week trial, MD&R uses each of these drills to drill 31 holes with a target diameter of three centimeters in one large carbon-steel alloy disk, then measures the diameter of each hole and records the results. MD&R's results are provided in the table that follows and are available in the file *meticulousdrills*. **LO 5**

DATA*file*
meticulousdrills

Hole Diameter					
T2005	**AZ100**	**T2005**	**AZ100**	**T2005**	**AZ100**
3.06	2.91	3.05	2.97	3.04	3.06
3.04	3.31	3.01	3.05	3.01	3.25
3.13	2.82	2.73	2.95	2.95	2.82
3.01	3.01	3.12	2.92	3.14	3.22
2.95	2.94	3.04	2.71	3.31	2.93
3.02	3.17	3.10	2.77	3.01	3.24
3.02	3.25	3.02	2.73	2.93	2.77
3.12	3.39	2.92	3.18	3.00	2.94
3.00	3.22	3.01	2.95	3.04	3.31
3.04	2.97	3.15	2.86		
3.03	2.93	2.69	3.16		

MD&R wants to consider both the accuracy (closeness of the diameter to three centimeters) and the precision (the variance of the diameter) of the holes drilled by the T2005 and the AZ100 when deciding which model to purchase.

Managerial Report

In making this assessment for MD&R, consider the following four questions:

1. Are the holes drilled by the T2005 or the AZ100 more accurate? That is, which model of drill produces holes with a mean diameter closer to three centimeters? Is a hypothesis test comparing these two means necessary? Why or why not?
2. Are the holes drilled by the T2005 or the AZ100 more precise? That is, which model of drill produces holes with a smaller variance?
3. Conduct a test of the hypothesis that the T2005 and the AZ100 are equally precise (that is, have equal variances) at $a = 0.05$. Discuss your findings.
4. Which drill do you recommend to MD&R? Why?

Chapter 12

Tests of Goodness of Fit, Independence, and Multiple Proportions

Contents

Statistics in Practice:
United Way

12.1 Goodness-of-Fit Test
Multinomial Probability Distribution
Using Excel to Conduct a Goodness-of-Fit Test

12.2 Test of Independence
Using Excel to Conduct a Test of Independence

12.3 Testing for Equality of Three or More Population Proportions
A Multiple Comparison Procedure
Using Excel to Conduct a Test of Multiple Proportions

Summary 563
Glossary 564
Key Formulas 564
Supplementary Exercises 565
Case Problem 1: A Bipartisan Agenda for Change 568
Case Problem 2: Fuentes Salty Snacks, Inc. 568
Case Problem 3: Fresno Board Games 569

Available in the Cengage eBook:
Appendix: Chi-Square Tests with R

Learning Objectives

After completing this chapter, you will be able to

LO 1 Conduct a goodness-of-fit test in which the population is hypothesized to have a multinomial distribution.

LO 2 Construct tables of observed and expected frequencies for a pair of categorical variables and conduct a chi-square test of independence.

LO 3 Conduct a hypothesis test about the equality of three or more population proportions using either the *p*-value approach or the critical value approach.

LO 4 Employ the Marascuilo procedure to execute a multiple pairwise comparisons test for three or more population proportions.

Statistics in Practice

United Way*

Rochester, New York

United Way of Greater Rochester is a nonprofit organization dedicated to improving the quality of life for all people in the seven counties it serves by meeting the community's most important human care needs.

The annual United Way/Red Cross fund-raising campaign funds hundreds of programs offered by more than 200 service providers. These providers meet a wide variety of human needs—physical, mental, and social—and serve people of all ages, backgrounds, and economic means.

The United Way of Greater Rochester decided to conduct a survey to learn more about community perceptions of charities. Focus-group interviews were held with professional, service, and general worker groups to obtain preliminary information on perceptions. The information obtained was then used to help develop the questionnaire for the survey. The questionnaire was pretested, modified, and distributed to 440 individuals.

A variety of descriptive statistics, including frequency distributions and crosstabulations, were provided from the data collected. An important part of the analysis involved the use of chi-square tests of independence. One use of such statistical tests was to determine whether perceptions of administrative expenses were independent of the occupation of the respondent.

The hypotheses for the test of independence were as follows:

H_0: Perception of United Way administrative expenses is independent of the occupation of the respondent.

H_a: Perception of United Way administrative expenses is not independent of the occupation of the respondent.

Two questions in the survey provided categorical data for the statistical test. One question obtained data on perceptions of the percentage of funds going to administrative expenses (up to 10%, 11–20%, and 21% or more). The other question asked for the occupation of the respondent.

The test of independence led to rejection of the null hypothesis and to the conclusion that perception of United Way administrative expenses is not independent of the occupation of the respondent. Actual administrative expenses were less than 9%, but 35% of the respondents perceived that administrative expenses were 21% or more. Hence, many respondents had inaccurate perceptions of administrative expenses. In this group, production-line, clerical, sales, and professional-technical employees had the more inaccurate perceptions.

The community perceptions study helped United Way of Rochester develop adjustments to its programs and fund-raising activities. In this chapter, you will learn how tests, such as described here, are conducted.

United Way programs meet the needs of children as well as adults. Jim West/age fotostock/Superstock

*The authors are indebted to Dr. Philip R. Tyler, marketing consultant to the United Way, for providing this Statistics in Practice.

In this chapter, we introduce three hypothesis testing procedures that extend our ability to make statistical inferences about populations. Specifically, we consider a test statistic based on the chi-square (χ^2) distribution. These tests are all based on comparing observed sample results with those that are expected when the null hypothesis is true. The hypothesis testing conclusion is based upon using a chi-square test statistic to determine how "close" the sample results are to the expected results.

In Chapter 11, we showed how the chi-square distribution can be used to compute an interval estimate and conduct hypothesis tests about a population variance.

All three hypothesis tests are designed for use with categorical data. In cases in which data are not naturally categorical, we define categories and consider the observation count in each category. The goodness-of-fit test in Section 12.1 is useful when we want to test whether a frequency distribution developed from categorical data is a good fit to a hypothesized probability distribution for the population. In Section 12.2, we show how the chi-square test of independence is used to determine whether two categorical variables sampled from one population are independent. Section 12.3 describes a chi-square test for multiple populations by showing how sample data from three or more populations can be used to determine whether the population proportions are equal.

12.1 Goodness-of-Fit Test

The chi-square **goodness-of-fit test** can be used to determine whether a random variable has a specific probability distribution. In this section, we show how to conduct a goodness-of-fit test for a random variable with a multinomial probability distribution.

Multinomial Probability Distribution

A **multinomial probability distribution** is an extension of the binomial probability distribution to the case where there are three or more categories of outcomes per trial. The category probabilities are the key parameters of the multinomial distribution. For an application of a goodness-of-fit test to a multinomial probability distribution, consider the market share study being conducted by Scott Marketing Research. Over the past year, market shares for a certain product have stabilized at 30% for company A, 50% for company B, and 20% for company C. Since each customer is classified as buying from one of these companies, we have a multinomial probability distribution with three possible categories of outcomes. The probability for each of the three categories is as follows.

$$p_A = \text{probability a customer purchases the company A product}$$
$$p_B = \text{probability a customer purchases the company B product}$$
$$p_C = \text{probability a customer purchases the company C product}$$

The sum of the probabilities for a multinomial probability distribution equals 1.

Using the historical market shares, we have a multinomial probability distribution with $p_A = 0.30$, $p_B = 0.50$, and $p_C = 0.20$.

Company C plans to introduce a "new and improved" product to replace its current entry in the market. Company C has retained Scott Marketing Research to determine whether the new product will alter or change the market shares for the three companies. Specifically, Scott Marketing Research will introduce a sample of customers to the new company C product and then ask the customers to indicate a preference for the company A product, the company B product, or the new company C product. Based on the sample data, the following hypothesis test can be used to determine whether the new company C product is likely to change the historical market shares for the three companies.

$$H_0\text{: } p_A = 0.30,\ p_B = 0.50, \text{ and } p_C = 0.20$$
$$H_a\text{: The probabilities are not } p_A = 0.30,\ p_B = 0.50, \text{ and } p_C = 0.20$$

The null hypothesis is based on the historical multinomial probability distribution for the market shares. If sample results lead to the rejection of H_0, Scott Marketing Research will have evidence to conclude that the introduction of the new company C product will change the market shares (the category probabilities for the multinomial distribution).

Let us assume that the market research firm has used a consumer panel of 200 customers. Each customer was asked to specify a purchase preference among the three alternatives: company A's product, company B's product, and company C's new product. The 200 responses are summarized in the following frequency distribution.

Category	Observed Frequency
Company A	48
Company B	98
Company C	54
Total	200

We now can perform a goodness-of-fit test to determine whether the sample of 200 customer purchase preferences is consistent with the null hypothesis. The goodness-of-fit test is based on a comparison of observed frequencies from the sample with the expected frequencies under the assumption that the null hypothesis is true. Hence, the next step is to compute expected purchase preferences for the 200 customers under the assumption that H_0: $p_A = 0.30$, $p_B = 0.50$, and $p_C = 0.20$ is true. Doing so provides the following expected frequency distribution.

Category	Expected Frequency
Company A	200(0.30) = 60
Company B	200(0.50) = 100
Company C	200(0.20) = 40
Total	200

Note that the expected frequency for each category is found by multiplying the sample size of 200 by the hypothesized probability for the category.

The goodness-of-fit test now focuses on the differences between the observed frequencies and the expected frequencies. Whether the differences between the observed and expected frequencies are "large" or "small" is a question answered with the aid of the following chi-square test statistic.

In equation (12.1), the difference between the observed (f_i) and expected (e_i) frequencies is squared; thus, χ^2 will never be negative.

Test Statistic for Goodness of Fit

$$\chi^2 = \sum_{i=1}^{k} \frac{(f_i - e_i)^2}{e_i} \tag{12.1}$$

where

f_i = observed frequency for category i

e_i = expected frequency for category i

k = the number of categories

Note: The test statistic has a chi-square distribution with $k - 1$ degrees of freedom provided that the expected frequencies are 5 *or more* for all categories.

Let us continue with the Scott Marketing Research example and use the sample data to test the hypothesis that the multinomial distribution has the market share probabilities $p_A = 0.30$, $p_B = 0.50$, and $p_C = 0.20$. We will use an $\alpha = 0.05$ level of significance. We proceed by using the observed and expected frequencies to compute the value of the test

Table 12.1 Computation of the Chi-Square Test Statistic for the Scott Marketing Research Market Share Study

Category	Hypothesized Probability	Observed Frequency (f_i)	Expected Frequency (e_i)	Difference ($f_i - e_i$)	Squared Difference $(f_i - e_i)^2$	Squared Difference Divided by Expected Frequency $(f_i - e_i)^2/e_i$
Company A	0.30	48	60	−12	144	2.40
Company B	0.50	98	100	−2	4	0.04
Company C	0.20	54	40	14	196	4.90
Total		200				$\chi^2 = 7.34$

statistic. With the expected frequencies all 5 or more, the computation of the chi-square test statistic is shown in Table 12.1. Thus, we have $\chi^2 = 7.34$.

The test for goodness of fit is always a one-tailed test, with the rejection occurring in the upper tail of the chi-square distribution.

We will reject the null hypothesis if the differences between the observed and expected frequencies are large. Thus the test of goodness of fit will always be an upper tail test. We can use the upper tail area for the test statistic and the p-value approach to determine whether the null hypothesis can be rejected. With $k - 1 = 3 - 1 = 2$ degrees of freedom, row two of the chi-square distribution Table 3 of Appendix B provides the following:

Area in Upper Tail	**0.10**	**0.05**	**0.025**	**0.01**	**0.005**
χ^2 Value (2 *df*)	4.605	5.991	7.378	9.210	10.597

$\chi^2 = 7.34$ (between 5.991 and 7.378)

The test statistic $\chi^2 = 7.34$ is between 5.991 and 7.378. Thus, the corresponding upper tail area or p-value must be between 0.05 and 0.025. With p-value ≤ 0.05, we reject H_0 and conclude that the introduction of the new product by company C will alter the historical market shares. In the Using Excel subsection which follows we will see that the p-value = 0.0255.

Instead of using the p-value, we could use the critical value approach to draw the same conclusion. With $\alpha = 0.05$ and 2 degrees of freedom, the critical value for the test statistic is $\chi^2_{.05} = 5.991$. The upper tail rejection rule becomes

$$\text{Reject } H_0 \text{ if } \chi^2 \geq 5.991$$

With $7.34 > 5.991$, we reject H_0. The p-value approach and critical value approach provide the same hypothesis testing conclusion.

Now that we have concluded that the introduction of a new company C product will alter the market shares for the three companies, we are interested in knowing more about how the market shares are likely to change. Using the historical market shares and the sample data, we summarize the data as follows:

Company	Historical Market Share (%)	Sample Data Market Share (%)
A	30	48/200 = 0.24, or 24
B	50	98/200 = 0.49, or 49
C	20	54/200 = 0.27, or 27

Figure 12.1 Bar Chart of Market Shares by Company Before and After the New Product for Company C

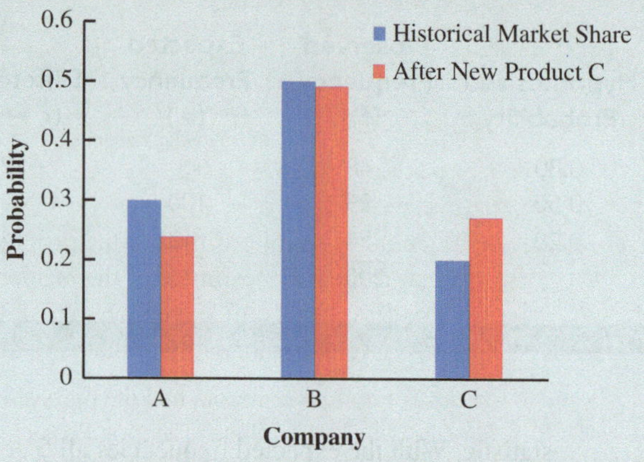

The historical market shares and the sample market shares are compared in the bar chart shown in Figure 12.1. The bar chart shows that the new product will likely increase the market share for company C. Comparisons for the other two companies indicate that company C's gain in market share will hurt company A more than company B.

Let us summarize the steps that can be used to conduct a goodness-of-fit test for a hypothesized multinomial probability distribution.

Multinomial Probability Distribution Goodness-of-Fit Test

1. State the null and alternative hypotheses.

   H_0: The population follows a multinomial probability distribution with specified probabilities for each of the k categories
   H_a: The population does not follow a multinomial probability distribution with the specified probabilities for each of the k categories

2. Select a random sample and record the observed frequencies f_i for each category.
3. Assume the null hypothesis is true and determine the expected frequency e_i in each category by multiplying the hypothesized category probability by the sample size.
4. If the expected frequency e_i is at least 5 for each category, compute the value of the test statistic.

$$\chi^2 = \sum_{i=1}^{k} \frac{(f_i - e_i)^2}{e_i}$$

5. Rejection rule:

   p-value approach: Reject H_0 if p-value $\leq \alpha$
   Critical value approach: Reject H_0 if $\chi^2 \geq \chi^2_\alpha$

   where α is the level of significance for the test and there are $k - 1$ degrees of freedom.

Figure 12.2 Excel Worksheet for the Goodness-of-Fit Test for the Scott Marketing Research Market Share Study

	A	B	C	D	E	F	G	H
1	Customer	Preference						
2	1	B						
3	2	A		Category	Observed Frequencies	Hypothesized Probability	Expected Frequency	
4	3	C		A	48	0.3	=F4*$E$7	
5	4	C		B	98	0.5	=F5*$E$7	
6	5	C		C	54	0.2	=F6*$E$7	
7	6	A		Grand Total	200			
8	7	A						
9	8	A		*p*-value	=CHISQ.TEST(E4:E6,G4:G6)			
10	9	C						
200	199	C						
201	200	C						
202								

	A	B	C	D	E	F	G	H
1	Customer	Preference						
2	1	B						
3	2	A		Category	Observed Frequencies	Hypothesized Probability	Expected Frequency	
4	3	C		A	48	0.3	60	
5	4	C		B	98	0.5	100	
6	5	C		C	54	0.2	40	
7	6	A		Grand Total	200			
8	7	A						
9	8	A		*p*-value	0.0255			
10	9	C						
200	199	C						
201	200	C						
202								

Note: Rows 11–199 are hidden.

Using Excel to Conduct a Goodness-of-Fit Test

Excel can be used to conduct a goodness-of-fit test for the market share study conducted by Scott Marketing Research. Refer to Figure 12.2 as we describe the tasks involved. The formula worksheet is in the background; the value worksheet is in the foreground.

DATA*file*
research

Enter/Access Data: Open the file *research*. The data are in cells B2:B201 and labels are in column A and cell B1. Values for the hypothesized category probabilities were entered into cells D10:D12.

Apply Tools: Cells D3:E7 show the results of using Excel's Recommended PivotTable tool (see Section 2.1 for details regarding how to use this tool) to construct a frequency distribution for the purchase preference data.

Enter Functions and Formulas: The Excel formulas in cells G4:G6 were used to compute the expected frequencies for each category by multiplying the hypothesized proportions by the sample size. Once the observed and expected frequencies have been computed, Excel's CHISQ.TEST function can be used to compute the p-value for a test of goodness of fit. The inputs to the CHISQ.TEST function are the range of values for the observed and expected frequencies. To compute the p-value for this test, we entered the following function into cell E9:

=CHISQ.TEST(E4:E6,G4:G6)

The value worksheet shows that the resulting p-value is 0.0255. Thus, with $\alpha = 0.05$, we reject H_0 and conclude that the introduction of the new product by company C will change the current market share structure.

Exercises

Methods

1. Test the following hypotheses for a multinomial probability distribution by using the χ^2 goodness-of-fit test.

$$H_0\text{: } p_A = 0.40,\ p_B = 0.40, \text{ and } p_C = 0.20$$

$$H_0\text{: The probabilities are not } p_A = 0.40,\ p_B = 0.40, \text{ and } p_C = 0.20$$

A sample of size 200 yielded 60 in category A, 120 in category B, and 20 in category C. Use $\alpha = 0.01$ and test to see whether the probabilities are as stated in H_0. **LO 1**
a. Use the p-value approach.
b. Repeat the test using the critical value approach.

2. Suppose we have a multinomial population with four categories: A, B, C, and D. The null hypothesis is that the proportion of items is the same in every category. The null hypothesis is

$$H_0: p_A = p_B = p_C = p_D = 0.25$$

A sample of size 300 yielded the following results.

A: 85 B: 95 C: 50 D: 70

Use $\alpha = 0.05$ to determine whether H_0 should be rejected. What is the p-value? **LO 1**

Applications

3. **Television Audiences Across Networks.** During the first 13 weeks of the television season, the Saturday evening 8:00 P.M. to 9:00 P.M. audience proportions were recorded as ABC 29%, CBS 28%, NBC 25%, and Independents 18%. A sample of 300 homes two weeks after a Saturday night schedule revision yielded the following viewing audience data: ABC 95 homes, CBS 70 homes, NBC 89 homes, and Independents 46 homes. Test with $\alpha = 0.05$ to determine whether the viewing audience proportions changed. **LO 1**

DATA*file*
mm

4. **M&M Candy Colors.** Mars, Inc. manufactures M&M's, one of the most popular candy treats in the world. The milk chocolate candies come in a variety of colors including blue, brown, green, orange, red, and yellow (M&M website). The overall proportions for the colors are 0.24 blue, 0.13 brown, 0.20 green, 0.16 orange, 0.13 red, and 0.14 yellow. In a sampling study, several bags of M&M milk chocolates were opened and the following color counts were obtained.

Blue	Brown	Green	Orange	Red	Yellow
105	72	89	84	70	80

Use a 0.05 level of significance and the sample data to test the hypothesis that the overall proportions for the colors are as stated above. What is your conclusion? **LO 1**

5. **America's Favorite Sports.** The *Harris Poll* tracks the favorite sport of Americans who follow at least one sport. Results of the poll show that professional football is the favorite sport of 33% of Americans who follow at least one sport, followed by baseball at 15%, men's college football at 10%, auto racing at 6%, men's professional basketball at 5%, and ice hockey at 5%, with other sports at 26%. Consider a survey in which 344 college undergraduates who follow at least one sport were asked to identify their favorite sport produced the following results:

Professional Football	Baseball	Men's College Football	Auto Racing	Men's Professional Basketball	Ice Hockey	Other Sports
111	39	46	14	6	20	108

Do college undergraduate students differ from the general public with regard to their favorite sports? Use $\alpha = 0.05$. **LO 1**

6. **Traffic Accidents by Day of Week.** The National Highway Traffic Safety Administration reports the percentage of traffic accidents occurring each day of the week. Assume that a sample of 420 accidents provided the following data. **LO 1**

Sunday	Monday	Tuesday	Wednesday	Thursday	Friday	Saturday
66	50	53	47	55	69	80

a. Conduct a hypothesis test to determine whether the proportion of traffic accidents is the same for each day of the week. What is the p-value? Using a 0.05 level of significance, what is your conclusion?

b. Compute the percentage of traffic accidents occurring on each day of the week. What day has the highest percentage of traffic accidents? Does this seem reasonable? Discuss.

12.2 Test of Independence

In this section we show how the chi-square test of independence can be used to determine whether two categorical variables sampled from one population are independent. Like the goodness-of-fit test, the test of independence is also based on comparing observed and expected frequencies. For this test, we take one sample from a single population and record the values for two categorical variables. We then summarize the data by counting the number of responses for each combination of a category for variable 1 and a category for variable 2. The null hypothesis for this test is that the two categorical variables are independent. Thus, the test is referred to as a **test of independence**. We will illustrate this test with the following example.

A beer industry association conducts a survey to determine the preferences of beer drinkers for light, regular, and dark beers. A sample of 200 beer drinkers is taken with each person in the sample asked to indicate a preference for one of the three types of beers: light, regular, or dark. At the end of the survey questionnaire, the respondent is asked to provide information on a variety of demographics including sex. In this survey of 200 beer drinkers, 132 respondents answered "male" and 68 respondents answered "female." A research question of interest to the association is whether preference for the three types of beer is independent of the sex of the beer drinker. If the two categorical variables, beer preference and sex, are independent, beer preference does not depend on sex and the preference for light, regular, and dark beer can be expected to be the same for male and female beer drinkers. However, if the test conclusion is that the two categorical variables are not independent, we have evidence that beer preference is associated with or dependent upon the sex of the beer drinker. As a result, we can expect beer preferences to differ for male and female beer drinkers. In this case, a beer manufacturer could use this information to customize its promotions and advertising for the different target markets of male and female beer drinkers.

The hypotheses for this test of independence are as follows:

H_0: Beer preference is independent of sex

H_a: Beer preference is not independent of sex

The two-way table used to summarize the data is also referred to as a contingency table.

The sample data will be summarized in a two-way table with beer preferences of light, regular, and dark as one of the variables and sex of male and female as the other variable. Since an objective of the study is to determine whether there is a difference between the beer preferences for male and female beer drinkers, we consider sex an explanatory variable and follow the usual practice of making the explanatory variable the column variable in the crosstabulation. The beer preference is the categorical response variable and is shown as the row variable. The sample results for the 200 beer drinkers in the study are summarized in Table 12.2.

The sample data are summarized based on the combination of beer preference and sex for the individual respondents. For example, 51 individuals in the study were males who preferred light beer, 56 individuals in the study were males who preferred regular beer, and so on. Let us now analyze the data in the table and test for independence of beer preference and sex.

Because we selected a sample of beer drinkers, summarizing the data for each variable separately will provide some insights into the characteristics of the beer drinker population.

DATA*file*
beerpreference

Table 12.2 Sample Results for Beer Preferences of Male and Female Beer Drinkers (Observed Frequencies)

		Sex		
		Male	Female	Total
Beer Preference	Light	51	39	90
	Regular	56	21	77
	Dark	25	8	33
	Total	132	68	200

For the categorical variable sex, 132 of the 200 beer drinkers in the sample are male. Thus, we estimate that 132/200 = 0.66, or 66%, of the beer drinker population is male. Similarly we estimate that 68/200 = 0.34, or 34%, of the beer drinker population is female. The sample data suggest that male beer drinkers outnumber female beer drinkers approximately 2 to 1. Sample proportions or percentages for the three types of beer are

Prefer Light Beer	90/200 = 0.450, or 45.0%
Prefer Regular Beer	77/200 = 0.385, or 38.5%
Prefer Dark Beer	33/200 = 0.165, or 16.5%

Across all beer drinkers in the sample, light beer is preferred most often and dark beer is preferred least often.

Let us now conduct the chi-square test to determine whether beer preference and sex are independent. The data in Table 12.2 are the observed frequencies for the two categories of sex and the three categories of beer preference.

A table of expected frequencies is developed based on the assumption that sex and beer preference are independent as stated in the null hypothesis. We showed above that for the sample of 200 beer drinkers, the proportions preferring light, regular, and dark beer are 0.450, 0.385, and 0.165, respectively. If the independence assumption is valid, we can conclude that these proportions must be applicable to both male and female beer drinkers. Thus, under the assumption of independence, we would expect that for the 132 male beer drinkers sampled that 0.450(132) = 59.40 would prefer light beer, 0.385(132) = 50.82 would prefer regular beer, and 0.165(132) = 21.78 would prefer dark beer. Application of the same proportions to the female beer drinkers leads to the expected frequencies shown in Table 12.3.

Let us generalize the approach to computing expected frequencies by letting e_{ij} denote the expected frequency in row i and column j of the table of expected frequencies. With this notation, let us reconsider the expected frequency calculation for light beer (row 1) and male beer drinkers (column 1), that is, the expected frequency e_{11}.

Table 12.3 Expected Frequencies If Beer Preference Is Independent of the Sex of the Beer Drinker

		Sex		
		Male	Female	Total
Beer Preference	Light	59.40	30.60	90
	Regular	50.82	26.18	77
	Dark	21.78	11.22	33
	Total	132.00	68.00	200

Note that 90 is the total number of light beer responses (row 1 total), 132 is the total number of male respondents in the sample (column 1 total), and 200 is the total sample size. Following the logic of the preceding paragraphs, we can compute the expected frequency in row 1 and column 1 as follows:

$$e_{11} = \left(\frac{\text{Row 1 Total}}{\text{Sample Size}}\right)(\text{Column 1 Total}) = \frac{90}{200}(132) = 59.40$$

Rewriting this expression slightly we obtain

$$e_{11} = \frac{(\text{Row 1 Total})\,(\text{Column 1 Total})}{\text{Sample Size}} = \frac{(90)(132)}{200} = 59.40$$

Generalizing this expression shows that the following formula can be used to compute the expected frequencies under the assumption that H_0 is true.

$$e_{ij} = \frac{(\text{Row } i \text{ Total})(\text{Column } j \text{ Total})}{\text{Sample Size}} \tag{12.2}$$

For example, $e_{11} = (90)(132)/200 = 59.40$ is the expected frequency for male beer drinkers who would prefer light beer if beer preference is independent of sex, $e_{12} = (90)(68)/200 = 30.60$, and so on. Show that equation (12.2) can be used to find the other expected frequencies shown in Table 12.3.

Using the table of observed frequencies (Table 12.2) and the table of expected frequencies (Table 12.3), we now wish to compute the chi-square statistic for our test of independence. Since the test of independence involves r rows and c columns, the formula for computing χ^2 involves a double summation.

$$\chi^2 = \sum_i \sum_j \frac{(f_{ij} - e_{ij})^2}{e_{ij}} \tag{12.3}$$

With r rows and c columns in the table, the chi-square distribution will have $(r - 1)(c - 1)$ degrees of freedom provided the expected frequency is at least 5 for each cell. Thus, in this application we will use a chi-square distribution with $(3 - 1)(2 - 1) = 2$ degrees of freedom. The complete steps to compute the chi-square test statistic are summarized in Table 12.4.

We can use the upper tail area of the chi-square distribution with 2 degrees of freedom and the p-value approach to determine whether the null hypothesis that beer preference

Table 12.4 Computation of the Chi-Square Test Statistic for the Test of Independence Between Beer Preference and Sex

Beer Preference	Sex	Observed Frequency f_{ij}	Expected Frequency e_{ij}	Difference $(f_{ij} - e_{ij})$	Squared Difference $(f_{ij} - e_{ij})^2$	Squared Difference Divided by Expected Frequency $(f_{ij} - e_{ij})^2/e_{ij}$
Light	Male	51	59.40	−8.40	70.56	1.19
Light	Female	39	30.60	8.40	70.56	2.31
Regular	Male	56	50.82	5.18	26.83	0.53
Regular	Female	21	26.18	−5.18	26.83	1.02
Dark	Male	25	21.78	3.22	10.37	0.48
Dark	Female	8	11.22	−3.22	10.37	0.92
	Total	200	200.00			$\chi^2 = 6.45$

is independent of sex can be rejected. Using row two of the chi-square distribution table shown in Table 3 of Appendix B, we have the following:

Area in Upper Tail	0.10	0.05	0.025	0.01	0.005
χ^2 Value (2 *df*)	4.605	5.991	7.378	9.210	10.597

$$\chi^2 = 6.45$$

Thus, we see the upper tail area at $\chi^2 = 6.45$ is between 0.05 and 0.025, and so the corresponding upper tail area or p-value must be between 0.05 and 0.025. With p-value ≤ 0.05, we reject H_0 and conclude that beer preference is not independent of the sex of the beer drinker. Stated another way, the study shows that beer preference can be expected to differ for male and female beer drinkers. In the Using Excel subsection that follows, we will see that the p-value $= 0.0398$.

Instead of using the p-value, we could use the critical value approach to draw the same conclusion. With $\alpha = 0.05$ and 2 degrees of freedom, the critical value for the chi-square test statistic is $\chi^2_{0.05} = 5.991$. The upper tail rejection region becomes

$$\text{Reject } H_0 \text{ if } \chi^2 \geq 5.991$$

With $6.45 \geq 5.991$, we reject H_0. Again we see that the p-value approach and the critical value approach provide the same conclusion.

While we now have evidence that beer preference and sex are not independent, we will need to gain additional insight from the data to assess the nature of the association between these two variables. One way to do this is to compute the probability of the beer preference responses for males and females separately. These calculations are as follows:

Beer Preference	Male	Female
Light	51/132 = 0.3864, or 38.64%	39/68 = 0.5735, or 57.35%
Regular	56/132 = 0.4242, or 42.42%	21/68 = 0.3088, or 30.88%
Dark	25/132 = 0.1894, or 18.94%	8/68 = 0.1176, or 11.76%

A bar chart showing the beer preference for male and female beer drinkers is shown in Figure 12.3.

Figure 12.3 Bar Chart Comparison of Beer Preference by Sex

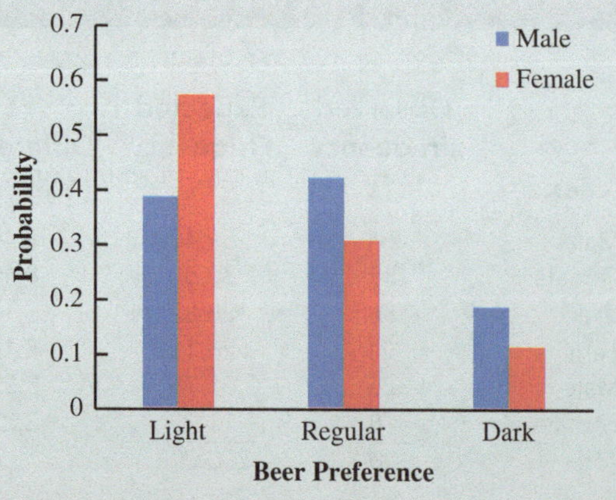

What observations can you make about the association between beer preference and sex? For female beer drinkers in the sample, the highest preference is for light beer at 57.35%. For male beer drinkers in the sample, regular beer is most frequently preferred at 42.42%. While female beer drinkers have a higher preference for light beer than males, male beer drinkers have a higher preference for both regular beer and dark beer. Data visualization through bar charts such as shown in Figure 12.3 is helpful in gaining insight as to how two categorical variables are associated.

Before we leave this discussion, we summarize the steps for a test of independence.

The expected frequencies must all be 5 or more for the chi-square test to be valid.

This chi-square test is a one-tailed test with rejection of H_0 occurring in the upper tail of a chi-square distribution with $(r - 1)(c - 1)$ degrees of freedom.

Chi-Square Test for Independence of Two Categorical Variables

1. State the null and alternative hypotheses.

   H_0: The two categorical variables are independent
   H_a: The two categorical variables are not independent

2. Select a random sample from the population and collect data for both variables for every element in the sample. Record the observed frequencies, f_{ij}, in a table with r rows and c columns.
3. Assume the null hypothesis is true and compute the expected frequencies, e_{ij}
4. If the expected frequency, e_{ij}, is 5 or more for each cell, compute the test statistic:

$$\chi^2 = \sum_i \sum_j \frac{(f_{ij} - e_{ij})^2}{e_{ij}}$$

5. Rejection rule:

   p-value approach: Reject H_0 if p-value $\leq \alpha$
   Critical value approach: Reject H_0 if $\chi^2 \geq \chi^2_\alpha$

   where the chi-square distribution has $(r - 1)(c - 1)$ degrees of freedom and α is the level of significance for the test.

Finally, if the null hypothesis of independence is rejected, summarizing the probabilities as shown in the above example will help the analyst determine where the association or dependence exists for the two categorical variables.

Using Excel to Conduct a Test of Independence

Excel can be used to conduct a test of independence for the beer preference example. Refer to Figure 12.4 as we describe the tasks involved. The formula worksheet is in the background; the value worksheet is in the foreground.

DATA*file*
beerpreference

Enter/Access Data: Open the file *beerpreference*. The data are in cells B2:C201 and labels are in column A and cells B1:C1.

Apply Tools: Cells E3:H8 show the contingency table resulting from using Excel's PivotTable tool (see Section 2.4 for details regarding how to use this tool) to construct a two-way table with beer preferences of dark, light, and regular as one of the variables and sex of male and female as the other variable.

Enter Functions and Formulas: The Excel formulas in cells F12:G14 were used to compute the expected frequencies for each row and column. Once the observed and expected frequencies have been computed, Excel's CHISQ.TEST function can be used to compute the *p*-value for a test of independence. The inputs to the CHISQ.TEST function are the

Figure 12.4 Excel Worksheet for the Beer Preference Test of Independence

	A	B	C	D	E	F	G	H	I
1	Beer Drinker	Preference	Sex						
2	1	Regular	Male						
3	2	Light	Female		Count of Beer Drinker	Sex			
4	3	Regular	Male		Preference	Female	Male	Grand Total	
5	4	Regular	Male		Dark	8	25	33	
6	5	Regular	Female		Light	39	51	90	
7	6	Regular	Male		Regular	21	56	77	
8	7	Dark	Male		Grand Total	68	132	200	
9	8	Dark	Male						
10	9	Dark	Male			Sex			
11	10	Light	Female		Preference	Female	Male		
12	11	Light	Male		Dark	=($H5*F$8)/$H$8	=($H5*G$8)/$H$8		
13	12	Dark	Female		Light	=($H6*F$8)/$H$8	=($H6*G$8)/$H$8		
14	13	Regular	Male		Regular	=($H7*F$8)/$H$8	=($H7*G$8)/$H$8		
15	14	Regular	Male						
16	15	Light	Male		*p*-value	=CHISQ.TEST(F5:G7,F12:G14)			
17	16	Regular	Male						
200	199	Light	Male						
201	200	Light	Male						
202									

	A	B	C	D	E	F	G	H	I
1	Beer Drinker	Preference	Sex						
2	1	Regular	Male						
3	2	Light	Female		Count of Beer Drinker	Sex			
4	3	Regular	Male		Preference	Female	Male	Grand Total	
5	4	Regular	Male		Dark	8	25	33	
6	5	Regular	Female		Light	39	51	90	
7	6	Regular	Male		Regular	21	56	77	
8	7	Dark	Male		Grand Total	68	132	200	
9	8	Dark	Male						
10	9	Dark	Male			Sex			
11	10	Light	Female		Preference	Female	Male		
12	11	Light	Male		Dark	11.22	21.78		
13	12	Dark	Female		Light	30.60	59.40		
14	13	Regular	Male		Regular	26.18	50.82		
15	14	Regular	Male						
16	15	Light	Male		*p*-value	0.0398			
17	16	Regular	Male						
200	199	Light	Male						
201	200	Light	Male						
202									

Note: Rows 18–199 are hidden.

range of values for the observed and expected frequencies. To compute the p-value for this test of independence, we entered the following function into cell F16:

$$=CHISQ.TEST(F5{:}G7,F12{:}G14)$$

The value worksheet shows that the resulting p-value is 0.0398. Thus, with $\alpha = 0.05$, we reject H_0 and conclude that beer preference is not independent of the sex of the beer drinker.

Notes + Comments

The test statistic for the chi-square tests in this chapter requires an expected frequency of 5 for each category. When a category has fewer than five, it is often appropriate to combine two adjacent categories to obtain an expected frequency of 5 or more in each category.

Exercises

Methods

7. The following table contains observed frequencies for a sample of 200. Test for independence of the row and column variables using $\alpha = 0.05$. **LO 2**

	Column Variable		
Row Variable	**A**	**B**	**C**
P	20	44	50
Q	30	26	30

8. The following table contains observed frequencies for a sample of 240. Test for independence of the row and column variables using $\alpha = 0.05$. **LO 2**

	Column Variable		
Row Variable	A	B	C
P	20	30	20
Q	30	60	25
R	10	15	30

Applications

9. **Airline Ticket Purchases for Domestic and International Flights.** A *Bloomberg Businessweek* subscriber study asked, "In the past 12 months, when traveling for business, what type of airline ticket did you purchase most often?" A second question asked if the type of flight was domestic or international travel. Sample data obtained are shown in the following table. **LO 2**

	Type of Flight	
Type of Ticket	Domestic	International
First Class	29	22
Business Class	95	121
Economy Class	518	135

a. Using a 0.05 level of significance, is the type of ticket purchased independent of the type of flight? What is your conclusion?
b. Discuss any dependence that exists between the type of ticket and type of flight.

DATA*file*
workforceplan

10. **Hiring and Firing Plans at Private and Public Companies.** A Deloitte employment survey asked a sample of human resource executives how their company planned to change its workforce over the next 12 months. A categorical response variable showed three options: The company plans to hire and add to the number of employees, the company plans no change in the number of employees, or the company plans to lay off and reduce the number of employees. Another categorical variable indicated if the company was private or public. Sample data for 180 companies are summarized as follows. **LO 2**

	Company	
Employment Plan	Private	Public
Add Employees	37	32
No Change	19	34
Lay Off Employees	16	42

a. Conduct a test of independence to determine whether the employment plan for the next 12 months is independent of the type of company. At a 0.05 level of significance, what is your conclusion?
b. Discuss any differences in the employment plans for private and public companies over the next 12 months.

DATA*file*
millennials

11. **Generational Differences in Work Place Attitudes.** Addison Group (a provider of professional staffing services) and Kelton (a global insights firm) surveyed the work preferences and attitudes of 1,006 working adults spread over three generations—baby boomers, Generation X, and millennials. In one question, individuals were asked if they would leave their current job to make more money at another job. The file *millennials* contains the sample data, which is also summarized in the following table.

	Generation		
Leave Job for More Money?	Baby Boomer	Generation X	Millennial
Yes	129	152	164
No	207	183	171

Conduct a test of independence to determine whether interest in leaving a current job for more money is independent of employee generation. What is the p-value? Using a 0.05 level of significance, what is your conclusion? **LO 2**

DATA*file*
autoquality

12. **Vehicle Quality Ratings.** A J.D. Power and Associates vehicle quality survey asked new owners a variety of questions about their recently purchased automobile. One question asked for the owner's rating of the vehicle using categorical responses of average, outstanding, and exceptional. Another question asked for the owner's education level with the categorical responses some high school, high school graduate, some college, and college graduate. Assume the sample data below are for 500 owners who had recently purchased an automobile. **LO 2**

	Education			
Quality Rating	Some HS	HS Grad	Some College	College Grad
Average	35	30	20	60
Outstanding	45	45	50	90
Exceptional	20	25	30	50

a. Use a 0.05 level of significance and a test of independence to determine whether a new owner's vehicle quality rating is independent of the owner's education. What is the p-value and what is your conclusion?
b. Use the overall percentage of average, outstanding, and exceptional ratings to comment on how new owners rate the quality of their recently purchased automobiles.

13. **Company Reputation and Management Quality Survey.** *The Wall Street Journal* Annual Corporate Perceptions Study surveys readers and asks how each rates the quality of management and the reputation of the company for over 250 worldwide corporations. Both the quality of management and the reputation of the company were rated on an excellent, good, and fair categorical scale. Assume the sample data for 200 respondents below applies to this study. **LO 2**

	Reputation of Company		
Quality of Management	Excellent	Good	Fair
Excellent	40	25	5
Good	35	35	10
Fair	25	10	15

a. Use a 0.05 level of significance and test for independence of the quality of management and the reputation of the company. What is the p-value and what is your conclusion?
b. If there is a dependence or association between the two ratings, discuss and use probabilities to justify your answer.

14. **Attitudes Toward New Nuclear Power Plants.** As the price of oil rises, there is increased worldwide interest in alternate sources of energy. The *Financial Times/Harris Poll* surveyed people in six countries to assess attitudes toward a variety of alternate forms of energy. The data in the following table are a portion of the poll's findings concerning whether people favor or oppose the building of new nuclear power plants. **LO 2**

	Country					
Response	Great Britain	France	Italy	Spain	Germany	United States
Strongly favor	141	161	298	133	128	204
Favor more than oppose	348	366	309	222	272	326
Oppose more than favor	381	334	219	311	322	316
Strongly oppose	217	215	219	443	389	174

a. How large was the sample in this poll?
b. Conduct a hypothesis test to determine whether people's attitude toward building new nuclear power plants is independent of country. What is your conclusion?
c. Using the percentage of respondents who "strongly favor" and "favor more than oppose," which country has the most favorable attitude toward building new nuclear power plants? Which country has the least favorable attitude?

15. **Research Classification of Higher Education.** The Carnegie Classification of Institutes of Higher Education categorizes colleges and universities on the basis of their research and degree-granting activities. Universities that grant doctoral degrees are placed into one of three classifications: highest research activity, higher research activity, or moderate research activity. The Carnegie classifications for public and not-for-profit private doctoral degree-granting universities follow.

	Carnegie Classification		
Type of University	Highest Research Activity	Higher Research Activity	Moderate Research Activity
Public	81	76	38
Not-For-Profit Private	34	31	58

Using a 0.05 level of significance, conduct a test of independence to determine whether Carnegie classification is independent of type of university for universities that grant doctoral degrees. What is the p-value and what is your conclusion? **LO 2**

16. **Movie Critic Opinions.** On a television program, two movie critics provide their reviews of recent movies and discuss. It is suspected that these hosts deliberately disagree in order to make the program more interesting for viewers. Each movie review is categorized as Pro ("thumbs up"), Con ("thumbs down"), or Mixed. The results of 160 movie ratings by the two hosts are shown here.

	Host B		
Host A	**Con**	**Mixed**	**Pro**
Con	24	8	13
Mixed	8	13	11
Pro	10	9	64

Use a test of independence with a 0.01 level of significance to analyze the data. What is your conclusion? **LO 2**

12.3 Testing for Equality of Three or More Population Proportions

We use the chi-square test statistic in a manner similar to the way we have used the normal (z) test statistic, t test statistic, and the F test statistic for hypothesis testing in Chapters 9, 10, and 11.

In this section, we show how the chi-square (χ^2) test statistic can be used to make statistical inferences about the equality of population proportions for three or more populations. The methodology is similar to that for the test of independence in Section 12.2 in the sense that we will compare a table of observed frequencies to a table of expected frequencies.

Using the notation

$$p_1 = \text{population proportion for population 1}$$

$$p_2 = \text{population proportion for population 2}$$

and

$$\vdots \qquad \qquad \vdots$$

$$p_k = \text{population proportion for population } k$$

the hypotheses for the equality of population proportions for $k \geq 3$ populations are as follows:

$$H_0\colon p_1 = p_2 = \cdots = p_k$$

$$H_a\colon \text{Not all population proportions are equal}$$

If the sample data and the chi-square test computations indicate H_0 cannot be rejected, we cannot detect a difference among the k population proportions. However, if the sample data and the chi-square test computations indicate H_0 can be rejected, we have statistical evidence to conclude that not all k population proportions are equal; that is, one or more population proportions differ from the other population proportions. Further analyses can be conducted to determine which population proportion or proportions are significantly different from others. Let us demonstrate this chi-square test by considering an application.

Organizations such as J.D. Power and Associates use the proportion of owners likely to repurchase a particular automobile as an indication of customer loyalty for the automobile. An automobile with a greater proportion of owners likely to repurchase is considered to have greater customer loyalty. Suppose that in a particular study we want to compare the customer loyalty for three automobiles: Chevrolet Impala, Ford Fusion, and Honda Accord. The current owners of each of the three automobiles form the three populations for the study. The three population proportions of interest are as follows:

p_1 = proportion likely to repurchase for the population of Chevrolet Impala owners

p_2 = proportion likely to repurchase for the population of Ford Fusion owners

p_3 = proportion likely to repurchase for the population of Honda Accord owners

The hypotheses are stated as follows:

$$H_0\colon p_1 = p_2 = p_3$$

$$H_a\colon \text{Not all population proportions are equal}$$

In studies such as these, we often use the same sample size for each population. We have chosen different sample sizes in this example to show that the chi-square test is not restricted to equal sample sizes for each of the k populations.

To conduct this hypothesis test we begin by taking a sample of owners from each of the three populations. Thus we will have a sample of Chevrolet Impala owners, a sample of Ford Fusion owners, and a sample of Honda Accord owners. Each sample provides categorical data indicating whether the respondents are likely or not likely to repurchase the automobile. The data for samples of 125 Chevrolet Impala owners, 200 Ford Fusion owners, and 175 Honda Accord owners are summarized in Table 12.5. This table has two rows for the responses Yes and No and three columns, one for each of the populations of automobile owners. The observed frequencies are summarized in the six cells of the table corresponding to each combination of the likely to repurchase responses and the three populations.

Using Table 12.5, we see that 69 of the 125 Chevrolet Impala owners said they were likely to repurchase a Chevrolet Impala; 120 of the 200 Ford Fusion owners said they were likely to repurchase a Ford Fusion; and 123 of the 175 Honda Accord owners said they were likely to repurchase a Honda Accord. Also, across all three samples, 312 of the 500 owners in the study indicated that they were likely to repurchase their current automobile. The question now is how to analyze the data in Table 12.5 to determine whether the hypothesis H_0: $p_1 = p_2 = p_3$ should be rejected.

The data in Table 12.5 are the *observed frequencies* for each of the six cells that represent the six combinations of the likely to repurchase response and the owner population. If we can determine the *expected frequencies under the assumption H_0 is true*, we can use a chi-square test statistic to determine whether there is a significant difference between the observed and expected frequencies. If a significant difference exists between the observed and expected frequencies, the hypothesis H_0 can be rejected and there is evidence that not all the population proportions are equal.

Expected frequencies for the six cells of the table are based on the following rationale. First, we assume that the null hypothesis of equal population proportions is true. Then we note that the three samples include a total of 500 owners; for this group, 312 owners indicated that they were likely to repurchase their current automobile. Thus, 312/500 = 0.624 is the overall proportion of owners indicating they are likely to repurchase their current automobile. If H_0: $p_1 = p_2 = p_3$ is true, 0.624 would be the best estimate of the proportion responding likely to repurchase for each of the automobile owner populations. So if the assumption of H_0 is true, we would expect 0.624 of the 125 Chevrolet Impala owners, or 0.624(125) = 78 owners to indicate they are likely to repurchase the Impala. Using the 0.624 overall proportion, we would expect 0.624(200) = 124.8 of the 200 Ford Fusion owners and 0.624(175) = 109.2 of the Honda Accord owners to respond that they are likely to repurchase their respective model of automobile.

The approach of computing a table of expected frequencies for this test of multiple proportions is essentially the same as we used for expected frequencies in Section 12.2. The following formula can be used to provide the expected frequencies under the assumption that the null hypothesis concerning equality of the population proportions is true.

DATA*file*
autoloyalty

Table 12.5 Sample Results of Likely to Repurchase for Three Populations of Automobile Owners (Observed Frequencies)

		Automobile Owners			
		Chevrolet Impala	**Ford Fusion**	**Honda Accord**	**Total**
Likely to Repurchase	**Yes**	69	120	123	312
	No	56	80	52	188
	Total	125	200	175	500

Expected Frequencies Under the Assumption H_0 Is True

$$e_{ij} = \frac{(\text{Row } i \text{ Total})(\text{Column } j \text{ Total})}{\text{Sum of Sample Sizes}} \tag{12.4}$$

Using equation (12.4), we see that the expected frequency of Yes responses (row 1) for Honda Accord owners (column 3) would be e_{13} = (Row 1 Total)(Column 3 Total)/(Sum of Sample Sizes) = (312)(175)/500 = 109.2. Use equation (12.4) to verify the other expected frequencies are as shown in Table 12.6.

The test procedure for comparing the observed frequencies of Table 12.5 with the expected frequencies of Table 12.6 involves the computation of the following chi-square statistic:

Chi-Square Test Statistic

$$\chi^2 = \sum_i \sum_j \frac{(f_{ij} - e_{ij})^2}{e_{ij}} \tag{12.5}$$

where

f_{ij} = observed frequency for the cell in row i and column j
e_{ij} = expected frequency for the cell in row i and column j under the assumption H_0 is true

Note: In a chi-square test involving the equality of k population proportions, the above test statistic has a chi-square distribution with $k - 1$ degrees of freedom provided the expected frequency is 5 *or more* for each cell.

Reviewing the expected frequencies in Table 12.6, we see that the expected frequency is at least five for each cell in the table. We therefore proceed with the computation of the chi-square test statistic. The calculations necessary to compute the value of the test statistic are shown in Table 12.7. In this case, we see that the value of the test statistic is $\chi^2 = 7.89$.

The chi-square test presented in this section is always a one-tailed test with the rejection of H_0 occurring in the upper tail of the chi-square distribution.

We can use the upper tail area of the appropriate chi-square distribution and the p-value approach to determine whether the null hypothesis can be rejected. In the automobile brand loyalty study, the three owner populations indicate that the appropriate chi-square distribution has $k - 1 = 3 - 1 = 2$ degrees of freedom. Using row two of the chi-square distribution table, we have the following:

Area in Upper Tail	**0.10**	**0.05**	**0.025**	**0.01**	**0.005**
χ^2 Value (2 *df*)	4.605	5.991	7.378	9.210	10.597

$\chi^2 = 7.89$ (falls between 7.378 and 9.210)

Table 12.6 Expected Frequencies for Likely to Repurchase for Three Populations of Automobile Owners If H_0 Is True

		Automobile Owners			
		Chevrolet Impala	**Ford Fusion**	**Honda Accord**	**Total**
Likely to Repurchase	**Yes**	78	124.8	109.2	312
	No	47	75.2	65.8	188
	Total	125	200.0	175.0	500

Table 12.7 Computation of the Chi-Square Test Statistic for the Test of Equal Population Proportions

Likely to Repurchase?	Automobile Owner	Observed Frequency (f_{ij})	Expected Frequency (e_{ij})	Difference ($f_{ij} - e_{ij}$)	Squared Difference $(f_{ij} - e_{ij})^2$	Squared Difference Divided by Expected Frequency $(f_{ij} - e_{ij})^2/e_{ij}$
Yes	Impala	69	78.0	−9.0	81.00	1.04
Yes	Fusion	120	124.8	−4.8	23.04	0.18
Yes	Accord	123	109.2	13.8	190.44	1.74
No	Impala	56	47.0	9.0	81.00	1.72
No	Fusion	80	75.2	4.8	23.04	0.31
No	Accord	52	65.8	−13.8	190.44	2.89
	Total	500	500.0			$\chi^2 = 7.89$

We see the upper tail area at $\chi^2 = 7.89$ is between 0.025 and 0.01. Thus, the corresponding upper tail area or p-value must be between 0.025 and 0.01. With p-value ≤ 0.05, we reject H_0 and conclude that the three population proportions are not all equal and thus there is a difference in brand loyalties among the Chevrolet Impala, Ford Fusion, and Honda Accord owners. In the Using Excel subsection that follows, we will see that the p-value $= 0.0193$.

Instead of using the p-value, we could use the critical value approach to draw the same conclusion. With $\alpha = 0.05$ and 2 degrees of freedom, the critical value for the chi-square test statistic is $\chi^2 = 5.991$. The upper tail rejection region becomes

$$\text{Reject } H_0 \text{ if } \chi^2 \geq 5.991$$

With $7.89 \geq 5.991$, we reject H_0. Thus, the p-value approach and the critical value approach provide the same hypothesis-testing conclusion.

Let us now summarize the general steps that can be used to conduct a chi-square test for the equality of the population proportions for three or more populations.

A Chi-Square Test for the Equality of Population Proportions for $K \geq 3$ Populations

1. State the null and alternative hypotheses:

$$H_0\colon p_1 = p_2 = \cdots = p_k$$
$$H_a\colon \text{Not all population proportions are equal}$$

2. Select a random sample from each of the populations and record the observed frequencies, f_{ij}, in a table with 2 rows and k columns.
3. Assume the null hypothesis is true and compute the expected frequencies, e_{ij}.
4. If the expected frequency, e_{ij}, is 5 or more for each cell, compute the test statistic:

$$\chi^2 = \sum_i \sum_j \frac{(f_{ij} - e_{ij})^2}{e_{ij}}$$

5. Rejection rule:

p-value approach: Reject H_0 if p-value $\leq \alpha$
Critical value approach: Reject H_0 if $\chi^2 \geq \chi^2_\alpha$

where the chi-square distribution has $k - 1$ degrees of freedom and α is the level of significance for the test.

Figure 12.5 Excel Worksheet for the Automobile Loyalty Study

	A	B	C	D	E	F	G	H	I
1	Owner	Automobile	Likely Repurchase						
2	1	Chevrolet Impala	Yes						
3	2	Chevrolet Impala	Yes		Count of Owner	Automobile			
4	3	Chevrolet Impala	No		Likely Repurchase	Chevrolet Impala	Ford Fusion	Honda Accord	Grand Total
5	4	Chevrolet Impala	Yes		No	56	80	52	188
6	5	Chevrolet Impala	Yes		Yes	69	120	123	312
7	6	Chevrolet Impala	Yes		Grand Total	125	200	175	500
8	7	Chevrolet Impala	Yes						
9	8	Chevrolet Impala	Yes						
10	9	Chevrolet Impala	No				Automobile		
11	10	Chevrolet Impala	Yes		Likely Repurchase	Chevrolet Impala	Ford Fusion	Honda Accord	Grand Total
12	11	Chevrolet Impala	Yes		No	=($I5*F$7)/$I$7	=($I5*G$7)/$I$7	=($I5*H$7)/$I$7	=($I5*I$7)/$I$7
13	12	Chevrolet Impala	No		Yes	=($I6*F$7)/$I$7	=($I6*G$7)/$I$7	=($I6*H$7)/$I$7	=($I6*I$7)/$I$7
14	13	Chevrolet Impala	Yes						
15	14	Chevrolet Impala	No		*p*-value	=CHISQ.TEST(F5:H6,F12:H13)			
16	15	Chevrolet Impala	No						
500	499	Honda Accord	No						
501	500	Honda Accord	No						
502									

	A	B	C	D	E	F	G	H	I
1	Owner	Automobile	Likely Repurchase						
2	1	Chevrolet Impala	Yes						
3	2	Chevrolet Impala	Yes		Count of Owner	Automobile			
4	3	Chevrolet Impala	No		Likely Repurchase	Chevrolet Impala	Ford Fusion	Honda Accord	Grand Total
5	4	Chevrolet Impala	Yes		No	56	80	52	188
6	5	Chevrolet Impala	Yes		Yes	69	120	123	312
7	6	Chevrolet Impala	Yes		Grand Total	125	200	175	500
8	7	Chevrolet Impala	Yes						
9	8	Chevrolet Impala	Yes						
10	9	Chevrolet Impala	No				Automobile		
11	10	Chevrolet Impala	Yes		Likely Repurchase	Chevrolet Impala	Ford Fusion	Honda Accord	Grand Total
12	11	Chevrolet Impala	Yes		No	47.0	75.2	65.8	188.0
13	12	Chevrolet Impala	No		Yes	78.0	124.8	109.2	312.0
14	13	Chevrolet Impala	Yes						
15	14	Chevrolet Impala	No		*p*-value	0.0193			
16	15	Chevrolet Impala	No						
500	499	Honda Accord	No						
501	500	Honda Accord	No						
502									

Note: Rows 17–499 are hidden.

Using Excel to Conduct a Test of Multiple Proportions

The Excel procedure used to test for the equality of three or more population proportions is essentially the same as the Excel procedure used to conduct a test of independence. The CHISQ.TEST function is used with the table of observed frequencies as one input and the table of expected frequencies as the other input. The function output is the p-value for the test. We illustrate using the automobile brand loyalty study. Refer to Figure 12.5 as we describe the tasks involved. The formula worksheet is in the background; the value worksheet is in the foreground.

DATA*file*
autoloyalty

Enter/Access Data: Open the file *autoloyalty*. The data are in cells B2:C501 and labels are in column A and cells B1:C1.

Apply Tools: The observed frequencies have been computed in cells F5:H6 using Excel's PivotTable tool (see Section 2.4 for details regarding how to use this tool).

Enter Functions and Formulas: The Excel formulas in cells F12:H13 were used to compute the expected frequencies for each category. Once the observed and expected frequencies have been computed, Excel's CHISQ.TEST function has been used in cell F15 to compute the p-value for the test. The value worksheet shows that the resulting p-value is 0.0193. With $\alpha = 0.05$, we reject the null hypothesis that the three population proportions are equal.

A Multiple Comparison Procedure

We have used a chi-square test to conclude that the population proportions for the three populations of automobile owners are not all equal. Thus, some differences among the population proportions exist and the study indicates that customer loyalties are not all the same for the Chevrolet Impala, Ford Fusion, and Honda Accord owners. To identify where the differences between population proportions exist, we can begin by computing the three sample proportions as follows:

Brand Loyalty Sample Proportions

Chevrolet Impala	$\bar{p}_1 = 69/125 = 0.5520$
Ford Fusion	$\bar{p}_2 = 120/200 = 0.6000$
Honda Accord	$\bar{p}_3 = 123/175 = 0.7029$

Since the chi-square test indicated that not all population proportions are equal, it is reasonable for us to proceed by attempting to determine where differences among the population proportions exist. For this we will rely on a multiple comparison procedure that can be used to conduct statistical tests between all pairs of population proportions. In the following, we discuss a multiple comparison procedure known as the **Marascuilo procedure**. This is a relatively straightforward procedure for making pairwise comparisons of all pairs of population proportions. We will demonstrate the computations required by this multiple comparison test procedure for the automobile customer loyalty study.

We begin by computing the absolute value of the pairwise difference between sample proportions for each pair of populations in the study. In the three-population automobile brand loyalty study, we compare populations 1 and 2, populations 1 and 3, and then populations 2 and 3 using the sample proportions as follows:

Chevrolet Impala and Ford Fusion

$$|\bar{p}_1 - \bar{p}_2| = |0.5520 - 0.6000| = 0.0480$$

Chevrolet Impala and Honda Accord

$$|\bar{p}_1 - \bar{p}_3| = |0.5520 - 0.7029| = 0.1509$$

Ford Fusion and Honda Accord

$$|\bar{p}_2 - \bar{p}_3| = |0.6000 - 0.7029| = 0.1029$$

In a second step, we select a level of significance and compute the corresponding critical value for each pairwise comparison using the following expression.

Critical Values for the Marascuilo Pairwise Comparison Procedure for *k* Population Proportions

For each pairwise comparison compute a critical value as follows:

$$CV_{ij} = \sqrt{\chi^2_\alpha}\sqrt{\frac{\bar{p}_i(1-\bar{p}_i)}{n_i} + \frac{\bar{p}_j(1-\bar{p}_j)}{n_j}} \qquad \textbf{(12.6)}$$

where

χ^2_α = chi-square with a level of significance α and $k - 1$ degrees of freedom

$\bar{p}_i$ and $\bar{p}_j$ = sample proportions for populations i and j

n_i and n_j = sample sizes for populations i and j

Using the chi-square distribution in Table 3 of Appendix B with $k - 1 = 3 - 1 = 2$ degrees of freedom, and a 0.05 level of significance, we have $\chi^2_{0.05} = 5.991$. Now using the sample proportions $\bar{p}_1 = 0.5520$, $\bar{p}_2 = 0.6000$, and $\bar{p}_3 = 0.7029$, the critical values for the three pairwise comparison tests are as follows:

Chevrolet Impala and Ford Fusion

$$CV_{12} = \sqrt{5.991}\sqrt{\frac{0.5520(1-0.5520)}{125} + \frac{0.6000(1-0.6000)}{200}} = 0.1380$$

Chevrolet Impala and Honda Accord

$$CV_{13} = \sqrt{5.991}\sqrt{\frac{0.5520(1-0.5520)}{125} + \frac{0.7029(1-0.7029)}{175}} = 0.1379$$

Table 12.8 Pairwise Comparison Tests for the Automobile Brand Loyalty Study

Pairwise Comparison	$\lvert \bar{p}_i - \bar{p}_j \rvert$	CV_{ij}	Significant If $\lvert \bar{p}_i - \bar{p}_j \rvert > CV_{ij}$
Chevrolet Impala vs. Ford Fusion	0.0480	0.1380	Not significant
Chevrolet Impala vs. Honda Accord	0.1509	0.1379	Significant
Ford Fusion vs. Honda Accord	0.1029	0.1198	Not significant

Ford Fusion and Honda Accord

$$CV_{23} = \sqrt{5.991}\sqrt{\frac{0.6000(1 - 0.6000)}{200} + \frac{0.7029(1 - 0.7029)}{175}} = 0.1198$$

If the absolute value of any pairwise sample proportion difference $\lvert \bar{p}_i - \bar{p}_j \rvert$ exceeds its corresponding critical value, CV_{ij}, the pairwise difference is significant at the 0.05 level of significance and we can conclude that the two corresponding population proportions are different. The final step of the pairwise comparison procedure is summarized in Table 12.8.

The file pairwisecomparisons *eases the computational burden of making multiple pairwise comparisons of the differences in proportions.*

DATA*file*
pairwisecomparisons

The conclusion from the pairwise comparison procedure is that the only significant difference in customer loyalty occurs between the Chevrolet Impala and the Honda Accord. Our sample results indicate that the Honda Accord had a greater population proportion of owners who say they are likely to repurchase the Honda Accord. Thus, we can conclude that the Honda Accord ($\bar{p}_3 = 0.7029$) has a greater customer loyalty than the Chevrolet Impala ($\bar{p}_1 = 0.5520$).

The results of the study are inconclusive as to the comparative loyalty of the Ford Fusion. While the Ford Fusion did not show significantly different results when compared to the Chevrolet Impala or Honda Accord, a larger sample may have revealed a significant difference between Ford Fusion and the other two automobiles in terms of customer loyalty. It is not uncommon for a multiple comparison procedure to show significance for some pairwise comparisons and yet not show significance for other pairwise comparisons in the study.

Notes + Comments

1. In Chapter 10, we used the standard normal distribution and the z test statistic to conduct hypothesis tests about the proportions of two populations. However, the chi-square test introduced in this section can also be used to conduct the hypothesis test that the proportions of two populations are equal. The results will be the same under both test procedures and the value of the test statistic χ^2 will be equal to the square of the value of the test statistic z. An advantage of the methodology in Chapter 10 is that it can be used for either a one-tailed or a two-tailed hypothesis about the proportions of two populations, whereas the chi-square test in this section can be used only for two-tailed tests.
2. Each of the k populations in this section had two response outcomes, Yes or No. In effect, each population had a binomial distribution with parameter p the population proportion of Yes responses. An extension of the chi-square procedure in this section applies when each of the k populations has three or more possible responses. In this case, each population is said to have a multinomial distribution. The chi-square calculations for the expected frequencies, e_{ij}, and the test statistic, χ^2, are the same as shown in expressions (12.4) and (12.5). The only difference is that the null hypothesis assumes that the multinomial distribution for the response variable is the same for all populations. With r responses for each of the k populations, the chi-square test statistic has $(r - 1)(k - 1)$ degrees of freedom.
3. The procedure for computing expected frequencies for the test of multiple proportions and for the test of independence in Section 12.2 are the same and both tests employ the same chi-square test statistic. But a key difference is that the test of independence is based on one sample from a single population. The test of multiple proportions is based on k independent samples from k populations. Thus, with the test of multiple proportions, we can control the sample size for each of the k population categories. With the test of independence, we control only the overall sample size.

Exercises

Methods

17. Use the sample data below to test the hypotheses

$$H_0: p_1 = p_2 = p_3$$
$$H_a: \text{Not all population proportions are equal}$$

where p_i is the population proportion of Yes responses for population i. Using a 0.05 level of significance, what is the p-value and what is your conclusion? **LO 3**

	Populations		
Response	**1**	**2**	**3**
Yes	150	150	96
No	100	150	104

18. Reconsider the observed frequencies in exercise 17. **LO 4**
    a. Compute the sample proportion for each population.
    b. Use the multiple comparison procedure to determine which population proportions differ significantly. Use a 0.05 level of significance.

Applications

19. **Late Flight Comparison Across Airlines.** The following sample data represent the number of late and on-time flights for Delta, United, and US Airways. **LO 3**

	Airline		
Flight	**Delta**	**United**	**US Airways**
Late	39	51	56
On Time	261	249	344

    a. Formulate the hypotheses for a test that will determine whether the population proportion of late flights is the same for all three airlines.
    b. Conduct the hypothesis test with a 0.05 level of significance. What is the p-value and what is your conclusion?
    c. Compute the sample proportion of late flights for each airline. What is the overall proportion of late flights for the three airlines?

20. **Electronic Component Supplier Quality Comparison.** Benson Manufacturing is considering ordering electronic components from three different suppliers. The suppliers may differ in terms of quality in that the proportion or percentage of defective components may differ among the suppliers. To evaluate the proportion of defective components for the suppliers, Benson has requested a sample shipment of 500 components from each supplier. The number of defective components and the number of good components found in each shipment are as follows. **LO 3, 4**

	Supplier		
Component	**A**	**B**	**C**
Defective	15	20	40
Good	485	480	460

a. Formulate the hypotheses that can be used to test for equal proportions of defective components provided by the three suppliers.
b. Using a 0.05 level of significance, conduct the hypothesis test. What is the p-value and what is your conclusion?
c. Conduct a multiple comparison test to determine whether there is an overall best supplier or if one supplier can be eliminated because of poor quality.

21. **Agricultural Contaminant Effect on Fish.** Kate Sanders, a researcher in the department of biology at IPFW University, studied the effect of agriculture contaminants on the stream fish population in northeastern Indiana. Specially designed traps collected samples of fish at each of four stream locations. A research question was, Did the differences in agricultural contaminants found at the four locations alter the proportion of the fish population by sex? Observed frequencies were as follows. **LO 3**

	Stream Locations			
Sex	A	B	C	D
Male	49	44	49	39
Female	41	46	36	44

a. Focusing on the proportion of male fish at each location, test the hypothesis that the population proportions are equal for all four locations. Use a 0.05 level of significance. What is the p-value and what is your conclusion?
b. Does it appear that differences in agricultural contaminants found at the four locations altered the fish population by sex?

Exercise 22 shows a chi-square test can be used when the hypothesis is about the equality of two population proportions.

22. **Error Rates in Tax Preparation.** A tax preparation firm is interested in comparing the quality of work at two of its regional offices. The observed frequencies showing the number of sampled returns with errors and the number of sampled returns that were correct are as follows. **LO 3**

	Regional Office	
Return	Office 1	Office 2
Error	35	27
Correct	215	273

a. What are the sample proportions of returns with errors at the two offices?
b. Use the chi-square test procedure to see if there is a significant difference between the population proportion of error rates for the two offices. Test the null hypothesis H_0: $p_1 = p_2$ with a 0.10 level of significance. What is the p-value and what is your conclusion? (*Note*: We generally use the chi-square test of equal proportions when there are three or more populations, but this example shows that the same chi-square test can be used for testing equal proportions with two populations.)
c. In Section 10.2, a z test was used to conduct the above test. Either a χ^2 test statistic or a z test statistic may be used to test the hypothesis. However, when we want to make inferences about the proportions for two populations, we generally prefer the z test statistic procedure. Refer to the Notes and Comments at the end of this section and comment on why the z test statistic provides the user with more options for inferences about the proportions of two populations.

DATA*file*
socialmedia

23. **Use of Social Media.** Social media is popular around the world. *Statista* provides estimate of the number of social media users in various countries in 2017 as well as the projections for 2022. Assume that the results for surveys in the United Kingdom, China, Russia, and the United States are as follows. **LO 3, 4**

Use Social Media	Country			
	United Kingdom	China	Russia	United States
Yes	480	215	343	640
No	320	285	357	360

a. Conduct a hypothesis test to determine whether the proportion of adults using social media is equal for all four countries. What is the p-value? Using a 0.05 level of significance, what is your conclusion?
b. What are the sample proportions for each of the four countries? Which country has the largest proportion of adults using social media?
c. Using a 0.05 level of significance, conduct multiple pairwise comparison tests among the four countries. What is your conclusion?

Exercise 24 shows a chi-square test can also be used for multiple population tests when the categorical response variable has three or more outcomes.

24. **Supplier Quality: Three Inspection Outcomes.** The Ertl Company is well-known for its high-quality die-cast metal alloy toy replicas of tractors and other farm equipment. As part of a periodic procurement evaluation, Ertl is considering purchasing parts for a toy tractor line from three different suppliers. The parts received from the suppliers are classified as having a minor defect, having a major defect, or being good. Test results from samples of parts received from each of the three suppliers are shown below. Note that any test with these data is no longer a test of proportions for the three supplier populations because the categorical response variable has three outcomes: minor defect, major defect, and good.

Part Tested	Supplier		
	A	B	C
Minor Defect	15	13	21
Major Defect	5	11	5
Good	130	126	124

Using the preceding data, conduct a hypothesis test to determine whether the distribution of defects is the same for the three suppliers. Use the chi-square test calculations as presented in this section with the exception that a table with r rows and c columns results in a chi-square test statistic with $(r - 1)(c - 1)$ degrees of freedom. Using a 0.05 level of significance, what is the p-value and what is your conclusion? **LO 3**

Summary

In this chapter, we have introduced hypothesis tests for the following applications.

1. Goodness-of-Fit Test. A test designed to determine whether the observed frequency distribution for a sample differs significantly from what we would expect given the hypothesized probabilities for each category.
2. Test of Independence. A test designed to determine whether the table of observed frequencies for a sample involving two categorical variables from the same population differs significantly from what we would expect if the two variables were independent as specified in the null hypothesis.

3. Test of Equality for Three or More Population Proportions. A test designed to determine whether three or more sample proportions differ significantly from what we would expect if the corresponding population proportions were equal as stated in the null hypothesis.

The first two tests are based on a single sample from a single population. The third test is based on independent samples from three or more different populations. All tests use a chi-square (χ^2) test statistic that is based on the differences between observed frequencies from a sample and the frequencies that we would expect if the null hypothesis was true. Large differences between observed and expected frequencies provide a large value for the chi-square test statistic and indicate that the null hypothesis should be rejected; thus, these chi-square tests are upper tailed tests.

Glossary

Goodness-of-fit test A chi-square test that can be used to test that a probability distribution has a specific historical or theoretical probability distribution. This test was demonstrated for a multinomial probability distribution.
Marascuilo procedure A multiple comparison procedure that can be used to test for a significant difference between pairs of population proportions. This test can be helpful in identifying differences between pairs of population proportions whenever the hypothesis of equal population proportions has been rejected.
Multinomial probability distribution A probability distribution where each outcome belongs to one of three or more categories. The multinomial probability distribution extends the binomial probability distribution from two to three or more outcomes per trial.
Test of independence A chi-square test that can be used to test for the independence of two random variables. If the hypothesis of independence is rejected, it can be concluded that the random variables are associated or dependent.

Key Formulas

Test Statistic for the Goodness-of-Fit Test

$$\chi^2 = \sum_{i=1}^{k} \frac{(f_i - e_i)^2}{e_i} \tag{12.1}$$

Expected Frequencies: Test of Independence

$$e_{ij} = \frac{(\text{Row } i \text{ Total})(\text{Column } j \text{ Total})}{\text{Sample Size}} \tag{12.2}$$

Chi-Square Test Statistic for Test of Independence and Test for Equality of Three or More Population Proportions

$$\chi^2 = \sum_i \sum_j \frac{(f_{ij} - e_{ij})^2}{e_{ij}} \tag{12.3 and 12.5}$$

Expected Frequencies: Test for Equality of Three or More Population Proportions

$$e_{ij} = \frac{(\text{Row } i \text{ Total})(\text{Column } j \text{ Total})}{\text{Sum of Sample Sizes}} \tag{12.4}$$

Critical Values for the Marascuilo Pairwise Comparison Procedure

$$CV_{ij} = \sqrt{\chi^2_\alpha}\sqrt{\frac{\bar{p}_i(1-\bar{p}_i)}{n_i} + \frac{\bar{p}_j(1-\bar{p}_j)}{n_j}} \tag{12.6}$$

Supplementary Exercises

DATA*file*
bbb

25. **Better Business Bureau.** Historically, the industries with the most complaints to the Better Business Bureau have been banks, cable and satellite television companies, collection agencies, cellular phone providers, and new car dealerships. The results for a sample of 200 complaints are contained in the file *bbb*. **LO 3**
    a. Construct a frequency distribution for the number of complaints by industry.
    b. Using $\alpha = 0.01$, conduct a hypothesis test to determine whether the probability of a complaint is the same for the five industries. What is your conclusion?
    c. Drop the industry with the most complaints. Using $\alpha = 0.05$, conduct a hypothesis test to determine whether the probability of a complaint is the same for the remaining four industries.

26. **Restaurant Entree Preferences.** Bistro 65 is a chain of Italian restaurants with locations in Ohio and Kentucky. The Bistro 65 menu has four categories of entrées: Pasta, Steak & Chops, Seafood, and Other (e.g., pizza, sandwiches). Historical data for the chain show that the probability a customer will order an entrée from one of the four categories is 0.4 for Pasta, 0.1 for Steak & Chops, 0.2 for Seafood, and 0.3 for Other. A new Bistro 65 restaurant has just opened in Dayton, Ohio, and the following purchase frequencies have been observed for the first 200 customers. **LO 1**

Category	Frequency
Pasta	70
Steak & Chops	30
Seafood	50
Other	50
Total	200

    a. Conduct a hypothesis test to determine whether the order pattern for the new restaurant in Dayton is the same as the historical pattern for the established Bistro 65 restaurants. Use $\alpha = 0.05$.
    b. If the difference in part (a) is significant, prepare a bar chart to show where the differences occur. Comment on any differences observed.

27. **Best-Selling Small Cars in America.** Based on 2017 sales, the six top-selling compact cars are the Honda Civic, Toyota Corolla, Nissan Sentra, Hyundai Elantra, Chevrolet Cruze, and Ford Focus (*New York Daily News*). The 2017 market shares are Honda Civic 20%, Toyota Corolla 17%, Nissan Sentra 12%, Hyundai Elantra 10%, Chevrolet Cruze 10%, and Ford Focus 8%, with other small car models comprising the remaining 23%. A sample of 400 compact car sales in Chicago showed the following number of vehicles sold.

Honda Civic	98
Toyota Corolla	72
Nissan Sentra	54
Hyundai Elantra	44
Chevrolet Cruze	42
Ford Focus	25
Others	65

Use a goodness-of-fit test to determine whether the sample data indicate that the market shares for cars in Chicago are different than the market shares suggested by nationwide 2017 sales. Using a 0.05 level of significance, what is the *p*-value and what is your conclusion? If the Chicago market appears to differ significantly from nationwide sales, which categories contribute most to this difference? **LO 1**

28. **Pace of Life Preference by Sex.** A Pew Research Center survey asked respondents if they would rather live in a place with a slower pace of life or a place with a faster pace of life. The survey also asked the respondent's sex. Consider the following sample data. LO 2

	Sex	
Preferred Pace of Life	**Male**	**Female**
Slower	230	218
No Preference	20	24
Faster	90	48

a. Is the preferred pace of life independent of sex? Using a 0.05 level of significance, what is the p-value and what is your conclusion?

b. Discuss any differences between the preferences of men and women.

DATA*file*
ambulance

29. **Church Attendance by Age Group.** Bara Research Group conducted a survey about church attendance. The survey respondents were asked about their church attendance and asked to indicate their age. Use the sample data to determine whether church attendance is independent of age. Using a 0.05 level of significance, what is the p-value and what is your conclusion? What conclusion can you draw about church attendance as individuals grow older? LO 2

	Age			
Church Attendance	**20 to 29**	**30 to 39**	**40 to 49**	**50 to 59**
Yes	31	63	94	72
No	69	87	106	78

30. **Ambulance Calls by Day of Week.** An ambulance service responds to emergency calls for two counties in Virginia. One county is an urban county and the other is a rural county. A sample of 471 ambulance calls over the past two years showed the county and the day of the week for each emergency call. Data are as follows.

	Day of Week						
County	**Sun**	**Mon**	**Tue**	**Wed**	**Thu**	**Fri**	**Sat**
Urban	61	48	50	55	63	73	43
Rural	7	9	16	13	9	14	10

Test for independence of the county and the day of the week. Using a 0.05 level of significance, what is the p-value and what is your conclusion? LO 2

31. **Where Millionaires Live in America.** In a 2018 study, Phoenix Marketing International identified Bridgeport, Connecticut; San Jose, California; Washington, DC; and Lexington Park, Maryland, as the four U.S. cities with the highest percentage of millionaires (Kiplinger website). Consider a sample of data that show the following number of millionaires for samples of individuals from each of the four cities. LO 3

	City			
Millionaire	Bridgeport, CT	San Jose, CA	Washington, DC	Lexington Park, MD
Yes	44	35	35	34
No	356	350	364	366

a. What is the estimate of the percentage of millionaires in each of these cities?
b. Using a 0.05 level of significance, test for the equality of the population proportion of millionaires for these four cities. What is the p-value and what is your conclusion?

32. **Quality Comparison Across Production Shifts.** Arconic Inc is a producer of aluminum components for the avionics and automotive industries. At its Davenport Works plant, an engineer has conducted a quality control test in which aluminum coils produced in each of the three shifts were inspected. The study was designed to determine whether the population proportion of good parts was the same for all three shifts. Sample data follow. **LO 3, 4**

	Production Shift		
Quality	First	Second	Third
Good	285	368	176
Defective	15	32	24

a. Using a 0.05 level of significance, conduct a hypothesis test to determine whether the population proportion of good parts is the same for all three shifts. What is the p-value and what is your conclusion?
b. If the conclusion is that the population proportions are not all equal, use a multiple comparison procedure to determine how the shifts differ in terms of quality. What shift or shifts need to improve the quality of parts produced?

33. **Ratings of Most Visited Art Museums.** As listed by *The Art Newspaper* Visitor Figures Survey, the five most visited art museums in the world are the Louvre Museum, the National Museum in China, the Metropolitan Museum of Art, the Vatican Museums, and the British Museum. Which of these five museums would visitors most frequently rate as spectacular? Samples of recent visitors of each of these museums were taken, and the results of these samples follow. **LO 3**

	Louvre Museum	National Museum in China	Metropolitan Museum of Art	Vatican Museums	British Museum
Spectacular	113	88	94	98	96
Not Spectacular	37	44	46	72	64

a. Use the sample data to calculate the point estimate of the population proportion of visitors who rated each of these museums as spectacular.

b. Conduct a hypothesis test to determine if the population proportion of visitors who rated the museum as spectacular is equal for these five museums. Using a 0.05 level of significance, what is the p-value and what is your conclusion?

Case Problem 1: A Bipartisan Agenda for Change

In a study conducted by Zogby International for the *Democrat and Chronicle,* more than 700 New Yorkers were polled to determine whether the New York State government works. Respondents surveyed were asked questions involving pay cuts for state legislators, restrictions on lobbyists, term limits for legislators, and whether state citizens should be able to put matters directly on the state ballot for a vote. The results regarding several proposed reforms had broad support, crossing all demographic and political lines.

Suppose that a follow-up survey of 100 individuals who live in the western region of New York was conducted. The party affiliation (Democrat, Independent, Republican) of each individual surveyed was recorded, as well as their responses to the following three questions.

1. Should legislative pay be cut for every day the state budget is late?
   Yes ____ No ____
2. Should there be more restrictions on lobbyists?
   Yes ____ No ____
3. Should there be term limits requiring that legislators serve a fixed number of years?
   Yes ____ No ____

DATA*file*
nyreform

The responses were coded using 1 for a Yes response and 2 for a No response. The complete data set is available in the file *nyreform.* **LO 2**

Managerial Report

1. Use descriptive statistics to summarize the data from this study. What are your preliminary conclusions about the independence of the response (Yes or No) and party affiliation for each of the three questions in the survey?
2. With regard to question 1, test for the independence of the response (Yes and No) and party affiliation. Use $\alpha = 0.05$.
3. With regard to question 2, test for the independence of the response (Yes and No) and party affiliation. Use $\alpha = 0.05$.
4. With regard to question 3, test for the independence of the response (Yes and No) and party affiliation. Use $\alpha = 0.05$.
5. Does it appear that there is broad support for change across all political lines? Explain.

Case Problem 2: Fuentes Salty Snacks, Inc.

Six months ago Fuentes Salty Snacks, Inc. added a new flavor to its line of potato chips. The new flavor, candied bacon, was introduced through a nationwide rollout supported by an extensive promotional campaign. Fuentes' management is convinced that quick penetration into grocery stores is a key to the successful introduction of a new salty snack product, and management now wants to determine whether availability of Fuentes' Candied Bacon Potato Chips is consistent in grocery stores across regions of the United States. Fuentes Marketing department has selected random samples of 40 grocery stores in each of its eight U.S. sales regions:

- New England (Connecticut, Maine, Massachusetts, New Hampshire, Rhode Island, and Vermont)
- Mid-Atlantic (New Jersey, New York, and Pennsylvania)
- Midwest (Illinois, Indiana, Michigan, Ohio, and Wisconsin)
- Great Plains (Iowa, Kansas, Minnesota, Missouri, Nebraska, North Dakota, Oklahoma, and South Dakota)

- South Atlantic (Delaware, Florida, Georgia, Maryland, North Carolina, South Carolina, Virginia, Washington, DC, and West Virginia)
- Deep South (Alabama, Arkansas, Kentucky, Louisiana, Mississippi, Tennessee, and Texas)
- Mountain (Arizona, Colorado, Idaho, Montana, Nevada, New Mexico, Utah, and Wyoming)
- Pacific (Alaska, California, Hawaii, Oregon, and Washington)

DATA*file*
fuenteschips

The stores in each sample were then contacted, and the manager of each store was asked whether the store currently carries Fuentes' Candied Bacon Potato Chips. The complete data set is available in the file *fuenteschips*.

Fuentes' senior management now wants to use these data to assess whether penetration of Fuentes' Candied Bacon Potato Chips in grocery stores is consistent across its eight U.S. sales regions. If penetration of Fuentes' Candied Bacon Potato Chips in grocery stores differs across its eight U.S. sales regions, Fuentes' management would also like to identify sales regions in which penetration of Fuentes' Candied Bacon Potato Chips is lower or higher than expected. **LO 3, 4**

Managerial Report

Prepare a managerial report that addresses the following issues.

1. Use descriptive statistics to summarize the data from Fuentes' study. Based on your descriptive statistics, what are your preliminary conclusions about penetration of Fuentes' Candied Bacon Potato Chips in grocery stores across its eight U.S. sales regions?
2. Use the data from Fuentes' study to test the hypothesis that the proportion of grocery stores that currently carries Fuentes' Candied Bacon Potato Chips is equal across its eight U.S. sales regions. Use $\alpha = 0.05$.
3. Do the results of your hypothesis test provide evidence that penetration of Fuentes' Candied Bacon Potato Chips in grocery stores differs across its eight U.S. sales regions? In which sales region(s) is penetration of Fuentes' Candied Bacon Potato Chips lower or higher than expected? Use the Marascuilo pairwise comparison procedure at $\alpha = 0.05$ to test for differences between regions.

Case Problem 3: Fresno Board Games

Fresno Board Games manufactures and sells several different board games online and through department stores nationwide. Fresno's most popular game, *¡Cabestrillo Cinco!*, is played with 5 six-sided dice. Fresno has purchased dice for this game from Box Cars, Ltd. for 25 years, but the company is now considering a move to Big Boss Gaming, Inc. (BBG), a new supplier that has offered to sell dice to Fresno at a substantially lower price. Fresno management is intrigued by the potential savings offered by BBG, but is also concerned about the quality of the dice produced by the new supplier. Fresno has a reputation for high integrity, and its management feels that it is imperative that the dice included with *¡Cabestrillo Cinco!* are fair.

DATA*file*
bbg

To alleviate concerns about the quality of the dice it produces, BBG allows Fresno's Manager of Product Quality to randomly sample five dice from its most recent production run. While being observed by several members of the BBG management team, Fresno's Manager of Product Quality rolls each of these five randomly selected dice 500 times and records each outcome. The results for each of these five randomly selected dicc are available in the file *bbg*.

Fresno management now wants to use these data to assess whether any of these 5 six-sided dice is not fair; i.e., does one outcome occur more frequently or less frequently than the other outcomes? **LO 1**

Managerial Report

Prepare a managerial report that addresses the following issues.

1. Use descriptive statistics to summarize the data collected by Fresno's Manager of Product Quality for each of the five randomly selected dice. Based on these descriptive statistics, what are your preliminary conclusions about the fairness of the five selected dice?
2. Use the data collected by Fresno's Manager of Product Quality to test the hypothesis that the first of the five randomly selected dice is fair, i.e., the distribution of outcomes for the first of the five randomly selected dice is multinomial with $p_1 = p_2 = p_3 = p_4 = p_5 = p_6 = 1/6$. Repeat this process for each of the other four randomly selected dice. Use $\alpha = 0.01$. Do the results of your hypothesis tests provide evidence that BBG is producing unfair dice?

Chapter 13

Experimental Design and Analysis of Variance

Contents

Statistics in Practice:
Burke, Inc.

13.1 An Introduction To Experimental Design And Analysis Of Variance
Data Collection
Assumptions for Analysis of Variance
Analysis of Variance: A Conceptual Overview

13.2 Analysis of Variance and the Completely Randomized Design
Between-Treatments Estimate of Population Variance
Within-Treatments Estimate of Population Variance
Comparing the Variance Estimates: The *F* Test
ANOVA Table
Using Excel
Testing for the Equality of *k* Population Means: An Observational Study

13.3 Multiple Comparison Procedures
Fisher's LSD
Type I Error Rates

13.4 Randomized Block Design
Air Traffic Controller Stress Test
ANOVA Procedure
Computations and Conclusions
Using Excel

13.5 Factorial Experiment
ANOVA Procedure
Computations and Conclusions
Using Excel

Summary 613
Glossary 614
Key Formulas 615
Supplementary Exercises 616
Case Problem 1: Wentworth Medical Center 621
Case Problem 2: Compensation For Sales Professionals 621
Case Problem 3: Touristopia Travel 622

Available in the Cengage eBook:
Appendix: Analysis Of Variance With R

Learning Objectives

After completing this chapter, you will be able to

LO 1 Compute the various components of an analysis of variance (ANOVA) table needed for testing of population means from a completely randomized design.

LO 2 Identify appropriate hypotheses to be tested with ANOVA.

LO 3 Test if the means of multiple populations are equal using ANOVA in a completely randomized design.

LO 4 Employ Fisher's least significant difference (LSD) procedure to conduct statistical comparisons between pairs of population means.

LO 5 Use Fisher's LSD procedure to estimate a confidence interval of the difference between means.

LO 6 Compute the various components of an ANOVA table needed for testing of population means from a randomized block design.

LO 7 Test if the means of multiple populations are equal using ANOVA in a randomized block design.

LO 8 Compute the various components of an ANOVA table needed for testing of population means from a factorial experiment.

LO 9 Test if the means of multiple populations are equal using ANOVA in a factorial experiment.

Statistics in Practice

Burke, Inc.*

Cincinnati, Ohio

Burke, Inc. is one of the most experienced market research firms in the industry. Burke writes more proposals, on more projects, every day than any other market research company in the world. Supported by state-of-the-art technology, Burke offers a wide variety of research capabilities, providing answers to nearly any marketing question.

In one study, a firm retained Burke to evaluate potential new versions of a children's dry cereal. To maintain confidentiality, we refer to the cereal manufacturer as the Anon Company. The four key factors that Anon's product developers thought would enhance the taste of the cereal were the following:

1. Ratio of wheat to corn in the cereal flake
2. Type of sweetener: sugar, honey, or artificial
3. Presence or absence of flavor bits with a fruit taste
4. Short or long cooking time

Burke designed an experiment to determine what effects these four factors had on cereal taste. For example, one test cereal was made with a specified ratio of wheat to corn, sugar as the sweetener, flavor bits, and a short cooking time; another test cereal was made with a different ratio of wheat to corn and the other three factors the same, and so on. Groups of children then taste-tested the cereals and stated what they thought about the taste of each.

*The authors are indebted to Dr. Ronald Tatham of Burke Inc. for providing this Statistics in Practice.

Burke uses taste tests to provide valuable statistical information on what customers want from a product.
Skydive Erick/Shutterstock.com

Analysis of variance was the statistical method used to study the data obtained from the taste tests. The results of the analysis showed the following:

- The flake composition and sweetener type were highly influential in taste evaluation.
- The flavor bits actually detracted from the taste of the cereal.
- The cooking time had no effect on the taste.

This information helped Anon identify the factors that would lead to the best-tasting cereal.

The experimental design employed by Burke and the subsequent analysis of variance were helpful in making a product design recommendation. In this chapter, we will see how such procedures are carried out.

In Chapter 1, we stated that statistical studies can be classified as either experimental or observational. In an experimental statistical study, an experiment is conducted to generate the data. An experiment begins with identifying a variable of interest. Then one or more other variables, thought to be related, are identified and controlled, and data are collected about how those variables influence the variable of interest.

In an observational study, data are usually obtained through sample surveys and not a controlled experiment. Good design principles are still employed, but the rigorous controls associated with an experimental statistical study are often not possible.

To illustrate the differences between an observational study and an experimental study, consider the product introduction options for a new high-intensity flashlight produced by the High Lumens Flashlight Company (HLFC). The new model, referred to as the HL5, is powered by a rechargeable lithium-ion battery. A large nationwide chain of sporting goods stores has agreed to help HLFC determine the best promotional strategy for the new flashlight. HLFC is considering three promotional strategies: giving each customer who purchases an HL5 a coupon for a 20% discount at checkout; giving each customer who purchases an HL5 a coupon for a free rechargeable battery; and no promotional offer. In order to assess the effect of these three strategies on sales, HLFC randomly selected 60 sporting goods stores to participate in the study. Two options for determining which promotional strategy to use in each of these stores are being considered:

- Allow each store to select any one of the three promotional strategies and then record sales for the 30-day trial period.
- Randomly assign each of the three promotional strategies to 20 of the 60 stores and then record sales for the 30-day trial period.

HLFC's first option is an **observational study**, because the 60 stores participating in the study are not each randomly assigned to one of the three promotional strategies. If HLFC employs this option, sales for the 30-day trial period may be systematically biased by factors other than the promotional strategy that is used at each store. For example, some store managers may have a bias against using the 20% discount at checkout promotion because they have not had great success with such promotions in the past. Other store managers may have a bias against offering a coupon for a free rechargeable battery because of the paperwork involved in processing such offers. HLFC will not be able to determine whether differences in sales can be explained by the effect of the type of promotion used.

HLFC's second option is an **experimental study**, because each of the 60 stores participating in the study is randomly assigned to one of the three promotional strategies. If HLFC uses this option, the likelihood of systematic biases affecting sales is greatly reduced. Therefore, if differences in sales are observed for the three strategies, HLFC will have a much stronger case for concluding that such differences can be explained by the effect of the type of promotion used.

It may be difficult and/or expensive to design and conduct an experimental study for some research questions. And, in some instances, it may be impractical or even impossible. For instance, in a study of the relationship between smoking and lung cancer, the researcher cannot randomly assign a smoking habit to each subject. The researcher is restricted to observing the outcomes for people who already smoke and the outcomes for people who do not already smoke and observing how frequently members of these two groups develop lung cancer. The design of this study prohibits the researcher from drawing a conclusion about whether smoking causes lung cancer; the researcher can only assess whether there is an association between smoking and lung cancer.

An association between two variables is necessary but not sufficient for establishing a causal relationship between the two variables.

In this chapter, we introduce three types of experimental designs: a completely randomized design, a randomized block design, and a factorial experiment. For each design we show how a statistical procedure called analysis of variance (ANOVA) can be used to analyze the data available. ANOVA can also be used to analyze the data obtained through an observational study. For instance, we will see that the ANOVA procedure used for a completely randomized experimental design also works for testing the equality of three or more population means when data are obtained through an observational study. In the following chapters, we will see that ANOVA plays a key role in analyzing the results of regression studies involving both experimental and observational data.

Sir Ronald Aylmer Fisher (1890–1962) invented the branch of statistics known as experimental design. In addition to being accomplished in statistics, he was a noted scientist in the field of genetics.

In the first section, we introduce the basic principles of an experimental study and show how they are employed in a completely randomized design. In the second section, we then show how ANOVA can be used to analyze the data from a completely randomized experimental design. In later sections, we discuss multiple comparison procedures and two other widely used experimental designs, the randomized block design and the factorial experiment.

13.1 An Introduction to Experimental Design and Analysis of Variance

Cause-and-effect relationships can be difficult to establish in observational studies; such relationships are easier to establish in experimental studies.

As an example of an experimental statistical study, let us consider the problem facing Chemitech, Inc. Chemitech developed a new filtration system for municipal water supplies. The components for the new filtration system will be purchased from several suppliers, and Chemitech will assemble the components at its plant in Columbia, South Carolina.

The industrial engineering group is responsible for determining the best assembly method for the new filtration system. After considering a variety of possible approaches, the group narrows the alternatives to three: method A, method B, and method C. These methods differ in the sequence of steps used to assemble the system. Managers at Chemitech want to determine which assembly method can produce the greatest number of filtration systems per week.

In the Chemitech experiment, assembly method is the independent variable or **factor**. Because three assembly methods correspond to this factor, we say that three treatments are associated with this experiment; each **treatment** corresponds to one of the three assembly methods. The Chemitech problem is an example of a **single-factor experiment**; it involves one categorical factor (method of assembly). More complex experiments may consist of multiple factors; some factors may be categorical and others may be quantitative.

The three assembly methods or treatments define the three populations of interest for the Chemitech experiment. One population is all Chemitech employees who use assembly method A, another is those who use method B, and the third is those who use method C. Note that for each population the dependent or **response variable** is the number of filtration systems assembled per week, and the primary statistical objective of the experiment is to determine whether the mean number of units produced per week is the same for all three populations (methods).

Randomization is the process of assigning the treatments to the experimental units at random. Prior to the work of Sir R. A. Fisher, treatments were assigned on a systematic or subjective basis.

Suppose a random sample of three employees is selected from all assembly workers at the Chemitech production facility. In experimental design terminology, the three randomly selected workers are the **experimental units**. The experimental design that we will use for the Chemitech problem is called a **completely randomized design**. This type of design requires that each of the three assembly methods or treatments be assigned randomly to one of the experimental units or workers. For example, method A might be randomly assigned to the second worker, method B to the first worker, and method C to the third worker. The concept of *randomization,* as illustrated in this example, is an important principle of all experimental designs.

Note that this experiment would result in only one measurement or number of units assembled for each treatment. To obtain additional data for each assembly method, we must repeat or replicate the basic experimental process. For example, suppose that instead of selecting just three workers at random, we selected 15 workers and then randomly assigned each of the three treatments to five of the workers. Because each method of assembly is assigned to five workers, we say that five replicates have been obtained. The process of *replication* is another important principle of experimental design. Figure 13.1 shows the completely randomized design for the Chemitech experiment.

Data Collection

Once we are satisfied with the experimental design, we proceed by collecting and analyzing the data. In the Chemitech case, the employees would be instructed in how to perform the assembly method assigned to them, and then would begin assembling the new filtration systems using that method. After this assignment and training, the number of units assembled by each employee during one week is as shown in Table 13.1. The sample means, sample variances, and sample standard deviations for each assembly method are also provided. Thus, the sample mean number of units produced using method A is 62; the sample mean using method B is 66; and the sample mean using method C is 52. From these data, method B appears to result in higher production rates than either of the other methods.

The real issue is whether the three sample means observed are different enough for us to conclude that the means of the populations corresponding to the three methods of assembly are different. To write this question in statistical terms, we introduce the following notation.

$$\mu_1 = \text{mean number of units produced per week using method A}$$
$$\mu_2 = \text{mean number of units produced per week using method B}$$
$$\mu_3 = \text{mean number of units produced per week using method C}$$

Figure 13.1 Completely Randomized Design for Evaluating the Chemitech Assembly Method Experiment

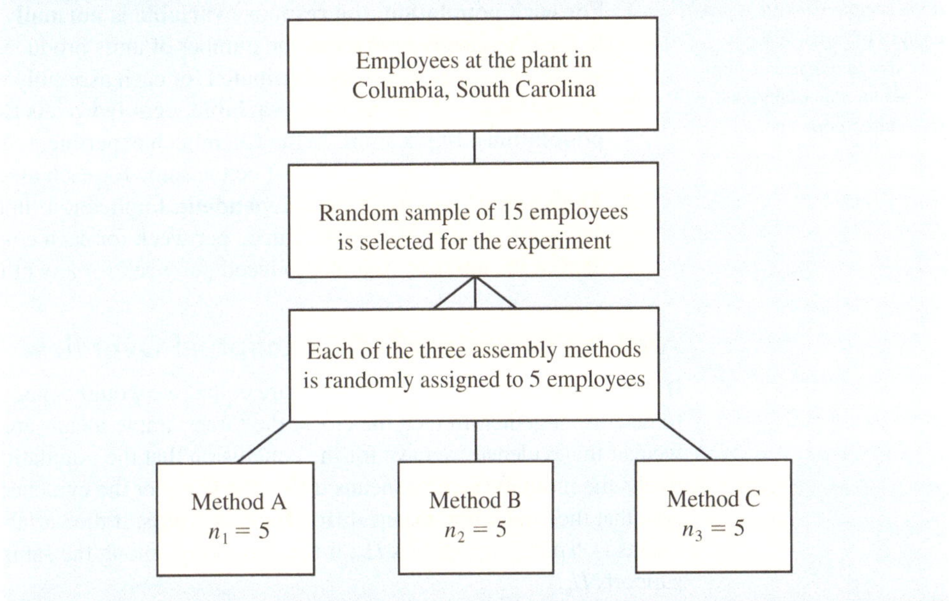

Although we will never know the actual values of μ_1, μ_2, and μ_3, we want to use the sample means to test the following hypotheses.

If H_0 is rejected, we cannot conclude that all population means are different. Rejecting H_0 means that at least two population means have different values.

$$H_0\colon \mu_1 = \mu_2 = \mu_3$$
$$H_a\colon \text{Not all population means are equal}$$

As we will demonstrate shortly, analysis of variance (ANOVA) is the statistical procedure used to determine whether the observed differences in the three sample means are large enough to reject H_0.

DATA*file*
chemitech

Table 13.1 Number of Units Produced by 15 Workers

	Method		
	A	B	C
	58	58	48
	64	69	57
	55	71	59
	66	64	47
	67	68	49
Sample mean	62	66	52
Sample variance	27.5	26.5	31.0
Sample standard deviation	5.244	5.148	5.568

Assumptions for Analysis of Variance

Three assumptions are required to use analysis of variance.

If the sample sizes are equal, analysis of variance is not sensitive to departures from the assumption of normally distributed populations.

1. **For each population, the response variable is normally distributed.** Implication: In the Chemitech experiment the number of units produced per week (response variable) must be normally distributed for each assembly method.
2. **The variance of the response variable, denoted σ^2, is the same for all of the populations.** Implication: In the Chemitech experiment, the variance of the number of units produced per week must be the same for each assembly method.
3. **The observations must be independent.** Implication: In the Chemitech experiment, the number of units produced per week for each employee must be independent of the number of units produced per week for any other employee.

Analysis of Variance: A Conceptual Overview

If the means for the three populations are equal, we would expect the three sample means to be close together. In fact, the closer the three sample means are to one another, the weaker the evidence we have for the conclusion that the population means differ. Alternatively, the more the sample means differ, the stronger the evidence we have for the conclusion that the population means differ. In other words, if the variability among the sample means is "small," it supports H_0; if the variability among the sample means is "large," it supports H_a.

If the null hypothesis, H_0: $\mu_1 = \mu_2 = \mu_3$, is true, we can use the variability among the sample means to develop an estimate of σ^2. First, note that if the assumptions for analysis of variance are satisfied and the null hypothesis is true, each sample will have come from the same normal distribution with mean μ and variance σ^2. Recall from Chapter 7 that the sampling distribution of the sample mean $\bar{x}$ for a simple random sample of size n from a normal population will be normally distributed with mean μ and variance σ^2/n. Figure 13.2 illustrates such a sampling distribution.

Thus, if the null hypothesis is true, we can think of each of the three sample means, $\bar{x}_1 = 62$, $\bar{x}_2 = 66$, and $\bar{x}_3 = 52$ from Table 13.1, as values drawn at random from the sampling distribution shown in Figure 13.2. In this case, the mean and variance of the three $\bar{x}$ values can be used to estimate the mean and variance of the sampling distribution. When the sample sizes are equal, as in the Chemitech experiment, the best estimate of the mean of the sampling

Figure 13.2 Sampling Distribution of $\bar{x}$ Given H_0 Is True

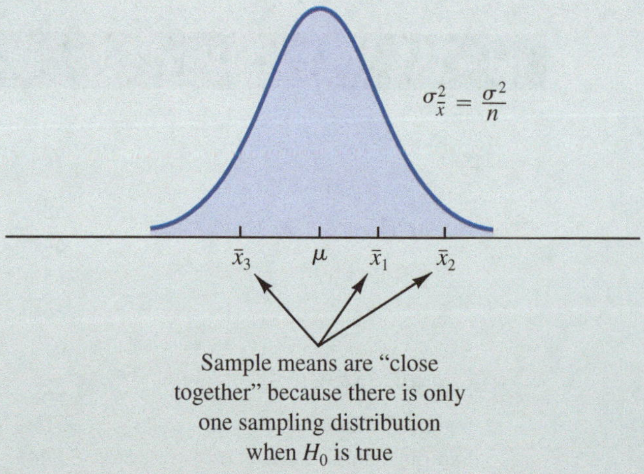

distribution of $\bar{x}$ is the mean or average of the sample means. In the Chemitech experiment, an estimate of the mean of the sampling distribution of $\bar{x}$ is $(62 + 66 + 52)/3 = 60$. We refer to this estimate as the *overall sample mean.* An estimate of the variance of the sampling distribution of $\bar{x}$, $\sigma^2_{\bar{x}}$, is provided by the variance of the three sample means.

$$s^2_{\bar{x}} = \frac{(62 - 60)^2 + (66 - 60)^2 + (52 - 60)^2}{3 - 1} = \frac{104}{2} = 52$$

Because $\sigma^2_{\bar{x}} = \sigma^2/n$, solving for σ^2 gives

$$\sigma^2 = n\sigma^2_{\bar{x}}$$

Hence,

$$\text{Estimate of } \sigma^2 = n\,(\text{Estimate of } \sigma^2_{\bar{x}}) = ns^2_{\bar{x}} = 5(52) = 260$$

The result, $ns^2_{\bar{x}} = 260$, is referred to as the *between-treatments* estimate of σ^2.

The between-treatments estimate of σ^2 is based on the assumption that the null hypothesis is true. In this case, each sample comes from the same population, and there is only one sampling distribution of $\bar{x}$. To illustrate what happens when H_0 is false, suppose the population means all differ. Note that because the three samples are from normal populations with different means, they will result in three different sampling distributions. Figure 13.3 shows that in this case, the sample means are not as close together as they were when H_0 was true. Thus, $s^2_{\bar{x}}$ will be larger, causing the between-treatments estimate of σ^2 to be larger. In general, when the population means are not equal, the between-treatments estimate will overestimate the population variance σ^2.

The variation within each of the samples also has an effect on the conclusion we reach in analysis of variance. When a random sample is selected from each population, each of the sample variances provides an unbiased estimate of σ^2. Hence, we can combine or pool the individual estimates of σ^2 into one overall estimate. The estimate of σ^2 obtained in this way is called the *pooled* or *within-treatments* estimate of σ^2. Because each sample variance provides an estimate of σ^2 based only on the variation within each sample, the within-treatments estimate of σ^2 is not affected by whether the population means are equal. When the sample sizes are equal, the within-treatments estimate of σ^2 can be obtained by computing the average of the individual sample variances. For the Chemitech experiment, we obtain

$$\text{Within-treatments estimate of } \sigma^2 = \frac{27.5 + 26.5 + 31.0}{3} = \frac{85}{3} = 28.33$$

Figure 13.3 Sampling Distributions of $\bar{x}$ Given H_0 Is False

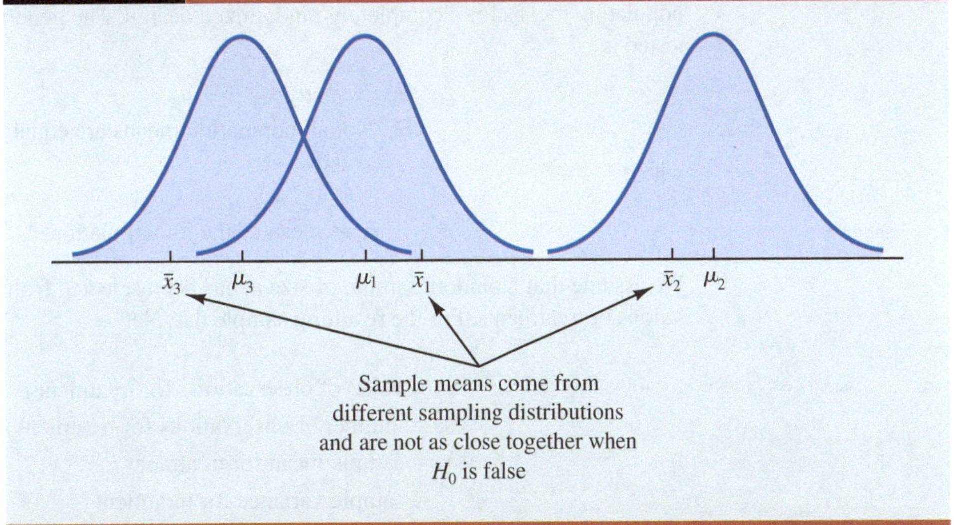

In the Chemitech experiment, the between-treatments estimate of σ^2 (260) is much larger than the within-treatments estimate of σ^2 (28.33). In fact, the ratio of these two estimates is 260/28.33 = 9.18. Recall, however, that the between-treatments approach provides a good estimate of σ^2 only if the null hypothesis is true; if the null hypothesis is false, the between-treatments approach overestimates σ^2. The within-treatments approach provides a good estimate of σ^2 in either case. Thus, if the null hypothesis is true, the two estimates will be similar and their ratio will be close to 1. If the null hypothesis is false, the between-treatments estimate will be larger than the within-treatments estimate, and their ratio will be large. In the next section, we will show how large this ratio must be to reject H_0.

In summary, the logic behind ANOVA is based on the development of two independent estimates of the common population variance σ^2. One estimate of σ^2 is based on the variability among the sample means themselves, and the other estimate of σ^2 is based on the variability of the data within each sample. By comparing these two estimates of σ^2, we will be able to determine whether the population means are equal.

Notes + Comments

1. Randomization in experimental design is the analog of probability sampling in an observational study.
2. In many medical experiments, potential bias is eliminated by using a double-blind experimental design. With this design, neither the physician applying the treatment nor the subject knows which treatment is being applied. Many other types of experiments could benefit from this type of design.
3. In this section, we provided a conceptual overview of how analysis of variance can be used to test for the equality of k population means for a completely randomized experimental design. We will see that the same procedure can also be used to test for the equality of k population means for an observational or nonexperimental study.
4. In Sections 10.1 and 10.2, we present statistical methods for testing the hypothesis that the means of two populations are equal. ANOVA can also be used to test the hypothesis that the means of two populations are equal. In practice, however, analysis of variance is usually not used except when dealing with three or more population means.

13.2 Analysis of Variance and the Completely Randomized Design

In this section, we show how analysis of variance can be used to test for the equality of k population means for a completely randomized design. The general form of the hypotheses tested is

$$H_0\colon \mu_1 = \mu_2 = \cdots = \mu_k$$
$$H_a\colon \text{Not all population means are equal}$$

where

$$\mu_j = \text{mean of the } j\text{th population}$$

We assume that a random sample of size n_j has been selected from each of the k populations or treatments. For the resulting sample data, let

$$x_{ij} = \text{value of observation } i \text{ for treatment } j$$
$$n_j = \text{number of observations for treatment } j$$
$$\bar{x}_j = \text{sample mean for treatment } j$$
$$s_j^2 = \text{sample variance for treatment } j$$
$$s_j = \text{sample standard deviation for treatment } j$$

The formulas for the sample mean and sample variance for treatment j are as follows.

$$\bar{x}_j = \frac{\sum_{i=1}^{n_j} x_{ij}}{n_j} \tag{13.1}$$

$$s_j^2 = \frac{\sum_{i=1}^{n_j} (x_{ij} - \bar{x}_j)^2}{n_j - 1} \tag{13.2}$$

The overall sample mean, denoted $\bar{\bar{x}}$, is the sum of all the observations divided by the total number of observations. That is,

$$\bar{\bar{x}} = \frac{\sum_{j=1}^{k}\sum_{i=1}^{n_j} x_{ij}}{n_T} \tag{13.3}$$

where

$$n_T = n_1 + n_2 + \cdots + n_k \tag{13.4}$$

If the size of each sample is n, $n_T = kn$; in this case, equation (13.3) reduces to

$$\bar{\bar{x}} = \frac{\sum_{j=1}^{k}\sum_{i=1}^{n_j} x_{ij}}{kn} = \frac{\sum_{j=1}^{k}\sum_{i=1}^{n_j} x_{ij}/n}{k} = \frac{\sum_{j=1}^{k} \bar{x}_j}{k} \tag{13.5}$$

In other words, whenever the sample sizes are the same, the overall sample mean is just the average of the k sample means.

Because each sample in the Chemitech experiment consists of $n = 5$ observations, the overall sample mean can be computed by using equation (13.5). For the data in Table 13.1, we obtained the following result.

$$\bar{\bar{x}} = \frac{62 + 66 + 52}{3} = 60$$

If the null hypothesis is true ($\mu_1 = \mu_2 = \mu_3 = \mu$), the overall sample mean of 60 is the best estimate of the population mean μ.

Between-Treatments Estimate of Population Variance

In the preceding section, we introduced the concept of a between-treatments estimate of σ^2 and showed how to compute it when the sample sizes were equal. This estimate of σ^2 is called the *mean square due to treatments* and is denoted MSTR. The general formula for computing MSTR is

$$\text{MSTR} = \frac{\sum_{j=1}^{k} n_j(\bar{x}_j - \bar{\bar{x}})^2}{k - 1} \tag{13.6}$$

The numerator in equation (13.6) is called the *sum of squares due to treatments* and is denoted SSTR. The denominator, $k - 1$, represents the degrees of freedom associated with SSTR. Hence, the mean square due to treatments can be computed using the following formula.

Mean Square Due to Treatments

$$\text{MSTR} = \frac{\text{SSTR}}{k - 1} \tag{13.7}$$

where

$$\text{SSTR} = \sum_{j=1}^{k} n_j(\bar{x}_j - \bar{\bar{x}})^2 \tag{13.8}$$

If H_0 is true, MSTR provides an unbiased estimate of σ^2. However, if the means of the k populations are not equal, MSTR is not an unbiased estimate of σ^2; in fact, in that case, MSTR should overestimate σ^2.

For the Chemitech data in Table 13.1, we obtain the following results.

$$\text{SSTR} = \sum_{j=1}^{k} n_j(\bar{x}_j - \bar{\bar{x}})^2 = 5(62 - 60)^2 + 5(66 - 60)^2 + 5(52 - 60)^2 = 520$$

$$\text{MSTR} = \frac{\text{SSTR}}{k - 1} = \frac{520}{2} = 260$$

Within-Treatments Estimate of Population Variance

Earlier, we introduced the concept of a within-treatments estimate of σ^2 and showed how to compute it when the sample sizes were equal. This estimate of σ^2 is called the *mean square due to error* and is denoted MSE. The general formula for computing MSE is

$$\text{MSE} = \frac{\sum_{j=1}^{k}(n_j - 1)s_j^2}{n_T - k} \tag{13.9}$$

The numerator in equation (13.9) is called the *sum of squares due to error* and is denoted SSE. The denominator of MSE is referred to as the degrees of freedom associated with SSE. Hence, the formula for MSE can also be stated as follows.

Mean Square Due to Error

$$\text{MSE} = \frac{\text{SSE}}{n_T - k} \tag{13.10}$$

where

$$\text{SSE} = \sum_{j=1}^{k}(n_j - 1)s_j^2 \tag{13.11}$$

Note that MSE is based on the variation within each of the treatments; it is not influenced by whether the null hypothesis is true. Thus, MSE always provides an unbiased estimate of σ^2.

For the Chemitech data in Table 13.1, we obtain the following results.

$$\text{SSE} = \sum_{j=1}^{k}(n_j - 1)s_j^2 = (5 - 1)27.5 + (5 - 1)26.5 + (5 - 1)31 = 340$$

$$\text{MSE} = \frac{\text{SSE}}{n_T - k} = \frac{340}{15 - 3} = \frac{340}{12} = 28.33$$

Comparing the Variance Estimates: The *F* Test

An introduction to the F distribution and the use of the F distribution table are presented in Section 11.2.

If the null hypothesis is true, MSTR and MSE provide two independent, unbiased estimates of σ^2. Based on the material covered in Chapter 11, we know that for normal populations, the sampling distribution of the ratio of two independent estimates of σ^2 follows an F distribution. Hence, if the null hypothesis is true and the ANOVA assumptions are valid, the sampling distribution of MSTR/MSE is an F distribution with numerator degrees of freedom equal to $k - 1$ and denominator degrees of freedom equal to $n_T - k$. In other words, if the null hypothesis is true, the value of MSTR/MSE should appear to have been selected from this F distribution.

However, if the null hypothesis is false, the value of MSTR/MSE will be inflated because MSTR overestimates σ^2. Hence, we will reject H_0 if the resulting value of MSTR/MSE appears to be too large to have been selected from an F distribution with $k - 1$ numerator degrees of freedom and $n_T - k$ denominator degrees of freedom. Because the decision to reject H_0 is based on the value of MSTR/MSE, the test statistic used to test for the equality of k population means is as follows.

Test Statistic for the Equality of *k* Population Means

$$F = \frac{\text{MSTR}}{\text{MSE}} \tag{13.12}$$

The test statistic follows an F distribution with $k - 1$ degrees of freedom in the numerator and $n_T - k$ degrees of freedom in the denominator.

Let us return to the Chemitech experiment and use a level of significance $\alpha = 0.05$ to conduct the hypothesis test. The value of the test statistic is

$$F = \frac{\text{MSTR}}{\text{MSE}} = \frac{260}{28.33} = 9.18$$

The numerator degrees of freedom is $k - 1 = 3 - 1 = 2$ and the denominator degrees of freedom is $n_T - k = 15 - 3 = 12$. Because we will only reject the null hypothesis for large values of the test statistic, the p-value is the upper tail area of the F distribution to the right of the test statistic $F = 9.18$. Figure 13.4 shows the sampling distribution of F = MSTR/ MSE, the value of the test statistic, and the upper tail area that is the p-value for the hypothesis test.

Figure 13.4 Computation of *p*-Value Using the Sampling Distribution of MSTR/MSE

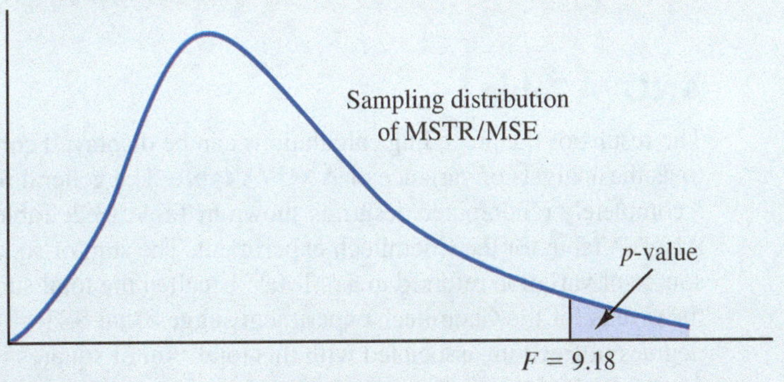

From Table 4 of Appendix B we find the following areas in the upper tail of an F distribution with 2 numerator degrees of freedom and 12 denominator degrees of freedom.

Area in Upper Tail	**0.10**	**0.05**	**0.025**	**0.01**
F Value ($df_1 = 2, df_2 = 12$)	2.81	3.89	5.10	6.93

$F = 9.18$

Because $F = 9.18$ is greater than 6.93, the area in the upper tail at $F = 9.18$ is less than 0.01. Thus, the p-value is less than 0.01. Excel can be used to show that the p-value is 0.004. With p-value $\leq \alpha = 0.05$, H_0 is rejected. The test provides sufficient evidence to conclude that the means of the three populations are not equal. In other words, analysis of variance supports the conclusion that the population mean number of units produced per week for the three assembly methods are not equal.

As with other hypothesis testing procedures, the critical value approach may also be used. With $\alpha = 0.05$, the critical F value occurs with an area of 0.05 in the upper tail of an F distribution with 2 and 12 degrees of freedom. From the F distribution table, we find $F_{0.05} = 3.89$. Hence, the appropriate upper tail rejection rule for the Chemitech experiment is

$$\text{Reject } H_0 \text{ if } F \geq 3.89$$

With $F = 9.18$, we reject H_0 and conclude that the means of the three populations are not equal. A summary of the overall procedure for testing for the equality of k population means follows.

Test for the Equality of *k* Population Means

$$H_0\colon \mu_1 = \mu_2 = \cdots = \mu_k$$
$$H_a\colon \text{Not all population means are equal}$$

Test Statistic

$$F = \frac{\text{MSTR}}{\text{MSE}}$$

Rejection Rule

p-value approach:	Reject H_0 if p-value $\leq \alpha$
Critical value approach:	Reject H_0 if $F \geq F_\alpha$

where the value of F is based on an F distribution with $k - 1$ numerator degrees of freedom and $n_T - k$ denominator degrees of freedom.

ANOVA Table

The results of the preceding calculations can be displayed conveniently in a table referred to as the analysis of variance or **ANOVA table**. The general form of the ANOVA table for a completely randomized design is shown in Table 13.2; Table 13.3 is the corresponding ANOVA table for the Chemitech experiment. The sum of squares associated with the source of variation referred to as "Total" is called the total sum of squares (SST). Note that the results for the Chemitech experiment suggest that SST = SSTR + SSE, and that the degrees of freedom associated with this total sum of squares is the sum of the degrees of freedom associated with the sum of squares due to treatments and the sum of squares due to error.

Table 13.2 ANOVA Table for a Completely Randomized Design

Source of Variation	Sum of Squares	Degrees of Freedom	Mean Square	F	p-Value
Treatments	SSTR	$k - 1$	$\text{MSTR} = \dfrac{\text{SSTR}}{k - 1}$	$\dfrac{\text{MSTR}}{\text{MSE}}$	
Error	SSE	$n_T - k$	$\text{MSE} = \dfrac{\text{SSE}}{n_T - k}$		
Total	SST	$n_T - 1$			

Table 13.3 Analysis of Variance Table for the Chemitech Experiment

Source of Variation	Sum of Squares	Degrees of Freedom	Mean Square	F	p-Value
Treatments	520	2	260.00	9.18	0.004
Error	340	12	28.33		
Total	860	14			

We point out that SST divided by its degrees of freedom $n_T - 1$ is nothing more than the overall sample variance that would be obtained if we treated the entire set of 15 observations as one data set. With the entire data set as one sample, the formula for computing the total sum of squares, SST, is

$$\text{SST} = \sum_{j=1}^{k} \sum_{i=1}^{n_j} (x_{ij} - \bar{\bar{x}})^2 \tag{13.13}$$

It can be shown that the results we observed for the analysis of variance table for the Chemitech experiment also apply to other problems. That is,

$$\text{SST} = \text{SSTR} + \text{SSE} \tag{13.14}$$

Analysis of variance can be thought of as a statistical procedure for partitioning the total sum of squares into separate components.

In other words, SST can be partitioned into two sums of squares: the sum of squares due to treatments and the sum of squares due to error. Note also that the degrees of freedom corresponding to SST, $n_T - 1$, can be partitioned into the degrees of freedom corresponding to SSTR, $k - 1$, and the degrees of freedom corresponding to SSE, $n_T - k$. The analysis of variance can be viewed as the process of **partitioning** the total sum of squares and the degrees of freedom into their corresponding sources: treatments and error. Dividing the sum of squares by the appropriate degrees of freedom provides the variance estimates, the F value, and the p-value used to test the hypothesis of equal population means.

Using Excel

Excel's Anova: Single Factor tool can be used to conduct a hypothesis test about the difference between the population means for the Chemitech experiment.

Enter/Access Data: Open the file *chemitech*. The data are in cells A2:C6 and labels are in cells A1:C1.

Apply Tools: The following steps describe how to use Excel's Anova: Single Factor tool to test the hypothesis that the mean number of units produced per week is the same for all three methods of assembly.

Figure 13.5 Excel's ANOVA: Single Factor Tool Dialog Box for the Chemitech Experiment

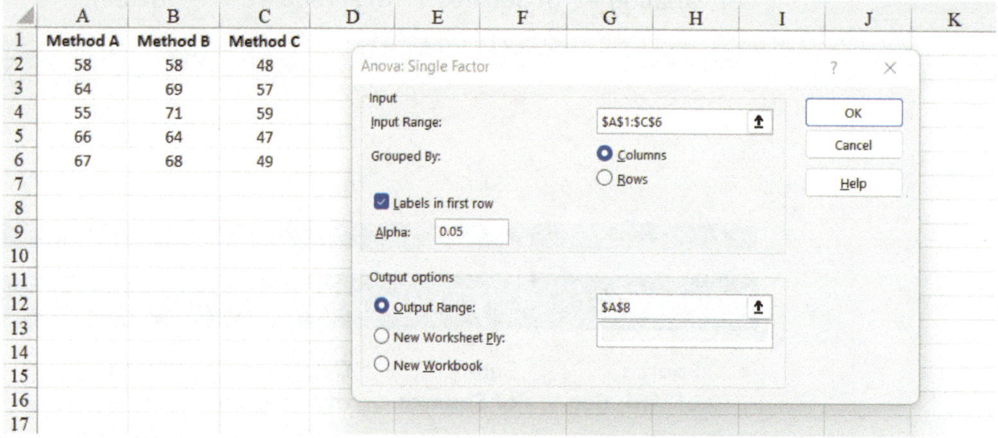

Source: Microsoft Corporation

Step 1. Click the **Data** tab on the Ribbon
Step 2. In the **Analyze** group, click **Data Analysis**
Step 3. Choose **Anova: Single Factor** from the list of Analysis Tools
Step 4. When the **Anova: Single Factor** dialog box appears (see Figure 13.5):
Enter *A1:C6* in the **Input Range:** box
Select **Columns** in the **Grouped By:** area
Select the check box for **Labels in First Row**
Enter *0.05* in the **Alpha:** box
Select **Output Range:** in the **Output options** area
Enter *A8* in the **Output Range:** box (to identify the upper-left corner of the section of the worksheet where the output will appear)
Click **OK**

The output, titled *Anova: Single Factor,* appears in cells A8:G22 of the worksheet shown in Figure 13.6. Cells A10:E14 provide a summary of the data. Note that the sample mean and sample variance for each method of assembly are the same as shown in Table 13.1. The ANOVA table, shown in cells A17:G22, is basically the same as the ANOVA table shown in Table 13.2. Excel identifies the treatments source of variation using the label *Between Groups* and the error source of variation using the label *Within Groups*. In addition, the Excel output provides the p-value associated with the test as well as the critical F value.

We can use the p-value shown in cell F19, 0.0038, to make the hypothesis testing decision. Thus, at the $\alpha = 0.05$ level of significance, we reject H_0 because the p-value $= 0.0038 < \alpha = 0.05$. Hence, using the p-value approach we still conclude that the mean number of units produced per week are not the same for the three assembly methods.

Testing for the Equality of *k* Population Means: An Observational Study

We have shown how analysis of variance can be used to test for the equality of k population means for a completely randomized experimental design. It is important to understand that ANOVA can also be used to test for the equality of three or more population means using data obtained from an observational study. As an example, let us consider the situation at National Computer Products, Inc. (NCP).

Figure 13.6 Excel's ANOVA: Single Factor Tool Output for the Chemitech Experiment

	A	B	C	D	E	F	G	H
1	**Method A**	**Method B**	**Method C**					
2	58	58	48					
3	64	69	57					
4	55	71	59					
5	66	64	47					
6	67	68	49					
7								
8	Anova: Single Factor							
9								
10	SUMMARY							
11	*Groups*	*Count*	*Sum*	*Average*	*Variance*			
12	Method A	5	310	62	27.5			
13	Method B	5	330	66	26.5			
14	Method C	5	260	52	31			
15								
16								
17	ANOVA							
18	*Source of Variation*	*SS*	*df*	*MS*	*F*	*P-value*	*F crit*	
19	Between Groups	520	2	260	9.1765	0.0038	3.8853	
20	Within Groups	340	12	28.3333				
21								
22	Total	860	14					
23								

NCP manufactures printers at plants located in Atlanta, Dallas, and Seattle. To measure how much employees at these plants know about quality management, a random sample of six employees was selected from each plant and the employees selected were given a quality awareness examination. The examination scores for these 18 employees are shown in Table 13.4. The sample means, sample variances, and sample standard

DATA*file*
ncp

Table 13.4 Examination Scores for 18 Employees

	Plant 1 Atlanta	Plant 2 Dallas	Plant 3 Seattle
	85	71	59
	75	75	64
	82	73	62
	76	74	69
	71	69	75
	85	82	67
Sample mean	79	74	66
Sample variance	34	20	32
Sample standard deviation	5.83	4.47	5.66

deviations for each group are also provided. Managers want to use these data to test the hypothesis that the mean examination score is the same for all three plants.

We define population 1 as all employees at the Atlanta plant, population 2 as all employees at the Dallas plant, and population 3 as all employees at the Seattle plant. Let

$$\mu_1 = \text{mean examination score for population 1}$$
$$\mu_2 = \text{mean examination score for population 2}$$
$$\mu_3 = \text{mean examination score for population 3}$$

Although we will never know the actual values of μ_1, μ_2, and μ_3, we want to use the sample results to test the following hypotheses.

$$H_0: \mu_1 = \mu_2 = \mu_3$$
$$H_a: \text{Not all population means are equal}$$

Note that the hypothesis test for the NCP observational study is exactly the same as the hypothesis test for the Chemitech experiment. Indeed, the same analysis of variance methodology we used to analyze the Chemitech experiment can also be used to analyze the data from the NCP observational study.

Even though the same ANOVA methodology is used for the analysis, it is worth noting how the NCP observational statistical study differs from the Chemitech experimental statistical study. The individuals who conducted the NCP study had no control over how the plants were assigned to individual employees. That is, the plants were already in operation and a particular employee worked at one of the three plants. All that NCP could do was to select a random sample of six employees from each plant and administer the quality awareness examination. To be classified as an experimental study, NCP would have had to be able to randomly select 18 employees and then assign the plants to each employee in a random fashion.

Notes + Comments

1. The overall sample mean can also be computed as a weighted average of the k sample means.

$$\bar{\bar{x}} = \frac{n_1\bar{x}_1 + n_2\bar{x}_2 + \ldots + n_k\bar{x}_k}{n_T}$$

In problems where the sample means are provided, this formula is simpler than equation (13.3) for computing the overall mean.

2. If each sample consists of n observations, equation (13.6) can be written as

$$\text{MSTR} = \frac{n\sum_{j=1}^{k}(\bar{x}_j - \bar{\bar{x}})^2}{k-1} = n\left[\frac{\sum_{j=1}^{k}(\bar{x}_j - \bar{\bar{x}})^2}{k-1}\right] = ns_{\bar{x}}^2$$

Note that this result is the same as what we presented in Section 13.1, when we introduced the concept of the between-treatments estimate of σ^2. Equation (13.6) is simply a generalization of this result to the unequal sample-size case.

3. If each sample has n observations, $n_T = kn$; thus, $n_T - k = k(n - 1)$, and equation (13.9) can be rewritten as

$$\text{MSE} = \frac{\sum_{j=1}^{k}(n-1)s_j^2}{k(n-1)} = \frac{(n-1)\sum_{j=1}^{k}s_j^2}{k(n-1)} = \frac{\sum_{j=1}^{k}s_j^2}{k}$$

In other words, if the sample sizes are the same, MSE is the average of the k sample variances. Note that it is the same result we used in Section 13.1 when we introduced the concept of the within-treatments estimate of σ^2.

Exercises

Methods

1. The following data are from a completely randomized design. **LO 1**

	Treatment		
	A	B	C
	162	142	126
	142	156	122
	165	124	138
	145	142	140
	148	136	150
	174	152	128
Sample mean	156	142	134
Sample variance	164.4	131.2	110.4

   a. Compute the sum of squares between treatments.
   b. Compute the mean square between treatments.
   c. Compute the sum of squares due to error.
   d. Compute the mean square due to error.
   e. Set up the ANOVA table for this problem.
   f. At the $\alpha = 0.05$ level of significance, test whether the means for the three treatments are equal.

2. In a completely randomized design, seven experimental units were used for each of the five levels of the factor. Complete the following ANOVA table. **LO 1, 3**

Source of Variation	Sum of Squares	Degrees of Freedom	Mean Square	F	p-Value
Treatments	300				
Error					
Total	460				

3. Refer to exercise 2. **LO 2, 3**
   a. What hypotheses are implied in this problem?
   b. At the $\alpha = 0.05$ level of significance, can we reject the null hypothesis in part (a)? Explain.

4. In an experiment designed to test the output levels of three different treatments, the following results were obtained: SST = 400, SSTR = 150, $n_T = 19$. Set up the ANOVA table and test for any significant difference between the mean output levels of the three treatments. Use $\alpha = 0.05$. **LO 1, 3**

5. In a completely randomized design, 12 experimental units were used for the first treatment, 15 for the second treatment, and 20 for the third treatment. Complete the following analysis of variance. At a 0.05 level of significance, is there a significant difference between the treatments? **LO 1, 3**

Source of Variation	Sum of Squares	Degrees of Freedom	Mean Square	F	p-Value
Treatments	1,200				
Error					
Total	1,800				

6. Develop the analysis of variance computations for the following completely randomized design. At $\alpha = 0.05$, is there a significant difference between the treatment means? **LO 1, 3**

DATA*file*
exer6

	Treatment		
	A	B	C
	136	107	92
	120	114	82
	113	125	85
	107	104	101
	131	107	89
	114	109	117
	129	97	110
	102	114	120
		104	98
		89	106
$\bar{x}_j$	119	107	100
s_j^2	146.86	96.44	173.78

Applications

7. **Product Assembly.** Three different methods for assembling a product were proposed by an industrial engineer. To investigate the number of units assembled correctly with each method, 30 employees were randomly selected and randomly assigned to the three proposed methods in such a way that each method was used by 10 workers. The number of units assembled correctly was recorded, and the analysis of variance procedure was applied to the resulting data set. The following results were obtained: SST = 10,800; SSTR = 4,560. **LO 1, 3**
   a. Set up the ANOVA table for this problem.
   b. Use $\alpha = 0.05$ to test for any significant difference in the means for the three assembly methods.

8. **Testing Quality Awareness.** Refer to the NCP data in Table 13.4. Set up the ANOVA table and test for any significant difference in the mean examination score for the three plants. Use $\alpha = 0.05$. **LO 1, 3**

9. **Temperature's Effect on a Chemical Process.** To study the effect of temperature on yield in a chemical process, five batches were produced at each of three temperature levels. The results follow. Construct an analysis of variance table. Use a 0.05 level of significance to test whether the temperature level has an effect on the mean yield of the process. **LO 1, 3**

Temperature		
50°C	60°C	70°C
34	30	23
24	31	28
36	34	28
39	23	30
32	27	31

10. **Auditing Errors.** Auditors must make judgments about various aspects of an audit on the basis of their own direct experience, indirect experience, or a combination of the two. In a study, auditors were asked to make judgments about the frequency of errors to be found in an audit. The judgments by the auditors were then compared to the actual results. Suppose the following data were obtained from a similar study; lower scores indicate better judgments. **LO 1, 3**

DATA*file*
audjudg

Direct	Indirect	Combination
17.0	16.6	25.2
18.5	22.2	24.0
15.8	20.5	21.5
18.2	18.3	26.8
20.2	24.2	27.5
16.0	19.8	25.8
13.3	21.2	24.2

Use $\alpha = 0.05$ to test to see whether the basis for the judgment affects the quality of the judgment. What is your conclusion? **LO 1, 3**

11. **Paint-Drying Robots.** How long it takes paint to dry can have an impact on the production capacity of a business. In May 2018, Deal's Auto Body & Paint in Prescott, Arizona, invested in a paint-drying robot to speed up its process (*The Daily Courier* website). An interesting question is, "Do all paint-drying robots have the same drying time?" To test this, suppose we sample five drying times for each of different brands of paint-drying robots. The time in minutes until the paint was dry enough for a second coat to be applied was recorded. The following data were obtained.

DATA*file*
paint

Robot 1	Robot 2	Robot 3	Robot 4
128	144	133	150
137	133	143	142
135	142	137	135
124	146	136	140
141	130	131	153

At the $\alpha = 0.05$ level of significance, test to see whether the mean drying time is the same for each brand of robot. **LO 1, 3**

12. **Restaurant Satisfaction.** The *Consumer Reports* Restaurant Customer Satisfaction Survey is based upon 148,599 visits to full-service restaurant chains (*Consumer Reports* website). One of the variables in the study is meal price, the average amount paid per person for dinner and drinks, minus the tip. Suppose a reporter for the *Sun Coast Times* thought that it would be of interest to her readers to conduct a similar study for restaurants located on the Grand Strand section in Myrtle Beach, South Carolina. The reporter selected a sample of eight seafood restaurants, eight Italian restaurants, and eight steakhouses. The following data show the meal prices ($) obtained for the 24 restaurants sampled. Use $\alpha = 0.05$ to test whether there is a significant difference among the mean meal price for the three types of restaurants. **LO 1, 3**

DATA*file*
grandstrand

Italian	Seafood	Steakhouse
$12	$16	$24
13	18	19
15	17	23
17	26	25
18	23	21
20	15	22
17	19	27
24	18	31

13.3 Multiple Comparison Procedures

When we use analysis of variance to test whether the means of k populations are equal, rejection of the null hypothesis allows us to conclude only that the population means are *not all equal.* In some cases, we will want to go a step further and determine where the differences among means occur. The purpose of this section is to show how **multiple comparison procedures** can be used to conduct statistical comparisons between pairs of population means.

Fisher's LSD

Suppose that analysis of variance provides statistical evidence to reject the null hypothesis of equal population means. In this case, Fisher's least significant difference (LSD) procedure can be used to determine where the differences occur. To illustrate the use of Fisher's LSD procedure in making pairwise comparisons of population means, recall the Chemitech experiment introduced in Section 13.1. Using analysis of variance, we concluded that the mean number of units produced per week are not the same for the three assembly methods. In this case, the follow-up question is: We believe the assembly methods differ, but where do the differences occur? That is, do the means of populations 1 and 2 differ? Or those of populations 1 and 3? Or those of populations 2 and 3? The following table summarizes Fisher's LSD procedure for comparing pairs of population means.

Fisher's Lsd Procedure

$$H_0\colon \mu_i = \mu_j$$
$$H_a\colon \mu_i \neq \mu_j$$

Test Statistic

$$t = \frac{\bar{x}_i - \bar{x}_j}{\sqrt{\text{MSE}\left(\dfrac{1}{n_i} + \dfrac{1}{n_j}\right)}} \tag{13.16}$$

Rejection Rule

p-value approach: Reject H_0 if p-value $\leq \alpha$

Critical value approach: Reject H_0 if $t \leq -t_{\alpha/2}$ or $t \geq t_{\alpha/2}$

where the value of $t_{\alpha/2}$ is based on a t distribution with $n_T - k$ degrees of freedom.

Let us now apply this procedure to determine whether there is a significant difference between the means of population 1 (method A) and population 2 (method B) at the $\alpha = 0.05$ level of significance. Table 13.1 showed that the sample mean is 62 for method A and 66 for method B. Table 13.3 showed that the value of MSE is 28.33; it is the estimate of σ^2 and is based on 12 degrees of freedom. For the Chemitech data, the value of the test statistic is

$$t = \frac{62 - 66}{\sqrt{28.33\left(\dfrac{1}{5} + \dfrac{1}{5}\right)}} = -1.19$$

Because we have a two-tailed test, the p-value is two times the area under the curve for the t distribution to the left of $t = -1.19$. Using Table 2 in Appendix B, the t distribution table for 12 degrees of freedom provides the following information.

Area in Upper Tail	0.20	0.10	0.05	0.025	0.01	0.005
***t* Value (12 *df*)**	0.873	1.356	1.782	2.179	2.681	3.055

$t = 1.19$

The t distribution table only contains positive t values. Because the t distribution is symmetric, however, we can find the area under the curve to the right of $t = 1.19$ and double it to find the p-value corresponding to $t = -1.19$. We see that $t = 1.19$ is between 0.20 and 0.10. Doubling these amounts, we see that the p-value must be between 0.40 and 0.20. Excel can be used to show that the p-value is 0.2571. Because the p-value is greater than $\alpha = 0.05$, we cannot reject the null hypothesis. Hence, we cannot conclude that the population mean number of units produced per week for method A is different from the population mean for method B.

Many practitioners find it easier to determine how large the difference between the sample means must be to reject H_0. In this case, the test statistic is $\bar{x}_i - \bar{x}_j$, and the test is conducted by the following procedure.

Fisher's Lsd Procedure Based on the Test Statistic $\bar{x}_i - \bar{x}_j$

$$H_0\colon \mu_i = \mu_j$$
$$H_a\colon \mu_i \neq \mu_j$$

Test Statistic

$$\bar{x}_i - \bar{x}_j$$

Rejection Rule at a Level of Significance α

$$\text{Reject } H_0 \text{ if } |\bar{x}_i - \bar{x}_j| \geq \text{LSD}$$

where

$$\text{LSD} = t_{\alpha/2}\sqrt{\text{MSE}\left(\frac{1}{n_i} + \frac{1}{n_j}\right)} \tag{13.17}$$

For the Chemitech experiment, the value of LSD is

$$\text{LSD} = 2.179\sqrt{28.33\left(\frac{1}{5} + \frac{1}{5}\right)} = 7.34$$

Note that when the sample sizes are equal, only one value for LSD is computed. In such cases, we can simply compare the magnitude of the difference between any two sample means with the value of LSD. For example, the difference between the sample means for population 1 (method A) and population 3 (method C) is $62 - 52 = 10$. This difference is greater than LSD $= 7.34$, which means we can reject the null hypothesis that the population mean number of units produced per week for method A is equal to the population mean for method C. Similarly, with the difference between the sample means for populations 2 and 3 of $66 - 52 = 14 > 7.34$, we can also reject the hypothesis that the population mean for method B is equal to the population mean for method C. In effect, our conclusion is that methods A and B both differ from method C.

Fisher's LSD can also be used to develop a confidence interval estimate of the difference between the means of two populations. The general procedure follows.

Confidence Interval Estimate of the Difference Between Two Population Means Using Fisher's Lsd Procedure

$$\bar{x}_i - \bar{x}_j \pm \text{LSD} \tag{13.18}$$

where

$$\text{LSD} = t_{\alpha/2}\sqrt{\text{MSE}\left(\frac{1}{n_i} + \frac{1}{n_j}\right)} \tag{13.19}$$

and $t_{\alpha/2}$ is based on a t distribution with $n_T - k$ degrees of freedom.

If the confidence interval in expression (13.18) includes the value zero, we cannot reject the hypothesis that the two population means are equal. However, if the confidence interval does not include the value zero, we conclude that there is a difference between the population means. For the Chemitech experiment, recall that LSD = 7.34 (corresponding to $t_{0.025} = 2.179$). Thus, a 95% confidence interval estimate of the difference between the means of populations 1 and 2 is $62 - 66 \pm 7.34 = -4 \pm 7.34 = -11.34$ to 3.34; because this interval includes zero, we cannot reject the hypothesis that the two population means are equal.

Type I Error Rates

We began the discussion of Fisher's LSD procedure with the premise that analysis of variance gave us statistical evidence to reject the null hypothesis of equal population means. We showed how Fisher's LSD procedure can be used in such cases to determine where the differences occur. Technically, it is referred to as a *protected* or *restricted* LSD test because it is employed only if we first find a significant F value by using analysis of variance. To see why this distinction is important in multiple comparison tests, we need to explain the difference between a *comparison-wise* Type I error rate and an *experiment-wise* Type I error rate.

In the Chemitech experiment, we used Fisher's LSD procedure to make three pairwise comparisons.

Test 1	Test 2	Test 3
$H_0\colon \mu_1 = \mu_2$	$H_0\colon \mu_1 = \mu_3$	$H_0\colon \mu_2 = \mu_3$
$H_a\colon \mu_1 \neq \mu_2$	$H_a\colon \mu_1 \neq \mu_3$	$H_a\colon \mu_2 \neq \mu_3$

In each case, we used a level of significance of $\alpha = 0.05$. Therefore, for each test, if the null hypothesis is true, the probability that we will make a Type I error is $\alpha = 0.05$; hence, the probability that we will not make a Type I error on each test is $1 - 0.05 = 0.95$. In discussing multiple comparison procedures we refer to this probability of a Type I error ($\alpha = 0.05$) as the **comparison-wise Type I error rate**; comparison-wise Type I error rates indicate the level of significance associated with a single pairwise comparison.

Let us now consider a slightly different question. What is the probability that in making three pairwise comparisons, we will commit a Type I error on at least one of the three tests? To answer this question, note that the probability that we will not make a Type I error on any of the three tests is $(0.95)(0.95)(0.95) = 0.8574$.[1] Therefore, the probability of making at least one Type I error is $1 - 0.8574 = 0.1426$. Thus, when we use Fisher's LSD procedure to make all three pairwise comparisons, the Type I error rate associated with this approach is not 0.05, but actually 0.1426; we refer to this error rate as the *overall* or **experiment-wise Type I error rate**. To avoid confusion, we denote the experimentwise Type I error rate as α_{EW}.

The experiment-wise Type I error rate gets larger for problems with more populations. For example, a problem with five populations has 10 possible pairwise comparisons. If we tested all possible pairwise comparisons by using Fisher's LSD with a comparisonwise error rate of $\alpha = 0.05$, the experiment-wise Type I error rate would be $1 - (1 - 0.05)^{10} = 0.40$. In such cases, practitioners look to alternatives that provide better control over the experimentwise error rate.

One alternative for controlling the overall experiment-wise error rate, referred to as the Bonferroni adjustment, involves using a smaller comparison-wise error rate for each test. For example, if we want to test C pairwise comparisons and want the maximum probability of making a Type I error for the overall experiment to be α_{EW}, we simply use a comparison-wise error rate equal to α_{EW}/C. In the Chemitech experiment, if we want to use Fisher's LSD procedure to test all three pairwise comparisons with a maximum experiment-wise

[1]The assumption is that the three tests are independent, and hence the joint probability of the three events can be obtained by simply multiplying the individual probabilities. In fact, the three tests are not independent because MSE is used in each test; therefore, the error involved is even greater than that shown.

error rate of $\alpha_{EW} = 0.05$, we set the comparison-wise error rate to be $\alpha = 0.05/3 = 0.017$. For a problem with five populations and 10 possible pairwise comparisons, the Bonferroni adjustment would suggest a comparison-wise error rate of $0.05/10 = 0.005$. Recall from our discussion of hypothesis testing in Chapter 9, that for a fixed sample size, any decrease in the probability of making a Type I error will result in an increase in the probability of making a Type II error, which corresponds to accepting the hypothesis that the two population means are equal when in fact they are not equal. As a result, many practitioners are reluctant to perform individual tests with a low comparison-wise Type I error rate because of the increased risk of making a Type II error.

Several other procedures, such as Tukey's procedure and Duncan's multiple range test, have been developed to help in such situations. However, there is considerable controversy in the statistical community as to which procedure is "best." The truth is that no one procedure is best for all types of problems.

Exercises

Methods

13. The following data are from a completely randomized design. **LO 3, 4, 5**

	Treatment A	Treatment B	Treatment C
	32	44	33
	30	43	36
	30	44	35
	26	46	36
	32	48	40
Sample mean	30	45	36
Sample variance	6.00	4.00	6.50

a. At the $\alpha = 0.05$ level of significance, can we reject the null hypothesis that the means of the three treatments are equal?
b. Use Fisher's LSD procedure to test whether there is a significant difference between the means for treatments A and B, treatments A and C, and treatments B and C. Use $\alpha = 0.05$.
c. Use Fisher's LSD procedure to develop a 95% confidence interval estimate of the difference between the means of treatments A and B.

14. The following data are from a completely randomized design. In the following calculations, use $\alpha = 0.05$. **LO 3, 4**

	Treatment 1	Treatment 2	Treatment 3
	63	82	69
	47	72	54
	54	88	61
	40	66	48
$\bar{x}_j$	51	77	58
s_j^2	96.67	97.34	81.99

a. Use analysis of variance to test for a significant difference among the means of the three treatments.
b. Use Fisher's LSD procedure to determine which means are different.

Applications

15. **Testing Chemical Processes.** To test whether the mean time needed to mix a batch of material is the same for machines produced by three manufacturers, the Jacobs Chemical Company obtained the following data on the time (in minutes) needed to mix the material. **LO 3, 4**

Manufacturer		
1	2	3
20	28	20
26	26	19
24	31	23
22	27	22

a. Use these data to test whether the population mean times for mixing a batch of material differ for the three manufacturers. Use $\alpha = 0.05$.

b. At the $\alpha = 0.05$ level of significance, use Fisher's LSD procedure to test for the equality of the means for manufacturers 1 and 3. What conclusion can you draw after carrying out this test?

16. **Confidence Intervals for Different Processes.** Refer to exercise 15. Use Fisher's LSD procedure to develop a 95% confidence interval estimate of the difference between the means for manufacturer 1 and manufacturer 2. **LO 5**

17. **Marketing Ethics.** In the digital age of marketing, special care must be taken to ensure that programmatic ads appear on websites aligned with a company's strategy, culture, and ethics. For example, in 2017, Nordstrom, Amazon, and Whole Foods each faced boycotts from social media users when automated ads for these companies showed up on the *Breitbart* website (*ChiefMarketer.com*). It is important for marketing professionals to understand a company's values and culture. The following data are from an experiment designed to investigate the perception of corporate ethical values among individuals specializing in marketing (higher scores indicate higher ethical values). **LO 3, 4**

Marketing Managers	Marketing Research	Advertising
6	5	6
5	5	7
4	4	6
5	4	5
6	5	6
4	4	6

a. Use $\alpha = 0.05$ to test for significant differences in perception among the three groups.

b. At the $\alpha = 0.05$ level of significance, we can conclude that there are differences in the perceptions for marketing managers, marketing research specialists, and advertising specialists. Use the procedures in this section to determine where the differences occur. Use $\alpha = 0.05$.

18. **Machine Breakdowns.** To test for any significant difference in the number of hours between breakdowns for four machines, the following data were obtained. **LO 3, 4**

Machine 1	Machine 2	Machine 3	Machine 4
6.4	8.7	11.1	9.9
7.8	7.4	10.3	12.8
5.3	9.4	9.7	12.1
7.4	10.1	10.3	10.8
8.4	9.2	9.2	11.3
7.3	9.8	8.8	11.5

a. At the $\alpha = 0.05$ level of significance, what is the difference, if any, in the population mean times among the four machines?
b. Use Fisher's LSD procedure to test for the equality of the means for machines 2 and 4. Use a 0.05 level of significance.

19. **Testing Time to Breakdown Between All Pairs of Machines.** Refer to exercise 18. Use the Bonferroni adjustment to test for a significant difference between all pairs of means. Assume that a maximum overall experimentwise error rate of 0.05 is desired. **LO 4**

20. **Minor League Baseball Attendance.** The International League of Triple-A minor league baseball consists of 14 teams organized into three divisions: North, South, and West. The following data show the average attendance for the 14 teams in the International League (The Biz of Baseball website). Also shown are the teams' records; W denotes the number of games won, L denotes the number of games lost, and PCT is the proportion of games played that were won. **LO 3, 4**

DATA*file*
triple-a

Team Name	Division	W	L	PCT	Attendance
Buffalo Bisons	North	66	77	0.462	8,812
Lehigh Valley IronPigs	North	55	89	0.382	8,479
Pawtucket Red Sox	North	85	58	0.594	9,097
Rochester Red Wings	North	74	70	0.514	6,913
Scranton-Wilkes Barre Yankees	North	88	56	0.611	7,147
Syracuse Chiefs	North	69	73	0.486	5,765
Charlotte Knights	South	63	78	0.447	4,526
Durham Bulls	South	74	70	0.514	6,995
Norfolk Tides	South	64	78	0.451	6,286
Richmond Braves	South	63	78	0.447	4,455
Columbus Clippers	West	69	73	0.486	7,795
Indianapolis Indians	West	68	76	0.472	8,538
Louisville Bats	West	88	56	0.611	9,152
Toledo Mud Hens	West	75	69	0.521	8,234

a. Use $\alpha = 0.05$ to test for any difference in the mean attendance for the three divisions.
b. Use Fisher's LSD procedure to determine where the differences occur. Use $\alpha = 0.05$.

13.4 Randomized Block Design

Thus far, we have considered the completely randomized experimental design. Recall that to test for a difference among treatment means, we computed an F value by using the ratio

$$F = \frac{\text{MSTR}}{\text{MSE}} \tag{13.20}$$

A completely randomized design is useful when the experimental units are homogeneous. If the experimental units are heterogeneous, ***blocking*** *is often used to form homogeneous groups.*

A problem can arise whenever differences due to extraneous factors (ones not considered in the experiment) cause the MSE term in this ratio to become large. In such cases, the F value in equation (13.20) can become small, signaling no difference among treatment means when in fact such a difference exists.

In this section, we present an experimental design known as a **randomized block design**. Its purpose is to control some of the extraneous sources of variation by removing such variation from the MSE term. This design tends to provide a better estimate of the true error variance and leads to a more powerful hypothesis test in terms of the ability to detect differences among treatment means. To illustrate, let us consider a stress study for air traffic controllers.

Air Traffic Controller Stress Test

A study measuring the fatigue and stress of air traffic controllers resulted in proposals for modification and redesign of the controller's workstation. After consideration of several designs for the workstation, three specific alternatives are selected as having the best potential for reducing controller stress. The key question is: To what extent do the three alternatives differ in terms of their effect on controller stress? To answer this question, we need to design an experiment that will provide measurements of air traffic controller stress under each alternative.

Experimental studies in business often involve experimental units that are highly heterogeneous; as a result, randomized block designs are often employed.

In a completely randomized design, a random sample of controllers would be assigned to each workstation alternative. However, controllers are believed to differ substantially in their ability to handle stressful situations. What is high stress to one controller might be only moderate or even low stress to another. Hence, when considering the within-group source of variation (MSE), we must realize that this variation includes both random error and error due to individual controller differences. In fact, managers expected controller variability to be a major contributor to the MSE term.

Blocking in experimental design is similar to stratification in sampling.

One way to separate the effect of the individual differences is to use a randomized block design. Such a design will identify the variability stemming from individual controller differences and remove it from the MSE term. The randomized block design calls for a single sample of controllers. Each controller in the sample is tested with each of the three workstation alternatives. In experimental design terminology, the workstation is the *factor of interest* and the controllers are the *blocks.* The three treatments or populations associated with the workstation factor correspond to the three workstation alternatives. For simplicity, we refer to the workstation alternatives as system A, system B, and system C.

The *randomized* aspect of the randomized block design is the random order in which the treatments (systems) are assigned to the controllers. If every controller were to test the three systems in the same order, any observed difference in systems might be due to the order of the test rather than to true differences in the systems.

To provide the necessary data, the three workstation alternatives were installed at the Cleveland Control Center in Oberlin, Ohio. Six controllers were selected at random and assigned to operate each of the systems. A follow-up interview and a medical examination of each controller participating in the study provided a measure of the stress for each controller on each system. The data are reported in Table 13.5.

Table 13.6 is a summary of the stress data collected. In this table we include column totals (treatments) and row totals (blocks) as well as some sample means that will be helpful in making the sum of squares computations for the ANOVA procedure. Because lower stress values are viewed as better, the sample data seem to favor system B with its mean stress rating of 13. However, the usual question remains: Do the sample results justify the conclusion that the population mean stress levels for the three systems differ? That is, are the differences statistically significant? An analysis of variance computation similar to the one performed for the completely randomized design can be used to answer this statistical question.

DATA*file*
airtraffic

Table 13.5 A Randomized Block Design for the Air Traffic Controller Stress Test

		Treatments		
		System A	**System B**	**System C**
Blocks	**Controller 1**	15	15	18
	Controller 2	14	14	14
	Controller 3	10	11	15
	Controller 4	13	12	17
	Controller 5	16	13	16
	Controller 6	13	13	13

Table 13.6 Summary of Stress Data for the Air Traffic Controller Stress Test

		Treatments				
		System A	System B	System C	Row or Block Totals	Block Means
Blocks	Controller 1	15	15	18	48	$\bar{x}_{1\cdot} = 48/3 = 16.0$
	Controller 2	14	14	14	42	$\bar{x}_{2\cdot} = 42/3 = 14.0$
	Controller 3	10	11	15	36	$\bar{x}_{3\cdot} = 36/3 = 12.0$
	Controller 4	13	12	17	42	$\bar{x}_{4\cdot} = 42/3 = 14.0$
	Controller 5	16	13	16	45	$\bar{x}_{5\cdot} = 45/3 = 15.0$
	Controller 6	13	13	13	39	$\bar{x}_{6\cdot} = 39/3 = 13.0$
Column or Treatment Totals		81	78	93	252	$\bar{\bar{x}} = \frac{252}{18} = 14.0$
Treatment Means		$\bar{x}_{\cdot 1} = \frac{81}{6} = 13.5$	$\bar{x}_{\cdot 2} = \frac{78}{6} = 13.0$	$\bar{x}_{\cdot 3} = \frac{93}{6} = 15.5$		

ANOVA Procedure

The ANOVA procedure for the randomized block design requires us to partition the sum of squares total (SST) into three groups: sum of squares due to treatments (SSTR), sum of squares due to blocks (SSBL), and sum of squares due to error (SSE). The formula for this partitioning follows.

$$\text{SST} = \text{SSTR} + \text{SSBL} + \text{SSE} \qquad \textbf{(13.21)}$$

This sum of squares partition is summarized in the ANOVA table for the randomized block design as shown in Table 13.7. The notation used in the table is

$$k = \text{the number of treatments}$$
$$b = \text{the number of blocks}$$
$$n_T = \text{the total sample size } (n_T = kb)$$

Note that the ANOVA table also shows how the $n_T - 1$ total degrees of freedom are partitioned such that $k - 1$ degrees of freedom go to treatments, $b - 1$ go to blocks, and $(k - 1)(b - 1)$ go to the error term. The mean square column shows the sum of squares

Table 13.7 ANOVA Table for the Randomized Block Design with *k* Treatments and *b* Blocks

Source of Variation	Sum of Squares	Degrees of Freedom	Mean Square	*F*	*p*-Value
Treatments	SSTR	$k - 1$	$\text{MSTR} = \frac{\text{SSTR}}{k - 1}$	$\frac{\text{MSTR}}{\text{MSE}}$	
Blocks	SSBL	$b - 1$	$\text{MSBL} = \frac{\text{SSBL}}{b - 1}$		
Error	SSE	$(k - 1)(b - 1)$	$\text{MSE} = \frac{\text{SSE}}{(k - 1)(b - 1)}$		
Total	SST	$n_T - 1$			

divided by the degrees of freedom, and F = MSTR/MSE is the F ratio used to test for a significant difference among the treatment means. The primary contribution of the randomized block design is that, by including blocks, we remove the individual controller differences from the MSE term and obtain a more powerful test for the stress differences in the three workstation alternatives.

Computations and Conclusions

To compute the F statistic needed to test for a difference among treatment means with a randomized block design, we need to compute MSTR and MSE. To calculate these two mean squares, we must first compute SSTR and SSE; in doing so, we will also compute SSBL and SST. To simplify the presentation, we perform the calculations in four steps. In addition to k, b, and n_T as previously defined, the following notation is used.

x_{ij} = value of the observation corresponding to treatment j in block i
$\bar{x}_{\cdot j}$ = sample mean of the jth treatment
$\bar{x}_{i\cdot}$ = sample mean for the ith block
$\bar{\bar{x}}$ = overall sample mean

Step 1. Compute the total sum of squares (SST).

$$\text{SST} = \sum_{i=1}^{b}\sum_{j=1}^{k}(x_{ij} - \bar{\bar{x}})^2 \tag{13.22}$$

Step 2. Compute the sum of squares due to treatments (SSTR).

$$\text{SSTR} = b\sum_{j=1}^{k}(\bar{x}_{\cdot j} - \bar{\bar{x}})^2 \tag{13.23}$$

Step 3. Compute the sum of squares due to blocks (SSBL).

$$\text{SSBL} = k\sum_{i=1}^{b}(\bar{x}_{i\cdot} - \bar{\bar{x}})^2 \tag{13.24}$$

Step 4. Compute the sum of squares due to error (SSE).

$$\text{SSE} = \text{SST} - \text{SSTR} - \text{SSBL} \tag{13.25}$$

For the air traffic controller data in Table 13.6, these steps lead to the following sums of squares.

Step 1. $\text{SST} = (15 - 14)^2 + (15 - 14)^2 + (18 - 14)^2 + \cdots + (13 - 14)^2 = 70$
Step 2. $\text{SSTR} = 6[(13.5 - 14)^2 + (13.0 - 14)^2 + (15.5 - 14)^2] = 21$
Step 3. $\text{SSBL} = 3[(16 - 14)^2 + (14 - 14)^2 + (12 - 14)^2 + (14 - 14)^2 + (15 - 14)^2 + (13 - 14)^2] = 30$
Step 4. $\text{SSE} = 70 - 21 - 30 = 19$

These sums of squares divided by their degrees of freedom provide the corresponding mean square values shown in Table 13.8.

Table 13.8 ANOVA Table for the Air Traffic Controller Stress Test

Source of Variation	Sum of Squares	Degrees of Freedom	Mean Square	F	p-Value
Treatments	21	2	10.5	10.5/1.9 = 5.53	0.024
Blocks	30	5	6.0		
Error	19	10	1.9		
Total	70	17			

Let us use a level of significance $\alpha = 0.05$ to conduct the hypothesis test. The value of the test statistic is

$$F = \frac{\text{MSTR}}{\text{MSE}} = \frac{10.5}{1.9} = 5.53$$

The numerator degrees of freedom is $k - 1 = 3 - 1 = 2$ and the denominator degrees of freedom is $(k - 1)(b - 1) = (3 - 1)(6 - 1) = 10$. Because we will only reject the null hypothesis for large values of the test statistic, the p-value is the area under the F distribution to the right of $F = 5.53$. From Table 4 of Appendix B we find that with the degrees of freedom 2 and 10, $F = 5.53$ is between $F_{0.025} = 5.46$ and $F_{0.01} = 7.56$. As a result, the area in the upper tail, or the p-value, is between 0.01 and 0.025. Alternatively, we can use Excel to show that the p-value for $F = 5.53$ is 0.024. With p-value $\leq \alpha = 0.05$, we reject the null hypothesis H_0: $\mu_1 = \mu_2 = \mu_3$ and conclude that the population mean stress levels differ for the three workstation alternatives.

Some general comments can be made about the randomized block design. The experimental design described in this section is a *complete* block design; the word "complete" indicates that each block is subjected to all k treatments. That is, all controllers (blocks) were tested with all three systems (treatments). Experimental designs in which some but not all treatments are applied to each block are referred to as *incomplete* block designs. A discussion of incomplete block designs is beyond the scope of this text.

Because each controller in the air traffic controller stress test was required to use all three systems, this approach guarantees a complete block design. In some cases, however, blocking is carried out with "similar" experimental units in each block. For example, assume that in a pretest of air traffic controllers, the population of controllers was divided into groups ranging from extremely high-stress individuals to extremely low-stress individuals. The blocking could still be accomplished by having three controllers from each of the stress classifications participate in the study. Each block would then consist of three controllers in the same stress group. The randomized aspect of the block design would be the random assignment of the three controllers in each block to the three systems.

Finally, note that the ANOVA table shown in Table 13.7 provides an F value to test for treatment effects but *not* for blocks. The reason is that the experiment was designed to test a single factor—workstation design. The blocking based on individual stress differences was conducted to remove such variation from the MSE term. However, the study was not designed to test specifically for individual differences in stress.

Some analysts compute $F = \text{MSB/MSE}$ and use that statistic to test for significance of the blocks. Then they use the result as a guide to whether the same type of blocking would be desired in future experiments. However, if individual stress difference is to be a factor in the study, a different experimental design should be used. A test of significance on blocks should not be performed as a basis for a conclusion about a second factor.

Using Excel

Excel's Anova: Two-Factor Without Replication tool can be used to test whether the mean stress levels for air traffic controllers are the same for the three systems.

Enter/Access Data: Open the file *airtraffic*. The data are in cells B2:D7 and labels are in column A and cells B1:D1.

Apply Tools: The following steps describe how to use Excel's Anova: Two-Factor Without Replication tool to test the hypothesis that the mean stress level score is the same for all three systems.

Step 1. Click the **Data** tab on the Ribbon
Step 2. In the **Analyze** group, click **Data Analysis**

Step 3. Choose **Anova: Two-Factor Without Replication** from the list of Analysis Tools

Step 4. When the **Anova: Two-Factor Without Replication** dialog box appears (see Figure 13.7):

Enter *A1:D7* in the **Input Range:** box
Select the check box for **Labels**
Enter *0.05* in the **Alpha:** box
Select **Output Range:** in the **Output options** area
Enter *A9* in the **Output Range:** box (to identify the upper-left corner of the section of the worksheet where the output will appear)
Click **OK**

The output, titled Anova: Two-Factor Without Replication, appears in cells A9:G30 of the worksheet shown in Figure 13.8. Cells A11:E21 provide a summary of the data. The ANOVA table shown in cells A24:G30 is basically the same as the ANOVA table shown in Table 13.8. The label Rows corresponds to the blocks in the problem, and the label Columns corresponds to the treatments. The Excel output provides the *p*-value associated with the test as well as the critical *F* value.

We can use the *p*-value shown in cell F27, 0.0242, to make the hypothesis testing decision. Thus, at the $\alpha = 0.05$ level of significance, we reject H_0 because the *p*-value $= 0.0242 < \alpha = 0.05$. Hence, we conclude that the mean stress scores differ among the three systems.

Figure 13.7 Excel's ANOVA: Two-Factor without Replication Tool Dialog Box for the Air Traffic Controller Stress Test

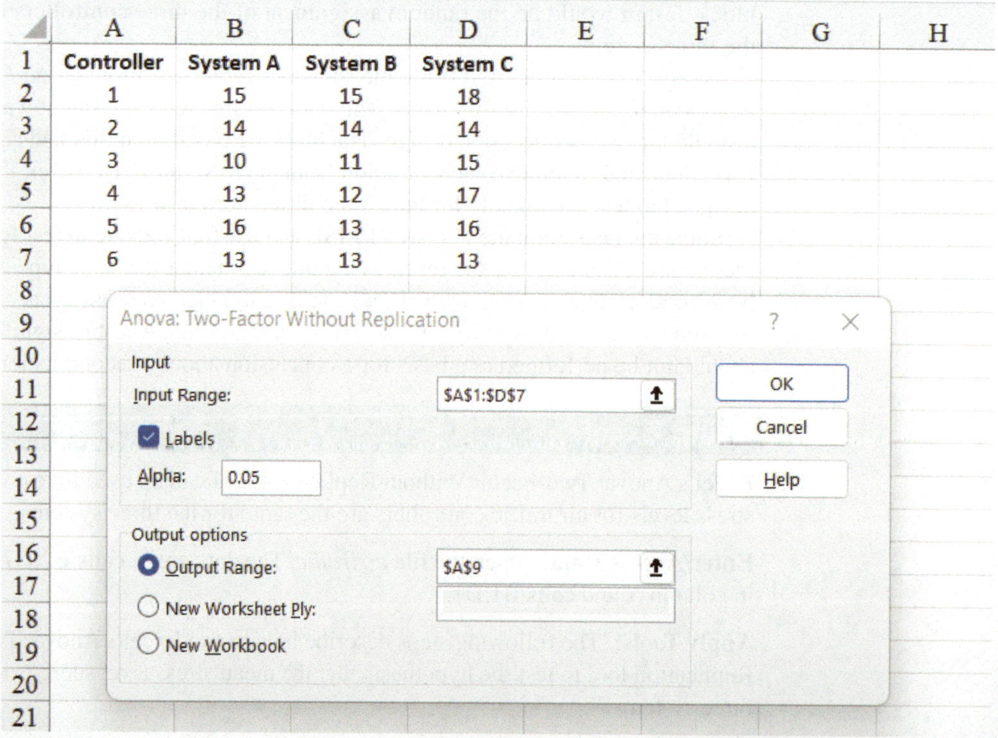

Source: Microsoft Corporation

Figure 13.8 Excel's ANOVA: Two-Factor without Replication Tool Output for the Air Traffic Controller Stress Test

	A	B	C	D	E	F	G	H
1	Controller	System A	System B	System C				
2	1	15	15	18				
3	2	14	14	14				
4	3	10	11	15				
5	4	13	12	17				
6	5	16	13	16				
7	6	13	13	13				
8								
9	Anova: Two-Factor Without Replication							
10								
11	*SUMMARY*	*Count*	*Sum*	*Average*	*Variance*			
12	1	3	48	16	3			
13	2	3	42	14	0			
14	3	3	36	12	7			
15	4	3	42	14	7			
16	5	3	45	15	3			
17	6	3	39	13	0			
18								
19	System A	6	81	13.5	4.3			
20	System B	6	78	13	2			
21	System C	6	93	15.5	3.5			
22								
23								
24	ANOVA							
25	*rce of Variat*	*SS*	*df*	*MS*	*F*	*P-value*	*F crit*	
26	Rows	30	5	6	3.1579	0.0574	3.3258	
27	Columns	21	2	10.5	5.5263	0.0242	4.1028	
28	Error	19	10	1.9				
29								
30	Total	70	17					

Note + Comment

The error degrees of freedom are less for a randomized block design than for a completely randomized design because $b - 1$ degrees of freedom are lost for the b blocks. If n is small, the potential effects due to blocks can be masked because of the loss of error degrees of freedom; for large n, the effects are minimized.

Exercises

Methods

21. Consider the experimental results for the following randomized block design. Make the calculations necessary to set up the analysis of variance table. **LO 6, 7**

		Treatments		
		A	B	C
Blocks	1	10	9	8
	2	12	6	5
	3	18	15	14
	4	20	18	18
	5	8	7	8

Use $\alpha = 0.05$ to test for any significant differences.

22. The following data were obtained for a randomized block design involving five treatments and three blocks: SST = 430, SSTR = 310, SSBL = 85. Set up the ANOVA table and test for any significant differences. Use $\alpha = 0.05$. **LO 6, 7**

23. An experiment has been conducted for four treatments with eight blocks. Complete the following analysis of variance table. **LO 6, 7**

Source of Variation	Sum of Squares	Degrees of Freedom	Mean Square	*F*
Treatments	900			
Blocks	400			
Error				
Total	1,800			

Use $\alpha = 0.05$ to test for any significant differences.

Applications

24. **Auto Tune-Ups.** An automobile dealer conducted a test to determine if the time in minutes needed to complete a minor engine tune-up depends on whether a computerized engine analyzer or an electronic analyzer is used. Because tune-up time varies among compact, intermediate, and full-sized cars, the three types of cars were used as blocks in the experiment. The data obtained follow. **LO 6, 7**

		Analyzer	
		Computerized	Electronic
Car	Compact	50	42
	Intermediate	55	44
	Full-sized	63	46

Use $\alpha = 0.05$ to test for any significant differences.

25. **Airfares on Travel Websites.** Are there differences in airfare depending on which travel agency website you utilize? The following data were collected on travel agency websites on July 9, 2018. The following table contains the prices in U.S. dollars for a one-way ticket between the cities listed on the left for each of the three travel agency websites. Here the pairs of cities are the blocks and the treatments are the different websites. Use $\alpha = 0.05$ to test for any significant differences in the mean price of a one-way airline ticket for the three travel agency websites. **LO 6, 7**

DATA*file* airfares

	Website		
Flight From–To	Expedia ($)	TripAdvisor ($)	Priceline ($)
Atlanta to Seattle	302	202	349
New York to Los Angeles	338	273	356
Cleveland to Orlando	53	50	58
Dallas to Indianapolis	177	190	177

26. **SAT Performance.** The Scholastic Aptitude Test (SAT) contains three parts: critical reading, mathematics, and writing. Each part is scored on an 800-point scale. Information on test scores for the 2009 version of the SAT is available at the College Board website. A sample of SAT scores for six students follows. LO 6, 7

DATA*file* satscores

Student	Critical Reading	Mathematics	Writing
1	526	534	530
2	594	590	586
3	465	464	445
4	561	566	553
5	436	478	430
6	430	458	420

a. Using a 0.05 level of significance, do students perform differently on the three portions of the SAT?
b. Which portion of the test seems to give the students the most trouble? Explain.

27. **Consumer Preferences.** In 2022, consumer goods giant Procter and Gamble (P&G) had more than 20 brands with more than $1 billion in annual sales (P&G website). How does a company like P&G create so many successful consumer products? P&G effectively invests in research and development to understand what consumers want. One method used to determine consumer preferences is called *conjoint analysis*. Conjoint analysis allows a company to ascertain the utility that a respondent in the conjoint study places on a design of a given product. The higher the utility, the more valuable a respondent finds the design. Suppose we have conducted a conjoint study and have the following estimated utilities (higher is preferred) for each of three different designs for a new whitening toothpaste. LO 6, 7

DATA*file* toothpaste

	Utilities		
Respondent	Design A	Design B	Design C
1	24.6	34.6	28.6
2	31.4	31.6	33.7
3	31.8	20.4	27.6
4	15.4	26.6	24.9
5	20.7	18.5	18.0
6	41.0	34.2	44.6
7	27.1	22.7	27.1
8	20.2	22.0	27.7
9	31.6	29.6	31.1
10	24.4	29.2	29.1

At the 0.05 level of significance, test for any significant differences.

13.5 Factorial Experiment

The experimental designs we have considered thus far enable us to draw statistical conclusions about one factor. However, in some experiments we want to draw conclusions about more than one variable or factor. A **factorial experiment** is an experimental design that allows simultaneous conclusions about two or more factors. The term *factorial* is used because the experimental conditions include all possible combinations of the factors. For example, for a levels of factor A and b levels of factor B, the experiment will involve collecting data on ab treatment combinations. In this section, we will show the analysis for a two-factor factorial experiment. The basic approach can be extended to experiments involving more than two factors.

As an illustration of a two-factor factorial experiment, we will consider a study involving the Graduate Management Admissions Test (GMAT), a standardized test used by graduate schools of business to evaluate an applicant's ability to pursue a graduate program in that field. Scores on the GMAT range from 200 to 800, with higher scores implying higher aptitude.

In an attempt to improve students' performance on the GMAT, a major Texas university is considering offering the following three GMAT preparation programs.

1. A three-hour review session covering the types of questions generally asked on the GMAT.
2. A one-day program covering relevant exam material, along with the taking and grading of a sample exam.
3. An intensive 10-week course involving the identification of each student's weaknesses and the setting up of individualized programs for improvement.

Hence, one factor in this study is the GMAT preparation program, which has three treatments: three-hour review, one-day program, and 10-week course. Before selecting the preparation program to adopt, further study will be conducted to determine how the proposed programs affect GMAT scores.

The GMAT is usually taken by students from three colleges: the College of Business, the College of Engineering, and the College of Arts and Sciences. Therefore, a second factor of interest in the experiment is whether a student's undergraduate college affects the GMAT score. This second factor, undergraduate college, also has three treatments: business, engineering, and arts and sciences. The factorial design for this experiment with three treatments corresponding to factor A, the preparation program, and three treatments corresponding to factor B, the undergraduate college, will have a total of $3 \times 3 = 9$ treatment combinations. These treatment combinations or experimental conditions are summarized in Table 13.9.

Assume that a sample of two students will be selected corresponding to each of the nine treatment combinations shown in Table 13.9: Two business students will take the three-hour review, two will take the one-day program, and two will take the 10-week course. In addition, two engineering students and two arts and sciences students will take each of the

Table 13.9 Nine Treatment Combinations for the Two-Factor GMAT Experiment

		Factor B: College		
		Business	**Engineering**	**Arts and Sciences**
Factor A: Preparation Program	**Three-hour review**	1	2	3
	One-day program	4	5	6
	10-week course	7	8	9

DATA*file*
gmatstudy

Table 13.10 GMAT Scores for the Two-Factor Experiment

		Factor B: College		
		Business	Engineering	Arts and Sciences
Factor A: Preparation Program	Three-hour review	500 580	540 460	480 400
	One-day program	460 540	560 620	420 480
	10-week course	560 600	600 580	480 410

three preparation programs. In experimental design terminology, the sample size of two for each treatment combination indicates that we have two **replications**. Additional replications and a larger sample size could easily be used, but we elect to minimize the computational aspects for this illustration.

This experimental design requires that six students who plan to attend graduate school be randomly selected from *each* of the three undergraduate colleges. Then, two students from each college should be assigned randomly to each preparation program, resulting in a total of 18 students being used in the study.

Let us assume that the randomly selected students participated in the preparation programs and then took the GMAT. The scores obtained are reported in Table 13.10.

The analysis of variance computations with the data in Table 13.10 will provide answers to the following questions.

- **Main effect (factor A):** Do the preparation programs differ in terms of effect on GMAT scores?
- **Main effect (factor B):** Do the undergraduate colleges differ in terms of effect on GMAT scores?
- **Interaction effect (factors A and B):** Do students in some colleges do better on one type of preparation program whereas others do better on a different type of preparation program?

The term **interaction** refers to a new effect that we can now study because we used a factorial experiment. If the interaction effect has a significant impact on the GMAT scores, we can conclude that the effect of the type of preparation program depends on the undergraduate college.

ANOVA Procedure

The ANOVA procedure for the two-factor factorial experiment requires us to partition the sum of squares total (SST) into four groups: sum of squares for factor A (SSA), sum of squares for factor B (SSB), sum of squares for interaction (SSAB), and sum of squares due to error (SSE). The formula for this partitioning follows.

$$\text{SST} = \text{SSA} + \text{SSB} + \text{SSAB} + \text{SSE} \tag{13.26}$$

The partitioning of the sum of squares and degrees of freedom is summarized in Table 13.11. The following notation is used.

a = number of levels of factor A
b = number of levels of factor B
r = number of replications
n_T = total number of observations taken in the experiment; $n_T = abr$

Table 13.11 ANOVA Table for the Two-Factor Factorial Experiment with r Replications

Source of Variation	Sum of Squares	Degrees of Freedom	Mean Square	F	p-Value
Factor A	SSA	$a - 1$	$\text{MSA} = \dfrac{\text{SSA}}{a-1}$	$\dfrac{\text{MSA}}{\text{MSE}}$	
Factor B	SSB	$b - 1$	$\text{MSB} = \dfrac{\text{SSB}}{b-1}$	$\dfrac{\text{MSB}}{\text{MSE}}$	
Interaction	SSAB	$(a-1)(b-1)$	$\text{MSAB} = \dfrac{\text{SSAB}}{(a-1)(b-1)}$	$\dfrac{\text{MSAB}}{\text{MSE}}$	
Error	SSE	$ab(r-1)$	$\text{MSE} = \dfrac{\text{SSE}}{ab(r-1)}$		
Total	SST	$n_T - 1$			

Computations and Conclusions

To compute the F statistics needed to test for the significance of factor A, factor B, and interaction, we need to compute MSA, MSB, MSAB, and MSE. To calculate these four mean squares, we must first compute SSA, SSB, SSAB, and SSE; in doing so, we will also compute SST. To simplify the presentation, we perform the calculations in five steps. In addition to a, b, r, and n_T as previously defined, the following notation is used.

x_{ijk} = observation corresponding to the kth replicate taken from treatment i of factor A and treatment j of factor B

$\bar{x}_{i\cdot}$ = sample mean for the observations in treatment i (factor A)

$\bar{x}_{\cdot j}$ = sample mean for the observations in treatment j (factor B)

$\bar{x}_{ij}$ = sample mean for the observations corresponding to the combination of treatment i (factor A) and treatment j (factor B)

$\bar{\bar{x}}$ = overall sample mean of all n_T observations

Step 1. Compute the total sum of squares.

$$\text{SST} = \sum_{i=1}^{a}\sum_{j=1}^{b}\sum_{k=1}^{r}(x_{ijk} - \bar{\bar{x}})^2 \tag{13.27}$$

Step 2. Compute the sum of squares for factor A.

$$\text{SSA} = br\sum_{i=1}^{a}(\bar{x}_{i\cdot} - \bar{\bar{x}})^2 \tag{13.28}$$

Step 3. Compute the sum of squares for factor B.

$$\text{SSB} = ar\sum_{j=1}^{b}(\bar{x}_{\cdot j} - \bar{\bar{x}})^2 \tag{13.29}$$

Step 4. Compute the sum of squares for interaction.

$$\text{SSAB} = r\sum_{i=1}^{a}\sum_{j=1}^{b}(\bar{x}_{ij} - \bar{x}_{i\cdot} - \bar{x}_{\cdot j} + \bar{\bar{x}})^2 \tag{13.30}$$

Step 5. Compute the sum of squares due to error.

$$\text{SSE} = \text{SST} - \text{SSA} - \text{SSB} - \text{SSAB} \quad \textbf{(13.31)}$$

Table 13.12 reports the data collected in the experiment and the various sums that will help us with the sum of squares computations. Using equations (13.27) through (13.31), we calculate the following sums of squares for the GMAT two-factor factorial experiment.

Step 1. $\text{SST} = (500 - 515)^2 + (580 - 515)^2 + (540 - 515)^2 + \cdots + (410 - 515)^2 = 82{,}450$

Step 2. $\text{SSA} = (3)(2)[(493.33 - 515)^2 + (513.33 - 515)^2 + (538.33 - 515)^2] = 6{,}100$

Step 3. $\text{SSB} = (3)(2)[(540 - 515)^2 + (560 - 515)^2 + (445 - 515)^2] = 45{,}300$

Step 4. $\text{SSAB} = 2[(540 - 493.33 - 540 + 515)^2 + (500 - 493.33 - 560 + 515)^2 + \cdots + (445 - 538.33 - 445 + 515)^2] = 11{,}200$

Step 5. $\text{SSE} = 82{,}450 - 6{,}100 - 45{,}300 - 11{,}200 = 19{,}850$

These sums of squares divided by their corresponding degrees of freedom provide the following mean square values for testing the two main effects (preparation program and undergraduate college) and interaction effect.

Factor A: $\text{MSA} = \dfrac{\text{SSA}}{a - 1} = \dfrac{6{,}100}{3 - 1} = 3{,}050$

Factor B: $\text{MSB} = \dfrac{\text{SSB}}{b - 1} = \dfrac{45{,}300}{3 - 1} = 22{,}650$

Interaction: $\text{MSAB} = \dfrac{\text{SSAB}}{(a - 1)(b - 1)} = \dfrac{11{,}200}{(3 - 1)(3 - 1)} = 2{,}800$

Error: $\text{MSE} = \dfrac{\text{SSE}}{ab(r - 1)} = \dfrac{19{,}850}{(3)(3)(2 - 1)} = 2205.5556$

Excel's F.DIST.RT function makes it easy to compute the p-value for each F value. For example, for factor A, p-value = F.DIST.RT(1.3829,2,9) = 0.2994.

Let us use a level of significance of $\alpha = 0.05$ to conduct the hypothesis tests for the two-factor GMAT study. The F ratio used to test for differences among preparation programs (factor A) is $F = \text{MSA/MSE} = 3{,}050/2{,}205.5556 = 1.3829$. We can use Excel to show that the p-value corresponding to $F = 1.3829$ is 0.2994. Because the p-value $> \alpha = 0.05$, we cannot reject the null hypothesis and must conclude that there is no significant difference among the three preparation programs. However, for the undergraduate college (factor B) effect, the p-value corresponding to $F = \text{MSB/MSE} = 22{,}650/2{,}205.5556 = 10.2695$ is 0.0048. Hence, the analysis of variance results enable us to conclude that the GMAT test scores do differ among the three undergraduate colleges; that is, the three undergraduate colleges do not provide the same preparation for performance on the GMAT. Finally, the interaction F value of $F = \text{MSAB/MSE} = 2{,}800/2{,}205.5556 = 1.2695$ and its corresponding p-value of 0.3503 mean we cannot identify a significant interaction effect. Therefore, we have no reason to believe that the three preparation programs differ in their ability to prepare students from the different colleges for the GMAT. The ANOVA table shown in Table 13.13 provides a summary of these results for the two-factor GMAT study.

Undergraduate college was found to be a significant factor. Checking the calculations in Table 13.12, we see that the sample means are business students $\bar{x}_{0.1} = 540$, engineering students $\bar{x}_{0.2} = 560$, and arts and sciences students $\bar{x}_{0.3} = 445$. Tests on individual treatment means can be conducted; yet after reviewing the three sample means, we would anticipate no difference in preparation for business and engineering graduates. However, the arts and sciences students appear to be significantly less prepared for the GMAT than students in the other colleges. Perhaps this observation will lead the university to consider other options for assisting these students in preparing for graduate management admission tests.

Table 13.12 GMAT Summary Data for the Two-Factor Experiment

		Factor B: College				
	Treatment combination totals	Business	Engineering	Arts and Sciences	Row Totals	Factor A Means
Factor A: Preparation Program	Three-hour review	500 580 1,080 $\bar{x}_{11} = \frac{1,080}{2} = 540$	540 460 1,000 $\bar{x}_{12} = \frac{1,000}{2} = 500$	480 400 880 $\bar{x}_{13} = \frac{880}{2} = 440$	2,960	$\bar{x}_{1\cdot} = \frac{2,960}{6} = 493.33$
	One-day program	460 540 1,000 $\bar{x}_{21} = \frac{1,000}{2} = 500$	560 620 1,180 $\bar{x}_{22} = \frac{1,180}{2} = 590$	420 480 900 $\bar{x}_{23} = \frac{900}{2} = 450$	3,080	$\bar{x}_{2\cdot} = \frac{3,080}{6} = 513.33$
	10-week course	560 600 1,160 $\bar{x}_{31} = \frac{1,160}{2} = 580$	600 580 1,180 $\bar{x}_{32} = \frac{1,180}{2} = 590$	480 410 890 $\bar{x}_{33} = \frac{890}{2} = 445$	3,230	$\bar{x}_{3\cdot} = \frac{3,230}{6} = 538.33$
	Column Totals	3,240	3,360	2,670	9,270 ← Overall total	
	Factor B Means	$\bar{x}_{\cdot 1} = \frac{3,240}{6} = 540$	$\bar{x}_{\cdot 2} = \frac{3,360}{6} = 560$	$\bar{x}_{\cdot 3} = \frac{2,670}{6} = 445$	$\bar{\bar{x}} = \frac{9,270}{18} = 515$	

Table 13.13 ANOVA Table for the Two-Factor GMAT Study

Source of Variation	Sum of Squares	Degrees of Freedom	Mean Square	*F*	*p*-Value
Factor A	6,100	2	3,050	3,050/2,205.5556 = 1.3829	0.2994
Factor B	45,300	2	22,650	22,650/2,205.5556 = 10.2695	0.0048
Interaction	11,200	4	2,800	2,800/2,205.5556 = 1.2695	0.3503
Error	19,850	9	2,205.5556		
Total	82,450	17			

Using Excel

Excel's Anova: Two-Factor With Replication tool can be used to analyze the data for the two-factor GMAT experiment. Refer to Figures 13.9 and 13.10 as we describe the tasks involved.

Enter/Access Data: Open the file *gmatstudy*. The data are in cells B2:D7 and labels are in cells A2:A7 and A1:D1.

Figure 13.9 Excel's ANOVA: Two-Factor with Replication Tool Output for the GMAT Experiment

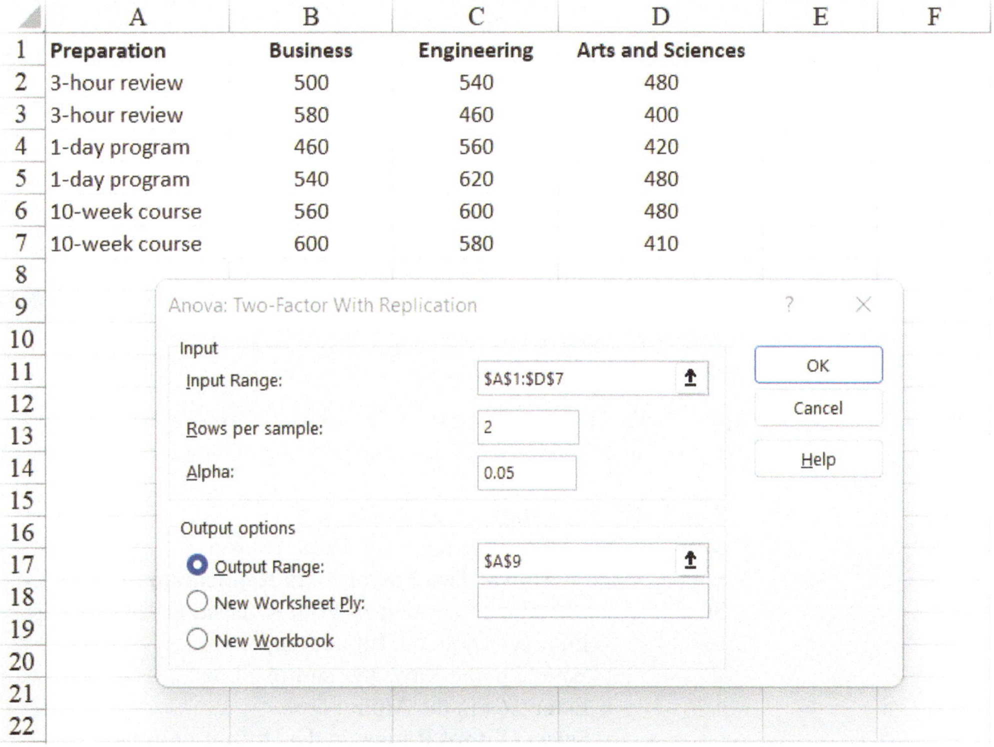

Source: Microsoft Corporation

Figure 13.10 Excel's ANOVA: Two-Factor with Replication Tool Output for the GMAT Experiment

	A	B	C	D	E	F	G	H
1	**Preparation**	**Business**	**Engineering**	**Arts and Sciences**				
2	3-hour review	500	540	480				
3	3-hour review	580	460	400				
4	1-day program	460	560	420				
5	1-day program	540	620	480				
6	10-week course	560	600	480				
7	10-week course	600	580	410				
8								
9	Anova: Two-Factor With Replication							
10								
11	SUMMARY	Business	Engineering	Arts and Sciences	Total			
12	*3-hour review*							
13	Count	2	2	2	6			
14	Sum	1080	1000	880	2960			
15	Average	540	500	440	493.3333			
16	Variance	3200	3200	3200	3946.6667			
17								
18	*1-day program*							
19	Count	2	2	2	6			
20	Sum	1000	1180	900	3080			
21	Average	500	590	450	513.3333			
22	Variance	3200	1800	1800	5386.6667			
23								
24	*10-week course*							
25	Count	2	2	2	6			
26	Sum	1160	1180	890	3230			
27	Average	580	590	445	538.3333			
28	Variance	800	200	2450	5936.6667			
29								
30	*Total*							
31	Count	6	6	6				
32	Sum	3240	3360	2670				
33	Average	540	560	445				
34	Variance	2720	3200	1510				
35								
36								
37	ANOVA							
38	*Source of Variation*	*SS*	*df*	*MS*	*F*	*P-value*	*F crit*	
39	Sample	6100	2	3050	1.3829	0.2994	4.2565	
40	Columns	45300	2	22650	10.2695	0.0048	4.2565	
41	Interaction	11200	4	2800	1.2695	0.3503	3.6331	
42	Within	19850	9	2205.555556				
43								
44	Total	82450	17					
45								
46								

Apply Tools: The following steps describe how Excel's Anova: Two-Factor With Replication tool can be used to analyze the data for the two-factor GMAT experiment.

Step 1. Click the **Data** tab on the Ribbon
Step 2. In the **Analyze** group, click **Data Analysis**
Step 3. Choose **Anova: Two-Factor With Replication** from the list of Analysis Tools
Step 4. When the **Anova: Two-Factor With Replication** dialog box appears (see Figure 13.9),
Enter *A1:D7* in the **Input Range:** box
Enter *2* in the **Rows per sample:** box
Enter *0.05* in the **Alpha:** box
Select **Output Range:** in the **Output options** area

Enter *A9* in the **Output Range:** box (to identify the upper-left corner of the section of the worksheet where the output will appear)
Click **OK**

The output, titled Anova: Two-Factor With Replication, appears in cells A9:G44 of the worksheet shown in Figure 13.10. Cells A11:E34 provide a summary of the data. The ANOVA table, shown in cells A37:G44, is basically the same as the ANOVA table shown in Table 13.13. The label Sample corresponds to factor A, the label Columns corresponds to factor B, and the label Within corresponds to error. The Excel output provides the p-value associated with each F test as well as the critical F values.

We can use the p-value of 0.2994 in cell F39 to make the hypothesis testing decision for factor A (Preparation Program). At the $\alpha = 0.05$ level of significance, we cannot reject H_0 because the p-value $= 0.2994 > \alpha = 0.05$. We can make the hypothesis testing decision for factor B (College) by using the p-value of 0.0048 shown in cell F40. At the $\alpha = 0.05$ level of significance, we reject H_0 because the p-value $= 0.0048 < \alpha = 0.05$. Finally, the interaction p-value of 0.3503 in cell F41 means that we cannot identify a significant interaction effect.

Exercises

Methods

28. A factorial experiment involving two levels of factor A and three levels of factor B resulted in the following data.

		Factor B		
		Level 1	Level 2	Level 3
Factor A	Level 1	135 165	90 66	75 93
	Level 2	125 95	127 105	120 136

Test for any significant main effects and any interaction. Use $\alpha = 0.05$. **LO 8, 9**

29. The calculations for a factorial experiment involving four levels of factor A, three levels of factor B, and three replications resulted in the following data: SST = 280, SSA = 26, SSB = 23, SSAB = 175. Set up the ANOVA table and test for any significant main effects and any interaction effect. Use $\alpha = 0.05$. **LO 8, 9**

Applications

30. **Mobile App Website Design.** Based on a 2018 study, the average elapsed time between when a user navigates to a website on a mobile device until its main content is available was 14.6 seconds. This is more than a 20% increase from 2017 (*searchenginejournal.com*). Responsiveness is certainly an important feature of any website and is perhaps even more important on a mobile device. What other web design factors need to be considered for a mobile device to make it more user friendly? Among other things, navigation menu placement and amount of text entry required are important on a mobile device. The following data provide the time (in seconds), it took randomly selected students (two for each factor combination), to perform a prespecified task with the different combinations of navigation menu placement and amount of text entry required. **LO 8, 9**

DATA*file*
mobileapps

		Amount of Text Entry Required	
		Low	High
Navigation Menu Position	Right	8	12
		12	8
	Middle	22	36
		14	20
	Left	10	18
		18	14

Use the ANOVA procedure for factorial designs to test for any significant effects resulting from navigation menu position and amount of text entry required. Use $\alpha = 0.05$. **LO 8, 9**

31. **Amusement Park Queues.** An amusement park studied methods for decreasing the waiting time (minutes) for rides by loading and unloading riders more efficiently. Two alternative loading/unloading methods have been proposed. To account for potential differences due to the type of ride and the possible interaction between the method of loading and unloading and the type of ride, a factorial experiment was designed. Use the following data to test for any significant effect due to the loading and unloading method, the type of ride, and interaction. Use $\alpha = 0.05$. **LO 8, 9**

	Type of Ride		
	Roller Coaster	Screaming Demon	Log Flume
Method 1	41	52	50
	43	44	46
Method 2	49	50	48
	51	46	44

32. **Auto Fuel Efficiency.** As part of a study designed to compare hybrid and similarly equipped conventional vehicles, *Consumer Reports* tested a variety of classes of hybrid and all-gas model cars and sport utility vehicles (SUVs). The following data show the miles-per-gallon rating *Consumer Reports* obtained for two hybrid small cars, two hybrid midsize cars, two hybrid small SUVs, and two hybrid midsize SUVs; also shown are the miles per gallon obtained for eight similarly equipped conventional models. **LO 8, 9**

DATA*file*
hybridtest

Make/Model	Class	Type	MPG
Honda Civic	Small Car	Hybrid	37
Honda Civic	Small Car	Conventional	28
Toyota Prius	Small Car	Hybrid	44
Toyota Corolla	Small Car	Conventional	32
Chevrolet Malibu	Midsize Car	Hybrid	27
Chevrolet Malibu	Midsize Car	Conventional	23
Nissan Altima	Midsize Car	Hybrid	32
Nissan Altima	Midsize Car	Conventional	25
Ford Escape	Small SUV	Hybrid	27
Ford Escape	Small SUV	Conventional	21
Saturn Vue	Small SUV	Hybrid	28
Saturn Vue	Small SUV	Conventional	22
Lexus RX	Midsize SUV	Hybrid	23
Lexus RX	Midsize SUV	Conventional	19
Toyota Highlander	Midsize SUV	Hybrid	24
Toyota Highlander	Midsize SUV	Conventional	18

At the $\alpha = 0.05$ level of significance, test for significant effects due to class, type, and interaction.

33. **Tax Research.** A study reported in *The Accounting Review* examined the separate and joint effects of two levels of time pressure (low and moderate) and three levels of knowledge (naive, declarative, and procedural) on key word selection behavior in tax research. Subjects were given a tax case containing a set of facts, a tax issue, and a key word index consisting of 1,336 key words. They were asked to select the key words they believed would refer them to a tax authority relevant to resolving the tax case. Prior to the experiment, a group of tax experts determined that the text contained 19 relevant key words. Subjects in the naive group had little or no declarative or procedural knowledge, subjects in the declarative group had significant declarative knowledge but little or no procedural knowledge, and subjects in the procedural group had significant declarative knowledge and procedural knowledge. Declarative knowledge consists of knowledge of both the applicable tax rules and the technical terms used to describe such rules. Procedural knowledge is knowledge of the rules that guide the tax researcher's search for relevant key words. Subjects in the low time pressure situation were told they had 25 minutes to complete the problem, an amount of time which should be "more than adequate" to complete the case; subjects in the moderate time pressure situation were told they would have "only" 11 minutes to complete the case. Suppose 25 subjects were selected for each of the six treatment combinations and the sample means for each treatment combination are as follows (standard deviations are in parentheses). **LO 8, 9**

		Knowledge		
		Naive	Declarative	Procedural
Time Pressure	Low	1.13 (1.12)	1.56 (1.33)	2.00 (1.54)
	Moderate	0.48 (0.80)	1.68 (1.36)	2.86 (1.80)

Use the ANOVA procedure to test for any significant differences due to time pressure, knowledge, and interaction. Use a 0.05 level of significance. Assume that the total sum of squares for this experiment is 327.50.

Summary

In this chapter, we showed how analysis of variance can be used to test for differences among means of several populations or treatments. We introduced the completely randomized design, the randomized block design, and the two-factor factorial experiment. The completely randomized design and the randomized block design are used to draw conclusions about differences in the means of a single factor. The primary purpose of blocking in the randomized block design is to remove extraneous sources of variation from the error term. Such blocking provides a better estimate of the true error variance and a better test to determine whether the population or treatment means of the factor differ significantly.

We showed that the basis for the statistical tests used in analysis of variance and experimental design is the development of two independent estimates of the population variance σ^2. In the single-factor case, one estimator is based on the variation between the treatments; this estimator provides an unbiased estimate of σ^2 only if the means $\mu_1, \mu_2, \ldots, \mu_k$ are all equal. A second estimator of σ^2 is based on the variation of the observations within each sample; this estimator will always provide an unbiased estimate of σ^2. By computing the ratio of these two estimators (the F statistic) we developed a rejection rule for determining whether to reject the null hypothesis that the population or treatment means are equal. In all the experimental designs considered, the partitioning of the sum of squares and degrees of freedom into their various sources enabled us to compute the appropriate values for the analysis of variance calculations and tests. We also showed how Fisher's LSD procedure and the Bonferroni adjustment can be used to perform pairwise comparisons to determine which means are different.

Glossary

ANOVA table A table used to summarize the analysis of variance computations and results. It contains columns showing the source of variation, the sum of squares, the degrees of freedom, the mean square, the F value(s), and the p-value(s).

Blocking The process of using the same or similar experimental units for all treatments. The purpose of blocking is to remove a source of variation from the error term and hence provide a more powerful test for a difference in population or treatment means.

Comparison-wise Type I error rate The probability of a Type I error associated with a single pairwise comparison.

Completely randomized design An experimental design in which the treatments are randomly assigned to the experimental units.

Experimental statistical study A study in which the investigator controls the values of one or more variables believed to be related to the outcome of interest, and then measures and records the outcome. The investigator's control over the values of variables believed to be related to the outcome of interest allows for possible conclusions about whether any of the manipulated variables might have a cause-and-effect relationship with the outcome.

Experimental units The objects of interest in the experiment.

Experiment-wise Type I error rate The probability of making a Type I error on at least one of several pairwise comparisons.

Factor Another word for the independent variable of interest.

Factorial experiment An experimental design that allows simultaneous conclusions about two or more factors.

Interaction The effect produced when the levels of one factor interact with the levels of another factor in influencing the response variable.

Multiple comparison procedures Statistical procedures that can be used to conduct statistical comparisons between pairs of population means.

Observational study A study in which the investigator observes the outcome of interest and possibly values of one or more variables believed to be related to the outcome without controlling the values of any variables, and then measures and records the outcome. The investigator's lack of control over the values of variables believed to be related to the outcome of interest allows only for possible conclusions about associations between the outcome and the variables.

Partitioning The process of allocating the total sum of squares and degrees of freedom to the various components.

Randomized block design An experimental design employing blocking.

Replications The number of times each experimental condition is repeated in an experiment.

Response variable Another word for the dependent variable of interest.

Single-factor experiment An experiment involving only one factor with k populations or treatments.

Treatments The different levels of a factor.

Key Formulas

Completely Randomized Design

Sample Mean for Treatment *j*

$$\bar{x}_j = \frac{\sum_{i=1}^{n_j} x_{ij}}{n_j} \tag{13.1}$$

Sample Variance for Treatment *j*

$$s_j^2 = \frac{\sum_{i=1}^{n_j} (x_{ij} - \bar{x}_j)^2}{n_j - 1} \tag{13.2}$$

Overall Sample Mean

$$\bar{\bar{x}} = \frac{\sum_{j=1}^{k} \sum_{i=1}^{n_j} x_{ij}}{n_T} \tag{13.3}$$

$$n_T = n_1 + n_2 + \cdots + n_k \tag{13.4}$$

Mean Square Due to Treatments

$$\text{MSTR} = \frac{\text{SSTR}}{k - 1} \tag{13.7}$$

Sum of Squares Due to Treatments

$$\text{SSTR} = \sum_{j=1}^{k} n_j(\bar{x}_j - \bar{\bar{x}})^2 \tag{13.8}$$

Mean Square Due to Error

$$\text{MSE} = \frac{\text{SSE}}{n_T - k} \tag{13.10}$$

Sum of Squares Due to Error

$$\text{SSE} = \sum_{j=1}^{k} (n_j - 1)s_j^2 \tag{13.11}$$

Test Statistic for the Equality of *k* Population Means

$$F = \frac{\text{MSTR}}{\text{MSE}} \tag{13.12}$$

Total Sum of Squares

$$\text{SST} = \sum_{j=1}^{k} \sum_{i=1}^{n_j} (x_{ij} - \bar{\bar{x}})^2 \tag{13.13}$$

Partitioning of Sum of Squares

$$\text{SST} = \text{SSTR} + \text{SSE} \tag{13.14}$$

Multiple Comparison Procedures

Test Statistic for Fisher's LSD Procedure

$$t = \frac{\bar{x}_i - \bar{x}_j}{\sqrt{\text{MSE}\left(\frac{1}{n_i} + \frac{1}{n_j}\right)}} \tag{13.16}$$

Fisher's LSD

$$\text{LSD} = t_{\alpha/2}\sqrt{\text{MSE}\left(\frac{1}{n_i} + \frac{1}{n_j}\right)} \tag{13.17}$$

Randomized Block Design

Total Sum of Squares

$$\text{SST} = \sum_{i=1}^{b}\sum_{j=1}^{k}(x_{ij} - \bar{\bar{x}})^2 \tag{13.22}$$

Sum of Squares Due to Treatments

$$\text{SSTR} = b\sum_{j=1}^{k}(\bar{x}_{\cdot j} - \bar{\bar{x}})^2 \tag{13.23}$$

Sum of Squares Due to Blocks

$$\text{SSBL} = k\sum_{i=1}^{b}(\bar{x}_{i\cdot} - \bar{\bar{x}})^2 \tag{13.24}$$

Sum of Squares Due to Error

$$\text{SSE} = \text{SST} - \text{SSTR} - \text{SSBL} \tag{13.25}$$

Factorial Experiment

Total Sum of Squares

$$\text{SST} = \sum_{i=1}^{a}\sum_{j=1}^{b}\sum_{k=1}^{r}(x_{ijk} - \bar{\bar{x}})^2 \tag{13.27}$$

Sum of Squares for Factor A

$$\text{SSA} = br\sum_{i=1}^{a}(\bar{x}_{i\cdot} - \bar{\bar{x}})^2 \tag{13.28}$$

Sum of Squares for Factor B

$$\text{SSB} = ar\sum_{j=1}^{b}(\bar{x}_{\cdot j} - \bar{\bar{x}})^2 \tag{13.29}$$

Sum of Squares for Interaction

$$\text{SSAB} = r\sum_{i=1}^{a}\sum_{j=1}^{b}(\bar{x}_{ij} - \bar{x}_{i\cdot} - \bar{x}_{\cdot j} + \bar{\bar{x}})^2 \tag{13.30}$$

Sum of Squares for Error

$$\text{SSE} = \text{SST} - \text{SSA} - \text{SSB} - \text{SSAB} \tag{13.31}$$

Supplementary Exercises

34. **Paper Towel Absorption.** In a completely randomized experimental design, three brands of paper towels were tested for their ability to absorb water. Equal-size towels were used, with four sections of towels tested per brand. The absorbency rating data follow. At a 0.05 level of significance, does there appear to be a difference in the ability of the brands to absorb water? **LO 1, 3**

	Brand	
x	y	z
91	99	83
100	96	88
88	94	89
89	99	76

35. **Job Satisfaction.** A study reported in the *Journal of Small Business Management* concluded that self-employed individuals do not experience higher job satisfaction than individuals who are not self-employed. In this study, job satisfaction is measured using 18 items, each of which is rated using a Likert-type scale with 1–5 response options ranging from strong agreement to strong disagreement. A higher score on this scale indicates a higher degree of job satisfaction. The sum of the ratings for the 18 items, ranging from 18 to 90, is used as the measure of job satisfaction. Suppose that this approach was used to measure the job satisfaction for lawyers, physical therapists, cabinetmakers, and systems analysts. The results obtained for a sample of 10 individuals from each profession follow. **LO 1, 3**

DATA*file*
satisjob

Lawyer	Physical Therapist	Cabinetmaker	Systems Analyst
44	55	54	44
42	78	65	73
74	80	79	71
42	86	69	60
53	60	79	64
50	59	64	66
45	62	59	41
48	52	78	55
64	55	84	76
38	50	60	62

At the $\alpha = 0.05$ level of significance, test for any difference in the job satisfaction among the four professions.

36. **Monitoring Air Pollution.** The U.S. Environmental Protection Agency (EPA) monitors levels of pollutants in the air for cities across the country. Ozone pollution levels are measured using a 500-point scale; lower scores indicate little health risk, and higher scores indicate greater health risk. The following data show the peak levels of ozone pollution in four cities (Birmingham, Alabama; Memphis, Tennessee; Little Rock, Arkansas; and Jackson, Mississippi) for 10 dates. **LO 6, 7**

DATA*file*
ozonelevels

	City			
Date	Birmingham AL	Memphis TN	Little Rock AR	Jackson MS
Jan 9	18	20	18	14
Jan17	23	31	22	30
Jan 18	19	25	22	21
Jan 31	29	36	28	35
Feb 1	27	31	28	24
Feb 6	26	31	31	25
Feb 14	31	24	19	25
Feb 17	31	31	28	28
Feb 20	33	35	35	34
Feb 29	20	42	42	21

Use $\alpha = 0.05$ to test for any significant difference in the mean peak ozone levels among the four cities.

DATA*file*
unemployment

37. **Regional Unemployment.** The file *unemployment* contains unemployment rates for a sample of metropolitan areas in four regions of the country (Northeast, Midwest, South, and West). The rates are for the month of October 2021 (U.S. Bureau of Labor Statistics). Use $\alpha = 0.05$ to test whether the unemployment rate is the same in all four regions. **LO 1, 3**

38. **Assembly Methods.** Three different assembly methods have been proposed for a new product. A completely randomized experimental design was chosen to determine which assembly method results in the greatest number of parts produced per hour, and 30 workers were randomly selected and assigned to use one of the proposed methods. The number of units produced by each worker follows. **LO 1, 3**

DATA*file*
assembly

Method		
A	B	C
97	93	99
73	100	94
93	93	87
100	55	66
73	77	59
91	91	75
100	85	84
86	73	72
92	90	88
95	83	86

Use these data and test to see whether the mean number of parts produced is the same with each method. Use $\alpha = 0.05$.

39. **Technology Company Regulation.** A 2021 Pew Research study showed that 56% of U.S. citizens believe that major technology companies should be more regulated than they are currently. Suppose we have the following sample data by political affiliation, where a higher number means that the person feels more strongly that more regulation is warranted. **LO 3, 4**

DATA*file*
techregulation

Republican	Independent	Democrat
4	6	5
5	3	7
6	5	5
3	4	7
3	3	4
4	6	6
5	5	5
4	5	7

a. Use $\alpha = 0.05$ to test for differences in the belief that more regulation of major technology companies is warranted for the three different political affiliations.
b. Use Fisher's LSD procedure to compare the belief that a person's job will be auto mated for Republicans and Independents.

40. **Fuel Efficiency of Gasoline Brands.** A research firm tests the miles-per-gallon characteristics of three brands of gasoline. Because of different gasoline performance

characteristics in different brands of automobiles, five brands of automobiles are selected and treated as blocks in the experiment; that is, each brand of automobile is tested with each type of gasoline. The results of the experiment (in miles per gallon) follow. **LO 1, 3, 6, 7**

		Gasoline Brands		
		I	II	III
Automobiles	A	18	21	20
	B	24	26	27
	C	30	29	34
	D	22	25	24
	E	20	23	24

a. At $\alpha = 0.05$, is there a significant difference in the mean miles-per-gallon characteristics of the three brands of gasoline?

b. Analyze the experimental data using the ANOVA procedure for completely randomized designs. Compare your findings with those obtained in part (a). What is the advantage of attempting to remove the block effect?

41. **Late-Night Talk Show Viewership.** *Jimmy Kimmel Live!* on ABC, *The Tonight Show Starring Jimmy Fallon* on NBC, and *The Late Show with Stephen Colbert* on CBS are three popular late-night talk shows. The following table shows the number of viewers in millions for a 10-week period during the spring for each of these shows (*TV by the Numbers* website). **LO 6, 7**

DATA*file*
talkshows

Week	*Jimmy Kimmel Live* (ABC)	*The Tonight Show Starring Jimmy Fallon* (NBC)	*The Late Show with Stephen Colbert* (CBS)
June 13–June 17	2.67	3.24	2.27
June 6–June 10	2.58	3.32	2.05
May 30–June 3	2.64	2.66	2.08
May 23–May 27	2.47	3.30	2.07
May 16–May 20	1.97	3.10	2.31
May 9–May 16	2.21	3.31	2.45
May 2–May 6	2.12	3.20	2.57
April 25–April 29	2.24	3.15	2.45
April 18–April 22	2.10	2.77	2.56
April 11–April 15	2.21	3.24	2.16

At the 0.05 level of significance, test for a difference in the mean number of viewers per week for the three late-night talk shows.

42. **Golf Club Design.** A major manufacturer of golf equipment is considering three designs for a new driver: Design A, Design B, and Design C. Each design differs slightly in terms of the material used to construct the driver's head and shaft. The company would like to know if there is any difference in the overall driving distance for the three designs. Twelve PGA Tour players who represent the company were asked to test each model. After a warmup period, each player hit a drive with one of the new designs in a randomly selected order, and the overall distance (in yards) was recorded. The results follow. **LO 6, 7**

DATA*file*
clubhead

Design A	Design B	Design C
306	323	320
279	313	289
293	318	314
277	288	282
281	286	287
272	312	283
297	326	332
271	306	284
279	325	294
323	319	289
301	307	293

At the 0.05 level of significance, test whether the mean driving distance is the same for the three designs.

43. **Language Translation.** A factorial experiment was designed to test for any significant differences in the time needed to perform English to foreign language translations with two computerized language translators. Because the type of language translated was also considered a significant factor, translations were made with both systems for three different languages: Spanish, French, and German. Use the following data for translation time in hours. **LO 8, 9**

	Language		
	Spanish	French	German
System 1	8 12	10 14	12 16
System 2	6 10	14 16	16 22

Test for any significant differences due to language translator, type of language, and interaction. Use $\alpha = 0.05$.

44. **Defective Parts.** A manufacturing company designed a factorial experiment to determine whether the number of defective parts produced by two machines differed and if the number of defective parts produced also depended on whether the raw material needed by each machine was loaded manually or by an automatic feed system. The following data give the numbers of defective parts produced. Use $\alpha = 0.05$ to test for any significant effect due to machine, loading system, and interaction. **LO 8, 9**

	Loading System	
	Manual	Automatic
Machine 1	30 34	30 26
Machine 2	20 22	24 28

Case Problem 1: Wentworth Medical Center

As part of a long-term study of individuals 65 years of age or older, sociologists and physicians at the Wentworth Medical Center in upstate New York investigated the relationship between geographic location and depression. A sample of 60 individuals, all in reasonably good health, was selected; 20 individuals were residents of Florida, 20 were residents of New York, and 20 were residents of North Carolina. Each of the individuals sampled was given a standardized test to measure depression. The data collected follow; higher test scores indicate higher levels of depression. These data are contained in the file *medical1*.

A second part of the study considered the relationship between geographic location and depression for individuals 65 years of age or older who had a chronic health condition such as arthritis, hypertension, and/or heart ailment. A sample of 60 individuals with such conditions was identified. Again, 20 were residents of Florida, 20 were residents of New York, and 20 were residents of North Carolina. The levels of depression recorded for this study follow. These data are contained in the file *medical2*. **LO 1, 2, 3**

DATA*file* medical1

DATA*file* medical2

Data from medical1			Data from medical2		
Florida	New York	North Carolina	Florida	New York	North Carolina
3	8	10	13	14	10
7	11	7	12	9	12
7	9	3	17	15	15
3	7	5	17	12	18
8	8	11	20	16	12
8	7	8	21	24	14
8	8	4	16	18	17
5	4	3	14	14	8
5	13	7	13	15	14
2	10	8	17	17	16
6	6	8	12	20	18
2	8	7	9	11	17
6	12	3	12	23	19
6	8	9	15	19	15
9	6	8	16	17	13
7	8	12	15	14	14
5	5	6	13	9	11
4	7	3	10	14	12
7	7	8	11	13	13
3	8	11	17	11	11

Managerial Report

1. Use descriptive statistics to summarize the data from the two studies. What are your preliminary observations about the depression scores?
2. Use analysis of variance on both data sets. State the hypotheses being tested in each case. What are your conclusions?
3. Use inferences about individual treatment means where appropriate. What are your conclusions?

Case Problem 2: Compensation for Sales Professionals

Suppose that a local chapter of sales professionals in the greater San Francisco area conducted a survey of its membership to study the relationship, if any, between the years of experience and salary for individuals employed in inside and outside sales positions. On the survey, respondents were asked to specify one of three levels of years of experience: low (1–10 years), medium (11–20 years), and high (21 or more years). A portion of the data obtained follows. The complete data set, consisting of 120 observations, is contained in the file *salessalary*. **LO 1, 3, 8, 9**

DATA*file*
salesalary

Observation	Salary $	Position	Experience
1	53,938	Inside	Medium
2	52,694	Inside	Medium
3	70,515	Outside	Low
4	52,031	Inside	Medium
5	62,283	Outside	Low
6	57,718	Inside	Low
7	79,081	Outside	High
8	48,621	Inside	Low
9	72,835	Outside	High
10	54,768	Inside	Medium
.	.	.	.
.	.	.	.
.	.	.	.
115	58,080	Inside	High
116	78,702	Outside	Medium
117	83,131	Outside	Medium
118	57,788	Inside	High
119	53,070	Inside	Medium
120	60,259	Outside	Low

Managerial Report

1. Use descriptive statistics to summarize the data.
2. Develop a 95% confidence interval estimate of the mean annual salary for all salespersons, regardless of years of experience and type of position.
3. Develop a 95% confidence interval estimate of the mean salary for inside salespersons.
4. Develop a 95% confidence interval estimate of the mean salary for outside salespersons.
5. Use analysis of variance to test for any significant differences due to position. Use a 0.05 level of significance, and for now, ignore the effect of years of experience.
6. Use analysis of variance to test for any significant differences due to years of experience. Use a 0.05 level of significance, and for now, ignore the effect of position.
7. At the 0.05 level of significance test for any significant differences due to position, years of experience, and interaction.

Case Problem 3: TourisTopia Travel

TourisTopia Travel (Triple T) is an online travel agency that specializes in trips to exotic locations around the world for groups of ten or more travelers. Triple T's marketing manager has been working on a major revision of the homepage of Triple T's website. The content for the homepage has been selected and the only remaining decisions involve the selection of the background color (white, green, or pink) and the type of font (Arial, Calibri, or Tahoma).

Triple T's IT group has designed prototype homepages featuring every combination of these background colors and fonts, and it has implemented computer code that will randomly direct each Triple T website visitor to one of these prototype homepages. For three weeks, the prototype homepage to which each visitor was directed and the amount of time in seconds spent at Triple T's website during each visit were recorded. Ten visitors to each of the prototype homepages were then selected randomly; the complete data set for these visitors is available in the file *touristopia*.

DATA*file*
touristopia

Triple T wants to use these data to determine if the time spent by visitors to Triple T's website differs by background color or font. It would also like to know if the time spent by visitors to the Triple T website differs by different combinations of background color and font. **LO 8, 9**

Managerial Report

Prepare a managerial report that addresses the following issues.

1. Use descriptive statistics to summarize the data from Triple T's study. Based on descriptive statistics, what are your preliminary conclusions about whether the time spent by visitors to the Triple T website differs by background color or font? What are your preliminary conclusions about whether time spent by visitors to the Triple T website differs by different combinations of background color and font?
2. Has Triple T used an observational study or a controlled experiment? Explain.
3. Use the data from Triple T's study to test the hypothesis that the time spent by visitors to the Triple T website is equal for the three background colors. Include both factors and their interaction in the ANOVA model, and use $\alpha = 0.05$.
4. Use the data from Triple T's study to test the hypothesis that the time spent by visitors to the Triple T website is equal for the three fonts. Include both factors and their interaction in the ANOVA model, and use $\alpha = 0.05$.
5. Use the data from Triple T's study to test the hypothesis that time spent by visitors to the Triple T website is equal for the nine combinations of background color and font. Include both factors and their interaction in the ANOVA model, and use $\alpha = 0.05$.
6. Do the results of your analysis of the data provide evidence that the time spent by visitors to the Triple T website differs by background color, font, or combination of background color and font? What is your recommendation?

Chapter 14

Simple Linear Regression

Contents

Statistics in Practice:
Walmart.com

14.1 Simple Linear Regression Model
Regression Model and Regression Equation
Estimated Regression Equation

14.2 Least Squares Method
Using Excel to Construct a Scatter Diagram, Display the Estimated Regression Line, and Display the Estimated Regression Equation

14.3 Coefficient of Determination
Using Excel to Compute the Coefficient of Determination
Correlation Coefficient

14.4 Model Assumptions

14.5 Testing for Significance
Estimate of σ^2
t Test
Confidence Interval for β_1
F Test
Some Cautions About the Interpretation of Significance Tests

14.6 Using the Estimated Regression Equation for Estimation and Prediction
Interval Estimation
Confidence Interval for the Mean Value of *y*
Prediction Interval for an Individual Value of *y*

14.7 Excel's Regression Tool
Using Excel's Regression Tool for the Armand's Pizza Parlors Example
Interpretation of Estimated Regression Equation Output
Interpretation of ANOVA Output
Interpretation of Regression Statistics Output

14.8 Residual Analysis: Validating Model Assumptions
Residual Plot Against *x*
Residual Plot Against $\hat{y}$
Standardized Residuals
Using Excel to Construct a Residual Plot
Normal Probability Plot

14.9 Outliers and Influential Observations
Detecting Outliers
Detecting Influential Observations

14.10 Practical Advice: Big Data and Hypothesis Testing in Simple Linear Regression

Summary 691
Glossary 691
Key Formulas 692
Supplementary Exercises 694
Case Problem 1: Measuring Stock Market Risk 704
Case Problem 2: U.S. Department of Transportation 705
Case Problem 3: Selecting a Point-and-Shoot Digital Camera 705
Case Problem 4: Finding the Best Car Value 707
Case Problem 5: Buckeye Creek Amusement Park 708

Appendixes
Appendix 14.1: Calculus-Based Derivation of Least Squares Formulas 709
Appendix 14.2: A Test for Significance Using Correlation 710

Available in the Cengage eBook:
Appendix: Simple Linear Regression with R

Learning Objectives

After completing this chapter, you will be able to

LO 1 Develop an equation that estimates how two variables are related based on sample data.

LO 2 Use a simple linear egression equation to predict the value of the dependent variable for a given value of the independent variable.

LO 3 Provide an interpretation of the intercept and slope of an estimated simple linear regression equation.

LO 4 Compute and interpret the coefficient of determination.

LO 5 Compute and interpret the sample correlation coefficient.

LO 6 Use the *t* test to assess the significance in a simple linear regression.

LO 7 Calculate the ANOVA table and use the *F* test to assess the significance in a simple linear regression.

LO 8 Develop a confidence interval for the mean value of the dependent variable *y* given a specific value of *x*.

LO 9 Develop a prediction interval for an individual value of the dependent variable *y* given a specific value of *x*.

LO 10 Use a residual plot to assess whether the assumptions of simple linear regression are valid.

LO 11 Use residual analysis to identify outliers and influential observations.

Statistics in Practice

Walmart.com*

Bentonville, Arkansas

With more than 10,000 stores across the globe, Walmart is the world's largest retailer. In response to increasing online shopping, Walmart launched its Internet site Walmart.com. To serve its online customers, Walmart created a network of distribution centers in the United States. One of these distribution centers, located in Carrollton, Georgia, was selected as the site for a study on how Walmart might better manage its packaging for online orders.

In its peak shipping season (November to December), the Walmart distribution center in Carrollton ships over 100,000 packages per day. The cost of fulfilling an order includes the material cost (the cost of the carton and packing material—paper that fills the empty space when the product is smaller than the volume of the box), labor for handling, and the shipping cost. The study conducted in Carrollton, called the Carton-mix Optimization Study, had as its objective to determine the number and size of cartons to have on hand for shipping Walmart's products to its online customers that would minimize raw material, labor, and shipping costs.

A number of constraints limited the possibilities for the variety of cartons to have on hand. For example, management provided a minimum and maximum carton size. In addition, for boxes automatically constructed (as opposed to manually built), a line would be limited to one size carton.

As with any study of this type, data had to be collected to build a cost model that could then be used to find the optimal carton mix. The material costs for existing cartons were known, but what about the cost of a carton in a size that is not currently used? Based on price quotes from its carton suppliers for a variety of sizes, a simple linear regression model was used to estimate the cost of any size carton based on its volume. The following model was used to estimate the material cost of a carton in dollars per carton (*y*) based

*Source: Based on S. Ahire, M. Malhotra, and J. Jensen, "Carton-Mix Optimization for Walmart.com Distribution Centers," *Interfaces*, Vol. 45, No. 4, July–August 2015, pp. 341–357.

on the volume of the carton measured in cubic inches per carton (x):

$$y = -0.11 + 0.0014x$$

For example, for a carton with volume of 2,800 cubic inches, we have $-0.11 + 0.0014(2{,}800) = 3.81$. Therefore, the estimated material cost for a carton of 2,800 cubic inches in volume is $3.81.

The simple linear regression model was imbedded into an optimization algorithm in Microsoft Excel to provide Walmart managers a recommendation on the optimal mix of carton sizes to carry at its Carrollton distribution center. The optimization model, based on this regression, provided documented savings of $600,000 in its first year of implementation. The model was later deployed across Walmart's other distribution centers with an estimated annual savings of $2 million.

In this chapter, we will study how to estimate a simple linear regression model, that is, a linear model in which a single variable is used to estimate the value of another variable.

Managerial decisions often are based on the relationship between two or more variables. For example, after considering the relationship between advertising expenditures and sales, a marketing manager might attempt to predict sales for a given level of advertising expenditures. In another case, a public utility might use the relationship between the daily high temperature and the demand for electricity to predict electricity usage on the basis of next month's anticipated daily high temperatures. Sometimes a manager will rely on intuition to judge how two variables are related. However, if data can be obtained, a statistical procedure called *regression analysis* can be used to develop an equation showing how the variables are related.

The statistical methods used in studying the relationship between two variables were first employed by Sir Francis Galton (1822–1911). Galton was interested in studying the relationship between a father's height and the son's height. Galton's disciple, Karl Pearson (1857–1936), analyzed the relationship between the father's height and the son's height for 1,078 pairs of subjects.

In regression terminology, the variable being predicted is called the **dependent variable**. The variable or variables being used to predict the value of the dependent variable are called the **independent variables**. For example, in analyzing the effect of advertising expenditures on sales, a marketing manager's desire to predict sales would suggest making sales the dependent variable. Advertising expenditure would be the independent variable used to help predict sales. In statistical notation, y denotes the dependent variable and x denotes the independent variable.

In this chapter, we consider the simplest type of regression analysis involving one independent variable and one dependent variable in which the relationship between the variables is approximated by a straight line. It is called **simple linear regression**. Regression analysis involving two or more independent variables is called multiple regression analysis; multiple regression and cases involving curvilinear relationships are covered in Chapters 15 and 16.

14.1 Simple Linear Regression Model

Armand's Pizza Parlors is a chain of Italian-food restaurants located in a five-state area. Armand's most successful locations are near college campuses. The managers believe that quarterly sales for these restaurants (denoted by y) are related positively to the size of the student population (denoted by x); that is, restaurants near campuses with a large student population tend to generate more sales than those located near campuses with a small student population. Using regression analysis, we can develop an equation showing how the dependent variable y is related to the independent variable x.

Regression Model and Regression Equation

In the Armand's Pizza Parlors example, the population consists of all the Armand's restaurants. For every restaurant in the population, there is a value of x (student population) and a corresponding value of y (quarterly sales). The equation that describes how y is related to x and an error term is called the **regression model**. The regression model used in simple linear regression follows.

Simple Linear Regression Model

$$y = \beta_0 + \beta_1 x + \epsilon \qquad \textbf{(14.1)}$$

β_0 and β_1 are referred to as the parameters of the model, and ϵ (the Greek letter epsilon) is a random variable referred to as the error term. The error term accounts for the variability in y that cannot be explained by the linear relationship between x and y.

The population of all Armand's restaurants can also be viewed as a collection of subpopulations, one for each distinct value of x. For example, one subpopulation consists of all Armand's restaurants located near college campuses with 8,000 students; another subpopulation consists of all Armand's restaurants located near college campuses with 9,000 students; and so on. Each subpopulation has a corresponding distribution of y values. Thus, a distribution of y values is associated with restaurants located near campuses with 8,000 students; a distribution of y values is associated with restaurants located near campuses with 9,000 students; and so on. Each distribution of y values has its own mean or expected value. The equation that describes how the expected value of y, denoted $E(y)$, is related to x is called the **regression equation**. The regression equation for simple linear regression follows.

Simple Linear Regression Equation

$$E(y) = \beta_0 + \beta_1 x \qquad \textbf{(14.2)}$$

The graph of the simple linear regression equation is a straight line; β_0 is the y-intercept of the regression line, β_1 is the slope, and $E(y)$ is the mean or expected value of y for a given value of x.

Examples of possible regression lines are shown in Figure 14.1. The regression line in Panel A shows that the mean value of y is related positively to x, with larger values of $E(y)$ associated with larger values of x. The regression line in Panel B shows the mean value of y is related negatively to x, with smaller values of $E(y)$ associated with larger values of x.

Figure 14.1 Possible Regression Lines in Simple Linear Regression

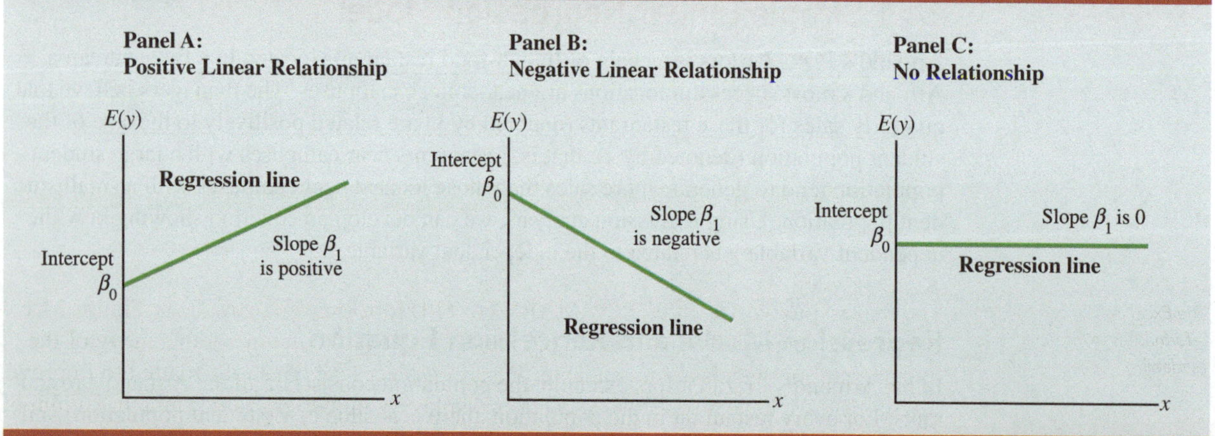

The regression line in Panel C shows the case in which the mean value of y is not related to x; that is, the mean value of y is the same for every value of x.

Estimated Regression Equation

If the values of the population parameters β_0 and β_1 were known, we could use equation (14.2) to compute the mean value of y for a given value of x. In practice, the parameter values are not known and must be estimated using sample data. Sample statistics (denoted b_0 and b_1) are computed as estimates of the population parameters β_0 and β_1. Substituting the values of the sample statistics b_0 and b_1 for β_0 and β_1 in the regression equation, we obtain the **estimated regression equation**. The estimated regression equation for simple linear regression follows.

Estimated Simple Linear Regression Equation

$$\hat{y} = b_0 + b_1 x \tag{14.3}$$

Figure 14.2 provides a summary of the estimation process for simple linear regression.

The graph of the estimated simple linear regression equation is called the *estimated regression line*; b_0 is the y-intercept and b_1 is the slope. In the next section, we show how the least squares method can be used to compute the values of b_0 and b_1 in the estimated regression equation.

The value of $\hat{y}$ provides both a point estimate of $E(y)$ for a given value of x and a prediction of an individual value of y for a given value of x.

In general, $\hat{y}$ is the point estimator of $E(y)$, the mean value of y for a given value of x. Thus, to estimate the mean or expected value of quarterly sales for all restaurants located near campuses with 10,000 students, Armand's would substitute the value of 10,000 for x in equation (14.3). In some cases, however, Armand's may be more interested in predicting sales for one particular restaurant. For example, suppose Armand's would like to

The estimation of β_0 and β_1 is a statistical process much like the estimation of μ discussed in Chapter 7. β_0 and β_1 are the unknown parameters of interest, and b_0 and b_1 are the sample statistics used to estimate the parameters.

Figure 14.2 The Estimation Process in Simple Linear Regression

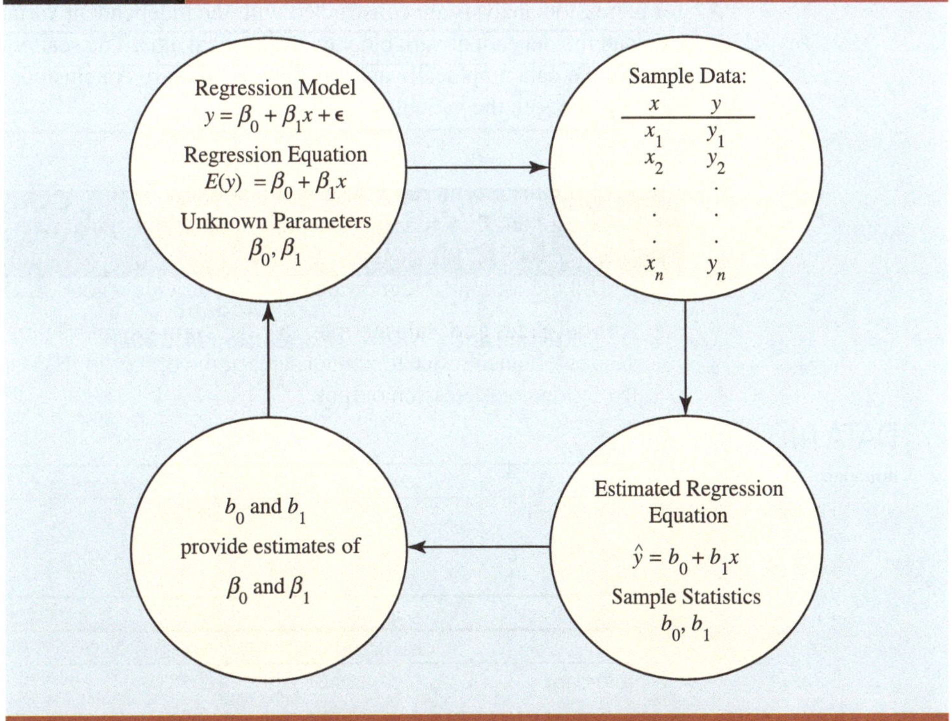

predict quarterly sales for the restaurant they are considering building near Talbot College, a school with 10,000 students. As it turns out, the best predictor of y for a given value of x is also provided by $\hat{y}$. Thus, to predict quarterly sales for the restaurant located near Talbot College, Armand's would also substitute the value of 10,000 for x in equation (14.3).

Notes + Comments

1. Regression analysis cannot be interpreted as a procedure for establishing a cause-and-effect relationship between variables. It can only indicate how or to what extent variables are associated with each other. Any conclusions about cause and effect must be based upon the judgment of those individuals most knowledgeable about the application.
2. The regression equation in simple linear regression is $E(y) = \beta_0 + \beta_1 x$. More advanced texts in regression analysis often write the regression equation as $E(y \mid x) = \beta_0 + \beta_1 x$ to emphasize that the regression equation provides the mean value of y for a given value of x.

14.2 Least Squares Method

In simple linear regression, each observation consists of two values: one for the independent variable and one for the dependent variable.

The **least squares method** is a procedure for using sample data to find the estimated regression equation. To illustrate the least squares method, suppose data were collected from a sample of 10 Armand's Pizza Parlor restaurants located near college campuses. For the ith observation or restaurant in the sample, x_i is the size of the student population (in thousands) and y_i is the quarterly sales (in thousands of dollars). The values of x_i and y_i for the 10 restaurants in the sample are summarized in Table 14.1. We see that restaurant 1, with $x_1 = 2$ and $y_1 = 58$, is near a campus with 2,000 students and has quarterly sales of \$58,000. Restaurant 2, with $x_2 = 6$ and $y_2 = 105$, is near a campus with 6,000 students and has quarterly sales of \$105,000. The largest sales value is for restaurant 10, which is near a campus with 26,000 students and has quarterly sales of \$202,000.

Figure 14.3 is a scatter diagram of the data in Table 14.1. Student population is shown on the horizontal axis and quarterly sales is shown on the vertical axis. **Scatter diagrams** for regression analysis are constructed with the independent variable x on the horizontal axis and the dependent variable y on the vertical axis. The scatter diagram enables us to observe the data graphically and to draw preliminary conclusions about the possible relationship between the variables.

DATA*file*
armands

Table 14.1 Student Population and Quarterly Sales Data for 10 Armand's Pizza Parlors

Restaurant i	Student Population (1,000s) x_i	Quarterly Sales ($1,000s) y_i
1	2	58
2	6	105
3	8	88
4	8	118
5	12	117
6	16	137
7	20	157
8	20	169
9	22	149
10	26	202

Figure 14.3 Scatter Diagram of Student Population and Quarterly Sales for Armand's Pizza Parlors

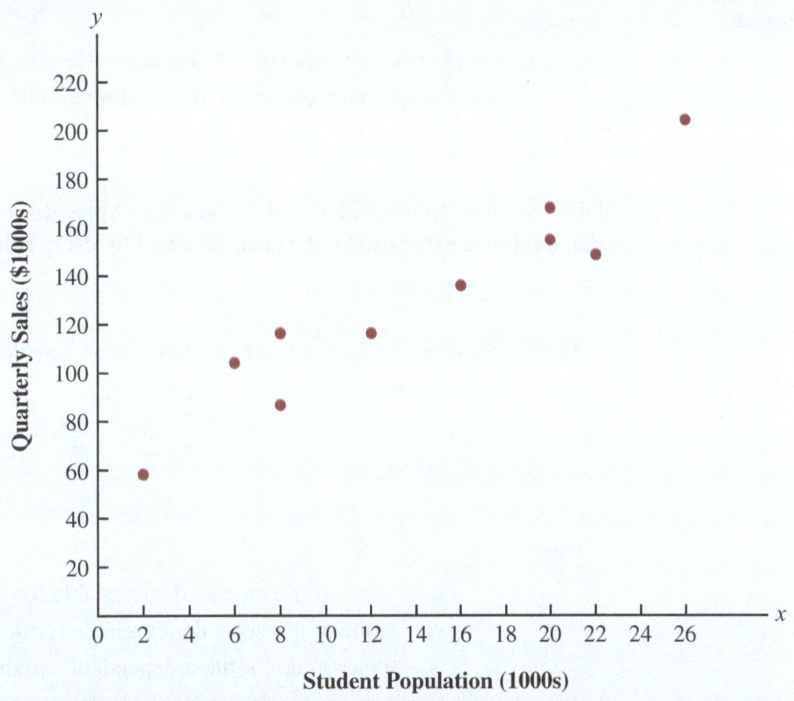

What preliminary conclusions can be drawn from Figure 14.3? Quarterly sales appear to be higher at campuses with larger student populations. In addition, for these data the relationship between the size of the student population and quarterly sales appears to be approximated by a straight line; indeed, a positive linear relationship is indicated between x and y. We therefore choose the simple linear regression model to represent the relationship between quarterly sales and student population. Given that choice, our next task is to use the sample data in Table 14.1 to determine the values of b_0 and b_1 in the estimated simple linear regression equation. For the ith restaurant, the estimated regression equation provides

$$\hat{y}_i = b_0 + b_1 x_i \tag{14.4}$$

where

$\hat{y}_i$ = predicted value of quarterly sales ($1,000s) for the ith restaurant
b_0 = y-intercept of the estimated regression line
b_1 = slope of the estimated regression line
x_i = size of the student population (1,000s) for the ith restaurant

With y_i denoting the observed (actual) sales for restaurant i and $\hat{y}_i$ in equation (14.4) representing the predicted value of sales for restaurant i, every restaurant in the sample will have an observed value of sales y_i and a predicted value of sales $\hat{y}_i$. For the estimated regression line to provide a good fit to the data, we want the differences between the observed sales values and the predicted sales values to be small.

The least squares method uses the sample data to provide the values of b_0 and b_1 that minimize the *sum of the squares of the deviations* between the observed values of the dependent variable y_i and the predicted values of the dependent variable $\hat{y}_i$. The criterion for the least squares method is given by expression (14.5).

Carl Friedrich Gauss (1777–1855) proposed the least squares method.

Least Squares Criterion

$$\min \sum (y_i - \hat{y}_i)^2 \tag{14.5}$$

where

y_i = observed value of the dependent variable for the ith observation
$\hat{y}_i$ = predicted value of the dependent variable for the ith observation

Differential calculus can be used to show (see Appendix 14.1) that the values of b_0 and b_1 that minimize expression (14.5) can be found by using equations (14.6) and (14.7).

Slope and y-Intercept for the Estimated Regression Equation[1]

$$b_1 = \frac{\sum (x_i - \bar{x})(y_i - \bar{y})}{\sum (x_i - \bar{x})^2} \tag{14.6}$$

$$b_0 = \bar{y} - b_1\bar{x} \tag{14.7}$$

where

x_i = value of the independent variable for the ith observation
y_i = value of the dependent variable for the ith observation
$\bar{x}$ = mean value for the independent variable
$\bar{y}$ = mean value for the dependent variable
n = total number of observations

Some of the calculations necessary to develop the least squares estimated regression equation for Armand's Pizza Parlors are shown in Table 14.2. With the sample of 10 restaurants, we have $n = 10$ observations. Because equations (14.6) and (14.7) require $\bar{x}$ and $\bar{y}$ we begin the calculations by computing $\bar{x}$ and $\bar{y}$.

$$\bar{x} = \frac{\sum x_i}{n} = \frac{140}{10} = 14$$

$$\bar{y} = \frac{\sum y_i}{n} = \frac{1{,}300}{10} = 130$$

Using equations (14.6) and (14.7) and the information in Table 14.2, we can compute the slope and intercept of the estimated regression equation for Armand's Pizza Parlors. The calculation of the slope (b_1) proceeds as follows:

$$\begin{aligned} b_1 &= \frac{\sum (x_i - \bar{x})(y_i - \bar{y})}{\sum (x_i - \bar{x})^2} \\ &= \frac{2{,}840}{568} \\ &= 5 \end{aligned}$$

[1]An alternate formula for b_1 is

$$b_1 = \frac{\sum x_i y_i - (\sum x_i \sum y_i)/n}{\sum x_i^2 - (\sum x_i)^2/n}$$

This form of equation (14.6) is often recommended when using a calculator to compute b_1.

Table 14.2 Calculations for the Least Squares Estimated Regression Equation for Armand's Pizza Parlors

Restaurant i	x_i	y_i	$x_i - \bar{x}$	$y_i - \bar{y}$	$(x_i - \bar{x})(y_i - \bar{y})$	$(x_i - \bar{x})^2$
1	2	58	−12	−72	864	144
2	6	105	−8	−25	200	64
3	8	88	−6	−42	252	36
4	8	118	−6	−12	72	36
5	12	117	−2	−13	26	4
6	16	137	2	7	14	4
7	20	157	6	27	162	36
8	20	169	6	39	234	36
9	22	149	8	19	152	64
10	26	202	12	72	864	144
Totals	140	1,300			2,840	568
	Σx_i	Σy_i			$\Sigma(x_i - \bar{x})(y_i - \bar{y})$	$\Sigma(x_i - \bar{x})^2$

The calculation of the y-intercept (b_0) follows.

$$b_0 = \bar{y} - b_1\bar{x}$$
$$= 130 - 5(14)$$
$$= 60$$

Thus, the estimated regression equation is

$$\hat{y} = 60 + 5x$$

Figure 14.4 shows the graph of this equation on the scatter diagram.

Figure 14.4 Graph of the Estimated Regression Equation for Armand's Pizza Parlors: $\hat{y} = 60 + 5x$

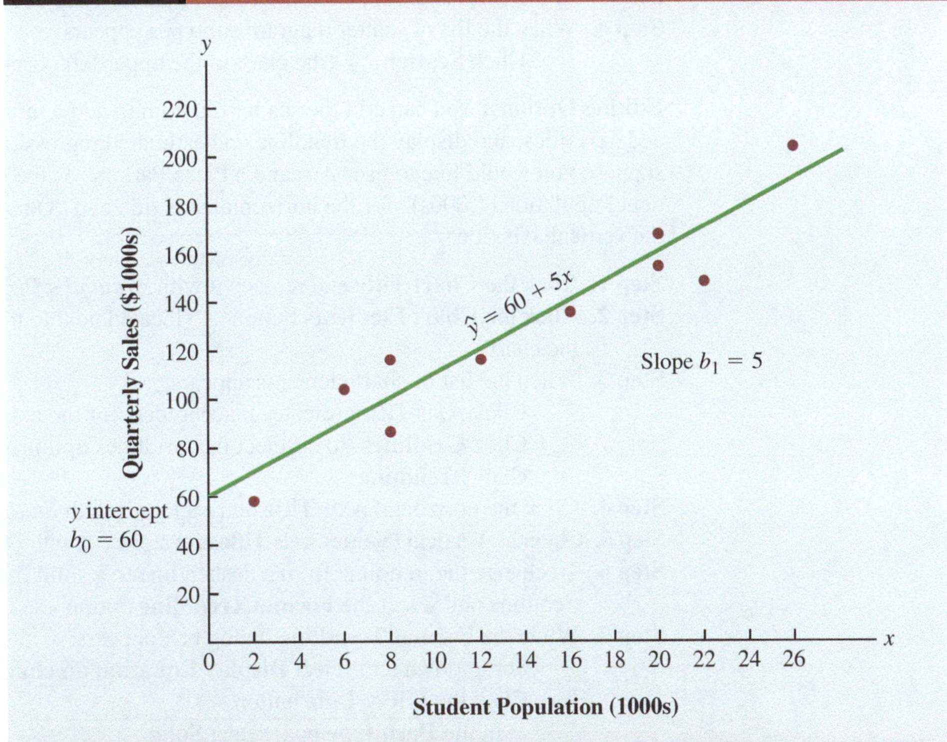

The slope of the estimated regression equation ($b_1 = 5$) is positive, implying that as student population increases, sales increase. In fact, we can conclude (based on sales measured in $1,000s and student population in 1,000s) that an increase in the student population of 1,000 is associated with an increase of $5,000 in expected sales; that is, quarterly sales are expected to increase by $5 per student.

If we believe the least squares estimated regression equation adequately describes the relationship between x and y, it would seem reasonable to use the estimated regression equation to predict the value of y for a given value of x. For example, if we wanted to predict quarterly sales for a restaurant to be located near a campus with 16,000 students, we would compute

Using the estimated regression equation to make predictions outside the range of the values of the independent variable should be done with caution because outside that range we cannot be sure that the same relationship is valid.

$$\hat{y} = 60 + 5(16) = 140$$

Hence, we would predict quarterly sales of $140,000 for this restaurant. In the following sections we will discuss methods for assessing the appropriateness of using the estimated regression equation for estimation and prediction.

Using Excel to Construct a Scatter Diagram, Display the Estimated Regression Line, and Display the Estimated Regression Equation

We can use Excel to construct a scatter diagram, display the estimated regression line, and display the estimated regression equation for the Armand's Pizza Parlors data appearing in Table 14.1. Refer to Figure 14.5 as we describe the tasks involved.

Enter/Access Data: Open the file *armands*. The data are in cells B2:C11 and labels appear in column A and cells B1:C1.

Apply Tools: The following steps describe how to construct a scatter diagram from the data in the worksheet.

Step 1. Select cells B2:C11
Step 2. Click the **Insert** tab on the Ribbon
Step 3. In the **Charts** group, click the **Insert Scatter (X,Y) or Bubble Chart**
Step 4. When the list of scatter diagram subtypes appears:
Click **Scatter** (the chart in the upper left corner)

Editing Options: You can edit the scatter diagram to add a more descriptive chart title, add axis titles, and display the trendline and estimated regression equation. For instance, suppose you would like to use "Armand's Pizza Parlors" as the chart title and insert "Student Population (1,000s)" for the horizontal axis title and "Quarterly Sales ($1,000s)" for the vertical axis title.

Step 1. Click the **Chart Title** and replace it with *Armand's Pizza Parlors*
Step 2. Click the **Chart Elements** button + (located next to the top-right corner of the chart)
Step 3. When the list of chart elements appears:
Click **Axis Titles** (creates placeholders for the axis titles)
Click **Gridlines** (to deselect the Gridlines option)
Click **Trendline**
Step 4. Click the horizontal **Axis Title** and replace it with *Student Population (1,000s)*
Step 5. Click the **Vertical (Value) Axis Title** and replace it with *Quarterly Sales ($1,000s)*
Step 6. To change the trendline from a dashed line to a solid line, right-click on the trendline and select the **Format Trendline** option
Step 7. When the **Format Trendline** dialog box appears:
Scroll down and select **Display Equation on chart**
Click the **Fill & Line** button
In the **Dash type** box, select **Solid**
Close the **Format Trendline** dialog box

Figure 14.5 Scatter Diagram, Estimated Regression Line, and the Estimated Regression Equation for Armand's Pizza Parlors

	A	B	C	D	E	F
1	Restaurant	Population	Sales			
2	1	2	58			
3	2	6	105			
4	3	8	88			
5	4	8	118			
6	5	12	117			
7	6	16	137			
8	7	20	157			
9	8	20	169			
10	9	22	149			
11	10	26	202			

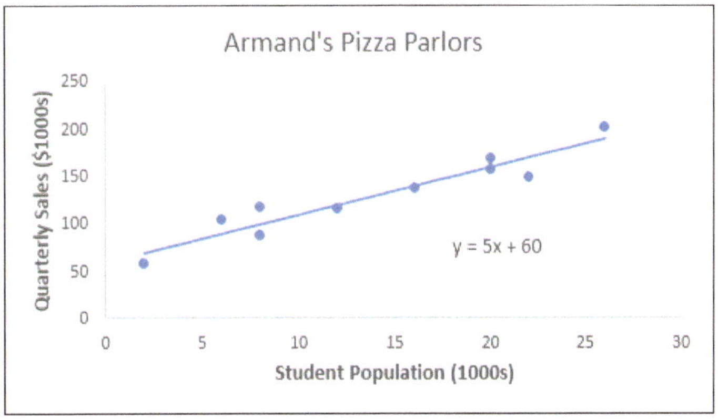

The worksheet displayed in Figure 14.5 shows the scatter diagram, the estimated regression line, and the estimated regression equation.

Note + Comment

The least squares method provides an estimated regression equation that minimizes the sum of squared deviations between the observed values of the dependent variable y_i and the predicted values of the dependent variable $\hat{y}_i$. This least squares criterion is used to choose the equation that provides the best fit. If some other criterion were used, such as minimizing the sum of the absolute deviations between y_i and $\hat{y}_i$, a different equation would be obtained. In practice, the least squares method is the most widely used.

Exercises

Methods

1. Given are five observations for two variables, x and y. **LO 1, 2**

x_i	1	2	3	4	5
y_i	3	7	5	11	14

a. Develop a scatter diagram for these data.

b. What does the scatter diagram developed in part (a) indicate about the relationship between the two variables?

c. Try to approximate the relationship between x and y by drawing a straight line through the data.
d. Develop the estimated regression equation by computing the values of b_0 and b_1 using equations (14.6) and (14.7).
e. Use the estimated regression equation to predict the value of y when $x = 4$.

2. Given are five observations for two variables, x and y. **LO 1, 2**

x_i	3	12	6	20	14
y_i	55	40	55	10	15

a. Develop a scatter diagram for these data.
b. What does the scatter diagram developed in part (a) indicate about the relationship between the two variables?
c. Try to approximate the relationship between x and y by drawing a straight line through the data.
d. Develop the estimated regression equation by computing the values of b_0 and b_1 using equations (14.6) and (14.7).
e. Use the estimated regression equation to predict the value of y when $x = 10$.

3. Given are five observations collected in a regression study on two variables. **LO 1, 2**

x_i	2	6	9	13	20
y_i	7	18	9	26	23

a. Develop a scatter diagram for these data.
b. Develop the estimated regression equation for these data.
c. Use the estimated regression equation to predict the value of y when $x = 6$.

Applications

4. **Retail and Trade: Female Managers.** The following data give the percentage of women working in five companies in the retail and trade industry. The percentage of management jobs held by women in each company is also shown. **LO 1, 2**

% Working	67	45	73	54	61
% Management	49	21	65	47	33

a. Develop a scatter diagram for these data with the percentage of women working in the company as the independent variable.
b. What does the scatter diagram developed in part (a) indicate about the relationship between the two variables?
c. Try to approximate the relationship between the percentage of women working in the company and the percentage of management jobs held by women in that company.
d. Develop the estimated regression equation by computing the values of b_0 and b_1.
e. Predict the percentage of management jobs held by women in a company that has 60% women employees.

5. **Production Line Speed and Quality Control.** Brawdy Plastics, Inc., produces plastic seat belt retainers for General Motors at their plant in Buffalo, New York. After final assembly and painting, the parts are placed on a conveyor belt that moves the parts past a final inspection station. How fast the parts move past the final inspection station depends upon the line speed of the conveyor belt (feet per minute). Although faster line speeds are desirable, management is concerned that increasing the line speed too much may not provide enough time for inspectors to identify which parts are actually defective. To test this theory, Brawdy Plastics conducted an experiment in which the same batch of parts, with a known number of defective parts, was inspected using a variety of line speeds. The following data were collected. **LO 1, 2**

Line Speed	Number of Defective Parts Found
20	23
20	21
30	19
30	16
40	15
40	17
50	14
50	11

a. Develop a scatter diagram with the line speed as the independent variable.
b. What does the scatter diagram developed in part (a) indicate about the relationship between the two variables?
c. Use the least squares method to develop the estimated regression equation.
d. Predict the number of defective parts found for a line speed of 25 feet per minute.

6. **Passing and Winning in the NFL.** The National Football League (NFL) records a variety of performance data for individuals and teams. To investigate the importance of passing on the percentage of games won by a team, the following data show the average number of passing yards per attempt (Yds/Att) and the percentage of games won in a season (WinPct) for a random sample of 10 NFL teams. **LO 1, 2, 3**

DATA*file*
nflpassing

Team	Yds/Att	WinPct
Arizona Cardinals	6.5	50
Atlanta Falcons	7.1	63
Carolina Panthers	7.4	38
Chicago Bears	6.4	50
Dallas Cowboys	7.4	50
New England Patriots	8.3	81
Philadelphia Eagles	7.4	50
Seattle Seahawks	6.1	44
St. Louis Rams	5.2	13
Tampa Bay Buccaneers	6.2	25

a. Develop a scatter diagram with the number of passing yards per attempt on the horizontal axis and the percentage of games won on the vertical axis.
b. What does the scatter diagram developed in part (a) indicate about the relationship between the two variables?
c. Develop the estimated regression equation that could be used to predict the percentage of games won given the average number of passing yards per attempt.
d. Provide an interpretation for the slope of the estimated regression equation.
e. For the 2011 season, the average number of passing yards per attempt for the Kansas City Chiefs was 6.2. Use the estimated regression equation developed in part (c) to predict the percentage of games won by the Kansas City Chiefs. (*Note:* For the 2011 season the Kansas City Chiefs' record was 7 wins and 9 losses.) Compare your prediction to the actual percentage of games won by the Kansas City Chiefs.

7. **Sales Experience and Performance.** A sales manager collected the following data on annual sales for new customer accounts and the number of years of experience for a sample of 10 salespersons. **LO 1, 2**

DATA*file*
sales

Salesperson	Years of Experience	Annual Sales ($1,000s)
1	1	80
2	3	97
3	4	92
4	4	102
5	6	103
6	8	111
7	10	119
8	10	123
9	11	117
10	13	136

a. Develop a scatter diagram for these data with years of experience as the independent variable.
b. Develop an estimated regression equation that can be used to predict annual sales given the years of experience.
c. Use the estimated regression equation to predict annual sales for a salesperson with nine years of experience.

8. **Broker Satisfaction.** The American Association of Individual Investors (AAII) On-Line Discount Broker Survey polls members on their experiences with discount brokers. As part of the survey, members were asked to rate the quality of the speed of execution with their broker as well as provide an overall satisfaction rating for electronic trades. Possible responses (scores) were no opinion (0), unsatisfied (l), somewhat satisfied (2), satisfied (3), and very satisfied (4). For each broker summary scores were computed by calculating a weighted average of the scores provided by each respondent. A portion of the survey results follow (AAII website). **LO 1, 2, 3**

DATA*file*
brokerratings

Brokerage	Speed	Satisfaction
Scottrade, Inc.	3.4	3.5
Charles Schwab	3.3	3.4
Fidelity Brokerage Services	3.4	3.9
TD Ameritrade	3.6	3.7
E*Trade Financial	3.2	2.9
Vanguard Brokerage Services	3.8	2.8
USAA Brokerage Services	3.8	3.6
Thinkorswim	2.6	2.6
Wells Fargo Investments	2.7	2.3
Interactive Brokers	4.0	4.0
Zecco.com	2.5	2.5

a. Develop a scatter diagram for these data with the speed of execution as the independent variable.
b. What does the scatter diagram developed in part (a) indicate about the relationship between the two variables?
c. Develop the least squares estimated regression equation.
d. Provide an interpretation for the slope of the estimated regression equation.
e. Suppose Zecco.com developed new software to increase their speed of execution rating. If the new software is able to increase their speed of execution rating from the current value of 2.5 to the average speed of execution rating for the other 10 brokerage firms that were surveyed, what value would you predict for the overall satisfaction rating?

DATA*file*
landscape

9. **Estimating Landscaping Expenditures.** David's Landscaping has collected data on home values (in thousands of $) and expenditures (in thousands of $) on landscaping with the hope of developing a predictive model to help marketing to potential new clients. Data for 14 households may be found in the file *landscape*. **LO 1, 2, 3**
   a. Develop a scatter diagram with home value as the independent variable.
   b. What does the scatter plot developed in part (a) indicate about the relationship between the two variables?
   c. Use the least squares method to develop the estimated regression equation.
   d. For every additional $1,000 in home value, estimate how much additional will be spent on landscaping.
   e. Use the equation estimated in part (c) to predict the landscaping expenditures for a home valued at $575,000.
10. **Age and the Price of Wine.** For a particular red wine, the following data show the auction price for a 750-milliliter bottle and the age of the wine as of June 2016 (WineX website). **LO 1, 3**

DATA*file*
wineprices

Age (years)	Price ($)
36	256
20	142
29	212
33	255
41	331
27	173
30	209
45	297
34	237
22	182

   a. Develop a scatter diagram for these data with age as the independent variable.
   b. What does the scatter diagram developed in part (a) indicate about the relationship between age and price?
   c. Develop the least squares estimated regression equation.
   d. Provide an interpretation for the slope of the estimated equation.
11. **Laptop Ratings.** To help consumers in purchasing a laptop computer, *Consumer Reports* calculates an overall test score for each computer tested based upon rating factors such as ergonomics, portability, performance, display, and battery life. Higher overall scores indicate better test results. The following data show the average retail price and the overall score for ten 13-inch models (*Consumer Reports* website). **LO 1, 2, 3**

DATA*file*
computer

Brand and Model	Price ($)	Overall Score
Samsung Ultrabook NP900X3C-A01US	1,250	83
Apple MacBook Air MC965LL/A	1,300	83
Apple MacBook Air MD231LL/A	1,200	82
HP ENVY 13-2050nr Spectre XT	950	79
Sony VAIO SVS13112FXB	800	77
Acer Aspire S5-391-9880 Ultrabook	1,200	74
Apple MacBook Pro MD101LL/A	1,200	74
Apple MacBook Pro MD313LL/A	1,000	73
Dell Inspiron I13Z-6591SLV	700	67
Samsung NP535U3C-A01US	600	63

a. Develop a scatter diagram with price as the independent variable.
b. What does the scatter diagram developed in part (a) indicate about the relationship between the two variables?
c. Use the least squares method to develop the estimated regression equation.
d. Provide an interpretation of the slope of the estimated regression equation.
e. Another laptop that *Consumer Reports* tested is the Acer Aspire S3-951-6646 Ultrabook; the price for this laptop was $700. Predict the overall score for this laptop using the estimated regression equation developed in part (c).

12. **Stock Beta.** In June 2016, Yahoo Finance reported the beta value for Coca-Cola was 0.82 (Yahoo Finance website). Betas for individual stocks are determined by simple linear regression. The dependent variable is the total return for the stock, and the independent variable is the total return for the stock market, such as the return of the S&P 500. The slope of this regression equation is referred to as the stock's *beta*. Many financial analysts prefer to measure the risk of a stock by computing the stock's beta value.

The data contained in the file *cocacola* show the monthly percentage returns for the S&P 500 and the Coca-Cola Company for 12 months. **LO 1, 3**

DATA*file*
cocacola

Month	S&P 500 % Return	Coca-Cola % Return
August	−3	3
September	8	6
October	0	1
November	−2	1
December	−5	0
January	0	0
February	7	8
March	0	−3
April	2	0
May	−5	−1

a. Develop a scatter diagram with the S&P % Return as the independent variable.
b. What does the scatter diagram developed in part (a) indicate about the relationship between the returns of the S&P 500 and those of the Coca-Cola Company?
c. Develop the least squares estimated regression equation.
d. Provide an interpretation for the slope of the estimated equation (i.e., the beta).
e. Is your beta estimate close to 0.82? If not, why might your estimate be different?

13. **Auditing Itemized Tax Deductions.** To the Internal Revenue Service (IRS), the reasonableness of total itemized deductions depends on the taxpayer's adjusted gross income. Large deductions, which include charity and medical deductions, are more reasonable for taxpayers with large adjusted gross incomes. If a taxpayer claims larger than average itemized deductions for a given level of income, the chances of an IRS audit are increased. Data (in thousands of dollars) on adjusted gross income and the average or reasonable amount of itemized deductions follow. **LO 1, 2**

Adjusted Gross Income ($1,000s)	Reasonable Amount of Itemized Deductions ($1,000s)
22	9.6
27	9.6
32	10.1
48	11.1
65	13.5
85	17.7
120	25.5

a. Develop a scatter diagram for these data with adjusted gross income as the independent variable.
b. Use the least squares method to develop the estimated regression equation.
c. Predict the reasonable level of total itemized deductions for a taxpayer with an adjusted gross income of \$52,500. If this taxpayer claimed itemized deductions of \$20,400, would the IRS agent's request for an audit appear justified? Explain.

14. **Distance and Absenteeism.** A large city hospital conducted a study to investigate the relationship between the number of unauthorized days that employees are absent per year and the distance (miles) between home and work for the employees. A sample of 10 employees was selected and the following data were collected. **LO 1, 2**

DATA*file*
absent

Distance to Work (miles)	Number of Days Absent
1	8
3	5
4	8
6	7
8	6
10	3
12	5
14	2
14	4
18	2

a. Develop a scatter diagram for these data. Does a linear relationship appear reasonable? Explain.
b. Develop the least squares estimated regression equation that relates the distance to work to the number of days absent.
c. Predict the number of days absent for an employee that lives five miles from the hospital.

14.3 Coefficient of Determination

For the Armand's Pizza Parlors example, we developed the estimated regression equation $\hat{y} = 60 + 5x$ to approximate the linear relationship between the size of the student population x and quarterly sales y. A question now is: How well does the estimated regression equation fit the data? In this section, we show that the **coefficient of determination** provides a measure of the goodness of fit for the estimated regression equation.

For the ith observation, the difference between the observed value of the dependent variable, y_i, and the predicted value of the dependent variable, $\hat{y}_i$, is called the ***i*th residual**. The ith residual represents the error in using $\hat{y}_i$ to estimate y_i. Thus, for the ith observation, the residual is $y_i - \hat{y}_i$. The sum of squares of these residuals or errors is the quantity that is minimized by the least squares method. This quantity, also known as the *sum of squares due to error,* is denoted by SSE.

Sum of Squares Due to Error

$$\text{SSE} = \Sigma(y_i - \hat{y}_i)^2 \qquad \textbf{(14.8)}$$

The value of SSE is a measure of the error in using the estimated regression equation to predict the values of the dependent variable in the sample.

Table 14.3 Calculation of SSE for Armand's Pizza Parlors

Restaurant i	x_i = Student Population (1,000s)	y_i = Quarterly Sales ($1,000s)	Predicted Sales $\hat{y}_i = 60 + 5x_i$	Error $y_i - \hat{y}_i$	Squared Error $(y_i - \hat{y}_i)^2$
1	2	58	70	−12	144
2	6	105	90	15	225
3	8	88	100	−12	144
4	8	118	100	18	324
5	12	117	120	−3	9
6	16	137	140	−3	9
7	20	157	160	−3	9
8	20	169	160	9	81
9	22	149	170	−21	441
10	26	202	190	12	144
					SSE = 1,530

In Table 14.3, we show the calculations required to compute the sum of squares due to error for the Armand's Pizza Parlors example. For instance, for restaurant 1 the values of the independent and dependent variables are $x_1 = 2$ and $y_1 = 58$. Using the estimated regression equation, we find that the predicted value of quarterly sales for restaurant 1 is $\hat{y}_1 = 60 + 5(2) = 70$. Thus, the error in using $\hat{y}_1$ to predict y_1 for restaurant 1 is $y_1 - \hat{y}_1 = 58 - 70 = -12$. The squared error, $(-12)^2 = 144$, is shown in the last column of Table 14.3. After computing and squaring the residuals for each restaurant in the sample, we sum them to obtain SSE = 1,530. Thus, SSE = 1,530 measures the error in using the estimated regression equation $\hat{y} = 60 + 5x$ to predict sales.

Now suppose we are asked to develop an estimate of quarterly sales without knowledge of the size of the student population. Without knowledge of any related variables, we would use the sample mean as an estimate of quarterly sales at any given restaurant. Table 14.2 showed that for the sales data, $\Sigma y_i = 1{,}300$. Hence, the mean value of quarterly sales for the sample of 10 Armand's restaurants is $\bar{y} = \Sigma y_i/n = 1{,}300/10 = 130$. In Table 14.4 we show the sum of squared deviations obtained by using the sample mean $\bar{y} = 130$ to predict the value of quarterly sales for each restaurant in the sample. For the ith restaurant in the sample, the difference $y_i - \bar{y}$ provides a measure of the error involved in using $\bar{y}$ to predict sales. The corresponding sum of squares, called the *total sum of squares,* is denoted SST.

Table 14.4 Computation of the Total Sum of Squares for Armand's Pizza Parlors

Restaurant i	x_i = Student Population (1,000s)	y_i = Quarterly Sales ($1,000s)	Deviation $y_i - \bar{y}$	Squared Deviation $(y_i - \bar{y})^2$
1	2	58	−72	5,184
2	6	105	−25	625
3	8	88	−42	1,764
4	8	118	−12	144
5	12	117	−13	169
6	16	137	7	49
7	20	157	27	729
8	20	169	39	1,521
9	22	149	19	361
10	26	202	72	5,184
				SST = 15,730

Total Sum of Squares

$$SST = \Sigma(y_i - \bar{y})^2 \quad (14.9)$$

With SST = 15,730 and SSE = 1,530, the estimated regression line provides a much better fit to the data than the line $y = \bar{y}$.

The sum at the bottom of the last column in Table 14.4 is the total sum of squares for Armand's Pizza Parlors; it is SST = 15,730.

In Figure 14.6 we show the estimated regression line $\hat{y} = 60 + 5x$ and the line corresponding to $\bar{y} = 130$. Note that the points cluster more closely around the estimated regression line than they do about the line $\bar{y} = 130$. For example, for the 10th restaurant in the sample we see that the error is much larger when $\bar{y} = 130$ is used to predict y_{10} than when $\hat{y}_{10} = 60 + 5(26) = 190$ is used. We can think of SST as a measure of how well the observations cluster about the $\bar{y}$ line and SSE as a measure of how well the observations cluster about the $\hat{y}$ line.

To measure how much the $\hat{y}$ values on the estimated regression line deviate from $\bar{y}$, another sum of squares is computed. This sum of squares, called the *sum of squares due to regression,* is denoted SSR.

Sum of Squares Due to Regression

$$SSR = \Sigma(\hat{y}_i - \bar{y})^2 \quad (14.10)$$

From the preceding discussion, we should expect that SST, SSR, and SSE are related. Indeed, the relationship among these three sums of squares provides one of the most important results in statistics.

Figure 14.6 Deviations About the Estimated Regression Line and the Line $y = \bar{y}$ for Armand's Pizza Parlors

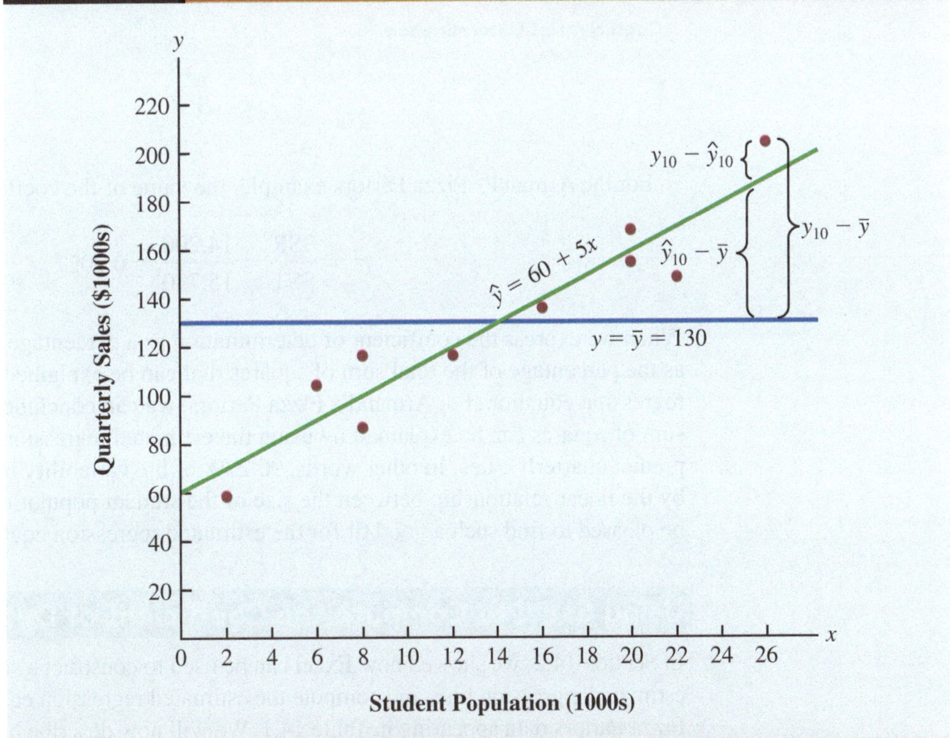

SSR can be thought of as the explained portion of SST, and SSE can be thought of as the unexplained portion of SST.

Relationship Among SST, SSR, and SSE

$$\text{SST} = \text{SSR} + \text{SSE} \tag{14.11}$$

where

SST = total sum of squares
SSR = sum of squares due to regression
SSE = sum of squares due to error

Equation (14.11) shows that the total sum of squares can be partitioned into two components, the sum of squares due to regression and the sum of squares due to error. Hence, if the values of any two of these sum of squares are known, the third sum of squares can be computed easily. For instance, in the Armand's Pizza Parlors example, we already know that SSE = 1,530 and SST = 15,730; therefore, solving for SSR in equation (14.11), we find that the sum of squares due to regression is

$$\text{SSR} = \text{SST} - \text{SSE} = 15{,}730 - 1{,}530 = 14{,}200$$

Now let us see how the three sums of squares, SST, SSR, and SSE, can be used to provide a measure of the goodness of fit for the estimated regression equation. The estimated regression equation would provide a perfect fit if every value of the dependent variable y_i happened to lie on the estimated regression line. In this case, $y_i - \hat{y}_i$ would be zero for each observation, resulting in SSE = 0. Because SST = SSR + SSE, we see that for a perfect fit SSR must equal SST, and the ratio (SSR/SST) must equal one. Poorer fits will result in larger values for SSE. Solving for SSE in equation (14.11), we see that SSE = SST − SSR. Hence, the largest value for SSE (and hence the poorest fit) occurs when SSR = 0 and SSE = SST.

The ratio SSR/SST, which will take values between zero and one, is used to evaluate the goodness of fit for the estimated regression equation. This ratio is called the *coefficient of determination* and is denoted by r^2.

Coefficient of Determination

$$r^2 = \frac{\text{SSR}}{\text{SST}} \tag{14.12}$$

For the Armand's Pizza Parlors example, the value of the coefficient of determination is

$$r^2 = \frac{\text{SSR}}{\text{SST}} = \frac{14{,}200}{15{,}730} = 0.9027$$

When we express the coefficient of determination as a percentage, r^2 can be interpreted as the percentage of the total sum of squares that can be explained by using the estimated regression equation. For Armand's Pizza Parlors, we can conclude that 90.27% of the total sum of squares can be explained by using the estimated regression equation $\hat{y} = 60 + 5x$ to predict quarterly sales. In other words, 90.27% of the variability in sales can be explained by the linear relationship between the size of the student population and sales. We should be pleased to find such a good fit for the estimated regression equation.

Using Excel to Compute the Coefficient of Determination

In Section 14.2, we showed how Excel can be used to construct a scatter diagram, display the estimated regression line, and compute the estimated regression equation for the Armand's Pizza Parlors data appearing in Table 14.1. We will now describe how to compute the coefficient of determination using the scatter diagram in Figure 14.5.

Figure 14.7 Using Excel's Chart Tools to Compute the Coefficient of Determination for Armand's Pizza Parlors

	A	B	C	D	E	F
1	Restaurant	Population	Sales			
2	1	2	58			
3	2	6	105			
4	3	8	88			
5	4	8	118			
6	5	12	117			
7	6	16	137			
8	7	20	157			
9	8	20	169			
10	9	22	149			
11	10	26	202			

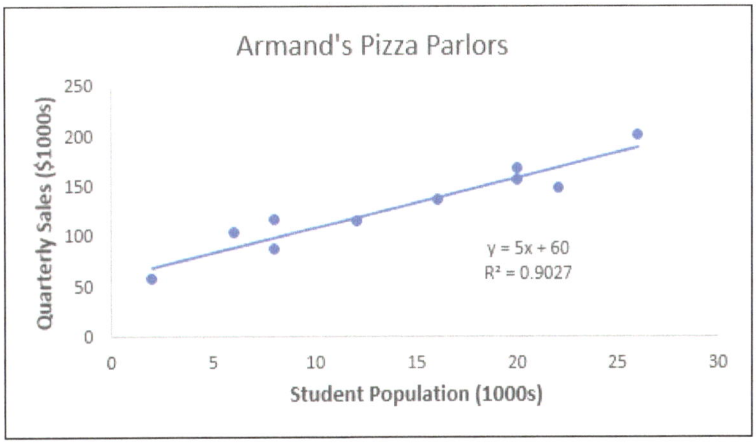

Step 1. Right-click on the trendline and select the **Format Trendline** option
Step 2. When the **Format Trendline** dialog box appears:
Scroll down and select **Display R-squared value on chart**
Close the **Format Trendline** dialog box

The worksheet displayed in Figure 14.7 shows the scatter diagram, the estimated regression line, and the estimated regression equation.

Correlation Coefficient

In Chapter 3, we introduced the **correlation coefficient** as a descriptive measure of the strength of linear association between two variables, x and y. Values of the correlation coefficient are always between -1 and $+1$. A value of $+1$ indicates that the two variables, x and y, are perfectly related in a positive linear sense. That is, all data points are on a straight line that has a positive slope. A value of -1 indicates that x and y are perfectly related in a negative linear sense, with all data points on a straight line that has a negative slope. Values of the correlation coefficient close to zero indicate that x and y are not linearly related.

In Section 3.5, we presented the equation for computing the sample correlation coefficient. If a regression analysis has already been performed and the coefficient of determination r^2 computed, the sample correlation coefficient can be computed as follows.

Sample Correlation Coefficient

$$
\begin{aligned}
r_{xy} &= (\text{sign of } b_1)\sqrt{\text{Coefficient of determination}} \\
&= (\text{sign of } b_1)\sqrt{r^2}
\end{aligned}
\tag{14.13}
$$

where

$$b_1 = \text{the slope of the estimated regression equation } \hat{y} = b_0 + b_1x$$

The sign for the sample correlation coefficient is positive if the estimated regression equation has a positive slope ($b_1 > 0$) and negative if the estimated regression equation has a negative slope ($b_1 < 0$).

For the Armand's Pizza Parlor example, the value of the coefficient of determination corresponding to the estimated regression equation $\hat{y} = 60 + 5x$ is 0.9027. Because the slope of the estimated regression equation is positive, equation (14.13) shows that the sample correlation coefficient is $+\sqrt{0.9027} = +0.9501$. With a sample correlation coefficient of $r_{xy} = +0.9501$, we would conclude that a strong positive linear association exists between x and y.

In the case of a linear relationship between two variables, both the coefficient of determination and the sample correlation coefficient provide measures of the strength of the relationship. The coefficient of determination provides a measure between zero and one, whereas the sample correlation coefficient provides a measure between -1 and $+1$. Although the sample correlation coefficient is restricted to a linear relationship between two variables, the coefficient of determination can be used for nonlinear relationships and for relationships that have two or more independent variables. Thus, the coefficient of determination provides a wider range of applicability.

Notes + Comments

1. In developing the least squares estimated regression equation and computing the coefficient of determination, we made no probabilistic assumptions about the error term ϵ, and no statistical tests for significance of the relationship between x and y were conducted. Larger values of r^2 imply that the least squares line provides a better fit to the data; that is, the observations are more closely grouped about the least squares line. But, using only r^2, we can draw no conclusion about whether the relationship between x and y is statistically significant. Such a conclusion must be based on considerations that involve the sample size and the properties of the appropriate sampling distributions of the least squares estimators.
2. As a practical matter, for typical data found in the social sciences, values of r^2 as low as 0.25 are often considered useful. For data in the physical and life sciences, r^2 values of 0.60 or greater are often found; in fact, in some cases, r^2 values greater than 0.90 can be found. In business applications, r^2 values vary greatly, depending on the unique characteristics of each application.

Exercises

Methods

15. The data from exercise 1 follow. **LO 4, 5**

x_i	1	2	3	4	5
y_i	3	7	5	11	14

The estimated regression equation for these data is $\hat{y} = 0.20 + 2.60x$.

a. Compute SSE, SST, and SSR using equations (14.8), (14.9), and (14.10).
b. Compute the coefficient of determination r^2. Comment on the goodness of fit.
c. Compute the sample correlation coefficient.

16. The data from exercise 2 follow. **LO 4, 5**

x_i	3	12	6	20	14
y_i	55	40	55	10	15

The estimated regression equation for these data is $\hat{y} = 68 - 3x$.
a. Compute SSE, SST, and SSR.
b. Compute the coefficient of determination r^2. Comment on the goodness of fit.
c. Compute the sample correlation coefficient.

17. The data from exercise 3 follow. **LO 4, 5**

x_i	2	6	9	13	20
y_i	7	18	9	26	23

The estimated regression equation for these data is $\hat{y} = 7.6 + 0.9x$. What percentage of the total sum of squares can be accounted for by the estimated regression equation? What is the value of the sample correlation coefficient?

Applications

18. **Price and Quality of Headphones.** The following data show the brand, price ($), and the overall score for six stereo headphones that were tested by *Consumer Reports* (*Consumer Reports* website). The overall score is based on sound quality and effectiveness of ambient noise reduction. Scores range from 0 (lowest) to 100 (highest). The estimated regression equation for these data is $\hat{y} = 23.194 + 0.318x$, where x = price ($) and y = overall score. **LO 4, 5**

DATA*file*
headphones

Brand	Price ($)	Score
Bose	180	76
Skullcandy	150	71
Koss	95	61
Phillips/O'Neill	70	56
Denon	70	40
JVC	35	26

a. Compute SST, SSR, and SSE.
b. Compute the coefficient of determination r^2. Comment on the goodness of fit.
c. What is the value of the sample correlation coefficient?

19. **Sales Experience and Sales Performance.** In exercise 7, a sales manager collected the following data on x = annual sales and y = years of experience. The estimated regression equation for these data is $\hat{y} = 80 + 4x$. **LO 4, 5**

DATA*file*
sales

Salesperson	Years of Experience	Annual Sales ($1,000s)
1	1	80
2	3	97
3	4	92
4	4	102
5	6	103
6	8	111
7	10	119
8	10	123
9	11	117
10	13	136

a. Compute SST, SSR, and SSE.
b. Compute the coefficient of determination r^2. Comment on the goodness of fit.
c. What is the value of the sample correlation coefficient?

20. **Price and Weight of Bicycles.** *Bicycling,* the world's leading cycling magazine, reviews hundreds of bicycles throughout the year. Their "Road-Race" category contains reviews of bikes used by riders primarily interested in racing. One of the most important factors in selecting a bike for racing is the weight of the bike. The following data show the weight (pounds) and price ($) for 10 racing bikes reviewed by the magazine (*Bicycling* website). **LO 1, 2, 4**

DATA*file*
racingbicycles

Brand	Weight	Price ($)
FELT F5	17.8	2,100
PINARELLO Paris	16.1	6,250
ORBEA Orca GDR	14.9	8,370
EDDY MERCKX EMX-7	15.9	6,200
BH RC1 Ultegra	17.2	4,000
BH Ultralight 386	13.1	8,600
CERVELO S5 Team	16.2	6,000
GIANT TCR Advanced 2	17.1	2,580
WILIER TRIESTINA Gran Turismo	17.6	3,400
SPECIALIZED S-Works Amira SL4	14.1	8,000

a. Use the data to develop an estimated regression equation that could be used to estimate the price for a bike given the weight.
b. Compute r^2. Did the estimated regression equation provide a good fit?
c. Predict the price for a bike that weighs 15 pounds.

21. **Cost Estimation.** An important application of regression analysis in accounting is in the estimation of cost. By collecting data on volume and cost and using the least squares method to develop an estimated regression equation relating volume and cost, an accountant can estimate the cost associated with a particular manufacturing volume. Consider the following sample of production volumes and total cost data for a manufacturing operation. **LO 1, 2, 3, 4**

Production Volume (units)	Total Cost ($)
400	4,000
450	5,000
550	5,400
600	5,900
700	6,400
750	7,000

a. Use these data to develop an estimated regression equation that could be used to predict the total cost for a given production volume.
b. What is the variable cost per unit produced?
c. Compute the coefficient of determination. What percentage of the variation in total cost can be explained by production volume?
d. The company's production schedule shows 500 units must be produced next month. Predict the total cost for this operation.

22. **Rental Car Revenue and Fleet Size.** The following data were used to investigate the relationship between the number of cars in service (1,000s) and the annual revenue ($ millions) for six smaller car rental companies (*Auto Rental News* website). **LO 3, 4**

Company	Cars (1,000s)	Revenue ($ millions)
U-Save Auto Rental System, Inc.	11.5	118
Payless Car Rental System, Inc.	10.0	135
ACE Rent A Car	9.0	100
Rent-A-Wreck of America	5.5	37
Triangle Rent-A-Car	4.2	40
Affordable/Sensible	3.3	32

With x = cars in service (1,000s) and y = annual revenue ($ millions), the estimated regression equation is $\hat{y} = -17.005 + 12.966x$. For these data SSE = 1,043.03.

a. Compute the coefficient of determination r^2.
b. Did the estimated regression equation provide a good fit? Explain.
c. What is the value of the sample correlation coefficient? Does it reflect a strong or weak relationship between the number of cars in service and the annual revenue?

14.4 Model Assumptions

In conducting a regression analysis, we begin by making an assumption about the appropriate model for the relationship between the dependent and independent variable(s). For the case of simple linear regression, the assumed regression model is

$$y = \beta_0 + \beta_1 x + \epsilon$$

Then the least squares method is used to develop values for b_0 and b_1, the estimates of the model parameters β_0 and β_1, respectively. The resulting estimated regression equation is

$$\hat{y} = b_0 + b_1 x$$

We saw that the value of the coefficient of determination (r^2) is a measure of the goodness of fit of the estimated regression equation. However, even with a large value of r^2, the estimated regression equation should not be used until further analysis of the appropriateness of the assumed model has been conducted. An important step in determining whether the assumed model is appropriate involves testing for the significance of the relationship. The tests of significance in regression analysis are based on the following assumptions about the error term ϵ.

Assumptions about the Error Term ϵ in the Regression Model

$$y = \beta_0 + \beta_1 x + \epsilon$$

1. The error term ϵ is a random variable with a mean or expected value of zero; that is, $E(\epsilon) = 0$.
   Implication: β_0 and β_1 are constants, therefore $E(\beta_0) = \beta_0$ and $E(\beta_1) = \beta_1$; thus, for a given value of x, the expected value of y is

$$E(y) = \beta_0 + \beta_1 x \qquad \textbf{(14.14)}$$

   As we indicated previously, equation (14.14) is referred to as the regression equation.
2. The variance of ϵ, denoted by σ^2, is the same for all values of x.
   Implication: The variance of y about the regression line equals σ^2 and is the same for all values of x.
3. The values of ϵ are independent.
   Implication: The value of ϵ for a particular value of x is not related to the value of ϵ for any other value of x; thus, the value of y for a particular value of x is not related to the value of y for any other value of x.
4. The error term ϵ is a normally distributed random variable for all values of x.
   Implication: Because y is a linear function of ϵ, y is also a normally distributed random variable for all values of x.

Figure 14.8 illustrates the model assumptions and their implications; note that in this graphical interpretation, the value of $E(y)$ changes according to the specific value of x

Figure 14.8 Assumptions for the Regression Model

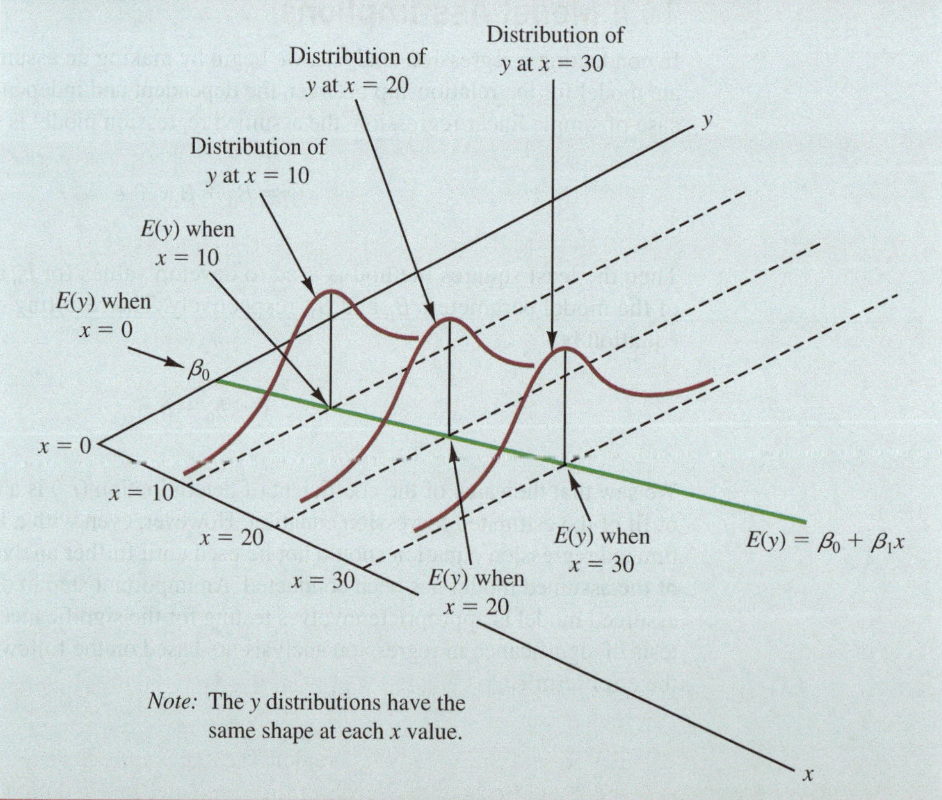

considered. However, regardless of the x value, the probability distribution of ϵ and hence the probability distributions of y are normally distributed, each with the same variance. The specific value of the error ϵ at any particular point depends on whether the actual value of y is greater than or less than $E(y)$.

At this point, we must keep in mind that we are also making an assumption or hypothesis about the form of the relationship between x and y. That is, we assume that a straight line represented by $\beta_0 + \beta_1 x$ is the basis for the relationship between the variables. We must not lose sight of the fact that some other model, for instance $y = \beta_0 + \beta_1 x^2 + \epsilon$, may turn out to be a better model for the underlying relationship.

14.5 Testing for Significance

In a simple linear regression equation, the mean or expected value of y is a linear function of x: $E(y) = \beta_0 + \beta_1 x$. If the value of β_1 is zero, $E(y) = \beta_0 + (0)x = \beta_0$. In this case, the mean value of y does not depend on the value of x and hence we would conclude that x and y are not linearly related. Alternatively, if the value of β_1 is not equal to zero, we would conclude that the two variables are related. Thus, to test for a significant regression relationship, we must conduct a hypothesis test to determine whether the value of β_1 is zero. Two tests are commonly used. Both require an estimate of σ^2, the variance of ϵ in the regression model.

Estimate of σ^2

From the regression model and its assumptions we can conclude that σ^2, the variance of ϵ, also represents the variance of the y values about the regression line. Recall that the deviations of the y values about the estimated regression line are called residuals. Thus, SSE, the sum of squared residuals, is a measure of the variability of the actual observations about the estimated regression line. The **mean square error (MSE)** provides the estimate of σ^2; it is SSE divided by its degrees of freedom.

With $\hat{y}_i = b_0 + b_1 x_i$, SSE can be written as

$$\text{SSE} = \Sigma(y_i - \hat{y}_i)^2 = \Sigma(y_i - b_0 - b_1 x_i)^2$$

Every sum of squares has associated with it a number called its degrees of freedom. Statisticians have shown that SSE has $n - 2$ degrees of freedom because two parameters (β_0 and β_1) must be estimated to compute SSE. Thus, the mean square error is computed by dividing SSE by $n - 2$. MSE provides an unbiased estimator of σ^2. Because the value of MSE provides an estimate of σ^2, the notation s^2 is also used.

Mean Square Error (Estimate of σ^2)

$$s^2 = \text{MSE} = \frac{\text{SSE}}{n - 2} \tag{14.15}$$

In Section 14.3, we showed that for the Armand's Pizza Parlors example, SSE = 1,530; hence,

$$s^2 = \text{MSE} = \frac{1{,}530}{8} = 191.25$$

provides an unbiased estimate of σ^2.

To estimate σ we take the square root of s^2. The resulting value, s, is referred to as the **standard error of the estimate**.

Standard Error of the Estimate

$$s = \sqrt{\text{MSE}} = \sqrt{\frac{\text{SSE}}{n-2}} \tag{14.16}$$

For the Armand's Pizza Parlors example, $s = \sqrt{\text{MSE}} = \sqrt{191.25} = 13.829$. In the following discussion, we use the standard error of the estimate in the tests for a significant relationship between x and y.

t Test

The simple linear regression model is $y = \beta_0 + \beta_1 x + \epsilon$. If x and y are linearly related, we must have $\beta_1 \neq 0$. The purpose of the t test is to see whether we can conclude that $\beta_1 \neq 0$. We will use the sample data to test the following hypotheses about the parameter β_1.

$$H_0\colon \beta_1 = 0$$
$$H_a\colon \beta_1 \neq 0$$

If H_0 is rejected, we will conclude that $\beta_1 \neq 0$ and that a statistically significant relationship exists between the two variables. However, if H_0 cannot be rejected, we will have insufficient evidence to conclude that a significant relationship exists. The properties of the sampling distribution of b_1, the least squares estimator of β_1, provide the basis for the hypothesis test.

First, let us consider what would happen if we used a different random sample for the same regression study. For example, suppose that Armand's Pizza Parlors used the sales records of a different sample of 10 restaurants. A regression analysis of this new sample might result in an estimated regression equation similar to our previous estimated regression equation $\hat{y} = 60 + 5x$. However, it is doubtful that we would obtain exactly the same equation (with an intercept of exactly 60 and a slope of exactly 5). Indeed, b_0 and b_1, the least squares estimators, are sample statistics with their own sampling distributions. The properties of the sampling distribution of b_1 follow.

Sampling Distribution of b_1

Expected Value: $E(b_1) = \beta_1$

Standard Deviation: $$\sigma_{b_1} = \frac{\sigma}{\sqrt{\Sigma(x_i - \bar{x})^2}} \tag{14.17}$$

Distribution Form: Normal

Note that the expected value of b_1 is equal to β_1, so b_1 is an unbiased estimator of β_1.

Because we do not know the value of σ, we develop an estimate of σ_{b_1}, denoted s_{b_1}, by estimating σ with s in equation (14.17). Thus, we obtain the following estimate of σ_{b_1}.

The standard deviation of b_1 is also referred to as the standard error of b_1. Thus, s_{b_1} provides an estimate of the standard error of b_1.

Estimated Standard Deviation of b_1

$$s_{b_1} = \frac{s}{\sqrt{\Sigma(x_i - \bar{x})^2}} \tag{14.18}$$

For Armand's Pizza Parlors, $s = 13.829$. Hence, using $\sum(x_i - \bar{x})^2 = 568$, as shown in Table 14.2, we have

$$s_{b_1} = \frac{13.829}{\sqrt{568}} = 0.5803$$

as the estimated standard deviation of b_1.

The t test for a significant relationship is based on the fact that the test statistic

$$\frac{b_1 - \beta_1}{s_{b_1}}$$

follows a t distribution with $n - 2$ degrees of freedom. If the null hypothesis is true, then $\beta_1 = 0$ and $t = b_1/s_{b_1}$.

Let us conduct this test of significance for Armand's Pizza Parlors at the $\alpha = 0.01$ level of significance. The test statistic is

$$t = \frac{b_1}{s_{b_1}} = \frac{5}{0.5803} = 8.62$$

The t distribution table (Table 2 of Appendix B) shows that with $n - 2 = 10 - 2 = 8$ degrees of freedom, $t = 3.355$ provides an area of 0.005 in the upper tail. Thus, the area in the upper tail of the t distribution corresponding to the test statistic $t = 8.62$ must be less than 0.005. Because this test is a two-tailed test, we double this value to conclude that the p-value associated with $t = 8.62$ must be less than $2(0.005) = 0.01$. Using Excel, the p-value $= 0.000$. Because the p-value is less than $\alpha = 0.01$, we reject H_0 and conclude that β_1 is not equal to zero. This evidence is sufficient to conclude that a significant relationship exists between student population and quarterly sales. A summary of the t test for significance in simple linear regression follows.

t Test For Significance in Simple Linear Regression

$$H_0\colon \beta_1 = 0$$
$$H_a\colon \beta_1 \neq 0$$

Test Statistic

$$t = \frac{b_1}{s_{b_1}} \tag{14.19}$$

Rejection Rule

p-value approach: Reject H_0 if p-value $\leq \alpha$

Critical value approach: Reject H_0 if $t \leq -t_{\alpha/2}$ or if $t \geq t_{\alpha/2}$

where $t_{\alpha/2}$ is based on a t distribution with $n - 2$ degrees of freedom.

Confidence Interval for β_1

The form of a confidence interval for β_1 is as follows:

$$b_1 \pm t_{\alpha/2}s_{b_1}$$

The point estimator is b_1 and the margin of error is $t_{\alpha/2}S_{b_1}$. The confidence coefficient associated with this interval is $1 - \alpha$, and $t_{\alpha/2}$ is the t value providing an area of $\alpha/2$ in the upper tail of a t distribution with $n - 2$ degrees of freedom. For example, suppose that we wanted to develop a 99% confidence interval estimate of β_1 for Armand's Pizza Parlors. From Table 2 of Appendix B we find that the t value corresponding to $\alpha = 0.01$

and $n - 2 = 10 - 2 = 8$ degrees of freedom is $t_{0.005} = 3.355$. Thus, the 99% confidence interval estimate of β_1 is

$$b_1 \pm t_{\alpha/2} s_{b_1} = 5 \pm 3.355(0.5803) = 5 \pm 1.95$$

or 3.05 to 6.95.

In using the t test for significance, the hypotheses tested were

$$H_0\colon \beta_1 = 0$$
$$H_a\colon \beta_1 \neq 0$$

At the $\alpha = 0.01$ level of significance, we can use the 99% confidence interval as an alternative for drawing the hypothesis testing conclusion for the Armand's data. Because 0, the hypothesized value of β_1, is not included in the confidence interval (3.05 to 6.95), we can reject H_0 and conclude that a significant statistical relationship exists between the size of the student population and quarterly sales. In general, a confidence interval can be used to test any two-sided hypothesis about β_1. If the hypothesized value of β_1 is contained in the confidence interval, do not reject H_0. Otherwise, reject H_0.

F Test

An F test, based on the F probability distribution, can also be used to test for significance in regression. With only one independent variable, the F test will provide the same conclusion as the t test; that is, if the t test indicates $\beta_1 \neq 0$ and hence a significant relationship, the F test will also indicate a significant relationship. But with more than one independent variable, only the F test can be used to test for an overall significant relationship.

The logic behind the use of the F test for determining whether the regression relationship is statistically significant is based on the development of two independent estimates of σ^2. We explained how MSE provides an estimate of σ^2. If the null hypothesis $H_0\colon \beta_1 = 0$ is true, the sum of squares due to regression, SSR, divided by its degrees of freedom provides another independent estimate of σ^2. This estimate is called the *mean square due to regression,* or simply the *mean square regression,* and is denoted MSR. In general,

$$\text{MSR} = \frac{\text{SSR}}{\text{Regression degrees of freedom}}$$

For the models we consider in this text, the regression degrees of freedom is always equal to the number of independent variables in the model:

$$\text{MSR} = \frac{\text{SSR}}{\text{Number of independent variables}} \tag{14.20}$$

Because we consider only regression models with one independent variable in this chapter, we have MSR = SSR/1 = SSR. Hence, for Armand's Pizza Parlors, MSR = SSR = 14,200.

If the null hypothesis ($H_0\colon \beta_1 = 0$) is true, MSR and MSE are two independent estimates of σ^2 and the sampling distribution of MSR/MSE follows an F distribution with numerator degrees of freedom equal to 1 and denominator degrees of freedom equal to $n - 2$. Therefore, when $\beta_1 = 0$, the value of MSR/MSE should be close to 1. However, if the null hypothesis is false ($\beta_1 \neq 0$), MSR will overestimate σ^2 and the value of MSR/MSE will be inflated; thus, large values of MSR/MSE lead to the rejection of H_0 and the conclusion that the relationship between x and y is statistically significant.

Let us conduct the F test for the Armand's Pizza Parlors example. The test statistic is

$$F = \frac{\text{MSR}}{\text{MSE}} = \frac{14{,}200}{191.25} = 74.25$$

The F test and the t test provide identical results for simple linear regression.

The F distribution table (Table 4 of Appendix B) shows that with 1 degree of freedom in the numerator and $n - 2 = 10 - 2 = 8$ degrees of freedom in the denominator, $F = 11.26$

provides an area of 0.01 in the upper tail. Thus, the area in the upper tail of the F distribution corresponding to the test statistic $F = 74.25$ must be less than 0.01. Thus, we conclude that the p-value must be less than 0.01. Using Excel, the p-value $= 0.000$. Because the p-value is less than $\alpha = 0.01$, we reject H_0 and conclude that a significant relationship exists between the size of the student population and quarterly sales. A summary of the F test for significance in simple linear regression follows.

If H_0 is false, MSE still provides an unbiased estimate of σ^2 and MSR overestimates σ^2. If H_0 is true, both MSE and MSR provide unbiased estimates of σ^2; in this case the value of MSR/MSE should be close to 1.

F Test For Significance In Simple Linear Regression

$$H_0\colon \beta_1 = 0$$
$$H_a\colon \beta_1 \neq 0$$

Test Statistic

$$F = \frac{\text{MSR}}{\text{MSE}} \tag{14.21}$$

Rejection Rule

p-value approach: Reject H_0 if p-value $\leq \alpha$
Critical value approach: Reject H_0 if $F \geq F_\alpha$

where F_α is based on an F distribution with 1 degree of freedom in the numerator and $n - 2$ degrees of freedom in the denominator.

In Chapter 13, we covered analysis of variance (ANOVA) and showed how an **ANOVA table** could be used to provide a convenient summary of the computational aspects of analysis of variance. A similar ANOVA table can be used to summarize the results of the F test for significance in regression. Table 14.5 is the general form of the ANOVA table for simple linear regression. Table 14.6 is the ANOVA table with the F test computations

In every analysis of variance table, the total sum of squares is the sum of the regression sum of squares and the error sum of squares; in addition, the total degrees of freedom is the sum of the regression degrees of freedom and the error degrees of freedom.

Table 14.5 General Form of the ANOVA Table for Simple Linear Regression

Source of Variation	Sum of Squares	Degrees of Freedom	Mean Square	F	p-Value
Regression	SSR	1	$\text{MSR} = \frac{\text{SSR}}{1}$	$F = \frac{\text{MSR}}{\text{MSE}}$	
Error	SSE	$n - 2$	$\text{MSE} = \frac{\text{SSE}}{n-2}$		
Total	SST	$n - 1$			

Table 14.6 ANOVA Table for the Armand's Pizza Parlors Problem

Source of Variation	Sum of Squares	Degrees of Freedom	Mean Square	F	p-Value
Regression	14,200	1	$\frac{14{,}200}{1} = 14{,}200$	$\frac{14{,}200}{191.25} = 74.25$	0.000
Error	1,530	8	$\frac{1{,}530}{8} = 191.25$		
Total	15,730	9			

performed for Armand's Pizza Parlors. Regression, Error, and Total are the labels for the three sources of variation, with SSR, SSE, and SST appearing as the corresponding sum of squares in column 2. The degrees of freedom, 1 for SSR, $n - 2$ for SSE, and $n - 1$ for SST, are shown in column 3. Column 4 contains the values of MSR and MSE, column 5 contains the value of $F = \text{MSR/MSE}$, and column 6 contains the p-value corresponding to the F value in column 5. Almost all computer printouts of regression analysis include an ANOVA table summary of the F test for significance.

Some Cautions About the Interpretation of Significance Tests

Regression analysis, which can be used to identify how variables are associated with one another, cannot be used as evidence of a cause-and-effect relationship.

Rejecting the null hypothesis H_0: $\beta_1 = 0$ and concluding that the relationship between x and y is significant do not enable us to conclude that a cause-and-effect relationship is present between x and y. Concluding a cause-and-effect relationship is warranted only if the analyst can provide some type of theoretical justification that the relationship is in fact causal. In the Armand's Pizza Parlors example, we can conclude that there is a significant relationship between the size of the student population x and quarterly sales y; moreover, the estimated regression equation $\hat{y} = 60 + 5x$ provides the least squares estimate of the relationship. We cannot, however, conclude that changes in student population x *cause* changes in quarterly sales y just because we identified a statistically significant relationship. The appropriateness of such a cause-and-effect conclusion is left to supporting theoretical justification and to good judgment on the part of the analyst. Armand's managers felt that increases in the student population were a likely cause of increased quarterly sales. Thus, the result of the significance test enabled them to conclude that a cause-and-effect relationship was present.

In addition, just because we are able to reject H_0: $\beta_1 = 0$ and demonstrate statistical significance does not enable us to conclude that the relationship between x and y is linear. We can state only that x and y are related and that a linear relationship explains a significant portion of the variability in y over the range of values for x observed in the sample. Figure 14.9 illustrates this situation. The test for significance calls for the rejection of the null hypothesis H_0: $\beta_1 = 0$ and leads to the conclusion that x and y are significantly related, but the figure shows that the actual relationship between x and y is not linear. Although the

Figure 14.9 Example of a Linear Approximation of a Nonlinear Relationship

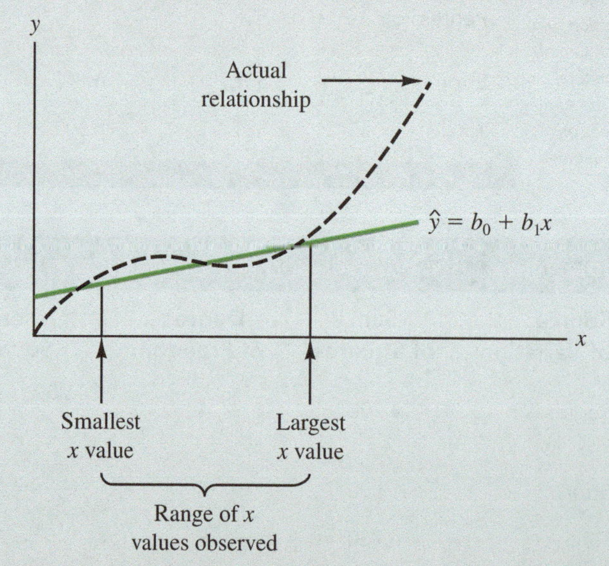

linear approximation provided by $\hat{y} = b_0 + b_1x$ is good over the range of x values observed in the sample, it becomes poor for x values outside that range.

Given a significant relationship, we should feel confident in using the estimated regression equation for predictions corresponding to x values within the range of the x values observed in the sample. For Armand's Pizza Parlors, this range corresponds to values of x between 2 and 26. Unless other reasons indicate that the model is valid beyond this range, predictions outside the range of the independent variable should be made with caution. For Armand's Pizza Parlors, because the regression relationship has been found significant at the 0.01 level, we should feel confident using it to predict sales for restaurants where the associated student population is between 2,000 and 26,000.

Notes + Comments

1. The assumptions made about the error term (Section 14.4) are what allow the tests of statistical significance in this section. The properties of the sampling distribution of b_1 and the subsequent t and F tests follow directly from these assumptions.
2. Do not confuse statistical significance with practical significance. With very large sample sizes, statistically significant results can be obtained for small values of b_1; in such cases, one must exercise care in concluding that the relationship has practical significance. We discuss this in more detail in Section 14.10.
3. A test of significance for a linear relationship between x and y can also be performed by using the sample correlation coefficient r_{xy}. With ρ_{xy} denoting the population correlation coefficient, the hypotheses are as follows.

$$H_0: \rho_{xy} = 0$$
$$H_a: \rho_{xy} \neq 0$$

A significant relationship can be concluded if H_0 is rejected. The details of this test are provided in Appendix 14.2. However, the t and F tests presented previously in this section give the same result as the test for significance using the correlation coefficient. Conducting a test for significance using the correlation coefficient therefore is not necessary if a t or F test has already been conducted.

Exercises

Methods

23. The data from exercise 1 follow. **LO 6, 7**

x_i	1	2	3	4	5
y_i	3	7	5	11	14

a. Compute the mean square error using equation (14.15).
b. Compute the standard error of the estimate using equation (14.16).
c. Compute the estimated standard deviation of b_1 using equation (14.18).
d. Use the t test to test the following hypotheses ($\alpha = 0.05$):

$$H_0: \beta_1 = 0$$
$$H_a: \beta_1 \neq 0$$

e. Use the F test to test the hypotheses in part (d) at a 0.05 level of significance. Present the results in the analysis of variance table format.

24. The data from exercise 2 follow. **LO 6, 7**

x_i	3	12	6	20	14
y_i	55	40	55	10	15

a. Compute the mean square error using equation (14.15).
b. Compute the standard error of the estimate using equation (14.16).
c. Compute the estimated standard deviation of b_1 using equation (14.18).

d. Use the t test to test the following hypotheses ($\alpha = 0.05$):

$$H_0: \beta_1 = 0$$
$$H_a: \beta_1 \neq 0$$

e. Use the F test to test the hypotheses in part (d) at a 0.05 level of significance. Present the results in the analysis of variance table format.

25. The data from exercise 3 follow. **LO 6, 7**

x_i	2	6	9	13	20
y_i	7	18	9	26	23

a. What is the value of the standard error of the estimate?
b. Test for a significant relationship by using the t test. Use $\alpha = 0.05$.
c. Use the F test to test for a significant relationship. Use $\alpha = 0.05$. What is your conclusion?

Applications

26. **Headphones Conclusion.** In exercise 18 the data on price ($) and the overall score for six stereo headphones tested by *Consumer Reports* were as follows (*Consumer Reports* website). **LO 6, 7**

Brand	Price ($)	Score
Bose	180	76
Skullcandy	150	71
Koss	95	61
Phillips/O'Neill	70	56
Denon	70	40
JVC	35	26

a. Does the t test indicate a significant relationship between price and the overall score? What is your conclusion? Use $\alpha = 0.05$.
b. Test for a significant relationship using the F test. What is your conclusion? Use $\alpha = 0.05$.
c. Show the ANOVA table for these data.

DATA*file*
gpasalary

27. **College GPA and Salary.** Do students with higher college grade point averages (GPAs) earn more than those graduates with lower GPAs (*CivicScience*)? Consider the college GPA and salary data (10 years after graduation) provided in the file *gpasalary*. **LO 1, 7**
a. Develop a scatter diagram for these data with college GPA as the independent variable. What does the scatter diagram indicate about the relationship between the two variables?
b. Use these data to develop an estimated regression equation that can be used to predict annual salary 10 years after graduation given college GPA.
c. At the 0.05 level of significance, test for a significant relationship using the F test. Does there appear to be a significant statistical relationship between the two variables?

DATA*file*
brokerratings

28. **Broker Satisfaction Conclusion.** In exercise 8, ratings data on x = the quality of the speed of execution and y = overall satisfaction with electronic trades provided the estimated regression equation $\hat{y} = 0.2046 + 0.9077x$ (AAII website). At the 0.05 level of significance, test whether speed of execution and overall satisfaction are related. Show the ANOVA table. What is your conclusion? **LO 6, 7**

29. **Cost Estimation Conclusion.** Refer to exercise 21, where data on production volume and cost were used to develop an estimated regression equation relating production volume and cost for a particular manufacturing operation. Use $\alpha = 0.05$ and the F test to determine whether the production volume is significantly related to the total cost. Show the ANOVA table. What is your conclusion? **LO 7**

30. **Rental Car Revenue and Fleet Size.** Companies in the U.S. car rental market vary greatly in terms of the size of the fleet, the number of locations, and annual revenue. The following data were used to investigate the relationship between the number of cars in service (1,000s) and the annual revenue ($ millions) for six smaller car rental companies (*Auto Rental News* website).

Company	Cars (1,000s)	Revenue ($ millions)
U-Save Auto Rental System, Inc.	11.5	118
Payless Car Rental System, Inc.	10.0	135
ACE Rent A Car	9.0	100
Rent-A-Wreck of America	5.5	37
Triangle Rent-A-Car	4.2	40
Affordable/Sensible	3.3	32

Source: Auto Rental News website, August 7, 2012.

With x = cars in service (1,000s) and y = annual revenue ($ millions), the estimated regression equation is $\hat{y} = -17.005 + 12.966x$. For these data, SSE = 1,043.03 and SST = 10,568. Use the t test to determine whether these results indicate a significant relationship between the number of cars in service and the annual revenue. **LO 6**

DATA*file*
racingbicycles

31. **Significance of Racing Bike Weight on Price.** In exercise 20, data on x = weight (pounds) and y = price ($) for 10 road-racing bikes provided the estimated regression equation $\hat{y} = 28{,}574 - 1{,}439x$ (*Bicycling* website). For these data SSE = 7,102,922.54 and SST = 52,120,800. Use the F test to determine whether the weight for a bike and the price are related at the 0.05 level of significance. **LO 7**

14.6 Using the Estimated Regression Equation for Estimation and Prediction

When using the simple linear regression model, we are making an assumption about the relationship between x and y. We then use the least squares method to obtain the estimated simple linear regression equation. If a significant relationship exists between x and y and the coefficient of determination shows that the fit is good, the estimated regression equation should be useful for estimation and prediction.

For the Armand's Pizza Parlors example, the estimated regression equation is $\hat{y} = 60 + 5x$. At the end of Section 14.1, we stated that $\hat{y}$ can be used as a *point estimator* of $E(y)$, the mean or expected value of y for a given value of x, and as a predictor of an individual value of y. For example, suppose Armand's managers want to estimate the mean quarterly sales for *all* restaurants located near college campuses with 10,000 students. Using the estimated regression equation $\hat{y} = 60 + 5x$, we see that for $x = 10$ (10,000 students), $\hat{y} = 60 + 5(10) = 110$. Thus, a *point estimate* of the mean quarterly sales for all restaurant locations near campuses with 10,000 students is $110,000. In this case, we are using $\hat{y}$ as the point estimator of the mean value of y when $x = 10$.

We can also use the estimated regression equation to *predict* an individual value of y for a given value of x. For example, to predict quarterly sales for a new restaurant Armand's is considering building near Talbot College, a campus with 10,000 students, we would compute $\hat{y} = 60 + 5(10) = 110$. Hence, we would predict quarterly sales of $110,000 for such a new restaurant. In this case, we are using $\hat{y}$ as the *predictor* of y for a new observation when $x = 10$.

When we are using the estimated regression equation to estimate the mean value of y or to predict an individual value of y, it is clear that the estimate or prediction depends on the given value of x. For this reason, as we discuss in more depth the issues concerning estimation and prediction, the following notation will help clarify matters.

x^* = the given value of the independent variable x

y^* = the random variable denoting the possible values of the dependent variable y when $x = x^*$

$E(y^*)$ = the mean or expected value of the dependent variable y when $x = x^*$

$\hat{y}^* = b_0 + b_1x^*$ = the point estimator of $E(y^*)$ and the predictor of an individual value of y^* when $x = x^*$

To illustrate the use of this notation, suppose we want to estimate the mean value of quarterly sales for *all* Armand's restaurants located near a campus with 10,000 students. For this case, $x^* = 10$ and $E(y^*)$ denotes the unknown mean value of quarterly sales for all restaurants where $x^* = 10$. Thus, the point estimate of $E(y^*)$ is provided by $\hat{y}^* = 60 + 5(10) = 110$, or $110,000. But, using this notation, $\hat{y}^* = 110$ is also the predictor of quarterly sales for the new restaurant located near Talbot College, a school with 10,000 students.

Interval Estimation

Confidence intervals and prediction intervals show the precision of the regression results. Narrower intervals provide a higher degree of precision.

Point estimators and predictors do not provide any information about the precision associated with the estimate and/or prediction. For that we must develop confidence intervals and prediction intervals. A **confidence interval** is an interval estimate of the *mean value of y* for a given value of x. A **prediction interval** is used whenever we want to *predict an individual value of y* for a new observation corresponding to a given value of x. Although the predictor of y for a given value of x is the same as the point estimator of the mean value of y for a given value of x, the interval estimates we obtain for the two cases are different. As we will show, the margin of error is larger for a prediction interval. We begin by showing how to develop an interval estimate of the mean value of y.

Confidence Interval for the Mean Value of y

In general, we cannot expect $\hat{y}^*$ to equal $E(y^*)$ exactly. If we want to make an inference about how close $\hat{y}^*$ is to the true mean value $E(y^*)$, we will have to estimate the variance of $\hat{y}^*$. The formula for estimating the variance of $\hat{y}^*$, denoted by $s^2_{\hat{y}^*}$, is

$$s^2_{\hat{y}^*} = s^2\left[\frac{1}{n} + \frac{(x^* - \bar{x})^2}{\Sigma(x_i - \bar{x})^2}\right] \tag{14.22}$$

The estimate of the standard deviation of $\hat{y}^*$ is given by the square root of equation (14.22).

$$s_{\hat{y}^*} = s\sqrt{\frac{1}{n} + \frac{(x^* - \bar{x})^2}{\Sigma(x_i - \bar{x})^2}} \tag{14.23}$$

The computational results for Armand's Pizza Parlors in Section 14.5 provided $s = 13.829$. With $x^* = 10$, $\bar{x} = 14$, and $\Sigma(x_i - \bar{x})^2 = 568$, we can use equation (14.23) to obtain

$$s_{\hat{y}^*} = 13.829\sqrt{\frac{1}{10} + \frac{(10 - 14)^2}{568}}$$

$$= 13.829\sqrt{0.1282} = 4.95$$

The general expression for a confidence interval follows.

The margin of error associated with this confidence interval is $t_{\alpha/2}s_{\hat{y}^*}$.

Confidence Interval for E(y*)

$$\hat{y}^* \pm t_{\alpha/2}s_{\hat{y}^*} \tag{14.24}$$

where the confidence coefficient is $1 - \alpha$ and $t_{\alpha/2}$ is based on the t distribution with $n - 2$ degrees of freedom.

Using expression (14.24) to develop a 95% confidence interval of the mean quarterly sales for all Armand's restaurants located near campuses with 10,000 students, we need the value of t for $\alpha/2 = 0.025$ and $n - 2 = 10 - 2 = 8$ degrees of freedom. Using Table 2 of Appendix B, we have $t_{.025} = 2.306$. Thus, with $\hat{y}^* = 110$ and a margin of error of $t_{\alpha/2}s_{\hat{y}^*} = 2.306(4.95) = 11.415$, the 95% confidence interval estimate is

$$110 \pm 11.415$$

In dollars, the 95% confidence interval for the mean quarterly sales of all restaurants near campuses with 10,000 students is \$110,000 ± \$11,415. Therefore, the 95% confidence interval for the mean quarterly sales when the student population is 10,000 is \$98,585 to \$121,415.

Note that the estimated standard deviation of $\hat{y}^*$ given by equation (14.23) is smallest when $x^* - \bar{x} = 0$. In this case, the estimated standard deviation of $\hat{y}^*$ becomes

$$s_{\hat{y}^*} = s\sqrt{\frac{1}{n} + \frac{(\bar{x} - \bar{x})^2}{\Sigma(x_i - \bar{x})^2}} = s\sqrt{\frac{1}{n}}$$

This result implies that we can make the best or most precise estimate of the mean value of y whenever $x^* = \bar{x}$. In fact, the further x^* is from $\bar{x}$, the larger $x^* - \bar{x}$ becomes. As a result, the confidence interval for the mean value of y will become wider as x^* deviates more from $\bar{x}$. This pattern is shown graphically in Figure 14.10.

Figure 14.10 Confidence Intervals for the Mean Sales y at Given Values of Student Population x

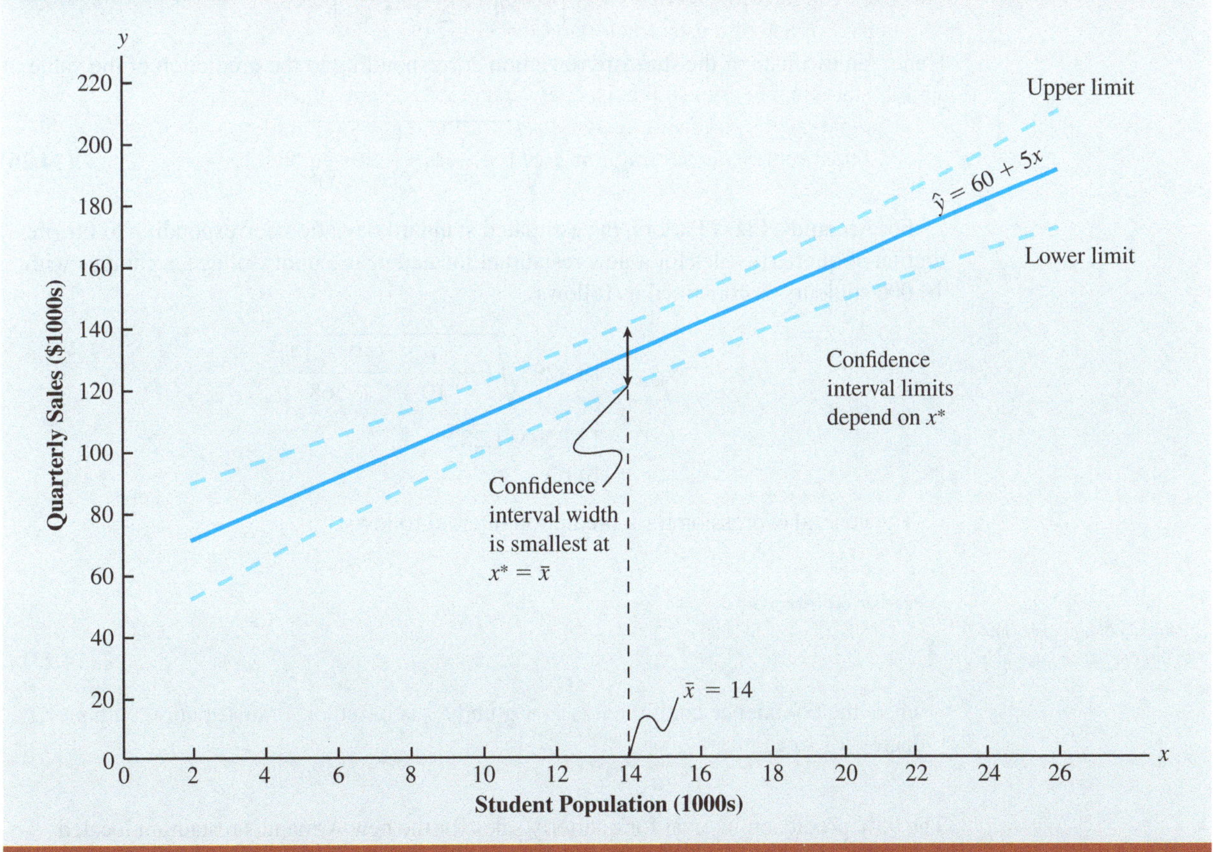

Prediction Interval for an Individual Value of y

Instead of estimating the mean value of quarterly sales for all Armand's restaurants located near campuses with 10,000 students, suppose we want to predict quarterly sales for a new restaurant Armand's is considering building near Talbot College, a campus with 10,000 students. As noted previously, the predictor of y^*, the value of y corresponding to the given x^*, is $\hat{y}^* = b_0 + b_1x^*$. For the new restaurant located near Talbot College, $x^* = 10$ and the prediction of quarterly sales is $\hat{y}^* = 60 + 5(10) = 110$, or \$110,000. Note that the prediction of quarterly sales for the new Armand's restaurant near Talbot College is the same as the point estimate of the mean sales for all Armand's restaurants located near campuses with 10,000 students.

To develop a prediction interval, let us first determine the variance associated with using $\hat{y}^*$ as a predictor of y when $x = x^*$. This variance is made up of the sum of the following two components.

1. The variance of the y^* values about the mean $E(y^*)$, an estimate of which is given by s^2
2. The variance associated with using $\hat{y}^*$ to estimate $E(y^*)$, an estimate of which is given by $s^2_{\hat{y}^*}$

The formula for estimating the variance corresponding to the prediction of the value of y when $x = x^*$, denoted s^2_{pred}, is

$$\begin{aligned} s^2_{\text{pred}} &= s^2 + s^2_{\hat{y}^*} \\ &= s^2 + s^2\left[\frac{1}{n} + \frac{(x^* - \bar{x})^2}{\Sigma(x_i - \bar{x})^2}\right] \\ &= s^2\left[1 + \frac{1}{n} + \frac{(x^* - \bar{x})^2}{\Sigma(x_i - \bar{x})^2}\right] \end{aligned} \tag{14.25}$$

Hence, an estimate of the standard deviation corresponding to the prediction of the value of y^* is

$$s_{\text{pred}} = s\sqrt{1 + \frac{1}{n} + \frac{(x^* - \bar{x})^2}{\Sigma(x_i - \bar{x})^2}} \tag{14.26}$$

For Armand's Pizza Parlors, the estimated standard deviation corresponding to the prediction of quarterly sales for a new restaurant located near Talbot College, a campus with 10,000 students, is computed as follows.

$$\begin{aligned} s_{\text{pred}} &= 13.829\sqrt{1 + \frac{1}{10} + \frac{(10 - 14)^2}{568}} \\ &= 13.829\sqrt{1.282} \\ &= 14.69 \end{aligned}$$

The general expression for a prediction interval follows.

The margin of error associated with this prediction interval is $t_{\alpha/2}s_{\text{pred}}$.

Prediction Interval for y^*

$$\hat{y}^* \pm t_{\alpha/2}s_{\text{pred}} \tag{14.27}$$

where the confidence coefficient is $1 - \alpha$ and $t_{\alpha/2}$ is based on a t distribution with $n - 2$ degrees of freedom.

The 95% prediction interval for quarterly sales for the new Armand's restaurant located near Talbot College can be found using $t\alpha_{/2} = t_{0.025} = 2.306$ and $s_{\text{pred}} = 14.69$. Thus, with

Figure 14.11 Confidence and Prediction Intervals for Sales y at Given Values of Student Population x

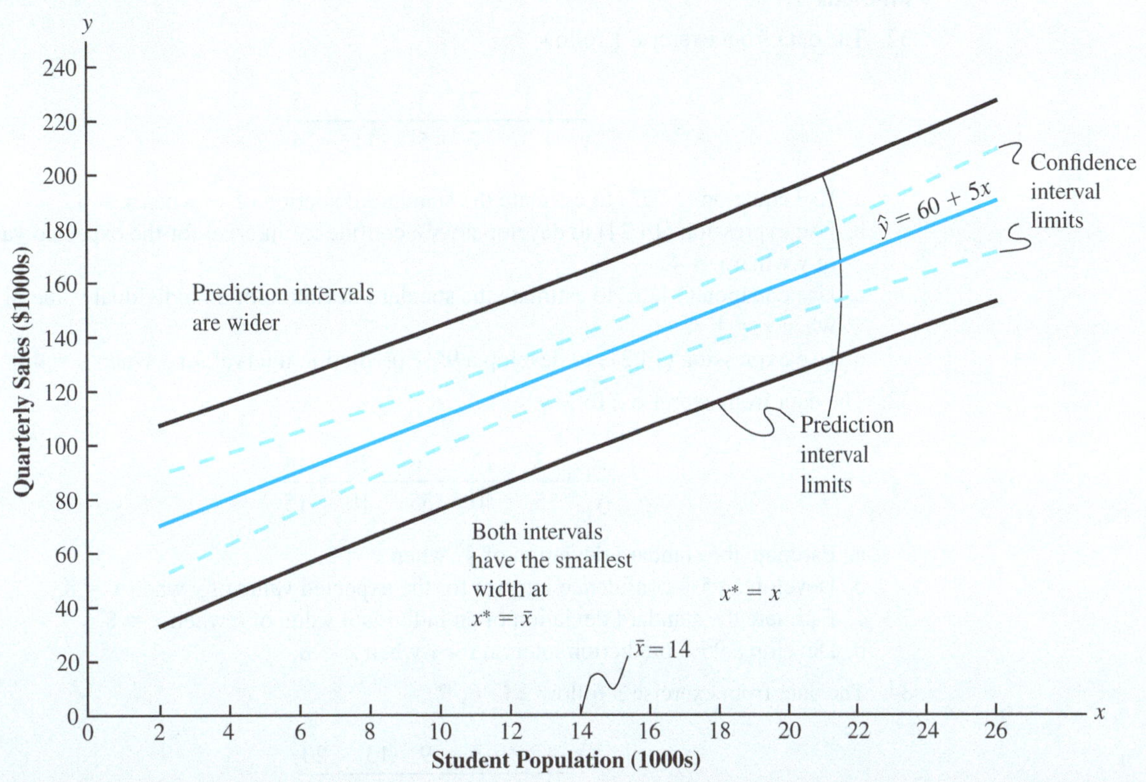

$\hat{y}^* = 110$ and a margin of error of $t_{0.025}s_{\text{pred}} = 2.306(14.69) = 33.875$, the 95% prediction interval is

$$110 \pm 33.875$$

In dollars, this prediction interval is $110,000 ± $33,875 or $76,125 to $143,875. Note that the prediction interval for the new restaurant located near Talbot College, a campus with 10,000 students, is wider than the confidence interval for the mean quarterly sales of all restaurants located near campuses with 10,000 students. The difference reflects the fact that we are able to estimate the mean value of y more precisely than we can predict an individual value of y.

In general, the lines for the confidence interval limits and the prediction interval limits both have curvature.

Confidence intervals and prediction intervals are both more precise when the value of the independent variable x^* is closer to $\bar{x}$. The general shapes of confidence intervals and the wider prediction intervals are shown together in Figure 14.11.

Note + Comment

A prediction interval is used to predict the value of the dependent variable y for a *new observation*. As an illustration, we showed how to develop a prediction interval of quarterly sales for a new restaurant that Armand's is considering building near Talbot College, a campus with 10,000 students. The fact that the value of $x = 10$ is not one of the values of student population for the Armand's sample data in Table 14.1 is not meant to imply that prediction intervals cannot be developed for values of x in the sample data. But, for the 10 restaurants that make up the data in Table 14.1, developing a prediction interval for quarterly sales for *one of these restaurants* does not make any sense because we already know the value of quarterly sales for each of these restaurants. In other words, a prediction interval only has meaning for something new, in this case, a new observation corresponding to a particular value of x that may or may not equal one of the values of x in the sample.

Exercises

Methods

32. The data from exercise 1 follow. **LO 8, 9**

x_i	1	2	3	4	5
y_i	3	7	5	11	14

a. Use equation (14.23) to estimate the standard deviation of $\hat{y}^*$ when $x = 4$.
b. Use expression (14.24) to develop a 95% confidence interval for the expected value of y when $x = 4$.
c. Use equation (14.26) to estimate the standard deviation of an individual value of y when $x = 4$.
d. Use expression (14.27) to develop a 95% prediction interval for y when $x = 4$.

33. The data from exercise 2 follow. **LO 8, 9**

x_i	3	12	6	20	14
y_i	55	40	55	10	15

a. Estimate the standard deviation of $\hat{y}^*$ when $x = 8$.
b. Develop a 95% confidence interval for the expected value of y when $x = 8$.
c. Estimate the standard deviation of an individual value of y when $x = 8$.
d. Develop a 95% prediction interval for y when $x = 8$.

34. The data from exercise 3 follow. **LO 8, 9**

x_i	2	6	9	13	20
y_i	7	18	9	26	23

Develop the 95% confidence and prediction intervals when $x = 12$. Explain why these two intervals are different.

Applications

DATA*file*
restaurantline

35. **Restaurant Lines.** Many small restaurants in Portland, Oregon, and other cities across the United States do not take reservations. Owners say that with smaller capacity, no-shows are costly, and they would rather have their staff focused on customer service rather than maintaining a reservation system (*pressherald.com*). However, it is important to be able to give reasonable estimates of waiting time when customers arrive and put their name on the waiting list. The file *restaurantline* contains 10 observations of number of people in line ahead of a customer (independent variable x) and actual waiting time (dependent variable y). The estimated regression equation is: $\hat{y} = 4.35 + 8.81x$ and MSE $= 94.42$. **LO 2, 8, 9**
a. Develop a point estimate for a customer who arrives with three people on the wait-list.
b. Develop a 95% confidence interval for the mean waiting time for a customer who arrives with three customers already in line.
c. Develop a 95% prediction interval for Roger and Sherry Davy's waiting time if there are three customers in line when they arrive.
d. Discuss the difference between parts (b) and (c).

DATA*file*
sales

36. **Sales Performance.** In exercise 7, the data on y = annual sales ($1,000s) for new customer accounts and x = number of years of experience for a sample of 10 salespersons provided the estimated regression equation $\hat{y} = 80 + 4x$. For these data $\bar{x} = 7$, $\Sigma(x_i - \bar{x})^2 = 142$, and $s = 4.6098$. **LO 8, 9**
a. Develop a 95% confidence interval for the mean annual sales for all salespersons with nine years of experience.

b. The company is considering hiring Tom Smart, a salesperson with nine years of experience. Develop a 95% prediction interval of annual sales for Tom Smart.
c. Discuss the differences in your answers to parts (a) and (b).

37. **Auditing Itemized Deductions.** In exercise 13, data were given on the adjusted gross income x and the amount of itemized deductions taken by taxpayers. Data were reported in thousands of dollars. With the estimated regression equation $\hat{y} = 4.68 + 0.16x$, the point estimate of a reasonable level of total itemized deductions for a taxpayer with an adjusted gross income of \$52,500 is \$13,080. **LO 8, 9**
a. Develop a 95% confidence interval for the mean amount of total itemized deductions for all taxpayers with an adjusted gross income of \$52,500.
b. Develop a 95% prediction interval estimate for the amount of total itemized deductions for a particular taxpayer with an adjusted gross income of \$52,500.
c. If the particular taxpayer referred to in part (b) claimed total itemized deductions of \$20,400, would the IRS agent's request for an audit appear to be justified?
d. Use your answer to part (b) to give the IRS agent a guideline as to the amount of total itemized deductions a taxpayer with an adjusted gross income of \$52,500 should claim before an audit is recommended.

38. **Prediction Intervals for Cost Estimation.** Refer to exercise 21, where data on the production volume x and total cost y for a particular manufacturing operation were used to develop the estimated regression equation $\hat{y} = 1{,}246.67 + 7.6x$. **LO 2, 9**
a. The company's production schedule shows that 500 units must be produced next month. Predict the total cost for next month.
b. Develop a 99% prediction interval for the total cost for next month.
c. If an accounting cost report at the end of next month shows that the actual production cost during the month was \$6,000, should managers be concerned about incurring such a high total cost for the month? Discuss.

39. **Entertainment Spend.** *The Wall Street Journal* asked Concur Technologies, Inc., an expense management company, to examine data from 8.3 million expense reports to provide insights regarding business travel expenses. Their analysis of the data showed that New York was the most expensive city. The following table shows the average daily hotel room rate (x) and the average amount spent on entertainment (y) for a random sample of 9 of the 25 most-visited U.S. cities. These data lead to the estimated regression equation $\hat{y} = 17.49 + 1.0334x$. For these data SSE = 1,541.4. **LO 2, 8, 9**

DATA*file*
businesstravel

City	Room Rate ($)	Entertainment ($)
Boston	148	161
Denver	96	105
Nashville	91	101
New Orleans	110	142
Phoenix	90	100
San Diego	102	120
San Francisco	136	167
San Jose	90	140
Tampa	82	98

a. Predict the amount spent on entertainment for a particular city that has a daily room rate of \$89.
b. Develop a 95% confidence interval for the mean amount spent on entertainment for all cities that have a daily room rate of \$89.
c. The average room rate in Chicago is \$128. Develop a 95% prediction interval for the amount spent on entertainment in Chicago.

14.7 Excel's Regression Tool

In previous sections of this chapter, we have shown how Excel's chart tools can be used for various tasks in a regression analysis. Excel also has a more comprehensive Regression tool. In this section, we will illustrate how Excel's Regression tool can be used to perform a complete regression analysis, including statistical tests of significance for the Armand's Pizza Parlors data in Table 14.2.

Using Excel's Regression Tool for the Armand's Pizza Parlors Example

Refer to Figures 14.12 and 14.13 as we describe the tasks involved to use Excel's Regression tool to perform the regression analysis computations for the Armand's data.

Enter/Access Data: Open the file *armands*. The data are in cells B2:C11 and labels are in column A and cells B1:C1.

Apply Tools: The following steps describe how to use Excel's Regression tool to perform the regression analysis computations performed in Sections 14.2–14.5.

Step 1. Click the **Data** tab on the Ribbon
Step 2. In the **Analyze** group, click **Data Analysis**
Step 3. Choose **Regression** from the list of Analysis Tools
Step 4. When the **Regression** dialog box appears (see Figure 14.12):
Enter *C1:C11* in the **Input Y Range:** box
Enter *B1:B11* in the **Input X Range:** box
Select the check box for **Labels**
Select the check box for **Confidence Level:**
Enter *99* in the **Confidence Level:** box
Select **Output Range:** in the **Output options** area
Enter *A13* in the **Output Range:** box (to identify the upper left corner of the section of the worksheet where the output will appear)
Click **OK**

Figure 14.12 Regression Tool Dialog Box for the Armand's Pizza Parlors Example

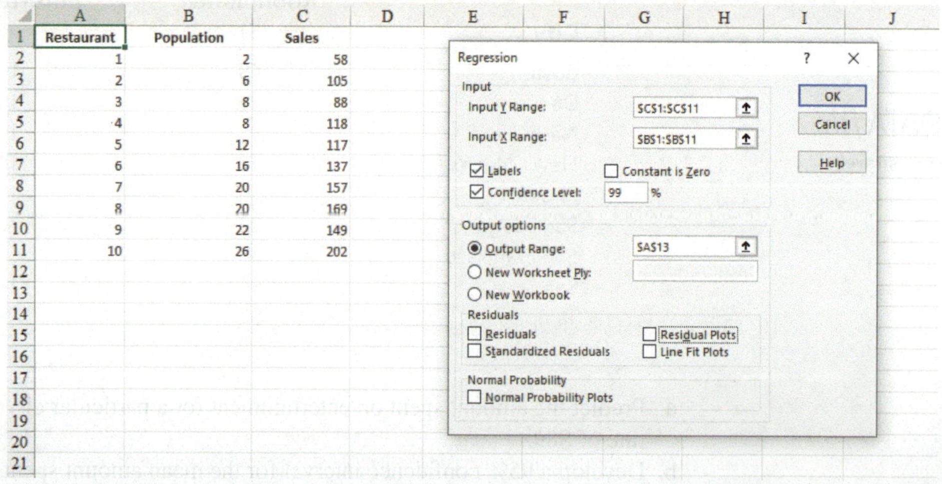

Source: Microsoft Corporation

Figure 14.13 Regression Tool Output for Armand's Pizza Parlors

	A	B	C	D	E	F	G	H	I	J
1	Restaurant	Population	Sales							
2	1	2	58							
3	2	6	105							
4	3	8	88							
5	4	8	118							
6	5	12	117							
7	6	16	137							
8	7	20	157							
9	8	20	169							
10	9	22	149							
11	10	26	202							
12										
13	SUMMARY OUTPUT									
14										
15	*Regression Statistics*									
16	Multiple R	0.9501								
17	R Square	0.9027								
18	Adjusted R Square	0.8906								
19	Standard Error	13.8293								
20	Observations	10								
21										
22	ANOVA									
23		*df*	*SS*	*MS*	*F*	*Significance F*				
24	Regression	1	14200	14200	74.2484	2.54887E-05				
25	Residual	8	1530	191.25						
26	Total	9	15730							
27										
28		*Coefficients*	*Standard Error*	*t Stat*	*P-value*	*Lower 95%*	*Upper 95%*	*Lower 99.0%*	*Upper 99.0%*	
29	Intercept	60	9.2260	6.5033	0.0002	38.7247	81.2753	29.0431	90.9569	
30	Population	5	0.5803	8.6167	0.0000	3.6619	6.3381	3.0530	6.9470	
31										

The Excel output can be reformatted to improve readability.

The regression output, titled SUMMARY OUTPUT, begins with row 13 in Figure 14.13. Because Excel initially displays the output using standard column widths, many of the row and column labels are unreadable. In several places we have reformatted to improve readability. We have also reformatted cells displaying numerical values to a maximum of four decimal places. Numbers displayed using scientific notation have not been modified. We reformat regression output in this way throughout this chapter.

The first section of the summary output, entitled *Regression Statistics,* contains summary statistics such as the coefficient of determination (R Square). The second section of the output, titled ANOVA, contains the analysis of variance table. The last section of the output, which is not titled, contains the estimated regression coefficients and related information. Let us begin our interpretation of the regression output with the information contained in rows 29 and 30.

Interpretation of Estimated Regression Equation Output

Row 29 contains information about the y-intercept of the estimated regression line. Row 30 contains information about the slope of the estimated regression line. The y-intercept of the estimated regression line, $b_0 = 60$, is shown in cell B29, and the slope of the estimated regression line, $b_1 = 5$, is shown in cell B30. The label *Intercept* in cell A29 and the label *Population* in cell A30 are used to identify these two values.

In Section 14.5, we showed that the estimated standard deviation of b_1 is $s_{b_1} = 0.5803$. Cell C30 contains the estimated standard deviation of b_1. As we indicated previously, the standard deviation of b_1 is also referred to as the standard error of b_1. Thus, s_{b_1} provides an estimate of the standard error of b_1. The label *Standard Error* in cell C28 is Excel's way of indicating that the value in cell C30 is the estimate of the standard error, or standard deviation, of b_1.

In Section 14.5, we stated that the form of the null and alternative hypotheses needed to test for a significant relationship between population and sales are as follows:

$$H_0\colon \beta_1 = 0$$
$$H_a\colon \beta_1 \neq 0$$

Recall that the t test for a significant relationship required the computation of the t statistic, $t = b_1/s_{b_1}$. For the Armand's data, the value of t that we computed was $t = 5/0.5803 = 8.62$. Note that after rounding, the value in cell D30 is 8.62. The label in cell D28, *t Stat,* reminds us that cell D30 contains the value of the t test statistic.

t Test The information in cell E30 provides a means for conducting a test of significance. The value in cell E30 is the p-value associated with the t test for significance. Excel has displayed the p-value using scientific notation. To obtain the decimal equivalent, we move the decimal point five places to the left; we obtain a p-value of 0.0000255. Thus, the p-value associated with the t test for significance is 0.0000255. Given the level of significance α, the decision of whether to reject H_0 can be made as follows:

$$\text{Reject } H_0 \text{ if } p\text{-value} \leq \alpha$$

Suppose the level of significance is $\alpha = 0.01$. Because the p-value $= 0.0000255 < \alpha = 0.01$, we can reject H_0 and conclude that we have a significant relationship between student population and sales. Because p-values are provided as part of the computer output for regression analysis, the p-value approach is most often used for hypothesis tests in regression analysis.

The information in cells F28:I30 can be used to develop confidence interval estimates of the y-intercept and slope of the estimated regression equation. Excel always provides the lower and upper limits for a 95% confidence interval. Recall that in the Regression dialog box (see Figure 14.12) we selected Confidence Level and entered 99 in the Confidence Level box. As a result, Excel's Regression tool also provides the lower and upper limits for a 99% confidence interval. For instance, the value in cell H30 is the lower limit for the 99% confidence interval estimate of β_1 and the value in cell I30 is the upper limit. Thus, after rounding, the 99% confidence interval estimate of β_1 is 3.05 to 6.95. The values in cells F30 and G30 provide the lower and upper limits for the 95% confidence interval. Thus, the 95% confidence interval is 3.66 to 6.34.

Interpretation of ANOVA Output

Excel refers to the error sum of squares as the residual sum of squares.

The information in cells A22:F26 summarizes the analysis of variance computations for the Armand's data. The three sources of variation are labeled *Regression*, *Residual*, and *Total*. The label *df* in cell B23 stands for degrees of freedom, the label *SS* in cell C23 stands for sum of squares, and the label *MS* in cell D23 stands for mean square. Looking at cells C24:C26, we see that the regression sum of squares is 14,200, the residual or error sum of squares is 1,530, and the total sum of squares is 15,730. The values in cells B24:B26 are the degrees of freedom corresponding to each sum of squares. Thus, the regression sum of squares has 1 degree of freedom, the residual or error sum of squares has 8 degrees of freedom, and the total sum of squares has 9 degrees of freedom. As we discussed previously, the regression degrees of freedom plus the residual degrees of freedom are equal to the total degrees of freedom, and the regression sum of squares plus the residual sum of squares are equal to the total sum of squares.

In Section 14.5, we stated that the mean square error, obtained by dividing the error or residual sum of squares by its degrees of freedom, provides an estimate of σ^2. The value in cell D25, 191.25, is the mean square error for the Armand's regression output. We also stated that the mean square regression is the sum of squares due to regression divided by the regression degrees of freedom. The value in cell D24, 14,200, is the mean square regression.

F Test In Section 14.5, we showed that an F test, based upon the F probability distribution, could also be used to test for significance in regression. The value in cell F24, 0.0000255, is the p-value associated with the F test for significance. Suppose the level of significance is $\alpha = 0.01$. Because the p-value $= 0.0000255 < \alpha = 0.01$, we can reject H_0 and conclude that we have a significant relationship between student population and sales. Note that it is the same conclusion that we obtained using the p-value approach for the t test for significance. In fact, because the t test for significance is equivalent to the F test for significance in simple linear regression, the p-values provided by both approaches are identical. The label Excel uses to identify the p-value for the F test for significance, shown in cell F23, is *Significance F.* In Chapter 9, we also stated that the p-value is often referred to as the observed level of significance. Thus, the label *Significance F* may be more meaningful if you think of the value in cell F24 as the observed level of significance for the F test.

Interpretation of Regression Statistics Output

Adjusted R Square, shown in cell B18 in Figure 4.13, is not meaningful for simple linear regression. Adjusted R Square will be discussed in more detail in chapter 15 where we discuss linear regression with more than one independent variable.

The output in cells A15:B20 summarizes the regression statistics. The number of observations in the data set, 10, is shown in cell B20. The coefficient of determination, 0.9027, appears in cell B17; the corresponding label, *R Square*, is shown in cell A17. The square root of the coefficient of determination provides the sample correlation coefficient of 0.9501 shown in cell B16. Note that Excel uses the label *Multiple R* (cell A16) to identify this value. In cell A19, the label *Standard Error* is used to identify the value of s, the estimate of σ. Cell B19 shows that the value of s is 13.8293. We caution the reader to keep in mind that in the Excel output, the label *Standard Error* appears in two different places. In the Regression Statistics section of the output the label *Standard Error* refers to s, the estimate of σ. In the Estimated Regression Equation section of the output, the label *Standard Error* refers to s_{b_1}, the estimated standard deviation of the sampling distribution of b_1.

Exercises

Applications

40. **Apartment Selling Price.** The commercial division of a real estate firm conducted a study to determine the extent of the relationship between annual gross rents ($1,000s) and the selling price ($1,000s) for apartment buildings. Data were collected on several properties sold, and Excel's Regression tool was used to develop an estimated regression equation. A portion of the regression output follows. **LO 1, 2, 7**
   a. How many apartment buildings were in the sample?

ANOVA

	df	*SS*	*MS*	*F*	*Significance F*
Regression	1	41587.3			
Residual	7				
Total	8	51984.1			

	Coefficients	*Standard Error*	*t Stat*	*P-value*
Intercept	20.000	3.2213	6.21	
Annual Gross Rents	7.210	1.3626	5.29	

   b. Write the estimated regression equation.
   c. Use the t test to determine whether the selling price is related to annual gross rents. Use $\alpha = 0.05$.
   d. Use the F test to determine whether the selling price is related to annual gross rents. Use $\alpha = 0.05$.
   e. Predict the selling price of an apartment building with gross annual rents of $50,000.

41. **Computer Maintenance.** Following is a portion of the regression output for an application relating maintenance expense (dollars per month) to usage (hours per week) for a particular brand of computer terminal. **LO 1, 2, 6**

ANOVA

	df	*SS*	*MS*	*F*	*Significance F*
Regression	1	1575.76			
Residual	8	349.14			
Total	9	1924.90			

	Coefficients	*Standard Error*	*t Stat*	*P-value*
Intercept	6.1092	0.9361		
Usage	0.8951	0.149		

a. Write the estimated regression equation.
b. Use a t test to determine whether monthly maintenance expense is related to usage at the 0.05 level of significance.
c. Did the estimated regression equation provide a good fit? Explain.

42. **Annual Sales and Salespeople.** A regression model relating the number of salespersons at a branch office to annual sales at the office (in thousands of dollars) provided the following regression output. **LO 1 2, 7**

ANOVA

	df	*SS*	*MS*	*F*	*Significance F*
Regression	1	6828.6			
Residual	28				
Total	29	9127.4			

	Coefficients	*Standard Error*	*t Stat*	*P-value*
Intercept	80.0	11.333		
	50.0	5.482		

a. Write the estimated regression equation.
b. Compute the F statistic and test the significance of the relationship at the 0.05 level of significance.
c. Compute the t statistic and test the significance of the relationship at the 0.05 level of significance.
d. Predict the annual sales at the Memphis branch office. This branch employs 12 salespersons.

43. **Estimating Setup Time.** Sherry is a production manager for a small manufacturing shop and is interested in developing a predictive model to estimate the time to produce an order of a given size—that is, the total time to produce a certain quantity of the product. She has collected data on the total time to produce 30 different orders of various quantities in the file *setup*. **LO 1, 3, 4, 6**

DATA*file*
setup

a. Develop a scatter diagram with quantity as the independent variable.
b. What does the scatter diagram developed in part (a) indicate about the relationship between the two variables?
c. Develop the estimated regression equation. Interpret the intercept and slope.
d. Test for a significant relationship. Use 0.05.
e. Did the estimated regression equation provide a good fit?

44. **Auto Racing Helmet.** Automobile racing, high-performance driving schools, and driver education programs run by automobile clubs continue to grow in popularity. All these activities require the participant to wear a helmet that is certified by the Snell

Memorial Foundation, a not-for-profit organization dedicated to research, education, testing, and development of helmet safety standards. Snell "SA" (Sports Application) rated professional helmets are designed for auto racing and provide extreme impact resistance and high fire protection. One of the key factors in selecting a helmet is weight, since lower-weight helmets tend to place less stress on the neck. The following data show the weight and price for 18 SA helmets (SoloRacer website). **LO 1, 4, 6**

DATA*file*
racehelmets

Helmet	Weight (oz)	Price ($)
Pyrotect Pro Airflow	64	248
Pyrotect Pro Airflow Graphics	64	278
RCi Full Face	64	200
RaceQuip RidgeLine	64	200
HJC AR-10	58	300
HJC Si-12	47	700
HJC HX-10	49	900
Impact Racing Super Sport	59	340
Zamp FSA-1	66	199
Zamp RZ-2	58	299
Zamp RZ-2 Ferrari	58	299
Zamp RZ-3 Sport	52	479
Zamp RZ-3 Sport Painted	52	479
Bell M2	63	369
Bell M4	62	369
Bell M4 Pro	54	559
G Force Pro Force 1	63	250
G Force Pro Force 1 Grafx	63	280

a. Develop a scatter diagram with weight as the independent variable.
b. Does there appear to be any relationship between these two variables?
c. Develop the estimated regression equation that could be used to predict the price given the weight.
d. Test for the significance of the relationship at the 0.05 level of significance.
e. Did the estimated regression equation provide a good fit? Explain.

14.8 Residual Analysis: Validating Model Assumptions

Residual analysis *is the primary tool for determining whether the assumed regression model is appropriate.*

As we noted previously, the *residual* for observation *i* is the difference between the observed value of the dependent variable (y_i) and the predicted value of the dependent variable ($\hat{y}_i$).

Residual for Observation *i*

$$y_i - \hat{y}_i \tag{14.28}$$

where

y_i is the observed value of the dependent variable
$\hat{y}_i$ is the predicted value of the dependent variable

In other words, the *i*th residual is the error resulting from using the estimated regression equation to predict the value of the dependent variable. The residuals for the Armand's Pizza Parlors example are computed in Table 14.7. The observed values of the dependent variable are in the second column and the predicted values of the dependent variable,

Table 14.7 Residuals for Armand's Pizza Parlors

Student Population x_i	Sales y_i	Predicted Sales $\hat{y}_i = 60 + 5x_i$	Residuals $y_i - \hat{y}_i$
2	58	70	−12
6	105	90	15
8	88	100	−12
8	118	100	18
12	117	120	−3
16	137	140	−3
20	157	160	−3
20	169	160	9
22	149	170	−21
26	202	190	12

obtained using the estimated regression equation $\hat{y} = 60 + 5x$, are in the third column. An analysis of the corresponding residuals in the fourth column will help determine whether the assumptions made about the regression model are appropriate.

Let us now review the regression assumptions for the Armand's Pizza Parlors example. A simple linear regression model was assumed.

$$y = \beta_0 + \beta_1 x + \epsilon \qquad \textbf{(14.29)}$$

This model indicates that we assumed quarterly sales (y) to be a linear function of the size of the student population (x) plus an error term ϵ. In Section 14.4, we made the following assumptions about the error term ϵ.

1. $E(\epsilon) = 0$.
2. The variance of ϵ, denoted by σ^2, is the same for all values of x.
3. The values of ϵ are independent.
4. The error term ϵ has a normal distribution.

These assumptions provide the theoretical basis for the t test and the F test used to determine whether the relationship between x and y is significant, and for the confidence and prediction interval estimates presented in Section 14.6. If the assumptions about the error term ϵ appear questionable, the hypothesis tests about the significance of the regression relationship and the interval estimation results may not be valid.

The residuals provide the best information about ϵ; hence an analysis of the residuals is an important step in determining whether the assumptions for ϵ are appropriate. Much of residual analysis is based on an examination of graphical plots. In this section, we discuss the following residual plots.

1. A plot of the residuals against values of the independent variable x
2. A plot of residuals against the predicted values of the dependent variable y
3. A standardized residual plot
4. A normal probability plot

Residual Plot Against x

A **residual plot** against the independent variable x is a graph in which the values of the independent variable are represented by the horizontal axis and the corresponding residual values are represented by the vertical axis. A point is plotted for each residual. The first coordinate for each point is given by the value of x_i and the second coordinate is given by the corresponding value of the residual $y_i - \hat{y}_i$. For a residual plot against x with the Armand's Pizza Parlors data from Table 14.7, the coordinates of the first point are $(2, -12)$, corresponding to $x_1 = 2$ and $y_1 - \hat{y}_1 = -12$; the coordinates of the second

Figure 14.14 Plot of the Residuals Against the Independent Variable x for Armand's Pizza Parlors

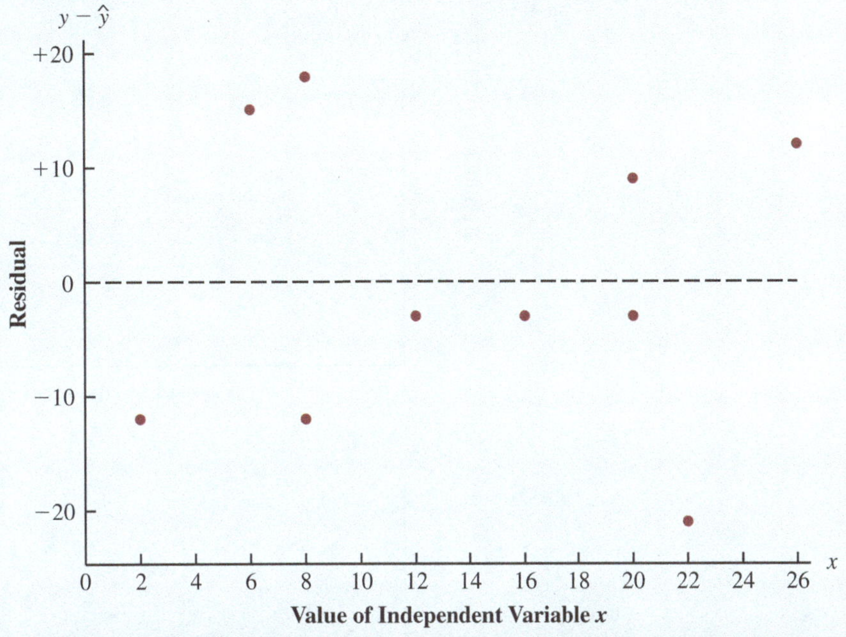

point are (6, 15), corresponding to $x_2 = 6$ and $y_2 - \hat{y}_2 = 15$; and so on. Figure 14.14 shows the resulting residual plot.

Before interpreting the results for this residual plot, let us consider some general patterns that might be observed in any residual plot. Three examples appear in Figure 14.15. If the assumption that the variance of ϵ is the same for all values of x and the assumed regression model is an adequate representation of the relationship between the variables, the residual plot should give an overall impression of a horizontal band of points such as the one in Panel A of Figure 14.15. However, if the variance of ϵ is not the same for all values of x—for example, if variability about the regression line is greater for larger values of x—a pattern such as the one in Panel B of Figure 14.15 could be observed. In this case, the assumption of a constant variance of ϵ is violated. Another possible residual plot is shown in Panel C. In this case, we would conclude that the assumed regression model is not an adequate representation of the relationship between the variables. A curvilinear regression model or multiple regression model should be considered.

Now let us return to the residual plot for Armand's Pizza Parlors shown in Figure 14.14. The residuals appear to approximate the horizontal pattern in Panel A of Figure 14.15. Hence, we conclude that the residual plot does not provide evidence that the assumptions made for Armand's regression model should be challenged. At this point, we are confident in the conclusion that Armand's simple linear regression model is valid.

Experience and good judgment are always factors in the effective interpretation of residual plots. Seldom does a residual plot conform precisely to one of the patterns in Figure 14.15. Yet analysts who frequently conduct regression studies and frequently review residual plots become adept at understanding the differences between patterns that are reasonable and patterns that indicate the assumptions of the model should be questioned. A residual plot provides one technique to assess the validity of the assumptions for a regression model.

Residual Plot Against $\hat{y}$

Another residual plot represents the predicted value of the dependent variable $\hat{y}$ on the horizontal axis and the residual values on the vertical axis. A point is plotted for each

Figure 14.15 Residual Plots from Three Regression Studies

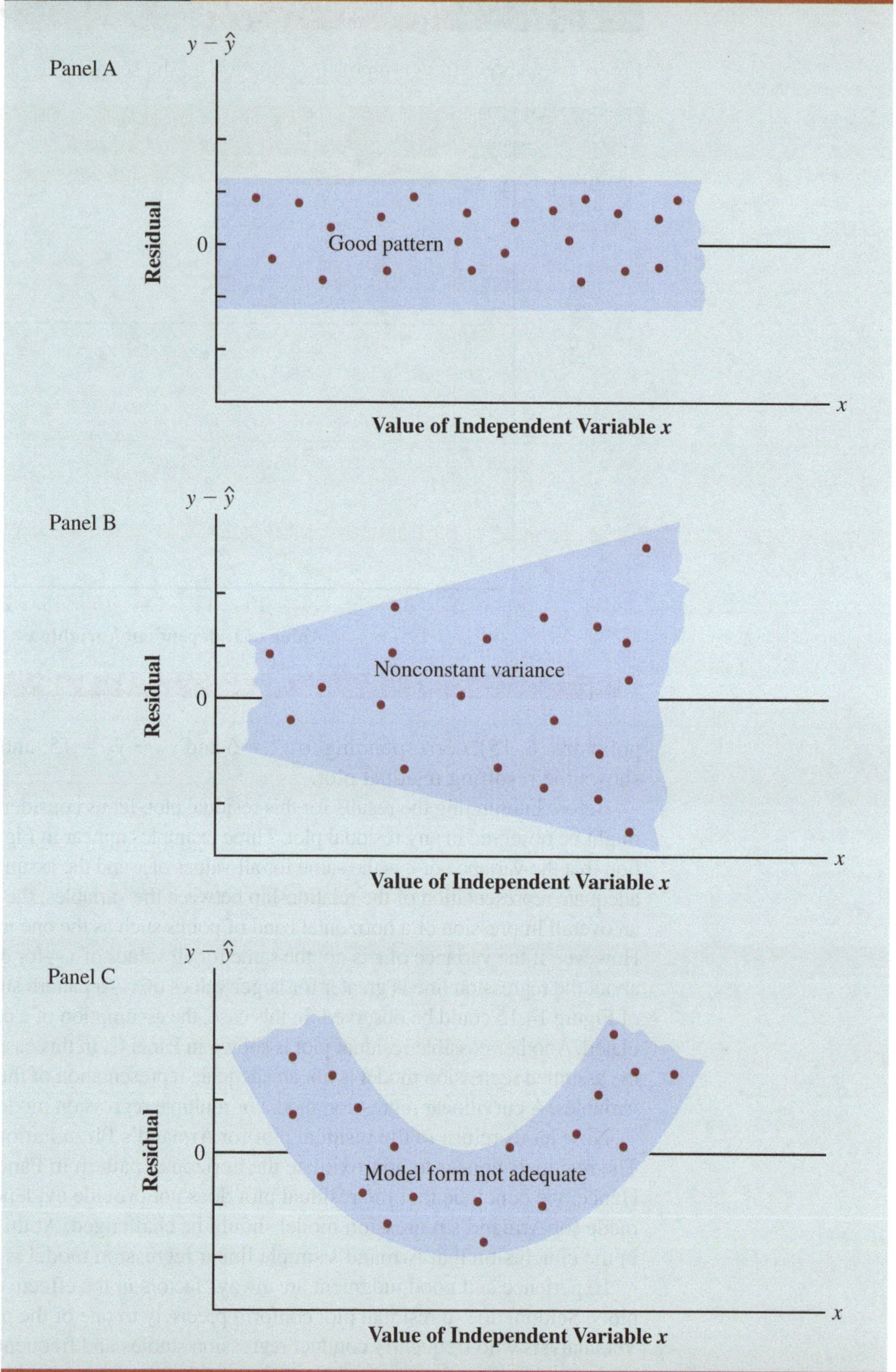

residual. The first coordinate for each point is given by $\hat{y}_i$ and the second coordinate is given by the corresponding value of the ith residual $y_i - \hat{y}_i$. With the Armand's data from Table 14.7, the coordinates of the first point are (70, −12), corresponding to $\hat{y}_1 = 70$ and $y_1 - \hat{y}_1 = -12$; the coordinates of the second point are (90, 15); and so on. Figure 14.16 provides the residual plot. Note that the pattern of this residual plot is the same as the

Figure 14.16 Plot of the Residuals Against the Predicted Values $\hat{y}$ for Armand's Pizza Parlors

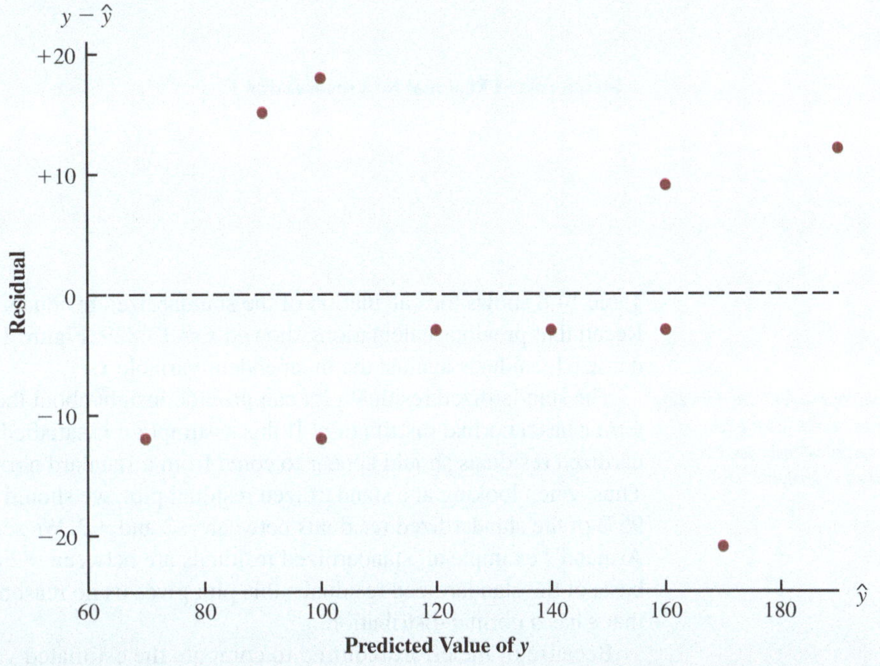

pattern of the residual plot against the independent variable x. It is not a pattern that would lead us to question the model assumptions. For simple linear regression, both the residual plot against x and the residual plot against $\hat{y}$ provide the same pattern. For multiple regression analysis, the residual plot against $\hat{y}$ is more widely used because of the presence of more than one independent variable.

Standardized Residuals

Many of the residual plots provided by computer software packages use a standardized version of the residuals. As demonstrated in preceding chapters, a random variable is standardized by subtracting its mean and dividing the result by its standard deviation. With the least squares method, the mean of the residuals is zero. Thus, simply dividing each residual by its standard deviation provides the **standardized residual**.

It can be shown that the standard deviation of residual i depends on the standard error of the estimate s and the corresponding value of the independent variable x_i.

Standard Deviation of the *i*th Residual[2]

$$s_{y_i - \hat{y}_i} = s\sqrt{1 - h_i} \tag{14.30}$$

where

$$s_{y_i - \hat{y}_i} = \text{the standard deviation of residual } i$$
$$s = \text{the standard error of the estimate}$$
$$h_i = \frac{1}{n} + \frac{(x_i - \bar{x})^2}{\Sigma(x_i - \bar{x})^2} \tag{14.31}$$

[2]This equation actually provides an estimate of the standard deviation of the *i*th residual, because *s* is used instead of σ.

Note that equation (14.30) shows that the standard deviation of the ith residual depends on x_i because of the presence of h_i in the formula.[3] Once the standard deviation of each residual is calculated, we can compute the standardized residual by dividing each residual by its corresponding standard deviation.

Standardized Residual for Observation *i*

$$\frac{y_i - \hat{y}_i}{s_{y_i - \hat{y}_i}} \tag{14.32}$$

Table 14.8 shows the calculation of the standardized residuals for Armand's Pizza Parlors. Recall that previous calculations showed $s = 13.829$. Figure 14.17 is the plot of the standardized residuals against the independent variable x.

Small departures from normality do not have a great effect on the statistical tests used in regression analysis.

The standardized residual plot can provide insight about the assumption that the error term ϵ has a normal distribution. If this assumption is satisfied, the distribution of the standardized residuals should appear to come from a standard normal probability distribution.[4] Thus, when looking at a standardized residual plot, we should expect to see approximately 95% of the standardized residuals between -2 and $+2$. We see in Figure 14.17 that for the Armand's example all standardized residuals are between -2 and $+2$. Therefore, on the basis of the standardized residuals, this plot gives us no reason to question the assumption that ϵ has a normal distribution.

Because of the effort required to compute the estimated values of $\hat{y}$, the residuals, and the standardized residuals, most statistical packages provide these values as optional regression output. Hence, residual plots can be easily obtained. For large problems, computer packages are the only practical means for developing the residual plots discussed in this section.

Table 14.8 Computation of Standardized Residuals for Armand's Pizza Parlors

Restaurant i	x_i	$x_i - \bar{x}$	$(x_i - \bar{x})^2$	$\frac{(x_i - \bar{x})^2}{\Sigma(x_i - \bar{x})^2}$	h_i	$s_{y_i - \hat{y}_i}$	$y_i - \hat{y}_i$	Standardized Residual
1	2	−12	144	0.2535	0.3535	11.1193	−12	−1.0792
2	6	−8	64	0.1127	0.2127	12.2709	15	1.2224
3	8	−6	36	0.0634	0.1634	12.6493	−12	−0.9487
4	8	−6	36	0.0634	0.1634	12.6493	18	1.4230
5	12	−2	4	0.0070	0.1070	13.0682	−3	−0.2296
6	16	2	4	0.0070	0.1070	13.0682	−3	−0.2296
7	20	6	36	0.0634	0.1634	12.6493	−3	−0.2372
8	20	6	36	0.0634	0.1634	12.6493	9	0.7115
9	22	8	64	0.1127	0.2127	12.2709	−21	−1.7114
10	26	12	144	0.2535	0.3535	11.1193	12	1.0792
		Total	568					

Note: The values of the residuals were computed in Table 14.7.

[3] h_i is referred to as the *leverage* of observation i. Leverage will be discussed further when we consider influential observations in Section 14.9.

[4] Because s is used instead of σ in equation (14.30), the probability distribution of the standardized residuals is not technically normal. However, in most regression studies, the sample size is large enough that a normal approximation is very good.

Figure 14.17 Plot of the Standardized Residuals Against the Independent Variable x for Armand's Pizza Parlors

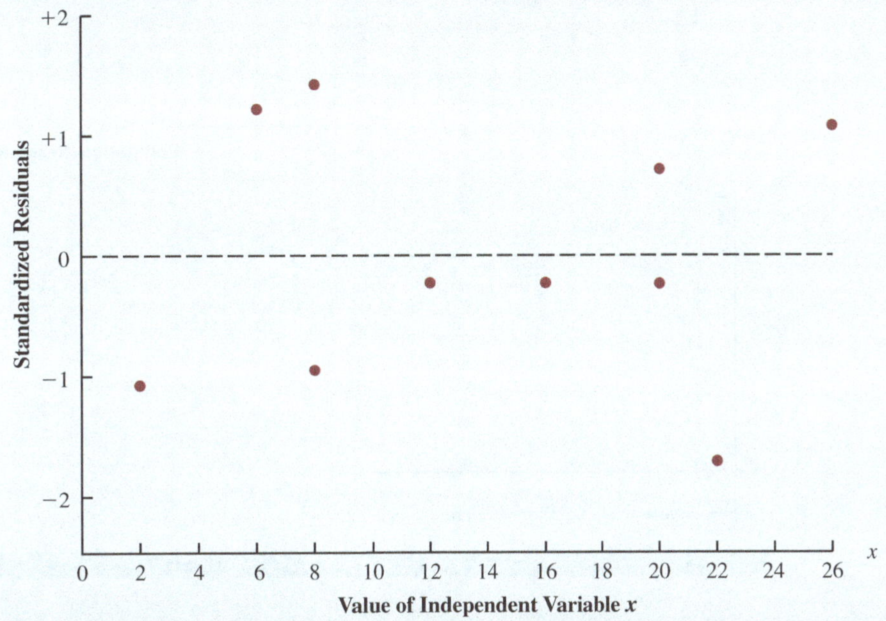

Using Excel to Construct a Residual Plot

In Section 14.7, we showed how Excel's Regression tool could be used for regression analysis. The Regression tool also provides the capability to obtain a residual plot against the independent variable x and, when used with Excel's chart tools, the Regression tool residual output can also be used to construct a residual plot against $\hat{y}$ as well as an Excel version of a standardized residual plot.

Residual Plot Against x To obtain a residual plot against x, the steps that we describe in Section 14.7 in order to obtain the regression output are performed with one change. When the Regression tool dialog box appears (see Figure 14.12), we must also select the Residual Plots option in the Residual section. The regression output will appear as described previously, and the worksheet will also contain a chart showing a plot of the residuals against the independent variable Population. In addition, a list of predicted values of y and the corresponding residual values are provided below the regression output. Figure 14.18 shows the residual output for the Armand's Pizza Parlors problem; note that rows 12–32, containing the standard Regression tool output, have been hidden to better focus on the residual portion of the output. We see that the shape of this plot is the same as shown previously in Figure 14.14.

Residual Plot Against $\hat{y}$ Using Excel's chart tools and the residual output provided in Figure 14.18, we can easily construct a residual plot against $\hat{y}$. The following steps describe how to use Excel's chart tools to construct the residual plot using the regression tool output in the worksheet.

Step 1. Select cells B37:C46
Step 2. Click the **Insert** tab on the Ribbon
Step 3. In the **Charts** group, click **Insert Scatter (X, Y) or Bubble Chart**
Step 4. When the list of scatter diagram subtypes appears:
Click **Scatter,**  (the chart in the upper-left corner)

Figure 14.18 Regression Tool Residual Output for the Armand's Pizza Parlors Problem

	A	B	C
1	Restaurant	Population	Sales
2	1	2	58
3	2	6	105
4	3	8	88
5	4	8	118
6	5	12	117
7	6	16	137
8	7	20	157
9	8	20	169
10	9	22	149
11	10	26	202
33			
34	RESIDUAL OUTPUT		
35			
36	*Observation*	*Predicted Sales*	*Residuals*
37	1	70	-12
38	2	90	15
39	3	100	-12
40	4	100	18
41	5	120	-3
42	6	140	-3
43	7	160	-3
44	8	160	9
45	9	170	-21
46	10	190	12
47			

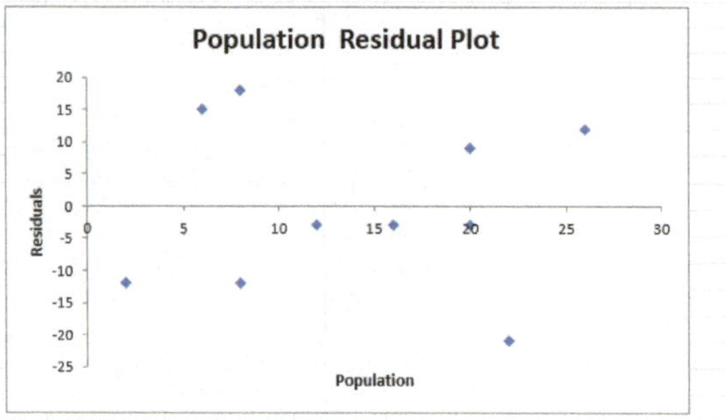

Note: Rows 12–32 are hidden.

The resulting chart will look similar to the residual plot shown in Figure 14.16. Adding a chart title, labels for the horizontal and vertical axes, as well as other formatting options can be easily done. Note that except for using different data to construct the chart as well as different labels for the chart output, the steps describing how to use Excel's chart tools to construct a residual plot against $\hat{y}$ are the same as the steps we used to construct a scatter diagram in Section 14.2.

Excel's Standardized Residual Plot Excel can be used to construct what it calls a standardized residual plot. Excel's standardized residual plot is really an approximation of the true standardized residual plot. In Excel, the standard deviation of the *i*th residual is not computed using equation (14.30). Instead, Excel estimates $s_{y_i - \hat{y}_i}$ using the standard deviation of the *n* residual values. Then, dividing each residual by this estimate, Excel obtains what it refers to as a standard residual. The plot of these standard residuals is what you get when you request a plot of the standardized residuals using Excel's Regression tool.

We will illustrate how to construct a standardized residual plot using Excel for the Armand's Pizza Parlors problem. The residuals for the Armand's Pizza Parlors problem are -12, 15, -12, 18, -3, -3, -3, 9, -21, and 12. Using Excel's STDEV.S function, we computed a standard deviation of 13.0384 for these 10 data values. To compute the standard residuals, Excel divides each residual by 13.0384; the results are shown in Table 14.9. Both the standardized residuals, computed in Table 14.8, and Excel's standard residuals are shown. There is not a great deal of difference between Excel's standard residuals and the true standardized residuals. In general, the differences get smaller as the sample size increases. Often we are interested only in identifying the general pattern of the points in a standardized residual plot; in such cases, the small differences between the standardized residuals and Excel's standard residuals will have little effect on the pattern observed. Thus these differences will not influence the conclusions reached when we use the residual plot to validate model assumptions.

The Regression tool and the chart tools can be used to obtain Excel's standardized residual plot. First, the steps that we described in Section 14.7 in order to conduct a

Table 14.9 Computation of Excel's Standard Residuals

	Values from Table 14.8			Values Using Excel	
Restaurant i	$y_i - \hat{y}$	$s_{y_i - \hat{y}_i}$	**Standardized Residual**	**Estimate of** $s_{y_i - \hat{y}_i}$	**Standard Residual**
1	−12	11.1193	−1.0792	13.0384	−0.9204
2	15	12.2709	1.2224	13.0384	1.1504
3	−12	12.6493	−0.9487	13.0384	−0.9204
4	18	12.6493	1.4230	13.0384	1.3805
5	−3	13.0682	−0.2296	13.0384	−0.2301
6	−3	13.0682	−0.2296	13.0384	−0.2301
7	−3	12.6493	−0.2372	13.0384	−0.2301
8	9	12.6493	0.7115	13.0384	0.6903
9	−21	12.2709	−1.7114	13.0384	−1.6106
10	12	11.1193	1.0792	13.0384	0.9204

regression analysis are performed with one change. When the Regression dialog box appears (see Figure 14.12), we must select the Standardized Residuals option. In addition to the regression output described previously, the output will contain a list of predicted values of y, residuals, and standard residuals, as shown in cells A34:D46 in Figure 14.19.

Figure 14.19 Standardized Residual Plot Against the Independent Variable Population for the Armand's Pizza Parlors Example

RESIDUAL OUTPUT

Observation	Predicted Sales	Residuals	Standard Residuals
1	70	-12	-0.9204
2	90	15	1.1504
3	100	-12	-0.9204
4	100	18	1.3805
5	120	-3	-0.2301
6	140	-3	-0.2301
7	160	-3	-0.2301
8	160	9	0.6903
9	170	-21	-1.6106
10	190	12	0.9204

Population	Standard Residuals
2	-0.9204
6	1.1504
8	-0.9204
8	1.3805
12	-0.2301
16	-0.2301
20	-0.2301
20	0.6903
22	-1.6106
26	0.9204

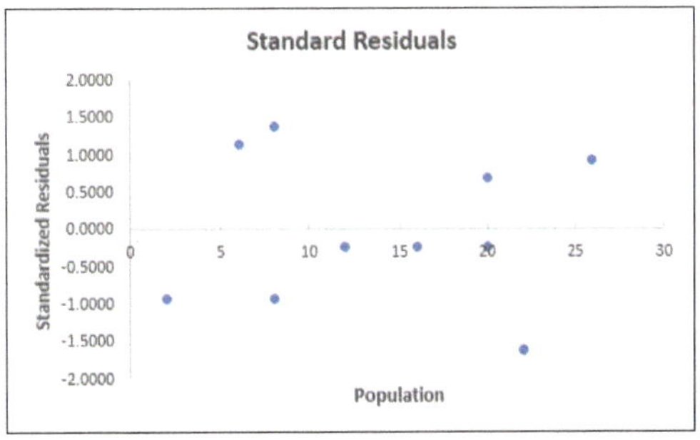

Note: Rows 1–33 are hidden.

The Standardized Residuals option does not automatically produce a standardized residual plot. But we can use Excel's chart tools to construct a scatter diagram in which the values of the independent variable are placed on the horizontal axis and the values of the standard residuals are placed on the vertical axis. The procedure that describes how to use Excel's chart tools to construct a standardized residual plot is similar to the steps we showed for using Excel's chart tools to construct a residual plot against $\hat{y}$. Because it is somewhat easier to plot two variables in Excel when the variables are in adjacent columns of the workbook, we copied the data and heading for the independent variable Population into cells F36:F46 and the data and heading for the standard residuals into cells G36:G46.

Using the data in cells F36:G46 and Excel's chart tools, we obtained the scatter diagram shown in Figure 14.19; this scatter diagram is Excel's version of the standardized residual plot for the Armand's Pizza Parlors example. Comparing Excel's version of the standardized residual plot to the standardized residual plot in Figure 14.16, we see the same pattern evident. All of the standardized residuals in both figures are between -2 and $+2$, indicating no reason to question the assumption that ϵ has a normal distribution.

Normal Probability Plot

Another approach for determining the validity of the assumption that the error term has a normal distribution is the **normal probability plot**. To show how a normal probability plot is developed, we introduce the concept of *normal scores.*

Suppose 10 values are selected randomly from a normal probability distribution with a mean of zero and a standard deviation of one, and that the sampling process is repeated over and over with the values in each sample of 10 ordered from smallest to largest. For now, let us consider only the smallest value in each sample. The random variable representing the smallest value obtained in repeated sampling is called the first-order statistic.

Statisticians show that for samples of size 10 from a standard normal probability distribution, the expected value of the first-order statistic is -1.55. This expected value is called a normal score. For the case with a sample of size $n = 10$, there are 10 order statistics and 10 normal scores (see Table 14.10). In general, a data set consisting of n observations will have n order statistics and hence n normal scores.

Let us now show how the 10 normal scores can be used to determine whether the standardized residuals for Armand's Pizza Parlors appear to come from a standard normal probability distribution. We begin by ordering the 10 standardized residuals from Table 14.8. The 10 normal scores and the ordered standardized residuals are shown together in Table 14.11. If the normality assumption is satisfied, the smallest standardized residual should be close to the smallest normal score, the next smallest standardized residual should be close to the next

Table 14.10 Normal Scores for $n = 10$

Order Statistic	Normal Score
1	−1.55
2	−1.00
3	−0.65
4	−0.37
5	−0.12
6	0.12
7	0.37
8	0.65
9	1.00
10	1.55

Table 14.11 Normal Scores and Ordered Standardized Residuals for Armand's Pizza Parlors

Normal Scores	Ordered Standardized Residuals
−1.55	−1.7114
−1.00	−1.0792
−0.65	−0.9487
−0.37	−0.2372
−0.12	−0.2296
0.12	−0.2296
0.37	0.7115
0.65	1.0792
1.00	1.2224
1.55	1.4230

smallest normal score, and so on. If we were to develop a plot with the normal scores on the horizontal axis and the corresponding standardized residuals on the vertical axis, the plotted points should cluster closely around a 45-degree line passing through the origin if the standardized residuals are approximately normally distributed. Such a plot is referred to as a *normal probability plot.*

Figure 14.20 is the normal probability plot for the Armand's Pizza Parlors example. Judgment is used to determine whether the pattern observed deviates from the line enough to conclude that the standardized residuals are not from a standard normal probability

Figure 14.20 Normal Probability Plot for Armand's Pizza Parlors

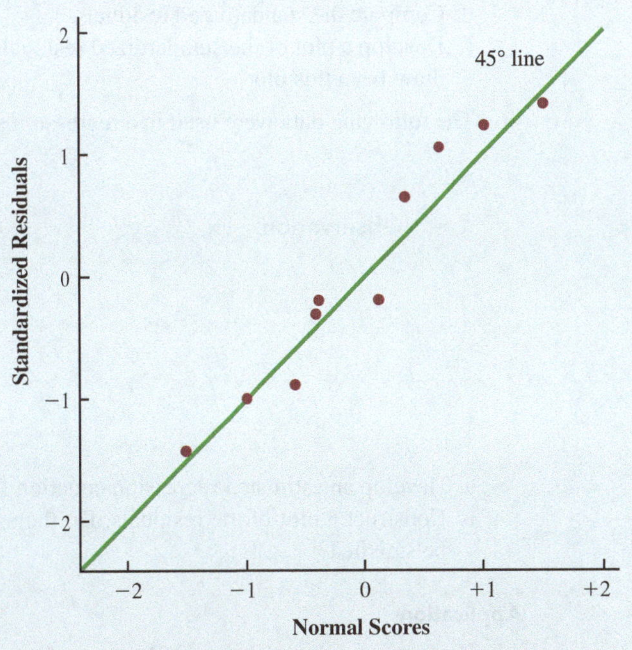

distribution. In Figure 14.20, we see that the points are grouped closely about the line. We therefore conclude that the assumption of the error term having a normal probability distribution is reasonable. In general, the more closely the points are clustered about the 45-degree line, the stronger the evidence supporting the normality assumption. Any substantial curvature in the normal probability plot is evidence that the residuals have not come from a normal distribution.

Notes + Comments

1. We use residual and normal probability plots to validate the assumptions of a regression model. If our review indicates that one or more assumptions are questionable, a different regression model or a transformation of the data should be considered. The appropriate corrective action when the assumptions are violated must be based on good judgment; recommendations from an experienced statistician can be valuable.
2. Analysis of residuals is the primary method statisticians use to verify that the assumptions associated with a regression model are valid. Even if no violations are found, it does not necessarily follow that the model will yield good predictions. However, if additional statistical tests support the conclusion of significance and the coefficient of determination is large, we should be able to develop good estimates and predictions using the estimated regression equation.

Exercises

Methods

45. Given are data for two variables, x and y. **LO 1, 10**

x_i	6	11	15	18	20
y_i	6	8	12	20	30

a. Develop an estimated regression equation for these data.
b. Compute the residuals.
c. Develop a plot of the residuals against the independent variable x. Do the assumptions about the error terms seem to be satisfied?
d. Compute the standardized residuals.
e. Develop a plot of the standardized residuals against $\hat{y}$. What conclusions can you draw from this plot?

46. The following data were used in a regression study. **LO 1, 10**

Observation	x_i	y_i	Observation	x_i	y_i
1	2	4	6	7	6
2	3	5	7	7	9
3	4	4	8	8	5
4	5	6	9	9	11
5	7	4			

a. Develop an estimated regression equation for these data.
b. Construct a plot of the residuals. Do the assumptions about the error term seem to be satisfied?

Applications

47. **Restaurant Advertising and Revenue.** Data on advertising expenditures and revenue (in thousands of dollars) for the Four Seasons Restaurant follow. **LO 1, 7, 10**

Advertising Expenditures	Revenue
1	19
2	32
4	44
6	40
10	52
14	53
20	54

a. Let x equal advertising expenditures and y equal revenue. Use the method of least squares to develop a straight line approximation of the relationship between the two variables.
b. Test whether revenue and advertising expenditures are related at a 0.05 level of significance using the F test.
c. Prepare a residual plot of $y - \hat{y}$ versus $\hat{y}$. Use the result from part (a) to obtain the values of $\hat{y}$.
d. What conclusions can you draw from residual analysis? Should this model be used, or should we look for a better one?

48. **Experience and Sales.** Refer to exercise 7, where an estimated regression equation relating years of experience and annual sales was developed. **LO 10**
a. Compute the residuals and construct a residual plot for this problem.
b. Do the assumptions about the error terms seem reasonable in light of the residual plot?

DATA*file*
costliving

49. **Cost of Living Index.** The file *costliving* contains the cost of living indexes and the population densities (number of people per square mile) for 61 cities in the United States. The cost of living index measures the cost of living in a particular city relative to the cost of living in New York City. San Francisco has an index of 112.15, meaning that it is 12.15% more expensive to live in San Francisco than New York City. Washington, DC, has an index of 84.64, which means that the cost to live in Washington, DC, is only 84.64% of what it costs to live in New York City (Numbeo website). **LO 1, 10**
a. Develop the estimated regression equation that can be used to predict the cost of living index for a U.S. city, given the city's population density.
b. Construct a residual plot against the independent variable.
c. Review the residual plot constructed in part (b). Do the assumptions of the error term and model form seem reasonable?

14.9 Outliers and Influential Observations

In this section, we discuss how to identify observations that can be classified as outliers or as being especially influential in determining the estimated regression equation. Some steps that should be taken when such observations are identified are provided.

Detecting Outliers

An **outlier** is a data point (observation) that does not fit the trend shown by the remaining data. Outliers represent observations that are suspect and warrant careful examination. They may represent erroneous data; if so, they should be corrected. They may signal a violation of model assumptions; if so, another model should be considered. Finally, they may simply be unusual values that have occurred by chance. In this case, they should be retained.

To illustrate the process of detecting outliers, consider the data set in Table 14.12; Figure 14.21 shows the scatter diagram for these data and a portion of the Regression tool output, including the tabular residual output obtained using the Standardized Residuals option. The estimated regression equation is $\hat{y} = 64.95 - 7.330x$ and R Square is 0.4968;

Table 14.12 Data Set Illustrating the Effect of an Outlier

x_i	y_i
1	45
1	55
2	50
3	75
3	40
3	45
4	30
4	35
5	25
6	15

Figure 14.21 Regression Tool Output for the Outlier Data Set

	A	B
1	x	y
2	1	45
3	1	55
4	2	50
5	3	75
6	3	40
7	3	45
8	4	30
9	4	35
10	5	25
11	6	15
12		
13	SUMMARY OUTPUT	
14		
15	*Regression Statistics*	
16	Multiple R	0.7049
17	R Square	0.4968
18	Adjusted R Square	0.4339
19	Standard Error	12.6704
20	Observations	10
21		
34	RESIDUAL OUTPUT	
35		

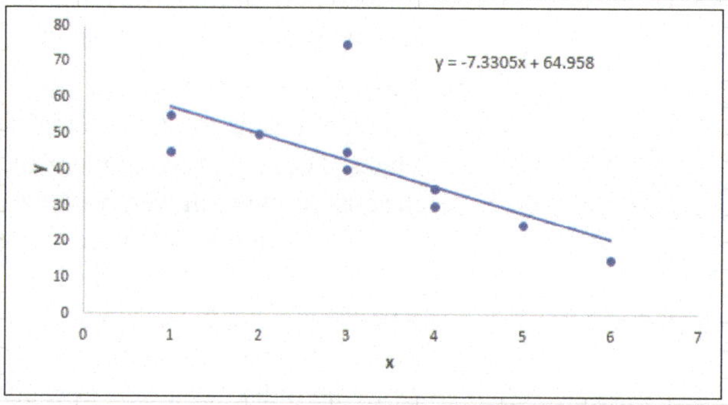

	Observation	*Predicted y*	*Residuals*	*Standard Residuals*
37	1	57.6271	-12.6271	-1.0570
38	2	57.6271	-2.6271	-0.2199
39	3	50.2966	-0.2966	-0.0248
40	4	42.9661	32.0339	2.6816
41	5	42.9661	-2.9661	-0.2483
42	6	42.9661	2.0339	0.1703
43	7	35.6356	-5.6356	-0.4718
44	8	35.6356	-0.6356	-0.0532
45	9	28.3051	-3.3051	-0.2767
46	10	20.9746	-5.9746	-0.5001
47				

The standardized residual for observation 4 is greater than +2. Hence, we consider observation 4 to be an outlier.

Note: Rows 22–33 are hidden.

thus, only 49.68% of the variability in the values of y is explained by the estimated regression equation. However, except for observation 4 ($x_4 = 3$, $y_4 = 75$), a pattern suggesting a strong negative linear relationship is apparent. Indeed, given the pattern of the rest of the data, we would have expected y_4 to be much smaller and hence would consider observation

4 to be an outlier. For the case of simple linear regression, one can often detect outliers by simply examining the scatter diagram.

The standardized residuals can also be used to identify outliers. If an observation deviates greatly from the pattern of the rest of the data, the corresponding standardized residual will be large in absolute value. We recommend considering any observation with a standardized residual of less than -2 or greater than $+2$ as an outlier. With normally distributed errors, standardized residuals should be outside these limits approximately 5% of the time. In the residual output section of Figure 14.21 we see that the standard residual value for observation 4 is 2.68; this value suggests we treat observation 4 as an outlier.

In deciding how to handle an outlier, we should first check to see whether it is a valid observation. Perhaps an error has been made in initially recording the data or in entering the data into the worksheet. For example, suppose that in checking the data in Table 14.11, we find that an error has been made and that the correct value for observation 4 is $x_4 = 3$, $y_4 = 30$. Figure 14.22 shows a portion of the Regression tool output after correction of the value of y_4. The estimated regression equation is $\hat{y} = 59.23 - 6.949x$ and R Square is 0.8380. Note also that no standard residuals are less than -2 or greater than $+2$; hence, the revised data contain no outliers. We see that using the incorrect data value had a substantial effect on the goodness of fit. With the correct data, the value of R Square has increased from 0.4968 to 0.8380 and the

Figure 14.22 Regression Tool Output for the Revised Outlier Data Set

	A	B
1	x	y
2	1	45
3	1	55
4	2	50
5	3	30
6	3	40
7	3	45
8	4	30
9	4	35
10	5	25
11	6	15
12		

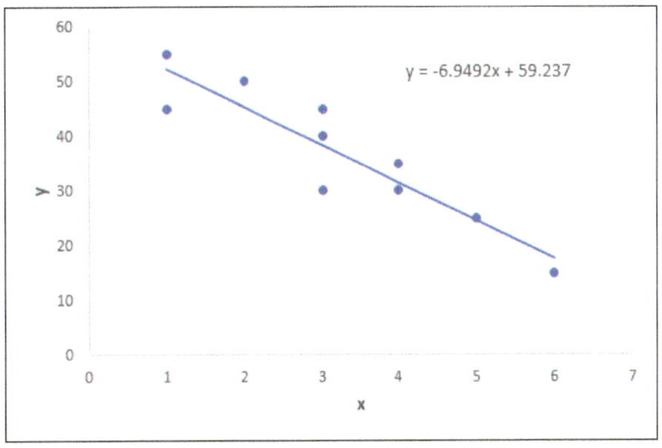

	A	B
13	SUMMARY OUTPUT	
14		
15	*Regression Statistics*	
16	Multiple R	0.9154
17	R Square	0.8380
18	Adjusted R Square	0.8177
19	Standard Error	5.2481
20	Observations	10
21		

	A	B	C	D
34	RESIDUAL OUTPUT			
35				
36	*Observation*	*Predicted y*	*Residuals*	*Standard Residuals*
37	1	52.2881	-7.2881	-1.4730
38	2	52.2881	2.7119	0.5481
39	3	45.3390	4.6610	0.9420
40	4	38.3898	-8.3898	-1.6956
41	5	38.3898	1.6102	0.3254
42	6	38.3898	6.6102	1.3359
43	7	31.4407	-1.4407	-0.2912
44	8	31.4407	3.5593	0.7194
45	9	24.4915	0.5085	0.1028
46	10	17.5424	-2.5424	-0.5138
47				

Note: Rows 22–33 are hidden.

value of b_0 has decreased from 64.95 to 59.23. The slope of the line has changed from −7.330 to −6.949. The identification of the outlier enables us to correct the data error and improve the regression results.

Detecting Influential Observations

An **influential observation** is an observation that has a strong influence on the regression results. An influential observation may be an outlier (an observation with a y value that deviates substantially from the trend of the remaining data), it may correspond to an x value far from its mean (extreme x value), or it may be caused by a combination of a somewhat off-trend y value and a somewhat extreme x value. Because influential observations may have such a dramatic effect on the estimated regression equation, they must be examined carefully. First, we should check to make sure no error has been made in collecting or recording the data. If such an error has occurred, it can be corrected and a new estimated regression equation developed. If the observation is valid, we might consider ourselves fortunate to have it. Such a point, if valid, can contribute to a better understanding of the appropriate model and can lead to a better estimated regression equation.

To illustrate the process of detecting influential observations, consider the data set in Table 14.13. The top part of Figure 14.23 shows the scatter diagram for these data and the graph of the corresponding estimated regression equation $\hat{y} = 127.4 - 0.425x$. The bottom part of Figure 14.23 shows the scatter diagram for the data in Table 14.13 with observation 7 ($x_7 = 70$, $y_7 = 100$) deleted; for these data the estimated regression equation is $\hat{y} = 138.1 - 1.090x$. With observation 7 deleted, the value of b_0 has increased from 127.4 to 138.1. The slope of the line has changed from −0.425 to −1.090. The effect of observation 7 on the regression results is dramatic and is confirmed by looking at the graphs of the two estimated regression equations. Clearly, observation 7 is influential.

Observations with extreme values for the independent variables are called **high leverage points**. Observation 7 in the data set shown in Table 14.13 (which we have identified as being influential) is a point with high leverage. The leverage of an observation is determined by how far the value of the independent variable is from its mean value. For the single-independent-variable case, the leverage of the ith observation, denoted h_i, can be computed using equation (14.33).

Leverage of Observation *i*

$$h_i = \frac{1}{n} + \frac{(x_i - \bar{x})^2}{\Sigma(x_i - \bar{x})^2} \tag{14.33}$$

Table 14.13 Data Set Illustrating the Effect of an Influential Observation

x_i	y_i
10	125
10	130
15	120
20	115
20	120
25	110
70	100

Figure 14.23 Scatter Diagrams for the Data Set with an Influential Observation

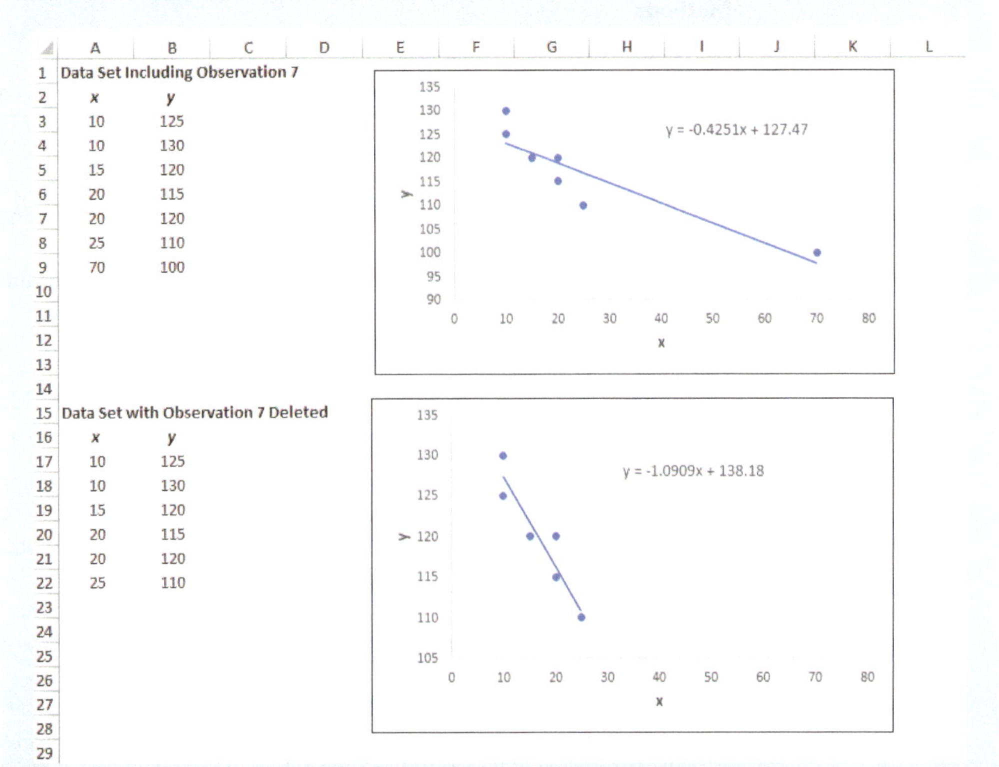

From the formula, it is clear that the farther x_i is from its mean $\bar{x}$, the higher the leverage of observation i. For the data in Table 14.13, the leverage of observation 7 is computed using equation (14.33) as follows:

$$h_i = \frac{1}{n} + \frac{(x_i - \bar{x})^2}{\sum(x_i - \bar{x})^2} = \frac{1}{7} + \frac{(70 - 24.286)^2}{2621.43} = 0.94$$

For simple linear regression, we consider observations as having high leverage if $h_i > 6/n$; for the data in Table 14.13, $6/n = 6/7 = 0.86$. Thus, because $h_i = 0.94 > 0.86$, observation 7 would be identified as having high leverage. Data points having high leverage are often influential. Influential observations that are caused by an interaction of somewhat large residuals and somewhat high leverage can be difficult to detect. Diagnostic procedures are available that take both into account in determining when an observation is influential. More advanced books on regression analysis discuss the use of such procedures. Excel does not have built-in capabilities for identifying outliers and high leverage points. Thus, we recommend reviewing the scatter diagram after fitting the regression line. For any point significantly off the line, rerun the regression analysis after deleting the observation. If the results change dramatically, the point in question is an influential observation.

Note + Comment

Once an observation is identified as potentially influential because of a large residual or high leverage, its impact on the estimated regression equation should be evaluated. More advanced texts discuss diagnostics for doing so. However, if one is not familiar with the more advanced material, a simple procedure is to run the regression analysis with and without the observation. This approach will reveal the influence of the observation on the results.

Exercises

Methods

50. Consider the following data for two variables, x and y. **LO 11**

x_i	135	110	130	145	175	160	120
y_i	145	100	120	120	130	130	110

a. Develop a scatter diagram for these data. Does the scatter diagram indicate any outliers in the data? In general, what implications does this finding have for simple linear regression?
b. Compute the standardized residuals for these data. Do the data include any outliers? Explain.

51. Consider the following data for two variables, x and y. **LO 11**

x_i	4	5	7	8	10	12	12	22
y_i	12	14	16	15	18	20	24	19

a. Develop a scatter diagram for these data. Does the scatter diagram indicate any influential observations? Explain.
b. Compute the standardized residuals for these data. Do the data include any outliers? Explain.
c. Compute the leverage values for these data. Does there appear to be any influential observations in these data? Explain.

Applications

52. **Predicting Charity Expenses.** Charity Navigator is America's leading independent charity evaluator. The following data show the total expenses ($), the percentage of the total budget spent on administrative expenses, the percentage spent on fundraising, and the percentage spent on program expenses for 10 supersized charities (Charity Navigator website). Administrative expenses include overhead, administrative staff and associated costs, and organizational meetings. Fundraising expenses are what a charity spends to raise money, and program expenses are what the charity spends on the programs and services it exists to deliver. The sum of the three percentages does not add to 100% because of rounding. **LO 1, 3, 11**

DATA*file*
charities

Charity	Total Expenses ($)	Administrative Expenses (%)	Fundraising Expenses (%)	Program Expenses (%)
American Red Cross	3,354,177,445	3.9	3.8	92.1
World Vision	1,205,887,020	4.0	7.5	88.3
Smithsonian Institution	1,080,995,083	23.5	2.6	73.7
Food For The Poor	1,050,829,851	0.7	2.4	96.8
American Cancer Society	1,003,781,897	6.1	22.2	71.6
Volunteers of America	929,158,968	8.6	1.9	89.4
Dana-Farber Cancer Institute	877,321,613	13.1	1.6	85.2
AmeriCares	854,604,824	0.4	0.7	98.8
ALSAC—St. Jude Children's Research Hospital	829,662,076	9.6	16.9	73.4
City of Hope	736,176,619	13.7	3.0	83.1

a. Develop a scatter diagram with fundraising expenses (%) on the horizontal axis and program expenses (%) on the vertical axis. Looking at the data, do there appear to be any outliers and/or influential observations?

b. Develop an estimated regression equation that could be used to predict program expenses (%) given fundraising expenses (%).
c. Does the value for the slope of the estimated regression equation make sense in the context of this problem situation?
d. Use residual analysis to determine whether any outliers and/or influential observations are present. Briefly summarize your findings and conclusions.

53. **Supermarket Checkout Lines.** Retail chain Kroger has more than 2,700 locations and is the largest supermarket in the United States based on revenue. Kroger has invested heavily in data, technology, and analytics. Feeding predictive models with data from an infrared sensor system called QueVision to anticipate when shoppers will reach the checkout counters, Kroger is able to alert workers to open more checkout lines as needed. This has allowed Kroger to lower its average checkout time from four minutes to less than 30 seconds (*Retail Touchpoints*).

DATA*file*
checkout

Consider the data in the file *checkout*. The file contains 32 observations. Each observation gives the arrival time (measured in minutes before 6 P.M.) and the shopping time (measured in minutes). **LO 1, 11**

a. Develop a scatter diagram for arrival time as the independent variable.
b. What does the scatter diagram developed in part (a) indicate about the relationship between the two variables? Do there appear to be any outliers or influential observations? Explain.
c. Using the entire data set, develop the estimated regression equation that can be used to predict the shopping time given the arrival time.
d. Use residual analysis to determine whether any outliers or influential observations are present.
e. After looking at the scatter diagram in part (a), suppose you were able to visually identify what appears to be an influential observation. Drop this observation from the data set and fit an estimated regression equation to the remaining data. Compare the estimated slope for the new estimated regression equation to the estimated slope obtained in part (c). Does this approach confirm the conclusion you reached in part (d)? Explain.

54. **Valuation of a Major League Baseball Team.** The following data show the annual revenue ($ millions) and the estimated team value ($ millions) for the 30 Major League Baseball teams (*Forbes* website). **LO 1, 11**

DATA*file*
mlbvalues

Team	Revenue ($ millions)	Value ($ millions)
Arizona Diamondbacks	195	584
Atlanta Braves	225	629
Baltimore Orioles	206	618
Boston Red Sox	336	1,312
Chicago Cubs	274	1,000
Chicago White Sox	216	692
Cincinnati Reds	202	546
Cleveland Guardians	186	559
Colorado Rockies	199	537
Detroit Tigers	238	643
Houston Astros	196	626
Kansas City Royals	169	457
Los Angeles Angels of Anaheim	239	718
Los Angeles Dodgers	245	1,615
Miami Marlins	195	520
Milwaukee Brewers	201	562

(continued)

Team	Revenue ($ millions)	Value ($ millions)
Minnesota Twins	214	578
New York Mets	232	811
New York Yankees	471	2,300
Oakland Athletics	173	468
Philadelphia Phillies	279	893
Pittsburgh Pirates	178	479
San Diego Padres	189	600
San Francisco Giants	262	786
Seattle Mariners	215	644
St. Louis Cardinals	239	716
Tampa Bay Rays	167	451
Texas Rangers	239	764
Toronto Blue Jays	203	568
Washington Nationals	225	631

a. Develop a scatter diagram with Revenue on the horizontal axis and Value on the vertical axis. Looking at the scatter diagram, does it appear that there are any outliers and/or influential observations in the data?
b. Develop the estimated regression equation that can be used to predict team value given the value of annual revenue.
c. Use residual analysis to determine whether any outliers and/or influential observations are present. Briefly summarize your findings and conclusions.

14.10 Practical Advice: Big Data and Hypothesis Testing in Simple Linear Regression

In Chapter 7, we observed that the standard errors of the sampling distributions of the sample mean $\bar{x}$ (shown in formula 7.2) and the sample proportion of $\bar{p}$ (shown in formula 7.5) decrease as the sample size increases. In Chapters 8 and 9, we observed that this results in narrower confidence interval estimates for μ and p and smaller p-values for the tests of the hypotheses H_0: $\mu \leq \mu_0$ and H_0: $p \leq p_0$ as the sample size increases. These results extend to simple linear regression. In simple linear regression, as the sample size increases,

- the p-value for the t test used to determine whether a significant relationship exists between the dependent variable and the independent decreases;
- the confidence interval for the slope parameter associated with the independent variable narrows;
- the confidence interval for the mean value of y narrows;
- the prediction interval for an individual value of y narrows.

Thus, as the sample size increases, we are more likely to reject the hypothesis that a relationship does not exist between the dependent variable and the independent variable and conclude that a relationship exists. The interval estimates for the slope parameter associated with the independent variable, the mean value of y, and predicted individual value of y will become more precise as the sample size increases. But this does not necessarily mean that these results become more reliable as the sample size increases.

No matter how large the sample used to estimate the simple linear regression equation, we must be concerned about the potential presence of nonsampling error in the data. It is important to carefully consider whether a random sample of the population of interest has actually been taken. If the data to be used for testing the hypothesis of no relationship between the independent and dependent variable are corrupted by nonsampling error, the likelihood of making a Type I or Type II error may be higher than if the sample data are free of nonsampling error. If the relationship between the independent and dependent variable is statistically significant, it is also important to consider whether the relationship in the simple linear regression equation is of *practical* significance.

Although simple linear regression is an extremely powerful statistical tool, it provides evidence that should be considered only in combination with information collected from other sources to make the most informed decision possible. No business decision should be based exclusively on inference in simple linear regression. Nonsampling error may lead to misleading results, and practical significance should always be considered in conjunction with statistical significance. This is particularly important when a hypothesis test is based on an extremely large sample because p-values in such cases can be extremely small. When executed properly, inference based on simple linear regression can be an important component in the business decision-making process.

Summary

In this chapter, we showed how regression analysis can be used to determine how a dependent variable y is related to an independent variable x. In simple linear regression, the regression model is $y = \beta_0 + \beta_1 x + \epsilon$. The simple linear regression equation $E(y) = \beta_0 + \beta_1 x$ describes how the mean or expected value of y is related to x. We used sample data and the least squares method to develop the estimated regression equation $\hat{y} = b_0 + b_1 x$. In effect, b_0 and b_1 are the sample statistics used to estimate the unknown model parameters β_0 and β_1.

The coefficient of determination was presented as a measure of the goodness of fit for the estimated regression equation; it can be interpreted as the proportion of the variation in the dependent variable y that can be explained by the estimated regression equation. We reviewed correlation as a descriptive measure of the strength of a linear relationship between two variables.

The assumptions about the regression model and its associated error term ϵ were discussed, and t and F tests, based on those assumptions, were presented as a means for determining whether the relationship between two variables is statistically significant. We showed how to use the estimated regression equation to develop confidence interval estimates of the mean value of y and prediction interval estimates of individual values of y.

The computer solution of regression problems and the use of residual analysis to validate the model assumptions and to identify outliers and influential observations were discussed. In the final section, we discussed the impact of big data on interpreting hypothesis tests in simple linear regression.

Glossary

ANOVA table The analysis of variance table used to summarize the computations associated with the F test for significance.

Coefficient of determination A measure of the goodness of fit of the estimated regression equation. It can be interpreted as the proportion of the variability in the dependent variable y that is explained by the estimated regression equation.

Confidence interval The interval estimate of the mean value of y for a given value of x.

Correlation coefficient A measure of the strength of the linear relationship between two variables (previously discussed in Chapter 3).

Dependent variable The variable that is being predicted or explained. It is denoted by y.

Estimated regression equation The estimate of the regression equation developed from sample data by using the least squares method. For simple linear regression, the estimated regression equation is $\hat{y} = b_0 + b_1 x$.

High leverage points Observations with extreme values for the independent variables.

Independent variable The variable that is doing the predicting or explaining. It is denoted by x.

Influential observation An observation that has a strong influence or effect on the regression results.

***i*th residual** The difference between the observed value of the dependent variable and the value predicted using the estimated regression equation; for the ith observation the ith residual is $y_i - \hat{y}_i$.

Least squares method A procedure used to develop the estimated regression equation. The objective is to minimize $\Sigma(y_i - \hat{y}_i)^2$.

Mean square error The unbiased estimate of the variance of the error term σ^2. It is denoted by MSE or s^2.

Normal probability plot A graph of the standardized residuals plotted against values of the normal scores. This plot helps determine whether the assumption that the error term has a normal probability distribution appears to be valid.

Outlier A data point or observation that does not fit the trend shown by the remaining data.

Prediction interval The interval estimate of an individual value of y for a given value of x.

Regression equation The equation that describes how the mean or expected value of the dependent variable is related to the independent variable; in simple linear regression, $E(y) = \beta_0 + \beta_1 x$.

Regression model The equation that describes how y is related to x and an error term; in simple linear regression, the regression model is $y = \beta_0 + \beta_1 x + \epsilon$.

Residual analysis The analysis of the residuals used to determine whether the assumptions made about the regression model appear to be valid. Residual analysis is also used to identify outliers and influential observations.

Residual plot Graphical representation of the residuals that can be used to determine whether the assumptions made about the regression model appear to be valid.

Scatter diagram A graph of bivariate data in which the independent variable is on the horizontal axis and the dependent variable is on the vertical axis.

Simple linear regression Regression analysis involving one independent variable and one dependent variable in which the relationship between the variables is approximated by a straight line.

Standard error of the estimate The square root of the mean square error, denoted by s. It is the estimate of σ, the standard deviation of the error term ϵ.

Standardized residual The value obtained by dividing a residual by its standard deviation.

Key Formulas

Simple Linear Regression Model

$$y = \beta_0 + \beta_1 x + \epsilon \qquad (14.1)$$

Simple Linear Regression Equation

$$E(y) = \beta_0 + \beta_1 x \qquad (14.2)$$

Estimated Simple Linear Regression Equation

$$\hat{y} = b_0 + b_1 x \qquad (14.3)$$

Least Squares Criterion

$$\min \Sigma(y_i - \hat{y}_i)^2 \qquad (14.5)$$

Slope and y-Intercept for the Estimated Regression Equation

$$b_1 = \frac{\Sigma(x_i - \bar{x})(y_i - \bar{y})}{\Sigma(x_i - \bar{x})^2} \qquad (14.6)$$

$$b_0 = \bar{y} - b_1 \bar{x} \qquad (14.7)$$

Sum of Squares Due to Error

$$\text{SSE} = \Sigma(y_i - \hat{y}_i)^2 \qquad (14.8)$$

Total Sum of Squares

$$\text{SST} = \Sigma(y_i - \bar{y})^2 \qquad (14.9)$$

Sum of Squares Due to Regression

$$\text{SSR} = \Sigma(\hat{y}_i - \bar{y})^2 \tag{14.10}$$

Relationship Among SST, SSR, and SSE

$$\text{SST} = \text{SSR} + \text{SSE} \tag{14.11}$$

Coefficient of Determination

$$r^2 = \frac{\text{SSR}}{\text{SST}} \tag{14.12}$$

Sample Correlation Coefficient

$$\begin{aligned} r_{xy} &= (\text{sign of } b_1)\sqrt{\text{Coefficient of determination}} \\ &= (\text{sign of } b_1)\sqrt{r^2} \end{aligned} \tag{14.13}$$

Mean Square Error (Estimate of σ^2)

$$s^2 = \text{MSE} = \frac{\text{SSE}}{n - 2} \tag{14.15}$$

Standard Error of the Estimate

$$s = \sqrt{\text{MSE}} = \sqrt{\frac{\text{SSE}}{n - 2}} \tag{14.16}$$

Standard Deviation of b_1

$$\sigma_{b_1} = \frac{\sigma}{\sqrt{\Sigma(x_i - \bar{x})^2}} \tag{14.17}$$

Estimated Standard Deviation of b_1

$$s_{b_1} = \frac{s}{\sqrt{\Sigma(x_i - \bar{x})^2}} \tag{14.18}$$

***t* Test Statistic**

$$t = \frac{b_1}{s_{b_1}} \tag{14.19}$$

Mean Square Regression

$$\text{MSR} = \frac{\text{SSR}}{\text{Number of independent variables}} \tag{14.20}$$

***F* Test Statistic**

$$F = \frac{\text{MSR}}{\text{MSE}} \tag{14.21}$$

Estimated Standard Deviation of $\hat{y}^*$

$$s_{\hat{y}^*} = s\sqrt{\frac{1}{n} + \frac{(x^* - \bar{x})^2}{\Sigma(x_i - \bar{x})^2}} \tag{14.23}$$

Confidence Interval for $E(y^*)$

$$\hat{y}^* \pm t_{\alpha/2} s_{\hat{y}^*} \tag{14.24}$$

Estimated Standard Deviation of an Individual Value

$$s_{\text{pred}} = s\sqrt{1 + \frac{1}{n} + \frac{(x^* - \bar{x})^2}{\Sigma(x_i - \bar{x})^2}} \tag{14.26}$$

Prediction Interval for y^*

$$\hat{y}^* \pm t_{\alpha/2} s_{\text{pred}} \tag{14.27}$$

Residual for Observation i

$$y_i - \hat{y}_i \tag{14.28}$$

Standard Deviation of the ith Residual

$$s_{y_i - \hat{y}_i} = s\sqrt{1 - h_i} \tag{14.30}$$

Standardized Residual for Observation i

$$\frac{y_i - \hat{y}_i}{s_{y_i - \hat{y}_i}} \tag{14.32}$$

Leverage of Observation i

$$h_i = \frac{1}{n} + \frac{(x_i - \bar{x})^2}{\Sigma(x_i - \bar{x})^2} \tag{14.33}$$

Supplementary Exercises

55. Does a high value of r^2 imply that two variables are causally related? Explain. **LO 4**
56. In your own words, explain the difference between an interval estimate of the mean value of y for a given x and an interval estimate for an individual value of y for a given x. **LO 8, 9**
57. What is the purpose of testing whether $\beta_1 = 0$? If we reject $\beta_1 = 0$, does it imply a good fit? **LO 6**
58. **Stock Market Performance.** The Dow Jones Industrial Average (DJIA) and the Standard & Poor's 500 (S&P 500) indexes are used as measures of overall movement in the stock market. The DJIA is based on the price movements of 30 large companies; the S&P 500 is an index composed of 500 stocks. Some say the S&P 500 is a better measure of stock market performance because it is broader based. The closing price for the DJIA and the S&P 500 for 15 weeks of a previous year follow (*Barron*'s website). **LO 1, 2, 4, 7, 9**

DATA*file*
djiasp500

Date	DJIA	S&P
January 6	12,360	1,278
January 13	12,422	1,289
January 20	12,720	1,315
January 27	12,660	1,316
February 3	12,862	1,345
February 10	12,801	1,343
February 17	12,950	1,362
February 24	12,983	1,366
March 2	12,978	1,370
March 9	12,922	1,371
March 16	13,233	1,404
March 23	13,081	1,397
March 30	13,212	1,408
April 5	13,060	1,398
April 13	12,850	1,370

a. Develop a scatter diagram with DJIA as the independent variable.
b. Develop the estimated regression equation.
c. Test for a significant relationship. Use $\alpha = 0.05$.
d. Did the estimated regression equation provide a good fit? Explain.
e. Suppose that the closing price for the DJIA is 13,500. Predict the closing price for the S&P 500.
f. Should we be concerned that the DJIA value of 13,500 used to predict the S&P 500 value in part (e) is beyond the range of the data used to develop the estimated regression equation?

59. **Home Size and Price.** Is the number of square feet of living space a good predictor of a house's selling price? The following data show the square footage and selling price for 15 houses in Winston Salem, North Carolina, in April 2015 (*Zillow.com*). **LO 1, 2, 4, 6, 9**

DATA*file*
wshouses

Size (1,000s sq. ft.)	Selling Price ($1,000s)
1.26	117.5
3.02	299.9
1.99	139.0
0.91	45.6
1.87	129.9
2.63	274.9
2.60	259.9
2.27	177.0
2.30	175.0
2.08	189.9
1.12	95.0
1.38	82.1
1.80	169.0
1.57	96.5
1.45	114.9

a. Develop a scatter diagram with square feet of living space as the independent variable and selling price as the dependent variable. What does the scatter diagram indicate about the relationship between the size of a house and the selling price?
b. Develop the estimated regression equation that could be used to predict the selling price given the number of square feet of living space.
c. At the 0.05 level, is there a significant relationship between the two variables?
d. Use the estimated regression equation to predict the selling price of a 2,000 square foot house in Winston Salem, North Carolina.
e. Do you believe the estimated regression equation developed in part (b) will provide a good prediction of selling price of a particular house in Winston Salem, North Carolina? Explain.
f. Would you be comfortable using the estimated regression equation developed in part (b) to predict the selling price of a particular house in Seattle, Washington? Why or why not?

60. **Online Education.** One of the biggest changes in higher education in recent years has been the growth of online universities. The Online Education Database is an independent organization whose mission is to build a comprehensive list of the top accredited online colleges. The following table shows the retention rate (%) and the graduation rate (%) for 29 online colleges. **LO 1, 4, 6, 11**

DATA*file*
onlineedu

Retention Rate (%)	Graduation Rate (%)
7	25
51	25
4	28
29	32
33	33
47	33
63	34
45	36
60	36
62	36
67	36
65	37
78	37
75	38
54	39
45	41
38	44
51	45
69	46
60	47
37	48
63	50
73	51
78	52
48	53
95	55
68	56
100	57
100	61

a. Develop a scatter diagram with retention rate as the independent variable. What does the scatter diagram indicate about the relationship between the two variables?
b. Develop the estimated regression equation.
c. Use a t test to determine whether there is a significant relationship. Use $\alpha = 0.05$.
d. Did the estimated regression equation provide a good fit?

61. **Machine Maintenance.** Jensen Tire & Auto is in the process of deciding whether to purchase a maintenance contract for its new computer wheel alignment and balancing machine. Managers feel that maintenance expense should be related to usage, and they collected the following information on weekly usage (hours) and annual maintenance expense (in hundreds of dollars). **LO 1, 2, 7, 9**

DATA*file*
jensen

Weekly Usage (hours)	Annual Maintenance Expense
13	17.0
10	22.0
20	30.0
28	37.0
32	47.0
17	30.5

(continued)

Weekly Usage (hours)	Annual Maintenance Expense
24	32.5
31	39.0
40	51.5
38	40.0

a. Develop the estimated regression equation that relates annual maintenance expense to weekly usage.
b. Test the significance of the relationship in part (a) at a 0.05 level of significance.
c. Jensen expects to use the new machine 30 hours per week. Develop a 95% prediction interval for the company's annual maintenance expense.
d. If the maintenance contract costs $3,000 per year, would you recommend purchasing it? Why or why not?

62. **Production Rate and Quality Control.** In a manufacturing process the assembly line speed (feet per minute) was thought to affect the number of defective parts found during the inspection process. To test this theory, managers devised a situation in which the same batch of parts was inspected visually at a variety of line speeds. They collected the following data. **LO 1, 4, 7, 8**

Line Speed	Number of Defective Parts Found
20	21
20	19
40	15
30	16
60	14
40	17

a. Develop the estimated regression equation that relates line speed to the number of defective parts found.
b. At a 0.05 level of significance, use the F test to determine whether line speed and number of defective parts found are related.
c. Did the estimated regression equation provide a good fit to the data?
d. Develop a 95% confidence interval to predict the mean number of defective parts for a line speed of 50 feet per minute.

63. **Absenteeism and Location.** A sociologist was hired by a large city hospital to investigate the relationship between the number of unauthorized days that employees are absent per year and the distance (miles) between home and work for the employees. A sample of 10 employees was chosen, and the following data were collected. **LO 1, 4, 7, 8**

DATA*file*
absent

Distance to Work (miles)	Number of Days Absent
1	8
3	5
4	8
6	7
8	6
10	3
12	5
14	2
14	4
18	2

a. Develop a scatter diagram for these data. Does a linear relationship appear reasonable? Explain.
b. Develop the least squares estimated regression equation.
c. Based on the F test, is there a significant relationship between the two variables? Use $\alpha = 0.05$.
d. Did the estimated regression equation provide a good fit? Explain.
e. Use the estimated regression equation developed in part (b) to develop a 95% confidence interval for the expected number of days absent for employees living five miles from the company.

64. **Bus Maintenance.** The regional transit authority for a major metropolitan area wants to determine whether there is any relationship between the age of a bus and the annual maintenance cost. A sample of 10 buses resulted in the following data. **LO 1, 4, 7, 9**

DATA*file*
agecost

Age of Bus (years)	Maintenance Cost ($)
1	350
2	370
2	480
2	520
2	590
3	550
4	750
4	800
5	790
5	950

a. Develop the least squares estimated regression equation.
b. Use the F test to determine whether the two variables are significantly related with $\alpha = 0.05$.
c. Did the least squares line provide a good fit to the observed data? Explain.
d. Develop a 95% prediction interval for the maintenance cost for a specific bus that is four years old.

65. **Studying and Grades.** A marketing professor at Givens College is interested in the relationship between hours spent studying and total points earned in a course. Data collected on 10 students who took the course last quarter follow. **LO 1, 2, 7, 9**

DATA*file*
hourspts

Hours Spent Studying	Total Points Earned
45	40
30	35
90	75
60	65
105	90
65	50
90	90
80	80
55	45
75	65

a. Develop an estimated regression equation showing how total points earned is related to hours spent studying.
b. Test the significance of the model with $\alpha = 0.05$.
c. Predict the total points earned by Mark Sweeney. He spent 95 hours studying.
d. Develop a 95% prediction interval for the total points earned by Mark Sweeney.

66. **Market Beta.** Market betas for individual stocks are determined by simple linear regression. For each stock, the dependent variable is its quarterly percentage return (capital appreciation plus dividends) minus the percentage return that could be obtained from a risk-free investment (the Treasury Bill rate is used as the risk-free rate). The independent variable is the quarterly percentage return (capital appreciation plus dividends) for the stock market (S&P 500) minus the percentage return from a risk-free investment. An estimated regression equation is developed with quarterly data; the market beta for the stock is the slope of the estimated regression equation (b_1). The value of the market beta is often interpreted as a measure of the risk associated with the stock. Market betas greater than 1 indicate that the stock is more volatile than the market average; market betas less than 1 indicate that the stock is less volatile than the market average. Suppose that the following figures are the differences between the percentage return and the risk-free return for 10 quarters for the S&P 500 and Horizon Technology. **LO 1, 3, 4, 6**

DATA*file*
mktbeta

S&P 500	Horizon
1.2	−0.7
−2.5	−2.0
−3.0	−5.5
2.0	4.7
5.0	1.8
1.2	4.1
3.0	2.6
−1.0	2.0
0.5	−1.3
2.5	5.5

a. Develop an estimated regression equation that can be used to predict the market beta for Horizon Technology. What is Horizon Technology's market beta?
b. Use the t test to assess whether there is a significant relationship at the 0.05 level of significance.
c. Did the estimated regression equation provide a good fit? Explain.

67. **Income and Percent Audited.** The Transactional Records Access Clearinghouse at Syracuse University reported data showing the odds of an Internal Revenue Service audit. The following table shows the average adjusted gross income reported and the percent of the returns that were audited for 20 selected IRS districts. **LO 1, 4, 6, 8**

District	Adjusted Gross Income ($)	Percent Audited
Los Angeles	36,664	1.3
Sacramento	38,845	1.1
Atlanta	34,886	1.1
Boise	32,512	1.1
Dallas	34,531	1.0
Providence	35,995	1.0

(continued)

DATA*file*
irsaudit

District	Adjusted Gross Income ($)	Percent Audited
San Jose	37,799	0.9
Cheyenne	33,876	0.9
Fargo	30,513	0.9
New Orleans	30,174	0.9
Oklahoma City	30,060	0.8
Houston	37,153	0.8
Portland	34,918	0.7
Phoenix	33,291	0.7
Augusta	31,504	0.7
Albuquerque	29,199	0.6
Greensboro	33,072	0.6
Columbia	30,859	0.5
Nashville	32,566	0.5
Buffalo	34,296	0.5

a. Develop the estimated regression equation that could be used to predict the percent audited given the average adjusted gross income reported.
b. At the 0.05 level of significance, use the t test to determine whether the adjusted gross income and the percent audited are related.
c. Did the estimated regression equation provide a good fit? Explain.
d. Use the estimated regression equation developed in part (a) to calculate a 95% confidence interval for the expected percent audited for districts with an average adjusted gross income of $35,000.

68. **Used Car Mileage and Price.** The Toyota Camry is one of the best-selling cars in North America. The cost of a previously owned Camry depends upon many factors, including the model year, mileage, and condition. To investigate the relationship between the car's mileage and the sales price for a 2007 model year Camry, the following data show the mileage and sale price for 19 sales (PriceHub website). **LO 1, 2, 3, 4, 6**

DATA*file*
camry

Miles (1,000s)	Price ($1,000s)
22	16.2
29	16.0
36	13.8
47	11.5
63	12.5
77	12.9
73	11.2
87	13.0
92	11.8
101	10.8
110	8.3
28	12.5
59	11.1
68	15.0
68	12.2
91	13.0
42	15.6
65	12.7
110	8.3

a. Develop a scatter diagram with the car mileage on the horizontal axis and the price on the vertical axis.
b. What does the scatter diagram developed in part (a) indicate about the relationship between the two variables?
c. Develop the estimated regression equation that could be used to predict the price ($1,000s) given the miles (1,000s).
d. Test for a significant relationship at the 0.05 level of significance.
e. Did the estimated regression equation provide a good fit? Explain.
f. Provide an interpretation for the slope of the estimated regression equation.
g. Suppose that you are considering purchasing a previously owned 2007 Camry that has been driven 60,000 miles. Using the estimated regression equation developed in part (c), predict the price for this car. Is this the price you would offer the seller?

69. **Used Farm Equipment Prices.** The following scatter chart shows the relationship between the price of a used tractor in dollars and the age of the tractor in years for 72 used tractors. **LO 2, 3, 4**

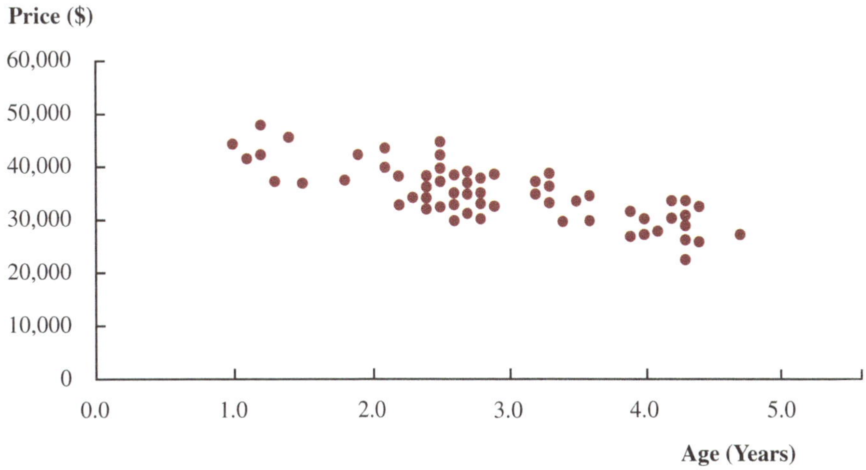

The regression output for these data is as follows:

Analysis of Variance

Source	DF	Adj SS	Adj MS	*F*-Value	*p*-Value
Regression	1	1069527379.3	1069527379.3	100.06	0.00
Error	70	748184308.9	10688347.3		
Total	71	1817711688.2			

Model Summary

S	R-sq	R-sq(adj)
3269.30	58.84%	58.25%

Coefficients

Term	Coef	SE Coef	*t* Value	*p*-Value
Constant	47315.67	1302.17	36.34	0.000
Age	−4251.89	425.05	−10.00	0.000

Regression Equation
Price = 47315.67 − 4251.89 Age

a. Interpret the constant term.
b. Interpret the slope (coefficient of Age).
c. Does this regression equation provide a good fit to the data? Explain.
d. Using the regression equation, predict the price of a tractor that is 4.2 years old.

70. **Used Farm Equipment Prices (Revisited).** Refer to problem 69 concerning the impact of age of a used tractor and its selling price. **LO 7, 10**
   a. At the 0.05 level of significance, use the *F* test to determine whether a significant statistical relationship exists between price and age of a tractor.
   b. Analyze the following residual plot for the regression model to assess whether the linear regression assumptions about the error terms are valid.

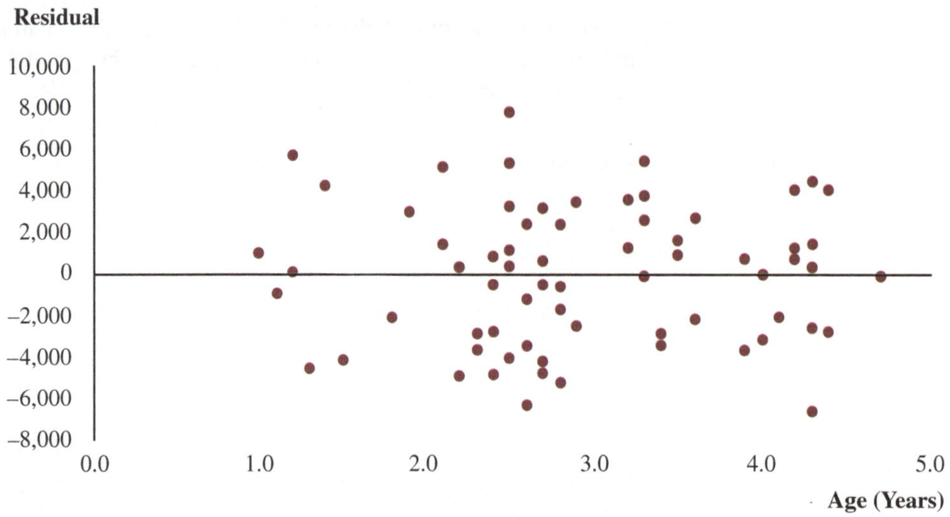

71. **Sales and Banner Ads.** An Internet-based apparel company, Jimmy-C, wishes to study the effectiveness of its banner ads. The marketing team has sales (in millions of dollars) and the amount spent on banner ads for a given week (in millions of dollars) for 200 weeks. These data appear in the scatter plot below. **LO 2, 3, 4**

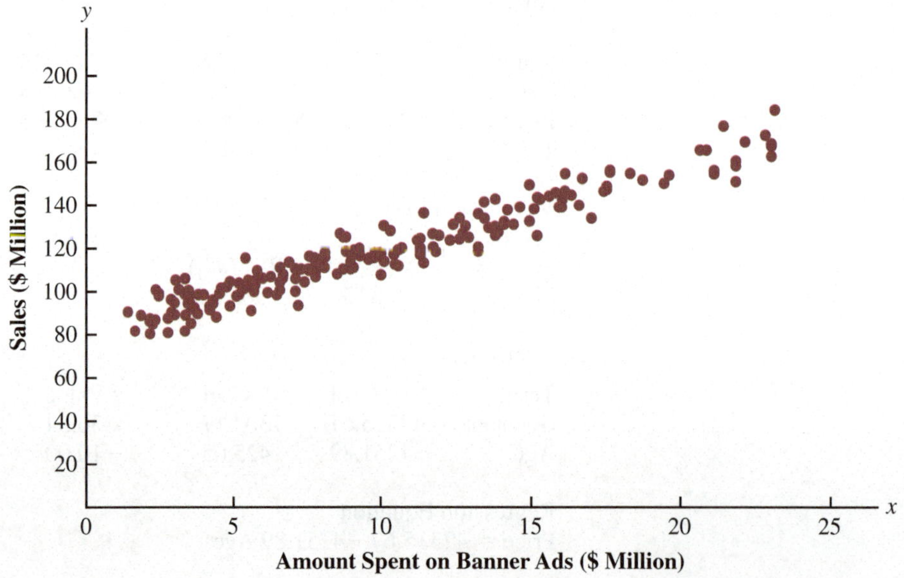

The regression output for these data is as follows:

Analysis of Variance

Source	DF	Adj SS	Adj MS	F-Value	p-Value
Regression	1	94074.4	94074.4	2655.8	0.00
Error	198	7013.5	35.4		
Total	199	101087.9			

Model Summary

S	R-sq	R-sq(adj)
5.95	93.06%	93.03%

Coefficients

Term	Coef	SE Coef	t Value	p-Value
Constant	81.11	0.85	95.90	0.000
Amount Spent on Banner Ads	3.87	0.08	51.53	0.000

Regression Equation
Sales = 81.11 + 3.87 Amount Spent on Banner Ads

a. Interpret the constant term.
b. Interpret the slope (coefficient of Amount Spent on Banner Ads).
c. Does this regression equation provide a good fit to the data? Explain.
d. Using the regression equation, predict the sales in a week when $15 million is spent on banner ads.

72. **Sales and Banner Ads (Revisited).** Refer to problem 71 and Jimmy-C's study of the effectiveness of banner ads. LO 7, 10
   a. At the 0.05 level of significance, use the F test to determine whether a significant statistical relationship exists between banner ad spend and sales.
   b. Analyze the following residual plot for the regression to assess whether the linear regression assumptions about the error terms are valid.

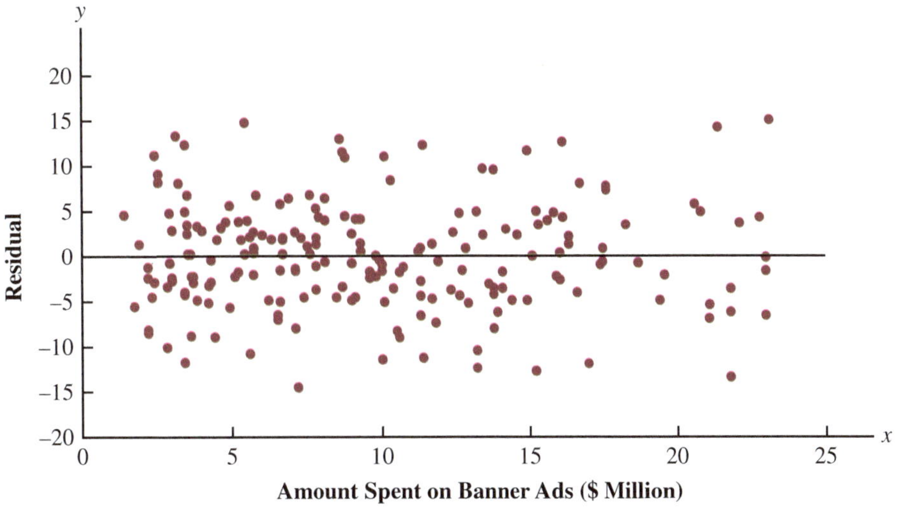

73. **On Base Percentage and Runs Scored.** As shown in the film *Moneyball*, the Oakland A's major league baseball team used analytics to their advantage in player

selection. By using techniques such as regression analysis, they were able to find new metrics that are important to success. One of those metrics the A's found to be helpful is "on-base percentage" (OBP). OBP is the number of times a player reaches a base divided by the number of plate appearances. The file *obp* contains OBP and total runs scored over the season for every major league baseball team over a 12-year period. **LO 1, 2, 3, 4**

DATA*file* obp

a. Construct a scatter plot. Does there appear to be a linear relationship between runs scored and OBP?
b. Using computer software, develop a regression equation with runs scored as the dependent variable and OBP as the independent variable.
c. Interpret the slope OBP. As OBP increases by 0.01, how is the number of runs scored predicted to change?
d. Does this regression equation provide a good fit to the data? Explain.
e. Using the regression equation, predict the runs scored in a season in which the OBP is 33% (0.33).

74. **On Base Percentage and Runs Scored (Revisited).** Refer to problem 73 and the baseball data on runs scored in a season and on base percentage. Develop a residual plot with residuals on the vertical axis and OBS on the horizontal axis. Based on this residual plot, do the assumptions about the error terms for this regression analysis seem reasonable? **LO 10**

Case Problem 1: Measuring Stock Market Risk

One measure of the risk or volatility of an individual stock is the standard deviation of the total return (capital appreciation plus dividends) over several periods of time. Although the standard deviation is easy to compute, it does not take into account the extent to which the price of a given stock varies as a function of a standard market index, such as the S&P 500. As a result, many financial analysts prefer to use another measure of risk referred to as *beta*.

DATA*file* beta

Betas for individual stocks are determined by simple linear regression. The dependent variable is the total return for the stock and the independent variable is the total return for the stock market.* For this case problem we will use the S&P 500 index as the measure of the total return for the stock market, and an estimated regression equation will be developed using monthly data. The beta for the stock is the slope of the estimated regression equation (b_1). The data contained in the file *beta* provides the total return (capital appreciation plus dividends) over 36 months for eight widely traded common stocks and the S&P 500.

The value of beta for the stock market will always be 1; thus, stocks that tend to rise and fall with the stock market will also have a beta close to 1. Betas greater than 1 indicate that the stock is more volatile than the market, and betas less than 1 indicate that the stock is less volatile than the market. For instance, if a stock has a beta of 1.4, it is 40% *more* volatile than the market, and if a stock has a beta of 0.4, it is 60% *less* volatile than the market. **LO 1, 3, 4**

Managerial Report

You have been assigned to analyze the risk characteristics of these stocks. Prepare a report that includes but is not limited to the following items.

a. Compute descriptive statistics for each stock and the S&P 500. Comment on your results. Which stocks are the most volatile?

*Various sources use different approaches for computing betas. For instance, some sources subtract the return that could be obtained from a risk-free investment (e.g., T-bills) from the dependent variable and the independent variable before computing the estimated regression equation. Some also use different indexes for the total return of the stock market; for instance, Value Line computes betas using the New York Stock Exchange composite index.

b. Compute the value of beta for each stock. Which of these stocks would you expect to perform best in an up market? Which would you expect to hold their value best in a down market?
c. Comment on how much of the return for the individual stocks is explained by the market.

Case Problem 2: U.S. Department of Transportation

As part of a study on transportation safety, the U.S. Department of Transportation collected data on the number of fatal accidents per 1,000 licenses and the percentage of licensed drivers under the age of 21 in a sample of 42 cities. Data collected over a one-year period follow. These data are contained in the file *safety*. **LO 1, 4, 7, 10, 11**

DATA*file*
safety

Percent Under 21	Fatal Accidents per 1,000 Licenses	Percent Under 21	Fatal Accidents per 1,000 Licenses
13	2.962	17	4.100
12	0.708	8	2.190
8	0.885	16	3.623
12	1.652	15	2.623
11	2.091	9	0.835
17	2.627	8	0.820
18	3.830	14	2.890
8	0.368	8	1.267
13	1.142	15	3.224
8	0.645	10	1.014
9	1.028	10	0.493
16	2.801	14	1.443
12	1.405	18	3.614
9	1.433	10	1.926
10	0.039	14	1.643
9	0.338	16	2.943
11	1.849	12	1.913
12	2.246	15	2.814
14	2.855	13	2.634
14	2.352	9	0.926
11	1.294	17	3.256

Managerial Report

1. Develop numerical and graphical summaries of the data.
2. Use regression analysis to investigate the relationship between the number of fatal accidents and the percentage of drivers under the age of 21. Discuss your findings.
3. What conclusion and recommendations can you derive from your analysis?

Case Problem 3: Selecting a Point-and-Shoot Digital Camera

Consumer Reports tested 166 different point-and-shoot digital cameras. Based upon factors such as the number of megapixels, weight (oz), image quality, and ease of use, they developed an overall score for each camera tested. The overall score ranges from 0 to 100, with higher scores indicating better overall test results. Selecting a camera with many options can be a difficult process, and price is certainly a key issue for most consumers. By spending more, will a consumer really get a superior camera? And, do cameras that

Table 14.15 Data for 28 Point-and-Shoot Digital Cameras

Camera	Brand	Price ($)	Megapixels	Weight (oz)	Score
1	Canon	330	10	7	66
2	Canon	200	12	5	66
3	Canon	300	12	7	65
4	Canon	200	10	6	62
5	Canon	180	12	5	62
6	Canon	200	12	7	61
7	Canon	200	14	5	60
8	Canon	130	10	7	60
9	Canon	130	12	5	59
10	Canon	110	16	5	55
11	Canon	90	14	5	52
12	Canon	100	10	6	51
13	Canon	90	12	7	46
14	Nikon	270	16	5	65
15	Nikon	300	16	7	63
16	Nikon	200	14	6	61
17	Nikon	400	14	7	59
18	Nikon	120	14	5	57
19	Nikon	170	16	6	56
20	Nikon	150	12	5	56
21	Nikon	230	14	6	55
22	Nikon	180	12	6	53
23	Nikon	130	12	6	53
24	Nikon	80	12	7	52
25	Nikon	80	14	7	50
26	Nikon	100	12	4	46
27	Nikon	110	12	5	45
28	Nikon	130	14	4	42

DATA*file*
cameras

have more megapixels, a factor often considered to be a good measure of picture quality, cost more than cameras with fewer megapixels? Table 14.15 shows the brand, average retail price ($), number of megapixels, weight (oz), and the overall score for 13 Canon and 15 Nikon subcompact cameras tested by *Consumer Reports* (*Consumer Reports* website). **LO 1, 4, 5, 7, 10, 11**

Managerial Report

1. Develop numerical summaries of the data.
2. Using overall score as the dependent variable, develop three scatter diagrams, one using price as the independent variable, one using the number of megapixels as the independent variable, and one using weight as the independent variable. Which of the three independent variables appears to be the best predictor of overall score?
3. Using simple linear regression, develop an estimated regression equation that could be used to predict the overall score given the price of the camera.
4. Analyze the data using only the observations for the Canon cameras. Discuss the appropriateness of using simple linear regression and make any recommendations regarding the prediction of overall score using just the price of the camera.

Case Problem 4: Finding the Best Car Value

When trying to decide what car to buy, real value is not necessarily determined by how much you spend on the initial purchase. Instead, cars that are reliable and don't cost much to own often represent the best values. But, no matter how reliable or inexpensive a car may cost to own, it must also perform well.

To measure value, *Consumer Reports* developed a statistic referred to as a value score. The value score is based upon five-year owner costs, overall road-test scores, and predicted reliability ratings. Five-year owner costs are based on the expenses incurred in the first five years of ownership, including depreciation, fuel, maintenance and repairs, and so on. Using a national average of 12,000 miles per year, an average cost per mile driven is used as the measure of five-year owner costs. Road-test scores are the results of more than 50 tests and evaluations and are based upon a 100-point scale, with higher scores indicating better performance, comfort, convenience, and fuel economy. The highest road-test score obtained in the tests conducted by *Consumer Reports* was a 99 for a Lexus LS 460L. Predicted-reliability ratings (1 = Poor, 2 = Fair, 3 = Good, 4 = Very Good, and 5 = Excellent) are based on data from *Consumer Reports'* Annual Auto Survey.

A car with a value score of 1.0 is considered to be "average-value." A car with a value score of 2.0 is considered to be twice as good a value as a car with a value score of 1.0; a car with a value score of 0.5 is considered half as good as average; and so on. The data for 20 family sedans, including the price ($) of each car tested, follow. **LO 1, 4, 7**

DATA*file*
familysadans

Car	Price ($)	Cost/Mile	Road-Test Score	Predicted Reliability	Value Score
Nissan Altima 2.5 S (4-cyl.)	23,970	0.59	91	4	1.75
Kia Optima LX (2.4)	21,885	0.58	81	4	1.73
Subaru Legacy 2.5i Premium	23,830	0.59	83	4	1.73
Ford Fusion Hybrid	32,360	0.63	84	5	1.70
Honda Accord LX-P (4-cyl.)	23,730	0.56	80	4	1.62
Mazda6 i Sport (4-cyl.)	22,035	0.58	73	4	1.60
Hyundai Sonata GLS (2.4)	21,800	0.56	89	3	1.58
Ford Fusion SE (4-cyl.)	23,625	0.57	76	4	1.55
Chevrolet Malibu LT (4-cyl.)	24,115	0.57	74	3	1.48
Kia Optima SX (2.0T)	29,050	0.72	84	4	1.43
Ford Fusion SEL (V6)	28,400	0.67	80	4	1.42
Nissan Altima 3.5 SR (V6)	30,335	0.69	93	4	1.42
Hyundai Sonata Limited (2.0T)	28,090	0.66	89	3	1.39
Honda Accord EX-L (V6)	28,695	0.67	90	3	1.36
Mazda6 s Grand Touring (V6)	30,790	0.74	81	4	1.34
Ford Fusion SEL (V6, AWD)	30,055	0.71	75	4	1.32
Subaru Legacy 3.6R Limited	30,094	0.71	88	3	1.29
Chevrolet Malibu LTZ (V6)	28,045	0.67	83	3	1.20
Chrysler 200 Limited (V6)	27,825	0.70	52	5	1.20
Chevrolet Impala LT (3.6)	28,995	0.67	63	3	1.05

Managerial Report

1. Develop numerical summaries of the data.
2. Use regression analysis to develop an estimated regression equation that could be used to predict the value score given the price of the car.
3. Use regression analysis to develop an estimated regression equation that could be used to predict the value score given the five-year owner costs (cost/mile).

4. Use regression analysis to develop an estimated regression equation that could be used to predict the value score given the road-test score.
5. Use regression analysis to develop an estimated regression equation that could be used to predict the value score given the predicted-reliability.
6. What conclusions can you derive from your analysis?

Case Problem 5: Buckeye Creek Amusement Park

Buckeye Creek Amusement Park is open from the beginning of May to the end of October. Buckeye Creek relies heavily on the sale of season passes. The sale of season passes brings in significant revenue prior to the park opening each season, and season pass holders contribute a substantial portion of the food, beverage, and novelty sales in the park. Greg Ross, director of marketing at Buckeye Creek, has been asked to develop a targeted marketing campaign to increase season pass sales.

Greg has data for last season that show the number of season pass holders for each zip code within 50 miles of Buckeye Creek. He has also obtained the total population of each zip code from the U.S. Census Bureau website. Greg thinks it may be possible to use regression analysis to predict the number of season pass holders in a zip code given the total population of a zip code. If this is possible, he could then conduct a direct mail campaign that would target zip codes that have fewer than the expected number of season pass holders. **LO 1, 4, 6, 10**

DATA*file*
buckeyecreek

Managerial Report

1. Compute descriptive statistics and construct a scatter diagram for the data. Discuss your findings.
2. Using simple linear regression, develop an estimated regression equation that could be used to predict the number of season pass holders in a zip code given the total population of the zip code.
3. Test for a significant relationship at the 0.05 level of significance.
4. Did the estimated regression equation provide a good fit?
5. Use residual analysis to determine whether the assumed regression model is appropriate.
6. Discuss if/how the estimated regression equation should be used to guide the marketing campaign.
7. What other data might be useful to predict the number of season pass holders in a zip code?

Chapter 14 Appendix

Appendix 14.1: Calculus-Based Derivation of Least Squares Formulas

As mentioned in the chapter, the least squares method is a procedure for determining the values of b_0 and b_1 that minimize the sum of squared residuals. The sum of squared residuals is given by

$$\Sigma(y_i - \hat{y}_i)^2$$

Substituting $\hat{y}_i = b_0 + b_1x_i$, we get

$$\Sigma(y_i - b_0 - b_1x_i)^2 \tag{14.34}$$

as the expression that must be minimized.

To minimize expression (14.34), we must take the partial derivatives with respect to b_0 and b_1, set them equal to zero, and solve. Doing so, we get

$$\frac{\partial\Sigma(y_i - b_0 - b_1x_i)^2}{\partial b_0} = -2\Sigma(y_i - b_0 - b_1x_i) = 0 \tag{14.35}$$

$$\frac{\partial\Sigma(y_i - b_0 - b_1x_i)^2}{\partial b_1} = -2\Sigma x_i(y_i - b_0 - b_1x_i) = 0 \tag{14.36}$$

Dividing equation (14.35) by two and summing each term individually yields

$$-\Sigma y_i + \Sigma b_0 + \Sigma b_1x_i = 0$$

Bringing Σy_i to the other side of the equal sign and noting that $\Sigma b_0 = nb_0$, we obtain

$$nb_0 + (\Sigma x_i)b_1 = \Sigma y_i \tag{14.37}$$

Similar algebraic simplification applied to equation (14.36) yields

$$(\Sigma x_i)b_0 + (\Sigma x_i^2)b_1 = \Sigma x_iy_i \tag{14.38}$$

Equations (14.37) and (14.38) are known as the *normal equations.* Solving equation (14.37) for b_0 yields

$$b_0 = \frac{\Sigma y_i}{n} - b_1\frac{\Sigma x_i}{n} \tag{14.39}$$

Using equation (14.39) to substitute for b_0 in equation (14.38) provides

$$\frac{\Sigma x_i\Sigma y_i}{n} - \frac{(\Sigma x_i)^2}{n}b_1 + (\Sigma x_i^2)b_1 = \Sigma x_iy_i \tag{14.40}$$

By rearranging the terms in equation (14.40), we obtain

$$b_1 = \frac{\Sigma x_iy_i - (\Sigma x_i\Sigma y_i)/n}{\Sigma x_i^2 - (\Sigma x_i)^2/n} = \frac{\Sigma(x_i - \bar{x})(y_i - \bar{y})}{\Sigma(x_i - \bar{x})^2} \tag{14.41}$$

Because $\bar{y} = \Sigma y_i/n$ and $\bar{x} = \Sigma x_i/n$, we can rewrite equation (14.39) as

$$b_0 = \bar{y} - b_1\bar{x} \tag{14.42}$$

Equations (14.41) and (14.42) are the formulas (14.6) and (14.7) we used in the chapter to compute the coefficients in the estimated regression equation.

Appendix 14.2: A Test for Significance Using Correlation

Using the sample correlation coefficient r_{xy}, we can determine whether the linear relationship between x and y is significant by testing the following hypotheses about the population correlation coefficient ρ_{xy}.

$$H_0: \rho_{xy} = 0$$
$$H_a: \rho_{xy} \neq 0$$

If H_0 is rejected, we can conclude that the population correlation coefficient is not equal to zero and that the linear relationship between the two variables is significant. This test for significance follows.

A Test for Significance Using Correlation

$$H_0: \rho_{xy} = 0$$
$$H_a: \rho_{xy} \neq 0$$

Test Statistic

$$t = r_{xy}\sqrt{\frac{n-2}{1-r_{xy}^2}} \tag{14.43}$$

Rejection Rule

p-value approach: Reject H_0 if *p*-value $\leq \alpha$

Critical value approach: Reject H_0 if $t \leq -t_{\alpha/2}$ or if $t \geq t_{\alpha/2}$

where $t_{\alpha/2}$ is based on a t distribution with $n - 2$ degrees of freedom.

In Section 14.3, we found that the sample with $n = 10$ provided the sample correlation coefficient for student population and quarterly sales of $r_{xy} = 0.9501$. The test statistic is

$$t = r_{xy}\sqrt{\frac{n-2}{1-r_{xy}^2}} = 0.9501\sqrt{\frac{10-2}{1-(0.9501)^2}} = 8.61$$

The t distribution table shows that with $n - 2 = 10 - 2 = 8$ degrees of freedom, $t = 3.355$ provides an area of 0.005 in the upper tail. Thus, the area in the upper tail of the t distribution corresponding to the test statistic $t = 8.61$ must be less than 0.005. Because this test is a two-tailed test, we double this value to conclude that the *p*-value associated with $t = 8.61$ must be less than $2(0.005) = 0.01$. Using Excel, the *p*-value $= 0.000$. Because the *p*-value is less than $\alpha = 0.01$, we reject H_0 and conclude that ρ_{xy} is not equal to zero. This evidence is sufficient to conclude that a significant linear relationship exists between student population and quarterly sales.

Note that except for rounding, the test statistic t and the conclusion of a significant relationship are identical to the results obtained in Section 14.5 for the t test conducted using Armand's estimated regression equation $\hat{y} = 60 + 5x$. Performing regression analysis provides the conclusion of a significant relationship between x and y and in addition provides the equation showing how the variables are related. Most analysts therefore use modern computer packages to perform regression analysis and find that using correlation as a test of significance is unnecessary.

Chapter 15

Multiple Regression

Contents

Statistics in Practice:
84.51°

15.1 Multiple Regression Model
Regression Model and Regression Equation
Estimated Multiple Regression Equation

15.2 Least Squares Method
An Example: Butler Trucking Company
Using Excel's Regression Tool to Develop the Estimated Multiple Regression Equation
Note on Interpretation of Coefficients

15.3 Multiple Coefficient of Determination

15.4 Model Assumptions

15.5 Testing for Significance
F Test
t Test
Multicollinearity

15.6 Using the Estimated Regression Equation for Estimation and Prediction

15.7 Categorical Independent Variables
An Example: Johnson Filtration, Inc.
Interpreting the Parameters
More Complex Categorical Variables

15.8 Residual Analysis
Residual Plot Against $\hat{y}$
Standardized Residual Plot Against $\hat{y}$

15.9 Practical Advice: Big Data and Hypothesis Testing in Multiple Regression

Summary 750
Glossary 750
Key Formulas 751
Supplementary Exercises 752
Case Problem 1: Consumer Research, Inc. 757
Case Problem 2: Predicting Winnings for NASCAR Drivers 758
Case Problem 3: Finding the Best Car Value 760

Available in the Cengage eBook:
Appendix: Multiple Linear Regression with R

Learning Objectives

After completing this chapter, you will be able to

LO 1 Develop a multiple linear regression equation that estimates how a dependent variable is related to multiple independent variables.

LO 2 Interpret the coefficients in a multiple linear regression analysis.

LO 3 Use a multiple linear regression model to predict the value of the dependent variable given values of the independent variables.

LO 4 Calculate and interpret the multiple coefficient of determination and adjusted multiple coefficient of determination as goodness-of-fit measures in a multiple regression analysis.

LO 5 Use the *t* test to assess the significance of individual coefficients in a multiple linear regression analysis.

LO 6 Use the *F* test to assess the overall significance of a multiple linear regression model.

LO 7 Determine if multicollinearity is present in a multiple linear regression analysis using the correlation between independent variables.

LO8 Develop a confidence interval for the mean value of the dependent variable given values of the independent variables.

LO 9 Develop a prediction interval for a particular value of the dependent variable given values of the independent variables.

LO 10 Develop a multiple linear regression equation that estimates how a dependent variable is related to categorical independent variables.

LO 11 Validate the assumptions of a multiple linear regression model using residual analysis.

LO 12 Identify outliers and influential observations for a multiple linear regression analysis.

Statistics in Practice

International Paper*

Purchase, New York

International Paper is the world's largest paper and forest products company. The company employs more than 45,000 people in its operations in nearly 50 countries, and exports its products to more than 130 nations. International Paper produces building materials such as lumber and plywood; consumer packaging materials such as disposable cups and containers; industrial packaging materials such as corrugated boxes and shipping containers; and a variety of papers for use in photocopiers, printers, books, and advertising materials.

To make paper products, pulp mills process wood chips and chemicals to produce wood pulp. The wood pulp is then used at a paper mill to produce paper products. In the production of white paper products, the pulp must be bleached to remove any discoloration. A key bleaching agent used in the process is chlorine dioxide, which, because of its combustible nature, is usually produced at a pulp mill facility and then piped in solution form into the bleaching tower of the pulp mill. To improve one of the processes used to produce chlorine dioxide, researchers studied the

Multiple regression analysis assisted in the development of a better bleaching process for making white paper products.
Prisma by Dukas Presseagentur GmbH/Alamy Stock Photo

process's control and efficiency. One aspect of the study looked at the chemical feed rate for chlorine dioxide production.

To produce the chlorine dioxide, four chemicals flow at metered rates into the chlorine dioxide generator. The chlorine dioxide produced in the generator flows to an absorber where chilled water absorbs the chlorine dioxide gas to form a chlorine dioxide solution. The solution is then piped into the paper mill. A key part of controlling the process involves the chemical feed rates. Historically, experienced operators set the chemical feed rates, but this approach led to overcontrol by the operators. Consequently, chemical engineers at the mill requested that a set of control equations, one for each chemical feed, be developed to aid the operators in setting the rates.

Using multiple regression analysis, statistical analysts developed an estimated multiple regression equation for each of the four chemicals used in the process. Each equation related the production of chlorine dioxide to the amount of chemical used and the concentration level of the chlorine dioxide solution. The resulting set of four equations was programmed into a computer at each mill. In the new system, operators enter the concentration of the chlorine dioxide solution and the desired production rate; the computer software then calculates the chemical feed needed to achieve the desired production rate. After the operators began using the control equations, the chlorine dioxide generator efficiency increased, and the number of times the concentrations fell within acceptable ranges increased significantly.

This example shows how multiple regression analysis can be used to develop a better bleaching process for producing white paper products. In this chapter, we will show how Excel can be used for such purposes. Most of the concepts introduced in Chapter 14 for simple linear regression can be directly extended to the multiple regression case.

*The authors are indebted to Marian Williams and Bill Griggs for providing this Statistics in Practice. This application was originally developed at Champion International Corporation, which became part of International Paper in 2000.

In Chapter 14, we presented simple linear regression and demonstrated its use in developing an estimated regression equation that describes the relationship between two variables. Recall that the variable being predicted or explained is called the *dependent variable* and the variable being used to predict or explain the dependent variable is called the *independent variable*. In this chapter, we continue our study of regression analysis by considering situations involving two or more independent variables. This subject area, called **multiple regression analysis**, enables us to consider more factors and thus obtain better predictions than are possible with simple linear regression.

15.1 Multiple Regression Model

Multiple regression analysis is the study of how a dependent variable y is related to two or more independent variables. In the general case, we will use p to denote the number of independent variables.

Regression Model and Regression Equation

The concepts of a regression model and a regression equation introduced in the preceding chapter are applicable in the multiple regression case. The equation that describes how the dependent variable y is related to the independent variables $x_1, x_2, \ldots, x_p$ and an error term is called the **multiple regression model**. We begin with the assumption that the multiple regression model takes the following form.

Multiple Regression Model

$$y = \beta_0 + \beta_1 x_1 + \beta_2 x_2 + \cdots + \beta_p x_p + \epsilon \qquad (15.1)$$

In the multiple regression model, $\beta_0, \beta_1, \beta_2, \ldots, \beta_p$ are the parameters and the error term ϵ (the Greek letter epsilon) is a random variable. A close examination of this model reveals that y is a linear function of $x_1, x_2, \ldots, x_p$ (the $\beta_0 + \beta_1 x_1 + \beta_2 x_2 + \cdots + \beta_p x_p$ part) plus the error term ϵ. The error term accounts for the variability in y that cannot be explained by the linear effect of the p independent variables.

In Section 15.4, we will discuss the assumptions for the multiple regression model and ϵ. One of the assumptions is that the mean or expected value of ϵ is zero. A consequence of this assumption is that the mean or expected value of y, denoted $E(y)$, is equal to $\beta_0 + \beta_1x_1 + \beta_2x_2 + \cdots + \beta_px_p$. The equation that describes how the mean value of y is related to $x_1, x_2, \ldots, x_p$ is called the **multiple regression equation**.

Multiple Regression Equation

$$E(y) = \beta_0 + \beta_1x_1 + \beta_2x_2 + \cdots + \beta_px_p \tag{15.2}$$

Estimated Multiple Regression Equation

If the values of $\beta_0, \beta_1, \beta_2, \ldots, \beta_p$ were known, equation (15.2) could be used to compute the mean value of y at given values of $x_1, x_2, \ldots, x_p$. Unfortunately, these parameter values will not, in general, be known and must be estimated from sample data. A simple random sample is used to compute sample statistics $b_0, b_1, b_2, \ldots, b_p$ that are used as the point estimators of the parameters $\beta_0, \beta_1, \beta_2, \ldots, \beta_p$. These sample statistics provide the following **estimated multiple regression equation**.

Estimated Multiple Regression Equation

$$\hat{y} = b_0 + b_1x_1 + b_2x_2 + \cdots + b_px_p \tag{15.3}$$

where

$b_0, b_1, b_2, \ldots, b_p$ are the estimates of $\beta_0, \beta_1, \beta_2, \ldots, \beta_p$
$\hat{y}$ = predicted value of the dependent variable

The estimation process for multiple regression is shown in Figure 15.1.

In simple linear regression, b_0 and b_1 were the sample statistics used to estimate the parameters β_0 and β_1. Multiple regression parallels this statistical inference process, with $b_0, b_1, b_2, \ldots, b_p$ denoting the sample statistics used to estimate the parameters $\beta_0, \beta_1, \beta_2, \ldots, \beta_p$.

Figure 15.1 The Estimation Process for Multiple Regression

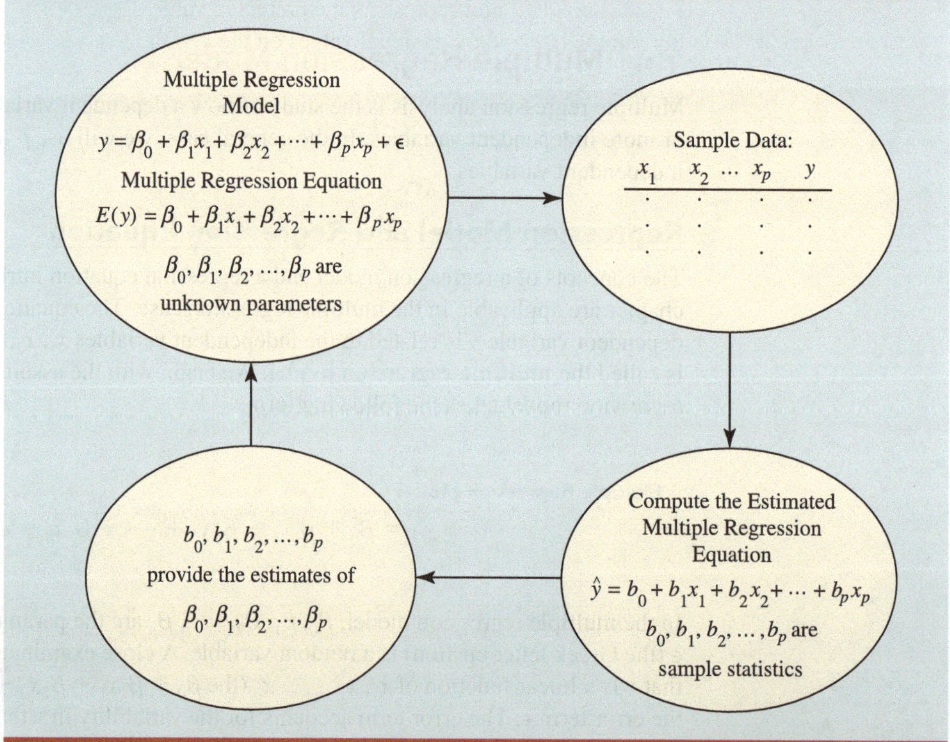

15.2 Least Squares Method

In Chapter 14, we used the **least squares method** to develop the estimated regression equation that best approximated the straight-line relationship between the dependent and independent variables. This same approach is used to develop the estimated multiple regression equation. The least squares criterion is restated as follows.

Least Squares Criterion

$$\min \Sigma(y_i - \hat{y}_i)^2 \tag{15.4}$$

where

y_i = observed value of the dependent variable for the ith observation
$\hat{y}_i$ = predicted value of the dependent variable for the ith observation

The predicted values of the dependent variable are computed by using the estimated multiple regression equation,

$$\hat{y} = b_0 + b_1x_1 + b_2x_2 + \cdots + b_px_p$$

As expression (15.4) shows, the least squares method uses sample data to provide the values of $b_0, b_1, b_2, \ldots, b_p$ that make the sum of squared residuals (the deviations between the observed values of the dependent variable (y_i) and the predicted values of the dependent variable $(\hat{y}_i)$) a minimum.

In Chapter 14, we presented formulas for computing the least squares estimators b_0 and b_1 for the estimated simple linear regression equation $\hat{y} = b_0 + b_1x$. With relatively small data sets, we were able to use those formulas to compute b_0 and b_1 by manual calculations. In multiple regression, however, the presentation of the formulas for the regression coefficients b_0, $b_1, b_2, \ldots, b_p$ involves the use of matrix algebra and is beyond the scope of this text. Therefore, in presenting multiple regression, we focus on how computer software packages can be used to obtain the estimated regression equation and other information. The emphasis will be on how to interpret the computer output rather than on how to make the multiple regression computations.

An Example: Butler Trucking Company

As an illustration of multiple regression analysis, we will consider a problem faced by the Butler Trucking Company, an independent trucking company in southern California. A major portion of Butler's business involves deliveries throughout its local area. To develop better work schedules, the managers want to predict the total daily travel time for their drivers.

Initially the managers believed that the total daily travel time would be closely related to the number of miles traveled in making the daily deliveries. A simple random sample of 10 driving assignments provided the data shown in Table 15.1 and the scatter diagram shown in Figure 15.2. After reviewing this scatter diagram, the managers hypothesized

DATA*file*
butler

Table 15.1 Preliminary Data for Butler Trucking

Driving Assignment	x_1 = Miles Traveled	y = Travel Time (hours)
1	100	9.3
2	50	4.8
3	100	8.9
4	100	6.5
5	50	4.2
6	80	6.2
7	75	7.4
8	65	6.0
9	90	7.6
10	90	6.1

Figure 15.2 Scatter Diagram of Preliminary Data for Butler Trucking

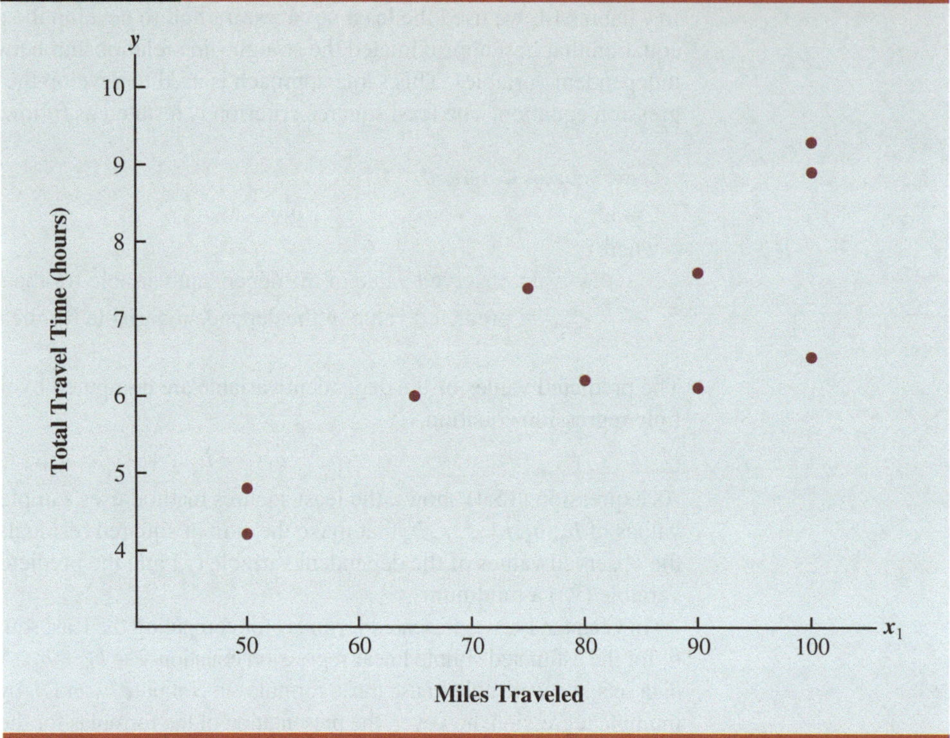

that the simple linear regression model $y = \beta_0 + \beta_1 x_1 + \epsilon$ could be used to describe the relationship between the total travel time (y) and the number of miles traveled (x_1). To estimate the parameters β_0 and β_1, the least squares method was used to develop the estimated regression equation.

$$\hat{y} = b_0 + b_1 x_1 \tag{15.5}$$

In Figure 15.3, we show the Excel Regression tool output[1] from applying simple linear regression to the data in Table 15.1. The estimated regression equation is

$$\hat{y} = 1.2739 + 0.0678x_1$$

At the 0.05 level of significance, the F value of 15.8146 and its corresponding p-value of 0.0041 indicate that the relationship is significant; that is, we can reject H_0: $\beta_1 = 0$ because the p-value is less than $\alpha = 0.05$. Note that the same conclusion is obtained from the t value of 3.9768 and its associated p-value of 0.0041. Thus, we can conclude that the relationship between the total travel time and the number of miles traveled is significant; longer travel times are associated with more miles traveled. With a coefficient of determination of R Square = 0.6641, we see that 66.41% of the variability in travel time can be explained by the linear effect of the number of miles traveled. This finding is fairly good, but the managers might want to consider adding a second independent variable to explain some of the remaining variability in the dependent variable.

[1]Excel's Regression tool was used to obtain the output. Section 14.7 describes how to use Excel's Regression tool for simple linear regression.

Figure 15.3 Regression Tool Output for Butler Trucking with One Independent Variable

	A	B	C	D	E	F	G	H	I	J
1	Assignment	Miles	Time							
2	1	100	9.3							
3	2	50	4.8							
4	3	100	8.9							
5	4	100	6.5							
6	5	50	4.2							
7	6	80	6.2							
8	7	75	7.4							
9	8	65	6.0							
10	9	90	7.6							
11	10	90	6.1							
12										
13	SUMMARY OUTPUT									
14										
15	*Regression Statistics*									
16	Multiple R	0.8149								
17	R Square	0.6641								
18	Adjusted R Square	0.6221								
19	Standard Error	1.0018								
20	Observations	10								
21										
22	ANOVA									
23		*df*	*SS*	*MS*	*F*	*Significance F*				
24	Regression	1	15.8713	15.8713	15.8146	0.0041				
25	Residual	8	8.0287	1.0036						
26	Total	9	23.9							
27										
28		*Coefficients*	*Standard Error*	*t Stat*	*P-value*	*Lower 95%*	*Upper 95%*	*Lower 99.0%*	*Upper 99.0%*	
29	Intercept	1.2739	1.4007	0.9095	0.3897	-1.9562	4.5040	-3.4261	5.9740	
30	Miles	0.0678	0.0171	3.9768	0.0041	0.0285	0.1072	0.0106	0.1251	
31										

In attempting to identify another independent variable, the managers felt that the number of deliveries could also contribute to the total travel time. The Butler Trucking data, with the number of deliveries added, are shown in Table 15.2. To develop the estimated multiple regression equation with both miles traveled (x_1) and number of deliveries (x_2) as independent variables, we will use Excel's Regression tool.

DATA*file*
butler

Table 15.2 Data for Butler Trucking with Miles Traveled (x_1) and Number of Deliveries (x_2) as the Independent Variables

Driving Assignment	x_1 = Miles Traveled	x_2 = Number of Deliveries	y = Travel Time (hours)
1	100	4	9.3
2	50	3	4.8
3	100	4	8.9
4	100	2	6.5
5	50	2	4.2
6	80	2	6.2
7	75	3	7.4
8	65	4	6.0
9	90	3	7.6
10	90	2	6.1

Using Excel's Regression Tool to Develop the Estimated Multiple Regression Equation

In Section 14.7, we showed how Excel's Regression tool could be used to determine the estimated regression equation for Armand's Pizza Parlors. We can use the same procedure with minor modifications to develop the estimated multiple regression equation for Butler Trucking. Refer to Figures 15.4 and 15.5 as we describe the tasks involved.

DATA*file*
butler

Enter/Access Data: Open the file *butler*. The data are in cells B2:D11 and labels are in column A and cells B1:D1.

Apply Tools: The following steps describe how to use Excel's Regression tool for multiple regression analysis.

Step 1. Click the **DATA** tab on the Ribbon
Step 2. In the **Analyze** group, click **Data Analysis**
Step 3. Choose **Regression** from the list of Analysis Tools
Step 4. When the **Regression** dialog box appears (see Figure 15.4):
Enter *D1:D11* in the **Input Y Range:** box
Enter *B1:C11* in the **Input X Range:** box
Select the check box for **Labels**
Select the check box for **Confidence Level**
Enter *99* in the **Confidence Level:** box
Select **Output Range:** in the **Output options** area
Enter *A13* in the **Output Range:** box (to identify the upper left corner of the section of the worksheet where the output will appear)
Click **OK**

Figure 15.4 Regression Tool Dialog Box for the Butler Trucking Example

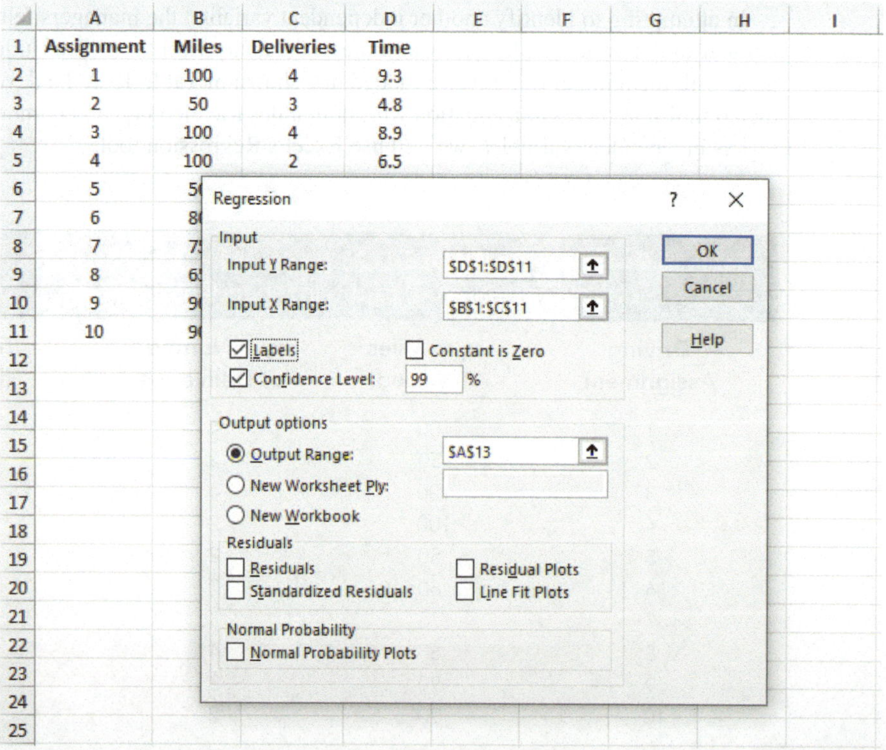

Figure 15.5 Regression Tool Output for Butler Trucking with Two Independent Variables

	A	B	C	D
1	Assignment	Miles	Deliveries	Time
2	1	100	4	9.3
3	2	50	3	4.8
4	3	100	4	8.9
5	4	100	2	6.5
6	5	50	2	4.2
7	6	80	2	6.2
8	7	75	3	7.4
9	8	65	4	6.0
10	9	90	3	7.6
11	10	90	2	6.1

SUMMARY OUTPUT

Regression Statistics	
Multiple R	0.9507
R Square	0.9038
Adjusted R Square	0.8763
Standard Error	0.5731
Observations	10

ANOVA

	df	*SS*	*MS*	*F*	*Significance F*
Regression	2	21.6006	10.8003	32.8784	0.0003
Residual	7	2.2994	0.3285		
Total	9	23.9			

	Coefficients	*Standard Error*	*t Stat*	*P-value*	*Lower 95%*	*Upper 95%*	*Lower 99.0%*	*Upper 99.0%*
Intercept	-0.8687	0.9515	-0.9129	0.3916	-3.1188	1.3814	-4.1986	2.4612
Miles	0.0611	0.0099	6.1824	0.0005	0.0378	0.0845	0.0265	0.0957
Deliveries	0.9234	0.2211	4.1763	0.0042	0.4006	1.4463	0.1496	1.6972

In the Excel output shown in Figure 15.5, the label for the independent variable x_1 is *Miles* (see cell A30), and the label for the independent variable x_2 is *Deliveries* (see cell A31). The estimated regression equation is

$$\hat{y} = -0.8687 + 0.0611x_1 + 0.9234x_2 \tag{15.6}$$

Note that using Excel's Regression tool for multiple regression is almost the same as using it for simple linear regression. The major difference is that in the multiple regression case a larger range of cells has to be provided in order to identify the independent variables.

In the next section, we will discuss the use of the coefficient of multiple determination in measuring how good a fit is provided by this estimated regression equation. Before doing so, let us examine more carefully the values of $b_1 = 0.0611$ and $b_2 = 0.9234$ in equation (15.6).

Note on Interpretation of Coefficients

One observation can be made at this point about the relationship between the estimated regression equation with only the miles traveled as an independent variable and the equation that includes the number of deliveries as a second independent variable. The value of b_1 is not the same in both cases. In simple linear regression, we interpret b_1 as an estimate of the change in y for a one-unit change in the independent variable. In multiple regression analysis, this interpretation must be modified somewhat. That is, in multiple regression analysis, we interpret each regression coefficient as follows: b_i represents an estimate of the change in y corresponding to a one-unit change in x_i when all other independent variables are held constant. In the Butler Trucking example involving two independent variables, $b_1 = 0.0611$. Thus, 0.0611 hours is an estimate of the expected increase in travel time corresponding to an increase of 1 mile in the distance traveled when the number of deliveries is held constant. Similarly, because $b_2 = 0.9234$, an estimate of the expected increase in travel time corresponding to an increase of one delivery when the number of miles traveled is held constant is 0.9234 hours.

Exercises

Note to student: The exercises involving data in this and subsequent sections were designed to be solved using a computer software package.

Methods

1. The estimated regression equation for a model involving two independent variables and 10 observations follows. **LO 2, 3**

$$\hat{y} = 29.1270 + 0.5906x_1 + 0.4980x_2$$

   a. Interpret b_1 and b_2 in this estimated regression equation.
   b. Predict y when $x_1 = 180$ and $x_2 = 310$.

2. Consider the following data for a dependent variable y and two independent variables, x_1 and x_2. **LO 1, 3**

DATA*file*
exer2

x_1	x_2	y
30	12	94
47	10	108
25	17	112
51	16	178
40	5	94
51	19	175
74	7	170
36	12	117
59	13	142
76	16	211

   a. Develop an estimated regression equation relating y to x_1. Predict y if $x_1 = 45$.
   b. Develop an estimated regression equation relating y to x_2. Predict y if $x_2 = 15$.
   c. Develop an estimated regression equation relating y to x_1 and x_2. Predict y if $x_1 = 45$ and $x_2 = 15$.

3. In a regression analysis involving 30 observations, the following estimated regression equation was obtained. **LO 2, 3**

$$\hat{y} = 17.6 + 3.8x_1 - 2.3x_2 + 7.6x_3 + 2.7x_4$$

   a. Interpret b_1, b_2, b_3, and b_4 in this estimated regression equation.
   b. Predict y when $x_1 = 10$, $x_2 = 5$, $x_3 = 1$, and $x_4 = 2$.

Applications

4. **Forecasting Shoe Sales.** A shoe store developed the following estimated regression equation relating sales to inventory investment and advertising expenditures. **LO 2, 3**

$$\hat{y} = 25 + 10x_1 + 8x_2$$

where

$$x_1 = \text{inventory investment (\$1,000s)}$$
$$x_2 = \text{advertising expenditures (\$1,000s)}$$
$$y = \text{sales (\$1,000s)}$$

   a. Predict the sales resulting from a $15,000 investment in inventory and an advertising budget of $10,000.
   b. Interpret b_1 and b_2 in this estimated regression equation.

5. **Predicting Theater Revenue.** The owner of Showtime Movie Theaters, Inc. would like to predict weekly gross revenue as a function of advertising expenditures. Historical data for a sample of eight weeks follow. LO 2, 3

DATA*file*
showtime

Weekly Gross Revenue ($1,000s)	Television Advertising ($1,000s)	Newspaper Advertising ($1,000s)
96	5.0	1.5
90	2.0	2.0
95	4.0	1.5
92	2.5	2.5
95	3.0	3.3
94	3.5	2.3
94	2.5	4.2
94	3.0	2.5

a. Develop an estimated regression equation with the amount of television advertising as the independent variable.
b. Develop an estimated regression equation with both television advertising and newspaper advertising as the independent variables.
c. Is the estimated regression equation coefficient for television advertising expenditures the same in part (a) and in part (b)? Interpret the coefficient in each case.
d. Predict weekly gross revenue for a week when $3,500 is spent on television advertising and $2,300 is spent on newspaper advertising?

6. **Predicting NFL Wins.** The National Football League (NFL) records a variety of performance data for individuals and teams. To investigate the importance of passing on the percentage of games won by a team, the following data show the conference (Conf), average number of passing yards per attempt (Yds/Att), the number of interceptions thrown per attempt (Int/Att), and the percentage of games won (Win%) for a random sample of 16 NFL teams for one full season. LO 1, 3

DATA*file*
passingnfl

Team	Conf	Yds/Att	Int/Att	Win%
Arizona Cardinals	NFC	6.5	0.042	50.0
Atlanta Falcons	NFC	7.1	0.022	62.5
Carolina Panthers	NFC	7.4	0.033	37.5
Cincinnati Bengals	AFC	6.2	0.026	56.3
Detroit Lions	NFC	7.2	0.024	62.5
Green Bay Packers	NFC	8.9	0.014	93.8
Houston Texans	AFC	7.5	0.019	62.5
Indianapolis Colts	AFC	5.6	0.026	12.5
Jacksonville Jaguars	AFC	4.6	0.032	31.3
Minnesota Vikings	NFC	5.8	0.033	18.8
New England Patriots	AFC	8.3	0.020	81.3
New Orleans Saints	NFC	8.1	0.021	81.3
Oakland Raiders	AFC	7.6	0.044	50.0
San Francisco 49ers	NFC	6.5	0.011	81.3
Tennessee Titans	AFC	6.7	0.024	56.3
Washington Redskins	NFC	6.4	0.041	31.3

a. Develop the estimated regression equation that could be used to predict the percentage of games won given the average number of passing yards per attempt.

b. Develop the estimated regression equation that could be used to predict the percentage of games won given the number of interceptions thrown per attempt.
c. Develop the estimated regression equation that could be used to predict the percentage of games won given the average number of passing yards per attempt and the number of interceptions thrown per attempt.
d. The average number of passing yards per attempt for the Kansas City Chiefs was 6.2 and the number of interceptions thrown per attempt was 0.036. Use the estimated regression equation developed in part (c) to predict the percentage of games won by the Kansas City Chiefs. (*Note:* For this season the Kansas City Chiefs' record was 7 wins and 9 losses.) Compare your prediction to the actual percentage of games won by the Kansas City Chiefs.

7. **Rating Computer Monitors.** *PC Magazine* provided ratings for several characteristics of computer monitors, including an overall rating (PC Magazine website). The following data show the rating for contrast ratio, resolution, and the overall rating for ten monitors tested using a 0–100 point scale. The highest rated monitor was the BenQ BL3201PH, with an overall rating of 87. **LO 1, 3**

DATA*file*
monitorratings

Model	Contrast Ratio	Resolution	Overall Rating
BenQ BL3201PH	78	89	87
AOC U2868PQU	98	87	86
NEC MultiSync PA322UHD	84	82	85
Acer XB280HK	78	77	82
Asus ROG Swift PG278Q	65	82	82
AOC E1759Fwu	57	78	82
Dell UltraSharp UZ2715H	56	83	81
NEC MultiSync EA244UHD	77	75	79
HP DreamColor Z27x	47	81	77
Dell UltraSharp UZ2315H	55	70	76

a. Develop the estimated regression equation that can be used to predict the Overall Rating using the Contrast Ratio Rating.
b. Develop the estimated regression equation that can be used to predict the Overall Rating using both the Contrast Ratio Rating and the Resolution Rating.
c. Predict the Overall Rating for a computer monitor computer that has a Contrast Ratio Rating of 85 and a Resolution Rating of 74.

8. **Scoring Cruise Ships.** The *Condé Nast Traveler* Gold List provides ratings for the top 20 small cruise ships. The following data shown are the scores each ship received based upon the results from *Condé Nast Traveler*'s annual Readers' Choice Survey. Each score represents the percentage of respondents who rated a ship as excellent or very good on several criteria, including Shore Excursions and Food/Dining. An overall score is also reported and used to rank the ships. The highest ranked ship, the *Seabourn Odyssey,* has an overall score of 94.4, the highest component of which is 97.8 for Food/Dining. **LO 1, 3**

Ship	Overall	Shore Excursions	Food/Dining
Seabourn Odyssey	94.4	90.9	97.8
Seabourn Pride	93.0	84.2	96.7
National Geographic Endeavor	92.9	100.0	88.5

DATA*file*
ships

Seabourn Sojourn	91.3	94.8	97.1
Paul Gauguin	90.5	87.9	91.2
Seabourn Legend	90.3	82.1	98.8
Seabourn Spirit	90.2	86.3	92.0
Silver Explorer	89.9	92.6	88.9
Silver Spirit	89.4	85.9	90.8
Seven Seas Navigator	89.2	83.3	90.5
Silver Whisperer	89.2	82.0	88.6
National Geographic Explorer	89.1	93.1	89.7
Silver Cloud	88.7	78.3	91.3
Celebrity Xpedition	87.2	91.7	73.6
Silver Shadow	87.2	75.0	89.7
Silver Wind	86.6	78.1	91.6
SeaDream II	86.2	77.4	90.9
Wind Star	86.1	76.5	91.5
Wind Surf	86.1	72.3	89.3
Wind Spirit	85.2	77.4	91.9

a. Determine an estimated regression equation that can be used to predict the overall score given the score for Shore Excursions.
b. Consider the addition of the independent variable Food/Dining. Develop the estimated regression equation that can be used to predict the overall score given the scores for Shore Excursions and Food/Dining.
c. Predict the overall score for a cruise ship with a Shore Excursions score of 80 and a Food/Dining Score of 90.

9. **House Prices.** Spring is a peak time for selling houses. The file *springhouses* contains the selling price, number of bathrooms, square footage, and number of bedrooms of 26 homes sold in Ft. Thomas, Kentucky, in spring 2018 (*realtor.com* website). **LO 1, 3**

DATA*file*
springhouses

a. Develop scatter plots of selling price versus number of bathrooms, selling price versus square footage, and selling price versus number of bedrooms. Comment on the relationship between selling price and these three variables.
b. Develop an estimated regression equation that can be used to predict the selling price given the three independent variables (number of baths, square footage, and number of bedrooms).
c. It is argued that we do not need both number of baths and number of bedrooms. Develop an estimated regression equation that can be used to predict selling price given square footage and the number of bedrooms.
d. Suppose your house has four bedrooms and is 2,650 square feet. What is the predicted selling price using the model developed in part (c).

10. **Predicting Baseball Pitcher Performance.** Major League Baseball (MLB) consists of teams that play in the American League and the National League. MLB collects a wide variety of team and player statistics. Some of the statistics often used to evaluate pitching performance are as follows:

ERA: The average number of earned runs given up by the pitcher per nine innings. An earned run is any run that the opponent scores off a particular pitcher except for runs scored as a result of errors.

SO/IP: The average number of strikeouts per inning pitched.

HR/IP: The average number of home runs per inning pitched.

R/IP: The number of runs given up per inning pitched.

The following data show values for these statistics for a random sample of 20 pitchers from the American League for a full season. **LO 1, 3**

DATA*file*
pitchingmlb

Player	Team	W	L	ERA	SO/IP	HR/IP	R/IP
Verlander, J	DET	24	5	2.40	1.00	0.10	0.29
Beckett, J	BOS	13	7	2.89	0.91	0.11	0.34
Wilson, C	TEX	16	7	2.94	0.92	0.07	0.40
Sabathia, C	NYY	19	8	3.00	0.97	0.07	0.37
Haren, D	LAA	16	10	3.17	0.81	0.08	0.38
McCarthy, B	OAK	9	9	3.32	0.72	0.06	0.43
Santana, E	LAA	11	12	3.38	0.78	0.11	0.42
Lester, J	BOS	15	9	3.47	0.95	0.10	0.40
Hernandez, F	SEA	14	14	3.47	0.95	0.08	0.42
Buehrle, M	CWS	13	9	3.59	0.53	0.10	0.45
Pineda, M	SEA	9	10	3.74	1.01	0.11	0.44
Colon, B	NYY	8	10	4.00	0.82	0.13	0.52
Tomlin, J	CLE	12	7	4.25	0.54	0.15	0.48
Pavano, C	MIN	9	13	4.30	0.46	0.10	0.55
Danks, J	CWS	8	12	4.33	0.79	0.11	0.52
Guthrie, J	BAL	9	17	4.33	0.63	0.13	0.54
Lewis, C	TEX	14	10	4.40	0.84	0.17	0.51
Scherzer, M	DET	15	9	4.43	0.89	0.15	0.52
Davis, W	TB	11	10	4.45	0.57	0.13	0.52
Porcello, R	DET	14	9	4.75	0.57	0.10	0.57

a. Develop an estimated regression equation that can be used to predict the average number of runs given up per inning given the average number of strikeouts per inning pitched.
b. Develop an estimated regression equation that can be used to predict the average number of runs given up per inning given the average number of home runs per inning pitched.
c. Develop an estimated regression equation that can be used to predict the average number of runs given up per inning given the average number of strikeouts per inning pitched and the average number of home runs per inning pitched.
d. A. J. Burnett, a pitcher for the New York Yankees, had an average number of strikeouts per inning pitched of 0.91 and an average number of home runs per inning of 0.16. Use the estimated regression equation developed in part (c) to predict the average number of runs given up per inning for A. J. Burnett. (*Note:* The actual value for R/IP was 0.6.)
e. Suppose a suggestion was made to also use the earned run average as another independent variable in part (c). What do you think of this suggestion?

15.3 Multiple Coefficient of Determination

In simple linear regression, we showed that the total sum of squares can be partitioned into two components: the sum of squares due to regression and the sum of squares due to error. The same procedure applies to the sum of squares in multiple regression.

Relationship Among SST, SSR, and SSE

$$SST = SSR + SSE \tag{15.7}$$

where

$$SST = \text{total sum of squares} = \Sigma(y_i - \bar{y})^2$$
$$SSR = \text{sum of squares due to regression} = \Sigma(\hat{y}_i - \bar{y})^2$$
$$SSE = \text{sum of squares due to error} = \Sigma(y_i - \hat{y}_i)^2$$

Because of the computational difficulty in computing the three sums of squares, we rely on computer packages to determine those values. The analysis of variance part of the Excel output in Figure 15.5 shows the three values for the Butler Trucking problem with two independent variables: SST = 23.9, SSR = 21.6006, and SSE = 2.2994. With only one independent variable (number of miles traveled), the Excel output in Figure 15.3 shows that SST = 23.9, SSR = 15.8713, and SSE = 8.0287. The value of SST is the same in both cases because it does not depend on $\hat{y}$, but SSR increases and SSE decreases when a second independent variable (number of deliveries) is added. The implication is that the estimated multiple regression equation provides a better fit for the observed data.

In Chapter 14, we used the coefficient of determination, $r^2 = \text{SSR/SST}$, to measure the goodness of fit for the estimated regression equation. The same concept applies to multiple regression. The term **multiple coefficient of determination** indicates that we are measuring the goodness of fit for the estimated multiple regression equation. The multiple coefficient of determination, denoted R^2, is computed as follows.

In the Excel Regression tool output the label R Square is used to identify the value of R^2.

Multiple Coefficient of Determination

$$R^2 = \frac{\text{SSR}}{\text{SST}} \tag{15.8}$$

The multiple coefficient of determination can be interpreted as the proportion of the variability in the dependent variable that can be explained by the estimated multiple regression equation. Hence, when multiplied by 100, it can be interpreted as the percentage of the variability in y that can be explained by the estimated regression equation.

In the two-independent-variable Butler Trucking example, with SSR = 21.6006 and SST = 23.9, we have

$$R^2 = \frac{21.6006}{23.9} = 0.9038$$

Adding independent variables causes the prediction errors (residuals) to become smaller, thus reducing the sum of squares due to error, SSE. Because SSR = SST − SSE, when SSE becomes smaller, SSR becomes larger, causing $R^2 = \text{SSR/SST}$ to increase.

Therefore, 90.38% of the variability in travel time y is explained by the estimated multiple regression equation with miles traveled and number of deliveries as the independent variables. In Figure 15.5, we see that the multiple coefficient of determination is also provided by the Excel output; it is denoted by R Square = 0.9038 (see cell B17).

Figure 15.3 shows that the R Square value for the estimated regression equation with only one independent variable, number of miles traveled (x_1), is 0.6641. Thus, the percentage of the variability in travel time that is explained by the estimated regression equation increases from 66.41% to 90.38% when number of deliveries is added as a second independent variable. In general, R^2 always increases as independent variables are added to the model.

Many analysts prefer adjusting R^2 for the number of independent variables to avoid overestimating the impact of adding an independent variable on the amount of variability explained by the estimated regression equation. With n denoting the number of observations and p denoting the number of independent variables, the **adjusted multiple coefficient of determination** is computed as follows.

If a variable is added to the model, R^2 becomes larger even if the variable added is not statistically significant. The adjusted multiple coefficient of determination compensates for the number of independent variables in the model.

Adjusted Multiple Coefficient of Determination

$$R_a^2 = 1 - (1 - R^2)\frac{n - 1}{n - p - 1} \tag{15.9}$$

For the Butler Trucking example with $n = 10$ and $p = 2$, we have

$$R_a^2 = 1 - (1 - 0.9038)\frac{10 - 1}{10 - 2 - 1} = 0.8763$$

Thus, after adjusting for the two independent variables, we have an adjusted multiple coefficient of determination of 0.8763. This value is provided by the Excel output in Figure 15.5 as Adjusted R Square = 0.8763 (see cell B18).

Exercises

Methods

11. In exercise 1, the following estimated regression equation based on 10 observations was presented. **LO 4**

$$\hat{y} = 29.1270 + 0.5906x_1 + 0.4980x_2$$

The values of SST and SSR are 6724.125 and 6216.375, respectively.
a. Find SSE.
b. Compute R^2.
c. Compute R_a^2.
d. Comment on the goodness of fit.

12. In exercise 2, 10 observations were provided for a dependent variable y and two independent variables x_1 and x_2; for these data SST = 15,182.9 and SSR = 14,052.2. **LO 4**
a. Compute R^2.
b. Compute R_a^2.
c. Does the estimated regression equation explain a large amount of the variability in the data? Explain.

13. In exercise 3, the following estimated regression equation based on 30 observations was presented. **LO 4**

$$\hat{y} = 17.6 + 3.8x_1 - 2.3x_2 + 7.6x_3 + 2.7x_4$$

The values of SST and SSR are 1,805 and 1,760, respectively.
a. Compute R^2.
b. Compute R_a^2.
c. Comment on the goodness of fit.

Applications

14. **R^2 in Shoe Sales Prediction.** In exercise 4, the following estimated regression equation relating sales to inventory investment and advertising expenditures was given. **LO 4**

$$\hat{y} = 25 + 10x_1 + 8x_2$$

The data used to develop the model came from a survey of 10 stores; for those data, SST = 16,000 and SSR = 12,000.
a. For the estimated regression equation given, compute R^2.
b. Compute R_a^2.
c. Does the model appear to explain a large amount of variability in the data? Explain.

15. **R^2 in Theater Revenue Prediction.** In exercise 5, the owner of Showtime Movie Theaters, Inc. used multiple regression analysis to predict gross revenue (y) as a function

of television advertising (x_1) and newspaper advertising (x_2). The estimated regression equation was

DATA*file* showtime

$$\hat{y} = 83.2 + 2.29x_1 + 1.30x_2$$

The computer solution provided SST = 25.5 and SSR = 23.435. **LO 4**

a. Compute and interpret R^2 and R_a^2.

b. When television advertising was the only independent variable, $R^2 = 0.653$ and $R_a^2 = 0.595$. Do you prefer the multiple regression results? Explain.

DATA*file* passingnfl

16. **Quality of Fit in Predicting NFL Wins.** In exercise 6, data were given on the average number of passing yards per attempt (Yds/Att), the number of interceptions thrown per attempt (Int/Att), and the percentage of games won (Win%) for a random sample of 16 National Football League (NFL) teams for one full season. **LO 4**

a. Did the estimated regression equation that uses only the average number of passing yards per attempt as the independent variable to predict the percentage of games won provide a good fit?

b. Discuss the benefit of using both the average number of passing yards per attempt and the number of interceptions thrown per attempt to predict the percentage of games won.

DATA*file* springhouses

17. **Quality of Fit in Predicting House Prices.** Revisit exercise 9, where we develop an estimated regression equation that can be used to predict the selling price given the number of bathrooms, square footage, and number of bedrooms in the house. **LO 4**

a. Does the estimated regression equation provide a good fit to the data? Explain.

b. In part (c) of exercise 9 you developed an estimated regression equation that predicts selling price given the square footage and number of bedrooms. Compare the fit for this simpler model to that of the model that also includes number of bathrooms as an independent variable.

DATA*file* pitchingmlb

18. **R^2 in Predicting Baseball Pitcher Performance.** Refer to exercise 10, where Major League Baseball (MLB) pitching statistics were reported for a random sample of 20 pitchers from the American League for one full season. **LO 4**

a. In part (c) of exercise 10, an estimated regression equation was developed relating the average number of runs given up per inning pitched given the average number of strikeouts per inning pitched and the average number of home runs per inning pitched. What are the values of R^2 and R_a^2?

b. Does the estimated regression equation provide a good fit to the data? Explain.

c. Suppose the earned run average (ERA) is used as the dependent variable in part (c) instead of the average number of runs given up per inning pitched. Does the estimated regression equation that uses the ERA provide a good fit to the data? Explain.

15.4 Model Assumptions

In Section 15.1, we introduced the following multiple regression model.

Multiple Regression Model

$$y = \beta_0 + \beta_1 x_1 + \beta_2 x_2 + \cdots + \beta_p x_p + \epsilon \qquad \textbf{(15.10)}$$

The assumptions about the error term ϵ in the multiple regression model parallel those for the simple linear regression model.

Assumptions about the Error Term ϵ in the Multiple Regression Model $y = \beta_0 + \beta_1 x_1 + \cdots + \beta_p x_p + \epsilon$

1. The error term ϵ is a random variable with mean or expected value of zero; that is, $E(\epsilon) = 0$.
   Implication: For given values of $x_1, x_2, \ldots, x_p$, the expected, or average, value of y is given by

   $$E(y) = \beta_0 + \beta_1 x_1 + \beta_2 x_2 + \cdots + \beta_p x_p \tag{15.11}$$

   Equation (15.11) is the multiple regression equation we introduced in Section 15.1. In this equation, $E(y)$ represents the average of all possible values of y that might occur for the given values of $x_1, x_2, \ldots, x_p$.
2. The variance of ϵ is denoted by σ^2 and is the same for all values of the independent variables $x_1, x_2, \ldots, x_p$.
   Implication: The variance of y about the regression line equals σ^2 and is the same for all values of $x_1, x_2, \ldots, x_p$.
3. The values of ϵ are independent.
   Implication: The value of ϵ for a particular set of values for the independent variables is not related to the value of ϵ for any other set of values.
4. The error term ϵ is a normally distributed random variable reflecting the deviation between the y value and the expected value of y given by $\beta_0 + \beta_1 x_1 + \beta_2 x_2 + \cdots + \beta_p x_p$.
   Implication: Because $\beta_0, \beta_1, \ldots, \beta_p$ are constants for the given values of $x_1, x_2, \ldots, x_p$, the dependent variable y is also a normally distributed random variable.

To obtain more insight about the form of the relationship given by equation (15.11), consider the following two-independent-variable multiple regression equation.

$$E(y) = \beta_0 + \beta_1 x_1 + \beta_2 x_2$$

The graph of this equation is a plane in three-dimensional space. Figure 15.6 provides an example of such a graph. Note that the value of ϵ shown is the difference between the actual y value and the expected value of y, $E(y)$, when $x_1 = x_1^*$ and $x_2 = x_2^*$

Figure 15.6 Graph of the Regression Equation for Multiple Regression Analysis with Two Independent Variables

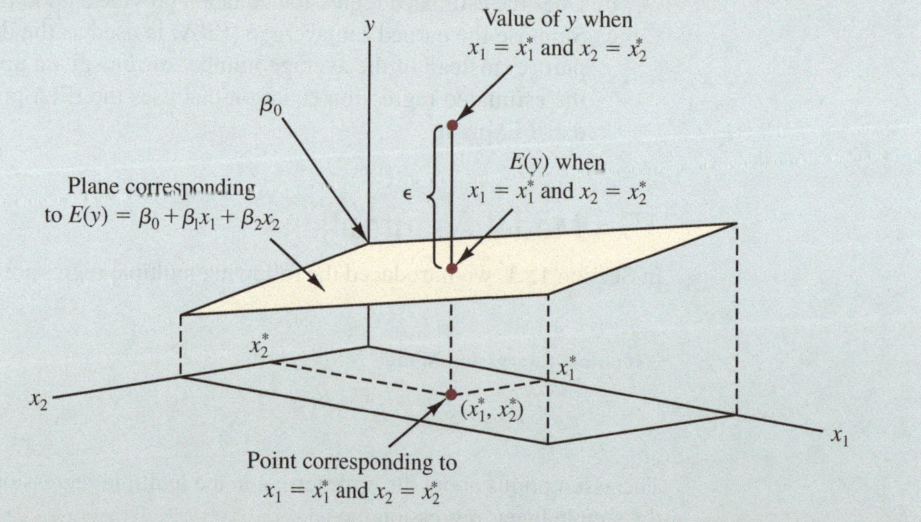

In regression analysis, the term *response variable* is often used in place of the term *dependent variable.* Furthermore, since the multiple regression equation generates a plane or surface, its graph is called a *response surface.*

15.5 Testing for Significance

In this section, we show how to conduct significance tests for a multiple regression relationship. The significance tests we used in simple linear regression were a t test and an F test. In simple linear regression, both tests provide the same conclusion; that is, if the null hypothesis is rejected, we conclude that $\beta_1 \neq 0$. In multiple regression, the t test and the F test have different purposes.

1. The F test is used to determine whether a significant relationship exists between the dependent variable and the set of all the independent variables; we will refer to the F test as the test for *overall significance.*
2. If the F test shows an overall significance, the t test is used to determine whether each of the individual independent variables is significant. A separate t test is conducted for each of the independent variables in the model; we refer to each of these t tests as a test for *individual significance.*

In the material that follows, we will explain the F test and the t test and apply each to the Butler Trucking Company example.

F Test

The multiple regression model as defined in Section 15.4 is

$$y = \beta_0 + \beta_1 x_1 + \beta_2 x_2 + \cdots + \beta_p x_p + \epsilon$$

The hypotheses for the F test involve the parameters of the multiple regression model.

$$H_0\colon \beta_1 = \beta_2 = \cdots = \beta_p = 0$$
$$H_a\colon \text{One or more of the parameters is not equal to zero}$$

If H_0 is rejected, the test gives us sufficient statistical evidence to conclude that one or more of the parameters is not equal to zero and that the overall relationship between y and the set of independent variables $x_1, x_2, \ldots, x_p$ is significant. However, if H_0 cannot be rejected, we do not have sufficient evidence to conclude that a significant relationship is present.

Before describing the steps of the F test, we need to review the concept of *mean square.* A mean square is a sum of squares divided by its corresponding degrees of freedom. In the multiple regression case, the total sum of squares has $n - 1$ degrees of freedom, the sum of squares due to regression (SSR) has p degrees of freedom, and the sum of squares due to error has $n - p - 1$ degrees of freedom. Hence, the mean square due to regression (MSR) is SSR/p and the mean square due to error (MSE) is SSE/$(n - p - 1)$.

$$\text{MSR} = \frac{\text{SSR}}{p} \tag{15.12}$$

and

$$\text{MSE} = \frac{\text{SSE}}{n - p - 1} \tag{15.13}$$

As discussed in Chapter 14, MSE provides an unbiased estimate of σ^2, the variance of the error term ϵ. If $H_0\colon \beta_1 = \beta_2 = \cdots = \beta_p = 0$ is true, MSR also provides an unbiased estimate of σ^2, and the value of MSR/MSE should be close to 1. However, if H_0 is false, MSR overestimates σ^2 and the value of MSR/MSE becomes larger. To determine how large the value of MSR/MSE must be to reject H_0, we make use of the fact that if H_0 is true and the assumptions about the multiple regression model are valid, the sampling distribution of MSR/MSE is an F distribution with p degrees of freedom in the numerator and $n - p - 1$ in the denominator. A summary of the F test for significance in multiple regression follows.

F Test for Overall Significance

$$H_0: \beta_1 = \beta_2 = \cdots = \beta_p = 0$$

H_a: One or more of the parameters is not equal to zero

Test Statistic

$$F = \frac{\text{MSR}}{\text{MSE}} \tag{15.14}$$

Rejection Rule

p-value approach: Reject H_0 if p-value $\leq \alpha$

Critical value approach: Reject H_0 if $F \geq F_\alpha$

where F_α is based on an F distribution with p degrees of freedom in the numerator and $n - p - 1$ degrees of freedom in the denominator.

Let us apply the F test to the Butler Trucking Company multiple regression problem. With two independent variables, the hypotheses are written as follows.

$$H_0: \beta_1 = \beta_2 = 0$$

H_a: β_1 and/or β_2 is not equal to zero

Figure 15.7 shows a portion of the Excel Regression tool output shown previously in Figure 15.5 with miles traveled (x_1) and number of deliveries (x_2) as the two independent variables.

Figure 15.7 Regression Tool Output for the Butler Trucking Example with Two Independent Variables

	A	B	C	D	E	F
1	Assignment	Miles	Deliveries	Time		
2	1	100	4	9.3		
3	2	50	3	4.8		
4	3	100	4	8.9		
5	4	100	2	6.5		
6	5	50	2	4.2		
7	6	80	2	6.2		
8	7	75	3	7.4		
9	8	65	4	6.0		
10	9	90	3	7.6		
11	10	90	2	6.1		
12						
13	SUMMARY OUTPUT					
14						
15	*Regression Statistics*					
16	Multiple R	0.9507				
17	R Square	0.9038				
18	Adjusted R Square	0.8763				
19	Standard Error	0.5731				
20	Observations	10				
21						
22	ANOVA					
23		*df*	*SS*	*MS*	*F*	*Significance F*
24	Regression	2	21.6006	10.8003	32.8784	0.0003
25	Residual	7	2.2994	0.3285		
26	Total	9	23.9			
27						
28		*Coefficients*	*Standard Error*	*t Stat*	*P-value*	
29	Intercept	-0.8687	0.9515	-0.9129	0.3916	
30	Miles	0.0611	0.0099	6.1824	0.0005	
31	Deliveries	0.9234	0.2211	4.1763	0.0042	
32						
33						

The *Significance F* value in cell F24 is the *p*-value used to test for overall

The *p*-value in cell E30 is used to test for the individual significance of Miles.

The *p*-value in cell E31 is used to test for the individual significance of Deliveries.

In the analysis of variance part of the output, we see that MSR = 10.8003 and MSE = 0.3285. Using equation (15.14), we obtain the test statistic.

$$F = \frac{10.8003}{0.3285} = 32.9$$

Note that the F value in the Excel output is $F = 32.8784$; the value we calculated differs because we used rounded values for MSR and MSE in the calculation. Using $\alpha = 0.01$, the p-value $= 0.0003$ in cell F24 indicates that we can reject H_0: $\beta_1 = \beta_2 = 0$ because the p-value is less than $\alpha = 0.01$. Alternatively, Table 4 of Appendix B shows that with 2 degrees of freedom in the numerator and 7 degrees of freedom in the denominator, $F_{0.01} = 9.55$. With $32.9 > 9.55$, we reject H_0: $\beta_1 = \beta_2 = 0$ and conclude that a significant relationship is present between travel time y and the two independent variables, miles traveled and number of deliveries.

The label Significance F in cell F23 is used to identify the p-value in cell F24.

As noted previously, MSE provides an unbiased estimate of σ^2, the variance of the error term ϵ. Thus, the estimate of σ^2 is MSE = 0.3285. The square root of MSE is the estimate of the standard deviation of the error term. As defined in Section 14.5, this standard deviation is called the standard error of the estimate and is denoted s. Hence, we have $s = \sqrt{\text{MSE}} = \sqrt{0.3285} = 0.5731$. Note that the value of the standard error of the estimate appears in cell B19 of Figure 15.7.

Table 15.3 is the general form of the ANOVA table for multiple regression. The value of the F test statistic and its corresponding p-value in the last column can be used to make the hypothesis test conclusion. By reviewing the Excel output for Butler Trucking Company in Figure 15.7, we see that Excel's analysis of variance table contains this information.

t Test

If the F test shows that the multiple regression relationship is significant, a t test can be conducted to determine the significance of each of the individual parameters. The t test for individual significance follows.

t Test for Individual Significance

For any parameter β_i

$$H_0\text{: } \beta_i = 0$$
$$H_a\text{: } \beta_i \neq 0$$

Test Statistic

$$t = \frac{b_i}{s_{b_i}} \tag{15.15}$$

Rejection Rule

p-value approach: Reject H_0 if p-value $\leq \alpha$

Critical value approach: Reject H_0 if $t \leq -t_{\alpha/2}$ or if $t \geq t_{\alpha/2}$

where $t_{\alpha/2}$ is based on a t distribution with $n - p - 1$ degrees of freedom.

Table 15.3 General Form of the ANOVA Table for Multiple Regression with p Independent Variables

Source	Sum of Squares	Degrees of Freedom	Mean Square	F	p-Value
Regression	SSR	p	$\text{MSR} = \frac{\text{SSR}}{p}$	$F = \frac{\text{MSR}}{\text{MSE}}$	
Error	SSE	$n - p - 1$	$\text{MSE} = \frac{\text{SSE}}{n - p - 1}$		
Total	SST	$n - 1$			

In the test statistic, s_{b_i} is the estimate of the standard deviation of b_i. The value of s_{b_i} will be provided by the computer software package.

Let us conduct the t test for the Butler Trucking regression problem. Refer to the section of Figure 15.7 that shows the Excel output for the t-ratio calculations. Values of b_1, b_2, s_{b_1}, and s_{b_2} are as follows.

$$b_1 = 0.0611 \quad s_{b_1} = 0.0099$$
$$b_2 = 0.9234 \quad s_{b_2} = 0.2211$$

Using equation (15.15), we obtain the test statistic for the hypotheses involving parameters β_1 and β_2.

$$t = 0.0611/.0099 = 6.1717$$
$$t = 0.9234/.2211 = 4.1764$$

The t values in the Regression tool output are 6.1824 and 4.1763. The difference is due to rounding.

Note that both of these t-ratio values and the corresponding p-values are provided by the Excel Regression tool output in Figure 15.7. Using $\alpha = 0.01$, the p-values of 0.0005 and 0.0042 on the Excel output indicate that we can reject H_0: $\beta_1 = 0$ and H_0: $\beta_2 = 0$. Hence, both parameters are statistically significant. Alternatively, Table 2 of Appendix B shows that with $n - p - 1 = 10 - 2 - 1 = 7$ degrees of freedom, $t_{0.005} = 3.499$. Because $6.1717 > 3.499$, we reject H_0: $\beta_1 = 0$. Similarly, with $4.1763 > 3.499$, we reject H_0: $\beta_2 = 0$.

Multicollinearity

We use the term *independent variable* in regression analysis to refer to any variable being used to predict or explain the value of the dependent variable. The term does not mean, however, that the independent variables themselves are independent in any statistical sense. On the contrary, most independent variables in a multiple regression problem are correlated to some degree with one another. For example, in the Butler Trucking example involving the two independent variables x_1 (miles traveled) and x_2 (number of deliveries), we could treat the miles traveled as the dependent variable and the number of deliveries as the independent variable to determine whether those two variables are themselves related. We could then compute the sample correlation coefficient $r_{x_1x_2}$ to determine the extent to which the variables are related. Doing so yields $r_{x_1x_2} = 0.16$. Thus, we find some degree of linear association between the two independent variables. In multiple regression analysis, **multicollinearity** refers to the correlation among the independent variables.

To provide a better perspective of the potential problems of multicollinearity, let us consider a modification of the Butler Trucking example. Instead of x_2 being the number of deliveries, let x_2 denote the number of gallons of gasoline consumed. Clearly, x_1 (the miles traveled) and x_2 are related; that is, we know that the number of gallons of gasoline used depends on the number of miles traveled. Hence, we would conclude logically that x_1 and x_2 are highly correlated independent variables.

Assume that we obtain the equation $\hat{y} = b_0 + b_1x_1 + b_2x_2$ and find that the F test shows the relationship to be significant. Then suppose we conduct a t test on β_1 to determine whether $\beta_1 \neq 0$, and we cannot reject H_0: $\beta_1 = 0$. Does this result mean that travel time is not related to miles traveled? Not necessarily. What it probably means is that with x_2 already in the model, x_1 does not make a significant contribution to determining the value of y. This interpretation makes sense in our example; if we know the amount of gasoline consumed, we do not gain much additional information useful in predicting y by knowing the miles traveled. Similarly, a t test might lead us to conclude $\beta_2 = 0$ on the grounds that, with x_1 in the model, knowledge of the amount of gasoline consumed does not add much. In addition, if multicollinearity is present the signs and magnitudes of the estimated slope coefficients can be misleading.

A sample correlation coefficient greater than +0.7 or less than −0.7 for two independent variables is a rule of thumb warning of potential problems with multicollinearity.

To summarize, in t tests for the significance of individual parameters, the difficulty caused by multicollinearity is that it is possible to conclude that none of the individual parameters are significantly different from zero when an F test on the overall multiple regression equation indicates a significant relationship. Furthermore, multicollinearity can cause the estimated slope coefficients to be misleading. These problems are avoided when there is little correlation among the independent variables.

Statisticians have developed several tests for determining whether multicollinearity is high enough to cause problems. According to the rule of thumb test, multicollinearity is a potential problem if the absolute value of the sample correlation coefficient exceeds 0.7 for any two of the independent variables. The other types of tests are more advanced and beyond the scope of this text.

When the independent variables are highly correlated, it is not possible to determine the separate effect of any particular independent variable on the dependent variable.

If possible, every attempt should be made to avoid including independent variables that are highly correlated. In practice, however, strict adherence to this policy is rarely possible. When decision makers have reason to believe substantial multicollinearity is present, they must realize that separating the effects of the individual independent variables on the dependent variable is difficult.

Notes + Comments

Ordinarily, multicollinearity does not affect the way in which we perform our regression analysis or interpret the output from a study. However, when multicollinearity is severe—that is, when two or more of the independent variables are highly correlated with one another—we can have difficulty interpreting the results of t tests on the individual parameters. In addition to the type of problem illustrated in this section, severe cases of multicollinearity have been shown to result in least squares estimates that have the wrong sign. That is, in simulated studies where researchers created the underlying regression model and then applied the least squares technique to develop estimates of β_0, β_1, β_2, and so on, it has been shown that under conditions of high multicollinearity the least squares estimates can have a sign opposite that of the parameter being estimated. For example, β_2 might actually be $+10$ and b_2, its estimate, might turn out to be -2. Thus, little faith can be placed in the individual coefficients if multicollinearity is present to a high degree.

Exercises

Methods

19. In exercise 1, the following estimated regression equation based on 10 observations was presented. **LO 5, 6**

$$\hat{y} = 29.1270 + 0.5906x_1 + 0.4980x_2$$

Here SST = 6724.125, SSR = 6216.375, $s_{b_1} = 0.0813$, and $s_{b_2} = 0.0567$.
a. Compute MSR and MSE.
b. Compute F and perform the appropriate F test. Use $\alpha = 0.05$.
c. Perform a t test for the significance of β_1. Use $\alpha = 0.05$.
d. Perform a t test for the significance of β_2. Use $\alpha = 0.05$.

20. Refer to the data presented in exercise 2. The estimated regression equation for these data is

$$\hat{y} = -18.4 + 2.01x_1 + 4.74x_2$$

Here SST = 15,182.9, SSR = 14,052.2, $s_{b_1} = 0.2471$, and $s_{b_2} = 0.9484$. **LO 5, 6**
a. Test for a significant relationship among x_1, x_2, and y. Use $\alpha = 0.05$.
b. Is β_1 significant? Use $\alpha = 0.05$.
c. Is β_2 significant? Use $\alpha = 0.05$.

21. The following estimated regression equation was developed for a model involving two independent variables.

$$\hat{y} = 40.7 + 8.63x_1 + 2.71x_2$$

After x_2 was dropped from the model, the least squares method was used to obtain an estimated regression equation involving only x_1 as an independent variable. **LO 2, 7**

$$\hat{y} = 42.0 + 9.01x_1$$

a. Give an interpretation of the coefficient of x_1 in both models.
b. Could multicollinearity explain why the coefficient of x_1 differs in the two models? If so, how?

Applications

22. **Testing Significance in Shoe Sales Prediction.** In exercise 4, the following estimated regression equation relating sales to inventory investment and advertising expenditures was given.

$$\hat{y} = 25 + 10x_1 + 8x_2$$

The data used to develop the model came from a survey of 10 stores; for these data SST = 16,000 and SSR = 12,000. **LO 6**

a. Compute SSE, MSE, and MSR.
b. Use an F test and a 0.05 level of significance to determine whether there is a relationship among the variables.

23. **Testing Significance in Theater Revenue.** Refer to exercise 5. **LO 5, 6**

a. Use $\alpha = 0.01$ to test the hypotheses

$$H_0\text{: } \beta_1 = \beta_2 = 0$$
$$H_a\text{: } \beta_1 \text{ and/or } \beta_2 \text{ is not equal to zero}$$

for the model $y = \beta_0 + \beta_1 x_1 + \beta_2 x_2 + \epsilon$, where

$$x_1 = \text{television advertising (\$1,000s)}$$
$$x_2 = \text{newspaper advertising (\$1,000s)}$$

b. Use $\alpha = 0.05$ to test the significance of β_1. Should x_1 be dropped from the model?
c. Use $\alpha = 0.05$ to test the significance of β_2. Should x_2 be dropped from the model?

24. **Testing Significance in Predicting NFL Wins.** The National Football League (NFL) records a variety of performance data for individuals and teams. A portion of the data showing the average number of passing yards obtained per game on offense (OffPassYds/G), the average number of yards given up per game on defense (DefYds/G), and the percentage of games won (Win%) for one full season follows. **LO 1, 5, 6**

DATA*file*
nfl2011

Team	OffPassYds/G	DefYds/G	Win%
Arizona	222.9	355.1	50.0
Atlanta	262.0	333.6	62.5
Baltimore	213.9	288.9	75.0
•	•	•	•
•	•	•	•
•	•	•	•
St. Louis	179.4	358.4	12.5
Tampa Bay	228.1	394.4	25.0
Tennessee	245.2	355.1	56.3
Washington	235.8	339.8	31.3

a. Develop an estimated regression equation that can be used to predict the percentage of games won given the average number of passing yards obtained per game on offense and the average number of yards given up per game on defense.

b. Use the F test to determine the overall significance of the relationship. What is your conclusion at the 0.05 level of significance?
c. Use the t test to determine the significance of each independent variable. What is your conclusion at the 0.05 level of significance?

DATA*file* autoresale

25. **Auto Resale Value.** The Honda Accord was named the best midsized car for resale value for 2018 by the Kelley Blue Book (*Kelley Blue Book* website). The file *autoresale* contains mileage, age, and selling price for a sample of 33 Honda Accords. **LO 1, 5, 6, 7**
 a. Develop an estimated regression equation that predicts the selling price of a used Honda Accord given the mileage and age of the car.
 b. Is multicollinearity an issue for this model? Find the correlation between the independent variables to answer this question.
 c. Use the F test to determine the overall significance of the relationship. What is your conclusion at the 0.05 level of significance?
 d. Use the t test to determine the significance of each independent variable. What is your conclusion at the 0.05 level of significance?

DATA*file* pitchingmlb

26. **Testing Significance in Baseball Pitcher Performance.** In exercise 10, data showing the values of several pitching statistics for a random sample of 20 pitchers from the American League of Major League Baseball were provided. In part (c) of this exercise an estimated regression equation was developed to predict the average number of runs given up per inning pitched (R/IP) given the average number of strikeouts per inning pitched (SO/IP) and the average number of home runs per inning pitched (HR/IP). **LO 5, 6**
 a. Use the F test to determine the overall significance of the relationship. What is your conclusion at the 0.05 level of significance?
 b. Use the t test to determine the significance of each independent variable. What is your conclusion at the 0.05 level of significance?

15.6 Using the Estimated Regression Equation for Estimation and Prediction

The procedures for estimating the mean value of y and predicting an individual value of y in multiple regression are similar to those in regression analysis involving one independent variable. First, recall that in Chapter 14 we showed that the estimated regression equation $\hat{y} = b_0 + b_1x$ can be used to estimate the mean value of y for a given value of x as well as to predict an individual value of y for a given value of x. In multiple regression we use the same procedure. That is, we substitute the value of $x_1, x_2, \ldots, x_p$ into the estimated regression equation and use the corresponding value of $\hat{y}$ to estimate the mean value of y given $x_1, x_2, \ldots, x_p$ as well as to predict an individual of y given $x_1, x_2, \ldots, x_p$.

To illustrate the procedure in multiple regression, suppose that for the Butler Trucking example we want to use the estimated regression equation involving x_1 (miles traveled) and x_2 (number of deliveries) to develop two interval estimates:

1. A *confidence interval* of the mean travel time for all trucks that travel 100 miles and make two deliveries
2. A *prediction interval* of the travel time for *one specific* truck that travels 100 miles and makes two deliveries

The Excel output in Figure 15.5 showed the estimated regression equation is

$$\hat{y} = -0.8687 + 0.0611x_1 + 0.9234x_2$$

With $x_1 = 100$ and $x_2 = 2$, we obtain the following value of $\hat{y}$:

$$\hat{y} = -0.8687 + 0.0611(100) + 0.9234(2) = 7.09$$

Hence a point estimate of the mean travel time for all trucks that travel 100 miles and make two deliveries is approximately 7 hours. And a prediction of the travel time for one specific truck that travels 100 miles and makes two deliveries is also 7 hours.

Table 15.4 The 95% Prediction Intervals for Butler Trucking

Value of x_1	Value of x_2	Prediction Interval Lower Limit	Prediction Interval Upper Limit
50	2	2.414	5.656
50	3	3.368	6.548
50	4	4.157	7.607
100	2	5.500	8.683
100	3	6.520	9.510
100	4	7.362	10.515

The formulas required to develop confidence and prediction intervals for multiple regression are beyond the scope of the text. And in multiple regression hand computation is simply not practical. Although Excel's Regression tool does not have an option for computing interval estimates, some software packages do provide confidence and prediction intervals. The interpretation of these intervals is the same as for simple linear regression. Table 15.4 shows the 95% prediction intervals for the Butler Trucking problem for selected values of x_1 and x_2. We see that the prediction interval of the travel time for *one specific* truck that travels 100 miles and makes two deliveries is approximately 5.5 to 8.7 hours.

Exercises

Methods

27. In exercise 1, the following estimated regression equation based on 10 observations was presented. **LO 3**

$$\hat{y} = 29.1270 + 0.5906x_1 + 0.4980x_2$$

a. Develop a point estimate of the mean value of y when $x_1 = 180$ and $x_2 = 310$.
b. Predict an individual value of y when $x_1 = 180$ and $x_2 = 310$.

DATA*file* exer2

28. Refer to the data in exercise 2. The estimated regression equation for those data follows. **LO 8, 9**

$$\hat{y} = -18.4 + 2.01x_1 + 4.74x_2$$

a. Develop a point estimate of the mean value of y when $x_1 = 45$ and $x_2 = 15$.
b. Develop a 95% prediction interval for y when $x_1 = 45$ and $x_2 = 15$.

Applications

29. **Confidence and Prediction Intervals for Theater Revenue.** In exercise 5, the owner of Showtime Movie Theaters, Inc. used multiple regression analysis to predict gross revenue (y) as a function of television advertising (x_1) and newspaper advertising (x_2). The estimated regression equation follows. **LO 3, 8, 9**

$$\hat{y} = 83.23 + 2.29x_1 + 1.30x_2$$

a. What is the gross revenue expected for a week when \$3,500 is spent on television advertising ($x_1 = 3.5$) and \$1,800 is spent on newspaper advertising ($x_2 = 1.8$)?
b. Provide a 95% prediction interval for next week's revenue, assuming that the advertising expenditures will be allocated as in part (a).

DATA*file* nfl2011

30. **Confidence and Prediction Intervals for NFL Wins.** In exercise 24, an estimated regression equation was developed relating the percentage of games won by a team in the National Football League during a complete season to the average number of passing yards obtained per game on offense and the average number of yards given up per game on defense during the season. **LO 3, 9**

a. Predict the percentage of games won for a particular team that averages 225 passing yards per game on offense and gives up an average of 300 yards per game on defense.
b. Develop a 95% prediction interval for the percentage of games won for a particular team that averages 225 passing yards per game on offense and gives up an average of 300 yards per game on defense.

DATA*file*
autoresale

31. **Confidence and Prediction Intervals for Auto Resale Value.** Refer to exercise 25. Use the estimated regression equation from part (a) to answer the following questions. **LO 3, 8, 9**
a. Estimate the selling price of a four-year-old Honda Accord with mileage of 40,000 miles.
b. Develop a 95% confidence interval for the selling price of a car with the data in part (a).
c. Develop a 95% prediction interval for the selling price of a particular car having the data in part (a).

15.7 Categorical Independent Variables

The independent variables may be categorical or quantitative.

Thus far, the examples we have considered involved quantitative independent variables such as student population, distance traveled, and number of deliveries. In many situations, however, we must work with **categorical independent variables** such as gender (male, female) and method of payment (cash, credit card, check). The purpose of this section is to show how categorical variables are handled in regression analysis. To illustrate the use and interpretation of a categorical independent variable, we will consider a problem facing the managers of Johnson Filtration, Inc.

An Example: Johnson Filtration, Inc.

Johnson Filtration, Inc., provides maintenance service for water-filtration systems throughout southern Florida. Customers contact Johnson with requests for maintenance service on their water-filtration systems. To estimate the service time and the service cost, Johnson's managers want to predict the repair time necessary for each maintenance request. Hence, repair time in hours is the dependent variable. Repair time is believed to be related to two factors, the number of months since the last maintenance service and the type of repair problem (mechanical or electrical). Data for a sample of 10 service calls are reported in Table 15.5.

Let y denote the repair time in hours and x_1 denote the number of months since the last maintenance service. The regression model that uses only x_1 to predict y is

$$y = \beta_0 + \beta_1 x_1 + \epsilon$$

Table 15.5 Data for the Johnson Filtration Example

Service Call	Months Since Last Service	Type of Repair	Repair Time in Hours
1	2	Electrical	2.9
2	6	Mechanical	3.0
3	8	Electrical	4.8
4	3	Mechanical	1.8
5	2	Electrical	2.9
6	7	Electrical	4.9
7	9	Mechanical	4.2
8	8	Mechanical	4.8
9	4	Electrical	4.4
10	6	Electrical	4.5

Using Excel's Regression tool to develop the estimated regression equation, we obtained the Excel output shown in Figure 15.8. The estimated regression equation is

$$\hat{y} = 2.1473 + 0.3041x_1 \quad \textbf{(15.16)}$$

At the 0.05 level of significance, the p-value of 0.0163 for the t (or F) test indicates that the number of months since the last service is significantly related to repair time. R Square = 0.5342 indicates that x_1 alone explains 53.42% of the variability in repair time.

To incorporate the type of repair into the regression model, we define the following variable.

$$x_2 = \begin{cases} 0 \text{ if the type of repair is mechanical} \\ 1 \text{ if the type of repair is electrical} \end{cases}$$

In regression analysis, x_2 is called a **dummy** or *indicator* **variable**. Using this dummy variable, we can write the multiple regression model as

$$y = \beta_0 + \beta_1 x_1 + \beta_2 x_2 + \epsilon$$

Table 15.6 is the revised data set that includes the values of the dummy variable. Using Excel and the data in Table 15.6, we can develop estimates of the model parameters. The Excel Regression tool output in Figure 15.9 shows that the estimated multiple regression equation is

$$\hat{y} = 0.9305 + 0.3876x_1 + 1.2627x_2 \quad \textbf{(15.17)}$$

At the 0.05 level of significance, the p-value of 0.0010 associated with the F test ($F = 21.357$) indicates that the regression relationship is significant. The t test part of the printout in Figure 15.9 shows that both months since last service (p-value = 0.0004) and type of repair (p-value = 0.0051) are statistically significant. In addition, R Square = 0.8952 and Adjusted R Square = 0.8190 indicate that the estimated regression equation does a good job of explaining the variability in repair times. Thus, equation (15.17) should prove helpful in predicting the repair time necessary for the various service calls.

Figure 15.8 Regression Tool Output for the Johnson Filtration Example with Months Since Last Service Call as the Independent Variable

The Excel Regression tool output appears in a new worksheet because we selected New Worksheet Ply as the Output option in the Regression dialog box.

	A	B	C	D	E	F	G
1	SUMMARY OUTPUT						
2							
3	*Regression Statistics*						
4	Multiple R	0.7309					
5	R Square	0.5342					
6	Adjusted R Square	0.4759					
7	Standard Error	0.7810					
8	Observations	10					
9							
10	ANOVA						
11		*df*	*SS*	*MS*	*F*	*Significance F*	
12	Regression	1	5.5960	5.5960	9.1739	0.0163	
13	Residual	8	4.8800	0.6100			
14	Total	9	10.476				
15							
16		*Coefficients*	*Standard Error*	*t Stat*	*P-value*		
17	Intercept	2.1473	0.6050	3.5493	0.0075		
18	Months Since Last Service	0.3041	0.1004	3.0288	0.0163		
19							

Table 15.6 Data for the Johnson Filtration Example with Type of Repair Indicated by a Dummy Variable ($x_2 = 0$ for Mechanical; $x_2 = 1$ for Electrical)

DATA*file*
johnson

Customer	Months Since Last Service (x_1)	Type of Repair (x_2)	Repair Time in Hours (y)
1	2	1	2.9
2	6	0	3.0
3	8	1	4.8
4	3	0	1.8
5	2	1	2.9
6	7	1	4.9
7	9	0	4.2
8	8	0	4.8
9	4	1	4.4
10	6	1	4.5

Figure 15.9 Regression Tool Output for the Johnson Filtration Example with Months Since Last Service Call and Type of Repair as the Independent Variables

	A	B	C	D	E	F	G
1	SUMMARY OUTPUT						
2							
3	*Regression Statistics*						
4	Multiple R	0.9269					
5	R Square	0.8592					
6	Adjusted R Square	0.8190					
7	Standard Error	0.4590					
8	Observations	10					
9							
10	ANOVA						
11		*df*	*SS*	*MS*	*F*	*Significance F*	
12	Regression	2	9.0009	4.5005	21.3570	0.0010	
13	Residual	7	1.4751	0.2107			
14	Total	9	10.476				
15							
16		*Coefficients*	*Standard Error*	*t Stat*	*P-value*		
17	Intercept	0.9305	0.4670	1.9926	0.0866		
18	Months Since Last Service	0.3876	0.0626	6.1954	0.0004		
19	Type of Repair	1.2627	0.3141	4.0197	0.0051		
20							

Interpreting the Parameters

The multiple regression equation for the Johnson Filtration example is

$$E(y) = \beta_0 + \beta_1 x_1 + \beta_2 x_2 \tag{15.18}$$

To understand how to interpret the parameters β_0, β_1, and β_2 when a categorical variable is present, consider the case when $x_2 = 0$ (mechanical repair). Using $E(y \mid \text{mechanical})$ to denote the mean or expected value of repair time *given* a mechanical repair, we have

$$E(y \mid \text{mechanical}) = \beta_0 + \beta_1 x_1 + \beta_2(0) = \beta_0 + \beta_1 x_1 \quad \textbf{(15.19)}$$

Similarly, for an electrical repair ($x_2 = 1$), we have

$$\begin{aligned} E(y \mid \text{electrical}) &= \beta_0 + \beta_1 x_1 + \beta_2(1) = \beta_0 + \beta_1 x_1 + \beta_2 \\ &= (\beta_0 + \beta_2) + \beta_1 x_1 \end{aligned} \quad \textbf{(15.20)}$$

Comparing equations (15.19) and (15.20), we see that the mean repair time is a linear function of x_1 for both mechanical and electrical repairs. The slope of both equations is β_1, but the y-intercept differs. The y-intercept is β_0 in equation (15.19) for mechanical repairs and $(\beta_0 + \beta_2)$ in equation (15.20) for electrical repairs. The interpretation of β_2 is that it indicates the difference between the mean repair time for an electrical repair and the mean repair time for a mechanical repair.

If β_2 is positive, the mean repair time for an electrical repair will be greater than that for a mechanical repair; if β_2 is negative, the mean repair time for an electrical repair will be less than that for a mechanical repair. Finally, if $\beta_2 = 0$, there is no difference in the mean repair time between electrical and mechanical repairs and the type of repair is not related to the repair time.

Using the estimated multiple regression equation $\hat{y} = 0.9305 + 0.3876x_1 + 1.2627x_2$, we see that 0.9305 is the estimate of β_0, 0.3876 is the estimate of β_1, and 1.2627 is the estimate of β_2. Thus, when $x_2 = 0$ (mechanical repair)

$$\hat{y} = 0.9305 + 0.3876x_1 \quad \textbf{(15.21)}$$

and when $x_2 = 1$ (electrical repair)

$$\begin{aligned} \hat{y} &= 0.9305 + 0.3876x_1 + 1.2627(1) \\ &= 2.1932 + 0.3876x_1 \end{aligned} \quad \textbf{(15.22)}$$

In effect, the use of a dummy variable for type of repair provides two estimated regression equations that can be used to predict the repair time, one corresponding to mechanical repairs and one corresponding to electrical repairs. In addition, with $b_2 = 1.2627$, we learn that, on average, electrical repairs require 1.2627 hours longer than mechanical repairs.

Figure 15.10 is the plot of the Johnson data from Table 13.6. Repair time in hours (y) is represented by the vertical axis and months since last service (x_1) is represented by the horizontal axis. A data point for a mechanical repair is indicated by an M and a data point for an electrical repair is indicated by an E. Equations (15.21) and (15.22) are plotted on the graph to show graphically the two equations that can be used to predict the repair time, one corresponding to mechanical repairs and one corresponding to electrical repairs.

More Complex Categorical Variables

A categorical variable with k levels must be modeled using k − 1 dummy variables. Care must be taken in defining and interpreting the dummy variables.

Because the categorical variable for the Johnson Filtration example had two levels (mechanical and electrical), defining a dummy variable with zero indicating a mechanical repair and one indicating an electrical repair was easy. However, when a categorical variable has more than two levels, care must be taken in both defining and interpreting the dummy variables. As we will show, if a categorical variable has k levels, $k - 1$ dummy variables are required, with each dummy variable being coded as 0 or 1.

For example, suppose a manufacturer of copy machines organized the sales territories for a particular state into three regions: A, B, and C. The managers want to use regression analysis to help predict the number of copiers sold per week. With the number of units sold

Figure 15.10 Scatter Diagram for the Johnson Filtration Repair Data from Table 15.6

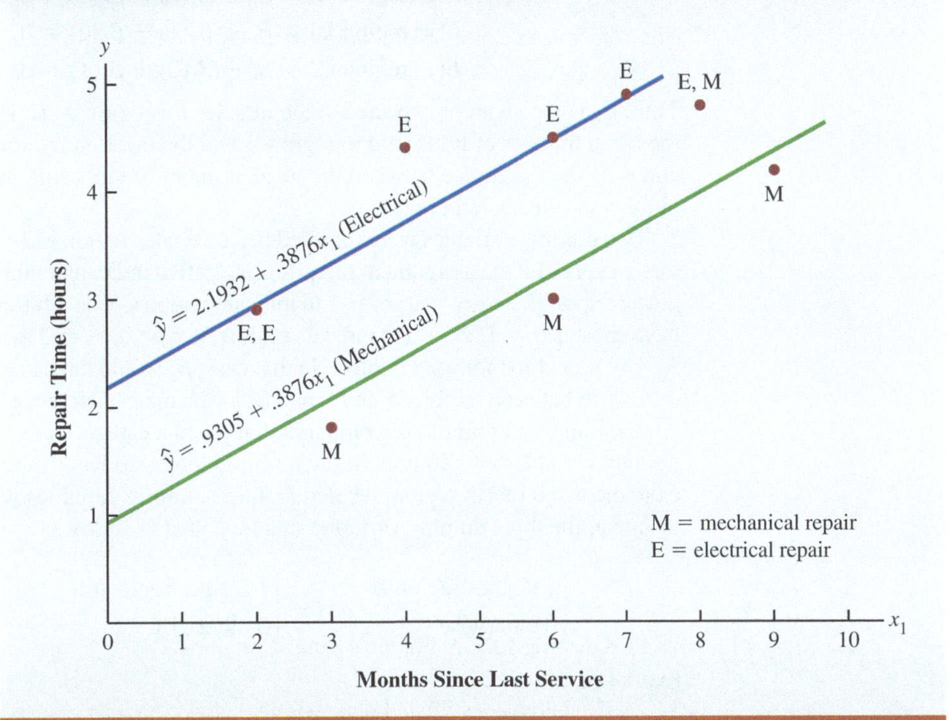

as the dependent variable, they are considering several independent variables (the number of sales personnel, advertising expenditures, and so on). Suppose the managers believe sales region is also an important factor in predicting the number of copiers sold. Because sales region is a categorical variable with three levels, A, B and C, we will need $3 - 1 = 2$ dummy variables to represent the sales region. Each variable can be coded 0 or 1 as follows.

$$x_1 = \begin{cases} 1 \text{ if sales region B} \\ 0 \text{ otherwise} \end{cases}$$

$$x_2 = \begin{cases} 1 \text{ if sales region C} \\ 0 \text{ otherwise} \end{cases}$$

With this definition, we have the following values of x_1 and x_2.

Region	x_1	x_2
A	0	0
B	1	0
C	0	1

Observations corresponding to region A would be coded $x_1 = 0$, $x_2 = 0$; observations corresponding to region B would be coded $x_1 = 1$, $x_2 = 0$; and observations corresponding to region C would be coded $x_1 = 0$, $x_2 = 1$.

The regression equation relating the expected value of the number of units sold, $E(y)$, to the dummy variables would be written as

$$E(y) = \beta_0 + \beta_1 x_1 + \beta_2 x_2$$

To help us interpret the parameters β_0, β_1, and β_2, consider the following three variations of the regression equation.

$$E(y \mid \text{region A}) = \beta_0 + \beta_1(0) + \beta_2(0) = \beta_0$$
$$E(y \mid \text{region B}) = \beta_0 + \beta_1(1) + \beta_2(0) = \beta_0 + \beta_1$$
$$E(y \mid \text{region C}) = \beta_0 + \beta_1(0) + \beta_2(1) = \beta_0 + \beta_2$$

Thus, β_0 is the mean or expected value of sales for region A; β_1 is the difference between the mean number of units sold in region B and the mean number of units sold in region A; and β_2 is the difference between the mean number of units sold in region C and the mean number of units sold in region A.

Two dummy variables were required because sales region is a categorical variable with three levels. But the assignment of $x_1 = 0, x_2 = 0$ to indicate region A, $x_1 = 1, x_2 = 0$ to indicate region B, and $x_1 = 0, x_2 = 1$ to indicate region C was arbitrary. For example, we could have chosen $x_1 = 1, x_2 = 0$ to indicate region A, $x_1 = 0, x_2 = 0$ to indicate region B, and $x_1 = 0, x_2 = 1$ to indicate region C. In that case, β_1 would have been interpreted as the mean difference between regions A and B and β_2 as the mean difference between regions C and B.

The important point to remember is that when a categorical variable has k levels, $k - 1$ dummy variables are required in the multiple regression analysis. Thus, if the sales region example had a fourth region, labeled D, three dummy variables would be necessary. For example, the three dummy variables can be coded as follows.

$$x_1 = \begin{cases} 1 \text{ if sales region B} \\ 0 \text{ otherwise} \end{cases} \quad x_2 = \begin{cases} 1 \text{ if sales region C} \\ 0 \text{ otherwise} \end{cases} \quad x_3 = \begin{cases} 1 \text{ if sales region D} \\ 0 \text{ otherwise} \end{cases}$$

Exercises

Methods

32. Consider a regression study involving a dependent variable y, a quantitative independent variable x_1, and a categorical independent variable with two levels (level 1 and level 2). **LO 2, 3, 10**
    a. Write a multiple regression equation relating x_1 and the categorical variable to y.
    b. What is the expected value of y corresponding to level 1 of the categorical variable?
    c. What is the expected value of y corresponding to level 2 of the categorical variable?
    d. Interpret the parameters in your regression equation.
33. Consider a regression study involving a dependent variable y, a quantitative independent variable x_1, and a categorical independent variable with three possible levels (level 1, level 2, and level 3). **LO 2, 10**
    a. How many dummy variables are required to represent the categorical variable?
    b. Write a multiple regression equation relating x_1 and the categorical variable to y.
    c. Interpret the parameters in your regression equation.

Applications

34. **Predicting Fast Food Sales.** Management proposed the following regression model to predict sales at a fast-food outlet.

$$y = \beta_0 + \beta_1 x_1 + \beta_2 x_2 + \beta_3 x_3 + \epsilon$$

where

$$x_1 = \text{number of competitors within one mile}$$
$$x_2 = \text{population within one mile (1,000s)}$$
$$x_3 = \begin{cases} 1 \text{ if drive-up window present} \\ 0 \text{ otherwise} \end{cases}$$
$$y = \text{sales (\$1,000s)}$$

The following estimated regression equation was developed after 20 outlets were surveyed. **LO 3, 10**

$$\hat{y} = 10.1 - 4.2x_1 + 6.8x_2 + 15.3x_3$$

a. What is the expected amount of sales attributable to the drive-up window?
b. Predict sales for a store with two competitors, a population of 8,000 within one mile, and no drive-up window.
c. Predict sales for a store with one competitor, a population of 3,000 within 1 mile, and a drive-up window.

35. **Predicting Repair Time.** Refer to the Johnson Filtration problem introduced in this section. Suppose that in addition to information on the number of months since the machine was serviced and whether a mechanical or an electrical repair was necessary, the managers obtained a list showing which repairperson performed the service. The revised data follow. **LO 4, 10**

DATA*file*
repair

Repair Time in Hours	Months Since Last Service	Type of Repair	Repairperson
2.9	2	Electrical	Dave Newton
3.0	6	Mechanical	Dave Newton
4.8	8	Electrical	Bob Jones
1.8	3	Mechanical	Dave Newton
2.9	2	Electrical	Dave Newton
4.9	7	Electrical	Bob Jones
4.2	9	Mechanical	Bob Jones
4.8	8	Mechanical	Bob Jones
4.4	4	Electrical	Bob Jones
4.5	6	Electrical	Dave Newton

a. Ignore for now the months since the last maintenance service (x_1) and the repairperson who performed the service. Develop the estimated simple linear regression equation to predict the repair time (y) given the type of repair (x_2). Recall that $x_2 = 0$ if the type of repair is mechanical and 1 if the type of repair is electrical.
b. Does the equation that you developed in part (a) provide a good fit for the observed data? Explain.
c. Ignore for now the months since the last maintenance service and the type of repair associated with the machine. Develop the estimated simple linear regression equation to predict the repair time given the repairperson who performed the service. Let $x_3 = 0$ if Bob Jones performed the service and $x_3 = 1$ if Dave Newton performed the service.
d. Does the equation that you developed in part (c) provide a good fit for the observed data? Explain.

36. **Model Extension for Predicting Repair Time.** This problem is an extension of the situation described in exercise 35. **LO 5, 6, 10**
a. Develop the estimated regression equation to predict the repair time given the number of months since the last maintenance service, the type of repair, and the repairperson who performed the service.
b. At the 0.05 level of significance, test whether the estimated regression equation developed in part (a) represents a significant relationship between the independent variables and the dependent variable.
c. Is the addition of the independent variable x_3, the repairperson who performed the service, statistically significant? Use $\alpha = 0.05$. What explanation can you give for the results observed?

37. **Pricing Refrigerators.** Best Buy, a nationwide retailer of electronics, computers, and appliances, sells several brands of refrigerators. A random sample of models of full

size refrigerators prices sold by Best Buy and the corresponding cubic feet (cu. ft.) and list price follow (Best Buy website). **LO 1, 5, 10**

DATA*file*
refrigerators

Model	Cu. Ft.	List Price
Frigidaire Gallery Custom-Flex Top-Freezer Refrigerator	18.3	$899.99
GE French Door Refrigerator	24.8	$1,599.99
GE Frost-Free Side-by-Side Refrigerator with Thru-the-Door Ice and Water	25.4	$1,599.99
Whirlpool Top-Freezer Refrigerator	19.3	$749.99
GE Frost-Free Top-Freezer Refrigerator	17.5	$599.99
Whirlpool French Door Refrigerator with Thru-the-Ice and Door Water	19.6	$1,619.99
Samsung French Door Refrigerator	25.0	$999.99
Samsung Side-by-Side Refrigerator	24.5	$1,299.99
Whirlpool Side-by-Side Refrigerator with Thru-the-Door Ice and Water	25.4	$1,299.99
Frigidaire Gallery Frost-Free Side-by-Side Refrigerator with Thru-the-Door Ice and Water	26.0	$1,299.99
Frigidaire Side-by-Side Refrigerator with Thru-the-Door Ice and Water	25.6	$1,099.99
Frigidaire Top-Freezer Refrigerator	18.0	$579.99
Whirlpool French Door Refrigerator with Thru-the-Door Ice and Water	25.0	$2,199.99
Whirlpool Top-Freezer Refrigerator	20.5	$849.99
GE Frost-Free Top-Freezer Refrigerator	15.5	$549.99
Samsung 4-Door French Door Refrigerator with Thru-the-Door Ice and Water	28.2	$2,599.99
Samsung Showcase 4-Door French Door Refrigerator	27.8	$2,999.99
Samsung 3-Door French Door Refrigerator with Thru-the-Door Ice and Water	24.6	$2,399.99
Frigidaire Side-by-Side Refrigerator with Thru-the-Door Ice and Water	22.6	$1,099.99
GE Side-by-Side Refrigerator with Thru-the-Door Ice and Water	21.8	$1,499.99
GE Bottom-Freezer Refrigerator	20.9	$1,649.99

a. Develop the estimated simple linear regression equation to show how list price is related to the independent variable cubic feet.

b. At the 0.05 level of significance, test whether the estimated regression equation developed in part (a) indicates a significant relationship between list price and cubic feet.

c. Develop a dummy variable that will account for whether the refrigerator has the thru-the-door ice and water feature. Code the dummy variable with a value of 1 if the refrigerator has the thru-the-door ice and water feature and with 0 otherwise. Use this dummy variable to develop the estimated multiple regression equation to show how list price is related to cubic feet and the thru-the-door ice and water feature.

d. At $\alpha = 0.05$, is the thru-the-door ice and water feature a significant factor in the list price of a refrigerator?

38. **Risk of a Stroke.** A 10-year study conducted by the American Heart Association provided data on how age, blood pressure, and smoking relate to the risk of strokes. Assume that the following data are from a portion of this study. Risk is interpreted as the probability (times 100) that the patient will have a stroke over the next 10-year period. For the smoker variable, 1 indicates a smoker and 0 indicates a nonsmoker. **LO 3, 5, 10**

DATA*file*
stroke

Risk	Age	Blood Presure	Smoker
12	57	152	0
24	67	163	0
13	58	155	0
56	86	177	1
28	59	196	0
51	76	189	1
18	56	155	1
31	78	120	0
37	80	135	1
15	78	98	0
22	71	152	0
36	70	173	1
15	67	135	1
48	77	209	1
15	60	199	0
36	82	119	1
8	66	166	0
34	80	125	1
3	62	117	0
37	59	207	1

a. Develop an estimated regression equation that relates risk of a stroke to the person's age, blood pressure, and whether the person is a smoker.
b. Is smoking a significant factor in the risk of a stroke? Explain. Use $\alpha = 0.05$.
c. What is the probability of a stroke over the next 10 years for Art Speen, a 68-year-old smoker who has blood pressure of 175? What action might the physician recommend for this patient?

15.8 Residual Analysis

In Chapter 14, we showed how a residual plot against the independent variable x can be used to validate the assumptions for a simple linear regression model. Because multiple regression analysis deals with two or more independent variables, we would have to examine a residual plot against each of the independent variables to use this approach. The more common approach in multiple regression analysis is to develop a residual plot against the predicted values $\hat{y}$.

Residual Plot Against $\hat{y}$

A residual plot against the predicted values $\hat{y}$ represents the predicted value of the dependent variable $\hat{y}$ on the horizontal axis and the residual values on the vertical axis. A point is plotted for each residual. The first coordinate for each point is given by $\hat{y}_i$ and the second coordinate is given by the corresponding value of the ith residual $y_i - \hat{y}_i$. For the Butler Trucking multiple regression example, the estimated regression equation that we developed using Excel (see Figure 15.5) is

$$\hat{y}_i = -0.8687 + 0.0611x_1 + 0.9234x_2$$

where x_1 = miles traveled and x_2 = number of deliveries. Table 15.7 shows the predicted values and residuals based on this equation. The residual plot against $\hat{y}$ for Butler Trucking is shown in Figure 15.11. The residual plot does not indicate any abnormalities.

A residual plot against $\hat{y}$ can also be used when performing residual analysis in simple linear regression. In fact, the pattern for a residual plot against $\hat{y}$ in simple linear regression

Table 15.7 Predicted Values and Residuals for Butler Trucking

Miles Traveled (x_1)	Deliveries (x_2)	Travel Time (y)	Predicted Time ($\hat{y}$)	Residual ($y - \hat{y}$)
100	4	9.3	8.9385	0.3615
50	3	4.8	4.9583	−0.1583
100	4	8.9	8.9385	−0.0385
100	2	6.5	7.0916	−0.5916
50	2	4.2	4.0349	0.1651
80	2	6.2	5.8689	0.3311
75	3	7.4	6.4867	0.9133
65	4	6.0	6.7987	−0.7987
90	3	7.6	7.4037	0.1963
90	2	6.1	6.4803	−0.3803

Figure 15.11 Residual Plot Against the Predicted Time $\hat{y}$ for Butler Trucking

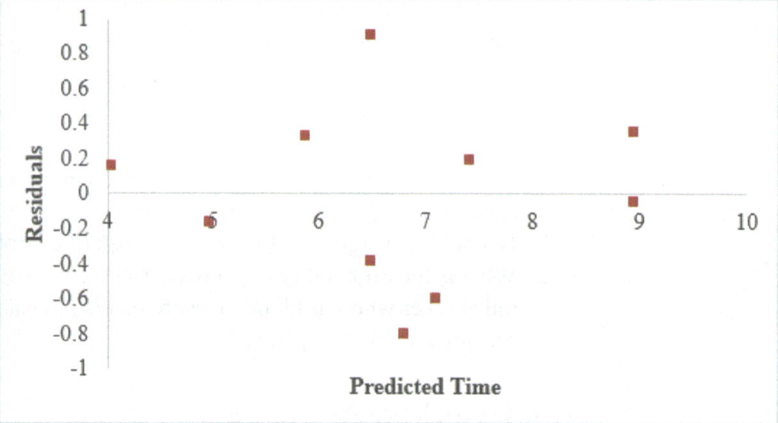

is the same as the pattern of the residual plot against x. Thus, for simple linear regression the residual plot against $\hat{y}$ and the residual plot against x provide the same information. In multiple regression analysis, however, it is preferable to use the residual plot against $\hat{y}$ to determine whether the model's assumptions are satisfied.

Standardized Residual Plot Against $\hat{y}$

In Chapter 14, we pointed out that standardized residuals were frequently used in residual plots. We showed how to construct a standardized residual plot against x and discussed how the standardized residual plot could be used to identify outliers and provide insight about the assumption that the error term ϵ has a normal distribution. Recall that we recommended considering any observation with a standardized residual of less than -2 or greater than $+2$ as an outlier. With normally distributed errors, standardized residuals should be outside these limits approximately 5% of the time.

In multiple regression analysis, the computation of the standardized residuals is too complex to be done by hand. As we showed in Section 14.8, Excel's Regression tool can be used to compute the standard residuals. In multiple regression analysis we use the same procedure to compute the standard residuals. Instead of developing a standardized residual plot against each of the independent variables, we will construct one standardized residual plot against the predicted values $\hat{y}$.

Figure 15.12 Standardized Residual Plot Against the Predicted Values $\hat{y}$ for Butler Trucking

Observation	Predicted Time	Residuals	Standard Residuals	Predicted Time	Standard Residuals
1	8.9385	0.3615	0.7153	8.9385	0.7153
2	4.9583	-0.1583	-0.3132	4.9583	-0.3132
3	8.9385	-0.0385	-0.0761	8.9385	-0.0761
4	7.0916	-0.5916	-1.1704	7.0916	-1.1704
5	4.0349	0.1651	0.3267	4.0349	0.3267
6	5.8689	0.3311	0.6550	5.8689	0.6550
7	6.4867	0.9133	1.8069	6.4867	1.8069
8	6.7987	-0.7987	-1.5802	6.7987	-1.5802
9	7.4037	0.1963	0.3884	7.4037	0.3884
10	6.4803	-0.3803	-0.7523	6.4803	-0.7523

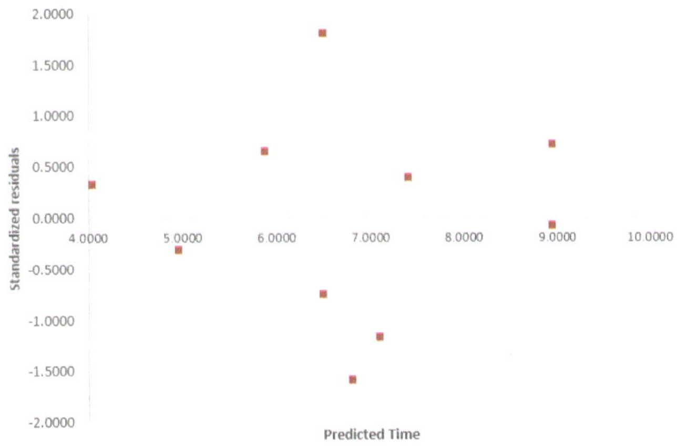

Note: Rows 1–34 are hidden.

Figure 15.12 shows the standard residuals and the corresponding standardized residual plot against $\hat{y}$ (Predicted Time) for Butler Trucking developed using Excel's Regression tool and Excel's chart tools. The standardized residual plot does not indicate any abnormalities, and no standard residual is less than -2 or greater than $+2$. Note that the pattern of the standardized residual plot against $\hat{y}$ is the same as the pattern of the residual plot against $\hat{y}$ shown in Figure 15.11. But the standardized residual plot is preferred because it enables us to check for outliers and determine whether the assumption of normality for the regression model is reasonable.

Exercises

Methods

39. Data for two variables, x and y, follow. **LO 1, 12**

x_i	1	2	3	4	5
y_i	3	7	5	11	14

a. Develop the estimated regression equation for these data.
b. Plot the residuals against $\hat{y}$. Does the residual plot support the assumptions about ϵ? Explain.
c. Plot the standardized residuals against $\hat{y}$. Do any outliers appear in these data? Explain.

40. Data for two variables, x and y, follow. **LO 1, 12**

x_i	22	24	26	28	40
y_i	12	21	31	35	70

a. Develop the estimated regression equation for these data.
b. Compute the standardized residuals for these data. Can any of these observations be classified as an outlier? Explain.
c. Develop a standardized residual plot against $\hat{y}$. Does the residual plot support the assumptions about ϵ? Explain.

Applications

41. **Detecting Outliers in Theater Revenue.** Exercise 5 gave the following data on weekly gross revenue ($1,000s), television advertising expenditures ($1,000s), and newspaper advertising expenditures ($1,000s) for Showtime Movie Theaters. **LO 1, 11, 12**

DATA*file* showtime

Weekly Gross Revenue ($1,000s)	Television Advertising ($1,000s)	Newspaper Advertising ($1,000s)
96	5.0	1.5
90	2.0	2.0
95	4.0	1.5
92	2.5	2.5
95	3.0	3.3
94	3.5	2.3
94	2.5	4.2
94	3.0	2.5

a. Find an estimated regression equation relating weekly gross revenue to television advertising expenditures and newspaper advertising expenditures.
b. Plot the standardized residuals against $\hat{y}$. Does the residual plot support the assumptions about ϵ? Explain.
c. Check for any outliers in these data. What are your conclusions?

42. **Predicting Sports Car Prices.** The following table reports the price, horsepower, and ¼-mile speed for 16 popular sports and GT cars. **LO 1, 11, 12**

DATA*file* auto2

Sports & GT Car	Price ($1,000s)	Curb Weight (lb.)	Horsepower	Speed at ¼ Mile (mph)
Accura Integra Type R	25.035	2,577	195	90.7
Accura NSX-T	93.758	3,066	290	108.0
BMW Z3 2.8	40.900	2,844	189	93.2
Chevrolet Camaro Z28	24.865	3,439	305	103.2
Chevrolet Corvette Convertible	50.144	3,246	345	102.1
Dodge Viper RT/10	69.742	3,319	450	116.2
Ford Mustang GT	23.200	3,227	225	91.7
Honda Prelude Type SH	26.382	3,042	195	89.7
Mercedes-Benz CLK320	44.988	3,240	215	93.0
Mercedes-Benz SLK230	42.762	3,025	185	92.3
Mitsubishi 3000GT VR-4	47.518	3,737	320	99.0
Nissan 240SX SE	25.066	2,862	155	84.6
Pontiac Firebird Trans Am	27.770	3,455	305	103.2
Porsche Boxster	45.560	2,822	201	93.2
Toyota Supra Turbo	40.989	3,505	320	105.0
Volvo C70	41.120	3,285	236	97.0

a. Find the estimated regression equation, which uses price and horsepower to predict ¼-mile speed.
b. Plot the standardized residuals against $\hat{y}$. Does the residual plot support the assumption about ϵ? Explain.
c. Check for any outliers. What are your conclusions?

DATA*file*
lpga2014

43. **Predicting Golf Scores.** The Ladies Professional Golfers Association (LPGA) maintains statistics on performance and earnings for members of the LPGA Tour. Year-end performance statistics for 134 golfers for 2014 appear in the file *lpga2014* (LPGA website). Earnings ($1,000s) is the total earnings in thousands of dollars; Scoring Avg. is the scoring average for all events; Greens in Reg. is the percentage of time a player is able to hit the greens in regulation; and Putting Avg. is the average number of putts taken on greens hit in regulation. A green is considered hit in regulation if any part of the ball is touching the putting surface and the difference between par for the hole and the number of strokes taken to hit the green is at least 2. **LO 1, 11, 12**
a. Develop an estimated regression equation that can be used to predict the scoring average given the percentage of time a player is able to hit the greens in regulation and the average number of putts taken on greens hit in regulation.
b. Plot the standardized residuals against $\hat{y}$. Does the residual plot support the assumption about ϵ? Explain.
c. Check for any outliers. What are your conclusions?
d. Are there any influential observations? Explain.

15.9 Practical Advice: Big Data and Hypothesis Testing in Multiple Regression

In Chapter 14, we observed that in simple linear regression, the p-value for the test of the hypothesis H_0: $\beta_1 = 0$ decreases as the sample size increases. Likewise, for a given level of confidence, the confidence interval for β_1, the confidence interval for the mean value of y, and the prediction interval for an individual value of y each narrows as the sample size increases. These results extend to multiple regression. As the sample size increases:

- the p-value for the F test used to determine whether a significant relationship exists between the dependent variable and the set of all independent variables in the regression model decreases;
- the p-value for each of t tests used to determine whether a significant relationship exists between the dependent variable and an individual independent variable in the regression model decreases;
- the confidence interval for the slope parameter associated with each individual independent variable narrows;
- the confidence interval for the mean value of y narrows;
- the prediction interval for an individual value of y narrows.

Thus, the interval estimates for the slope parameter associated with each individual independent variable, the mean value of y, and predicted individual value of y will become more precise as the sample size increases. And we are more likely to reject the hypothesis that a relationship does not exist between the dependent variable and the set of all individual independent variables in the model as the sample size increases. And for each individual independent variable, we are more likely to reject the hypothesis that a relationship does not exist between the dependent variable and the individual independent variable as the sample size increases. Even when severe multicollinearity is present, if the sample is sufficiently large, independent variables that are highly correlated may each have a significant relationship with the dependent variable. But this does not necessarily mean that these results become more reliable as the sample size increases.

No matter how large the sample used to estimate the multiple regression model, we must be concerned about the potential presence of nonsampling error in the data. It is important to carefully consider whether a random sample of the population of interest has actually been taken. If nonsampling error is introduced in the data collection process, the likelihood of making a Type I or Type II error on hypothesis tests in multiple regression may be higher than if the sample data are free of nonsampling error. Furthermore, multicollinearity may cause the estimated slope coefficients to be misleading; this problem persists as the size of the sample used to estimate the multiple regression model increases. Finally, it is important to consider whether the statistically significant relationship(s) in the multiple regression model are of practical significance.

Although multiple regression is an extremely powerful statistical tool, no business decision should be based exclusively on hypothesis testing in multiple regression. Nonsampling error may lead to misleading results. If severe multicollinearity is present, we must be cautious in interpreting the estimated slope coefficients. And practical significance should always be considered in conjunction with statistical significance; this is particularly important when a hypothesis test is based on an extremely large sample, because *p*-values in such cases can be extremely small. When executed properly, hypothesis tests in multiple regression provide evidence that should be considered in combination with information collected from other sources to make the most informed decision possible.

Summary

In this chapter, we introduced multiple regression analysis as an extension of simple linear regression analysis presented in Chapter 14. Multiple regression analysis enables us to understand how a dependent variable is related to two or more independent variables. The regression equation $E(y) = \beta_0 + \beta_1x_1 + \beta_2x_2 + \cdots + \beta_px_p$ shows that the expected value or mean value of the dependent variable y is related to the values of the independent variables x_1, $x_2, \ldots, x_p$. Sample data and the least squares method are used to develop the estimated regression equation $\hat{y} = b_0 + b_1x_1 + b_2x_2 + \cdots + b_px_p$. In effect, $b_0, b_1, b_2, \ldots, b_p$ are sample statistics used to estimate the unknown model parameters $\beta_0, \beta_1, \beta_2, \ldots, \beta_p$. Excel output was used throughout the chapter to emphasize the fact that computer software packages are the only realistic means of performing the numerous computations required in multiple regression analysis.

The multiple coefficient of determination was presented as a measure of the goodness of fit of the estimated regression equation. It determines the proportion of the variation of y that can be explained by the estimated regression equation. The adjusted multiple coefficient of determination is a similar measure of goodness of fit that adjusts for the number of independent variables and thus avoids overestimating the impact of adding more independent variables.

An F test and a t test were presented as ways to determine statistically whether the relationship among the variables is significant. The F test is used to determine whether there is a significant overall relationship between the dependent variable and the set of all independent variables. The t test is used to determine whether there is a significant relationship between the dependent variable and an individual independent variable given the other independent variables in the regression model. Correlation among the independent variables, known as multicollinearity, was discussed.

The section on categorical independent variables showed how dummy variables can be used to incorporate categorical data into multiple regression analysis. The section on residual analysis showed how residual analysis can be used to validate the model assumptions and detect outliers. Finally, we discussed the implications of large data sets on the application and interpretation of multiple regression analysis.

Glossary

Adjusted multiple coefficient of determination A measure of the goodness of fit of the estimated multiple regression equation that adjusts for the number of independent variables in the model and thus avoids overestimating the impact of adding more independent variables.

Categorical independent variable An independent variable with categorical data.

Dummy variable A variable used to model the effect of categorical independent variables. A dummy variable may take only the value zero or one.

Estimated multiple regression equation The estimate of the multiple regression equation based on sample data and the least squares method; it is $\hat{y} = b_0 + b_1x_1 + b_2x_2 + \cdots + b_px_p$.
Least squares method The method used to develop the estimated regression equation. It minimizes the sum of squared residuals (the deviations between the observed values of the dependent variable, y_i, and the estimated values of the dependent variable, $\hat{y}_i$).
Multicollinearity The term used to describe the correlation among the independent variables.
Multiple coefficient of determination A measure of the goodness of fit of the estimated multiple regression equation. It can be interpreted as the proportion of the variability in the dependent variable that is explained by the estimated regression equation.
Multiple regression analysis Regression analysis involving two or more independent variables.
Multiple regression equation The mathematical equation relating the expected value or mean value of the dependent variable to the values of the independent variables; that is, $E(y) = \beta_0 + \beta_1x_1 + \beta_2x_2 + \cdots + \beta_px_p$.
Multiple regression model The mathematical equation that describes how the dependent variable y is related to the independent variables $x_1, x_2, \ldots, x_p$ and an error term ϵ.

Key Formulas

Multiple Regression Model

$$y = \beta_0 + \beta_1x_1 + \beta_2x_2 + \cdots + \beta_px_p + \epsilon \qquad \textbf{(15.1)}$$

Multiple Regression Equation

$$E(y) = \beta_0 + \beta_1x_1 + \beta_2x_2 + \cdots + \beta_px_p \qquad \textbf{(15.2)}$$

Estimated Multiple Regression Equation

$$\hat{y} = b_0 + b_1x_1 + b_2x_2 + \cdots + b_px_p \qquad \textbf{(15.3)}$$

Least Squares Criterion

$$\min \Sigma(y_i - \hat{y}_i)^2 \qquad \textbf{(15.4)}$$

Relationship Among SST, SSR, and SSE

$$\text{SST} = \text{SSR} + \text{SSE} \qquad \textbf{(15.7)}$$

Multiple Coefficient of Determination

$$R^2 = \frac{\text{SSR}}{\text{SST}} \qquad \textbf{(15.8)}$$

Adjusted Multiple Coefficient of Determination

$$R_a^2 = 1 - (1 - R^2)\frac{n - 1}{n - p - 1} \qquad \textbf{(15.9)}$$

Mean Square Due to Regression

$$\text{MSR} = \frac{\text{SSR}}{p} \qquad \textbf{(15.12)}$$

Mean Square Due to Error

$$\text{MSE} = \frac{\text{SSE}}{n - p - 1} \qquad \textbf{(15.13)}$$

***F* Test Statistic**

$$F = \frac{\text{MSR}}{\text{MSE}} \qquad \textbf{(15.14)}$$

***t* Test Statistic**

$$t = \frac{b_i}{s_{b_i}} \qquad \textbf{(15.15)}$$

Supplementary Exercises

44. **Predicting College Grade Point Average.** The admissions officer for Clearwater College developed the following estimated regression equation relating the final college GPA to the student's SAT mathematics score and high-school GPA. **LO 2, 3**

$$\hat{y} = -1.41 + 0.0235x_1 + 0.00486x_2$$

where

x_1 = high-school grade point average
x_2 = SAT mathematics score
y = final college grade point average

a. Interpret the coefficients in this estimated regression equation.
b. Predict the final college GPA for a student who has a high-school average of 84 and a score of 540 on the SAT mathematics test.

45. **Predicting Job Satisfaction.** The personnel director for Electronics Associates developed the following estimated regression equation relating an employee's score on a job satisfaction test to his or her length of service and wage rate. **LO 2, 3**

$$\hat{y} = 14.4 - 8.69x_1 + 13.5x_2$$

where

x_1 = length of service (years)
x_2 = wage rate (dollars)
y = job satisfaction test score (higher scores indicate greater job satisfaction)

a. Interpret the coefficients in this estimated regression equation.
b. Predict the job satisfaction test score for an employee who has four years of service and makes $6.50 per hour.

46. A partial computer output from a regression analysis using Excel's Regression tool follows. **LO 4, 5, 6**

	A	B	C	D	E	F	G
1	SUMMARY OUTPUT						
2							
3	*Regression Statistics*						
4	Multiple R						
5	R Square	0.923					
6	Adjusted R Square						
7	Standard Error	3.35					
8	Observations						
9							
10	ANOVA						
11		*df*	*SS*	*MS*	*F*	*Significance F*	
12	Regression		1612				
13	Residual	12					
14	Total						
15							
16		*Coefficients*	*Standard Error*	*t Stat*	*P-value*		
17	Intercept	8.103	2.667				
18	X1	7.602	2.105				
19	X2	3.111	0.613				
20							

a. Compute the missing entries in this output.
b. Using $\alpha = 0.05$, test for overall significance.
c. Use the t test and $\alpha = 0.05$ to test H_0: $\beta_1 = 0$ and H_0: $\beta_2 = 0$.

47. **Analyzing College Grad Point Average.** Recall that in exercise 44, the admissions officer for Clearwater College developed the following estimated regression equation relating final college GPA to the student's SAT mathematics score and high-school GPA.

$$\hat{y} = -1.41 + 0.0235x_1 + 0.00486x_2$$

where

x_1 = high-school grade point average
x_2 = SAT mathematics score
y = final college grade point average

A portion of the Excel Regression tool output follows. **LO 4, 5, 6**

	A	B	C	D	E	F	G
1	SUMMARY OUTPUT						
2							
3	*Regression Statistics*						
4	Multiple R						
5	R Square						
6	Adjusted R Square						
7	Standard Error						
8	Observations						
9							
10	ANOVA						
11		*df*	*SS*	*MS*	*F*	*Significance F*	
12	Regression		1.76209				
13	Residual						
14	Total	9	1.88				
15							
16		*Coefficients*	*Standard Error*	*t Stat*	*P-value*		
17	Intercept	-1.4053	0.4848				
18	X1	0.023467	0.0086666				
19	X2	0.00486	0.001077				
20							

a. Complete the missing entries in this output.
b. Using $\alpha = 0.05$, test for overall significance.
c. Did the estimated regression equation provide a good fit to the data? Explain.
d. Use the t test and $\alpha = 0.05$ to test H_0: $\beta_1 = 0$ and H_0: $\beta_2 = 0$.

48. **Analyzing Job Satisfaction.** Recall that in exercise 45 the personnel director for Electronics Associates developed the following estimated regression equation relating an employee's score on a job satisfaction test to length of service and wage rate.

$$\hat{y} = 14.4 - 8.69x_1 + 13.5x_2$$

where

x_1 = length of service (years)
x_2 = wage rate (dollars)
y = job satisfaction test score (higher scores indicate greater job satisfaction)

A portion of the output follows. **LO 4, 5, 6**

a. Complete the missing entries in this output.
b. Using $\alpha = 0.05$, test for overall significance.
c. Did the estimated regression equation provide a good fit to the data? Explain.
d. Use the t test and $\alpha = 0.05$ to test H_0: $\beta_1 = 0$ and H_0: $\beta_2 = 0$.

	A	B	C	D	E	F	G
1	SUMMARY OUTPUT						
2							
3	*Regression Statistics*						
4	Multiple R						
5	R Square						
6	Adjusted R Square						
7	Standard Error	3.773					
8	Observations						
9							
10	ANOVA						
11		*df*	*SS*	*MS*	*F*	*Significance F*	
12	Regression						
13	Residual		77.17				
14	Total		720				
15							
16		*Coefficients*	*Standard Error*	*t Stat*	*P-value*		
17	Intercept	14.4	8.191				
18	X1	-8.69	1.555				
19	X2	13.517	2.085				
20							

49. **Analyzing Repeat Purchases.** The Tire Rack, America's leading online distributor of tires and wheels, conducts extensive testing to provide customers with products that are right for their vehicle, driving style, and driving conditions. In addition, the Tire Rack maintains an independent consumer survey to help drivers help each other by sharing their long-term tire experiences. The following data show survey ratings (1 to 10 scale with 10 the highest rating) for 18 maximum performance summer tires. The variable Steering rates the tire's steering responsiveness, Tread Wear rates quickness of wear based on the driver's expectations, and Buy Again rates the driver's overall tire satisfaction and desire to purchase the same tire again. **LO 1, 4, 5**

DATA*file*
tirerack

Tire	Steering	Tread Wear	Buy Again
Goodyear Assurance TripleTred	8.9	8.5	8.1
Michelin HydroEdge	8.9	9.0	8.3
Michelin Harmony	8.3	8.8	8.2
Dunlop SP 60	8.2	8.5	7.9
Goodyear Assurance ComforTred	7.9	7.7	7.1
Yokohama Y372	8.4	8.2	8.9
Yokohama Aegis LS4	7.9	7.0	7.1
Kumho Power Star 758	7.9	7.9	8.3
Goodyear Assurance	7.6	5.8	4.5
Hankook H406	7.8	6.8	6.2
Michelin Energy I X4	7.1	5.7	4.8
Michelin MX4	7.0	6.5	5.3
Michelin Symmetry	6.9	5.7	4.2
Kumho 722	7.2	6.6	5.0
Dunlop SP 40 A/S	6.2	4.2	3.4
Bridgestone Insignia SE200	5.7	5.5	3.6
Goodyear Integrity	5.7	5.4	2.9
Dunlop SP20 FE	5.7	5.0	3.3

a. Develop an estimated regression equation that can be used to predict the Buy Again rating given based on the Steering rating. At the 0.05 level of significance, test for a significant relationship.

b. Did the estimated regression equation developed in part (a) provide a good fit to the data? Explain.
c. Develop an estimated regression equation that can be used to predict the Buy Again rating given the Steering rating and the Tread Wear rating.
d. Is the addition of the Tread Wear independent variable significant? Use $\alpha = 0.05$.

50. **Zoo Attendance.** The Cincinnati Zoo and Botanical Gardens had a record attendance of 1.87 million visitors in 2017 (*Cincinnati Business Courier* website). Nonprofit organizations such as zoos and museums are becoming more sophisticated in their use of data to improve the customer experience. Being able to better estimate expected revenue is one use of analytics that allows nonprofits to better manage their operations.

DATA*file*
zoospend

The file *zoospend* contains sample data on zoo attendance. The file contains the following data on 125 visits by families to the zoo: amount spent, size of the family, the distance the family lives from the zoo (the gate attendee asks for the zip code of each family entering the zoo), and whether or not the family has a zoo membership (1 = yes, 0 = no). **LO 3, 5, 6, 10**

a. Develop an estimated regression equation that predicts the amount of money spent by a family given family size, whether or not it has a zoo membership, and the distance the family lives from the zoo.
b. Test the significance of the zoo membership independent variable at the 0.05 level.
c. Give an explanation for the sign of the estimate you tested in part (b).
d. Test the overall significance of the model at the 0.05 level.
e. Estimate the amount of money spent in a visit by a family of five that lives 125 miles from the zoo and does not have a zoo membership.

51. **Mutual Fund Returns.** A portion of a data set containing information for 45 mutual funds that are part of the *Morningstar Funds 500* follows. The complete data set is available in the file *mutualfunds*. The data set includes the following five variables: **LO 3, 4, 5, 6, 10**

Fund Type: The type of fund, labeled DE (Domestic Equity), IE (International Equity), and FI (Fixed Income)

Net Asset Value ($): The closing price per share on December 31, 2007

5-Year Average Return (%): The average annual return for the fund over the past five years

Expense Ratio (%): The percentage of assets deducted each fiscal year for fund expenses

Morningstar Rank: The risk adjusted star rating for each fund; Morningstar ranks go from a low of 1-Star to a high of 5-Stars

DATA*file*
mutualfunds

Fund Name	Fund Type	Net Asset Value ($)	5-Year Average Return (%)	Expense Ratio (%)	Morningstar Rank
Amer Cent Inc & Growth Inv	DE	28.88	12.39	0.67	2-Star
American Century Intl. Disc	IE	14.37	30.53	1.41	3-Star
American Century Tax-Free Bond	FI	10.73	3.34	0.49	4-Star
American Century Ultra	DE	24.94	10.88	0.99	3-Star
Ariel	DE	46.39	11.32	1.03	2-Star
Artisan Intl Val	IE	25.52	24.95	1.23	3-Star
Artisan Small Cap	DE	16.92	15.67	1.18	3-Star
Baron Asset	DE	50.67	16.77	1.31	5-Star
Brandywine	DE	36.58	18.14	1.08	4-Star
⋮	⋮	⋮	⋮	⋮	⋮

a. Develop an estimated regression equation that can be used to predict the 5-year average return given the type of fund. At the 0.05 level of significance, test for a significant relationship.
b. Did the estimated regression equation developed in part (a) provide a good fit to the data? Explain.
c. Develop the estimated regression equation that can be used to predict the 5-year average return given the type of fund, the net asset value, and the expense ratio. At the 0.05 level of significance, test for a significant relationship. Do you think any variables should be deleted from the estimated regression equation? Explain.
d. Morningstar Rank is a categorical variable. Because the data set contains only funds with four ranks (2-Star through 5-Star), use the following dummy variables: 3StarRank = 1 for a 3-Star fund, 0 otherwise; 4StarRank = 1 for a 4-Star fund, 0 otherwise; and 5StarRank = 1 for a 5-Star fund, 0 otherwise. Develop an estimated regression equation that can be used to predict the 5-year average return given the type of fund, the expense ratio, and the Morningstar Rank. Using $\alpha = 0.05$, remove any independent variables that are not significant.
e. Use the estimated regression equation developed in part (d) to predict the five-year average return for a domestic equity fund with an expense ratio of 1.05% and a 3-Star Morningstar Rank.

DATA*file*
giftcards

52. **Gift Card Sales.** For the holiday season of 2017, nearly 59% of consumers planned to buy gift cards. According to the National Retail Federation, millennials like to purchase gift cards (*Dayton Daily News* website). Consider the sample data in the file *giftcards*. The following data are given for a sample of 600 millennials: the amount they reported spending on gift cards over the last year, annual income, marital status (1 = yes, 0 = no), and whether they are male (1 = yes, 0 = no). **LO 5, 6, 10**
a. Develop an estimated regression equation that predicts annual spend on gift cards given annual income, marital status, and gender.
b. Test the overall significance at the 0.05 level.
c. Test the significance of each individual variable using a 0.05 level of significance.

DATA*file*
moneyballruns

53. **Moneyball.** As depicted in the film *Moneyball*, the Oakland A's major league baseball team used analytics to their advantage in player selection. By using techniques such as multiple regression analysis, they were able to find exceptional players that other teams overlooked. They did this by finding important success factors that were traditionally not considered in drafting players. The file *moneyballruns* contains the following data for each major league team for four years, a total of 120 data points (*baseball-reference.com*). **LO 1, 2, 4, 7**

- Runs Scored (RS): Total runs scored by the team in that year
- Batting Average (BA): The ratio of hits to at-bats for the team that year
- On-Base Percentage (OBP): The percentage of plate appearances in which a batter reaches base
- Slugging Percentage (SLG): Total number of bases a player records per at-bat

a. Develop three scatter plots: *RS* versus *BA*, *RS* versus *OBP*, and *RS* versus *SLG*. Comment on each of the three relationships.
b. Develop a multiple regression equation with *RS* as the dependent variable and *BA*, *OBP* and *SLG* as the independent variables. How well does this equation fit the data?
c. Comment on the signs of the estimated coefficients, given the scatter plots developed in part (a). Check for multicollinearity by computing the pairwise correlations between the independent variables. Which variables if any, seem to be highly correlated?
d. Estimate a multiple regression equation with *RS* as the dependent variable and *OBP* and *SLG* as the independent variables. How well does this equation fit the data?

e. Which equation would you recommend, the one developed in part (b) or part (d)? Explain.

54. **Moneyball (Revisited), Residual Analysis.** Refer to problem 53 and the estimated equation in part (d) with *RS* as the dependent variable and *OBS* and *SLG* as the independent variables. **LO 6, 11**
   a. At the 0.05 level of significance, does the model appear to be significant?
   b. Develop a residual plot with the predicted value of the dependent variable on the horizontal axis and the standardized residuals on the vertical axis. Given the plot, do the assumptions that the error terms are random and have a constant variance seem reasonable?

DATA*file*
iowahouses

55. **Iowa Housing Prices**. Realtors speculate on how a variety of a house's characteristics may affect its selling price. The file *iowahouses* contains a sample of 1,198 house sales in Iowa (Source: *Journal of Statistics Education*). For each house sold, the following data listed are provided. **LO 1, 2, 4, 7**

   - *LotArea* = Lot size in square feet
   - *CentralAir* = 1 has central air-conditioning, 0 does not have central air-conditioning
   - *GrLivArea* = Above grade (ground) living area in square feet
   - *FullBath* = Full bathrooms above ground
   - *HalfBath* = Half bathrooms above ground
   - *BedroomAbvGr* = Bedrooms above ground
   - *GarageCars* = Size of the garage in car capacity
   - *Age* = Age of the house when sold (in years)
   - *SalePrice* = Selling price of the house

   a. Develop a multiple regression equation with *SalePrice* as the dependent variable and the other eight variables as the independent variables. How well does this equation fit the data?
   b. Are any of the signs of the estimated coefficients counterintuitive? Compute the correlation between each pair of independent variables. Is there evidence of multicollinearity?
   c. Estimate a multiple regression equation with *SalePrice* as the dependent variable and *LotArea*, *CentralAir*, *GrLivArea*, *GarageCars*, and *Age* as the independent variables. How well does this equation fit the data?
   d. Which equation would you recommend, that developed in part (a) or part (c)? Explain.

56. **Iowa Housing Prices (Revisited), Residual Analysis**. Refer to problem 55 and the estimated equation in part (c) with *SalePrice* as the dependent variable and *LotArea*, *CentralAir*, *GrLivArea*, *GarageCars*, and *Age* as independent variables. **LO 6, 11**
   a. At the 0.05 level of significance, does the model appear to be significant?
   b. Develop a residual plot with the predicted value of the dependent variable on the horizontal axis and the standardized residuals on the vertical axis. Given the plot, do the assumptions that the error terms are random and have a constant variance seem reasonable?

Case Problem 1: Consumer Research, Inc.

Consumer Research, Inc., is an independent agency that conducts research on consumer attitudes and behaviors for a variety of firms. In one study, a client asked for an investigation of consumer characteristics that can be used to predict the amount charged by credit card users. Data were collected on annual income, household size, and annual credit card charges for a sample of 50 consumers. The following data are contained in the file *consumer*. **LO 1, 3, 4, 5, 11**

DATA*file*

consumer

Income ($1,000s)	Household Size	Amount Charged ($)	Income ($1,000s)	Household Size	Amount Charged ($)
54	3	4,016	54	6	5,573
30	2	3,159	30	1	2,583
32	4	5,100	48	2	3,866
50	5	4,742	34	5	3,586
31	2	1,864	67	4	5,037
55	2	4,070	50	2	3,605
37	1	2,731	67	5	5,345
40	2	3,348	55	6	5,370
66	4	4,764	52	2	3,890
51	3	4,110	62	3	4,705
25	3	4,208	64	2	4,157
48	4	4,219	22	3	3,579
27	1	2,477	29	4	3,890
33	2	2,514	39	2	2,972
65	3	4,214	35	1	3,121
63	4	4,965	39	4	4,183
42	6	4,412	54	3	3,730
21	2	2,448	23	6	4,127
44	1	2,995	27	2	2,921
37	5	4,171	26	7	4,603
62	6	5,678	61	2	4,273
21	3	3,623	30	2	3,067
55	7	5,301	22	4	3,074
42	2	3,020	46	5	4,820
41	7	4,828	66	4	5,149

Managerial Report

1. Use methods of descriptive statistics to summarize the data. Comment on the findings.
2. Develop estimated regression equations, first using annual income as the independent variable and then using household size as the independent variable. Which variable is the better predictor of annual credit card charges? Discuss your findings.
3. Develop an estimated regression equation with annual income and household size as the independent variables. Discuss your findings.
4. What is the predicted annual credit card charge for a three-person household with an annual income of $40,000?
5. Discuss the need for other independent variables that could be added to the model. What additional variables might be helpful?

Case Problem 2: Predicting Winnings for NASCAR Drivers

Matt Kenseth won the 2012 Daytona 500, the most important race of the NASCAR season. His win was no surprise because for the 2011 season he finished fourth in the point standings with 2,330 points, behind Tony Stewart (2,403 points), Carl Edwards (2,403 points), and Kevin Harvick (2,345 points). In 2011, he earned $6,183,580 by winning three Poles (fastest driver in qualifying), winning three races, finishing in the top five 12 times, and finishing in the top ten 20 times. NASCAR's point system in 2011 allocated 43 points to the driver who finished first, 42 points to the driver who finished second, and so on down to 1 point for the driver who finished in the 43rd position. In addition, any driver who led a lap received 1 bonus point, the driver who led the most laps received an additional bonus point, and the race winner was awarded 3 bonus points. But the maximum number of points a driver could earn in any race was 48. Table 15.8 shows data for the 2011 season for the top 35 drivers (NASCAR website). **LO 1, 2, 4, 5, 7**

DATA*file*
nascar

Table 15.8 NASCAR Results for the 2011 Season

Driver	Points	Poles	Wins	Top 5	Top 10	Winnings ($)
Tony Stewart	2,403	1	5	9	19	6,529,870
Carl Edwards	2,403	3	1	19	26	8,485,990
Kevin Harvick	2,345	0	4	9	19	6,197,140
Matt Kenseth	2,330	3	3	12	20	6,183,580
Brad Keselowski	2,319	1	3	10	14	5,087,740
Jimmie Johnson	2,304	0	2	14	21	6,296,360
Dale Earnhardt Jr.	2,290	1	0	4	12	4,163,690
Jeff Gordon	2,287	1	3	13	18	5,912,830
Denny Hamlin	2,284	0	1	5	14	5,401,190
Ryan Newman	2,284	3	1	9	17	5,303,020
Kurt Busch	2,262	3	2	8	16	5,936,470
Kyle Busch	2,246	1	4	14	18	6,161,020
Clint Bowyer	1,047	0	1	4	16	5,633,950
Kasey Kahne	1,041	2	1	8	15	4,775,160
A. J. Allmendinger	1,013	0	0	1	10	4,825,560
Greg Biffle	997	3	0	3	10	4,318,050
Paul Menard	947	0	1	4	8	3,853,690
Martin Truex Jr.	937	1	0	3	12	3,955,560
Marcos Ambrose	936	0	1	5	12	4,750,390
Jeff Burton	935	0	0	2	5	3,807,780
Juan Montoya	932	2	0	2	8	5,020,780
Mark Martin	930	2	0	2	10	3,830,910
David Ragan	906	2	1	4	8	4,203,660
Joey Logano	902	2	0	4	6	3,856,010
Brian Vickers	846	0	0	3	7	4,301,880
Regan Smith	820	0	1	2	5	4,579,860
Jamie McMurray	795	1	0	2	4	4,794,770
David Reutimann	757	1	0	1	3	4,374,770
Bobby Labonte	670	0	0	1	2	4,505,650
David Gilliland	572	0	0	1	2	3,878,390
Casey Mears	541	0	0	0	0	2,838,320
Dave Blaney	508	0	0	1	1	3,229,210
Andy Lally	398	0	0	0	0	2,868,220
Robby Gordon	268	0	0	0	0	2,271,890
J. J. Yeley	192	0	0	0	0	2,559,500

Managerial Report

1. Suppose you wanted to predict Winnings ($) using only the number of poles won (Poles), the number of wins (Wins), the number of top five finishes (Top 5), or the number of top ten finishes (Top 10). Which of these four variables provides the best single predictor of winnings?
2. Develop an estimated regression equation that can be used to predict Winnings ($) given the number of poles won (Poles), the number of wins (Wins), the number of top five finishes (Top 5), and the number of top ten (Top 10) finishes. Test for individual significance and discuss your findings and conclusions.

3. Create two new independent variables: Top 2–5 and Top 6–10. Top 2–5 represents the number of times the driver finished between second and fifth place and Top 6–10 represents the number of times the driver finished between sixth and tenth place. Develop an estimated regression equation that can be used to predict Winnings ($) using Poles, Wins, Top 2–5, and Top 6–10. Test for individual significance and discuss your findings and conclusions.
4. Based upon the results of your analysis, what estimated regression equation would you recommend using to predict Winnings ($)? Provide an interpretation of the estimated regression coefficients for this equation.

Case Problem 3: Finding the Best Car Value

When trying to decide what car to buy, real value is not necessarily determined by how much you spend on the initial purchase. Instead, cars that are reliable and don't cost much to own often represent the best values. But no matter how reliable or inexpensive a car may be to own, it must also perform well.

To measure value, *Consumer Reports* developed a statistic referred to as a value score. The value score is based upon five-year owner costs, overall road-test scores, and predicted-reliability ratings. Five-year owner costs are based upon the expenses incurred in the first five years of ownership, including depreciation, fuel, maintenance and repairs, and so on. Using a national average of 12,000 miles per year, an average cost per mile driven is used as the measure of five-year owner costs. Road-test scores are the results of more than 50 tests and evaluations and are based on a 100-point scale, with higher scores indicating better performance, comfort, convenience, and fuel economy. The highest road-test score obtained in the tests conducted by *Consumer Reports* was a 99 for a Lexus LS 460L. Predicted-reliability ratings (1 = Poor, 2 = Fair, 3 = Good, 4 = Very Good, and 5 = Excellent) are based upon data from *Consumer Reports*' Annual Auto Survey.

DATA*file*
carvalues

A car with a value score of 1.0 is considered to be an "average-value" car. A car with a value score of 2.0 is considered to be twice as good a value as a car with a value score of 1.0; a car with a value score of 0.5 is considered half as good as average; and so on. The data for three sizes of cars (13 small sedans, 20 family sedans, and 21 upscale sedans), including the price ($) of each car tested, are contained in the file *carvalues* (*Consumer Reports* website). To incorporate the effect of size of car, a categorical variable with three values (small sedan, family sedan, and upscale sedan), use the following dummy variables. **LO 1, 2, 4, 5, 10**

$$\text{Family-Sedan} = \begin{cases} 1 \text{ if the car is a Family Sedan} \\ 0 \text{ otherwise} \end{cases}$$

$$\text{Upscale-Sedan} = \begin{cases} 1 \text{ if the car is an Upscale Sedan} \\ 0 \text{ otherwise} \end{cases}$$

Managerial Report

1. Treating Cost/Mile as the dependent variable, develop an estimated regression with Family-Sedan and Upscale-Sedan as the independent variables. Discuss your findings.
2. Treating Value Score as the dependent variable, develop an estimated regression equation using Cost/Mile, Road-Test Score, Predicted Reliability, Family-Sedan, and Upscale-Sedan as the independent variables.
3. Delete any independent variables that are not significant from the estimated regression equation developed in part 2 using a 0.05 level of significance. After deleting any independent variables that are not significant, develop a new estimated regression equation.
4. Suppose someone claims that "smaller cars provide better values than larger cars." For the data in this case, the Small Sedans represent the smallest type of car and the Upscale Sedans represent the largest type of car. Does your analysis support this claim?

Chapter 16

Regression Analysis: Model Building

Contents

Statistics in Practice:
BASF

16.1 General Linear Model
Modeling Curvilinear Relationships
Interaction
Transformations Involving the Dependent Variable
Nonlinear Models That Are Intrinsically Linear

16.2 Determining When to Add or Delete Variables
General Case

16.3 Variable Selection Procedures
Regression Analysis of Cravens Example
Stepwise Regression
Forward Selection
Backward Elimination
Best-Subsets Regression

16.4 Multiple Regression Approach to Experimental Design

16.5 Autocorrelation and the Durbin–Watson Test
Jefe de Cocina Example

Summary 799
Glossary 800
Key Formulas 800
Supplementary Exercises 801
Case Problem 1: Analysis of LPGA Tour Statistics 804
Case Problem 2: Rating Wines from the Piedmont Region of Italy 804

Available in the Cengage eBook:
Appendix: Linear Regression Variable Selection Procedures with R

Learning Objectives

After completing this chapter, you will be able to

LO 1 Identify a curvilinear relationship between variables and construct a curvilinear relationship in the general linear model.

LO 2 Explain the concept of interaction between variables and construct an interaction effect in the general linear model.

LO 3 Identify circumstances motivating the transformation of the dependent variable in the general linear model and fit an estimated regression model using a transformed dependent variable.

LO 4 Employ an *F* test to determine when to add or delete one or more variables from regression model.

LO 5 Employ variable selection procedures to identify a set of independent variables for a regression model.

LO 6 Formulate experimental design problems with multiple regression.

LO 7 Employ the Durbin-Watson test to assess autocorrelation in the residuals of an estimated linear regression model.

Statistics in Practice

BASF

Ludwigshafen, Germany

BASF SE is a German multinational chemical company comprising subsidiaries and joint ventures in more than 90 countries with customers in over 190 countries. The animal nutrition division of BASF is a global supplier of innovative feed additives for livestock, aquaculture, and companion animals.

BASF's animal nutrition division manufactures and markets a methionine supplement used in poultry, swine, and cattle feed products. Because poultry growers work with high volumes and low profit margins, cost-effective poultry feed products with the best possible nutrition value are needed. Optimal feed composition will result in rapid growth and high final body weight for a given level of feed intake. The chemical industry works closely with poultry growers to optimize poultry feed products. Ultimately, success depends on keeping the cost of poultry low in comparison with the cost of beef and other meat products.

Researchers used regression analysis to model the relationship between body weight y and the amount of methionine x added to the poultry feed. Initially, the following simple linear estimated regression equation was developed.

$$\hat{y} = 0.21 + 0.42x$$

This estimated regression equation proved statistically significant; however, the analysis of the residuals indicated that a curvilinear relationship would be a better model of the relationship between body weight and methionine.

Researchers used regression analysis to develop an optimal feed composition for poultry growers.
Source: monticello/Shutterstock.com

Further research showed that although small amounts of methionine tended to increase body weight, at some point body weight leveled off and additional amounts of the methionine were of little or no benefit. In fact, when the amount of methionine increased beyond nutritional requirements, body weight tended to decline. The following estimated multiple regression equation was used to model the curvilinear relationship between body weight and methionine.

$$\hat{y} = -1.89 + 1.32x - 0.506x^2$$

The regression model determines the optimal level of methionine to be used in poultry feed products.

In this chapter, we will extend the discussion of regression analysis by showing how curvilinear models can be developed. In addition, we will describe a variety of tools that help determine which independent variables lead to the best estimated regression equation.

Model building is the process of developing an estimated regression equation that describes the relationship between a dependent variable and one or more independent variables. The major issues in model building are finding the proper functional form of the relationship and selecting the independent variables to be included in the model. In Section 16.1, we establish the framework for model building by introducing the concept of a general linear model. Section 16.2, which provides the foundation for the more sophisticated procedures, introduces a general approach for determining when to add or delete independent variables. In Section 16.3, we consider a larger regression problem involving eight independent variables; this problem is used to illustrate variable selection procedures, including stepwise regression, the forward selection procedure, the backward elimination procedure, and best-subsets regression. In Section 16.4, we show how to use dummy variables in a multiple regression equation for experimental design problems. To conclude, Section 16.5 demonstrates the Durbin–Watson test for autocorrelation.

16.1 General Linear Model

Suppose we have collected data for one dependent variable y and k independent variables $x_1, x_2, \ldots, x_k$. Our objective is to use these data to develop an estimated regression equation that provides the best relationship between the dependent and the independent variables. As a general framework for developing more complex relationships among the independent variables, we introduce the concept of a **general linear model** involving p independent variables.

If you can write a regression model in the form of equation (16.1), the standard multiple regression procedures described in Chapter 15 are applicable.

General Linear Model

$$y = \beta_0 + \beta_1 z_1 + \beta_2 z_2 + \cdots + \beta_p z_p + \epsilon \tag{16.1}$$

In equation (16.1), each of the independent variables z_j (where $j = 1, 2, \ldots, p$) is a function of $x_1, x_2, \ldots, x_k$ (the variables for which data have been collected). In some cases, each z_j may be a function of only one x variable. The simplest case is when we have collected data for just one variable (x_1) and want to estimate y by using a straight-line relationship. In this case $z_1 = x_1$, and equation (16.1) becomes

Equation (16.2) is the simple linear regression model introduced in Chapter 14 with the exception that the independent variable is labeled x_1 instead of x.

$$y = \beta_0 + \beta_1 x_1 + \epsilon \tag{16.2}$$

In the statistical modeling literature, equation (16.2) is called a *simple first-order model with one predictor variable.*

Modeling Curvilinear Relationships

In this section, we consider a **curvilinear relationship** in which the association between an independent variable and dependent variable changes as the values of the variables change and this is captured with a smooth, nonlinear curve. This is a more complex relationship than modeled by equation (16.1) in which the relationship between an independent variable z_i and dependent variable remains constant at a value of β_i. To illustrate, let us consider the problem facing Reynolds, Inc., a manufacturer of industrial scales and laboratory equipment. Managers at Reynolds want to investigate the relationship between length of employment of their salespeople and the number of electronic laboratory scales sold. Table 16.1 gives the number of months each salesperson has been employed by the firm and the number of scales sold by 15 randomly selected salespeople for the most recent sales period. Figure 16.1 is the scatter diagram for these data. The scatter diagram indicates

DATA*file*
reynolds

Table 16.1 Data for the Reynolds Example

Months Employed	Scales Sold
41	275
106	296
76	317
104	376
22	162
12	150
85	367
111	308
40	189
51	235
9	83
12	112
6	67
56	325
19	189

Figure 16.1 Scatter Diagram for the Reynolds Example

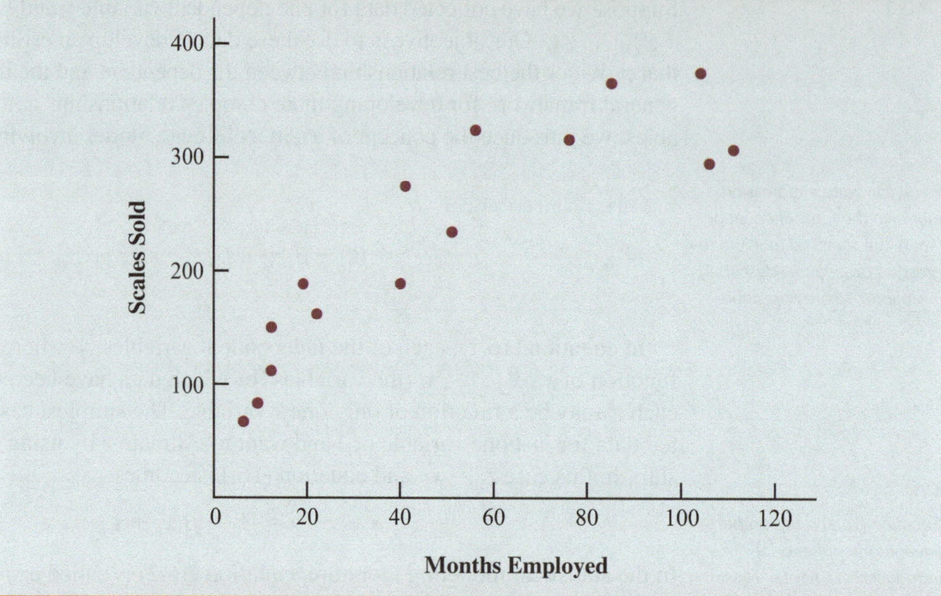

a possible curvilinear relationship between the length of time employed and the number of units sold. Before considering how to develop a curvilinear relationship for Reynolds, let us consider the Excel Regression tool output in Figure 16.2, corresponding to a simple first-order model; the estimated regression equation is

$$\text{Sales} = 111.2279 + 2.3768 \text{ Months}$$

where

$$\text{Sales} = \text{number of electronic laboratory scales sold}$$
$$\text{Months} = \text{the number of months the salesperson has been employed}$$

A standardized residual plot against $\hat{y}$ (predicted Sales) is also displayed. Although the Excel output shows that a linear relationship explains a high percentage of the variability in sales (R Square = 0.7812), the standardized residual plot suggests that a curvilinear relationship is present.

To account for the curvilinear relationship, we set $z_1 = x_1$ and $z_2 = x_1^2$ in equation (16.1) to obtain the model

$$y = \beta_0 + \beta_1 x_1 + \beta_2 x_1^2 + \epsilon \qquad \textbf{(16.3)}$$

This model is called a *second-order model with one predictor variable.* To develop an estimated regression equation corresponding to this second-order model, Excel's Regression tool needs the original data in Table 16.1, as well as those data corresponding to adding a second independent variable that is the square of the number of months the employee has been with the firm. In Figure 16.3 we show the Excel Regression tool output corresponding to the second-order model (the months squared data are in column B); the estimated regression equation is

$$\text{Sales} = 45.3476 + 6.3448 \text{ Months} - 0.0345 \text{ MonthsSq}$$

where

$$\text{MonthsSq} = \text{the square of the number of months the salesperson has been employed}$$

Figure 16.2 Regression Tool Output for the Reynolds Example: First-Order Model

Months	Sales
41	275
106	296
76	317
104	376
22	162
12	150
85	367
111	308
40	189
51	235
9	83
12	112
6	67
56	325
19	189

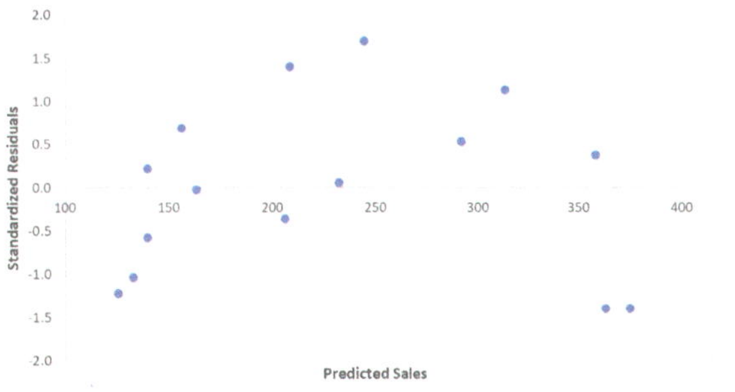

SUMMARY OUTPUT

Regression Statistics	
Multiple R	0.8838
R Square	0.7812
Adjusted R Square	0.7643
Standard Error	49.5158
Observations	15

ANOVA

	df	*SS*	*MS*	*F*	*Significance F*
Regression	1	113,783.3447	113,783.3447	46.4078	0.0000
Residual	13	31,873.5886	2,451.8145		
Total	14	145,656.9333			

	Coefficients	*Standard Error*	*t Stat*	*P-value*	*Lower 95%*	*Upper 95%*	*Lower 99.0%*	*Upper 99.0%*
Intercept	111.2279	21.6280	5.1428	0.0002	64.5035	157.9524	46.0784	176.3774
Months	2.3768	0.3489	6.8123	0.0000	1.6230	3.1305	1.3258	3.4277

The corresponding standardized residual plot is also shown in Figure 16.3. It shows that the previous curvilinear pattern has been removed. At the 0.05 level of significance, the Excel output shows that the overall model is significant (p-value for the F test is 8.75E-07). Note also that the p-value $= 0.0023$ corresponding to the t Stat value for MonthsSq is less than 0.05. Thus, we can conclude that adding MonthsSq to the model involving Months is statistically significant. Further, this second-order model achieves an Adjusted R Square value of 0.8859, which is an improvement of the Adjusted R Square value of 0.7643 of the first-order model with only the Months variable. Thus, we see how easy it is to handle curvilinear relationships in regression analysis.

Many types of relationships can be modeled by using equation (16.1). The regression techniques with which we have been working are definitely not limited to linear, or straight-line, relationships. In multiple regression analysis the word *linear* in the term *general linear model* refers only to the fact that $\beta_0, \beta_1, \ldots, \beta_p$ all have exponents of one; it does not imply that the relationship between y and the underlying x_i variables is linear. Indeed, in this section we have seen one example of equation (16.1) being used to model a curvilinear relationship.

Interaction

The term x_1x_2 is sometimes referred to as a cross-product term.

If the original data set consists of observations for y and two independent variables x_1 and x_2, we can develop a second-order model with two predictor variables by substituting $z_1 = x_1$, $z_2 = x_2$, $z_3 = x_1^2$, $z_4 = x_2^2$, and $z_5 = x_1x_2$ into the general linear model of equation (16.1). The model obtained is

$$y = \beta_0 + \beta_1x_1 + \beta_2x_2 + \beta_3x_1^2 + \beta_4x_2^2 + \beta_5x_1x_2 + \epsilon \tag{16.4}$$

Figure 16.3 Regression Tool Output for the Reynolds Example: Second-Order Model

	A	B	C
1	Months	MonthsSq	Sales
2	41	1,681	275
3	106	11,236	296
4	76	5,776	317
5	104	10,816	376
6	22	484	162
7	12	144	150
8	85	7,225	367
9	111	12,321	308
10	40	1,600	189
11	51	2,601	235
12	9	81	83
13	12	144	112
14	6	36	67
15	56	3,136	325
16	19	361	189

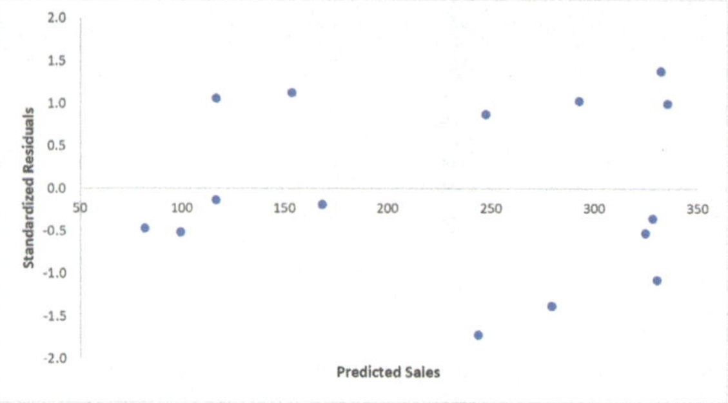

SUMMARY OUTPUT

Regression Statistics	
Multiple R	0.9498
R Square	0.9022
Adjusted R Square	0.8859
Standard Error	34.4528
Observations	15

ANOVA

	df	*SS*	*MS*	*F*	*Significance F*
Regression	2	131,413.0156	65,706.5078	55.3554	0.0000
Residual	12	14,243.9177	1,186.9931		
Total	14	145,656.9333			

	Coefficients	*Standard Error*	*t Stat*	*P-value*	*Lower 95%*	*Upper 95%*	*Lower 99.0%*	*Upper 99.0%*
Intercept	45.3476	22.7747	1.9911	0.0697	-4.2741	94.9693	-24.2185	114.9137
Months	6.3448	1.0579	5.9978	0.0001	4.0399	8.6497	3.1136	9.5761
MonthsSq	-0.0345	0.0089	-3.8539	0.0023	-0.0540	-0.0150	-0.0618	-0.0072

In this second-order model, the variable $z_5 = x_1x_2$ is added to account for the potential effects of the two variables acting together. This type of effect is called **interaction**.

To provide an illustration of interaction and what it means, let us review the regression study conducted by Tyler Personal Care for one of its new shampoo products. Two factors believed to have the most influence on sales are unit selling price and advertising expenditure. To investigate the effects of these two variables on sales, prices of \$2.00, \$2.50, and \$3.00 were paired with advertising expenditures of \$50,000 and \$100,000 in 24 test markets. The unit sales that were observed (in 1,000s) are reported in Table 16.2.

Table 16.3 is a summary of these data. Note that the mean sales corresponding to a price of \$2.00 and an advertising expenditure of \$50,000 is 461,000, and the mean sales corresponding to a price of \$2.00 and an advertising expenditure of \$100,000 is 808,000. Hence, with price held constant at \$2.00, the difference in mean sales between advertising expenditures of \$50,000 and \$100,000 is 808,000 − 461,000 = 347,000 units. When the price of the product is \$2.50, the difference in mean sales is 646,000 − 364,000 = 282,000 units. Finally, when the price is \$3.00, the difference in mean sales is 375,000 − 332,000 = 43,000 units. Clearly, the difference in mean sales between advertising expenditures of \$50,000 and \$100,000 depends on the price of the product. In other words, at higher selling prices, the effect of increased advertising expenditure diminishes. These observations provide evidence of interaction between the price and advertising expenditure variables.

To provide another perspective of interaction, Figure 16.4 shows a graph of the mean sales for the six price-advertising expenditure combinations. This graph also shows that the effect of advertising expenditure on mean sales depends on the price of the product; we again see the effect of interaction. When interaction between two variables is present,

DATA *file*
tyler

Table 16.2 Data for the Tyler Personal Care Example

Price ($)	Advertising Expenditure ($1,000s)	Sales (1,000s)	Price ($)	Advertising Expenditure ($1,000s)	Sales (1,000s)
2.00	50	478	2.00	100	810
2.50	50	373	2.50	100	653
3.00	50	335	3.00	100	345
2.00	50	473	2.00	100	832
2.50	50	358	2.50	100	641
3.00	50	329	3.00	100	372
2.00	50	456	2.00	100	800
2.50	50	360	2.50	100	620
3.00	50	322	3.00	100	390
2.00	50	437	2.00	100	790
2.50	50	365	2.50	100	670
3.00	50	342	3.00	100	393

Table 16.3 Mean Sales (1,000s) for the Tyler Personal Care Example

		Price		
		$2.00	$2.50	$3.00
Advertising Expenditure	$50,000	461	364	332
	$100,000	808	646	375

Mean sales of 808 thousand units when price = $2.00 and advertising expenditure = $100,000

we cannot study the effect of one variable on the response y independently of the other variable. In other words, meaningful conclusions can be developed only if we consider the joint effect that both variables have on the response.

To account for the effect of interaction, we will use the following regression model.

$$y = \beta_0 + \beta_1 x_1 + \beta_2 x_2 + \beta_3 x_1 x_2 + \epsilon \tag{16.5}$$

where

$$y = \text{unit sales (1,000s)}$$
$$x_1 = \text{price (\$)}$$
$$x_2 = \text{advertising expenditure (\$1,000s)}$$

Note that equation (16.5) reflects Tyler's belief that the number of units sold depends linearly on selling price and advertising expenditure (accounted for by the $\beta_1 x_1$ and $\beta_2 x_2$ terms), and that there is interaction between the two variables (accounted for by the $\beta_3 x_1 x_2$ term).

Figure 16.4 Mean Sales as a Function of Selling Price ($) and Advertising Expenditure

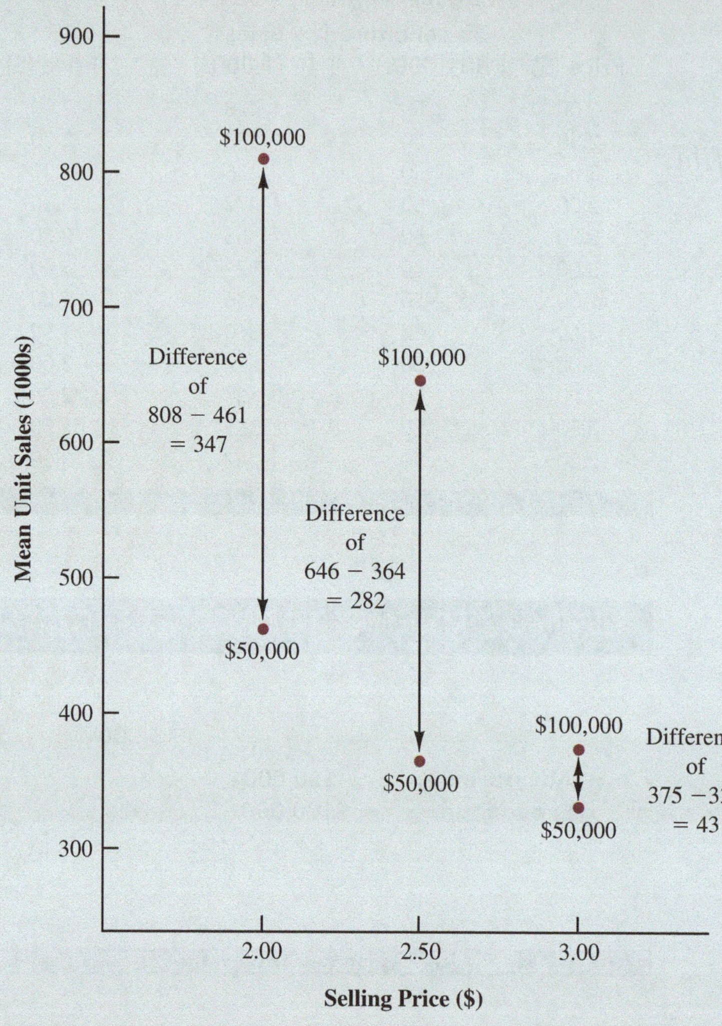

To develop an estimated regression equation, a general linear model involving three independent variables (z_1, z_2, and z_3) is used.

$$y = \beta_0 + \beta_1 z_1 + \beta_2 z_2 + \beta_3 z_3 + \epsilon \tag{16.6}$$

where

$$z_1 = x_1$$
$$z_2 = x_2$$
$$z_3 = x_1 x_2$$

Figure 16.5 is the Excel Regression tool output corresponding to the interaction model for the Tyler Personal Care example. The resulting estimated regression equation is

$$\text{Sales} = -275.8333 + 175 \text{ Price} + 19.68 \text{ AdvExp} - 6.08 \text{ PriceAdv}$$

Figure 16.5 Regression Tool Output for the Tyler Personal Care Example

Note that rows 5 through 22 are hidden.

	A	B	C	D	E	F	G	H	I
1	**Price**	**AdvExp**	**PriceAdv**	**Sales**					
2	2.0	50	100	478					
3	2.5	50	125	373					
4	3.0	50	150	335					
23	2.0	100	200	790					
24	2.5	100	250	670					
25	3.0	100	300	393					
26									
27	SUMMARY OUTPUT								
28									
29	*Regression Statistics*								
30	Multiple R	0.9890							
31	R Square	0.9781							
32	Adjusted R Square	0.9748							
33	Standard Error	28.1739							
34	Observations	24							
35									
36	ANOVA								
37		*df*	*SS*	*MS*	*F*	*Significance F*			
38	Regression	3	709,316.0000	236,438.6667	297.8692	0.0000			
39	Residual	20	15,875.3333	793.7667					
40	Total	23	725,191.3333						
41									
42		*Coefficients*	*Standard Error*	*t Stat*	*P-value*	*Lower 95%*	*Upper 95%*	*Lower 99.0%*	*Upper 99.0%*
43	Intercept	-275.8333	112.8421	-2.4444	0.0239	-511.2178	-40.4488	-596.9075	45.2408
44	Price	175.0000	44.5468	3.9285	0.0008	82.0770	267.9230	48.2492	301.7508
45	AdvExp	19.6800	1.4274	13.7878	0.0000	16.7026	22.6574	15.6187	23.7413
46	PriceAdv	-6.0800	0.5635	-10.7901	0.0000	-7.2554	-4.9046	-7.6833	-4.4767
47									

where

$$\begin{aligned} \text{Sales} &= \text{unit sales (1,000s)} \\ \text{Price} &= \text{price of the product (\$)} \\ \text{AdvExp} &= \text{advertising expenditure (\$1,000s)} \\ \text{PriceAdv} &= \text{interaction term (Price times AdvExp)} \end{aligned}$$

Because the p-value corresponding to the t test for PriceAdv is 0.0000, we conclude that interaction is significant given the linear effect of the price of the product and the advertising expenditure. Thus, the regression results show that the effect of advertising expenditure on sales depends on the price.

Transformations Involving the Dependent Variable

In showing how the general linear model can be used to model a variety of possible relationships between the independent variables and the dependent variable, we have focused attention on transformations involving one or more of the independent variables. Often it is worthwhile to consider transformations involving the dependent variable y. As an illustration of when we might want to transform the dependent variable, consider the data in Table 16.4, the weight and miles-per-gallon rating for 12 automobiles. The scatter diagram in Figure 16.6 shows a negative linear relationship between these two variables. Therefore, we use a simple first-order model to relate the two variables. The Excel Regression tool output is in Figure 16.7; the resulting estimated regression equation is

$$\text{MPG} = 56.0957 - 0.0116\ \text{Weight}$$

DATA*file*
mpg

Table 16.4 Weight and Miles-per-Gallon Rating for 12 Automobiles

Weight (pounds)	Miles per Gallon
2,289	28.7
2,113	29.2
2,180	34.2
2,448	27.9
2,026	33.3
2,702	26.4
2,657	23.9
2,106	30.5
3,226	18.1
3,213	19.5
3,607	14.3
2,888	20.9

Figure 16.6 Scatter Diagram for the Miles-per-Gallon Example

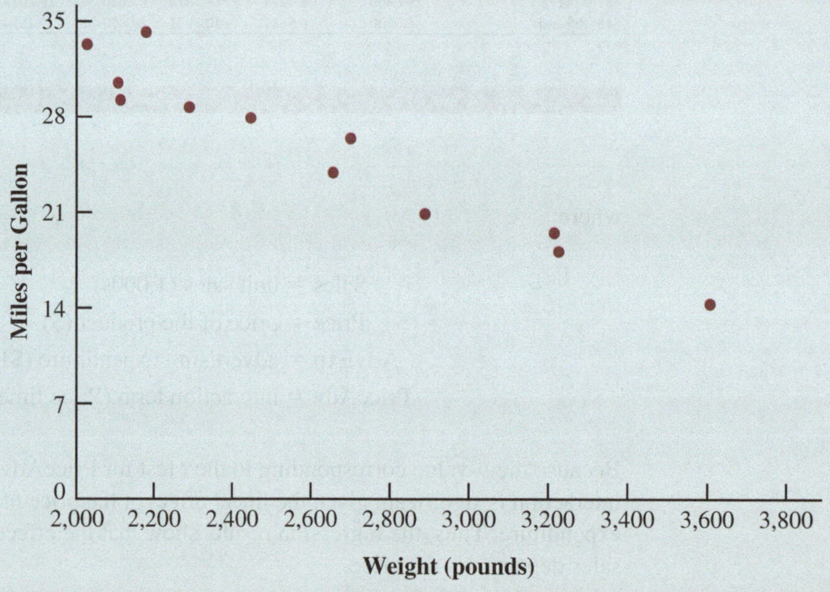

where

$$\text{MPG} = \text{miles-per-gallon rating}$$
$$\text{Weight} = \text{weight of the car in pounds}$$

The model is significant (*Significance F* or *p*-value for the *F* test is 0.000) and the fit is very good (R Square = 0.9354).

We provide detailed coverage of residual analysis, including detecting nonconstant variance in residual plots, in Chapters 14 and 15.

A standardized residual plot is also displayed. The pattern we observe does not look like the horizontal band we should expect to find if the assumptions about the error term are valid. Instead, the variability in the residuals appears to increase as the value of $\hat{y}$ (weight) increases. In other words, we have the wedge-shaped pattern indicative of a nonconstant variance. We are not justified in reaching any conclusions about the statistical significance

Figure 16.7 Regression Tool Output for the Miles-per-Gallon Example

	A	B
1	Weight	MPG
2	2289	28.7
3	2113	29.2
4	2180	34.2
5	2448	27.9
6	2026	33.3
7	2702	26.4
8	2657	23.9
9	2106	30.5
10	3226	18.1
11	3213	19.5
12	3607	14.3
13	2888	20.9

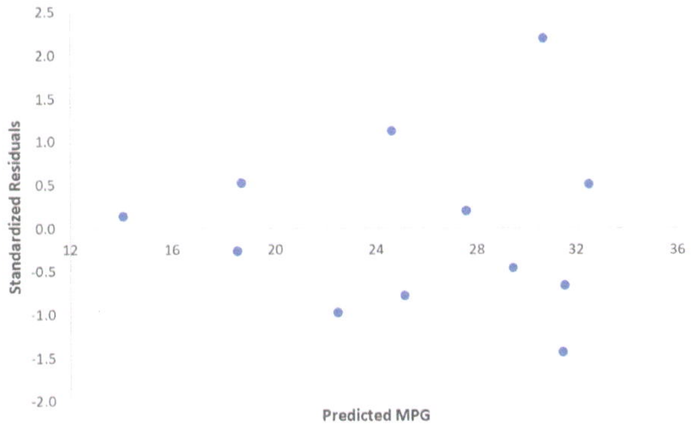

15 SUMMARY OUTPUT

	Regression Statistics	
18	Multiple R	0.9672
19	R Square	0.9354
20	Adjusted R Square	0.9289
21	Standard Error	1.6705
22	Observations	12

24 ANOVA

25		*df*	*SS*	*MS*	*F*	*Significance F*
26	Regression	1	403.9759	403.9759	144.7601	0.0000
27	Residual	10	27.9066	2.7907		
28	Total	11	431.8825			

30		*Coefficients*	*Standard Error*	*t Stat*	*P-value*	*Lower 95%*	*Upper 95%*	*Lower 99.0%*	*Upper 99.0%*
31	Intercept	56.0957	2.5821	21.7245	0.0000	50.3423	61.8490	47.9122	64.2792
32	Weight	-0.0116	0.0010	-12.0316	0.0000	-0.0138	-0.0095	-0.0147	-0.0086

of the resulting estimated regression equation when the underlying assumptions for the tests of significance do not appear to be satisfied.

Often the problem of nonconstant variance can be corrected by transforming the dependent variable to a different scale. For instance, if we work with the logarithm of the dependent variable instead of the original dependent variable, the effect will be to compress the values of the dependent variable and thus diminish the effects of nonconstant variance. Excel provides the ability to apply logarithmic transformations using either the base 10 common logarithm, $\log_{10}$, or the base $e = 2.71828\ldots$ natural logarithm, ln. In Figure 16.8, we applied a natural logarithmic transformation to the miles-per-gallon data and developed the estimated regression equation relating weight to the natural logarithm of miles-per-gallon rating. The value in cell C2 of Figure 16.8 is computed using the Excel formula =LN(B2). Then, this formula was copied to cells C3:C13 to produce the rest of the values in column C shown in Figure 16.8. The regression results obtained by using the natural logarithm of miles-per-gallon rating as the dependent variable, labeled LnMPG in the output, are in Figure 16.8.

Looking at the standardized residual plot in Figure 16.8, we see that the wedge-shaped pattern has now disappeared. The model with the logarithm of miles per gallon as the dependent variable is statistically significant and provides an excellent fit to the observed data. Hence, we would recommend using the estimated regression equation

$$\text{LnMPG} = 4.5242 - 0.0005 \text{ Weight}$$

To estimate the miles-per-gallon rating for an automobile that weighs 2,500 pounds, we first develop an estimate of the logarithm of the miles-per-gallon rating.

$$\text{LnMPG} = 4.5242 - 0.0005(2500) = 3.27$$

Figure 16.8 Regression Tool Output for the Miles-per-Gallon Example: Logarithmic Transformation

	A	B	C
1	Weight	MPG	LnMPG
2	2289	28.7	3.3569
3	2113	29.2	3.3742
4	2180	34.2	3.5322
5	2448	27.9	3.3286
6	2026	33.3	3.5056
7	2702	26.4	3.2734
8	2657	23.9	3.1739
9	2106	30.5	3.4177
10	3226	18.1	2.8959
11	3213	19.5	2.9704
12	3607	14.3	2.6603
13	2888	20.9	3.0397

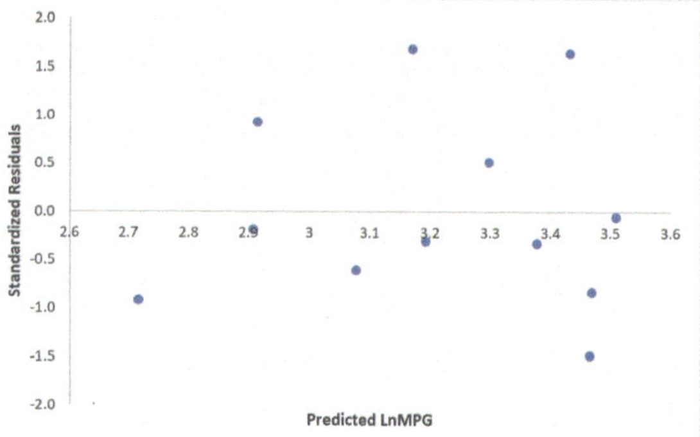

14		
15	SUMMARY OUTPUT	
16		
17	*Regression Statistics*	
18	Multiple R	0.9735
19	R Square	0.9477
20	Adjusted R Square	0.9425
21	Standard Error	0.0643
22	Observations	12
23		
24	ANOVA	

25		*df*	*SS*	*MS*	*F*	*Significance F*
26	Regression	1	0.7482	0.7482	181.2244	0.0000
27	Residual	10	0.0413	0.0041		
28	Total	11	0.7895			
29						

30		*Coefficients*	*Standard Error*	*t Stat*	*P-value*	*Lower 95%*	*Upper 95%*	*Lower 99.0%*	*Upper 99.0%*
31	Intercept	4.5242	0.0993	45.5527	0.0000	4.3029	4.7455	4.2095	4.8390
32	Weight	-0.0005	0.0000	-13.4620	0.0000	-0.0006	-0.0004	-0.0006	-0.0004
33									

The miles-per-gallon estimate is obtained by finding the number whose natural logarithm is 3.27. Using Excel's exponential function EXP, or raising e to the power 3.27, we obtain 26.3 miles per gallon.

Another approach to problems of nonconstant variance is to use $1/y$ as the dependent variable instead of y. This type of transformation is called a *reciprocal transformation.* For instance, if the dependent variable is measured in miles per gallon, the reciprocal transformation would result in a new dependent variable whose units would be 1/(miles per gallon) or gallons per mile. In general, there is no way to determine whether a logarithmic transformation or a reciprocal transformation will perform best without actually trying each of them.

When considering a model with a transformed dependent variable, care must be taken when comparing it to a model that uses the untransformed (original) dependent variable or to a model that uses a different transformation of the dependent variable. Reconsider the miles-per-gallon example in this section. The R Square = 0.9354 of the model MPG = 56.0957− 0.0116 Weight in Figure 16.7 should not be compared to the R Square = 0.9477 of the model LnMPG = 4.5242 − 0.0005 Weight in Figure 16.8. This comparison is not valid because the units used to compute the R Square in Figure 16.7 are measured in miles per gallon, but the units used to compute the R Square in Figure 16.8 are measured in (natural) logged miles per gallon. Due to this difference in scale, the R Square measures are not comparable.

To compare the fit of a model with a transformed dependent variable with one based on the original dependent variable, the estimated transformed model can be transformed back into the units of the original dependent variable. The fit can then be compared to a model based on the original dependent variable. For the miles-per-gallon example, raising each side of the fitted regression equation LnMPG = 4.5242 − 0.0005 Weight to the power of e, we obtain

$$\text{MPG} = e^{4.5242-0.0005\ \text{Weight}} = 92.2e^{-0.0005\ \text{Weight}}$$

Figure 16.9 Comparing Simple Linear Model and Logarithmic Transformed Model for the Miles-Per-Gallon Example

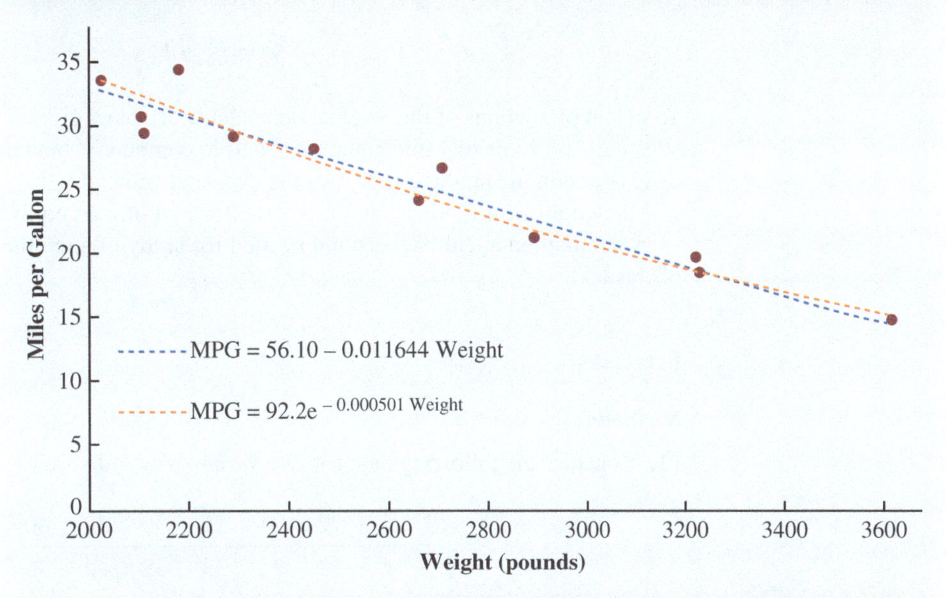

In Chapter 17, we discuss the computation of accuracy measures such as the mean absolute error, mean squared error, and mean absolute percentage error.

The error resulting from the predicted values from MPG $= 92.2e^{-0.0005\text{ Weight}}$ can then be compared to the error resulting from the predicted values of MPG $= 56.0957 - 0.0116$ Weight. Figure 16.9 displays these two respective fitted curves.

Nonlinear Models That Are Intrinsically Linear

The **exponential model** involves the following regression equation.

$$E(y) = \beta_0\beta_1^x \tag{16.7}$$

This regression equation is appropriate when the dependent variable y increases or decreases by a constant percentage, instead of by a fixed amount, as x increases.

As an example, suppose sales for a product y are related to advertising expenditure x (in thousands of dollars) according to the following regression equation.

$$E(y) = 500(1.2)^x$$

Thus, for $x = 1$, $E(y) = 500(1.2)^1 = 600$; for $x = 2$, $E(y) = 500(1.2)^2 = 720$; and for $x = 3$, $E(y) = 500(1.2)^3 = 864$. Note that $E(y)$ is not increasing by a constant amount in this case, but by a constant percentage; the percentage increase is 20%.

Models in which the parameters ($\beta_0, \beta_1, \ldots, \beta_p$) have exponents other than 1 are called nonlinear models. However, for the case of the exponential model, we can perform a transformation of variables that will enable us to perform regression analysis with equation (16.1), the general linear model. We can transform this nonlinear regression equation to a linear regression equation by taking the natural logarithm of both sides of equation (16.7).

$$\ln E(y) = \ln \beta_0 + x \ln \beta_1 \tag{16.8}$$

Now if we let $y' = \ln E(y)$ $\beta_0' = \ln \beta_0$, and $\beta_1' = \ln \beta_1$, we can rewrite equation (16.8) as

$$y' = \beta_0' + \beta_1' x$$

The formulas for simple linear regression can now be used to develop estimates of β_0' and β_1'. Denoting the estimates as b_0' and b_1' leads to the following estimated regression equation.

$$\hat{y}' = b_0' + b_1' x \tag{16.9}$$

To obtain predictions of the original dependent variable y given a value of x, we would first substitute the value of x into equation (16.9) to compute $\hat{y}'$, and then raise e to the power of $\hat{y}'$ to obtain the prediction of y, or the expected value of y, in its original units.

Many nonlinear models cannot be transformed into an equivalent linear model. However, the mathematical background needed for study of such models is beyond the scope of this text.

Exercises

Methods

1. Consider the following data for two variables, x and y. **LO 1**

x	22	24	26	30	35	40
y	12	21	33	35	40	36

   a. Develop an estimated regression equation for the data of the form $\hat{y} = b_0 + b_1x$.
   b. Using the results from part (a), test for a significant relationship between x and y; use $\alpha = 0.05$.
   c. Develop a scatter diagram for the data. Does the scatter diagram suggest an estimated regression equation of the form $\hat{y} = b_0 + b_1x + b_2x^2$? Explain.
   d. Develop an estimated regression equation for the data of the form $\hat{y} = b_0 + b_1x + b_2x^2$.
   e. Refer to part (d). Is the relationship between x, x^2, and y significant? Use $\alpha = 0.05$.
   f. Predict the value of y when $x = 25$.

2. Consider the following data for two variables, x and y. **LO 1**

x	9	32	18	15	26
y	10	20	21	16	22

   a. Develop an estimated regression equation for the data of the form $\hat{y} = b_0 + b_1x$. Comment on the adequacy of this equation for predicting y.
   b. Develop an estimated regression equation for the data of the form $\hat{y} = b_0 + b_1x + b_2x^2$. Comment on the adequacy of this equation for predicting y.
   c. Predict the value of y when $x = 20$.

3. Consider the following data for two variables, x and y. **LO 3**

x	2	3	4	5	7	7	7	8	9
y	4	5	4	6	4	6	9	5	11

   a. Does there appear to be a linear relationship between x and y? Explain.
   b. Develop the estimated regression equation relating x and y.
   c. Plot the standardized residuals versus $\hat{y}$ for the estimated regression equation developed in part (b). Do the model assumptions appear to be satisfied? Explain.
   d. Perform a logarithmic transformation on the dependent variable y. Develop an estimated regression equation using the transformed dependent variable. Do the model assumptions appear to be satisfied by using the transformed dependent variable? Does a reciprocal transformation work better in this case? Explain.

Applications

4. **Vehicle Speed and Traffic Flow.** A highway department is studying the relationship between traffic flow and speed. The following model has been hypothesized.

$$y = \beta_0 + \beta_1 x + \epsilon$$

DATA*file* traffic

where

y = traffic flow in vehicles per hour
x = vehicle speed in miles per hour

The following data were collected during rush hour for six highways leading out of the city. LO 1

Traffic Flow (y)	Vehicle Speed (x)
1,256	35
1,329	40
1,226	30
1,335	45
1,349	50
1,124	25

a. Develop an estimated regression equation for the data.
b. Construct a standardized residual plot. Based on the standardized residual plot, is there any indication that a curvilinear relationship may exist?

5. **Curvilinear Relationship Between Vehicle Speed and Traffic Flow.** In working further with the data in problem 4, statisticians suggested the use of the following curvilinear estimated regression equation. LO 1

$$\hat{y} = b_0 + b_1 x + b_2 x^2$$

a. Use the data in problem 4 to compute the coefficients of this estimated regression equation.
b. Using $\alpha = 0.01$, test for a significant relationship.
c. Estimate the traffic flow in vehicles per hour at a speed of 38 miles per hour.

6. **Emergency Facilities and Distance to Service.** A study of emergency service facilities investigated the relationship between the number of facilities and the average distance traveled to provide the emergency service. The following table gives the data collected. LO 1

DATA*file* emergency

Number of Facilities	Average Distance (miles)
9	1.66
11	1.12
16	0.83
21	0.62
27	0.51
30	0.47

a. Develop a scatter diagram for these data, treating average distance traveled as the dependent variable.
b. Does a simple linear model appear to be appropriate? Explain.
c. Develop an estimated regression equation for the data that you believe will best explain the relationship between these two variables.

7. **Washing Machine Capacity and Price.** Home Depot, a nationwide home improvement retailer, sells several brands of washing machines. A sample of 24 models of full-size washing machines sold by Home Depot and the corresponding capacity (in cubic feet) and list price (in $) follow (Home Depot website). **LO 1**

DATA*file*
washingmachines

Model	Capacity (ft^3)	List Price ($)
Maytag High-Efficiency Top Loading Washer with Steam	4.8	749
Samsung High-Efficiency Top Loading Washer with Active Wash and Integrated Touch Controls	5.0	999
Whirlpool High-Efficiency Front Loading Washer with Steam	4.2	1,299
Maytag High-Efficiency Top Loading Washer	4.3	649
Whirlpool High-Efficiency Top Loading Washer	4.3	599
Samsung High-Efficiency Front Loading Washer	4.2	799
Samsung High-Efficiency Front Loading Washer with AddWash Door	4.5	999
Whirlpool High-Efficiency Front Loading Washer	4.5	799
Whirlpool High-Efficiency Top Loading Washer with Steam	4.8	799
Samsung High-Efficiency Top Loading Washer with ActiveWash	4.8	899
Whirlpool High-Efficiency Top Loading Washer	4.8	699
Maytag High-Efficiency Front Loading Washer with Steam	4.3	799
Whirlpool High-Efficiency Front Loading Washer with Steam	4.5	1,099
Maytag High-Efficiency Top Loading Washer	5.3	899
Samsung High-Efficiency Top Loading Washer	4.8	799
Maytag High-Efficiency Front Loading Washer with Steam	4.5	999
Samsung High-Efficiency Top Loading Washer with ActiveWash and Integrated Touch Controls	4.5	849
Samsung High-Efficiency Top Loading Washer	4.5	699
Samsung High-Efficiency Front Loading Washer with Steam	5.6	1,599
Whirlpool High-Efficiency Front Loading Washer with Steam	4.5	1,099
Whirlpool High-Efficiency Front Loading Washer	4.2	799
Samsung High-Efficiency Top Loading Washer with ActiveWash	5.2	1,199
Maytag High-Efficiency Top Loading Washer with Steam	5.3	1,099
Whirlpool High-Efficiency Top Loading Washer with Steam	5.3	1,199

a. Develop a scatter diagram for these data, treating cubic feet as the independent variable. Does a simple linear regression model appear to be appropriate?
b. Use a simple linear regression model to develop an estimated regression equation to predict the list price given the cubic feet. Construct a standardized residual plot. Based upon the standardized residual plot, does a simple linear regression model appear to be appropriate?
c. Using a second-order model, develop an estimated regression equation to predict the list price given the cubic feet.
d. Do you prefer the estimated regression equation developed in part (b) or part (c)? Explain.
e. Are there other factors that should be considered for inclusion as independent variables in this regression?

8. **Classic Car Rating and Price.** Corvette, Ferrari, and Jaguar produced a variety of classic cars that continue to increase in value. The following data, based upon the Martin Rating System for Collectible Cars, show the rarity rating (1–20) and the high price ($1,000) for 15 classic cars. **LO 1, 3**

DATA*file*
classiccars

Year	Make	Model	Rating	Price ($1,000s)
1984	Chevrolet	Corvette	18	1,600
1956	Chevrolet	Corvette 265/225-hp	19	4,000
1963	Chevrolet	Corvette coupe (340-bhp 4-speed)	18	1,000
1978	Chevrolet	Corvette coupe Silver Anniversary	19	1,300
1960–1963	Ferrari	250 GTE 2+2	16	350
1962–1964	Ferrari	250 GTL Lusso	19	2,650
1962	Ferrari	250 GTO	18	375
1967–1968	Ferrari	275 GTB/4 NART Spyder	17	450
1968–1973	Ferrari	365 GTB/4 Daytona	17	140
1962–1967	Jaguar	E-type OTS	15	77.5
1969–1971	Jaguar	E-type Series II OTS	14	62
1971–1974	Jaguar	E-type Series III OTS	16	125
1951–1954	Jaguar	XK 120 roadster (steel)	17	400
1950–1953	Jaguar	XK C-type	16	250
1956–1957	Jaguar	XKSS	13	70

a. Develop a scatter diagram of the data using the rarity rating as the independent variable and price as the dependent variable. Does a simple linear regression model appear to be appropriate?
b. Develop an estimated multiple regression equation with x = rarity rating and x^2 as the two independent variables.
c. Consider the nonlinear relationship shown by equation (16.7). Use logarithms to develop an estimated regression equation for this model.
d. Plot the fitted curve from part (b) on the scatter diagram from part (a). Plot the fitted curve from part (c) on the scatter diagram from part (a). Do you prefer the estimated regression equation developed in part (b) or part (c)? Explain.

DATA*file*
rottentomatoes

9. **Movie Ratings.** As of September 4, 2016, the film *Suicide Squad* had an average rating of 3.7 out of 5 based on 117,323 viewer ratings (Rotten Tomatoes website). How are the viewer ratings of *Suicide Squad* related to the viewer age and the viewer ratings of *The Secret Life of Pets*? The file *rottentomatoes* contains a sample of data containing viewer ages and their ratings of *Suicide Squad* and *The Secret Life of Pets*. **LO 1**
a. Develop a scatter diagram for these data with the viewers' ages as the independent variable and their ratings of *Suicide Squad* as the dependent variable. Does a simple linear regression model appear to be appropriate?
b. Use the data provided to develop the regression equation for estimating the viewer ratings of *Suicide Squad* that is suggested by the scatter diagram in part (a).
c. Include the viewer rating of *The Secret Life of Pets* as an independent variable in the regression model developed in part (b). Interpret the regression coefficient for the viewer rating of *The Secret Life of Pets*.
d. Is the regression equation developed in part (b) or the regression equation developed in part (c) superior? Explain.
e. Suppose a 31-year-old viewer gave *The Secret Life of Pets* a rating of 4. Use the model you selected in part (d) to predict that viewer's rating of *Suicide Squad*.

16.2 Determining When to Add or Delete Variables

In this section we will show how an F test can be used to determine whether it is advantageous to add one or more independent variables to a multiple regression model. This test is based on a determination of the amount of reduction in the error sum of squares resulting from adding one or more independent variables to the model. We will first illustrate how the test can be used in the context of the Butler Trucking example.

We provide a more thorough discussion of the regression analysis for the Butler Trucking example in Chapter 15.

Butler Trucking Company wanted to improve how it creates delivery schedules for its drivers. The managers wanted to develop an estimated regression equation to predict total daily travel time for trucks using two independent variables: miles traveled and number of deliveries. With miles traveled, x_1, as the only independent variable, the least squares procedure provided the following estimated regression equation.

$$\hat{y} = 1.2739 + 0.0678x_1$$

The error sum of squares for this model is SSE $= 8.0287$. When x_2, the number of deliveries, was added as a second independent variable, we obtained the following estimated regression equation.

$$\hat{y} = -0.8687 + 0.0611x_1 + 0.9234x_2$$

The error sum of squares for this model is SSE $= 2.2994$. Clearly, adding x_2 resulted in a reduction of SSE. The question we want to answer is: Does adding the variable x_2 lead to a *significant* reduction in SSE?

We use the notation SSE(x_1) to denote the error sum of squares when x_1 is the only independent variable in the model, SSE(x_1, x_2) to denote the error sum of squares when x_1 and x_2 are both in the model, and so on. Hence, the reduction in SSE resulting from adding x_2 to the Butler Trucking model involving just x_1 is

$$\text{SSE}(x_1) - \text{SSE}(x_1, x_2) = 8.0287 - 2.2994 = 5.7293$$

An F test is conducted to determine whether this reduction is significant.

The numerator of the F statistic is the reduction in SSE divided by the number of independent variables added to the original model. Here only one variable, x_2, has been added; thus, the numerator of the F statistic is

$$\frac{\text{SSE}(x_1) - \text{SSE}(x_1, x_2)}{1} = 5.7293$$

The numerator is a measure of the reduction in SSE per independent variable added to the model. The denominator of the F statistic is the mean square error for the model that includes all of the independent variables. For Butler Trucking, this corresponds to the model containing both x_1 and x_2; thus, $p = 2$ and

$$\text{MSE} = \frac{\text{SSE}(x_1, x_2)}{n - p - 1} = \frac{2.2994}{7} = 0.3285$$

The following F statistic provides the basis for testing whether the addition of x_2 is statistically significant.

$$F = \frac{\dfrac{\text{SSE}(x_1) - \text{SSE}(x_1, x_2)}{1}}{\dfrac{\text{SSE}(x_1, x_2)}{n - p - 1}} \qquad \textbf{(16.10)}$$

The numerator degrees of freedom for this F test is equal to the number of variables added to the model, and the denominator degrees of freedom is equal to $n - p - 1$.

For the Butler Trucking example, we obtain

$$F = \frac{\dfrac{5.7293}{1}}{\dfrac{2.2994}{7}} = \frac{5.7293}{0.3285} = 17.44$$

Using Excel, p-value = F.DIST.RT(17.44,1,7) = 0.0042.

Excel can be used to show that $F = 17.44$ provides a p-value $= 0.0042$. For a level of significance of $\alpha = 0.05$, we can reject the null hypothesis that x_2 is not statistically significant because the p-value $= 0.0042 < \alpha = 0.05$; in other words, adding x_2 to the model involving only x_1 results in a significant reduction in the error sum of squares.

When we want to test for the significance of adding only one independent variable to a model, the result found using the F test just described could also be obtained by using the t test for the significance of an individual parameter (described in Section 15.5). Indeed, the F statistic we just computed is the square of the t statistic used to test the significance of an individual parameter.

Because the t test is equivalent to the F test when only one independent variable is being added to the model, we can now further clarify the proper use of the t test for testing the significance of an individual parameter. If the t test shows that only one parameter is not significant, the corresponding variable can be dropped from the model. However, if the t test shows that two or more parameters are not significant, no more than one independent variable can ever be dropped from a model on the basis of a t test; if one variable is dropped, another variable that was not significant initially might become significant.

We now turn to a consideration of whether the addition of more than one independent variable—as a set—results in a significant reduction in the error sum of squares.

General Case

Consider the following multiple regression model involving q independent variables, where $q < p$.

$$y = \beta_0 + \beta_1 x_1 + \beta_2 x_2 + \cdots + \beta_q x_q + \epsilon \tag{16.11}$$

If we add variables $x_{q+1}, x_{q+2}, \ldots, x_p$ to this model, we obtain a model involving p independent variables.

$$\begin{aligned} y = \beta_0 &+ \beta_1 x_1 + \beta_2 x_2 + \cdots + \beta_q x_q \\ &+ \beta_{q+1} x_{q+1} + \beta_{q+2} x_{q+2} + \cdots + \beta_p x_p + \epsilon \end{aligned} \tag{16.12}$$

To test whether the addition of $x_{q+1}, x_{q+2}, \ldots, x_p$ is statistically significant, the null and alternative hypotheses can be stated as follows.

H_0: $\beta_{q+1} = \beta_{q+2} = \cdots = \beta_p = 0$

H_a: One or more of the parameters are not equal to zero

The following F statistic provides the basis for testing whether the additional independent variables are statistically significant.

$$F = \frac{\dfrac{\text{SSE}(x_1, x_2, \ldots, x_q) - \text{SSE}(x_1, x_2, \ldots, x_q, x_{q+1}, \ldots, x_p)}{p - q}}{\dfrac{\text{SSE}(x_1, x_2, \ldots, x_q, x_{q+1}, \ldots, x_p)}{n - p - 1}} \tag{16.13}$$

This F statistic has $p - q$ numerator degrees of freedom and $n - p - 1$ denominator degrees of freedom. If the corresponding p-value $\leq \alpha$ or $F > F_\alpha$, we reject H_0 and conclude that the set of additional independent variables is statistically significant. Note that for the special case where $q = 1$ and $p = 2$, equation (16.13) reduces to equation (16.10).

Many students find equation (16.13) somewhat complex. To provide a simpler description of this F statistic, we can refer to the model with the smaller number of independent variables as the reduced model and the model with the larger number of independent variables as the full model. If we let SSE(reduced) denote the error sum of squares for the reduced model and SSE(full) denote the error sum of squares for the full model, we can write the numerator of equation (16.13) as

$$\frac{\text{SSE(reduced)} - \text{SSE(full)}}{\text{Number of extra terms}} \tag{16.14}$$

Note that "Number of extra terms" in equation (16.14) denotes the difference between the number of independent variables in the full model and the number of independent variables in the reduced model. The denominator of equation (16.13) is the error sum of squares for the full model divided by the corresponding degrees of freedom; in other words, the denominator is the mean square error for the full model. Denoting the mean square error for the full model as MSE(full) enables us to write the F statistic as

$$F = \frac{\dfrac{\text{SSE(reduced)} - \text{SSE(full)}}{\text{Number of extra terms}}}{\text{MSE(full)}} \tag{16.15}$$

To illustrate the use of this F statistic, suppose we have a regression problem involving 30 observations. One model with the independent variables x_1, x_2, and x_3 has an error sum of squares of 150 and a second model with the independent variables x_1, x_2, x_3, x_4, and x_5 has an error sum of squares of 100. Did the addition of the two independent variables x_4 and x_5 result in a significant reduction in the error sum of squares?

First, note that the degrees of freedom for SST is $30 - 1 = 29$ and that the degrees of freedom for the regression sum of squares for the full model is 5 (the number of independent variables in the full model). Thus, the degrees of freedom for the error sum of squares for the full model is $n - p - 1 = 30 - 5 - 1 = 24$, and hence MSE(full) $= 0.100/24 = 4.17$. Therefore, the F statistic is

$$F = \frac{\dfrac{150 - 100}{2}}{4.17} = 6.00$$

Using Excel, p-value = F.DIST.RT(6,2,24) = 0.0077.

This computed F value is compared with the F value with 2 numerator and 24 denominator degrees of freedom. Excel can be used to show that $F = 6.00$ provides a p-value $= 0.0077$. Suppose the level of significance is $\alpha = 0.05$. Because the p-value $= 0.0077 < \alpha = 0.05$, we conclude that the addition of variables x_4 and x_5 is statistically significant.

Notes + Comments

Computation of the F statistic can also be based on the difference in the regression sums of squares. To show this form of the F statistic, we first note that

$$\text{SSE(reduced)} = \text{SST} - \text{SSR(reduced)}$$
$$\text{SSE(full)} = \text{SST} - \text{SSR(full)}$$

Hence

$$\begin{aligned}\text{SSE(reduced)} - \text{SSE(full)} &= [\text{SST} - \text{SSR(reduced)}] - [\text{SST} - \text{SSR(full)}] \\ &= \text{SSR(full)} - \text{SSR(reduced)}\end{aligned}$$

Thus,

$$F = \frac{\dfrac{\text{SSR(full)} - \text{SSR(reduced)}}{\text{Number of extra terms}}}{\text{MSE(full)}}$$

Exercises

Methods

10. In a regression analysis involving 27 observations, the following estimated regression equation was developed.

$$\hat{y} = 25.2 + 5.5x_1$$

For this estimated regression equation SST = 1,550 and SSE = 520. **LO 4**

a. At $\alpha = 0.05$, test whether x_1 is significant.

b. Suppose that variables x_2 and x_3 are added to the model and the following regression equation is obtained.

$$\hat{y} = 16.3 + 2.3x_1 + 12.1x_2 - 5.8x_3$$

For this estimated regression equation SST = 1,550 and SSE = 100.

c. Use an F test and a 0.05 level of significance to determine whether x_2 and x_3 together contribute significantly to the model.

11. In a regression analysis involving 30 observations, the following estimated regression equation was obtained.

$$\hat{y} = 17.6 + 3.8x_1 - 2.3x_2 + 7.6x_3 + 2.7x_4$$

For this estimated regression equation SST = 1,805 and SSR = 1,760. **LO 4**

a. At $\alpha = 0.05$, test the significance of the relationship among the variables.

Suppose variables x_1 and x_4 are dropped from the model and the following estimated regression equation is obtained.

$$\hat{y} = 11.1 - 3.6x_2 + 8.1x_3$$

For this model SST = 1,805 and SSR = 1,705.

b. Compute SSE(x_1, x_2, x_3, x_4).

c. Compute SSE(x_2, x_3).

d. Use an F test and a 0.05 level of significance to determine whether x_1 and x_4 contribute significantly to the model.

Applications

DATA*file*
stats_lpga

12. **Predicting LPGA Player's Average Score.** The Ladies Professional Golfers Association (LPGA) maintains statistics on performance and earnings for members of the LPGA Tour. Year-end performance statistics for 134 golfers appear in the file *stats_lpga* (LPGA website). Earnings ($1000s) is the total earnings in thousands of dollars; Scoring Avg. is the average score for all events; Greens in Reg. is the percentage of time a player is able to hit the greens in regulation; Putting Avg. is the average number of putts taken on greens hit in regulation; and Drive Accuracy is the percentage of times a tee shot comes to rest in the fairway. A green is considered hit in regulation if any part of the ball is touching the putting surface and the difference between the value of par for the hole and the number of strokes taken to hit the green is at least 2. **LO 4**

a. Develop an estimated regression equation that can be used to predict the average score for all events given the average number of putts taken on greens hit in regulation.

b. Develop an estimated regression equation that can be used to predict the average score for all events given the percentage of time a player is able to hit the greens in regulation, the average number of putts taken on greens hit in regulation, and the percentage of times a player's tee shot comes to rest in the fairway.

c. At the 0.05 level of significance, test whether the two independent variables added in part (b), the percentage of time a player is able to hit the greens in regulation and the percentage of times a player's tee shot comes to rest in the fairway, contribute significantly to the estimated regression equation developed in part (a). Explain.

DATA*file*
stats_lpga

13. **Predicting LPGA Player's Total Earnings.** Refer to the description in problem 12. **LO 4**
    a. Develop an estimated regression equation that can be used to predict the total earnings for all events given the average number of putts taken on greens hit in regulation.
    b. Develop an estimated regression equation that can be used to predict the total earnings for all events given the average number of putts taken on greens hit in regulation, the percentage of time a player is able to hit the greens in regulation, and the percentage of times a player's tee shot comes to rest in the fairway.
    c. At the 0.05 level of significance, test whether the two independent variables added in part (b), the percentage of time a player is able to hit the greens in regulation and the percentage of times a player's tee shot comes to rest in the fairway, contribute significantly to the estimated regression equation developed in part (a). Explain.
    d. In general, lower scores should lead to higher earnings. To investigate this option for predicting total earnings, develop an estimated regression equation that can be used to predict total earnings for all events given the average score for all events. Would you prefer to use this equation to predict total earnings, or would you prefer to use the estimated regression equation developed in part (b)? Explain.

14. **Predicting the Risk of Stroke.** A 10-year study conducted by the American Heart Association provided data on how age, systolic blood pressure, and smoking relate to the risk of strokes. Data from a portion of this study follow. Risk is interpreted as the probability (times 100) that a person will have a stroke over the next 10-year period. For the smoker variable, 1 indicates a smoker and 0 indicates a nonsmoker. **LO 2, 4**

DATA*file*
stroke

Risk	Age (years)	Systolic Blood Pressure (mmHg)	Smoker
12	57	152	0
24	67	163	0
13	58	155	0
56	86	177	1
28	59	196	0
51	76	189	1
18	56	155	1
31	78	120	0
37	80	135	1
15	78	98	0
22	71	152	0
36	70	173	1
15	67	135	1
48	77	209	1
15	60	199	0
36	82	119	1
8	66	166	0
34	80	125	1
3	62	117	0
37	59	207	1

a. Develop an estimated regression equation that can be used to predict the risk of stroke given the age and blood-pressure level.
b. Consider adding two independent variables to the model developed in part (a), one for the interaction between age and blood-pressure level and the other for whether the person is a smoker. Develop an estimated regression equation using these four independent variables.
c. At a 0.05 level of significance, test to see whether the addition of the interaction term and the smoker variable contribute significantly to the estimated regression equation developed in part (a).

15. **Natural Gas Utility Bills.** The average monthly residential gas bill for Black Hills Energy customers in Cheyenne, Wyoming, is $67.95 (Wyoming Public Service Commission website). How is the average monthly gas bill for a Cheyenne residence related to the square footage, number of rooms, and age of the residence? The following data show the average monthly gas bill for last year, square footage, number of rooms, and age for 20 typical Cheyenne residences. LO 4

DATA*file*
naturalgas

Average Monthly Gas Bill for Last Year ($)	Age	Square Footage	Number of Rooms
70.20	16	2,537	6
81.33	2	3,437	8
45.86	27	976	6
59.21	11	1,713	7
117.88	16	3,979	11
57.78	2	1,328	7
47.01	27	1,251	6
52.89	4	827	5
32.90	12	645	4
67.04	29	2,849	5
76.76	1	2,392	7
60.40	26	900	5
44.07	14	1,386	5
26.68	20	1,299	4
62.70	17	1,441	6
45.37	13	562	4
38.09	10	2,140	4
45.31	22	908	6
52.45	24	1,568	5
96.11	27	1,140	10

a. Develop an estimated regression equation that can be used to predict a residence's average monthly gas bill for last year given its age.
b. Develop an estimated regression equation that can be used to predict a residence's average monthly gas bill for last year given its age, square footage, and number of rooms.
c. At the 0.05 level of significance, test whether the two independent variables added in part (b), the square footage and the number of rooms, contribute significantly to the estimated regression equation developed in part (a).

16.3 Variable Selection Procedures

Variable selection procedures are particularly useful in the early stages of building a model, but they cannot substitute for experience and judgment on the part of the analyst.

In this section, we discuss four variable selection procedures: stepwise regression, forward selection, backward elimination, and best-subsets regression. Given a data set with several possible independent variables, we can use these procedures to identify which independent variables provide the best model. The first three procedures are iterative; at each step of the procedure a single independent variable is added or deleted and the new model is evaluated. The process continues until a stopping criterion indicates that the procedure cannot find a better model. The last procedure (best subsets) is not a one-variable-at-a-time procedure; it evaluates regression models involving all possible subsets of the specified independent variables.

In the stepwise regression, forward selection, and backward elimination procedures, the criterion for selecting an independent variable to add or delete from the model at each step is based on the F statistic introduced in Section 16.2. Suppose, for instance, that we are considering adding x_2 to a model involving x_1 or deleting x_2 from a model involving x_1 and x_2. To test whether the addition or deletion of x_2 is statistically significant, the null and alternative hypotheses can be stated as follows:

$$H_0\colon \beta_2 = 0$$
$$H_a\colon \beta_2 \neq 0$$

In Section 16.2, (see equation (16.10)) we showed that

$$F = \frac{\dfrac{\text{SSE}(x_1) - \text{SSE}(x_1, x_2)}{1}}{\dfrac{\text{SSE}(x_1, x_2)}{n - p - 1}}$$

can be used as a criterion for determining whether the presence of x_2 in the model causes a significant reduction in the error sum of squares. The p-value corresponding to this F statistic is the criterion used to determine whether an independent variable should be added or deleted from the regression model. The usual rejection rule applies: Reject H_0 if p-value $\leq \alpha$.

To provide an illustration of variable selection procedures, we introduce the Cravens data set consisting of 25 observations on eight independent variables.[1]

Regression Analysis of Cravens Example

The Cravens data are for a company that sells products in several sales territories, each of which is assigned to a single sales representative. A regression analysis was conducted to determine whether a variety of predictor (independent) variables could explain sales in each territory. A random sample of 25 sales territories resulted in the data in Table 16.5; the variable definitions are given in Table 16.6.

To access the correlation tool, click **Data Analysis** *in the* **Analysis** *group on the* **Data** *tab.*

As a preliminary step, let us consider the sample correlation coefficients between each pair of variables. Figure 16.10 is the correlation matrix obtained by using Excel's Correlation tool. The sample correlation coefficient between Sales and Time is 0.623, between Sales and Poten it is 0.598, and so on.

Looking at the sample correlation coefficients between the independent variables, we see that the correlation between Time and Accounts is 0.758; hence, if Accounts were used as an independent variable, Time would not add much more explanatory power to the model. Recall the rule-of-thumb test from the discussion of multicollinearity in Section 15.5: Multicollinearity can cause problems if the absolute value of the sample correlation coefficient exceeds 0.7 for any two of the independent variables. If possible, then, we should avoid including both Time and Accounts in the same regression model. The sample correlation coefficient of 0.549 between Change and Rating is also high and may warrant further consideration.

Looking at the sample correlation coefficients between Sales and each of the independent variables can give us a quick indication of which independent variables are, by themselves, good predictors. We see that the single best predictor of Sales is Accounts, because it has the highest sample correlation coefficient (0.754). Recall that for the case of one independent variable, the square of the sample correlation coefficient is the coefficient of determination. Thus, Accounts can explain $(0.754)^2(100)$, or 56.85%, of the variability in Sales. The next most important independent variables are Time, Poten, and AdvExp, each with a sample correlation coefficient of approximately 0.6.

Although the potential for multicollinearity problems is present, let us consider developing an estimated regression equation using all eight independent variables.

[1]For details see David W. Cravens, Robert B. Woodruff, and Joe C. Stamper, "An Analytical Approach for Evaluating Sales Territory Performance," *Journal of Marketing*, 36 (January 1972): 31–37. Copyright © 1972 American Marketing Association.

DATA*file*
cravens

Table 16.5 The Cravens Data

Sales	Time	Poten	AdvExp	Share	Change	Accounts	Work	Rating
3,669.88	43.10	74,065.1	4,582.9	2.51	0.34	74.86	15.05	4.9
3,473.95	108.13	58,117.3	5,539.8	5.51	0.15	107.32	19.97	5.1
2,295.10	13.82	21,118.5	2,950.4	10.91	−0.72	96.75	17.34	2.9
4,675.56	186.18	68,521.3	2,243.1	8.27	0.17	195.12	13.40	3.4
6,125.96	161.79	57,805.1	7,747.1	9.15	0.50	180.44	17.64	4.6
2,134.94	8.94	37,806.9	402.4	5.51	0.15	104.88	16.22	4.5
5,031.66	365.04	50,935.3	3,140.6	8.54	0.55	256.10	18.80	4.6
3,367.45	220.32	35,602.1	2,086.2	7.07	−0.49	126.83	19.86	2.3
6,519.45	127.64	46,176.8	8,846.2	12.54	1.24	203.25	17.42	4.9
4,876.37	105.69	42,053.2	5,673.1	8.85	0.31	119.51	21.41	2.8
2,468.27	57.72	36,829.7	2,761.8	5.38	0.37	116.26	16.32	3.1
2,533.31	23.58	33,612.7	1,991.8	5.43	−0.65	142.28	14.51	4.2
2,408.11	13.82	21,412.8	1,971.5	8.48	0.64	89.43	19.35	4.3
2,337.38	13.82	20,416.9	1,737.4	7.80	1.01	84.55	20.02	4.2
4,586.95	86.99	36,272.0	10,694.2	10.34	0.11	119.51	15.26	5.5
2,729.24	165.85	23,093.3	8,618.6	5.15	0.04	80.49	15.87	3.6
3,289.40	116.26	26,878.6	7,747.9	6.64	0.68	136.58	7.81	3.4
2,800.78	42.28	39,572.0	4,565.8	5.45	0.66	78.86	16.00	4.2
3,264.20	52.84	51,866.1	6,022.7	6.31	−0.10	136.58	17.44	3.6
3,453.62	165.04	58,749.8	3,721.1	6.35	−0.03	138.21	17.98	3.1
1,741.45	10.57	23,990.8	861.0	7.37	−1.63	75.61	20.99	1.6
2,035.75	13.82	25,694.9	3,571.5	8.39	−0.43	102.44	21.66	3.4
1,578.00	8.13	23,736.3	2,845.5	5.15	0.04	76.42	21.46	2.7
4,167.44	58.44	34,314.3	5,060.1	12.88	0.22	136.58	24.78	2.8
2,799.97	21.14	22,809.5	3,552.0	9.14	−0.74	88.62	24.96	3.9

Table 16.6 Variable Definitions for the Cravens Data

Variable	Definition
Sales	Total sales credited to the sales representative
Time	Length of time employed in months
Poten	Market potential; total industry sales in units for the sales territory*
AdvExp	Advertising expenditure in the sales territory
Share	Market share; weighted average for the past four years
Change	Change in the market share over the previous four years
Accounts	Number of accounts assigned to the sales representative*
Work	Workload; a weighted index based on annual purchases and concentrations of accounts
Rating	Sales representative overall rating on eight performance dimensions; an aggregate rating on a 1–7 scale

*These data were coded to preserve confidentiality.

Excel's Regression tool provided the results in Figure 16.11. The eight-variable multiple regression model has an adjusted coefficient of determination (Adjusted R Square) of 0.8331. Note, however, that the *P-value* column (the *p*-values for the *t* tests of individual parameters) shows that only Poten, AdvExp, and Share are significant at the $\alpha = 0.05$ level, given the effect of all the other variables. Hence, we might be inclined to investigate the results that

Figure 16.10 Sample Correlation Coefficients for the Cravens Data

	Sales	Time	Poten	AdvExp	Share	Change	Accounts	Work
Time	0.623							
Poten	0.598	0.454						
AdvExp	0.596	0.249	0.174					
Share	0.484	0.106	−0.211	0.264				
Change	0.489	0.251	0.268	0.377	0.085			
Accounts	0.754	0.758	0.479	0.200	0.403	0.327		
Work	−0.117	−0.179	−0.259	−0.272	0.349	−0.288	−0.199	
Rating	0.402	0.101	0.359	0.411	−0.024	0.549	0.229	-0.277

Figure 16.11 Regression Tool Output Using All Eight Independent Variables

	A	B	C	D	E	F	G	H	I
1	SUMMARY OUTPUT								
2									
3	*Regression Statistics*								
4	Multiple R	0.9602							
5	R Square	0.9220							
6	Adjusted R Square	0.8831							
7	Standard Error	449.0154							
8	Observations	25							
9									
10	ANOVA								
11		*df*	*SS*	*MS*	*F*	*Significance F*			
12	Regression	8	38,153,712.1137	4,769,214.0142	23.6551	0.0000			
13	Residual	16	3,225,836.8131	201,614.8008					
14	Total	24	41,379,548.9269						
15									
16		*Coefficients*	*Standard Error*	*t Stat*	*P-value*	*Lower 95%*	*Upper 95%*	*Lower 99.0%*	*Upper 99.0%*
17	Intercept	-1,507.8358	778.6084	-1.9366	0.0707	-3,158.4119	142.7403	-3,781.9809	766.3094
18	Time	2.0101	1.9305	1.0412	0.3132	-2.0824	6.1026	-3.6285	7.6487
19	Poten	0.0372	0.0082	4.5361	0.0003	0.0198	0.0546	0.0132	0.0612
20	AdvExp	0.1510	0.0471	3.2051	0.0055	0.0511	0.2508	0.0134	0.2886
21	Share	199.0402	67.0291	2.9695	0.0090	56.9447	341.1356	3.2627	394.8177
22	Change	290.8666	186.7769	1.5573	0.1390	-105.0827	686.8159	-254.6679	836.4010
23	Accounts	5.5497	4.7754	1.1621	0.2622	-4.5737	15.6732	-8.3983	19.4978
24	Work	19.7939	33.6752	0.5878	0.5649	-51.5943	91.1821	-78.5639	118.1517
25	Rating	8.1890	128.4985	0.0637	0.9500	-264.2155	280.5936	-367.1269	383.5050
26									

would be obtained if we used just those three variables. Figure 16.12 shows the Excel results obtained for the estimated regression equation with those three variables. We see that the estimated regression equation has an adjusted coefficient of determination of 0.8274, which is almost as high as that for the eight-independent-variable estimated regression equation.

How can we find an estimated regression equation that will do the best job given the data available? One approach is to compute all possible regressions. That is, we could develop 8 one-variable estimated regression equations (each of which corresponds to one of the independent variables), 28 two-variable estimated regression equations (the number of combinations of eight variables taken two at a time), and so on. In all, for the Cravens data, 255 different estimated regression equations involving one or more independent variables would have to be fitted to the data.

With the powerful statistical software packages available today, it is possible to compute all possible regressions. But doing so involves a substantial amount of computation and requires the model builder to review a large volume of computer output, much of which is associated with obviously poor models. Statisticians prefer a more systematic approach

Figure 16.12 Regression Tool Output Using Three Independent Variables: Poten, AdvExp, and Share

	A	B	C	D	E	F	G	H	I	J
1	SUMMARY OUTPUT									
2										
3	*Regression Statistics*									
4	Multiple R	0.9214								
5	R Square	0.8490								
6	Adjusted R Square	0.8274								
7	Standard Error	545.5151								
8	Observations	25								
9										
10	ANOVA									
11		*df*	*SS*	*MS*	*F*	*Significance F*				
12	Regression	3	35,130,228.2856	11,710,076.0952	39.3501	0.0000				
13	Residual	21	6,249,320.6413	297,586.6972						
14	Total	24	41,379,548.9269							
15										
16		*Coefficients*	*Standard Error*	*t Stat*	*P-value*	*Lower 95%*	*Upper 95%*	*Lower 99.0%*	*Upper 99.0%*	
17	Intercept	-1,603.5821	505.5509	-3.1719	0.0046	-2,654.9328	-552.2315	-3,034.9786	-172.1857	
18	Poten	0.0543	0.0075	7.2632	0.0000	0.0387	0.0698	0.0331	0.0754	
19	AdvExp	0.1675	0.0443	3.7829	0.0011	0.0754	0.2596	0.0421	0.2928	
20	Share	282.7469	48.7556	5.7993	0.0000	181.3541	384.1398	144.7023	420.7916	
21										

to selecting the subset of independent variables that provide the best estimated regression equation. In the next section, we introduce some of the more popular approaches.

Stepwise Regression

Excel does not have built-in capabilities for performing the stepwise regression, forward selection, and backward elimination procedures.

The **stepwise regression** procedure begins each step by determining whether any of the variables already in the model should be removed. It does so by first computing an F statistic (as shown previously) and corresponding p-value for each independent variable in the model. Here we refer to the level of significance α for determining whether an independent variable should be removed from the model as *p Value to Leave*. If the p-value for any independent variable is greater than *p Value to Leave,* the independent variable with the largest p-value is removed from the model and the stepwise regression procedure begins a new step.

If no independent variable can be removed from the model, the procedure attempts to enter another independent variable into the model. It does so by first computing an F statistic and corresponding p-value for each independent variable that is not in the model. We refer to the level of significance α for determining whether an independent variable should be entered into the model as *p Value to Enter.* The independent variable with the smallest p-value is entered into the model provided its p-value is less than *p Value to Enter*. The procedure continues in this manner until no independent variables can be deleted from or added to the model.

Because the one-at-a time procedures do not consider every possible subset for a given number of independent variables, they will not necessarily select the model with the highest R-Square value.

In summary, at each step of the stepwise regression procedure the first consideration is to see whether any independent variable can be removed from the current model. If none of the independent variables can be removed from the model, the procedure checks to see whether any of the independent variables that are not currently in the model can be entered. Because of the nature of the stepwise regression procedure, an independent variable can enter the model at one step, be removed at a subsequent step, and then enter the model at a later step. The procedure stops when no independent variables can be removed from or entered into the model.

Forward Selection

The **forward selection** procedure starts with no independent variables. It adds variables one at a time using the same procedure as stepwise regression for determining whether an independent variable should be entered into the model. However, the forward selection procedure does not permit a variable to be removed from the model once it has been entered. The procedure stops when the p-value for each of the independent variables not in the model is greater than *p Value to Enter*.

Backward Elimination

The **backward elimination** procedure begins with a model that includes all the independent variables. It then deletes one independent variable at a time using the same procedure as stepwise regression. However, the backward elimination procedure does not permit an independent variable to be reentered once it has been removed. The procedure stops when none of the independent variables in the model has a *p*-value greater than *p Value to Leave.*

Forward selection and backward elimination may lead to different models.

Forward selection and backward elimination are the two extremes of model building; the forward selection procedure starts with no independent variables in the model and adds independent variables one at a time, whereas the backward elimination procedure starts with all independent variables in the model and deletes variables one at a time. The two procedures may lead to the same estimated regression equation. It is possible, however, for them to lead to two different estimated regression equations. Deciding which estimated regression equation to use remains a topic for discussion. Ultimately, the analyst's judgment must be applied.

Best-Subsets Regression

Stepwise regression, forward selection, and backward elimination are approaches to choosing the regression model by adding or deleting independent variables one at a time. Hence, they offer no guarantee that the best model for a given number of variables will be found. These one-variable-at-a-time procedures are properly viewed as heuristics for selecting a good regression model.

Many statistical software packages have a procedure called **best-subsets regression** that enables the user to find, given a specified number of independent variables, the best regression equation. Typical output from such packages will enable the user to identify the two best one-variable estimated regression equations, the two best two-variable regression equations, the two best three-variable regression equations, and so on. The criterion used in determining which estimated regression equations are best for any number of predictors is usually the value of the coefficient of determination.

Notes + Comments

1. Functions of the independent variables can be used to create new independent variables for use with any of the procedures in this section. For instance, if we wanted x_1x_2 in the model to account for interaction, we would use the data for x_1 and x_2 to create the data for $z = x_1x_2$.
2. None of the procedures that add or delete variables one at a time can be guaranteed to identify the best regression model. But they are excellent approaches to finding good models—especially when little multicollinearity is present.
3. The stepwise, forward selection, backward elimination, and best-subsets approaches to building a regression model can be implemented in Excel. However, this would be very inefficient as each approach would potentially require several steps in which various models based on what was learned in the previous step would have to be estimated. Most statistical software (including JMP and R) are capable of implementing each of these algorithms automatically.

16.4 Multiple Regression Approach to Experimental Design

In Chapter 13, we discuss experimental design, and specifically the application of the completely randomized design to the Chemitech example.

In Section 15.7, we discussed the use of dummy variables in multiple regression analysis. In this section we show how the use of dummy variables in a multiple regression equation can provide another approach to solving experimental design problems. We will demonstrate the multiple regression approach to experimental design by applying it to the Chemitech, Inc., completely randomized design.

Chemitech has developed a new filtration system for municipal water supplies. The components for the new filtration system will be purchased from several suppliers, and

Table 16.7 Number of Units Produced by 15 Workers

	Method	
A	B	C
58	58	48
64	69	57
55	71	59
66	64	47
67	68	49

Chemitech will assemble the components at its plant in Columbia, South Carolina. Three different assembly methods, referred to as methods A, B, and C, have been proposed. Managers at Chemitech want to determine which assembly method can produce the greatest number of filtration systems per week.

A random sample of 15 employees was selected, and each of the three assembly methods was randomly assigned to 5 employees. The number of units assembled by each employee is shown in Table 16.7. The sample mean number of units produced with each of the three assembly methods is as follows:

Assembly Method	Mean Number Produced
A	62
B	66
C	52

Although method B appears to result in higher production rates than either of the other methods, the issue is whether the three sample means observed are different enough for us to conclude that the means of the populations corresponding to the three methods of assembly are different.

We begin the regression approach to this problem by defining dummy variables that will be used to indicate which assembly method is used. Because the Chemitech problem has three assembly methods or treatments, we need two dummy variables. In general, if the factor being investigated involves k distinct levels or treatments, we need to define $k - 1$ dummy variables. For the Chemitech experiment we define dummy variables A and B as shown in Table 16.8.

We can use the dummy variables to relate the number of units produced per week, y, to the method of assembly the employee uses.

$$\begin{aligned} E(y) &= \text{Expected value of the number of units produced per week} \\ &= \beta_0 + \beta_1\text{A} + \beta_2\text{B} \end{aligned}$$

Table 16.8 Dummy Variables for the Chemitech Experiment

A	B	
1	0	Observation is associated with assembly method A
0	1	Observation is associated with assembly method B
0	0	Observation is associated with assembly method C

Thus, if we are interested in the expected value of the number of units assembled per week for an employee who uses method C, our procedure for assigning numerical values to the dummy variables would result in setting A = B = 0. The multiple regression equation then reduces to

$$E(y) = \beta_0 + \beta_1(0) + \beta_2(0) = \beta_0$$

We can interpret β_0 as the expected value of the number of units assembled per week for an employee who uses method C. In other words, β_0 is the mean number of units assembled per week using method C.

Next let us consider the forms of the multiple regression equation for each of the other methods. For method A, the values of the dummy variables are A = 1 and B = 0, and

$$E(y) = \beta_0 + \beta_1(1) + \beta_2(0) = \beta_0 + \beta_1$$

For method B, we set A = 0 and B = 1, and

$$E(y) = \beta_0 + \beta_1(0) + \beta_2(1) = \beta_0 + \beta_2$$

We see that $\beta_0 + \beta_1$ represents the mean number of units assembled per week using method A, and $\beta_0 + \beta_2$ represents the mean number of units assembled per week using method B.

We now want to estimate the coefficient of β_0, β_1, and β_2 and hence develop an estimate of the mean number of units assembled per week for each method. Table 16.9 shows the sample data, and Figure 16.13 shows a portion of the corresponding Excel Regression tool multiple regression output. We see that the estimates of β_0, β_1, and β_2 are $b_0 = 52$, $b_1 = 10$, and $b_2 = 14$. Thus, the best estimate of the mean number of units assembled per week for each assembly method is as follows:

Assembly Method	Estimate of $E(y)$
A	$b_0 + b_1 = 52 + 10 = 62$
B	$b_0 + b_2 = 52 + 14 = 66$
C	$b_0 = 52$

Note that the estimate of the mean number of units produced with each of the three assembly methods obtained from the regression analysis is the same as the sample mean shown previously.

Table 16.9 Input Data for the Chemitech Completely Randomized Design

A	B	y
1	0	58
1	0	64
1	0	55
1	0	66
1	0	67
0	1	58
0	1	69
0	1	71
0	1	64
0	1	68
0	0	48
0	0	57
0	0	59
0	0	47
0	0	49

DATA*file*
chemitech2

The file chemitech2 contains the data from the chemitech file reorganized for a linear regression analysis.

Figure 16.13 Multiple Regression Output for the Chemitech Completely Randomized Design

	A	B	C	D	E	F	G	H	I	J
1	SUMMARY OUTPUT									
2										
3	*Regression Statistics*									
4	Multiple R	0.7776								
5	R Square	0.6047								
6	Adjusted R Square	0.5388								
7	Standard Error	5.3229								
8	Observations	15								
9										
10	ANOVA									
11		*df*	*SS*	*MS*	*F*	*Significance F*				
12	Regression	2	520.0000	260.0000	9.1765	0.0038				
13	Residual	12	340.0000	28.3333						
14	Total	14	860.0000							
15										
16		*Coefficients*	*Standard Error*	*t Stat*	*P-value*	*Lower 95%*	*Upper 95%*	*Lower 99.0%*	*Upper 99.0%*	
17	Intercept	52.0000	2.3805	21.8444	0.0000	46.8134	57.1866	44.7287	59.2713	
18	A	10.0000	3.3665	2.9704	0.0117	2.6650	17.3350	-0.2831	20.2831	
19	B	14.0000	3.3665	4.1586	0.0013	6.6650	21.3350	3.7169	24.2831	
20										

Now let us see how we can use the output from the multiple regression analysis to perform the ANOVA test on the difference among the means for the three plants. First, we observe that if the means do not differ

$$E(y) \text{ for method A} - E(y) \text{ for method C} = 0$$
$$E(y) \text{ for method B} - E(y) \text{ for method C} = 0$$

Because β_0 equals $E(y)$ for method C and $\beta_0 + \beta_1$ equals $E(y)$ for method A, the first difference is equal to $(\beta_0 + \beta_1) - \beta_0 = \beta_1$. Moreover, because $\beta_0 + \beta_2$ equals $E(y)$ for method B, the second difference is equal to $(\beta_0 + \beta_2) - \beta_0 = \beta_2$. We would conclude that the three methods do not differ if $\beta_1 = 0$ and $\beta_2 = 0$. Hence, the null hypothesis for a test for difference of means can be stated as

$$H_0\colon \beta_1 = \beta_2 = 0$$

Suppose the level of significance is $\alpha = 0.05$. Recall that to test this type of null hypothesis about the significance of the regression relationship we use the F test for overall significance. The Excel output in Figure 16.13 shows that the p-value corresponding to $F = 9.1765$ is 0.0038. Because the p-value $= 0.0038 < \alpha = 0.05$, we reject $H_0\colon \beta_1 = \beta_2 = 0$ and conclude that the means for the three assembly methods are not the same. Because the F test shows that the multiple regression relationship is significant, a t test can be conducted to determine the significance of the individual parameters, β_1 and β_2. Using $\alpha = 0.05$, the p-values of 0.0117 and 0.0013 on the Excel output indicate that we can reject $H_0\colon \beta_1 = 0$ and $H_0\colon \beta_2 = 0$. Hence, both parameters are statistically significant. Thus, we can also conclude that the means for methods A and C are different and that the means for methods B and C are different.

Exercises

Methods

16. Consider a completely randomized design involving three treatments: A, B, and C. Write a multiple regression equation that can be used to analyze these data. Define all variables. **LO 6**

17. Consider a completely randomized design involving four treatments: A, B, C, and D. Write a multiple regression equation that can be used to analyze these data. Define all variables. **LO 6**

18. Write a multiple regression equation that can be used to analyze the data for a randomized block design involving three treatments and two blocks. Define all variables. **LO 6**

19. Write a multiple regression equation that can be used to analyze the data for a two-factorial design with two levels for factor A and three levels for factor B. Define all variables. **LO 6**

Applications

DATA*file*
jacobs

20. **Estimating Process Time on Different Mixer Machines.** The Jacobs Chemical Company wants to estimate the mean time (minutes) required to process a batch of material on mixer machines produced by three different manufacturers. To limit the cost of testing, four batches of material were mixed on machines produced by each of the three manufacturers. The times needed to mix the material follow. **LO 6**

Manufacturer 1	Manufacturer 2	Manufacturer 3
20	28	20
26	26	19
24	31	23
22	27	22

a. Write a multiple regression equation that can be used to analyze the data.
b. What are the best estimates of the coefficients in your regression equation?
c. In terms of the regression equation coefficients, what hypotheses must we test to see whether the mean time to mix a batch of material is the same for all three manufacturers?
d. For an $\alpha = 0.05$ level of significance, what conclusion should be drawn?

21. **Estimating Drying Time of Different Paints.** Four different paints are advertised as having the same drying time. To check the manufacturers' claims, five samples were tested for each of the paints. The time in minutes until the paint was dry enough for a second coat to be applied was recorded for each sample. The data obtained follow. **LO 6**

DATA*file*
paint

Paint 1	Paint 2	Paint 3	Paint 4
128	144	133	150
137	133	143	142
135	142	137	135
124	146	136	140
141	130	131	153

a. Use $\alpha = 0.05$ to test for any significant differences in mean drying time among the paints.
b. What is your estimate of mean drying time for paint 2? How is it obtained from the computer output?

DATA*file*
tuneup

22. **Car Tune-Up Times.** An automobile dealer conducted a test to determine whether the time needed to complete a minor engine tune-up depends on whether a computerized engine analyzer or an electronic analyzer is used. Because tune-up time varies among compact, intermediate, and full-sized cars, the three types of cars were used as blocks in the experiment. The data (time in minutes) obtained follow. **LO 6**

		Car		
		Compact	Intermediate	Full Size
Analyzer	Computerized	50	55	63
	Electronic	42	44	46

Use $\alpha = 0.05$ to test for any significant differences.

DATA*file*
bannerads

23. **Effect of Banner Ad Size and Design.** Mbuy is a media consulting firm that provides advice to companies on how to allocate their advertising budgets. Mbuy designed a factorial experiment to test the effect of the size of a banner ad on a website and the ad design on the number (in thousands) of product inquiries received. Three advertising designs and two sizes of advertisements were considered. The following data were obtained. Test for any significant effects due to type of design, size of advertisement, or interaction. Use $\alpha = 0.05$. **LO 6**

		Size of Advertisement	
		Small	Large
Design	A	8	12
		12	8
	B	22	26
		14	30
	C	10	18
		18	14

16.5 Autocorrelation and the Durbin–Watson Test

Often, the data used for regression studies are collected over time. It is not uncommon for the value of y at time t, denoted by y_t, to be related to the value of y at previous time periods. In such cases, we say **autocorrelation** (also called **serial correlation**) is present in the data. If the value of y in time period t is related to its value in time period $t - 1$, first-order autocorrelation is present. If the value of y in time period t is related to the value of y in time period $t - 2$, second-order autocorrelation is present, and so on.

When autocorrelation is present, one of the assumptions of the regression model is violated: the error terms are not independent. In the case of first-order autocorrelation, the error at time t, denoted ϵ_t, will be related to the error at time period $t - 1$, denoted ϵ_{t-1}. Two cases of first-order autocorrelation are illustrated in Figure 16.14. Panel A is the case of positive autocorrelation; panel B is the case of negative autocorrelation. With positive autocorrelation we expect a positive residual in one period to be followed by a positive residual in the next period, a negative residual in one period to be followed by a negative residual in the next period, and so on. With negative autocorrelation, we expect a positive residual in one period to be followed by a negative residual in the next period, then a positive residual, and so on.

When autocorrelation is present, serious errors can be made in performing tests of statistical significance based upon the assumed regression model. It is therefore important to be able to detect autocorrelation and take corrective action. We will show how the Durbin–Watson statistic can be used to detect first-order autocorrelation.

Suppose the values of ϵ are not independent but are related in the following manner:

$$\epsilon_t = \rho\epsilon_{t-1} + z_t \tag{16.16}$$

where ρ is a parameter with an absolute value less than one and z_t is a normally and independently distributed random variable with a mean of zero and a variance of σ^2.

Figure 16.14 Two Data Sets with First-Order Autocorrelation

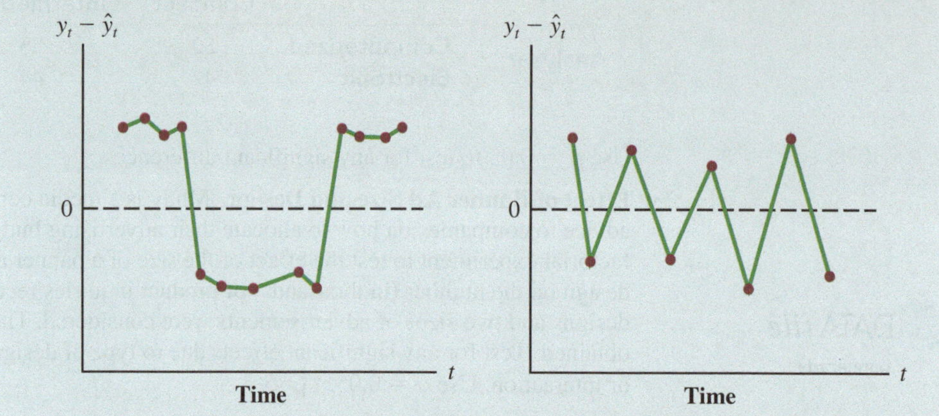

Panel A. Positive Autocorrelation **Panel B. Negative Autocorrelation**

From equation (16.16) we see that if $\rho = 0$, the error terms are not related, and each has a mean of zero and a variance of σ^2. In this case, there is no autocorrelation and the regression assumptions are satisfied. If $\rho > 0$, we have positive autocorrelation; if $\rho < 0$, we have negative autocorrelation. In either of these cases, the regression assumptions about the error term are violated.

The **Durbin–Watson test** for autocorrelation uses the residuals to determine whether $\rho = 0$. To simplify the notation for the Durbin–Watson statistic, we denote the tth residual by $e_t = y_t - \hat{y}_t$. The Durbin–Watson test statistic is computed as follows.

Durbin–Watson Test Statistic

$$d = \frac{\sum_{t=2}^{n}(e_t - e_{t-1})^2}{\sum_{t=1}^{n} e_t^2} \tag{16.17}$$

If successive values of the residuals are close together (positive autocorrelation), the value of the Durbin–Watson test statistic will be small. If successive values of the residuals are far apart (negative autocorrelation), the value of the Durbin–Watson statistic will be large.

The Durbin–Watson test statistic ranges in value from zero to four, with a value of two indicating no autocorrelation is present. Durbin and Watson developed tables that can be used to determine when their test statistic indicates the presence of autocorrelation. Table 16.10 shows lower and upper bounds (d_L and d_U) for hypothesis tests using $\alpha = 0.05$; n denotes the number of observations. The null hypothesis to be tested is always that there is no autocorrelation.

$$H_0: \rho = 0$$

The alternative hypothesis to test for positive autocorrelation is

$$H_a: \rho > 0$$

Table 16.10 Critical Values for the Durbin–Watson Test for Autocorrelation

Note: Entries in the table are the critical values for a one-tailed Durbin–Watson test for autocorrelation. For a two-tailed test, the level of significance is doubled.

Significance Points of d_L and d_U: $\alpha = 0.05$
Number of Independent Variables

	1		2		3		4		5	
n^*	d_L	d_U	d_L	d_U	d_L	d_U	d_L	d_U	d_L	d_U
15	1.08	1.36	0.95	1.54	0.82	1.75	0.69	1.97	0.56	2.21
20	1.20	1.41	1.10	1.54	1.00	1.68	0.90	1.83	0.79	1.99
25	1.29	1.45	1.21	1.55	1.12	1.66	1.04	1.77	0.95	1.89
30	1.35	1.49	1.28	1.57	1.21	1.65	1.14	1.74	1.07	1.83
40	1.44	1.54	1.39	1.60	1.34	1.66	1.29	1.72	1.23	1.79
50	1.50	1.59	1.46	1.63	1.42	1.67	1.38	1.72	1.34	1.77
70	1.58	1.64	1.55	1.67	1.52	1.70	1.49	1.74	1.46	1.77
100	1.65	1.69	1.63	1.72	1.61	1.74	1.59	1.76	1.57	1.78

*Interpolate linearly for intermediate *n* values.

The alternative hypothesis to test for negative autocorrelation is

$$H_a\colon \rho < 0$$

A two-sided test is also possible. In this case the alternative hypothesis is

$$H_a\colon \rho \neq 0$$

Figure 16.15 shows how the values of d_L and d_U in Table 16.10 are used to test for autocorrelation. Panel A illustrates the test for positive autocorrelation. If $d < d_L$, we conclude that positive autocorrelation is present. If $d_L \leq d \leq d_U$, we say the test is inconclusive. If $d > d_U$, we conclude that there is no evidence of positive autocorrelation.

Panel B illustrates the test for negative autocorrelation. If $d > 4 - d_L$, we conclude that negative autocorrelation is present. If $4 - d_U \leq d \leq 4 - d_L$, we say the test is inconclusive. If $d < 4 - d_U$, we conclude that there is no evidence of negative autocorrelation.

Panel C illustrates the two-sided test. If $d < d_L$ or $d > 4 - d_L$, we reject H_0 and conclude that autocorrelation is present. If $d_L \leq d \leq d_U$ or $4 - d_U \leq d \leq 4 - d_L$, we say the test is inconclusive. If $d_U < d < 4 - d_U$, we conclude that there is no evidence of autocorrelation.

If significant autocorrelation is identified, we should investigate whether we omitted one or more key independent variables that have time-ordered effects on the dependent variable. If no such variables can be identified, including an independent variable that measures the time of the observation (for instance, the value of this variable could be one for the first observation, two for the second observation, and so on) will sometimes eliminate or reduce the autocorrelation. When these attempts to reduce or remove autocorrelation do not work, transformations on the dependent or independent variables can prove helpful; a discussion of such transformations can be found in more advanced texts on regression analysis.

Note that the Durbin–Watson tables list the smallest sample size as 15. The reason is that the test is generally inconclusive for smaller sample sizes; in fact, many statisticians believe the sample size should be at least 50 for the test to produce worthwhile results.

Figure 16.15 Hypothesis Test for Autocorrelation Using the Durbin–Watson Test

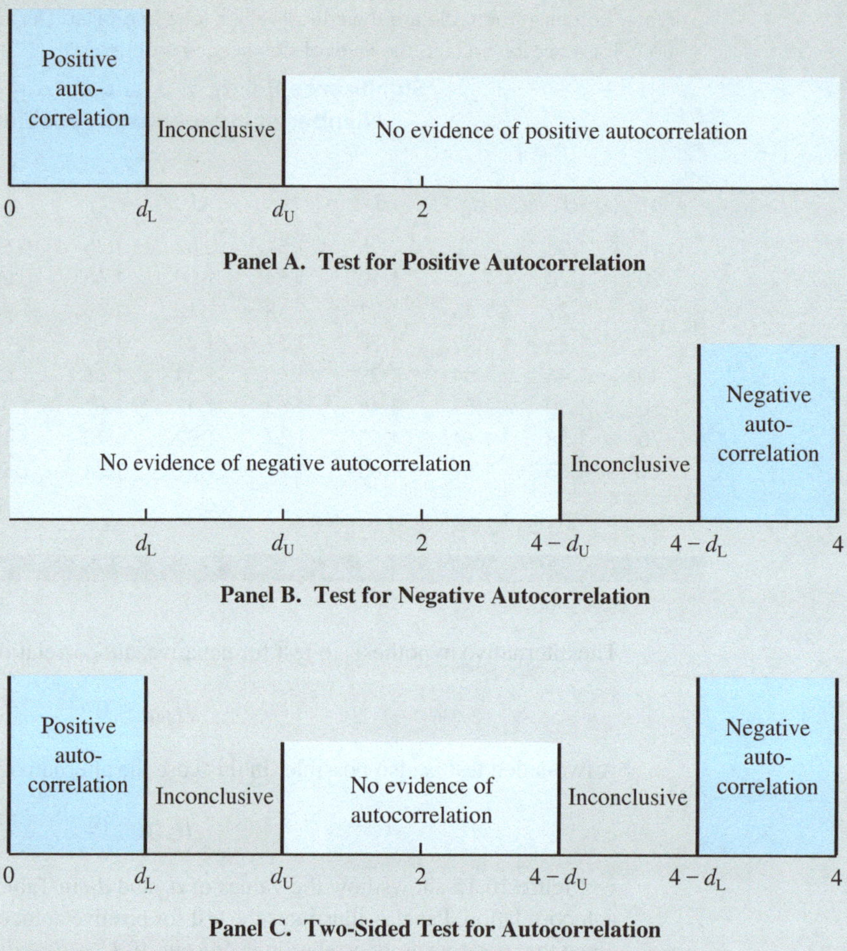

Jefe de Cocina Example

As a company advocating for sustainable living, Jefe de Cocina provides delicious, locally sourced meals to households in waste-free packaging. Table 16.11 contains data on Jefe de Cocina's sales (in \$ million) over the 20-year history of the company and the median income in the region which it operates.

Using the data in Table 16.11, an industry analyst has estimated the regression model:

$$\text{Sales} = -12.60671 + 0.00028 \text{ Income}$$

This model achieves an R Square = 0.97 on these data. The industry analyst is encouraged that this model supports the theory that Jefe de Cocina's sales have been boosted by increase in the disposable income of people living in its sales region. However, the industry analyst recalls that in order for inference based on a regression model to be valid, residuals should not exhibit any signs of systemic misprediction. Because these data have been collected over time, the industry analyst is particularly wary about the presence of strong autocorrelation in the residuals.

Using the regression model, the industry analyst can compute the residuals resulting from the prediction of each year's sales. For example, the residual for Year 1 is

$$e_1 = 3.31 - (-12.60671 + 0.00028 \times 59{,}317) = -0.79$$

refer to Figure 16.16 displays the residuals corresponding to all 20 years of sales. Signs of positive autocorrelation are present, motivating the industry analyst to conduct a formal test.

Table 16.11 Jefe de Cocina Sales Data

Year	Sales ($ million)	Income ($)
1	3.31	59,317
2	3.56	60,280
3	3.61	60,555
4	3.72	59,737
5	4.04	60,453
6	4.13	60,056
7	4.27	59,564
8	4.58	60,240
9	5.09	60,490
10	5.72	62,834
11	6.36	65,100
12	6.77	67,532
13	7.29	69,189
14	8.18	71,829
15	8.84	74,026
16	9.25	77,294
17	10.01	80,246
18	11.22	83,148
19	12.55	90,119
20	13.11	94,429

Figure 16.16 Residual Plot of Jefe de Cocina Regression Model

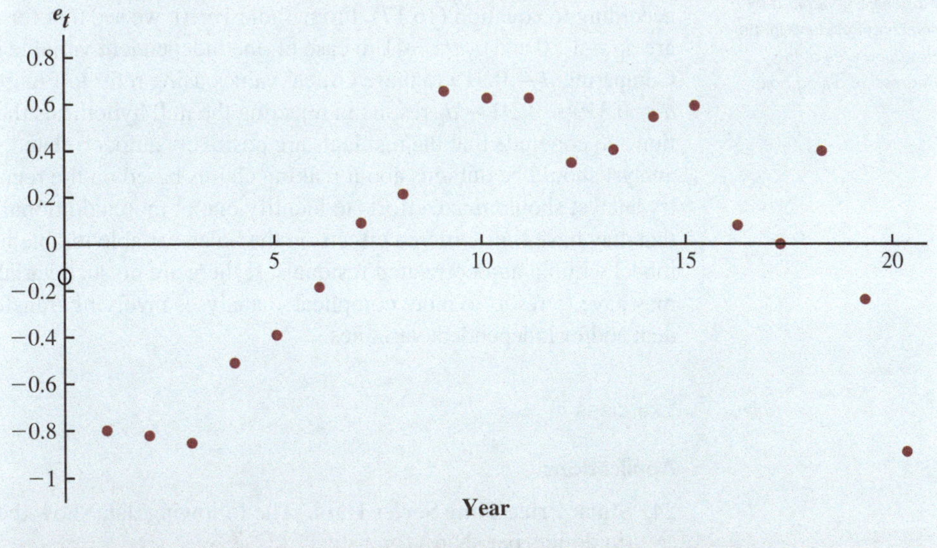

In Excel's Regression tool, the residual plot for a regression model are generated by selecting ***Residual Plots*** *in the* ***Residuals*** *area of the* ***Regression*** *dialog box.*

Table 16.12 Jefe de Cocina Regression Model Predictions and Durbin-Watson Calculations

Year	Sales ($ million)	Predicted Sales ($ million)	e_t	$(e_t - e_{t-1})^2$	e_t^2
1	3.31	4.10	−0.79		0.6241
2	3.56	4.37	−0.81	0.0004	0.6561
3	3.61	4.45	−0.84	0.0009	0.7056
4	3.72	4.22	−0.50	0.1156	0.25
5	4.04	4.42	−0.38	0.0144	0.1444
6	4.13	4.31	−0.18	0.0400	0.0324
7	4.27	4.17	0.10	0.0784	0.01
8	4.58	4.36	0.22	0.0144	0.0484
9	5.09	4.43	0.66	0.1936	0.4356
10	5.72	5.09	0.63	0.0009	0.3969
11	6.36	5.73	0.63	0.0000	0.3969
12	6.77	6.42	0.35	0.0784	0.1225
13	7.29	6.88	0.41	0.0036	0.1681
14	8.18	7.63	0.55	0.0196	0.3025
15	8.84	8.25	0.59	0.0016	0.3481
16	9.25	9.17	0.08	0.2601	0.0064
17	10.01	10.00	0.01	0.0049	0.0001
18	11.22	10.82	0.40	0.1521	0.16
19	12.55	12.78	−0.23	0.3969	0.0529
20	13.11	13.99	−0.88	0.4225	0.7744
				1.798	5.635

$d = 1.798/5.635 = 0.319$

In Excel's Regression tool, the residuals for a regression model are generated by selecting ***Residuals*** *in the* ***Residuals*** *area of the* ***Regression*** *dialog box.*

Table 16.12 contains predicted sales for each of the 20 years as well as the residual calculations necessary to compute the Durbin-Watson test statistic $d = 1.798/5.635 = 0.319$ according to equation (16.17). From Table 16.10, we see that for $n = 20$, the critical values are $d_L = 1.20$ and $d_U = 1.41$ in case of one independent variable (in our case, Income). Comparing $d = 0.319$ to these critical values using refer to Figure 16.15, we observe that $d = 0.319 < 1.20 = d_L$ results in rejecting the null hypothesis that there is no autocorrelation and conclude that the residuals are positively autocorrelated. Therefore, the industry analyst should be dubious about making claims based on the regression model. The industry analyst should make efforts to identify one or more additional independent variables that may have time-ordered effects on the Sales variable to obtain a more robust regression model without autocorrelated residuals. If there are no such variables, the industry analyst may have to resort to more complicated analyses involving transformations of the dependent and/or independent variables.

Exercises

Applications

24. **Stock Price Time Series Data.** The following data show the daily closing prices (in dollars per share) for a stock. **LO 7**

DATA*file*
closingprice

Date	Price ($)
November 3	82.87
November 4	83.00
November 7	83.61
November 8	83.15
November 9	82.84
November 10	83.99
November 11	84.55
November 14	84.36
November 15	85.53
November 16	86.54
November 17	86.89
November 18	87.77
November 21	87.29
November 22	87.99
November 23	88.80
November 25	88.80
November 28	89.11
November 29	89.10
November 30	88.90
December 1	89.21

a. Define the independent variable Period, where Period = 1 corresponds to the data for November 3, Period = 2 corresponds to the data for November 4, and so on. Develop the estimated regression equation that can be used to predict the closing price given the value of Period.
b. At the 0.05 level of significance, test for any positive autocorrelation in the residuals of the regression model.

DATA*file*
meangreens

25. **Nutritional Supplement Sales Time Series Data.** Mean Greens is a nutritional supplement company specializing in products made from a blend of dried and powdered vegetables and fruits, probiotics, digestive enzymes, vitamins, and minerals. The file *meangreens* contains data on the monthly sales and advertising expenditures for Mean Greens. **LO 7**
a. Using these data, construct the estimated regression equation to predict monthly sales given advertising expenditures.
b. At the 0.05 level of significance, test for any positive autocorrelation in the residuals of the regression model.

Summary

In this chapter we discussed several concepts used by model builders to help identify the best estimated regression equation. First, we introduced the concept of a general linear model to show how a model which is linear with respect to its regression parameters, $\beta_0, \beta_1, \beta_2, \ldots, \beta_p$, could be extended to handle curvilinear relationships and interaction effects. Then we discussed how transformations involving the dependent variable could be used to account for problems such as nonconstant variance in the error term.

In many applications of regression analysis, a large number of independent variables are considered. We presented a general approach based on an F statistic for adding or deleting variables from a regression model. We then discussed several different variable selection methods to find the best subset of independent variables to use in a regression model: stepwise regression, forward selection, backward elimination, and best-subsets regression.

In Section 16.4, we showed how the use of dummy variables in a multiple regression equation can provide another approach to solving experimental design problems. The chapter concluded with an application of residual analysis to show the Durbin–Watson test for autocorrelation.

Glossary

Autocorrelation (serial correlation) The degree of association between a variable's current value and the values at previous points in time.
Backward elimination Variable selection procedure that begins with model with all independent variables and removes one variable at a time based on the p-value of the corresponding F statistic.
Best-subsets regression Variable selection procedure that considers all possible models resulting from a combination of specified independent variables.
Curvilinear relationship An association between an independent variable and dependent variable that changes as the values of the variables change modeled with a smooth, nonlinear curve.
Durbin–Watson test A test to determine whether first-order autocorrelation is present.
Exponential model A relationship between an independent variable and dependent variable such that a unit change in the independent variable results in a constant percentage change in the dependent variable.
Forward selection Variable selection procedure that begins with model with no independent variables and adds one variable at a time based on the p-value of the corresponding F statistic.
General linear model A model of the form $y = \beta_0 + \beta_1 z_1 + \beta_2 z_2 + \cdots + \beta_p z_p + \epsilon$, where each of the independent variables z_j $(j = 1, 2, \ldots, p)$ is a function of $x_1, x_2, \ldots, x_k$, the variables for which data have been collected.
Interaction The effect of two independent variables acting together.
Stepwise regression Variable selection procedure that considers the iterative removal and addition of independent variables based on the p-value of the corresponding F statistic.

Key Formulas

General Linear Model

$$y = \beta_0 + \beta_1 z_1 + \beta_2 z_2 + \cdots + \beta_p z_p + \epsilon \tag{16.1}$$

F Test Statistic for Adding or Deleting $p - q$ Variables

$$F = \frac{\dfrac{\text{SSE}(x_1, x_2, \ldots, x_q) - \text{SSE}(x_1, x_2, \ldots, x_q, x_{q+1}, \ldots, x_p)}{p - q}}{\dfrac{\text{SSE}(x_1, x_2, \ldots, x_q, x_{q+1}, \ldots, x_p)}{n - p - 1}} \tag{16.13}$$

First-Order Autocorrelation

$$\epsilon_t = \rho\epsilon_{t-1} + z_t \tag{16.16}$$

Durbin–Watson Test Statistic

$$d = \frac{\sum_{t=2}^{n}(e_t - e_{t-1})^2}{\sum_{t=1}^{n} e_t^2} \tag{16.17}$$

Supplementary Exercises

DATA*file*
corporatebonds

26. **Years to Maturity and Bond Yield.** A sample containing years to maturity and yield (%) for 40 corporate bonds is contained in the file *corporatebonds*. LO 1
    a. Develop a scatter diagram of the data using x = years to maturity as the independent variable. Does a simple linear regression model appear to be appropriate?
    b. Develop an estimated regression equation with x = years to maturity and x^2 as the independent variables.
    c. As an alternative to fitting a second-order model, fit a model using the natural logarithm of price as the independent variable; that is, $\hat{y} = b_0 + b_1\ln(x)$. Does the estimated regression using the natural logarithm of x provide a better fit than the estimated regression developed in part (b)? Explain.

27. **Bike Prices.** *Consumer Reports* tested 19 different brands and models of road, fitness, and comfort bikes. Road bikes are designed for long road trips; fitness bikes are designed for regular workouts or daily commutes; and comfort bikes are designed for leisure rides on typically flat roads. The following data show the type, weight (lbs), and price ($) for the 19 bicycles tested. LO 1, 2

DATA*file*
bikes

Brand and Model	Type	Weight (lbs)	Price ($)
Klein Reve V	Road	20	1,800
Giant OCR Composite 3	Road	22	1,800
Giant OCR 1	Road	22	1,000
Specialized Roubaix	Road	21	1,300
Trek Pilot 2.1	Road	21	1,320
Cannondale Synapse 4	Road	21	1,050
LeMond Poprad	Road	22	1,350
Raleigh Cadent 1.0	Road	24	650
Giant FCR3	Fitness	23	630
Schwinn Super Sport GS	Fitness	23	700
Fuji Absolute 2.0	Fitness	24	700
Jamis Coda Comp	Fitness	26	830
Cannondale Road Warrior 400	Fitness	25	700
Schwinn Sierra GS	Comfort	31	340
Mongoose Switchback SX	Comfort	32	280
Giant Sedona DX	Comfort	32	360
Jamis Explorer 4.0	Comfort	35	600
Diamondback Wildwood Deluxe	Comfort	34	350
Specialized Crossroads Sport	Comfort	31	330

    a. Develop a scatter diagram with weight as the independent variable and price as the dependent variable. Does a simple linear regression model appear to be appropriate?
    b. Develop an estimated multiple regression equation with x = weight and x^2 as the two independent variables.
    c. Use the following dummy variables to develop an estimated regression equation that can be used to predict the price given the type of bike: Type_Fitness = 1 if the bike is a fitness bike, 0 otherwise; and Type_Comfort = 1 if the bike is a comfort bike; 0 otherwise. Compare the results obtained to the results obtained in part (b).
    d. To account for possible interaction between the type of bike and the weight of the bike, develop a new estimated regression equation that can be used to predict the price of the bike given the type, the weight of the bike, and any interaction between weight and each of the dummy variables defined in part (c). What estimated regression equation appears to be the best predictor of price? Explain.

DATA*file*
auditdelays

28. **Delays in Company Audits.** A study investigated the relationship between audit delay and variables that describe the client and the auditor. The file *auditdelays* contains data from a sample of 40 companies on the following set of variables. LO 1, 5

Delay	The length of time from a company's fiscal year-end to the date of the auditor's report
Industry	A dummy variable coded 1 if the firm was an industrial company or 0 if the firm was a bank, savings and loan, or insurance company.
Public	A dummy variable coded 1 if the company was traded on an organized exchange or over the counter; otherwise coded 0.
Quality	A measure of overall quality of internal controls, as judged by the auditor, on a five-point scale ranging from "virtually none" (1) to "excellent" (5).
Finished	A measure ranging from 1 to 4, as judged by the auditor, where 1 indicates "all work performed subsequent to year-end" and 4 indicates "most work performed prior to year-end."

a. Develop the estimated regression equation using all of the independent variables.
b. Did the estimated regression equation developed in part (a) provide a good fit? Explain.
c. Develop a scatter diagram showing Delay as a function of Finished. What does this scatter diagram indicate about the relationship between Delay and Finished?
d. On the basis of your observations about the relationship between Delay and Finished, develop an alternative estimated regression equation to the one developed in part (a) to explain as much of the variability in Delay as possible.

DATA*file*
gelato

29. **Gelato Sales Time Series Data.** Basta LLC produces and sells gelato, an Italian frozen dessert similar to ice cream. The file *gelato* contains data on Basta's weekly sales of gelato (in pints), the sales price of gelato (in dollars per pint), the median family annual income (in $1,000s), and the average temperature in the sales region. LO 7
a. Using these data, construct the estimated regression equation to predict weekly sales of gelato given the sales price, family income, and temperature.
b. At the 0.05 level of significance, test for any positive autocorrelation in the residuals of the regression model.

DATA*file*
pork

30. **Pork Industry Time Series Data.** Pork is the meat provided by domesticated pigs (hogs) for dietary consumption. The state of Iowa produces more pork than any other state in the United States. Economic leaders in Iowa are interested in investigating relationships between hog price and factors such as hog supply, corn price, corn supply, and farm wage. To facilitate this analysis, the file *pork* contains indices for these variables that have been constructed by pork industry experts using variable transformations. LO 7
a. Develop an estimated regression equation that can be used to predict Hog Price given Hog Supply, Corn Price, Corn Supply, and Farm Wage.
b. At the 0.05 level of significance, test for any positive autocorrelation in the residuals of the regression model.

31. **Predicting ERA in Major League Baseball.** In baseball, an earned run is any run that the opposing team scores off a pitcher except for a run scored as a result of fielding errors. The earned run average (ERA) is a statistic commonly used to compare the performance of pitchers; the ERA of a pitcher is computed as

$$\text{ERA} = \left(\frac{\text{earned runs allowed}}{\text{innings pitched}}\right) \times 9$$

DATA*file*
pitching_mlb

Note that ERA is the average number of earned runs per inning pitched multiplied by nine (the number of innings in a regulation baseball game). Thus, ERA represents the average number of runs the pitcher gives up per nine innings. To investigate the relationship between ERA and other measures of pitching performance, data for 109 pitchers for the 2017 Major League Baseball (MLB) season appear in the file *pitching_mlb*, which contains the variables in the following table. **LO 4, 5**

Player	Name of MLB pitcher
ERA	Earned run average
Wins	Number of games won
Losses	Number of games lost
H/9	Average number of hits allowed per nine innings
HR/9	Average number of home runs allowed per nine innings
BB/9	Average number of bases on balls (walks) allowed per nine innings
SO/9	Average number of batters struck out per nine innings
WHIP	Walks plus hits divided by innings pitched

a. Develop an estimated regression equation that can be used to predict ERA given the average number of hits allowed per nine innings.
b. Develop an estimated regression equation that can be used to predict ERA given the average number of hits allowed per nine innings, the average number of home runs allowed per nine innings, the average number of bases on balls allowed per nine innings, the average number of batters struck out per nine innings, and WHIP.
c. At the 0.01 level of significance, test whether the four independent variables added in part (b) contribute significantly to the estimated regression equation developed in part (a).
d. Compute the correlation between each pair of potential independent variables. With the correlation results in mind, apply a variable selection procedure to identify a model that reliably predicts ERA.

32. **Shopper Comfort and Level of Browsing Activity.** A study was conducted to investigate browsing activity by shoppers. Shoppers were classified as nonbrowsers, light browsers, and heavy browsers. For each shopper in the study, a measure was obtained to determine how comfortable the shopper was in the store. Higher scores indicated greater comfort. Assume that the following data are from this study. Use a 0.05 level of significance to test for differences in comfort levels among the three types of browsers. **LO 6**

DATA*file*
browsing

Nonbrowser	Light Browser	Heavy Browser
4	5	5
5	6	7
6	5	5
3	4	7
3	7	4
4	4	6
5	6	5
4	5	7

DATA*file*
fueleconomy2019

33. **Estimating Fuel Mileage by Car Size.** The U.S. Department of Energy's *Fuel Economy Guide* provides fuel efficiency data for cars and trucks (www.fueleconomy.gov). The file *fueleconomy2019* provides a portion of the data for 387 vehicles from the 2019 model year. The column labeled Class identifies the category of the vehicle (Two Seaters, Minicompact Cars, etc.). The column labeled Combined MPG shows the fuel efficiency rating based on 55% city driving and 45% highway driving in terms of miles per gallon. Use $\alpha = 0.05$ and test for any significant difference in the mean fuel efficiency rating for highway driving among the 10 different classes of cars. **LO 6**

Case Problem 1: Analysis of LPGA Tour Statistics

DATA*file*
tour_lpga

The Ladies Professional Golf Association (LPGA) maintains data on performance for members of the LPGA Tour. Scoring average is generally considered the most important statistic in terms of a player's success. To investigate the relationship between scoring average and variables such as driving distance, driving accuracy, greens in regulation, sand saves, and average putts per round, year-end performance data for 140 players on the LPGA Tour are contained in the file *tour_lpga* (LPGA website). Each row of the data set corresponds to an LPGA Tour player. Descriptions for the variables in the data set follow. **LO 5**

Scoring Average	The average number of strokes per completed round.
DrDist (Driving Distance)	The average number of yards per measured drive. On the LPGA Tour, driving distance is measured on two holes per round. Care is taken to select two holes which face in opposite directions to counteract the effect of wind. Drives are measured to the point at which they come to rest regardless of whether they are in the fairway or not.
DrAccu (Driving Accuracy)	The percentage of time a tee shot comes to rest in the fairway. Driving accuracy is measured on every hole, excluding holes which have par of 3.
GIR (Greens in Regulation)	The percentage of time a player was able to hit the green in regulation. A green is considered hit in regulation if any portion of the ball is touching the putting surface after the GIR stroke has been taken. The GIR stroke is determined by subtracting 2 from par (1st stroke on a par 3, 2nd on a par 4, 3rd on a par 5). In other words, a green is considered hit in regulation if the player has reached the putting surface in par minus two strokes.
Sand Saves	The percentage of time a player was able to get "up and down" once in a greenside sand bunker (regardless of score). "Up and down" indicates it took the player two shots or less to put the ball in the hole from a greenside sand bunker.
PPR (Putts per Round)	The average number of putts per round.

Managerial Report

Suppose that you have been hired by the commissioner of the LPGA to analyze the data for a presentation to be made at the annual LPGA Tour meeting. The commissioner has asked whether it would be possible to use these data to determine the performance measures that are the best predictors of a player's average score. Use the methods presented in this and previous chapters to analyze the data. Prepare a report that summarizes your analysis, including key statistical results, conclusions, and recommendations.

Case Problem 2: Rating Wines from the Piedmont Region of Italy

Wine Spectator magazine contains articles and reviews on every aspect of the wine industry, including ratings of wine from around the world. In a recent issue they reviewed and scored 475 wines from the Piedmont region of Italy using a 100-point scale.

The following table shows how the *Wine Spectator* score each wine received is used to rate each wine as being classic, outstanding, very good, good, mediocre, or not recommended.

Score	Rating
95–100	Classic: a great wine
90–94	Outstanding: a wine of superior character and style
85–89	Very good: a wine with special qualities
80–84	Good: a solid, well-made wine
75–79	Mediocre: a drinkable wine that may have minor flaws
below 75	Not recommended

DATA*file*
wineratings

A key question for most consumers is whether paying more for a bottle of wine will result in a better wine. To investigate this question for wines from the Piedmont region we selected a random sample of 100 wines from the 475 wines that *Wine Spectator* reviewed. The data, contained in the file *wineratings*, shows the price ($), the *Wine Spectator* score, and the rating for each wine. **LO 1**

Managerial Report

1. Develop a table that shows the number of wines that were classified as classic, outstanding, very good, good, mediocre, and not recommended and the average price. Does there appear to be any relationship between the price of the wine and the *Wine Spectator* rating? Are there any other aspects of your initial summary of the data that stand out?
2. Develop a scatter diagram with price on the horizontal axis and the Wine Spectator score on the vertical axis. Does the relationship between price and score appear to be linear?
3. Using linear regression, develop an estimated regression equation that can be used to predict the score given the price of the wine.
4. Using a second-order model, develop an estimated regression equation that can be used to predict the score given the price of the wine.
5. Compare the results from fitting a linear model and fitting a second-order model.
6. As an alternative to fitting a second-order model, fit a model using the natural logarithm of price as the independent variable. Compare the results with the second-order model.
7. Based upon your analysis, would you say that spending more for a bottle of wine will provide a better wine?
8. Suppose that you want to spend a maximum of $30 for a bottle of wine. In this case, will spending closer to your upper limit for price result in a better wine than a much lower price?

Chapter 17

Time Series Analysis and Forecasting

Contents

Statistics in Practice:
Nevada Occupational Health Clinic

17.1 Time Series Patterns
- Horizontal Pattern
- Trend Pattern
- Seasonal Pattern
- Trend and Seasonal Pattern
- Cyclical Pattern
- Using Excel's Chart Tools to Construct a Time Series Plot
- Selecting a Forecasting Method

17.2 Forecast Accuracy

17.3 Moving Averages and Exponential Smoothing
- Moving Averages
- Using Excel's Moving Average Tool
- Weighted Moving Averages
- Exponential Smoothing
- Using Excel's Exponential Smoothing Tool

17.4 Trend Projection
- Linear Trend Regression
- Using Excel's Regression Tool to Compute a Linear Trend Equation
- Nonlinear Trend Regression
- Using Excel's Regression Tool to Compute a Quadratic Trend Equation
- Using Excel's Regression Tool to Compute an Exponential Trend Equation
- Using Excel's Chart Tools for Trend Projection

17.5 Seasonality and Trend
- Seasonality Without Trend
- Seasonality and Trend
- Models Based on Monthly Data

17.6 Time Series Decomposition
- Calculating the Seasonal Indexes
- Deseasonalizing the Time Series
- Using the Deseasonalized Time Series to Identify Trend
- Seasonal Adjustments
- Models Based on Monthly Data
- Cyclical Component

Summary 868
Glossary 868
Key Formulas 869
Supplementary Exercises 870
Case Problem 1: Forecasting Food and Beverage Sales 874
Case Problem 2: Forecasting Lost Sales 875

Available in the Cengage eBook:
Appendix: Forecasting with R

Learning Objectives

After completing this chapter, you will be able to

LO 1 Calculate measures of forecasting accuracy, including mean absolute error, mean squared error and mean absolute percentage error.

LO 2 Use measures of forecasting error to choose an appropriate forecasting model.

LO 3 Identify an underlying pattern from a time-series plot of data.

LO 4 Use smoothing techniques such as moving average and exponential smoothing to forecast a time series that exhibits a horizontal pattern.

LO 5 Use simple linear regression to forecast a time series that exhibits a linear trend.

LO 6 Develop a quadratic trend equation to forecast a time series with a curvilinear or nonlinear trend.

LO 7 Develop an exponential trend equation to forecast a time series with a curvilinear or nonlinear trend.

LO 8 Use regression analysis with binary variables to develop a forecast for a time series that exhibits a seasonal pattern.

LO 9 Compute seasonal indexes and de-seasonalize a time series.

LO 10 Decompose a time series into seasonal, trend, and irregular components and develop a forecast for a time series using these components.

Statistics in Practice

Nevada Occupational Health Clinic*

Sparks, Nevada

Nevada Occupational Health Clinic is a privately owned medical clinic in Sparks, Nevada. The clinic specializes in industrial medicine. Operating at the same site for more than 20 years, the clinic had been in a rapid growth phase. Monthly billings increased from $57,000 to more than $300,000 in 26 months, when the main clinic building burned to the ground.

The clinic's insurance policy covered physical property and equipment as well as loss of income due to the interruption of regular business operations. Settling the property insurance claim was a relatively straightforward matter of determining the value of the physical property and equipment lost during the fire. However, determining the value of the income lost during the seven months that it took to rebuild the clinic was a complicated matter involving negotiations between the business owners and the insurance company. No preestablished rules could help calculate "what would have happened" to the clinic's billings if the fire had not occurred. To estimate the lost income, the clinic used a forecasting method to project the growth in business that would have been realized during the seven-month lost-business period. The actual history of billings prior to the fire provided the basis for a forecasting model with linear trend and seasonal components as discussed in this chapter. This forecasting model enabled the clinic to establish an accurate estimate of the loss, which was eventually accepted by the insurance company.

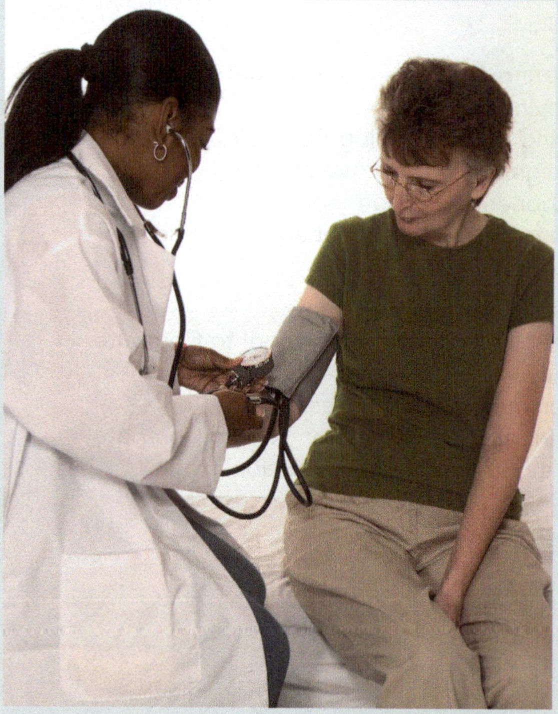

A physician checks a patient's blood pressure at the Nevada Occupational Health Clinic. Bob Pardue—Medical Bob Pardue/Medical Lifestyle/Alamy Stock Photo

*The authors are indebted to Bard Betz, Director of Operations, and Curtis Brauer, Executive Administrative Assistant, Nevada Occupational Health Clinic, for providing this Statistics in Practice.

A forecast is simply a prediction of what will happen in the future. Managers must learn to accept that regardless of the technique used, they will not be able to develop perfect forecasts.

The purpose of this chapter is to provide an introduction to time series analysis and forecasting. Suppose we are asked to provide quarterly forecasts of sales for one of our company's products over the coming one-year period. Production schedules, raw material purchasing, inventory policies, and sales quotas will all be affected by the quarterly forecasts we provide. Consequently, poor forecasts may result in poor planning and increased costs for the company. How should we go about providing the quarterly sales forecasts? Good judgment, intuition, and an awareness of the state of the economy may give us a rough idea or "feeling" of what is likely to happen in the future, but converting that feeling into a number that can be used as next year's sales forecast is difficult.

Forecasting methods can be classified as qualitative or quantitative. Qualitative methods generally involve the use of expert judgment to develop forecasts. Such methods are appropriate when historical data on the variable being forecast are either not applicable or unavailable. Quantitative forecasting methods can be used when (1) past information about the variable being forecast is available, (2) the information can be quantified, and (3) it is reasonable to assume that the pattern of the past will continue into the future. In such cases, a forecast can be developed using a time series method or a causal method. We will focus exclusively on quantitative forecasting methods in this chapter.

If the historical data are restricted to past values of the variable to be forecast, the forecasting procedure is called a *time series method* and the historical data are referred to as a time series. The objective of time series analysis is to discover a pattern in the historical data or time series and then extrapolate the pattern into the future; the forecast is based solely on past values of the variable and/or on past forecast errors.

Causal forecasting methods are based on the assumption that the variable we are forecasting has a cause-effect relationship with one or more other variables. In standard regression analysis, one or more independent variables can be used to predict the value of a single dependent variable. Looking at regression analysis as a forecasting tool, we can view the time series value that we want to forecast as the dependent variable. Hence, if we can identify a good set of related independent, or explanatory, variables, we may be able to develop an estimated regression equation for predicting or forecasting the time series. For instance, the sales for many products are influenced by advertising expenditures, so regression analysis may be used to develop an equation showing how sales and advertising are related. Once the advertising budget for the next period is determined, we could substitute this value into the equation to develop a prediction or forecast of the sales volume for that period. Note that if a time series method were used to develop the forecast, advertising expenditures would not be considered; that is, a time series method would base the forecast solely on past sales.

We discuss regression analysis in detail in chapters 14, 15 and 16.

By treating time as the independent variable and the time series as a dependent variable, regression analysis can also be used as a time series method. To help differentiate the application of regression analysis in these two cases, we use the terms *cross-sectional regression* and *time series regression*. Thus, time series regression refers to the use of regression analysis when the independent variable is time. Because our focus in this chapter is on time series methods, we leave the discussion of the application of regression analysis as a causal forecasting method to more advanced texts on forecasting.

17.1 Time Series Patterns

A **time series** is a sequence of observations on a variable measured at successive points in time or over successive periods of time. The measurements may be taken every hour, day, week, month, or year, or at any other regular interval.[1] The pattern of the data is an important factor in understanding how the time series has behaved in the past. If such behavior can be expected to continue in the future, we can use the past pattern to guide us in selecting an appropriate forecasting method.

To identify the underlying pattern in the data, a useful first step is to construct a **time series plot**. A time series plot is a graphical presentation of the relationship between time

[1]We limit our discussion to time series in which the values of the series are recorded at equal intervals. Cases in which the observations are made at unequal intervals are beyond the scope of this text.

Table 17.1 Gasoline Sales Time Series

Week	Sales (1,000s of gallons)
1	17
2	21
3	19
4	23
5	18
6	16
7	20
8	18
9	22
10	20
11	15
12	22

DATA*file*
gasolinesales

and the time series variable; time is on the horizontal axis and the time series values are shown on the vertical axis. Let us review some of the common types of data patterns that can be identified when examining a time series plot.

Horizontal Pattern

A **horizontal pattern** exists when the data fluctuate around a constant mean. To illustrate a time series with a horizontal pattern, consider the 12 weeks of data in Table 17.1. These data are the number of gallons of gasoline sold by a gasoline distributor in Bennington, Vermont, over the past 12 weeks. The average value or mean for this time series is 19.25 or 19,250 gallons per week. Figure 17.1 shows a time series plot for these data. Note how the data fluctuate around the sample mean of 19,250 gallons. Although random variability is present, we would say that these data follow a horizontal pattern.

Figure 17.1 Gasoline Sales Time Series Plot

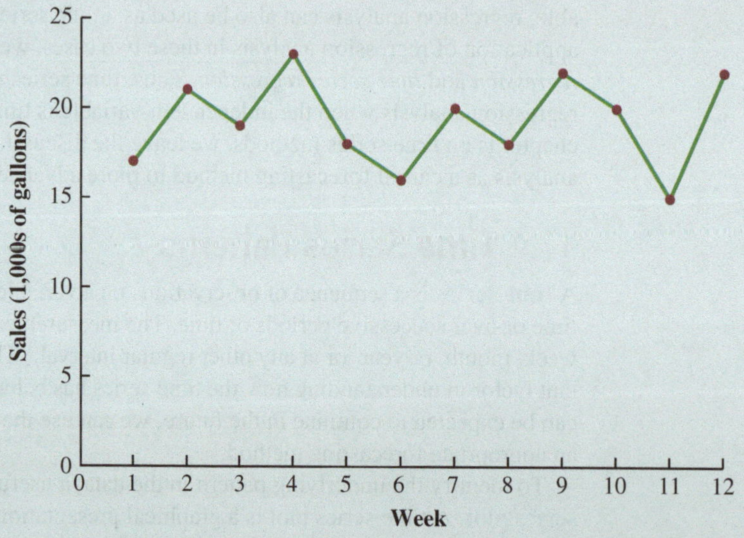

The term **stationary time series**[2] is used to denote a time series whose statistical properties are independent of time. In particular this means that

1. The process generating the data has a constant mean.
2. The variability of the time series is constant over time.

A time series plot for a stationary time series will always exhibit a horizontal pattern. But simply observing a horizontal pattern is not sufficient evidence to conclude that the time series is stationary. More advanced texts on forecasting discuss procedures for determining if a time series is stationary and provide methods for transforming a time series that is not stationary into a stationary series.

Changes in business conditions can often result in a time series that has a horizontal pattern shifting to a new level. For instance, suppose the gasoline distributor signs a contract with the Vermont State Police to provide gasoline for state police cars located in southern Vermont. With this new contract, the distributor expects to see a major increase in weekly sales starting in week 13. Table 17.2 shows the number of gallons of gasoline sold for the original time series and for the 10 weeks after signing the new contract. Figure 17.2 shows the corresponding time series plot. Note the increased level of the time series beginning in week 13. This change in the level of the time series makes it more difficult to choose an appropriate forecasting method. Selecting a forecasting method that adapts well to changes in the level of a time series is an important consideration in many practical applications.

DATA*file*
gasolinerevised

Table 17.2 Gasoline Sales Time Series After Obtaining the Contract with the Vermont State Police

Week	Sales (1,000s of gallons)
1	17
2	21
3	19
4	23
5	18
6	16
7	20
8	18
9	22
10	20
11	15
12	22
13	31
14	34
15	31
16	33
17	28
18	32
19	30
20	29
21	34
22	33

[2]For a formal definition of stationary see K. Ord and R. Fildes, *Principles of Business Forecasting* (Mason, OH: Cengage Learning, 2012), p. 155.

Figure 17.2 Gasoline Sales Time Series Plot After Obtaining the Contract with the Vermont State Police

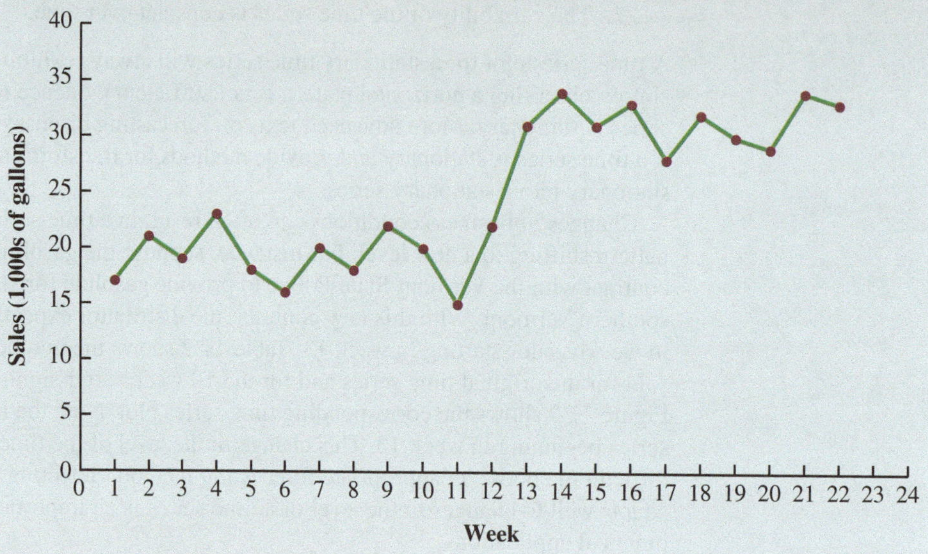

Trend Pattern

Although time series data generally exhibit random fluctuations, a time series may also show gradual shifts or movements to relatively higher or lower values over a longer period of time. If a time series plot exhibits this type of behavior, we say that a **trend pattern** exists. A trend is usually the result of long-term factors such as population increases or decreases, changing demographic characteristics of the population, technology, and/or consumer preferences.

To illustrate a time series with a trend pattern, consider the time series of bicycle sales for a particular manufacturer over the past 10 years, as shown in Table 17.3 and Figure 17.3. Note that 21,600 bicycles were sold in Year 1, 22,900 were sold in Year 2, and so on. In Year 10, the most recent year, 31,400 bicycles were sold. Visual inspection of the time series plot shows some up and down movement over the past 10 years, but the time series also seems to have a systematically increasing or upward trend.

The trend for the bicycle sales time series appears to be linear and increasing over time, but sometimes a trend can be described better by other types of patterns. For instance, the

DATA*file*
bicyclesales

Table 17.3 Bicycle Sales Time Series

Year	Sales (1,000s)
1	21.6
2	22.9
3	25.5
4	21.9
5	23.9
6	27.5
7	31.5
8	29.7
9	28.6
10	31.4

Figure 17.3 Bicycle Sales Time Series Plot

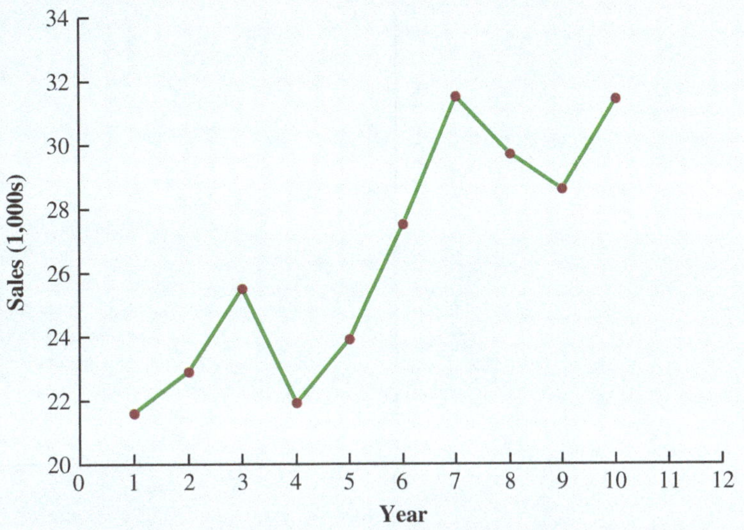

data in Table 17.4 and the corresponding time series plot in Figure 17.4 show the sales for a cholesterol drug since the company won FDA approval for it 10 years ago. The time series increases in a nonlinear fashion; that is, the rate of change of revenue does not increase by a constant amount from one year to the next. In fact, the revenue appears to be growing in an exponential fashion. Exponential relationships such as this are appropriate when the percentage change from one period to the next is relatively constant.

Seasonal Pattern

The trend of a time series can be identified by analyzing multiyear movements in historical data. Seasonal patterns are recognized by seeing the same repeating patterns over successive periods of time. For example, a manufacturer of swimming pools expects low sales activity in the fall and winter months, with peak sales in the spring and summer months. Manufacturers of snow removal equipment and heavy clothing, however, expect just the opposite yearly pattern. Not surprisingly, the pattern for a time series plot that exhibits a repeating pattern over a one-year period due to seasonal influences is called a **seasonal pattern**. While we generally think of seasonal movement in a time series as occurring

DATA*file*
cholesterolrevenue

Table 17.4 Cholesterol Revenue Time Series ($millions)

Year	Revenue
1	23.1
2	21.3
3	27.4
4	34.6
5	33.8
6	43.2
7	59.5
8	64.4
9	74.2
10	99.3

Figure 17.4 Cholesterol Revenue Time Series Plot ($millions)

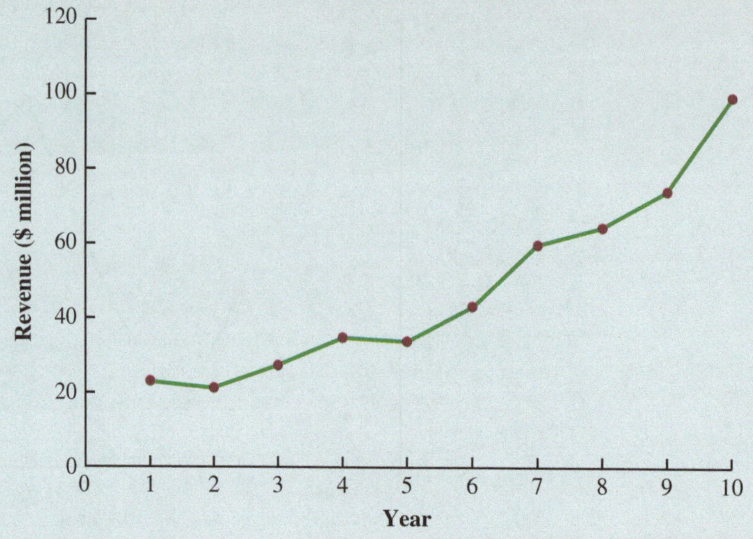

within one year, time series data can also exhibit seasonal patterns of less than one year in duration. For example, daily traffic volume shows within-the-day "seasonal" behavior, with peak levels occurring during rush hours, moderate flow during the rest of the day and early evening, and light flow from midnight to early morning.

As an example of a seasonal pattern, consider the number of umbrellas sold at a clothing store over the past five years. Table 17.5 shows the time series and Figure 17.5 shows the corresponding time series plot. The time series plot does not indicate any long-term

DATA*file*
umbrellasales

Table 17.5 Umbrella Sales Time Series

Year	Quarter	Sales
1	1	125
	2	153
	3	106
	4	88
2	1	118
	2	161
	3	133
	4	102
3	1	138
	2	144
	3	113
	4	80
4	1	109
	2	137
	3	125
	4	109
5	1	130
	2	165
	3	128
	4	96

Figure 17.5 Umbrella Sales Time Series Plot

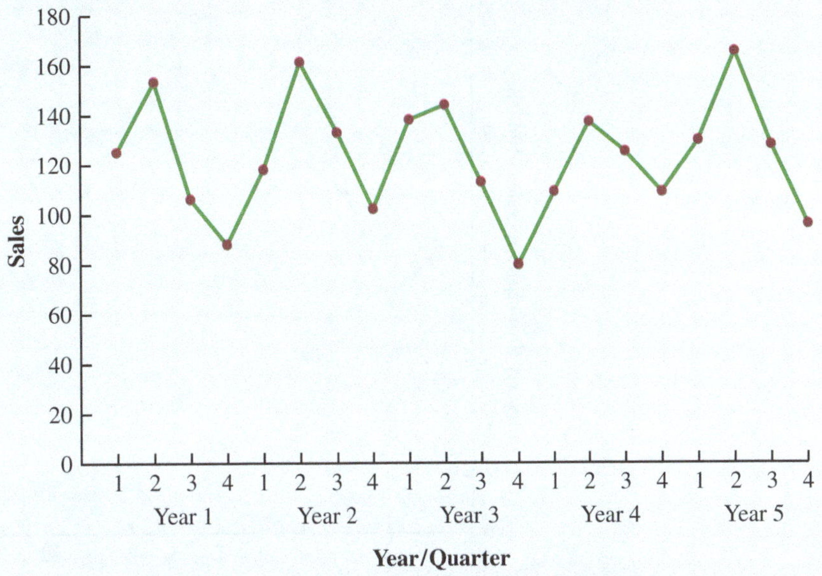

trend in sales. In fact, unless you look carefully at the data, you might conclude that the data follow a horizontal pattern. But closer inspection of the time series plot reveals a regular pattern in the data. That is, the first and third quarters have moderate sales, the second quarter has the highest sales, and the fourth quarter tends to have the lowest sales volume. Thus, we would conclude that a quarterly seasonal pattern is present.

Trend and Seasonal Pattern

Some time series include a combination of a trend and seasonal pattern. For instance, the data in Table 17.6 and the corresponding time series plot in Figure 17.6 show smartphone

DATA*file*
smartphonesales

Table 17.6 Quarterly Smartphone Sales Time Series

Year	Quarter	Sales (1,000s)
1	1	4.8
	2	4.1
	3	6.0
	4	6.5
2	1	5.8
	2	5.2
	3	6.8
	4	7.4
3	1	6.0
	2	5.6
	3	7.5
	4	7.8
4	1	6.3
	2	5.9
	3	8.0
	4	8.4

Figure 17.6 Quarterly Smartphone Sales Time Series Plot

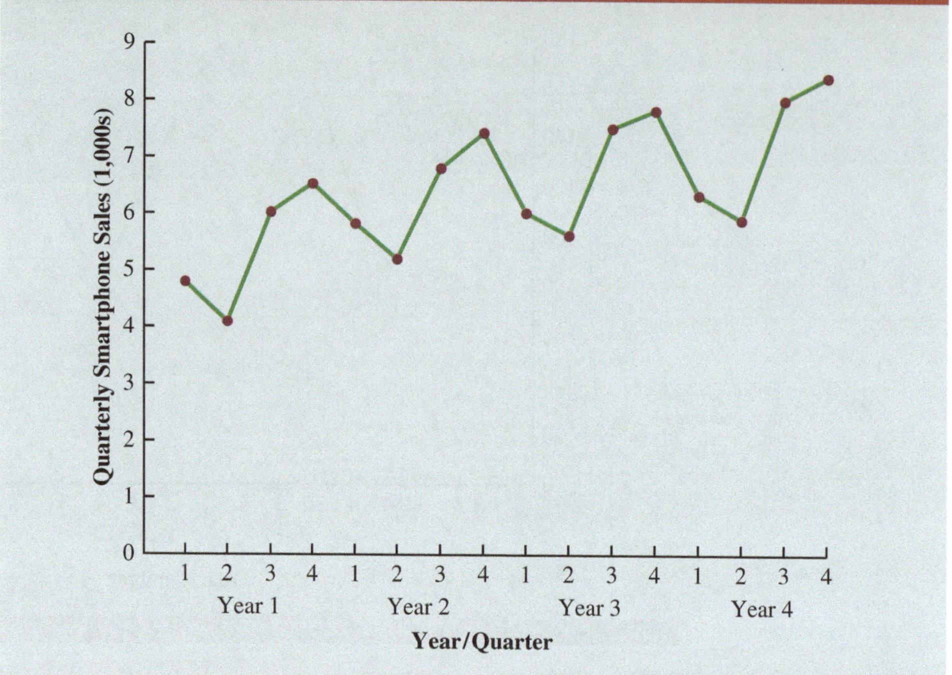

sales for a particular manufacturer over the past four years. Clearly, an increasing trend is present. But Figure 17.6 also indicates that sales are lowest in the second quarter of each year and increase in quarters 3 and 4. Thus, we conclude that a seasonal pattern also exists for smartphone sales. In such cases, we need to use a forecasting method that has the capability to deal with both trend and seasonality.

Cyclical Pattern

A **cyclical pattern** exists if the time series plot shows an alternating sequence of points below and above the trend line lasting more than one year. Many economic time series exhibit cyclical behavior with regular runs of observations below and above the trend line. Often, the cyclical component of a time series is due to multiyear business cycles. For example, periods of moderate inflation followed by periods of rapid inflation can lead to time series that alternate below and above a generally increasing trend line (e.g., a time series for housing costs). Business cycles are extremely difficult, if not impossible, to forecast. As a result, cyclical effects are often combined with long-term trend effects and referred to as trend-cycle effects. In this chapter, we do not deal with cyclical effects that may be present in the time series.

Using Excel's Chart Tools to Construct a Time Series Plot

We can use Excel's Chart tools to construct a time series plot for the gasoline time series in Table 17.1.

DATA*file*
gasolinesales

Enter/Access Data: Open the file *gasolinesales*. The data are in cells A2:B13 and labels are in cells A1:B1.

Apply Tools: The following steps describe how to use Excel's Chart tools to construct a time series plot from the data in the worksheet. Refer to Figure 17.7 as we describe the tasks involved.

Figure 17.7 Time Series Plot for the Gasoline Sales Time Series Using Excel's Charts Tools

	A	B
1	Week	Sales
2	1	17
3	2	21
4	3	19
5	4	23
6	5	18
7	6	16
8	7	20
9	8	18
10	9	22
11	10	20
12	11	15
13	12	22

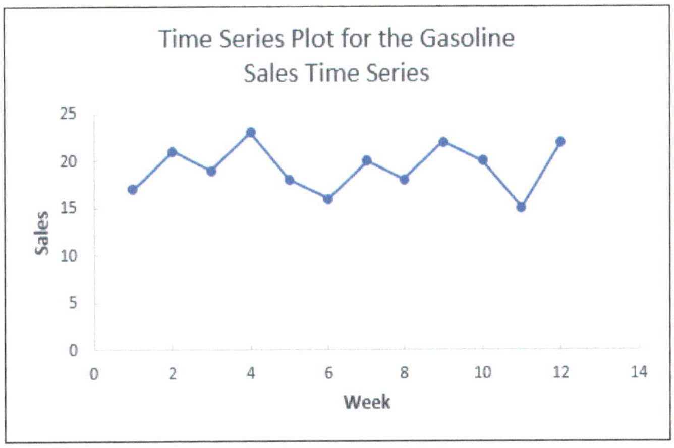

A time series plot is simply a scatter diagram with lines connecting the points. We discuss how to construct and edit a scatter diagram in Chapter 2.

Step 1. Select cells A2:B13
Step 2. Click the **Insert** tab on the Ribbon
Step 3. In the **Charts** group, click the **Insert Scatter (X,Y) or Bubble Chart** button
Step 4. When the list of scatter diagram subtypes appears:
Click the **Scatter with Straight Lines and Markers** button

The time series plot produced by Excel will appear in the same worksheet.

Editing Options: The time series plot can be edited to display a different chart title and axis titles as shown in Figure 17.7.

Selecting a Forecasting Method

The underlying pattern in the time series is an important factor in selecting a forecasting method. Thus, a time series plot should be one of the first things developed when trying to determine which forecasting method to use. If we see a horizontal pattern, then we need to select a method appropriate for this type of pattern. Similarly, if we observe a trend in the data, then we need to use a forecasting method that has the capability to handle trend effectively. The next two sections illustrate methods that can be used in situations where the underlying pattern is horizontal; in other words, no trend or seasonal effects are present. We then consider methods appropriate when trend and/or seasonality are present in the data.

17.2 Forecast Accuracy

In this section, we begin by developing forecasts for the gasoline time series shown in Table 17.1 using the simplest of all the forecasting methods: an approach that uses the most recent week's sales volume as the forecast for the next week. For instance, the distributor sold 17 thousand gallons of gasoline in week 1; this value is used as the forecast for week 2. Next, we use 21, the actual value of sales in week 2, as the forecast for week 3, and so on. The forecasts obtained for the historical data using this method are shown in Table 17.7 in the column labeled Forecast. Because of its simplicity, this method is often referred to as a *naive* forecasting method.

How accurate are the forecasts obtained using this *naive* forecasting method? To answer this question we will introduce several measures of forecast accuracy. These measures are used to determine how well a particular forecasting method is able to reproduce the time series data that are already available. By selecting the method that has the best accuracy for the data already known, we hope to increase the likelihood that we will obtain better forecasts for future time periods.

The key concept associated with measuring forecast accuracy is **forecast error**, defined as

$$\text{Forecast Error} = \text{Actual Value} - \text{Forecast}$$

For instance, because the distributor actually sold 21 thousand gallons of gasoline in week 2 and the forecast, using the sales volume in week 1, was 17 thousand gallons, the forecast error in week 2 is

$$\text{Forecast Error in week 2} = 21 - 17 = 4$$

The fact that the forecast error is positive indicates that in week 2 the forecasting method underestimated the actual value of sales. Next, we use 21, the actual value of sales in week 2, as the forecast for week 3. Since the actual value of sales in week 3 is 19, the forecast error for week 3 is $19 - 21 = -2$. In this case, the negative forecast error indicates that in week 3 the forecast overestimated the actual value. Thus, the forecast error may be positive or negative, depending on whether the forecast is too low or too high. A complete summary of the forecast errors for this naive forecasting method is shown in Table 17.7 in the column labeled Forecast Error.

In regression analysis, a residual is defined as the difference between the observed value of the dependent variable and the estimated value. The forecast errors are analogous to the residuals in regression analysis.

A simple measure of forecast accuracy is the mean or average of the forecast errors. Table 17.7 shows that the sum of the forecast errors for the gasoline sales time series is 5; thus, the mean or average forecast error is $5/11 = 0.45$. Note that although the gasoline time series consists of 12 values, to compute the mean error we divided the sum of the forecast errors by 11 because there are only 11 forecast errors. Because the mean forecast error is positive, the method is underforecasting; in other words, the observed values tend to be greater than the forecasted values. Because positive and negative forecast errors tend

Table 17.7 Computing Forecasts and Measures of Forecast Accuracy Using the Most Recent Value as the Forecast for the Next Period

Week	Time Series Value	Forecast	Forecast Error	Absolute Value of Forecast Error	Squared Forecast Error	Percentage Error	Absolute Value of Percentage Error
1	17						
2	21	17	4	4	16	19.05	19.05
3	19	21	−2	2	4	−10.53	10.53
4	23	19	4	4	16	17.39	17.39
5	18	23	−5	5	25	−27.78	27.78
6	16	18	−2	2	4	−12.50	12.50
7	20	16	4	4	16	20.00	20.00
8	18	20	−2	2	4	−11.11	11.11
9	22	18	4	4	16	18.18	18.18
10	20	22	−2	2	4	−10.00	10.00
11	15	20	−5	5	25	−33.33	33.33
12	22	15	7	7	49	31.82	31.82
		Totals	5	41	179	1.19	211.69

to offset one another, the mean error is likely to be small; thus, the mean error is not a very useful measure of forecast accuracy.

The **mean absolute error**, denoted **MAE**, is a measure of forecast accuracy that avoids the problem of positive and negative forecast errors offsetting one another. As you might expect given its name, MAE is the average of the absolute values of the forecast errors. Table 17.7 shows that the sum of the absolute values of the forecast errors is 41; thus,

$$\text{MAE} = \text{average of the absolute value of forecast errors} = \frac{41}{11} = 3.73$$

In regression analysis, the mean square error (MSE) is the residual sum of squares divided by its degrees of freedom. In forecasting, MSE is the average of the sum of squared forecast errors.

Another measure that avoids the problem of positive and negative forecast errors offsetting each other is obtained by computing the average of the squared forecast errors. This measure of forecast accuracy, referred to as the **mean squared error**, is denoted **MSE**. From Table 17.7, the sum of the squared errors is 179; hence,

$$\text{MSE} = \text{average of the sum of squared forecast errors} = \frac{179}{11} = 16.27$$

The size of MAE and MSE depends upon the scale of the data. As a result, it is difficult to make comparisons for different time intervals, such as comparing a method of forecasting monthly gasoline sales to a method of forecasting weekly sales, or to make comparisons across different time series. To make comparisons like these we need to work with relative or percentage error measures. The **mean absolute percentage error**, denoted **MAPE**, is such a measure. To compute MAPE we must first compute the percentage error for each forecast. For example, the percentage error corresponding to the forecast of 17 in week 2 is computed by dividing the forecast error in week 2 by the actual value in week 2 and multiplying the result by 100. For week 2, the percentage error is computed as follows:

$$\text{Percentage error for week 2} = \frac{4}{21}(100) = 19.05\%$$

Thus, the forecast error for week 2 is 19.05% of the observed value in week 2. A complete summary of the percentage errors is shown in Table 17.7 in the column labeled Percentage Error. In the next column, we show the absolute value of the percentage error.

Table 17.7 shows that the sum of the absolute values of the percentage errors is 211.69; thus,

$$\text{MAPE} = \text{average of the absolute value of percentage forecast errors} = \frac{211.69}{11} = 19.24\%$$

Summarizing, using the naive (most recent observation) forecasting method, we obtained the following measures of forecast accuracy:

$$\text{MAE} = 3.73$$
$$\text{MSE} = 16.27$$
$$\text{MAPE} = 19.24\%$$

These measures of forecast accuracy simply measure how well the forecasting method is able to forecast historical values of the time series. Now, suppose we want to forecast sales for a future time period, such as week 13. In this case, the forecast for week 13 is 22, the actual value of the time series in week 12. Is this an accurate estimate of sales for week 13? Unfortunately, there is no way to address the issue of accuracy associated with forecasts for future time periods. But, if we select a forecasting method that works well for the historical data, and we think that the historical pattern will continue into the future, we should obtain results that will ultimately be shown to be good.

Before closing this section, let's consider another method for forecasting the gasoline sales time series in Table 17.1. Suppose we use the average of all the historical data available as the forecast for the next period. We begin by developing a forecast for week 2.

Since there is only one historical value available prior to week 2, the forecast for week 2 is just the time series value in week 1; thus, the forecast for week 2 is 17,000 gallons of gasoline. To compute the forecast for week 3, we take the average of the sales values in weeks 1 and 2. Thus,

$$\text{Forecast for week 3} = \frac{17 + 21}{2} = 19$$

Similarly, the forecast for week 4 is

$$\text{Forecast for week 4} = \frac{17 + 21 + 19}{3} = 19$$

The forecasts obtained using this method for the gasoline time series are shown in Table 17.8 in the column labeled Forecast. Using the results shown in Table 17.8, we obtained the following values of MAE, MSE, and MAPE:

$$\text{MAE} = \frac{26.81}{11} = 2.44$$

$$\text{MSE} = \frac{89.07}{11} = 8.10$$

$$\text{MAPE} = \frac{141.34}{11} = 12.85\%$$

We can now compare the accuracy of the two forecasting methods we have considered in this section by comparing the values of MAE, MSE, and MAPE for each method.

	Naive Method	Average of Past Values
MAE	3.73	2.44
MSE	16.27	8.10
MAPE	19.24%	12.85%

Table 17.8 Computing Forecasts and Measures of Forecast Accuracy Using the Average of All the Historical Data as the Forecast for the Next Period

Week	Time Series Value	Forecast	Forecast Error	Absolute Value of Forecast Error	Squared Forecast Error	Percentage Error	Absolute Value of Percentage Error
1	17						
2	21	17.00	4.00	4.00	16.00	19.05	19.05
3	19	19.00	0.00	0.00	0.00	0.00	0.00
4	23	19.00	4.00	4.00	16.00	17.39	17.39
5	18	20.00	−2.00	2.00	4.00	−11.11	11.11
6	16	19.60	−3.60	3.60	12.96	−22.50	22.50
7	20	19.00	1.00	1.00	1.00	5.00	5.00
8	18	19.14	−1.14	1.14	1.31	−6.35	6.35
9	22	19.00	3.00	3.00	9.00	13.64	13.64
10	20	19.33	0.67	0.67	0.44	3.33	3.33
11	15	19.40	−4.40	4.40	19.36	−29.33	29.33
12	22	19.00	3.00	3.00	9.00	13.64	13.64
		Totals	4.53	26.81	89.07	2.76	141.34

For every measure, the average of past values provides more accurate forecasts than using the most recent observation as the forecast for the next period. In general, if the underlying time series is stationary, the average of all the historical data will always provide the best results.

But suppose that the underlying time series is not stationary. In Section 17.1, we mentioned that changes in business conditions can often result in a time series that has a horizontal pattern shifting to a new level. We discussed a situation in which the gasoline distributor signed a contract with the Vermont State Police to provide gasoline for state police cars located in southern Vermont. Table 17.2 shows the number of gallons of gasoline sold for the original time series and the 10 weeks after signing the new contract, and Figure 17.2 shows the corresponding time series plot. Note the change in level in week 13 for the resulting time series. When a shift to a new level like this occurs, it takes a long time for the forecasting method that uses the average of all the historical data to adjust to the new level of the time series. But, in this case, the simple naive method adjusts very rapidly to the change in level because it uses the most recent observation available as the forecast.

Measures of forecast accuracy are important factors in comparing different forecasting methods, but we have to be careful not to rely upon them too heavily. Good judgment and knowledge about business conditions that might affect the forecast also have to be carefully considered when selecting a method. And historical forecast accuracy is not the only consideration, especially if the time series is likely to change in the future.

In the next section, we will introduce more sophisticated methods for developing forecasts for a time series that exhibits a horizontal pattern. Using the measures of forecast accuracy developed here, we will be able to determine if such methods provide more accurate forecasts than we obtained using the simple approaches illustrated in this section. The methods that we will introduce also have the advantage of adapting well in situations where the time series changes to a new level. The ability of a forecasting method to adapt quickly to changes in level is an important consideration, especially in short-term forecasting situations.

Exercises

Methods

1. Consider the following time series data.

Week	1	2	3	4	5	6
Value	18	13	16	11	17	14

Using the naive method (most recent value) as the forecast for the next week, compute the following measures of forecast accuracy. **LO 1**

a. Mean absolute error.
b. Mean squared error.
c. Mean absolute percentage error.
d. What is the forecast for week 7?

2. Refer to the time series data in exercise 1. Using the average of all the historical data as a forecast for the next period, compute the following measures of forecast accuracy. **LO 1**

a. Mean absolute error.
b. Mean squared error.
c. Mean absolute percentage error.
d. What is the forecast for week 7?

3. Exercises 1 and 2 used different forecasting methods. Which method appears to provide the more accurate forecasts for the historical data? Explain. **LO 2**

4. Consider the following time series data. **LO 1, 2**

Month	1	2	3	4	5	6	7
Value	24	13	20	12	19	23	15

a. Compute MSE using the most recent value as the forecast for the next period. What is the forecast for month 8?
b. Compute MSE using the average of all the data available as the forecast for the next period. What is the forecast for month 8?
c. Which method appears to provide the better forecast?

17.3 Moving Averages and Exponential Smoothing

In this section, we discuss three forecasting methods that are appropriate for a time series with a horizontal pattern: moving averages, weighted moving averages, and exponential smoothing. These methods also adapt well to changes in the level of a horizontal pattern such as we saw with the extended gasoline sales time series (Table 17.2 and Figure 17.2). However, without modification they are not appropriate when significant trend, cyclical, or seasonal effects are present. Because the objective of each of these methods is to "smooth out" the random fluctuations in the time series, they are referred to as smoothing methods. These methods are easy to use and generally provide a high level of accuracy for short-range forecasts, such as a forecast for the next time period.

Moving Averages

The **moving averages** method uses the average of the most recent k data values in the time series as the forecast for the next period. Mathematically, a moving average forecast of order k is as follows:

Moving Average Forecast of Order k

$$F_{t+1} = \frac{\sum(\text{most recent } k \text{ data values})}{k} = \frac{Y_t + Y_{t-1} + \cdots + Y_{t-k+1}}{k} \quad \textbf{(17.1)}$$

where

F_{t+1} = forecast of the time series for period $t + 1$
Y_t = actual value of the time series in period t

The term *moving* is used because every time a new observation becomes available for the time series, it replaces the oldest observation in the equation and a new average is computed. As a result, the average will change, or move, as new observations become available.

To illustrate the moving averages method, let us return to the gasoline sales data in Table 17.1 and Figure 17.1. The time series plot in Figure 17.1 indicates that the gasoline sales time series has a horizontal pattern. Thus, the smoothing methods of this section are applicable.

To use moving averages to forecast a time series, we must first select the order, or number of time series values, to be included in the moving average. If only the most recent values of the time series are considered relevant, a small value of k is preferred. If more past values are considered relevant, then a larger value of k is better. As mentioned earlier, a time series with a horizontal pattern can shift to a new level over time. A moving average will adapt to the new level of the series and resume providing good forecasts in k periods. Thus, a smaller value of k will track shifts in a time series more quickly. But larger values of k will be more effective in smoothing out the random fluctuations over time. So managerial judgment based on an understanding of the behavior of a time series is helpful in choosing a good value for k.

To illustrate how moving averages can be used to forecast gasoline sales, we will use a three-week moving average ($k = 3$). We begin by computing the forecast of sales in week 4 using the average of the time series values in weeks 1–3.

$$F_4 = \text{average of weeks 1–3} = \frac{17 + 21 + 19}{3} = 19$$

Thus, the moving average forecast of sales in week 4 is 19 or 19,000 gallons of gasoline. Because the actual value observed in week 4 is 23, the forecast error in week 4 is $23 - 19 = 4$.

Next, we compute the forecast of sales in week 5 by averaging the time series values in weeks 2–4.

$$F_5 = \text{average of weeks 2–4} = \frac{21 + 19 + 23}{3} = 21$$

Hence, the forecast of sales in week 5 is 21 and the error associated with this forecast is $18 - 21 = -3$. A complete summary of the three-week moving average forecasts for the gasoline sales time series is provided in Table 17.9. Figure 17.8 shows the original time series plot and the three-week moving average forecasts. Note how the graph of the moving average forecasts has tended to smooth out the random fluctuations in the time series.

To forecast sales in week 13, the next time period in the future, we simply compute the average of the time series values in weeks 10, 11, and 12.

$$F_{13} = \text{average of weeks 10–12} = \frac{20 + 15 + 22}{3} = 19$$

Thus, the forecast for week 13 is 19, or 19,000 gallons of gasoline.

Table 17.9 Summary of Three-Week Moving Average Calculations

Week	Time Series Value	Forecast	Forecast Error	Absolute Value of Forecast Error	Squared Forecast Error	Percentage Error	Absolute Value of Percentage Error
1	17						
2	21						
3	19						
4	23	19	4	4	16	17.39	17.39
5	18	21	−3	3	9	−16.67	16.67
6	16	20	−4	4	16	−25.00	25.00
7	20	19	1	1	1	5.00	5.00
8	18	18	0	0	0	0.00	0.00
9	22	18	4	4	16	18.18	18.18
10	20	20	0	0	0	0.00	0.00
11	15	20	−5	5	25	−33.33	33.33
12	22	19	3	3	9	13.64	13.64
		Totals	0	24	92	−20.79	129.21

Figure 17.8 Gasoline Sales Time Series Plot and Three-Week Moving Average Forecasts

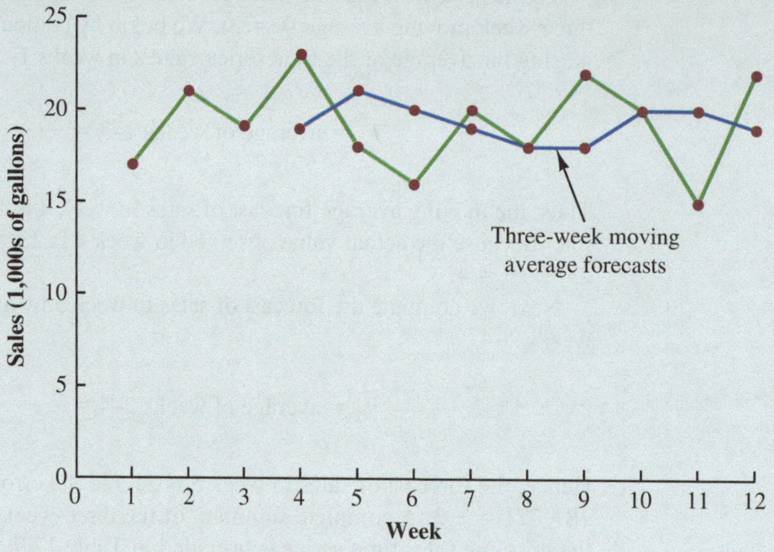

Using Excel's Moving Average Tool

We can use Excel's Moving Average tool to develop the three-week moving average forecasts for the gasoline sales time series in Table 17.1.

DATA*file*
gasolinesales

Enter/Access Data: Open the file *gasolinesales*. The data are in cells A2:B13 and labels are in cells A1:B1.

Apply Tools: The following steps describe how to use Excel's Moving Average tool to develop the three-week moving average forecasts for the gasoline sales time series in Table 17.1. Refer to Figure 17.9 as we describe the tasks involved.

Figure 17.9 Three-Week Moving Average Forecasts for the Gasoline Time Series Using Excel's Moving Average Tool

	A	B	C
1	Week	Sales	
2	1	17	
3	2	21	#N/A
4	3	19	#N/A
5	4	23	19
6	5	18	21
7	6	16	20
8	7	20	19
9	8	18	18
10	9	22	18
11	10	20	20
12	11	15	20
13	12	22	19
14			
15			

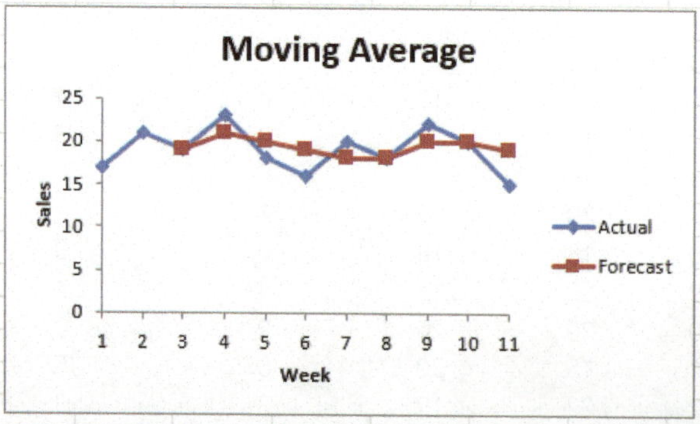

Step 1. Click the **Data** tab on the Ribbon
Step 2. In the **Analyze** group, click **Data Analysis**
Step 3. Choose **Moving Average** from the list of **Analysis Tools**
Click **OK**
Step 4. When the **Moving Average** dialog box appears:
Enter *B2:B13* in the **Input Range:** box
Enter *3* in the **Interval:** box
Enter *C3* in the **Output Range:** box
Select the check box for **Chart Output**
Click **OK**

The three-week moving average forecasts appear in column C of the worksheet; a chart showing the actual values of the time series and the forecasted values also appears. Forecasts for periods of other length can be computed easily by entering a different value in the interval box.

Forecast Accuracy In Section 17.2, we discussed three measures of forecast accuracy: MAE, MSE, and MAPE. Using the three-week moving average calculations in Table 17.9, the values for these three measures of forecast accuracy are

$$\text{MAE} = \frac{24}{9} = 2.67$$

$$\text{MSE} = \frac{92}{9} = 10.22$$

$$\text{MAPE} = \frac{129.21}{9} = 14.36\%$$

In situations where you need to compare forecasting methods for different time periods, such as comparing a forecast of weekly sales to a forecast of monthly sales, relative measures such as MAPE are preferred.

In Section 17.2, we also showed that using the most recent observation as the forecast for the next week (a moving average of order $k = 1$) resulted in values of MAE $= 3.73$, MSE $= 16.27$, and MAPE $= 19.24\%$. Thus, in each case the three-week moving average approach provided more accurate forecasts than simply using the most recent observation as the forecast.

To determine if a moving average with a different order k can provide more accurate forecasts, we recommend using trial and error to determine the value of k that minimizes MSE. For the gasoline sales time series, it can be shown that the minimum value of MSE corresponds to a moving average of order $k = 6$ with MSE $= 6.79$. If we are willing to assume that the order of the moving average that is best for the historical data will also be best for future values of the time series, the most accurate moving average forecasts of gasoline sales can be obtained using a moving average of order $k = 6$.

Weighted Moving Averages

A moving average forecast of order k = 3 is just a special case of the weighted moving averages method in which each weight is equal to 1/3.

In the moving averages method, each observation in the moving average calculation receives the same weight. One variation, known as **weighted moving averages**, involves selecting a different weight for each data value and then computing a weighted average of the most recent k values as the forecast. In most cases, the most recent observation receives the most weight, and the weight decreases for older data values. Let us use the gasoline sales time series to illustrate the computation of a weighted three-week moving average. We assign a weight of 3/6 to the most recent observation, a weight of 2/6 to the second most recent observation, and a weight of 1/6 to the third most recent observation. Using this weighted average, our forecast for week 4 is computed as follows:

$$\text{Forecast for week 4} = \tfrac{1}{6}(17) + \tfrac{2}{6}(21) + \tfrac{3}{6}(19) = 19.33$$

Note that for the weighted moving average method the sum of the weights is equal to 1.

Forecast Accuracy To use the weighted moving averages method, we must first select the number of data values to be included in the weighted moving average and then choose weights for each of the data values. In general, if we believe that the recent past is a better predictor of the future than the distant past, larger weights should be given to the more recent observations. However, when the time series is highly variable, selecting approximately equal weights for the data values may be best. The only requirement in selecting the weights is that their sum must equal 1. To determine whether one particular combination of number of data values and weights provides a more accurate forecast than another combination, we recommend using MSE as the measure of forecast accuracy. That is, if we assume that the combination that is best for the past will also be best for the future, we would use the combination of number of data values and weights that minimizes MSE for the historical time series to forecast the next value in the time series.

Exponential Smoothing

There are a number of exponential smoothing procedures. The method presented here is often referred to as single exponential smoothing. In the next section we show how an exponential smoothing method that uses two smoothing constants can be used to forecast a time series with a linear trend.

Exponential smoothing also uses a weighted average of past time series values as a forecast; it is a special case of the weighted moving averages method in which we select only one weight—the weight for the most recent observation. The weights for the other data values are computed automatically and become smaller as the observations move farther into the past. The exponential smoothing equation follows.

Exponential Smoothing Forecast

$$F_{t+1} = \alpha Y_t + (1 - \alpha)F_t \qquad \textbf{(17.2)}$$

where

F_{t+1} = forecast of the time series for period $t = 1$
Y_t = actual value of the time series in period t
F_t = forecast of the time series for period t
α = smoothing constant $(0 \le \alpha \le 1)$

Equation (17.2) shows that the forecast for period $t + 1$ is a weighted average of the actual value in period t and the forecast for period t. The weight given to the actual value in period t is the **smoothing constant** α and the weight given to the forecast in period t is $1 - \alpha$. It turns out that the exponential smoothing forecast for any period is actually a weighted average of *all the previous actual values* of the time series. Let us illustrate by working with a time series involving only three periods of data: Y_1, Y_2, and Y_3.

To initiate the calculations, we let F_1 equal the actual value of the time series in period 1; that is, $F_1 = Y_1$. Hence, the forecast for period 2 is

$$\begin{aligned} F_2 &= \alpha Y_1 + (1 - \alpha)F_1 \\ &= \alpha Y_1 + (1 - \alpha)Y_1 \\ &= Y_1 \end{aligned}$$

We see that the exponential smoothing forecast for period 2 is equal to the actual value of the time series in period 1.

The forecast for period 3 is

$$F_3 = \alpha Y_2 + (1 - \alpha)F_2 = \alpha Y_2 + (1 - \alpha)Y_1$$

Finally, substituting this expression for F_3 in the expression for F_4, we obtain

$$\begin{aligned} F_4 &= \alpha Y_3 + (1 - \alpha)F_3 \\ &= \alpha Y_3 + (1 - \alpha)[\alpha Y_2 + (1 - \alpha)Y_1] \\ &= \alpha Y_3 + \alpha(1 - \alpha)Y_2 + (1 - \alpha)^2 Y_1 \end{aligned}$$

The term exponential smoothing comes from the exponential nature of the weighting scheme for the historical values.

We now see that F_4 is a weighted average of the first three time series values. The sum of the coefficients, or weights, for Y_1, Y_2, and Y_3 equals 1. A similar argument can be made to show that, in general, any forecast F_{t+1} is a weighted average of all the previous time series values.

Despite the fact that exponential smoothing provides a forecast that is a weighted average of all past observations, all past data do not need to be saved to compute the forecast for the next period. In fact, equation (17.2) shows that once the value for the smoothing constant α is selected, only two pieces of information are needed to compute the forecast: Y_t, the actual value of the time series in period t, and F_t, the forecast for period t.

To illustrate the exponential smoothing approach, let us again consider the gasoline sales time series in Table 17.1 and Figure 17.1. As indicated previously, to start the calculations we set the exponential smoothing forecast for period 2 equal to the actual value of the time series in period 1. Thus, with $Y_1 = 17$, we set $F_2 = 17$ to initiate the computations. Referring to the time series data in Table 17.1, we find an actual time series value in period 2 of $Y_2 = 21$. Thus, period 2 has a forecast error of $21 - 17 = 4$.

Continuing with the exponential smoothing computations using a smoothing constant of $\alpha = 0.2$, we obtain the following forecast for period 3:

$$F_3 = 0.2Y_2 + 0.8F_2 = 0.2(21) + 0.8(17) = 17.8$$

Once the actual time series value in period 3, $Y_3 = 19$, is known, we can generate a forecast for period 4 as follows:

$$F_4 = 0.2Y_3 + 0.8F_3 = 0.2(19) + 0.8(17.8) = 18.04$$

Continuing the exponential smoothing calculations, we obtain the weekly forecast values shown in Table 17.10. Note that we have not shown an exponential smoothing forecast or a forecast error for week 1 because no forecast was made. For week 12, we have $Y_{12} = 22$ and $F_{12} = 18.48$. We can use this information to generate a forecast for week 13.

$$F_{13} = 0.2Y_{12} + 0.8F_{12} = 0.2(22) + 0.8(18.48) = 19.18$$

Thus, the exponential smoothing forecast of the amount sold in week 13 is 19.18, or 19,180 gallons of gasoline. With this forecast, the firm can make plans and decisions accordingly.

Figure 17.10 shows the time series plot of the actual and forecast time series values. Note in particular how the forecasts "smooth out" the irregular or random fluctuations in the time series.

Table 17.10 Summary of the Exponential Smoothing Forecasts and Forecast Errors for the Gasoline Sales Time Series with Smoothing Constant $\alpha = 0.2$

Week	Time Series Value	Forecast	Forecast Error	Squared Forecast Error
1	17			
2	21	17.00	4.00	16.00
3	19	17.80	1.20	1.44
4	23	18.04	4.96	24.60
5	18	19.03	−1.03	1.06
6	16	18.83	−2.83	8.01
7	20	18.26	1.74	3.03
8	18	18.61	−0.61	0.37
9	22	18.49	3.51	12.32
10	20	19.19	0.81	0.66
11	15	19.35	−4.35	18.92
12	22	18.48	3.52	12.39
		Totals	10.92	98.80

Figure 17.10 Actual and Forecast Gasoline Sales Time Series with Smoothing Constant $\alpha = 0.2$

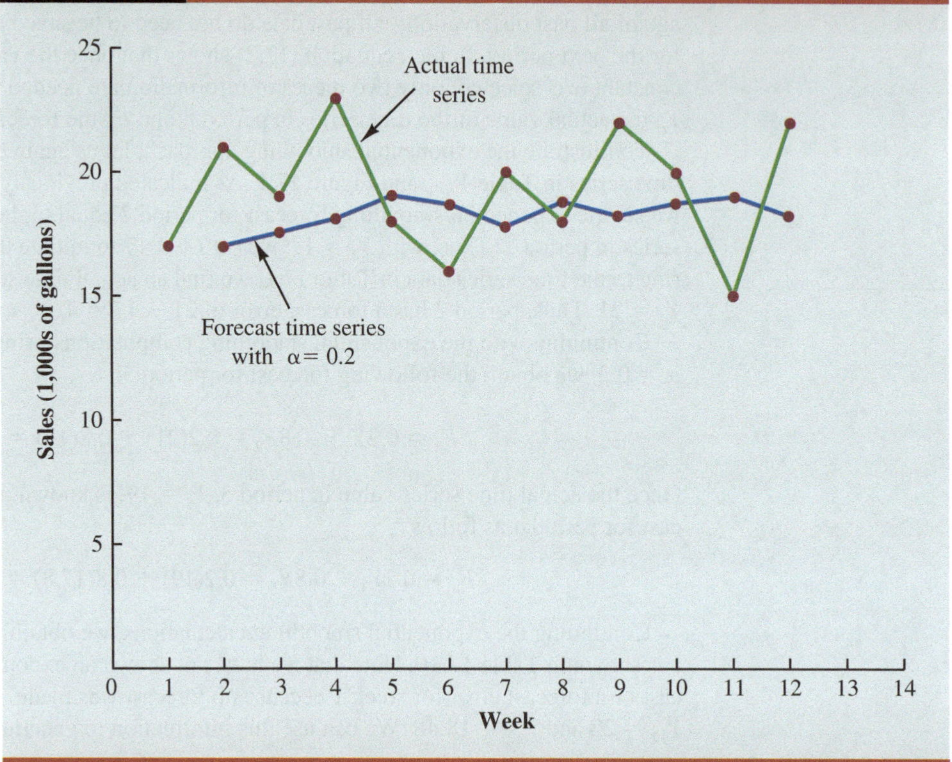

Using Excel's Exponential Smoothing Tool

We can use Excel's Exponential Smoothing tool to develop forecasts for the gasoline sales time series in Table 17.1 using a smoothing constant of $\alpha = 0.2$.

DATA*file* gasolinesales

Enter/Access Data: Open the file *gasolinesales*. The data are in cells A2:B13 and labels are in cells A1:B1.

Apply Tools: The following steps describe how to use Excel's Exponential Smoothing tool to develop forecasts for the gasoline sales time series in Table 17.1 using a smoothing constant of $\alpha = 0.2$. Refer to Figure 17.11 as we describe the tasks involved.

Step 1. Click the **Data** tab on the Ribbon
Step 2. In the **Analyze** group, click **Data Analysis**
Step 3. Choose **Exponential Smoothing** from the list of **Analysis Tools**
Click **OK**
Step 4. When the **Exponential Smoothing** dialog box appears:
Enter *B2:B13* in the **Input Range:** box
Enter *0.8* in the **Damping factor:** box
Enter *C2* in the **Output Range:** box
Select the check box for **Chart Output**
Click **OK**

The exponential smoothing forecasts appear in column C of the worksheet; a chart showing the actual values of the time series and the forecasted values also appears. Note that the value we entered in the Damping factor box is $1 - \alpha$; forecasting for other smoothing constants can be computed easily by entering a different value for $1 - \alpha$ in the Damping Factor box.

Figure 17.11 Exponential Smoothing Forecasts with $\alpha = 0.2$ for the Gasoline Time Series Using Excel's Exponential Smoothing Tool

	A	B	C
1	Week	Sales	
2	1	17	#N/A
3	2	21	17
4	3	19	17.8
5	4	23	18.04
6	5	18	19.032
7	6	16	18.8256
8	7	20	18.2605
9	8	18	18.6084
10	9	22	18.4867
11	10	20	19.1894
12	11	15	19.3515
13	12	22	18.4812
14			
15			

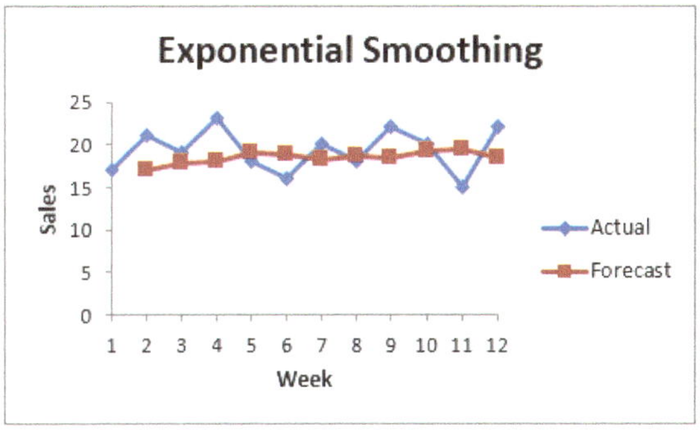

Forecast Accuracy In the preceding exponential smoothing calculations, we used a smoothing constant of $\alpha = 0.2$. Although any value of α between 0 and 1 is acceptable, some values will yield better forecasts than others. Insight into choosing a good value for α can be obtained by rewriting the basic exponential smoothing model as follows:

$$F_{t+1} = \alpha Y_t + (1 - \alpha)F_t$$
$$F_{t+1} = \alpha Y_t + F_t - \alpha F_t$$
$$F_{t+1} = F_t + \alpha(Y_t - F_t) \quad \textbf{(17.3)}$$

Thus, the new forecast F_{t+1} is equal to the previous forecast F_t plus an adjustment, which is the smoothing constant α times the most recent forecast error, $Y_t - F_t$. That is, the forecast in period $t + 1$ is obtained by adjusting the forecast in period t by a fraction of the forecast error. If the time series contains substantial random variability, a small value of the smoothing constant is preferred. The reason for this choice is that if much of the forecast error is due to random variability, we do not want to overreact and adjust the forecasts too quickly. For a time series with relatively little random variability, forecast errors are more likely to represent a change in the level of the series. Thus, larger values of the smoothing constant provide the advantage of quickly adjusting the forecasts; this allows the forecasts to react more quickly to changing conditions.

The criterion we will use to determine a desirable value for the smoothing constant α is the same as the criterion we proposed for determining the order or number of periods of data to include in the moving averages calculation. That is, we choose the value of α that minimizes the MSE. A summary of the MSE calculations for the exponential smoothing forecast of gasoline sales with $\alpha = 0.2$ is shown in Table 17.10. Note that there is one less squared error term than the number of time periods because we had no past values with which to make a forecast for period 1. The value of the sum of squared forecast errors is 98.80; hence MSE = 98.80/11 = 8.98. Would a different value of α provide better results in terms of a lower MSE value? Perhaps the most straightforward way to answer this question is simply to try another value for α. We will then compare its mean squared error with the MSE value of 8.98 obtained by using a smoothing constant of $\alpha = 0.2$.

The exponential smoothing results with $\alpha = 0.3$ are shown in Table 17.11. The value of the sum of squared forecast errors is 102.83; hence MSE = 102.83/11 = 9.35. With MSE = 9.35, we see that, for the current data set, a smoothing constant of $\alpha = 0.3$ results in less forecast accuracy than a smoothing constant of $\alpha = 0.2$. Thus, we would be inclined

Table 17.11 Summary of the Exponential Smoothing Forecasts and Forecast Errors for the Gasoline Sales Time Series with Smoothing Constant $\alpha = 0.3$

Week	Time Series Value	Forecast	Forecast Error	Squared Forecast Error
1	17			
2	21	17.00	4.00	16.00
3	19	18.20	0.80	0.64
4	23	18.44	4.56	20.79
5	18	19.81	−1.81	3.28
6	16	19.27	−3.27	10.69
7	20	18.29	1.71	2.92
8	18	18.80	−0.80	0.64
9	22	18.56	3.44	11.83
10	20	19.59	0.41	0.17
11	15	19.71	−4.71	22.18
12	22	18.30	3.70	13.69
		Totals	8.03	102.83

to prefer the original smoothing constant of $\alpha = 0.2$. Using a trial-and-error calculation with other values of α, we can find a "good" value for the smoothing constant. This value can be used in the exponential smoothing model to provide forecasts for the future. At a later date, after new time series observations are obtained, we analyze the newly collected time series data to determine whether the smoothing constant should be revised to provide better forecasting results.

Notes + Comments

1. Spreadsheet packages are an effective aid in choosing a good value of α for exponential smoothing. With the time series data and the forecasting formulas in a spreadsheet, you can experiment with different values of α and choose the value that provides the smallest forecast error using one or more of the measures of forecast accuracy (MAE, MSE, or MAPE).
2. We presented the moving average and exponential smoothing methods in the context of a stationary time series. These methods can also be used to forecast a nonstationary time series which shifts in level but exhibits no trend or seasonality. Moving averages with small values of k adapt more quickly than moving averages with larger values of k. Exponential smoothing models with smoothing constants closer to one adapt more quickly than models with smaller values of the smoothing constant.

Exercises

Methods

5. Consider the following time series data. **LO 1, 2, 3, 4**

Week	1	2	3	4	5	6
Value	18	13	16	11	17	14

a. Construct a time series plot. What type of pattern exists in the data?

b. Develop the three-week moving average forecasts for this time series. Compute MSE and a forecast for week 7.

c. Use $\alpha = 0.2$ to compute the exponential smoothing forecasts for the time series. Compute MSE and a forecast for week 7.
d. Compare the three-week moving average approach with the exponential smoothing approach using $\alpha = 0.2$. Which appears to provide more accurate forecasts based on MSE? Explain.
e. Use a smoothing constant of $\alpha = 0.4$ to compute the exponential smoothing forecasts. Does a smoothing constant of 0.2 or 0.4 appear to provide more accurate forecasts based on MSE? Explain.

6. Consider the following time series data. **LO 1, 2, 3, 4**

Month	1	2	3	4	5	6	7
Value	24	13	20	12	19	23	15

Construct a time series plot. What type of pattern exists in the data?
a. Develop the three-week moving average forecasts for this time series. Compute MSE and a forecast for week 8.
b. Use $\alpha = 0.2$ to compute the exponential smoothing forecasts for the time series. Compute MSE and a forecast for week 8.
c. Compare the three-week moving average approach with the exponential smoothing approach using $\alpha = 0.2$. Which appears to provide more accurate forecasts based on MSE?
d. Use a smoothing constant of $\alpha = 0.4$ to compute the exponential smoothing forecasts. Does a smoothing constant of 0.2 or 0.4 appear to provide more accurate forecasts based on MSE? Explain.

DATA*file*
gasolinesales

7. Refer to the gasoline sales time series data in Table 17.1. **LO 1, 2, 4**
a. Compute four-week and five-week moving averages for the time series.
b. Compute the MSE for the four-week and five-week moving average forecasts.
c. What appears to be the best number of weeks of past data (three, four, or five) to use in the moving average computation? Recall that MSE for the three-week moving average is 10.22.

DATA*file*
gasolinesales

8. Refer again to the gasoline sales time series data in Table 17.1. **LO 1, 2, 4**
a. Using a weight of 1/2 for the most recent observation, 1/3 for the second most recent observation, and 1/6 for third most recent observation, compute a three-week weighted moving average for the time series.
b. Compute the MSE for the weighted moving average in part (a). Do you prefer this weighted moving average to the unweighted moving average? Remember that the MSE for the unweighted moving average is 10.22.
c. Suppose you are allowed to choose any weights as long as they sum to 1. Could you always find a set of weights that would make the MSE at least as small for a weighted moving average than for an unweighted moving average? Why or why not?

DATA*file*
gasolinesales

9. With the gasoline time series data from Table 17.1, show the exponential smoothing forecasts using $\alpha = 0.1$. **LO 1, 2, 4**
a. Applying the MSE measure of forecast accuracy, would you prefer a smoothing constant of $\alpha = 0.1$ or $\alpha = 0.2$ for the gasoline sales time series?
b. Are the results the same if you apply MAE as the measure of accuracy?
c. What are the results if MAPE is used?

10. With a smoothing constant of $\alpha = 0.2$, equation (17.2) shows that the forecast for week 13 of the gasoline sales data from Table 17.1 is given by $F_{13} = 0.2Y_{12} + 0.8F_{12}$. However, the forecast for week 12 is given by $F_{12} = 0.2Y_{11} + 0.8F_{11}$. Thus, the forecast for week 13 can be written

$$F_{13} = 0.2Y_{12} + 0.8(0.2Y_{11} + 0.8F_{11}) = 0.2Y_{12} + 0.16Y_{11} + 0.64F_{11}$$

by combining these two expressions for F_{13} and F_{12}. **LO 4**

a. Making use of the fact that $F_{11} = 0.2Y_{10} + 0.8F_{10}$ (and similarly for F_{10} and F_9), continue to expand the expression for F_{13} until it is written in terms of the past data values Y_{12}, Y_{11}, Y_{10}, Y_9, Y_8, and the forecast for period 8.
b. Refer to the coefficients or weights for the past values Y_{12}, Y_{11}, Y_{10}, Y_9, Y_8. What observation can you make about how exponential smoothing weights past data values in arriving at new forecasts? Compare this weighting pattern with the weighting pattern of the moving averages method.

Applications

11. **On-time Shipments.** For the Hawkins Company, the monthly percentages of all shipments received on time over the past 12 months are 80, 82, 84, 83, 83, 84, 85, 84, 82, 83, 84, and 83. **LO 1, 2, 3, 4**
    a. Construct a time series plot. What type of pattern exists in the data?
    b. Compare the three-month moving average approach with the exponential smoothing approach for $\alpha = 0.2$. Which provides more accurate forecasts using MSE as the measure of forecast accuracy?
    c. What is the forecast for next month?
12. **Bond Interest Rates.** Corporate triple-A bond interest rates for 12 consecutive months follow. **LO 1, 2, 3, 4**

    9.5 9.3 9.4 9.6 9.8 9.7 9.8 10.5 9.9 9.7 9.6 9.6

    a. Construct a time series plot. What type of pattern exists in the data?
    b. Develop three and four-month moving averages for this time series. Does the three-month or four-month moving average provide more accurate forecasts based on MSE? Explain.
    c. What is the moving average forecast for the next month?
13. **Building Contracts.** The values of Alabama building contracts (in $ millions) for a 12-month period follow. **LO 1, 2, 3, 4**

    240 350 230 260 280 320 220 310 240 310 240 230

    a. Construct a time series plot. What type of pattern exists in the data?
    b. Compare the three-month moving average approach with the exponential smoothing forecast using $\alpha = 0.2$. Which provides more accurate forecasts based on MSE?
    c. What is the forecast for the next month?
14. **Sales Forecasts.** The following time series shows the sales of a particular product over the past 12 months. **LO 1, 2, 3, 4**

DATA*file*
productsales

Month	Sales	Month	Sales
1	105	7	145
2	135	8	140
3	120	9	100
4	105	10	80
5	90	11	100
6	120	12	110

    a. Construct a time series plot. What type of pattern exists in the data?
    b. Use $\alpha = 0.3$ to compute the exponential smoothing forecasts for the time series.
    c. Use a smoothing constant of $\alpha = 0.5$ to compute the exponential smoothing forecasts. Does a smoothing constant of 0.3 or 0.5 appear to provide more accurate forecasts based on MSE?

15. **Commodity Futures Index.** Ten weeks of data on the Commodity Futures Index are 7.35, 7.40, 7.55, 7.56, 7.60, 7.52, 7.52, 7.70, 7.62, and 7.55. **LO 1, 2, 3, 4**
    a. Construct a time series plot. What type of pattern exists in the data?
    b. Compute the exponential smoothing forecasts for $\alpha = 0.2$.
    c. Compute the exponential smoothing forecasts for $\alpha = 0.3$.
    d. Which exponential smoothing constant provides more accurate forecasts based on MSE? Forecast week 11.

16. **Home Prices.** The U.S. Census Bureau tracks the median price for new home sales by month of year. The median prices for April for the years 1990 to 2011 follow (U.S. Census Bureau website). **LO 1, 2, 3, 4**

DATA*file*
homeprices

Year	Price ($1,000s)	Year	Price ($1,000s)
1	130.0	12	175.2
2	121.0	13	187.1
3	120.0	14	189.5
4	127.0	15	222.3
5	129.0	16	236.3
6	134.0	17	257.0
7	140.0	18	242.5
8	150.0	19	246.4
9	148.0	20	219.2
10	159.9	21	208.3
11	162.6	22	224.7

    a. Construct a time series plot. Comment on any pattern you observe. Discuss some of the factors that may have resulted in this time series plot.
    b. Given the time series plot in part (a), do you think the forecasting methods developed in this section are appropriate for this time series? Explain.
    c. To forecast a value for year 23, how much of the past data would you use? Explain.

17.4 Trend Projection

In this section, we present two forecasting methods that are appropriate for time series exhibiting a trend pattern. First, we show how simple linear regression can be used to forecast a time series with a linear trend. We then show how the curve-fitting capability of regression analysis can also be used to forecast time series with a curvilinear or nonlinear trend.

Linear Trend Regression

In Section 17.1, we used the bicycle sales time series in Table 17.3 and Figure 17.3 to illustrate a time series with a trend pattern. Let us now use this time series to illustrate how simple linear regression can be used to forecast a time series with a linear trend. The data for the bicycle time series are repeated in Table 17.12 and Figure 17.12.

Although the time series plot in Figure 17.12 shows some up and down movement over the past 10 years, we might agree that the linear trend line shown in Figure 17.13 provides a reasonable approximation of the long-run movement in the series. We can use the methods of simple linear regression to develop such a linear trend line for the bicycle sales time series.

In Chapter 14, we describe simple linear regression in more detail.

The estimated regression equation describing a straight-line relationship between an independent variable x and a dependent variable y is written as

$$\hat{y} = b_0 + b_1x$$

Table 17.12 Bicycle Sales Time Series

DATA*file*
bicyclesales

Year	Sales (1,000s)
1	21.6
2	22.9
3	25.5
4	21.9
5	23.9
6	27.5
7	31.5
8	29.7
9	28.6
10	31.4

Figure 17.12 Bicycle Sales Time Series Plot

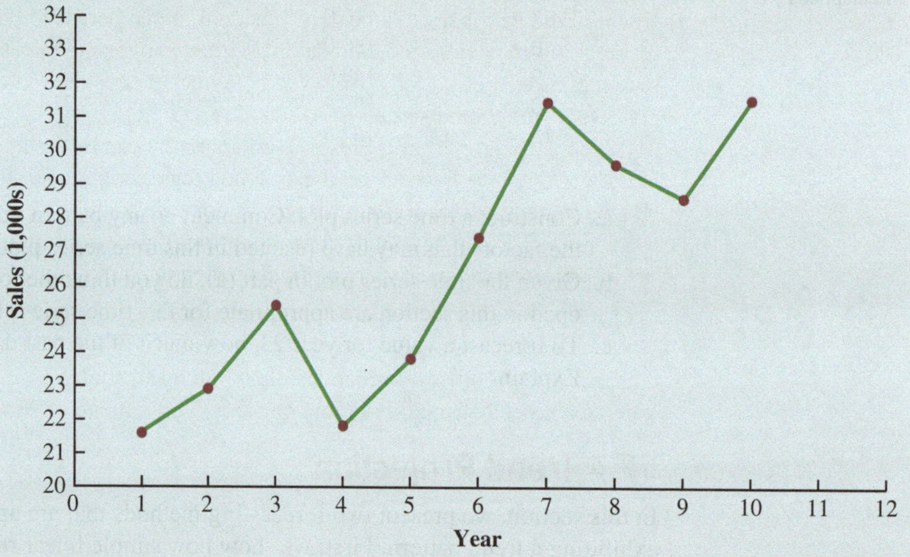

where $\hat{y}$ is the estimated or predicted value of y. To emphasize the fact that in forecasting the independent variable is time, we will replace x with t and $\hat{y}$ with T_t to emphasize that we are estimating the trend for a time series. Thus, for estimating the linear trend in a time series we will use the following estimated regression equation.

Linear Trend Equation

$$T_t = b_0 + b_1 t \tag{17.4}$$

where

T_t = linear trend forecast in period t
b_0 = intercept of the linear trend line
b_1 = slope of the linear trend line
t = time period

Figure 17.13 Trend Represented by a Linear Function for the Bicycle Sales Time Series

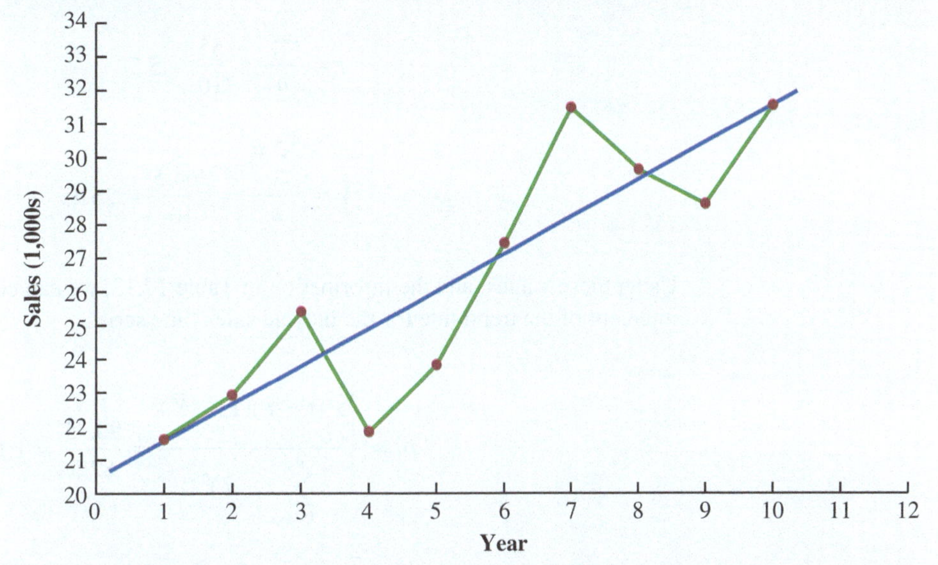

In equation (17.4), the time variable begins at $t = 1$ corresponding to the first time series observation (Year 1 for the bicycle sales time series) and continues until $t = n$ corresponding to the most recent time series observation (year 10 for the bicycle sales time series). Thus, for the bicycle sales time series $t = 1$ corresponds to the oldest time series value and $t = 10$ corresponds to the most recent year.

Formulas for computing the estimated regression coefficients (b_1 and b_0) in equation (17.4) follow.

Computing the Slope and Intercept for a Linear Trend*

$$b_1 = \frac{\sum_{t=1}^{n}(t - \bar{t})(Y_t - \bar{Y})}{\sum_{t=1}^{n}(t - \bar{t})^2} \quad \textbf{(17.5)}$$

$$b_0 = \bar{Y} - b_1\bar{t} \quad \textbf{(17.6)}$$

where

Y_t = value of the time series in period t
n = number of time periods (number of observations)
$\bar{Y}$ = average value of the time series
$\bar{t}$ = average value of t

*An alternate formula for b_1 is

$$b_1 = \frac{\sum_{t=1}^{n} tY_t - \left(\sum_{t=1}^{n} t \sum_{t=1}^{n} Y_t\right)/n}{\sum_{t=1}^{n} t^2 - \left(\sum_{t=1}^{n} t\right)^2/n}$$

This form of equation (17.5) is often recommended when using a calculator to compute b_1.

To compute the linear trend equation for the bicycle sales time series, we begin the calculations by computing $\bar{t}$ and $\bar{Y}$ using the information in Table 17.12.

$$\bar{t} = \frac{\sum_{t=1}^{n} t}{n} = \frac{55}{10} = 5.5$$

$$\bar{Y} = \frac{\sum_{t=1}^{n} Y_t}{n} = \frac{264.5}{10} = 26.45$$

Using these values, and the information in Table 17.13, we can compute the slope and intercept of the trend line for the bicycle sales time series.

$$b_1 = \frac{\sum_{t=1}^{n} (t - \bar{t})(Y_t - \bar{Y})}{\sum_{t=1}^{n} (t - \bar{t})^2} = \frac{90.75}{82.5} = 1.1$$

$$b_0 = \bar{Y} - b_1\bar{t} = 26.45 - 1.1(5.5) = 20.4$$

Therefore, the linear trend equation is

$$T_t = 20.4 + 1.1t$$

The slope of 1.1 indicates that over the past 10 years the firm experienced an average growth in sales of about 1,100 units per year. If we assume that the past 10-year trend in sales is a good indicator of the future, this trend equation can be used to develop forecasts for future time periods. For example, substituting $t = 11$ into the equation yields next year's trend projection or forecast, T_{11}.

$$T_{11} = 20.4 + 1.1(11) = 32.5$$

Thus, using trend projection, we would forecast sales of 32,500 bicycles next year.

Table 17.13 Summary of Linear Trend Calculations for the Bicycle Sales Time Series

	t	Y_t	$t - \bar{t}$	$Y_t - \bar{Y}$	$(t - \bar{t})(Y_t - \bar{Y})$	$(t - \bar{t})^2$
	1	21.6	−4.5	−4.85	21.825	20.25
	2	22.9	−3.5	−3.55	12.425	12.25
	3	25.5	−2.5	−0.95	2.375	6.25
	4	21.9	−1.5	−4.55	6.825	2.25
	5	23.9	−0.5	−2.55	1.275	0.25
	6	27.5	0.5	1.05	0.525	0.25
	7	31.5	1.5	5.05	7.575	2.25
	8	29.7	2.5	3.25	8.125	6.25
	9	28.6	3.5	2.15	7.525	12.25
	10	31.4	4.5	4.95	22.275	20.25
Totals	55	264.5			90.750	82.50

Table 17.14 Summary of the Linear Trend Forecasts and Forecast Errors for the Bicycle Sales Time Series

Year	Sales (1,000s) Y_t	Forecast T_t	Forecast Error	Squared Forecast Error
1	21.6	21.5	0.1	0.01
2	22.9	22.6	0.3	0.09
3	25.5	23.7	1.8	3.24
4	21.9	24.8	−2.9	8.41
5	23.9	25.9	−2.0	4.00
6	27.5	27.0	0.5	0.25
7	31.5	28.1	3.4	11.56
8	29.7	29.2	0.5	0.25
9	28.6	30.3	−1.7	2.89
10	31.4	31.4	0.0	0.00
			Total	30.70

To compute the accuracy associated with the trend projection forecasting method, we will use the MSE. Table 17.14 shows the computation of the sum of squared errors for the bicycle sales time series. Thus, for the bicycle sales time series,

$$\text{MSE} = \frac{\sum_{t=1}^{n}(Y_t - F_t)^2}{n} = \frac{30.7}{10} = 3.07$$

Using Excel's Regression Tool to Compute a Linear Trend Equation

In Section 14.6, we showed how Excel's Regression tool can be used to perform a complete regression analysis. The same procedure can be used to compute a linear trend equation. We illustrate using the bicycle sales time series in Table 17.12.

DATA*file*
bicyclesales

Enter/Access Data: Open the file *bicyclesales*. The data are in cells A2:B11 and labels are in cells A1:B1.

Apply Tools: The following steps describe how to use Excel's Regression tool to compute a linear trend equation for the bicycle sales time. Refer to Figure 17.14 as we describe the tasks involved.

Step 1. Click the **Data** tab on the Ribbon
Step 2. In the **Analyze** group, click **Data Analysis**
Step 3. Choose **Regression** from the list of **Analysis Tools**
Step 4. When the Regression dialog box appears:
Enter *B1:B11* in the **Input Y Range:** box
Enter *A1:A11* in the **Input X Range:** box
Select the check box for **Labels**
Select the check box for **Confidence Level:**
Select **Output Range:**
Enter *A13* in the **Output Range:** box (to identify the upper-left corner of the section of the worksheet where the output will appear)
Click **OK**

Figure 17.14 Excel's Regression Tool Output for the Bicycle Sales Time Series

	A	B	C	D	E	F	G	H
1	Year	Sales						
2	1	21.6						
3	2	22.9						
4	3	25.5						
5	4	21.9						
6	5	23.9						
7	6	27.5						
8	7	31.5						
9	8	29.7						
10	9	28.6						
11	10	31.4						
12								
13	SUMMARY OUTPUT							
14								
15	*Regression Statistics*							
16	Multiple R	0.8745						
17	R Square	0.7648						
18	Adjusted R Square	0.7354						
19	Standard Error	1.9590						
20	Observations	10						
21								
22	ANOVA							
23		*df*	*SS*	*MS*	*F*	*Significance F*		
24	Regression	1	99.825	99.825	26.0130	0.0009		
25	Residual	8	30.7	3.8375				
26	Total	9	130.525					
27								
28		*Coefficients*	*Standard Error*	*t Stat*	*P-value*	*Lower 95%*	*Upper 95%*	
29	Intercept	20.4	1.3382	15.2441	0.0000	17.3141	23.4859	
30	Year	1.1	0.2157	5.1003	0.0009	0.6027	1.5973	
31								

The Excel Regression tool output shows that the value of the intercept of the trend line is 20.4 (cell B29) and that the slope of the trend line is 1.1 (cell B30), the same values we obtained using hand calculation. But in the regression output the value of MSE (cell D25) is

$$\text{MSE} = \frac{\text{Sum of Squares Due to Error}}{\text{Degrees of Freedom}} = \frac{30.7}{8} = 3.8375$$

This value of MSE differs from the value we computed previously because in regression analysis the sum of squared errors is divided by 8 (degrees of freedom) instead of 10 (number of observations). Thus, MSE computed using Excel's Regression tool is not the average of the squared forecast errors. Most forecasting packages, however, compute MSE by taking the average of the forecast errors.

Nonlinear Trend Regression

The use of a linear function to model trend is common. However, as we discussed previously, sometimes time series have a curvilinear or nonlinear trend. As an example, consider the annual revenue in millions of dollars for a cholesterol drug for the first 10 years of sales. Table 17.15 shows the time series and Figure 17.15 shows the corresponding time series plot. For instance, revenue in Year 1 was $23.1 million; revenue in Year 2 was $21.3 million; and so on. The time series plot indicates an overall increasing or upward trend. But, unlike the bicycle sales time series, a linear trend does not appear to be appropriate. Instead, a curvilinear function appears to be needed to model the long-term trend.

DATA*file*
cholesterolrevenue

Table 17.15 Cholesterol Revenue Time Series ($millions)

Year (t)	Revenue ($millions)
1	23.1
2	21.3
3	27.4
4	34.6
5	33.8
6	43.2
7	59.5
8	64.4
9	74.2
10	99.3

Figure 17.15 Cholesterol Revenue Time Series Plot ($millions)

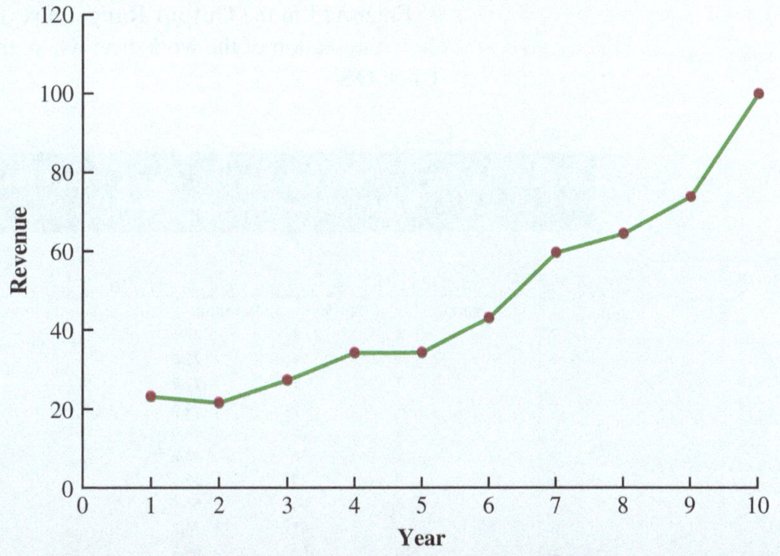

Quadratic Trend Equation A variety of nonlinear functions can be used to develop an estimate of the trend for the cholesterol time series. For instance, consider the following quadratic trend equation:

$$T_t = b_0 + b_1 t + b_2 t^2 \quad \textbf{(17.7)}$$

For the cholesterol time series, $t = 1$ corresponds to Year 1, $t = 2$ corresponds to Year 2, and so on.

Using Excel's Regression Tool to Compute a Quadratic Trend Equation

We can use Excel's Regression tool to compute a quadratic trend equation by creating a multiple regression model consisting of two *independent* variables, year and year squared. We illustrate using the cholesterol revenue time series in Table 17.15.

DATA*file*
cholesterolrevenue

Enter/Access Data: Open the file *cholesterolrevenue*. The data are in cells A2:B11 and labels are in cells A1:B1. To place the values of year squared in the column next to the values of year, we must first move the values in column B to column C. We then enter the label *YearSq* into cell B1 and place the values of year squared into cells B2:B11. The revised data set is shown in Figure 17.16. Note that the first observation is 1, 1, 23.1; the second observation is 2, 4, 21.3; the third observation is 3, 9, 27.4; and so on.

Apply Tools: The following steps describe how to use Excel's Regression tool to compute a quadratic trend equation for the cholesterol revenue time series. Refer to Figure 17.16 as we describe the tasks involved.

Step 1. Click the **Data** tab on the Ribbon
Step 2. In the **Analyze** group, click **Data Analysis**
Step 3. Choose **Regression** from the list of **Analysis Tools**
Step 4. When the **Regression** dialog box appears:
Enter *C1:C11* in the **Input Y Range:** box
Enter *A1:B11* in the **Input X Range:** box
Select the check box for **Labels**
Select the check box for **Confidence Level:**
Select **Output Range:**
Enter *A13* in the **Output Range:** box (to identify the upper-left corner of the section of the worksheet where the output will appear)
Click **OK**

Figure 17.16 Excel's Regression Tool Output for a Quadratic Model for the Cholesterol Revenue Time Series

	A	B	C	D	E	F	G	H
1	Year	YearSq	Revenue					
2	1	1	23.1					
3	2	4	21.3					
4	3	9	27.4					
5	4	16	34.6					
6	5	25	33.8					
7	6	36	43.2					
8	7	49	59.5					
9	8	64	64.4					
10	9	81	74.2					
11	10	100	99.3					
12								
13	SUMMARY OUTPUT							
14								
15	*Regression Statistics*							
16	Multiple R	0.9905						
17	R Square	0.9812						
18	Adjusted R Square	0.9758						
19	Standard Error	3.9758						
20	Observations	10						
21								
22	ANOVA							
23		*df*	*SS*	*MS*	*F*	*Significance F*		
24	Regression	2	5770.1281	2885.0640	182.5199	0.0000		
25	Residual	7	110.6479	15.8068				
26	Total	9	5880.776					
27								
28		*Coefficients*	*Standard Error*	*t Stat*	*P-value*	*Lower 95%*	*Upper 95%*	
29	Intercept	24.1817	4.6761	5.1713	0.0013	13.1244	35.2389	
30	Year	-2.1060	1.9529	-1.0784	0.3166	-6.7240	2.5120	
31	YearSq	0.9216	0.1730	5.3264	0.0011	0.5125	1.3307	
32								

The Excel Regression tool output shows that the values of b_0, b_1, and b_2 are 24.1817 (cell B29), −2.1060 (cell B30), and 0.9216 (cell B31). Thus, the estimated regression equation is

$$T_t = 24.1817 - 2.1060t + 0.9216t^2$$

The forecast of sales revenue for year 11 is

$$T_{11} = 24.1817 - 2.1060(11) + 0.9216(11)^2 = 112.53$$

or approximately \$112.5 million.

Exponential Trend Equation Another alternative that can be used to model the nonlinear pattern exhibited by the cholesterol time series is to fit an exponential model to the data. For instance, consider the following exponential trend equation:

$$T_t = b_0\, e^{b_1 t} \tag{17.8}$$

To better understand this exponential trend equation, suppose $b_0 = 16.71$ and $b_1 = 0.1697$. Then, for $t = 1$, $T_1 = 16.71\, e^{0.1697(1)} = 19.80$; for $t = 2$, $T_2 = 16.71e^{0.1697(2)} = 23.46$; for $t = 3$, $T_3 = 16.71\, e^{0.1697(3)} = 27.80$, and so forth for higher values of t. Note that T_t is not increasing by a constant amount as in the case of the linear trend model but by a constant percentage. In this exponential trend model, the multiplicative factor is $e^{0.1697(1)} = 1.185$, so the constant percentage increase from time period to time period is 18.5%.

Many statistical software packages have the capability to compute an exponential trend equation directly. Some software packages only provide linear trend, but by applying a natural log transformation to both sides of the equality in equation (17.8) we can apply the equivalent linear form:

$$\ln(T_t) = \ln(b_o) + b_1\, t \tag{17.9}$$

Figure 17.17 shows the graphical output of an exponential trend equation based on equation (17.8) for the cholesterol revenue time series.

Figure 17.17 Time Series Exponential Growth Trend Analysis Output for the Cholesterol Revenue Time Series

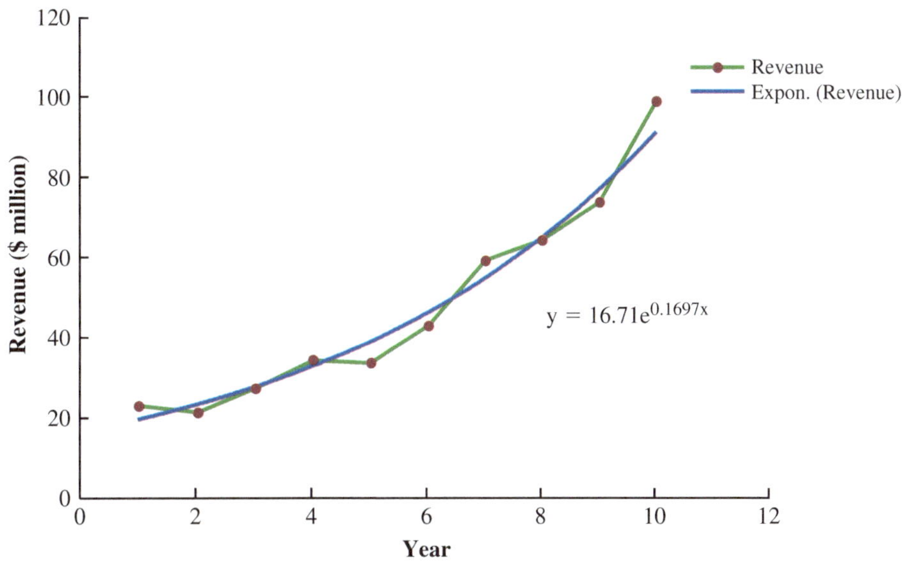

Using Excel's Regression Tool to Compute an Exponential Trend Equation

We can use Excel's Regression tool to compute an exponential trend equation by using the linear form given in equation (17.9). We illustrate using the cholesterol revenue time series in Table 17.15.

Enter/Access Data: Open the file *cholesterolrevenue*. The data are in cells A2:B11 and labels are in cells A1:B1. To place the values of ln(Revenue) in the column next to the values of Revenue, enter the label LN(Revenue) into cell C1 and the formula =LN(B2) in cell C2. Copy the formula in cell C2 to cells C3 through C11.The revised data set is shown in Figure 17.18. Note that the first observation is 1, 23.1, 3.1398; the second observation is 2, 21.3, 3.0857; and so on.

Apply Tools: The following steps describe how to use Excel's Regression tool to compute an exponential trend equation for the cholesterol revenue time series. Refer to Figure 17.18 as we describe the tasks involved.

Step 1. Click the **Data** tab on the Ribbon
Step 2. In the **Analyze** group, click **Data Analysis**
Step 3. Choose **Regression** from the list of **Analysis Tools**

Figure 17.18 Excel's Regression Tool Output for the Exponential Model for the Cholesterol Revenue Time Series

	A	B	C	D	E	F	G	H
1	Year	Revenue	LN(Revenue)					
2	1	23.1	3.1398					
3	2	21.3	3.0587					
4	3	27.4	3.3105					
5	4	34.6	3.5439					
6	5	33.8	3.5205					
7	6	43.2	3.7658					
8	7	59.5	4.0860					
9	8	64.4	4.1651					
10	9	74.2	4.3068					
11	10	99.3	4.5981					
12								
13	SUMMARY OUTPUT							
14								
15	*Regression Statistics*							
16	Multiple R	0.9843						
17	R Square	0.9688						
18	Adjusted R Square	0.9649						
19	Standard Error	0.0978						
20	Observations	10						
21								
22	ANOVA							
23		*df*	*SS*	*MS*	*F*	*Significance F*		
24	Regression	1	2.3767	2.3767	248.4262	2.62338E-07		
25	Residual	8	0.0765	0.0096				
26	Total	9	2.4533					
27								
28		*Coefficients*	*Standard Error*	*t Stat*	*P-value*	*Lower 95%*	*Upper 95%*	
29	Intercept	2.8160	0.0668	42.1440	0.0000	2.6619	2.9701	
30	Year	0.1697	0.0108	15.7615	0.0000	0.1449	0.1946	
31								

Step 4. When the **Regression** dialog box appears:
Enter *C1:C11* in the **Input Y Range:** box
Enter *A1:A11* in the **Input X Range:** box
Select the check box for **Labels**
Select the check box for **Confidence Level:**
Select **Output Range:**
Enter *A13* in the **Output Range:** box (to identify the upper-left corner of the section of the Worksheet where the output will appear)
Click **OK**

In the regression output, the Intercept = $\ln(b_0) = 2.816$ and $b_1 = 0.1697$. Using these estimates equation (17.9) is

$$\ln(T_t) = 2.816 + 0.1697t$$

We may convert $\ln(T_t) = 2.816 + 0.1697t$ to equation (17.8) by raising both sides of the equation to the power of the number e. Noting that $e^{2.816} = 16.7098$, equation (17.8) is:

$$T_t = 16.7098\, e^{0.1697t}$$

The forecast for Year 11 is:

$$T_{11} = 16.7098\, e^{0.1697(11)} = 108.0609.$$

Using Excel's Chart Tools for Trend Projection

In closing this section, we show how Excel's Chart tools can be used to develop a variety of trend equations, including linear, polynomial, and exponential. We illustrate by computing a quadratic trend equation for the cholesterol drug revenue time series in Table 17.15.

DATA*file*
cholesterolrevenue

Enter/Access Data: Open the file *cholesterolrevenue*. The data are in cells A2:B11 and labels are in cells A1:B1.

Apply Tools: Refer to Figure 17.19 as we describe the tasks involved in developing a quadratic trend line for the cholesterol time series.

Figure 17.19 Using Excel's Chart Tools to Compute a Time Series Plot for the Cholesterol Revenue Time Series

	A	B
1	Year	Revenue
2	1	23.1
3	2	21.3
4	3	27.4
5	4	34.6
6	5	33.8
7	6	43.2
8	7	59.5
9	8	64.4
10	9	74.2
11	10	99.3
12		
13		
14		
15		
16		

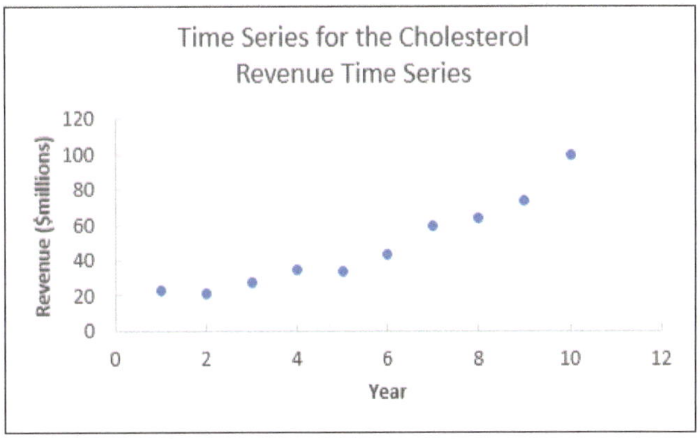

Step 1. Select cells B2:B11
Step 2. Click the **Insert** tab on the Ribbon
Step 3. In the **Charts** group, click the **Insert Scatter (X,Y) or Bubble Chart** button
Step 4. When the list of scatter diagram subtypes appears:
Click the **Scatter** button (the chart in the upper-left corner)
Step 5. Click **OK**; the scatter diagram will appear in the current worksheet (see Figure 17.19)
Step 6. Position the mouse pointer over any data point in the scatter diagram and right-click to display a list of options; choose **Add Trendline**
Step 7. When the **Format Trendline** dialog box appears (see Figure 17.20):
Choose **Polynomial** from the **Trend/Regression Type** list
Enter *2* in the **Order** box
Choose **Display Equation on chart**

A quadratic trend equation is simply a second-degree polynomial function.

Figure 17.20 shows that there are 6 trendline options. Choosing the polynomial option with order 2 indicates that we want to fit a quadratic trend equation (a second degree polynomial) to the data. The worksheet displayed in Figure 17.21 shows the time series plot, the quadratic trend equation, and the graph of the trend equation.

Figure 17.20 Excel's Format Trendline Dialog Box for the Cholesterol Revenue Time Series

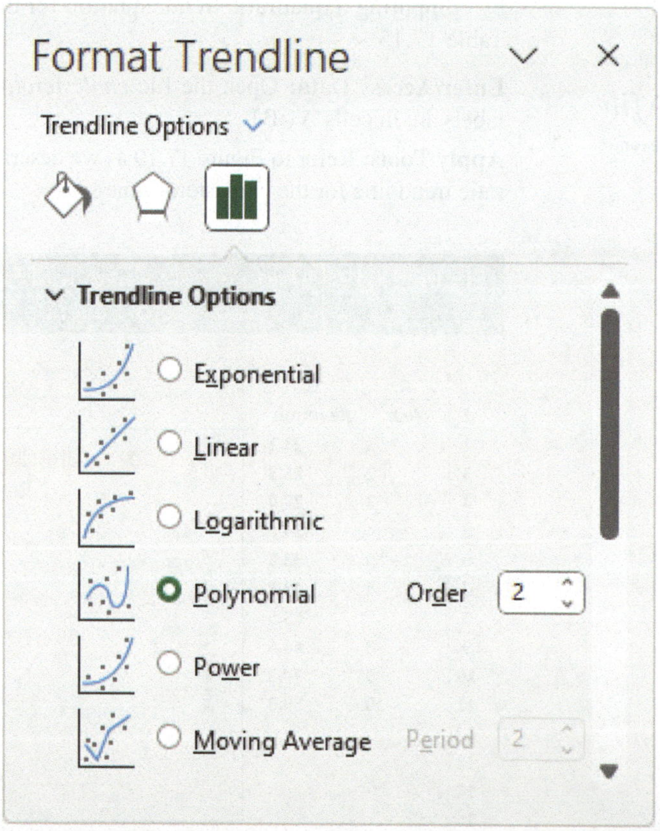

Figure 17.21 Using Excel's Chart Tools to Compute a Quadratic Trend Equation for the Cholesterol Revenue Time Series

	A	B
1	Year	Revenue
2	1	23.1
3	2	21.3
4	3	27.4
5	4	34.6
6	5	33.8
7	6	43.2
8	7	59.5
9	8	64.4
10	9	74.2
11	10	99.3

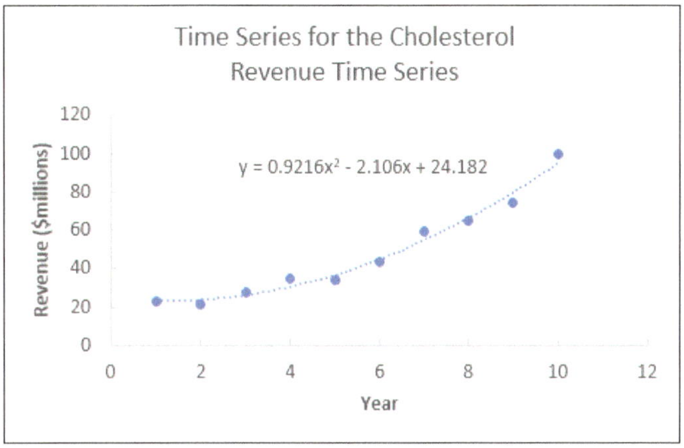

Except for rounding, the trend equation computed using Excel's Chart tools is the same as the trend equation we computed using Excel's Regression tool. And it is much easier to fit a variety of trend lines to a time series using this approach. However, the advantage of using Excel's Regression tool for trend projection is that it provides additional output that can be used to determine the statistical significance of the trend equation as well as determine how good a fit the estimated regression equation provides.

Notes + Comments

1. As discussed in Chapter 16, care must be taken when comparing a model with a transformed dependent variable with a model that uses the original dependent variable. In the case of an exponential model for the cholesterol data, if the natural log of the dependent variable is used to estimate an exponential trend, the units of the R^2 value are not commensurable with the units of the original dependent variable. Therefore, one should not compare the R^2 of a model using the natural log of the dependent variable to the R^2 of a quadratic model or any model that is based on the original dependent variable.
2. To compare the fit of a model with a transformed dependent variable with a model based on the original dependent variable, the estimated transformed model first needs to be transformed back to the original dependent variable. Then, the errors can be recalculated in the units of the original dependent variable so MAE, MSE, or MAPE can be used as measures of model comparison.

Exercises

Methods

17. Consider the following time series data. **LO 3, 5**

t	1	2	3	4	5
Y_t	6	11	9	14	15

a. Construct a time series plot. What type of pattern exists in the data?
b. Develop the linear trend equation for this time series.
c. What is the forecast for $t = 6$?

18. Refer to the time series in exercise 17. Suppose the values of the time series for the next two time periods are 13 in period 6 and 10 in period 7. **LO 3, 5**
    a. Construct a time series plot for the updated time series. What type of pattern exists in the data?
    b. Develop the quadratic trend equation for the updated time series.
    c. Use the quadratic trend equation developed in part (b) to compute the forecast for $t = 8$.
    d. Use the linear trend equation developed in exercise 17 to compute the forecast for $t = 8$. Comment on the difference between the linear trend forecast and the quadratic trend forecast and what needs to be done as new time series data become available.
19. Consider the following time series. **LO 3, 5**

t	1	2	3	4	5	6	7
Y_t	120	110	100	96	94	92	88

    a. Construct a time series plot. What type of pattern exists in the data?
    b. Develop the linear trend equation for this time series.
    c. What is the forecast for $t = 8$?
20. Consider the following time series. **LO 3, 6**

t	1	2	3	4	5	6	7
Y_t	82	60	44	35	30	29	35

    a. Construct a time series plot. What type of pattern exists in the data?
    b. Develop the quadratic trend equation for the time series.
    c. What is the forecast for $t = 8$?

Applications

DATA*file*
kyrevenue

21. **Kentucky State Revenue.** The general fund revenue receipts for the state of Kentucky for 2003 (period 1) to 2021 (period 19) are in the file *kyrevenue* (*ky.gov* website). **LO 3, 5**
    a. Construct a time-series plot. What type of pattern exists in the data?
    b. Develop a linear trend equation for this time series.
    c. What is the forecast for period 20?
22. **Administrative Expenses.** The Seneca Children's Fund (SCF) is a local charity that runs a summer camp for disadvantaged children. The fund's board of directors has been working very hard in recent years to decrease the amount of overhead expenses, a major factor in how charities are rated by independent agencies. The following data show the percentage of the money SCF has raised that was spent on administrative and fund-raising expenses for 2006–2012. **LO 3, 5**

Year	Period (t)	Expense (%)
2006	1	13.9
2007	2	12.2
2008	3	10.5
2009	4	10.4
2010	5	11.5
2011	6	10.0
2012	7	8.5

    a. Construct a time series plot. What type of pattern exists in the data?
    b. Develop the linear trend equation for this time series.
    c. Forecast the percentage of administrative expenses for 2013.
    d. If SCF can maintain their current trend in reducing administrative expenses, how long will it take them to achieve a level of 5% or less?

DATA*file*
nikerevenue

23. **Nike Revenue.** Headquartered in Beaverton, Oregon, Nike sells athletic footwear, apparel, and equipment. The file *nikerevenue* contains annual revenue for Nike from 2012 to 2021. **LO 3, 5**
    a. Construct a time-series plot. What type of pattern exists in the data?
    b. Develop a linear trend equation for this time series.
    c. What is the forecast for sales for period 11?

24. **Mortgage Interest Rates.** The following data show the average interest rate (%) for a 30-year fixed-rate mortgage over a 10-year period (FreddieMac website). **LO 2, 3, 5, 6**

DATA*file*
mortgage

Period	Interest Rate (%)
1	6.41
2	6.34
3	6.03
4	5.04
5	4.69
6	4.45
7	3.66
8	3.98
9	4.17
10	3.85

    a. Construct a time series plot. Do you think a linear trend or a quadratic trend will provide a better fit for this time series? Why?
    b. Develop the linear trend equation for this time series. Using this linear trend equation, forecast the average interest rate for period 11.
    c. Develop the quadratic trend equation for this time series. Using this quadratic trend equation, forecast the average interest rate for period 11.
    d. Compare your answers to parts (b) and (c). Which model would you recommend? Why?

25. **Netflix Subscribers.** The file *netflixsubscribers* contains the number of Netflix subscribers worldwide for the years 2001 (period 1) to 2020 (period 20) (datawrapper website). **LO 3, 6, 7**

DATA*file*
netflixsubscribers

    a. Construct a time-series plot. What type of pattern exists in the data?
    b. Develop a quadratic trend equation for this time series.
    c. Develop an exponential trend equation for this time series.
    d. Use the models in parts (b) and (c) to forecast subscribers for 2021.
    e. Which of the two forecasts in part (d) would you use? Explain.

26. **Forecasting Revenue.** Giovanni Food Products produces and sells frozen pizzas to public schools throughout the eastern United States. Using a very aggressive marketing strategy they have been able to increase their annual revenue by approximately $10 million over the past 10 years. But increased competition has slowed their growth rate in the past few years. The annual revenue, in millions of dollars, for the previous 10 years is shown. **LO 3, 6**

DATA*file*
pasta

Year	Revenue
1	8.53
2	10.84
3	12.98
4	14.11
5	16.31
6	17.21
7	18.37
8	18.45
9	18.40
10	18.43

a. Construct a time series plot. Comment on the appropriateness of a linear trend.
b. Develop a quadratic trend equation that can be used to forecast revenue.
c. Using the trend equation developed in part (b), forecast revenue in Year 11.

27. **Google Revenue.** The following data show Google revenue from 2011 (period 1) to 2020 (period 10) in billions of dollars (Alphabet, Inc. annual reports). These data are in the file *googlerevenue*. **LO 3, 6**

DATA*file*
googlerevenue

Year	Period	Annual Revenue (in $ billion)
2011	1	37.91
2012	2	50.18
2013	3	55.50
2014	4	66.00
2015	5	74.99
2016	6	90.27
2017	7	110.86
2018	8	136.82
2019	9	161.86
2020	10	182.53

a. Construct a time-series plot. What type of pattern exists?
b. Develop a quadratic trend equation.

17.5 Seasonality and Trend

In this section, we show how to develop forecasts for a time series that has a seasonal pattern. To the extent that seasonality exists, we need to incorporate it into our forecasting models to ensure accurate forecasts. We begin by considering a seasonal time series with no trend and then discuss how to model seasonality with trend.

Seasonality Without Trend

As an example, consider the number of umbrellas sold at a clothing store over the past five years. Table 17.16 shows the time series and Figure 17.22 shows the corresponding time series plot. The time series plot does not indicate any long-term trend in sales. In fact, unless you look carefully at the data, you might conclude that the data follow a horizontal pattern and that single exponential smoothing could be used to forecast sales. But closer inspection of the time series plot reveals a pattern in the data. That is, the first and third quarters have moderate sales, the second quarter has the highest sales, and the fourth quarter tends to be the lowest quarter in terms of sales volume. Thus, we would conclude that a quarterly seasonal pattern is present.

In Chapter 15, we describe how dummy variables can be used to deal with categorical independent variables in a regression model.

Just like using dummy variables to deal with an independent variable in a standard regression analysis, we can use the same approach to model a time series with a seasonal pattern by treating the season as a categorical variable. Recall that when a categorical variable has k levels, $k - 1$ dummy variables are required. So, if there are four seasons, we need three dummy variables. For instance, in the umbrella sales time series season is a categorical variable with four levels: quarter 1, quarter 2, quarter 3, and quarter 4. Thus, to model the seasonal effects in the umbrella time series we need $4 - 1 = 3$ dummy variables. The three dummy variables can be coded as follows:

$$\text{Qtr1} = \begin{cases} 1 \text{ if Quarter 1} \\ 0 \text{ otherwise} \end{cases} \quad \text{Qtr2} = \begin{cases} 1 \text{ if Quarter 2} \\ 0 \text{ otherwise} \end{cases} \quad \text{Qtr3} = \begin{cases} 1 \text{ if Quarter 3} \\ 0 \text{ otherwise} \end{cases}$$

Using $\hat{Y}$ to denote the estimated or forecasted value of sales, the general form of the estimated regression equation relating the number of umbrellas sold to the quarter the sales take place follows:

$$\hat{Y} = b_0 + b_1 \text{ Qtr1} + b_2 \text{ Qtr2} + b_3 \text{ Qtr3}$$

DATA*file*
umbrellasales

Table 17.16 Umbrella Sales Time Series

Year	Quarter	Sales
1	1	125
	2	153
	3	106
	4	88
2	1	118
	2	161
	3	133
	4	102
3	1	138
	2	144
	3	113
	4	80
4	1	109
	2	137
	3	125
	4	109
5	1	130
	2	165
	3	128
	4	96

Figure 17.22 Umbrella Sales Time Series Plot

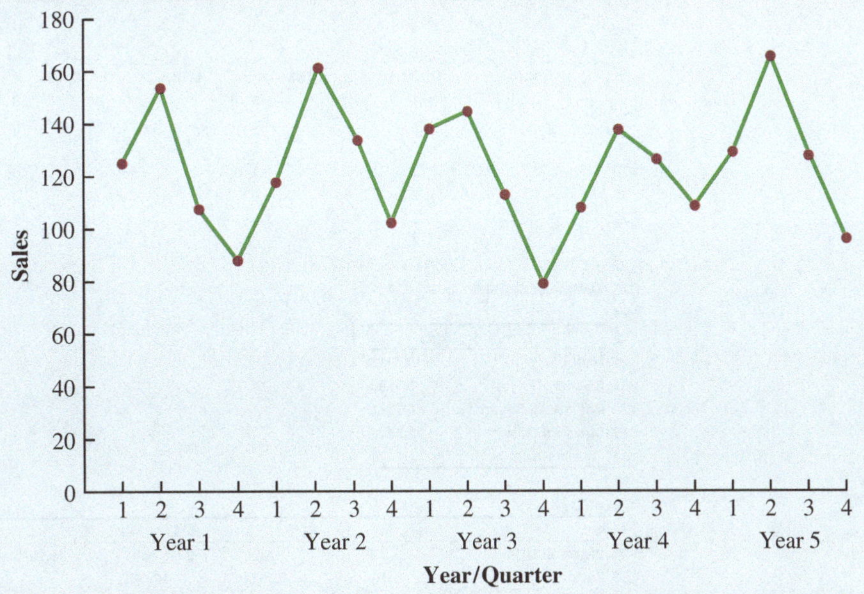

Table 17.17 is the umbrella sales time series with the coded values of the dummy variables shown. Using the data in Table 17.17 and Excel's Regression tool, we obtained the computer output shown in Figure 17.23. The estimated multiple regression equation obtained is

$$\text{Sales} = 95.0 + 29.0\ \text{Qtr1} + 57.0\ \text{Qtr2} + 26.0\ \text{Qtr3}$$

Table 17.17 Umbrella Sales Time Series with Dummy Variables

Year	Quarter	Qtr1	Qtr2	Qtr3	Sales
1	1	1	0	0	125
	2	0	1	0	153
	3	0	0	1	106
	4	0	0	0	88
2	1	1	0	0	118
	2	0	1	0	161
	3	0	0	1	133
	4	0	0	0	102
3	1	1	0	0	138
	2	0	1	0	144
	3	0	0	1	113
	4	0	0	0	80
4	1	1	0	0	109
	2	0	1	0	137
	3	0	0	1	125
	4	0	0	0	109
5	1	1	0	0	130
	2	0	1	0	165
	3	0	0	1	128
	4	0	0	0	96

DATA*file*
umbrellasales_dummy_vars

Figure 17.23 Excel's Regression Tool Output for the Umbrella Sales Time Series

	A	B	C	D	E	F	G	H
1	Year	Quarter	QTR1	QTR2	QTR3	Sales		
2	1	1	1	0	0	125		
3		2	0	1	0	153		
4		3	0	0	1	106		
18	5	1	1	0	0	130		
19		2	0	1	0	165		
20		3	0	0	1	128		
21		4	0	0	0	96		
22								
23	SUMMARY OUTPUT							
24								
25	*Regression Statistics*							
26	Multiple R	0.8938						
27	R Square	0.7989						
28	Adjusted R Square	0.7611						
29	Standard Error	11.3248						
30	Observations	20						
31								
32	ANOVA							
33		*df*	*SS*	*MS*	*F*	*Significance F*		
34	Regression	3	8150	2716.6667	21.1826	8.1036E-06		
35	Residual	16	2052	128.25				
36	Total	19	10202					
37								
38		*Coefficients*	*Standard Error*	*t Stat*	*P-value*	*Lower 95%*	*Upper 95%*	
39	Intercept	95	5.0646	18.7577	2.5659E-12	84.2636	105.7364	
40	QTR1	29	7.1624	4.0489	0.0009	13.8164	44.1836	
41	QTR2	57	7.1624	7.9582	5.9348E-07	41.8164	72.1836	
42	QTR3	26	7.1624	3.6301	0.0023	10.8164	41.1836	
43								

We can use this equation to forecast quarterly sales for next year.

$$\text{Quarter 1: Sales} = 95.0 + 29.0(1) + 57.0(0) + 26.0(0) = 124$$
$$\text{Quarter 2: Sales} = 95.0 + 29.0(0) + 57.0(1) + 26.0(0) = 152$$
$$\text{Quarter 3: Sales} = 95.0 + 29.0(0) + 57.0(0) + 26.0(1) = 121$$
$$\text{Quarter 4: Sales} = 95.0 + 29.0(0) + 57.0(0) + 26.0(0) = 95$$

It is interesting to note that we could have obtained the quarterly forecasts for next year simply by computing the average number of umbrellas sold in each quarter, as shown in the following table.

Year	Quarter 1	Quarter 2	Quarter 3	Quarter 4
1	125	153	106	88
2	118	161	133	102
3	138	144	113	80
4	109	137	125	109
5	130	165	128	96
Average	124	152	121	95

Nonetheless, the regression output shown in Figure 17.23 provides additional information that can be used to assess the accuracy of the forecast and determine the significance of the results. And, for more complex types of problem situations, such as dealing with a time series that has both trend and seasonal effects, this simple averaging approach will not work.

Seasonality and Trend

Let us now extend the regression approach to include situations where the time series contains both a seasonal effect and a linear trend by showing how to forecast the quarterly smartphone sales time series introduced in Section 17.1. The data for the smartphone time series are shown in Table 17.18. The time series plot in Figure 17.24 indicates that sales are lowest in the second quarter of each year and increase in quarters 3 and 4. Thus, we conclude that a seasonal pattern exists for smartphone sales. But the time series also has an upward linear trend that will need to be accounted for in order to develop accurate forecasts

DATA*file*
smartphonesales

Table 17.18 Smartphone Sales Time Series

Year	Quarter	Sales (1,000s)
1	1	4.8
	2	4.1
	3	6.0
	4	6.5
2	1	5.8
	2	5.2
	3	6.8
	4	7.4
3	1	6.0
	2	5.6
	3	7.5
	4	7.8
4	1	6.3
	2	5.9
	3	8.0
	4	8.4

Figure 17.24 Smartphone Sales Time Series Plot

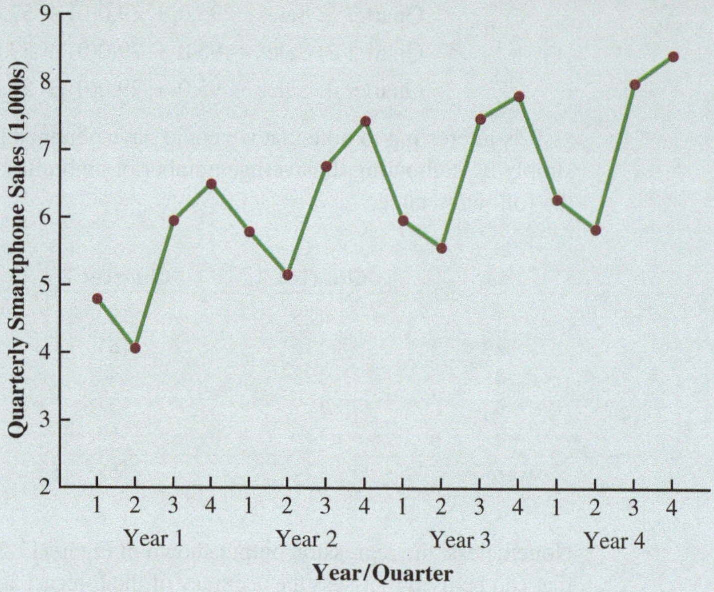

of quarterly sales. This is easily handled by combining the dummy variable approach for seasonality with the time series regression approach we discussed in Section 17.3 for handling linear trend.

The general form of the estimated multiple regression equation for modeling both the quarterly seasonal effects and the linear trend in the smartphone time series is as follows:

$$\hat{Y}_t = b_0 + b_1 \text{ Qtr1} + b_2 \text{ Qtr2} + b_3 \text{ Qtr3} + b_4 t$$

where

$\hat{Y}_t$ = estimate or forecast of sales in period t
Qtr1 = 1 if time period t corresponds to the first quarter of the year; 0 otherwise
Qtr2 = 1 if time period t corresponds to the second quarter of the year; 0 otherwise
Qtr3 = 1 if time period t corresponds to the third quarter of the year; 0 otherwise
t = time period

Table 17.19 is the revised smartphone sales time series that includes the coded values of the dummy variables and the time period t. Using the data in Table 17.19 and Excel's Regression tool, we obtained the computer output shown in Figure 17.25. The estimated multiple regression equation is

$$\text{Sales} = 6.07 - 1.36 \text{ Qtr1} - 2.03 \text{ Qtr2} - 0.304 \text{ Qtr3} + 0.146t \qquad \textbf{(17.10)}$$

We can now use equation (17.10) to forecast quarterly sales for next year. Next year is year 5 for the smartphone sales time series; that is, time periods 17, 18, 19, and 20.

Forecast for Time Period 17 (Quarter 1 in Year 5)

$$\text{Sales} = 6.07 - 1.36(1) - 2.03(0) - 0.304(0) + 0.146(17) = 7.19$$

Forecast for Time Period 18 (Quarter 2 in Year 5)

$$\text{Sales} = 6.07 - 1.36(0) - 2.03(1) - 0.304(0) + 0.146(18) = 6.67$$

Table 17.19 Smartphone Sales Time Series with Dummy Variables and Time Period

DATA*file*
smartphonesales_dummy_vars

Year	Quarter	Qtr1	Qtr2	Qtr3	Period	Sales (1,000s)
1	1	1	0	0	1	4.8
	2	0	1	0	2	4.1
	3	0	0	1	3	6.0
	4	0	0	0	4	6.5
2	1	1	0	0	5	5.8
	2	0	1	0	6	5.2
	3	0	0	1	7	6.8
	4	0	0	0	8	7.4
3	1	1	0	0	9	6.0
	2	0	1	0	10	5.6
	3	0	0	1	11	7.5
	4	0	0	0	12	7.8
4	1	1	0	0	13	6.3
	2	0	1	0	14	5.9
	3	0	0	1	15	8.0
	4	0	0	0	16	8.4

Figure 17.25 Excel's Regression Tool Output for the Smartphone Sales Time Series

	A	B	C	D	E	F	G	H
1	Year	Quarter	QTR1	QTR2	QTR3	Period	Sales (1000s)	
2	1	1	1	0	0	1	4.8	
3	1	2	0	1	0	2	4.1	
4	1	3	0	0	1	3	6.0	
5	1	4	0	0	0	4	6.5	
14	4	1	1	0	0	13	6.3	
15	4	2	0	1	0	14	5.9	
16	4	3	0	0	1	15	8.0	
17	4	4	0	0	0	16	8.4	
18								
19	SUMMARY OUTPUT							
20								
21	*Regression Statistics*							
22	Multiple R	0.9881						
23	R Square	0.9763						
24	Adjusted R Square	0.9676						
25	Standard Error	0.2167						
26	Observations	16						
27								
28	ANOVA							
29		*df*	*SS*	*MS*	*F*	*Significance F*		
30	Regression	4	21.248	5.312	113.1581	7.37582E-09		
31	Residual	11	0.5164	0.0469				
32	Total	15	21.7644					
33								
34		*Coefficients*	*Standard Error*	*t Stat*	*P-value*	*Lower 95%*	*Upper 95%*	
35	Intercept	6.0688	0.1625	37.3467	6.12289E-13	5.7111	6.4264	
36	QTR1	-1.3631	0.1575	-8.6573	3.05975E-06	-1.7097	-1.0166	
37	QTR2	-2.0338	0.1551	-13.1119	4.65532E-08	-2.3751	-1.6924	
38	QTR3	-0.3044	0.1537	-1.9805	0.0732	-0.6426	0.0339	
39	Period	0.1456	0.0121	12.0233	1.14029E-07	0.1190	0.1723	
40								

Forecast for Time Period 19 (Quarter 3 in Year 5)

$$\text{Sales} = 6.07 - 1.36(0) - 2.03(0) - 0.304(1) + 0.146(19) = 8.54$$

Forecast for Time Period 20 (Quarter 4 in Year 5)

$$\text{Sales} = 6.07 - 1.36(0) - 2.03(0) - 0.304(0) + 0.146(20) = 8.99$$

Thus, accounting for the seasonal effects and the linear trend in smartphone sales, the estimates of quarterly sales in year 5 are 7,190, 6,670, 8,540, and 8,990.

The dummy variables in the estimated multiple regression equation actually provide four estimated multiple regression equations, one for each quarter. For instance, if time period t corresponds to quarter 1, the estimate of quarterly sales is

$$\text{Quarter 1: Sales} = 6.07 - 1.36(1) - 2.03(0) - 0.304(0) + 0.146t = 4.71 + 0.146t$$

Similarly, if time period t corresponds to quarters 2, 3, and 4, the estimates of quarterly sales are

$$\text{Quarter 2: Sales} = 6.07 - 1.36(0) - 2.03(1) - 0.304(0) + 0.146t = 4.04 + 0.146t$$
$$\text{Quarter 3: Sales} = 6.07 - 1.36(0) - 2.03(0) - 0.304(1) + 0.146t = 5.77 + 0.146t$$
$$\text{Quarter 4: Sales} = 6.07 - 1.36(0) - 2.03(0) - 0.304(0) + 0.146t = 6.07 + 0.146t$$

The slope of the trend line for each quarterly forecast equation is 0.146, indicating a growth in sales of about 146 smartphones per quarter. The only difference in the four equations is that they have different intercepts. For instance, the intercept for the quarter 1 equation is 4.71 and the intercept for the quarter 4 equation is 6.07. Thus, sales in quarter 1 are $4.71 - 6.07 = -1.36$ or 1,360 smartphones less than in quarter 4. In other words, the estimated regression coefficient for Qtr1 in equation (17.10) provides an estimate of the difference in sales between quarter 1 and quarter 4. Similar interpretations can be provided for -2.03, the estimated regression coefficient for dummy variable Qtr2, and -0.304, the estimated regression coefficient for dummy variable Qtr3.

Models Based on Monthly Data

Whenever a categorical variable such as season has k levels, k − 1 dummy variables are required.

In the preceding smartphone sales example, we showed how dummy variables can be used to account for the quarterly seasonal effects in the time series. Because there were four levels for the categorical variable season, three dummy variables were required. However, many businesses use monthly rather than quarterly forecasts. For monthly data, season is a categorical variable with 12 levels and thus $12 - 1 = 11$ dummy variables are required. For example, the 11 dummy variables could be coded as follows:

$$\text{Month1} = \begin{cases} 1 \text{ if January} \\ 0 \text{ otherwise} \end{cases}$$

$$\text{Month2} = \begin{cases} 1 \text{ if February} \\ 0 \text{ otherwise} \end{cases}$$

$$\vdots$$

$$\text{Month11} = \begin{cases} 1 \text{ if November} \\ 0 \text{ otherwise} \end{cases}$$

Other than this change, the multiple regression approach for handling seasonality remains the same.

Exercises

Methods

28. Consider the following time series. **LO 3, 8**

Quarter	Year 1	Year 2	Year 3
1	71	68	62
2	49	41	51
3	58	60	53
4	78	81	72

a. Construct a time series plot. What type of pattern exists in the data?
b. Use the following dummy variables to develop an estimated regression equation to account for seasonal effects in the data: Qtr1 = 1 if Quarter 1, 0 otherwise; Qtr2 = 1 if Quarter 2, 0 otherwise; Qtr3 = 1 if Quarter 3, 0 otherwise.
c. Compute the quarterly forecasts for next year.

29. Consider the following time series data. **LO 3, 8**

Quarter	Year 1	Year 2	Year 3
1	4	6	7
2	2	3	6
3	3	5	6
4	5	7	8

a. Construct a time series plot. What type of pattern exists in the data?
b. Use the following dummy variables to develop an estimated regression equation to account for any seasonal and linear trend effects in the data: Qtr1 = 1 if Quarter 1, 0 otherwise; Qtr2 = 1 if Quarter 2, 0 otherwise; Qtr3 = 1 if Quarter 3, 0 otherwise.
c. Compute the quarterly forecasts for next year.

Applications

30. **Textbook Sales.** The quarterly sales data (number of copies sold) for a college textbook over the past three years follow. **LO 3, 8**

DATA*file*
textbooks

Quarter	Year 1	Year 2	Year 3
1	1,690	1,800	1,850
2	940	900	1,100
3	2,625	2,900	2,930
4	2,500	2,360	2,615

a. Construct a time series plot. What type of pattern exists in the data?
b. Use the following dummy variables to develop an estimated regression equation to account for any seasonal effects in the data: Qtr1 = 1 if Quarter 1, 0 otherwise; Qtr2 = 1 if Quarter 2, 0 otherwise; Qtr3 = 1 if Quarter 3, 0 otherwise.
c. Compute the quarterly forecasts for next year.
d. Let $t = 1$ to refer to the observation in quarter 1 of year 1; $t = 2$ to refer to the observation in quarter 2 of year 1; . . . and $t = 12$ to refer to the observation in quarter 4 of year 3. Using the dummy variables defined in part (b) and t, develop an estimated regression equation to account for seasonal effects and any linear trend in the time series. Based upon the seasonal effects in the data and linear trend, compute the quarterly forecasts for next year.

31. **Air Pollution.** Air pollution control specialists in southern California monitor the amount of ozone, carbon dioxide, and nitrogen dioxide in the air on an hourly basis. The hourly time series data exhibit seasonality, with the levels of pollutants showing patterns that vary over the hours in the day. On July 15, 16, and 17, the following levels of nitrogen dioxide were observed for the 12 hours from 6:00 A.M. to 6:00 P.M. **LO 3, 8**

DATA*file*
pollution

July 15:	25	28	35	50	60	60	40	35	30	25	25	20
July 16:	28	30	35	48	60	65	50	40	35	25	20	20
July 17:	35	42	45	70	72	75	60	45	40	25	25	25

a. Construct a time series plot. What type of pattern exists in the data?
b. Use the following dummy variables to develop an estimated regression equation to account for the seasonal effects in the data.

Hour1 = 1 if the reading was made between 6:00 A.M. and 7:00 A.M.;
0 otherwise
Hour2 = 1 if the reading was made between 7:00 A.M. and 8:00 A.M.;
0 otherwise
.
.
.
Hour11 = 1 if the reading was made between 4:00 P.M. and 5:00 P.M.,
0 otherwise.

Note that when the values of the 11 dummy variables are equal to 0, the observation corresponds to the 5:00 P.M. to 6:00 P.M. hour.

c. Using the estimated regression equation developed in part (a), compute estimates of the levels of nitrogen dioxide for July 18.
d. Let $t = 1$ to refer to the observation in hour 1 on July 15; $t = 2$ to refer to the observation in hour 2 of July 15; . . . and $t = 36$ to refer to the observation in hour 12 of July 17. Using the dummy variables defined in part (b) and t, develop an estimated regression equation to account for seasonal effects and any linear trend in the time series. Based upon the seasonal effects in the data and linear trend, compute estimates of the levels of nitrogen dioxide for July 18.

32. **Seasonal Sales.** South Shore Construction builds permanent docks and seawalls along the southern shore of Long Island, New York. Although the firm has been in business only five years, revenue has increased from $308,000 in the first year of operation to $1,084,000 in the most recent year. The following data show the quarterly sales revenue in thousands of dollars. **LO 3, 8**

DATA*file*
southshore

Quarter	Year 1	Year 2	Year 3	Year 4	Year 5
1	20	37	75	92	176
2	100	136	155	202	282
3	175	245	326	384	445
4	13	26	48	82	181

a. Construct a time series plot. What type of pattern exists in the data?
b. Use the following dummy variables to develop an estimated regression equation to account for seasonal effects in the data. Qtr1 = 1 if Quarter 1, 0 otherwise; Qtr2 = 1 if Quarter 2, 0 otherwise; Qtr3 = 1 if Quarter 3, 0 otherwise. Based only on the seasonal effects in the data, compute estimates of quarterly sales for Year 6.
c. Let Period = 1 to refer to the observation in quarter 1 of year 1; Period = 2 to refer to the observation in quarter 2 of year 1; . . . and Period = 20 to refer to the observation in quarter 4 of Year 5. Using the dummy variables defined in part (b)

and Period, develop an estimated regression equation to account for seasonal effects and any linear trend in the time series. Based upon the seasonal effects in the data and linear trend, compute estimates of quarterly sales for Year 6.

33. **Power Consumption.** Electric power consumption is measured in kilowatt-hours (kWh). The local utility company offers an interrupt program whereby commercial customers that participate receive favorable rates but must agree to cut back consumption if the utility requests them to do so. Timko Products has agreed to cut back consumption from noon to 8:00 P.M. on Thursday. To determine Timko's savings, the utility must estimate Timko's normal power usage for this period of time. Data on Timko's electric power consumption for the previous 72 hours are shown in the following table. LO 3, 8

DATA*file*
power

Time Period	Monday	Tuesday	Wednesday	Thursday
12–4 A.M.	—	19,281	31,209	27,330
4–8 A.M.	—	33,195	37,014	32,715
8–12 noon	—	99,516	119,968	152,465
12–4 P.M.	124,299	123,666	156,033	
4–8 P.M.	113,545	111,717	128,889	
8–12 midnight	41,300	48,112	73,923	

a. Construct a time series plot. What type of pattern exists in the data?
b. Use the following dummy variables to develop an estimated regression equation to account for any seasonal effects in the data.

Time1 = 1 for time period 12–4 A.M.; 0 otherwise
Time2 = 1 for time period 4–8 A.M.; 0 otherwise
Time3 = 1 for time period 8–12 noon; 0 otherwise
Time4 = 1 for time period 12–4 P.M.; 0 otherwise
Time5 = 1 for time period 4–8 P.M.; 0 otherwise

c. Use the estimated regression equation developed in part (b) to estimate Timko's normal usage over the period of interrupted service.
d. Let Period = 1 to refer to the observation for Monday in the time period 12–4 P.M.; Period = 2 to refer to the observation for Monday in the time period 4–8 P.M.; . . . and Period = 18 to refer to the observation for Thursday in the time period 8–12 noon. Using the dummy variables defined in part (b) and Period, develop an estimated regression equation to account for seasonal effects and any linear trend in the time series.
e. Using the estimated regression equation developed in part (d), estimate Timko's normal usage over the period of interrupted service.

34. **Lawn Maintenance.** Three years of monthly lawn-maintenance expenses ($) for a six-unit apartment house in southern Florida follow. LO 3, 8

DATA*file*
aptexp

Month	Year 1	Year 2	Year 3
January	170	180	195
February	180	205	210
March	205	215	230
April	230	245	280
May	240	265	290
June	315	330	390
July	360	400	420
August	290	335	330
September	240	260	290
October	240	270	295
November	230	255	280
December	195	220	250

a. Construct a time series plot. What type of pattern exists in the data?
b. Develop an estimated regression equation that can be used to account for any seasonal and linear trend effects in the data. Use the following dummy variables to account for the seasonal effects in the data: Jan = 1 if January, 0 otherwise; Feb = 1 if February, 0 otherwise; Mar = 1 if March, 0 otherwise; . . . Nov = 1 if November, 0 otherwise. Note that using this coding method, when all the 11 dummy variables are 0, the observation corresponds to an expense in December.
c. Compute the monthly forecasts for next year based upon both trend and seasonal effects.

17.6 Time Series Decomposition

In this section, we turn our attention to what is called **time series decomposition**. Time series decomposition can be used to separate or decompose a time series into seasonal, trend, and irregular components. While this method can be used for forecasting, its primary applicability is to get a better understanding of the time series. Many business and economic time series are maintained and published by government agencies such as the Census Bureau and the Bureau of Labor Statistics. These agencies use time series decomposition to create deseasonalized time series.

Understanding what is really going on with a time series often depends upon the use of deseasonalized data. For instance, we might be interested in learning whether electrical power consumption is increasing in our area. Suppose we learn that electric power consumption in September is down 3% from the previous month. Care must be exercised in using such information, because whenever a seasonal influence is present, such comparisons may be misleading if the data have not been deseasonalized. The fact that electric power consumption is down 3% from August to September might be only the seasonal effect associated with a decrease in the use of air conditioning and not because of a long-term decline in the use of electric power. Indeed, after adjusting for the seasonal effect, we might even find that the use of electric power increased. Many other time series, such as unemployment statistics, home sales, and retail sales, are subject to strong seasonal influences. It is important to deseasonalize such data before making a judgment about any long-term trend.

Time series decomposition methods assume that Y_t, the actual time series value at period t, is a function of three components: a trend component; a seasonal component; and an irregular or error component. How these three components are combined to generate the observed values of the time series depends upon whether we assume the relationship is best described by an additive or a multiplicative model.

An **additive decomposition model** takes the following form:

$$Y_t = \text{Trend}_t + \text{Seasonal}_t + \text{Irregular}_t \tag{17.11}$$

where

$$\begin{aligned} \text{Trend}_t &= \text{trend value at time period } t \\ \text{Seasonal}_t &= \text{seasonal value at time period } t \\ \text{Irregular}_t &= \text{irregular value at time period } t \end{aligned}$$

The irregular component corresponds to the error term ϵ in the simple linear regression model discussed in Chapter 14.

In an additive model, the values for the three components are simply added together to obtain the actual time series value Y_t. The irregular or error component accounts for the variability in the time series that cannot be explained by the trend and seasonal components.

An additive model is appropriate in situations where the seasonal fluctuations do not depend upon the level of the time series. The regression model for incorporating seasonal and trend effects in Section 17.5 is an additive model. If the sizes of the seasonal fluctuations in earlier time periods are about the same as the sizes of the seasonal fluctuations in later time periods, an additive model is appropriate. However, if the seasonal fluctuations change over time, growing larger as the sales volume increases because of a long-term linear trend, then a multiplicative model should be used. Many business and economic time series follow this pattern.

A **multiplicative decomposition model** takes the following form:

$$Y_t = \text{Trend}_t \times \text{Seasonal}_t \times \text{Irregular}_t \qquad \textbf{(17.12)}$$

where

$$\text{Trend}_t = \text{trend value at time period } t$$
$$\text{Seasonal}_t = \text{seasonal index at time period } t$$
$$\text{Irregular}_t = \text{irregular index at time period } t$$

The Census Bureau uses a multiplicative model in conjunction with its methodology for deseasonalizing time series.

In this model, the trend and seasonal and irregular components are multiplied to give the value of the time series. Trend is measured in units of the item being forecast. However, the seasonal and irregular components are measured in relative terms, with values above 1.00 indicating effects above the trend and values below 1.00 indicating effects below the trend.

Because this is the method most often used in practice, we will restrict our discussion of time series decomposition to showing how to develop estimates of the trend and seasonal components for a multiplicative model. As an illustration, we will work with the quarterly smartphone sales time series introduced in Section 17.5; the quarterly sales data are shown in Table 17.18 and the corresponding time series plot is presented in Figure 17.24. After demonstrating how to decompose a time series using the multiplicative model, we will show how the seasonal indices and trend component can be recombined to develop a forecast.

Calculating the Seasonal Indexes

Figure 17.24 indicates that sales are lowest in the second quarter of each year and increase in quarters 3 and 4. Thus, we conclude that a seasonal pattern exists for the smartphone sales time series. The computational procedure used to identify each quarter's seasonal influence begins by computing a moving average to remove the combined seasonal and irregular effects from the data, leaving us with a time series that contains only trend and any remaining random variation not removed by the moving average calculations.

Because we are working with a quarterly series, we will use four data values in each moving average. The moving average calculation for the first four quarters of the smartphone sales data is

$$\text{First moving average} = \frac{4.8 + 4.1 + 6.0 + 6.5}{4} = \frac{21.4}{4} = 5.35$$

Note that the moving average calculation for the first four quarters yields the average quarterly sales over Year 1 of the time series. Continuing the moving average calculations, we next add the 5.8 value for the first quarter of Year 2 and drop the 4.8 for the first quarter of Year 1. Thus, the second moving average is

$$\text{Second moving average} = \frac{4.1 + 6.0 + 6.5 + 5.8}{4} = \frac{22.4}{4} = 5.60$$

Similarly, the third moving average calculation is $(6.0 + 6.5 + 5.8 + 5.2)/4 = 5.875$.

Before we proceed with the moving average calculations for the entire time series, let us return to the first moving average calculation, which resulted in a value of 5.35. The 5.35 value is the average quarterly sales volume for Year 1. As we look back at the calculation of the 5.35 value, associating 5.35 with the "middle" of the moving average group makes sense. Note, however, that with four quarters in the moving average, there is no middle period. The 5.35 value really corresponds to period 2.5, the last half of quarter 2 and the first half of quarter 3. Similarly, if we go to the next moving average value of 5.60, the middle period corresponds to period 3.5, the last half of quarter 3 and the first half of quarter 4.

The two moving average values we computed do not correspond directly to the original quarters of the time series. We can resolve this difficulty by computing the average of the two moving averages. Since the center of the first moving average is period 2.5 (half a period or quarter early) and the center of the second moving average is period 3.5 (half a period or quarter late), the average of the two moving averages is centered at quarter 3, exactly where it should be. This moving average is referred to as a *centered moving average*. Thus, the centered moving average for period 3 is $(5.35 + 5.60)/2 = 5.475$. Similarly, the centered moving average value for period 4 is $(5.60 + 5.875)/2 = 5.738$. Table 17.20 shows a complete summary of the moving average and centered moving average calculations for the smartphone sales data.

Table 17.20 Centered Moving Average Calculations for the Smartphone Sales Time Series

Year	Quarter	Sales (1,000s)	Four-Quarter Moving Average	Centered Moving Average
1	1	4.8		
1	2	4.1		
			5.350	
1	3	6.0		5.475
			5.600	
1	4	6.5		5.738
			5.875	
2	1	5.8		5.975
			6.075	
2	2	5.2		6.188
			6.300	
2	3	6.8		6.325
			6.350	
2	4	7.4		6.400
			6.450	
3	1	6.0		6.538
			6.625	
3	2	5.6		6.675
			6.725	
3	3	7.5		6.763
			6.800	
3	4	7.8		6.838
			6.875	
4	1	6.3		6.938
			7.000	
4	2	5.9		7.075
			7.150	
4	3	8.0		
4	4	8.4		

Figure 17.26 Quarterly Smartphone Sales Time Series and Centered Moving Average

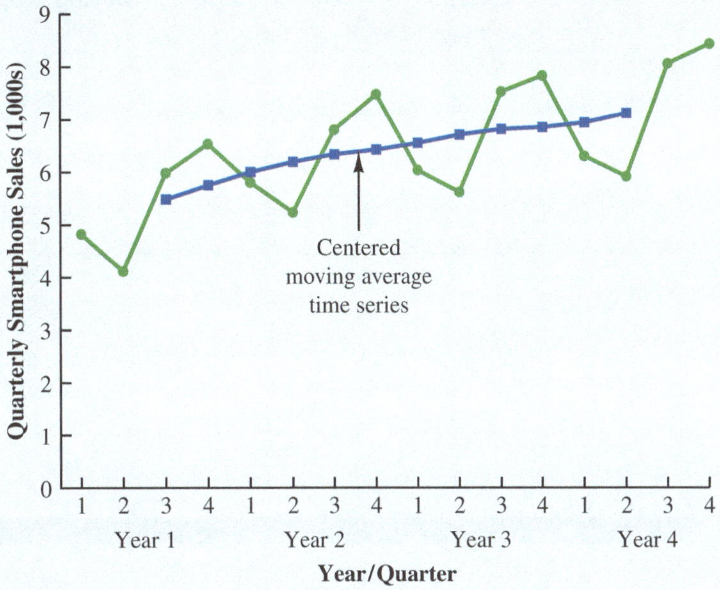

What do the centered moving averages in Table 17.20 tell us about this time series? Figure 17.26 shows a time series plot of the actual time series values and the centered moving average values. Note particularly how the centered moving average values tend to "smooth out" both the seasonal and irregular fluctuations in the time series. The centered moving averages represent the trend in the data and any random variation that was not removed by using moving averages to smooth the data.

Previously we showed that the multiplicative decomposition model is

$$Y_t = \text{Trend}_t \times \text{Seasonal}_t \times \text{Irregular}_t$$

By dividing each side of this equation by the trend component Trend_t, we can identify the combined seasonal-irregular effect in the time series.

The seasonal-irregular values are often referred to as the de-trended values of the time series.

$$\frac{Y_t}{\text{Trend}_t} = \frac{\text{Trend}_t \times \text{Seasonal}_t \times \text{Irregular}_t}{\text{Trend}_t} = \text{Seasonal}_t \times \text{Irregular}_t$$

For example, the third quarter of year 1 shows a trend value of 5.475 (the centered moving average). So 6.0/5.475 = 1.096 is the combined seasonal-irregular value. Table 17.21 summarizes the seasonal-irregular values for the entire time series.

Consider the seasonal-irregular values for the third quarter: 1.096, 1.075, and 1.109. Seasonal-irregular values greater than 1.00 indicate effects above the trend estimate and values below 1.00 indicate effects below the trend estimate. Thus, the three seasonal-irregular values for quarter 3 show an above-average effect in the third quarter. Since the year-to-year fluctuations in the seasonal-irregular values are primarily due to random error, we can average the computed values to eliminate the irregular influence and obtain an estimate of the third-quarter seasonal influence.

$$\text{Seasonal effect of quarter 3} = \frac{1.096 + 1.075 + 1.109}{3} = 1.09$$

Table 17.21 Seasonal Irregular Values for the Smartphone Sales Time Series

Year	Quarter	Sales (1,000s)	Centered Moving Average	Seasonal-Irregular Value
1	1	4.8		
1	2	4.1		
1	3	6.0	5.475	1.096
1	4	6.5	5.738	1.133
2	1	5.8	5.975	0.971
2	2	5.2	6.188	0.840
2	3	6.8	6.325	1.075
2	4	7.4	6.400	1.156
3	1	6.0	6.538	0.918
3	2	5.6	6.675	0.839
3	3	7.5	6.763	1.109
3	4	7.8	6.838	1.141
4	1	6.3	6.938	0.908
4	2	5.9	7.075	0.834
4	3	8.0		
4	4	8.4		

We refer to 1.09 as the *seasonal index* for the third quarter. Table 17.22 summarizes the calculations involved in computing the seasonal indexes for the smartphone sales time series. The seasonal indexes for the four quarters are 0.93, 0.84, 1.09, and 1.14.

Interpretation of the seasonal indexes in Table 17.22 provides some insight about the seasonal component in smartphone sales. The best sales quarter is the fourth quarter, with sales averaging 14% above the trend estimate. The worst, or slowest, sales quarter is the second quarter; its seasonal index of 0.84 shows that the sales average is 16% below the trend estimate. The seasonal component corresponds clearly to the intuitive expectation that smartphone sales increase when a new school year begins (quarter 3) and for the holiday season (quarter 4).

One final adjustment is sometimes necessary in obtaining the seasonal indexes. Because the multiplicative model requires that the average seasonal index equal 1.00, the sum of the four seasonal indexes in Table 17.22 must equal 4.00. In other words, the seasonal effects must even out over the year. The average of the seasonal indexes in our example is equal to 1.00, and hence this type of adjustment is not necessary. In other cases, a slight adjustment may be necessary. To make the adjustment, multiply each seasonal index by the number of seasons divided by the sum of the unadjusted seasonal indexes. For instance, for quarterly data, multiply each seasonal index by 4/(sum of the unadjusted seasonal indexes). Some of the exercises will require this adjustment to obtain the appropriate seasonal indexes.

Table 17.22 Seasonal Index Calculations for the Smartphone Sales Time Series

Quarter	Seasonal-Irregular Values			Seasonal Index
1	0.971	0.918	0.908	0.93
2	0.840	0.839	0.834	0.84
3	1.096	1.075	1.109	1.09
4	1.133	1.156	1.141	1.14

Deseasonalizing the Time Series

A time series that has had the seasonal effects removed is referred to as a **deseasonalized time series**, and the process of using the seasonal indexes to remove the seasonal effects from a time series is referred to as deseasonalizing the time series. Using a multiplicative decomposition model, we deseasonalize a time series by dividing each observation by its corresponding seasonal index. The multiplicative decomposition model is

Economic time series adjusted for seasonal variations are often reported in publications such as the Survey of Current Business, The Wall Street Journal, *and* Bloomberg Businessweek.

$$Y_t = \text{Trend}_t \times \text{Seasonal}_t \times \text{Irregular}_t$$

So, when we divide each time series observation (Y_t) by its corresponding seasonal index, the resulting data show only trend and random variability (the irregular component). The deseasonalized time series for smartphone sales is summarized in Table 17.23. A graph of the deseasonalized time series is shown in Figure 17.27.

Using the Deseasonalized Time Series to Identify Trend

The graph of the deseasonalized smartphone sales time series shown in Figure 17.27 appears to have an upward linear trend. To identify this trend, we will fit a linear trend equation to the deseasonalized time series using the same method shown in Section 17.4. The only difference is that we will be fitting a trend line to the deseasonalized data instead of the original data.

Recall that for a linear trend, the estimated regression equation can be written as

$$T_t = b_0 + b_1 t$$

where

$$\begin{aligned} T_t &= \text{linear trend forecast in period } t \\ b_0 &= \text{intercept of the linear trend line} \\ b_1 &= \text{slope of the trend line} \\ t &= \text{time period} \end{aligned}$$

Table 17.23 Deseasonalized Values for the Smartphone Sales Time Series

Year	Quarter	Time Period	Sales (1,000s)	Seasonal Index	Deseasonalized Sales
1	1	1	4.8	0.93	5.16
	2	2	4.1	0.84	4.88
	3	3	6.0	1.09	5.50
	4	4	6.5	1.14	5.70
2	1	5	5.8	0.93	6.24
	2	6	5.2	0.84	6.19
	3	7	6.8	1.09	6.24
	4	8	7.4	1.14	6.49
3	1	9	6.0	0.93	6.45
	2	10	5.6	0.84	6.67
	3	11	7.5	1.09	6.88
	4	12	7.8	1.14	6.84
4	1	13	6.3	0.93	6.77
	2	14	5.9	0.84	7.02
	3	15	8.0	1.09	7.34
	4	16	8.4	1.14	7.37

Figure 17.27 Deseasonalized Smartphone Sales Time Series

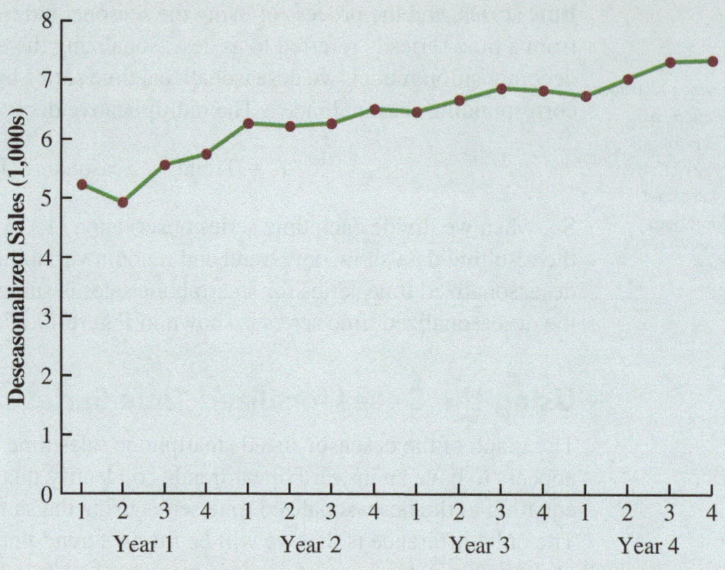

In Section 17.4, we provide formulas for computing the values of b_0 and b_1.

To fit a linear trend line to the deseasonalized data in Table 17.23, the only change is that the deseasonalized time series values are used instead of the observed values Y_t in computing b_0 and b_1. Using Excel's Regression tool, the estimated linear trend equation is

$$\text{Deseasonalized Sales} = 5.10 + 0.148t$$

The slope of 0.148 indicates that over the past 16 quarters, the firm averaged a deseasonalized growth in sales of about 148 smartphones per quarter. If we assume that the past 16-quarter trend in sales data is a reasonably good indicator of the future, this equation can be used to develop a trend projection for future quarters. For example, substituting $t = 17$ into the equation yields next quarter's deseasonalized trend projection, T_{17}.

$$T_{17} = 5.10 + 0.148(17) = 7.616$$

Thus, using the deseasonalized data, the linear trend forecast for next quarter (period 17) is 7,616 smartphones. Similarly, the deseasonalized trend forecasts for the next three quarters (periods 18, 19, and 20) are 7,764, 7,912, and 8,060 smartphones, respectively.

Seasonal Adjustments

The final step in developing the forecast when both trend and seasonal components are present is to use the seasonal indexes to adjust the deseasonalized trend projections. Returning to the smartphone sales example, we have a deseasonalized trend projection for the next four quarters. Now we must adjust the forecast for the seasonal effect. The seasonal index for the first quarter of Year 5 ($t = 17$) is 0.93, so we obtain the quarterly forecast by multiplying the deseasonalized forecast based on trend ($T_{17} = 7{,}616$) by the seasonal index (0.93). Thus, the forecast for the next quarter is 7,616(0.93) = 7,083. Table 17.24 shows the quarterly forecast for quarters 17 through 20. The high-volume fourth quarter has a 9,188-unit forecast, and the low-volume second quarter has a 6,522-unit forecast.

Table 17.24 Quarterly Forecasts for the Smartphone Sales Time Series

Year	Quarter	Deseasonalized Trend Forecast	Seasonal Index	Quarterly Forecast
5	1	7,616	0.93	(7,616)(0.93) = 7,083
	2	7,764	0.84	(7,764)(0.84) = 6,522
	3	7,912	1.09	(7,912)(1.09) = 8,624
	4	8,060	1.14	(8,060)(1.14) = 9,188

Models Based on Monthly Data

In the preceding smartphone sales example, we used quarterly data to illustrate the computation of seasonal indexes. However, many businesses use monthly rather than quarterly forecasts. In such cases, the procedures introduced in this section can be applied with minor modifications. First, a 12-month moving average replaces the four-quarter moving average; second, 12 monthly seasonal indexes, rather than four quarterly seasonal indexes, must be computed. Other than these changes, the computational and forecasting procedures are identical.

Cyclical Component

Mathematically, the multiplicative model of equation (17.12) can be expanded to include a cyclical component.

$$Y_t = \text{Trend}_t \times \text{Cyclical}_t \times \text{Seasonal}_t \times \text{Irregular}_t \qquad \textbf{(17.13)}$$

The cyclical component, like the seasonal component, is expressed as a percentage of trend. As mentioned in Section 17.1, this component is attributable to multiyear cycles in the time series. It is analogous to the seasonal component, but over a longer period of time. However, because of the length of time involved, obtaining enough relevant data to estimate the cyclical component is often difficult. Another difficulty is that cycles usually vary in length. Because it is so difficult to identify and/or separate cyclical effects from long-term trend effects, in practice these effects are often combined and referred to as a combined trend-cycle component. We leave further discussion of the cyclical component to specialized texts on forecasting methods.

Notes + Comments

1. There are a number of different approaches to computing the seasonal indexes. In this section, each seasonal index was computed by averaging the corresponding seasonal-irregular values. Another approach is to use the median of the seasonal-irregular values as the seasonal index.
2. Calendar adjustments are often made before deseasonalizing a time series. For example, if a time series consists of monthly sales values, the value for February sales may be less than for another month simply because there are fewer days in February. To account for this factor, we would first divide each month's sales value by the number of days in the month to obtain a daily average. Since the average number of days in a month is approximately 365/12 = 30.4167, we then multiply the daily averages by 30.4167 to obtain adjusted monthly values. For the examples and exercises in this chapter, you can assume that any required calendar adjustments have already been made.

Exercises

Methods

35. Consider the following time series data. **LO 3, 9**

Quarter	Year 1	Year 2	Year 3
1	4	6	7
2	2	3	6
3	3	5	6
4	5	7	8

a. Construct a time series plot. What type of pattern exists in the data?
b. Show the four-quarter and centered moving average values for this time series.
c. Compute seasonal indexes and adjusted seasonal indexes for the four quarters.

36. Refer to exercise 35. **LO 9, 10**
a. Deseasonalize the time series using the adjusted seasonal indexes computed in part (c) of exercise 35.
b. Compute the linear trend regression equation for the deseasonalized data.
c. Compute the deseasonalized quarterly trend forecast for Year 4.
d. Use the seasonal indexes to adjust the deseasonalized trend forecasts computed in part (c).

Applications

37. **Seasonal Textbook Sales Using Deseasonalization.** The quarterly sales data (number of copies sold) for a college textbook over the past three years follow. **LO 3, 9, 10**

DATA*file*
textsales

Quarter	Year 1	Year 2	Year 3
1	1,690	1,800	1,850
2	940	900	1,100
3	2,625	2,900	2,930
4	2,500	2,360	2,615

a. Construct a time series plot. What type of pattern exists in the data?
b. Show the four-quarter and centered moving average values for this time series.
c. Compute the seasonal and adjusted seasonal indexes for the four quarters.
d. When does the publisher have the largest seasonal index? Does this result appear reasonable? Explain.
e. Deseasonalize the time series.
f. Compute the linear trend equation for the deseasonalized data and forecast sales using the linear trend equation.
g. Adjust the linear trend forecasts using the adjusted seasonal indexes computed in part (c).

38. **Lawn Maintenance Expenses Using Deseasonalization.** Three years of monthly lawn-maintenance expenses ($) for a six-unit apartment house in southern Florida follow. **LO 3, 9, 10**
a. Construct a time series plot. What type of pattern exists in the data?
b. Identify the monthly seasonal indexes for the three years of lawn-maintenance expenses for the apartment house in southern Florida as given here. Use a 12-month moving average calculation.
c. Deseasonalize the time series.
d. Compute the linear trend equation for the deseasonalized data.
e. Compute the deseasonalized trend forecasts and then adjust the trend forecasts using the seasonal indexes to provide a forecast for monthly expenses in Year 4.

DATA*file*
aptexp

Month	Year 1	Year 2	Year 3
January	170	180	195
February	180	205	210
March	205	215	230
April	230	245	280
May	240	265	290
June	315	330	390
July	360	400	420
August	290	335	330
September	240	260	290
October	240	270	295
November	230	255	280
December	195	220	250

39. **Air Pollution Using Deseasonalization.** Air pollution control specialists in southern California monitor the amount of ozone, carbon dioxide, and nitrogen dioxide in the air on an hourly basis. The hourly time series data exhibit seasonality, with the levels of pollutants showing patterns over the hours in the day. On July 15, 16, and 17, the following levels of nitrogen dioxide were observed in the downtown area for the 12 hours from 6:00 A.M. to 6:00 P.M. **LO 3, 9, 10**

DATA*file*
pollution

July 15:	25	28	35	50	60	60	40	35	30	25	25	20
July 16:	28	30	35	48	60	65	50	40	35	25	20	20
July 17:	35	42	45	70	72	75	60	45	40	25	25	25

a. Construct a time series plot. What type of pattern exists in the data?
b. Identify the hourly seasonal indexes for the 12 readings each day.
c. Deseasonalize the time series.
d. Compute the linear trend equation for the deseasonalized data.
e. Compute the deseasonalized trend forecasts for the 12 hours for July 18 and then adjust the trend forecasts using the seasonal indexes computed in part (b).

40. **Electricity Consumption Using Deseasonalization.** Electric power consumption is measured in kilowatt-hours (kWh). The local utility company offers an interrupt program whereby commercial customers that participate receive favorable rates but must agree to cut back consumption if the utility requests them to do so. Timko Products cut back consumption at 12:00 noon Thursday. To assess the savings, the utility must estimate Timko's usage without the interrupt. The period of interrupted service was from noon to 8:00 P.M. Data on electric power consumption for the previous 72 hours are available. **LO 3, 9, 10**

DATA*file*
power

Time Period	Monday	Tuesday	Wednesday	Thursday
12–4 A.M.	—	19,281	31,209	27,330
4–8 A.M.	—	33,195	37,014	32,715
8–12 noon	—	99,516	119,968	152,465
12–4 P.M.	124,299	123,666	156,033	
4–8 P.M.	113,545	111,717	128,889	
8–12 midnight	41,300	48,112	73,923	

a. Is there a seasonal effect over the 24-hour period?
b. Compute seasonal indexes for the six 4-hour periods.
c. Use trend adjusted for seasonal indexes to estimate Timko's normal usage over the period of interrupted service.

Summary

In this chapter, we provided an introduction to the basic methods of time series analysis and forecasting. First, we showed that the underlying pattern in the time series can often be identified by constructing a time series plot. Several types of data patterns can be distinguished, including a horizontal pattern, a trend pattern, and a seasonal pattern. The forecasting methods we have discussed are based on which of these patterns are present in the time series.

For a time series with a horizontal pattern, we showed how moving averages and exponential smoothing can be used to develop a forecast. The moving averages method consists of computing an average of past data values and then using that average as the forecast for the next period. In the exponential smoothing method, a weighted average of past time series values is used to compute a forecast. These methods also adapt well when a horizontal pattern shifts to a different level and resumes a horizontal pattern.

An important factor in determining what forecasting method to use involves the accuracy of the method. We discussed three measures of forecast accuracy: mean absolute error (MAE), mean squared error (MSE), and mean absolute percentage error (MAPE). Each of these measures is designed to determine how well a particular forecasting method is able to reproduce the time series data that are already available. By selecting a method that has the best accuracy for the data already known, we hope to increase the likelihood that we will obtain better forecasts for future time periods.

For time series that have only a long-term linear trend, we showed how simple time series regression can be used to make trend projections. For a time series with a curvilinear or nonlinear trend, we showed how multiple regression can be used to fit a quadratic trend equation to the data.

For a time series with a seasonal pattern, we showed how the use of dummy variables in a multiple regression model can be used to develop an estimated regression equation with seasonal effects. We then extended the regression approach to include situations where the time series contains both a seasonal and a linear trend effect by showing how to combine the dummy variable approach for handling seasonality with the time series regression approach for handling linear trend.

In the last section of the chapter, we showed how time series decomposition can be used to separate or decompose a time series into seasonal and trend components and then to deseasonalize the time series. We showed how to compute seasonal indexes for a multiplicative model, how to use the seasonal indexes to deseasonalize the time series, and how to use regression analysis on the deseasonalized data to estimate the trend component. The final step in developing a forecast when both trend and seasonal components are present is to use the seasonal indexes to adjust the trend projections.

Glossary

Additive decomposition model In an additive decomposition model the actual time series value at time period *t* is obtained by adding the values of a trend component, a seasonal component, and an irregular component.

Cyclical pattern A cyclical pattern exists if the time series plot shows an alternating sequence of points below and above the trend line lasting more than one year.

Deseasonalized time series A time series from which the effect of season has been removed by dividing each original time series observation by the corresponding seasonal index.

Exponential smoothing A forecasting method that uses a weighted average of past time series values as the forecast; it is a special case of the weighted moving averages method in which we select only one weight—the weight for the most recent observation.

Forecast error The difference between the actual time series value and the forecast.

Horizontal pattern A horizontal pattern exists when the data fluctuate around a constant mean.

Mean absolute error (MAE) The average of the absolute values of the forecast errors.
Mean absolute percentage error (MAPE) The average of the absolute values of the percentage forecast errors.
Mean squared error (MSE) The average of the sum of squared forecast errors.
Moving averages A forecasting method that uses the average of the most recent *k* data values in the time series as the forecast for the next period.
Multiplicative decomposition model In a multiplicative decomposition model the actual time series value at time period *t* is obtained by multiplying the values of a trend component, a seasonal component, and an irregular component.
Seasonal pattern A seasonal pattern exists if the time series plot exhibits a repeating pattern over successive periods. The successive periods are often one-year intervals, which is where the name seasonal pattern comes from.
Smoothing constant A parameter of the exponential smoothing model that provides the weight given to the most recent time series value in the calculation of the forecast value.
Stationary time series A time series whose statistical properties are independent of time. For a stationary time series the process generating the data has a constant mean and the variability of the time series is constant over time.
Time series A sequence of observations on a variable measured at successive points in time or over successive periods of time.
Time series decomposition A time series method that is used to separate or decompose a time series into seasonal and trend components.
Time series plot A graphical presentation of the relationship between time and the time series variable. Time is shown on the horizontal axis and the time series values are shown on the vertical axis.
Trend pattern A trend pattern exists if the time series plot shows gradual shifts or movements to relatively higher or lower values over a longer period of time.
Weighted moving averages A forecasting method that involves selecting a different weight for the most recent *k* data values in the time series and then computing a weighted average of the values. The sum of the weights must equal one.

Key Formulas

Moving Average Forecast of Order *k*

$$F_{t+1} = \frac{\sum(\text{most recent } k \text{ data values})}{k} \tag{17.1}$$

Exponential Smoothing Forecast

$$F_{t+1} = \alpha Y_t + (1 - \alpha) F_t \tag{17.2}$$

Linear Trend Equation

$$T_t = b_0 + b_1 t \tag{17.4}$$

where

$$b_1 = \frac{\sum_{t=1}^{n} (t - \bar{t})(Y_t - \bar{Y})}{\sum_{t=1}^{n} (t - \bar{t})^2} \tag{17.5}$$

$$b_0 = \bar{Y} - b_1 \bar{t} \tag{17.6}$$

Quadratic Trend Equation

$$T_t = b_0 + b_1 t + b_2 t^2 \quad (17.7)$$

Exponential Trend Equation

$$T_t = b_0 e^{b_1 t} \quad (17.8)$$

Additive Decomposition Model

$$Y_t = \text{Trend}_t + \text{Seasonal}_t + \text{Irregular}_t \quad (17.11)$$

Multiplicative Decomposition Model

$$Y_t = \text{Trend}_t \times \text{Seasonal}_t \times \text{Irregular}_t \quad (17.12)$$

Supplementary Exercises

41. **Demand for Consumer Goods.** The weekly demand (in cases) for a particular brand of automatic dishwasher detergent for a chain of grocery stores located in Columbus, Ohio, follows. **LO 1, 2, 3, 4**

DATA*file*
dishwasher

Week	Demand	Week	Demand
1	22	6	24
2	18	7	20
3	23	8	19
4	21	9	18
5	17	10	21

a. Construct a time series plot. What type of pattern exists in the data?
b. Use a three-week moving average to develop a forecast for week 11.
c. Use exponential smoothing with a smoothing constant of $\alpha = 0.2$ to develop a forecast for week 11.
d. Which of the two methods do you prefer? Why?

42. **Portfolio Composition.** The following table reports the percentage of stocks in a portfolio for nine quarters from 2011 to 2013. **LO 1, 2, 3, 4**

DATA*file*
portfolio

Quarter	Stock %
1st—Year 1	29.8
2nd—Year 1	31.0
3rd—Year 1	29.9
4th—Year 1	30.1
1st—Year 2	32.2
2nd—Year 2	31.5
3rd—Year 2	32.0
4th—Year 2	31.9
1st—Year 3	30.0

a. Construct a time series plot. What type of pattern exists in the data?
b. Use exponential smoothing to forecast this time series. Consider smoothing constants of $\alpha = 0.2$, 0.3, and 0.4. What value of the smoothing constant provides the most accurate forecasts?
c. What is the forecast of the percentage of stocks in a typical portfolio for the second quarter of Year 3?

43. **Demand for Dairy Products.** United Dairies, Inc., supplies milk to several independent grocers throughout Dade County, Florida. Managers at United Dairies want to develop a forecast of the number of half-gallons of milk sold per week. Sales data for the past 12 weeks follow. **LO 3, 4**

DATA*file*
udfmilk

Week	Sales	Week	Sales
1	2,750	7	3,300
2	3,100	8	3,100
3	3,250	9	2,950
4	2,800	10	3,000
5	2,900	11	3,200
6	3,050	12	3,150

a. Construct a time series plot. What type of pattern exists in the data?
b. Use exponential smoothing with $\alpha = 0.4$ to develop a forecast of demand for week 13.

44. **Crude Oil Cost.** The data contained in the file *crudecost* show the U.S. refiner acquisition cost of crude oil in dollars per barrel (Energy Information Administration website). **LO 1, 2, 3, 5, 6**

DATA*file*
crudecost

a. Construct a time series plot. What type of pattern exists in the data?
b. Compute the linear trend equation for the time series. Use the linear trend equation to forecast the crude cost for period 49.
c. Compute the quadratic trend equation for the time series. Use the quadratic trend equation to forecast the crude cost for period 49.
d. Using MSE, which approach provides the most accurate forecasts for the historical data?

45. **Tesla Sales.** Tesla is an electric vehicle manufacturer based in Austin, Texas. The file *teslasales* contains the annual sales of Tesla vehicles from 2013 to 2020. **LO 3, 5**

DATA*file*
teslasales

Year	Period	Sales (Units)
2013	1	22,442
2014	2	31,655
2015	3	50,517
2016	4	76,243
2017	5	103,091
2018	6	245,491
2019	7	367,656
2020	8	499,535

a. Construct a time series plot. What type of pattern exists in the data?
b. Develop an exponential trend equation for this time series.
c. Use the equation developed in part (b) to forecast sales in 2021 (period 9).

46. **Lost Sales.** The Mayfair Department Store in Davenport, Iowa, is trying to determine the amount of sales lost while it was shut down during July and August because of damage caused by the Mississippi River flood. Sales data for January through June follow. **LO 4, 5**

Month	Sales ($1,000s)	Month	Sales ($1,000s)
January	185.72	April	210.36
February	167.84	May	255.57
March	205.11	June	261.19

a. Use exponential smoothing, with $\alpha = 0.4$, to develop a forecast for July and August. (*Hint*: Use the forecast for July as the actual sales in July in developing the August forecast.) Comment on the use of exponential smoothing for forecasts more than one period into the future.
b. Use trend projection to forecast sales for July and August.
c. Mayfair's insurance company proposed a settlement based on lost sales of $240,000 in July and August. Is this amount fair? If not, what amount would you recommend as a counteroffer?

47. **Disney Price of Admission.** The following data show the price in dollars for a general admission ticket to the Magic Kingdom at Disney World from the year 2000 (period 1) to 2020 (period 21). These data are in the file *disneyprices* (Source: *Travel + Leisure* website). **LO 2, 3**

DATA*file*
disneyprices

Year	Period	Price of Admission ($)
2000	1	46.00
2001	2	48.00
2002	3	50.00
2003	4	52.00
2004	5	54.75
2005	6	59.75
2006	7	67.00
2007	8	71.00
2008	9	75.00
2009	10	79.00
2010	11	82.00
2011	12	85.00
2012	13	89.00
2013	14	95.00
2014	15	99.00
2015	16	106.00
2016	17	110.00
2017	18	115.00
2018	19	119.00
2019	20	125.00
2020	21	125.00

a. Construct a time-series plot. What type of pattern exists?
b. Develop an appropriate trend equation. Explain your choice of trend equation.
c. Compare the predicted price for 2020 (period 21) with the actual.

48. **Musical Instrument Sales.** The Costello Music Company has been in business for five years. During that time, sales of pianos increased from 12 units in the first year to 76 units in the most recent year. Fred Costello, the firm's owner, wants to develop a forecast of piano sales for the coming year. The historical data follow. **LO 3, 5**

Year	1	2	3	4	5
Sales	12	28	34	50	76

a. Construct a time series plot. What type of pattern exists in the data?
b. Develop the linear trend equation for the time series. What is the average increase in sales that the firm has been realizing per year?
c. Forecast sales for Years 6 and 7.

49. **Musical Instrument Sales with Seasonality.** Consider the Costello Music Company problem in exercise 48. The quarterly sales data follow. **LO 8**

DATA*file*
pianosales

Year	Quarter 1	Quarter 2	Quarter 3	Quarter 4	Total Yearly Sales
1	4	2	1	5	12
2	6	4	4	14	28
3	10	3	5	16	34
4	12	9	7	22	50
5	18	10	13	35	76

a. Use the following dummy variables to develop an estimated regression equation to account for any seasonal and linear trend effects in the data: Qtr1 = 1 if Quarter 1, 0 otherwise; Qtr2 = 1 if Quarter 2, 0 otherwise; and Qtr3 = 1 if Quarter 3, 0 otherwise.
b. Compute the quarterly forecasts for next year.

50. **Musical Instrument Sales with Decomposition.** Refer to the Costello Music Company problem in exercise 49. **LO 9**
a. Using time series decomposition, compute the seasonal indexes for the four quarters.
b. When does Costello Music experience the largest seasonal effect? Does this result appear reasonable? Explain.

51. **Musical Instrument Sales Using Trend and Seasonality.** Refer to the Costello Music Company time series in exercise 49. **LO 9, 10**
a. Deseasonalize the data and use the deseasonalized time series to identify the trend.
b. Use the results of part (a) to develop a quarterly forecast for next year based on trend.
c. Use the seasonal indexes developed in exercise 50 to adjust the forecasts developed in part (b) to account for the effect of season.

52. **Boat Trailer Sales.** Hudson Marine provides boats sales, service, and maintenance. Boat trailers are one of its top sales items. The following table reports the number of trailers sold each year. **LO 3, 5**

Year	1	2	3	4	5	6	7
Number Sold	35	50	75	90	105	110	130

a. Construct a time series plot. Does a linear trend appear to be present?
b. Compute the linear trend equation for this time series.
c. Use the linear trend equation developed in part (b) to develop a forecast for annual sales in Year 8.

53. **Boat Trailer Sales with Seasonality.** Refer to the Hudson Marine problem in exercise 52. Suppose the quarterly sales values for the seven years of historical data are as follows. **LO 8**

DATA*file*
hudsonmarine

Year	Quarter 1	Quarter 2	Quarter 3	Quarter 4	Total Yearly Sales
1	6	15	10	4	35
2	10	18	15	7	50
3	14	26	23	12	75
4	19	28	25	18	90
5	22	34	28	21	105
6	24	36	30	20	110
7	28	40	35	27	130

a. Use the following dummy variables to develop an estimated regression equation to account for any season and linear trend effects in the data: Qtr1 = 1 if Quarter 1, 0 otherwise; Qtr2 = 1 if Quarter 2, 0 otherwise; and Qtr3 = 1 if Quarter 3, 0 otherwise.
b. Compute the quarterly forecasts for next year.

54. **Estimating Seasonal Effects in Boat Trailer Sales.** Refer to the Hudson Marine problem in exercise 53. **LO 9**
    a. Compute the centered moving average values for this time series.
    b. Construct a time series plot that also shows the centered moving average and original time series on the same graph. Discuss the differences between the original time series plot and the centered moving average time series.
    c. Compute the seasonal indexes for the four quarters.
    d. When does Hudson Marine experience the largest seasonal effect? Does this result seem reasonable? Explain.

55. **Deseasonalizing Boat Trailer Sales Data.** Refer to the Hudson Marine data in exercise 53. **LO 9, 10**
    a. Deseasonalize the data and use the deseasonalized time series to identify the trend.
    b. Use the results of part (a) to develop a quarterly forecast for next year based on trend.
    c. Use the seasonal indexes developed in exercise 54 to adjust the forecasts developed in part (b) to account for the effect of season.

Case Problem 1: Forecasting Food and Beverage Sales

The Vintage Restaurant, on Captiva Island near Fort Myers, Florida, is owned and operated by Karen Payne. The restaurant just completed its third year of operation. Since opening her restaurant, Karen has sought to establish a reputation for the Vintage as a high-quality dining establishment that specializes in fresh seafood. Through the efforts of Karen and her staff, her restaurant has become one of the best and fastest growing restaurants on the island.

To better plan for future growth of the restaurant, Karen needs to develop a system that will enable her to forecast food and beverage sales by month for up to one year in advance. Table 17.25 shows the value of food and beverage sales ($1,000s) for the first three years of operation. **LO 3, 8, 9, 10**

Managerial Report

Perform an analysis of the sales data for the Vintage Restaurant. Prepare a report for Karen that summarizes your findings, forecasts, and recommendations. Include the following:

1. A time series plot. Comment on the underlying pattern in the time series.
2. An analysis of the seasonality of the data. Indicate the seasonal indexes for each month, and comment on the high and low seasonal sales months. Do the seasonal indexes make intuitive sense? Discuss.
3. Deseasonalize the time series. Does there appear to be any trend in the deseasonalized time series?

Table 17.25 Food and Beverage Sales for the Vintage Restaurant ($1,000s)

Month	First Year	Second Year	Third Year
January	242	263	282
February	235	238	255
March	232	247	265
April	178	193	205
May	184	193	210
June	140	149	160
July	145	157	166
August	152	161	174
September	110	122	126
October	130	130	148
November	152	167	173
December	206	230	235

DATA*file*
vintage

4. Using the time series decomposition method, forecast sales for January through December of the fourth year.
5. Using the dummy variable regression approach, forecast sales for January through December of the fourth year.
6. Provide summary tables of your calculations and any graphs in the appendix of your report.

Assume that January sales for the fourth year turn out to be $295,000. What was your forecast error? If this error is large, Karen may be puzzled about the difference between your forecast and the actual sales value. What can you do to resolve her uncertainty in the forecasting procedure?

Case Problem 2: Forecasting Lost Sales

The Carlson Department Store suffered heavy damage when a hurricane struck on August 31. The store was closed for four months (September through December), and Carlson is now involved in a dispute with its insurance company about the amount of lost sales during the time the store was closed. Two key issues must be resolved: (1) the amount of sales Carlson would have made if the hurricane had not struck and (2) whether Carlson is entitled to any compensation for excess sales due to increased business activity after the storm. More than $8 billion in federal disaster relief and insurance money came into the county, resulting in increased sales at department stores and numerous other businesses.

Table 17.26 gives Carlson's sales data for the 48 months preceding the storm. Table 17.27 reports total sales for the 48 months preceding the storm for all department stores in the county, as well as the total sales in the county for the four months the Carlson Department Store was closed. Carlson's managers asked you to analyze these data and develop estimates of the lost sales at the Carlson Department Store for the months of September through December. They also asked you to determine whether a case can be made for excess storm-related sales during the same period. If such a case can be made, Carlson is entitled to compensation for excess sales it would have earned in addition to ordinary sales. **LO 9, 10**

Managerial Report

Prepare a report for the managers of the Carlson Department Store that summarizes your findings, forecasts, and recommendations. Include the following:

1. An estimate of sales for Carlson Department Store had there been no hurricane.
2. An estimate of countywide department store sales had there been no hurricane.
3. An estimate of lost sales for the Carlson Department Store for September through December.

DATA*file*
carlsonsales

Table 17.26 Sales for Carlson Department Store ($millions)

Month	Year 1	Year 2	Year 3	Year 4	Year 5
January		1.45	2.31	2.31	2.56
February		1.80	1.89	1.99	2.28
March		2.03	2.02	2.42	2.69
April		1.99	2.23	2.45	2.48
May		2.32	2.39	2.57	2.73
June		2.20	2.14	2.42	2.37
July		2.13	2.27	2.40	2.31
August		2.43	2.21	2.50	2.23
September	1.71	1.90	1.89	2.09	
October	1.90	2.13	2.29	2.54	
November	2.74	2.56	2.83	2.97	
December	4.20	4.16	4.04	4.35	

DATA*file*
countysales

Table 17.27 Department Store Sales for the County ($millions)

Month	Year 1	Year 2	Year 3	Year 4	Year 5
January		46.80	46.80	43.80	48.00
February		48.00	48.60	45.60	51.60
March		60.00	59.40	57.60	57.60
April		57.60	58.20	53.40	58.20
May		61.80	60.60	56.40	60.00
June		58.20	55.20	52.80	57.00
July		56.40	51.00	54.00	57.60
August		63.00	58.80	60.60	61.80
September	55.80	57.60	49.80	47.40	69.00
October	56.40	53.40	54.60	54.60	75.00
November	71.40	71.40	65.40	67.80	85.20
December	117.60	114.00	102.00	100.20	121.80

Chapter 18

Nonparametric Methods

Contents

Statistics in Practice:
West Shell Realtors

18.1 Sign Test
Hypothesis Test About a Population Median
Hypothesis Test with Matched Samples

18.2 Wilcoxon Signed-Rank Test

18.3 Mann–Whitney– Wilcoxon Test

18.4 Kruskal–Wallis Test

18.5 Rank Correlation

Summary 912
Glossary 913
Key Formulas 913
Supplementary Exercises 914
Case Problem: RainOrShine.Com 917

Available in the Cengage eBook:
Appendix: The Sign Test with R
Appendix: The Wilcoxon Signed-Rank Test with R
Appendix: The Mann-Whitney-Wilcoxon Test with R
Appendix: The Kruskal-Wallis Test with R
Appendix: The Spearman Rank Correlation Coefficient with R

Learning Objectives

After completing this chapter, you will be able to

LO 1 Test hypotheses about a population median using the sign test and interpret the results.

LO 2 Use the sign test to test hypotheses about the difference between two populations using matched samples and interpret the results.

LO 3 Use the Wilcoxon signed-rank test to test hypotheses about the difference between two populations using matched samples and interpret the results.

LO 4 Use the Mann-Whitney-Wilcoxon test to test hypotheses about the difference between two populations using independent samples and interpret the results.

LO 5 Use the Kruskal-Wallis test to test hypotheses about differences among three or more populations using independent samples and interpret the results.

LO 6 Compute and use the Spearman rank-correlation coefficient to assess the association and test hypotheses about between two variables based on rank-ordered data and interpret the results.

Statistics in Practice

West Shell Realtors*

Cincinnati, Ohio

West Shell Realtors was founded in 1958 with one office and a sales staff of three people. In 1964, the company began a long-term expansion program, with new offices added almost yearly. Over the years, West Shell grew to become one of the largest realtors in Greater Cincinnati, with offices in southwest Ohio, southeast Indiana, and northern Kentucky. The company was eventually acquired by Coldwell Banker Residential Brokerage.

Statistical analysis helps real estate firms such as West Shell monitor sales performance. Monthly reports are generated for each of West Shell's offices as well as for the total company. Statistical summaries of total sales dollars, number of units sold, and median selling price per unit are essential in keeping both office managers and the company's top management informed of progress and trouble spots in the organization.

In addition to monthly summaries of ongoing operations, the company uses statistical considerations to guide corporate plans and strategies. West Shell has implemented a strategy of planned expansion. Each time an expansion plan calls for the establishment of a new sales office, the company must address the question of office location. Selling prices of homes, turnover rates, and forecast sales volumes are the types of data used in evaluating and comparing alternative locations.

In one instance, West Shell identified two neighborhoods, Clifton and Roselawn, as prime candidates for a new office. A variety of factors were considered in comparing the two areas, including selling prices of homes. West Shell employed nonparametric statistical methods to help identify any differences in sales patterns for the two areas.

Samples of 25 sales in the Clifton area and 18 sales in the Roselawn area were taken, and the Mann–Whitney–Wilcoxon rank-sum test was chosen as an appropriate statistical test of the difference in the pattern of selling prices. At the 0.05 level of significance, the Mann–Whitney–Wilcoxon test did not allow rejection of the null hypothesis that the two populations of selling prices were identical. Thus, West Shell was able to focus on criteria other than selling prices of homes in the site selection process.

West Shell uses statistical analysis of home sales to remain competitive. Richard Clement/Bloomberg/Getty Images

In this chapter we will show how nonparametric statistical tests such as the Mann–Whitney–Wilcoxon test are applied. We will also discuss the proper interpretation of such tests.

*The authors are indebted to Rodney Fightmaster of West Shell Realtors for providing this Statistics in Practice.

The statistical methods for inference presented previously in the text are generally known as **parametric methods**. These methods begin with an assumption about the probability distribution of the population which is often that the population has a normal distribution. Based upon this assumption, statisticians are able to derive the sampling distribution that can be used to make inferences about one or more parameters of the population, such as the population mean μ or the population standard deviation σ. For example, a parametric method can be used to make an inference about a population mean based on an assumption that the sampling distribution of $\bar{x}$ is normally distributed (which is true if the population is normally distributed or the sample size is sufficiently large) with unknown parameters μ

The parametric method described here is introduced in Chapter 9.

and σ. Using the sample standard deviation s to estimate the population standard deviation σ, the test statistic for making an inference about the population has a t distribution. As a result, the t distribution is used to compute confidence intervals and conduct hypothesis tests about the mean of a normally distributed population.

In this chapter, we present **nonparametric methods** which can be used to make inferences about a population without requiring an assumption about the specific form of the population's probability distribution. For this reason, these nonparametric methods are also called **distribution-free methods**.

Most of the statistical methods referred to as parametric methods require quantitative data, whereas nonparametric methods allow inferences based on either categorical or quantitative data. However, the computations used in the nonparametric methods are generally done with categorical data. Whenever the data are quantitative, we will transform the data into categorical data in order to conduct the nonparametric test. In the first section of the chapter, we show how the binomial distribution uses two categories of data to make an inference about a population median. In the next three sections, we show how rank-ordered data are used in nonparametric tests about two or more populations. In the final section, we use rank-ordered data to compute the rank correlation for two variables.

18.1 Sign Test

The **sign test** is a versatile nonparametric method for hypothesis testing that uses the binomial distribution with $p = 0.50$ as the sampling distribution. It does not require an assumption about the distribution of the population. In this section, we present two applications of the sign test: one involving a hypothesis test about a population median and one involving a matched-sample test about the difference between two populations.

Hypothesis Test About a Population Median

In Chapter 9, we describe how to conduct hypothesis tests about a population mean.

In this section, we show how the sign test can be used to conduct a hypothesis test about a population median. If we consider a population where no data value is exactly equal to the median, the median is the measure of central tendency that divides the population so that 50% of the values are greater than the median and 50% of the values are less than the median. Whenever a population distribution is skewed, the median is often preferred over the mean as the best measure of central location for the population. The sign test provides a nonparametric procedure for testing a hypothesis about the value of a population median.

In order to demonstrate the sign test, we consider the weekly sales of Cape May Potato Chips by the Lawler Grocery Store chain. Lawler's management made the decision to carry the new potato chip product based on the manufacturer's estimate that the median sales should be \$450 per week on a per store basis. After carrying the product for three months, Lawler's management requested the following hypothesis test about the population median weekly sales.

$$H_0\text{: Median} = 450$$
$$H_a\text{: Median} \neq 450$$

Data showing one-week sales at 10 randomly selected Lawler's stores are provided in Table 18.1.

Observations equal to the hypothesized value are discarded and the analysis proceeds with the observations having either a plus sign or a minus sign.

In conducting the sign test, we compare each sample observation to the hypothesized value of the population median. If the observation is greater than the hypothesized value, we record a plus sign "+." If the observation is less than the hypothesized value, we record a minus sign "−." If an observation is exactly equal to the hypothesized value, the observation is eliminated from the sample and the analysis proceeds with the smaller sample size, using only the observations where a plus sign or a minus sign has been recorded. It is the

Table 18.1 One-Week Sales of Cape May Potato Chips at 10 Lawler Grocery Stores

Store Number	Weekly Sales ($)	Store Number	Weekly Sales ($)
56	485	63	474
19	562	39	662
36	415	84	380
128	860	102	515
12	426	44	721

conversion of the sample data to either a plus sign or a minus sign that gives the nonparametric method its name: the sign test.

Consider the sample data in Table 18.1. The first observation, 485, is greater than the hypothesized median 450; a plus sign is recorded. The second observation, 562, is greater than the hypothesized median 450; a plus sign is recorded. Continuing with the 10 observations in the sample provides the plus and minus signs as shown in Table 18.2. Note that there are seven plus signs and three minus signs.

The assigning of the plus signs and minus signs has made the situation a binomial distribution application. The sample size $n = 10$ is the number of trials. There are two outcomes possible per trial, a plus sign or a minus sign, and the trials are independent. Let p denote the probability of a plus sign. If the population median is 450, p would equal 0.50 as there should be 50% plus signs and 50% minus signs in the population. Thus, in terms of the binomial probability p, the sign test hypotheses about the population median

$$H_0\text{: Median} = 450$$
$$H_a\text{: Median} \neq 450$$

are converted to the following hypotheses about the binomial probability p.

$$H_0\text{: } p = 0.50$$
$$H_a\text{: } p \neq 0.50$$

If H_0 cannot be rejected, we cannot conclude that p is different from 0.50 and thus we cannot conclude that the population median is different from 450. However, if H_0 is rejected, we can conclude that p is not equal to 0.50 and thus the population median is not equal to 450.

With $n = 10$ stores or trials and $p = 0.50$, we can use Excel's BINOM.DIST function to obtain the binomial probabilities for the number of plus signs under the assumption H_0 is true. These probabilities are shown in Table 18.3. Figure 18.1 shows a graphical representation of this binomial distribution.

The BINOM.DIST function is discussed in Chapter 5.

Table 18.2 Lawler Sample Data for the Sign Test About the Population Median Weekly Sales

Store Number	Weekly Sales ($)	Sign	Store Number	Weekly Sales ($)	Sign
56	485	+	63	474	+
19	562	+	39	662	+
36	415	−	84	380	−
128	860	+	102	515	+
12	426	−	44	721	+

Table 18.3 Binomial Probabilities with $n = 10$ and $p = 0.50$

Number of Plus Signs	Probability
0	0.0010
1	0.0098
2	0.0439
3	0.1172
4	0.2051
5	0.2461
6	0.2051
7	0.1172
8	0.0439
9	0.0098
10	0.0010

Figure 18.1 Binomial Sampling Distribution for the Number of Plus Signs When $n = 10$ and $p = 0.50$

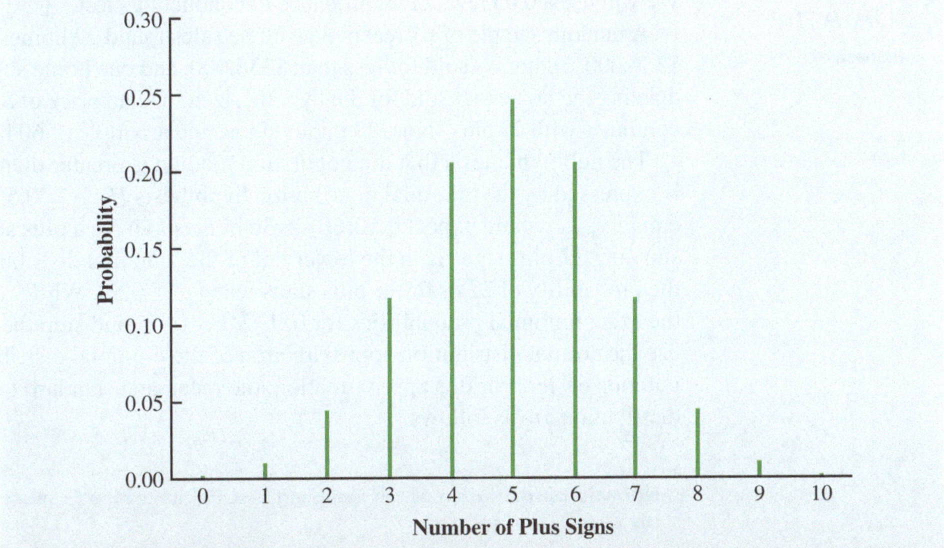

Let us proceed to show how the binomial distribution can be used to test the hypothesis about the population median. We will use a 0.10 level of significance for the test. Since the observed number of plus signs for the sample data, 7, is in the upper tail of the binomial distribution, we begin by computing the probability of obtaining 7 or more plus signs. This probability is the probability of 7, 8, 9, or 10 plus signs. Adding these probabilities shown in Table 18.3, we have $0.1172 + 0.0439 + 0.0098 + 0.0010 = 0.1719$. Since we are using a two-tailed hypothesis test, this upper tail probability is doubled to obtain the p-value $= 2(0.1719) = 0.3438$. With p-value $> \alpha$, we cannot reject H_0. In terms of the binomial probability p, we cannot reject H_0: $p = 0.50$, and thus we cannot reject the hypothesis that the population median is \$450.

In this example, the hypothesis test about the population median was formulated as a two-tailed test. However, one-tailed sign tests about a population median are also possible.

For example, we could have formulated the hypotheses as an upper tail test so that the null and alternative hypotheses would be written as follows:

$$H_0\text{: Median} \leq 450$$
$$H_a\text{: Median} > 450$$

The corresponding p-value is equal to the binomial probability that the number of plus signs is greater than or equal to 7 found in the sample. This one-tailed p-value would have been $0.1172 + 0.0439 + 0.0098 + 0.0010 = 0.1719$. If the example were converted to a lower tail test, the p-value would have been the probability of obtaining 7 or fewer plus signs.

The application we have just described used Excel's BINOM.DIST function to compute the binomial probabilities required to obtain the p-value. With larger sample sizes, the normal distribution approximation of the binomial distribution can also be used to compute the p-value. A large sample application of the sign test is illustrated in the following example.

One year ago the median price of a new home was \$336,000. However, a current downturn in the economy has real estate firms using sample data on recent home sales to determine if the population median price of a new home is less today than it was a year ago. The hypothesis test about the population median price of a new home is as follows:

$$H_0\text{: Median} \geq 336{,}000$$
$$H_a\text{: Median} < 336{,}000$$

DATA*file*
homesales

We will use a 0.05 level of significance to conduct this test.

A random sample of 61 recent new home sales found 22 homes sold for more than \$336,000, 38 homes sold for less than \$336,000, and one home sold for \$336,000. After deleting the home that sold for the hypothesized median price of \$336,000, the sign test continues with 22 plus signs, 38 minus signs, and a sample of 60 homes.

The null hypothesis that the population median is greater than or equal to \$336,000 is expressed by the binomial distribution hypothesis H_0: $p \geq 0.50$. If H_0 were true as an equality, we would expect $0.50(60) = 30$ homes to have a plus sign. The sample result showing 22 plus signs is in the lower tail of the binomial distribution. Thus, the p-value is the probability of 22 or fewer plus signs when $p = 0.50$. While it is possible to compute the exact binomial probabilities for 0, 1, 2, . . . to 22 and sum these probabilities, we will use the normal distribution approximation of the binomial distribution to make this computation easier. For this approximation, the mean and standard deviation of the normal distribution are as follows.

Normal Approximation of the Sampling Distribution of the Number of Plus Signs When H_0: $p = 0.50$

$$\text{Mean: } \mu = 0.50n \quad \textbf{(18.1)}$$

$$\text{Standard deviation: } \sigma = \sqrt{0.25n} \quad \textbf{(18.2)}$$

Distribution form: Approximately normal for $n > 20$

Using equations (18.1) and (18.2) with $n = 60$ homes and $p = 0.50$, the sampling distribution of the number of plus signs can be approximated by a normal distribution with

$$\mu = 0.50n = 0.50(60) = 30$$
$$\sigma = \sqrt{0.25n} = \sqrt{0.25(60)} = 3.873$$

Let us now use the normal distribution to approximate the binomial probability of 22 or fewer plus signs. Before we proceed, remember that the binomial probability distribution

Figure 18.2 Normal Distribution Approximation of the *p*-Value for the Sign Test About the Median Price of New Homes

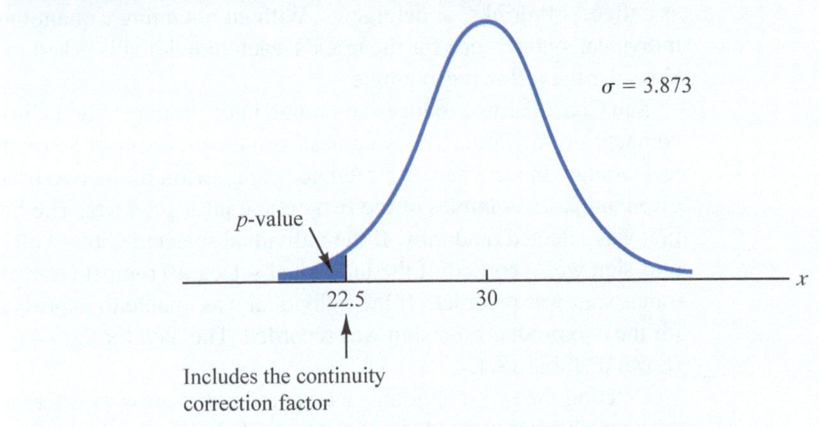

is discrete and the normal probability distribution is continuous. To account for this, the binomial probability of 22 is computed by the normal probability interval 21.5 to 22.5. The 0.5 added to and subtracted from 22 is called the continuity correction factor. Thus, to compute the p-value for 22 or fewer plus signs we use the normal distribution with $\mu = 30$ and $\sigma = 3.873$ to compute the probability that the normal random variable, x, has a value less than or equal to 22.5. A graph of this p-value is shown in Figure 18.2.

Using this normal distribution, we compute the p-value as follows:

$$p\text{-value} = P(x \leq 22.5) = P\left(z \leq \frac{22.5 - 30}{3.873}\right) = P(z \leq -1.94)$$

Using Excel's NORM.S.DIST function, the cumulative probability for $z = 1.94$ is 0.0262; thus the p-value $= 0.0262$. With $0.0262 < 0.05$, we reject the null hypothesis and conclude that the median price of a new home is less than the \$336,000 median price a year ago.

Notes + Comments

The examples used to illustrate a hypothesis test about a population median involved weekly sales data and home price data. The probability distributions for these types of variables are usually not symmetrical and are most often skewed to the right. In such cases, the population median rather than the population mean becomes the preferred measure of central location. In general, when the population is not symmetrical, the nonparametric sign test for the population median is the more appropriate statistical test.

Hypothesis Test with Matched Samples

This parametric test is introduced in Chapter 10.

Consider a matched-sample experimental design where each of n experimental units provides a pair of observations, one from population 1 and one from population 2. A parametric test for comparing the means of these matched samples is to use quantitative data and assume that the differences between the pairs of matched observations are normally distributed. Then the t distribution can be used to make an inference about the difference between the means of the two populations.

In the following example we will use the nonparametric sign test to analyze matched-sample data. Unlike the t distribution procedure, which requires quantitative data and the assumption that the differences were normally distributed, the sign test enables us to analyze categorical as well as quantitative data and requires no assumption about the distribution of the differences. This type of matched-sample design occurs in market research when a sample of n potential customers is asked to compare two brands of a product such as coffee, soft drinks, or detergents. Without obtaining a quantitative measure of each individual's preference for the brands, each individual is asked to state a brand preference. Consider the following example.

Sun Coast Farms produces an orange juice product called Citrus Valley. The primary competition for Citrus Valley comes from the producer of an orange juice known as Tropical Orange. In a consumer preference comparison of the two brands, 14 individuals were given unmarked samples of the two orange juice products. The brand each individual tasted first was selected randomly. If the individual selected Citrus Valley as the more preferred, a plus sign was recorded. If the individual selected Tropical Orange as the more preferred, a minus sign was recorded. If the individual was unable to express a difference in preference for the two products, no sign was recorded. The data for the 14 individuals in the study are shown in Table 18.4.

Deleting the two individuals who could not express a preference for either brand, the data have been converted to a sign test with 2 plus signs and 10 minus signs for the $n = 12$ individuals who could express a preference for one of the two brands. Letting p indicate the proportion of the population of customers who prefer Citrus Valley orange juice, we want to test the hypotheses that there is no difference between the preferences for the two brands as follows:

$$H_0: p = 0.50$$
$$H_a: p \neq 0.50$$

If H_0 cannot be rejected, we cannot conclude that there is a difference in preference for the two brands. However, if H_0 can be rejected, we can conclude that the consumer preferences differ for the two brands. We will use a 0.05 level of significance for this hypothesis test.

We will conduct the sign test exactly as we did earlier in this section. The sampling distribution for the number of plus signs is a binomial distribution with $p = 0.50$ and $n = 12$. Using Excel's BINOM.DIST function, we obtain the binomial probabilities for the number of plus signs, as shown in Table 18.5. Under the assumption H_0 is true, we would expect $0.50n = 0.50(12) = 6$ plus signs. With only two plus signs in the sample, the results are in the lower tail of the binomial distribution. To compute the p-value for this two-tailed test, we first compute the probability of 2 or fewer plus signs and then double this value. Using the binomial probabilities of 0, 1, and 2 shown in Table 18.5, the p-value is $2(0.0002 + 0.0029 + 0.0161) = 0.0384$. With $0.0384 < 0.05$, we reject H_0. The taste test provides evidence that consumer preference differs significantly for the two brands of orange juice. We would advise Sun Coast Farms of this result and conclude that the competitor's Tropical Orange product is the more preferred. Sun Coast Farms can then pursue a strategy to address this issue.

Table 18.4 Preference Data for the Sun Coast Farms Taste Test

Individual	Preference	Sign	Individual	Preference	Sign
1	Tropical Orange	−	8	Tropical Orange	−
2	Tropical Orange	−	9	Tropical Orange	−
3	Citrus Valley	+	10	No Preference	
4	Tropical Orange	−	11	Tropical Orange	−
5	Tropical Orange	−	12	Citrus Valley	+
6	No Preference		13	Tropical Orange	−
7	Tropical Orange	−	14	Tropical Orange	−

Table 18.5 Binomial Probabilities with $n = 12$ and $p = 0.50$

Number of Plus Signs	Probability
0	0.0002
1	0.0029
2	0.0161
3	0.0537
4	0.1208
5	0.1934
6	0.2256
7	0.1934
8	0.1208
9	0.0537
10	0.0161
11	0.0029
12	0.0002

Similar to other uses of the sign test, one-tailed tests may be used depending upon the application. Also, as the sample size becomes large, the normal distribution approximation of the binomial distribution as shown earlier in this section can be used. While the Sun Coast Farms sign test for matched samples used categorical preference data, the sign test for matched samples can be used with quantitative data as well. This would be particularly helpful if the paired differences are not normally distributed and are skewed. In this case a positive difference is assigned a plus sign, a negative difference is assigned a minus sign, and a zero difference is removed from the sample. The sign test computations proceed as before.

Using Excel

Excel does not have an option for the sign test in its Data Analysis ToolPak. But it is easy to use Excel's BINOM.DIST function to compute the appropriate p-values for a sign test. Here we show how to compute lower tail, upper tail, and two-tailed p-values.

Lower Tail p-Values In a sign test, the lower tail p-value is given by the cumulative probability for the number of plus signs. The cumulative probability for the number of plus signs, p-value (Lower tail), is computed by entering the following formula into a cell of an Excel worksheet.

$$= BINOM.DIST(PlusSigns, Trials, 0.50, TRUE)$$

where

PlusSigns = the number of plus signs in the sign test
Trials = the total number of plus and minus signs in the sign test

Upper Tail p-Values The upper tail p-value is given by entering the following formula into a cell of an Excel worksheet.

$$= 1 - BINOM.DIST(PlusSigns - 1, Trials, 0.50, TRUE)$$

Note that, since the binomial distribution is discrete, (PlusSigns − 1) is used in the upper-tail probability calculation. For example, the upper tail probability for 7 plus signs is $P(\text{PlusSigns} \geq 7) = 1 - P(\text{PlusSigns} - 1 \leq 6)$.

Two-Tailed *p*-Values The *p*-value for a two-tailed sign test is found by first determining whether the number of plus signs is in the lower or upper tail of the binomial distribution. Then we double the area in that tail to get the *p*-value (two tail). Let us illustrate using the Lawler Grocery Store hypothesis test about a population median. We have seven plus signs and three minus signs for the sample of 10 stores. The number of plus signs is in the upper tail, so we compute

$$p\text{-value (Upper tail)} = 1 - \text{BINOM.DIST(PlusSigns} - 1\text{,Trials,0.50,TRUE)}$$
$$= 1 - \textit{BINOM.DIST(6,10,0.50,TRUE)} = 0.1719$$

Since this is a two-tailed hypothesis test, we have p-value $= 2(0.1719) = 0.3438$.

Exercises

Methods

1. The following hypothesis test is to be conducted.

$$H_0\text{: Median} \leq 150$$
$$H_a\text{: Median} > 150$$

A sample of 30 provided 22 observations greater than 150, 3 observations equal to 150, and 5 observations less than 150. Use $\alpha = 0.01$. What is your conclusion? **LO 1**

2. Ten individuals participated in a taste test involving two brands of a product. Sample results show 7 preferred brand A, 2 preferred brand B, and 1 was unable to state a preference. With $\alpha = 0.05$, test for a significant difference in the preferences for the two brands. What is your conclusion? **LO 2**

Applications

3. **Employees at Fast-Food Restaurants.** The median number of part-time employees at fast-food restaurants in a particular city was known to be 18 last year. City officials think the use of part-time employees may be increasing. A sample of nine fast-food restaurants showed that seven restaurants were employing more than 18 part-time employees, one restaurant was employing exactly 18 part-time employees, and one restaurant was employing fewer than 18 part-time employees. Can it be concluded that the median number of part-time employees has increased? Test using $\alpha = 0.05$. **LO 1**

4. **Assets of Stock Mutual Funds.** Net assets for the 50 largest stock mutual funds show a median of $15 billion. A sample of 10 of the 50 largest bond mutual funds follows.

Bond Fund	Net Assets	Bond Fund	Net Assets
Fidelity Intl Bond	6.1	T. Rowe Price New Income	6.9
Franklin CA TF	11.7	Vanguard GNMA	15.0
American Funds	22.4	Oppenheimer Intl Bond	6.6
Vanguard Short Term	9.6	Dodge & Cox Income	14.5
PIMCO: Real Return	4.9	iShares: TIPS Bond	9.6

Using the median, can it be concluded that bond mutual funds are smaller and have fewer net assets than stock mutual funds? Use $\alpha = 0.05$. **LO 2**

a. What are the hypotheses for this test?
b. What is the *p*-value? What is your conclusion?

5. **Median Price of Homes in Austin.** In 2022, the median price of homes in Austin, Texas, was $580,000 (*Realtor.com* website). A sample of 200 homes sold in the south Austin suburb of Westlake Hills found 111 homes with sales prices over $580,000 and 89 homes with sales prices under $580,000. Can you conclude that the median price of homes in Westlake Hills differs from the median price of homes in Austin? Use $\alpha = 0.05$. **LO 1**

DATA*file*
chicagoincome

6. **Median Annual Income in Chicago.** According to *FinancialSamuri.com*, the median annual income for families living in the United States is $73,000. Annual incomes in thousands of dollars for a sample of 50 families living in Chicago, Illinois, are shown. Use the sample data to see if it can be concluded that the families living in Chicago have a median annual income greater than $73,000. Use $\alpha = 0.05$. What is your conclusion? LO 1

Annual Income ($1,000s)

83.4	77.3	67.0	92.5	90.8
82.8	78.2	140.9	74.4	65.6
91.1	163.4	92.2	60.8	104.0
76.8	81.3	73.0	66.0	126.7
56.9	78.0	96.8	59.4	69.7
78.0	50.6	78.8	71.8	112.3
87.5	50.9	74.9	100.6	73.6
68.4	50.0	104.6	60.7	80.3
65.8	96.2	79.0	70.5	73.0
74.1	66.7	126.6	69.2	91.7

7. **Profitability of Stock Splits.** Are stock splits beneficial to stockholders? SNL Financial studied stock splits in the banking industry over an 18-month period. For a sample of 20 stock splits, 14 led to an increase in investment value, 4 led to a decrease in investment value, and 2 resulted in no change. Conduct a sign test to determine if it can be concluded that stock splits are beneficial for holders of bank stocks. LO 2
   a. What are the null and alternative hypotheses?
   b. Using $\alpha = 0.05$, what is your conclusion?

8. **Ideal Pace of Life.** A Pew Research Center survey asked adults if their ideal place to live would have a faster pace of life or a slower pace of life. A preliminary sample of 16 respondents showed 4 preferred a faster pace of life, 11 preferred a slower place of life, and 1 said it did not matter. LO 2
   a. Are these data sufficient to conclude there is a difference between the preferences for a faster pace of life or a slower pace of life? Use $\alpha = 0.05$. What is your conclusion?
   b. Considering the entire sample of 16 respondents, what is the percentage who would like a faster pace of life? What is the percentage who would like a slower pace of life? What recommendation do you have for the study?

9. **Economic Conditions and Children's Futures.** In a recent poll, six hundred adults were asked a series of questions about the state of the economy and their children's future. One question was, "Do you expect your children to have a better life than you have had, a worse life, or a life about the same as yours?" The responses showed 242 better, 310 worse, and 48 about the same. Use the sign test and $\alpha = 0.05$ to determine whether there is a difference between the number of adults who feel their children will have a better life compared to a worse life. What is your conclusion? LO 1

10. **Favorite Prime-Time Network Series.** *The Hollywood Reporter* identified *Grey's Anatomy* and *This is Us* as the two top-rated prime-time television series. In a local television preference survey, 750 individuals were asked to indicate their favorite prime-time television series: Three hundred thirty selected *This is Us,* 270 selected *Grey's Anatomy,* and 150 selected another television show. Use a 0.05 level of significance to test the hypothesis that there is no difference in the preference for *This is Us* and *Grey's Anatomy*. What is your conclusion? LO 1

11. **Share of Desktop Computer Market.** Competition in the desktop computer market is intense. A sample of 450 purchases showed 202 Brand A computers, 175 Brand B computers, and 73 other computers. Use a 0.05 level of significance to test the null hypothesis that Brand A and Brand B have the same share of the desktop computer market. What is your conclusion? LO 1

18.2 Wilcoxon Signed-Rank Test

This parametric test is introduced in Chapter 10.

Consider a matched-sample experimental design where each of n experimental units provided a pair of observations, one from population 1 and one from population 2. The parametric test for this experiment requires quantitative data and the assumption that the differences between the paired observations are normally distributed. The t distribution can then be used to make an inference about the difference between the means of the two populations.

If the population of differences is skewed, the sign test for matched samples presented in Section 18.1 is recommended.

The **Wilcoxon signed-rank test** is a nonparametric procedure for analyzing data from a matched-sample experiment. The test uses quantitative data but does not require the assumption that the differences between the paired observations are normally distributed. It only requires the assumption that the differences between the paired observations have a symmetric distribution. This occurs whenever the shapes of the two populations are the same and the focus is on determining if there is a difference between the medians of the two populations. Let us demonstrate the Wilcoxon signed-rank test with the following example.

Consider a manufacturing firm that is attempting to determine whether two production methods differ in terms of task completion time. Using a matched-samples experimental design, 11 randomly selected workers completed the production task two times, once using method A and once using method B. The production method that the worker used first was randomly selected. The completion times for the two methods and the differences between the completion times are shown in Table 18.6. A positive difference indicates that method A required more time; a negative difference indicates that method B required more time. Do the data indicate that the two production methods differ significantly in terms of completion times? If we assume that the differences have a symmetric distribution but not necessarily a normal distribution, the Wilcoxon signed-rank test applies.

In particular, we will use the Wilcoxon signed-rank test for the difference between the median completion times for the two production methods. The hypotheses are as follows:

The examples in this section take the point of view that the two populations have the same shape and if they do differ, it is only in location. This enables the hypotheses for the Wilcoxon signed-rank test to be stated in terms of the population medians.

$$H_0\text{: Median for method A} - \text{Median for method B} = 0$$
$$H_a\text{: Median for method A} - \text{Median for method B} \neq 0$$

If H_0 cannot be rejected, we will not be able to conclude that the median completion times are different. However, if H_0 is rejected, we will conclude that the median completion times are different. We will use a 0.05 level of significance for the test.

Table 18.6 Production Task Completion Times (Minutes)

	Method		
Worker	A	B	Difference
1	10.2	9.5	0.7
2	9.6	9.8	−0.2
3	9.2	8.8	0.4
4	10.6	10.1	0.5
5	9.9	10.3	−0.4
6	10.2	9.3	0.9
7	10.6	10.5	0.1
8	10.0	10.0	0.0
9	11.2	10.6	0.6
10	10.7	10.2	0.5
11	10.6	9.8	0.8

Table 18.7 Ranking the Absolute Differences and the Signed Ranks for the Production Task Completion Times

Worker	Difference	Absolute Difference	Rank	Signed Ranks Negative	Signed Ranks Positive
1	0.7	0.7	8		8
2	−0.2	0.2	2	−2	
3	0.4	0.4	3.5		3.5
4	0.5	0.5	5.5		5.5
5	−0.4	0.4	3.5	−3.5	
6	0.9	0.9	10		10
7	0.1	0.1	1		1
8	0.0				
9	0.6	0.6	7		7
10	0.5	0.5	5.5		5.5
11	0.8	0.8	9		9
			Sum of Positive Signed Ranks		$T^+ = 49.5$

Differences of 0 are discarded and the analysis continues with the smaller sample size involving the nonzero differences.

Ties among absolute differences are assigned the average of their ranks.

The first step in the Wilcoxon signed-rank test is to discard the difference of zero for worker 8 and then compute the absolute value of the differences for the remaining 10 workers as shown in column 3 of Table 18.7. Next, we rank these absolute differences from lowest to highest as shown in column 4. The smallest absolute difference of 0.1 for worker 7 is assigned the rank of 1. The second smallest absolute difference of 0.2 for worker 2 is assigned the rank of 2. This ranking of absolute differences continues with the largest absolute difference of 0.9 for worker 6 being assigned the rank of 10. The tied absolute differences of 0.4 for workers 3 and 5 are assigned the average rank of 3.5. Similarly, the tied absolute differences of 0.5 for workers 4 and 10 are assigned the average rank of 5.5.

Once the ranks of the absolute differences have been determined, each rank is given the *sign* of the original difference for the worker. The negative signed ranks are placed in column 5 and the positive signed ranks are placed in column 6 (see Table 18.7). For example, the difference for worker 1 was a positive 0.7 (see column 2) and the rank of the absolute difference was 8 (see column 4). Thus, the rank for worker 1 is shown as a positive signed rank in column 6. The difference for worker 2 was a negative 0.2 and the rank of the absolute difference was 2. Thus, the rank for worker 2 is shown as a negative signed rank of −2 in column 5. Continuing this process generates the negative and positive signed ranks as shown in Table 18.7.

Let T^+ denote the sum of the positive signed ranks, which is $T^+ = 49.5$. To conduct the Wilcoxon signed-rank test, we will use T^+ as the test statistic. If the medians of the two populations are equal and the number of matched pairs is 10 or more, the sampling distribution of T^+ can be approximated by a normal distribution as follows.

Sampling Distribution of T^+ for the Wilcoxon Signed-Rank Test

$$\text{Mean: } \mu_{T^+} = \frac{n(n+1)}{4} \quad \textbf{(18.3)}$$

$$\text{Standard deviation: } \sigma_{T^+} = \sqrt{\frac{n(n+1)(2n+1)}{24}} \quad \textbf{(18.4)}$$

Distribution form: Approximately normal for $n \geq 10$

After discarding the observation of a zero difference for worker 8, the analysis continues with the $n = 10$ matched pairs. Using equations (18.3) and (18.4), we have

$$\mu_{T^+} = \frac{n(n+1)}{4} = \frac{10(10+1)}{4} = 27.5$$

$$\sigma_{T^+} = \sqrt{\frac{n(n+1)(2n+1)}{24}} = \sqrt{\frac{10(10+1)(20+1)}{24}} = \sqrt{\frac{2310}{24}} = 9.8107$$

Figure 18.3 shows the sampling distribution of the T^+ test statistic.

Let us compute the two-tailed p-value for the hypothesis that the median completion times for the two production methods are equal. Since the test statistic $T^+ = 49.5$ is in the upper tail of the sampling distribution, we begin by computing the upper tail probability $P(T^+ \geq 49.5)$. Since the sum of the positive ranks T^+ is discrete and the normal distribution is continuous, we will obtain the best approximation by including the continuity correction factor. Thus, the discrete probability of $T^+ = 49.5$ is approximated by the normal probability interval, 49 to 50, and the probability that $T^+ \geq 49.5$ is approximated by

$$P(T^+ \leq 49.5) = P\left(z \geq \frac{49 - 27.5}{9.8107}\right) = P(z \geq 2.19)$$

Using Excel's NORM.S.DIST function, the cumulative probability for $z = 2.19$ is 0.9857; thus, the p-value $= 2(1 - 0.9857) = 0.0286$. With the p-value ≤ 0.05, we reject H_0 and conclude that the median completion times for the two production methods are not equal. With T^+ being in the upper tail of the sampling distribution, we see that method A led to the longer completion times. We would expect management to conclude that method B is the faster or better production method.

One-tailed Wilcoxon signed-rank tests are possible. For example, if initially we had been looking for statistical evidence to conclude method A has the larger median completion time and method B has the smaller median completion time, we would have formulated an upper tail hypothesis test as follows:

$$H_0\text{: Median for method A} - \text{Median for method B} \leq 0$$
$$H_a\text{: Median for method A} - \text{Median for method B} > 0$$

Rejecting H_0 would provide the conclusion that method A has the greater median completion time and method B has the smaller median completion time. Lower tail hypothesis tests are also possible.

Figure 18.3 Sampling Distribution of T^+ for the Production Task Completion Time Example

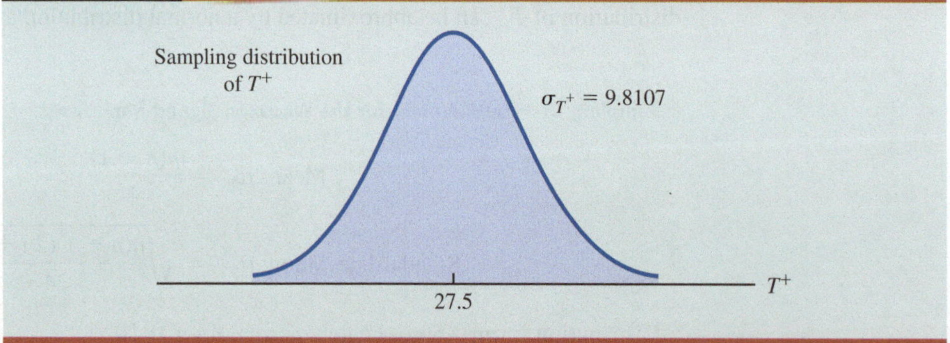

The Wilcoxon signed-rank test can be used to test the hypothesis about the median of a symmetric population. If the population is skewed, the sign test presented in Section 18.1 is preferred.

As a final note, in Section 18.1 we showed how the sign test could be used for both a hypothesis test about a population median and a hypothesis test with matched samples. In this section, we have demonstrated the use of the Wilcoxon signed-rank test for a hypothesis test with matched samples. However, the Wilcoxon signed-rank test can also be used for a nonparametric test about a population median. This test makes no assumption about the population distribution other than that it is symmetric. If this assumption is appropriate, the Wilcoxon signed-rank test is the preferred nonparametric test for a population median. However, if the population is skewed, the sign test presented in Section 18.1 is preferred. With the Wilcoxon signed-rank test, the differences between the observations and the hypothesized value of the population median are used instead of the differences between the matched-pair observations. Otherwise the calculations are exactly as shown in this section.

Notes + Comments

1. The Wilcoxon signed-rank test for a population median is based on the assumption that the population is symmetric. With this assumption, the population median is equal to the population mean. Thus, the Wilcoxon signed-rank test can also be used as a test about the mean of a symmetric population.
2. The Wilcoxon signed-rank procedure can also be used to compute a confidence interval for the median of a symmetric population. However, the computations are rather complex and would rarely be done by hand. Statistical packages can be used to obtain this confidence interval.

Exercises

Applications

In the following exercises involving paired differences, consider that it is reasonable to assume the populations being compared have approximately the same shape and that the distribution of paired differences is approximately symmetric.

12. **Comparing Fuel Additives.** Two fuel additives are tested to determine their effect on miles per gallon for passenger cars. Test results for 12 cars follow; each car was tested with both fuel additives. Use $\alpha = 0.05$ and the Wilcoxon signed-rank test to see whether there is a significant difference between the median miles per gallon for the additives. **LO 3**

DATA*file*
additive

	Additive			Additive	
Car	**1**	**2**	**Car**	**1**	**2**
1	20.12	18.05	7	16.16	17.20
2	23.56	21.77	8	18.55	14.98
3	22.03	22.57	9	21.87	20.03
4	19.15	17.06	10	24.23	21.15
5	21.23	21.22	11	23.21	22.78
6	24.77	23.80	12	25.02	23.70

13. **Time Needed to Fall Asleep.** A sample of 10 men was used in a study to test the effects of a relaxant on the time required to fall asleep. Data for 10 subjects showing the number of minutes required to fall asleep with and without the relaxant follow. Use a 0.05 level of significance to determine whether the relaxant reduces the median time required to fall asleep. What is your conclusion? **LO 3**

DATA*file* relaxant

	Relaxant			Relaxant	
Subject	No	Yes	Subject	No	Yes
1	15	10	6	7	5
2	12	10	7	8	10
3	22	12	8	10	7
4	8	11	9	14	11
5	10	9	10	9	6

14. **On-Time Arrivals at Busy Airports.** Percents of on-time arrivals for flights in the past two years were collected for 11 randomly selected airports. Data for these airports follow. Use $\alpha = 0.05$ to test the hypothesis that there is no difference between the median percent of on-time arrivals for the two years. What is your conclusion? **LO 3**

DATA*file* ontime

	Percent On Time	
Airport	Two Years Ago	Last Year
Boston Logan	71.78	69.69
Chicago O'Hare	68.23	65.88
Chicago Midway	77.98	78.40
Denver	78.71	75.78
Fort Lauderdale	77.59	73.45
Houston	77.67	78.68
Los Angeles	76.67	76.38
Miami	76.29	70.98
New York (JFK)	69.39	62.84
Orlando	79.91	76.49
Washington (Dulles)	75.55	72.42

15. **Speed of Overnight Delivery Services.** A test was conducted for two overnight mail delivery services. Two samples of identical deliveries were set up so that both delivery services were notified of the need for a delivery at the same time. The hours required to make each delivery follow. Do the data shown suggest a difference in the median delivery times for the two services? Use a 0.05 level of significance for the test. **LO 3**

DATA*file* overnight

	Service	
Delivery	1	2
1	24.5	28.0
2	26.0	25.5
3	28.0	32.0
4	21.0	20.0
5	18.0	19.5
6	36.0	28.0
7	25.0	29.0
8	21.0	22.0
9	24.0	23.5
10	26.0	29.5
11	31.0	30.0

16. **Scores on the First Two Rounds in an LPGA Tournament.** The Ladies Professional Golf Association (LPGA) Drive On Championship was held in February 2022 at the Crown Colony Golf & Country Club in Fort Meyers, Florida. Shown here are first-round

and second-round scores for a random sample of 13 golfers. Use $\alpha = 0.05$ to determine whether the first- and second-round median scores for golfers in the LPGA Drive On Championship differed significantly. What is your conclusion? LO 3

DATA*file*
lpga_driveon

Golfer	Round 1	Round 2
Carlota Ciganda	72	71
Brittany Lincicome	73	69
Amy Yang	70	72
Giulia Molinaro	68	74
Cydney Clanton	70	70
Pajaree Anannarukarn	70	73
Alison Lee	69	74
Angela Stanford	77	65
Hye-Jin Choi	71	69
Lauren Stephenson	72	65
Bianca Pagdanganan	70	71
Perrine Delacour	73	67
Lexi Thompson	69	67

17. **SAT Writing Scores.** The Scholastic Aptitude Test (SAT) consists of two sections: Math and Evidence-Based Reading and Writing. Each section is scored on a 200- to 800-point scale with a median of approximately 520. Scores for each part of the test can be assumed to be symmetric. Use the following data to test the hypothesis that the population median score for the students taking the Evidence-Based Reading and Writing section of the SAT is 520. Using $\alpha = 0.05$, what is your conclusion? LO 3

DATA*file*
writingscore

655	721	459	467	484
522	425	473	491	496
467	610	357	407	534

18.3 Mann–Whitney–Wilcoxon Test

In Chapter 10, we introduced a procedure for conducting a hypothesis test about the difference between the means of two populations using two independent samples, one from population 1 and one from population 2. This parametric test required quantitative data and the assumption that both populations had a normal distribution. In the case where the population standard deviations σ_1 and σ_2 were unknown, the sample standard deviations s_1 and s_2 provided estimates of σ_1 and σ_2 and the t distribution was used to make an inference about the difference between the means of the two populations.

Ordinal data are categorical data that can be rank ordered. Ordinal data are also discussed in Chapter 1.

In this section we present a nonparametric test for the difference between two populations based on two independent samples. Advantages of this nonparametric procedure are that it can be used with either ordinal data or quantitative data and it does not require the assumption that the populations have a normal distribution. Versions of the test were developed jointly by Mann and Whitney and also by Wilcoxon. As a result, the test has been referred to as the Mann–Whitney test and the Wilcoxon rank-sum test. The tests are equivalent and both versions provide the same conclusion. In this section, we will refer to this nonparametric test as the **Mann–Whitney–Wilcoxon (MWW) test**.

We begin the MWW test by stating the most general form of the null and alternative hypotheses as follows:

H_0: The two populations are identical

H_a: The two populations are not identical

Figure 18.4 Two Populations Are Not Identical, with Population 1 Tending to Provide the Smaller Values

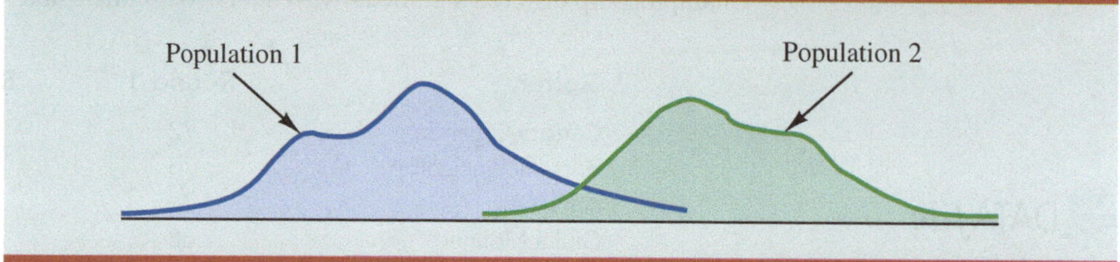

The alternative hypothesis that the two populations are not identical requires some clarification. If H_0 is rejected, we are using the test to conclude that the populations are not identical and that population 1 tends to provide either smaller or larger values than population 2. A situation where population 1 tends to provide smaller values than population 2 is shown in Figure 18.4. Note that it is not necessary that all values from population 1 be less than all values from population 2. However, the figure correctly shows, the conclusion that H_a is true; the two populations are not identical and population 1 tends to provide smaller values than population 2. In a two-tailed test, we consider the alternative hypothesis that either population may provide the smaller or larger values. One-tailed versions of the test can be formulated with the alternative hypothesis that population 1 provides either the smaller or the larger values compared to population 2.

We will first illustrate the MWW test using small samples with rank-ordered data. This will give you an understanding of how the rank-sum statistic is computed and how it is used to determine whether to reject the null hypothesis that the two populations are identical. Later in the section, we will introduce a large-sample approximation based on the normal distribution that will simplify the calculations required by the MWW test.

Let us consider the on-the-job performance ratings for employees at a Showtime Cinemas 20-screen multiplex movie theater. During an employee performance review, the theater manager rated all 35 employees from best (rating 1) to worst (rating 35) in the theater's annual report. Knowing that the part-time employees were primarily college and high school students, the district manager asked if there was evidence of a significant difference in performance for college students compared to high school students. In terms of the population of college students and the population of high school students who could be considered for employment at the theater, the hypotheses were stated as follows:

H_0: College and high school student populations are identical in terms of performance

H_a: College and high school student populations are not identical in terms of performance

We will use a 0.05 level of significance for this test.

We begin by selecting a random sample of four college students and a random sample of five high school students working at Showtime Cinemas. The theater manager's overall performance rating based on all 35 employees was recorded for each of these employees, as shown in Table 18.8. The first college student selected was rated 15th in the manager's annual performance report, the second college student selected was rated 3rd in the manager's annual performance report, and so on.

The data in this example show how the MWW test can be used with ordinal (rank-ordered) data.

The next step in the MWW procedure is to rank the *combined* samples from low to high. Since there is a total of 9 students, we rank the performance rating data in Table 18.8 from 1 to 9. The lowest value of 3 for college student 2 receives a rank of 1 and the second lowest value of 8 for college student 4 receives a rank of 2. The highest value of 32 for high school student 3 receives a rank of 9. The combined-sample ranks for all 9 students are shown in Table 18.9.

Next we sum the ranks for each sample as shown in Table 18.9. The MWW procedure may use the sum of the ranks for either sample. However, in our application of the MWW test we will follow the common practice of using the first sample which is the sample of

Table 18.8 Performance Ratings for a Sample of College Students and a Sample of High School Students Working at Showtime Cinemas

College Student	Manager's Performance Rating	High School Student	Manager's Performance Rating
1	15	1	18
2	3	2	20
3	23	3	32
4	8	4	9
		5	25

Table 18.9 Ranks for the Nine Students in the Showtime Cinemas Combined Samples

College Student	Manager's Performance Rating	Rank	High School Student	Manager's Performance Rating	Rank
1	15	4	1	18	5
2	3	1	2	20	6
3	23	7	3	32	9
4	8	2	4	9	3
	Sum of Ranks	14	5	25	8
				Sum of Ranks	31

four college students. The sum of ranks for the first sample will be the test statistic W for the MWW test. This sum, as shown in Table 18.9, is $W = 4 + 1 + 7 + 2 = 14$.

Let us consider why the sum of the ranks will help us select between the two hypotheses: H_0: The two populations are identical and H_a: The two populations are not identical. Letting C denote a college student and H denote a high school student, suppose the ranks of the nine students had the following order with the four college students having the four lowest ranks.

Rank	1	2	3	4	5	6	7	8	9
Student	C	C	C	C	H	H	H	H	H

Notice that this permutation or ordering separates the two samples, with the college students all having a lower rank than the high school students. This is a strong indication that the two populations are not identical. The sum of ranks for the college students in this case is $W = 1 + 2 + 3 + 4 = 10$.

Now consider a ranking where the four college students have the four highest ranks.

Rank	1	2	3	4	5	6	7	8	9
Student	H	H	H	H	H	C	C	C	C

Notice that this permutation or ordering separates the two samples again, but this time the college students all have a higher rank than the high school students. This is another strong indication that the two populations are not identical. The sum of ranks for the college students in this case is $W = 6 + 7 + 8 + 9 = 30$. Thus, we see that the sum of the ranks for the college students must be between 10 and 30. Values of W near 10 imply that college students have lower ranks than the high school students, whereas values of W near 30 imply that college students have higher ranks than the high school students. Either of these

Figure 18.5 Exact Sampling Distribution of the Sum of the Ranks for the Sample of College Students

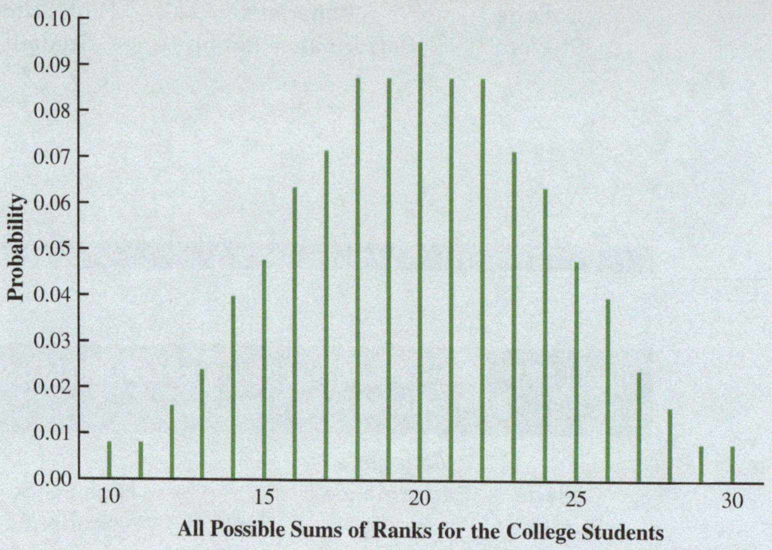

extremes would signal the two populations are not identical. However, if the two populations are identical, we would expect a mix in the ordering of the C's and H's so that the sum of ranks W is closer to the average of the two extremes, or nearer to $(10 + 30)/2 = 20$.

Making the assumption that the two populations are identical, we compute all possible orderings for the nine students. For each ordering, we computed the sum of the ranks for the college students. This provided the probability distribution showing the exact sampling distribution of W in Figure 18.5. The exact probabilities associated with the values of W are summarized in Table 18.10. While we will not ask you to generate this exact sampling distribution, we will use it to test the hypothesis that the two populations of students are identical.

Let us use the sampling distribution of W in Figure 18.5 to compute the p-value for the test just as we have done using other sampling distributions. Table 18.9 shows that the sum of ranks

Table 18.10 Probabilities for the Exact Sampling Distribution of the Sum of the Ranks for the Sample of College Students

W	Probability	*W*	Probability
10	0.0079	20	0.0952
11	0.0079	21	0.0873
12	0.0159	22	0.0873
13	0.0238	23	0.0714
14	0.0397	24	0.0635
15	0.0476	25	0.0476
16	0.0635	26	0.0397
17	0.0714	27	0.0238
18	0.0873	28	0.0159
19	0.0873	29	0.0079
		30	0.0079

for the four college student is $W = 14$. Because this value of W is in the lower tail of the sampling distribution, we begin by computing the lower tail probability $P(W \leq 14)$. Thus, we have

$$P(W \leq 14) = P(10) + P(11) + P(12) + P(13) + P(14)$$
$$= 0.0079 + 0.0079 + 0.0159 + 0.0238 + 0.0397 = 0.0952$$

The two-tailed p-value $= 2(0.0952) = 0.1904$. With $\alpha = 0.05$ as the level of significance and p-value > 0.05, the MWW test conclusion is that we cannot reject the null hypothesis that the populations of college and high school students are identical. While the sample of four college students and the sample of five high school students did not provide statistical evidence to conclude there is a difference between the two populations, this is an ideal time to suggest withholding judgment. Further study with larger samples should be considered before drawing a final conclusion.

Most applications of the MWW test involve larger sample sizes than shown in this first example. For such applications, a large sample approximation of the sampling distribution of W based on the normal distribution is employed. In fact, note that the sampling distribution of W in Figure 18.5 shows a normal distribution is a pretty good approximation for sample sizes as small as four and five. We will use the same combined-sample ranking procedure that we used in the previous example but will use the normal distribution approximation rather than the exact sampling distribution of W to compute the p-value and draw the conclusion.

Doing the ranking of the combined samples by hand will take some time. Excel's Sort and Filter capability can be used to do this ranking quickly and efficiently.

We illustrate the use of the normal distribution approximation for the MWW test by considering the situation at Third National Bank. The bank manager is monitoring the balances maintained in checking accounts at two branch banks and is wondering if the populations of account balances at the two branch banks are identical. Two independent samples of checking accounts are taken with sample sizes $n_1 = 12$ at branch 1 and $n_2 = 10$ at branch 2. The data are shown in Table 18.11 and provided in the file *thirdnational*.

As before, the first step in the MWW test is to rank the combined data from the lowest to highest values. Using the combined 22 observations in Table 18.11, we find the smallest value of \$1,750 (Branch 2 Account 6) and assign it a rank of 1. The second smallest value of \$1,800 (Branch 2 Account 5) is assigned a rank of 2. The third smallest value of \$1,805 (Branch 1 Account 7) is assigned a rank of 3, and so on. In ranking the combined data, we may find that two or more values are the same. In that case, the tied values are assigned the *average* rank of their positions in the combined data set. For example, the balance of \$1,950 occurs for both Branch 1 Account 6 and Branch 2 Account 4. In the combined

DATA*file*
thirdnational

Table 18.11 Account Balances for Two Branches of Third National Bank

Branch 1		Branch 2	
Account	Balance (\$)	Account	Balance (\$)
1	2,095	1	1,885
2	1,955	2	1,850
3	2,200	3	1,915
4	2,195	4	1,950
5	1,925	5	1,800
6	1,950	6	1,750
7	1,805	7	1,865
8	1,945	8	2,000
9	1,875	9	2,050
10	2,055	10	1,935
11	2,025		
12	1,975		

Table 18.12 Assigned Ranks for the Combined Account Balance Samples

Branch	Account	Balance ($)	Rank
2	6	1,750	1
2	5	1,800	2
1	7	1,805	3
2	2	1,850	4
2	7	1,865	5
1	9	1,875	6
2	1	1,885	7
2	3	1,915	8
1	5	1,925	9
2	10	1,935	10
1	8	1,945	11
1	6	1,950	12.5
2	4	1,950	12.5
1	2	1,955	14
1	12	1,975	15
2	8	2,000	16
1	11	2,025	17
2	9	2,050	18
1	10	2,055	19
1	1	2,095	20
1	4	2,195	21
1	3	2,200	22

data set, the two values of $1,950 are in positions 12 and 13 when the combined data are ranked from low to high. As a result, these two accounts are assigned the average rank $(12 + 13)/2 = 12.5$. Table 18.12 shows the assigned ranks for the combined samples.

We now return to the two separate samples and show the ranks from Table 18.12 for each account balance. These results are provided in Table 18.13. The next step is to sum the ranks

Table 18.13 Combined Ranking of the Data in the Two Samples from Third National Bank

Branch 1			Branch 2		
Account	Balance ($)	Rank	Account	Balance ($)	Rank
1	2,095	20	1	1,885	7
2	1,955	14	2	1,850	4
3	2,200	22	3	1,915	8
4	2,195	21	4	1,950	12.5
5	1,925	9	5	1,800	2
6	1,950	12.5	6	1,750	1
7	1,805	3	7	1,865	5
8	1,945	11	8	2,000	16
9	1,875	6	9	2,050	18
10	2,055	19	10	1,935	10
11	2,025	17		Sum of Ranks	83.5
12	1,975	15			
	Sum of Ranks	169.5			

for each sample: 169.5 for sample 1 and 83.5 for sample 2 are shown. As stated previously, we will always follow the procedure of using the sum of the ranks for sample 1 as the test statistic W. Thus, we have $W = 169.5$. When both sample sizes are 7 or more, a normal approximation of the sampling distribution of W can be used. Under the assumption that the null hypothesis is true and the populations are identical, the sampling distribution of the test statistic W is as follows.

Sampling Distribution of *W* with Identical Populations

$$\text{Mean: } \mu_W = (1/2)n_1(n_1 + n_2 + 1) \quad \textbf{(18.5)}$$

$$\text{Standard deviation: } \sigma_W = \sqrt{(1/12)n_1 n_2(n_1 + n_2 + 1)} \quad \textbf{(18.6)}$$

Distribution form: Approximately normal provided $n_1 \geq 7$ and $n_2 \geq 7$

Given the sample sizes $n_1 = 12$ and $n_2 = 10$, equations (18.5) and (18.6) provide the following mean and standard deviation for the sampling distribution:

$$\mu_W = (1/2)n_1(n_1 + n_2 + 1) = (1/2)(12)(12 + 10 + 1) = 138$$

$$\sigma_W = \sqrt{(1/12)n_1 n_2(n_1 + n_2 + 1)} = \sqrt{(1/12)(12)(10)(12 + 10 + 1)} = 15.1658$$

Figure 18.6 shows the normal distribution used for the sampling distribution of W.

Let us proceed with the MWW test and use a 0.05 level of significance to draw a conclusion. Since the test statistic W is discrete and the normal distribution is continuous, we will again use the continuity correction factor for the normal distribution approximation. With $W = 169.5$ in the upper tail of the sampling distribution, we have the following p-value calculation:

$$P(W \geq 169.5) = P\left(z \geq \frac{169 - 138}{15.1658}\right) = P(z \geq 2.04)$$

Using Excel's NORM.S.DIST function, the cumulative probability for $z = 2.04$ is 0.9793; thus, the two-tailed p-value $= 2(1 - 0.9793) = 0.0414$. With p-value ≤ 0.05, reject H_0 and conclude that the two populations of account balances are not identical. The upper tail value for test statistic W indicates that the population of account balances at branch 1 tends to be larger.

If the assumption can be made that the two populations have the same shape, the MWW test becomes a test about the difference between the medians of the two populations.

As a final comment, some applications of the MWW test make it appropriate to assume that the two populations have identical shapes and if the populations differ, it is only by a shift in the location of the distributions. If the two populations have the same shape, the hypothesis test may be stated in terms of the difference between the two population medians. Any difference between the medians can be interpreted as the shift in location of one

Figure 18.6 Sampling Distribution of *W* for the Third National Bank Example

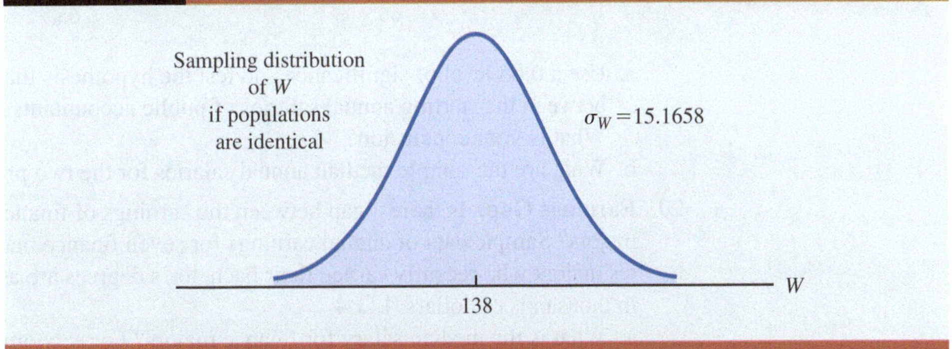

population compared to the other. In this case, the three forms of the MWW test about the medians of the two populations are as follows:

Two-Tailed Test	Lower Tail Test	Upper Tail Test
H_0: $\text{Median}_1 - \text{Median}_2 = 0$	H_0: $\text{Median}_1 - \text{Median}_2 \geq 0$	H_0: $\text{Median}_1 - \text{Median}_2 \leq 0$
H_a: $\text{Median}_1 - \text{Median}_2 \neq 0$	H_a: $\text{Median}_1 - \text{Median}_2 < 0$	H_a: $\text{Median}_1 - \text{Median}_2 > 0$

Exercises

Applications

18. **Fuel Additives and Mileage.** Two fuel additives are being tested to determine their effect on gasoline mileage. Seven cars were tested with additive 1 and nine cars were tested with additive 2. The following data show the miles per gallon obtained with the two additives. Use $\alpha = 0.05$ and the MWW test to see whether there is a significant difference between gasoline mileage for the two additives. **LO 4**

Additive 1	Additive 2
27.3	28.7
28.4	27.8
29.1	35.3
26.7	31.0
28.2	36.1
28.6	28.7
27.5	29.8
	30.7
	30.2

19. **Beginning Salaries for Public Accountants and Financial Planners.** Samples of starting annual salaries for individuals entering the public accounting and financial planning professions follow. Annual salaries are shown in thousands of dollars. **LO 4**

DATA*file*
acctplanners

Annual Salaries ($1,000s)	
Public Accountant	**Financial Planner**
65.2	64.0
73.8	64.2
71.3	68.1
73.2	70.9
69.2	66.9
70.0	68.6
65.9	64.7
74.5	68.9
72.0	66.8
66.9	63.9

a. Use a 0.05 level of significance and test the hypothesis that there is no difference between the starting annual salaries of public accountants and financial planners. What is your conclusion?
b. What are the sample median annual salaries for the two professions?

20. **Earnings Gap.** Is there a gap between the earnings of finance majors and economics majors? Sample data of annual earnings for seven finance majors and seven ecomomics majors who recently earned their bachelor's degrees are as follows. Data are shown in thousands of dollars. **LO 4**
a. What is the median salary for finance majors? For economics majors?
b. Use $\alpha = 0.05$ and conduct the hypothesis test for identical population distributions. What is your conclusion?

Annual Earnings ($1,000s)	
Finance Majors	Economics Majors
35.6	49.5
80.5	40.4
50.2	32.9
67.2	45.5
43.2	30.8
54.9	52.5
60.3	29.8

21. **Chief Executive Officer Salaries.** In a 2018 survey of 10,508 CEOs by *PayScale.com*, the range of annual salaries reported was from $73,187 to $336,550. But do CEO salaries differ across the two most populous states in the United States? Consider the salaries for CEOs who work for companies headquartered in California and Texas as provided in the following table. **LO 4**

DATA*file*
ceosalaries

CEO Salaries ($1,000s)	
California	Texas
$321	$125
$94	$186
$121	$133
$212	$204
$138	$275
$158	$88
$182	$305
$247	$177
$316	$225
$199	$210
$263	$196
$304	$107

Use $\alpha = 0.05$ and test to determine whether the population of CEO salaries is the same for California and Texas. What is your conclusion?

22. **P/E Ratios for Japanese and U.S. Companies.** Each year *Bloomberg Businessweek* publishes statistics on the world's 1,000 largest companies. A company's price/earnings (P/E) ratio is the company's current stock price divided by the latest 12 months' earnings per share. The following table shows the P/E ratios for a sample of 10 Japanese companies and 12 U.S. companies. Is the difference between the P/E ratios for the two countries significant? Use the MWW test and $\alpha = 0.01$ to support your conclusion. **LO 4**

DATA*file*
japan_us

Japan		United States	
Company	P/E Ratio	Company	P/E Ratio
Sumitomo Corp.	153	Gannet	19
Kinden	21	Motorola	24
Heiwa	18	Schlumberger	24
NCR Japan	125	Oracle Systems	43
Suzuki Motor	31	Gap	22
Fuji Bank	213	Winn-Dixie	14
Sumintomo Chemical	64	Ingersoll-Rand	21
Seibu Railway	666	American Electric	14
Shiseido	33	Hercules	21
Toho Gas	68	Times Mirror	38
		WellPoint Health	15
		Northern States Power	14

23. **Crime in Winter vs. Summer.** Police records show the following numbers of daily crime reports for a sample of days during the winter months and a sample of days during the summer months. Use a 0.05 level of significance to determine whether there is a significant difference between the winter and summer months in terms of the number of crime reports. What is your conclusion? **LO 4**

DATA*file*
policerecords

Number of Crimes

Winter	Summer
18	28
20	18
15	24
16	32
21	18
20	29
12	23
16	38
19	28
20	18

24. **Microwave Oven Prices in Dallas vs. San Antonio.** A certain brand of microwave oven was priced at 10 stores in Dallas and 13 stores in San Antonio. The data follow. Use a 0.05 level of significance and test whether prices (in \$) for the microwave oven are the same in the two cities. **LO 4**

DATA*file*
microwave

Price ($)

Dallas	San Antonio
445	460
489	451
405	435
485	479
439	475
449	445
436	429
420	434
430	410
405	422
	425
	459
	430

25. **Delayed Flights at Newark Liberty and LaGuardia.** Newark Liberty International Airport and LaGuardia Airport are the U.S. airports with the worst percentage of delayed flights in 2021 according to *TripSavvy.com*. But when flights are delayed, do these two airports experience delays of the same length? The delay times in minutes for seven recent, randomly selected delayed flights departing from each of these airports are as follows.

DATA*file*
delayedflights

Delay Time (minutes)

Newark Liberty International Airport	LaGuardia Airport
68	105
99	35
42	34
31	87
54	73
25	41
49	57

Use the MWW test to determine if there is a difference in length of flight delays for these two airports. Use $\alpha = 0.05$. What is the p-value? What is your conclusion? **LO 4**

18.4 Kruskal–Wallis Test

Chapter 13 introduces a parametric test for this situation that uses quantitative data and assumes that the populations have normal distributions with the same standard deviations. Based on an independent random sample from each population, the F distribution is used to test for differences among the population means.

In this section we extend the nonparametric procedures to hypothesis tests involving three or more populations. The nonparametric **Kruskal–Wallis test** is based on the analysis of independent random samples from each of k populations. This procedure can be used with either ordinal data or quantitative data and does not require the assumption that the populations have normal distributions. The general form of the null and alternative hypotheses is as follows:

H_0: All populations are identical
H_a: Not all populations are identical

If H_0 is rejected, we will conclude that there is a difference among the populations with one or more populations tending to provide smaller or larger values compared to the other populations. We will demonstrate the Kruskal–Wallis test using the following example.

Williams Manufacturing Company hires employees for its management staff from three different colleges. Recently, the company's personnel director began reviewing the annual performance reports for the management staff in an attempt to determine whether there are differences in the performance ratings among the managers who graduated from the three colleges. Performance rating data are available for independent samples of seven managers who graduated from college A, six managers who graduated from college B, and seven managers who graduated from college C. These data are summarized in Table 18.14. The performance rating shown for each manger is recorded on a scale from 0 to 100, with 100 being the highest possible rating. Suppose we want to test whether the three populations of managers are identical in terms of performance ratings. We will use a 0.05 level of significance for the test.

The first step in the Kruskal–Wallis procedure is to rank the combined samples from lowest to highest values. Using all 20 observations in Table 18.14, the lowest rating of 15 for the 4th manager in the college B sample receives a rank of 1. The highest rating of 95 for the 5th manager in the college A sample receives a rank of 20. The performance rating data and their assigned ranks are shown in Table 18.15. Note that we assigned the average ranks to tied performance ratings of 60, 70, 80, and 90. Table 18.15 also shows the sum of ranks for each of the three samples.

Table 18.14 Performance Evaluation Ratings for 20 Williams Employees

College A	College B	College C
25	60	50
70	20	70
60	30	60
85	15	80
95	40	90
90	35	70
80		75

Table 18.15 Combined Rankings for the Three Samples

College A	Rank	College B	Rank	College C	Rank
25	3	60	9	50	7
70	12	20	2	70	12
60	9	30	4	60	9
85	17	15	1	80	15.5
95	20	40	6	90	18.5
90	18.5	35	5	70	12
80	15.5			75	14
Sum of Ranks	95	Sum of Ranks	27	Sum of Ranks	88

The Kruskal–Wallis test statistic uses the sum of the ranks for the three samples and is computed as follows.

Kruskal–Wallis Test Statistic

$$H = \left[\frac{12}{n_T(n_T + 1)} \sum_{i=1}^{k} \frac{R_i^2}{n_i}\right] - 3(n_T + 1) \tag{18.7}$$

where

k = the number of populations

n_i = the number of observations in sample i

$n_T = \sum_{i=1}^{k} n_i$ = the total number of observations in all samples

R_i = the sum of the ranks for sample i

Kruskal and Wallis were able to show that, under the null hypothesis assumption of identical populations, the sampling distribution of H can be approximated by a chi-square distribution with $(k - 1)$ degrees of freedom. This approximation is generally acceptable if the sample sizes for each of the k populations are all greater than or equal to five. The null hypothesis of identical populations will be rejected if the test statistic H is large. As a result, the Kruskal–Wallis test is always expressed as an upper tail test. The computation of the test statistic for the sample data in Table 18.15 is as follows.

The sample sizes are

$$n_1 = 7 \qquad n_2 = 6 \qquad n_3 = 7$$

and

$$n_T = \sum_{i=1}^{3} n_i = 7 + 6 + 7 = 20$$

Using the sum of ranks for each sample, the value of the Kruskal–Wallis test statistic is as follows:

$$H = \left[\frac{12}{n_T(n_T + 1)} \sum_{i=1}^{k} \frac{R_i^2}{n_i}\right] - 3(n_T + 1) = \frac{12}{20(21)}\left[\frac{(95)^2}{7} + \frac{(27)^2}{6} + \frac{(88)^2}{7}\right] - 3(20 + 1) = 8.92$$

We can now use the chi-square distribution table (Table 3 of Appendix B) to determine the p-value for the test. Using $k - 1 = 3 - 1 = 2$ degrees of freedom, we find $\chi^2 = 7.378$

has an area of 0.025 in the upper tail of the chi-square distribution and $\chi^2 = 9.21$ has an area of 0.01 in the upper tail of the chi-square distribution. With $H = 8.92$ between 7.378 and 9.21, we can conclude that the area in the upper tail of the chi-square distribution is between 0.025 and 0.01. Because this is an upper tail test, we conclude that the p-value is between 0.025 and 0.01. Using Excel will show the exact p-value for $\chi^2 = 8.92$ is 0.0116. Because p-value $\leq \alpha = 0.05$, we reject H_0 and conclude that the three populations are not all the same. The three populations of performance ratings are not identical and differ significantly depending upon the college. Because the sum of the ranks is relatively low for the sample of managers who graduated from college B, it would be reasonable for the company to either reduce its recruiting from college B, or at least evaluate the college B graduates more thoroughly before making a hiring decision.

Using Excel: p-value =CHISQ.DIST.RT(2,8.92) = 0.0116.

As a final comment, we note that in some applications of the Kruskal–Wallis test it may be appropriate to make the assumption that the populations have identical shapes and if they differ, it is only by a shift in location for one or more of the populations. If the k populations are assumed to have the same shape, the hypothesis test can be stated in terms of the population medians. In this case, the hypotheses for the Kruskal–Wallis test would be written as follows:

If the assumption can be made that the populations all have the same shape, the Kruskal–Wallis test becomes a test about the medians of the k populations.

$$H_0\text{: Median}_1 = \text{Median}_2 = \cdots = \text{Median}_k$$
$$H_a\text{: Not all medians are equal}$$

Note + Comment

The example in this section uses quantitative data on employee performance ratings to conduct the Kruskal–Wallis test. This test could also have been used if the data were the ordinal rankings of the 20 employees in terms of performance. In this case, the test would use the ordinal data directly. The step of converting the quantitative data into rank-ordered data would not be necessary.

Exercises

Applications

26. **Consumer Ratings for Three Products.** A sample of 15 consumers provided the following product ratings for three different products. Five consumers were randomly assigned to test and rate each product. Use the Kruskal–Wallis test and $\alpha = 0.05$ to determine whether there is a significant difference among the ratings for the products. **LO 5**

	Product	
A	B	C
50	80	60
62	95	45
75	98	30
48	87	58
65	90	57

DATA*file*
testprepare

27. **College Admission Test-Prep Programs.** Three admission test preparation programs are being evaluated. The scores obtained by a sample of 20 people who used the programs provided the following data. Use the Kruskal–Wallis test to determine whether there is a significant difference among the three test preparation programs. Use $\alpha = 0.05$. **LO 5**

Program		
A	B	C
540	450	600
400	540	630
490	400	580
530	410	490
490	480	590
610	370	620
	550	570

28. **Calories Burned During Different Types of Workouts.** Forty-minute workouts of one of the following activities (swimming, tennis, cycling) three days a week will burn a substantial amount of calories. The following sample data show the number of calories burned during 40-minute workouts for three different activities. Do these data indicate differences in the amount of calories burned for the three activities? Use a 0.05 level of significance. What is your conclusion? **LO 5**

Swimming	Tennis	Cycling
408	415	385
380	485	250
425	450	295
400	420	402
427	530	268

29. **NFL Draft Positions by College Football Conference.** The National Football League (NFL) holds its annual draft of the nation's best college football players in April each year. Prior to the draft, various sporting news services project the players who will be drafted along with the order in which each will be selected, in what are called mock drafts. Players who are considered to have superior potential as professional football players are selected earlier in the draft. The following table shows, for the 2022 NFL draft, projections by CBS Sports of what position in the first round players from the Atlantic Coast Conference (ACC), the Big Ten Conference (Big 10), the Pac-12 Conference (PAC-12), and the Southeastern Conference (SEC) will be selected.

DATA*file*
mocknfldraft2022

ACC		Big 10		PAC-12		SEC	
College Attended	Projected Draft Position	College Attended	Projected Draft Position	College Attended	Projected Draft Position	College Attended	Projected Draft Position
NC State	3	Michigan	2	Oregon	1	Alabama	4
Pittsburgh	6	Purdue	12	USC	8	Mississippi State	5
Florida State	15	Ohio State	17	Utah	9	LSU	10
Clemson	16	Iowa	23	Washington	25	Georgia	14
Boston College	19	Michigan	26			Ole Miss	18
North Carolina	20	Ohio State	27			Alabama	21
		Minnesota	28			Georgia	22
						Arkansas	24
						Texas A&M	31
						Georgia	32

Use the Kruskal–Wallis test to determine if there is any difference among NFL teams for players from these four conferences. Use $\alpha = 0.05$. What is the p-value? What is your conclusion? **LO 5**

30. **Supervisory Skills Developed by Off-Site Training Courses.** A large corporation sends many of its first-level managers to an off-site supervisory skills training course. Four different management development centers offer this course. The director of human resources would like to know whether there is a difference among the quality of training provided at the four centers. An independent random sample of five employees was chosen from each training center. The employees were then ranked 1 to 20 in terms of supervisory skills. A rank of 1 was assigned to the employee with the best supervisory skills. The ranks are shown. Use $\alpha = 0.05$ and test whether there is a significant difference among the quality of training provided by the four programs. **LO 5**

Course			
A	B	C	D
3	2	19	20
14	7	16	4
10	1	9	15
12	5	18	6
13	11	17	8

31. **Calories in Popular Candies.** The better-selling candies are often high in calories. Assume that the following data show the calorie content from samples of M&M, Kit Kat, and Milky Way candies. Test for significant differences among the calorie content of these three candies. At a 0.05 level of significance, what is your conclusion? **LO 5**

Calories		
M&M	Kit Kat	Milky Way
230	225	200
210	205	208
240	245	202
250	235	190
230	220	180

18.5 Rank Correlation

The Pearson product moment correlation coefficient is introduced in Chapter 3.

The Pearson product moment correlation coefficient is a measure of the linear association between two variables using quantitative data. In this section, we provide a correlation measure of association between two variables when ordinal or rank-ordered data are available. The **Spearman rank-correlation coefficient** has been developed for this purpose.

Spearman Rank-Correlation Coefficient

$$r_s = 1 - \frac{6\sum_{i=1}^{n} d_i^2}{n(n^2 - 1)} \quad \textbf{(18.8)}$$

where

n = the number of observations in the sample
x_i = the rank of observation i with respect to the first variable
y_i = the rank of observation i with respect to the second variable
$d_i = x_i - y_i$

Table 18.16 Sales Potential and Actual Two-Year Sales Data

Salesperson	Ranking of Potential	Two-Year Sales (units)	Ranking According to Two-Year Sales
A	2	400	1
B	4	360	3
C	7	300	5
D	1	295	6
E	6	280	7
F	3	350	4
G	10	200	10
H	9	260	8
I	8	220	9
J	5	385	2

DATA*file*
potentialactual

Let us illustrate the use of the Spearman rank-correlation coefficient. A company wants to determine whether individuals who had a greater potential at the time of employment turn out to have higher sales records. To investigate, the personnel director reviewed the original job interview reports, academic records, and letters of recommendation for 10 current members of the sales force. After the review, the director ranked the 10 individuals in terms of their potential for success at the time of employment and assigned the individual who had the most potential the rank of 1. Data were then collected on the actual sales for each individual during their first two years of employment. On the basis of the actual sales records, a second ranking of the 10 individuals based on sales performance was obtained. Table 18.16 provides the ranks based on potential as well as the ranks based on the actual performance.

Let us compute the Spearman rank-correlation coefficient for the data in Table 18.16. The computations are summarized in Table 18.17. We first compute the difference between the two ranks for each salesperson, d_i, as shown in column 4. The sum of the d_i^2 in column 5 is 44. This value and the sample size $n = 10$ are used to compute the rank-correlation coefficient $r_s = 0.733$ shown in Table 18.17.

Table 18.17 Computation of the Spearman Rank-Correlation Coefficient for Sales Potential and Sales Performance

Salesperson	x_i = Ranking of Potential	y_i = Ranking of Sales Performance	$d_i = x_i - y_i$	d_i^2
A	2	1	1	1
B	4	3	1	1
C	7	5	2	4
D	1	6	5	25
E	6	7	−1	1
F	3	4	−1	1
G	10	10	0	0
H	9	8	1	1
I	8	9	−1	1
J	5	2	3	9
				$\sum d_i^2 = 44$

$$r_s = 1 - \frac{6\sum d_i^2}{n(n^2 - 1)} = 1 - \frac{6(44)}{10(100 - 1)} = 0.733$$

The Spearman rank-correlation coefficient ranges from -1.0 to $+1.0$ and its interpretation is similar to the Pearson product moment correlation coefficient for quantitative data. A rank-correlation coefficient near $+1.0$ indicates a strong positive association between the ranks for the two variables, while a rank-correlation coefficient near -1.0 indicates a strong negative association between the ranks for the two variables. A rank-correlation coefficient of 0 indicates no association between the ranks for the two variables. In the example, $r_s = 0.733$ indicates a positive correlation between the ranks based on potential and the ranks based on sales performance. Individuals who ranked higher in potential at the time of employment tended to rank higher in two-year sales performance.

At this point, we may want to use the sample rank correlation r_s to make an inference about the population rank correlation coefficient ρ_s. To do this, we test the following hypotheses:

$$H_0\colon \rho_s = 0$$
$$H_a\colon \rho_s \neq 0$$

Under the assumption that the null hypothesis is true and the population rank-correlation coefficient is 0, the following sampling distribution of r_s can be used to conduct the test.

Sampling Distribution of r_s

$$\text{Mean: } \mu_{rs} = 0 \tag{18.9}$$

$$\text{Standard deviation: } \sigma_{rs} = \sqrt{\frac{1}{n-1}} \tag{18.10}$$

Distribution form: Approximately normal provided $n \geq 10$

The sample rank-correlation coefficient for sales potential and sales performance is $r_s = 0.733$. Using equation (18.9), we have $\mu_{r_s} = 0$, and using equation (18.10), we have $\sigma_{r_s} = \sqrt{1/(10-1)} = 0.333$. With the sampling distribution of r_s approximated by a normal distribution, the standard normal random variable z becomes the test statistic with

$$z = \frac{r_s - \mu_{rs}}{\sigma_{rs}} = \frac{0.733 - 0}{0.333} = 2.20$$

Using Excel's NORM.S.DIST function, the cumulative probability for $z = 2.20$ is 0.9861; thus, the p-value $= 2(1 - 0.9861) = 0.0278$. With a 0.05 level of significance, p-value $\leq \alpha$. Thus, we reject the null hypothesis that the population rank-correlation coefficient is zero. The test result shows that there is a significant rank correlation between potential at the time of employment and actual sales performance.

Using Excel

DATA*file*
potentialactual

Excel does not have a specific procedure for computing the Spearman rank-correlation coefficient. However, this correlation coefficient is the same as the Pearson correlation coefficient provided you are using rank-ordered data. As a result, we can compute the Spearman rank-correlation coefficient by applying Excel's Pearson correlation coefficient procedure to the rank-ordered data. We illustrate using the data on sales potential and actual two-year sales from Section 18.5. The file *potentialactual* provides the ranking of the 10 individuals in terms of potential in column B and the ranking of the 10 individuals in terms of actual two-year sales in column C. The following steps provide the Spearman rank-correlation coefficient.

Step 1. Click the **Data** tab on the Ribbon
Step 2. In the **Analyze** group, click **Data Analysis**
Step 3. Choose **Correlation** from the list of Analysis Tools
Step 4. When the **Correlation** dialog box appears:
Enter *B1:C11* in the **Input Range:** box
Select **Columns** for **Grouped By:**
Select the check box for **Labels in First Row**
Select **Output Range:** for **Output options** and enter *D1* in the box
Click **OK**

The Spearman rank-correlation coefficient of 0.7333 will appear in cell E3.

Notes + Comments

The Spearman rank-correlation coefficient provides the same value that is obtained by using the Pearson product moment correlation coefficient procedure with the rank-ordered data.

Exercises

Methods

32. Consider the following set of rankings for a sample of 10 elements. **LO 6**

Element	x	y	Element	x	y
1	10	8	6	2	7
2	6	4	7	8	6
3	7	10	8	5	3
4	3	2	9	1	1
5	4	5	10	9	9

a. Compute the Spearman rank-correlation coefficient for the data.
b. Use $\alpha = 0.05$ and test for significant rank correlation. What is your conclusion?

33. Consider the following two sets of rankings for six items.

	Case One			Case Two	
Item	First Ranking	Second Ranking	Item	First Ranking	Second Ranking
A	1	1	A	1	6
B	2	2	B	2	5
C	3	3	C	3	4
D	4	4	D	4	3
E	5	5	E	5	2
F	6	6	F	6	1

Note that in the first case the rankings are identical, whereas in the second case the rankings are exactly opposite. What value should you expect for the Spearman rank-correlation coefficient for each of these cases? Explain. Calculate the rank-correlation coefficient for each case. **LO 6**

Applications

34. **Expenditure per Student and Student–Teacher Ratio.** The following data show the rankings of 11 states based on expenditure per student (ranked 1 highest to 11 lowest) and student–teacher ratio (ranked 1 lowest to 11 highest). **LO 6**

DATA*file*
student

State	Expenditure per Student	Student–Teacher Ratio
Arizona	9	10
Colorado	5	8
Florida	4	6
Idaho	2	11
Iowa	6	4
Louisiana	11	3
Massachusetts	1	1
Nebraska	7	2
North Dakota	8	7
South Dakota	10	5
Washington	3	9

a. What is the rank correlation between expenditure per student and student–teacher ratio? Discuss.

b. At the $\alpha = 0.05$ level, does there appear to be a relationship between expenditure per student and student–teacher ratio?

35. **Technology Company Reputations and Investor Willingness to Purchase Stock.** A national study by Harris Interactive, Inc., evaluated the top technology companies and their reputations. The following shows how 10 technology companies ranked in reputation and how the companies ranked in percentage of respondents who said they would purchase the company's stock. A positive rank correlation is anticipated because it seems reasonable to expect that a company with a higher reputation would have the more desirable stock to purchase. **LO 6**

DATA*file*
techs

Company	Reputation	Stock Purchase
Microsoft	1	3
Intel	2	4
Dell	3	1
Lucent	4	2
Texas Instruments	5	9
Cisco Systems	6	5
Hewlett-Packard	7	10
IBM	8	6
Motorola	9	7
Yahoo	10	8

a. Compute the rank correlation between reputation and stock purchase.

b. Test for a significant positive rank correlation. What is the p-value?

c. At $\alpha = 0.05$, what is your conclusion?

36. **Golfer Driving Distances and Putting Proficiencies.** The relative rankings of a sample of professional golfers in both driving distance and putting are shown. What is the rank correlation between driving distance and putting for these golfers? Test for significance of the correlation coefficient at the 0.10 level of significance. **LO 6**

DATA*file*
driveputt2022

Golfer	Driving Distance	Putting
Charl Schwartzel	6	10
Chan Kim	2	9
Scott Gutschewski	5	8
Louis Oosthuizen	3	7
Matthias Schwab	8	1
J.J. Spaun	7	3
Jason Dufner	10	2
Cameron Champ	1	6
Emiliano Grillo	4	5
Henrik Norlander	9	4

37. **Quality of Teaching Assessments.** A student organization surveyed both current students and recent graduates to obtain information on the quality of teaching at a particular university. An analysis of the responses provided the following teaching-ability rankings. Do the rankings given by the current students agree with the rankings given by the recent graduates? Use $\alpha = 0.10$ and test for a significant rank correlation. **LO 6**

DATA*file*
professors

Professor	Current Students	Recent Graduates
1	4	6
2	6	8
3	8	5
4	3	1
5	1	2
6	2	3
7	5	7
8	10	9
9	7	4
10	9	10

Summary

In this chapter, we have presented statistical procedures that are classified as nonparametric methods. Because these methods can be applied to categorical data as well as quantitative data and because they do not require an assumption about the distribution of the population, they expand the number of situations that can be subjected to statistical analysis.

The sign test is a nonparametric procedure for testing a hypothesis about a population median or for testing a hypothesis with matched samples. The data must be summarized in two categories, one denoted by a plus sign and one denoted by a minus sign. The Wilcoxon signed-rank test analyzes matched samples from two populations when quantitative data are available. No assumption is required other than the distribution of the paired differences is symmetric. The Wilcoxon signed-rank test is used to determine if the median of the population of paired differences is zero. This test can also be used to make inferences about the median of a symmetric population.

The Mann–Whitney–Wilcoxon test is a nonparametric procedure for the difference between two populations based on two independent samples. It is an alternative to the parametric t test for the difference between the means of the two populations. The combined ranks for the data from the two samples are obtained and the test statistic for the MWW test is the sum of ranks for the first sample. In most applications, the samples sizes are large enough to use a normal approximation with the continuity correction factor in conducting the hypothesis test. If no assumption is made about the populations, the MWW procedure tests whether the two populations are identical. If the assumption can be made that the two populations have the same shape, the test provides an inference about the difference between the medians of the two populations.

The Kruskal–Wallis test extends the MWW test to three or more populations. It is an alternative to the parametric analysis of variance test for the differences among the means of three or more normally distributed populations. The Kruskal–Wallis test does not require any assumption about the distribution of the populations and uses the null hypothesis that the k populations are identical. If the assumption can be made that the populations have the same shape, the test provides an inference about differences among the medians of the k populations. In the last section of the chapter we introduced the Spearman rank-correlation coefficient as a measure of association between two variables based on rank-ordered data.

Glossary

Distribution-free methods Statistical methods that make no assumption about the probability distribution of the population.

Kruskal–Wallis test A nonparametric test for the differences among three or more populations based on the analysis of an independent sample from each population. The null hypothesis is that the populations are identical. If the assumption can be made that the populations have the same shape, this test provides an inference about the differences among the medians of the populations.

Mann–Whitney–Wilcoxon (MWW) test A nonparametric test for the difference between two populations based on an independent sample from each population. The null hypothesis is that the two populations are identical. If the assumption can be made that the populations have the same shape, this test provides an inference about the difference between the medians of the two populations.

Nonparametric methods Statistical methods that require no assumption about the form of the probability distribution of the population and are often referred to as distribution-free methods. Several of the methods can be applied with categorical as well as quantitative data.

Parametric methods Statistical methods that begin with an assumption about the probability distribution of the population which is often that the population has a normal distribution. A sampling distribution for the test statistic can then be derived and used to make an inference about one or more parameters of the population such as the population mean μ or the population standard deviation σ.

Sign test A nonparametric test for a hypothesis about a population median or for identifying differences between two populations based on matched samples. The data are summarized in two categories, denoted by a plus sign or a minus sign, and the binomial distribution with $p = 0.50$ provides the sampling distribution for the test statistic.

Spearman rank-correlation coefficient A correlation measure of the association between two variables based on rank-ordered data.

Wilcoxon signed-rank test A nonparametric test for the difference between the medians of two populations based on matched samples. The procedure uses quantitative data and is based on the assumption that the distribution of differences is symmetric. The paired-difference data are used to make an inference about the medians of the two populations. This test can also be used to make inferences about the median of a symmetric population.

Key Formulas

Sign Test: Normal Approximation

$$\text{Mean: } \mu = 0.50n \qquad \textbf{(18.1)}$$

$$\text{Standard Deviation: } \sigma = \sqrt{0.25n} \qquad \textbf{(18.2)}$$

Wilcoxon Signed-Rank Test: Normal Approximation

$$\text{Mean: } \mu_{T^+} = \frac{n(n+1)}{4} \tag{18.3}$$

$$\text{Standard deviation: } \sigma_{T^+} = \sqrt{\frac{n(n+1)(2n+1)}{24}} \tag{18.4}$$

Mann–Whitney–Wilcoxon Test: Normal Approximation

$$\text{Mean: } \mu_W = (1/12)(n_1 + n_2 + 1) \tag{18.5}$$

$$\text{Standard deviation: } \sigma_W = \sqrt{(1/12)(n_1 n_2(n_1 + n_2 + 1)} \tag{18.6}$$

Kruskal–Wallis Test Statistic

$$H = \left[\frac{12}{n_T(n_T+1)} \sum_{i=1}^{k} \frac{R_i^2}{n_i}\right] - 3(n_T + 1) \tag{18.7}$$

Spearman Rank-Correlation Coefficient

$$r_s = 1 - \frac{6 \sum_{i=1}^{n} d_i^2}{n(n^2 - 1)} \tag{18.8}$$

Supplementary Exercises

38. **Survey on School Voucher Programs.** A survey asked the following question: Do you favor or oppose providing tax-funded vouchers or tax deductions to parents who send their children to private schools? Of the 2010 individuals surveyed, 905 favored the proposal, 1,045 opposed the proposal, and 60 offered no opinion. Do the data indicate a significant difference in the preferences for the financial support of parents who send their children to private schools? Use a 0.05 level of significance. **LO 1**

39. **Sales Prices for Single-Family Homes.** According to the National Association of Realtors website, the national median sales price for single-family homes was $254,000 in 2018. Assume that the following data were obtained from samples of recent sales of single-family homes in St. Louis and Denver. **LO 1**

Metropolitan Area	Less Than $254,000	Equal to $254,000	Greater Than $254,000
St. Louis	32	2	18
Denver	13	1	27

a. Is the median sales price in St. Louis significantly lower than the national median of $254,000? Use a statistical test with $\alpha = 0.05$ to support your conclusion.

b. Is the median sales price in Denver significantly higher than the national median of $254,000? Use a statistical test with $\alpha = 0.05$ to support your conclusion.

40. **Refrigerator Prices.** Twelve survey respondents were asked to estimate the retail selling price of two models of refrigerators. Their estimates of selling price are shown in the following table. Use these data and test at the 0.05 level of significance to

determine whether there is a difference between the two models in terms of respondents' perceptions of selling price. **LO 3**

DATA*file* refrigerators

Respondent	Model 1	Model 2	Respondent	Model 1	Model 2
1	\$850	\$1,100	7	\$900	\$1,090
2	\$960	\$920	8	\$890	\$1,120
3	\$940	\$890	9	\$1,100	\$1,200
4	\$900	\$1,050	10	\$700	\$890
5	\$790	\$1,120	11	\$810	\$900
6	\$820	\$1,000	12	\$920	\$900

41. **Effectiveness of a New Poultry Feed.** A study was designed to evaluate the weight-gain potential of a new poultry feed. A sample of 12 chickens was used in a six-week study. The weight of each chicken was recorded before and after the six-week test period. The differences between the before and after weights of the 12 chickens are as follows: 1.5, 1.2, −0.2, 0.0, 0.5, 0.7, 0.8, 1.0, 0.0, 0.6, 0.2, −0.01. A positive difference indicates a weight gain and a negative difference indicates a weight loss. Use a 0.05 level of significance to determine if the new feed provides a significant weight gain for the chickens. **LO 3**

42. **Weights of an Item Produced on Two Different Lines.** The following data are product weights (in kilograms) for the same items produced on two different production lines. Test for a difference between the product weights for the two lines. Use $\alpha = 0.05$. **LO 4**

DATA*file* productweights

Product Weights (kilograms)

Line 1	Line 2
13.6	13.7
13.8	14.1
14.0	14.2
13.9	14.0
13.4	14.6
13.2	13.5
13.3	14.4
13.6	14.8
12.9	14.5
14.4	14.3
	15.0
	14.9

43. **Comparison of Program Evaluation Methods.** A client wants to determine whether there is a significant difference in the time required to complete a program evaluation with the three different methods that are in common use. The times (in hours) required for each of 18 evaluators to conduct a program evaluation follow. Use $\alpha = 0.05$ and test to see whether there is a significant difference in the time required by the three methods. **LO 5**

DATA*file* methods

Time Required (hours)

Method 1	Method 2	Method 3
68	62	58
74	73	67
65	75	69
76	68	57
77	72	59
72	70	62

44. **Evaluating Managerial Potential.** A sample of 20 engineers employed with a company for three years has been rank ordered with respect to managerial potential. Some of the engineers attended the company's management-development course, others attended an off-site management-development program at a local university, and the remainder did not attend any program. Use the following rankings and $\alpha = 0.025$ to test for a significant difference in the managerial potential of the three groups. **LO 5**

DATA*file* programs

No Program	Company Program	Off-Site Program
16	12	7
9	20	1
10	17	4
15	19	2
11	6	3
13	18	8
	14	5

45. **Instructor Course Evaluations.** Course evaluation ratings for four college instructors are shown in the following table. Use $\alpha = 0.05$ and test for a significant difference among the rating for these instructors. What is your conclusion? **LO 5**

DATA*file* evaluations

Instructor			
Black	Jennings	Swanson	Wilson
88	87	88	80
80	78	76	85
79	82	68	56
68	85	82	71
96	99	85	89
69	99	82	87
	85	84	
	94	83	
		81	

46. **Midterm and Final Exam Scores.** A sample of 15 students received the following rankings on midterm and final examinations in a statistics course. Compute the Spearman rank-correlation coefficient for the data and test for a significant correlation with $\alpha = 0.10$. What is the p-value and what is your conclusion? **LO 6**

DATA*file* exams

Rank		Rank		Rank	
Midterm	Final	Midterm	Final	Midterm	Final
1	4	6	2	11	14
2	7	7	5	12	15
3	1	8	12	13	11
4	3	9	6	14	10
5	8	10	9	15	13

47. **Network TV Series Viewership.** Nielsen Research provides weekly ratings of nationally broadcast television programs. The mean weekly number of viewers for the 207 prime-time programs broadcast by five major televisions networks (ABC, CBS, FOX, NBC, and CW) for the 2017–2018 television season are provided in the file *viewership2017_18*. Shown in the following table are the mean weekly number of viewers for 12 shows in the file. Do these data suggest that the overall ratings for the

five networks differ significantly? Use the Kruskal–Wallis test with a 0.10 level of significance. What is the p-value, and what is your conclusion? **LO 5**

DATA*file* viewership2017_18

Program	Network	Mean Weekly Number of Viewers (millions)
9-1-1 (Fri)	FOX	2.317
Valor	CW	1.431
The Amazing Race	CBS	7.702
Modern Family	ABC	7.099
Quantico	ABC	3.215
Undercover Boss	CBS	4.813
The Good Doctor	ABC	15.610
The Brave	NBC	7.683
The Exorcist	FOX	1.937
Bull	CBS	14.374
Shark Tank	ABC	5.507
Lucifer	FOX	4.161

Case: RainOrShine.Com

RainOrShine.Com is an online provider of weather forecasts and information. The organization is putting together a weather-preparedness program to increase its audience's understanding of severe weather. As part of this program, RainOrShine.Com would like to be able to warn its audience if there are seasonal differences in the number of fatal lightning strikes in the United States.

To test for possible seasonal differences, RainOrShine.Com has collected data from the National Weather Service, which maintains an online database that provides information on lightning strike fatalities by month. Because only monthly data are available, RainOrShine.Com has defined the four seasons as follows.

Season	Months
Winter	January, February, March
Spring	April, May, June
Summer	July, August, September
Fall	October, November, December

The data collected on the number of lightning strike fatalities for each season from 2008 through 2017 by RainOrShine.Com from the National Weather Service are provided in the following table. **LO 5**

DATA*file* rainorshine

	Season			
Year	Winter	Spring	Summer	Fall
2017	0	4	12	0
2016	2	9	28	1
2015	0	17	11	0
2014	0	8	17	1
2013	0	8	15	0
2012	1	5	22	1
2011	0	6	19	1
2010	0	11	17	1
2009	1	15	18	1
2008	2	12	15	0

Managerial Report

Use the methods described in this chapter to provide a report that addresses the following questions.

1. Based on these data, should RainOrShine.Com warn its audience of seasonal differences in the numbers of fatal lightning strikes in the United States? Use the $\alpha = 0.05$ level of significance.
2. If the data suggest there are seasonal differences in fatal lightning strikes in the United States, during which season are fatal lightning strikes most common in the United States?
3. Are you concerned about RainOrShine.Com's definitions of seasons? Explain why or why not.

Chapter 19

Statistical Methods for Quality Control

Contents

Statistics in Practice:
Ocean Spray

19.1 Philosophies and Frameworks
Malcolm Baldrige National Quality Award
ISO 9001
Six Sigma
Quality in the Service Sector

19.2 Statistical Process Control
Control Charts
$\bar{x}$ Chart: Process Mean and Standard Deviation Known
$\bar{x}$ Chart: Process Mean and Standard Deviation Unknown
R Chart
p Chart
np Chart
Interpretation of Control Charts

19.3 Acceptance Sampling
KALI, Inc.: An Example of Acceptance Sampling
Computing the Probability of Accepting a Lot
Selecting an Acceptance Sampling Plan
Multiple Sampling Plans

Summary 946
Glossary 946
Key Formulas 947
Supplementary Exercises 948

Available in the Cengage eBook:
Appendix: Control Charts with R

Learning Objectives

After completing this chapter, you will be able to

LO 1 Construct and interpret an $\bar{x}$ control chart with known and unknown standard deviations.

LO 2 Construct and interpret an *R* control chart.

LO 3 Construct and interpret a *p* control chart.

LO 4 Construct and interpret an *np* control chart.

LO 5 Calculate the probability of accepting a lot for a sampling plan.

LO 6 Construct and interpret an operating characteristic curve.

LO 7 Calculate and interpret producer's risk and consumer's risk for a sampling plan.

LO 8 Select a sampling plan based on producer and consumer risk.

Statistics in Practice

Ocean Spray*

Lakeville-Middleborough, Massachusetts

Ocean Spray is an American agricultural cooperative. A cooperative business is owned and controlled by a group of people typically known as "member-owners" who collectively own the company. Earnings from the cooperative are shared by its member-owners.

Three cranberry growers, Marcus Urann, John Makepeace, and Elizabeth Lee, founded the Ocean Spray cooperative in 1930 and shortly thereafter introduced their first product, cranberry sauce. Ocean Spray has grown to more than 700 member-owners who grow cranberries and grapefruit. With over 2,000 employees and annual revenue of $2 billion, Ocean Spray distributes over 1,000 products including a variety of juices, cranberry sauce, supplements, and fresh and dried fruit products.

Ocean Spray is strategically focused on customer satisfaction, product quality, and continuous improvement in all their production processes. Ensuring efficient and stable production processes translates to more-consistent product quality. Historically, Ocean Spray relied on manual data collection and report generation to monitor their production. Partnering with statistical process control (SPC) software company InfinityQS®, Ocean Spray was able to automate the collection and analysis of its production process data and realize significant benefits.

Working with InfinityQS®, Ocean Spray first implemented the automated data collection and reporting at their plant in Markham, Washington. The SPC software was tested on the Craisins® dried cranberry production process at the Markham plant. Automated data collection resulted in fewer recording errors. Automated reports, consisting of charts and graphs, show process data over time. The control charts show process data and control limits, so that when the process data drifts beyond the control limits, corrective action can be taken. With the automated system, process control charts are available in real time, which shortens the time delay before action can be taken to address a process that is drifting out of control.

Ocean Spray saw a 50% improvement of the stability of their process in just one month. Ocean Spray has now implemented the SPC software in all of their plants with similar benefits, and the company has created a culture of continuous improvement among its workforce.

In this chapter, we show how control charts, like those used by Ocean Spray, can be developed. We will also discuss methods of quality control for situations in which a decision to accept or reject a group of items is based on a sample.

*This Statistics in Practice is based on "Ocean Spray and SPC: Growing Together," *InfinityQA.com*.

The American Society for Quality (ASQ) defines quality as "the characteristics of a product or service that bear on its ability to satisfy stated or implied needs.[1]" In other words, quality measures how well a product or service meets customer needs. Organizations recognize that to be competitive in today's global economy, they must strive for a high level of quality. As a result, they place increased emphasis on methods for monitoring and maintaining quality.

Today, the customer-driven focus that is fundamental to high-performing organizations has changed the scope that quality issues encompass, from simply eliminating defects on a production line to developing broad-based corporate quality strategies. Broadening the scope of quality naturally leads to the concept of **total quality (TQ)**.

> Total Quality (TQ) is a people-focused management system that aims at continual increase in customer satisfaction at continually lower real cost. TQ is a total system approach (not a separate area or work program) and an integral part of high-level strategy; it works horizontally across function and departments, involves all employees, top to bottom, and extends backward

[1]From the Quality Glossary of the ASQ.org website.

and forward to include the supply chain and the customer chain. TQ stresses learning and adaptation to continual change as keys to organization success.[2]

Regardless of how it is implemented in different organizations, total quality is based on three fundamental principles: a focus on customers and stakeholders; participation and teamwork throughout the organization; and a focus on continuous improvement and learning. In the first section of the chapter, we provide a brief introduction to three quality management frameworks: the Malcolm Baldrige Quality Award, ISO 9001 standards, and the Six Sigma philosophy. In the last two sections, we introduce two statistical tools that can be used to monitor quality: statistical process control and acceptance sampling.

19.1 Philosophies and Frameworks

After World War II, Dr. W. Edwards Deming became a consultant to Japanese industry; he is credited with being the person who convinced top managers in Japan to use the methods of statistical quality control.

In the early twentieth century, quality control practices were limited to inspecting finished products and removing defective items. But this all changed as the result of the pioneering efforts of a young engineer named Walter A. Shewhart. After completing his doctorate in physics from the University of California in 1917, Dr. Shewhart joined the Western Electric Company, working in the inspection engineering department. In 1924 Dr. Shewhart prepared a memorandum that included a set of principles that are the basis for what is known today as process control. His memo also contained a diagram that would be recognized as a statistical control chart. Continuing his work in quality at Bell Telephone Laboratories until his retirement in 1956, he brought together the disciplines of statistics, engineering, and economics and in doing so changed the course of industrial history. Dr. Shewhart is recognized as the father of statistical quality control and was the first honorary member of the ASQ.

Two other individuals who have had great influence on quality are Dr. W. Edwards Deming, a student of Dr. Shewhart, and Joseph Juran. They helped educate the Japanese in quality management shortly after World War II. Although quality is everybody's job, Deming stressed that the focus on quality must be led by managers. He developed a list of 14 points that he believed represent the key responsibilities of managers. For instance, Deming stated that managers must cease dependence on mass inspection; must end the practice of awarding business solely on the basis of price; must seek continual improvement in all production processes and service; must foster a team-oriented environment; and must eliminate goals, slogans, and work standards that prescribe numerical quotas. Perhaps most important, managers must create a work environment in which a commitment to quality and productivity is maintained at all times.

Juran proposed a simple definition of quality: *fitness for use.* Juran's approach to quality focused on three quality processes: quality planning, quality control, and quality improvement. In contrast to Deming's philosophy, which required a major cultural change in the organization, Juran's programs were designed to improve quality by working within the current organizational system. Nonetheless, the two philosophies are similar in that they both focus on the need for top management to be involved and stress the need for continuous improvement, the importance of training, and the use of quality control techniques.

Many other individuals played significant roles in the quality movement, including Philip B. Crosby, A. V. Feigenbaum, Karou Ishikawa, and Genichi Taguchi. More specialized texts dealing exclusively with quality provide details of the contributions of each of these individuals. The contributions of all individuals involved in the quality movement helped define a set of best practices and led to numerous awards and certification programs. Some of the most significant quality-management programs are the U.S. Malcolm Baldrige National Quality Award, the international ISO 9001 certification process, and Six Sigma methodologies.

[2]J. R. Evans and W. M. Lindsay, *Managing for Quality and High Performance*, 11th ed. (Cincinnati, OH: Cengage Learning, 2020), p. 16.

Malcolm Baldrige National Quality Award

The U.S. Commerce Department's National Institute of Standards and Technology (NIST) manages the Baldrige National Quality Program. More information can be obtained at the NIST.gov website.

The Malcolm Baldrige National Quality Award is given by the president of the United States to organizations that apply and are judged to be outstanding in seven areas: leadership; strategy; customers measurement, analysis, and knowledge management; workforce; operations; and results. Congress established the award program in 1987 to recognize U.S. organizations for their achievements in quality and performance and to raise awareness about the importance of quality as a competitive edge. The award is named for Malcolm Baldrige, who served as secretary of commerce from 1981 until his death in 1987.

Since the presentation of the first awards in 1988, the Baldrige National Quality Program (BNQP) has grown in stature and impact. More than 4 million copies of the criteria have been distributed since 1988. Bob Barnett, executive vice president of Motorola, Inc., said, "We applied for the Award, not with the idea of winning, but with the goal of receiving the evaluation of the Baldrige Examiners. That evaluation was comprehensive, professional, and insightful . . . making it perhaps the most cost-effective, value-added business consultation available anywhere in the world today."

ISO 9001

ISO 9001 is also referred to as the ISO 9000 Family of Quality Management Systems.

ISO 9001 defines the requirements and criteria that helps organizations ensure that their products and services meet the quality standards of their customers and regulatory requirements. ISO 9001 is the current evolution of ISO 9000 which is a series of five international standards published in 1987 by the International Organization for Standardization (ISO), Geneva, Switzerland. Companies can use the standards defined in ISO 9001 to help determine what is needed to maintain an efficient quality conformance system. For example, the standards describe the need for an effective quality system, for ensuring that measuring and testing equipment is calibrated regularly, and for maintaining an adequate record-keeping system. ISO 9001 certification determines whether a company complies with its own quality system.

Six Sigma

In the late 1980s, Motorola recognized the need to improve the quality of its products and services; their goal was to achieve a level of quality so good that for every million opportunities no more than 3.4 defects will occur. This level of quality is referred to as the six sigma level of quality, and the methodology created to reach this quality goal is referred to as **Six Sigma**.

An organization may undertake two kinds of Six Sigma projects:

- DMAIC (Define, Measure, Analyze, Improve, and Control) to help redesign existing processes
- DFSS (Design for Six Sigma) to design new products, processes, or services

In helping to redesign existing processes and design new processes, Six Sigma places a heavy emphasis on statistical analysis and careful measurement. Today, Six Sigma is a major tool in helping organizations achieve Baldrige levels of business performance and process quality. Many Baldrige examiners view Six Sigma as the ideal approach for implementing Baldrige improvement programs.

Six Sigma Limits and Defects per Million Opportunities In Six Sigma terminology, a *defect* is any mistake or error that is passed on to the customer. The Six Sigma process defines quality performance as defects per million opportunities (dpmo). Six Sigma represents a quality level of at most 3.4 dpmo. To illustrate how this quality level is measured, let us consider the situation at KJW Packaging.

KJW operates a production line where boxes of cereal are filled. The filling process has a mean of $\mu = 16.05$ ounces and a standard deviation of $\sigma = 0.10$ ounces. It is reasonable to assume the filling weights are normally distributed. The distribution of filling weights is shown in Figure 19.1. Suppose management considers 15.45 to

Figure 19.1 Normal Distribution of Cereal Box Filling Weights with a Process Mean $\mu = 16.05$

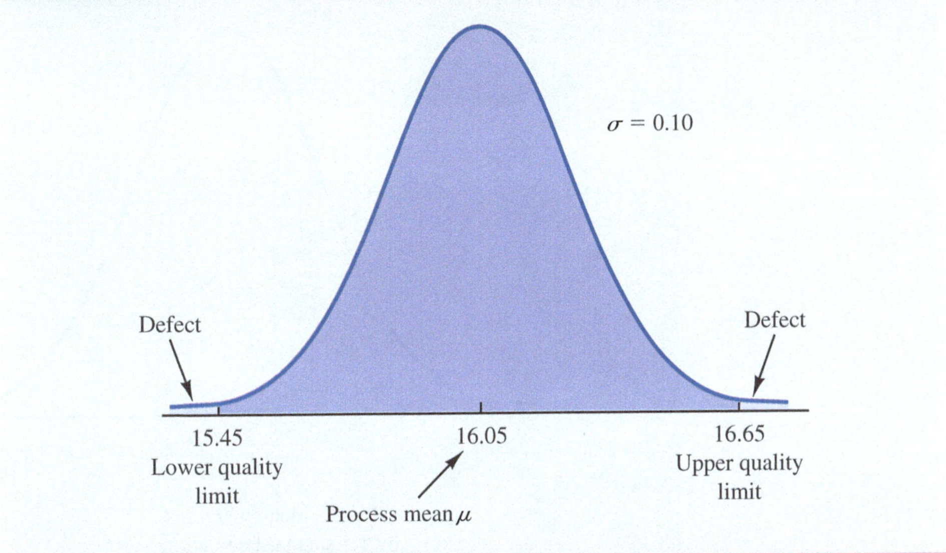

16.65 ounces to be acceptable quality limits for the filling process. Thus, any box of cereal that contains less than 15.45 or more than 16.65 ounces is considered to be a defect. Using Excel, it can be shown that 99.9999998% of the boxes filled will have between $16.05 - 6(0.10) = 15.45$ ounces and $16.05 + 6(0.10) = 16.65$ ounces. In other words, only 0.0000002% of the boxes filled will contain less than 15.45 ounces or more than 16.65 ounces. Thus, the likelihood of obtaining a defective box of cereal from the filling process appears to be extremely unlikely, because on average only two boxes in 10 million will be defective.

Using Excel, NORM.S.DIST(6,TRUE) − NORM.S.DIST(−6,TRUE) = 0.999999998.

Motorola's early work on Six Sigma convinced them that a process mean can shift on average by as much as 1.5 standard deviations. For instance, suppose that the process mean for KJW increases by 1.5 standard deviations or $1.5(0.10) = 0.15$ ounces. With such a shift, the normal distribution of filling weights would now be centered at $\mu = 16.05 + 0.15 = 16.20$ ounces. With a process mean of $\mu = 16.05$ ounces, the probability of obtaining a box of cereal with more than 16.65 ounces is extremely small. But how does this probability change if the mean of the process shifts up to $\mu = 16.20$ ounces? Figure 19.2 shows that for this case, the upper quality limit of 16.65 is 4.5 standard deviations to the right of the new mean $\mu = 16.20$ ounces. Using this mean and Excel, we find that the probability of obtaining a box with more than 16.65 ounces is 0.0000034. Thus, if the process mean shifts up by 1.5 standard deviations, approximately $1{,}000{,}000(0.0000034) = 3.4$ boxes of cereal will exceed the upper limit of 16.65 ounces. In Six Sigma terminology, the quality level of the process is said to be 3.4 defects per million opportunities. If management of KJW considers 15.45 to 16.65 ounces to be acceptable quality limits for the filling process, the KJW filling process would be considered a Six Sigma process. Thus, if the process mean stays within 1.5 standard deviations of its target value $\mu = 16.05$ ounces, a maximum of only 3.4 defects per million boxes filled can be expected.

Using Excel, 1 − NORM.S.DIST(4.5,TRUE) = 0.0000034.

Organizations that want to achieve and maintain a Six Sigma level of quality must emphasize methods for monitoring and maintaining quality. *Quality assurance* refers to the entire system of policies, procedures, and guidelines established by an organization to achieve and maintain quality. Quality assurance consists of two principal functions: quality engineering and quality control. The objective of *quality engineering* is to include

Figure 19.2 Normal Distribution of Cereal Box Filling Weights with a Process Mean $\mu = 16.20$

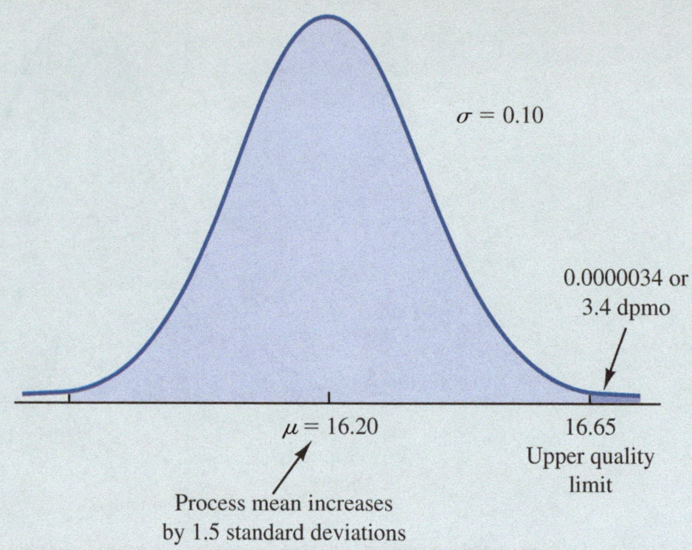

quality in the design of products and processes and to identify quality problems prior to production. **Quality control** consists of a series of inspections and measurements used to determine whether quality standards are being met. If quality standards are not being met, corrective or preventive action can be taken to achieve and maintain conformance. In the next two sections, we present two statistical methods used in quality control. The first method, *statistical process control,* uses graphical displays known as control charts to monitor a process; the goal is to determine whether the process can be continued or whether corrective action should be taken to achieve a desired quality level. The second method, *acceptance sampling,* is used in situations where a decision to accept or reject a group of items must be based on the quality found in a sample.

Quality in the Service Sector

While its roots are in manufacturing, quality control is also very important for businesses that focus primarily on providing services. Examples of businesses that are primarily involved in providing services are healthcare providers, law firms, hotels, airlines, restaurants, and banks. Businesses focused on providing services are a very important part of the U.S. economy.

Rather than a focus on measuring defects in a production process, quality efforts in the service sector focus on ensuring customer satisfaction and improving the customer experience. Because it is generally much less costly to retain a customer than it is to acquire a new one, quality control processes that are designed to improve customer service are critical to a service business. Customer satisfaction is the key to success in any service-oriented business.

Service businesses are very different from manufacturing businesses and this has an impact on how quality is measured and ensured. Services provided are often intangible (e.g., advice from a residence hall adviser). Because customer satisfaction is very subjective, it can be challenging to measure quality in services. However, quality can be monitored by measuring such things as timeliness of providing service as well as by conducting customer satisfaction surveys. This is why some dry cleaners guarantee one-hour service and why automobile service centers, airlines, and restaurants ask you to fill out a survey about your service experience. It is also why businesses use customer loyalty cards. By tracking your buying behavior, they can better understand the wants and needs of their customers and consequently provide better service.

Quality management in healthcare services is extremely important. Many errors that occur in hospitals and clinics are preventable. Medical errors lead to excessive costs and can lead to negative outcomes for patients. Healthcare administrators focus on quality management programs to improve patient outcomes and reduce costs in health care.

19.2 Statistical Process Control

In this section, we consider quality control procedures for a production process whereby goods are manufactured continuously. On the basis of sampling and inspection of production output, a decision will be made to either continue the production process or adjust it to bring the items or goods being produced up to acceptable quality standards.

Continuous improvement is one of the most important concepts of total quality management. The most important use of a control chart is in improving the process.

Despite high standards of quality in manufacturing and production operations, machine tools will invariably wear out, vibrations will throw machine settings out of adjustment, purchased materials will be defective, and human operators will make mistakes. Any or all of these factors can result in poor quality output. Fortunately, procedures are available for monitoring production output so that poor quality can be detected early and the production process can be adjusted or corrected.

If the variation in the quality of the production output is due to **assignable causes** such as tools wearing out, incorrect machine settings, poor quality raw materials, or operator error, the process should be adjusted or corrected as soon as possible. Alternatively, if the variation is due to what are called **common causes**—that is, randomly occurring variations in materials, temperature, humidity, and so on, which the manufacturer cannot possibly control—the process does not need to be adjusted. The main objective of statistical process control is to determine whether variations in output are due to assignable causes or common causes.

Whenever assignable causes are detected, we conclude that the process is *out of control.* In that case, corrective action will be taken to bring the process back to an acceptable level of quality. However, if the variation in the output of a production process is due only to common causes, we conclude that the process is *in statistical control,* or simply *in control;* in such cases, no changes or adjustments are necessary.

Process control procedures are closely related to hypothesis testing procedures introduced in Chapter 9. Control charts provide an ongoing test of the hypothesis that the process is in control.

The null hypothesis H_0 is formulated in terms of the production process being in control. The alternative hypothesis H_a is formulated in terms of the production process being out of control. Table 19.1 shows that correct decisions to continue an in-control process and adjust an out-of-control process are possible. However, as with other hypothesis testing

Table 19.1 The Outcomes of Statistical Process Control

		State of Production Process	
		H_0 True Process in Control	H_0 False Process Out of Control
Decision	Continue Process	Correct decision	Type II error (allowing an out-of-control process to continue)
	Adjust Process	Type I error (adjusting an in-control process)	Correct decision

procedures, both a Type I error (adjusting an in-control process) and a Type II error (allowing an out-of-control process to continue) are also possible.

Control Charts

A **control chart** provides a basis for deciding whether the variation in the output is due to common causes (in control) or assignable causes (out of control). Whenever an out-of-control situation is detected, adjustments or other corrective action will be taken to bring the process back into control.

Control charts can be classified by the type of data they contain. An **$\bar{x}$ chart** is used if the quality of the output of the process is measured in terms of a variable such as length, weight, and temperature. In that case, the decision to continue or to adjust the production process will be based on the mean value found in a sample of the output. To introduce some of the concepts common to all control charts, let us consider some specific features of an $\bar{x}$ chart.

Figure 19.3 shows the general structure of an $\bar{x}$ chart. The center line of the chart corresponds to the mean of the process when the process is *in control.* The vertical line identifies the scale of measurement for the variable of interest. Each time a sample is taken from the production process, a value of the sample mean $\bar{x}$ is computed and a data point showing the value of $\bar{x}$ is plotted on the control chart.

The two lines labeled UCL and LCL are important in determining whether the process is in control or out of control. The lines are called the *upper control limit* (UCL) and the *lower control limit* (LCL), respectively. They are chosen so that when the process is in control, there will be a high probability that the value of $\bar{x}$ will be between the two control limits. Values outside the control limits provide strong statistical evidence that the process is out of control and corrective action should be taken.

Over time, more and more data points will be added to the control chart. The order of the data points will be from left to right as the process is sampled. In essence, every time a point is plotted on the control chart, we are carrying out a hypothesis test to determine whether the process is in control.

In addition to the $\bar{x}$ chart, other control charts can be used to monitor the range of the measurements in the sample (***R* chart**), the proportion defective in the sample (***p* chart**), and the number of defective items in the sample (***np* chart**). In each case, the control chart has an LCL, a center line, and a UCL similar to the $\bar{x}$ chart in Figure 19.3. The major difference among the charts is what the vertical axis measures; for instance, in a *p* chart the measurement scale denotes the proportion of defective items in the sample instead of the sample mean. In the following discussion, we will illustrate the construction and use of the $\bar{x}$ chart, *R* chart, *p* chart, and *np* chart.

Figure 19.3 $\bar{x}$ Chart Structure

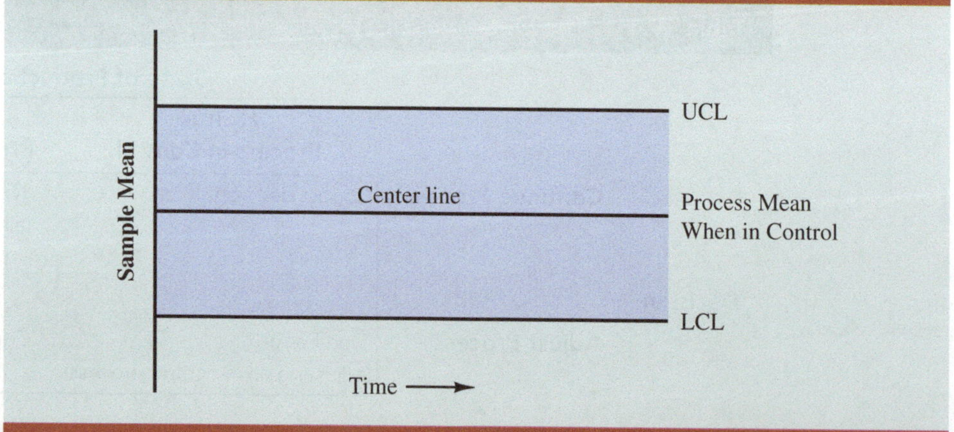

$\bar{x}$ Chart: Process Mean and Standard Deviation Known

To illustrate the construction of an $\bar{x}$ chart, let us reconsider the situation at KJW Packaging. Recall that KJW operates a production line where cartons of cereal are filled. When the process is operating correctly—and hence the system is in control—the mean filling weight is $\mu = 16.05$ ounces, and the process standard deviation is $\sigma = 0.10$ ounces. In addition, the filling weights are assumed to be normally distributed. This distribution is shown in Figure 19.4.

The sampling distribution of $\bar{x}$ is discussed in Chapter 7.

The sampling distribution of $\bar{x}$ can be used to determine the variation that can be expected in $\bar{x}$ values for a process that is in control. Let us first briefly review the properties of the sampling distribution of $\bar{x}$. First, recall that the expected value or mean of $\bar{x}$ is equal to μ, the mean filling weight when the production line is in control. For samples of size n, the equation for the standard deviation of $\bar{x}$, called the standard error of the mean, is

$$\sigma_{\bar{x}} = \frac{\sigma}{\sqrt{n}} \qquad \textbf{(19.1)}$$

In addition, because the filling weights are normally distributed, the sampling distribution of $\bar{x}$ is normally distributed for any sample size. Thus, the sampling distribution of $\bar{x}$ is a normal distribution with mean μ and standard deviation $\sigma_{\bar{x}}$. This distribution is shown in Figure 19.5.

The sampling distribution of $\bar{x}$ is used to determine what values of $\bar{x}$ are reasonable if the process is in control. The general practice in quality control is to define as reasonable any value of $\bar{x}$ that is within three standard deviations, or standard errors, above or below the mean value. Recall from the study of the normal probability distribution that approximately 99.7% of the values of a normally distributed random variable are within ± 3 standard deviations of its mean value. Thus, if a value of $\bar{x}$ is within the interval $\mu - 3\sigma_{\bar{x}}$ to $\mu + 3\sigma_{\bar{x}}$, we will assume that the process is in control. In summary, then, the control limits for an $\bar{x}$ chart are as follows.

Control Limits for An $\bar{x}$ Chart: Process Mean and Standard Deviation Known

$$\text{UCL} = \mu + 3\sigma_{\bar{x}} \qquad \textbf{(19.2)}$$

$$\text{LCL} = \mu - 3\sigma_{\bar{x}} \qquad \textbf{(19.3)}$$

Figure 19.4 Normal Distribution of Cereal Carton Filling Weights

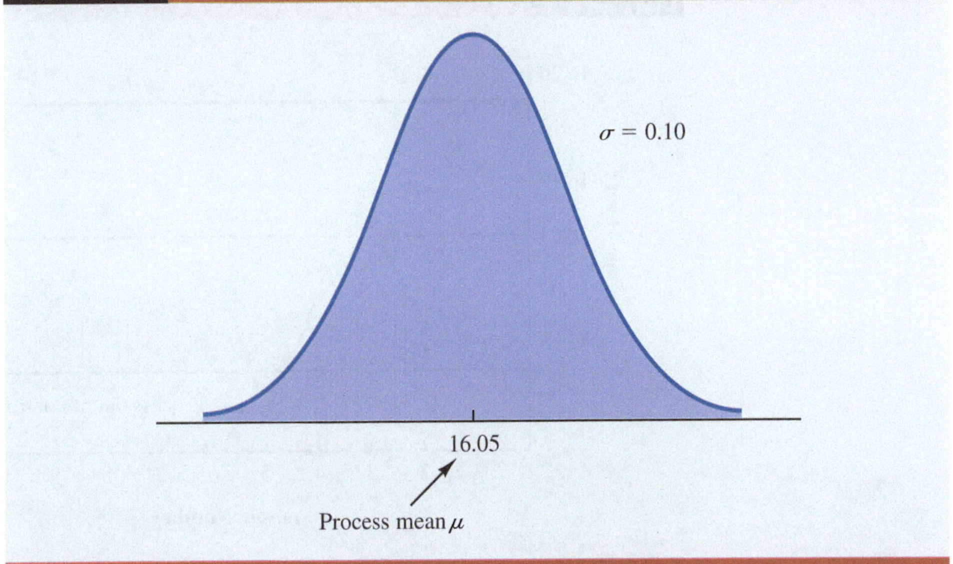

Figure 19.5 Sampling Distribution of $\bar{x}$ for a Sample of n Filling Weights

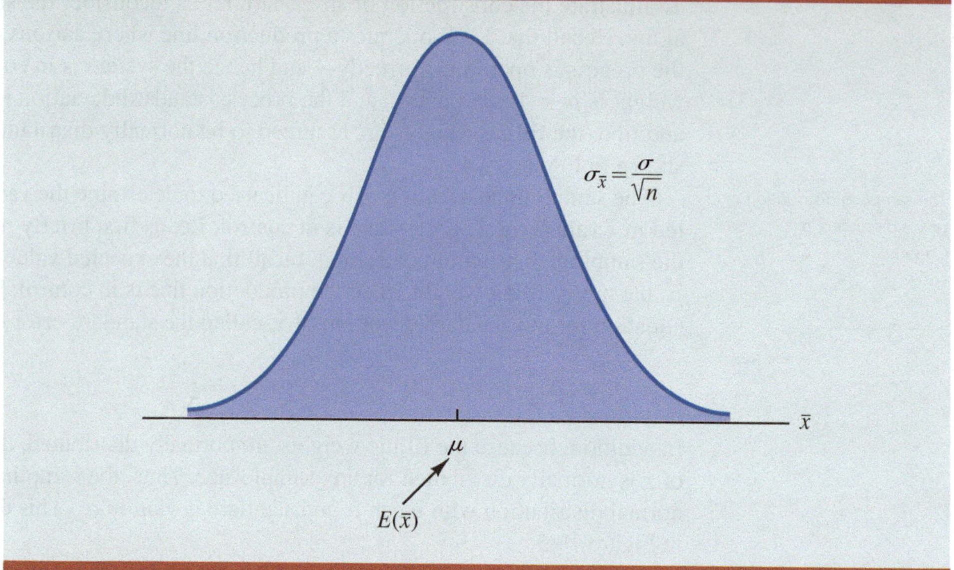

Reconsider the KJW Packaging example with the process distribution of filling weights shown in Figure 19.4 and the sampling distribution of $\bar{x}$ shown in Figure 19.5. Assume that a quality control inspector periodically samples six cartons and uses the sample mean filling weight to determine whether the process is in control or out of control. Using equation (19.1), we find that the standard error of the mean is $\sigma_{\bar{x}} = \sigma\sqrt{n} = 0.10/\sqrt{6} = 0.04$. Thus, with the process mean at 16.05, the control limits are UCL $= 16.05 + 3(0.04) = 16.17$ and LCL $= 16.05 - 3(0.04) = 15.93$. Figure 19.6 is the control chart with the results of 10 samples taken over a 10-hour period. For ease of reading, the sample numbers 1 through 10 are listed below the chart.

Note that the mean for the fifth sample in Figure 19.6 shows there is strong evidence that the process is out of control. The fifth sample mean is below the LCL, indicating that

Figure 19.6 The $\bar{x}$ Chart for the Cereal Carton Filling Process

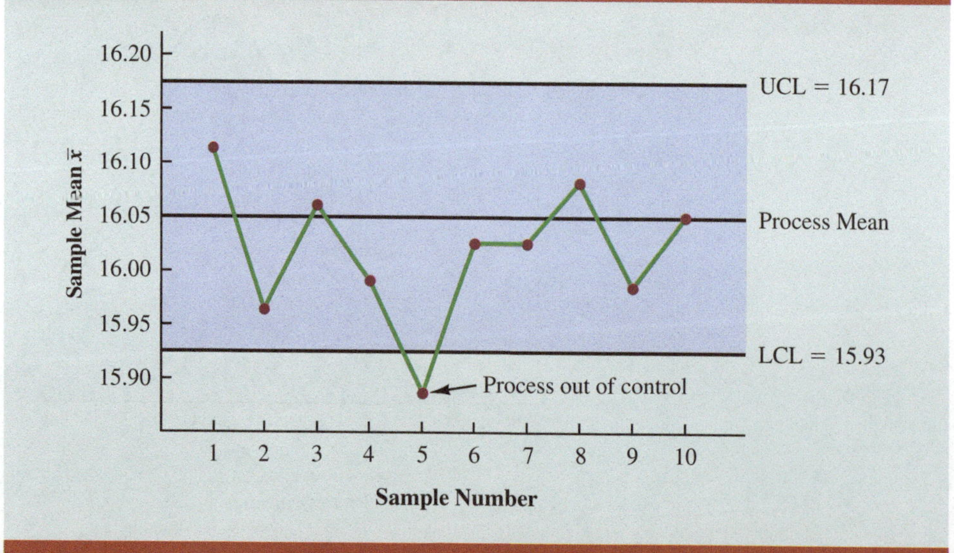

assignable causes of output variation are present and that underfilling is occurring. As a result, corrective action was taken at this point to bring the process back into control. The fact that the remaining points on the $\bar{x}$ chart are within the upper and lower control limits indicates that the corrective action was successful.

$\bar{x}$ Chart: Process Mean and Standard Deviation Unknown

In the KJW Packaging example, we showed how an $\bar{x}$ chart can be developed when the mean and standard deviation of the process are known. In most situations, the process mean and standard deviation must be estimated by using samples that are selected from the process when it is in control. For instance, KJW might select a random sample of five boxes each morning and five boxes each afternoon for 10 days of in-control operation. For each subgroup, or sample, the mean and standard deviation of the sample are computed. The overall averages of both the sample means and the sample standard deviations are used to construct control charts for both the process mean and the process standard deviation.

It is important to maintain control over both the mean and the variability of a process.

In practice, it is more common to monitor the variability of the process by using the range instead of the standard deviation because the range is easier to compute. The range can be used to provide good estimates of the process standard deviation; thus it can be used to construct upper and lower control limits for the $\bar{x}$ chart with little computational effort. To illustrate, let us consider the problem facing Jensen Computer Supplies, Inc.

Jensen Computer Supplies (JCS) manufactures solid-state drives; they just finished adjusting their production process so that it is operating in control. Suppose random samples of five drives were selected during the first hour of operation, five drives were selected during the second hour of operation, and so on, until 20 samples were obtained. Table 19.2 provides the diameter of each drive sampled as well as the mean $\bar{x}_j$ and range R_j for each of the samples.

The estimate of the process mean μ is given by the overall sample mean.

Overall Sample Mean

$$\bar{\bar{x}} = \frac{\bar{x}_1 + \bar{x}_2 + \cdots + \bar{x}_k}{k} \tag{19.4}$$

where

$\bar{x}_j$ = mean of the jth sample $j = 1, 2, \ldots, k$
k = number of samples

For the JCS data in Table 19.2, the overall sample mean is $\bar{\bar{x}} = 3.4995$. This value will be the center line for the $\bar{x}$ chart. The range of each sample, denoted R_j, is simply the difference between the largest and smallest values in each sample. The average range for k samples is computed as follows.

Average Range

$$\bar{R} = \frac{R_1 + R_2 + \cdots + R_k}{k} \tag{19.5}$$

where

R_j = range of the jth sample, $j = 1, 2, \ldots, k$
k = number of samples

For the JCS data in Table 19.2, the average range is $\bar{R} = 0.0253$.

Table 19.2 Data for the Jensen Computer Supplies Problem

DATA*file* jensen

Sample Number	Observations					Sample Mean $\bar{x}_j$	Sample Range R_j
1	3.5056	3.5086	3.5144	3.5009	3.5030	3.5065	0.0135
2	3.4882	3.5085	3.4884	3.5250	3.5031	3.5026	0.0368
3	3.4897	3.4898	3.4995	3.5130	3.4969	3.4978	0.0233
4	3.5153	3.5120	3.4989	3.4900	3.4837	3.5000	0.0316
5	3.5059	3.5113	3.5011	3.4773	3.4801	3.4951	0.0340
6	3.4977	3.4961	3.5050	3.5014	3.5060	3.5012	0.0099
7	3.4910	3.4913	3.4976	3.4831	3.5044	3.4935	0.0213
8	3.4991	3.4853	3.4830	3.5083	3.5094	3.4970	0.0264
9	3.5099	3.5162	3.5228	3.4958	3.5004	3.5090	0.0270
10	3.4880	3.5015	3.5094	3.5102	3.5146	3.5047	0.0266
11	3.4881	3.4887	3.5141	3.5175	3.4863	3.4989	0.0312
12	3.5043	3.4867	3.4946	3.5018	3.4784	3.4932	0.0259
13	3.5043	3.4769	3.4944	3.5014	3.4904	3.4935	0.0274
14	3.5004	3.5030	3.5082	3.5045	3.5234	3.5079	0.0230
15	3.4846	3.4938	3.5065	3.5089	3.5011	3.4990	0.0243
16	3.5145	3.4832	3.5188	3.4935	3.4989	3.5018	0.0356
17	3.5004	3.5042	3.4954	3.5020	3.4889	3.4982	0.0153
18	3.4959	3.4823	3.4964	3.5082	3.4871	3.4940	0.0259
19	3.4878	3.4864	3.4960	3.5070	3.4984	3.4951	0.0206
20	3.4969	3.5144	3.5053	3.4985	3.4885	3.5007	0.0259

In the preceding section, we showed that the upper and lower control limits for the $\bar{x}$ chart are

$$\bar{\bar{x}} \pm 3\frac{\sigma}{\sqrt{n}} \tag{19.6}$$

The overall sample mean $\bar{\bar{x}}$ is used to estimate μ and the sample ranges are used to develop an estimate of σ.

Hence, to construct the control limits for the $\bar{x}$ chart, we need to estimate μ and σ, the mean and standard deviation of the process. An estimate of μ is given by $\bar{\bar{x}}$. An estimate of σ can be developed by using the range data.

It can be shown that an estimator of the process standard deviation σ is the average range divided by d_2, a constant that depends on the sample size n. That is,

$$\text{Estimator of } \sigma = \frac{\bar{R}}{d_2} \tag{19.7}$$

The *American Society for Testing and Materials Manual on Presentation of Data and Control Chart Analysis* provides values for d_2 as shown in Table 19.3. For instance, when $n = 5$, $d_2 = 2.326$, and the estimate of σ is the average range divided by 2.326. If we substitute $\bar{R}/d_2$ for σ in expression (19.6), we can write the control limits for the $\bar{x}$ chart as

$$\bar{\bar{x}} \pm 3\frac{\bar{R}/d_2}{\sqrt{n}} = \bar{\bar{x}} \pm \frac{3}{d_2\sqrt{n}}\bar{R} = \bar{\bar{x}} \pm A_2\bar{R} \tag{19.8}$$

Note that $A_2 = 3/(d_2\sqrt{n})$ is a constant that depends only on the sample size. Values for A_2 are provided in Table 19.3. For $n = 5$, $A_2 = 0.577$; thus, the control limits for the $\bar{x}$ chart are

$$3.4995 \pm (0.577)(0.0253) = 3.4995 \pm 0.0146$$

Hence, UCL = 3.514 and LCL = 3.485.

Table 19.3 Factors for $\bar{x}$ and R Control Charts

Observations in Sample, n	d_2	A_2	d_3	D_3	D_4
2	1.128	1.880	0.853	0	3.267
3	1.693	1.023	0.888	0	2.574
4	2.059	0.729	0.880	0	2.282
5	2.326	0.577	0.864	0	2.114
6	2.534	0.483	0.848	0	2.004
7	2.704	0.419	0.833	0.076	1.924
8	2.847	0.373	0.820	0.136	1.864
9	2.970	0.337	0.808	0.184	1.816
10	3.078	0.308	0.797	0.223	1.777
11	3.173	0.285	0.787	0.256	1.744
12	3.258	0.266	0.778	0.283	1.717
13	3.336	0.249	0.770	0.307	1.693
14	3.407	0.235	0.763	0.328	1.672
15	3.472	0.223	0.756	0.347	1.653
16	3.532	0.212	0.750	0.363	1.637
17	3.588	0.203	0.744	0.378	1.622
18	3.640	0.194	0.739	0.391	1.608
19	3.689	0.187	0.734	0.403	1.597
20	3.735	0.180	0.729	0.415	1.585
21	3.778	0.173	0.724	0.425	1.575
22	3.819	0.167	0.720	0.434	1.566
23	3.858	0.162	0.716	0.443	1.557
24	3.895	0.157	0.712	0.451	1.548
25	3.931	0.153	0.708	0.459	1.541

Source: Reprinted with permission from Table 27 of ASTM STP 15D, *ASTM Manual on Presentation of Data and Control Chart Analysis*, Copyright ASTM International, 100 Barr Harbor Drive, West Conshohocken, PA 19428.

Figure 19.7 shows the $\bar{x}$ chart for the Jensen Computer Supplies problem. We used the data in Table 19.2 to construct the chart. The center line is shown at the overall sample mean $\bar{\bar{x}} = 3.4995$. The upper control limit (UCL) is 3.514 and the lower control limit (LCL) is 3.485. The $\bar{x}$ chart shows the 20 sample means plotted over time. Because all 20 sample means are within the control limits, we confirm that the process mean was in control during the sampling period.

R Chart

Let us now consider a range chart (R chart) that can be used to control the variability of a process. To develop the R chart, we need to think of the range of a sample as a random variable with its own mean and standard deviation. The average range $\bar{R}$ provides an estimate of the mean of this random variable. Moreover, it can be shown that an estimate of the standard deviation of the range is

$$\hat{\sigma}_R = d_3 \frac{\bar{R}}{d_2} \tag{19.9}$$

where d_2 and d_3 are constants that depend on the sample size; values of d_2 and d_3 are provided in Table 19.3. Thus, the UCL for the R chart is given by

$$\bar{R} + 3\hat{\sigma}_R = \bar{R}\left(1 + 3\frac{d_3}{d_2}\right) \tag{19.10}$$

Figure 19.7 $\bar{x}$ Chart for the Jensen Computer Supplies Problem

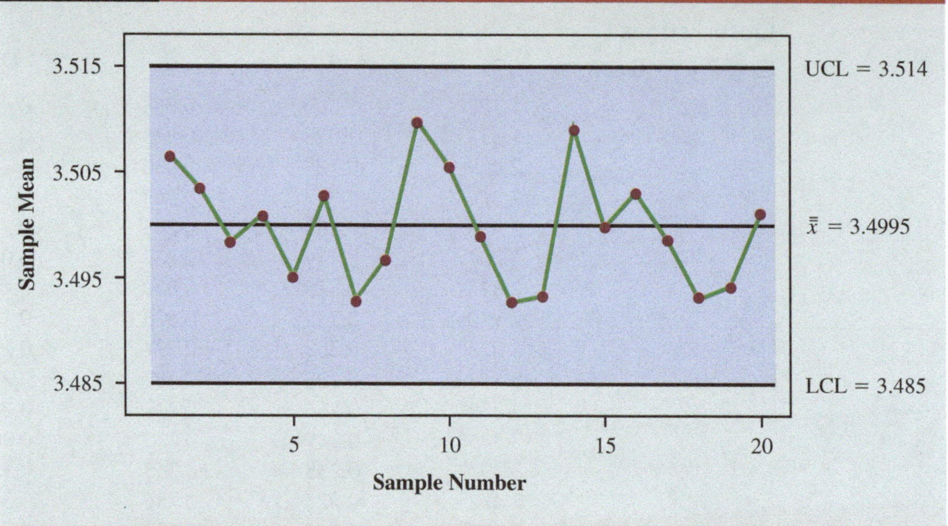

and the LCL is

$$\bar{R} - 3\hat{\sigma}_R = \bar{R}\left(1 - 3\frac{d_3}{d_2}\right) \qquad \textbf{(19.11)}$$

If we let

$$D_4 = 1 + 3\frac{d_3}{d_2} \qquad \textbf{(19.12)}$$

$$D_3 = 1 - 3\frac{d_3}{d_2} \qquad \textbf{(19.13)}$$

we can write the control limits for the *R* chart as

$$\text{UCL} = \bar{R}D_4 \qquad \textbf{(19.14)}$$

$$\text{LCL} = \bar{R}D_3 \qquad \textbf{(19.15)}$$

Values for D_3 and D_4 are also provided in Table 19.3. Note that for $n = 5$, $D_3 = 0$ and $D_4 = 2.114$. Thus, with $\bar{R} = 0.0253$, the control limits are

$$\text{UCL} = 0.0253(2.114) = 0.053$$
$$\text{LCL} = 0.0253(0) = 0$$

If the R chart indicates that the process is out of control, the $\bar{x}$ chart should not be interpreted until the R chart indicates the process variability is in control.

Figure 19.8 shows the *R* chart for the Jensen Computer Supplies problem. We used the data in Table 19.2 to construct the chart. The center line is shown at the overall mean of the 20 sample ranges, $\bar{R} = 0.0253$. The UCL is 0.053 and the LCL is 0.000. The *R* chart shows the 20 sample ranges plotted over time. Because all 20 sample ranges are within the control limits, we confirm that the process variability was in control during the sampling period.

p Chart

Let us consider the case in which the output quality is measured by either nondefective or defective items. The decision to continue or to adjust the production process will be

Figure 19.8 *R* Chart for the Jensen Computer Supplies Problem

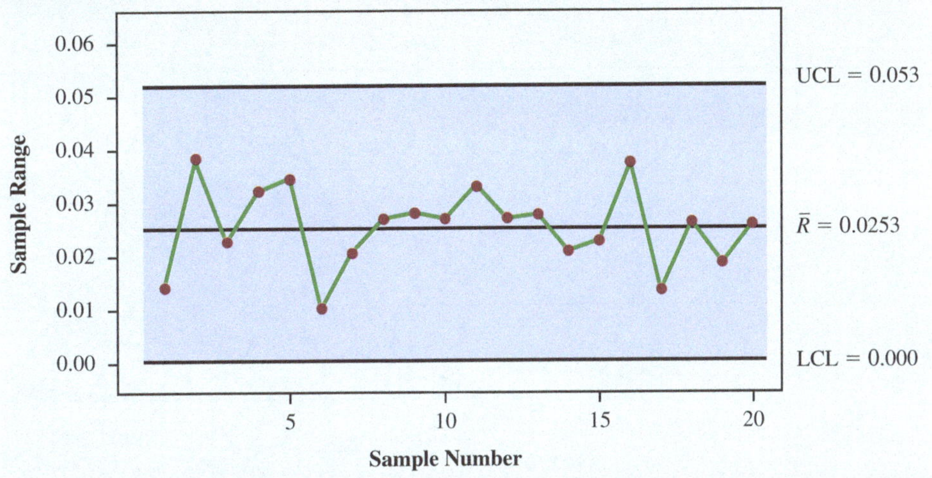

based on $\bar{p}$, the proportion of defective items found in a sample. The control chart used for proportion-defective data is called a *p* chart.

To illustrate the construction of a *p* chart, consider the use of automated mail-sorting machines in a post office. These automated machines scan the zip codes on letters and divert each letter to its proper carrier route. Even when a machine is operating properly, some letters are diverted to incorrect routes. Assume that when a machine is operating correctly, or in a state of control, 3% of the letters are incorrectly diverted. Thus *p*, the proportion of letters incorrectly diverted when the process is in control, is 0.03.

Sampling distributions are discussed in Chapter 7.

The sampling distribution of $\bar{p}$ can be used to determine the variation that can be expected in $\bar{p}$ values for a process that is in control. Recall that the expected value or mean of $\bar{p}$ is *p*, the proportion defective when the process is in control. With samples of size *n*, the formula for the standard deviation of $\bar{p}$, called the standard error of the proportion, is

$$\sigma_{\bar{p}} = \sqrt{\frac{p(1-p)}{n}} \tag{19.16}$$

The sampling distribution of $\bar{p}$ can be approximated by a normal distribution whenever the sample size is large. With $\bar{p}$, the sample size can be considered large whenever the following two conditions are satisfied.

$$np \geq 5$$
$$n(1-p) \geq 5$$

In summary, whenever the sample size is large, the sampling distribution of $\bar{p}$ can be approximated by a normal distribution with mean *p* and standard deviation $\sigma_{\bar{p}}$. This distribution is shown in Figure 19.9.

To establish control limits for a *p* chart, we follow the same procedure we used to establish control limits for an $\bar{x}$ chart. That is, the limits for the control chart are set at three standard deviations, or standard errors, above and below the proportion defective when the process is in control. Thus, we have the following control limits.

Control Limits for a *p* Chart

$$\text{UCL} = p + 3\sigma_{\bar{p}} \tag{19.17}$$
$$\text{LCL} = p - 3\sigma_{\bar{p}} \tag{19.18}$$

Figure 19.9 Sampling Distribution of $\bar{p}$

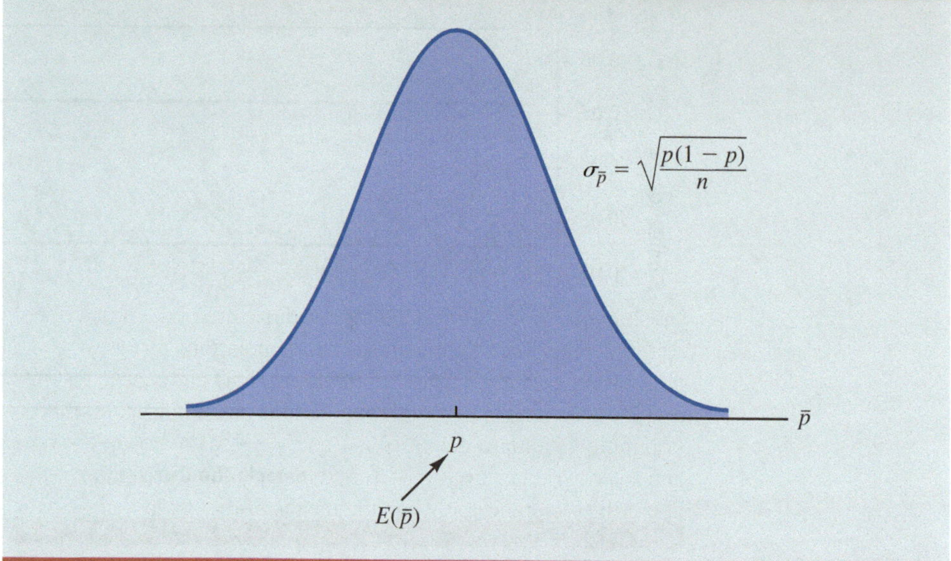

With $p = 0.03$ and samples of size $n = 200$, equation (19.16) shows that the standard error is

$$\sigma_{\bar{p}} = \sqrt{\frac{0.03(1 - 0.03)}{200}} = 0.0121$$

Hence, the control limits are UCL $= 0.03 + 3(0.0121) = 0.0663$ and LCL $= 0.03 - 3(0.0121) = -0.0063$. Whenever equation (19.18) provides a negative value for LCL, LCL is set equal to zero in the control chart.

Figure 19.10 is the p chart for the mail-sorting process. The points plotted show the sample proportion defective found in samples of letters taken from the process. All points are within the control limits, providing no evidence to conclude that the sorting process is out of control.

If the proportion of defective items for a process that is in control is not known, that value is first estimated by using sample data. Suppose, for example, that k different

Figure 19.10 p Chart for the Proportion Defective in a Mail-Sorting Process

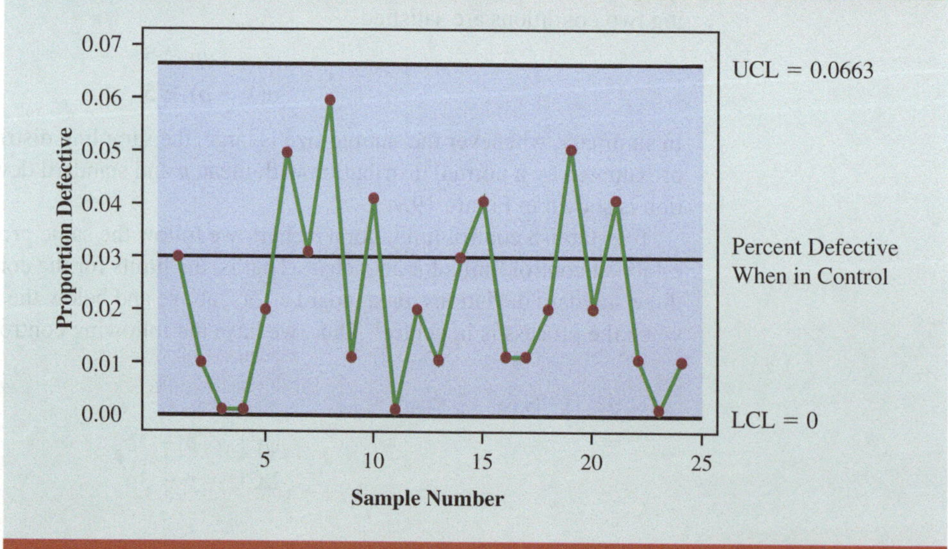

samples, each of size n, are selected from a process that is in control. The fraction or proportion of defective items in each sample is then determined. Treating all the data collected as one large sample, we can compute the proportion of defective items for all the data; that value can then be used to estimate p, the proportion of defective items observed when the process is in control. Note that this estimate of p also enables us to estimate the standard error of the proportion; upper and lower control limits can then be established.

np Chart

An np chart is a control chart developed for the number of defective items in a sample. In this case, n is the sample size and p is the probability of observing a defective item when the process is in control. Whenever the sample size is large, that is, when $np \geq 5$ and $n(1 - p) \geq 5$, the distribution of the number of defective items observed in a sample of size n can be approximated by a normal distribution with mean np and standard deviation $\sqrt{np(1 - p)}$. Thus, for the mail-sorting example, with $n = 200$ and $p = 0.03$, the number of defective items observed in a sample of 200 letters can be approximated by a normal distribution with a mean of $200(0.03) = 6$ and a standard deviation of $\sqrt{200(0.03)(0.97)} = 2.4125$.

The control limits for an np chart are set at three standard deviations above and below the expected number of defective items observed when the process is in control. Thus, we have the following control limits.

Control Limits for an *NP* Chart

$$\text{UCL} = np + 3\sqrt{np(1 - p)} \qquad \textbf{(19.19)}$$

$$\text{LCL} = np - 3\sqrt{np(1 - p)} \qquad \textbf{(19.20)}$$

For the mail-sorting process example, with $p = 0.03$ and $n = 200$, the control limits are $\text{UCL} = 6 + 3(2.4125) = 13.2375$ and $\text{LCL} = 6 - 3(2.4125) = -1.2375$. When LCL is negative, LCL is set equal to zero in the control chart. Hence, if the number of letters diverted to incorrect routes is greater than 13, the process is concluded to be out of control.

The information provided by an np chart is equivalent to the information provided by the p chart; the only difference is that the np chart is a plot of the number of defective items observed, whereas the p chart is a plot of the proportion of defective items observed. Thus, if we were to conclude that a particular process is out of control on the basis of a p chart, the process would also be concluded to be out of control on the basis of an np chart.

Interpretation of Control Charts

The location and pattern of points in a control chart enable us to determine, with a small probability of error, whether a process is in statistical control. A primary indication that a process may be out of control is a data point outside the control limits, such as point 5 in Figure 19.6. Finding such a point is statistical evidence that the process is out of control; in such cases, corrective action should be taken as soon as possible.

In addition to points outside the control limits, certain patterns of the points within the control limits can be warning signals of quality control problems. For example, assume that all the data points are within the control limits but that a large number of points are on one side of the center line. This pattern may indicate that an equipment problem, a change in materials, or some other assignable cause of a shift in quality has occurred. Careful investigation of the production process should be undertaken to determine whether quality has changed.

Even if all points are within the upper and lower control limits, a process may not be in control. Trends in the sample data points or unusually long runs above or below the center line may also indicate out-of-control conditions.

Another pattern to watch for in control charts is a gradual shift, or trend, over time. For example, as tools wear out, the dimensions of machined parts will gradually deviate from their designed levels. Gradual changes in temperature or humidity, general equipment deterioration, dirt buildup, or operator fatigue may also result in a trend pattern in control charts. Six or seven points in a row that indicate either an increasing or decreasing trend should be cause for concern, even if the data points are all within the control limits. When such a pattern occurs, the process should be reviewed for possible changes or shifts in quality. Corrective action to bring the process back into control may be necessary.

Notes + Comments

1. Because the control limits for the $\bar{x}$ chart depend on the value of the average range, these limits will not have much meaning unless the process variability is in control. In practice, the R chart is usually constructed before the $\bar{x}$ chart; if the R chart indicates that the process variability is in control, then the $\bar{x}$ chart is constructed.
2. An np chart is used to monitor a process in terms of the number of defects. The Motorola Six Sigma Quality Level sets a goal of producing no more than 3.4 defects per million operations; this goal implies $p = 0.0000034$.

Exercises

Methods

1. A process that is in control has a mean of $\mu = 12.5$ and a standard deviation of $\sigma = 0.8$. **LO 1**
   a. Construct the $\bar{x}$ control chart for this process if samples of size 4 are to be used.
   b. Repeat part (a) for samples of size 8 and 16.
   c. What happens to the limits of the control chart as the sample size is increased? Discuss why this is reasonable.
2. Twenty-five samples, each of size 5, were selected from a process that was in control. The sum of all the data collected was 677.5 pounds. **LO 1**
   a. What is an estimate of the process mean (in terms of pounds per unit) when the process is in control?
   b. Develop the $\bar{x}$ control chart for this process if samples of size 5 will be used. Assume that the process standard deviation is 0.5 when the process is in control, and that the mean of the process is the estimate developed in part (a).
3. Twenty-five samples of 100 items each were inspected when a process was considered to be operating satisfactorily. In the 25 samples, a total of 135 items were found to be defective. **LO 3**
   a. What is an estimate of the proportion defective when the process is in control?
   b. What is the standard error of the proportion if samples of size 100 will be used for statistical process control?
   c. Compute the upper and lower control limits for the control chart.
4. A process sampled 20 times with a sample of size 8 resulted in $\bar{\bar{x}} = 28.5$ and $\bar{R} = 1.6$. Compute the upper and lower control limits for the $\bar{x}$ and R charts for this process. **LO 1, 2**

Applications

5. **Production Process Temperature.** Temperature is used to measure the output of a production process. When the process is in control, the mean of the process is $\mu = 128.5$ and the standard deviation is $\sigma = 0.4$. **LO 1**
   a. Construct the $\bar{x}$ chart for this process if samples of size 6 are to be used.
   b. Is the process in control for a sample providing the following data?

128.8	128.2	129.1	128.7	128.4	129.2

   c. Is the process in control for a sample providing the following data?

129.3	128.7	128.6	129.2	129.5	129.0

6. **Plant-Based Burgers.** The sales of plant-based dairy and meat alternative foods are expected to increase fivefold from 2021 to 2030 (*Fortune.com*). Consider a food processing plant that makes quarter-pound plant-based burgers. The director of quality control must ensure that the burgers are close enough to 0.25 pounds to satisfy consumers. If the burger's weight is between 0.245 pounds and 0.255 pounds it is considered acceptable, but outside that range the burger is considered defective. When the processing system is in control, only

2.6% of the burgers are defective (either too heavy or too light). Samples of 200 burgers are taken from the production line and individually weighed. **LO 3, 4**

a. Calculate the standard error of the proportion defective.
b. Calculate the upper and lower control limits for a chart.
c. Five samples of 200 burgers have been taken with the following proportion defective: 0.01, 0.02, 0.04, 0.03, and 0.05. Create a p chart.
d. Does the process appear to be in control or out of control?

7. **Tire Tread Tests.** The Goodman Tire and Rubber Company periodically tests its tires for tread wear under simulated road conditions. To study and control the manufacturing process, 20 samples, each containing three radial tires, were chosen from different shifts over several days of operation, with the following results. Assuming that these data were collected when the manufacturing process was believed to be operating in control, develop the R and $\bar{x}$ charts. **LO 1, 2**

DATA*file*
tires

Sample	Tread Wear (hundredths of inch)		
1	31	42	28
2	26	18	35
3	25	30	34
4	17	25	21
5	38	29	35
6	41	42	36
7	21	17	29
8	32	26	28
9	41	34	33
10	29	17	30
11	26	31	40
12	23	19	25
13	17	24	32
14	43	35	17
15	18	25	29
16	30	42	31
17	28	36	32
18	40	29	31
19	18	29	28
20	22	34	26

8. **Tennis String Breaking Strength.** Over several weeks of normal, or in-control, operation, 20 samples of 150 packages each of synthetic-gut tennis strings were tested for breaking strength. A total of 141 packages of the 3,000 tested failed to conform to the manufacturer's specifications. **LO 3, 4**

a. What is an estimate of the process proportion defective when the system is in control?
b. Compute the upper and lower control limits for a p chart.
c. With the results of part (b), what conclusion should be made about the process if tests on a new sample of 150 packages find 12 defective? Do there appear to be assignable causes in this situation?
d. Compute the upper and lower control limits for an np chart.
e. Answer part (c) using the results of part (d).
f. Which control chart would be preferred in this situation? Explain.

9. **Airline Call Center.** An airline operates a call center to handle customer questions and complaints. The airline monitors a sample of calls to help ensure that the service being provided is of high quality. Ten random samples of 100 calls each were monitored under normal conditions. The center can be thought of as being in control when these 10 samples were taken. The number of calls in each sample not resulting in a satisfactory resolution for the customer is as follows. **LO 3, 4**

4	5	3	2	3	3	4	6	4	7

a. What is an estimate of the proportion of calls not resulting in a satisfactory outcome for the customer when the center is in control?
b. Construct the upper and lower limits for a *p* chart for the manufacturing process, assuming each sample has 100 calls.
c. With the results of part (b), what conclusion should be made if a sample of 100 has 12 calls not resulting in a satisfactory resolution for the customer?
d. Compute the upper and lower limits for the *np* chart.
e. With the results of part (d), what conclusion should be made if a sample of 100 calls has 12 not resulting in a satisfactory conclusion for the customer?

19.3 Acceptance Sampling

In acceptance sampling, the items of interest can be incoming shipments of raw materials or purchased parts as well as finished goods from final assembly. Suppose we want to decide whether to accept or reject a group of items on the basis of specified quality characteristics. In quality control terminology, the group of items is a **lot**, and **acceptance sampling** is a statistical method that enables us to base the accept-reject decision on the inspection of a sample of items from the lot.

The general steps of acceptance sampling are shown in Figure 19.11. After a lot is received, a sample of items is selected for inspection. The results of the inspection are compared to specified quality characteristics. If the quality characteristics are satisfied, the lot is accepted and sent to production or shipped to customers. If the lot is rejected, managers must decide on its disposition. In some cases, the decision may be to keep the lot and remove the unacceptable or nonconforming items. In other cases, the lot may be returned to the supplier at the supplier's expense; the extra work and cost placed on the supplier can motivate

Figure 19.11 Acceptance Sampling Procedure

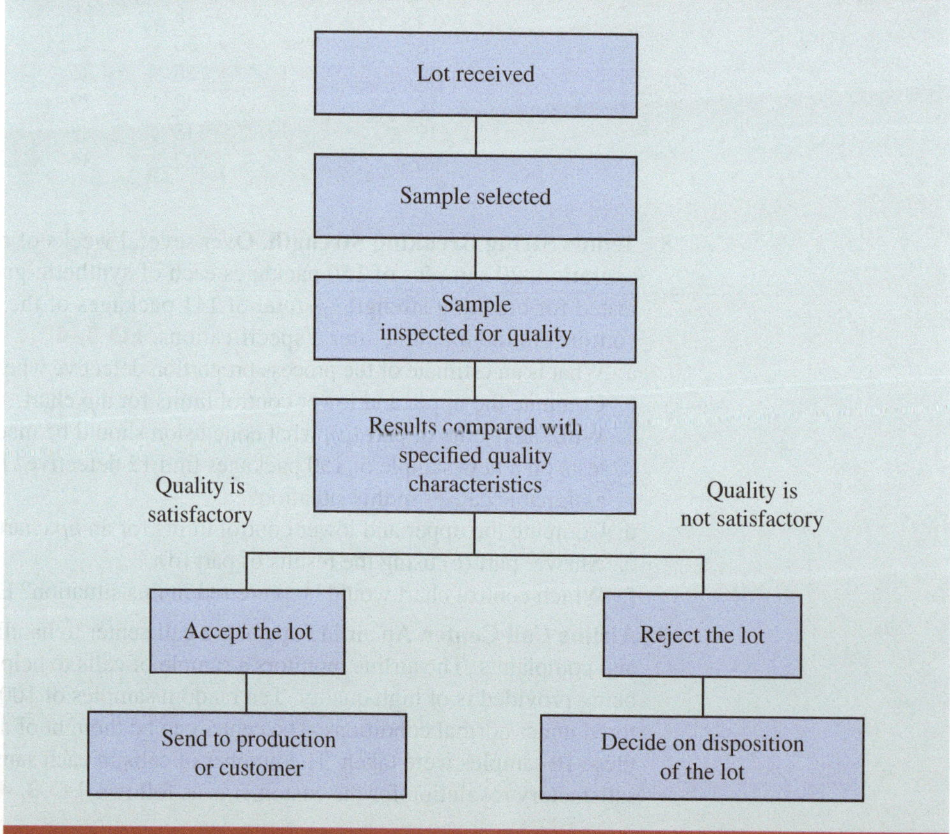

Table 19.4 The Outcomes of Acceptance Sampling

		State of the Lot	
		H_0 True Good-Quality Lot	H_0 False Poor-Quality Lot
Decision	Accept the Lot	Correct decision	Type II error (accepting a poor-quality lot)
	Reject the Lot	Type I error (rejecting a good-quality lot)	Correct decision

the supplier to provide high-quality lots. Finally, if the rejected lot consists of finished goods, the goods must be scrapped or reworked to meet acceptable quality standards.

Hypothesis testing was introduced in Chapter 9.

The statistical procedure of acceptance sampling uses the null and alternative hypotheses stated as follows.

H_0: Good-quality lot
H_a: Poor-quality lot

Table 19.4 shows the results of the hypothesis testing procedure. Note that correct decisions correspond to accepting a good-quality lot and rejecting a poor-quality lot. However, as with other hypothesis testing procedures, we need to be aware of the possibilities of making a Type I error (rejecting a good-quality lot) or a Type II error (accepting a poor-quality lot).

The probability of a Type I error creates a risk for the producer of the lot and is known as the **producer's risk**. For example, a producer's risk of 0.05 indicates a 5% chance that a good-quality lot will be erroneously rejected. The probability of a Type II error, on the other hand, creates a risk for the consumer of the lot and is known as the **consumer's risk**. For example, a consumer's risk of 0.10 means a 10% chance that a poor-quality lot will be erroneously accepted and thus used in production or shipped to the customer. Specific values for the producer's risk and the consumer's risk can be controlled by the person designing the acceptance sampling procedure. To illustrate how to assign risk values, let us consider the problem faced by KALI, Inc.

KALI, Inc.: An Example of Acceptance Sampling

KALI, Inc., manufactures home appliances that are marketed under a variety of trade names. However, KALI does not manufacture every component used in its products. Several components are purchased directly from suppliers. For example, one of the components that KALI purchases for use in home air conditioners is an overload protector, a device that turns off the compressor if it overheats. The compressor can be seriously damaged if the overload protector does not function properly, and therefore KALI is concerned about the quality of the overload protectors. One way to ensure quality would be to test every component received through an approach known as 100% inspection. However, to determine proper functioning of an overload protector, the device must be subjected to time-consuming and expensive tests, and KALI cannot justify testing every overload protector it receives.

Instead, KALI uses an acceptance sampling plan to monitor the quality of the overload protectors. The acceptance sampling plan requires that KALI's quality control inspectors select and test a sample of overload protectors from each shipment. If very few defective units are found in the sample, the lot is probably of good quality and should be accepted. However, if a large number of defective units are found in the sample, the lot is probably of poor quality and should be rejected.

An acceptance sampling plan consists of a sample size n and an acceptance criterion c. The **acceptance criterion** is the maximum number of defective items that can be found in the sample and still indicate an acceptable lot. For example, for the KALI problem let us assume that a sample of 15 items will be selected from each incoming shipment or lot. Furthermore, assume that the manager of quality control states that the lot can be accepted only if no defective items are found. In this case, the acceptance sampling plan established by the quality control manager is $n = 15$ and $c = 0$.

This acceptance sampling plan is easy for the quality control inspector to implement. The inspector simply selects a sample of 15 items, performs the tests, and reaches a conclusion based on the following decision rule.

- *Accept the lot* if zero defective items are found.
- *Reject the lot* if one or more defective items are found.

Before implementing this acceptance sampling plan, the quality control manager wants to evaluate the risks or errors possible under the plan. The plan will be implemented only if both the producer's risk (Type I error) and the consumer's risk (Type II error) are controlled at reasonable levels.

Computing the Probability of Accepting a Lot

The key to analyzing both the producer's risk and the consumer's risk is a "what-if" type of analysis. That is, we will assume that a lot has some known percentage of defective items and compute the probability of accepting the lot for a given sampling plan. By varying the assumed percentage of defective items, we can examine the effect of the sampling plan on both types of risks.

The binomial probability function is introduced in Chapter 5.

Let us begin by assuming that a large shipment of overload protectors has been received and that 5% of the overload protectors in the shipment are defective. For a shipment or lot with 5% of the items defective, what is the probability that the $n = 15$, $c = 0$ sampling plan will lead us to accept the lot? Because each overload protector tested will be either defective or nondefective and because the lot size is large, the number of defective items in a sample of 15 has a binomial distribution. The binomial probability function is as follows.

Binomial Probability Function for Acceptance Sampling

$$f(x) = \frac{n!}{x!(n-x)!}p^x(1-p)^{(n-x)} \tag{19.21}$$

where

n = the sample size
p = the proportion of defective items in the lot
x = the number of defective items in the sample
$f(x)$ = the probability of x defective items in the sample

For the KALI acceptance sampling plan, $n = 15$; thus, for a lot with 5% defective ($p = 0.05$), we have

$$f(x) = \frac{15!}{x!(15-x)!}(0.05)^x(1-0.05)^{(15-x)} \tag{19.22}$$

Using equation (19.22), $f(0)$ will provide the probability that zero overload protectors will be defective and the lot will be accepted. In using equation (19.22), recall that $0! = 1$. Thus, the probability computation for $f(0)$ is

$$f(0) = \frac{15!}{0!(15-0)!}(0.05)^0(1-0.05)^{(15-0)}$$

$$= \frac{15!}{0!(15)!}(0.05)^0(0.95)^{15} = (0.95)^{15} = 0.4633$$

Table 19.5 Probability of Accepting the Lot for the KALI Problem with $n = 15$ and $c = 0$

Percent Defective in the Lot	Probability of Accepting the Lot
1	0.8601
2	0.7386
3	0.6333
4	0.5421
5	0.4633
10	0.2059
15	0.0874
20	0.0352
25	0.0134

We now know that the $n = 15$, $c = 0$ sampling plan has a 0.4633 probability of accepting a lot with 5% defective items. Hence, there must be a corresponding $1 - 0.4633 = 0.5367$ probability of rejecting a lot with 5% defective items.

Excel's BINOM.DIST function can be used to simplify making these binomial probability calculations. Using this function, we can determine that if the lot contains 10% defective items, there is a 0.2059 probability that the $n = 15$, $c = 0$ sampling plan will indicate an acceptable lot. The probability that the $n = 15$, $c = 0$ sampling plan will lead to the acceptance of lots with 1%, 2%, 3%, . . . defective items is summarized in Table 19.5.

Using the probabilities in Table 19.5, a graph of the probability of accepting the lot versus the percent defective in the lot can be drawn as shown in Figure 19.12. This graph, or curve, is called the **operating characteristic (OC) curve** for the $n = 15$, $c = 0$ acceptance sampling plan.

Figure 19.12 Operating Characteristic Curve for the $n = 15$, $c = 0$ Acceptance Sampling Plan

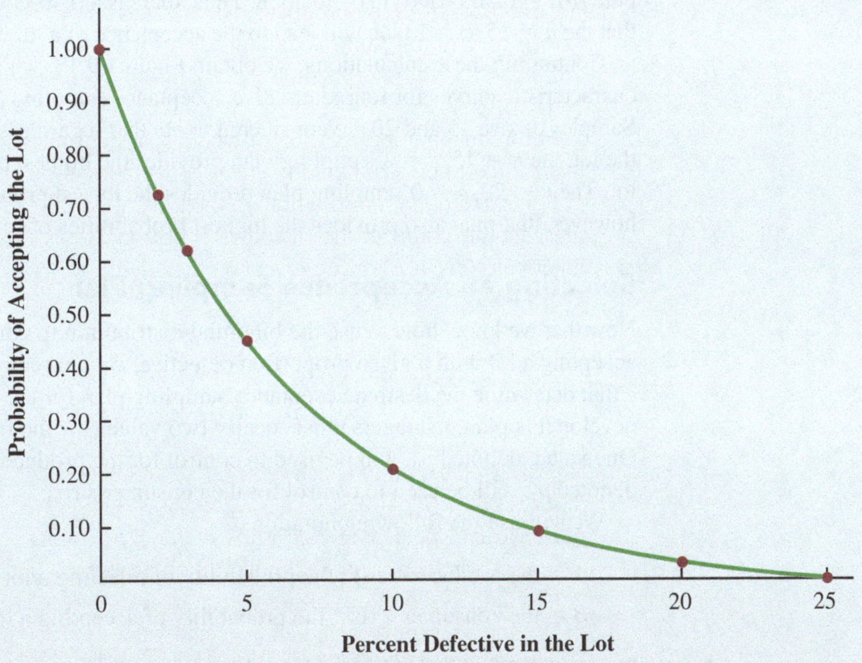

Figure 19.13 Operating Characteristic Curves for Four Acceptance Sampling Plans

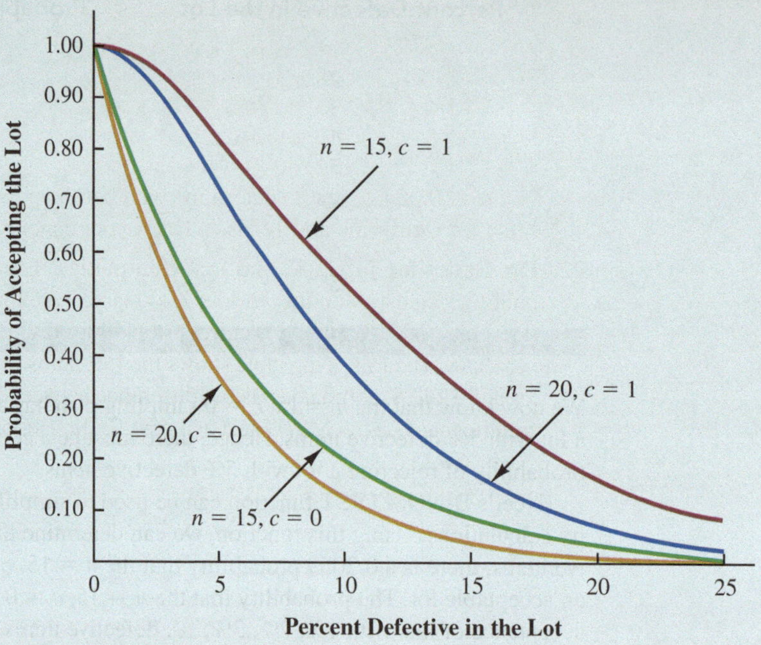

We can also use Excel's BINOM.DIST function to compute these probabilities.

Perhaps we should consider other sampling plans, ones with different sample sizes n or different acceptance criteria c. First consider the case in which the sample size remains $n = 15$ but the acceptance criterion increases from $c = 0$ to $c = 1$. That is, we will now accept the lot if zero or one defective component is found in the sample. For a lot with 5% defective items ($p = 0.05$), the binomial probability function in equation (19.21) can be used to compute $f(0) = 0.4633$ and $f(1) = 0.3658$. Thus, there is a $0.4633 + 0.3658 = 0.8291$ probability that the $n = 15$, $c = 1$ plan will lead to the acceptance of a lot with 5% defective items.

Continuing these calculations, we obtain Figure 19.13, which shows the operating characteristic curves for four alternative acceptance sampling plans for the KALI problem. Samples of size 15 and 20 are considered. Note that regardless of the proportion defective in the lot, the $n = 15$, $c = 1$ sampling plan provides the highest probabilities of accepting the lot. The $n = 20$, $c = 0$ sampling plan provides the lowest probabilities of accepting the lot; however, that plan also provides the highest probabilities of rejecting the lot.

Selecting an Acceptance Sampling Plan

Now that we know how to use the binomial distribution to compute the probability of accepting a lot with a given proportion defective, we are ready to select the values of n and c that determine the desired acceptance sampling plan for the application being studied. To develop this plan, managers must specify two values for the fraction defective in the lot. One value, denoted p_0, will be used to control for the producer's risk, and the other value, denoted p_1, will be used to control for the consumer's risk.

We will use the following notation.

α = the producer's risk; the probability of rejecting a lot with p_0 defective items

β = the consumer's risk; the probability of accepting a lot with p_1 defective items

Suppose that for the KALI problem, the managers specify that $p_0 = 0.03$ and $p_1 = 0.15$. From the OC curve for $n = 15$, $c = 0$ in Figure 19.14, we see that $p_0 = 0.03$ provides a

Figure 19.14 Operating Characteristic Curve for $n = 15$, $c = 0$ with $p_0 = 0.03$ and $p_1 = 0.15$

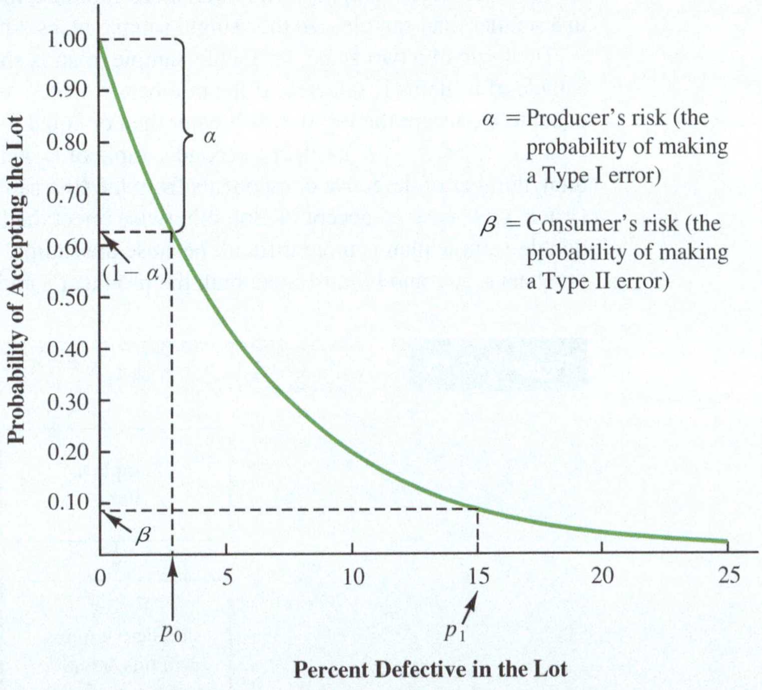

producer's risk of approximately $1 - 0.63 = 0.37$, and $p_1 = 0.15$ provides a consumer's risk of approximately 0.09. Thus, if the managers are willing to tolerate both a 0.37 probability of rejecting a lot with 3% defective items (producer's risk) and a 0.09 probability of accepting a lot with 15% defective items (consumer's risk), the $n = 15$, $c = 0$ acceptance sampling plan would be acceptable.

Suppose, however, that the managers request a producer's risk of $\alpha = 0.10$ and a consumer's risk of $\beta = 0.19$. We see that now the $n = 15$, $c = 0$ sampling plan has a better-than-desired consumer's risk but an unacceptably large producer's risk. The fact that $\alpha = 0.37$ indicates that 37% of the lots will be erroneously rejected when only 3% of the items in them are defective. The producer's risk is too high, and a different acceptance sampling plan should be considered.

Using $p_0 = 0.03$, $\alpha = 0.10$, $p_1 = 0.15$, and $\beta = 0.20$, Figure 19.13 shows that the acceptance sampling plan with $n = 20$ and $c = 1$ comes closest to meeting both the producer's and the consumer's risk requirements.

As shown in this section, several computations and several operating characteristic curves may need to be considered to determine the sampling plan with the desired producer's and consumer's risk. Fortunately, tables of sampling plans are published. For example, the American Military Standard Table, MIL-STD-105D, provides information helpful in designing acceptance sampling plans. More advanced texts on quality control, such as those listed in the bibliography, describe the use of such tables. The advanced texts also discuss the role of sampling costs in determining the optimal sampling plan.

Multiple Sampling Plans

The acceptance sampling procedure we presented for the KALI problem is a *single-sample* plan. It is called a single-sample plan because only one sample or sampling stage is used. After the number of defective components in the sample is determined, a decision must be made to accept or reject the lot. An alternative to the single-sample plan is a **multiple sampling plan**, in which two or more stages of sampling are used. At each stage a decision is made among three possibilities: stop sampling and accept the lot, stop sampling and reject the lot, or continue sampling. Although more complex, multiple sampling plans often result in a smaller total sample size than single-sample plans with the same α and β probabilities.

The logic of a two-stage, or double-sample, plan is shown in Figure 19.15. Initially a sample of n_1 items is selected. If the number of defective components x_1 is less than or equal to c_1, accept the lot. If x_1 is greater than or equal to c_2, reject the lot. If x_1 is between c_1 and c_2 ($c_1 < x_1 < c_2$), select a second sample of n_2 items. Determine the combined, or total, number of defective components from the first sample (x_1) and the second sample (x_2). If $x_1 + x_2 \leq c_3$, accept the lot; otherwise reject the lot. The development of the double-sample plan is more difficult because the sample sizes n_1 and n_2 and the acceptance numbers c_1, c_2, and c_3 must meet both the producer's and consumer's risks desired.

Figure 19.15 A Two-Stage Acceptance Sampling Plan

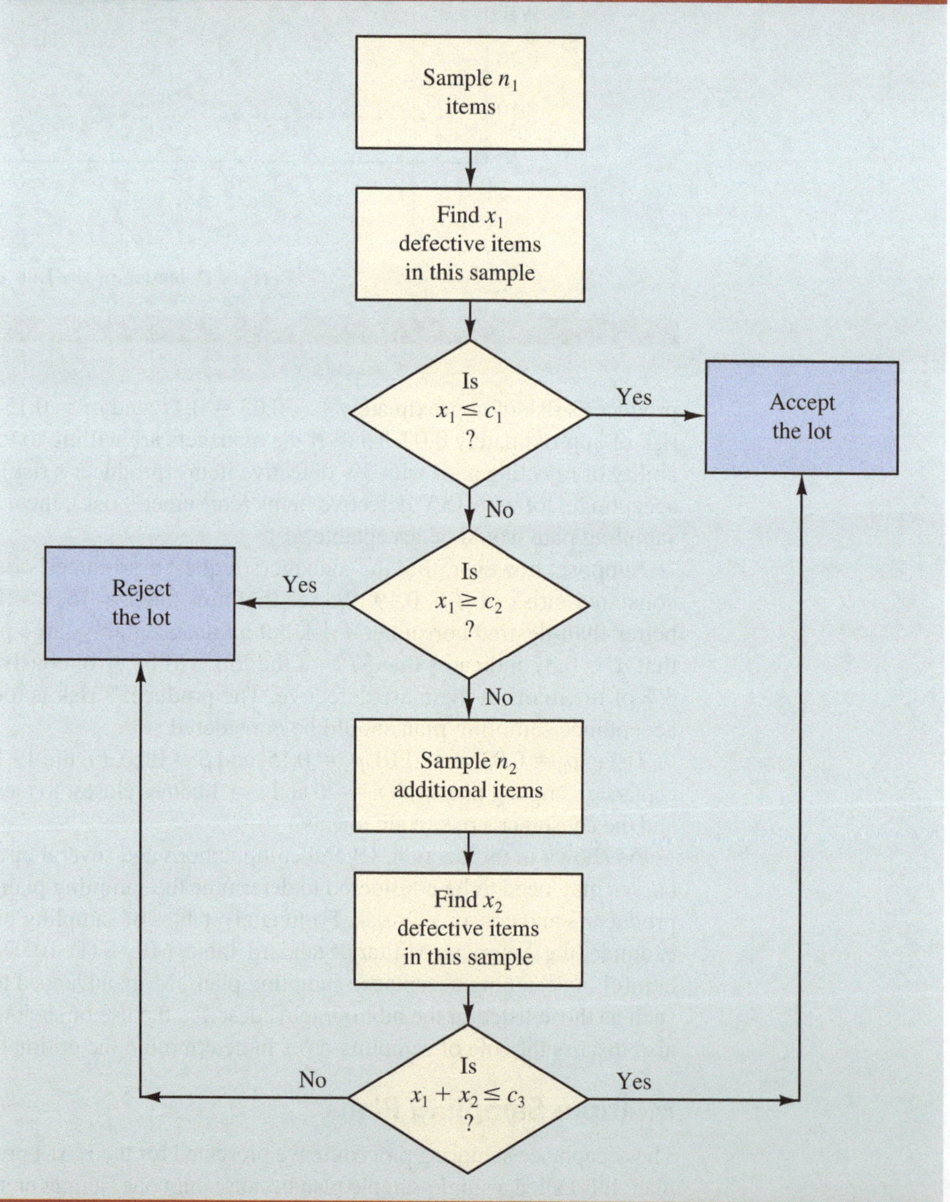

Notes + Comments

1. Acceptance sampling has the following advantages over 100% inspection: (a) usually less expensive; (b) less product damage due to less handling and testing; (c) fewer inspectors required; (d) it is the only approach possible if destructive testing must be used.
2. The use of the binomial distribution for acceptance sampling is based on the assumption of large lots. If the lot size is small, the hypergeometric distribution is appropriate.
3. In the MIL-STD-105D sampling tables, p_0 is called the acceptable quality level (AQL). In some sampling tables, p_1 is called the lot tolerance percent defective (LTPD) or the rejectable quality level (RQL). Many of the published sampling plans also use quality indexes such as the indifference quality level (IQL) and the average outgoing quality limit (AOQL). The more advanced texts listed in the bibliography provide a complete discussion of these other indexes.
4. In this section, we provided an introduction to *attributes sampling plans*. In these plans, each item sampled is classified as nondefective or defective. In *variables sampling plans*, a sample is taken and a measurement of the quality characteristic is taken. For example, for gold jewelry a measurement of quality may be the amount of gold it contains. A simple statistic such as the average amount of gold in the sample jewelry is computed and compared with an allowable value to determine whether to accept or reject the lot.

Exercises

Methods

10. For an acceptance sampling plan with $n = 25$ and $c = 0$, find the probability of accepting a lot that has a defect rate of 2%. What is the probability of accepting the lot if the defect rate is 6%? **LO 5**
11. Consider an acceptance sampling plan with $n = 20$ and $c = 0$. Compute the producer's risk for each of the following cases. **LO 7**
    a. The lot has a defect rate of 2%.
    b. The lot has a defect rate of 6%.
12. Repeat exercise 11 for the acceptance sampling plan with $n = 20$ and $c = 1$. What happens to the producer's risk as the acceptance number c is increased? Explain. **LO 7**

Applications

13. **KALI Home Appliance Manufacturer.** Refer to the KALI problem presented in this section. The quality control manager requested a producer's risk of 0.10 when p_0 was 0.03 and a consumer's risk of 0.20 when p_1 was 0.15. Consider the acceptance sampling plan based on a sample size of 20 and an acceptance number of 1. Answer the following questions. **LO 7**
    a. What is the producer's risk for the $n = 20$, $c = 1$ sampling plan?
    b. What is the consumer's risk for the $n = 20$, $c = 1$ sampling plan?
    c. Does the $n = 20$, $c = 1$ sampling plan satisfy the risks requested by the quality control manager? Discuss.
14. **Incoming Shipments of Raw Materials.** To inspect incoming shipments of raw materials, a manufacturer is considering samples of sizes 10, 15, and 19. Use Excel's BINOM.DIST function to select a sampling plan that provides a producer's risk of $\alpha = 0.03$ when p_0 is 0.05 and a consumer's risk of $\beta = 0.12$ when p_1 is 0.30. **LO 7, 8**
15. **Quartz Crystals.** A domestic manufacturer of watches purchases quartz crystals from a Swiss firm. The crystals are shipped in lots of 1000. The acceptance sampling procedure uses 20 randomly selected crystals. **LO 6, 7**
    a. Construct operating characteristic curves for acceptance numbers of 0, 1, and 2.
    b. If p_0 is 0.01 and $p_1 = 0.08$, what are the producer's and consumer's risks for each sampling plan in part (a)?

Summary

In this chapter, we discussed how statistical methods can be used to assist in the control of quality. We first introduced some quality-management philosophies such as the Malcolm Baldrige National Quality Award, ISO 9001, and Six Sigma. We then presented the $\bar{x}$, R, p, and np control charts as graphical aids in monitoring process quality. Control limits are established for each chart; samples are selected periodically, and the data points plotted on the control chart. Data points outside the control limits indicate that the process is out of control and that corrective action should be taken. Patterns of data points within the control limits can also indicate potential quality control problems and suggest that corrective action may be warranted.

We also considered the technique known as acceptance sampling. With this procedure, a sample is selected and inspected. The number of defective items in the sample provides the basis for accepting or rejecting the lot. The sample size and the acceptance criterion can be adjusted to control both the producer's risk (Type I error) and the consumer's risk (Type II error).

Glossary

Acceptance criterion The maximum number of defective items that can be found in the sample and still indicate an acceptable lot.

Acceptance sampling A statistical method in which the number of defective items found in a sample is used to determine whether a lot should be accepted or rejected.

Assignable causes Variations in process outputs that are due to factors such as machine tools wearing out, incorrect machine settings, poor-quality raw materials, and operator error. Corrective action should be taken when assignable causes of output variation are detected.

Common causes Normal or natural variations in process outputs that are due purely to chance. No corrective action is necessary when output variations are due to common causes.

Consumer's risk The risk of accepting a poor-quality lot; a Type II error.

Control chart A graphical tool used to help determine whether a process is in control or out of control.

Lot A group of items such as incoming shipments of raw materials or purchased parts as well as finished goods from final assembly.

Multiple sampling plan A form of acceptance sampling in which more than one sample or stage is used. On the basis of the number of defective items found in a sample, a decision will be made to accept the lot, reject the lot, or continue sampling.

***np* chart** A control chart used to monitor the quality of the output of a process in terms of the number of defective items.

Operating characteristic (OC) curve A graph showing the probability of accepting the lot as a function of the percentage defective in the lot. This curve can be used to help determine whether a particular acceptance sampling plan meets both the producer's and the consumer's risk requirements.

***p* chart** A control chart used when the quality of the output of a process is measured in terms of the proportion defective.

Producer's risk The risk of rejecting a good-quality lot; a Type I error.

Quality control A series of inspections and measurements that determine whether quality standards are being met.

***R* chart** A control chart used when the quality of the output of a process is measured in terms of the range of a variable.

Six Sigma A methodology that uses measurement and statistical analysis to achieve a level of quality so good that for every million opportunities no more than 3.4 defects will occur.

Total quality (TQ) A total system approach to improving customer satisfaction and lowering real cost through a strategy of continuous improvement and learning.

$\bar{x}$ chart A control chart used when the quality of the output of a process is measured in terms of the mean value of a variable such as a length, weight, or temperature.

Key Formulas

Standard Error of the Mean

$$\sigma_{\bar{x}} = \frac{\sigma}{\sqrt{n}} \tag{19.1}$$

Control Limits for an x Chart: Process Mean and Standard Deviation Known

$$\text{UCL} = \mu + 3\sigma_{\bar{x}} \tag{19.2}$$
$$\text{LCL} = \mu - 3\sigma_{\bar{x}} \tag{19.3}$$

Overall Sample Mean

$$\bar{\bar{x}} = \frac{\bar{x}_1 + \bar{x}_2 + \cdots + \bar{x}_k}{k} \tag{19.4}$$

Average Range

$$\bar{R} = \frac{R_1 + R_2 + \cdots + R_k}{k} \tag{19.5}$$

Control Limits for an $\bar{x}$ Chart: Process Mean and Standard Deviation Unknown

$$\text{UCL} = \bar{\bar{x}} + A_2\bar{R} \tag{19.8}$$
$$\text{LCL} = \bar{\bar{x}} - A_2\bar{R}$$

Control Limits for an R Chart

$$\text{UCL} = \bar{R}D_4 \tag{19.14}$$
$$\text{LCL} = \bar{R}D_3 \tag{19.15}$$

Standard Error of the Proportion

$$\sigma_{\bar{p}} = \sqrt{\frac{p(1-p)}{n}} \tag{19.16}$$

Control Limits for a p Chart

$$\text{UCL} = p + 3\sigma_{\bar{p}} \tag{19.17}$$
$$\text{LCL} = p - 3\sigma_{\bar{p}} \tag{19.18}$$

Control Limits for an np Chart

$$\text{UCL} = np + 3\sqrt{np(1-p)} \tag{19.19}$$
$$\text{LCL} = np - 3\sqrt{np(1-p)} \tag{19.20}$$

Binomial Probability Function for Acceptance Sampling

$$f(x) = \frac{n!}{x!(n-x)!}p^x(1-p)^{(n-x)} \tag{19.21}$$

Supplementary Exercises

16. **Production Quality.** Samples of size 5 provided the following 20 sample means for a production process that is believed to be in control. **LO 1**

DATA*file*
productionquality

95.72	95.24	95.18
95.44	95.46	95.32
95.40	95.44	95.08
95.50	95.80	95.22
95.56	95.22	95.04
95.72	94.82	95.46
95.60	95.78	

a. Based on these data, what is an estimate of the mean when the process is in control?
b. Assume that the process standard deviation is $\sigma = 0.50$. Develop the $\bar{x}$ control chart for this production process. Assume that the mean of the process is the estimate developed in part (a).
c. Do any of the 20 sample means indicate that the process was out of control?

17. **Filling Rates.** Product filling weights are normally distributed with a mean of 350 grams and a standard deviation of 15 grams. **LO 1**
a. Develop the control limits for the $\bar{x}$ chart for samples of size 10, 20, and 30.
b. What happens to the control limits as the sample size is increased?
c. What happens when a Type I error is made?
d. What happens when a Type II error is made?
e. What is the probability of a Type I error for samples of size 10, 20, and 30?
f. What is the advantage of increasing the sample size for control chart purposes? What error probability is reduced as the sample size is increased?

18. **Control Limits.** Twenty-five samples of size 5 resulted in $\bar{\bar{x}} = 5.42$ and $\bar{R} = 2.0$. Compute control limits for the $\bar{x}$ and R charts, and estimate the standard deviation of the process. **LO 1, 2**

19. **Temperature for a Chemical Manufacturing Process.** The following are quality control data for a manufacturing process at Kensport Chemical Company. The data show the temperature in degrees centigrade at five points in time during a manufacturing cycle. The company is interested in using control charts to monitor the temperature of its manufacturing process. The data are in the file *kensport*. Construct the $\bar{x}$ chart and R chart. What conclusions can be made about the quality of the process? **LO 1, 2**

DATA*file*
kensport

Sample	$\bar{x}$	R	Sample	$\bar{x}$	R
1	95.72	1.0	11	95.80	0.6
2	95.24	0.9	12	95.22	0.2
3	95.18	0.8	13	95.56	1.3
4	95.44	0.4	14	95.22	0.5
5	95.46	0.5	15	95.04	0.8
6	95.32	1.1	16	95.72	1.1
7	95.40	0.9	17	94.82	0.6
8	95.44	0.3	18	95.46	0.5
9	95.08	0.2	19	95.60	0.4
10	95.50	0.6	20	95.74	0.6

20. **Filling Weights for a Coffee Production Process.** The following were collected for the Master Blend Coffee production process. The data show the filling weights based on samples of three-pound cans of coffee. Use these data to construct the $\bar{x}$ and R charts. What conclusions can be made about the quality of the production process? **LO 1, 2**

DATA*file*
coffee

	Observations				
Sample	1	2	3	4	5
1	3.05	3.08	3.07	3.11	3.11
2	3.13	3.07	3.05	3.10	3.10
3	3.06	3.04	3.12	3.11	3.10
4	3.09	3.08	3.09	3.09	3.07
5	3.10	3.06	3.06	3.07	3.08
6	3.08	3.10	3.13	3.03	3.06
7	3.06	3.06	3.08	3.10	3.08
8	3.11	3.08	3.07	3.07	3.07
9	3.09	3.09	3.08	3.07	3.09
10	3.06	3.11	3.07	3.09	3.07

21. **Processing Insurance Claims.** An insurance company samples claim forms for errors created by its employees as well as the amount of time it takes to process a claim. **LO 1, 3**
    a. When the process is in control, the proportion of claims with an error is 0.033. A p chart has LCL $= 0$ and UCL $= 0.068$. Plot the following seven sample results: 0.035, 0.062, 0.055, 0.049, 0.058, 0.066, and 0.055. Comment on whether there might be concern about the quality of the process.
    b. An $\bar{x}$ chart for the mean processing time has LCL $= 22.2$ and UCL $= 24.5$. The mean is $\mu = 23.35$ when the claim process is in control. Plot the following seven sample results: 22.4, 22.6, 22.65, 23.2, 23.4, 23.85, and 24.1. Comment on whether there might be concern about the quality of the process.
22. **Retail Restocking.** Managers of 1,200 different retail outlets make twice-a-month restocking orders from a central warehouse. Past experience shows that 4% of the orders result in one or more errors such as wrong item shipped, wrong quantity shipped, and item requested but not shipped. Random samples of 200 orders are selected monthly and checked for accuracy. **LO 3**
    a. Construct a control chart for this situation.
    b. Six months of data show the following numbers of orders with one or more errors: 10, 15, 6, 13, 8, and 17. Plot the data on the control chart. What does your plot indicate about the order process?

DATA*file*
callrouting

23. **Call Routing.** Carson Airlines uses a voice-recognition program to route passenger calls to its consumer hotline to various problem specialists. Based on customer voice responses, the call is routed to a specialist in a given problem-area (delayed flight, lost luggage, etc.). Based on testing, the probability of a defective routing when the program is in control is 0.025. The file *callrouting* contains ten samples of 250 calls each, along with the number of incorrect routings. **LO 4**
    a. Calculate the upper and lower control limits for an np chart.
    b. Construct an np chart using the upper and lower control limits calculated in part (a) and the ten samples.
    c. Comment on whether there might be concern. Does the process appear to be in control or out of control for these ten samples?
24. **Producer and Consumer Risk.** An $n = 10$, $c = 2$ acceptance sampling plan is being considered; assume that $p_0 = 0.05$ and $p_1 = 0.20$. **LO 7, 8**
    a. Compute both producer's and consumer's risk for this acceptance sampling plan.
    b. Would the producer, the consumer, or both be unhappy with the proposed sampling plan?
    c. What change in the sampling plan, if any, would you recommend?

25. **Calculating Consumer Risk.** An acceptance sampling plan with $n = 15$ and $c = 1$ has been designed with a producer's risk of 0.075. **LO 5, 7**
   a. Which of the following was the value of p_0: 0.01, 0.02, 0.03, 0.04, or 0.05? What does this value mean?
   b. What is the consumer's risk associated with this plan if p_1 is 0.25?
26. **Acceptance Sampling in Food Production.** A manufacturer produces lots of a canned food product. Let p denote the proportion of the lots that do not meet the product quality specifications. An $n = 25$, $c = 0$ acceptance sampling plan will be used. **LO 5, 6**
   a. Compute points on the operating characteristic curve when $p = 0.01, 0.03, 0.10$, and 0.20.
   b. Plot the operating characteristic curve.
   c. What is the probability that the acceptance sampling plan will reject a lot containing 0.01 defective?

Chapter 20

Decision Analysis

Contents

Statistics In Practice:
U.S. Centers for Disease Control and Prevention

20.1 Problem Formulation
Payoff Tables
Decision Trees

20.2 Decision Making with Probabilities
Expected Value Approach
Expected Value of Perfect Information

20.3 Decision Analysis with Sample Information
Decision Tree
Decision Strategy
Expected Value of Sample Information

20.4 Computing Branch Probabilities Using Bayes' Theorem

Summary 977
Glossary 977
Key Formulas 978
Supplementary Exercises 978
Case Problem 1: Lawsuit Defense Strategy 982
Case Problem 2: Property Purchase Strategy 983

Learning Objectives

After completing this chapter, you will be able to

LO 1 Construct and interpret payoff tables and decision trees for a decision problem.

LO 2 Use the expected value approach to determine the optimal decision for a decision maker.

LO 3 Calculate and interpret the expected value of perfect information for a decision problem.

LO 4 Calculate and interpret the expected value of sample information for a decision problem.

LO 5 Use Bayes' theorem to calculate and interpret posterior probabilities for a decision problem.

Statistics in Practice

U.S. Centers for Disease Control and Prevention*

Over the course of history, polio has been one of the most terrifying diseases known to humans. Polio is caused by the poliovirus. Wild polioviruses (WPVs) refer to polioviruses that exist in the wild, rather than viruses that are derived from vaccines. WPVs are typically transmitted when contaminated water or food is ingested by an uninfected person, which can be common in areas with poor hygiene or poor sanitation. In the 1950s, polio vaccines were developed separately by Jonas Salk and Albert Sabin. These vaccines led to the eradication of WPV transmission in the United States by 1979 and throughout the western hemisphere by 1991. However, polio remains endemic to several countries around the world, which puts all other populations at risk of infection.

The Global Polio Eradication Initiative (GPEI) seeks to eradicate polio worldwide. It is financed by a variety of public and private donors including the World Health Organization, the U.S. Centers for Disease Control and Prevention (CDC), and the Bill & Melinda Gates Foundation. The CDC collaborated with Kid Risk, Inc. to use analytics tools to evaluate the policy options available for pursuing global polio eradication in terms of benefits, risks, and costs. The researchers used a variety of decision analysis tools, including decision trees, to consider the many different options available to potentially eradicate polio around the world. These policy decisions include such options as using oral poliovirus vaccines (OPVs), inactivated poliovirus vaccines (IPVs), and whether to continue routine vaccinations after WPV-transmission has been eradicated. The decision trees allowed the researchers to capture much of the complexity inherent in such a large-scale decision problem and to evaluate the relative risks, benefits, and costs of different policy options. The uncertainties in costs were modeled using 47 different probability distributions for cost inputs, and cost data were collected through extensive data collection efforts led by the Global Polio Laboratory Network.

The findings from the decision analysis model led researchers to understand that the speed with which medical professionals respond to a polio outbreak can be more effective than having extremely high rates of WPV immunity through vaccinations. The models also allowed the researchers to calculate the cost tradeoffs of eradicating polio worldwide versus responding to greater polio outbreaks. The research provided extensive evidence of the value of the GPEI by showing that net benefits of countries covered by the GPEI approach \$40–\$50 billion. The work done by these researchers was recognized with the 2014 INFORMS Franz Edelman Award based on the enormous financial and global health impacts from these analytical models and the derived insights.

*Source: Based on K. M. Thompson, R. J. Duintjer Tebbens, M. A. Pallansch, S. G. F. Wassilak, S. L. Cochi, "Polio Eradicators Use Integrated Analytical Models to Make Better Decisions," Interfaces, 45, no. 1, (January-February 2015), 1–16.

Decision analysis can be used to develop an optimal decision strategy when a decision maker is faced with several decision alternatives and an uncertain or risk-filled pattern of future events. We begin the study of decision analysis by considering decision problems that involve reasonably few decision alternatives and reasonably few future events. Payoff tables are introduced to provide a structure for decision problems. We then introduce decision trees to show the sequential nature of the problems. Decision trees are used to analyze more complex problems and to identify an optimal sequence of decisions, referred to as an optimal decision strategy. In the last section, we show how Bayes' theorem can be used to compute branch probabilities for decision trees.

Bayes' theorem was first introduced in Chapter 4.

20.1 Problem Formulation

The first step in the decision analysis process is problem formulation. We begin with a verbal statement of the problem. We then identify the decision alternatives, the uncertain future events, referred to as **chance events**, and the **consequences** associated with each decision alternative and each chance event outcome. Let us begin by considering a construction project for the Pittsburgh Development Corporation.

Pittsburgh Development Corporation (PDC) purchased land that will be the site of a new luxury condominium complex. The location provides a spectacular view of downtown Pittsburgh and the Golden Triangle where the Allegheny and Monongahela Rivers meet to form the Ohio River. PDC plans to price the individual condominium units between \$300,000 and \$1,400,000.

PDC commissioned preliminary architectural drawings for three different-sized projects: one with 30 condominiums, one with 60 condominiums, and one with 90 condominiums. The financial success of the project depends upon the size of the condominium complex and the chance event concerning the demand for the condominiums. The statement of the PDC decision problem is to select the size of the new luxury condominium project that will lead to the largest profit given the uncertainty concerning the demand for the condominiums.

Given the statement of the problem, it is clear that the decision is to select the best size for the condominium complex. PDC has the following three decision alternatives:

d_1 = a small complex with 30 condominiums
d_2 = a medium complex with 60 condominiums
d_3 = a large complex with 90 condominiums

A factor in selecting the best decision alternative is the uncertainty associated with the chance event concerning the demand for the condominiums. When asked about the possible demand for the condominiums, PDC's president acknowledged a wide range of possibilities but decided that it would be adequate to consider two possible chance event outcomes: a strong demand and a weak demand.

In decision analysis, the possible outcomes for a chance event are referred to as the **states of nature**. The states of nature are defined so that one and only one of the possible states of nature will occur. For the PDC problem, the chance event concerning the demand for the condominiums has two states of nature:

s_1 = strong demand for the condominiums
s_2 = weak demand for the condominiums

Management must first select a decision alternative (complex size), then a state of nature follows (demand for the condominiums), and finally a consequence will occur. In this case, the consequence is PDC's profit.

Payoff Tables

Given the three decision alternatives and the two states of nature, which complex size should PDC choose? To answer this question, PDC will need to know the consequence associated with each decision alternative and each state of nature. In decision analysis, we refer to the consequence resulting from a specific combination of a decision alternative and a state of nature as a **payoff**. A table showing payoffs for all combinations of decision alternatives and states of nature is a **payoff table**.

Payoffs can be expressed in terms of profit, cost, time, distance, or any other measure appropriate for the decision problem being analyzed.

Because PDC wants to select the complex size that provides the largest profit, profit is used as the consequence. The payoff table with profits expressed in millions of dollars is shown in Table 20.1. Note, for example, that if a medium complex is built and demand turns out to be strong, a profit of \$14 million will be realized. We will use the notation V_{ij} to denote the payoff associated with decision alternative i and state of nature j. Using Table 20.1, $V_{31} = 20$ indicates a payoff of \$20 million occurs if the decision is to build a large complex (d_3) and the strong demand state of nature (s_1) occurs. Similarly, $V_{32} = -9$ indicates a loss of \$9 million if the decision is to build a large complex (d_3) and the weak demand state of nature (s_2) occurs.

Table 20.1 Payoff Table for the PDC Condominium Project (Payoffs in $ Millions)

	State of Nature	
Decision Alternative	**Strong Demand, s_1**	**Weak Demand, s_2**
Small complex, d_1	8	7
Medium complex, d_2	14	5
Large complex, d_3	20	−9

Decision Trees

A **decision tree** graphically shows the sequential nature of the decision-making process. Figure 20.1 presents a decision tree for the PDC problem, demonstrating the natural or logical progression that will occur over time. First, PDC must make a decision regarding the size of the condominium complex (d_1, d_2, or d_3). Then, after the decision is implemented, either state of nature s_1 or s_2 will occur. The number at each end point of the tree indicates the payoff associated with a particular sequence. For example, the topmost payoff of 8 indicates that an $8 million profit is anticipated if PDC constructs a small condominium complex (d_1) and demand turns out to be strong (s_1). The next payoff of 7 indicates an anticipated profit of $7 million if PDC constructs a small condominium complex (d_1) and demand turns out to be weak (s_2). Thus, the decision tree shows graphically the sequences of decision alternatives and states of nature that provide the six possible payoffs.

The decision tree in Figure 20.1 has four **nodes**, numbered 1–4, that represent the decisions and chance events. Squares are used to depict **decision nodes** and circles are used

Figure 20.1 Decision Tree for the PDC Condominium Project (Payoffs in $ Millions)

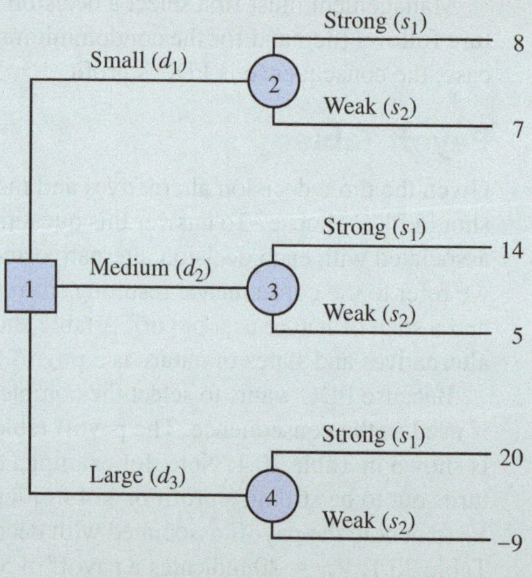

to depict **chance nodes**. Thus, node 1 is a decision node, and nodes 2, 3, and 4 are chance nodes. The **branches** leaving the decision node correspond to the decision alternatives. The branches leaving each chance node correspond to the states of nature. The payoffs are shown at the end of the states-of-nature branches. We now turn to the question: How can the decision maker use the information in the payoff table or the decision tree to select the best decision alternative? Several possible approaches are covered in the remaining sections of this chapter.

Notes + Comments

1. The first step in solving a complex problem is to decompose it into a series of smaller subproblems. Decision trees provide a useful way to show how a problem can be decomposed and the sequential nature of the decision process.
2. People often view the same problem from different perspectives. Thus, the discussion regarding the development of a decision tree may provide additional insight about the problem.

20.2 Decision Making with Probabilities

These methods of assigning probabilities are discussed in Chapter 4.

Once we define the decision alternatives and the states of nature for the chance events, we can focus on determining probabilities for the states of nature. The classical method, the relative frequency method, or the subjective method of assigning probabilities may be used to identify these probabilities. After determining the appropriate probabilities, we show how to use the **expected value approach** to identify the best, or recommended, decision alternative for the problem.

Expected Value Approach

We begin by defining the expected value of a decision alternative. Let

$$N = \text{the number of states of nature}$$
$$P(s_j) = \text{the probability of state of nature } s_j$$

The probabilities for the states of nature must satisfy the basic requirements for assigning probabilities introduced in Chapter 4.

Because one and only one of the N states of nature can occur, the probabilities must satisfy two conditions:

$$P(s_j) \geq 0 \qquad \text{for all states of nature} \tag{20.1}$$

$$\sum_{j=1}^{N} P(s_j) = P(s_1) + P(s_2) + \cdots + P(s_N) = 1 \tag{20.2}$$

The **expected value (EV)** of decision alternative d_i is as follows.

Expected Value

$$\text{EV}(d_i) = \sum_{j=1}^{N} P(s_j)V_{ij} \tag{20.3}$$

where

$$V_{ij} = \text{the value of the payoff for decision alternative } d_i \text{ and state of nature } s_j$$

In words, the expected value of a decision alternative is the sum of weighted payoffs for the decision alternative. The weight for a payoff is the probability of the associated state of nature and therefore the probability that the payoff will occur. Let us return to the PDC problem to see how the expected value approach can be applied.

PDC is optimistic about the potential for the luxury high-rise condominium complex. Suppose that this optimism leads to an initial subjective probability assessment of 0.8 that demand will be strong (s_1) and a corresponding probability of 0.2 that demand will be weak (s_2). Thus, $P(s_1) = 0.8$ and $P(s_2) = 0.2$. Using the payoff values in Table 20.1 and equation (20.3), we compute the expected value for each of the three decision alternatives as follows:

$$\begin{aligned} \text{EV}(d_1) &= 0.8(8) + 0.2(7) = 7.8 \\ \text{EV}(d_2) &= 0.8(14) + 0.2(5) = 12.2 \\ \text{EV}(d_3) &= 0.8(20) + 0.2(-9) = 14.2 \end{aligned}$$

Thus, using the expected value approach, we find that the large condominium complex, with an expected value of \$14.2 million, is the recommended decision.

The calculations required to identify the decision alternative with the best expected value can be conveniently carried out on a decision tree. Figure 20.2 shows the decision tree for the PDC problem with state-of-nature branch probabilities. Working backward through the decision tree, we first compute the expected value at each chance node; that is, at each chance node, we weight each possible payoff by its probability of occurrence. By doing so, we obtain the expected values for nodes 2, 3, and 4, as shown in Figure 20.3.

Because the decision maker controls the branch leaving decision node 1, and because we are trying to maximize the expected profit, the best decision alternative at node 1 is d_3. Thus, the decision tree analysis leads to a recommendation of d_3 with an expected value of \$14.2 million. Note that this recommendation is also obtained with the expected value approach in conjunction with the payoff table.

Computer software packages are available to help in constructing more complex decision trees.

Other decision problems may be substantially more complex than the PDC problem, but if a reasonable number of decision alternatives and states of nature are present, you can use the decision tree approach outlined here. First, draw a decision tree consisting of decision nodes, chance nodes, and branches that describe the sequential nature of the problem. If you use the expected value approach, the next step is to determine the probabilities

Figure 20.2 PDC Decision Tree with State-of-Nature Branch Probabilities

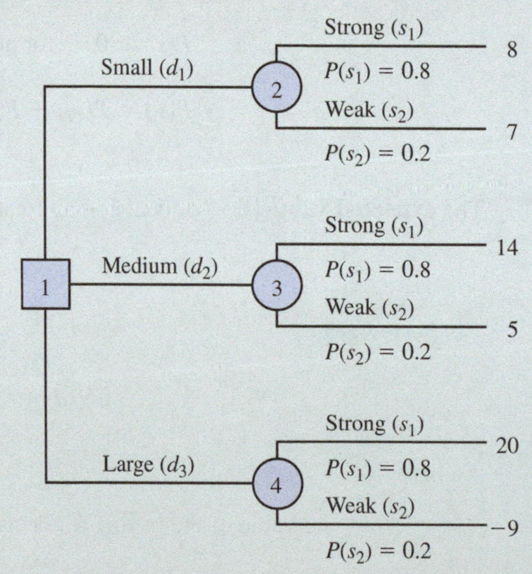

Figure 20.3 Applying the Expected Value Approach Using Decision Trees

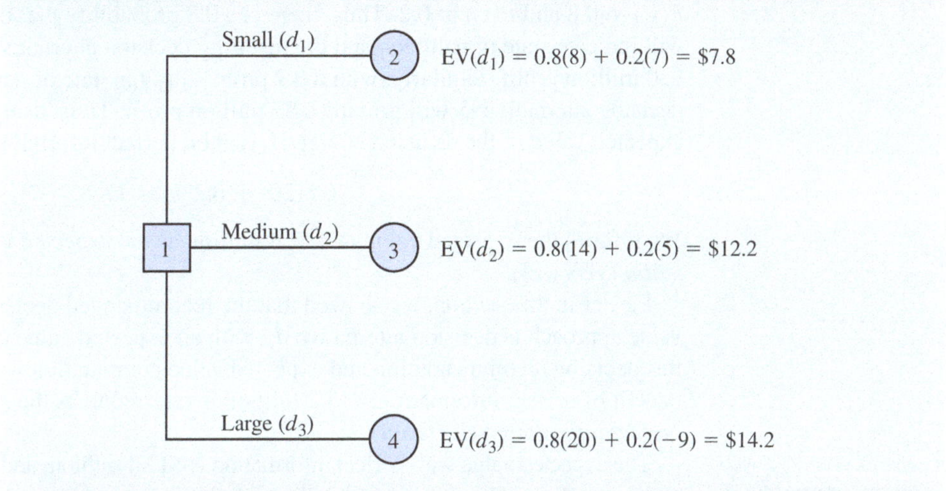

for each of the states of nature and compute the expected value at each chance node. Then select the decision branch leading to the chance node with the best expected value. The decision alternative associated with this branch is the recommended decision.

Expected Value of Perfect Information

Suppose that PDC has the opportunity to conduct a market research study that would help evaluate buyer interest in the condominium project and provide information that management could use to improve the probability assessments for the states of nature. To determine the potential value of this information, we begin by supposing that the study could provide *perfect information* regarding the states of nature; that is, we assume for the moment that PDC could determine with certainty, prior to making a decision, which state of nature is going to occur. To make use of this perfect information, we will develop a decision strategy that PDC should follow once it knows which state of nature will occur. A decision strategy is simply a decision rule that specifies the decision alternative to be selected after new information becomes available.

To help determine the decision strategy for PDC, we reproduce PDC's payoff table in Table 20.2. Note that, if PDC knew for sure that state of nature s_1 would occur, the best decision alternative would be d_3, with a payoff of \$20 million. Similarly, if PDC knew for sure that state of nature s_2 would occur, the best decision alternative would be d_1, with a payoff of \$7 million. Thus, we can state PDC's optimal decision strategy if the perfect information becomes available as follows:

If s_1, select d_3 and receive a payoff of \$20 million.
If s_2, select d_1 and receive a payoff of \$7 million.

Table 20.2 Payoff Table for the PDC Condominium Project ($ Millions)

	State of Nature	
Decision Alternative	**Strong Demand, s_1**	**Weak Demand, s_2**
Small complex, d_1	8	7
Medium complex, d_2	14	5
Large complex, d_3	20	−9

What is the expected value for this decision strategy? To compute the expected value with perfect information, we return to the original probabilities for the states of nature: $P(s_1) = 0.8$ and $P(s_2) = 0.2$. Thus, there is a 0.8 probability that the perfect information will indicate state of nature s_1 and the resulting decision alternative d_3 will provide a \$20 million profit. Similarly, with a 0.2 probability for state of nature s_2, the optimal decision alternative d_1 will provide a \$7 million profit. Thus, using equation (20.3), the expected value of the decision strategy based on perfect information is

$$0.8(20) + 0.2(7) = 17.4$$

We refer to the expected value of \$17.4 million as the *expected value with perfect information* (EVwPI).

Earlier in this section, we showed that the recommended decision using the expected value approach is decision alternative d_3, with an expected value of \$14.2 million. Because this decision recommendation and expected value computation were made without the benefit of perfect information, \$14.2 million is referred to as the *expected value without perfect information* (EVwoPI).

It would be worth \$3.2 million for PDC to learn the level of market acceptance before selecting a decision alternative.

The expected value with perfect information is \$17.4 million, and the expected value without perfect information is \$14.2; therefore, the expected value of the perfect information (EVPI) is \$17.4 − \$14.2 = \$3.2 million. In other words, \$3.2 million represents the additional expected value that can be obtained if perfect information were available about the states of nature. Generally speaking, a market research study will not provide "perfect" information; however, if the market research study is a good one, the information gathered might be worth a sizable portion of the \$3.2 million. Given the EVPI of \$3.2 million, PDC might seriously consider a market survey as a way to obtain more information about the states of nature.

In general, the **expected value of perfect information (EVPI)** is computed as follows:

Expected Value of Perfect Information

$$\text{EVPI} = |\text{EVwPI} - \text{EVwoPI}| \quad \textbf{(20.4)}$$

where

EVPI = expected value of perfect information
EVwPI = expected value *with* perfect information about the states of nature
EVwoPI = expected value *without* perfect information about the states of nature

Note the role of the absolute value in equation (20.4). For minimization problems, information helps reduce or lower cost; thus the expected value with perfect information is less than or equal to the expected value without perfect information. In this case, EVPI is the magnitude of the difference between EVwPI and EVwoPI, or the absolute value of the difference as shown in equation (20.4).

Exercises

Methods

1. The following payoff table shows profit for a decision analysis problem with two decision alternatives and three states of nature. **LO 1, 2**

Decision Alternative	State of Nature s_1	s_2	s_3
d_1	250	100	25
d_2	100	100	75

a. Construct a decision tree for this problem.
b. Suppose that the decision maker obtains the probabilities $P(s_1) = 0.65$, $P(s_2) = 0.15$, and $P(s_3) = 0.20$. Use the expected value approach to determine the optimal decision.

2. A decision maker faced with four decision alternatives and four states of nature develops the following profit payoff table.

	State of Nature			
Decision Alternative	s_1	s_2	s_3	s_4
d_1	14	9	10	5
d_2	11	10	8	7
d_3	9	10	10	11
d_4	8	10	11	13

The decision maker obtains information that enables the following probabilities assessments: $P(s_1) = 0.5$, $P(s_2) = 0.2$, $P(s_3) = 0.2$, and $P(s_4) = 0.1$. **LO 1, 2**
a. Use the expected value approach to determine the optimal solution.
b. Now assume that the entries in the payoff table are costs. Use the expected value approach to determine the optimal decision.

Applications

3. **Market Segment Stock Market Returns.** Investment advisors estimated the stock market returns for four market segments: technology, financial, manufacturing, and pharmaceuticals. Annual return projections vary depending on whether the general economic conditions are improving, stable, or declining. The anticipated annual return percentages for each market segment under each economic condition are follow. **LO 2**

	Economic Condition		
Market Segment	**Improving**	**Stable**	**Declining**
Technology	10	2	−4
Financial	8	5	−3
Manufacturing	6	4	−2
Pharmaceuticals	6	5	−1

a. Assume that an individual investor wants to select one market segment for a new investment. A forecast shows improving to declining economic conditions with the following probabilities: improving (0.2), stable (0.5), and declining (0.3). What is the preferred market segment for the investor, and what is the expected return percentage?
b. At a later date, a revised forecast shows a potential for an improvement in economic conditions. New probabilities are as follows: improving (0.4), stable (0.4), and declining (0.2). What is the preferred market segment for the investor based on these new probabilities? What is the expected return percentage?

4. **Air Service from Cleveland to Myrtle Beach.** Myrtle Air Express decided to offer direct service from Cleveland to Myrtle Beach. Management must decide between a full price service using the company's new fleet of jet aircraft and a discount service using smaller capacity commuter planes. It is clear that the best choice depends on the market reaction to the service Myrtle Air offers. Management developed estimates of the contribution to profit for each type of service based upon two possible levels of demand for service to Myrtle Beach: strong and weak. The following table shows the estimated quarterly profits (in thousands of dollars). **LO 1, 2**

	Demand for Service	
Service	Strong	Weak
Full price	$960	−$490
Discount	$670	$320

a. What is the decision to be made, what is the chance event, and what is the consequence for this problem? How many decision alternatives are there? How many outcomes are there for the chance event?
b. Suppose that management of Myrtle Air Express believes that the probability of strong demand is 0.7 and the probability of weak demand is 0.3. Use the expected value approach to determine an optimal decision.
c. Suppose that the probability of strong demand is 0.8 and the probability of weak demand is 0.2. What is the optimal decision using the expected value approach?

5. **Augmented Reality Application Investment**. Software applications that use augmented reality can provide an enhanced version of the real world by adding digital elements such as visual graphics, sounds, and other sensory feedback to the user. Augmented reality (AR) has been applied to settings such as health care, military, and entertainment. According to a 2022 article by *Yahoo! Finance*, the global market size of augmented reality software applications is estimated to surpass $332 billion in 2028. However, there is considerable uncertainty in this estimated market size because the technologies to support augmented reality are still being developed and there is little history on its use.

Consider the case of AR Ventures, a venture-capital firm that provides support for start-up companies using augmented reality technology. AR Ventures has the opportunity to invest in one of two start-ups utilizing AR technology: one that is developing a healthcare application and one that is developing an entertainment application. The healthcare application uses AR to help train medical students, and the entertainment application allows people to compete virtually in the sport of badminton. AR Ventures believes that the potential market size of the healthcare application is larger, but that the technology needed for this application is unproven. The technology used for the entertainment application is more well established, but the market size is likely smaller.

Suppose that demand for the entertainment application is estimated to be High, Medium, or Low with the following associated probabilities, revenues, and costs.

		Demand	
Entertainment Application	High	Medium	Low
Revenue ($ million)	1.80	1.00	0.25
Cost ($ million)	1.10	0.80	0.60
Probability	0.40	0.30	0.30

The costs associated with the healthcare application are largely dependent on the success of one particular new device that would be worn by medical students. If the current protype of the device proves to be successful, the costs will be significantly lower than if the prototype device is not successful. The estimated revenues, costs, and probabilities of different demand scenarios for each possibility follow. AR Ventures would like to make the decision of which application in which to invest, based on expected profit (revenue – cost). **LO 1, 2**

Healthcare Application (if prototype is successful)	High	Medium	Low
		Demand	
Revenue ($ million)	6.50	4.00	2.50
Cost ($ million)	4.30	3.40	2.80
Probability	0.30	0.50	0.20

Healthcare Application (if prototype is unsuccessful)	High	Medium	Low
		Demand	
Revenue ($ million)	6.50	4.00	2.50
Cost ($ million)	5.90	4.10	3.60
Probability	0.30	0.50	0.20

a. Develop a decision tree for the AR Ventures problem.
b. Suppose that AR Ventures believes it is equally likely that the healthcare application device prototype will be successful as it is that the prototype will be unsuccessful. Using an expected value approach, would you recommend that AR Ventures invest in the entertainment application or the healthcare application?
c. Would your recommendation in part (b) change if the probability of the prototype being successful is only 0.25? Why or why not?

6. **Choice of Grapes for a New Vineyard.** A 2017 survey of sommeliers ranked the Finger Lakes region of New York state as the top wine region to visit (*Thrillist* website). Finger Lakes vineyards typically specialize in growing grapes for white wines such as Chardonnay and Riesling. Seneca Hill Winery recently purchased land for the purpose of establishing a new vineyard. Management is considering two varieties of white grapes for the new vineyard: Chardonnay and Riesling. The Chardonnay grapes would be used to produce a dry Chardonnay wine, and the Riesling grapes would be used to produce a semi-dry Riesling wine. It takes approximately four years from the time of planting before new grapes can be harvested. This length of time creates a great deal of uncertainty concerning future demand and makes the decision concerning the type of grapes to plant difficult. Three possibilities are being considered: Chardonnay grapes only, Riesling grapes only, and both Chardonnay and Riesling grapes. Seneca management decided that for planning purposes it would be adequate to consider only two demand possibilities for each type of wine: strong or weak. With two possibilities for each type of wine, it was necessary to assess four probabilities. With the help of some forecasts in industry publications management made the following probability assessments.

	Riesling Demand	
Chardonnay Demand	Weak	Strong
Weak	0.05	0.50
Strong	0.25	0.20

Revenue projections show an annual contribution to profit of $20,000 if Seneca Hill only plants Chardonnay grapes and demand is weak for Chardonnay wine, and $70,000 if they only plant Chardonnay grapes and demand is strong for Chardonnay wine. If they only plant Riesling grapes, the annual profit projection is $25,000 if demand is weak for Riesling grapes and $45,000 if demand is strong for Riesling grapes. If Seneca plants both types of grapes, the annual profit projections are shown in the following table. **LO 1, 2**

	Riesling Demand	
Chardonnay Demand	Weak	Strong
Weak	$22,000	$40,000
Strong	$26,000	$60,000

a. What is the decision to be made, what is the chance event, and what is the consequence? Identify the alternatives for the decisions and the possible outcomes for the chance events.
b. Develop a decision tree.
c. Use the expected value approach to recommend which alternative Seneca Hill Winery should follow in order to maximize expected annual profit.
d. Suppose management is concerned about the probability assessments when demand for Chardonnay wine is strong. Some believe it is likely for Riesling demand to also be strong in this case. Suppose the probability of strong demand for Chardonnay and weak demand for Riesling is 0.05 and that the probability of strong demand for Chardonnay and strong demand for Riesling is 0.40. How does this change the recommended decision? Assume that the probabilities when Chardonnay demand is weak are still 0.05 and 0.50.
e. Other members of the management team expect the Chardonnay market to become saturated at some point in the future, causing a fall in prices. Suppose that the annual profit projections fall to $50,000 when demand for Chardonnay is strong and Chardonnay grapes only are planted. Using the original probability assessments, determine how this change would affect the optimal decision.

7. **New Community Center in Lake Placid.** The Lake Placid Town Council has decided to build a new community center to be used for conventions, concerts, and other public events, but considerable controversy surrounds the appropriate size. Many influential citizens want a large center that would be a showcase for the area, but the mayor feels that if demand does not support such a center, the community will lose a large amount of money. To provide structure for the decision process, the council narrowed the building alternatives to three sizes: small, medium, and large. Everybody agreed that the critical factor in choosing the best size is the number of people who will want to use the new facility. A regional planning consultant provided demand estimates under three scenarios: worst case, base case, and best case. The worst-case scenario corresponds to a situation in which tourism drops significantly, the base-case scenario corresponds to a situation in which Lake Placid continues to attract visitors at current levels, and the best-case scenario corresponds to a significant increase in tourism. The consultant has provided probability assessments of 0.10, 0.60, and 0.30 for the worst-case, base-case, and best-case scenarios, respectively.

   The town council suggested using net cash flow over a five-year planning horizon as the criterion for deciding on the best size. A consultant developed the following projections of net cash flow (in thousands of dollars) for a five-year planning horizon. All costs, including the consultant's fee, are included. **LO 2, 3**

	Demand Scenario		
Center Size	Worst Case	Base Case	Best Case
Small	400	500	660
Medium	−250	650	800
Large	−400	580	990

a. What decision should Lake Placid make using the expected value approach?
b. Compute the expected value of perfect information. Do you think it would be worth trying to obtain additional information concerning which scenario is likely to occur?
c. Suppose the probability of the worst-case scenario increases to 0.2, the probability of the base-case scenario decreases to 0.5, and the probability of the best-case scenario remains at 0.3. What effect, if any, would these changes have on the decision recommendation?
d. The consultant suggested that an expenditure of $150,000 on a promotional campaign over the planning horizon will effectively reduce the probability of the worst-case scenario to zero. If the campaign can be expected to also increase the probability of the best-case scenario to 0.4, is it a good investment?

20.3 Decision Analysis with Sample Information

In applying the expected value approach, we showed how probability information about the states of nature affects the expected value calculations and thus, the decision recommendation. Frequently, decision makers have preliminary or **prior probability** assessments for the states of nature that are the best probability values available at that time. However, to make the best possible decision, the decision maker may want to seek additional information about the states of nature. This new information can be used to revise or update the prior probabilities so that the final decision is based on more accurate probabilities for the states of nature. Usually, additional information is obtained through experiments designed to provide **sample information** about the states of nature. Raw material sampling, product testing, and market research studies are examples of experiments (or studies) that may enable management to revise or update the state-of-nature probabilities. These revised probabilities are called **posterior probabilities**.

Let us return to the PDC problem and assume that management is considering a six-month market research study designed to learn more about potential market acceptance of the PDC condominium project. Management anticipates that the market research study will provide one of the following two results:

1. Favorable report: A significant number of the individuals contacted express interest in purchasing a PDC condominium.
2. Unfavorable report: Very few of the individuals contacted express interest in purchasing a PDC condominium.

Decision Tree

The decision tree for the PDC problem with sample information shows the logical sequence for the decisions and the chance events in Figure 20.4. First, PDC's management must decide whether the market research should be conducted. If it is conducted, PDC's management must be prepared to make a decision about the size of the condominium project if the market research report is favorable and, possibly, a different decision about the size of the condominium project if the market research report is unfavorable.

In Figure 20.4, the squares are decision nodes and the circles are chance nodes. At each decision node, the branch of the tree that is taken is based on the decision made. At each chance node, the branch of the tree that is taken is based on probability or chance. For example, decision node 1 shows that PDC must first make the decision whether to conduct the market research study. If the market research study is undertaken, chance node 2 indicates that both the favorable report branch and the unfavorable report branch are not under PDC's control and will be determined by chance. Node 3 is a decision node, indicating that PDC must make the decision to construct the small, medium, or large complex if the market research report is favorable. Node 4 is a decision node showing that PDC must make the decision to construct the small, medium, or large complex if the market research report is unfavorable. Node 5 is a decision

Figure 20.4 The PDC Decision Tree Including the Market Research Study

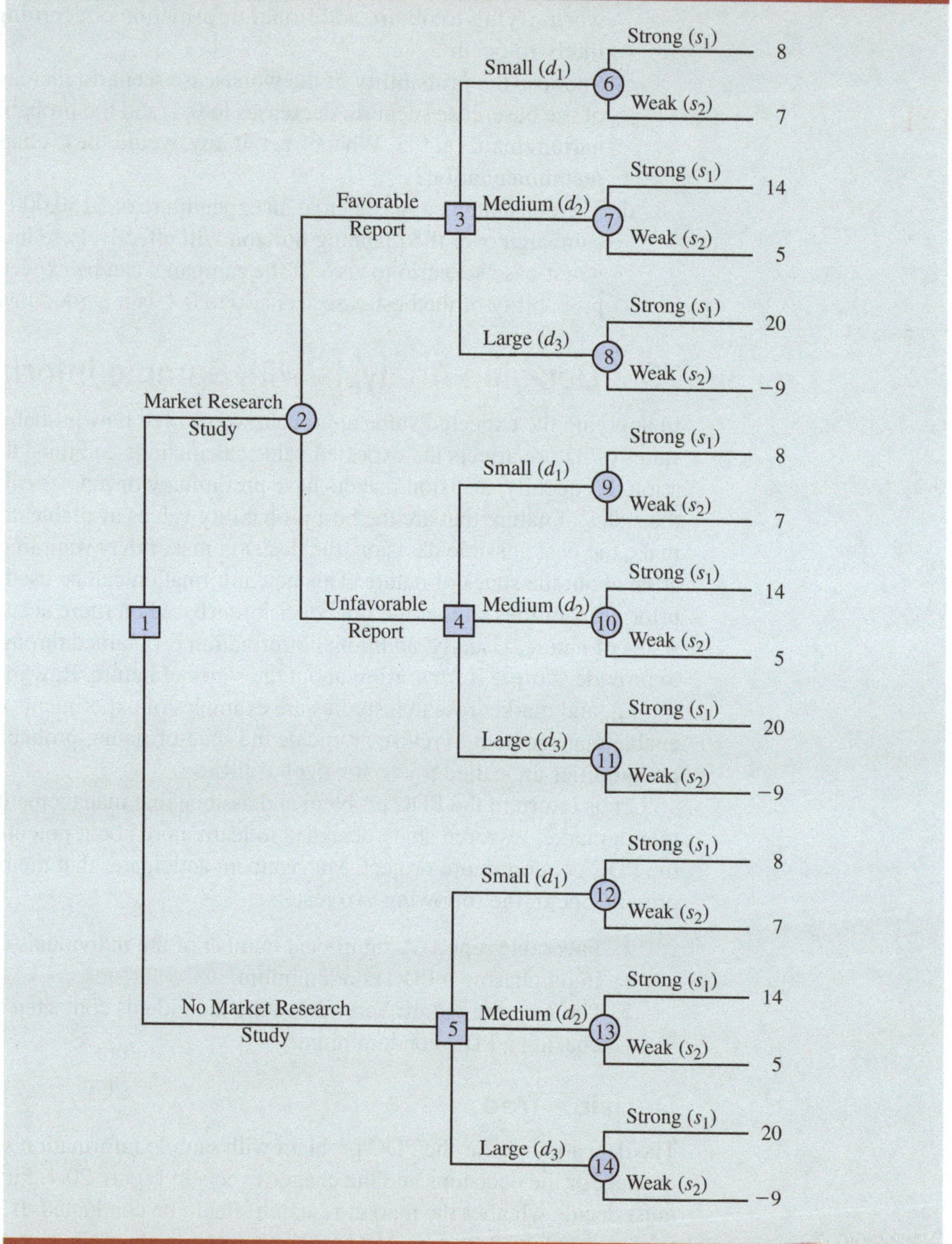

node indicating that PDC must make the decision to construct the small, medium, or large complex if the market research is not undertaken. Nodes 6 to 14 are chance nodes indicating that the strong demand or weak demand state-of-nature branches will be determined by chance.

In Section 20.4, we explain how these probabilities can be developed.

Analysis of the decision tree and the choice of an optimal strategy requires that we know the branch probabilities corresponding to all chance nodes. PDC developed the following branch probabilities.

If the market research study is undertaken,

$$P(\text{Favorable report}) = P(F) = 0.77$$
$$P(\text{Unfavorable report}) = P(U) = 0.23$$

If the market research report is favorable,

$$P(\text{Strong demand given a favorable report}) = P(s_1 \mid F) = 0.94$$
$$P(\text{Weak demand given a favorable report}) = P(s_2 \mid F) = 0.06$$

If the market research report is unfavorable,

$$P(\text{Strong demand given an unfavorable report}) = P(s_1 \mid U) = 0.35$$
$$P(\text{Weak demand given an unfavorable report}) = P(s_2 \mid U) = 0.65$$

If the market research report is not undertaken, the prior probabilities are applicable.

$$P(\text{Strong demand}) = P(s_1) = 0.80$$
$$P(\text{Weak demand}) = P(s_2) = 0.20$$

The branch probabilities are shown on the decision tree in Figure 20.5.

Figure 20.5 The PDC Decision Tree with Branch Probabilities

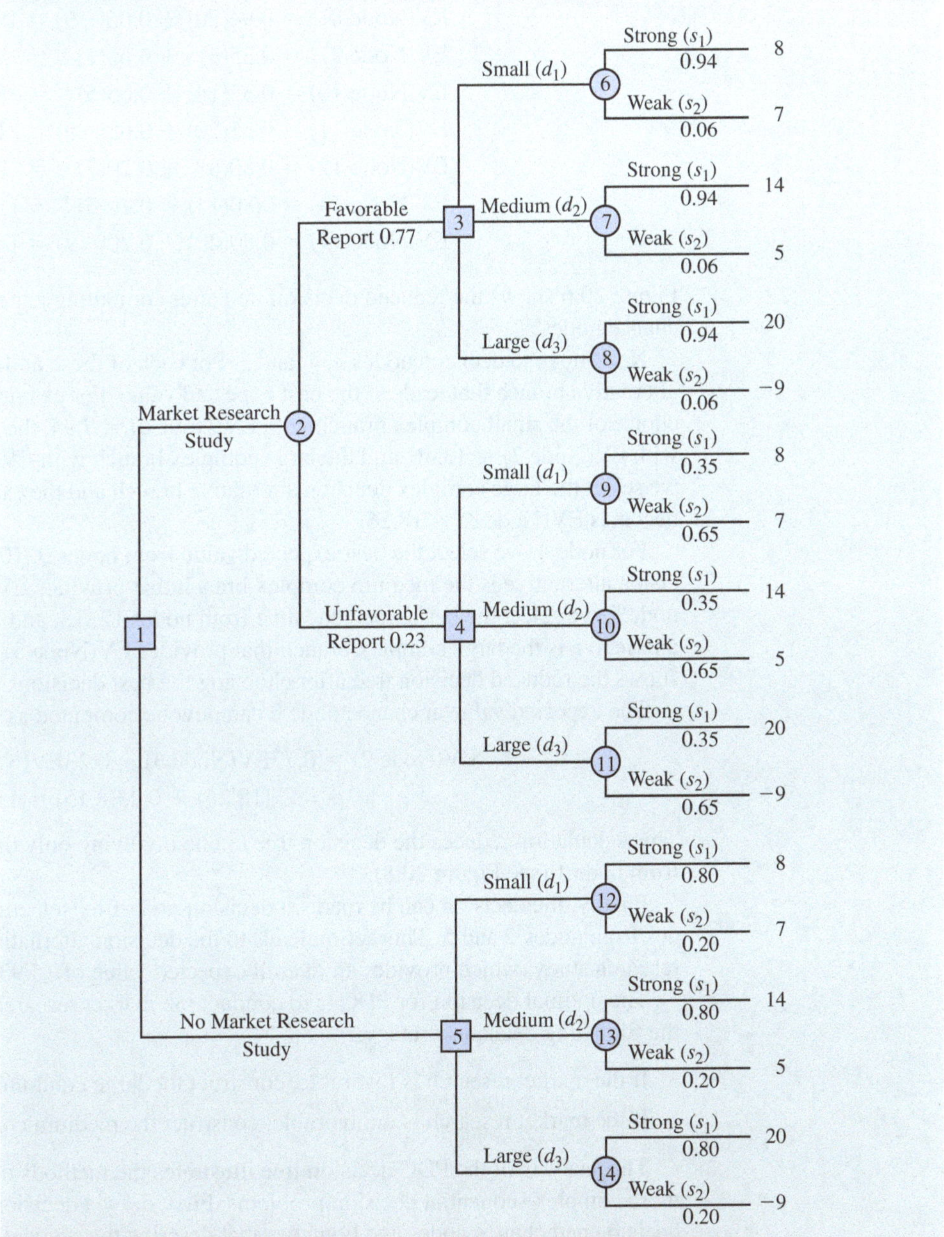

Decision Strategy

A **decision strategy** is a sequence of decisions and chance outcomes where the decisions chosen depend on the yet-to-be-determined outcomes of chance events. The approach used to determine the optimal decision strategy is based on a backward pass through the decision tree using the following steps:

1. At chance nodes, compute the expected value by multiplying the payoff at the end of each branch by the corresponding branch probability.
2. At decision nodes, select the decision branch that leads to the best expected value. This expected value becomes the expected value at the decision node.

Starting the backward pass calculations by computing the expected values at chance nodes 6 to 14 provides the following results.

$$
\begin{aligned}
EV(\text{Node } 6) &= 0.94(8) + 0.06(7) = 7.94\\
EV(\text{Node } 7) &= 0.94(14) + 0.06(5) = 13.46\\
EV(\text{Node } 8) &= 0.94(20) + 0.06(-9) = 18.26\\
EV(\text{Node } 9) &= 0.35(8) + 0.65(7) = 7.35\\
EV(\text{Node } 10) &= 0.35(14) + 0.65(5) = 8.15\\
EV(\text{Node } 11) &= 0.35(20) + 0.65(-9) = 1.15\\
EV(\text{Node } 12) &= 0.80(8) + 0.20(7) = 7.80\\
EV(\text{Node } 13) &= 0.80(14) + 0.20(5) = 12.20\\
EV(\text{Node } 14) &= 0.80(20) + 0.20(-9) = 14.20
\end{aligned}
$$

Figure 20.6 shows the reduced decision tree after computing expected values at these chance nodes.

Next move to decision nodes 3, 4, and 5. For each of these nodes, we select the decision alternative branch that leads to the best expected value. For example, at node 3 we have the choice of the small complex branch with EV(Node 6) = 7.94, the medium complex branch with EV(Node 7) = 13.46, and the large complex branch with EV(Node 8) = 18.26. Thus, we select the large complex decision alternative branch and the expected value at node 3 becomes EV(Node 3) = 18.26.

For node 4, we select the best expected value from nodes 9, 10, and 11. The best decision alternative is the medium complex branch that provides EV(Node 4) = 8.15. For node 5, we select the best expected value from nodes 12, 13, and 14. The best decision alternative is the large complex branch that provides EV(Node 5) = 14.20. Figure 20.7 shows the reduced decision tree after choosing the best decisions at nodes 3, 4, and 5.

The expected value at chance node 2 can now be computed as follows:

$$
\begin{aligned}
EV(\text{Node } 2) &= 0.77EV(\text{Node } 3) + 0.23EV(\text{Node } 4)\\
&= 0.77(18.26) + 0.23(8.15) = 15.93
\end{aligned}
$$

This calculation reduces the decision tree to one involving only the two decision branches from node 1 (see Figure 20.8).

Finally, the decision can be made at decision node 1 by selecting the best expected values from nodes 2 and 5. This action leads to the decision alternative to conduct the market research study, which provides an overall expected value of 15.93.

The optimal decision for PDC is to conduct the market research study and then carry out the following decision strategy:

If the market research is favorable, construct the large condominium complex.

If the market research is unfavorable, construct the medium condominium complex.

The analysis of the PDC decision tree illustrates the methods that can be used to analyze more complex sequential decision problems. First, draw a decision tree consisting of decision and chance nodes and branches that describe the sequential nature of the problem.

Figure 20.6 PDC Decision Tree After Computing Expected Values at Chance Nodes 6 to 14

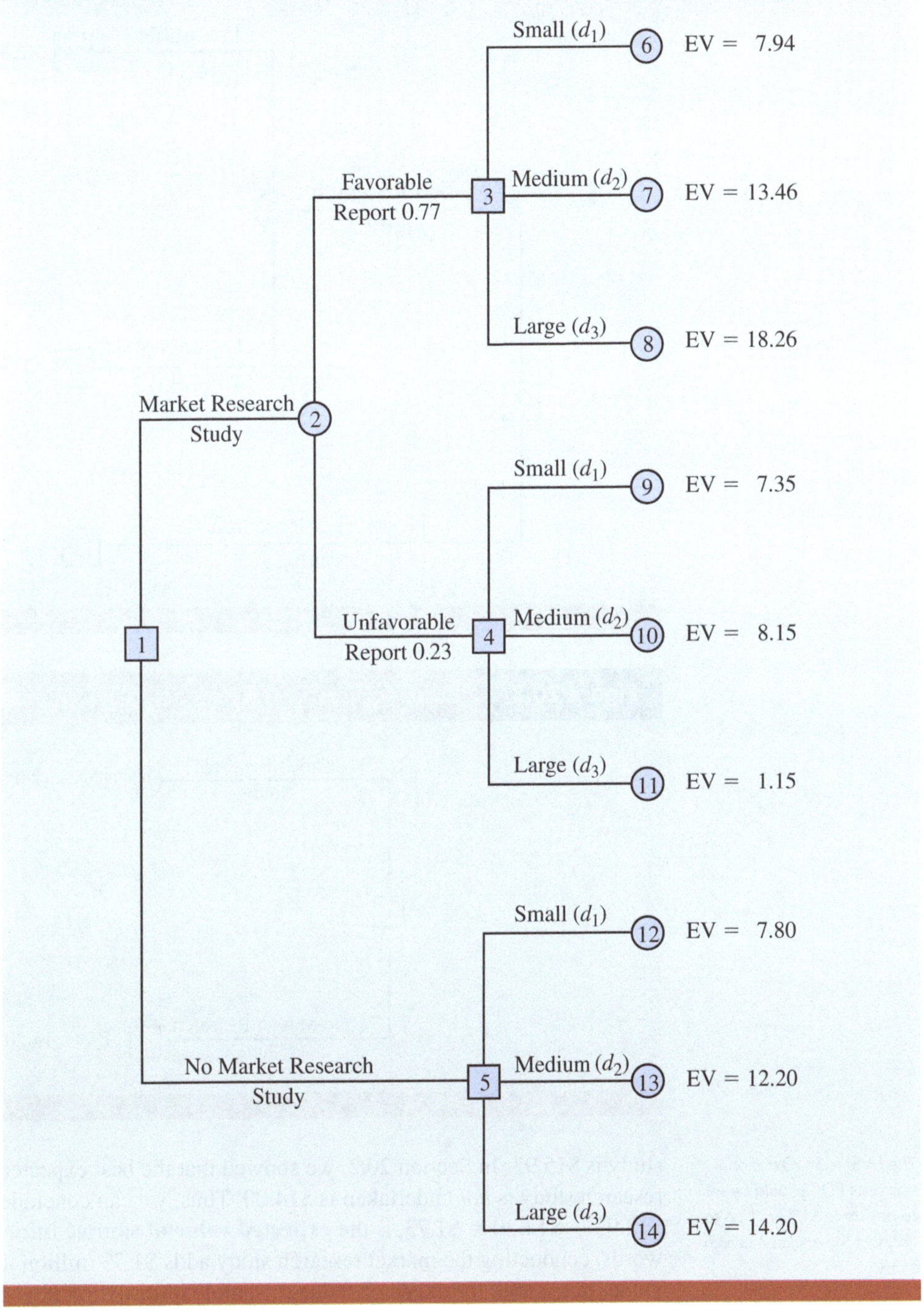

Determine the probabilities for all chance outcomes. Then, by working backward through the tree, compute expected values at all chance nodes and select the best decision branch at all decision nodes. The sequence of optimal decision branches determines the optimal decision strategy for the problem.

Expected Value of Sample Information

In the PDC problem, the market research study is the sample information used to determine the optimal decision strategy. The expected value associated with the market research

Figure 20.7 PDC Decision Tree After Choosing Best Decisions at Nodes 3, 4, and 5

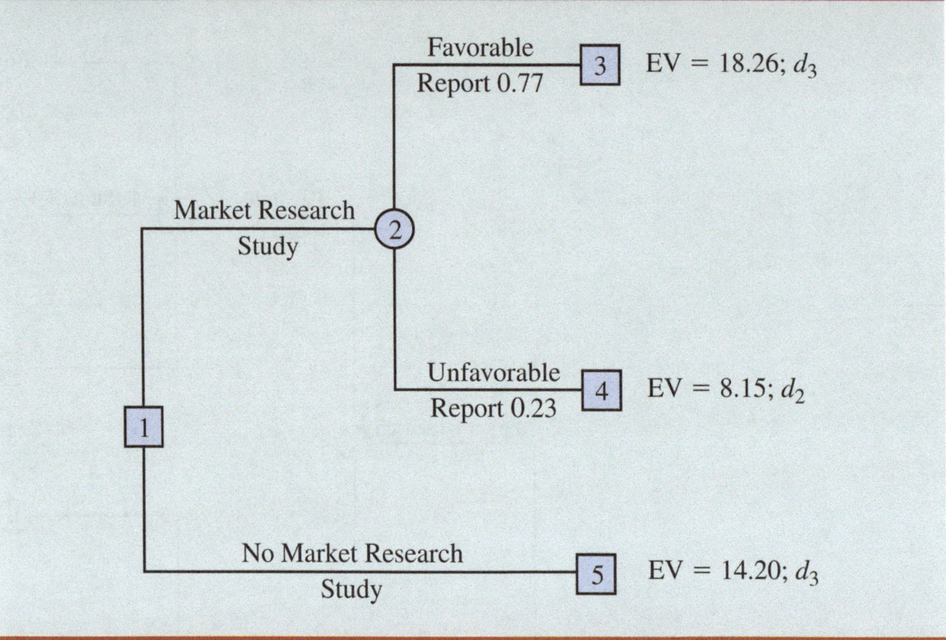

Figure 20.8 PDC Decision Tree Reduced to Two Decision Branches

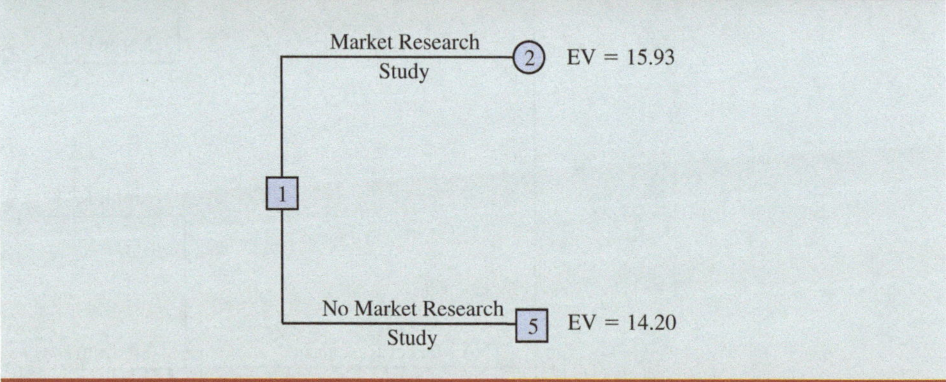

The EVSI = $1.73 million suggests PDC should be willing to pay up to $1.73 million to conduct the market research study.

study is $15.93. In Section 20.2, we showed that the best expected value if the market research study is *not* undertaken is $14.20. Thus, we can conclude that the difference, $15.93 − $14.20 = $1.73, is the **expected value of sample information (EVSI)**. In other words, conducting the market research study adds $1.73 million to the PDC expected value. In general, the expected value of sample information is as follows.

Expected Value of Sample Information

$$\text{EVSI} = |\text{EVwSI} - \text{EVwoSI}| \tag{20.5}$$

where

EVSI = expected value of sample information

EVwSI = expected value *with* sample information about the states of nature

EVwoSI = expected value *without* sample information about the states of nature

Note the role of the absolute value in equation (20.5). For minimization problems, the expected value with sample information is always less than or equal to the expected value without sample information. In this case, EVSI is the magnitude of the difference between EVwSI and EVwoSI; thus, by taking the absolute value of the difference as shown in equation (20.5), we can handle both the maximization and minimization cases with one equation.

Exercises

Methods

8. Consider a variation of the PDC decision tree shown in Figure 20.5. The company must first decide whether to undertake the market research study. If the market research study is conducted, the outcome will either be favorable (F) or unfavorable (U). Assume there are only two decision alternatives d_1 and d_2 and two states of nature s_1 and s_2. The payoff table showing profit follows. **LO 1, 2**

	State of Nature	
Decision Alternative	s_1	s_2
d_1	100	300
d_2	400	200

a. Show the decision tree.
b. Use the following probabilities. What is the optimal decision strategy?

$P(F) = 0.56$	$P(s_1 \mid F) = 0.57$	$P(s_1 \mid U) = 0.18$	$P(s_1) = 0.40$
$P(U) = 0.44$	$P(s_2 \mid F) = 0.43$	$P(s_2 \mid U) = 0.82$	$P(s_2) = 0.60$

Applications

9. **Prepositioning Supplies for Hurricane Response.** In 2017, the American Red Cross had to make decisions related to preparations for Hurricane Irma which was threatening the United States including Florida, Puerto Rico, and the U.S. Virgin Islands. To prepare for such disasters, organizations such as the Red Cross must make decisions about when and where to preposition relief supplies such as water, food, and medical supplies. Suppose that the Red Cross can choose to stock supplies for a possible hurricane that hits Florida either in a central distribution center that is protected from possible hurricane disaster or in regional distribution centers that are closer to where damage is expected, but run the risk of being destroyed by severe hurricanes. The following table displays the costs (in $ millions) of the different decision alternatives under three possible states of nature: no hurricane landfall, moderate hurricane landfall, severe hurricane landfall. Note that because these values represent costs, they are all displayed as negative values.

		State of Nature	
Decision Alternatives	No Landfall, s_1	Moderate Landfall, s_2	Severe Landfall, s_3
Stock Centralized Distribution Center, d_1	−30	−18	−65
Stock Regional Distribution Centers, d_2	−15	−40	−50

The probabilities for the states of nature are $P(s_1) = 0.5$, $P(s_2) = 0.35$, $P(s_3) = 0.15$. The Red Cross can also wait an additional 48 hours during which time an additional "hurricane hunter" flight will collect additional data on the hurricane. By waiting, the Red Cross gathers additional sample data on whether the hurricane will make a turn toward Florida or away from Florida. The probabilities associated with these scenarios follow. **LO 1, 2, 4**

P(Toward Florida) = 0.6	$P(s_1 \mid \text{Toward Florida}) = 0.2$	$P(s_1 \mid \text{Away From Florida}) = 0.75$
P(Away From Florida) = 0.4	$P(s_2 \mid \text{Toward Florida}) = 0.55$	$P(s_2 \mid \text{Away From Florida}) = 0.2$
	$P(s_3 \mid \text{Toward Florida}) = 0.25$	$P(s_3 \mid \text{Away From Florida}) = 0.05$

a. Construct a decision tree for this problem.
b. What is the recommended decision if the Red Cross does not wait to make a decision? What is the expected value of this decision?
c. What is the optimal decision strategy if the Red Cross waits an additional 48 hours? What is the expected value of this decision?
d. What is the expected value of the sample data?

10. **Bidding on Rights to Construct a New Office Building Complex.** Dante Development Corporation is considering bidding on a contract for a new office building complex. Figure 20.9 shows the decision tree prepared by one of Dante's analysts. At node 1, the company must decide whether to bid on the contract. The cost of preparing the bid is \$200,000. The upper branch from node 2 shows that the company has a 0.8 probability of winning the contract if it submits a bid. If the company wins the bid, it will have to pay \$2,000,000 to become a partner in the project. Node 3 shows that the company will then consider doing a market research study to forecast demand for the office units prior to beginning construction. The cost of this study is \$150,000. Node 4 is a chance node showing the possible outcomes of the market research study.

Nodes 5, 6, and 7 are similar in that they are the decision nodes for Dante to either build the office complex or sell the rights in the project to another developer. The decision to

Figure 20.9 Decision Tree for the Dante Development Corporation

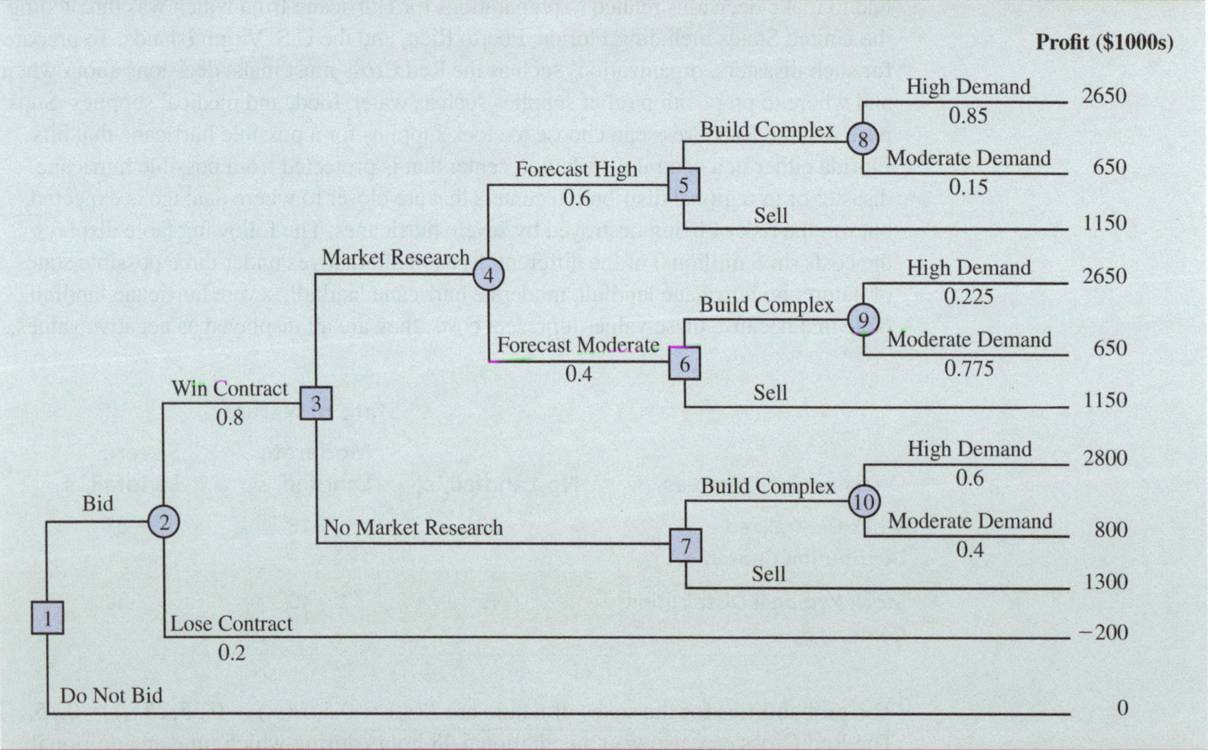

build the complex will result in an income of \$5,000,000 if demand is high and \$3,000,000 if demand is moderate. If Dante chooses to sell its rights in the project to another developer, income from the sale is estimated to be \$3,500,000. The probabilities shown at nodes 4, 8, and 9 are based on the projected outcomes of the market research study. **LO 2, 4**

a. Verify Dante's profit projections shown at the ending branches of the decision tree by calculating the payoffs of \$2,650,000 and \$650,000 for first two outcomes.
b. What is the optimal decision strategy for Dante, and what is the expected profit for this project?
c. What would the cost of the market research study have to be before Dante would change its decision about conducting the study?

11. **Producing a Pilot for a New Comedy Series.** There were more than 500 scripted television series available for viewing in 2018 (*Hollywood Reporter* website). New series typically start by producing a pilot episode that can be evaluated by networks before agreeing to pick up the series for production. Hale's TV Productions is considering producing a pilot for a comedy series in the hope of selling it to a major television network. The network may decide to reject the series, but it may also decide to purchase the rights to the series for either one or two years. At this point in time, Hale may either produce the pilot and wait for the network's decision or transfer the rights for the pilot and series to a competitor for \$100,000. Hale's decision alternatives and profits (in thousands of dollars) follow:

	State of Nature		
Decision Alternative	Reject, s_1	1 Year, s_2	2 Years, s_3
Produce pilot, d_1	−100	50	150
Sell to competitor, d_2	100	100	100

The probabilities for the states of nature are $P(s_1) = 0.2$, $P(s_2) = 0.3$, and $P(s_3) = 0.5$. For a consulting fee of \$5,000, an agency will review the plans for the comedy series and indicate the overall chances of a favorable network reaction to the series. Assume that the agency review will result in a favorable (F) or an unfavorable (U) review and that the following probabilities are relevant. **LO 1, 2, 3, 4**

$$P(F) = 0.69 \quad P(s_1 \mid F) = 0.09 \quad P(s_1 \mid U) = 0.45$$
$$P(U) = 0.31 \quad P(s_2 \mid F) = 0.26 \quad P(s_2 \mid U) = 0.39$$
$$P(s_3 \mid F) = 0.65 \quad P(s_3 \mid U) = 0.16$$

a. Construct a decision tree for this problem.
b. What is the recommended decision if the agency opinion is not used? What is the expected value?
c. What is the expected value of perfect information?
d. What is Hale's optimal decision strategy assuming the agency's information is used?
e. What is the expected value of the agency's information?
f. Is the agency's information worth the \$5,000 fee? What is the maximum that Hale should be willing to pay for the information?
g. What is the recommended decision?

12. **Entering the Snowplowing Business.** Martin's Service Station is considering entering the snowplowing business for the coming winter season. Martin can purchase either a snowplow blade attachment for the station's pick-up truck or a new heavy-duty snowplow truck. After analyzing the situation, Martin believes that either alternative would be a profitable investment if the snowfall is heavy. Smaller profits would result if the snowfall is moderate, and losses would result if the snowfall is light. The following profits/losses apply.

	State of Nature		
Decision Alternative	**Heavy, s_1**	**Moderate, s_2**	**Light, s_3**
Blade attachment, d_1	3,500	1,000	−1,500
New snowplow, d_2	7,000	2,000	−9,000

The probabilities for the states of nature are $P(s_1) = 0.4$, $P(s_2) = 0.3$, and $P(s_3) = 0.3$. Suppose that Martin decides to wait until September before making a final decision. Assessments of the probabilities associated with a normal (N) or unseasonably cold (U) September follow. **LO 1, 2, 3**

$P(N) = 0.8$	$P(s_1 \mid N) = 0.35$	$P(s_1 \mid U) = 0.62$
$P(U) = 0.2$	$P(s_2 \mid N) = 0.30$	$P(s_2 \mid U) = 0.31$
	$P(s_3 \mid N) = 0.35$	$P(s_3 \mid U) = 0.07$

a. Construct a decision tree for this problem.
b. What is the recommended decision if Martin does not wait until September? What is the expected value?
c. What is the expected value of perfect information?
d. What is Martin's optimal decision strategy if the decision is not made until the September weather is determined? What is the expected value of this decision strategy?

13. **Buying Decision for a Seasonal Product.** Lawson's Department Store faces a buying decision for a seasonal product for which demand can be high, medium, or low. The purchaser for Lawson's can order 1, 2, or 3 lots of the product before the season begins but cannot reorder later. Profit projections (in thousands of dollars) are shown. **LO 1, 2, 3, 4**

	State of Nature		
Decision Alternative	**High Demand, s_1**	**Medium Demand, s_2**	**Low Demand, s_3**
Order 1 lot, d_1	60	60	50
Order 2 lots, d_2	80	80	30
Order 3 lots, d_3	100	70	10

a. If the prior probabilities for the three states of nature are 0.3, 0.3, and 0.4, respectively, what is the recommended order quantity?
b. At each preseason sales meeting, the vice president of sales provides a personal opinion regarding potential demand for this product. Because of the vice president's enthusiasm and optimistic nature, the predictions of market conditions have always been either "excellent" (E) or "very good" (V). Probabilities are as follows. What is the optimal decision strategy?

$P(E) = 0.7$	$P(s_1 \mid E) = 0.34$	$P(s_1 \mid V) = 0.20$
$P(V) = 0.3$	$P(s_2 \mid E) = 0.32$	$P(s_2 \mid V) = 0.26$
	$P(s_3 \mid E) = 0.34$	$P(s_3 \mid V) = 0.54$

c. Compute EVPI and EVSI. Discuss whether the firm should consider a consulting expert who could provide independent forecasts of market conditions for the product.

20.4 Computing Branch Probabilities Using Bayes' Theorem

Bayes' theorem is introduced in Chapter 4.

In Section 20.3, the branch probabilities for the PDC decision tree chance nodes were specified in the problem description. No computations were required to determine these probabilities. In this section, we show how **Bayes' theorem** can be used to compute branch probabilities for decision trees.

The PDC decision tree is shown again in Figure 20.10. Let

F = Favorable market research report

U = Unfavorable market research report

s_1 = Strong demand (state of nature 1)

s_2 = Weak demand (state of nature 2)

At chance node 2, we need to know the branch probabilities $P(F)$ and $P(U)$. At chance nodes 6, 7, and 8, we need to know the branch probabilities $P(s_1 \mid F)$, the probability of state of nature 1 given a favorable market research report, and $P(s_2 \mid F)$, the probability of state of nature 2 given a favorable market research report. $P(s_1 \mid F)$ and $P(s_2 \mid F)$ are referred to as *posterior probabilities* because they are conditional probabilities based on the outcome of the sample information. At chance nodes 9, 10, and 11, we need to know the branch probabilities $P(s_1 \mid U)$ and $P(s_2 \mid U)$; note that these are also posterior probabilities, denoting the probabilities of the two states of nature *given* that the market research report is unfavorable. Finally at chance nodes 12, 13, and 14, we need the probabilities for the states of nature, $P(s_1)$ and $P(s_2)$, if the market research study is not undertaken.

In making the probability computations, we need to know PDC's assessment of the probabilities for the two states of nature, $P(s_1)$ and $P(s_2)$, which are the prior probabilities as discussed earlier. In addition, we must know the **conditional probability** of the market research outcomes (the sample information) *given* each state of nature. For example, we need to know the conditional probability of a favorable market research report given that strong demand exists for the PDC project; note that this conditional probability of F given state of nature s_1 is written $P(F \mid s_1)$. To carry out the probability calculations, we will need conditional probabilities for all sample outcomes given all states of nature, that is, $P(F \mid s_1)$, $P(F \mid s_2)$, $P(U \mid s_1)$, and $P(U \mid s_2)$. In the PDC problem, we assume that the following assessments are available for these conditional probabilities.

	Market Research	
State of Nature	**Favorable, F**	**Unfavorable, U**
Strong demand, s_1	$P(F \mid s_1) = 0.90$	$P(U \mid s_1) = 0.10$
Weak demand, s_2	$P(F \mid s_2) = 0.25$	$P(U \mid s_2) = 0.75$

Note that the preceding probability assessments provide a reasonable degree of confidence in the market research study. If the true state of nature is s_1, the probability of a favorable market research report is 0.90, and the probability of an unfavorable market research report is 0.10. If the true state of nature is s_2, the probability of a favorable market research report is 0.25, and the probability of an unfavorable market research report is 0.75. The reason for a 0.25 probability of a potentially misleading favorable market research report for state of nature s_2 is that when some potential buyers first hear about the new condominium project, their enthusiasm may lead them to overstate their real interest in it. A potential buyer's initial favorable response can change quickly to a "no thank you" when later faced with the reality of signing a purchase contract and making a down payment.

In the following discussion, we present a tabular approach as a convenient method for carrying out the probability computations. The computations for the PDC problem based

Figure 20.10 The PDC Decision Tree

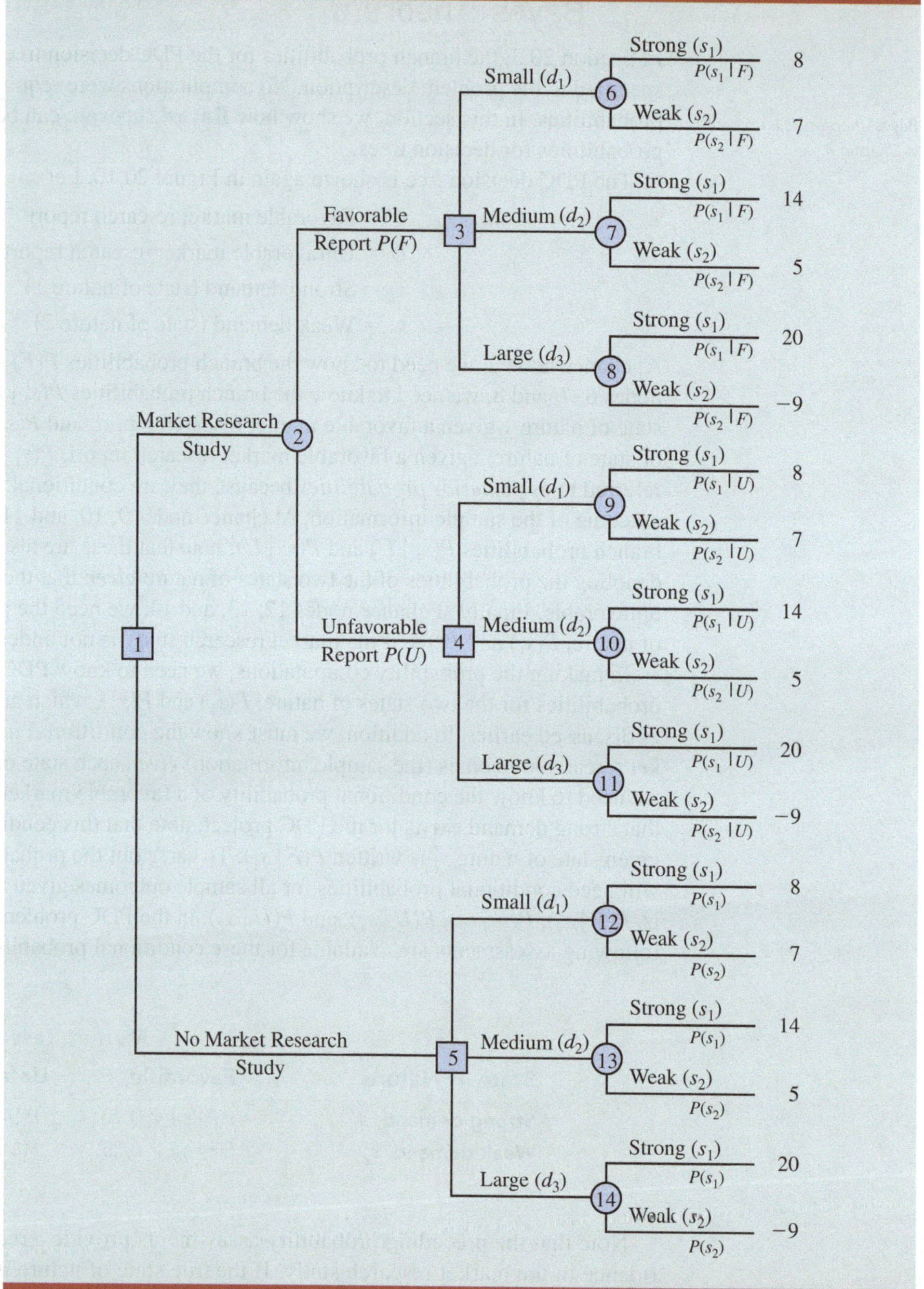

on a favorable market research report (F) are summarized in Table 20.3. The steps used to develop this table are as follows.

Step 1. In column 1, enter the states of nature. In column 2, enter the *prior probabilities* for the states of nature. In column 3, enter the *conditional probabilities* of a favorable market research report (F) given each state of nature.

Step 2. In column 4, compute the **joint probabilities** by multiplying the prior probability values in column 2 by the corresponding conditional probability values in column 3.

Table 20.3 Branch Probabilities for the PDC Condominium Project Based on a Favorable Market Research Report

States of Nature s_j	Prior Probabilities $P(s_j)$	Conditional Probabilities $P(F \mid s_j)$	Joint Probabilities $P(F \cap s_j)$	Posterior Probabilities $P(s_j \mid F)$
s_1	0.8	0.90	0.72	0.94
s_2	0.2	0.25	0.05	0.06
	1.0		$P(F) = 0.77$	1.00

Table 20.4 Branch Probabilities for the PDC Condominium Project Based on an Unfavorable Market Research Report

States of Nature s_j	Prior Probabilities $P(s_j)$	Conditional Probabilities $P(U \mid s_j)$	Joint Probabilities $P(F \cap s_j)$	Posterior Probabilities $P(s_j \mid U)$
s_1	0.8	0.10	0.08	0.35
s_2	0.2	0.75	0.15	0.65
	1.0		$P(U) = 0.23$	1.00

Step 3. Sum the joint probabilities in column 4 to obtain the probability of a favorable market research report, $P(F)$.

Step 4. Divide each joint probability in column 4 by $P(F) = 0.77$ to obtain the revised or *posterior probabilities,* $P(s_1 \mid F)$ and $P(s_2 \mid F)$.

Table 20.3 shows that the probability of obtaining a favorable market research report is $P(F) = 0.77$. In addition, $P(s_1 \mid F) = 0.94$ and $P(s_2 \mid F) = 0.06$. In particular, note that a favorable market research report will prompt a revised or posterior probability of 0.94 that the market demand of the condominium will be strong, s_1.

The tabular probability computation procedure must be repeated for each possible sample information outcome. Thus, Table 20.4 shows the computations of the branch probabilities of the PDC problem based on an unfavorable market research report. Note that the probability of obtaining an unfavorable market research report is $P(U) = 0.23$. If an unfavorable report is obtained, the posterior probability of a strong market demand, s_1, is 0.35 and of a weak market demand, s_2, is 0.65. The branch probabilities from Tables 20.3 and 20.4 were shown on the PDC decision tree in Figure 20.5.

The discussion in this section shows an underlying relationship between the probabilities on the various branches in a decision tree. To assume different prior probabilities, $P(s_1)$ and $P(s_2)$, without determining how these changes would alter $P(F)$ and $P(U)$, as well as the posterior probabilities $P(s_1 \mid F)$, $P(s_2 \mid F)$, $P(s_1 \mid U)$, and $P(s_2 \mid U)$, would be inappropriate.

Exercises

Methods

14. Suppose that you are given a decision situation with three possible states of nature: s_1, s_2, and s_3. The prior probabilities are $P(s_1) = 0.2$, $P(s_2) = 0.5$, and $P(s_3) = 0.3$. With sample information I, $P(I \mid s_1) = 0.1$, $P(I \mid s_2) = 0.05$, and $P(I \mid s_3) = 0.2$. Compute the revised or posterior probabilities: $P(s_1 \mid I)$, $P(s_2 \mid I)$, and $P(s_3 \mid I)$. **LO 5**
15. In the following profit payoff table for a decision problem with two states of nature and three decision alternatives, the prior probabilities for s_1 and s_2 are $P(s_1) = 0.8$ and $P(s_2) = 0.2$. **LO 2, 3, 5**

Decision Alternative	State of Nature s_1	s_2
d_1	15	10
d_2	10	12
d_3	8	20

a. What is the optimal decision?
b. Find the EVPI.
c. Suppose that sample information I is obtained, with $P(I \mid s_1) = 0.20$ and $P(I \mid s_2) = 0.75$. Find the posterior probabilities $P(s_1 \mid I)$ and $P(s_2 \mid I)$. Recommend a decision alternative based on these probabilities.

Applications

16. **Choosing a Route for Carpooling.** To save on expenses, Rona and Jerry agreed to form a carpool for traveling to and from work. Rona preferred to use the somewhat longer but more consistent Queen City Avenue. Although Jerry preferred the quicker expressway, he agreed with Rona that they should take Queen City Avenue, if the expressway had a traffic jam. The following payoff table provides the one-way time estimate in minutes for traveling to and from work.

Decision Alternative	State of Nature: Expressway Open s_1	Expressway Jammed s_2
Queen City Avenue, d_1	30	30
Expressway, d_2	25	45

Based on their experience with traffic problems, Rona and Jerry agreed on a 0.15 probability that the expressway would be jammed.

In addition, they agreed that weather seemed to affect the traffic conditions on the expressway. Let

C = clear
O = overcast
R = rain

The following conditional probabilities apply. **LO 1, 2, 5**

$P(C \mid s_1) = 0.8$ $P(O \mid s_1) = 0.2$ $P(R \mid s_1) = 0.0$
$P(C \mid s_2) = 0.1$ $P(O \mid s_2) = 0.3$ $P(R \mid s_2) = 0.6$

a. Use Bayes' theorem for probability revision to compute the probability of each weather condition and the conditional probability of the expressway open, s_1, or jammed, s_2, given each weather condition.
b. Show the decision tree for this problem.
c. What is the optimal decision strategy, and what is the expected travel time?

17. **Manufacture or Outsource.** The Gorman Manufacturing Company must decide whether to manufacture a component part at its Milan, Michigan, plant or purchase the component part from a supplier. The resulting profit is dependent upon the demand for the product. The following payoff table shows the projected profit (in thousands of dollars).

	State of Nature		
	Low Demand	Medium Demand	High Demand
Decision Alternative	s_1	s_2	s_3
Manufacture, d_1	−20	40	100
Purchase, d_2	10	45	70

The state-of-nature probabilities are $P(s_1) = 0.35$, $P(s_2) = 0.35$, and $P(s_3) = 0.30$.
LO 1, 2, 3, 4, 5

a. Use a decision tree to recommend a decision.
b. Use EVPI to determine whether Gorman should attempt to obtain a better estimate of demand.
c. A test market study of the potential demand for the product is expected to report either a favorable (F) or unfavorable (U) condition. The relevant conditional probabilities are as follows:

$$P(F \mid s_1) = 0.10 \qquad P(U \mid s_1) = 0.90$$
$$P(F \mid s_2) = 0.40 \qquad P(U \mid s_2) = 0.60$$
$$P(F \mid s_3) = 0.60 \qquad P(U \mid s_3) = 0.40$$

What is the probability that the market research report will be favorable?
d. What is Gorman's optimal decision strategy?
e. What is the expected value of the market research information?

Summary

Decision analysis can be used to determine a recommended decision alternative or an optimal decision strategy when a decision maker is faced with an uncertain and risk-filled pattern of future events. The goal of decision analysis is to identify the best decision alternative or the optimal decision strategy given information about the uncertain events and the possible consequences or payoffs. The uncertain future events are called chance events and the outcomes of the chance events are called states of nature.

We showed how payoff tables and decision trees could be used to structure a decision problem and describe the relationships among the decisions, the chance events, and the consequences. With probability assessments provided for the states of nature, the expected value approach was used to identify the recommended decision alternative or decision strategy.

In cases where sample information about the chance events is available, a sequence of decisions can be made. First we decide whether to obtain the sample information. If the answer to this decision is yes, an optimal decision strategy based on the specific sample information must be developed. In this situation, decision trees and the expected value approach can be used to determine the optimal decision strategy.

Glossary

Bayes' theorem A theorem that enables the use of sample information to revise prior probabilities.
Branch Lines showing the alternatives from decision nodes and the outcomes from chance nodes.
Chance event An uncertain future event affecting the consequence, or payoff, associated with a decision.
Chance nodes Nodes indicating points where an uncertain event will occur.

Conditional probabilities The probability of one event given the known outcome of a (possibly) related event.
Consequence The result obtained when a decision alternative is chosen and a chance event occurs. A measure of the consequence is often called a payoff.
Decision nodes Nodes indicating points where a decision is made.
Decision strategy A strategy involving a sequence of decisions and chance outcomes to provide the optimal solution to a decision problem.
Decision tree A graphical representation of the decision problem that shows the sequential nature of the decision-making process.
Expected value (EV) For a chance node, it is the weighted average of the payoffs. The weights are the state-of-nature probabilities.
Expected value approach An approach to choosing a decision alternative that is based on the expected value of each decision alternative. The recommended decision alternative is the one that provides the best expected value.
Expected value of perfect information (EVPI) The expected value of information that would tell the decision maker exactly which state of nature is going to occur (i.e., perfect information).
Expected value of sample information (EVSI) The difference between the expected value of an optimal strategy based on sample information and the "best" expected value without any sample information.
Joint probabilities The probabilities of both sample information and a particular state of nature occurring simultaneously.
Node An intersection or junction point of an influence diagram or a decision tree.
Payoff A measure of the consequence of a decision, such as profit, cost, or time. Each combination of a decision alternative and a state of nature has an associated payoff (consequence).
Payoff table A tabular representation of the payoffs for a decision problem.
Posterior (revised) probabilities The probabilities of the states of nature after revising the prior probabilities based on sample information.
Prior probabilities The probabilities of the states of nature prior to obtaining sample information.
Sample information New information obtained through research or experimentation that enables an updating or revision of the state-of-nature probabilities.
States of nature The possible outcomes for chance events that affect the payoff associated with a decision alternative.

Key Formulas

Expected Value

$$\text{EV}(d_i) = \sum_{j-1}^{N} P(s_j)V_{ij} \tag{20.3}$$

Expected Value of Perfect Information

$$\text{EVPI} = |\text{EVwPI} - \text{EVwoPI}| \tag{20.4}$$

Expected Value of Sample Information

$$\text{EVSI} = |\text{EVwSI} - \text{EVwoSI}| \tag{20.5}$$

Supplementary Exercises

18. **Selecting Mutual Funds.** An investor wants to select one of seven mutual funds for the coming year. Data showing the percentage annual return for each fund during five

typical one-year periods are shown here. The assumption is that one of these five-year periods will occur again during the coming year. Thus, years A, B, C, D, and E are the states of nature for the mutual fund decision. **LO 2**

	State of Nature				
Mutual Fund	**Year A**	**Year B**	**Year C**	**Year D**	**Year E**
Large-Cap Stock	35.3	20.0	28.3	10.4	−9.3
Mid-Cap Stock	32.3	23.2	−0.9	49.3	−22.8
Small-Cap Stock	20.8	22.5	6.0	33.3	6.1
Energy/Resources Sector	25.3	33.9	−20.5	20.9	−2.5
Health Sector	49.1	5.5	29.7	77.7	−24.9
Technology Sector	46.2	21.7	45.7	93.1	−20.1
Real Estate Sector	20.5	44.0	−21.1	2.6	5.1

a. Suppose that an experienced financial analyst reviews the five states of nature and provides the following probabilities: 0.1, 0.3, 0.1, 0.1, and 0.4. Using the expected value approach, what is the recommended mutual fund? What is the expected annual return? Using this mutual fund, what are the minimum and maximum annual returns?
b. A conservative investor notes that the Small-Cap mutual fund is the only fund that does not have the possibility of a loss. In fact, if the Small-Cap fund is chosen, the investor is guaranteed a return of at least 6%. What is the expected annual return for this fund?
c. Considering the mutual funds recommended in parts (a) and (b), which fund appears to have more risk? Why? Is the expected annual return greater for the mutual fund with more risk?
d. What mutual fund would you recommend to the investor? Explain.

19. **Determining Which Car to Lease.** Warren Lloyd is interested in leasing a new car and has contacted three automobile dealers for pricing information. Each dealer offered Warren a closed-end 36-month lease with no down payment due at the time of signing. Each lease includes a monthly charge and a mileage allowance. Additional miles receive a surcharge on a per-mile basis. The monthly lease cost, the mileage allowance, and the cost for additional miles follow:

Dealer	**Monthly Cost**	**Mileage Allowance**	**Cost per Additional Mile**
Forno Automotive	$299	36,000	$0.15
Midtown Motors	$310	45,000	$0.20
Hopkins Automotive	$325	54,000	$0.15

Warren decided to choose the lease option that will minimize his total 36-month cost. The difficulty is that Warren is not sure how many miles he will drive over the next three years. For purposes of this decision he believes it is reasonable to assume that he will drive 12,000 miles per year, 15,000 miles per year, or 18,000 miles per year. With this assumption Warren estimated his total costs for the three lease options. For example, he figures that the Forno Automotive lease will cost him $10,764 if he drives 12,000 miles per year; $12,114 if he drives 15,000 miles per year; or $13,464 if he drives 18,000 miles per year. **LO 1, 2**

a. What is the decision, and what is the chance event?
b. Construct a payoff table.
c. Suppose that the probabilities that Warren drives 12,000, 15,000, and 18,000 miles per year are 0.5, 0.4, and 0.1, respectively. What dealer should Warren choose?

d. Suppose that after further consideration, Warren concludes that the probabilities that he will drive 12,000, 15,000, and 18,000 miles per year are 0.3, 0.4, and 0.3, respectively. What dealer should Warren select?

20. **R&D Project Investment Decision.** Hemmingway, Inc., is considering a $5 million research and development (R&D) project. Profit projections appear promising, but Hemmingway's president is concerned because the probability that the R&D project will be successful is only 0.50. Secondly, the president knows that even if the project is successful, it will require that the company build a new production facility at a cost of $20 million in order to manufacture the product. If the facility is built, uncertainty remains about the demand and thus uncertainty about the profit that will be realized. Another option is that if the R&D project is successful, the company could sell the rights to the product for an estimated $25 million. Under this option, the company would not build the $20 million production facility.

The decision tree is shown in Figure 20.11. The profit projection for each outcome is shown at the end of the branches. For example, the revenue projection for the high-demand outcome is $59 million. However, the cost of the R&D project ($5 million) and the cost of the production facility ($20 million) show the profit of this outcome to be $59 − $5 − $20 = $34 million. Branch probabilities are also shown for the chance events. **LO 1, 2**

a. Analyze the decision tree to determine whether the company should undertake the R&D project. If it does, and if the R&D project is successful, what should the company do? What is the expected value of your strategy?

b. What must the selling price be for the company to consider selling the rights to the product?

21. **Medical Decision Making for Cancer Patients**. Cancer patients and their physicians face many decisions related to treatment options. Depending on the type of cancer, the location of the cancer, and patient history, treatment options can include surgery, chemotherapy, radiation therapy, and immunotherapy. The probability of the success of these treatments is affected by many factors based on the type of cancer and

Figure 20.11 Decision Tree for Hemmingway, Inc.

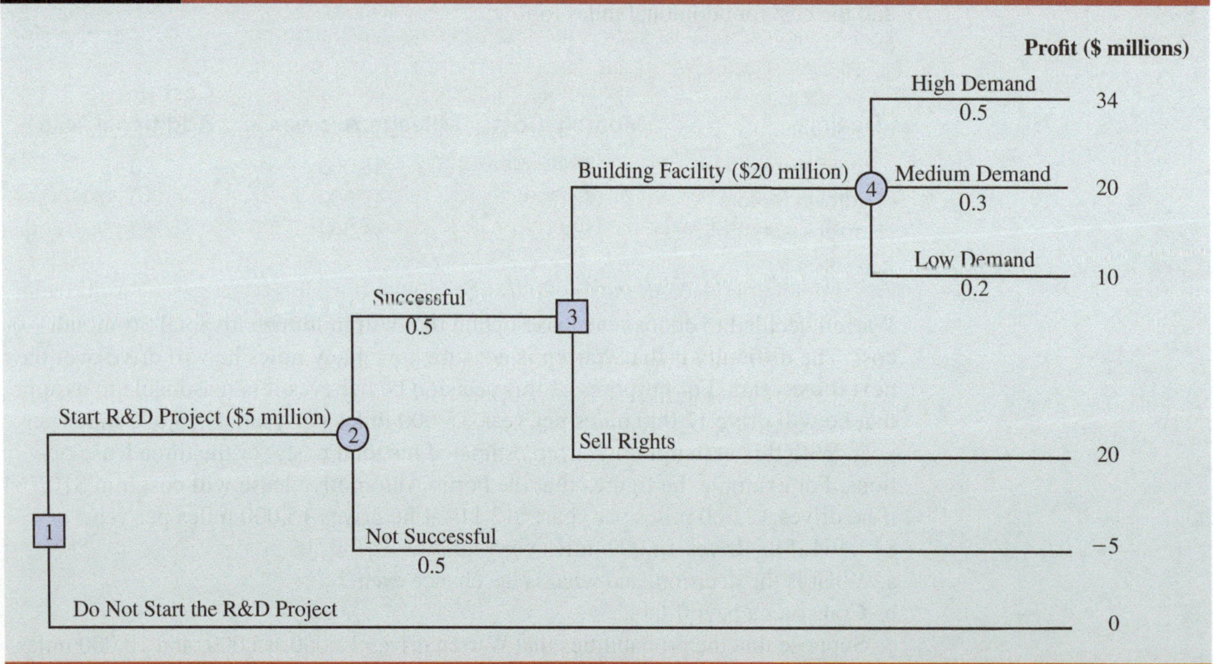

overall health of the patient. Medical decision makers often measure the expected effectiveness of different types of treatments using a metric called quality adjusted life year (QALY). One QALY is equivalent to one year of life in perfect health. Decision makers use QALYs to approximate the possible outcomes on the patient from different treatment options.

Suppose that a physician is working with a cancer patient to determine the best course of treatment. The physician and patient need to decide whether to have an exploratory surgery procedure to determine the spread of the cancer or to follow an active surveillance strategy in which no surgery is performed but the patient has regular tests to track progression of the cancer. If exploratory surgery is chosen, the results of the surgery can be favorable (F), unfavorable (U), or show that no further treatment is needed (N). Past data suggests that $P(F) = 0.5$, $P(U) = 0.2$, and $P(N) = 0.3$. If the exploratory surgery is favorable or unfavorable, then one of two treatments will be used, Treatment A (A) or Treatment B (B), using the following conditional probabilities:

$$P(A \mid F) = 0.4 \qquad P(A \mid U) = 0.8$$

$$P(B \mid F) = 0.6 \qquad P(B \mid U) = 0.2$$

Possible patient outcomes are measured using QALYs, and this depends on both the result of the exploratory surgery and the treatment option required, as shown in the following table.

Outcome of Exploratory Surgery	Treatment Option Required	Resulting QALYs
Favorable	A	22
Favorable	B	26
Unfavorable	A	14
Unfavorable	B	17
No Treatment Needed	None	35

If active surveillance is chosen, then the cancer can either progress (P) or not progress (NP), where $P(P) = 0.4$ and $P(NP) = 0.6$. If the cancer does not progress, then no further treatment is needed. If the cancer does progress, then either Treatment A or Treatment B will be required where $P(A|P) = 0.7$ and $P(B|P) = 0.3$. The possible resulting QALYs for this decision alternative follow. **LO 1, 2**

Outcome of Active Surveillance	Treatment Option Required	Resulting QALYs
Progress	A	15
Progress	B	20
Not Progress	None	35

a. Construct a decision tree for this problem.
b. Using the expected value approach and QALYs as the outcome measure, would you recommend exploratory surgery or active surveillance? What is the expected QALYs associated with this decision?

22. **Semiconductor Fabrication.** The integrated circuit (IC) chips used to power computers, phones, and many other devices are produced through a semiconductor fabrication

process. Blank discs made of silicon called wafers undergo processing steps that include etching and masking to create the transistors of extremely small size necessary for the integrated circuit. The processing takes place in clean rooms to prevent contamination, and the processes have extremely small tolerances to meet quality requirements.

Axeon Labs is considering production of a new type of IC chip for a customer. The customer has placed a one-time order, so Axeon must decide whether to produce or not to produce the order. Based on its previous experience, Axeon believes that the probability the chips will be acceptable (event A) to the customer if they produce them is $P(A) = 0.74$ and the probability the chips will be unacceptable (event U) is $P(U) = 0.26$. If Axeon produces the chips and they are acceptable, they will make a profit of $2.3 million If Axeon produces the chips and they are unacceptable, they will lose $1.1 million (profit = −$1.1 million). If Axeon does not produce the chips, the profit is $0.

Before making the decision of whether or not to begin production, Axeon has the opportunity to do a full quality check of its fabrication processes. This quality check will give additional information on the likelihood of Axeon producing acceptable or unacceptable chips for the customer. If Axeon chooses to do the quality check, it can either pass (event P) or fail (event F) the quality check. The revised probabilities are shown below.

$$P(A \mid P) = 0.93 \qquad P(A \mid F) = 0.11$$

$$P(U \mid P) = 0.07 \qquad P(U \mid F) = 0.89$$

The cost of the quality check is $15,000, and the probability of failing the quality check is 0.3 ($P(F) = 0.3$). **LO 1, 2, 3, 4**

a. Construct a decision tree for this problem assuming Axeon will first make a decision of whether or not to do the full quality check and then will make the decision of whether to produce or not.
b. Use the decision tree and an expected value approach to determine the optimal decision strategy for Axeon. Should Axeon do the full quality check?
c. What is the expected value of the sample information provided by the full quality check? What does this suggest about the maximum Axeon should be prepared to spend on a full quality check?
d. What is the expected value of perfect information for this decision problem? What does this suggest for Axeon?

Case Problem 1: Lawsuit Defense Strategy

John Campbell, an employee of Manhattan Construction Company, claims to have suffered a back injury as a result of a fall while repairing the roof at one of the Eastview apartment buildings. In a lawsuit asking for damages of $1,500,000, filed against Estella Reynaud, the owner of Eastview Apartments, John claims that the roof had rotten sections and that his fall could have been prevented if Estella had told Manhattan Construction about the problem. Allied Insurance represents Estella and Eastview Apartments, so Allied must decide what action to take regarding the lawsuit.

Following some depositions and a series of discussions between the two sides, John Campbell offered to accept a settlement of $750,000. Thus, one option is for Allied to pay John $750,000 to settle the claim. Allied is also considering making John a counteroffer of $400,000 in the hope that he will accept a lesser amount to avoid the time and cost of going to trial. Allied's preliminary investigation shows that John has a strong case; Allied is concerned that John may reject their counteroffer and request a jury trial. Allied's lawyers spent some time exploring John's likely reaction if they make a counteroffer of $400,000. The lawyers concluded that it is adequate to consider three possible outcomes to represent John's possible reaction to a counteroffer of $400,000: (1) John will accept the counteroffer and the case will be closed; (2) John will reject the counteroffer and elect to have a jury decide the settlement amount; or (3) John will make a counteroffer to Allied of $600,000. If John does make a counteroffer, Allied has decided that they will not make additional counteroffers. They will either accept John's counteroffer of $600,000 or go to trial.

If the case goes to a jury trial, Allied considers three outcomes possible: (1) The jury rejects John's claim and Allied will not be required to pay any damages; (2) the jury finds in favor of John and awards him $750,000 in damages; or (3) the jury concludes that John has a strong case and awards him the full amount of $1,500,000.

As Allied develops its strategy for disposing of the case, key considerations are the probabilities associated with John's response to an Allied counteroffer of $400,000, and the probabilities associated with the three possible trial outcomes. Allied's lawyers believe the probability that John will accept a counteroffer of $400,000 is 0.10, the probability that John will reject a counteroffer of $400,000 is 0.40, and the probability that John will, himself, make a counteroffer to Allied of $600,000 is 0.50. If the case goes to court, they believe that the probability the jury will award John damages of $1,500,000 is 0.30, the probability that the jury will award John damages of $750,000 is 0.50, and the probability that the jury will award John nothing is 0.20. **LO 1, 2**

Managerial Report

Perform an analysis of the problem facing Allied Insurance and prepare a report that summarizes your findings and recommendations. Be sure to include the following items:

1. A decision tree
2. A recommendation regarding whether Allied should accept John's initial offer to settle the claim for $750,000
3. A decision strategy that Allied should follow if they decide to make John a counteroffer of $400,000
4. A risk profile for your recommended strategy

Case Problem 2: Property Purchase Strategy

Hamed Namavari, president of Oceanview Development Corporation, is considering submitting a bid to purchase property that will be sold by sealed-bid auction at a county tax foreclosure. Hamed's initial judgment is to submit a bid of $5 million. Based on previous experience, Hamed estimates that a bid of $5 million will have a 0.2 probability of being the highest bid and securing the property for Oceanview. The current date is June 1. Sealed bids for the property must be submitted by August 15. The winning bid will be announced on September 1.

If Oceanview submits the highest bid and obtains the property, the firm plans to build and sell a complex of luxury condominiums. However, a complicating factor is that the property is currently zoned for single-family residences only. Hamed believes that a referendum could be placed on the voting ballot in time for the November election. Passage of the referendum would change the zoning of the property and permit construction of the condominiums.

The sealed-bid procedure requires the bid to be submitted with a certified check for 10% of the amount bid. If the bid is rejected, the deposit is refunded. If the bid is accepted, the deposit is the down payment for the property. However, if the bid is accepted and the bidder does not follow through with the purchase and meet the remainder of the financial obligation within six months, the deposit will be forfeited. In this case, the county will offer the property to the next highest bidder.

To determine whether Oceanview should submit the $5 million bid, Hamed conducted some preliminary analysis. This preliminary work provided an assessment that the referendum for a zoning change will be approved with 0.3 probability. Furthermore, the following estimates of the costs and revenues that will be incurred if the condominiums are built:

Costs and Revenue Estimates	
Revenue from condominium sales	\$15,000,000
Costs	
Property	\$5,000,000
Construction expenses	\$8,000,000

If Oceanview obtains the property and the zoning change is rejected in November, Hamed believes that the best option would be for the firm not to complete the purchase of the property. In this case, Oceanview would forfeit the 10% deposit that accompanied the bid.

Because the likelihood that the zoning referendum will be approved is such an important factor in the decision process, Hamed suggested that the firm hire a market research service to conduct a survey of voters. The survey would provide a better estimate of the likelihood that the referendum for a zoning change would be approved. The market research firm that Oceanview Development has worked with in the past has agreed to do the study for \$15,000. The results of the study will be available August 1, so that Oceanview will have this information before the August 15 bid deadline. The results of the survey will be a prediction either that the zoning change will be approved or that the zoning change will be rejected. After considering the record of the market research service in previous studies conducted for Oceanview, Hamed developed the following probability estimates concerning the accuracy of the market research information:

$$P(A \mid s_1) = 0.9 \qquad P(N \mid s_1) = 0.1$$
$$P(A \mid s_2) = 0.2 \qquad P(N \mid s_2) = 0.8$$

where

A = prediction of zoning change approval
N = prediction that zoning change will not be approved
s_1 = the zoning change is approved by the voters
s_2 = the zoning change is rejected by the voters

Managerial Report

Perform an analysis of the problem facing the Oceanview Development Corporation, and prepare a report that summarizes your findings and recommendations. Include the following items in your report. **LO 1, 2, 4**

1. A decision tree that shows the logical sequence of the decision problem
2. A recommendation regarding what Oceanview should do if the market research information is not available
3. A decision strategy that Oceanview should follow if the market research is conducted
4. A recommendation as to whether Oceanview should employ the market research firm, along with the value of the information provided by the market research firm

Include the details of your analysis as an appendix to your report.

Chapter 21

Sample Survey

Contents

Statistics in Practice:
Duke Energy

21.1 Terminology Used in Sample Surveys
21.2 Types of Surveys and Sampling Methods
21.3 Survey Errors
Nonsampling Error
Sampling Error
21.4 Simple Random Sampling
Population Mean
Population Total
Population Proportion
Using Excel for Simple Random Sampling
Determining the Sample Size
21.5 Stratified Simple Random Sampling
Population Mean
Using Excel: Population Mean
Population Total
Population Proportion
Using Excel: Population Proportion
Determining the Sample Size
21.6 Cluster Sampling
Population Mean
Population Total
Population Proportion
Using Excel for Cluster Sampling
Determining the Sample Size
21.7 Systematic Sampling

Summary 1014
Glossary 1015
Key Formulas 1015
Supplementary Exercises 1018
Case: Medicament's Predicament 1020

Learning Objectives

After completing this chapter, you will be able to

LO 1 Explain how nonsampling error might bias the results of a survey.

LO 2 Calculate the point estimate, standard error, and interval estimate of the population mean, population total, and population proportion at a given level of confidence for a simple random sample.

LO 3 Determine the sample size necessary to provide interval estimates of the population mean and the population total with a desired margin of error at a specified confidence level for a simple random sample.

LO 4 Calculate the point estimate, standard error, and interval estimate of the population mean, population total, and population proportion at a given level of confidence for a stratified random sample, and determine how many elements should be sampled in each stratum.

LO 5 Determine the sample size necessary to provide interval estimates of the population mean and the population total with a desired margin of error at a specified confidence level for a stratified simple random sample.

LO 6 Calculate the point estimate, standard error, and interval estimate of the population mean, population total, and population proportion at a given level of confidence for a cluster sample.

Statistics in Practice

Duke Energy*

Charlotte, North Carolina

Duke Energy is a diversified energy company with a portfolio of natural gas and electric businesses and an affiliated real estate company. Duke Energy is one of North America's largest energy companies, with assets totaling more than $180 billion. Today, Duke Energy serves more than 8.2 million electric and gas customers in North Carolina, South Carolina, Ohio, Florida, Indiana, and Kentucky.

To improve service to its customers, Duke Energy continually looks for emerging customer needs. In the following example, we discuss how the company used a Building Characteristics Survey to learn about the energy requirements of commercial buildings in the Cincinnati, Ohio, service area.

A variety of information concerning commercial buildings was sought, such as the floor space, number of employees, energy end use, age of the building, type of building materials, and energy conservation measures. During preparations for the survey, analysts determined that approximately 27,000 commercial buildings were in operation in the Cincinnati service area. Based on available funds and the precision desired in the results, a sample of 616 commercial buildings was recommended.

The sample design chosen was stratified simple random sampling. Total electrical usage over the past year for each commercial building in the service area was available from company records, and because many of the building characteristics of interest (size, number of employees, etc.) were related to usage, it was the criterion used to divide the population of buildings into six strata.

The first stratum contained the commercial buildings for the 100 largest energy users; each building in this stratum was included in the sample. Although these buildings constituted only 0.2% of the population, they accounted for 14.4% of the total electrical usage. For the other strata, the number of buildings sampled was determined on the basis of obtaining the greatest precision possible per unit cost.

A sample survey of energy requirements for commercial buildings was conducted in Cincinnati, Ohio. Rudy Balasko/Shutterstock.com

A questionnaire was developed and pretested before the actual survey was conducted. Data were collected through personal interviews. Completed surveys totaled 526 out of the sample of 616 commercial buildings. This response rate of 85.4% was considered to be excellent. The company used the survey results to improve the forecasts of energy demand and to improve service to its commercial customers.

In this chapter you will learn about the issues that statisticians consider in the design and execution of a sample survey such as the one conducted by Duke Energy. Sample surveys are often used to develop profiles of a company's customers; they are also used by the government and other agencies to learn about various segments of the population.

*The authors are indebted to Jim Riddle, formerly of Duke Energy, for providing this Statistics in Practice.

21.1 Terminology Used in Sample Surveys

These definitions are first introduced in Chapter 1.

The following are the definitions of an element, a population, and a sample.

- An **element** is the entity on which data are collected.
- A **population** is the collection of all the elements of interest.
- A **sample** is a subset of the population.

To illustrate these concepts, consider the following situation. Dunning Microsystems, Inc. (DMI), a manufacturer of personal computers and peripherals, would like to collect data about the characteristics of individuals who purchased a DMI personal computer. To obtain such data, a sample survey of DMI personal computer owners could be conducted.

The *elements* in this sample survey would be individuals who purchased a DMI personal computer. The *population* would be the collection of all people who purchased a DMI personal computer, and the *sample* would be the subset of DMI personal computer owners who are surveyed.

In sample surveys it is necessary to distinguish between the target population and the sampled population. The **target population** is the population we want to make inferences about, while the **sampled population** is the population from which the sample is actually selected. It is important to understand that these two populations are not always the same. In the DMI example, the target population consists of all people who purchased a DMI personal computer. The sampled population, however, might be all owners who sent warranty registration cards back to DMI. Not every person who buys a DMI personal computer sends in the warranty card, so the sampled population would differ from the target population.

If inferences from a sample are to be valid, the sampled population must be representative of the target population.

Conclusions drawn from a sample survey apply only to the sampled population. Whether these conclusions can be extended to the target population depends on the judgment of the analyst. The key issue is whether the correspondence between the sampled population and the target population on the characteristics of interest is close enough to allow this extension.

Before sampling, the population must be divided into **sampling units**. In some cases, the sampling units are simply the elements. In other cases, the sampling units are groups of the elements. For example, suppose we want to survey certified professional engineers who are involved in the design of heating and air conditioning systems for commercial buildings. If a list of all professional engineers involved in such work were available, the sampling units would be the professional engineers we want to survey. If such a list is not available, we must find an alternative approach. An Internet search might provide a list of all engineering firms involved in the design of heating and air conditioning systems. Given this list, we could select a sample of the engineering firms to survey; then, for each firm surveyed, we might interview all the professional engineers. In this case, the engineering firms would be the sampling units and the engineers interviewed would be the elements.

A list of the sampling units for a particular study is called a **frame**. In the sample survey of professional engineers, the frame is defined as all engineering firms found through an Internet search; the frame is not a list of all professional engineers because no such list is available. The choice of a particular frame and hence the definition of the sampling units is often determined by the availability and reliability of a list. In practice, the development of the frame can be one of the most difficult and important steps in conducting a sample survey.

21.2 Types of Surveys and Sampling Methods

The most common types of surveys are mail surveys, e-mail surveys, Internet surveys, telephone surveys, and personal interview surveys; each of these types involves the design and administration of a questionnaire. Other types of surveys used to collect data do not involve questionnaires. For example, accounting firms are often hired to sample a company's inventory of goods to estimate the value of inventory on the company's balance sheet. In such surveys, someone simply counts the items and records the results.

In surveys that use questionnaires, the design of the questionnaire is critical. The designer must resist the temptation to include questions that *might* be of interest, because every question adds to the length of the questionnaire. Long questionnaires lead not only to respondent fatigue, but also to interviewer fatigue, especially in mail and telephone surveys. However, if personal interviews are to be used, a longer and more complex questionnaire is feasible. A large body of knowledge exists concerning the phrasing, sequencing, and grouping of questions for a questionnaire. These issues are discussed in more comprehensive books on survey sampling; several sources for this type of information are listed in the bibliography.

Sample surveys can also be classified in terms of the sampling method used. With **probabilistic sampling**, the probability of obtaining each possible sample can be computed; with a **nonprobabilistic sampling**, this probability is unknown. Nonprobabilistic sampling methods should not be used if the researcher wants to make statements about the precision of the estimates. In contrast, probabilistic sampling methods can be used to develop confidence intervals that provide bounds on the sampling error. In the following sections, four of the most popular probabilistic sampling methods are discussed: simple random sampling, stratified simple random sampling, cluster sampling, and systematic sampling.

Although statisticians prefer to use a probabilistic sampling method, nonprobabilistic sampling methods often are necessary. The advantages of nonprobabilistic sampling methods are their low expense and ease of implementation. The disadvantage is that statistically valid statements cannot be made about the precision of the estimates. Two of the more common nonprobabilistic methods are convenience sampling and judgment sampling.

With **convenience sampling**, the units included in the sample are chosen because of accessibility. For example, a professor conducting a research study at a university may ask student volunteers to participate in the study simply because they are in the professor's class; in this case, the sample of students is referred to as a convenience sample. In some situations, convenience sampling is the only practical approach. For example, to sample a shipment of oranges, an inspector might select oranges haphazardly from several crates since labeling each orange in the entire shipment to create a frame and employing a probabilistic sampling method would be impractical. Wildlife captures and volunteer panels for consumer research are other examples of convenience samples.

Although convenience sampling is a relatively easy approach to sample selection and data gathering, it is impossible to evaluate the "goodness" of the sample statistics obtained in terms of their ability to estimate the population parameters of interest. A convenience sample may provide good results or it may not; there is no statistically justified procedure for making any statistical inferences from the sample results. Nevertheless, at times some researchers apply a statistical method designed for a probability sample to the data gathered from a convenience sample. In doing so, the researcher may argue that the convenience sample can be treated as though it were a random sample in the sense that it is representative of the population. However, this argument should be questioned; one should be cautious in using a convenience sample to make statistical inferences about population parameters.

In using the nonprobability sampling technique referred to as **judgment sampling**, a person knowledgeable on the subject of the study selects sampling units that he or she feels are most representative of the population. Although judgment sampling is often a relatively easy way to select samples, users of the survey results must recognize that the quality of the results is dependent on the judgment of the person selecting the sample. Consequently, caution must be exercised in using judgment samples to make statistical inferences about a population parameter. In general, no statistical statements should be made about the precision of the results from a judgment sample.

With a nonprobabilistic sampling method, if methods can be employed to ensure that a representative sample is obtained, point estimates based on the sample can be useful. However, even then the precision of the results is unknown.

Both probabilistic and nonprobabilistic sampling methods can be used to select a sample. The advantage of nonprobabilistic methods is that they are generally inexpensive and easy to use. However, if it is necessary to provide statements about the precision of the estimates, a probabilistic sampling method must be used. Almost all large sample surveys employ probabilistic sampling methods.

21.3 Survey Errors

Two types of errors can occur in conducting a survey. One type, **sampling error**, is defined as the magnitude of the difference between an unbiased point estimator developed from the sample and the population parameter. In other words, sampling error is the error that occurs because not every element in the population is surveyed. The second type, **nonsampling**

error, refers to all other types of errors that can occur when a survey is conducted, such as measurement error, interviewer error, and processing error. Although sampling error can occur only in a sample survey, nonsampling errors can occur in both a census and a sample survey.

Nonsampling Error

Nonsampling error can be minimized by proper interviewer training, good questionnaire design, pretesting, and careful management of the process of coding and transferring the data to the computer.

One of the most common types of nonsampling error occurs whenever we incorrectly measure the characteristic of interest. Measurement error can occur in a census or a sample survey. For either type of survey, the researcher must exercise care to ensure that any measuring instruments (e.g., the questionnaire) are properly calibrated and that the people who take the measurements are properly trained. Attention to detail is the best precaution in most situations.

Errors due to nonresponse are a concern to both the statistician responsible for designing the survey and the manager using the results. This type of nonsampling error occurs when data cannot be obtained for some of the units surveyed or when only partial data are obtained. The problem is most serious when a bias is created. For example, if a survey is conducted to measure potential voter preferences on a particular upcoming election, and the survey is conducted by calling only landline phones, this will create a bias because the responses will likely miss many younger individuals who use only a cell phone.

Nonsampling errors due to lack of respondent knowledge are common in technical surveys. For example, suppose building managers were surveyed to obtain detailed information about the types of ventilation systems used in office buildings. Managers of large office buildings may be especially knowledgeable about such systems because they may attend training seminars and have support staff to help keep them current. In contrast, managers of smaller office buildings may be less knowledgeable about such systems because of the wide variety of duties they must perform. This difference in knowledge can significantly affect the survey results.

Two other types of nonsampling error are selection error and processing error. Selection errors occur when an inappropriate sampling unit is surveyed. Suppose a sample survey was designed to develop a profile of video game players; if some interviewers interpreted the statement "video game players" to mean only those who play video games on a console or personal computer while other interviewers included those who play video games on their phones, the resulting data would be flawed. Processing errors occur whenever data are incorrectly recorded or incorrectly transferred from recording forms, such as from questionnaires to computer files.

Although some nonsampling errors will occur in most surveys, they can be minimized by careful planning. Care should be taken to ensure that the sampled population corresponds closely to the target population, that good questionnaire design principles are followed, that interviewers are well trained, and so on. The final report on a survey should include some discussion of the likely impact of nonsampling errors on the results.

Sampling Error

Recall the Dunning Microsystems (DMI) sample survey mentioned previously. Suppose DMI wants to estimate the mean age of people who have purchased a DMI personal computer. If the entire population of DMI personal computer owners could be surveyed (a census) and nonsampling errors were not present, we could determine the mean age exactly. But what if less than 100% of the population of DMI owners can be surveyed? In this case, there will most likely be a difference between the sample mean and the population mean; the absolute value of this difference is the sampling error. In practice, it is not possible to know what the sampling error will be for any one particular sample because the population mean is unknown; however, it is possible to provide probability statements about the size of the sampling error.

Sampling error is minimized by proper choice of a sample design.

As stated, sampling error occurs because a sample, and not the entire population, is surveyed. Even though sampling error cannot be avoided, it can be controlled. Selecting an appropriate sampling method or design is one important way to control this type of error. In the following sections we will discuss four probabilistic sampling methods: simple random sampling, stratified simple random sampling, cluster sampling, and systematic sampling.

21.4 Simple Random Sampling

Simple random sampling is first introduced in Chapter 7.

The definition of simple random sampling is:

> A simple random sample of size n from a finite population of size N is a sample selected such that every possible sample of size n has the same probability of being selected.

To conduct a sample survey using **simple random sampling**, we begin by developing a frame or list of all elements in the sampled population. Then a selection procedure, based on the use of random numbers, is used to ensure that each element in the sampled population has the same probability of being selected. In this section we show how estimates of a population mean, total, and proportion are made for sample surveys that use simple random sampling.

Population Mean

Properties of the sample mean are introduced in Chapter 8.

The sample mean $\bar{x}$ is an estimate of the population mean μ, and the sample standard deviation s is an estimate of the population standard deviation σ. For a sample of size n, the t distribution can be used to provide the following interval estimate of μ.

$$\bar{x} \pm t_{\alpha/2}\frac{s}{\sqrt{n}} \qquad \textbf{(21.1)}$$

In expression (21.1), $s/\sqrt{n}$ is the estimate of $\sigma_{\bar{x}}$, the standard error of the mean.

When a simple random sample of size n is selected from a finite population of size N, an estimate of the standard error of the mean is

$$s_{\bar{x}} = \sqrt{\frac{N-n}{N}}\left(\frac{s}{\sqrt{n}}\right) \qquad \textbf{(21.2)}$$

Using $s_{\bar{x}}$ as an estimate of $\sigma_{\bar{x}}$, the interval estimate of the population mean becomes

$$\bar{x} \pm t_{\alpha/2}s_{\bar{x}} \qquad \textbf{(21.3)}$$

In a sample survey, it is common practice to use a value of $t = 2$ when developing interval estimates. Thus, when simple random sampling is used, an approximate 95% confidence interval estimate of the population mean is given by the following expression.

Approximate 95% Confidence Interval Estimate of the Population Mean

$$\bar{x} \pm 2s_{\bar{x}} \qquad \textbf{(21.4)}$$

As an example, consider the situation of the publisher of *Great Lakes Recreation,* a regional magazine specializing in articles on boating and fishing. The magazine currently has $N = 8{,}000$ subscribers. A simple random sample of $n = 484$ subscribers shows mean annual income to be \$60,500 with a standard deviation of \$7,040. An unbiased estimate of the mean annual income of all subscribers is given by $\bar{x} = \$60{,}500$. Using the sample results and equation (21.2), we obtain the following estimate of the standard error of the mean.

$$s_{\bar{x}} = \sqrt{\frac{8{,}000-484}{8{,}000}}\left(\frac{7{,}040}{\sqrt{484}}\right) = 310$$

Therefore, using formula (21.4), we find that an approximate 95% confidence interval estimate of the mean annual income for the magazine subscribers is

$$60{,}500 \pm 2(310) = 60{,}500 \pm 620$$

or \$59,880 to \$61,120.

The number added to and subtracted from a point estimate to create an interval estimate is called the **bound on the sampling error**. For example, in the *Great Lakes Recreation* sample survey, an estimate of the standard error of the point estimator is $s_{\bar{x}} = \$310$, and the bound on the sampling error is 2(\$310) = \$620.

The preceding procedure can be used to compute an interval estimate for other population parameters such as the population total or the population proportion. In these cases, the approximate 95% confidence interval can be written as

$$\text{Point estimator} \pm 2(\text{Estimate of the standard error of the point estimator})$$

Population Total

DATA*file*
neg

Consider the problem facing Northeast Electric and Gas (NEG). As part of an energy usage study, NEG needs to estimate the *total* square footage for the 500 public schools in its service area. We will denote the total square footage for the 500 schools as X; in other words, X denotes the population total. Note that if μ, the mean square footage for the 500 public schools, were known, the value of X could be computed by multiplying N times μ. However, because μ is unknown, a point estimate of X is obtained by multiplying N times $\bar{x}$. We will denote the point estimator of X as $\hat{X}$.

Point Estimator of a Population Total

$$\hat{X} = N\bar{x} \tag{21.5}$$

An estimate of the standard error of this point estimator is given by

$$s_{\hat{X}} = Ns_{\bar{x}} \tag{21.6}$$

where

$$s_{\bar{x}} = \sqrt{\frac{N-n}{N}}\left(\frac{s}{\sqrt{n}}\right) \tag{21.7}$$

Note that equation (21.7) is the formula for the estimated standard error of the mean. With this standard error and equation (21.6), an approximate 95% confidence interval for the population total is given by the following expression.

Approximate 95% Confidence Interval Estimate of the Population Total

$$N\bar{x} \pm 2s_{\hat{X}} \tag{21.8}$$

Suppose that in the NEG study a simple random sample of $n = 50$ public schools is selected from the population of $N = 500$ schools; the sample mean is $\bar{x} = 22{,}000$ square feet and the sample standard deviation is $s = 4{,}000$ square feet. Using equation (21.5), we find that the point estimator of the population total is

$$\hat{X} = (500)(22{,}000) = 11{,}000{,}000$$

Equation (21.7) can be used to compute an estimate of the standard error of the mean.

$$s_{\bar{x}} = \sqrt{\frac{500-50}{500}}\left(\frac{4{,}000}{\sqrt{50}}\right) = 536.66$$

Then, using equation (21.6), we can obtain an estimate of the standard error of $\hat{X}$.

$$s_{\hat{X}} = (500)(536.66) = 268{,}330$$

Therefore, using expression (21.8), we find that an approximate 95% confidence interval estimate of the total square footage for the 500 public schools in NEG's service area is

$$11{,}000{,}000 \pm 2(268{,}330) = 11{,}000{,}000 \pm 536{,}660$$

or 10,463,340 to 11,536,660 square feet.

Population Proportion

The population proportion p is the fraction of the elements in the population with some characteristic of interest. In a market research study, for example, one might be interested in the proportion of consumers preferring a certain brand of product. The sample proportion $\bar{p}$ is an unbiased point estimator of the population proportion. An estimate of the standard error of the proportion is given by

$$s_{\bar{p}} = \sqrt{\left(\frac{N-n}{N}\right)\left(\frac{\bar{p}(1-\bar{p})}{n-1}\right)} \quad \textbf{(21.9)}$$

An approximate 95% confidence interval estimate of the population proportion is given by the following expression.

Approximate 95% Confidence Interval Estimate of the Population Proportion

$$\bar{p} \pm 2s_{\bar{p}} \quad \textbf{(21.10)}$$

As an illustration, suppose that in the Northeast Electric and Gas sampling problem, NEG would also like to estimate the proportion of the 500 public schools in its service area that use natural gas as fuel for heating. If 35 of the 50 sampled schools indicate the use of natural gas, the point estimate of the proportion of the 500 schools in the population that use natural gas is $\bar{p} = 35/50 = 0.70$. Using equation (21.9), we can compute an estimate of the standard error of the proportion.

$$s_p = \sqrt{\left(\frac{500-50}{500}\right)\left(\frac{0.7(1-0.7)}{50-1}\right)} = 0.0621$$

Therefore, using expression (21.10), we find that an approximate 95% confidence interval for the population proportion is

$$0.7 \pm 2(0.0621) = 0.7 \pm 0.1242$$

or 0.5758 to 0.8242.

As this example shows, the width of the confidence interval can be rather large when one is estimating a population proportion. In general, large sample sizes are needed to obtain precise estimates of population proportions.

Using Excel for Simple Random Sampling

We assume the Excel procedure described in Chapter 7 has been used to select the sample.

To show how Excel can be used to summarize the results for sample surveys that use simple random sampling, we will construct an approximate 95% confidence interval of the population mean, population total, and population proportion for the NEG study. We begin with the population total case. Refer to Figure 21.1 as we describe the tasks involved. The formula worksheet is in the background; the value worksheet appears in the foreground.

Enter/Access Data: Open the file *neg*. In Figure 21.1, column A identifies the school in the sample and column B shows the number of square feet in the school.

Enter Functions and Formulas: The population size is entered in cell E3 and the descriptive statistics needed are provided in cells E4:E6. Excel's COUNT, AVERAGE, and STDEV.S functions are used to compute the sample size, sample mean, and sample standard deviation, respectively.

Cells E8:E10 are used to compute the standard error of the mean, standard error of the total, and the bound on the sampling error. The standard error of the mean was computed

Figure 21.1 Excel Worksheet for the Population Total in the NEG Example

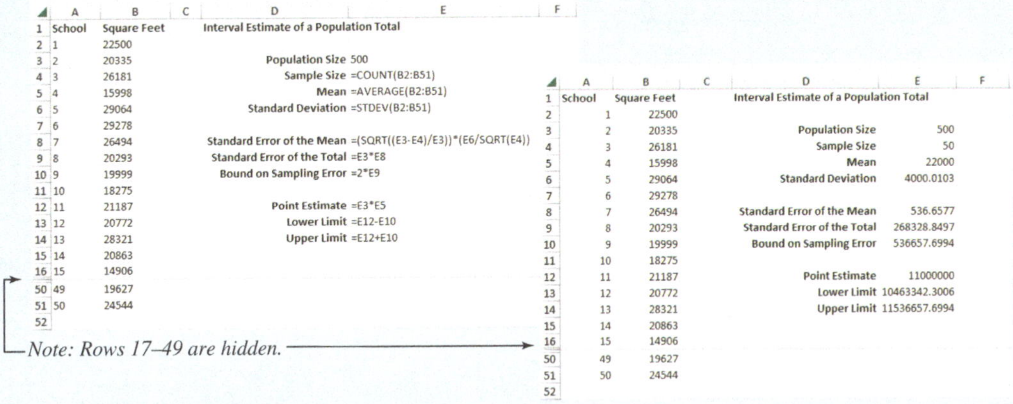

	A	B	C	D	E	F
1	School	Square Feet		Interval Estimate of a Population Total		
2	1	22500				
3	2	20335		Population Size	500	
4	3	26181		Sample Size	=COUNT(B2:B51)	
5	4	15998		Mean	=AVERAGE(B2:B51)	
6	5	29064		Standard Deviation	=STDEV(B2:B51)	
7	6	29278				
8	7	26494		Standard Error of the Mean	=(SQRT((E3-E4)/E3))*(E6/SQRT(E4))	
9	8	20293		Standard Error of the Total	=E3*E8	
10	9	19999		Bound on Sampling Error	=2*E9	
11	10	18275				
12	11	21187		Point Estimate	=E3*E5	
13	12	20772		Lower Limit	=E12-E10	
14	13	28321		Upper Limit	=E12+E10	
15	14	20863				
16	15	14906				
50	49	19627				
51	50	24544				
52						

	A	B	C	D	E	F
1	School	Square Feet		Interval Estimate of a Population Total		
2	1	22500				
3	2	20335		Population Size	500	
4	3	26181		Sample Size	50	
5	4	15998		Mean	22000	
6	5	29064		Standard Deviation	4000.0103	
7	6	29278				
8	7	26494		Standard Error of the Mean	536.6577	
9	8	20293		Standard Error of the Total	268328.8497	
10	9	19999		Bound on Sampling Error	536657.6994	
11	10	18275				
12	11	21187		Point Estimate	11000000	
13	12	20772		Lower Limit	10463342.3006	
14	13	28321		Upper Limit	11536657.6994	
15	14	20863				
16	15	14906				
50	49	19627				
51	50	24544				
52						

Note: Rows 17–49 are hidden.

DATA*file*
neg

using equation (21.2) by entering the formula *=(SQRT((E3-E4)/E3))*(E6/SQRT(E4))* in cell E8. The standard error of the total was computed using equation (21.6) by entering the formula *=E3*E8* in cell E9, and the bound on the sampling error was computed in cell E10 by entering the formula *=2*E9*. The value worksheet shows that the standard error of the mean is 536.6577, the standard error of the total is 268,328.8497, and the bound on the sampling error is 536,657.6994.

Cells E12:E14 provide the point estimate and the lower and upper limits for the confidence interval. Because the point estimate of the population total is just the population size times the sample mean, we entered the formula *=E3*E5* in cell E12. To compute the lower limit of the 95% confidence interval, the formula *=E12-E10* was entered in cell E13; to compute the upper limit, the formula *=E12+E10* was entered in cell E14. The value worksheet shows that the point estimate of the population total is 11,000,000 and that the 95% approximate interval is 10,463,342 to 11,536,658. The differences in the Excel values and the hand calculations we computed previously are due to the fact that in doing the hand calculations we rounded the intermediate calculations to simplify the presentation.

It is easy to compute an approximate 95% confidence interval for the population mean in the NEG study by modifying the worksheet developed to compute the approximate 95% confidence interval of the population total. For this case, the point estimate shown in cell E12 is just the sample mean in cell E5; thus, we would enter the formula *=E5* in cell E12. The bound on the sampling error would be two times the standard error of the mean in cell E8; thus, we would enter the formula *=2*E8* in cell E10. The resulting lower and upper limits in cells E13:E14 would be the upper and lower limits of the approximate 95% confidence interval of the population mean.

To show how Excel can be used to compute an approximate 95% confidence interval for the population proportion, we will compute an approximate 95% confidence interval of the proportion of schools in the NEG example that use natural gas as fuel for heating. Refer to Figure 21.2 as we describe the tasks involved. The formula worksheet is in the background; the value worksheet appears in the foreground.

Enter/Access Data: Open the file named *neg*. In Figure 21.2, column A identifies the school and column B indicates whether the school uses natural gas as fuel for heating.

Enter Functions and Formulas: The descriptive statistics needed are provided in cells E4, E6, and E7. The population size and response of interest are typed in cells E3 and E5. Excel's COUNTA and COUNTIF functions are used to compute the sample size and the

Figure 21.2 Excel Worksheet for the NEG Study: Population Proportion

	A	B	C	D	E	F
1	School	Natural Gas?		Interval Estimate of a Population Proportion		
2	1	No				
3	2	Yes		Population Size	500	
4	3	Yes		Sample Size	=COUNTA(B2:B51)	
5	4	Yes		Response of Interest	Yes	
6	5	No		Count for Response	=COUNTIF(B2:B51,E5)	
7	6	Yes		Sample Proportion	=E6/E4	
8	7	Yes				
9	8	Yes		Standard Error of the Proportion	=SQRT(((E3-E4)/E3)*(E7*(1-E7)/(E4-1)))	
10	9	Yes		Bound on Sampling Error	=2*E9	
11	10	Yes				
12	11	Yes		Point Estimate	=E7	
13	12	Yes		Lower Limit	=E12-E10	
14	13	No		Upper Limit	=E12+E10	
15	14	No				
16	15	No				
50	49	Yes				
51	50	Yes				
52						

	A	B	C	D	E	F
1	School	Natural Gas?		Interval Estimate of a Population Proportion		
2	1	No				
3	2	Yes		Population Size	500	
4	3	Yes		Sample Size	50	
5	4	Yes		Response of Interest	Yes	
6	5	No		Count for Response	35	
7	6	Yes		Sample Proportion	0.7	
8	7	Yes				
9	8	Yes		Standard Error of the Proportion	0.0621	
10	9	Yes		Bound on Sampling Error	0.1242	
11	10	Yes				
12	11	Yes		Point Estimate	0.7	
13	12	Yes		Lower Limit	0.5758	
14	13	No		Upper Limit	0.8242	
15	14	No				
16	15	No				
50	49	Yes				
51	50	Yes				
52						

Note: Rows 17–49 are hidden.

number of schools in the sample that use natural gas. The value worksheet shows that 35 schools use natural gas and that the sample proportion is 0.7.

Cells E9:E10 are used to compute the standard error of the proportion and the bound on the sampling error. The standard error of the proportion was computed using equation (21.9) by entering the formula *=SQRT(((E3-E4)/E3)*(E7*(1-E7))/(E4-1))* in cell E9. The bound on the sampling error was computed in cell E10 by entering the formula *=2*E9*. The value worksheet shows that the value of the standard error of the proportion is 0.0621 and that the bound on the sampling error is 0.1242.

Cells E12:E14 provide the point estimate and the lower and upper limits for the confidence interval. Because the point estimate of the population proportion is just the sample proportion, we entered the formula *=E7* in cell E12. To compute the lower limit of the 95% confidence interval, the formula *=E12-E10* was entered in cell E13; to compute the upper limit, the formula *=E12+E10* was entered in cell E14. The value worksheet shows that the point estimate of the population proportion is 0.7 and that the 95% approximate interval is 0.5758 to 0.8242.

Determining the Sample Size

An important consideration in sample design is the choice of sample size. The best choice usually involves a trade-off between cost and precision. Larger samples provide greater precision (tighter bounds on the sampling error) but are more costly. Often the budget for a study will dictate how large the sample can be. In other cases, the size of the sample must be large enough to provide a specified level of precision.

A common approach to choosing the sample size is to first specify the precision desired and then determine the smallest sample size providing that precision. In this context, the term *precision* refers to the size of the approximate confidence interval; smaller confidence intervals provide more precision. Because the size of the approximate confidence interval depends on the bound B on the sampling error, choosing a level of precision amounts to choosing a value for B. Let us see how this approach works in choosing the sample size necessary to estimate the population mean.

Equation (21.2) showed that the estimate of the standard error of the mean is

$$s_{\bar{x}} = \sqrt{\frac{N-n}{N}}\left(\frac{s}{\sqrt{n}}\right)$$

Recall that the bound on the sampling error is "2 times the estimate of the standard error of the point estimator." Thus,

$$B = 2\sqrt{\frac{N-n}{N}}\left(\frac{s}{\sqrt{n}}\right) \tag{21.11}$$

Solving equation (21.11) for n will provide a bound on the sampling error equal to B. Doing so yields

$$n = \frac{Ns^2}{N\left(\frac{B^2}{4}\right) + s^2} \tag{21.12}$$

Once a desired level of precision has been selected (by choosing a value for B), equation (21.12) can be used to find the value of n that will provide the desired level of precision. Using equation (21.12) to choose n for a practical study presents problems, however. In addition to specifying the desired bound on the sampling error B, one must know the sample variance s^2, but s^2 will not be known until the sample is actually taken.

Cochran[1] suggests several ways to develop an estimate of s^2 in practice. Three of them are stated as the following:

1. Take the sample in two stages. Use the value of s^2 found in stage 1 in equation (21.12); the resulting value of n is what the size of the total sample must be. Then, select the number of additional units needed at stage 2 to provide the total sample size determined in stage 1.
2. Use the results of a pilot survey or pretest to estimate s^2.
3. Use information from a previous sample.

Let us now consider an example involving the estimate of the population mean for monthly starting salaries of graduates of a particular university. Suppose, with $N = 5{,}000$ graduates, we want to develop an approximate 95% confidence interval with a width of at most $1,000. To provide such a confidence interval, $B = 500$. Before using equation (21.12) to determine the sample size, we need an estimate of s^2. Suppose a study of starting salaries conducted last year found that $s = \$4{,}600$. We can use the data from this previous sample to estimate s^2. Using $B = 500$, $s = 4{,}600$, and $N = 5{,}000$, we can now use equation (21.12) to determine the sample size.

$$n = \frac{5{,}000(4{,}600)^2}{5{,}000\left(\frac{(500)^2}{4}\right) + (4{,}600)^2}$$
$$= 317.09$$

Rounding up, we see that a sample size of 318 will provide an approximate 95% confidence interval of width $1,000. Keep in mind, however, that this calculation is based on the initial estimate of $s = \$4{,}600$. If s turns out to be larger in this year's sample survey, the resulting approximate confidence interval will have a width greater than $1,000. Consequently, if cost considerations permit, the survey designer might choose a sample size of, say, 350 or 400 to provide added assurance that the final approximate 95% confidence interval will have a width less than $1,000.

The formula for determining the sample size necessary for estimating a population total with a bound B on the sampling error is as follows.

$$n = \frac{Ns^2}{\left(\frac{B^2}{4N}\right) + s^2} \tag{21.13}$$

In the previous example, we wanted to estimate the mean starting salary with a bound on the sampling error of $B = 500$. Suppose we are also interested in estimating the total

[1]William G. Cochran, *Sampling Techniques*, 3rd ed., Wiley, 1977.

salary of all 5,000 graduates with a bound of \$2 million. We can use equation (21.13) with $B = 2{,}000{,}000$ to find the sample size needed to provide such a bound on the population total.

$$n = \frac{5{,}000(4{,}600)^2}{\dfrac{(2{,}000{,}000)^2}{4(5{,}000)} + (4{,}600)^2}$$
$$= 478.39$$

Rounding up, we see that a sample size of 479 is necessary to provide an approximate 95% confidence interval with a bound of \$2 million. We note here that if the same survey is expected to provide a bound of \$500 on the population mean and a bound of \$2 million on the population total, a sample size of at least 479 must be used. This size will provide a tighter bound than necessary on the population mean, while providing the minimum desired precision for the population total.

To choose the sample size for estimating a population proportion, we use a formula similar to the one for the population mean. We simply substitute $\bar{p}(1 - \bar{p})$ for s^2 in equation (21.12) to obtain

$$n = \frac{N\bar{p}(1 - \bar{p})}{N\left(\dfrac{B^2}{4}\right) + \bar{p}(1 - \bar{p})} \tag{21.14}$$

To use equation (21.14), we must specify the desired bound B and provide an estimate of $\bar{p}$. If a good estimate of $\bar{p}$ is not available, we can use $\bar{p} = 0.5$; it will ensure that the resulting approximate confidence interval will have a bound on the sampling error at least as small as desired.

Exercises

Methods

1. Simple random sampling was used to obtain a sample of $n = 50$ elements from a population of $N = 800$. The sample mean was $\bar{x} = 215$, and the sample standard deviation was found to be $s = 20$. **LO 2**
   a. Estimate the population mean.
   b. Estimate the standard error of the mean.
   c. Develop an approximate 95% confidence interval for the population mean.
2. Simple random sampling was used to obtain a sample of $n = 80$ elements from a population of $N = 400$. The sample mean was $\bar{x} = 75$, and the sample standard deviation was found to be $s = 8$. **LO 2**
   a. Estimate the population total.
   b. Estimate the standard error of the population total.
   c. Develop an approximate 95% confidence interval for the population total.
3. Simple random sampling was used to obtain a sample of $n = 100$ elements from a population of $N = 1{,}000$. The sample proportion was $\bar{p} = 0.30$. **LO 2**
   a. Estimate the population proportion.
   b. Estimate the standard error of the proportion.
   c. Develop an approximate 95% confidence interval for the population proportion.
4. A sample is to be taken to develop an approximate 95% confidence interval estimate of the population mean. The population consists of 450 elements, and a pilot study resulted in $s = 70$. How large must the sample be if we want to develop an approximate 95% confidence interval with a width of 30? **LO 3**

Applications

5. **MLB Salaries.** On opening day of 2022, there were 750 players on the rosters of major league baseball teams. Suppose a sample of 65 major league baseball players

showed an average annual salary \$4,170,000 with a standard deviation of \$1,950,240 and that 13 of the players in the sample were pitchers. **LO 2**

a. Develop an approximate 95% confidence interval for the population mean annual income or major league baseball players.
b. Develop an approximate 95% confidence interval for the total value of all 750 major league baseball player salaries.
c. In the sample, 13 of the 65 players are pitchers. Develop an approximate 95% confidence interval for the proportion of major league players who are pitchers.

6. **California State Tax Returns.** A county in California had 724 corporate tax returns filed. The mean annual income reported was \$161,220 with a standard deviation of \$31,300. How large a sample will be necessary next year to develop an approximate 95% confidence interval for mean annual corporate earnings? The precision required is an interval width of no more than \$5,000. **LO 3**

21.5 Stratified Simple Random Sampling

In **stratified simple random sampling**, the population is first divided into H groups, called strata. Then for stratum h, a simple random sample of size n_h is selected. The data from the H simple random samples are combined to develop an estimate of a population parameter such as the population mean, total, or proportion.

If the variability within each stratum is smaller than the variability across the strata, a stratified simple random sample can lead to greater precision (narrower interval estimates of the population parameters). The basis for forming the various strata depends on the judgment of the designer of the sample. Depending on the application, a population might be stratified by department, location, age, product type, industry type, sales levels, and so on.

DATA*file*
lakeland

As an example, suppose the College of Business at Lakeland College wants to conduct a survey of this year's graduating class to learn about their starting salaries. There are five majors in the college: accounting, finance, information systems, marketing, and operations management. Of the $N = 1{,}500$ students who graduated this year, there were $N_1 = 500$ accounting majors, $N_2 = 350$ finance majors, $N_3 = 200$ information systems majors, $N_4 = 300$ marketing majors, and $N_5 = 150$ operations management majors. Analysis of previous salary data suggests more variability in starting salaries across majors than within each major. As a result, a stratified simple random sample of $n = 180$ students is selected; 45 of the 180 students majored in accounting ($n_1 = 45$), 40 majored in finance ($n_2 = 40$), 30 majored in information systems ($n_3 = 30$), 35 majored in marketing ($n_4 = 35$), and 30 majored in operations management ($n_5 = 30$).

Population Mean

In stratified sampling an unbiased estimate of the population mean is obtained by computing a weighted average of the sample means for each stratum. The weights used are the fraction of the population in each stratum. The resulting point estimator, denoted $\bar{x}_{\text{st}}$, is defined as follows. For stratified simple random sampling, the formula for computing an estimate of the standard error of the mean is a function of s_h, the sample standard deviation for stratum h.

Point Estimator of the Population Mean

$$\bar{x}_{\text{st}} = \sum_{h=1}^{H} \left(\frac{N_h}{N}\right)\bar{x}_h \qquad \textbf{(21.15)}$$

where

H = number of strata
$\bar{x}_h$ = sample mean for stratum h
N_h = number of elements in the population in stratum h
N = total number of elements in the population: $N = N_1 + N_2 + \cdots + N_H$

$$s_{\bar{x}_{st}} = \sqrt{\frac{1}{N^2}\sum_{h=1}^{H} N_h(N_h - n_h)\frac{s_h^2}{n_h}} \quad \textbf{(21.16)}$$

Using these results, we see that an approximate 95% confidence interval estimate of the population mean is given by the following expression.

Approximate 95% Confidence Interval Estimate of the Population Mean

$$\bar{x}_{st} \pm 2s_{\bar{x}_{st}} \quad \textbf{(21.17)}$$

Suppose the survey of 180 graduates of the College of Business at Lakeland College provided the sample results shown in Table 21.1. The sample means for each major, or stratum, are $49,000 for accounting, $48,500 for finance, $56,500 for information systems, $44,000 for marketing, and $51,000 for operations management. Using these results and equation (21.15), we can compute a point estimate of the population mean.

$$\bar{x}_{st} = \left(\frac{500}{1,500}\right)(49,000) + \left(\frac{350}{1,500}\right)(48,500) + \left(\frac{200}{1,500}\right)(56,500)$$
$$+ \left(\frac{300}{1,500}\right)(44,000) + \left(\frac{150}{1,500}\right)(51,000) = 49,083$$

In Table 21.2, we show a portion of the calculations needed to estimate the standard error; note that

$$\sum_{h=1}^{5} N_h(N_h - n_h)\frac{s_h^2}{n_h} = 42,909,037,698$$

Thus,

$$s_{\bar{x}_{st}} = \sqrt{\left(\frac{1}{(1,500)^2}\right)(42,909,037,698)} = \sqrt{19,070.68} = 138$$

Hence, using equation (21.17), we find that an approximate 95% confidence interval estimate of the population mean is 49,083 ± 2(138) = 49,083 ± 276, or $48,807 to $49,359.

Using Excel: Population Mean

To show how Excel can be used for sample surveys that use stratified simple random sampling we will construct an approximate 95% confidence interval of the population mean for the Lakeland Community College sample survey. In a separate worksheet for each stratum (major), we have computed the sample mean and sample standard deviation for that stratum. Another worksheet is used to summarize the calculations needed to compute an approximate 95% confidence interval of the population mean. A copy of this

Table 21.1 Lakeland College Sample Survey of Starting Salaries of Graduates

Major (h)	$\bar{x}_h$	s_h	N_h	n_h
Accounting	$49,000	2,000	500	45
Finance	$48,500	1,700	350	40
Information systems	$56,500	2,300	200	30
Marketing	$44,000	1,600	300	35
Operations management	$51,000	2,250	150	30

Table 21.2 Partial Calculations for the Estimate of the Standard Error of the Mean for the Lakeland College Sample Survey

Major	h	$N_h(N_h - n_h)\dfrac{s_h^2}{n_h}$
Accounting	1	$500(500-45)\dfrac{(2{,}000)^2}{45} = 20{,}222{,}222{,}222$
Finance	2	$350(350-40)\dfrac{(1{,}700)^2}{40} = 7{,}839{,}125{,}000$
Information systems	3	$200(200-30)\dfrac{(2{,}300)^2}{30} = 5{,}995{,}333{,}333$
Marketing	4	$300(300-35)\dfrac{(1600)^2}{35} = 5{,}814{,}857{,}143$
Operations management	5	$150(150-30)\dfrac{(2{,}250)^2}{30} = 3{,}037{,}500{,}000$
		$\sum_{h=1}^{5} N_h(N_h - n_h)\dfrac{s_h^2}{n_h} = 42{,}909{,}037{,}698$

summary worksheet is shown in Figure 21.3. The formula worksheet is in the background; the value worksheet appears in the foreground.

DATA*file*
lakeland

Enter/Access Data: Open the file *lakeland*. The worksheet shown in Figure 21.3 summarizes the starting salary data that appear in the worksheets for the separate strata of the Lakeland data set. Note that the standard deviations shown in cells C3:C7 were rounded to the nearest dollar.

Figure 21.3 Summary Worksheet for the Lakeland Community College Stratified Sample: Population Mean

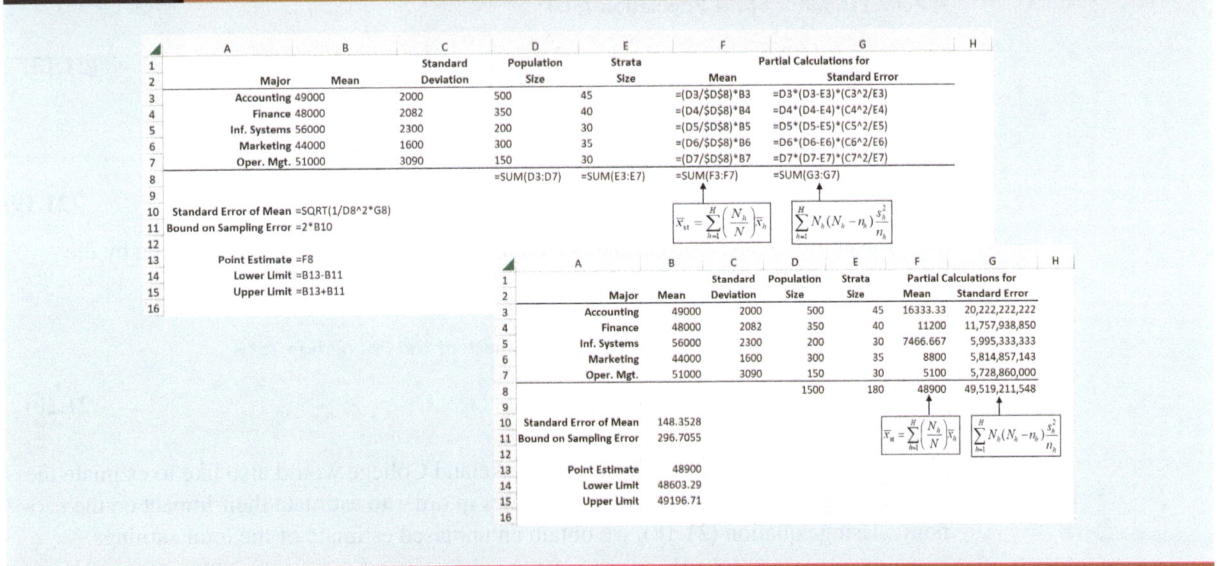

	A	B	C	D	E	F	G	H
1			Standard	Population	Strata	Partial Calculations for		
2	Major	Mean	Deviation	Size	Size	Mean	Standard Error	
3	Accounting	49000	2000	500	45	=(D3/$D$8)*B3	=D3*(D3-E3)*(C3^2/E3)	
4	Finance	48000	2082	350	40	=(D4/$D$8)*B4	=D4*(D4-E4)*(C4^2/E4)	
5	Inf. Systems	56000	2300	200	30	=(D5/$D$8)*B5	=D5*(D5-E5)*(C5^2/E5)	
6	Marketing	44000	1600	300	35	=(D6/$D$8)*B6	=D6*(D6-E6)*(C6^2/E6)	
7	Oper. Mgt.	51000	3090	150	30	=(D7/$D$8)*B7	=D7*(D7-E7)*(C7^2/E7)	
8				=SUM(D3:D7)	=SUM(E3:E7)	=SUM(F3:F7)	=SUM(G3:G7)	
9								
10	Standard Error of Mean	=SQRT(1/D8^2*G8)						
11	Bound on Sampling Error	=2*B10						
12								
13	Point Estimate	=F8						
14	Lower Limit	=B13-B11						
15	Upper Limit	=B13+B11						
16								

	A	B	C	D	E	F	G	H
1			Standard	Population	Strata	Partial Calculations for		
2	Major	Mean	Deviation	Size	Size	Mean	Standard Error	
3	Accounting	49000	2000	500	45	16333.33	20,222,222,222	
4	Finance	48000	2082	350	40	11200	11,757,938,850	
5	Inf. Systems	56000	2300	200	30	7466.667	5,995,333,333	
6	Marketing	44000	1600	300	35	8800	5,814,857,143	
7	Oper. Mgt.	51000	3090	150	30	5100	5,728,860,000	
8				1500	180	48900	49,519,211,548	
9								
10	Standard Error of Mean	148.3528						
11	Bound on Sampling Error	296.7055						
12								
13	Point Estimate	48900						
14	Lower Limit	48603.29						
15	Upper Limit	49196.71						
16								

$$\bar{x}_{st} = \sum_{h=1}^{H}\left(\frac{N_h}{N}\right)\bar{x}_h \qquad \sum_{h=1}^{H} N_h(N_h - n_h)\frac{s_h^2}{n_h}$$

Enter Functions and Formulas: The descriptive statistics needed are provided in cells B3:E7. The strata sample means and standard deviations were calculated in the separate worksheets for each major and entered as constants in the summary worksheet. Cells F3:G7 represent partial calculations required to compute the point estimate of the population mean and the estimate of the standard error of the mean. To compute the weighted sample mean for the accounting majors we entered the formula *=(D3/$D$8)*B3* in cell F3; we then copied this formula in cells F4:F7 to compute the weighted sample means for each of the other majors. The formula *=SUM(F3:F7)* was entered in cell F8 to compute the point estimate of the population mean. The computations in cells G3:G7 correspond to the calculations shown in Table 21.2. For instance, the formula *=D3*(D3-E3)*(C3^2/E3)* was entered in cell G3 to compute the value of

Cells F3:F7 computed $\bar{x}_{st}$ using equation (21.15).

$$N_h(N_h - n_h)\frac{s_h^2}{n_h}$$

for the accounting majors; copying this formula in cells G4:G7 provided similar values for each of the other majors. In cell G8 we entered the cell formula *=SUM(G3:G7)* to compute

$$\sum_{h=1}^{5} N_h(N_h - n_h)\frac{s_h^2}{n_h}$$

Note that the value worksheet shows that this partial calculation is 49,519,211,548. To compute the standard error of the mean we entered the formula *=SQRT(1/D8^2*G8)* in cell B10; we then computed the bound on the sampling error by entering the formula *=2*B10* in cell B11. The value worksheet shows 148.3528 for the standard error of the mean and 296.7055 for the bound on the sampling error.

Cells B13:B15 provide the point estimate and the lower and upper limits for the confidence interval. Because the point estimate of the population mean was computed in cell F8, we entered the formula *=F8* in cell B13. To compute the lower limit of the 95% confidence interval, the formula *=B13-B11* was entered in cell B14; to compute the upper limit, the formula *=B13+B11* was entered in cell B15. The value worksheet shows that the point estimate of the population mean is 48,900 and that the 95% approximate confidence interval is 48,603.29 to 49,196.17.

Population Total

The point estimator of the population total (X) is obtained by multiplying N times $\bar{x}_{st}$.

Point Estimator of the Population Total

$$\hat{X} = N\bar{x}_{st} \tag{21.18}$$

An estimate of the standard error of this point estimator is

$$s_{\hat{X}} = Ns_{\bar{x}_{st}} \tag{21.19}$$

Thus, an approximate 95% confidence interval for the population total is given by the following expression.

Approximate 95% Confidence Interval Estimate of the Population Total

$$N\bar{x}_{st} \pm 2s_{\hat{X}} \tag{21.20}$$

Now suppose the College of Business at Lakeland College would also like to estimate the total earnings of the 1,500 business graduates in order to estimate their impact on the economy. Using equation (21.18), we obtain an unbiased estimate of the total earnings.

$$\hat{X} = (1{,}500)49{,}083 = 73{,}624{,}500$$

Using equation (21.19), we obtain an estimate of the standard error of the population total.

$$s_{\hat{X}} = 1{,}500(138) = 207{,}000$$

Thus, using expression (21.20), we find that an approximate 95% confidence interval estimate of the total earnings of the 1,500 graduates is 73,624,500 ± 2(207,000) = 73,624,500 ± 414,000 or \$73,210,500 to \$74,038,500.

Population Proportion

An unbiased estimate of the population proportion, p, for stratified simple random sampling is a weighted average of the proportions for each stratum. The weights used are the fraction of the population in each stratum. The resulting point estimator, denoted $\bar{p}_{\text{st}}$, is defined as follows.

Point Estimator of the Population Proportion

$$\bar{p}_{\text{st}} = \sum_{h=1}^{H}\left(\frac{N_h}{N}\right)\bar{p}_h \tag{21.21}$$

where

H = the number of strata
$\bar{p}_h$ = the sample proportion for stratum h
N_h = the number of elements in the population in stratum h
N = the total number of elements in the population: $N = N_1 + N_2 + \cdots + N_H$

An estimate of the standard error of $\bar{p}_{\text{st}}$ is given by

$$s_{\bar{p}_{\text{st}}} = \sqrt{\frac{1}{N^2}\sum_{h=1}^{H} N_h(N_h - n_h)\left[\frac{\bar{p}_h(1-\bar{p}_h)}{n_h - 1}\right]} \tag{21.22}$$

Thus, an approximate 95% confidence interval estimate of the population proportion is given by the following expression.

Approximate 95% Confidence Interval Estimate of the Population Proportion

$$\bar{p}_{\text{st}} \pm 2s_{\bar{p}_{\text{st}}} \tag{21.23}$$

In the Lakeland College survey, the college wants to know the proportion of graduates receiving a starting salary of \$52,000 or more. The results of the sample survey of 180 graduates show that 63 received starting salaries of \$52,000 or more and that 16 of the 63 majored in accounting, 3 majored in finance, 29 majored in information systems, 0 majored in marketing, and 15 majored in operations management.

Using equation (21.21), we can compute the point estimate of the proportion receiving starting salaries of \$52,000 or more.

$$\begin{aligned}\bar{p}_{\text{st}} &= \left(\frac{500}{1{,}500}\right)\left(\frac{16}{45}\right) + \left(\frac{350}{1{,}500}\right)\left(\frac{3}{40}\right) + \left(\frac{200}{1{,}500}\right)\left(\frac{29}{30}\right) + \left(\frac{300}{1{,}500}\right)\left(\frac{0}{35}\right) + \left(\frac{150}{1{,}500}\right)\left(\frac{15}{30}\right) \\ &= 0.3149\end{aligned}$$

In Table 21.3, we show a portion of the calculations needed to estimate the standard error; note that

$$\sum_{h=1}^{5} N_h(N_h - n_h)\left[\frac{\bar{p}_h(1-\bar{p}_h)}{n_h - 1}\right] = 1{,}570.6913$$

Table 21.3 Partial Calculations for the Estimate of the Standard Error of $\bar{p}_{st}$ for the Lakeland College Sample Survey

Major	h	$N_v(N_h - n_h)\left[\frac{\bar{p}_h(1-\bar{p}_h)}{n_h - 1}\right]$
Accounting	1	$500(500-45)\left[\frac{(16/45)(29/45)}{45-1}\right] = 1{,}184.7363$
Finance	2	$350(350-40)\left[\frac{(3/40)(37/40)}{40-1}\right] = 193.0048$
Information systems	3	$200(200-30)\left[\frac{(29/30)(1/30)}{30-1}\right] = 37.7778$
Marketing	4	$300(300-35)\left[\frac{(0/35)(35/35)}{35-1}\right] = 0.0000$
Operations management	5	$150(150-30)\left[\frac{(15/30)(15/30)}{30-1}\right] = 155.1724$
$\sum_{h=1}^{5} N_h(N_h - n_h)\left[\frac{\bar{p}_h(1-\bar{p}_h)}{n_h - 1}\right]$		1,570.6913

Thus,

$$s_{\bar{p}_{st}} = \sqrt{\frac{1}{(1{,}500)^2}(1{,}570.6913)}$$
$$= 0.0264$$

Using expression (21.23), we find that an approximate 95% confidence interval for the proportion of graduates receiving starting salaries of \$52,000 or more is $0.3149 \pm 2(0.0264) = 0.3149 \pm 0.0528$, or 0.2621 to 0.3677.

Using Excel: Population Proportion

The worksheet used to compute an approximate 95% confidence interval of the population mean for the Lakeland Community College sample survey can be modified in order to compute an approximate 95% confidence interval estimate of the proportion of graduates receiving a starting salary of \$36,000 or more. First, using the original data, we must determine for each major the proportion of graduates in the sample that received a starting salary of \$36,000 or more. This calculation can be easily made using Excel's COUNTIF function. For instance, in the file *lakeland,* the salary data for the accounting majors appear in the worksheet named Accounting in cells A2:A46. We can compute the number of accounting graduates who received a starting salary of \$52,000 or more by entering the function *=COUNTIF(A2:A46,">=52000")* in any empty cell of the worksheet; the result is 16. Once the sample proportions for each stratum are obtained, it is a simple matter to modify the formulas shown in Figure 21.3 in order to display the partial calculations for the sample proportion and the standard error of the sample proportion based upon equations (21.21) and (21.22).

Determining the Sample Size

With stratified simple random sampling we can think of choosing a sample size as a two-step process. First, a total sample size n must be chosen. Second, we must decide how to assign the sampled units to the various strata. Alternatively, we could first decide how large a sample to take in each stratum and then sum the stratum sample sizes to obtain the total sample size. It is often of interest to develop estimates of the mean, total, and proportion for the individual strata; therefore a combination of these two approaches is often employed. An overall sample size n and an allocation that will provide the necessary precision for the overall population parameter of interest are found. Then, if the sample sizes in some of the strata are not large enough to provide the precision necessary for the estimates within the strata, the sample sizes for those strata are adjusted upward as necessary. In this subsection, we discuss some of the issues pertinent to allocating the total sample to the various strata and present a method for choosing the total sample size and making the allocation.

The allocation task is to decide what fraction of the total sample should be assigned to each stratum. This fraction determines how large the simple random sample will be in each stratum. The factors considered most important in making the allocation follow:

1. The number of elements in each stratum
2. The variance of the elements within each stratum
3. The cost of selecting elements within each stratum

Generally, larger samples should be assigned to the larger strata and to the strata with larger variances. Conversely, to get the most information for a given cost, smaller samples should be allocated to the strata where the cost per unit of sampling is greatest.

The individual stratum variances often differ greatly. For example, suppose that in a particular study we are interested in determining the mean number of employees per building; because variability is greater in a stratum with larger buildings than in one with smaller buildings, a proportionately larger sample should be taken in such a stratum. The cost of selection can be an important consideration when significant interviewer travel between sampled units is necessary in some of the strata but not in others; this issue frequently arises when some of the strata involve rural areas and others involve cities.

In many surveys, the cost per unit of sampling is approximately the same for each stratum (e.g., mail and telephone surveys); in such cases, the cost of sampling can be ignored in making the allocation. We present here the appropriate formulas for choosing the sample size and making the allocation in such cases. More advanced texts on sampling provide formulas for the case when sampling costs vary significantly across strata. The formulas we present in this section will minimize the total sampling cost for a given level of precision. This method allocates the total sample n to the various strata as follows.

This method of allocation for stratified sampling is known as Neymann allocation.

$$n_h = n\left(\frac{N_h s_h}{\sum_{h=1}^{H} N_h s_h}\right) \tag{21.24}$$

Equation (21.24) shows that the number of units allocated to a stratum increases with the stratum size and standard deviation. Note that to make this allocation, we need to first determine the total sample size n. Given a specified level of precision B, we can use the following formulas to choose the total sample size when estimating the population mean and the population total.

Sample Size When Estimating the Population Mean

$$n = \frac{\left(\sum_{h=1}^{H} N_h s_h\right)^2}{N^2\left(\frac{B^2}{4}\right) + \sum_{h=1}^{H} N_h s_h^2} \tag{21.25}$$

Sample Size When Estimating the Population Total

$$n = \frac{\left(\sum_{h=1}^{H} N_h s_h\right)^2}{\frac{B^2}{4} + \sum_{h=1}^{H} N_h s_h^2} \tag{21.26}$$

As an example, suppose a Chevrolet dealer wants to survey the customers who purchased a Traverse, Equinox, or Silverado to obtain information the dealer feels will be helpful in determining future advertising. In particular, suppose the dealer wants to estimate the mean monthly income for these customers with a bound on the sampling error of \$100. The dealer's 600 Traverse, Equinox, and Silverado customers are divided into three strata: 100 Traverse owners, 200 Equinox owners, and 300 Silverado owners. A pilot survey was used to estimate the standard deviation in each stratum; the results are $s_1 = \$1{,}300$, $s_2 = \$900$, and $s_3 = \$500$ for the Traverse, Equinox, and Silverado owners, respectively.

The first step in choosing a sample size for this survey is to use equation (21.25) to determine the total sample size necessary to provide a bound of $B = \$100$ on the estimate of the population mean. First, we compute

$$\sum_{h=1}^{3} N_h s_h = 100(1{,}300) + 200(900) + 300(500) = 460{,}000$$

Next, we compute

$$\sum_{h=1}^{3} N_h s_h^2 = 100(1{,}300)^2 + 200(900)^2 + 300(500)^2 = 406{,}000{,}000$$

Substituting these values into equation (21.25), we can determine the total sample size needed to provide a bound on the sampling error of $B = \$100$.

$$n = \frac{(460{,}000)^2}{\dfrac{(600)^2(100)^2}{4} + 406{,}000{,}000} = 162$$

Thus, a total sample size of 162 will provide the precision desired. To allocate the total sample to the three strata, we use equation (21.24).

$$n_1 = 162\left(\frac{100(1{,}300)}{460{,}000}\right) = 46$$

$$n_2 = 162\left(\frac{200(900)}{460{,}000}\right) = 63$$

$$n_3 = 162\left(\frac{300(500)}{460{,}000}\right) = 53$$

We would therefore recommend sampling 46 Traverse owners, 63 Equinox owners, and 53 Silverado owners for a total sample size of 162 customers.

To determine the sample size when estimating a population proportion, we simply substitute $\sqrt{\bar{p}_h(1 - \bar{p}_h)}$ for s_h in equation (21.25); the result is

$$n = \frac{\left(\sum_{h=1}^{H} N_h \sqrt{\bar{p}_h(1 - \bar{p}_h)}\right)^2}{N^2\left(\dfrac{B^2}{4}\right) + \sum_{h=1}^{H} N_h \bar{p}_h(1 - \bar{p}_h)} \qquad \textbf{(21.27)}$$

Once the total sample size for the population proportion estimate has been determined, allocation to the various strata is again made by using equation (21.24) with $\sqrt{\bar{p}_h(1 - \bar{p}_h)}$ substituted for s_h.

Notes + Comments

1. An advantage of stratified simple random sampling is that estimates of population parameters for each stratum are automatically available as a by-product of the sampling procedure. For example, besides obtaining an estimate of the average starting salary for all graduates in the Lakeland College sampling problem, we obtained an estimate of the average starting salary for each major. Because each of the starting salary estimates was based on a simple

random sample from each stratum, the procedure for developing an approximate confidence interval estimate when a simple random sample is selected (see equation (21.4)) can be used to compute an approximate 95% confidence interval estimate for the mean in each stratum. In a similar manner, interval estimates for the population total and the population proportion for each stratum can be developed by using equations (21.8) and (21.10), respectively.

2. Another type of allocation that is sometimes used with stratified simple random sampling is called *proportional allocation*. In this approach, the sample size allocated to each stratum is given by the following formula.

$$n_h = n\left(\frac{N_h}{N}\right) \tag{21.28}$$

Proportional allocation is appropriate when the stratum variances are approximately equal and the cost per unit of sampling is about the same across strata. In the case where the stratum variances are equal, proportional allocation and the Neyman procedure result in the same allocation.

Exercises

Methods

7. A stratified simple random sample was taken with the following results. **LO 2, 4**

Stratum (h)	$\bar{x}_h$	s_h	$\bar{p}_h$	N_h	n_h
1	138	30	0.50	200	20
2	103	25	0.78	250	30
3	210	50	0.21	100	25

a. Develop an estimate of the population mean for each stratum.
b. Develop an approximate 95% confidence interval for the population mean in each stratum.
c. Develop an approximate 95% confidence interval for the overall population mean.

8. Reconsider the sample results in exercise 7. **LO 2, 4**
a. Develop an estimate of the population total for each stratum.
b. Develop a point estimate of the total for all 550 elements in the population.
c. Develop an approximate 95% confidence interval for the population total.

9. Reconsider the sample results in exercise 7. **LO 2, 4**
a. Develop an approximate 95% confidence interval for the proportion in each stratum.
b. Develop a point estimate of the population proportion for the 550 elements in the population.
c. Estimate the standard error of the population proportion.
d. Develop an approximate 95% confidence interval for the population proportion.

10. A population was divided into three strata with $N_1 = 300$, with $N_2 = 600$, and with $N_3 = 500$. From a past survey, the following estimates for the standard deviations in the three strata are available: $s_1 = 150$, $s_2 = 75$, $s_3 = 100$. **LO 5**
a. Suppose an estimate of the population mean with a bound on the error of estimate of $B = 20$ is required. How large must the sample be? How many elements should be allocated to each stratum?
b. Suppose a bound of $B = 10$ is desired. How large must the sample be? How many elements should be allocated to each stratum?
c. Suppose an estimate of the population total with a bound of $B = 15{,}000$ is requested. How large must the sample be? How many elements should be allocated to each stratum?

Applications

11. **Estimating Mean Store Sales for a Drugstore Chain.** A drugstore chain has stores in four cities: 38 stores in Indianapolis, 45 in Louisville, 80 in St. Louis, and 70 in Memphis. Pharmacy sales in the four cities vary considerably because of the competition. The following sales data (in thousands of dollars) are available from a sample

survey. Each of the cities was considered a separate stratum, and a stratified simple random sample was taken. **LO 2, 4**

DATA*file*
drugstorechain

Indianapolis	Louisville	St. Louis	Memphis
50.3	48.7	16.7	14.7
41.2	59.8	38.4	88.3
15.7	28.9	51.6	94.2
22.5	36.5	42.7	76.8
26.7	89.8	45.0	35.1
20.8	96.0	59.7	48.2
	77.2	80.0	57.9
	81.3	27.6	18.8
			22.0
			74.3

a. Estimate the mean pharmacy sales for each city (stratum).
b. Develop an approximate 95% confidence interval for the mean pharmacy sales in each city.
c. Estimate the proportion of stores with sales of $50,000 or more.
d. Develop an approximate 95% confidence interval for the proportion of stores with sales of $50,000 or more.

12. **Estimating Total Sales for a Drugstore Chain.** Reconsider the sample survey results in exercise 11. **LO 2, 4**

DATA*file*
drugstorechain

a. Estimate the population total pharmacy sales for St. Louis.
b. Estimate the population total pharmacy sales for Indianapolis.
c. Develop an approximate 95% confidence interval for mean pharmacy sales for the drugstore chain.
d. Develop an approximate 95% confidence interval for total pharmacy sales for the drugstore chain.

13. **Surveying an Accounting Firm's Clients.** An accounting firm works for a number of clients in the banking, insurance, and brokerage industries: $N_1 = 50$ banks, $N_2 = 38$ insurance companies, and $N_3 = 35$ brokerage firms. A marketing research firm has been hired to survey the accounting firm's clients in these three industries. The survey will ask a variety of questions about both the clients' businesses and their satisfaction with services provided by the accounting firm. Suppose an approximate 95% confidence interval is requested for the mean number of employees for the 123 clients with a bound on the error of estimation of $B = 30$. **LO 5**
a. Suppose a pilot study finds $s_1 = 80$, $s_2 = 150$, and $s_3 = 45$. Choose a total sample size, and explain how the sample size should be allocated to the three strata.
b. Suppose the pilot test is called into question and a decision is made to assume the stratum standard deviations are all equal to 100 in choosing the sample size. Choose a total sample size, and determine how many elements should be sampled in each stratum.

21.6 Cluster Sampling

Cluster sampling requires that the population be divided into N groups of elements called clusters such that each element in the population belongs to one and only one cluster. For example, suppose we want to survey registered voters in the state of Ohio. One approach would be to develop a frame consisting of all registered voters in the state of Ohio and then select a simple random sample of voters from this frame. Alternatively, in cluster sampling, we might choose to define the frame as the list of the $N = 88$ counties in the state (see Figure 21.4). In this approach, each county or cluster would consist of a group of registered voters, and each registered voter in the state would belong to one and only one cluster.

Figure 21.4 Counties of the State of Ohio Used as Clusters of Registered Voters

Suppose we select a simple random sample of $n = 12$ of the 88 counties. At this point, we could collect data for *all* registered voters in each of the 12 sampled clusters, an approach referred to as *single-stage cluster sampling,* or we could select a simple random sample of registered voters from each of the 12 sampled clusters, an approach referred to as *two-stage cluster sampling.* In either case, formulas are available for using the sample results to develop point and interval estimates of population parameters such as the population mean, total, or proportion. In this chapter, however, we consider only single-stage cluster sampling; more advanced texts on sampling present results for two-stage cluster sampling.

In the sense that both stratified and cluster sampling divide the population into groups of elements, the two sampling procedures are similar. The reasons for choosing cluster sampling, however, differ from the reasons for choosing stratified sampling. Cluster sampling tends to provide better results when the elements within the clusters are heterogeneous (not alike). In the ideal case, each cluster would be a small-scale version of the entire population. In this case, sampling a small number of clusters would provide good information about the characteristics of the entire population.

One of the primary applications of cluster sampling involves area sampling, where the clusters are counties, townships, city blocks, or other well-defined geographic sections of the population. Because data are collected from only a sample of the total geographic areas or clusters available, and the elements within the clusters are typically close to one another, significant savings in time and cost can be realized when a data collector or interviewer is sent to a sampled unit. As a result, even if a larger total sample size is required, cluster sampling may be less costly than either simple random sampling or stratified simple random sampling. In addition, cluster sampling can minimize the time and cost associated with developing the frame or list of elements to be sampled because cluster sampling does not require that a list of every element in the population be developed. One needs only a list of the elements in the clusters sampled.

All the elements in the population do not need to be listed. With cluster sampling, one needs only a list of the elements in the clusters sampled.

To illustrate cluster sampling, let us consider a survey conducted by the American Institute of Certified Public Accountants (AICPA) of the 12,000 practicing certified public accountants (CPAs) in a particular state. As part of the survey, the AICPA collected information on income, gender, and factors related to the CPA's lifestyle. Because personal interviews were needed to obtain all the desired information, the AICPA used a cluster sample to minimize the total travel and interviewing cost. The frame consisted of all CPA firms that were registered to practice accounting in the state. Suppose there are $N = 1{,}000$ clusters, or CPA firms, registered to practice accounting in the state, and that a simple random sample of $n = 10$ CPA firms is to be selected.

In presenting the formulas for cluster sampling that are needed to develop approximate 95% confidence interval estimates of the population mean, total, and proportion, we will use the following notation.

N = number of clusters in the population
n = number of clusters selected in the sample
M_i = number of elements in cluster i
M = number of elements in the population: $M = M_1 + M_2 + \cdots + M_N$
$\bar{M} = M/N$ = average number of elements in a cluster
x_i = total of all observations in cluster i
a_i = number of observations in cluster i with a certain characteristic

For the AICPA sample survey we have the following information.

$$N = 1{,}000$$
$$n = 10$$
$$M = 12{,}000$$
$$\bar{M} = 12{,}000/1{,}000 = 12$$

Table 21.4 shows the values of M_i and x_i for each of the sampled clusters as well as the number of senior CPAs in the sampled firms (a_i), which is defined as CPAs who have a minimum of 15 years of experience.

Population Mean

The point estimator of the population mean obtained from cluster sampling is given by the following formula.

Point Estimator of the Population Mean

$$\bar{x}_c = \frac{\sum_{i=1}^{n} x_i}{\sum_{i=1}^{n} M_i} \tag{21.29}$$

Table 21.4 Results of CPA Sample Survey

DATA*file* cpasample

Firm (i)	CPAs (M_i)	Total Salary ($1,000s) for Firm i (x_i)	Senior CPAs (a_i)
1	8	704	2
2	25	2,350	8
3	4	308	0
4	17	1,537	6
5	7	576	1
6	3	251	2
7	15	1,361	2
8	4	336	0
9	12	1,057	5
10	33	3,200	9
Totals	128	11,680	35

An estimate of the standard error of this point estimator is

$$s_{\bar{x}_c} = \sqrt{\left(\frac{N-n}{Nn\bar{M}^2}\right)\frac{\sum_{i=1}^{n}(x_i - \bar{x}_c M_i)^2}{n-1}} \tag{21.30}$$

Thus, the following expression gives an approximate 95% confidence interval estimate of the population mean.

Approximate 95% Confidence Interval Estimate of the Population Mean

$$\bar{x}_c \pm 2s_{\bar{x}_c} \tag{21.31}$$

Using the data in Table 21.4, we obtain an estimate of the mean salary for practicing certified public accountants.

$$\bar{x}_c = \frac{11{,}680}{128} = 91.250$$

The salary data in Table 21.4, listed in thousands of dollars, indicate an estimate of the mean salary for practicing certified public accountants in the state is $91,250.

In Table 21.5, we show a portion of the calculations needed to estimate the standard error; note that

$$\sum_{i=1}^{n}(x_i - \bar{x}_c M_i)^2 = 51{,}281.375$$

Thus,

$$s_{\bar{x}_c} = \sqrt{\left[\frac{1{,}000 - 10}{(1{,}000)(10)(12)^2}\right]\frac{51{,}281.378}{10-1}} = 1.979$$

Hence, the standard error is $1,979. Using expression (21.31), we find that an approximate 95% confidence interval estimate for the mean annual salary is 91,250 ± 2(1,979) = 91,250 ± 3,958 or $87,292 to $95,208.

Population Total

The point estimator of the population total X is obtained by multiplying M times $\bar{x}_c$.

Table 21.5 Partial Calculations for the Estimate of the Standard Error of the Mean for the CPA Sample Survey Where $\bar{x}_c = 91.250$

Firm (i)	M_i	x_i	$(x_i - 91.250M_i)^2$
1	8	704	$[704 - 91.250(8)]^2 =$ 676.000
2	25	2,350	$[2,350 - 91.250(25)]^2 =$ 4,726.563
3	4	308	$[308 - 91.250(4)]^2 =$ 3,249.000
4	17	1,537	$[1,537 - 91.250(17)]^2 =$ 203.063
5	7	576	$[576 - 91.250(7)]^2 =$ 3,937.563
6	3	251	$[251 - 91.250(3)]^2 =$ 517.563
7	15	1,361	$[1,361 - 91.250(15)]^2 =$ 60.063
8	4	336	$[336 - 91.250(4)]^2 =$ 841.000
9	12	1,057	$[1,057 - 91.250(12)]^2 =$ 1,444.000
10	33	3,200	$[3,200 - 91.250(33)]^2 =$ 35,626.563
Totals	128	11,680	51,281.378

$\sum_{i=1}^{n}(x_i - \bar{x}_c M_i)^2$ → 51,281.378

Point Estimator of the Population Total

$$\hat{X} = M\bar{x}_c \tag{21.32}$$

An estimate of the standard error of this point estimator is

$$s_{\hat{X}} = Ms_{\bar{x}_c} \tag{21.33}$$

Thus, an approximate 95% confidence interval estimate for the population total is given by the following expression.

Approximate 95% Confidence Interval Estimate of the Population Total

$$M\bar{x}_c \pm 2s_{\hat{X}} \tag{21.34}$$

For the CPA sample survey,

$$\hat{X} = M\bar{x}_c = 12,000(91,250) = \$1,095,000,000$$
$$s_{\hat{X}} = Ms_{\bar{x}_c} = 12,000(1,979) = \$23,748,000$$

Thus, using expression (21.34), we find that an approximate 95% confidence interval is \$1,095,000,000 ± 2(\$23,748,000) = \$1,095,000,000 ± \$47,496,000 or \$1,047,504,000 to \$1,142,496,000.

Population Proportion

The point estimator of the population proportion obtained from cluster sampling follows.

Point Estimator of the Population Proportion

$$\bar{p}_c = \frac{\sum_{i=1}^{n} a_i}{\sum_{i=1}^{n} M_i} \tag{21.35}$$

where

a_i = number of elements in cluster i with the characteristic of interest

An estimate of the standard error of this point estimator is

$$s_{\bar{p}_c} = \sqrt{\left(\frac{N - n}{Nn\bar{M}^2}\right)\frac{\sum_{i=1}^{n}(a_i - \bar{p}_c M_i)^2}{n - 1}} \tag{21.36}$$

Thus, an approximate 95% confidence interval estimate for the population proportion is given by the following expression.

Approximate 95% Confidence Interval Estimate of the Population Proportion

$$\bar{p}_c \pm 2s_{\bar{p}_c} \tag{21.37}$$

For the CPA sample survey, we can use equation (21.35) and the data in Table 21.4 to develop an estimate of the proportion of practicing certified public accountants who have at least 15 years of experience and are therefore classified as senior CPAs.

$$\bar{p}_c = \frac{2 + 8 + \cdots + 9}{8 + 25 + \cdots + 33} = \frac{35}{128} = 0.2734$$

In Table 21.6, we show a portion of the calculations needed to estimate the standard error; note that

$$\sum_{i=1}^{n}(a_i - \bar{p}_c M_i)^2 = 15.2098$$

Thus,

$$s_{\bar{p}_c} = \sqrt{\left[\frac{1{,}000 - 10}{(1{,}000)(10)(12)^2}\right]\frac{15.2098}{10 - 1}} = 0.0341$$

Hence, using expression (21.37), we find that an approximate 95% confidence interval for the proportion of practicing CPAs who have at least 15 years of experience is 0.2734 ± 2(0.0341) = 0.2734 ± 0.0682 or 0.2052 to 0.3416.

Using Excel for Cluster Sampling

The calculations required to develop an approximate 95% confidence interval of the population mean, population total, and population proportion for cluster sampling can be easily

Table 21.6 Partial Calculations for the Estimate of the Standard Error of $\bar{p}_c$ for the CPA Sample Survey Where $\bar{p}_c = 0.2734$

Firm (i)	M_i	a_i	$(a_i - 0.2734M_i)^2$
1	8	2	$[2 - 0.2734(8)]^2 =$ 0.0350
2	25	8	$[8 - 0.2734(25)]^2 =$ 1.3572
3	4	0	$[0 - 0.2734(4)]^2 =$ 1.1960
4	17	6	$[6 - 0.2734(17)]^2 =$ 1.8284
5	7	1	$[1 - 0.2734(7)]^2 =$ 0.8350
6	3	2	$[2 - 0.2734(3)]^2 =$ 1.3919
7	15	2	$[2 - 0.2734(15)]^2 =$ 4.4142
8	4	0	$[0 - 0.2734(4)]^2 =$ 1.1960
9	12	5	$[5 - 0.2734(12)]^2 =$ 2.9556
10	33	9	$[9 - 0.2734(33)]^2 =$ 0.0005
Totals	128	35	15.2098

$\sum_{i=1}^{n}(a_i - \bar{p}_c M_i)^2$ → 15.2098

made in an Excel worksheet. For instance, to compute an approximate 95% confidence interval estimate of the population mean for the CPA sample survey, we simply develop a worksheet similar in appearance to Table 21.5. Using the partial output from this worksheet, cell formulas for equations (21.29) and (21.30) can be entered into the worksheet in order to compute point estimates of the population mean and standard error of the mean. The bound on the sampling error can then be computed and used to develop the lower and upper limits for the confidence interval. Although the details vary somewhat for developing interval estimates for estimating the population total and the population proportion, similar worksheets can also be developed for these two cases.

Determining the Sample Size

Once the clusters are formed, the primary issue in choosing a sample size is selecting the number of clusters n. The procedure for cluster sampling is similar to that for other methods of sampling. An acceptable level of precision is specified by choosing a value for B, the bound on the sampling error. Then a formula is developed for finding the value of n that will provide the desired precision.

The average cluster size and the variance between clusters are key factors in deciding how many clusters to include in the sample. If the clusters are similar, the variance between them will be small and the number of clusters sampled can be smaller. Also, if the average number of elements per cluster is larger, the number of clusters sampled can be smaller. The formulas for making an exact determination of sample size are included in more advanced texts on sampling.

Exercises

Methods

14. A sample of four clusters is to be taken from a population with $N = 25$ clusters and $M = 300$ elements. The values of M_i, x_i, and a_i for each cluster in the sample follow. **LO 6**

Cluster (i)	M_i	x_i	a_i
1	7	95	1
2	18	325	6
3	15	190	6
4	10	140	2
Totals	50	750	15

a. Develop point estimates of the population mean, total, and proportion.
b. Estimate the standard error for the estimates in part (a).
c. Develop an approximate 95% confidence interval for the population mean.
d. Develop an approximate 95% confidence interval for the population total.
e. Develop an approximate 95% confidence interval for the population proportion.

15. A sample of six clusters is to be taken from a population with $N = 30$ clusters and $M = 600$ elements. The following table shows values of M_i, x_i, and a_i for each cluster in the sample. **LO 6**

Cluster (i)	M_i	x_i	a_i
1	35	3,500	3
2	15	965	0
3	12	960	1
4	23	2,070	4
5	20	1,100	3
6	25	1,805	2
Totals	130	10,400	13

a. Develop point estimates of the population mean, total, and proportion.
b. Develop an approximate 95% confidence interval for the population mean.
c. Develop an approximate 95% confidence interval for the population total.
d. Develop an approximate 95% confidence interval for the population proportion.

Applications

16. **Public Utility HVAC Survey.** A public utility is conducting a survey of mechanical engineers to learn more about the factors influencing the choice of heating, ventilation, and air conditioning (HVAC) equipment for new commercial buildings. A total of 120 firms in the utility's service area are engaged in designing HVAC systems. The sampling plan is to use cluster sampling with each firm representing a cluster. For each firm in the sample, all of the mechanical engineers will be interviewed. Approximately 500 mechanical engineers are believed to be employed by the 120 firms. A sample of 10 firms was taken. Among other things, the age of each respondent was recorded as well as whether the respondent had attended the local university. **LO 6**

DATA*file*
hvac

Cluster (i)	M_i	Total of Respondents' Ages	Number Attending Local University
1	12	520	8
2	1	33	0
3	2	70	1
4	1	29	1
5	6	270	3
6	3	129	2
7	2	102	0
8	1	48	1
9	9	337	7
10	13	462	12
Totals	50	2000	35

a. Estimate the mean age of mechanical engineers engaged in this type of work.
b. Estimate the proportion of mechanical engineers in the utility's service area who attended the local university.
c. Develop an approximate 95% confidence interval for the mean age of mechanical engineers designing HVAC systems for commercial buildings.
d. Develop an approximate 95% confidence interval for the proportion of mechanical engineers in the utility's service area who attended the local university.

17. **Employee Attitudes.** A national real estate company just acquired a smaller firm with 150 offices and 6,000 agents in Los Angeles and other parts of Southern California. The national firm conducted a sample survey to learn about attitudes and other characteristics of its new employees. In a sample of eight offices, all of the agents completed the questionnaire. Results of the survey for the eight offices follow. **LO 6**

DATA*file*
employeeattitudes

Office	Agents	Average Age	College Graduates	Male Agents
1	17	37	3	4
2	35	32	14	12
3	26	36	8	7
4	66	30	38	28
5	43	41	18	12
6	12	52	2	6
7	48	35	20	17
8	57	44	25	26

a. Estimate the mean age of the agents.
b. Estimate the proportion of agents who are college graduates and the proportion who are male.
c. Develop an approximate 95% confidence interval for the mean age of the agents.
d. Develop an approximate 95% confidence interval for the proportion of agents who are college graduates.
e. Develop an approximate 95% confidence interval for the proportion of agents who are male.

21.7 Systematic Sampling

Systematic sampling is often used as an alternative to simple random sampling. In some sampling situations, especially those with large populations, it can be time consuming to select a simple random sample by first finding a random number and then counting or searching through the frame until the corresponding element is found. Systematic sampling offers an alternative to simple random sampling in such cases. For example, if a sample size of 50 from a population containing 5,000 elements is desired, we might sample one element for every 5,000/50 = 100 elements in the population. A systematic sample for this case would involve randomly selecting one of the first 100 elements from the frame. The remaining sample elements are identified by starting with the first sampled element and then selecting every 100th element that follows in the frame. In effect, the sample of 50 is identified by moving systematically through the population and identifying every 100th element after the first randomly selected element. The sample of 50 will often be easier to select in this manner than it would be if simple random sampling were used. The first element selected is a random choice, allowing for the assumption that a systematic sample has the properties of a simple random sample. This assumption is usually appropriate when the frame is a random ordering of the elements in the population.

Summary

We provided a brief introduction to the field of survey sampling. The purpose of survey sampling is to collect data for the purpose of making estimates of population parameters such as the population mean, total, or proportion. Survey sampling as a method of data collection can be contrasted with conducting experiments to generate data. When survey sampling is used, the design of the sampling plan is of critical importance in determining which existing data will be collected. When experiments are employed, experimental design issues are of critical importance in determining which data will be generated, or created.

Two types of errors can occur with sample surveys: sampling error and nonsampling error. Sampling error is the error that occurs because a sample, and not the entire population, is used to estimate a population parameter. Nonsampling error refers to all the other types of errors that can occur, such as measurement, interviewer, nonresponse, and processing error. Nonsampling errors are controlled by proper questionnaire design, thorough training of interviewers, careful verification of data, and so on. Sampling errors are minimized by a proper choice of sample design and by selecting an appropriate sample size.

We discussed four commonly used sample designs in this chapter: simple random sampling, stratified simple random sampling, cluster sampling, and systematic sampling. The objective of sample design is to get the most precise estimates for the least cost. When the population can be divided into strata so that the elements within each stratum are relatively homogeneous, stratified simple random sampling will provide more precision (smaller approximate confidence intervals) than simple random sampling. When the elements can be grouped in clusters so that all the elements in a cluster are close together geographically, cluster sampling often reduces interviewer cost; in these situations, cluster sampling will often provide the most precision per dollar. Systematic random sampling was presented as an alternative to simple random sampling.

Glossary

Bound on the sampling error A number added to and subtracted from a point estimate to create an approximate 95% confidence interval. It is given by two times the standard error of the point estimator.
Cluster sampling A probabilistic method of sampling in which the population is first divided into clusters and then one or more clusters are selected for sampling. In single-stage cluster sampling, every element in each selected cluster is sampled; in two-stage cluster sampling, a sample of the elements in each selected cluster is collected.
Convenience sampling A nonprobabilistic method of sampling whereby elements are selected on the basis of convenience.
Element The entity on which data are collected.
Frame A list of the sampling units for a study. The sample is drawn by selecting units from the frame.
Judgment sampling A nonprobabilistic method of sampling whereby element selection is based on the judgment of the person doing the study.
Nonprobabilistic sampling Any method of sampling for which the probability of selecting a sample cannot be computed.
Nonsampling error All types of errors other than sampling error, such as measurement error, interviewer error, and processing error.
Population The collection of all elements of interest.
Probabilistic sampling Any method of sampling for which the probability of each possible sample can be computed.
Sample A subset of the population.
Sampled population The population from which the sample is taken.
Sampling error The error that occurs because a sample, and not the entire population, is used to estimate a population parameter.
Sampling unit The units selected for sampling. A sampling unit may include several elements.
Simple random sample A sample selected in such a manner that each sample of size n has the same probability of being selected.
Stratified simple random sampling A probabilistic method of selecting a sample in which the population is first divided into strata and a simple random sample is then taken from each stratum.
Systematic sampling A method of choosing a sample by randomly selecting the first element and then selecting every kth element thereafter.
Target population The population about which inferences are made.

Key Formulas

Simple Random Sampling

Interval Estimate of the Population Mean

$$\bar{x} \pm t_{\alpha/2}\frac{s}{\sqrt{n}} \tag{21.1}$$

Estimate of the Standard Error of the Mean

$$s_{\bar{x}} = \sqrt{\frac{N-n}{N}}\left(\frac{s}{\sqrt{n}}\right) \tag{21.2}$$

Interval Estimate of the Population Mean

$$\bar{x} \pm t_{\alpha/2}s_{\bar{x}} \tag{21.3}$$

Approximate 95% Confidence Interval Estimate of the Population Mean

$$\bar{x} \pm 2s_{\bar{x}} \tag{21.4}$$

Point Estimator of a Population Total

$$\hat{X} = N\bar{x} \tag{21.5}$$

Estimate of the Standard Error of $\hat{X}$

$$s_{\hat{X}} = N s_{\bar{x}} \tag{21.6}$$

Approximate 95% Confidence Interval Estimate of the Population Total

$$N\bar{x} \pm 2s_{\hat{X}} \tag{21.8}$$

Estimate of the Standard Error of the Proportion

$$s_{\bar{p}} = \sqrt{\left(\frac{N-n}{N}\right)\left(\frac{\bar{p}(1-\bar{p})}{n-1}\right)} \tag{21.9}$$

Approximate 95% Confidence Interval Estimate of the Population Proportion

$$\bar{p} \pm 2s_{\bar{p}} \tag{21.10}$$

Sample Size for an Estimate of the Population Mean

$$n = \frac{Ns^2}{N\left(\frac{B^2}{4}\right) + s^2} \tag{21.12}$$

Sample Size for an Estimate of the Population Total

$$n = \frac{Ns^2}{\left(\frac{B^2}{4N}\right) + s^2} \tag{21.13}$$

Sample Size for an Estimate of the Population Proportion

$$n = \frac{N\bar{p}(1-\bar{p})}{N\left(\frac{B^2}{4}\right) + \bar{p}(1-\bar{p})} \tag{21.14}$$

Stratified Simple Random Sampling

Point Estimator of the Population Mean

$$\bar{x}_{\text{st}} = \sum_{h=1}^{H}\left(\frac{N_h}{N}\right)\bar{x}_h \tag{21.15}$$

Estimate of the Standard Error of the Mean

$$s_{\bar{x}_{\text{st}}} = \sqrt{\frac{1}{N^2}\sum_{h=1}^{H} N_h(N_h - n_h)\frac{s_h^2}{n_h}} \tag{21.16}$$

Approximate 95% Confidence Interval Estimate of the Population Mean

$$\bar{x}_{\text{st}} \pm 2s_{\bar{x}_{\text{st}}} \tag{21.17}$$

Point Estimator of the Population Total

$$\hat{X} = N\bar{x}_{\text{st}} \tag{21.18}$$

Estimate of the Standard Error of $\hat{X}$

$$s_{\hat{X}} = N s_{\bar{x}_{\text{st}}} \tag{21.19}$$

Approximate 95% Confidence Interval Estimate of the Population Total

$$N\bar{x}_{\text{st}} \pm 2s_{\hat{X}} \tag{21.20}$$

Point Estimator of the Population Proportion

$$\bar{p}_{\text{st}} = \sum_{h=1}^{H} \left(\frac{N_h}{N}\right) \bar{p}_h \tag{21.21}$$

Estimate of the Standard Error of p_{st}

$$s_{\bar{p}_{\text{st}}} = \sqrt{\frac{1}{N^2} \sum_{h=1}^{H} N_h(N_h - n_h)\left[\frac{\bar{p}_h(1 - \bar{p}_h)}{n_h - 1}\right]} \tag{21.22}$$

Approximate 95% Confidence Interval Estimate of the Population Proportion

$$\bar{p}_{\text{st}} \pm 2s_{\bar{p}_{\text{st}}} \tag{21.23}$$

Allocating the Total Sample n to the Strata: Neyman Allocation

$$n_h = n\left(\frac{N_h s_h}{\sum_{h=1}^{H} N_h s_h}\right) \tag{21.24}$$

Sample Size When Estimating the Population Mean

$$n = \frac{\left(\sum_{h=1}^{H} N_h s_h\right)^2}{N^2\left(\frac{B^2}{4}\right) + \sum_{h=1}^{H} N_h s_h^2} \tag{21.25}$$

Sample Size When Estimating the Population Total

$$n = \frac{\left(\sum_{h=1}^{H} N_h s_h\right)^2}{\frac{B^2}{4} + \sum_{h=1}^{H} N_h s_h^2} \tag{21.26}$$

Sample Size for the Estimate of the Population Proportion

$$n = \frac{\left(\sum_{h=1}^{H} N_h \sqrt{\bar{p}_h(1 - \bar{p}_h)}\right)^2}{N^2\left(\frac{B^2}{4}\right) + \sum_{h=1}^{H} N_h \bar{p}_h(1 - \bar{p}_h)} \tag{21.27}$$

Proportional Allocation of Sample n to the Strata

$$n_h = n\left(\frac{N_h}{N}\right) \tag{21.28}$$

Cluster Sampling

Point Estimator of the Population Mean

$$\bar{x}_{\text{c}} = \frac{\sum_{i=1}^{n} x_i}{\sum_{i=1}^{n} M_i} \tag{21.29}$$

Estimate of the Standard Error of the Mean

$$s_{\bar{x}_{\text{c}}} = \sqrt{\left(\frac{N - n}{Nn\bar{M}^2}\right) \frac{\sum_{i=1}^{n} (x_i - \bar{x}_{\text{c}} M_i)^2}{n - 1}} \tag{21.30}$$

Approximate 95% Confidence Interval Estimate of the Population Mean

$$\bar{x}_c \pm 2s_{\bar{x}_c} \tag{21.31}$$

Point Estimator of the Population Total

$$\hat{X} = M\bar{x}_c \tag{21.32}$$

Estimate of the Standard Error of $\hat{X}$

$$s_{\hat{X}} = Ms_{\bar{x}_c} \tag{21.33}$$

Approximate 95% Confidence Interval Estimate of the Population Total

$$M\bar{x}_c \pm 2s_{\hat{X}} \tag{21.34}$$

Point Estimator of the Population Proportion

$$\bar{p}_c = \frac{\sum_{i=1}^{n} a_i}{\sum_{i=1}^{n} M_i} \tag{21.35}$$

Estimate of the Standard Error of p_c

$$s_{\bar{p}_c} = \sqrt{\left(\frac{N-n}{NnM^2}\right)\frac{\sum_{i=1}^{n}(a_i - \bar{p}_c M_i)^2}{n-1}} \tag{21.36}$$

Approximate 95% Confidence Interval Estimate of the Population Proportion

$$\bar{p}_c \pm 2s_{\bar{p}_c} \tag{21.37}$$

Supplementary Exercises

18. **Beer Ad Acceptance.** To assess consumer acceptance of a new series of ads for Miller Lite Beer, Louis Harris conducted a nationwide poll of 363 adults who had seen the Miller Lite ads. The following responses are based on that survey. *Note:* Because the survey sampled only a small fraction of all adults, assume $(N - n)/N = 1$ in any formulas involving the standard error. **LO 1, 2**
    a. Nineteen percent of all respondents indicated they liked the ads a lot. Develop a 95% confidence interval for the population proportion.
    b. Thirty-one percent of the respondents disliked the new ads. Develop a 95% confidence interval for the population proportion.
    c. Seventeen percent of the respondents felt the ads are very effective. Develop a 95% confidence interval for the proportion of adults who think the ads are very effective.
    d. Louis Harris reported that the "margin of error is five percentage points." What does this statement mean and how do you think they arrived at this number?
    e. How might nonsampling error bias the results of such a survey?
19. **CEO Compensation.** In a 2017 study conducted by *The Wall Street Journal,* 200 large U.S. companies were asked how they compensated their CEOs. One question asked if the companies included appreciation awards (stock options and stock appreciation rights) in their CEO compensation packages; 45% said they did. Another question asked if the companies included performance-based awards in their CEO compensation package; 77% said they did. **LO 2**
    a. Develop an estimate of the standard error of the proportion for the proportion that includes appreciation awards.
    b. Develop an estimate of the standard error of the proportion for the proportion that includes performance-based awards.

c. Are the estimates of the standard error the same in parts (a) and (b)? If they differ, explain why.
d. Develop an approximate 95% confidence interval for the proportion that includes appreciation awards.
e. Develop an approximate 95% confidence interval for the proportion that includes performance-based awards.

20. **Employee Quality of Life.** A quality of life survey was conducted with employees of a manufacturing firm. Of the firm's 3,000 employees, a sample of 300 were sent questionnaires. Two hundred usable questionnaires were obtained for a response rate of 67%. **LO 1, 2**
 a. The mean annual salary for the sample was $\bar{x}$ = \$23,200 with s = \$3,000. Develop an approximate 95% confidence interval for the mean annual salary of the population.
 b. Use the information in part (a) to develop an approximate 95% confidence interval for the total salary of all 3,000 employees.
 c. Seventy-three percent of respondents reported that they were "generally satisfied" with their job. Develop an approximate 95% confidence interval for the population proportion.
 d. Comment on whether you think the results in part (c) might be biased. Would your opinion change if you knew the respondents were guaranteed anonymity?

21. **Homicides by Shooting.** A U.S. Senate Judiciary Committee report showed the number of homicides in each state. In Indiana, Ohio, and Kentucky, the number of homicides was, respectively, 380, 760, and 260. Suppose a stratified random sample with the following results was taken to learn more about the victims and the cause of death. **LO 2, 4**

Stratum	Sample Size	Shootings	Beatings	Urban Victims
Indiana	30	10	9	21
Ohio	45	19	12	34
Kentucky	25	7	11	15

 a. Develop an approximate 95% confidence interval for the proportion of shooting homicides in Indiana.
 b. Develop an estimate for the total number of shooting homicides in Ohio.
 c. Develop an approximate 95% confidence interval for the proportion of shooting homicides in Ohio.
 d. Develop an approximate 95% confidence interval for the proportion of shooting homicides across all three states.

22. **Homicides by Beating.** Refer again to the data in exercise 21. **LO 4**
 a. Develop an estimate of the total number of homicides (in the three states) due to beatings.
 b. Develop an approximate 95% confidence interval for the proportion of homicides across all three states due to beatings.
 c. Develop an approximate 95% confidence interval for the proportion of homicide by beating victims who are urban.
 d. Develop an estimate of the total number of urban victims of homicide.

23. **Bank Customer Attitudes.** A stratified simple random sample is to be taken of a bank's customers to learn about a variety of attitudinal and demographic issues. The stratification is to be based on savings account balances as of January 30 of this year. A frequency distribution showing the number of accounts in each stratum, together with the standard deviation of account balances by stratum, follows. **LO 5**
 a. Assuming the cost per unit sampled is approximately equal across strata, determine the total number of persons to include in the sample. Assume we want a bound

on the error of estimate of the population mean for savings account balances of $B = \$20$.

b. Use the Neyman allocation procedure to determine the number to be sampled for each stratum.

DATA*file*
bankcustomerattitudes

Stratum ($)	Accounts	Standard Deviation of Account Balances
0.00–1,000.00	3,000	80
1,000.01–2,000.00	600	150
2,000.01–5,000.00	250	220
5,000.01–10,000.00	100	700
over 10,000.00	50	3,000

24. **Assisted Living Home Residents.** A public agency is interested in learning more about the persons living in assisted living homes in a particular city. A total of 100 assisted living homes are caring for 4,800 people in the city and a cluster sample of six homes has been taken. Each person in the six assisted living homes has been interviewed. A portion of the sample results follows. **LO 6**

DATA*file*
assistedliving_ages

Home	Residents	Average Age of Residents	Long Term Care Residents
1	14	61	12
2	7	74	2
3	96	78	30
4	23	69	8
5	71	73	10
6	29	84	22

a. Develop an estimate of the mean age of assisted living home residents in this city.
b. Develop an approximate 95% confidence interval for the proportion of long term care residents in the city's assisted living homes.
c. Estimate the total number of long term care residents in assisted living homes in this city.

Case: Medicament's Predicament

Medicament, Inc., is a supplier of replacement parts for medical equipment that sells its products to four types of hospitals: rehabilitation hospitals, children's hospitals, geriatric hospitals, and long-term acute-care facilities. The types of hospitals to which Medicament sells its parts are distributed as follows:

Rehabilitation Hospitals	Children's Hospitals	Geriatric Hospitals	Long-Term Acute-Care Facilities
250	275	400	225

To plan for the next year, Medicament's management needs to estimate its total dollar sales over that period. Medicament has found that it is difficult to obtain estimates of future purchases from a hospital, so it has decided to collect estimates from a sample of the hospitals to which it sells parts.

From a past survey, the following estimates for the standard deviations of annual dollar sales in these four types of hospitals are available as shown below. **LO 5**

Rehabilitation Hospitals	Children's Hospitals	Geriatric Hospitals	Long-Term Acute-Care Facilities
1,100	900	250	335

Managerial Report

Perform an analysis that will help Medicament design a sample survey to estimate sales over the next year. Prepare a report that answers the four specific questions that follow.

1. Medicament wants an estimate of the population mean with a bound on the error of estimate of $150. How large must the sample be? How many elements should be allocated to each stratum?
2. Medicament also wants to consider a bound of $100 on its estimated population mean. How large must the sample now be? How many elements should now be allocated to each stratum?
3. Medicament wants an estimate of the population total with a bound of $75,000. How large must the sample now be? How many elements should now be allocated to each stratum?
4. If Medicament wants an estimate of the population mean with a bound of $100 and an estimate of the population total with a bound of $75,000, how large must the sample be? How many elements should be allocated to each stratum?

Include the details of your analysis as an appendix to your report.

Appendixes

Contents

Appendix A–References and Bibliography

General

Freedman, D., R. Pisani, and R. Purves. *Statistics*, 4th ed. W. W. Norton, 2007.

Hogg R. V., E. A. Tanis, and D. L. Zimmerman. *Probability and Statistical Inference*, 10th ed. Prentice Hall, 2018.

McKean, J. W., R. V. Hogg, and A. T. Craig. *Introduction to Mathematical Statistics*, 8th ed. Prentice Hall, 2019.

Miller, I., and M. Miller. *John E. Freund's Mathematical Statistics*, 8th ed. Pearson Prentice Hall, 2012.

Moore, D. S., G. P. McCabe, and B. Craig. *Introduction to the Practice of Statistics*, 10th ed. Freeman, 2021.

Wackerly, D. D., W. Mendenhall, and R. L. Scheaffer. *Mathematical Statistics with Applications*, 7th ed. Cengage Learning, 2008.

Experimental Design

Cochran, W. G., and G. M. Cox. *Experimental Designs*, 2nd ed. Wiley, 1992.

Hicks, C. R., and K. V. Turner. *Fundamental Concepts in the Design of Experiments*, 5th ed. Oxford University Press, 1999.

Montgomery, D. C. *Design and Analysis of Experiments*, 10th ed. Wiley, 2019.

Winer, B. J., K. M. Michels, and D. R. Brown. *Statistical Principles in Experimental Design*, 3rd ed. McGraw Hill, 1991.

Wu, C. F. Jeff, and M. Hamada. *Experiments: Planning, Analysis, and Optimization*, 3rd ed. Wiley, 2021.

Time Series and Forecasting

Bowerman, B. L., R. T. O'Connell, and A. Koehler. *Forecasting and Time Series: An Applied Approach*, 4th ed. Thomson Learning, 2004.

Box, G. E. P., G. M. Jenkins, and G. C. Reinsel. *Time Series Analysis: Forecasting and Control*, 5th ed. Wiley, 2015.

Makridakis, S. G., S. C. Wheelwright, and R. J. Hyndman. *Forecasting Methods and Applications*, 3rd ed. Wiley, 1997.

Wilson, J. H., B. Keating, and John Galt Solutions, Inc. *Business Forecasting with Accompanying Excel-Based Forecast X^{TM}*, 6th ed. McGraw Hill/Irwin, 2008.

Nonparametric Methods

Conover, W. J. *Practical Nonparametric Statistics*, 3rd ed. Wiley, 1999.

Corder, G. W., and D. I. Foreman. *Nonparametric Statistics: A Step-by-Step Approach*, 2nd ed. Wiley, 2014.

Gibbons, J. D., and S. Chakraborti. *Nonparametric Statistical Inference*, 6th ed. CRC Press, 2021.

Higgins, J. J. *Introduction to Modern Nonparametric Statistics*. Thomson-Brooks/Cole, 2003.

Hollander, M., D. A. Wolfe, and E. Chicken. *Non-Parametric Statistical Methods*, 3rd ed. Wiley, 2013.

Jureckova, J., P. K. Sen, and J. Picek. *Methodology in Robust and Nonparametric Statistics*, 7th ed. CRC Press, 2012.

Probability

Hogg R. V., E. A. Tanis, and D. L. Zimmerman. *Probability and Statistical Inference*, 10th ed. Pearson, 2018.

Ross, S. M. *Introduction to Probability Models*, 12th ed. Academic Press, 2019.

Wackerly, D. D., W. Mendenhall, and R. L. Scheaffer. *Mathematical Statistics with Applications*, 7th ed. Cengage Learning, 2008.

Quality Control

DeFeo, J. A., and J. M. Juran, *Juran's Quality Handbook*, 7th ed. McGraw Hill, 2016.

Evans, J. R., and W. M. Lindsay. *Managing for Quality and Performance Excellence,* 11th ed., Cengage, 2020.

Montgomery, D. C. *Introduction to Statistical Quality Control*, 8th ed. Wiley, 2019.

Regression Analysis

Chatterjee, S., and A. S. Hadi. *Regression Analysis by Example*, 5th ed. Wiley, 2012.

Draper, N. R., and H. Smith. *Applied Regression Analysis*, 3rd ed. Wiley, 1998.

Graybill, F. A., and H. K. Iyer. *Regression Analysis: Concepts and Applications*. Wadsworth, 1994.

Hosmer, D. W., and S. Lemeshow. *Applied Logistic Regression*, 3rd ed. Wiley, 2013.

Kleinbaum, D. G., L. L. Kupper, and K. E. Muller. *Applied Regression Analysis and Other Multivariate Methods*, 4th ed. Cengage Learning, 2007.

Neter, J., W. Wasserman, M. H. Kutner, and C. Nashtsheim. *Applied Linear Statistical Models*, 5th ed. McGraw Hill, 2004.

Mendenhall, M., T. Sincich., and T. R. Dye. *A Second Course in Statistics: Regression Analysis*, 8th ed. Prentice Hall, 2020.

Decision Analysis

Clemen, R. T., and T. Reilly. *Making Hard Decisions with Decision Tools*, 3rd ed. Cengage Learning, 2014.

Goodwin, P., and G. Wright. *Decision Analysis for Management Judgment*, 5th ed. Wiley, 2014.

Pratt, J. W., H. Raiffa, and R. Schlaifer. *Introduction to Statistical Decision Theory*. MIT Press, 2008.

Sampling

Cochran, W. G. *Sampling Techniques*, 3rd ed. Wiley, 1977.

Hansen, M. H., W. N. Hurwitz, W. G. Madow, and M. N. Hanson. *Sample Survey Methods and Theory.* Wiley, 1993.

Kish, L. *Survey Sampling.* Wiley, 2008.

Levy, P. S., and S. Lemeshow. *Sampling of Populations: Methods and Applications*, 4th ed. Wiley, 2009.

Scheaffer, R. L., W. Mendenhall, and L. Ott. *Elementary Survey Sampling*, 7th ed. Duxbury Press, 2011.

Data Visualization

Camm, J. D., J. J. Cochran, M. J. Fry, and J. W. Ohlmann. *Data Visualization: Exploring and Explaining with Data*, 1st ed. Cengage Learning, 2021.

Cleveland, W. S. *Visualizing Data.* Hobart Press, 1993.

Cleveland, W. S. *The Elements of Graphing Data*, 2nd ed. Hobart Press, 1994.

Few, S. *Show Me the Numbers: Designing Tables and Graphs to Enlighten*, 2nd ed. Analytics Press, 2012.

Few, S. *Information Dashboard Design: The Effective Visual Communication of Data*, 2nd ed. O'Reilly Media, 2012.

Few, S. *Now You See It: Simple Visualization Techniques for Quantitative Analysis.* Analytics Press, 2009.

Fry, B. *Visualizing Data: Exploring and Explaining Data with the Processing Environment.* O'Reilly Media, 2008.

Knaflic, C., N. *Storytelling with Data: A Data Visualization Guide for Business Professionals,* Wiley, 2015.

Robbins, N. B. *Creating More Effective Graphs.* Chart House, 2013.

Telea, A. C. *Data Visualization Principles and Practice,* 2nd ed. A.K. Peters Ltd., 2014.

Tufte, E. R. *Envisioning Information.* Graphics Press, 1990.

Tufte, E. R. *The Visual Display of Quantitative Information*, 2nd ed. Graphics Press, 1990.

Tufte, E. R. *Visual Explanations: Images and Quantities, Evidence and Narrative.* Graphics Press, 1997.

Tufte, E. R. *Visual and Statistical Thinking: Displays of Evidence for Making Decisions.* Graphics Press, 2009.

Tufte, E. R. *Beautiful Evidence.* Graphics Press, 2006.

Wong, D. M. *The Wall Street Journal Guide to Information Graphics.* W. W. Norton & Company, 2013.

Young, F. W., P. M. Valero-Mora, and M. Friendly. *Visual Statistics: Seeing Data with Dynamic Interactive Graphics.* Wiley, 2006.

Business Analytics

Camm, J. D., J. J. Cochran, M. J. Fry, J. W. Ohlmann. *Business Analytics*, 5th ed. Cengage Learning, 2024.

Appendix B–Tables

Table 1 Cumulative Probabilities for the Standard Normal Distribution

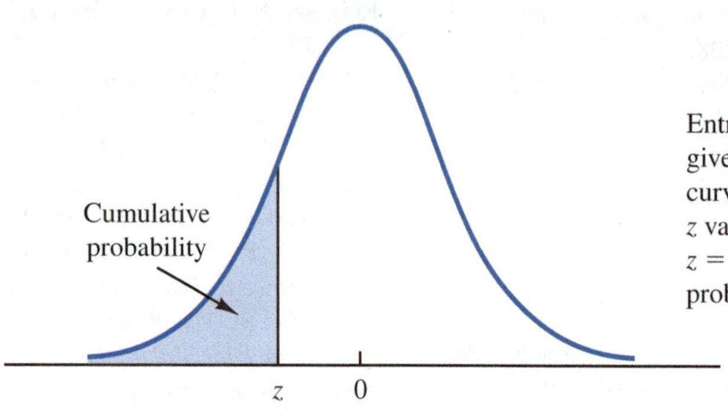

Entries in the table give the area under the curve to the left of the z value. For example, for $z = -.85$, the cumulative probability is .1977.

z	.00	.01	.02	.03	.04	.05	.06	.07	.08	.09
−3.0	.0013	.0013	.0013	.0012	.0012	.0011	.0011	.0011	.0010	.0010
−2.9	.0019	.0018	.0018	.0017	.0016	.0016	.0015	.0015	.0014	.0014
−2.8	.0026	.0025	.0024	.0023	.0023	.0022	.0021	.0021	.0020	.0019
−2.7	.0035	.0034	.0033	.0032	.0031	.0030	.0029	.0028	.0027	.0026
−2.6	.0047	.0045	.0044	.0043	.0041	.0040	.0039	.0038	.0037	.0036
−2.5	.0062	.0060	.0059	.0057	.0055	.0054	.0052	.0051	.0049	.0048
−2.4	.0082	.0080	.0078	.0075	.0073	.0071	.0069	.0068	.0066	.0064
−2.3	.0107	.0104	.0102	.0099	.0096	.0094	.0091	.0089	.0087	.0084
−2.2	.0139	.0136	.0132	.0129	.0125	.0122	.0119	.0116	.0113	.0110
−2.1	.0179	.0174	.0170	.0166	.0162	.0158	.0154	.0150	.0146	.0143
−2.0	.0228	.0222	.0217	.0212	.0207	.0202	.0197	.0192	.0188	.0183
−1.9	.0287	.0281	.0274	.0268	.0262	.0256	.0250	.0244	.0239	.0233
−1.8	.0359	.0351	.0344	.0336	.0329	.0322	.0314	.0307	.0301	.0294
−1.7	.0446	.0436	.0427	.0418	.0409	.0401	.0392	.0384	.0375	.0367
−1.6	.0548	.0537	.0526	.0516	.0505	.0495	.0485	.0475	.0465	.0455
−1.5	.0668	.0655	.0643	.0630	.0618	.0606	.0594	.0582	.0571	.0559
−1.4	.0808	.0793	.0778	.0764	.0749	.0735	.0721	.0708	.0694	.0681
−1.3	.0968	.0951	.0934	.0918	.0901	.0885	.0869	.0853	.0838	.0823
−1.2	.1151	.1131	.1112	.1093	.1075	.1056	.1038	.1020	.1003	.0985
−1.1	.1357	.1335	.1314	.1292	.1271	.1251	.1230	.1210	.1190	.1170
−1.0	.1587	.1562	.1539	.1515	.1492	.1469	.1446	.1423	.1401	.1379
−.9	.1841	.1814	.1788	.1762	.1736	.1711	.1685	.1660	.1635	.1611
−.8	.2119	.2090	.2061	.2033	.2005	.1977	.1949	.1922	.1894	.1867
−.7	.2420	.2389	.2358	.2327	.2296	.2266	.2236	.2206	.2177	.2148
−.6	.2743	.2709	.2676	.2643	.2611	.2578	.2546	.2514	.2483	.2451
−.5	.3085	.3050	.3015	.2981	.2946	.2912	.2877	.2843	.2810	.2776
−.4	.3446	.3409	.3372	.3336	.3300	.3264	.3228	.3192	.3156	.3121
−.3	.3821	.3783	.3745	.3707	.3669	.3632	.3594	.3557	.3520	.3483
−.2	.4207	.4168	.4129	.4090	.4052	.4013	.3974	.3936	.3897	.3859
−.1	.4602	.4562	.4522	.4483	.4443	.4404	.4364	.4325	.4286	.4247
−.0	.5000	.4960	.4920	.4880	.4840	.4801	.4761	.4721	.4681	.4641

Table 1 Cumulative Probabilities for the Standard Normal Distribution (*Continued*)

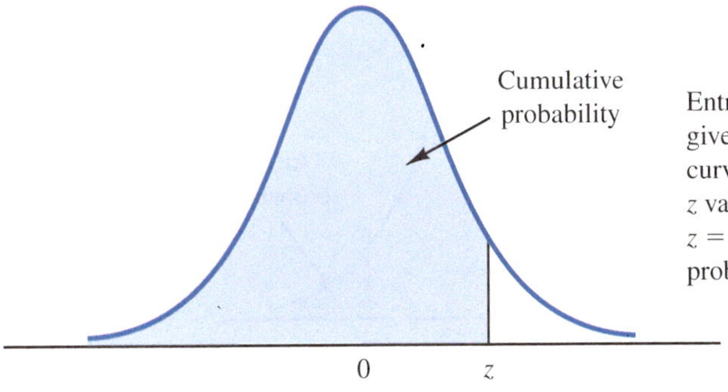

Entries in the table give the area under the curve to the left of the z value. For example, for $z = 1.25$, the cumulative probability is .8944.

z	.00	.01	.02	.03	.04	.05	.06	.07	.08	.09
.0	.5000	.5040	.5080	.5120	.5160	.5199	.5239	.5279	.5319	.5359
.1	.5398	.5438	.5478	.5517	.5557	.5596	.5636	.5675	.5714	.5753
.2	.5793	.5832	.5871	.5910	.5948	.5987	.6026	.6064	.6103	.6141
.3	.6179	.6217	.6255	.6293	.6331	.6368	.6406	.6443	.6480	.6517
.4	.6554	.6591	.6628	.6664	.6700	.6736	.6772	.6808	.6844	.6879
.5	.6915	.6950	.6985	.7019	.7054	.7088	.7123	.7157	.7190	.7224
.6	.7257	.7291	.7324	.7357	.7389	.7422	.7454	.7486	.7517	.7549
.7	.7580	.7611	.7642	.7673	.7704	.7734	.7764	.7794	.7823	.7852
.8	.7881	.7910	.7939	.7967	.7995	.8023	.8051	.8078	.8106	.8133
.9	.8159	.8186	.8212	.8238	.8264	.8289	.8315	.8340	.8365	.8389
1.0	.8413	.8438	.8461	.8485	.8508	.8531	.8554	.8577	.8599	.8621
1.1	.8643	.8665	.8686	.8708	.8729	.8749	.8770	.8790	.8810	.8830
1.2	.8849	.8869	.8888	.8907	.8925	.8944	.8962	.8980	.8997	.9015
1.3	.9032	.9049	.9066	.9082	.9099	.9115	.9131	.9147	.9162	.9177
1.4	.9192	.9207	.9222	.9236	.9251	.9265	.9279	.9292	.9306	.9319
1.5	.9332	.9345	.9357	.9370	.9382	.9394	.9406	.9418	.9429	.9441
1.6	.9452	.9463	.9474	.9484	.9495	.9505	.9515	.9525	.9535	.9545
1.7	.9554	.9564	.9573	.9582	.9591	.9599	.9608	.9616	.9625	.9633
1.8	.9641	.9649	.9656	.9664	.9671	.9678	.9686	.9693	.9699	.9706
1.9	.9713	.9719	.9726	.9732	.9738	.9744	.9750	.9756	.9761	.9767
2.0	.9772	.9778	.9783	.9788	.9793	.9798	.9803	.9808	.9812	.9817
2.1	.9821	.9826	.9830	.9834	.9838	.9842	.9846	.9850	.9854	.9857
2.2	.9861	.9864	.9868	.9871	.9875	.9878	.9881	.9884	.9887	.9890
2.3	.9893	.9896	.9898	.9901	.9904	.9906	.9909	.9911	.9913	.9916
2.4	.9918	.9920	.9922	.9925	.9927	.9929	.9931	.9932	.9934	.9936
2.5	.9938	.9940	.9941	.9943	.9945	.9946	.9948	.9949	.9951	.9952
2.6	.9953	.9955	.9956	.9957	.9959	.9960	.9961	.9962	.9963	.9964
2.7	.9965	.9966	.9967	.9968	.9969	.9970	.9971	.9972	.9973	.9974
2.8	.9974	.9975	.9976	.9977	.9977	.9978	.9979	.9979	.9980	.9981
2.9	.9981	.9982	.9982	.9983	.9984	.9984	.9985	.9985	.9986	.9986
3.0	.9987	.9987	.9987	.9988	.9988	.9989	.9989	.9989	.9990	.9990

Table 2 *t* Distribution

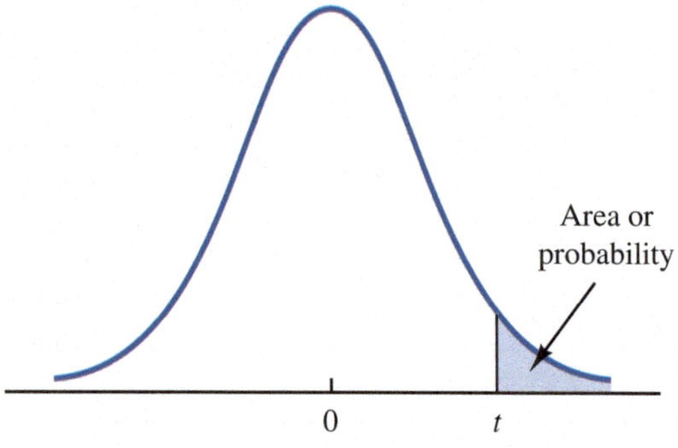

Entries in the table give *t* values for an area or probability in the upper tail of the *t* distribution. For example, with 10 degrees of freedom and a .05 area in the upper tail, $t_{.05} = 1.812$.

Degrees of Freedom	Area in Upper Tail					
	.20	.10	.05	.025	.01	.005
1	1.376	3.078	6.314	12.706	31.821	63.656
2	1.061	1.886	2.920	4.303	6.965	9.925
3	.978	1.638	2.353	3.182	4.541	5.841
4	.941	1.533	2.132	2.776	3.747	4.604
5	.920	1.476	2.015	2.571	3.365	4.032
6	.906	1.440	1.943	2.447	3.143	3.707
7	.896	1.415	1.895	2.365	2.998	3.499
8	.889	1.397	1.860	2.306	2.896	3.355
9	.883	1.383	1.833	2.262	2.821	3.250
10	.879	1.372	1.812	2.228	2.764	3.169
11	.876	1.363	1.796	2.201	2.718	3.106
12	.873	1.356	1.782	2.179	2.681	3.055
13	.870	1.350	1.771	2.160	2.650	3.012
14	.868	1.345	1.761	2.145	2.624	2.977
15	.866	1.341	1.753	2.131	2.602	2.947
16	.865	1.337	1.746	2.120	2.583	2.921
17	.863	1.333	1.740	2.110	2.567	2.898
18	.862	1.330	1.734	2.101	2.552	2.878
19	.861	1.328	1.729	2.093	2.539	2.861
20	.860	1.325	1.725	2.086	2.528	2.845
21	.859	1.323	1.721	2.080	2.518	2.831
22	.858	1.321	1.717	2.074	2.508	2.819
23	.858	1.319	1.714	2.069	2.500	2.807
24	.857	1.318	1.711	2.064	2.492	2.797
25	.856	1.316	1.708	2.060	2.485	2.787
26	.856	1.315	1.706	2.056	2.479	2.779
27	.855	1.314	1.703	2.052	2.473	2.771
28	.855	1.313	1.701	2.048	2.467	2.763
29	.854	1.311	1.699	2.045	2.462	2.756
30	.854	1.310	1.697	2.042	2.457	2.750
31	.853	1.309	1.696	2.040	2.453	2.744
32	.853	1.309	1.694	2.037	2.449	2.738
33	.853	1.308	1.692	2.035	2.445	2.733
34	.852	1.307	1.691	2.032	2.441	2.728

Table 2 *t* Distribution (*Continued*)

Degrees of Freedom	Area in Upper Tail .20	.10	.05	.025	.01	.005
35	.852	1.306	1.690	2.030	2.438	2.724
36	.852	1.306	1.688	2.028	2.434	2.719
37	.851	1.305	1.687	2.026	2.431	2.715
38	.851	1.304	1.686	2.024	2.429	2.712
39	.851	1.304	1.685	2.023	2.426	2.708
40	.851	1.303	1.684	2.021	2.423	2.704
41	.850	1.303	1.683	2.020	2.421	2.701
42	.850	1.302	1.682	2.018	2.418	2.698
43	.850	1.302	1.681	2.017	2.416	2.695
44	.850	1.301	1.680	2.015	2.414	2.692
45	.850	1.301	1.679	2.014	2.412	2.690
46	.850	1.300	1.679	2.013	2.410	2.687
47	.849	1.300	1.678	2.012	2.408	2.685
48	.849	1.299	1.677	2.011	2.407	2.682
49	.849	1.299	1.677	2.010	2.405	2.680
50	.849	1.299	1.676	2.009	2.403	2.678
51	.849	1.298	1.675	2.008	2.402	2.676
52	.849	1.298	1.675	2.007	2.400	2.674
53	.848	1.298	1.674	2.006	2.399	2.672
54	.848	1.297	1.674	2.005	2.397	2.670
55	.848	1.297	1.673	2.004	2.396	2.668
56	.848	1.297	1.673	2.003	2.395	2.667
57	.848	1.297	1.672	2.002	2.394	2.665
58	.848	1.296	1.672	2.002	2.392	2.663
59	.848	1.296	1.671	2.001	2.391	2.662
60	.848	1.296	1.671	2.000	2.390	2.660
61	.848	1.296	1.670	2.000	2.389	2.659
62	.847	1.295	1.670	1.999	2.388	2.657
63	.847	1.295	1.669	1.998	2.387	2.656
64	.847	1.295	1.669	1.998	2.386	2.655
65	.847	1.295	1.669	1.997	2.385	2.654
66	.847	1.295	1.668	1.997	2.384	2.652
67	.847	1.294	1.668	1.996	2.383	2.651
68	.847	1.294	1.668	1.995	2.382	2.650
69	.847	1.294	1.667	1.995	2.382	2.649
70	.847	1.294	1.667	1.994	2.381	2.648
71	.847	1.294	1.667	1.994	2.380	2.647
72	.847	1.293	1.666	1.993	2.379	2.646
73	.847	1.293	1.666	1.993	2.379	2.645
74	.847	1.293	1.666	1.993	2.378	2.644
75	.846	1.293	1.665	1.992	2.377	2.643
76	.846	1.293	1.665	1.992	2.376	2.642
77	.846	1.293	1.665	1.991	2.376	2.641
78	.846	1.292	1.665	1.991	2.375	2.640
79	.846	1.292	1.664	1.990	2.374	2.639

Table 2 *t* Distribution (*Continued*)

Degrees of Freedom	Area in Upper Tail					
	.20	.10	.05	.025	.01	.005
80	.846	1.292	1.664	1.990	2.374	2.639
81	.846	1.292	1.664	1.990	2.373	2.638
82	.846	1.292	1.664	1.989	2.373	2.637
83	.846	1.292	1.663	1.989	2.372	2.636
84	.846	1.292	1.663	1.989	2.372	2.636
85	.846	1.292	1.663	1.988	2.371	2.635
86	.846	1.291	1.663	1.988	2.370	2.634
87	.846	1.291	1.663	1.988	2.370	2.634
88	.846	1.291	1.662	1.987	2.369	2.633
89	.846	1.291	1.662	1.987	2.369	2.632
90	.846	1.291	1.662	1.987	2.368	2.632
91	.846	1.291	1.662	1.986	2.368	2.631
92	.846	1.291	1.662	1.986	2.368	2.630
93	.846	1.291	1.661	1.986	2.367	2.630
94	.845	1.291	1.661	1.986	2.367	2.629
95	.845	1.291	1.661	1.985	2.366	2.629
96	.845	1.290	1.661	1.985	2.366	2.628
97	.845	1.290	1.661	1.985	2.365	2.627
98	.845	1.290	1.661	1.984	2.365	2.627
99	.845	1.290	1.660	1.984	2.364	2.626
100	.845	1.290	1.660	1.984	2.364	2.626
∞	.842	1.282	1.645	1.960	2.326	2.576

Table 3 Chi-Square Distribution

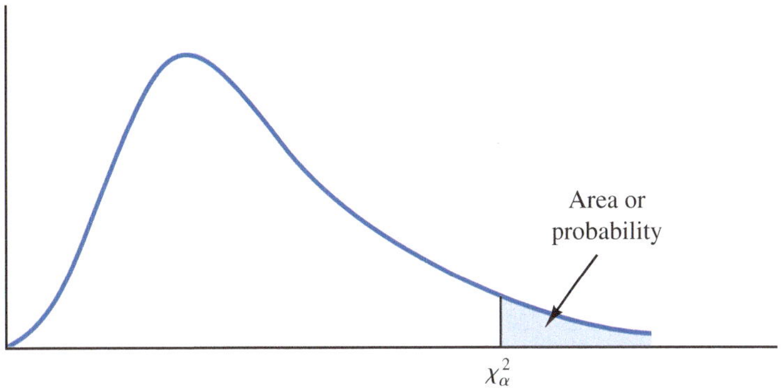

Entries in the table give χ^2_α values, where α is the area or probability in the upper tail of the chi-square distribution. For example, with 10 degrees of freedom and a .01 area in the upper tail, $\chi^2_{.01} = 23.209$.

Degrees of Freedom	Area in Upper Tail									
	.995	.99	.975	.95	.90	.10	.05	.025	.01	.005
1	.000	.000	.001	.004	.016	2.706	3.841	5.024	6.635	7.879
2	.010	.020	.051	.103	.211	4.605	5.991	7.378	9.210	10.597
3	.072	.115	.216	.352	.584	6.251	7.815	9.348	11.345	12.838
4	.207	.297	.484	.711	1.064	7.779	9.488	11.143	13.277	14.860
5	.412	.554	.831	1.145	1.610	9.236	11.070	12.832	15.086	16.750
6	.676	.872	1.237	1.635	2.204	10.645	12.592	14.449	16.812	18.548
7	.989	1.239	1.690	2.167	2.833	12.017	14.067	16.013	18.475	20.278
8	1.344	1.647	2.180	2.733	3.490	13.362	15.507	17.535	20.090	21.955
9	1.735	2.088	2.700	3.325	4.168	14.684	16.919	19.023	21.666	23.589
10	2.156	2.558	3.247	3.940	4.865	15.987	18.307	20.483	23.209	25.188
11	2.603	3.053	3.816	4.575	5.578	17.275	19.675	21.920	24.725	26.757
12	3.074	3.571	4.404	5.226	6.304	18.549	21.026	23.337	26.217	28.300
13	3.565	4.107	5.009	5.892	7.041	19.812	22.362	24.736	27.688	29.819
14	4.075	4.660	5.629	6.571	7.790	21.064	23.685	26.119	29.141	31.319
15	4.601	5.229	6.262	7.261	8.547	22.307	24.996	27.488	30.578	32.801
16	5.142	5.812	6.908	7.962	9.312	23.542	26.296	28.845	32.000	34.267
17	5.697	6.408	7.564	8.672	10.085	24.769	27.587	30.191	33.409	35.718
18	6.265	7.015	8.231	9.390	10.865	25.989	28.869	31.526	34.805	37.156
19	6.844	7.633	8.907	10.117	11.651	27.204	30.144	32.852	36.191	38.582
20	7.434	8.260	9.591	10.851	12.443	28.412	31.410	34.170	37.566	39.997
21	8.034	8.897	10.283	11.591	13.240	29.615	32.671	35.479	38.932	41.401
22	8.643	9.542	10.982	12.338	14.041	30.813	33.924	36.781	40.289	42.796
23	9.260	10.196	11.689	13.091	14.848	32.007	35.172	38.076	41.638	44.181
24	9.886	10.856	12.401	13.848	15.659	33.196	36.415	39.364	42.980	45.558
25	10.520	11.524	13.120	14.611	16.473	34.382	37.652	40.646	44.314	46.928
26	11.160	12.198	13.844	15.379	17.292	35.563	38.885	41.923	45.642	48.290
27	11.808	12.878	14.573	16.151	18.114	36.741	40.113	43.195	46.963	49.645
28	12.461	13.565	15.308	16.928	18.939	37.916	41.337	44.461	48.278	50.994
29	13.121	14.256	16.047	17.708	19.768	39.087	42.557	45.722	49.588	52.335

Table 3 Chi-Square Distribution (*Continued*)

Degrees of Freedom	Area in Upper Tail									
	.995	.99	.975	.95	.90	.10	.05	.025	.01	.005
30	13.787	14.953	16.791	18.493	20.599	40.256	43.773	46.979	50.892	53.672
35	17.192	18.509	20.569	22.465	24.797	46.059	49.802	53.203	57.342	60.275
40	20.707	22.164	24.433	26.509	29.051	51.805	55.758	59.342	63.691	66.766
45	24.311	25.901	28.366	30.612	33.350	57.505	61.656	65.410	69.957	73.166
50	27.991	29.707	32.357	34.764	37.689	63.167	67.505	71.420	76.154	79.490
55	31.735	33.571	36.398	38.958	42.060	68.796	73.311	77.380	82.292	85.749
60	35.534	37.485	40.482	43.188	46.459	74.397	79.082	83.298	88.379	91.952
65	39.383	41.444	44.603	47.450	50.883	79.973	84.821	89.177	94.422	98.105
70	43.275	45.442	48.758	51.739	55.329	85.527	90.531	95.023	100.425	104.215
75	47.206	49.475	52.942	56.054	59.795	91.061	96.217	100.839	106.393	110.285
80	51.172	53.540	57.153	60.391	64.278	96.578	101.879	106.629	112.329	116.321
85	55.170	57.634	61.389	64.749	68.777	102.079	107.522	112.393	118.236	122.324
90	59.196	61.754	65.647	69.126	73.291	107.565	113.145	118.136	124.116	128.299
95	63.250	65.898	69.925	73.520	77.818	113.038	118.752	123.858	129.973	134.247
100	67.328	70.065	74.222	77.929	82.358	118.498	124.342	129.561	135.807	140.170

Table 4 *F* Distribution

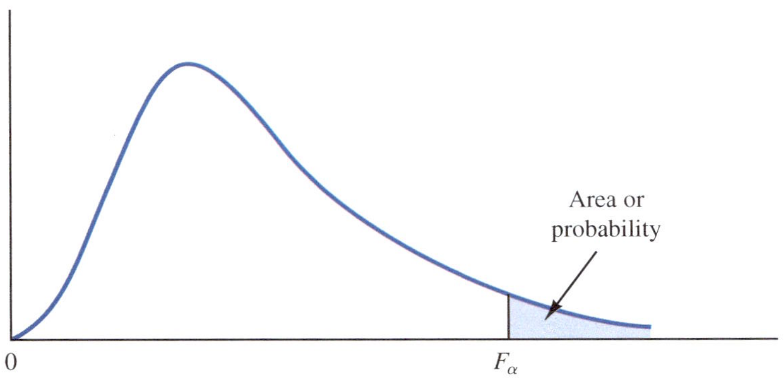

Entries in the table give F_α values, where α is the area or probability in the upper tail of the F distribution. For example, with 4 numerator degrees of freedom, 8 denominator degrees of freedom, and a .05 area in the upper tail, $F_{.05} = 3.84$.

Denominator Degrees of Freedom	Area in Upper Tail	Numerator Degrees of Freedom																	
		1	2	3	4	5	6	7	8	9	10	15	20	25	30	40	60	100	1000
1	.10	39.86	49.50	53.59	55.83	57.24	58.20	58.91	59.44	59.86	60.19	61.22	61.74	62.05	62.26	62.53	62.79	63.01	63.30
	.05	161.45	199.50	215.71	224.58	230.16	233.99	236.77	238.88	240.54	241.88	245.95	248.02	249.26	250.10	251.14	252.20	253.04	254.19
	.025	647.79	799.48	864.15	899.60	921.83	937.11	948.20	956.64	963.28	968.63	984.87	993.08	998.09	1001.40	1005.60	1009.79	1013.16	1017.76
	.01	4052.18	4999.34	5403.53	5624.26	5763.96	5858.95	5928.33	5980.95	6022.40	6055.93	6156.97	6208.66	6239.86	6260.35	6286.43	6312.97	6333.92	6362.80
2	.10	8.53	9.00	9.16	9.24	9.29	9.33	9.35	9.37	9.38	9.39	9.42	9.44	9.45	9.46	9.47	9.47	9.48	9.49
	.05	18.51	19.00	19.16	19.25	19.30	19.33	19.35	19.37	19.38	19.40	19.43	19.45	19.46	19.46	19.47	19.48	19.49	19.49
	.025	38.51	39.00	39.17	39.25	39.30	39.33	39.36	39.37	39.39	39.40	39.43	39.45	39.46	39.46	39.47	39.48	39.49	39.50
	.01	98.50	99.00	99.16	99.25	99.30	99.33	99.36	99.38	99.39	99.40	99.43	99.45	99.46	99.47	99.48	99.48	99.49	99.50
3	.10	5.54	5.46	5.39	5.34	5.31	5.28	5.27	5.25	5.24	5.23	5.20	5.18	5.17	5.17	5.16	5.15	5.14	5.13
	.05	10.13	9.55	9.28	9.12	9.01	8.94	8.89	8.85	8.81	8.79	8.70	8.66	8.63	8.62	8.59	8.57	8.55	8.53
	.025	17.44	16.04	15.44	15.10	14.88	14.73	14.62	14.54	14.47	14.42	14.25	14.17	14.12	14.08	14.04	13.99	13.96	13.91
	.01	34.12	30.82	29.46	28.71	28.24	27.91	27.67	27.49	27.34	27.23	26.87	26.69	26.58	26.50	26.41	26.32	26.24	26.14
4	.10	4.54	4.32	4.19	4.11	4.05	4.01	3.98	3.95	3.94	3.92	3.87	3.84	3.83	3.82	3.80	3.79	3.78	3.76
	.05	7.71	6.94	6.59	6.39	6.26	6.16	6.09	6.04	6.00	5.96	5.86	5.80	5.77	5.75	5.72	5.69	5.66	5.63
	.025	12.22	10.65	9.98	9.60	9.36	9.20	9.07	8.98	8.90	8.84	8.66	8.56	8.50	8.46	8.41	8.36	8.32	8.26
	.01	21.20	18.00	16.69	15.98	15.52	15.21	14.98	14.80	14.66	14.55	14.20	14.02	13.91	13.84	13.75	13.65	13.58	13.47
5	.10	4.06	3.78	3.62	3.52	3.45	3.40	3.37	3.34	3.32	3.30	3.324	3.21	3.19	3.17	3.16	3.14	3.13	3.11
	.05	6.61	5.79	5.41	5.19	5.05	4.95	4.88	4.82	4.77	4.74	4.62	4.56	4.52	4.50	4.46	4.43	4.41	4.37
	.025	10.01	8.43	7.76	7.39	7.15	6.98	6.85	6.76	6.68	6.62	6.43	6.33	6.27	6.23	6.18	6.12	6.08	6.02
	.01	16.26	13.27	12.06	11.39	10.97	10.67	10.46	10.29	10.16	10.05	9.72	9.55	9.45	9.38	9.29	9.20	9.13	9.03

Table 4 *F* Distribution (*Continued*)

Denominator Degrees of Freedom	Area in Upper Tail	Numerator Degrees of Freedom																	
		1	2	3	4	5	6	7	8	9	10	15	20	25	30	40	60	100	1000
6	.10	3.78	3.46	3.29	3.18	3.11	3.05	3.01	2.98	2.96	2.94	2.87	2.84	2.81	2.80	2.78	2.76	2.75	2.72
	.05	5.99	5.14	4.76	4.53	4.39	4.28	4.21	4.15	4.10	4.06	3.94	3.87	3.83	3.81	3.77	3.74	3.71	3.67
	.025	8.81	7.26	6.60	6.23	5.99	5.82	5.70	5.60	5.52	5.46	5.27	5.17	5.11	5.07	5.01	4.96	4.92	4.86
	.01	13.75	10.92	9.78	9.15	8.75	8.47	8.26	8.10	7.98	7.87	7.56	7.40	7.30	7.23	7.14	7.06	6.99	6.89
7	.10	3.59	3.26	3.07	2.96	2.88	2.83	2.78	2.75	2.72	2.70	2.63	2.59	2.57	2.56	2.54	2.51	2.50	2.47
	.05	5.59	4.74	4.35	4.12	3.97	3.87	3.79	3.73	3.68	3.64	3.51	3.44	3.40	3.38	3.34	3.30	3.27	3.23
	.025	8.07	6.54	5.89	5.52	5.29	5.12	4.99	4.90	4.82	4.76	4.57	4.47	4.40	4.36	4.31	4.25	4.21	4.15
	.01	12.25	9.55	8.45	7.85	7.46	7.19	6.99	6.84	6.72	6.62	6.31	6.16	6.06	5.99	5.91	5.82	5.75	5.66
8	.10	3.46	3.11	2.92	2.81	2.73	2.67	2.62	2.59	2.56	2.54	2.46	2.42	2.40	2.38	2.36	2.34	2.32	2.30
	.05	5.32	4.46	4.07	3.84	3.69	3.58	3.50	3.44	3.39	3.35	3.22	3.15	3.11	3.08	3.04	3.01	2.97	2.93
	.025	7.57	6.06	5.42	5.05	4.82	4.65	4.53	4.43	4.36	4.30	4.10	4.00	3.94	3.89	3.84	3.78	3.74	3.68
	.01	11.26	8.65	7.59	7.01	6.63	6.37	6.18	6.03	5.91	5.81	5.52	5.36	5.26	5.20	5.12	5.03	4.96	4.87
9	.10	3.36	3.01	2.81	2.69	2.61	2.55	2.51	2.47	2.44	2.42	2.34	2.30	2.27	2.25	2.23	2.21	2.19	2.16
	.05	5.12	4.26	3.86	3.63	3.48	3.37	3.29	3.23	3.18	3.14	3.01	2.94	2.89	2.86	2.83	2.79	2.76	2.71
	.025	7.21	5.71	5.08	4.72	4.48	4.32	4.20	4.10	4.03	3.96	3.77	3.67	3.60	3.56	3.51	3.45	3.40	3.34
	.01	10.56	8.02	6.99	6.42	6.06	5.80	5.61	5.47	5.35	5.26	4.96	4.81	4.71	4.65	4.57	4.48	4.41	4.32
10	.10	3.29	2.92	2.73	2.61	2.52	2.46	2.41	2.38	2.35	2.32	2.24	2.20	2.17	2.16	2.13	2.11	2.09	2.06
	.05	4.96	4.10	3.71	3.48	3.33	3.22	3.14	3.07	3.02	2.98	2.85	2.77	2.73	2.70	2.66	2.62	2.59	2.54
	.025	6.94	5.46	4.83	4.47	4.24	4.07	3.95	3.85	3.78	3.72	3.52	3.42	3.35	3.31	3.26	3.20	3.15	3.09
	.01	10.04	7.56	6.55	5.99	5.64	5.39	5.20	5.06	4.94	4.85	4.56	4.41	4.31	4.25	4.17	4.08	4.01	3.92
11	.10	3.23	2.86	2.66	2.54	2.45	2.39	2.34	2.30	2.27	2.25	2.17	2.12	2.10	2.08	2.05	2.03	2.01	1.98
	.05	4.84	3.98	3.59	3.36	3.20	3.09	3.01	2.95	2.90	2.85	2.72	2.65	2.60	2.57	2.53	2.49	2.46	2.41
	.025	6.72	5.26	4.63	4.28	4.04	3.88	3.76	3.66	3.59	3.53	3.33	3.23	3.16	3.12	3.06	3.00	2.96	2.89
	.01	9.65	7.21	6.22	5.67	5.32	5.07	4.89	4.74	4.63	4.54	4.25	4.10	4.01	3.94	3.86	3.78	3.71	3.61
12	.10	3.18	2.81	2.61	2.48	2.39	2.33	2.28	2.24	2.21	2.19	2.10	2.06	2.03	2.01	1.99	1.96	1.94	1.91
	.05	4.75	3.89	3.49	3.26	3.11	3.00	2.91	2.85	2.80	2.75	2.62	2.54	2.50	2.47	2.43	2.38	2.35	2.30
	.025	6.55	5.10	4.47	4.12	3.89	3.73	3.61	3.51	3.44	3.37	3.18	3.07	3.01	2.96	2.91	2.85	2.80	2.73
	.01	9.33	6.93	5.95	5.41	5.06	4.82	4.64	4.50	4.39	4.30	4.01	3.86	3.76	3.70	3.62	3.54	3.47	3.37
13	.10	3.14	2.76	2.56	2.43	2.35	2.28	2.23	2.20	2.16	2.14	2.05	2.01	1.98	1.96	1.93	1.90	1.88	1.85
	.05	4.67	3.81	3.41	3.18	3.03	2.92	2.83	2.77	2.71	2.67	2.53	2.46	2.41	2.38	2.34	2.30	2.26	2.21
	.025	6.41	4.97	4.35	4.00	3.77	3.60	3.48	3.39	3.31	3.25	3.05	2.95	2.88	2.84	2.78	2.72	2.67	2.60
	.01	9.07	6.70	5.74	5.21	4.86	4.62	4.44	4.30	4.19	4.10	3.82	3.66	3.57	3.51	3.43	3.34	3.27	3.18
14	.10	3.10	2.73	2.52	2.39	2.31	2.24	2.19	2.15	2.12	2.10	2.01	1.96	1.93	1.99	1.89	1.86	1.83	1.80
	.05	4.60	3.74	3.34	3.11	2.96	2.85	2.76	2.70	2.65	2.60	2.46	2.39	2.34	2.31	2.27	2.22	2.19	2.14
	.025	6.30	4.86	4.24	3.89	3.66	3.50	3.38	3.29	3.21	3.15	2.95	2.84	2.78	2.73	2.67	2.61	2.56	2.50
	.01	8.86	6.51	5.56	5.04	4.69	4.46	4.28	4.14	4.03	3.94	3.66	3.51	3.41	3.35	3.27	3.18	3.11	3.02
15	.10	3.07	2.70	2.49	2.36	2.27	2.21	2.16	2.12	2.09	2.06	1.97	1.92	1.89	1.87	1.85	1.82	1.79	1.76
	.05	4.54	3.68	3.29	3.06	2.90	2.79	2.71	2.64	2.59	2.54	2.40	2.33	2.28	2.25	2.20	2.16	2.12	2.07
	.025	6.20	4.77	4.15	3.80	3.58	3.41	3.29	3.20	3.12	3.06	2.86	2.76	2.69	2.64	2.59	2.52	2.47	2.40
	.01	8.68	6.36	5.42	4.89	4.56	4.32	4.14	4.00	3.89	3.80	3.52	3.37	3.28	3.21	3.13	3.05	2.98	2.88

Denominator Degrees of Freedom	Area in Upper Tail	Numerator Degrees of Freedom																	
		1	2	3	4	5	6	7	8	9	10	15	20	25	30	40	60	100	1000
16	.10	3.05	2.67	2.46	2.33	2.24	2.18	2.13	2.09	2.06	2.03	1.94	1.89	1.86	1.84	1.81	1.78	1.76	1.72
	.05	4.49	3.63	3.24	3.01	2.85	2.74	2.66	2.59	2.54	2.49	2.35	2.28	2.23	2.19	2.15	2.11	2.07	2.02
	.025	6.12	4.69	4.08	3.73	3.50	3.34	3.22	3.12	3.05	2.99	2.79	2.68	2.61	2.57	2.51	2.45	2.40	2.32
	.01	8.53	6.23	5.29	4.77	4.44	4.20	4.03	3.89	3.78	3.69	3.41	3.26	3.16	3.10	3.02	2.93	2.86	2.76
17	.10	3.03	2.64	2.44	2.31	2.22	2.15	2.10	2.06	2.03	2.00	1.91	1.86	1.83	1.81	1.78	1.75	1.73	1.69
	.05	4.45	3.59	3.20	2.96	2.81	2.70	2.61	2.55	2.49	2.45	2.31	2.23	2.18	2.15	2.10	2.06	2.02	1.97
	.025	6.04	4.62	4.01	3.66	3.44	3.28	3.16	3.06	2.98	2.92	2.72	2.62	2.55	2.50	2.44	2.38	2.33	2.26
	.01	8.40	6.11	5.19	4.67	4.34	4.10	3.93	3.79	3.68	3.59	3.31	3.16	3.07	3.00	2.92	2.83	2.76	2.66
18	.10	3.01	2.62	2.42	2.29	2.20	2.13	2.08	2.04	2.00	1.98	1.89	1.84	1.80	1.78	1.75	1.72	1.70	1.66
	.05	4.41	3.55	3.16	2.93	2.77	2.66	2.58	2.51	2.46	2.41	2.27	2.19	2.14	2.11	2.06	2.02	1.98	1.92
	.025	5.98	4.56	3.95	3.61	3.38	3.22	3.10	3.01	2.93	2.87	2.67	2.56	2.49	2.44	2.38	2.32	2.27	2.20
	.01	8.29	6.01	5.09	4.58	4.25	4.01	3.84	3.71	3.60	3.51	3.23	3.08	2.98	2.92	2.84	2.75	2.68	2.58
19	.10	2.99	2.61	2.40	2.27	2.18	2.11	2.06	2.02	1.98	1.96	1.86	1.81	1.78	1.76	1.73	1.70	1.67	1.64
	.05	4.38	3.52	3.13	2.90	2.74	2.63	2.54	2.48	2.42	2.38	2.23	2.16	2.11	2.07	2.03	1.98	1.94	1.88
	.025	5.92	4.51	3.90	3.56	3.33	3.17	3.05	2.96	2.88	2.82	2.62	2.51	2.44	2.39	2.33	2.27	2.22	2.14
	.01	8.18	5.93	5.01	4.50	4.17	3.94	3.77	3.63	3.52	3.43	3.15	3.00	2.91	2.84	2.76	2.67	2.60	2.50
20	.10	2.97	2.59	2.38	2.25	2.16	2.09	2.04	2.00	1.96	1.94	1.84	1.79	1.76	1.74	1.71	1.68	1.65	1.61
	.05	4.35	3.49	3.10	2.87	2.71	2.60	2.51	2.45	2.39	2.35	2.20	2.12	2.07	2.04	1.99	1.95	1.91	1.85
	.025	5.87	4.46	3.86	3.51	3.29	3.13	3.01	2.91	2.84	2.77	2.57	2.46	2.40	2.35	2.29	2.22	2.17	2.09
	.01	8.10	5.85	4.94	4.43	4.10	3.87	3.70	3.56	3.46	3.37	3.09	2.94	2.84	2.78	2.69	2.61	2.54	2.43
21	.10	2.96	2.57	2.36	2.23	2.14	2.08	2.02	1.98	1.95	1.92	1.83	1.78	1.74	1.72	1.69	1.66	1.63	1.59
	.05	4.32	3.47	3.07	2.84	2.68	2.57	2.49	2.42	2.37	2.32	2.18	2.10	2.05	2.01	1.96	1.92	1.88	1.82
	.025	5.83	4.42	3.82	3.48	3.25	3.09	2.97	2.87	2.80	2.73	2.53	2.42	2.36	2.31	2.25	2.18	2.13	2.05
	.01	8.02	5.78	4.87	4.37	4.04	3.81	3.64	3.51	3.40	3.31	3.03	2.88	2.79	2.72	2.64	2.55	2.48	2.37
22	.10	2.95	2.56	2.35	2.22	2.13	2.06	2.01	1.97	1.93	1.90	1.81	1.76	1.73	1.70	1.67	1.64	1.61	1.57
	.05	4.30	3.44	3.05	2.82	2.66	2.55	2.46	2.40	2.34	2.30	2.15	2.07	2.02	1.98	1.94	1.89	1.85	1.79
	.025	5.79	4.38	3.78	3.44	3.22	3.05	2.93	2.84	2.76	2.70	2.50	2.39	2.32	2.27	2.21	2.14	2.09	2.01
	.01	7.95	5.72	4.82	4.31	3.99	3.76	3.59	3.45	3.35	3.26	2.98	2.83	2.73	2.67	2.58	2.50	2.42	2.32
23	.10	2.94	2.55	2.34	2.21	2.11	2.05	1.99	1.95	1.92	1.89	1.80	1.74	1.71	1.69	1.66	1.62	1.59	1.55
	.05	4.28	3.42	3.03	2.80	2.64	2.53	2.44	2.37	2.32	2.27	2.13	2.05	2.00	1.96	1.91	1.86	1.82	1.76
	.025	5.75	4.35	3.75	3.41	3.18	3.02	2.90	2.81	2.73	2.67	2.47	2.36	2.29	2.24	2.18	2.11	2.06	1.98
	.01	7.88	5.66	4.76	4.26	3.94	3.71	3.54	3.41	3.30	3.21	2.93	2.78	2.69	2.62	2.54	2.45	2.37	2.27
24	.10	2.93	2.54	2.33	2.19	2.10	2.04	1.98	1.94	1.91	1.88	1.78	1.73	1.70	1.67	1.64	1.61	1.58	1.54
	.05	4.26	3.40	3.01	2.78	2.62	2.51	2.42	2.36	2.30	2.25	2.11	2.03	1.97	1.94	1.89	1.84	1.80	1.74
	.025	5.72	4.32	3.72	3.38	3.15	2.99	2.87	2.78	2.70	2.64	2.44	2.33	2.26	2.21	2.15	2.08	2.02	1.94
	.01	7.82	5.61	4.72	4.22	3.90	3.67	3.50	3.36	3.26	3.17	2.89	2.74	2.64	2.58	2.49	2.40	2.33	2.22

Table 4 *F* Distribution (*Continued*)

Denominator Degrees of Freedom	Area in Upper Tail	Numerator Degrees of Freedom																	
		1	2	3	4	5	6	7	8	9	10	15	20	25	30	40	60	100	1000
25	.10	2.92	2.53	2.32	2.18	2.09	2.02	1.97	1.93	1.89	1.87	1.77	1.72	1.68	1.66	1.63	1.59	1.56	1.52
	.05	4.24	3.39	2.99	2.76	2.60	2.49	2.40	2.34	2.28	2.24	2.09	2.01	1.96	1.92	1.87	1.82	1.78	1.72
	.025	5.69	4.29	3.69	3.35	3.13	2.97	2.85	2.75	2.68	2.61	2.41	2.30	2.23	2.18	2.12	2.05	2.00	1.91
	.01	7.77	5.57	4.68	4.18	3.85	3.63	3.46	3.32	3.22	3.13	2.85	2.70	2.60	2.54	2.45	2.36	2.29	2.18
26	.10	2.91	2.52	2.31	2.17	2.08	2.01	1.96	1.92	1.88	1.86	1.76	1.71	1.67	1.65	1.61	1.58	1.55	1.51
	.05	4.23	3.37	2.98	2.74	2.59	2.47	2.39	2.32	2.27	2.22	2.07	1.99	1.94	1.90	1.85	1.80	1.76	1.70
	.025	5.66	4.27	3.67	3.33	3.10	2.94	2.82	2.73	2.65	2.59	2.39	2.28	2.21	2.16	2.09	2.03	1.97	1.89
	.01	7.72	5.53	4.64	4.14	3.82	3.59	3.42	3.29	3.18	3.09	2.81	2.66	2.57	2.50	2.42	2.33	2.25	2.14
27	.10	2.90	2.51	2.30	2.17	2.07	2.00	1.95	1.91	1.87	1.85	1.75	1.70	1.66	1.64	1.60	1.57	1.54	1.50
	.05	4.21	3.35	2.96	2.73	2.57	2.46	2.37	2.31	2.25	2.20	2.06	1.97	1.92	1.88	1.84	1.79	1.74	1.68
	.025	5.63	4.24	3.65	3.31	3.08	2.92	2.80	2.71	2.63	2.57	2.36	2.25	2.18	2.13	2.07	2.00	1.94	1.86
	.01	7.68	5.49	4.60	4.11	3.78	3.56	3.39	3.26	3.15	3.06	2.78	2.63	2.54	2.47	2.38	2.29	2.22	2.11
28	.10	2.89	2.50	2.29	2.16	2.06	2.00	1.94	1.90	1.87	1.84	1.74	1.69	1.65	1.63	1.59	1.56	1.53	1.48
	.05	4.20	3.34	2.95	2.71	2.56	2.45	2.36	2.29	2.24	2.19	2.04	1.96	1.91	1.87	1.82	1.77	1.73	1.66
	.025	5.61	4.22	3.63	3.29	3.06	2.90	2.78	2.69	2.61	2.55	2.34	2.23	2.16	2.11	2.05	1.98	1.92	1.84
	.01	7.64	5.45	4.57	4.07	3.75	3.53	3.36	3.23	3.12	3.03	2.75	2.60	2.51	2.44	2.35	2.26	2.19	2.08
29	.10	2.89	2.50	2.28	2.15	2.06	1.99	1.93	1.89	1.86	1.83	1.73	1.68	1.64	1.62	1.58	1.55	1.52	1.47
	.05	4.18	3.33	2.93	2.70	2.55	2.43	2.35	2.28	2.22	2.18	2.03	1.94	1.89	1.85	1.81	1.75	1.71	1.65
	.025	5.59	4.20	3.61	3.27	3.04	2.88	2.76	2.67	2.59	2.53	2.32	2.21	2.14	2.09	2.03	1.96	1.90	1.82
	.01	7.60	5.42	4.54	4.04	3.73	3.50	3.33	3.20	3.09	3.00	2.73	2.57	2.48	2.41	2.33	2.23	2.16	2.05
30	.10	2.88	2.49	2.28	2.14	2.05	1.98	1.93	1.88	1.85	1.82	1.72	1.67	1.63	1.61	1.57	1.54	1.51	1.46
	.05	4.17	3.32	2.92	2.69	2.53	2.42	2.33	2.27	2.21	2.16	2.01	1.93	1.88	1.84	1.79	1.74	1.70	1.63
	.025	5.57	4.18	3.59	3.25	3.03	2.87	2.75	2.65	2.57	2.51	2.31	2.20	2.12	2.07	2.01	1.94	1.88	1.80
	.01	7.56	5.39	4.51	4.02	3.70	3.47	3.30	3.17	3.07	2.98	2.70	2.55	2.45	2.39	2.30	2.21	2.13	2.02
40	.10	2.84	2.44	2.23	2.09	2.00	1.93	1.87	1.83	1.79	1.76	1.66	1.61	1.57	1.54	1.51	1.47	1.43	1.38
	.05	4.08	3.23	2.84	2.61	2.45	2.34	2.25	2.18	2.12	2.08	1.92	1.84	1.78	1.74	1.69	1.64	1.59	1.52
	.025	5.42	4.05	3.46	3.13	2.90	2.74	2.62	2.53	2.45	2.39	2.18	2.07	1.99	1.94	1.88	1.80	1.74	1.65
	.01	7.31	5.18	4.31	3.83	3.51	3.29	3.12	2.99	2.89	2.80	2.52	2.37	2.27	2.20	2.11	2.02	1.94	1.82
60	.10	2.79	2.39	2.18	2.04	1.95	1.87	1.82	1.77	1.74	1.71	1.60	1.54	1.50	1.48	1.44	1.40	1.36	1.30
	.05	4.00	3.15	2.76	2.53	2.37	2.25	2.17	2.10	2.04	1.99	1.84	1.75	1.69	1.65	1.59	1.53	1.48	1.40
	.025	5.29	3.93	3.34	3.01	2.79	2.63	2.51	2.41	2.33	2.27	2.06	1.94	1.87	1.82	1.74	1.67	1.60	1.49
	.01	7.08	4.98	4.13	3.65	3.34	3.12	2.95	2.82	2.72	2.63	2.35	2.20	2.10	2.03	1.94	1.84	1.75	1.62
100	.10	2.76	2.36	2.14	2.00	1.91	1.83	1.78	1.73	1.69	1.66	1.56	1.49	1.45	1.42	1.38	1.34	1.29	1.22
	.05	3.94	3.09	2.70	2.46	2.31	2.19	2.10	2.03	1.97	1.93	1.77	1.68	1.62	1.57	1.52	1.45	1.39	1.30
	.025	5.18	3.83	3.25	2.92	2.70	2.54	2.42	2.32	2.24	2.18	1.97	1.85	1.77	1.71	1.64	1.56	1.48	1.36
	.01	6.90	4.82	3.98	3.51	3.21	2.99	2.82	2.69	2.59	2.50	2.22	2.07	1.97	1.89	1.80	1.69	1.60	1.45
1000	.10	2.71	2.31	2.09	1.95	1.85	1.78	1.72	1.68	1.64	1.61	1.49	1.43	1.38	1.35	1.30	1.25	1.20	1.08
	.05	3.85	3.00	2.61	2.38	2.22	2.11	2.02	1.95	1.89	1.84	1.68	1.58	1.52	1.47	1.41	1.33	1.26	1.11
	.025	5.04	3.70	3.13	2.80	2.58	2.42	2.30	2.20	2.13	2.06	1.85	1.72	1.64	1.58	1.50	1.41	1.32	1.13
	.01	6.66	4.63	3.80	3.34	3.04	2.82	2.66	2.53	2.43	2.34	2.06	1.90	1.79	1.72	1.61	1.50	1.38	1.16

Appendix C—Summation Notation

Summations

Definition

$$\sum_{i=1}^{n} x_i = x_1 + x_2 + \cdots + x_n \tag{C.1}$$

Example for $x_1 = 5, x_2 = 8, x_3 = 14$:

$$\begin{aligned}\sum_{i=1}^{3} x_i &= x_1 + x_2 + x_3 \\ &= 5 + 8 + 14 \\ &= 27\end{aligned}$$

Result 1

For a constant c:

$$\sum_{i=1}^{n} c = \underbrace{(c + c + \cdots + c)}_{n \text{ times}} = nc \tag{C.2}$$

Example for $c = 5, n = 10$:

$$\sum_{i=1}^{10} 5 = 10(5) = 50$$

Example for $c = \bar{x}$:

$$\sum_{i=1}^{n} \bar{x} = n\bar{x}$$

Result 2

$$\begin{aligned}\sum_{i=1}^{n} cx_i &= cx_1 + cx_2 + \cdots + cx_n \\ &= c(x_1 + x_2 + \cdots + x_n) = c\sum_{i=1}^{n} x_i \qquad \text{(C.3)}\end{aligned}$$

Example for $x_1 = 5, x_2 = 8, x_3 = 14, c = 2$:

$$\sum_{i=1}^{3} 2x_i = 2\sum_{i=1}^{3} x_i = 2(27) = 54$$

Result 3

$$\sum_{i=1}^{n} (ax_i + by_i) = a\sum_{i=1}^{n} x_i + b\sum_{i=1}^{n} y_i \tag{C.4}$$

Example for $x_1 = 5, x_2 = 8, x_3 = 14, a = 2, y_1 = 7, y_2 = 3, y_3 = 8, b = 4$:

$$\sum_{i=1}^{3}(2x_i + 4y_i) = 2\sum_{i=1}^{3}x_i + 4\sum_{i=1}^{3}y_i$$
$$= 2(27) + 4(18)$$
$$= 54 + 72$$
$$= 126$$

Double Summations

Consider the following data involving the variable x_{ij}, where i is the subscript denoting the row position and j is the subscript denoting the column position:

		Column		
		1	2	3
Row	1	$x_{11} = 10$	$x_{12} = 8$	$x_{13} = 6$
	2	$x_{21} = 7$	$x_{22} = 4$	$x_{23} = 12$

Definition

$$\sum_{i=1}^{n}\sum_{j=1}^{m}x_{ij} = (x_{11} + x_{12} + \cdots + x_{1m}) + (x_{21} + x_{22} + \cdots + x_{2m})$$
$$+ (x_{31} + x_{32} + \cdots + x_{3m}) + \cdots + (x_{n1} + x_{n2} + \cdots + x_{nm}) \quad \textbf{(C.5)}$$

Example:

$$\sum_{i=1}^{2}\sum_{j=1}^{3}x_{ij} = x_{11} + x_{12} + x_{13} + x_{21} + x_{22} + x_{23}$$
$$= 10 + 8 + 6 + 7 + 4 + 12$$
$$= 47$$

Definition

$$\sum_{i=1}^{n}x_{ij} = x_{1j} + x_{2j} + \cdots + x_{nj} \quad \textbf{(C.6)}$$

Example:

$$\sum_{i=1}^{2}x_{i2} = x_{12} + x_{22}$$
$$= 8 + 4$$
$$= 12$$

Shorthand Notation

Sometimes when a summation is for all values of the subscript, we use the following shorthand notations:

$$\sum_{i=1}^{n}x_i = \sum x_i \quad \textbf{(C.7)}$$

$$\sum_{i=1}^{n}\sum_{j=1}^{m}x_{ij} = \sum\sum x_{ij} \quad \textbf{(C.8)}$$

$$\sum_{i=1}^{n}x_{ij} = \sum_{i}x_{ij} \quad \textbf{(C.9)}$$

Appendix D—Microsoft Excel and Tools for Statistical Analysis

Microsoft Excel is a spreadsheet program that can be used to organize and analyze data, perform complex calculations, and create a wide variety of graphical displays. We assume that readers are familiar with basic Excel operations such as selecting cells, entering formulas, copying, and so on. But we do not assume readers are familiar with Excel or the use of Excel for statistical analysis.

The purpose of this appendix is twofold. First, we provide an overview of Excel and discuss the basic operations needed to work with Excel workbooks and worksheets. Second, we provide an overview of the tools that are available for conducting statistical analysis with Excel. These include Excel functions and formulas that allow users to conduct their own analyses and add-ins that provide more comprehensive analysis tools.

Excel's Data Analysis add-in, included with the basic Excel system, is a valuable tool for conducting statistical analysis. In the last section of this appendix, we provide instruction for installing the Data Analysis add-in.

Overview of Microsoft Excel

A workbook is a file containing one or more worksheets.

When using Excel for statistical analysis, data is displayed in workbooks, each of which contains a series of worksheets that typically include the original data as well as any resulting analysis, including charts. Figure D.1 shows the layout of a blank workbook created each time Excel is opened. The workbook is named Book1, and contains one worksheet named Sheet1. Excel highlights the worksheet currently displayed (Sheet1) by setting the name on the worksheet tab in bold. Note that cell A1 is initially selected.

The wide bar located across the top of the workbook is referred to as the Ribbon. Tabs, located at the top of the Ribbon, provide quick access to groups of related commands. The Ribbon contains a variety of tabs, including File, Home, Insert, Formulas, and Data as shown in Figure D.1. Note that the Home tab is selected when Excel is opened. Clicking on the Home tab displays a variety of groups including Clipboard, Font, Alignment, Number, Styles, Cells, Editing, and Analysis (See Figure D.2). Commands are arranged within each group. For example, to change selected text to boldface, click the **Home** tab and click the Bold **B** button in the **Font** group.

Figure D.3 illustrates the location of the Quick Access Toolbar and the Formula Bar. The Quick Access Toolbar allows you to quickly access workbook options. To add or remove features on the Quick Access Toolbar, click the **Customize Quick Access Toolbar** button ⩢ at the end of the **Quick Access Toolbar**.

The Formula Bar (see Figure D.3) contains a Name box, the Insert Function button *fx*, and a Formula box. In Figure D.3, "A1" appears in the name box because cell A1 is selected. You can select any other cell in the worksheet by using the mouse to move the cursor to another cell and clicking or by typing the new cell location in the Name box. The Formula box is used to display the formula in the currently selected cell. For instance, if you enter *=A1+A2* into cell A3, whenever you select cell A3, the formula =A1+A2 will be shown in the Formula box. This feature makes it very easy to see and edit a formula in a particular cell. The Insert Function button allows you to quickly access all the functions available in Excel. Later we show how to find and use a particular function.

Basic Workbook Operations

Figure D.4 illustrates the worksheet options that can be performed after right-clicking on a worksheet tab. For instance, to change the name of the current worksheet from "Sheet1" to

Figure D.1 Blank Workbook Created When Excel Is Opened

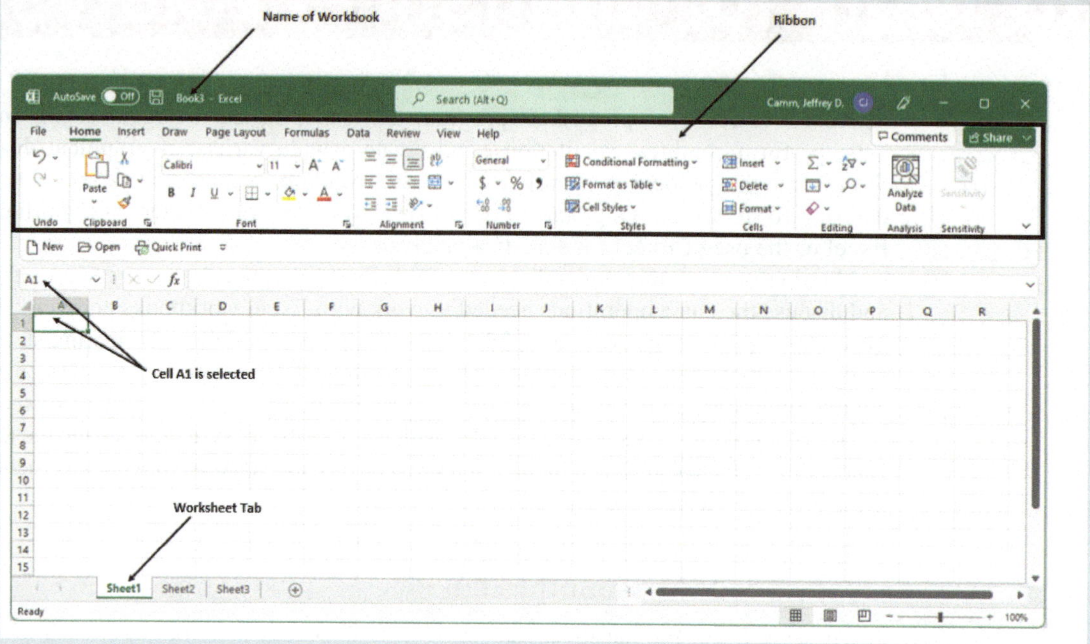

Source: Microsoft Corporation

"Data," right-click the worksheet tab named "Sheet1" and select the **Rename** option. The current worksheet name (Sheet1) will be highlighted. Then, simply type the new name *Data* and press the **Enter** key to rename the worksheet.

Suppose that you wanted to create a copy of "Sheet1." After right-clicking the tab named "Sheet1," select the **Move or Copy** option. When the **Move or Copy** dialog box appears,

Figure D.2 Portion of the Home Tab

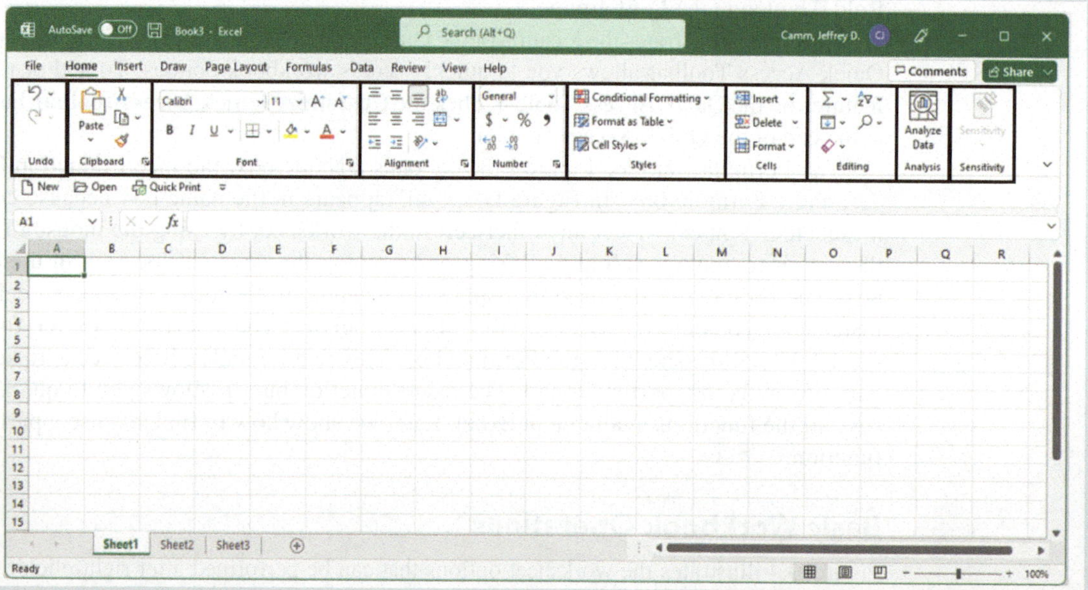

Source: Microsoft Corporation

Figure D.3 Excel Quick Access Toolbar and Formula Bar

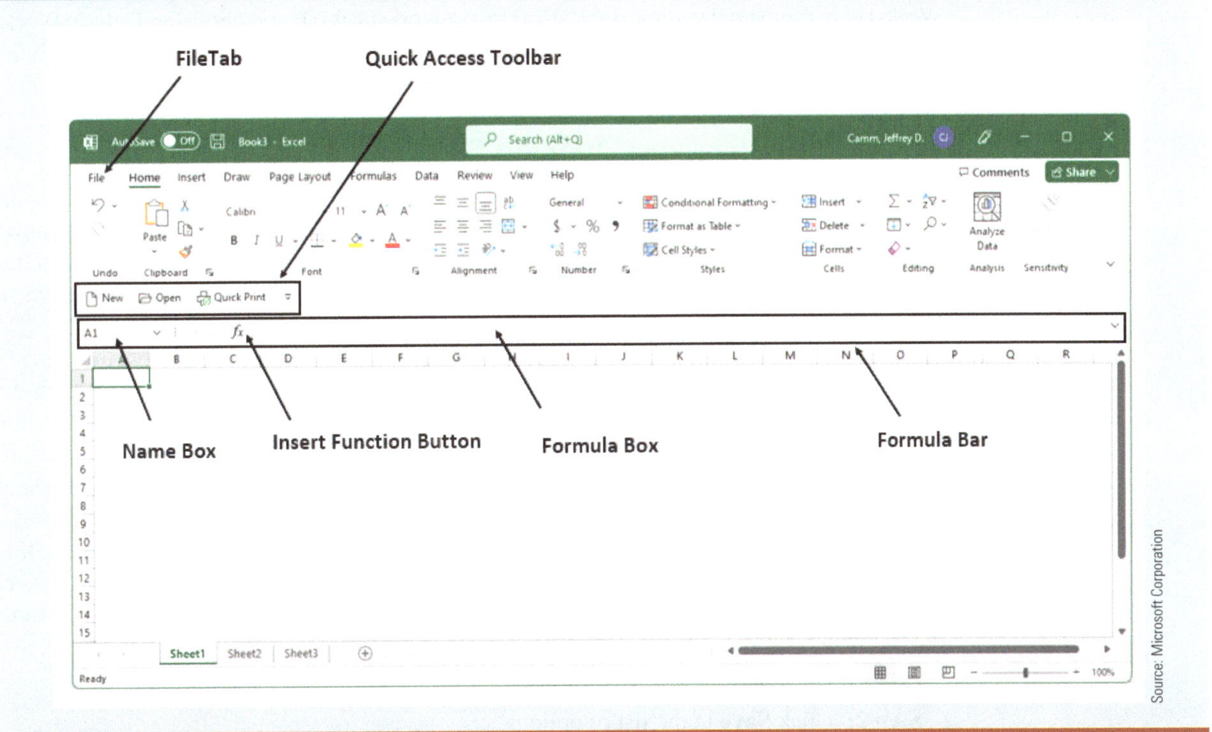

select **Create a Copy** and click **OK**. The name of the copied worksheet will appear as **"Sheet1 (2)."** You can then rename it, if desired.

To add a new worksheet to the workbook, right-click any worksheet tab and select the **Insert** option; when the **Insert** dialog box appears, select **Worksheet** and click **OK**. An addi-

Figure D.4 Worksheet Options Obtained after Right-Clicking on a Worksheet Tab

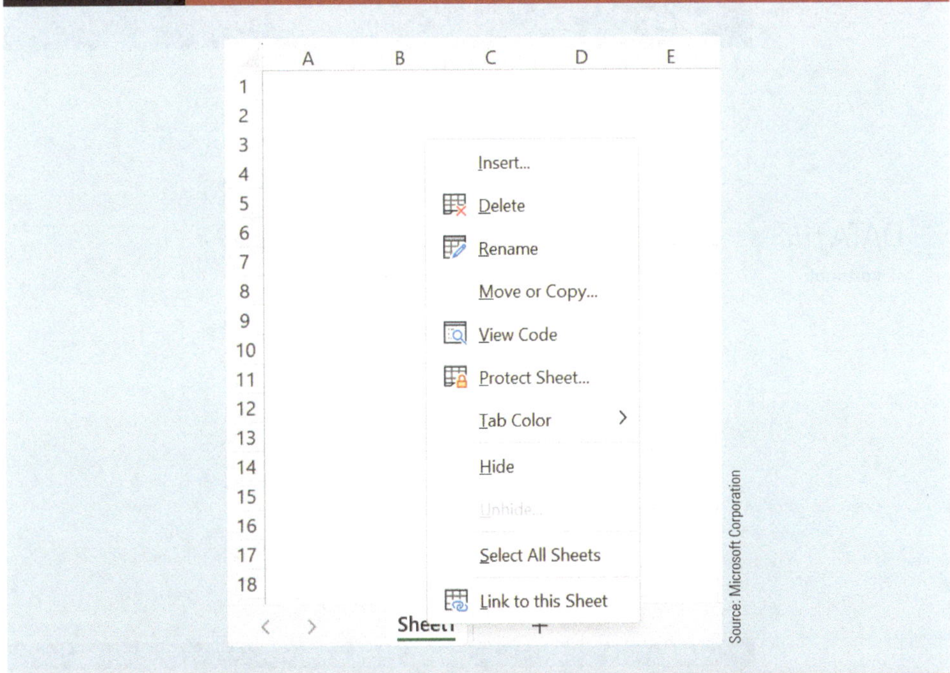

tional blank worksheet will appear in the workbook. You can also insert a new worksheet by clicking the **New** sheet button ⊕ that appears to the right of the last worksheet tab displayed. Worksheets can be deleted by right-clicking the worksheet tab and choosing **Delete**. Worksheets can also be moved to other workbooks or a different position in the current workbook by using the Move or Copy option.

Creating, Saving, and Opening Files

Data can be entered into an Excel worksheet by manually entering the data into the worksheet or by opening another workbook that already contains the data. As an illustration of manually entering, saving, and opening a file, we will use the example from Chapter 2 involving data for a sample of 50 soft drink purchases. The original data are shown in Table D.1.

Suppose we want to enter the data for the sample of 50 soft drink purchases into Sheet1 of the new workbook. First, we enter the label "Brand Purchased" into cell A1; then we enter the data for the 50 soft drink purchases into cells A2:A51. As a reminder that this worksheet contains the data, we will change the name of the worksheet from "Sheet1" to "Data" using the procedure described previously. Figure D.5 shows the data worksheet that we just developed.

Before doing any analysis with these data, we recommend that you first save the file; this will prevent you from having to reenter the data in case something happens that causes Excel to close. To save the file as an Excel workbook using the filename "softdrink" we perform the following steps:

Step 1: Click the **File** tab in the Ribbon
Step 2: Click **Save** in the list of options
Step 3: When the **Save As** window appears:
Select **Browse**
Select the location where you want to save the file
Type the filename *softdrink* in the **File name:** box
Click **Save**

DATA*file*
softdrink

Table D.1 Data from a Sample of 50 Soft Drink Purchases

Coca-Cola	Sprite	Pepsi
Diet Coke	Coca-Cola	Coca-Cola
Pepsi	Diet Coke	Coca-Cola
Diet Coke	Coca-Cola	Coca-Cola
Coca-Cola	Diet Coke	Pepsi
Coca-Cola	Coca-Cola	Dr. Pepper
Dr. Pepper	Sprite	Coca-Cola
Diet Coke	Pepsi	Diet Coke
Pepsi	Coca-Cola	Pepsi
Pepsi	Coca-Cola	Pepsi
Coca-Cola	Coca-Cola	Pepsi
Dr. Pepper	Pepsi	Pepsi
Sprite	Coca-Cola	Coca-Cola
Coca-Cola	Sprite	Dr. Pepper
Diet Coke	Dr. Pepper	Pepsi
Coca-Cola	Pepsi	Sprite
Coca-Cola	Diet Coke	

Figure D.5 Worksheet Containing the Soft Drink Data

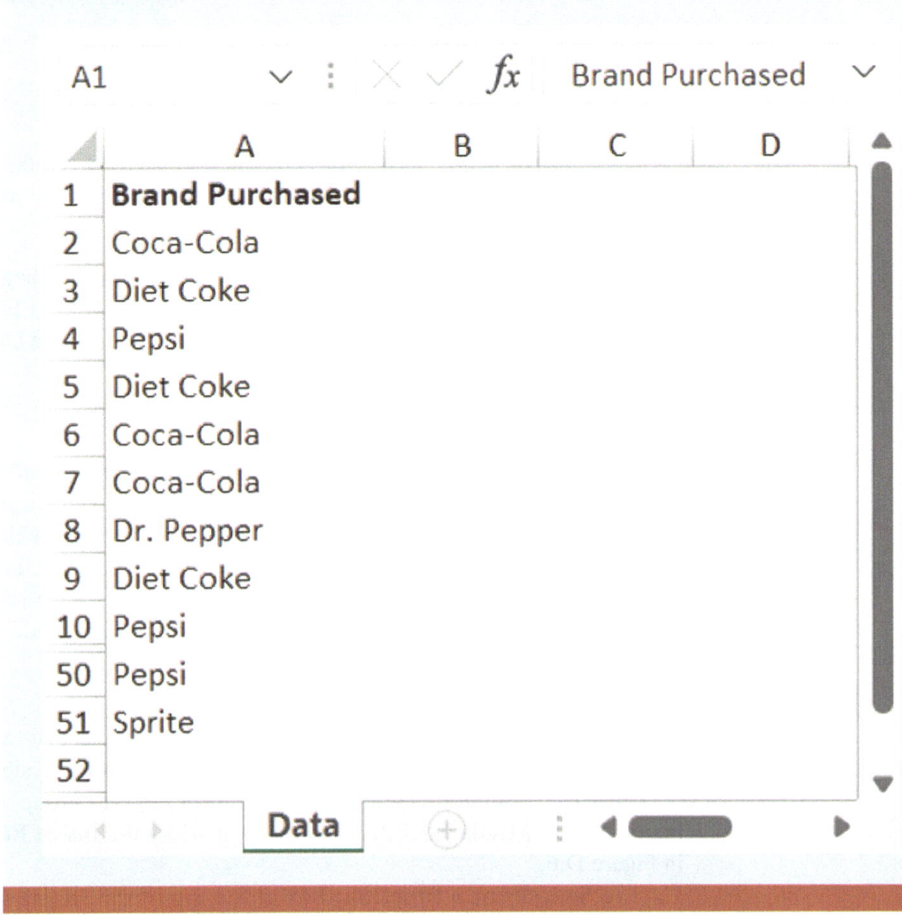

Source: Microsoft Corporation

Note: Rows 11–49 are hidden.

Keyboard shortcut: To save the file, press **CTRL+S.**

As you work with the file to do statistical analysis you should follow the practice of periodically saving the file so you will not lose any statistical analysis you may have performed. You can also click the **Save** icon in the **Quick Analysis** Toolbar to quickly save a file.

Sometimes you may want to create a copy of an existing file. For instance, suppose you would like to save the soft drink data and any resulting statistical analysis in a new file named "softdrink analysis." The following steps show how to create a copy of the softdrink workbook and analysis with the new filename, "softdrink analysis."

Step 1: Click the **File** tab
Step 2: Click **Save As**
Step 3: When the **Save As** window appears:
Select **Browse**
Select the location where you want to save the file
Type the filename *softdrink_analysis* in the **File name:** box
Click **Save**

Once the workbook has been saved, you can continue to work with the data to perform whatever type of statistical analysis is appropriate. When you are finished working with the file, simply click the **File** tab and then click **close** in the list of options. To access the *softdrink_analysis* file at another point in time, you can open the file by performing the following steps after launching Excel:

Step 1: Click the **File** tab
Step 2: Click **Open**
Step 3: When the Open window appears:
Select **Browse**
Select the location where you previously saved the file
Enter the filename *softdrink_analysis* in the **File name:** box
Click **Open**

The procedures we showed for saving or opening a workbook begin by clicking the **File** tab to access the Save and Open commands. Once you have used Excel for a while, you will probably find it more convenient to add these commands to the Quick Access Toolbar.

Using Excel Functions

Excel provides a wealth of functions for data management and statistical analysis. If we know which function is needed, and how to use it, we can simply enter the function into the appropriate worksheet cell. However, if we are not sure which functions are available to accomplish a task, or are not sure how to use a particular function, Excel can provide assistance. Many new functions for statistical analysis have been added with Excel. To illustrate, we will use the *softdrink_analysis* workbook created in the previous subsection.

Finding the Right Excel Function

To identify the functions available in Excel, select the cell where you want to insert the function; we have selected cell D2. Click the **Formulas** tab on the Ribbon and then click the **Insert Function** button in the **Function Library** group. Alternatively, click the *fx* button on the formula bar. Either approach provides the **Insert Function** dialog box shown in Figure D.6.

The **Search for a function:** box at the top of the **Insert Function** dialog box enables us to type a brief description of what we want to do. After doing so and clicking **Go**, Excel will search for and display, in the **Select a function:** box, the functions that may accomplish our task. In many situations, however, we may want to browse through an entire category of functions to see what is available. For this task, the **Or select a category:** box is helpful. It contains a drop-down list of several categories of functions provided by Excel. Figure D.6 shows that we selected the **Statistical** category. As a result, Excel's statistical functions appear in alphabetic order in the **Select a function:** box. We see the AVEDEV function listed first, followed by the AVERAGE function, and so on.

The AVEDEV function is highlighted in Figure D.6, indicating it is the function currently selected. The proper syntax for the function and a brief description of the function appear below the **Select a function:** box. We can scroll through the list in the **Select a function** box to display the syntax and a brief description for each of the statistical functions that are available. For instance, scrolling down farther, we select the **COUNTIF** function as shown in Figure D.7. Note that COUNTIF is now highlighted, and that immediately below the **Select a function:** box we see **COUNTIF(range,criteria)**, which indicates that the COUNTIF function contains two inputs: range and criteria. In addition, we see that the description of the COUNTIF function is "Counts the number of cells within a range that meet the given condition."

If the function selected (highlighted) is the one we want to use, we click **OK**; the **Function Arguments** dialog box then appears. The **Function Arguments** dialog box for

Figure D.6 Insert Function Dialog Box

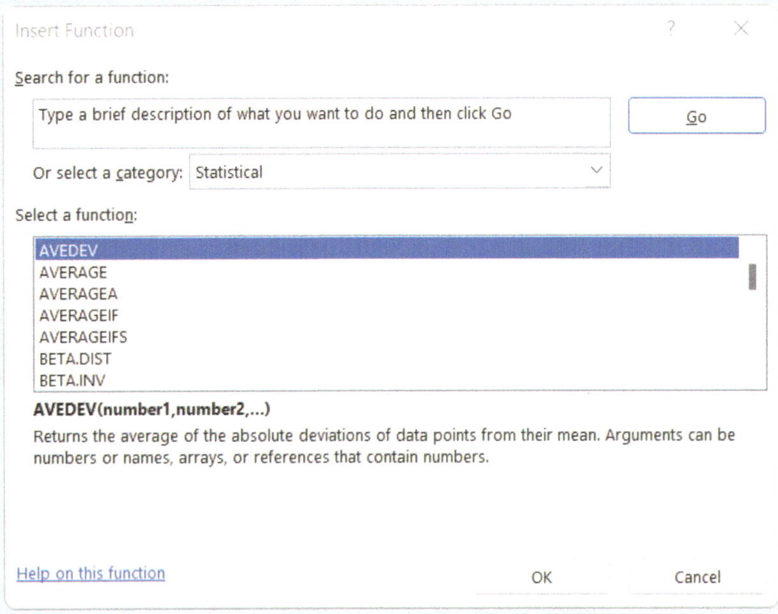

Source: Microsoft Corporation

Figure D.7 Description of the Countif Function in the Insert Function Dialog Box

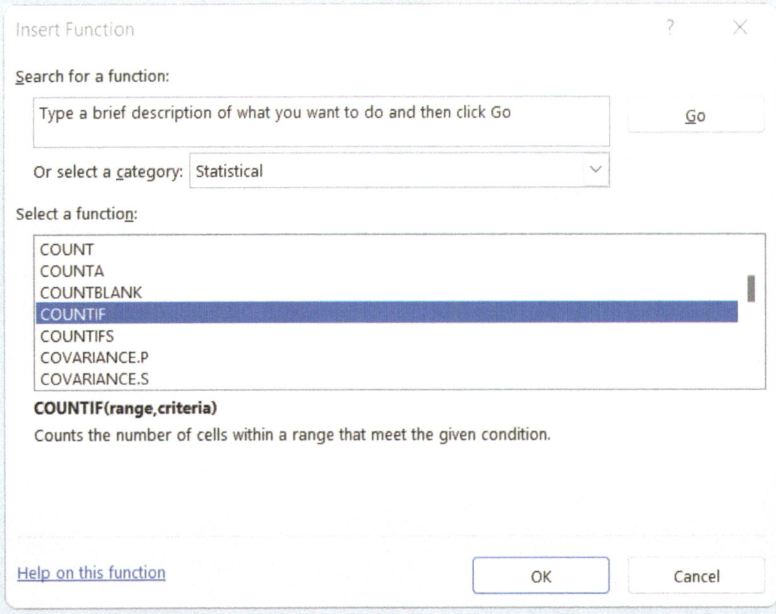

Source: Microsoft Corporation

Figure D.8 Function Arguments Dialog Box for the Countif Function

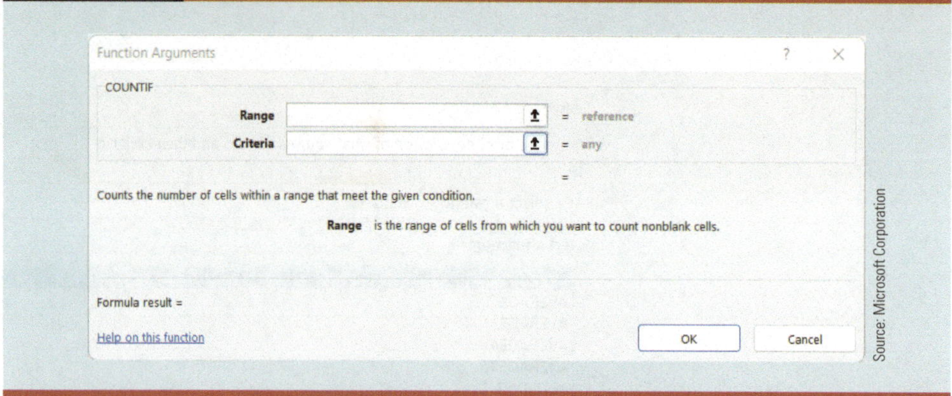

Source: Microsoft Corporation

the COUNTIF function is shown in Figure D.8. This dialog box assists in creating the appropriate arguments (inputs) for the function selected. When finished entering the arguments, click **OK**; Excel then inserts the function into a worksheet cell.

Using Excel Add-Ins

Excel's Data Analysis Add-In

Excel's Data Analysis add-in is a valuable tool for conducting statistical analysis. Before you can use the Data Analysis add-in it must be installed. To see if the Data Analysis add-in has already been installed, click the **Data** tab on the Ribbon. In the **Analyze** group, you should see the **Data Analysis** button. If you do not have an **Analyze** group and/or the Data Analysis button does not appear in the **Analyze** group, you will need to install the Data Analysis add-in. The steps needed to install the Data Analysis add-in are as follows:

*You may need to click **More...** to reveal **Options** in step 2.*

Step 1. Click the **File** tab
Step 2. Click **Options**
Step 3. When the **Excel Options** dialog box appears:
Select **Add-ins** from the list of options (on the pane on the left)
In the **Manage:** box, select **Excel Add-ins**
Click **Go...**
Step 4. When the **Add-ins** dialog box appears:
Select the check box for **Analysis ToolPak**
Click **OK**

Appendix E–Microsoft Excel Online and Tools for Statistical Analysis

Microsoft Excel Online is a spreadsheet program that can be used to organize and analyze data, perform complex calculations, and create a wide variety of graphical displays. With Microsoft Excel Online, you can use your web browser to create, edit, view, and share workbooks stored on OneDrive. We assume that readers are familiar with basic Excel operations such as selecting cells, entering formulas, and copying. But we do not assume readers are familiar with Excel Online or the use of Excel for statistical analysis.

Appendix D covers the basics of working with desktop versions of Excel.

The purpose of this appendix is to give a brief overview of Excel Online and contrast it with desktop versions of Excel. Excel Online is very similar in many ways to desktop Excel, but there are also some important differences for those that are familiar with using desktop Excel. For instance, Excel's Data Analysis add-in, a valuable tool for conducting statistical analysis that is included with desktop versions of Excel is not available with Excel Online. Some add-ins that are useful for statistical analysis are available through the Office Store. To find a list of add-ins that are available for Excel Online, click on the **Insert** tab and select **Office Add-ins** in the **Add-ins** group. When the **Office Add-ins** window opens, click on **Office Store**.

Overview of Microsoft Excel Online

When using Excel Online for statistical analysis, data is displayed in workbooks, each of which contains a series of worksheets that typically include the original data as well as any resulting analysis, including charts. Figure E.1 shows the layout of a blank workbook that can be opened in Excel Online. The workbook is named "Book 1" and contains one worksheet named "Sheet1." Excel Online highlights the worksheet currently displayed (Sheet1) by setting the name on the worksheet tab in bold. Note that cell A1 is initially selected.

Excel Online's Clipboard tab contains several of the features in desktop Excel's Quick Access Toolbar.

The wide bar located across the top of the workbook is referred to as the Ribbon. Tabs, located at the top of the Ribbon, provide quick access to groups of related commands. There are several tabs shown on the workbook in Figure E.1, including: File; Home; Insert; Draw; Page Layout; Formulas; Data; Review; View; and Help. Each tab contains a series of groups of related commands. Note that the Home tab is selected when Excel Online is opened. Figure E.2 displays the groups available when the Home tab is selected. Under the Home tab there are several groups, including: Undo; Clipboard; Font; Alignment; Number; Styles; Cells; Editing; and Analysis. Commands are arranged within each group.

The Formula Bar (see Figure E.3) contains a Name box, the Insert Function button fx, and a Formula box. In Figure E.3, "A1" appears in the name box because cell A1 is selected. You can select any other cell in the worksheet by using the mouse to move the cursor to another cell and clicking or by typing the new cell location in the Name box. The Formula box is used to display the formula in the currently selected cell. For instance, if you enter $=A1+A2$ into cell A3, whenever you select cell A3, the formula =A1+A2 will be shown in the Formula box. This feature makes it very easy to see and edit a formula in a particular cell. The Insert Function button fx allows you to quickly access all the functions available in Excel Online. Later, we show how to find and use a particular function.

Figure E.1 Blank Workbook Created with Excel Online

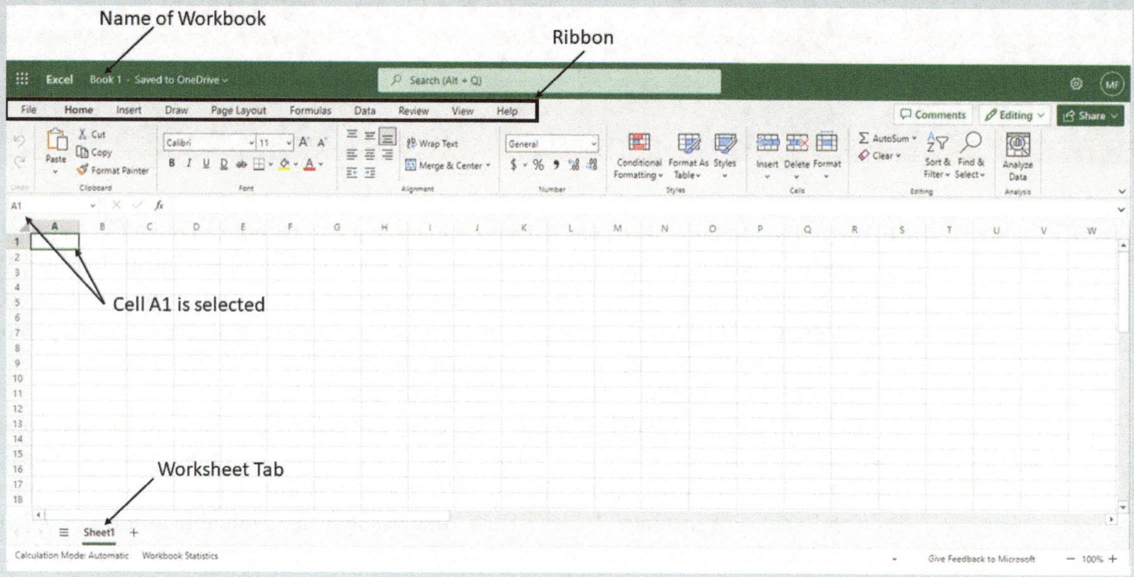

Source: Microsoft Corporation

Basic Workbook Operations

Figure E.4 illustrates the worksheet options that can be performed after right-clicking on a worksheet tab. For instance, to change the name of the current worksheet from "Sheet1" to "Data," right-click the worksheet tab named "Sheet1" and select the **Rename** option. The current worksheet name (Sheet1) will be highlighted. Then, simply type the new name, *Data*, and press the **Enter** key to rename the worksheet.

Suppose that you wanted to create a copy of "Sheet1." After right-clicking the tab named "Sheet1," select the **Duplicate** option. The name of the copied worksheet will appear as "Sheet1 (2)." You can then rename it, if desired.

Figure E.2 Portion of the Home Tab

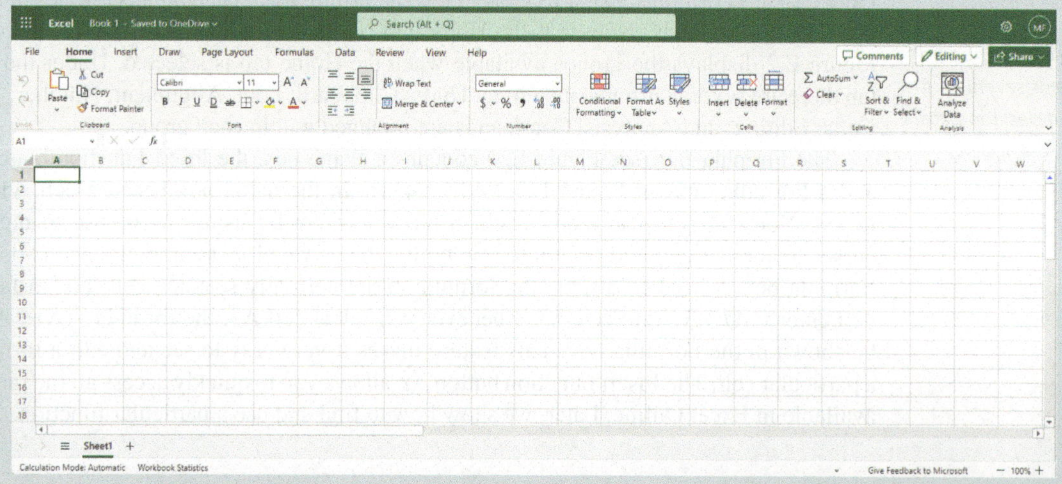

Source: Microsoft Corporation

Figure E.3 Excel Online Formula Bar

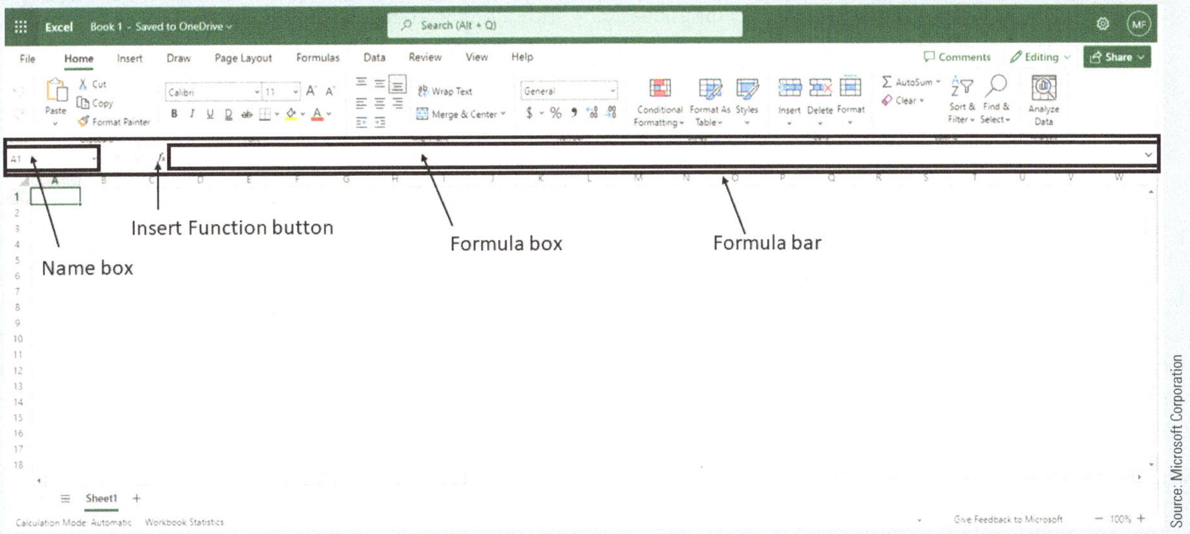

To add a new worksheet to the workbook, right-click any worksheet tab and select the **Insert** option. An additional blank worksheet will appear in the workbook. You can also insert a new worksheet by clicking the **New sheet** button ⊕ that appears to the right of the last worksheet tab displayed. Worksheets can be deleted by right-clicking the worksheet tab and choosing **Delete**. Worksheets can also be copied in the current workbook by using the **Duplicate** option.

Figure E.4 Worksheet Options Obtained After Right-Clicking on a Worksheet Tab

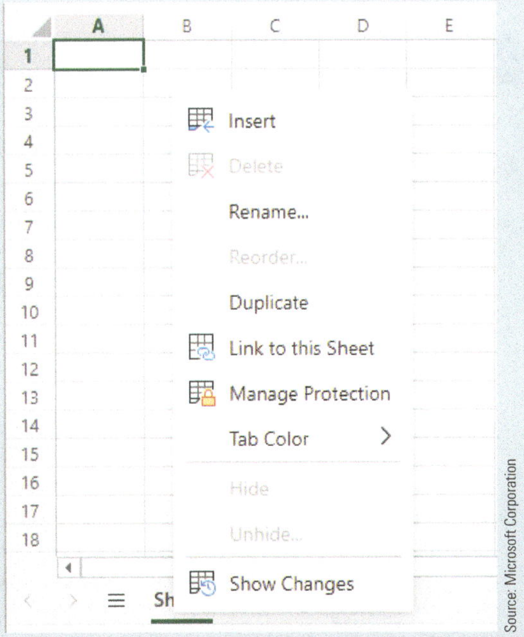

Creating, Saving, Opening, and Uploading Files

Data can be entered into an Excel Online worksheet by manually entering the data into the worksheet or by opening another workbook that already contains the data. As an illustration of manually entering, saving, and opening a file, we will use data for a sample of 50 soft drink purchases. The original data are shown in Table E.1.

Suppose we want to enter the data for the sample of 50 soft drink purchases into Sheet1 of the new workbook. First we enter the label "Brand Purchased" into cell A1; then we enter the data for the 50 soft drink purchases into cells A2:A51. As a reminder that this worksheet contains the data, we will change the name of the worksheet from "Sheet1" to "Data" using the procedure described previously. Figure E.5 shows the Data worksheet that we just developed.

OneDrive is Microsoft's storage service for hosting files in the cloud for an owner of a Microsoft account.

Make sure that your Internet connection is active when you close the Excel Online file so all of your changes are saved in the OneDrive file.

Excel Online does not have a Save button. Any changes you make to the Excel Online spreadsheet will automatically be saved to the existing file in OneDrive. However, you may wish to give the file a more descriptive name than what Excel Online has assigned by default. To change the name of the Excel Online file on OneDrive, we perform the following steps:

Step 1: Click the **File** tab
Step 2: Click **Save As** in the list of options
Step 3: When the **Save As** window appears:
  Select **Rename**
  Type the filename *softdrinkpurchases* in the **Rename** box
  Click **OK**

The current Excel Online file is now saved on OneDrive under the file name *softdrinkpurchases*.

We may also want to save a copy of an Excel file to our computer's hard drive. Excel Online's Download a Copy command is designed to save an Excel Online file to your computer's hard drive as an Excel workbook. To save the Excel Online file to your computer's hard drive as an Excel workbook using the filename *softdrinkpurchases*, we perform the following steps:

Step 1: Click the **File** tab
Step 2: Click **Save As** in the list of options
Step 3: When the **Save As** window appears, select **Download a Copy**

You may want to create a copy of an existing file. For instance, suppose you would like to save the soft drink data and any resulting statistical analysis in a new file named

DATA*file*
softdrinkpurchases

Table E.1 Data from a Sample of 50 Soft Drink Purchases

Coca-Cola	Sprite	Pepsi
Diet Coke	Coca-Cola	Coca-Cola
Pepsi	Diet Coke	Coca-Cola
Diet Coke	Coca-Cola	Coca-Cola
Coca-Cola	Diet Coke	Pepsi
Coca-Cola	Coca-Cola	Dr. Pepper
Dr. Pepper	Sprite	Coca-Cola
Diet Coke	Pepsi	Diet Coke
Pepsi	Coca-Cola	Pepsi
Pepsi	Coca-Cola	Pepsi
Coca-Cola	Coca-Cola	Pepsi
Dr. Pepper	Pepsi	Pepsi
Sprite	Coca-Cola	Coca-Cola
Coca-Cola	Sprite	Dr. Pepper
Diet Coke	Dr. Pepper	Pepsi
Coca-Cola	Pepsi	Sprite
Coca-Cola	Diet Coke	

Figure E.5 Worksheet Containing the Soft Drink Data

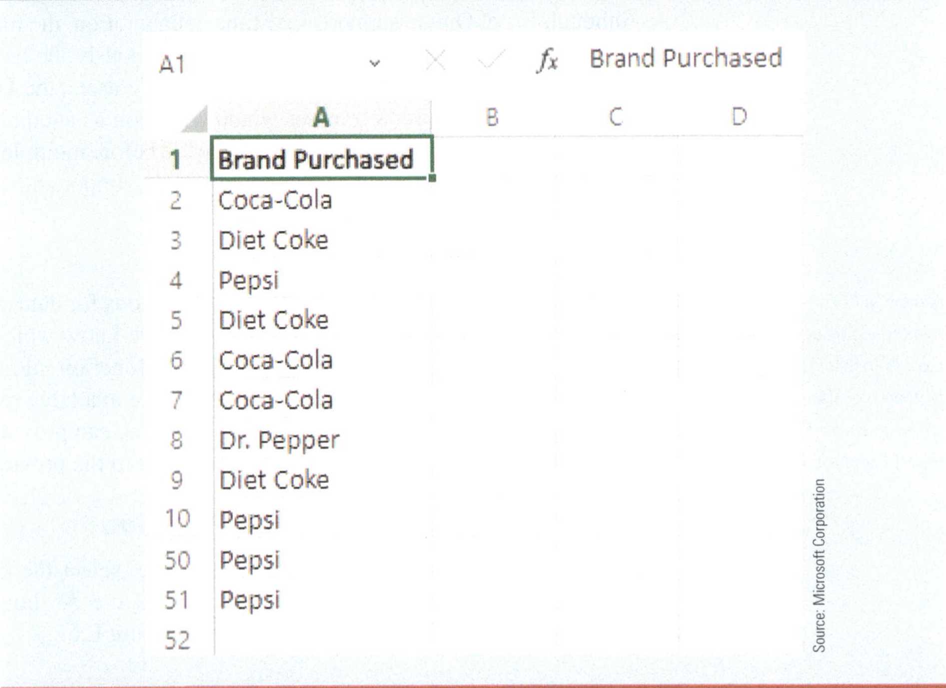

Note: Rows 11–49 are hidden.

softdrink_analysis. The following steps show how to create a copy of the *softdrinkpurchases* Excel Online workbook and analysis on OneDrive as a new Excel Online file with the new filename, *softdrink_analysis*.

Step 1: Click the **File** tab
Step 2: Click **Save As**
Step 3: When the **My files** window appears:
Select the OneDrive location where you want to save the file, and type the filename *softdrink_analysis* in the **Enter a name for this copy:** box
Click **Save**

Once the workbook has been saved to OneDrive, you can continue to work with the data to perform whatever type of statistical analysis is appropriate.

One important feature of Excel Online is the ability for multiple users to open, view, and edit a worksheet simultaneously; this is called co-authoring. When you and other users co-author, you can see each other's changes quickly, and this supports real-time collaboration. You may want to upload an Excel file from your computer to OneDrive in order to co-author with one or more other people on a worksheet. To upload an existing Excel file to OneDrive, sign into your OneDrive account, open the Excel file you want to upload to OneDrive, and perform the following steps:

Step 1: Click the **File** tab
Step 2: Click **Save As**
Step 3: When the **My files** window appears:
Select the OneDrive location to which you want to upload the file
Click **Save**

The current Excel file is now saved on OneDrive and can simultaneously be opened and edited by several users.

Although Excel Online supports real-time collaboration, the manner in which worksheets can be edited changes when multiple users simultaneously the have Excel Online file open. When a workbook is simultaneously open by multiple users, the **Undo** and **Redo** commands are not available in one user's browser window as soon as another user makes a change. We suggest saving a backup copy of an Excel Online file before multiple users simultaneously open and edit the file, to protect against inadvertently losing important features of the original file.

Using Excel Functions

Almost all of the functions available through desktop Excel's Insert Function button are also available through Excel Online's Insert Function button fx.

Excel Online provides many, but not all of the functions for data management and statistical analysis provided in desktop versions of Excel. If we know which Excel Office function is needed, and how to use it, we can simply enter the function into the appropriate worksheet cell. However, if we are not sure which functions are available to accomplish a task, or are not sure how to use a particular function, Excel Online can provide assistance. To illustrate, we will use the *softdrink_analysis* workbook created in the previous subsection.

Finding the Right Excel Online Function

To identify the functions available in Excel Online, select the cell in which you want to insert the function; we have selected cell D2. Click the *fx* button on the formula bar to access the **Insert Function** dialog box shown in Figure E.6.

Figure E.6 Insert Function Dialog Box

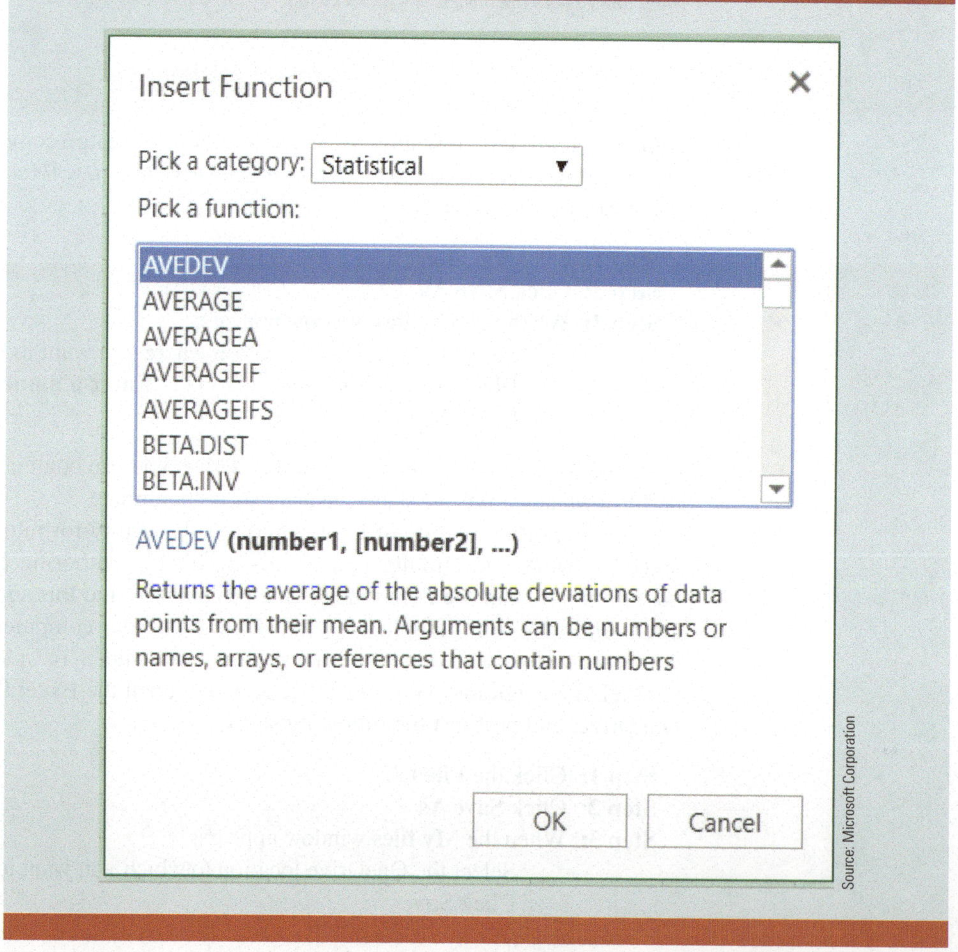

Source: Microsoft Corporation

Excel Online does not currently feature the ***Search for a function*** *box in the* ***Insert Dialog*** *box that is available in desktop Excel.*

We can scroll through the options in the **Pick a function:** box to browse for the functions to find an available function that may accomplish our task. In many situations, however, we may want to browse through an entire category of functions to see which functions are available. For this task, the **Pick a category:** box is helpful. It contains a drop-down list of several categories of functions provided by Excel Online. Figure E.6 shows that we selected the **Statistical** category. As a result, Excel Online's statistical functions in this category appear in alphabetic order in the **Pick a function:** box. We see the AVEDEV function listed first, followed by the AVERAGE function, and so on.

The AVEDEV function is highlighted in Figure E.6, indicating it is the function currently selected. The proper syntax for the function and a brief description of the function appear below the **Pick a function:** box. We can scroll through the list in the **Pick a function:** box to display the syntax and a brief description for each of the statistical functions that are available. For instance, scrolling down farther, we select the COUNTIF function, as shown in Figure E.7. Note that COUNTIF is now highlighted, and that immediately below the **Pick a function:** box we see **COUNTIF(range,criteria)**, which indicates that the COUNTIF function contains two inputs: range and criteria. In addition, we see that the description of the COUNTIF function is "Counts the number of cells within a range that meet the given condition."

Figure E.7 Description of the COUNTIF Function in the Insert Function Dialog Box

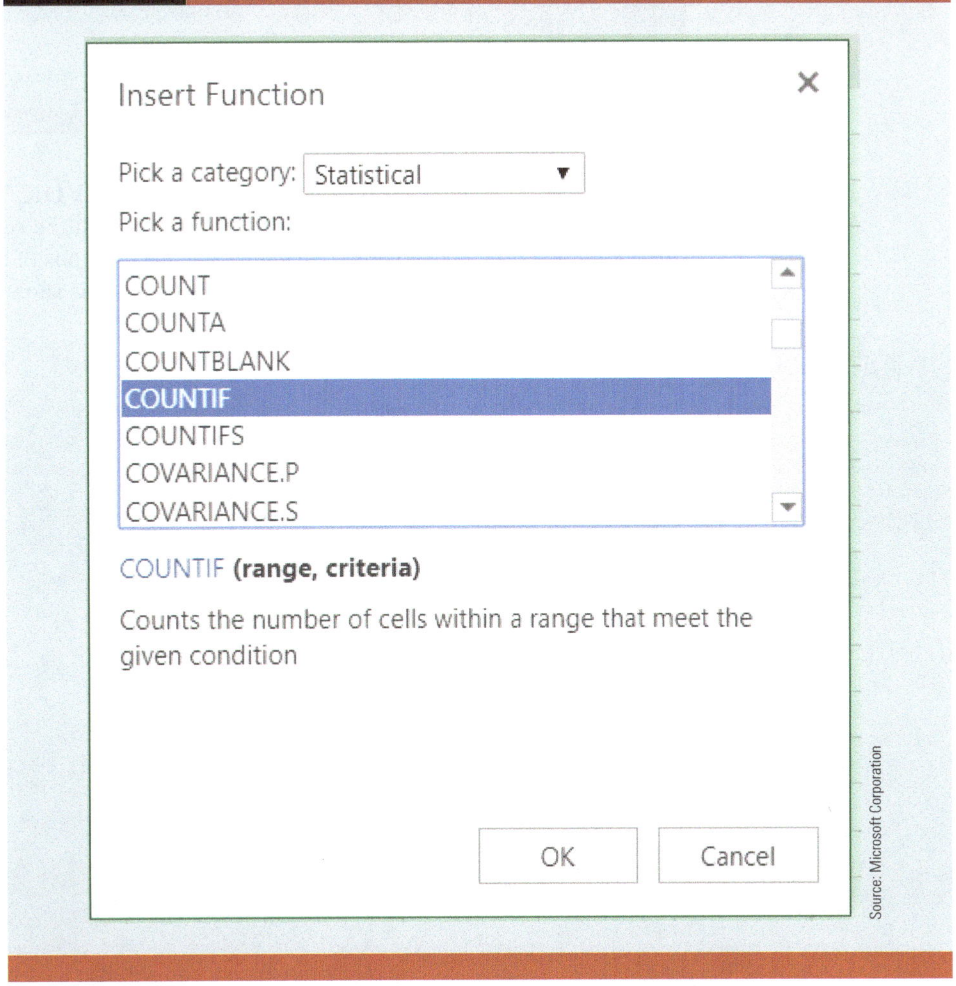

Source: Microsoft Corporation

Figure E.8 COUNTIF Function in Cell D2 of the *softdrink_analysis* Excel Online File

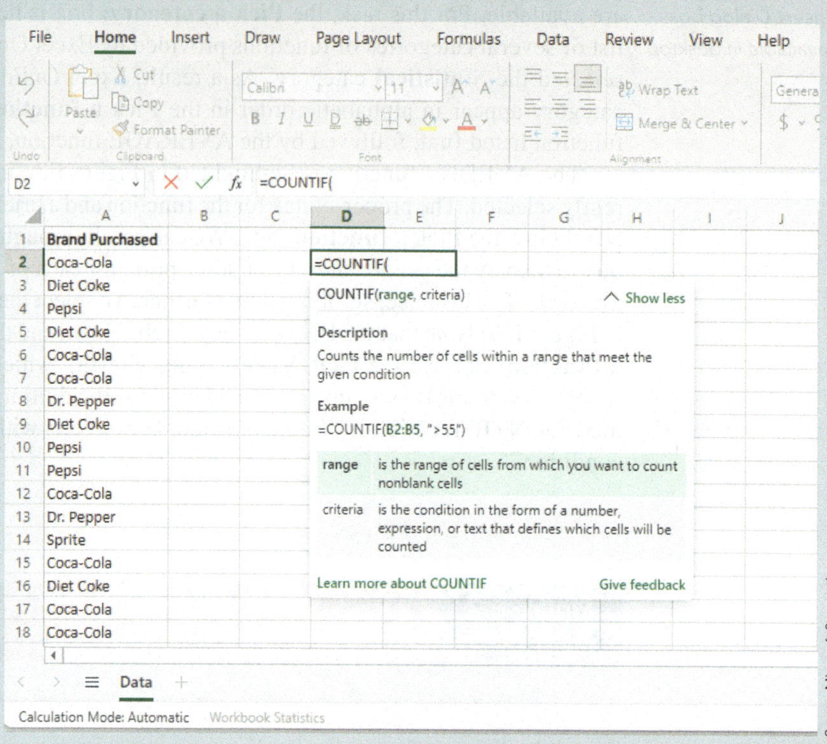

Source: Microsoft Corporation

If the function selected is the one we want to use, click **OK**. The function then appears in the cell originally selected (cell D2 here). Underneath the selected cell, Excel Online provides a pop-up box that shows the names and descriptions of the inputs for the function and a hyperlink to a learn more about the function. This is shown in Figure E.8.

Index

A

Acceptable quality level (AQL), 945
Acceptance criterion, 939–940
Acceptance sampling, 924
  acceptance sampling plan, selecting, 942–943
  binomial probability function for, 947
  example of, 939–940
  introduction to, 938–939
  multiple sampling plans, 943–944
  probability of accepting a lot, computing, 940–942
Accounting applications, 3
Addition law, 202–205, 223
Additive decomposition models, 858, 870
Adjusted multiple coefficient of determination, 725, 750
AICPA (American Institute of Certified Public Accountants), 1008
Air traffic controller stress test, 596, 597
Alternative hypotheses, 416, 419, 424
American Institute of Certified Public Accountants (AICPA), 1008
American Society for Quality (ASQ), 920
American Statistical Association, 22
Analysis of variance (ANOVA), 576. *See also* ANOVA procedure; ANOVA procedure assumptions for; ANOVA tables
  between-treatments estimate of population variance, 579, 580
  comparing variance estimates, *F* test, 581, 582
  completely randomized design, 578, 589
  conceptual overview, 576, 578
  example of, 731
  introduction to, 573–578
  output, interpretation of, 668–669
  summary, 613–614
  testing for the equality of *k* population means, 584, 586
Analytics, 19–20
Animal nutrition, 762
ANOVA procedure
  in air traffic controller stress test, 596
  ANOVA table and, 597, 598
  Excel used for, 599, 601, 609, 611
  overview of, 605, 606
ANOVA tables
  ANOVA procedure and, 597, 599
  example of, 609, 655–656
  overview of, 582, 586
  for two-factor factorial experiment, 606
AOQL (Average outgoing quality limit), 945
Approximate class width, 103
AQL (Acceptable quality level), 945
Area as a measure of probability, 292, 293
  normal distribution, 295, 309
  standard normal distribution, 297, 301
Assignable causes, 925
Association between two variables
  correlation coefficient, 162–164
  covariance, 157–165
  covariance, interpretation of, 159–160
  measures of, 157–165
  multinomial probability distribution, 560
AT&T, 21
Attributes sampling plans, 945
Autocorrelation, 793–798
AVERAGE function, 19
Average of past values, 820
Average outgoing quality limit (AOQL), 945
Average range, 929, 947

B

Backward elimination, 788
Baldrige, Malcolm, 922
Baldrige National Quality Program (BNQP), 922
Bar charts
  example of, 97–98
  Excel used to create, 43–44
  histograms and, 60
  introduction to, 41–42
  side-by-side bar chart, 95–96
Barnett, Bob, 922
BASF SE, 762
Basic requirements for assigning probabilities, 192–195
Bayes, Reverend Thomas, 217
Bayes' theorem, 193
  applications of, 952
  branch probabilities computed using, 973, 975
  formula, 223
  overview of, 215–219
  tabular approach, 218–219
Bell-shaped curve, 295
Bell-shaped distribution, 147
Bernoulli, Jakob, 259
Bernoulli process, 259
Best-subsets regression, 788
Between-treatments estimate, 577
Bias in selection, 329, 330
Big data, 20–22, 358–361, 402, 404
  confidence intervals, precision of, 402, 403
  errors in sampling, 356–362
  hypothesis tests, 452, 454
  implications of, 359–361, 403, 404, 454
  p-values and, 452, 454
  simple linear regression, 690–691
Bimodal data, 121
Binomial experiment
  example of, 260–263
  Excel used to compute, 264–265
  expected value and variance, 265–266
  overview of, 258–260
Binomial probability distribution
  binomial experiment, 258–260
  example of, 260–263
  Excel used to compute, 264–266
  expected value and variance, 265–266
  multinomial probability distribution, 539
  normal distribution and, 349
  sign test and, 881–882
Binomial probability function, 259, 262–263, 280, 940, 947
Biodiversity preservation, 91
Bivariate probability distribution, 249–255
Blocking, 595–596, 599
Blocks, 596, 599
Bloomberg Businessweek, 2
BNQP (Baldrige National Quality Program), 922
Bonferroni adjustment, 593
Boxplot, 155–157
  comparative analysis, using Excel to construct, 153–154
  Excel used to create, 152–153
  overview of, 151
Branches, of decision tree, 955, 956, 963, 964–965
Branch probabilities, Bayes' theorem for computing of, 973, 975
Burke Inc, 572
Business applications, 3–4
BusinessWeek, 2

C

Cartogram, 89–90
Cash flow management, 116
Categorical data, 7, 37
Categorical independent variables
  example of, 737–740
  interpreting the parameters, 739–740
  more complex categorical variables, 740–742
Categorical variable, 7
  applications, 45–48
  bar charts, 41–48
  frequency distribution, 37–38
  methods, 45
  percent frequency distribution, 37–38
  pie charts, 41–48
  relative frequency distribution, 38–40
  summarizing data for, 37–48
Causal forecasting methods, 809
Cause-and-effect relationships, 630, 656
Census, 15
Centered moving average, 860–861
Center for Drug Evaluation and Research (CDER), 466
Central limit theorem, 340–342, 429
Certified public accountants (CPAs), 1008
Chance events, 952
Chance nodes, 955
Chebyshev's theorem, 146, 148
Chi-square (x^2) distribution
  hypothesis testing and, 517–518
  hypothesis tests, 560
  interval estimation and, 511–520
  testing for equality of population proportions, 557
  test of independence and, 547, 549
  test of independence and test for equality, 564
  test statistics, 541, 550
Chi-square test statistic
  equality of population proportions, testing for, 554, 557
  testing for, 556, 557
Choropleth map, 86–89
  using excel to construct, 87–89
Cincinnati Zoo and Botanical Garden, 98–100
Classical method for assigning probabilities, 199
Classical method for assigning probabilities, 192, 238
Class limits, 49–50, 60
Class midpoint, 49
Class width, 49
Cluster sampling, 322, 330, 354–355, 1006–1014, 1017–1018
  Excel used to, 1011
Cochran, William G., 995
Coefficient of determination, 641–646
  correlation coefficient, 645–646
  Excel used to compute, 644–645
  multiple regression, 724–726
  relationship among SST, SSR, and SSE, 644
  sum of squares due to error (SSE), 641–643
  sum of squares due to regression (SSR), 643
  total sum of squares (SST), 642
Coefficient of variation, 138–140, 172
Coefficients, interpretation of, 719–720
Colgate-Palmolive Company, 36–37
Column chart, 42
Combinations, 190–191, 195
Common causes, 925
Comparisons, displays for, 96
Comparisonwise Type I error rate, 592, 593
Complements, 201–202
Complete block design, 599
Completely randomized design
  equality of population means, testing for, 584
Completely randomized design
  ANOVA table for, 582, 586
  between-treatments estimateof population variance, 580
  definition of, 574
  equality of population means, testing for, 586
  F test, 581
  introduction to, 578
  overview of, 574
  population variance, 579
  within-treatments estimate of population variance, 580

Conditional probability, 207–212, 973
formula, 223
independent events, 210
multiplication law, 211–212
Confidence
hypothesis testing and, 433, 435
precision, 403
precision of, 402
usefulness, 403
usefulness of, 404
Confidence coefficient, 377
Confidence intervals, 377, 380, 387, 390, 392, 399. *See also* Interval estimation
approximate 95% estimate of population mean, 998, 1009
approximate 95% estimate of population proportion, 992, 1001, 1011
approximate 95% estimate of population total, 1010
estimated regression equation, 660–661, 663, 735
estimate of population total, 991
Excel used to construct, 515–516
formula, 693
significance tests, 653–654
Confidence levels, 377, 378
Consequences, 952
Consumer's risk, 939
Continuous improvement, 921, 925
Continuous probability distributions, 313
exponential probability distribution, 309, 313
normal probability distribution, 295, 309
summary, 314
uniform probability distribution, 291, 295
Continuous random variables, 235–236
Control charts, 926
np chart, 926, 935
p chart, 926, 932–935
R chart, 931–932
x-chart, 926
Convenience sampling, 355, 362, 988
Correlation between random variables, 263
Correlation coefficient, 160–162. *See also* Sample correlation coefficient
coefficient of determination and, 645–646
Excel used to compute, 164
interpretation of, 162–164
for two random variables, 254
Counting rules, 188–192
for combinations, 188–189, 195, 222
for multiple-step experiments, 188–189
for permutations, 191–192, 222
Covariance, 157–159
discrete probability distributions, 249–255
Excel used to compute, 164
interpretation of, 159–160
of random variables, 252, 280
Coverage error, 357
CPAs (Certified public accountants), 1008
Cravens, David W., 784, 785
Critical value approach
for Marascuilo pairwise comparison procedure, 564
one-tailed tests, 428
overview of, 433
p-value approach *versus,* 448
rejection rule, 541, 549, 582, 590, 653, 655, 710, 730–731
t test for significance in simple linear regression, 653
two-tailed tests, 430, 431
Crosby, Philip B., 921
Cross-sectional data, 8–10
Cross-sectional regression, 809
Crosstabulation, 67–70
Excel used to create, 68–69
Cumulative frequency distribution, 56–57, 60
Cumulative percent frequency distribution, 55–56
Cumulative probabilities, 314
Cumulative relative frequency distribution, 57
Curvilinear relationships, 763–765
Cyclical pattern, 816–817

D

Dashboards. *See* Data dashboards
Data, 5–10
acquisition errors, 13
big data and data mining, 20–22
categorical and quantitative, 7–8
collection of, 574, 575
cross-sectional, 8–10
definition of, 5
elements, variables, and observations, 5
existing sources, 10–11
experiments, 12
observational study, 11–12
scales of measurement, 5–7
sources of, 10–13
summary, 24
time and cost issues, 13
time series, 8
Data analytics, 19–20
Data dashboards, 97–100, 167–170
DATA.GOV, 11
Data mining, 21–22
Data set, 5–6
Data visualization, 37, 92–100
Data warehousing, 21
Deciles, 128
Decision analysis
decision trees, 954, 955, 963, 967, 968, 974
description of, 219
payoff tables, 953, 954
problem formulation, 955
with sample information, 962, 973
Decision analysis, 917–949
decision trees, 967
Decision making with probabilities
expected value approach, 955, 957
information, 957, 958
Decision nodes, 954
Decision strategy, 966
Decision trees, 954, 955, 963, 967, 968, 974
Decomposition. *See* Time series decomposition
Defects, 922
Defects per million opportunities (dpmo), 922
Degrees of freedom
of chi-square distribution, 497, 512–513, 547
definition of, 382
error, 601
of *F* distribution, 523–524
of *t* distribution, 477, 478, 482, 487
of *t* distribution with two independent random samples, 504
Deming, W. Edwards, 921
de Moivre, Abraham, 295
Dependent events, 210
Dependent variables, 627, 729, 769–773
Descriptive analytics, 20
Descriptive statistics
association between two variables, measures of, 157–165
boxplot, 152–155
data dashboards, 167–170
distribution shape and relative location, measures of, 143–151
five-number summary, 151
location, measures of, 117–134
numerical measures, 115–184
outliers, detecting, 147–148
overview of, 13–15
variability, measures of, 134–143
Descriptive Statistics tool, 139–140
exponential probability distribution, 311, 312
hypothesis tests, 431, 432, 441, 443
interval estimate, 379
interval estimation, 386, 387
interval estimation of population proportion, 396, 398
normal probabilities, 304, 306
Deseasonalized time series, 863
Deviation about the mean, 135
Difference between two population proportions, 494, 496
Difference of population means
hypothesis tests, 471, 474, 480
interval estimate, 504
interval estimation, 467, 471, 477, 478
Difference of population means
hypothesis tests, 483
Discrete probability distributions, 233–288
binomial experiment, 258–260
bivariate probability distribution, 249–255
covariance, 249–255
developing, 238–243
expected value, 243
financial applications, 252–255
hypergeometric probability distribution, 274–276
Poisson probability distribution, 268–272
random variables, 235–237
required conditions for, 239
summary, 278–279
variance, 243–245
Discrete random variable, 235
Discrete uniform probability distribution, 239, 280
Dispersion, measures of, 117, 134, 170, 243–245
Distance intervals, 270
Distribution-free methods, 879
Distribution of data, displays for, 97–98
Distribution shape, measures of, 143–144
DMI (Dunning Microsystems, Inc.), 986, 989
Dot plots, 52–53, 96, 118
Double-blind experimental design, 578
Dow, 2
Dow Jones & Company, 10
Dow Jones Industrial Average Index, 8
Drug efficacy testing, 466
Duke Energy, 986
Dummy variables
complex categorical variables, 740–742
experimental design, 788–793
in regression analysis, 738
seasonality without trend, 748–758
Dun & Bradstreet, 10
Dunning Microsystems, Inc. (DMI), 986–987
Durbin–Watson test, 793–798
Durbin–Watson test statistic, 800

E

Economic applications, 4
Electoral vote maps, 91
Elements, 986–987
Elements of data, 5, 322
Empirical discrete distribution, 238
Empirical rule, 147
Equalarea cartogram, 90
Equality
testing for the equality of *k* population means, 584, 586
testing for three or more population proportions, 554
Errors in sampling, 356–362
Error term ∈, 649–650, 728
Estimated multiple regression
Excel used to create, 718–719
Estimated multiple regression equation, 714, 751
Estimated regression equation, 634–635
ANOVA output, interpretation of, 668–669
confidence intervals, 660–661
for estimation and prediction, 659–665
formula, 672–674
interpretation of output, 667–668
interval estimation, 660
prediction interval, 662–663
regression statistics output, interpretation of, 669
simple linear regression model, 629–630

F

G

H

I

International Organization for Standardization (ISO), 922
International Paper, 712–713
Interquartile range (IQR), 135, 172
Intersection of *A* and *B*, 203
Intersection of two events, 203
Interval estimate
  definition of, 374
  difference between two population proportions, 504
  margin of error, 383, 387
  of population mean known, 405
  of population mean unknown, 405
  of population proportion, 405
  summary, 405
Interval estimation, 660
  big data and, 402, 404
  difference between population means known, 504
  difference between two population means, 489
  of difference of population means, 467, 471, 477, 478
  of difference of population means unknown, 504
  of difference of population proportions, 494, 497
  hypothesis tests and, 433, 435
  margin of error, 374, 380
  population mean known, 374, 382
  population mean unknown, 382, 392
  population proportion, 395, 402
  population variances, 523–527
  sample size, determining, 392, 395, 398, 399
  summary, 389
Interval scale, 7
Intranets, 4
IQL (Indifference quality level), 945
IQR (Interquartile range), 135, 172
IRI, 4, 10
Ishikawa, Karou, 921
ISO 9000, 922
ISO (International Organization for Standardization), 922
  *i*th observation, 630
*i*th observation, 117, 632, 641, 715
*i*th residual, 641, 671, 674, 676, 678, 745, 794

J

John Morrell & Company, 416
Joint probabilities, 208–209, 974
Judgment sampling, 356, 362, 988
Juran, Joseph, 921

K

Key performance indicators (KPIs), 97, 167
Key performance metrics (KPMs), 97
k population, 584, 586
Kruskal–Wallis
  population proportion, 447, 448
  p-values and, 453
Kruskal–Wallis test, 903–907, 914

L

LCL (lower control limit), 926
Leaf unit, 60
Least squares criterion, 632, 635, 692, 715–719, 751
Least squares method
  coefficients, interpretation of, 719–720
  example of, 715–719
  multiple regression, 718–724
  simple linear regression, 630
Length intervals, 270
Levels of significance (alpha), 377–378, 421, 424
Leverage of observation *i,* 694
Leverage points, 686
LIFO (last-in, first-out) method of inventory valuation, 374
Linear trend equation, 833–838, 869
Linear trend regression, 833–838
Local area networks (LANs), 4
Location, measures of
  geometric mean, 123–125
  mean, 117–119, 128
  median, 119–120, 128
  mode, 120–121
  percentiles, 125–126
  quartiles, 126–127
  weighted mean, 122–123
Location of the *p*th percentile, 172
Lots, 938
Lot tolerance percent defective (LTPD), 945
Lower class limits, 48
Lower control limit (LCL), 926
Lower tail test
  population mean, 423, 425, 428, 472
  population proportion, 446
  p-value approach, 885
LTPD (Lot tolerance percent defective), 945

M

MAE (Mean absolute error), 140, 819–820, 825
Malcolm Baldrige National Quality Award, 922
Mann–Whitney–Wilcoxon (MWW), 914
  test, 893–903
MAPE (Mean absolute percentage error), 819–820, 825
Marascuilo procedure, 559–560, 564
Marascuilo procedureAnalysis of variance (ANOVA)
  example of, 572
Marginal probabilities, 209
Margin of error
  interval estimate and, 383, 387
  interval estimation and, 468
  introduction to, 374, 375
  population mean, 374, 380, 390
  population proportion, 395, 396
  sample size, 393, 398, 399
Marketing applications, 4
Market research, 416
Matched sample design, 487, 491
Matched sample(s), 500
  definition of, 487
  hypothesis tests, 497, 500, 504
  population means, inferences about difference between, 487, 494
McDonald's Inc., 8
Mean, 117–119, 128, 144–145, 296, 302
Mean absolute error (MAE), 140, 819–820
Mean absolute percentage error (MAPE), 819–820, 825
Mean square due to error (MSE)
  data sets and Excel worksheets, 17–18
  forecast accuracy, 819–820, 825
  formula, 693, 750–751
  F test, 730–731
  randomized block design, 595, 596, 598, 599
  statistical analysis using, 16–19
  testing for significance, 651–652
Mean square due to error (MSE)
  ANOVA procedure, 607
  formula, 615
  population variance, 580
Mean square due to treatments (MSTR), 579, 580, 595, 598, 599, 615
Mean square regression (MSR), 654, 730–731, 751
  formula, 693
Measurement, scales of, 5, 7
Measurement error, 357
Median, 119–120, 129, 144–145, 296
Microsoft, 2–4
Microsoft Exce
  ANOVA table, 583
Microsoft Excel
  ANOVA procedure, 599, 601, 609, 611
  ANOVA table, 584
  bar and pie charts, 43–44
  binomial probabilities, 264–266
  boxplot, 152–153
  for cluster sampling, 1011–1012
  coefficient of determination, 644–645
  comparative analysis using boxplots constructed using, 153–154
  confidence intervals, 469, 471, 478, 480, 496, 497, 515–516
  construct choropleth map, 87–89
  covariance and correlation coefficient, 164
  crosstabulation, 69–70
  estimated multiple regression equation, 718–719
  estimated regression equation, displaying, 634–635
  estimated regression line, displaying, 634–635
  expected value, 244–245
  exponential smoothing tool, 828–830
  frequency distribution, 39–40, 50–52
  geometric mean, 125–127
  goodness of fit test, 543
  histogram, 55–56
  hypergeometric probability distribution, 275–276
  hypothesis tests, 482, 483, 489, 490, 499, 500, 518–520
  linear trend equation, 837–838
  mean, median, and mode, 121–125
  moving average tool, 824–825
  NORM.DIST function, 350–351, 361
  percent frequency distribution, 39–40
  percentiles and quartiles, 127–128
  Poisson probability distribution, 270–272
  population mean, 998–1000
  population proportion, 1002
  for population total in NEG, 993
  for the Population Total in the NEG, 992–994
  quadratic trend equation, using regression tool to compute, 837–843
  regression tool, 666–671
  relative frequency distribution, 39–40
  residual plot, 677–680
  scatter diagram, 77–80, 634–635
  side-by-side bar chart and stacked bar chart, 82–83
  sign test, 885–886
  simple random sample, 324, 329
  for simple random sampling, 992–994
  Spearman rank-correlation coefficient, 909–912
  standard deviation, 138, 244–245
  test of independence, 549, 550
  test of multiple proportions, 558
  time series plots, 816
  trendline, 77–80
  trend projection, chart tools used for, 843–845
  variance, 138, 243–244
Mode, 120–121, 128, 129, 296
Monthly data, 854, 865
Motorola, 922–923
Moving averages, 822–825, 869
MSE. *See* Mean square due to error (MSE)
MSR (Mean square regression), 654, 693, 730–731, 751
MSTR (Mean square due to treatments), 579, 580, 595, 598, 599, 615
Multicollinearity, 732–733, 749–750, 784
Multimodal data, 121
Multinomial probability distribution, 539, 545
Multiple coefficient of determination, 724–726, 750
Multiple comparison procedures
  Fisher's LSD, 590, 592
  Type I error rates, 592–593
Multiple experiments, 188–190
Multiple proportions
  equality, testing for, 554
  Excel used to conduct, 558
Multiple regression
  big data and hypothesis testing in, 749–750
  categorical independent variables, 737–745

F

G

H

I

International Organization for Standardization (ISO), 922
International Paper, 712–713
Interquartile range (IQR), 135, 172
Intersection of *A* and *B*, 203
Intersection of two events, 203
Interval estimate
  definition of, 374
  difference between two population proportions, 504
  margin of error, 383, 387
  of population mean known, 405
  of population mean unknown, 405
  of population proportion, 405
  summary, 405
Interval estimation, 660
  big data and, 402, 404
  difference between population means known, 504
  difference between two population means, 489
  of difference of population means, 467, 471, 477, 478
  of difference of population means unknown, 504
  of difference of population proportions, 494, 497
  hypothesis tests and, 433, 435
  margin of error, 374, 380
  population mean known, 374, 382
  population mean unknown, 382, 392
  population proportion, 395, 402
  population variances, 523–527
  sample size, determining, 392, 395, 398, 399
  summary, 389
Interval scale, 7
Intranets, 4
IQL (Indifference quality level), 945
IQR (Interquartile range), 135, 172
IRI, 4, 10
Ishikawa, Karou, 921
ISO 9000, 922
ISO (International Organization for Standardization), 922
  *i*th observation, 630
*i*th observation, 117, 632, 641, 715
*i*th residual, 641, 671, 674, 676, 678, 745, 794

J

John Morrell & Company, 416
Joint probabilities, 208–209, 974
Judgment sampling, 356, 362, 988
Juran, Joseph, 921

K

Key performance indicators (KPIs), 97, 167
Key performance metrics (KPMs), 97
k population, 584, 586
Kruskal–Wallis
  population proportion, 447, 448
  p-values and, 453
Kruskal–Wallis test, 903–907, 914

L

LCL (lower control limit), 926
Leaf unit, 60
Least squares criterion, 632, 635, 692, 715–719, 751
Least squares method
  coefficients, interpretation of, 719–720
  example of, 715–719
  multiple regression, 718–724
  simple linear regression, 630
Length intervals, 270
Levels of significance (alpha), 377–378, 421, 424
Leverage of observation *i,* 694
Leverage points, 686
LIFO (last-in, first-out) method of inventory valuation, 374
Linear trend equation, 833–838, 869
Linear trend regression, 833–838
Local area networks (LANs), 4
Location, measures of
  geometric mean, 123–125
  mean, 117–119, 128
  median, 119–120, 128
  mode, 120–121
  percentiles, 125–126
  quartiles, 126–127
  weighted mean, 122–123
Location of the *p*th percentile, 172
Lots, 938
Lot tolerance percent defective (LTPD), 945
Lower class limits, 48
Lower control limit (LCL), 926
Lower tail test
  population mean, 423, 425, 428, 472
  population proportion, 446
  p-value approach, 885
LTPD (Lot tolerance percent defective), 945

M

MAE (Mean absolute error), 140, 819–820, 825
Malcolm Baldrige National Quality Award, 922
Mann–Whitney–Wilcoxon (MWW), 914
  test, 893–903
MAPE (Mean absolute percentage error), 819–820, 825
Marascuilo procedure, 559–560, 564
Marascuilo procedureAnalysis of variance (ANOVA)
  example of, 572
Marginal probabilities, 209
Margin of error
  interval estimate and, 383, 387
  interval estimation and, 468
  introduction to, 374, 375
  population mean, 374, 380, 390
  population proportion, 395, 396
  sample size, 393, 398, 399
Marketing applications, 4
Market research, 416
Matched sample design, 487, 491
Matched sample(s), 500
  definition of, 487
  hypothesis tests, 497, 500, 504
  population means, inferences about difference between, 487, 494
McDonald's Inc., 8
Mean, 117–119, 128, 144–145, 296, 302
Mean absolute error (MAE), 140, 819–820
Mean absolute percentage error (MAPE), 819–820, 825
Mean square due to error (MSE)
  data sets and Excel worksheets, 17–18
  forecast accuracy, 819–820, 825
  formula, 693, 750–751
  F test, 730–731
  randomized block design, 595, 596, 598, 599
  statistical analysis using, 16–19
  testing for significance, 651–652
Mean square due to error (MSE)
  ANOVA procedure, 607
  formula, 615
  population variance, 580
Mean square due to treatments (MSTR), 579, 580, 595, 598, 599, 615
Mean square regression (MSR), 654, 730–731, 751
  formula, 693
Measurement, scales of, 5, 7
Measurement error, 357
Median, 119–120, 129, 144–145, 296
Microsoft, 2–4
Microsoft Exce
  ANOVA table, 583
Microsoft Excel
  ANOVA procedure, 599, 601, 609, 611
  ANOVA table, 584
  bar and pie charts, 43–44
  binomial probabilities, 264–266
  boxplot, 152–153
  for cluster sampling, 1011–1012
  coefficient of determination, 644–645
  comparative analysis using boxplots constructed using, 153–154
  confidence intervals, 469, 471, 478, 480, 496, 497, 515–516
  construct choropleth map, 87–89
  covariance and correlation coefficient, 164
  crosstabulation, 69–70
  estimated multiple regression equation, 718–719
  estimated regression equation, displaying, 634–635
  estimated regression line, displaying, 634–635
  expected value, 244–245
  exponential smoothing tool, 828–830
  frequency distribution, 39–40, 50–52
  geometric mean, 125–127
  goodness of fit test, 543
  histogram, 55–56
  hypergeometric probability distribution, 275–276
  hypothesis tests, 482, 483, 489, 490, 499, 500, 518–520
  linear trend equation, 837–838
  mean, median, and mode, 121–125
  moving average tool, 824–825
  NORM.DIST function, 350–351, 361
  percent frequency distribution, 39–40
  percentiles and quartiles, 127–128
  Poisson probability distribution, 270–272
  population mean, 998–1000
  population proportion, 1002
  for population total in NEG, 993
  for the Population Total in the NEG, 992–994
  quadratic trend equation, using regression tool to compute, 837–843
  regression tool, 666–671
  relative frequency distribution, 39–40
  residual plot, 677–680
  scatter diagram, 77–80, 634–635
  side-by-side bar chart and stacked bar chart, 82–83
  sign test, 885–886
  simple random sample, 324, 329
  for simple random sampling, 992–994
  Spearman rank-correlation coefficient, 909–912
  standard deviation, 138, 244–245
  test of independence, 549, 550
  test of multiple proportions, 558
  time series plots, 816
  trendline, 77–80
  trend projection, chart tools used for, 843–845
  variance, 138, 243–244
Mode, 120–121, 128, 129, 296
Monthly data, 854, 865
Motorola, 922–923
Moving averages, 822–825, 869
MSE. *See* Mean square due to error (MSE)
MSR (Mean square regression), 654, 693, 730–731, 751
MSTR (Mean square due to treatments), 579, 580, 595, 598, 599, 615
Multicollinearity, 732–733, 749–750, 784
Multimodal data, 121
Multinomial probability distribution, 539, 545
Multiple coefficient of determination, 724–726, 750
Multiple comparison procedures
  Fisher's LSD, 590, 592
  Type I error rates, 592–593
Multiple experiments, 188–190
Multiple proportions
  equality, testing for, 554
  Excel used to conduct, 558
Multiple regression
  big data and hypothesis testing in, 749–750
  categorical independent variables, 737–745

estimated regression equation, using for estimation and prediction, 735–737
experimental design, 788–791
least squares method, 718–724
model assumptions, 727–729
model of, 713–714, 727–729, 751
multiple coefficient of determination, 724–726
residual analysis, 745–749
summary, 750
testing for significance, 729–735
Multiple regression analysis, 713
Multiple regression equation, 713, 751
Multiple sampling plans, 943–944
Multiplication law, 211–212, 223
Multiplicative decomposition model, 859–862, 870
Mutually exclusive events, 205, 212
MWW (Mann–Whitney–Wilcoxon) test, 893–903, 914

N

Naive forecasting method, 817–818, 820
Nasdaq, 2
National Aeronautics and Space Administration (NASA), 186
NEG (Northeast Electric and Gas), 991
Network segments, 4
Nevada Occupational Health Clinic, 808
Neyman allocation, 1017
Nielsen Company, The, 4, 10
Nonlinear models, 773–774
Nonlinear trend regression, 837–838
Nonparametric methods, 877–918
definition of, 879
introduction to, 878–879
Kruskal–Wallis test, 903–907
Mann–Whitney–Wilcoxon (MWW) test, 893–903
rank correlation, 907–913
summary, 912–913
Wilcoxon signed-rank test, 888–893
Nonprobabilistic sampling, 988
Nonprobability sampling technique, 355, 362
Nonresponse error, 357
Nonsampling error, 356–358, 690, 988–989
Nonstationary time series, 830
Normal approximation of the sampling distribution of the number of plus signs when $H0$: $p = 0.50$, 882–883
Normal curve, 295, 297
Normal probability density function, 296, 315
Normal probability distribution, 349
computing, 301–302
distribution, 301
example of, 302, 306
Excel used to compute, 304, 306
normal curve, 297
standard normal probability distribution, 297
Normal probability plot, 680–682
Normal scores, 680–681
NORM.DIST function, 344
Northeast Electric and Gas (NEG), 991
np chart, 926, 935
Null hypotheses, 416, 419, 424
Numerical measures
adding to data dashboards, 167–170
association between two variables, measures of, 157–165
boxplot, 152–155
data dashboards, 167–170
distribution shape and relative location, measures of, 143–144
five-number summary, 151
location, measures of, 117–134
outliers, detecting, 147–148
variability, measures of, 134–143

O

Observational study, 11–12, 573
Observations of data, 5, 7
Observed level of significance, 427
Ocean Spray, 920
One-tailed tests, 419, 423, 428, 439, 885
one-tailed tests, 428
Online dating sites, 2
Open-end class, 60
Operating characteristic (OC) curve, 941–942
Oracle, 22
Ordinal scale, 5
Outliers, 147–148, 151, 683–686
Out of control process, 925
Overall sample mean, 577, 615, 929, 947
Overall significance, 729

P

p (Population correlation coefficient), 160–162, 657, 710
Pairwise comparisons, 559–560, 590, 592
Parameters of a sampling population, 324
Parameters of regression model (ß), 628–629, 651–652
Parametric methods, 878–879
Partitioned scatter diagram, 160
Partitioning, 583
of sum of squares, 615
Pascal, Blaise, 186
Payoff tables, 953–954
p chart, 926, 932–935
Pearson, Karl, 627
Pearson product moment correlation coefficient, 160–162, 172
Per Capita GDP, 5–7, 14–15
Percent frequency distribution, 38–40
categorical variable, 38–40
Excel used to create, 39–40
quantitative variable, 50–51
Percentiles, 125–126
Perfect information, expected value, 957, 958
Permutations, 191–192
Pie charts, 41–48, 96
Excel used to create, 43–44
Pivot point, 118
Planning value for s, 393
Point estimates, 333
Point estimation, 332–334
Point estimators, 117, 332–333, 336, 339, 468, 991
approximate 95% confidence interval estimate, 991
difference between two population means, 504
difference between two population proportions, 494–495, 504
estimated regression equation, 660
of population mean, 997, 1016, 1017
population proportion, 1001, 1017
of population total, 1010, 1016–1018
of population variance, 523
Poisson, Siméon, 269
Poisson probability distribution, 234, 268–272
Excel used to compute, 270–272
exponential distributions, relationship between, 311, 312
length or distance intervals example, 270
population proportion, 448, 449
time intervals example, 269–270
Poisson probability function, 269, 280
Polio, 952
Pooled estimates, 504, 577
Pooled estimators of population proportions, 498
Pooled sample variance, 484
Population, 15, 322–323, 986–987
sampled, 987
target, 987
Population correlation coefficient (*p*), 160–162, 657, 710
Population covariance, 159, 172
Population mean (*m*), 990–991, 1008–1009
approximate 95% confidence interval estimate, 998, 1015, 1016, 1018
Excel used to, 998–1000
formula, 172
interval estimate, 1015
known, 423, 438
matched samples, inference about difference between, 487, 494
in null and alternative hypotheses, 419
one-tailed tests, 423
point estimator of, 997, 1017
population proportions, inference about difference between, 494, 502
sample size for estimate, 1016, 1017
sampling error, 356
small sample, 387, 389
standard deviation, 244, 296, 302
two-tailed tests, 433
unknown, 438, 446
σ_1 and σ_2 known, inference about difference between, 467
σ_1 and σ_2 unknown, inference between difference between, 476, 487
Population mean: σ known, 374, 382
Excel for, 379
margin of error and the interval estimate, 374, 380
practical advice, 380
Population mean: σ unknown, 382, 392
Excel for, 386, 387
interval estimation procedures, 389
introduction to, 382–383
margin of error and the interval estimate, 383, 387
practical advice, 387
small sample, 387, 389
Population means: σ_1 and σ_2 unknown, difference between, 476
Population parameters, 117
cluster sampling, 354–355
confidence intervals, 402–403
estimated regression equation, 629
hypothesis tests, 419, 435
point estimator, 333
sampling methods, 323, 324
Population proportions, 992, 1001–1002, 1010–1012
approximate 95% confidence interval estimate, 1016, 1017, 1018
Excel for, 396, 398
Excel used to, 1002
hypothesis tests, 395, 396, 446, 452
in null and alternative hypotheses, 419
point estimator, 1001
sample size, 398, 399
sample size for estimate, 1016, 1017
testing for equality of three or more, 554
Population total, 991, 1000–1001, 1009–1010
approximate 95% confidence interval estimate, 1000, 1016, 1018
point estimator, 1000, 1016, 1018
sample size estimating, 1003, 1016–1017
Population variances (σ_2), 135–136, 516–520
between-treatments estimate of, 579, 580
formula, 172
inferences about, 523–535
interval estimation, 523–529
within-treatments estimate of, 580
Posterior probabilities, 215, 217, 973, 975
Practical significance, 454
Precision, 994
Prediction interval, 662–663, 694, 735
Predictive analytics, 20
Predictive models, 22
Prescriptive analytics, 20
Prior probability, 215, 962, 974
Probabilistic sampling, 988

Probability
addition law, 202–205
assigning, 192–193
basic relationships of, 201–207
Bayes' theorem, 215–219
complement of an event, 201–202
computing using the complement, 222
conditional, 207–212
counting rules, combinations, and permutations, 189–194
definition of, 186
events and, 197–201
example of, 193–194
experiments, 187–188
introduction to, 186–187
multiple, 189–190, 189–194
relative frequency method, 238
subjective method, 238
summary, 221
Probability density function *f(x)*, 291, 293
Probability distributions, 238
Probability functions, 238
Probability of accepting a lot, 940–942
Probability sampling techniques, 355, 362
Probability tree, 216–217. *See also* Tree diagrams
Problem formulation
decision trees, 954
overview of, 952
payoff tables, 953, 954
Problem formulation decision trees, 957
Procter & Gamble (P&G), 290
Producer Price Index, 4
Producer's risk, 939
Production applications, 4
Proportional allocation, 1005
Protected LSD test, 591
*p*th percentile, 125
p-value, 435, 452, 454, 472, 517–518, 541, 548, 581, 583, 653, 749
p-value approach, 425
chi-square test, 547, 557
critical value approach *versus,* 448
hypothesis tests, 517
one-tailed tests, 425, 426
rejection rule, 541, 549, 582, 590, 653, 655, 710, 730–731
t test for significance in simple linear regression, 653
two-tailed tests, 429–430, 433

Q

Quadratic trend equation, 837–843, 870
Qualitative forecasting methods, 809
Quality assurance, 923
Quality control, 4
acceptance sampling, 938–945
ISO 9000, 922
Malcolm Baldrige National Quality Award, 922
philosophies and frameworks, 921–925
in service sector, 924–925
Six Sigma, 922–924
statistical process control, 925–938
summary, 946
Quality engineering, 923
Quantitative data, 7, 37, 60
Quantitative forecasting methods, 809
Quantitative variable, 7
cumulative distributions, 56–57
dot plot, 52–53
frequency distribution, 48–49
histogram, 53–56
percent frequency distribution, 50–52
relative frequency distribution, 50–52
stem-and-leaf display, 56–60
summarizing data for, 48–66
Quartiles, 126–127, 148
Quintiles, 128

R

Random experiments, 195
Randomization, 574, 578
Randomized block design
air traffic controller stress test, 596, 597
ANOVA procedure, 597–598
computations and conclusions, 598, 601
Random numbers, 325
Random sample, 323, 329–330, 356, 474, 477
Random variables, 235–237, 280, 293
Range, 135
Rank correlation, 907–913
Ratio scale of measurement, 7
R chart, 926, 931–932
Reciprocal transformation, 771–772
Regression analysis, 762. *See also* Backwar delimination; Best-subsets regression; Forward selection; Multiple regression; Simple linear regression; Stepwise regression
autocorrelation, 793–798
Durbin–Watson test, 793–798
general linear model, 763–774
Independent variables, 778–780
multiple regression approach to experimental design, 788–791
summary, 799–800
Regression equation, 627–629
estimated, linear, 629, 634–635, 692
estimated, multiple, 713–714, 718–719, 751
Regression models, 627–630
multiple, 713–714, 727–729, 751
simple linear, 627–630, 692
Regression statistics output, interpretation of, 669
Rejectable quality level (RQL), 945
Rejection rule, 426, 428, 541, 549, 557, 582, 590, 591, 653, 655, 710, 730–731
Relationships, displays for, 96
Relative frequency, 38, 103
Relative frequency distribution
categorical variable, 38–40
crosstabulation and, 67, 67–70
definition of, 38
example of, 143–144
Excel used to create, 39–40
quantitative variable, 50–52
Relative frequency method, 192–193, 238
Relative location, 145
Replication, 574, 605
Rescue methods, 186
Research hypothesis, 416, 418
Residual analysis, 671–683
introduction to, 671–672
multiple regression, 745–749
normal probability plot, 680–682
residual plot, 672–673
standardized residuals, 675–676
Residual for observation *i*, 671, 694
Residual plots, 672–673, 677–680, 682, 745–746
Response surface, 729
Response variables, 574, 576, 729
Restricted LSD test, 592
Return on equity (ROE), 11
Rounding errors, 140
RQL (Rejectable quality level), 945

S

Sabin, Albert, 952
Salk, Jonas, 952
Sample, 15, 323, 986–987
Sample correlation coefficient, 160–162, 164, 693
Sample covariance, 158, 161, 164, 172
Sampled population, 323, 987
Sample information, decision analysis with, 962, 973
Sample mean, 356
example of, 342, 345
expected value of, 338–339
form of the sampling distribution of *x*, 342, 990
formula, 172
introduction to, 336–338
overall, 929
practical value of, 342–344
sample size and sampling distribution of, 344–345
standard deviation of, 339–340
standard deviation of for treatment *j*, 615
Sample points, 187, 189–190
Sample proportion, 348–353
expected value of, 348
introduction to, 336–337
practical value of, 350–351
sampling distribution of, 350
standard deviation of, 349
Sample size
determining, 392, 395, 398, 399, 994–996, 1002–1005, 1012
estimating population mean, 1003, 1016
estimating population proportion, 1016
estimating population total, 1003, 1016
hypothesis tests, 474
interval estimate and, 380
for interval estimate of population mean, 405
for interval estimate of population proportion, 405
sampling distribution and, 344–345
in multiple regression, 749
Sample space, 187–188, 199
Sample statistics, 117, 332
Sample survey, 985–1021
formulas, 1015–1018
summary, 1014
terminology used, 986–987
types of surveys and sampling methods, 987–988
Sample surveys, 15
Sample variances
Excel for, 138
formula, 140, 172
interval estimation, 511–514
pooled sample variance, 484
population variances and, 135–136, 514
standard deviation, 137–138
for treatment *j*, 615
Sampling
big data and, 356–362
convenience, 988
errors in, 356–362
example problem, 323–324
from finite population, 325, 329
from infinite population, 329, 330
introduction to, 323–324
judgment, 988
nonprobabilistic, 988
point estimation, 332–334
probabilistic, 988
sample selection, 325, 331
simple random, 990–996
single-stage cluster, 1007
summary, 365
systematic, 1014
two-stage cluster, 1007
Sampling distributions
big data and errors in sampling, 356–362
definition of, 337
form of, 340–345
inferences about two population variances, 523–529
introduction to, 336–337
judgment sampling, 356
other sampling methods, 353–356
of population variance, 514
practical value of, 342–344
of sample mean, 338–345, 514
sample proportion, 348–353
sample size and, 344–345
standard deviation of, 339–340
summary, 365
t test, 652–653
for Wilcoxon signed-rank test, 889–890
Sampling errors, 323–324, 356–362, 402, 989
bound on, 990
Sampling methods, 324
Sampling units, 987
SAS, 22
SAT scores, 7
Scales of measurement, 5, 7

Scatter diagram and trendline
Excel used to create, 77–80, 634–635
least squares method, 630–631
overview of, 77–78
perfect positive linear relationship, 163
to show relationships, 96
in time series analysis, 83
Seasonal indexes, 859–862, 865
Seasonality and trend, 851–854
Seasonality without trend, 748–751
Seasonal pattern, 813–815
Second-order models, 764, 765
Selection bias, 329, 330
Serial correlation of data, 793
Service sector, quality in, 924–925
Shewhart, Walter A., 921–925
Side-by-side bar chart
description of, 80–82, 95–96, 98
Excel used to create, 82–83
Significance, levels, 377, 421–422
Significance tests, 421
confidence intervals, 653–654
F test, 654–656
interpretation of, 656–657
mean square error, 651–652
multiple regression, 729–735
simple linear regression, 651–657
t test, 652–653
Sign test, 879–888
hypothesis test about population median, 879–883
hypothesis test with matched samples, 883–885
normal approximation, 913
Simple first-order model, 763
Simple linear regression
big data and hypothesis testing in, 690–691
coefficient of determination, 641–649
definition of, 627
equation, 692
estimated regression equation used for estimation and prediction, 659–665
estimation process, 609
influential observation, 686–687
least squares method, 630–641
model assumptions, 649–651
model of, 627–630, 692
outliers, 683–686
parameters, 628–629, 650, 652
residual analysis, 671–683
Smoothing constant, 829
summary, 691
testing for significance, 649–659
Simple random sample, 317–318, 325, 328, 330, 355, 376
Simple random sampling, 990–996
Excel used to compute, 992–994
formulas, 1015–1017
population mean, 990–991
population total, 991
stratified, 997–2005, 1016–1017
Simpson's paradox, 71–72
Single exponential smoothing, 826, 848
Single-factor experiment, 574
Single-stage cluster sampling, 1007
Six Sigma, 922–924
Skewness of distributions, 143–144, 312, 390
Slope, 632–634, 692, 835
Small Fry Design, 116
Smoothing constant, 826
Social media, 21, 358
S&P 500, 2, 4
Spearman rank-correlation coefficient, 165, 907–913, 914
SSA. *See* Sum of squares for factor A (SSA)
SSAB
See Sum of squares for interaction (SSAB)
SSB. *See* Sum of squares for factor B (SSB)
SSBL. *See* Sum of squares due to blocks (SSBL)
SSE. *See* Sum of squares due to error (SSE)
SSR. *See* Sum of squares due to regression (SSR)
SST. *See* Sum of squares total (SST); Total sum of squares (SST)
SSTR. *See* Sum of squares due to treatments (SSTR)
Stacked bar chart
description of, 80–82, 96
Excel used to create, 82–83
Standard deviation (σ), 148, 244, 296, 302, 693
Excel used to compute, 244–245
in financial applications, 252–255
formula, 172
introduction to, 137–138
of *i*th residual, 694
as measure of risk, 139
population, 137, 244, 302, 484
of sample mean, 339–340, 366
of sample proportion, 349–350, 366
Standard error
confidence intervals, 403
of the estimate, 652, 693
formula, 366, 504
hypothesis tests, 498
interval estimation, 468, 495
of the mean, 340, 344, 348, 349
of the proportion, 349
sampling and nonsampling error, 356–362
Standard error of the mean, 947, 1015–1018
Standard error of the proportion, 947, 1016
Standardized residuals, 675–680, 688, 694, 745–746, 771
Standardized value, 148
Standard normal density function, 297
Standard normal probability distribution, 560
Standard normal probability distribution, 297, 301
Standard normal random variable, 302, 315
States of nature, 953, 963
Stationarity assumption, 260
Stationary time series, 811
Statistical analysis using Microsoft Excel, 16–19
Statistical inference, 15–16, 333, 362
Statistical process control, 924–925
control charts, 926
interpretation of, 935–936
np chart, 935
p chart, 932–935
process mean and standard deviation known, 927–929
process mean and standard deviation unknown, 929–931
R chart, 931–932
Statistical significance, practical significance *versus,* 657, 690
Statistics
business applications of, 3–4
definition of, 3
descriptive (*See* Descriptive statistics)
economics applications of, 3
ethical guidelines for, 22–23
introduction to, 2–3
in practice, 2
summary, 24
Statistics in practice
Bloomberg Businessweek, 2
Colgate-Palmolive Company, 37
Duke Energy, 986
International Paper, 712–713
Ocean Spray, 920
Small Fry Design, 116
Walmart.com, 626
West Shell Realtors, 878
Stem-and-leaf display, 57–60, 96
Stepwise regression procedures, 787
Strata, 354
proportional allocation of sample *n,* 1017
total sample *n* to, 1017
Stratified random sampling, 330, 354, 356
Stratified simple random sampling, 997–1005
population mean, 997–998
Subjective method for assigning probabilities, 193, 238
Summarizing data, graphical displays for
best practices for, 92–100
data dashboards, 97–98
examples of, 98–100
scatter diagram, 77–78
side-by-side bar chart, 80–82
stacked bar chart, 80–82
trendline, 77–78
two variables, 77–86
type of, selecting, 96
Summation sign (σ), 117
Sum of squares due to blocks (SSBL), 597, 598, 616
Sum of squares due to error (SSE)
ANOVA procedure, 597, 598, 605, 606
ANOVA table, 582, 583
coefficient of determination, 641–644
formula, 615, 616, 692
multiple coefficient of determination, 724–725
significance tests, 651
variables, adding and deleting, 778
within-treatments estimate of population variance, 580
Sum of squares due to regression (SSR), 643, 654, 692, 724–725
Sum of squares due to treatments (SSTR), 579, 582–583, 597–598, 615–616
Sum of squares for factor A (SSA), 605, 607, 616
Sum of squares for factor B (SSB), 605, 607, 616
Sum of squares for interaction (SSAB), 605, 607, 616
Sum of squares total (SST), 605, 607
Sum of the squares of the deviations, 631
Survey errors, 988–989
Symmetric distribution, 143–144
Systematic sampling, 330, 355, 1014

T

Tables for summarizing data
crosstabulation, 67–70
Simpson's paradox, 71–72
two variables, 66
Taguchi, Genichi, 921
Tall data, 359
Target population, 333, 987
t distribution, 382, 384, 388, 440, 477, 482, 489, 517
Teradata, 22
Test for equality, 564
Test statistic, hypothesis tests about population mean: ó known
chi-square tests, 550
description of, 425
equality of *k* population means, 581, 582, 615
Fisher's LSD procedure, 590, 591, 616
goodness of fit, 540–541, 564
hypothesis tests, 471, 480–481, 498, 504
hypothesis tests about population mean: ó unknown, 456
hypothesis tests about population proportion, 456
hypothesis tests about population variance, 516–517, 525
hypothesis tests about the difference between two population means: $ó_1$ and $ó_2$ unknown, 690–691
hypothesis tests involving matched samples, 488, 504
Kruskal–Wallis, 904
one-tailed tests, 424, 425
Thearling, Kurt, 21
The Economist, 2
The Wall Wall Street Journal, 2–3
Time intervals, 269–270
Time series analysis and forecasting
exponential smoothing, 826–833
forecast accuracy, 817–821
introduction to, 809–810
moving averages, 822–825
seasonality and trend, 851–854
summary, 868
time series decomposition (*See* Time series decomposition)
time series patterns (*See* Time series patterns)
trend projection, 833–848
weighted moving averages, 825–826

Time series data, 8–10, 83
Time series decomposition, 858–868
 cyclical component, 865
 deseasonalized time series, 863
 models based on monthly data, 865
 seasonal adjustments, 864
 seasonal indexes, calculating, 859–862
 using deseasonalized time series to identify trend, 863–864
Time series method, 809
Time series patterns, 809–817
 cyclical pattern, 816–817
 forecasting method, selection of, 817
 horizontal pattern, 810–811
 seasonal pattern, 813–815
 trend and seasonal pattern, 815–816
 trend pattern, 812–813
Time series plots, 809–817
 Excel used to construct, 816–817
Time series regression, 809
Total quality (TQ), 920–921
Total sample
 n to strata, 1017
Total sum of squares (SST), 582–583, 597–598, 615–616, 642–643, 692, 724–725
TQ (Total quality), 920–921
Treatments, 574
Tree diagrams, 216–217, 260
Trend and seasonal pattern, 815–816
Trendlines, 77–78, 86
 Excel used to create, 77–80
Trend pattern, 812–813
Trend projection, 833–848
 linear trend regression, 833–838
 nonlinear trend regression, 837–838
Trimmed mean, 128
t test, 652–653, 668, 672, 731–732, 749
t test statistics, 693, 751
Two-stage cluster sampling, 1007
Two-tailed tests, 428
 confidence intervals, 433
 hypothesis testing, 489
 hypothesis tests, 499
 null and alternative hypotheses, 419
 overview of, 428, 433
 population mean: *s* unknown, 440, 442
 population proportion, 446
 population variance, 518
 p-value, 886, 890
 p-value approach, 425
Type I and Type II errors, 420, 423, 427, 454, 592, 593, 690, 750

U

UCL (Upper control limit), 926
Unbiased estimators, 339
Uniform probability density function, 291, 314
Uniform probability distribution
 area as measure of probability, 292, 293
 description of, 291, 295
Union of A and B, 202
Union of two events, 202–203
United Way, 538
Upper class limits, 48, 56
Upper control limit (UCL), 926
Upper tail test
 chi-square distributions, 557
 goodness of fit test, 541
 population mean: *s* known, 423, 428
 population proportion, 446
 population variance, 518
 p-value, 482, 499, 885
 t distribution, 489
 test of independence, 547, 548
U.S. Bureau of Labor Statistics, 11
U.S. Department of Interior, 510
U.S. Food and Drug Administration, 466
U.S. Food and Drug Administration, 422, 466
U.S. Government Accountability Office, 510
U.S. Travel Association, 11
US Centers for Disease Control and Prevention, 952
 voter waiting times in elections, 234

V

Validity of data, 148
Value worksheet, 19
Variability, measures of, 134–143
 coefficient of variation, 139–140
 interquartile range (IQR), 135
 introduction to, 134
 range, 135
 standard deviation, 137–138
 variance, 135–136
Variables, 5–7, 738, 778–780
Variable selection procedures, 783–788
Variables sampling plans, 945
Variance, 135–136, 243–245
 for binomial distribution, 265–266, 280
 of discrete random variable, 280
 Excel used to compute, 244–245
 in financial applications, 253–254
 for hypergeometric distribution, 281
 of linear combination of random variables, 280
Variety, 21
Velocity, 21
Venn diagram, 201–202, 210
Volume, 21
Voter waiting times in elections, 234

W

Walmart.com, 626–627
Warehousing data, 21
Weighted mean, 122, 129, 172
Weighted moving averages, 825–826
West Shell Realtors, 878
Whiskers, 152–153
Wide area networks (WANs), 4
Wide data, 359
Wilcoxon rank-sum test. *See* Mann-Whitney-Wilcoxon (MWW) test
Wilcoxon signed-rank test, 888–893, 914
Wild polioviruses, 952
Williams, Walter, 422
Within-treatments estimate, 577
World Trade Organization (WTO), 5–8, 13, 17–18
WTO Status, 5–7, 18

X

x-chart, 3, 926–931

Y

y-intercept, 632–633, 692
Yottabytes, 358

Z

z-scores, 145, 148, 172
z test statistic, 560